MUSICAL INSTRUMENTS

A Comprehensive Dictionary

MUSICAL INSTRUMENTS

A Comprehensive Dictionary

by

SIBYL MARCUSE

The Norton Library

W·W·NORTON & COMPANY·INC·

NEW YORK

CORRECTED EDITION COPYRIGHT © 1975 BY SIBYL MARCUSE
COPYRIGHT 1964 BY SIBYL MARCUSE
First published in the Norton Library 1975

Books That Live
The Norton imprint on a book means that in the publisher's
estimation it is a book not for a single season but for the years.
W. W. Norton & Company, Inc.

Library of Congress Cataloging in Publication Data
Marcuse, Sibyl.
  Musical instruments.
  (The Norton Library; N758)
  1. Musical instruments—Dictionaries.
ML102.I5M37   1975   781.9′1′03   74-30050
ISBN 0-393-00758-8

Printed in the United States of America
4 5 6 7 8 9 0

PREFACE

The publication of Curt Sachs's *Reallexikon der Musikinstrumente* just half a century ago—the first work to deal exclusively with musical instruments of all peoples and times—not only was a milestone in the history of organology, but also marked the beginning of an entirely new era in this science. Today we can speak of a pre-Sachs and a post-Sachs period. And it is both a fitting tribute to his genius and proof of the increasingly wide interest accorded musical instruments that the work he jokingly referred to in his maturer years as his *Jugendsünde* should have been reprinted in 1962.

For the English-language reader the *Reallexikon* has the obvious disadvantage of being written in German, and the present volume was written with the intention of providing such readers with a comparable reference tool, and at the same time of presenting some of the results of post-1913 organological research. By including translations into English of foreign names of instruments, *termini technici*, and the more important instrument parts, I have hoped to make the book of assistance to those who have a reading knowledge of other languages.

At the onset I must point out that this dictionary is incomplete. Of necessity so. The late Jaap Kunst listed well over five thousand books and papers on non-European and folk instruments alone; it is of course impossible for any individual to peruse all of them; limits of time and availability of material preclude such an undertaking. Furthermore, in order to keep the material presented here within the bounds of a one-volume edition, it has been necessary in many instances to reduce to skeletal proportions the information given.

Sound producers that by nature are not primarily musical instruments, such as sirens, foghorns, popguns, tables used for drumming on, etc., have been excluded from this dictionary, despite the fact that they may occasionally serve musical purposes. On the other hand, "talking drums" (signaling devices), bull-roarers, and certain other sound producers are included—illogically perhaps—because of their great ethnomusicological or sociological importance.

In preparing the material for this book I have retraced some of Sachs's steps (and so come to realize his great debt to Carl Engel and to Charles Mahillon), and have covered a portion of the newer literature. Sources repeatedly referred to appear as round-bracketed numbers at the end of the entries and are listed in numerical order at the end of this volume. In most instances it has been impossible to differentiate the various authors cited within a given entry, and to distinguish quoted material from original material.

It remains for me to express my gratitude to the many persons who have facilitated my work, and particularly to the librarians and staffs of Basel University, the British Museum, the Horniman Museum, the Yale University School of Music, for their many courtesies and assistance extended, and to the following persons for their kindness in supplying information and/or putting material at my disposition: Dr. Ernst Emsheimer, Stockholm; Mrs. Jean Jenkins, London; Dr. Walter Nef, Basel; Mr.

Jack Pfeiffer, New York; Señor J. Ricart-Matas, Barcelona; Mr. Rembert Wurlitzer, New York; Professor Walter Senn, Innsbruck; Dr. K. P. Wachsmann, London. For the loan of trade catalogues I am also indebted to Boosey & Hawkes, Ltd., London; Goldie's Music Shop, New Haven, Connecticut; Hug & Co., Basel.

USE OF THE DICTIONARY

Alphabetization. Entries are arranged in strictly alphabetical order, headings of more than one word being treated as though they were but one word; for instance, *Altobasso* precedes *Alto clarinet*. The umlaut of German words is not taken into consideration: *Flöte* is alphabetized as *Flote*.

An **asterisk** (*) placed before a word or words indicates that there is an entry for the word or words so starred.

Brackets. Both square and round brackets are used. The square brackets contain etymological data. Round brackets following a heading serve: to identify the language of a given heading, as *"Clairon* (Fr.)"; to contain translations into foreign languages of a heading, as *"Harp* (Fr.: *harpe;* Ger.: *Harfe;* It., Sp.: *arpa)";* or to contain a translation into English of a foreign term, as *"Ni gen kin* (2-stringed kin)." Round brackets placed at the end of an entry indicate the source or sources.

Geographical terms. To designate the territory, including Mexico, between North and South America, I have used the term Central America (though this expression is nearly obsolete in the United States), for the more modern term Meso-America covers only the area between the Rio Grande and the Gulf of Fonseca.

Orthography. In general, spellings of proper names and of names of non-European instruments are those of the sources cited, except in those instances in which it has been necessary to make changes for the sake of conformity. As spellings of some instrument names (particularly African ones) vary considerably according to whether an author writes in French, English, or German, cross-references are furnished wherever deemed necessary. As to names of African peoples, the authors' original orthographies have been retained in most instances (resulting, to be sure, in such inconsistencies as mention of both the Luba and the Baluba), but in order to maintain uniformity as far as possible, readily identifiable variants have been changed to agree with the spellings used in George Peter Murdock's *Africa* (McGraw-Hill, 1959). The Dutch and Flemish *tj* have systematically been changed to *ch,* the *oe* to *u.* The *tx* sometimes encountered in the rather flexible Basque orthography has been changed to *ch.*

Sources. As noted under Brackets, above, the numbers placed inside round brackets at the end of many entries correspond to those of a list of sources repeatedly referred to, appended to this volume.

Basel, May 1962

NOTE

Corrections have been made throughout the text for the Norton Library edition.

CONTENTS

PITCH NAMES

Pitch letters printed without further identification, as C, E♭, etc., do not connote any definite pitch. Definite pitches are indicated as in the following chart.

TONAL POSITIONS OF INSTRUMENTS

octave bb^1 or c^2

sopranino eb^1 or f^1

soprano bb^0 or c^1

alto eb^0 or f^0

tenor Bb^0 or c^0

baritone Bb^0 or c^0

bass Eb^0 or F^0

contrabass Bb^1 or C^0

subbass Eb^1 or F^1

sub-contrabass Bb^2 or C^1

ABBREVIATIONS

abbr.   abbreviation, abbreviated
A.C.   After Christ
Akk.   Akkadian
Alb.   Albanian
Alem.   Alemannic
Amer.   American
Amh.   Amharic
Arab.   Arabic
Aram.   Aramaic
Ass.   Assyrian
aug.   augmentative
B.C.   before Christ
Beng.   Bengali
Brit.   British
Bulg.   Bulgarian
c.   century
C.   Central
Cast.   Castilian
Cat.   Catalonian
Chin.   Chinese
coll.   colloquial
corr.   corruption
cps.   cycles per second
d.   died
Dan.   Danish
dial.   dialect
diam.   diameter
dim.   diminutive
Du.   Dutch
E.   East, Eastern
Engl.   English
etym.   etymology
fl.   flourished
Flem.   Flemish
Fr.   French
Gael.   Gaelic
Gal.   Galician
Gasc.   Gascon
Ger.   German
Gk.   Greek

H.   High
Heb.   Hebrew
HGer.   High German
Hindust.   Hindustani
Hung.   Hungarian
instr.   instrument
It.   Italian
Jap.   Japanese
Kan.   Kanarese
Kurd.   Kurdish
Kym.   Kymric
l.   low
Lat.   Latin
LGer.   Low German
Lith.   Lithuanian
M   Middle
Mac.   Macassarese
Mal.   Malayan
Mar.   Marathi
max.   maximum
med.   medieval
MEngl.   Middle English
MFr.   Middle French
MGer.   Middle German
MHGer.   Middle High German
MLGer.   Middle Low German
N.   North, Northern
Nor.   Norwegian
O   Old
obs.   obsolete
oct.   octave
ODu.   Old Dutch
OEngl.   Old English
OFr.   Old French
OHGer.   Old High German
onom.   onomatopoeic
OProv.   Old Provençal
OSlav.   Old Slavonic
OSp.   Old Spanish
Pahl.   Pahlevi

Pers.   Persian
pl.   plural
Pol.   Polish
pop.   popular
Port.   Portuguese
pron.   pronounced
Prov.   Provençal
Punj.   Punjabi
Rom.   Romanian
Russ.   Russian
Ruth.   Ruthenian
S.   South, Southern
Sans.   Sanskrit
Scot.   Scottish
SE.   Southeast, Southeastern
Serb.   Serbo-Croatian

sing.   singular
Slav.   Slavonic
Slov.   Slovenian
Sp.   Spanish
Sum.   Sumerian
SW.   Southwest, Southwestern
Swah.   Swahili
Swed.   Swedish
syn.   synonymous
Tel.   Telugu
Turk.   Turkish
U.   Unknown
var.   variant
vulg.   vulgar
W.   West, Western
Yugo.   Yugoslav

MUSICAL INSTRUMENTS

A Comprehensive Dictionary

A

A, *percussion tube of Korea, made of a bamboo segment nearly 2 m. (6½ ft.) long, thinned at both ends, thicker at the middle, where it is covered with leather, balanced horizontally so that the ends hit alternately against the ground (66).

Aba [Fr. *hautbois*], a large modern oboe of Egypt (170).

Ababas, see: abobas.

Abacus, Lat.: keyboard (170).

Abada, single-headed Afro-Brazilian drum of the Babasue of Belém do Pará, slightly conical, made of a hollowed palm trunk. The head is stretched over a hoop and is laced to the base of the drum by means of 4 metal hooks. See also: abita (6, 152).

Ab-a-fu, Jew's-harp of the Igorot of the Philippine Islands, made of bamboo or brass, 8–10 cm. (3–4 in.) long (176).

Aballa [Sp. *aballar*, to move], Basque *disc buzzer, consisting of a piece of paper inserted into a twisted string *ca.* 30 cm. (12 in.) long; the string is attached to a stone, and the whole contraption is then thrown in the air. The paper whirrs as it falls to earth (57).

Abanangbweli, bell of the Azande of the Congo, made of 2 pieces of sheet metal soldered together, with a clapper suspended from an oval ring. It announces the chief's presence, is sounded at meetings when he drinks or smokes, etc. Also called abivadongbwali (132).

Abendair, pl. **ibindiren,** Shauja and Kabyl equivalent of *bandair.

Abeng (Twi: animal horn), **1.** generic name in Twi (a Sudanic language) for wind instrs. made of horn or animal tusk; **2.** mirliton of the Fang of Gabon Republic, made of a piece of cane closed at one end by a spider's-egg membrane, and inserted into one nostril. An efam, a small piece of horn, is inserted into the other nostril (165).

Abi, var. of ibi in Santrokofi and Onitsha (Sudanic languages) (93).

Abiba, *barrel drum of the Momboutou of the Congo, with one head slightly smaller than the other. Both are laced (30).

Abida deni, drum of the Walengola of the Congo (30).

Abilosen adar [*ibili,* to go + *adar,* horn], Basque horn sounded at night to frighten away wild animals; syn. of gau adar.

Abita, conical drum of the Bapopoie of the Congo, with laced heads (19).

Abitin, pl. **ebitin,** generic name for drums among the Timne of Sierra Leone (176).

Abivadongbwali, syn. of abanangbweli.

Abobas, reedpipe of ancient Syria. See also: abuba, imbubu (89).

Abole, stopped *end-blown flute of the Labwor of Uganda, made from the top of a gourd and devoid of fingerholes. *Ca.* 10 cm. (4 in.) long (195).

Abombo, small drum of the Bangelima of the Congo (30).

Abowa mokindja, drum of the Walengola of the Congo (30).

Abrégé (Fr.), **1.** roller; **2.** roller action.

Abruzzi oboe, see: ciaramella.

Abstract, 1. syn. of sticker in the organ; **2.** vertical wooden stick connecting key to whippen in an upright piano.

Abstrakt, Ger.: sticker.

Abuba (Heb.), reedpipe of ancient Israel, possibly a double-reed instr., frowned upon by the Temple authorities, translated in the Septuagint as *aulos. Probably of Syrian origin: Sachs considered the abuba to be the Syrian equivalent of gingras. See also: abobas, imbubu, 'ugab (84, 89, 170).

Abuboyo, sansa of the Ababua of the Congo (132).

Abumi, var. of ebumi.

Abu qurun (Arab.: father of horns), large med. Arab. horn also known to Moorish Spain (89, 144).

Abwaq, pl. of būq.

Abzug (Ger.), 1. the off-board strings of lutes, etc.; 2. tracker.

Acciarino [dim. of It. *acciaio*, steel], It.: triangle. The modern word is *triangolo.*

Accopiamento, It.: coupler.

Accordéon, Fr.: accordion.

Accordéon à pédales, Fr.: pedal accordion.

Accordéon à pistons (Fr.: valve accordion), accordion patented by Jacob Alexandre of Paris in 1846, with piston valves enabling one or more tones to be played by one key (204).

Accordéon-flûtina (Fr.), accordion with one or more rows of flue pipes, patented by the Parisian *luthier* Leroy on Feb. 8, 1855 (204).

Accordéon-orgue (Fr.), accordion with organ keyboard, in shape of a box, invented by Busson of Paris and patented by Titeaux and Rousseau on Aug. 16, 1853. It was held on the seated performer's lap, his left hand working the bellows.

Accordéon-piano, Fr.: piano accordion.

Accordéon-symphonica, see: symphonica.

Accordéophone-orchestre (Fr.), accordion patented on Apr. 11, 1884, by Neveux of Paris. According to the terms of the patent, it was capable of "instantaneous transposition" (204).

Accord-Flöte (Ger.), circular pitch pipe with free reeds, like a small round mouth organ. Triads of each of the 24 scales are produced in rotation. Not to be confused with the Akkordflöte.

Accordio, 19th-c. It. term for accordion.

Accordion (Fr.: *accordéon;* Ger.: *Ziehharmonika;* It.: *armonica a manticino*), portable, keyed free-reed instr. consisting largely of an expandable bellows worked by the player's arm and supplying wind to the free reeds by pressure or by suction, depending on whether it is compressed or expanded. The accordion is provided with a variable number of melody keys or buttons, and bass keys or chord buttons. Simple models have 10 melody keys and 2 bass keys, but far more elaborate ones are built. Each key opens a valve that controls 2 reeds, 1 of which works on pressure and the other on suction. Stops are provided for connecting different reeds so that several may be played by one key. The player's left hand works the bellows and plays the bass accompaniment—usually consisting of tonic and dominant chords—while his right hand plays the melody. The chord buttons work in a manner similar to that of the melody keys except that they act on 3 reeds simultaneously. The accordion was invented in 1822 by Friedrich Buschmann of Berlin, who named his instr. "Handäoline." On May 23, 1829, a privilege was granted to Cyril Demian of Vienna and his sons Carl and Guido, for an "Akkordion," an improvement of Buschmann's instr., and the invention of the accordion is thus usually credited to Demian. The new instr. was so successful that it was promptly copied, despite the terms of Demian's privilege, its imitators calling their output "Handharmonika." An 1835 tutor by Adolph Müller already lists 6 varieties of accordion. Built originally as a diatonic instr., mostly in C, D, or G, it became chromatic *ca.* 1855. See also: autophone, bandoniphone, bayan, chromatine, éoli-Courtier, flûtina, haitari, Handharmonika, Handorgel, hanuri, harmoniflûte, karmon, melophone, mélophonorgue, muzekan, pedal accordion, piano accordion, polka, sanfoña, symphonica. *Cf.* concertina (117, 132, 151, 169).

Accordo (It.), a chord, hence also a mixture (organ stop).

Accouplement, Fr.: coupler.

Acetabula (Lat.: vinegar containers), cymbals of ancient Rome made of brass, silver, or other metal, mentioned *i.a.*, by Suida and Isidore of Seville. Two could be clashed together, or one was struck with a stick (48, 176).

A chang, bowed long zither of Korea, with 7 strings, played with a very short bow. It corresponds to the Chin. la ch'in (66).

Achelette (Fr.), 15th- and 16th-c. var. of echelette (82).

Acheré, 1. Afro-Cuban term to designate any form of rattle used for ritual purposes; **2.** Afro-Cuban *vessel rattle that assumes different forms, some being made of dried fruit pods with the seeds left inside; often painted red and white (152).

Achhrautī, Hindust. name of the sitār.

Achik saz, the next to largest of the Anatolian saz, with 9 strings (89).

Achilliaca (Gk.), mentioned by Homer in the tenth book of the *Iliad*, and by Venantius Fortunatus *ca.* 600 A.C. in connection with instrs. Not an instr., but "songs of Achilles" (185A).

Achordion [Gk.: *a*, without + *chorde*, strings], 19th-c. automatophone built by Cornelius van Oeckelen of Breda (d. 1865) (176).

Achromatic horn (Ger.: *achromatisches Horn*), horn in cornet form invented by Johann Riedel of Pressburg (Bratislava) in 1854, with 4 valves and a compass G^1–g^2 (176).

Acocotl, wooden trumpet of the ancient Incas and of Mexico today, named for the wood (*acocotl*) of which it is made. *Ca.* 3 m. (10 ft.) long with a very narrow bore, a bell, and a mouthpiece. Nowadays called clarín (38, 176).

Acoustic bass, organ stop of 64′, 32′, or 16′ pitch, the product of resultant tones. It is created, for example, by playing a 16′ stop with a *quint 2⅔′ and obtaining the differential or resultant tone of 32′. This can be accomplished either by a 2-rank stop or by adding pipes to the pedal compass of a 1-rank stop and coupling the pedal pipes in 5ths. The object of such procedures is to avoid the expense of very large pipes. The phenomenon known as resultant tone was discovered by Tartini and first introduced into the organ by Abbé Vogler (1749–1814) in his *simplification system. Also called gravitone, harmonic bass, resultant bass, tonitru (101, 186).

Action (Fr.: *mécanique;* Ger.: *Mechanik;* It.: *meccanica*), **1.** the intermediary mechanism between the keyboard and the strings or pipes of a keyboard instr.; **2.** the pitch-controlling devices of a pedal harp; **3.** in a larger sense any device that actuates an instr.

Acucryptophone, automatic instr. with secret action in shape of a lyre, invented in 1822 by Charles Wheatstone of London. It was wound with a key and imitated the sounds of orchestral instrs. (176, 204).

Acuta, acuta vox (Lat.) (Du.: *scherp;* Ger.: *Scharf*), mixture organ stop composed of 3–5 ranks of high-pitched pipes, either with or without a tierce, and repeating. It corresponds to the Fr. *cymbale* (133, 198).

Acute mixture, see: acuta, acuta vox.

Adabatram, war and executioner's drum of the Ewe of Ghana (176).

Adabo, 2-headed *cylindrical drum, short and wide, of the Malagasy Republic (171).

Adamādalā [Beng. *āda*, width + *mādalā*, drum], drum of Bengal, as long as it is wide (176).

A-da-pa (Sum.), square frame drum of ancient Babylon which first appears in the third millennium B.C. It corresponds to the adapu (89 Galpin).

Adapu, Akkad : adapa.

Adar (Basque: horn), Basque horn

made of cow horn. Also called tuhunta, tuta.

Adarturanta [Basque: *adar*, horn + *turanta*, onom.], valveless French horn of the Labourd district of the Basque country.

Adedura [?Arab. *adedar*, drum sound], med. Sp. drum, mentioned in the 14th c. by Juan Ruiz, believed to have corresponded to the darabuka (176).

Adeudeu, *arched harp of the Teso of Uganda, with very slim, elongated body and 6 strings (195).

Adewu [*ade*, hunter + *wu*, drum], drum used by Ewe hunters in Ghana before setting out for the hunt (93).

Adiaphone [Gk.: *a*, without + *diaphonos*, discord], *tuning-fork piano invented by Fischer & Fritz of Leipzig and patented in 1882, in which the strings of an upright piano were replaced by a series of tuning forks. These lay horizontally in a frame and were struck from below and simultaneously pressed against a soundboard. An improved version was supplied with a second tuning fork for each note, tuned to the octave. The name implies that it would not go out of tune. Compass F^0–f^3 or C^1–c^5 (178).

Adiaphonon, keyboard instr. invented by a Viennese clockmaker named Franz Schuster, patented 1819, in which the strings were replaced by vertical steel bars. It had a 6-oct. compass (176).

Adil, trumpet of the Garo of Assam, made of a bamboo tube to which a curved buffalo horn is attached (172).

Adingili, *musical bow of the Alur of Uganda, corresponding to the adungu. It is played by women only (195).

Adja, **1.** small Afro-Brazilian metal bell, possibly of Yoruba origin, used in voodoo rites of Bahia and Recife (6); **2.** Afro-Brazilian rattle made of 2 tin-plate cones soldered together at the widest part, perforated with holes, and furnished with a handle (7).

Adjulona, name given to several wind instrs. of the Carajá Indians of Brazil: **1.** pipe consisting of a narrow, spirally twisted blade of muriti-palm leaf, pressed flat, ca. 3 cm. (1¼ in.) wide, 1–2½ cm. (⅜–1¼ in.) long; this is also found among the Savaje Indians; **2.** trumpet made of a tube of *taquara* wood, with lateral blowhole, terminating in a gourd bell 40 cm. (16 in.) long. The tube is ca. 45 cm. (17½ in.) long (105).

Adufe [Arab. **duff*], **1.** obs. Sp. *frame drum; **2.** in Brazil a square frame drum (7, 154).

Adufo, name of the cuíca in Alagoas, Brazil (7).

Adungu, **1.** *musical bow of the Acoli of Uganda, with bow bent into a U shape and the string laced through it so as to form a Z. The bottom of the U rests on a gourd not connected to the bow and placed open side down on the player's lap. The chin rests against the top section of the string, thereby stopping it, and all 3 sections of it are plucked. It is played by women only; **2.** *arched harp of the Alur of Uganda, with triangular body, neck fitted into a hole cut in the side of the body, and 7 strings (195).

Adya oro, small *bull-roarer of the Ibo of Nigeria (152).

Aelyau, large *frame drum of Greenland, held by a handle. The frame, not the membrane, is struck (176).

Aeola [Aeolus, god of wind], improved concertina in octagonal form, made by Charles Wheatstone of London, in 3 sizes: treble g^0–c^4 or higher, tenor c^0–c^4, baritone G^0–c^3 (176).

Aeol-harmonica (Ger.: *Äolsharmonika*), free-reed keyboard instr., invented in the 1820's by Reinlein in France—a precursor of the harmonium. It was played in public in Stuttgart in 1828 (176, 204).

Aeolian, organ stop; see: aeoline, 2.

Aeolian bells (Fr.: *cloches éoliennes;* Ger.: *Äolsglocken*), bells suspended in the open and sounded by the wind. They are found in E. Asia and E. Africa today and were known to classical antiquity. In the sanctuary of Zeus in Dodona bells were suspended from chains and set in motion by the wind; and bells were hung over the grave of the Etruscan Porsenna so that the wind might sound them and banish evil spirits. Flavius Josephus relates that Solomon had bells hung from the Temple roof to keep birds away (21, 176).

Aeolian bow, *musical bow sounded by the wind. It occurs in various forms: suspended from a tree, swung by hand (Java, Malaya, W. Africa), or attached to a kite (China, Japan, Korea, parts of Indonesia). One Far Eastern type (*yao ch'in) has 7 bows attached to a frame tied to a kite. See also: feng cheng, sundaren, yao ch'in, yao p'ien (149).

Aeolian flute, see: aeolian pipe.

Aeolian harp (Fr.: *harpe d'Éole;* Ger.: *Äolsharfe;* It.: *arpa d'Eolo*), box zither strung with gut strings of identical length and pitch but of different thicknesses. Usually the box is some 1½ m. (5 ft.) long, provided with soundholes and a dozen strings or so that pass over 2 bridges between hitch pins and tuning pins. The strings are set in vibration by the action of the wind, sounding in chords because of their different thicknesses. The box is usually placed in a window or suspended elsewhere so as to catch the breeze. The principle of the aeolian harp was known in biblical times (King David's lyre sounded in the N. wind at night), but the Middle Ages regarded such phenomena with the greatest suspicion: St. Dunstan (d. 988) was suspected of sorcery for having experimented with a harp that played by itself. From then on we hear nothing more of it until the mid-16th c., when Giovanni Battista Porta, writing in Naples in 1558, mentions strings sounded by the wind. He is followed by Athanasius Kircher, who from 1646 on designed elaborate wind catchers and who aroused a measure of theoretical and practical interest in the Aeolian harp. A c. later the poet James Thomson discussed the aeolian harp (1746), after which the "ghostly sound of chords" took a definite place in 18th-c. *Affekten* and

the instr. became popular enough to warrant a history of the aeolian harp by Jean-Georges Kastner in 1856. See also: anémocorde, armonica meteorologicale, arpa gigantesca (149, 170, 178).

Aeolian kite, see: aeolian bow.

Aeolian lyre, syn. of aeolian harp.

Aeolian piano, see: Äolsklavier.

Aeolian pipe (Fr.: *flûte éolienne;* Ger.: *Äolspfeife, Windpfeife*), pipe sounded by the wind. It may be stationary (attached to a tree or building) or mobile: a *pigeon whistle. Such pipes are made of bamboo, wood, or shell and are found predominantly in SE. Asia, but also in the New Hebrides. See also: bulu pārinda, bulu ribut, hsiao tse, ko ling, ko tse, sundari (77).

Aeolian tube zither, idiochord *tube zither of bamboo, suspended from treetops and found in Malaya and Guiana. In Guiana there is a variety made of palm stalk, up to 3 m. (10 ft.) in length, one end of which is stuck in the ground (148).

Aeoline (Fr.: *éoline;* Ger.: *Äoline*), **1.** free-reed keyboard instr. invented by Bernhard Eschenbach of Königshofen *ca.* 1815, a precursor of the harmonium. Bellows and a swell were controlled by the player's knees, the swell permitting dynamic gradations of tone. The 6-oct. compass varied from flute tone in the treble to contrabassoon tone in the bass. The aeoline shared its slow speech with the *anémocorde, of which it may conceivably have been a development. According to the *Allgemeine Musikalische Zeitung,* Eschenbach gave details of his invention to Voit, who produced the first of a series of imitations of the aeoline under the name of *aeolodicon. In 1841 Bollermann of Dresden combined the aeoline with a piano. See also: aeolodicon, Äolsklavier, physharmonica, which are developments of the aeoline;

2. organ stop imitative of the above, with free reeds originally, and so found in Ger. organs, at 16′ or 8′ pitch. Now it is made of open flue pipes of very small scale, usually of metal, in which case it is at 8' or 4' pitch, but also of wood when it is at 16' or 8'; **3.** see: Handäoline (115, 176, 186).

Aeolodicon (Ger.: *Äolodikon*), **1.** name given to several improvements and imitations of the aeoline: a) by Voit of Schweinfurt *ca.* 1818 (Eschenbach had given him details of his invention); b) by Van Raay of Amsterdam, *ca.* 1825; c) by Friedrich Sturm of Suhl *ca.* 1830. His instr. had 2 rows of reeds, at 8' and 4' pitches, and a 6-oct. compass, F^1–f^4. Sturm claimed originality for his instr. and denied that it was merely an improved aeoline. Also called Windharmonika; **2.** organ stop, invented by Walcker, of free reeds usually at 16' pitch, occasionally at 8' pitch, imitative of the keyboard instr. of that name (133).

Aeolodion, var. of aeolodicon.

Aeolo melodicon, compact reed organ designed by Prof. Hoffmann of Warsaw, built and patented in 1824 by Fidelis Brunner, also of Warsaw, in which metal tubes were affixed to the reeds. Crescendo could be obtained by more powerful working of the bellows. See also: choraleon (176).

Aeolopantalon [*Pantaleon*], a combined aeolo-melodicon and piano, invented by Józe Dlugosz of Warsaw, who obtained a 5-year patent for it in 1824. Each instr. could be played separately, or both could be played together. Chopin performed on it in public in 1825 (89, 176).

Aéro-clavicorde (Fr.), name suggested by the *Journal de Paris* in its supplement of Jan. 30, 1790, for a keyboard instr. with strings set in motion by wind, said to have been invented by Schell (*sic*) and Schirski. This was Johann Jacob Schnell's recently invented anémocorde. In Italy it became known as aero-clavicordio (176, 204).

Aerophone, a musical instr. in which tone is generated by means of air set in vibration. Aerophones may be divided into 4 basic categories: **1.** free aero-

phones, in which the vibrating air is not contained in the body of the instr., such as ribbon reeds, certain organ reed stops, bull-roarers, the gora. In the following categories the vibrating air is contained within the instr.: **2.** flutes, where air impinges upon the sharp edge of an aperture; **3.** reedpipes, in which air is set in motion by a vibrating reed; **4.** lip-vibrated instrs.: the trumpets and horns (Von Hornborstel and Sachs in 80 XIV).

Aérophone, a small free-reed organ, actually an improved physharmonica, invented by Johann Christian Dietz, Jr., by 1830 (176, 204).

Aerophor, device that permits indefinite sustaining of tone on a wind instr., invented by Bernhard Samuels of Schwerin in 1911 and patented by him in 1912. Wind from a foot-controlled bellows is fed through a tube to the player's mouth, whence it enters the instr. quite independently of the player's breathing (89, 176).

Aetheria, see: harmonia aetherea.

Aetherophone, syn. of theremin.

Afosangu [*afo,* foot + **sangu*], sansa in Agu (Sudanic) dialect, so named from the method of playing it, *i.e.,* held between the feet while it is plucked. See also: sangu, tresangu (93).

African nail violin, European name for the sansa.

Agaita [?*ghaita*], wooden trumpet of N. Cameroun (120).

Aganga, pl. **igangat** [**ganga*], *cylindrical drum in Kambali (a Sudanic language) and Tamashek. See also: ganga (74, 93, 176).

Agau, small bell of the Mentawei (Indonesia) islanders (173).

Agbé (bottle gourd), Afro-Cuban gourd rattle, covered with a network of percussive objects. Also called aggüé, chekeré, piano de cuia (152).

Agblo, drum of the Ewe of Ghana, carved out of a tree trunk and played with sticks having knobbed heads (109).

Agbosí, Afro-Cuban *barrel drum with nailed heads, used only for liturgical purposes; 30–50 cm. (12–20 in.) long (152).

Agé, var. of agüé (7).

Ageng, see: gong ageng.

Aggüé, syn. of agbé (152).

Aghanim, woodwind instr. of the Moroccan Zummur people, with double reed inserted in a mouthpiece of beeswax (144 Chottin).

Aghāta, **aghāti**, Sans. word occurring in the Rig-Veda and believed to have been a drum or clappers (170).

Aghiz tanburasi, Turk.: Jew's-harp. An instr. apparently unknown in the Near East. The Turk. is a translation of a European term (76).

Agiosideron (Gk.: holy iron), a metal semanterion (169).

Agiosimandre [Gk. *agios*, holy + *semanterion*], obs. Fr.: semanterion (82).

Agith, idiochord bamboo *tube zither of Wetar Island, Moluccas (119).

Agógo, Afro-Cuban ritual hand bell made in various shapes, often conical, tapering to a handle. Others are multiple bells, several being strung on a vertical or horizontal handle. Some specimens have clappers; those which do not are beaten with sticks (152).

Agogó, Afro-Brazilian hand bell, tulip-shaped, of iron or tin, riveted, used in voodoo rites in Rio de Janeiro, Bahia, and Pernambuco. It lacks a clapper and is struck with a metal rod. The agogó also occurs as a double clapper bell with common handle. Also called gã, gan in Bahia, Brazil (7).

Agong, idiochord *tube zither of the Philippine Islands; it is simultaneously plucked and drummed. See also: tagong (149, 173).

Agonga [*ganga], *cylindrical drum of the Tuareg. See also: ganga (93).

Agongo (Akasele) [*ganga], *cylindrical drum of Togoland (74, 176).

Agüé, syn. of piano de cuia.

Agung, 1. gong of the Bagobo of S. Mindanao, Philippine Islands of Chin. origin, having a central boss; 2. gong of

the Hanunoo of the Philippine Islands (103, 176).

Agwāl, *goblet drum of N. Africa, of Berber origin, similar to the darabuka, with single painted head and clay body, known since med. times. Twice the size of the ta'riya (89 Farmer, 144 Chottin).

Ah tu, metal trumpet of China, played with a cup mouthpiece having almost the shape of a double reed (89 Galpin).

Ahuri'au, straight trumpet of San Cristoval, Solomon Islands, made of bamboo and half-stopped, the lower end closed by a node in which a small hole is pierced (77).

Aïda trumpet (Fr.: *trompette thébaine;* Ger.: *Aïdatrompete*), a straight, slender B or A♭ trumpet with 1–3 piston valves, made for stage purposes. A variety with single winding also exists. See also: herald's trumpet (89, 176).

Aidye or **aiǧe**, *bull-roarer of the Bororo of C. Brazil. *Cf.* adya oro (105).

'Air (Arab.), drum according to Al-Shalahi, 1301; Farmer suggests that it may rather be a misreading of *kabar (75 II).

Aiuton, or "Evertuned Organ"; *tuning fork piano invented *ca.* 1790 by Charles Claggett of London, with a series of tuning forks replacing the strings. They were pressed against a rotating horizontal metal cone. Compass 3–5 octs. (89, 176).

Ajabeba [Arab. *ash-shabbaba*], med. Sp. *end-blown flute introduced by the Moors, mentioned in the first half of the 14th c.; as *axabeba, it is recorded from 1294 on. *Cf.* shabbāba (44, 170).

Ajacaxtli, see: ayacachtli.

Aje, drum of the Marshall Islands, made from the wood of a breadfruit tree (144).

Ajjub burusi, horn of Turkey (144).

Ajoute, Fr.: crook.

Ajrās, pl. of jaras.

Ajulona, see: adjulona.

Akacence, rattle of the Kiga of Uganda, identical with the ensegu (195).

Akache (little one), drum of the Lala of N. Rhodesia (109).

Akadinda, xylophone of the Ganda of Uganda, now extremely rare. Formerly with 22 slabs, nowadays reduced to 17, set on 2 banana stems and separated from one another by small sticks (195).

Akadingidi, idiochord *stick zither of the Ganda of Uganda, with single string, used as a child's toy (195).

Akadongo k'abaluru (little instr. of the Alur), sansa of Bantu Uganda, of recent importation (195).

Akakyenkye, rattle of the Nkole of Uganda, identical with the ensegu. Also called ruganira (195).

Akalumbe, pl. **ekalumbe,** Timne: harp (176).

Akasitori, pl. **ukusitori,** mirliton of the Rundi of Urundi, a toy made of a cane segment, each end closed by a spider's-egg membrane or similar material; it is blown through a central blowhole (176).

Akata vakia, *ribbon reed of the Sakaraha region of the Malagasy Republic (171).

Akatuba k'abakuru, *trough zither of the Konjo of Uganda. Also called enanga (195).

Akawunde, syn. of eggwara, 1 (195).

Akayamba, rattle of the Toro of Uganda, identical with the ensegu (195).

Akbele [*akwa,* calabash], Ibo name of a long calabash flute. The name was later transferred to the ivory horn (93).

Akene, Twi (Sudanic) name for drum. Also called akyene (93).

Akengere, see: kengere.

Akete, Afro-Cuban drum of Matanzas Province, Cuba, played with 2 small sticks (152).

Akidi, *board zither of the Momvu of the Congo, with resonator (128).

Akikiri koto, koto made of *kiri* wood (176).

Akimbi, *board zither of the Budu of the Congo, with resonator (128).

Akkord (Ger.), accessory organ stop consisting of several tuned bells struck with hammers. Also called Glockenakkord (133).

Akkordflöte, Ger.: chord flute.

Akkordgitarre (Ger.), mid-19th-c. guitar in which the strings were not stopped by the fingers directly, but indirectly by means of 15 buttons bearing on a leather-covered roller. The guitar had 16 strings and a proportionately wide neck. *Cf.* keyed guitar (149, 176).

Akkordion, obs. Ger.: accordion (name given to the instr. invented by Cyril Demian).

Akkordklarinette, Ger.: double clarinet.

Akkordzither, Ger.: chord zither.

Akofe, var. of kofen among the Ewe of Ghana. The term occurs also in Dahomey (93).

Akonde, pl. **ekonde** (Timne), fiddle of the Susu of Sierra Leone (176).

Akora, syn. of antsiva.

Akpataré [Yoruba *okpá,* stick + *te,* adore + *ere,* image, idol], syn. of págugu (152).

Akpossi, drum of the Nago of Dahomey (103).

Akunde, *friction drum of the Bari of Uele district, Congo, identical with the maroto (132).

Akyene, var. of akene.

Ala (Lat.: wing), med. psaltery. Paulus Paulirinus, writing *ca.* 1460, says that it is either triangular (he calls this form *ala integra*) or semitriangular (*media ala*), strung with wire strings and played with a plectrum. *Cf.* canon and micanon.

Ala bohemica (Lat.: Bohemian wing), name given in modern times to a med. psaltery of C. Europe, held upright, usually in form of a long rectangle with flat circular head and variable number of strings.

Alābu-sārangī (gourd *sārangī*), sārangī similar to the European violin. It has a gourd body with thin wooden belly, pinched waist, F holes, neck with a scroll, and with a violin-like bridge and tailpiece. The scroll, F holes, and fittings show definite European influence. The 4 strings are tuned in 5ths: $B\flat^0 f^0 c^1 g^1$. It also has 7 or 9 sympathetic strings tuned $g^1 a^1 b^1 c^2 d^2 e^2 f^2$. *Ca.* 52 cm. (20½ in.) long.

Alagbagovu, drum of the Ewe of Ghana, made of giant acorns. Single-headed, they are used as practice instrs. (109).

Ala integra, see: ala.

A-lal (Sum.), drum of ancient Sumer, first mentioned *ca.* 2200 B.C., equivalent of the Akk. alū, and until recently identified as a cymbal (170).

Alambre, Sp.: bell worn by draft animals.

Alamiré, Port.: tuning fork. Also called lamiré.

Alamoru, 1. *end-blown flute of the Karamojong of Uganda, with 2 finger-holes near the lower end, which is cut off obliquely; **2.** similar instr. of the Acholi of Uganda, made of bamboo, with 4 fingerholes; **3.** short flute of the Teso of Uganda, *ca.* 50 cm. (20 in.) long, and a larger one *ca.* 117 cm. (46 in.) long, held obliquely, with 4 fingerholes. A gourd attached to the lower end forms a bell (195).

Alapini vīnā, vīnā of Bengal, with calabash body, played with a plectrum. *Alapini* is the name of a microtone of the *sruti* scale; *alapa* means adagio. The vīnā is used for playing adagio pieces, but *alapini* seems the more likely etym. (173).

Alapu vīnā, syn. of sur vāhara.

Alaude [Arab. *al-ud*], Port.: lute.

Alaunut, friction *idiophone of Lamekot, New Ireland. For details see: nunut (77).

Albion, bichord upright piano with downstriking action, patented by Robert Wornum of London on Feb. 15, 1842 (176).

Albisifono, metal *bass flute invented in 1910 by Abelardo Albisi of Milan, pitched in C, an oct. lower than the ordinary flute, with a B foot. In order to bring the widely spaced fingerholes within reach, the flute is built with a vertical body and an embouchure set in a short horizontal tube, somewhat like the letter T. The keys are worked by exten-sion rods. Over-all length is reduced by means of a winding in the upper end of the tube. Its original cylindrical bore of 39 mm. required too much breath and was subsequently reduced. The Boehm system of fingering is employed. *Ca.* 2½-oct. compass (89, 170, 176).

Albogón (aug. of *albogue*), OSp.: shawm. The word occurs from the 13th c. on, but had changed to albogue by Lope de Vega's day (d. 1635) (44).

Albogue [Arab. *al-*būq*], **1.** obs. shawm of Spain, called albogón up to the time of Lope de Vega (d. 1635), albogue thereafter. The word survives in the Basque country as *alboka (a hornpipe); **2.** in the 16th and 17th c. a metal cymbal. In his *Don Quijote,* Cervantes identifies albogues as clappers (44, 176).

Alboka [Arab. *al-*būq*], double horn-pipe of the Basque country, consisting of 2 parallel, cylindrical cane pipes *ca.* 14 cm. (5½ in.) long, tied together and cradled in a wooden gutter, with idioglott beating reeds protected by a horn mouth bell. The lower end terminates in a common cow-horn bell. The left pipe has 5 fingerholes, the right pipe 3. As the player inhales while playing, the sound is continuous. Also called zinburruna (13; *Anuario musical,* 1956).

Alboquea, var. of alboka.

Al-būq, see: būq.

Aldaba, Sp.: clappers (56).

Alduf, Cat. equivalent of adufe.

Alexandre organ (Fr.: *orgue Alexandre*), an improved *American organ built by Jacob Alexandre and his son in Paris in 1874, with wider and stronger reeds than the ordinary American organ and 2 interconnected wind channels above them. It was popularly known as the *orgue à cent francs*—the hundred-franc organ (176, 204).

Alfandoque, *vessel rattle of Esmeraldas Province, Ecuador, made of a bamboo internode closed at both ends, with small rattling objects introduced through a longitudinal slit. It is held in both hands and shaken (152).

Algaita, pl. **algaitu** (Hausa) [Arab. **ghaita*], shawm of the Hausa and Tuareg, made of wood with conical bore and 5 or 6 front fingerholes and played with a metal, wooden, or gourd *pirouette. It corresponds to the N. African ghaita and was formerly called by this name. *Ca.* 45 cm. (17½ in.) long (176).

Algaitaru [Arab. **ghaita*], Ful (Sudanic) name of the Arab. ghaita (93).

Al-gar (Sum.: music maker), lyre of Babylon that first appeared in the third millennium B.C. and is probably of Semitic origin (89 Galpin, 147 Farmer).

Algeta [Arab. **ghaita*], Nupe (Sudanic) name of the Arab. ghaita (93).

Algoja, Hindust. equivalent of algōsa.

Algōsa (Arab.), beaked *whistle flute of India, made of wood or bamboo, with 5–8 fingerholes, occasionally a rear thumbhole, of very soft tone; 27–42 cm. (10½–17 in.) long (176).

Alguoji, Kan. equivalent of algōsa.

Aligeta [Arab. **ghaita*], name of the ghaita in Hausa colonies of N. Togo (93).

Alindi, drum of the Bakumu of the Congo, with a goatskin head, played with bare hands during dances. Also called lukumbi (30).

Aliquodium, sound chamber for the Elegiezither, consisting of 3 soundboards and 24 sympathetic strings, tuned chromatically. Built *ca.* 1873 by Heidegger of Passau (176).

Aliquot piano (Ger.: *Aliquotflügel*), name given by Blüthner of Leipzig to their pianos with sympathetic strings (one per note) strung above the ordinary strings. These are tuned an octave higher, except in the treble, where they are at unison pitch with the main strings. This device has been used by several other makers of the late 19th c. and of the 20th c.

Aliquot-Streichflöte (Ger.: aliquot bowed flute), improved *nail violin, patented 1888 by P. J. Brambach of Marburg, with bent iron nails raised by the motion of keys to an aperture in the lid, where they were bowed with a violin bow.

The instr. was named for its flute-like tone. Compass c^1–a^3 (176).

Aliquot stringing, term applied to pianos in which: **1.** a double length of string is passed around a hitch pin and the ends are fastened to tuning pins (early pianos were strung like harpsichords, with each length of string looped separately over a hitch pin); **2.** the "dead" end of each string in the center and treble range is of a length calculated to sound a harmonic of the string's speaking length.

Allgäuisches Waldhorn (Ger.: horn of the Allgau), Austrian term for an alphorn in trumpet form; also for a 16th-c. alphorn with helical coils and a tube *ca.* 3 m. (10 ft.) long (117).

Allonge, Fr.: crook.

Allun, the bandair of the N. African Berbers (89 Farmer).

Almadurie (Fr.), mentioned 1379 in *Jean de Brie* and assumed to be a corr. of *mandore (53).

Almain whistle [Fr.: *allemand*, German], 17th-c. expression for the cross flute (169).

Almérie (Fr.), a variety of lute invented by Jean Lemaire (d. *ca.* 1650), *Almérie* being an anagram of his name (127).

Almonie, var. of armonie.

Al nafīr (pron. annafir), see: nafīr.

Al naqqāra, see: naqqāra.

Alonge, obs. spelling of allonge.

Alpa, obs. var. of arpa.

Alpbüchel [*Bürke,* birch], a name of the alphorn in C. and E. Switzerland. *Cf.* Bürkel.

Alpenhorn (Ger.), syn. of alphorn.

Alphorn (Fr.: *cor des Alpes;* Ger.: *Alphorn;* It.: *corno delli Alpi*), **1.** shepherds' trumpet of considerable age, found in the Alps, Carpathians, Lithuania, Pyrenees, and Scandinavia; always made of wood but assuming different shapes. The oldest form is straight, with a slight flare at the lower end; it is also made in straight form with upturned bell, as well as S-shaped or in form of a natural trumpet; the bore is always conical. The instr. is *ca.* 1½–4 m. (5–13 ft.) long. Nowadays a turned wooden mouthpiece or a trumpet mouthpiece is inserted into Alpine instrs., but up to the mid-19th c. the mouthpiece was turned in the instr. proper. The Swiss alphorn yields from the second to the eighth harmonic or more, the fourth harmonic being characteristically too high ("alphorn fa"). According to a 1689 description of alphorn making, it was fashioned from a log split lengthwise into 2 sections; the bore was then marked and hollowed out, then the sections were glued together with pitch and wound with cherry bark. In the 19th c. methods changed: the bore was burned out of a single log (a young fir being preferred) and bound with bark or fir roots or even cane. The bell was made separately and fitted on, and the whole instr. measured *ca.* 3 m. (10 ft.), except in the Bavarian Alps, where it was shorter and had a wider bore. The alphorn was known to the Romans: Tacitus called it *cornu alpinus. According to Swiss tradition, it was used as a signal instr. in certain villages in the 14th c. Its length in the 16th c. is given as 11 ft., at which time it is also depicted as a straight instr. held vertically. The familiar upturned-bell form is typical of Swiss alphorns and developed in the 18th c. In Austria the older, straight form was able to maintain itself until the 19th c. The idea of making such instrs. in different sizes, tuned for performing part music, seems to have originated with Ferdinand Huber of Switzerland, who had 3 alphorns tuned for ensemble playing in 1826. Two- and three-part playing was also practiced in Styria in the 19th c. Because of its great carrying power the alphorn has traditionally been a signal instr.; in the 19th c. it was still played in Catholic Alpine districts as a signal for evening prayer. Today it is chiefly a tourist and music-hall attraction, for both solo and ensemble music. See also: allgäuisches Waldhorn, Alpbüchel, Büchel, bucium, Bürkel, cornu alpinus, fakurst,

Flatsche, ligawka, liti, lituus alpinus, lur, 2, Stockbüchel, Stockhorn, trembita, trîmbiţă, truba, tulnic, Waldhorn, Waldtuter, Wurzhorn;

2. organ stop of reed pipes with very wide resonators, closed completely; or of conical flue pipes, in which case it is a syn. of the gemshorn stop (117, 133, 187).

Alpicordo, var. of arpicordo.

Al shaqira (Arab.), according to Farmer, a musical instr. mentioned by Al-Shaqandi, an Arab. writer of the 13th c. Other Arabists deny its existence as a musical instr. (75 I, 170).

Alt, Du.: viola.

Alt . . . , Ger.: alto . . .

Al tambor, see: tambor.

Alta-viola, see: alto-viola.

Altgeige (Ger.), **1.** obs. expression for the viola, now called Bratsche; **2.** a name of the viola alta.

Althorn (Fr.: *alto en mi♭, bugle alto;* Engl.: *tenor horn;* Ger.: *Althorn;* It.: *flicorno contralto, genis*), valved brass instr. of the cornet family, of alto range, invented in Austria *ca.* 1830 and, according to Eichborn, descended from the valved trumpet. Now built in F and E♭, formerly also in D. Its conical bore is narrower than that of the flugelhorn and terminates in a medium-sized bell. The tube may be coiled in trumpet, tuba, or helicon form and is fitted with 3 valves. The althorn in helicon shape is known in the U.S. as mellophone, mellohorn, ballad horn, or concert horn (the last a misnomer to be avoided); it is also called alto horn, sometimes abbr. to alto. Compasses B♭⁰/A⁰–f²/e♭², both notated f♯⁰–c³.

The Bavarian althorn in low C or B♭ is in reality a tenor horn; the E♭ althorn is also known in Germany as Alttuba; in England the same instr. is called tenor horn in E♭. In the U.S. the E♭ alto saxhorn is also called althorn. In England the (instr. called) althorn is the same as the (Engl.) baritone. See also: baryton aigu.

Althorn-Obligat (Ger.), althorn in E♭, F, C, or D, either in helicon shape or with parallel tubes, invented by Vaclav F. Červeny of Königgrätz (Hradec Králové) in 1859, intended for solo work, as its name implies. Compass e^0–g^2 (176).

Alto, 1. modern Fr., It., Port.: viola; **2.** a U.S. name of the althorn.

Altobasso (It.: high-low), obs. N. It. equivalent of the tambourin à cordes, folk zither with rectangular body strung with a few strings tuned to tonic and dominant. Giuseppi Zarlino (*Sopplimenti*, 1588) informs us that these were of gut and that altobasso is a Venetian name. The strings were struck with a little stick. Often the player would suspend it from one arm, thus having one hand free to strike the strings, the other to hold a small flute. Praetorius is in error in identifying it with the *instromento di porco*. See also: chorus.

Alto clarinet (Fr.: *clarinette alto;* Ger.: *Altklarinette;* It.: *clarinetto contralto*). A clarinet that in the late 18th c. was pitched in G, later in F or E♭, a 5th or 6th below the ordinary clarinet. It never gained a foothold in the orchestra, but became a military band instr. In appearance it resembles the *basset horn, with which it is often confused. Older specimens were often made entirely of wood. The bell of modern instrs. usually points up, whereas on older ones it pointed down. The alto clarinet is notated a 5th or 6th higher than it sounds. *Ca.* 75–90 cm. (30–36 in.) long. The alto clarinet in F is called tenor clarinet in England; that in E♭ is called alto in England. See also: mélodore (89 Rendall, 169).

Alto en mi♭, Fr.: althorn (tenor horn in England).

Alto fagotto, a Scot. bandmaster, William Meikle of Strathaven, Lanarkshire, invented *ca.* 1830 a wind instr. in bassoon shape with conical bore, played with a single reed, which he called Caledonica. An improved version was subsequently made by George Wood of London, and because of its shape and pitch was called alto fagotto. Meikle's original model is

preserved at the University of Edinburgh. The alto fagotto has bore, shape, and key work similar to those of the bassoon and was made in several sizes. The only surviving specimen, in the Museum of Fine Arts, Boston, is in C, an oct. above the ordinary bassoon (89 Langwill).

Alto flute (Fr.: *flûte contralto;* Ger.: *Altflöte*), orchestral flute pitched in G, a 4th below the ordinary, or concert, flute, and known in England as the *bass flute. Agricola is the earliest author to have mentioned (in 1528) an alto cross flute. In the 16th and early 17th c. its compass was d^1–d^3; it now is g^0–g^3. The alto flute is treated as a transposing instr. *Ca.* 86 cm. (34 in.) long (14, 170).

Alto horn, see: althorn.

Alto-moderne (Fr.), a large viola held like a violoncello, introduced by R. Farramon of Barcelona in the 1930's. Also called viole-ténor (Scholes: *Oxford Companion to Music,* 1955).

Alto-piano (Fr.), viola to which a mélotétraphone is adapted.

Alto-ténor (Fr.), **1.** large viola of fanciful shape, made by Charles Henri (Carolus Henry) of Paris in 1854, with the bass side of the body larger than the treble side; **2.** a very squat, almost square viola made by Jean-Baptiste Vuillaume in 1845 (Catalogue of the Paris 1900 Exposition).

Alto trumpet, a name given in the first half of the 19th c. to trumpets in E♭ or lower pitches, and also occasionally to those in high B♭ or A♭ because they were known as "tromba in B alto." Not identical with the tromba contralta in fa (176).

Alto tuba, 1. a false designation of the B♭ *Wagner tuba; **2.** in Germany the E♭ althorn is also called alto tuba (Alttuba) (25).

Alto-viola, alto-viole, obs. Fr. terms for viola.

Alto violin, 1. the viola; **2.** see: violonalto.

Alto violoncello, see: violoncello alto.

Altówka (Pol.), viola.

Al tubel, syn. of gangatan.

Alt-Violine, obs. Ger. term for viola.

Altviool, Du.: viola.

Alu, Akk. equivalent of a-lal (170).

Al-'ud or **el-'ud,** see: 'ud.

Aluminophone, metallophone with aluminum bars, formerly used during recording sessions as a substitute for the xylophone because the latter had too much echo (176).

Alumnaxkáki, panpipes of the Simacu Indians of Peru, with 10–12 pipes (104).

Alungu, *board zither of the Butuku plains of Lake Albert region, Africa (195).

Aluut, side-blown horn of the Karamojong of Uganda, made of animal horn and used by herdboys to frighten off hyenas (195).

Al yarā, see: yarā.

Amadinda (the keys), present-day name of the entaala of the Ganda of Uganda. Also called madinda (195).

Amafohlwane, ankle rattle of the S. African Zulu: **1.** several small basketry boxes woven of palm leaf and containing pebbles are attached to a fiber cord and tied around dancers' ankles; **2.** a number of moth cocoons containing small stones are bunched together on plaited fiber and tied to dancers' legs. This latter type is also called umfece (116).

Amagala, *percussion sticks of Amba and Madi, Uganda. In Amba they consist of 7 or more pieces of wood 70–140 cm. (28–56 in.) long. The sticks are used at circumcision rites, when an initiate holds one stick under the arm and beats it with a drumstick, and are kept for only a short time after the ceremony (195).

Amagemfe, pl. of igemfe.

Amagwara, Ganda word now used for European brass instrs. (195).

Amahahlazo, dancers' rattles of the S. African Pondo, made of small basketry boxes woven from palm leaf and containing pebbles. They are threaded on cords and tied to the dancers' ankles (116).

Amalé, name given to the ganzá, **1,** in Bahia, Brazil (7).

Amang, idiochord bamboo *tube zither of the Semang of the Malay Peninsula (119).

Aman-khuur, syn. of temür-khuur.

Amanqashele, ankle rattles of the S. African Xhosa, made of goatskin (116).

Amata, pottery kettledrum of the Yavapai Indians of Arizona, U.S., with buckskin head. The drum is partly filled with water and is beaten with a stick (105).

Amatambo, clappers of the S. African Zulu, made of cattle rib bones, similar to the European "bones" and quite possibly an imitation of them (116).

Amateur voice horn, see: ballad horn.

Amban, *hourglass drum of Siassi Island, Bismarck Archipelago, similar to the *oñ (28).

Ambilta, gigantic bamboo flutes of Gamo and Konso provinces, Ethiopia, end-blown, without fingerholes, held obliquely and played in sets of 5 or so. Each flute yields only one tone but can overblow the octave. Flutes comprising a set are tuned to the tones required for melodic purposes (A. E. Jensen: *Im Lande des Gada,* 1936).

Ambira, 1. sansa of Mozambique; **2.** 9-pronged African sansa mentioned by João dos Santos in 1586; **3.** Dos Santos' name for a xylophone of the Karanga of Ethiopia, with gourd resonators and spider's-egg membrane. He reported that the treble keys were on the left and were struck with beaters having knobs made of balls of sinew. Today the beaters have rubber heads and the instr. is known as mbila, a var. of ambira (116).

Ambnuba [*ambaúwa,* tree], bamboo *stamping tube of the Indians of São Gabriel, Brazil; the upper end is open. Sometimes the tube is struck with a palm-leaf beater (130).

Amboss, Ger.: anvil.

Âme, Fr.: soundpost.

Amejoni, *slit drum of the Agomé of Togoland (42).

Amelé, syn. of piano de cuia (7).

Ame no nori koto (Jap.: heavenly oracle koto), syn. of wagon.

American banjo, name formerly given in England to the 5-stringed banjo (89).

American organ (Fr.: *orgue américain;* Ger.: *amerikanische Orgel*), free-reed keyboard instr. working on suction wind, *i.e.,* wind drawn inward through the reeds by means of suction bellows. This feature distinguishes it from the harmonium, which works on pressure wind. Otherwise the 2 are identical. The principle of suction bellows is said to have been invented by a workman employed by Jacob Alexandre of Paris. The workman immigrated to the U.S., where harmoniums with suction wind were constructed from 1856 on by Estey of Brattleboro, Vt., and from 1861 by Mason and Hamlin of Boston. Since then practically all American-built reed organs have been constructed on the vacuum principle. The earliest ones were known as melodeon or melodium. These were followed by the *Alexandre organ and many others. American organ reeds are smaller than harmonium reeds and more highly curved, thus yielding a softer tone. The number of manuals, presence or absence of a coupler, number and type of stops vary from maker to maker. Swell and tremolo, even pedals, were adapted to the instr. in the course of time. At an early date it was even made to work automatically. *Cf.* cartonium. See also: Alexandre organ, aspirophone, cartonium, melodeon, melodium, Saugluftharmonium, seraphine (89, 151, 170, 176).

Amg'ad, see: amz'ad.

Amma-no-fuye (Jap.: double flute), *double flute of Japan, made of 2 bamboo tubes glued together lengthwise; used by blind masseurs to announce their presence; 14–20 cm. (5½–8 in.) long (176).

Amokoderi, side-blown antelope horn of the Bahaya of Tanganyika, played in sets of 5 or more. Single horns are also used for hunting and are then called olukula (108).

Amor, 2-headed drum of the Alur of E. Africa, with cowhide heads, a symbol of royalty (30).

Amorosa (Lat.), a name occasionally given in the 18th and 19th c. to such organ stops as the flauto amabile, Dolzflöte, flûte allemande. The expression *vox amorosa* was also used (12, 131, 133).

Amorschall (Ger.) (Fr.: *taille d'amour*), the earliest recorded keyed horn, an invention of the Russian court horn player Kölbel, a much-traveled Bohemian who returned to St. Petersburg by 1754 and then spent 10 years perfecting his instr., according to Ernst Ludwig Gerber. The keys, probably 2 in number, were located close to the bell, which was hemispheric, of *amore* form. The bell was provided with a lid (another hemisphere pierced with numerous small holes) that lowered the pitch when closed, probably by a semitone. This attempt at creating a more flexible instr. was short-lived, as the *Inventionshorn had already been created and was to come into general use. The Amorschall is identical with the taille d'amour, for which Johann Christian Bach wrote parts (*i.a., Temistocle,* first performed in 1772). The *Avant-Coureur* of June 24, 1771, wrote of the taille d'amour as follows: *"C'est une espece de cor-de-chasse mais avec des touches pratiquées dans le tuyau, qui se replie en quarté. Au moyen de ces touches on en tire des sons différemment modulés, comme dans les clarinettes; cet instrument est très flatteur, il participe . . . du cor-de-chasse ordinaire, du cor Anglais, et du Hautbois"* (83, 169, 204).

Amphicord, syn. of lyra barberina (Note: confused with *accordo in the Encyclopédie méthodique*) (124).

Ampicordo, misreading of arpicordo.

Ampondokaka, horn of the Malagasy Republic (171).

Amponga, 1. generic Malagasy term for drum; **2.** specifically a 2-headed *cylindrical drum; **3.** a Malagasy *ground zither (171).

Ampongabē, drum of the Malagasy Republic, similar to the langoro, and imitative of the European bass drum (176).

Amponga fantrotrarana (couch-grass drum), *ground zither of the Malagasy Republic, played by children (128).

Ampongakely, side drum of the Malagasy Republic (176).

Ampongalava, elongated kettledrum of the Sakalava of the Malagasy Republic. It is let down into a clay pot that serves as resonator (176).

Amponga-tany, *ground zither of the Malagasy Republic (128).

Ampongavilany, kettledrum of the Malagasy Republic, with clay body and laced oxhide head, played with bare hands (176).

Amrita, *spike fiddle of India of the rebab type, said to be of great antiquity. It corresponds to the t'i ch'in of China, sō-i of Laos, sō luang of Thailand, cai ñi of Vietnam (47, 176).

Amz'ad, *spike fiddle of the N. African Tuareg, with a large gourd body covered with goatskin, which is laced around the bottom, and a slim handle that pierces the body to emerge as a projecting stub. A single horsehair string passes over a bridge to a notch in the end of the handle; farther down it is looped to the handle to form a nut. The belly is often painted. Two soundholes are cut in it. The amz'ad can be either bowed or plucked. In at least one area of the Sahara it is played by women only. *Cf.* ribab (176, 193).

Ana-batching (Mac.), *percussion sticks of the Celebes, made of iron with flat square ends. Their function is to drive devils away (112).

Anacaire (Fr.) [Arab. *al *naqqāra*], syn. of nacaire. The term was used from 1214 to the 17th c.

Anacaria, Lat.: kettledrum (176).

Anafil, Cat., Port.: equivalent of añafil.

Añafil [Arab. *al *nafīr*], OSp. name of the Arab. nafīr, a straight, cylindrical trumpet with bell, documented from the mid-13th c. on, also became known as trompeta morisca. An OProv. glossary defined it as *"parva tuba cum voce alta."* Its high pitch seems to be confirmed by Nicot, who, writing in 1606, says that the

"clairon" (*i.e.,* clarin), still played by the Moors, served as treble to trumpets sounding tenor and bass (see text under clairon). The añafil corresponds to the cor sarrazinois, danafil, nafil, nafīr, senafil (35, 170).

Anafim, Cat., Port.: var. of anafil.

Anaka [Arab. *naqqāra*], kettledrum of Bengal, with body of clay (176).

Anakidory, a small dory some 20–25 cm. (8–10 in.) in diam., always played in pairs (171).

Ānanda laharī (Beng.: lightning of delight), plucked chordophone of Bengal, consisting of a wooden bucket open at the top and closed at the bottom by a membrane. A gut string fastened to the center of the membrane passes through the bucket, its far end being tied to a miniature replica of the bucket or to a wooden knob furnished with a membrane. The bucket is wedged under the player's left arm; the small recipient in his left hand holds the string taut while it is being plucked with a plectrum held in the right hand. Today it is an instr. of mendicant monks who use it for vocal accompaniment. The pitch varies according to the voice it accompanies. *Cf.* plucked drum (132, 173).

Ananta vijaya (Sans.: immense victory), *marine-shell trumpet of India (176).

Anata, *whistle flute of Bolivia and Argentina, with 6 fingerholes, narrow bore, and thick walls (192).

Anche, Fr.: reed.

Anche à ruban, Fr.: ribbon reed.

Anche battante, Fr.: beating reed.

Anche double, Fr.: double reed.

Anche libre, Fr.: free reed.

Anche simple, Fr.: single reed.

Ancia, It.: reed.

Ancia battante, It.: beating reed.

Ancia doppia, It.: double reed.

Ancia libera, It.: free reed.

Ancia semplice, It.: single reed.

Andobu, *musical bow of the Bakongo Pygmies of the Congo, with a tuning loop (128).

Android [Gk.: *androeides*, of man's form], name given to musical automata in human form which play real instrs. The outstanding makers of androids were Jacques de Vaucanson (1709–82); the Jacquet-Droz family (18th c.), whose instrs. are still played in Neuchâtel, Switzerland; and Cornelius van Oeckelen of Breda (1798–1865). In 1958, 3 electronically actuated androids were built by the Fr. engineer Didier Jouas-Poutrel; they play the saxophone, piano-accordion, and percussion (37, 144, 176).

Andulón, horn of the Carajá Indians of Brazil, made of animal horn (176).

Anémocorde [Gk. *anemos*, wind + *chorde*, string], stringed keyboard instr. invented by Johann Jacob Schnell of Paris in 1789, actually an *aeolian harp controlled from a keyboard. When the corresponding key was depressed, the trichord strings were set in vibration by wind conducted through tubes leading from the bellows. Dynamic variations were made possible by registers, but the tone remained soft and required a slow tempo. In 1803 the instr. was purchased by the Brit. physicist Robertson. Compass 5 octs. *Cf.* aéro-clavicorde (27, 169).

Anemometer [Gk. *anemos*, wind], syn. of wind gauge.

Anfur, pl. of nafīr.

Angang-angang, see: gong angang-angang.

Angangvena, female *cross flute of Finschhafen, New Guinea, made of cane (176).

Angelica (Fr.: *angélique*), *archlute of the 17th and 18th c., with a long neck, 16 or 17 strings, and 2 pegboxes. The strings were of gut, tuned diatonically. Samuel Pepys mentioned the angelica in 1660, and Johann Mattheson (*Orchester*, 1713) said that it was easier to play than a lute, having more courses. The angelica was favored by amateurs because it required no tablature. For the organ stop see: vox angelica (80 Lesure, 169).

Angelic organ, set of *musical glasses played with sticks, invented by Richard

Pockrich in 1741. He became a virtuoso player, but after successful concert tours both inventor and instr. perished in a fire in 1759 (113, 176).

Angélophone, 1. an instr. of this name of unknown construction was patented by Leferme in France on Feb. 28, 1859; **2.** a folding harmonium patented by H. Christophe and Étienne in France on July 29, 1891 (204).

Angenehm . . . (Ger.), the same as Lieblich . . .

Ang en tsuma, *nose flute of Ponape, Micronesia (203).

Angklung, 1. tubular chime of E. Java, with 12–14 bamboo tubes, cut back longitudinally at the top so as to leave a tongue, and closed at the lower end by a node. The tubes, graduated according to size, are tied to a wooden frame, and the frame is set up in a slanting position against a wall and is played with 2 small hammers; **2.** *sliding rattle of W. Java (formerly of all Java), consisting of 2 or 3 bamboo tubes cut back to form a tongue at one end and closed by a node at the other; these are suspended vertically, while retaining their mobility, in a bamboo frame that is shaken to and fro. The tubes are tuned in octaves. A number of angklungs, 9–14, all of different sizes, form a set with a pentatonic tone sequence. Also called kechruk. *Cf.* grantang (121).

Angong, iron dog-bell of the Fan, Yaunde, and other peoples of the Congo and S. Cameroun (176).

Angremut, *slit drum of Oceania; see: garamut (77).

Angūahuasi [*angua*, water], larger variety of angūarai (105).

Angūarai, large kettledrum of the Chiriguano Indians of Brazil, made of a mortar and partly filled with water before it is played (105).

Angular harp (Fr.: *harpe angulaire;* Ger.: *Winkelharfe*), harp in which neck and resonator form a right angle or an acute angle. Angular harps are believed to be younger than *arched harps.

Angun (cane), cane *nose flute of Truk, Micronesia. The same word is used for a mouth-blown flute (203).

Anim, *nose flute of Truk, Micronesia. Some specimens have no fingerholes, others have 3. The nose-blown flutes of Truk are larger than the mouth-blown ones and are made of mangrove root or bamboo (203).

Anima (It.: soul), It.: **1.** soundpost; **2.** block (of flue pipes).

Animochord, var. of anémocorde.

Anjomara [Swah. *zomari,* from Arab. *zamr*], shawm of the Malagasy Republic (171).

Anjomary varahina, trumpet of the Malagasy Republic (171).

Anjombo, horn of the Malagasy Republic (171).

Anjombona, *marine-shell trumpet, side-blown, of the Merina of the Malagasy Republic (171).

Ankárana, syn. of antsiva.

Anklung, see: angklung.

Ankóra, syn. of antsiva.

Annexe-piano, piano attachment devised by the Alexandres (reed-organ builders) of Paris in the second half of the 19th c., consisting of a 3-oct. keyboard and 3 registers of reeds: flute, oboe, voix céleste. It could be fitted under the keyboard of an ordinary piano (204).

Anoin, bamboo Jew's-harp of the Orang Seman of Malaya (173).

Anqa, obs. long-necked Arab. lute first mentioned by Avicenna in the 11th c. (89 Farmer).

Antanatra, slit drum of the SW. Malagasy Republic (171).

Antara (Quechua), panpipes of the S. Amer. Andes, made of cane or clay, often in the form of double panpipes. See also: atala, ayarichi, sico (80 XII).

Anthropoglossa, syn. of vox humana (organ stop).

Antilopenhorn (Ger.), bugle in C, made of antelope horn, with a cornet mouthpiece, suggested by Hermann Schulz, a Berlin musician, and made by the firm of C. W. Moritz of Berlin in 1896. Said to have had superior carrying power, the instr. was adopted by a Prussian military band; 1 m. (40 in.) long (176).

Antiphonel, automatic player attachment for harmoniums and organs, invented by Alexandre Debain of Paris in 1846, intended for use in small provincial churches. Instead of pinning the music on cylinders, Debain pinned it on an oblong board called *planchette* by means of iron pegs. When the device was set in motion by a hand crank, the pegs engaged a series of jacks that acted on the keys. The device was in form of a large rectangular box and had a 5-oct. compass. In 1852, Martin de Corteuil patented a perforated cardboard strip to replace the *planchette,* thereby considerably simplifying it. See also: musique perforée, piano mécanique (37, 176, 204).

Antoniophone [inventor's name], brass bombardon invented by Antoine Courtois of Paris in the mid-19th c., with close coils, 3 valves placed in the center of the coils, and a detachable bell (176).

Antsiva, *marine-shell trumpet with lateral blowhole, of the Merina, Betsileo, and Sakalava of the Malagasy Republic. In the Belo district this name is also applied to the antsivambazaha. Also called: akora, ankárana, ankóra (171).

Antsiva láhy, antsiva váry, male and female antsivas of the Antandroy of the Malagasy Republic (171).

Antsivambazaha (white man's trumpet), a long, slender trumpet of the Androy area of the Malagasy Republic, made of bamboo, cane, or papaya wood, with a bell of cattle horn. The instr. was introduced after the arrival of the French. In the Belo district it is called simply antsiva (171).

Antsódina, syn. of sódina.

Anukué, Afro-Cuban double *vessel rattle of metal, now rare. Each rattle is made of 2 cones joined at their widest part and contains seeds or pellets (152).

Anuman, wooden whistle of the Baoule of the Ivory Coast Republic (103).

Anvil (Fr.: *enclume;* Ger.: *Amboss;* It.: *incudine*), percussion instr. of indefinite pitch, mentioned by Virdung in 1511 and still in occasional use. Although a true anvil is sometimes provided, 1 or 2 metal bars now more often act as replacements (89, 194).

Anzang, xylophone of the Bakela and Fan of Gabon Republic, without resonators (42).

Anzel, small iron bell of the W. African Fan (176).

Anzolo, bracelet or anklet rattles worn by Azande dancers in the Congo, made of sheet-iron *pellet bells of an average size of 7½ cm. (3 in.) (132).

Äoline, see: aeoline.

Äolo . . . , see: aeolo . . .

Äolsflöte, Ger.: aeolian pipe.

Äolsglocken, Ger.: aeolian bells.

Äolsharfe, Ger.: aeolian harp.

Äolsharmonika, Ger.: aeol-harmonica.

Äolsklavier (Ger.), keyboard instr. invented by Schortmann of Buttelstedt, Germany, *ca.* 1822, in which tone was generated by the action of wind upon small, upright wooden bars, the wind being supplied by bellows controlled by a pedal. The tone was extremely soft. The Äolsklavier is one of the numerous improvements or imitations of the aeoline (176, 204).

Äolspfeife, Ger.: aeolian pipe.

Ao yü, a broad variety of mu yü, used chiefly by Taoists (the ao is a sea monster) (142).

Apaché, var. of arpa-ché.

Apänkal, pl. **epankal,** harp of the Timne of Sierra Leone (176).

Apeau, var. of appeau.

Apfelregal (Ger.: apple regal), *regal organ stop at 8′ pitch, occasionally at 4′, the thin pipes of which were surmounted by apple-shaped (*i.e.,* globular) resonators pierced with holes. According to Praetorius, the whole pipe was some 4 Brunswick inches high. Also called Knopf-regal, Kugelregal (133, 159).

Apiau, 14th-c. var. of appeau.

Aping, bamboo Jew's-harp of the Ka-

yan of Borneo, pointed at one end. *Ca.* 35 cm. (14 in.) long (176).

Apito, Port. *whistle flute, equivalent of the pito. *Cf.* pitu, 2.

Apollina [Apollo], guitar-like instr. in form of a kithara, built by Wilhelm Ferdinand Rong of Berlin and shown there in 1802. Its builder intended it to be a woman's instr. (176).

Apolliricon [Apollo + *lyra*], *lyra piano built by Franz Weiss, who took out an Austrian patent for it in March 1826. Also called Apollonium (92, 149).

Apollo guitar, syn. of the lyre-guitar.

Apollo lyre (Fr.: *lyre d'Apollon;* Ger.: *Apollolyra*), **1.** free-reed wind instr. invented by Ernst Leopold Schmidt of Heiligenstadt in Eichsfeld in 1832, in shape of a kithara. The flat wooden body had a brass blowpipe fitted to the top, and 44 free reeds controlled by keys. A contemporary source identifies it as an improved Psallmelodikon. It had 16 keys, 4 tone holes, and a 4-oct. compass, F^0–f^3, and was small enough to be set on a table. It could imitate the sound of the violin, clarinet, oboe, horn, and bassoon; **2.** a name by which the lyre-guitar was known in England (178, 184).

Apollon, lute-like instr. invented by Prompt of Paris in 1677, with 20 strings for playing accompaniments in all tonalities (176).

Apollonicon, a large orchestrion built by Flight & Robson of London between 1812 and 1817 at a cost of £10,000 and first exhibited in June 1817. It was 7.2 m. (24 ft.) high, 6 m. (20 ft.) wide, and 6 m. (20 ft.) deep, had about 1900 pipes disposed in 46 registers, a compass G^2–a^3, and 5 keyboards, playable either manually or automatically. The keyboards were detached from the main body of the instr. to permit manual playing by 5 performers, all facing the public. Four of the manuals had each a 2-oct. compass; the fifth (in the center) had a 5-oct. compass, and its player also disposed of a 2-oct. pedalboard. Automatic playing was accomplished by means of 3 barrels, each 2.40 m. (8 ft.) long, pinned spirally so as to permit the playing of longer pieces. Although it attracted a great deal of attention, the Apollonicon was not a financial success, and its makers demolished it *ca.* 1840 (89, 176).

Apollonion, 2-manual *giraffe piano, with organ attachment and automaton in form of a boy playing a flute, built by Johann Heinrich Völler of Angersbach in 1800. The instr. was about 3.30 m. (11 ft.) high and had a compass of over 5 octs., F^1–a^3. The organ part consisted of flue pipe stops at 8′, 4′, and 2′ pitches. The Apollonion could be played manually or automatically, but it was not successful and its maker soon destroyed it (92, 176).

Apollonium, syn. of the Apolliricon.

Apolo, clapperless iron bell of the Nzakara of the Union of Central African Republics, consisting of 2 bells united by a U-shaped handle and played with a knobbed stick (42).

Aporo, 1. double bell of the Azande of the Congo. The bells are of equal length but of unequal diam., connected by a handle in form of an arch, bound with rattan. Made of sheet iron soldered down the side, clapperless, and struck with a wooden stick; 22 cm. (8½ in.) high (132). **2.** tube of the Labwor of Uganda, played by women only, made of *aporo* wood, cylindrical, without mouthpiece. The player blows into it from either end with expanded cheeks. The sound is like that of a low foghorn. *Ca.* 90 cm. (3 ft.) long (195).

Appalachian dulcimer, folk zither of the Appalachian highlands of the U.S., similar to the bûche, with up to 5, but usually 3, metal strings: 1 melody string and 2 drone strings, tuned $C^0 f^0 c^0$ or $C^0 g^0 c^0$. The melody (highest) string is stretched over fixed frets. All strings are strummed by the player's right hand while the left hand stops them with a turkey quill or small stick. Also called dulcimer, mountain zither (89).

Appeau [Fr. *appel,* call], **1.** Fr. word in use from the 14th c. to the 16th for a clapperless bell, struck on the outside by a hammer and used as bell chime, carillon, tower bell, clockwork. The *Dictionnaire de Trévoux* of 1771 says that it was a small bell for sounding the quarter and half hours, and that laymen called it *timbre;* **2.** from 1380 on, a decoy whistle for imitating and attracting birds. Randle Cotgrave (in 1611) calls it "the reed or little pipe wherewith fowlers call sillie birds . . ." In this sense appeau is still in use today (82, 132, 204).

Appiaulx, var. of appeau.

Appo (Mac.), percussion instr. of S. Celebes, a bamboo pole some 1.5–1.8 m. (5–6 ft.) long, split at one end. Used for ritual purposes only (112).

Apunga, ivory horn of Angola, with lateral mouthpiece. Also called ponga (185).

Äqual [Lat. *aequalis,* equal], Ger.: any organ stop at 8′ pitch (133).

Aqwal, see: agwāl.

Arababu [Arab. *rabāb*], name of the rabāb on Halmahera, Moluccas, with coconut body and single string of vegetable fiber, but otherwise similar to the rabāb. Although it is usually bowed, it is sometimes plucked with bare fingers (112, 173).

Arabana [*rabāna*], *frame drum of the Kai Islands, Indonesia, introduced from Macassar. Most specimens are round, but octagonal ones are also found. Some are provided with jingles. *Ca.* 28–35 cm. (11–14 in.) in diam. (119).

Arāghil, pl. of argūl.

Arain(e) (OFr.) [*airain,* bronze], **1.** an abbr. of cor d'araine, a med. horn of metal. The word occurs from the 12th c. on and is often mentioned together with trompes; **2.** in the 15th c. pellet bells that were sewn on garments. Araigne, haraine, etc., occur as vars. (82, 176, 204).

Arará, Cuban word designating a drum built by Negroes from Dahomey or their descendants. The drums follow several traditional models, each of which has a single head. The membrane is usually laced to wooden pegs (152).

Aratz, Basque *cylindrical drum, approximately our *tenor drum. Also spelled arratz.

Arba, OSp. var. of arpa.

Arbab [*rabāb], name of the rabāb in Sumatra, where it has a heart-shaped body of calabash, a glued belly, 2 silk strings, and rear pegs (178).

Arbana [*rabāna], var. of arabana.

Arbu, bracelet rattle made of snail shells strung on a piece of bark fiber and worn by dancers on Paris Island, New Guinea (132).

Arc-en-terre, Fr.: *ground bow.

Archcittern (Fr.: archicistre, cistrethéorbe; Ger.: Erzcister, Cisthertheorbe; It.: archicetera), bass cittern in use chiefly in France and Germany during the 18th c., but also known in the 17th c., patterned on the theorbo, with 2 pegboxes for on-board and off-board strings. Praetorius describes one of 12 courses. Most surviving specimens are Fr., from the late 18th c. and have gut strings. A typical tuning was $A^0 B^0 c\sharp^0 d^0 d\sharp^0/ e^0 a^0 c\sharp^1 e^1 a^1 c\sharp^2 e^2$. Ca. 1 m. (40 in.) long. Cf. bijuga cither, syron (144, 178).

Arched harp (Fr.: harpe arquée; Ger.: Bogenharfe), harp with a curved neck rising away from the resonator, first appearing in Egypt in the middle of the third millennium B.C. The most ancient ones have a spoon-shaped resonator. The horizontally played type appears before the vertically played one. The arched harp disappeared from ancient Egypt and made way for the *angular harp, passing briefly to Greece and Rome. It is now believed to be older than the angular harp. Today it survives among the Abchas of the Caucasus, the Vogul, and some other W. Siberian peoples, also in Africa and Farther India. On most Asiatic instrs. the strings are attached to tuning rings, on African ones to pegs that are fixed. In some African instrs. the neck rests loosely against the bottom of the resonator until the tension of the strings

holds it taut against the underside of the belly. The performer holds it on his lap with the neck pointing away from him (97, 118, 144, 168, 195).

Arched viol, on Oct. 5, 1664, Samuel Pepys described the "arched viall"—a "new instrument" he had seen displayed at the Royal Society—a gut-strung bowed keyboard instr., presumably a Geigenwerk or an imitation thereof. It was a disappointment to him, in as much as after 3 hours it could not be "fixed in tune."

Archet [Lat. arcus], Fr.: bow. The word first occurs in the 12th c.

Archicembalo, see: arcicembalo.

Archicetera, It.: archcittern.

Archicistre, Fr.: archcittern.

Archicymbalum, see: arcicembalo.

Archiluth, Fr.: archlute.

Archiviole, Fr.: *bowed keyboard instr.

Archlute (Fr.: archiluth; Ger.: Erzlaute; It.: arciliuto), a large bass lute created in the 16th c. to meet the lutanist's need for additional bass strings. As the reach of his hand was limited, the fingerboard could not be widened indefinitely, and therefore a number of open bass strings were placed off-board and secured to a separate pegbox. Their tuning varied according to the requirements of the piece to be played. The archlute assumed 3 forms: those of chitarrone, theorbo, and theorbo-lute. See also: angelica; bandoura (170).

Arcicembalo (It.), term applied to the *enharmonic harpsichord.

Arcichitarra, syn. of chitarrone.

Arciliuto, It.: archlute.

Arcimandola, syn. of mandolone.

Arcimandora, see: mandolone.

Arciorgano (It.), term applied to an *enharmonic organ.

Arciviolata lira, syn. of lira da gamba.

Arc musical, Fr.: *musical bow.

Arco, It., Port., Sp.: bow.

Arco musical, Sp.: *musical bow.

Arçon [Lat. arcionum, from· arcum], OFr.: bow. The word was used in the

13th c., when it was superseded by archet (204).

Arco sonoro, It.: musical bow.

Arc sonore, Fr.: *musical bow. Nowadays the term arc musical is preferred.

Ardablis [Gk. *hydraulos*], Heb. term for the organ. *Cf.* hirdolis, magrepha (170).

Ardin, also **Ardine,** *angular harp of the Moors of Mauretania, with 10–12 strings and a calabash resonator covered with a tanned skin. The neck rests against one end of the resonator and is maintained in position by the tension of the strings. Often the neck is surmounted by an iron plaque to which rattling metal rings are affixed. The strings are plucked while the membrane is drummed upon. Played by women only (103, 193).

Areng'as, obs. vertical stopped pipe of the Links tribe of the Korana Hottentots, SW. Transvaal, made from the shinbone of a springbok (116).

Arfa, Pol., Russ., Ruth., Serb., Slov.: harp.

Arghan [Gk. *organon*], unidentified instr. with 16 strings and large compass, of Gk. origin, known to 9th-c. Byzantium (71).

Arghanum [Gk. *organon*], Arab. name for the Byzantine organ. According to Ibn Khurdādhbih, writing in the 9th c., it had bellows of skin and iron, and the word *arghanum* was interpreted as meaning 1000 voices. Another early Arab. writer says: "When 1000 men . . . sing . . . with different sounds . . . that state of things they call arghanum." Farmer has suggested that "1000 voices" was a nickname for the organ. The Byzantines reputedly used the arghanum to disconcert their enemies, and it is said to have been audible 60 miles away. Also called urghanum (71).

Argūl, pl. **arāghil** (Arab.) [*urghān*, from Gk. *organon*], a soft-toned double pipe of the Near East, composed of 2 idioglott, parallel cylindrical pipes—a melody pipe and a drone pipe, the drone usually longer than the melody pipe. (If both pipes are of the same length, the instr. is called a qurmah.) Generally the melody pipe has 6 fingerholes, the drone none. Instrs. having fewer fingerholes are either children's toys or folk instrs. The drone pipe is made up of several detachable extensions so that its pitch can be adjusted according to requirements. The beating reeds are upcut. They are larger than those of the *zummāra and are taken completely into the player's mouth, which serves as an air chamber. In Egypt the argūl has been known since ancient times. Similar instrs. are found in the Balkans and Sardinia. See also: argun, mashūra, yaroul (89, 144).

Argūl-al-asgar, a small argūl with one extension on the drone pipe, *ca.* 40 cm. (16 in.) long (168).

Argūl-al-kabīr (Arab.: great argūl), argūl with 3 extensions on the drone pipe, *ca.* 1.40 m. (55 in.) long (144, 168).

Argūl-as-sogaiji, a medium-sized argūl with 2 extensions on the drone pipe, *ca.* 1 m. (40 in.) long. Also called maussil (144, 168).

Argun [Arab. *argūl*], *double pipe of S. Anatolia, with single beating reeds (89).

Ari, *slit tube of the Trans-Fly region of New Guinea and of the Marind-Anim of New Guinea, made of a bamboo internode up to 60 cm. (2 ft.) long. The player's breath is directed against a lengthwise slit, thereby causing it to open and close rapidly (77).

Arigot, var. of larigot.

Arion zither [Gk. Arion], **1.** zither invented by Curt Schulz of London in 1880; **2.** zither invented by V. J. Schunda of Pest in 1880, in lyra form; **3.** a large zither with the right-hand section of the body in circular form (22, 149).

Ariston, free-reed *music box made by P. and F. E. Ehrlich of Gohlis in the 19th c., hand-cranked, with perforated disc (37, 178).

Arka(tu) (Akk.), unidentified instr. of ancient Mesopotamia (147).

Armandine, name given by Pascal Taskin of Paris to a gut-strung psaltery in harpsichord form which he built in 1790 for the singer Anne-Aimée Armand, and now preserved in the museum of the Paris Conservatoire.

Armeeposaune (Ger.: army trombone), family of brass instrs. invented by Vaclav F. Červeny of Königgrätz (Hradec Králové) in 1867, akin to the trombone but with somewhat larger bore, built either with down-pointing bell or in helicon shape. He made all sizes from the alto in F and Eb to the subbass in F¹ (25, 176).

Armgeige, obs. Ger.: viola da braccio.

Armonica (It.), Benjamin Franklin's name for his invention, which we now call *glass harmonica.

Armonica a bocca, It.: mouth organ.

Armonica a cembalo, It.: *keyed harmonica.

Armonica a manticino, It.: accordion.

Armonica de gura, Rom.: mouth organ.

Armonica meteorologicale (It.), *aeolian harp of Abbate G. C. Gattoni of Como, in 1785, consisting of 15 strings of different diam. which he had strung between his house and a tower, set in vibration by the wind, but because of atmospheric influences it seems to have been more successful as a barometer than as a musical instr. Also called arpa gigantesca (176).

Armonie [U.], word occurring in Fr. literature from the 12th to the 14th c., identified by Sachs as a hurdy-gurdy. But, as it is mentioned together with the chifonie, this seems unlikely. The word also appears as almonie (53, 176).

Armonio, armonium, It.: harmonium.

Armonipiano, piano invented by Ricordi & Fanzi, improved by W. Hlawatsch, with a second set of small hammers to keep the strings in vibration so that the tone may be sustained at the player's pleasure. See also: melopiano (176).

Arnaba, modern Egyptian *spike fiddle, equivalent of the kāmanja (89).

Arnolo, a form of viola d'amore invented ca. 1900 by Contal, with 4 pairs of strings and as many sympathetic strings, shown at the 1900 Paris Exposition (204).

Arol, a small bell suspended from the neck of a mule in the Basque country.

Arpa, 1. Basque, It., Sp.: harp; **2.** drum of New Guinea, of elongated hourglass shape and single, glued head. The other end is left open and is sometimes fashioned in the form of a crocodile mouth. A handle is generally attached at the waist; 50–150 cm. (20–60 in.) long (176).

Arpa a cembalo, It.: clavicytherium (176).

Arpa a nottolini, arpa ad uncinetti, It.: hook harp.

Arpa a pedali, It.: pedal harp.

Arpa-ché, *musical bow of the Kekchi Indians of Guatemala, some 1.80 m. (6 ft.) long, struck with a stick while the player's mouth serves as a resonator. A tuning loop is provided. Also called apaché, caramba, marimba-ché, narimba-ché (105).

Arpa con doppio movimento, It.: double-action harp.

Arpa d'Eolo, It.: aeolian harp.

Arpa di vetro, It.: glass harp.

Arpa doppia, It.: double harp.

Arpa gigantesca, syn. of armonica meteorologicale.

Arpanetta (It.) (Ger.: *Spitzharfe, Harfenett*), **1.** an upright double psaltery with a soundboard between 2 rows of strings: steel on one side for the treble, brass on the other for the bass. Harp-shaped, it could be set on a table and was pop. in the 17th and 18th c., chiefly in Germany. The tuning pins are set in the base, from which 2 sides rise perpendicularly. The strings pass over a bridge and a nut and are played with bare fingers. The arpanetta is believed to have evolved from the med. cruit (rotte); from the 13th c. on it appears to have been played on both sides of the soundboard. Occasionally it is called *David's harp. See also: consonnante (132, 169, 178);

2. mechanical zither invented by L. Hupfeld of Leipzig in 1895, in which the 36 strings were plucked by mechanical plectra controlled by perforated paper strips set in motion by a hand crank (149).

Arpeggione [aug. of It. *arpeggio*], *bowed guitar invented by Georg Staufer of Vienna in 1823, the size of a violoncello, with 24 fixed frets on the fingerboard and a smooth guitar waist. Its 6 strings are tuned $E^0 A^0 d^0 g^0 b^0 e^1$. It proved sufficiently pop. to warrant imitation. A tutor for it was written by Vincenz Schuster; Franz Schubert wrote a sonata for it. Also called chitarra d'amore, guitare d'amour, guitar violoncello (89, 176).

Arpicordo (It.) [*arpa*, harp + *chorde*, string] (Lat.: *harpichordum*), early name of the polygonal spinet of Italy. Scaliger (1484–1558), one of the earliest authors to mention it, says that the spinet was called "harpichordum" (he writes in Latin) when he was a boy. A *maistro d'arpicordi* is mentioned in the Venetian state archives of 1515; "*uno arpicordo cum la cassa dipenta de uerde*" (with case painted green) was played in Verona in 1543. Innocenzio Ringhieri in 1551 lists the *alpicordo* together with monocordo (*i.e.*, clavichord) and clavicembalo. Vincenzo Galilei, writing in 1581, confirms its having been a keyboard instr. of square, not of grand, form, as does Tommaso Garzoni in 1585. Zarlino mentions it together with the harpsichord. In the 17th c. Banchieri (in 1609) and an Este inventory of 1625 also refer to it (the inventory lists "*8 arpicordi grandi*"). Despite the general confusion of early keyboard nomenclature, one gathers that the arpicordo was a spinet rather than a virginal. Praetorius confuses the issue by describing it as a "Symphony or virginal" with a special stop consisting of brass hooks placed under the strings to give a "harping" sound. Here he is probably influenced by Virdung, who had written in 1511 of an instr. of recent invention with gut strings and nails "which make it harp" (Virdung called it clavicimbalum). The Germanic references to "harping" tone encountered sporadically in the literature may stem from an interpretation of *arpicordo* as harp-sounding instead of harp-shaped. After Praetorius the word occurs in a historical sense only, as, *e.g.*, Comenius (Komensky), in his *Orbis sensualium pictus quadrilinguis* of 1664, who translates the Lat. *sambuca* as *arpicordo* in It., *manicordion* in Fr., *Hackbrett* in Ger. His source was obviously Junius (1575), who is cited by Victor Gay as translating *sambuca* as *harpecorde* and *Hackbrett*.

Arpi-guitare (Fr.), guitar in form of a small harp, with an elongated, narrow body and a fretted fingerboard in lieu of a pillar, with 7 strings, and a pegbox terminating in a carved animal head. A large rose is set in the soundhole. The strings are secured to a guitar-type string fastener. A creation of the 19th c. (132).

Arpilegno, It.: xylophone.

Arpone [aug. of It. *arpa*], a gut-strung upright piano built by Michele Barbici of Palermo (d. 1790), according to Valdrighi (*Nomocheliurgrafia*). As it is said to have sounded pizzicato, it may have been an upright harpsichord.

Arrabil [*rabil*], obs. Port.: rebec.

Arrabita, Basque pop. term for violin (56).

Arrain-beharri, Basque: *marine-shell trumpet (56).

Arran, 1. *whirled friction drum of Gascony and Guienne, made of cane. A horsehair string passes through 2 holes in the membrane (16); **2.** a Basque herd-animal bell (56).

Arrancadera, Sp.: the bell of a bell-wether.

Arratz, var. of aratz.

'Artaba (Arab.), another name for the lute, according to Al-Shalahi (in 1391) (75 II).

Arub, drum of the Berg-Dama of S. Africa, similar to a wooden bucket, covered with skin of goat, calf, or steinbok, tied down by thongs. The drum is beaten with the thumbs and is used only when the medicine man is called to treat a sick person (116).

Arunu, drum of the Timne of Sierra Leone (176).

Arupepe, side-blown trumpet of the Karamojong of Uganda, straight, conical, made of 2 hollowed sections of wood covered with leather (195).

Arxalu-ak, Basque: castanet (56).

Arxouxelas, large *pellet bells affixed to the tambourine in Galicia, Spain (57).

Asaf (Arab.), according to Al-Shalahi (in 1391), a single-headed drum (75 II).

Asakasaka [Arab. *shaqshaq], generic name for rattles among the Ibo of Nigeria (93).

Asambori, pl. **esambori,** drum of the Timne of Sierra Leone (176).

Ascaules (Lat.) [Gk. *aski, bag], bag-pipe of ancient Rome, of Eastern origin. *Cf.* askaulos (147).

A'seh, drum of ancient Egypt (89 Farmer).

Asiko, rectangular *frame drum of the Yoruba of Nigeria, with single head, largest of their 3 frame drums, the 2 smaller sizes being called samba (108).

As-it, double pipe of ancient Egypt, formerly identified as clarinets, now considered to have been flutes. A museum specimen in Berlin has 4 fingerholes in each pipe, no mouthpiece, is 25 cm. (10 in.) long (144).

Askaulos [*aski], syn. of aski and tulumi. *Cf.* ascaules.

Aski (Gk.: bag), syn. of tulumi (13).

Asmari, name of the cherewata in Shoa Province, Ethiopia (45).

Asobi-daiko, children's *frame drum of Japan, with single head and a handle (176).

Asok, tubular rattle filled with dried seeds, of the Pangwe children of Gabon Republic and Cameroun (176).

Asokoben [*aso,* elephant + *kofen*], ivory horn of the Ashanti of W. Africa (93).

Asopi, syn. of kachapi, 1, among the Batak of Sumatra (176).

'Asor (ten), instr. mentioned in the Bible and presumed to have been the Phoenician 10-stringed psaltery with rectangular frame, plucked with bare fingers. *Cf.* psalterium decachordum (170).

Aspirophone, presumably an *American organ; Alexandre Debain of Paris took out a patent for this instr. on July 29, 1870 (204).

Assat, corr. of nazard.

Assogui, basketwork rattle of the Ndasa and Mbamba of Okondja, Gabon Republic, used for accompanying dances during circumcision rites (185).

Asson, Haitian maraca rattle, covered with a network of small percussive objects: a ritual instr. (152).

Asukusuk, wooden trumpet of the Teso of Uganda, with an oblong gourd attached to one end; 140 cm. (55 in.) long (195).

Asvar, pl. of sūr.

'Atab, Arab. for nut, and, by extension, fret. The term was used in the 9th c. See also: dastan (75 II).

Atabal [Arab. *tabl* via *tabal*], OSp. and modern Basque: *cylindrical drum, now the equivalent of the modern bass drum.

Atabale [Arab. *tabl* via *tabal*], Fr. and Port., 16th and 17th c.: kettledrum (82).

Atabal turqués (Sp.: Turkish drum), Sp. name for the *tabl turki, which was formerly called *Turkish drum—ancestor of the bass drum.

Atabaque [*tabl*], generic name for elongated, single-headed drums in Bahia, Rio de Janeiro, and São Paulo states, Brazil, including those in form of a truncated barrel with laced heads stretched over hoops; believed to be of African origin. See also: tabaq, tabaqa, tabaque, tambaque. Also called ilú in Bahia, Brazil (6, 7).

Atabule, pl. **etabule** (Timne) [Arab.: *tabl*], *hourglass drum of the Yela of Sierra Leone; the chieftain's drum (176).

Atala, panpipes of the Nahuqua Indians of C. America. *Cf.* antara (105).

Atama, pl. **etama** (Timne), a small atabule. *Cf.* atāmo (176).

Atambor, atamor [Pers. **tabir*], OSp.: drum; mentioned by Juan Ruiz in the 14th c. *Cf.* danbore.

Atāmo (Amh.), Ethiopian *frame drum, made in different sizes and used for accompanying dancers. *Cf.* atama (74, 176).

Atari gane, a small brass gong of Japan, with turned rim, suspended by a cord or held in the player's hand, and struck with a bone mallet on its inner surface. Different tones are obtained by striking it in different spots. It serves in *kabuki* and at folk music festivals. *Cf.* hitotsu gane (135).

Atata-tsang, drum of Burma, the right end of which is closed (176).

Atata-witata, drum of Burma, closed at both ends (176).

Atecocolli, *marine-shell trumpet of the Nahuatls and Aztecs (137, 144).

Atoke, gong of the Ewe of Ghana, small, scaphoid, made of beaten iron, of an indefinite high pitch; it is struck with a metal rod (109).

Atoros, name given to the asukusuk by the Toro of Uganda (195).

Atranata, var. of antanatra.

Atsimevu, master drum of the Ewe of Ghana, barrel-shaped, single-headed, painted with bright colors, and encircled by iron hoops. The bottom remains open. It stands *ca.* 1.50 m. (5 ft.) high. The duiker-skin head is sewn to a wooden hoop slightly larger than the drum. Before tuning the drum is wetted on the inside. Lowest-pitched of the Ewe drums, it is played with 2 drumsticks (109).

Atukpani [Arab. **tabl*], drum of the Ewe of Ghana, played in pairs of male and female. *Cf.* atumpani (176).

Atumpani, pl. **ntumpani** [Arab. **tabl*], *"talking drum" of the Ashanti of Ghana. According to Hause, both drum and name are borrowed, the latter presumably from the Mandingo. *Cf.* ntumpani, "talking drum" (93, 162).

Atuñsa, flute of the Motilon Indians of

the Sierra de Perija, Colombia, with attached air duct set at an angle and 4 fingerholes. *Ca.* 110 cm. (43 in.) long (105).

Aturma, pl. **eturma,** a small horn of the Timne of Sierra Leone (176).

Atvur, *marine-shell trumpet of the Kai Islands, Indonesia, made from the *Charonia tritonis* (119).

Aufeda, idiophone of Sulabesi, Moluccas, consisting of a bamboo segment split from both ends toward the center, which is left intact. Attached to spinning wheels (173).

Auferion, var. of orpharion.

Aufschlagidiophon, Ger.: percussion idiophone.

Aufschlagplatte, Ger.: percussion plaque.

Aufschlagröhre, Ger.: percussion tube.

Aufschlagzunge, Ger.: beating reed.

Aufschnitt, Ger.: *cutup, mouth (of an organ pipe).

Aufsteckbogen, Ger.: crook.

Aulodion [Gk. **aulos*], a small automatic organ made by the Kaufmann family of Dresden (176).

Auloi elymoi (Gk.), divergent *double pipes of ancient Greece, of unequal length, the longer one being curved and terminating in a bell originally of animal horn. The fingerholes are in different positions on each pipe. Also known as *Phrygian auloi, they were taken over by the Romans as tibiae impares or tibiae phrygiae. See also: aulos (170, 199).

Auloi hyperteleioi (Gk.: superperfect **auloi*), the bass auloi of ancient Greece, used in temples (89, 176).

Auloi kitharisterioi (Gk.: *kithara **auloi*), auloi of ancient Greece at kithara pitch (89, 176).

Auloi paidikoi (Gk.: boy's **auloi*), the alto auloi of ancient Greece, apparently the commonest; used at entertainments (89, 170).

Auloi parthenoi (Gk.: girl's **auloi*), the soprano auloi of ancient Greece, used by young pupils and at funerals (89, 170).

Auloi teleoi (Gk.: perfect *auloi*), the tenor auloi of ancient Greece, used at contests (176).

Aulos, pl. **auloi** (Gk.), literally "pipe," the divergent *double pipe of the ancient Greeks, most important of their wind instrs., later called *tibia* by the Romans. The aulos consisted of a slender cylindrical tube usually of wood or ivory (the *bombyx*), with an ovoid barrel called *holmos* at the upper end, generally continued by a short conical *hypholmion* in which the reeds (*glottai*) were inserted. Apparently both single and double reeds were employed. The number of fingerholes during the classical period is stated to have been 4; this number was later increased. From the 5th c. B.C. on, the number and arrangement of fingerholes permitted playing in the 3 major Gk. tonalities: Dorian, Phrygian, and Lydian. The removable reeds were kept in a small, box-shaped container often depicted at the side of the player's aulos bag. The player held one pipe in each hand; frequently he is depicted wearing a *phorbeia, also called *peristomion* (the *capistrum* of the Romans), a band that passed across his mouth and cheeks and was tied at the back of his head, with a slit for the mouth. As the player took the large reed completely in his mouth and inflated his cheeks, breathing through the nose while playing (as in the East today), the phorbeia gave support to the cheeks.

The double pipe appears in Asia Minor at a considerably earlier date than in Greece: a Sum. specimen from Ur of *ca.* 2700 B.C., now in the Museum of the University of Pennsylvania, Philadelphia, is of silver and measures about 25 cm. (10 in.). By the second millennium B.C. it had been introduced to Egypt. Some 50-odd pipes have been recovered from Egyptian tombs; they are very slender cylindrical tubes of cane, most of them with 3 or 4 equidistant fingerholes. The Gk. aulos is a descendant of these Near Eastern pipes, the Greeks themselves attributing its origin to Asia. Several ivory pipes dating from the second half of the 7th c. B.C. were found in Sparta, and as far as they can be pieced together they show 3 front fingerholes and 1 rear fingerhole, but it is possible that 1 front hole is missing. The only complete specimens of the classical age which have survived are 2 wooden pipes found in a tomb near Athens, at present dated from between the 4th and the 1st c. B.C., now preserved in the British Museum. They measure *ca.* 35 cm. (14 in.) and have 5 front fingerholes. Later examples have been found in Pompeii and in Meroë, Sudan. These have a larger number of fingerholes. Those from Meroë resemble the Pompeian ones fairly closely and are now in Boston. Unfortunately not a single one of the Meroë pipes survived intact, but there are sections of at least 9 auloi, some of which are of ivory with an outer casing of bronze, others of wood, also with an outer casing. Several of these later auloi have rotary sleeves permitting a given fingerhole to be opened or closed as needed. The sleeves were provided with knobs (*keras*) for ease of handling. Classical auloi were in pairs of equal length. Those of unequal length or of conical bore, as well as single pipes, are postclassical developments. Auloi are not found on vase paintings prior to 700 B.C. and only sparingly for some time thereafter. They never enjoyed the prestige that the major string instrs. had among the Greeks. See also: giglaros, gingras, Lydian pipes, monaulos, photinx, Phrygian auloi, plagiaulos, tibiae (21, 89 Baines, 144 Wegner; Bodley, in: *North American Journal of Archaeology*, X, 1946).

Aura (Lat.: breath), **1.** name of an early *mouth organ patented by Friedrich Buschmann of Berlin in 1821; **2.** device invented by Johann Heinrich Scheibler of Krefeld in 1816, by which 3, 4, or 5 Jew's-harps of different pitches could be combined in a frame, thus permitting rapid change of tonality. He seems to have combined subsequently a larger number of tongues in one frame (15, 117).

Auslösung, Ger.: escapement.

Ausschlagende Zunge, Ger.: retreating reed.

Auszug, Ger.: slide, 1.

Auto-accordéon-orgue (Fr.), a small free-reed organ that presumably could be played automatically, patented by Gallet of Rouen on June 5, 1858 (204).

Auto-harmonique-flûte (Fr.), a small flue-pipe organ that presumably could be played automatically, patented by Gallet of Rouen on June 5, 1858 (204).

Autoharp, *chord zither invented by C. A. Gütter of Markneukirchen in the last quarter of the 19th c., furnished with a series of chord bars that lie across all the strings; when these are depressed, the unwanted strings are damped, thus permitting persons of no musical ability to play in chords. It is still played in the U.S. (176).

Automatic . . . see the instr. in question.

Automatophone, an instr. which goeth by itself, to use a 16th-c. definition. Automatophones do not form a separate organological category, but are classed as flutes, virginals, carillons, or whatever the instr. may be that is played automatically. Such instrs. have been pop. since antiquity: Heron of Alexandria describes an organ actuated by a windmill; the forces of sun, water, clockwork, and cranks have been used to set instrs. playing. Pinned cylinders carrying musical notation were invented in the 14th c., as far as we know. See also: electrophonic instrs., Spieluhr.

Autopanphones [Gk. *auto,* self + *pan,* all + *phone,* sound], mechanical keyboard instrs. patented by Claude-Félix Seytre of Lyon on Jan. 24, 1842, consisting of pianos that contained each an organ, or harmonica, or accordion action that played tunes by means of perforated cardboard strips controlled by a treadle (92, 204).

Autophone, a small automatic accordion made by the Autophone Co. of Ithaca, N.Y., from 1880 on, in form of an upright frame with bellows hanging from it. The upper portion of the instr. contained free reeds controlled by a perforated cardboard strip (37, 204).

Auwi kakweng (mature woman), *piston flute of Papua, used at circumcision rites (176).

Avanaddha, generic name for drums on the Indian subcontinent (147).

Avicinum (Lat.), see: nightingale.

Awe, generic term for horn in Agni (a Sudanic language), hence also for the instr. (93).

Awunene, *ground bow of the Teso of Uganda, used as a children's toy (195).

'Awwada, flute of the N. African Berbers, with 6 equidistant fingerholes and a rear thumbhole (89 Farmer, 127).

Axabeba, early form of the word ajabeba, first mentioned in 1294 (44).

Axatse, rattle of the Ewe of Ghana, made of a calabash covered with a mesh of string, beads, and pieces of bamboo (109).

Axmāl, gourd rattle of the Yuma Indians of the Western U.S. (52).

Ayābi, pl. **eyābi,** Timne: horn; pipe (176).

Ayacachtli, gourd rattle of the Aztecs (105).

Ayarichi (Aymara), large antara or flute of ancient Peru (80 XII).

Ayi, West Ewe (Ghana) dialect for a small drum.

Ayíguí [Yoruba: *adyi,* awaken + *igui,* stick], syn. of págugu (152).

Aykhori, *double flute of Bolivia, made of cane, with one large pipe and one small (89).

Ayon chicuaztli, *stick rattle of ancient C. America, used for ritual purposes (170).

Ayotl, scraper of ancient and modern C. America, consisting of a turtle's carapace scraped with a stag's antler. Today it is generally suspended from the player's neck and is struck on both sides like a drum, producing sounds of at least 2 different pitches a 4th or 5th apart. It is used in Mexico and Guatemala. *Cf.* jicotea (137).

Aza rag, goat's or bull's horn of ancient Latvia, with 3 or 5 fingerholes, played with a mouthpiece like that of a modern brass instr. (89).

'Azf, pl. **ma'azif,** Arab. instr. with open strings, mentioned in the 9th c. but not described, and mentioned again by Al-Shalahi in 1301, again without details (75 II).

Azibwasi, rattle of the Azande of the Congo, made of dried fruit shells strung on a cord and worn by dancers as bracelets or anklets or on their upper calves (132).

Azkonadar, syn. of adar.

"Aztec flute," see: tlapiztalli.

Azuma fuye (Jap.: Eastern flute), obs. form of *yamato fuye, made of thinner bamboo, now replaced by the koma fuye (157).

Azuma koto (Jap.: Eastern koto), syn. of wagon (144).

Azzurinu, triangle of Sicily (169).

B

Baarpijp (Du.), organ stop corresponding to the Offenflöte or Hellflöte at 8' or 4' pitch. As a Hellflöte, it was also made of stopped pipes in the 16th c. Not identical with the Bärpfeife (133).

Babakungbu (onom.), ground bow of the Mamvu of the Congo (128).

Babakungu (onom.), ground bow of the Mari Andosi and Apanga of the Congo (128).

Babandi, large bossless gong of SE. Borneo. Also called pahawang (176).

Babarangan, 1-row bonang of Bali, tuned an octave higher than the trompong (121).

Babulá, syn. of bambulá (152).

Baby grand piano, (Fr.: *piano à queue mignon;* Ger.: *Stutzflügel*), smallest-sized grand piano.

Bacchias [Prov. *bachas*], Prov. drum. *Cf.* bachas (204).

Bacciocolo [It. *bacioccolo,* vase], percussion folk instr. of Tuscany: a vaselike container is held in the left hand and struck with a stick 10 cm. (4 in.) long (176, 204).

Bachas (Prov.), bass drum of the Comtat Venaissin, France. *Cf.* bacchias (23).

Bachflöte, organ stop; the name is given to modern copies of the cylindrical Gemshorn 2' (133).

Bachi, generic name for plectra and drumsticks in Japan.

Bachin, bacin (OFr.), early forms of bassin.

Bach trumpet, term applied to various models of trumpets made in the 19th and 20th c. either to facilitate performance of high 18th-c. trumpet parts or in the belief that they constituted a reconstruction of the early-18th-c. trumpet (whereas they actually sounded an oct., 10th, or 13th higher). Among them should be mentioned: **1.** sopranino in D made in straight form by Mahillon of Brussels, introduced in the 1890's and since abandoned. It measured *ca.* 107 cm. (42 in.); **2.** straight trumpet in A with 2 valves, made for trumpeter Julius Koslek and used by him from 1884 on, supposedly representing an instr. of Bach's day. It measured *ca.* 142 cm. (56 in.) (89 Baines, 170).

Badajo, Sp.: clapper (of a bell).

Badalo, Port.: clapper (of a bell).

Badosa, var. of baldosa.

Baerpijp (Du.), organ stop of reed pipes which originated in the Low Countries and spread from there by the mid-16th c. to N. Germany. Made in a number of forms, imitative of the flue Rohrpfeife. Called Bärpfeife in Ger. (133).

Bagana, lyre of Ethiopia, a survival of the ancient Gk. kithara, with a round wooden body and a yoke of 2 straight arms joined by a crossbar. The strings are held by tuning rings on the crossbar. Ethiopians believe it to be the harp of David. The 5 strings are tuned: $d^2 g^1 a^1 b^1 e^2$; over a century ago Villoteau gave the following tuning for a 10-stringed instr.: $d^1 b^1 e^2 d^2 g^1 a^1 e^1 g^1 a^1 b^1$. The bagana serves chiefly for vocal accompaniments and is played with a plectrum. Total height *ca.* 75 cm. (30 in.), body 25–30 cm. (10–12 in.) high and 30–35 cm. (12–14 in.) wide (15 Wachsmann, 89 Baines).

Bagezege, rattle of the Ababua women of the Congo, made of 2 small gourds filled with hard objects and tied together by a cord (176).

Bagili, *musical bow of the Basiri of the Uele region of the Congo, with lozenge-shaped resonator. A small pellet bell called nzolo is attached to the upper end of the bow (132).

Baglama, second smallest of the Anatolian saz, with 3 pairs of strings tuned e¹ d¹ a¹. Also called tanbūr baglama (89, 132).

Baglamas (Turk.), string instr. of modern Greece. *Cf.* baglama (144).

Bagpipe, wind instr. characterized by being played with a reed and having an air reservoir. It can be either mouth-blown or bellows-blown. In either case air reaches the reed in a steady stream, causing the instr. to sound continuously. In mouth-blown specimens the air is blown through a narrow blowpipe furnished with a nonreturn valve into a bag held under the player's left arm; the arm acts as a bellows by exercising appropriate pressure. Attached to the bag by means of stocks are a melody pipe called chanter (or 2 melody pipes called double chanter) and often 1–3 drone pipes. The reed is either a single beating reed or a double reed. In some types of instrs. both are used. Bellows are not found outside Europe; they are known to have existed in the 16th c. and are also worked by the player's left arm, sometimes being strapped to his body. The bag has traditionally been made of the skin of sheep, goat, or kid, hence one finds goats' heads carved on many chanter stocks, and names such as *Bock, *chevrette, *koza, etc., are given to the instr. Usually the bag is made of 2 pieces of skin cut to the required shape. Stocks are wooden sockets into which the pipes are fitted and that protect the reeds. The chanter normally has 8 fingerholes (7 front and 1 rear). The drone was known by the 13th c.; its bore is cylindrical, made in 2 or 3 joints with tenons to facilitate tuning ("stepped bore"); even if the joints vary in diam., the bore is considered cylindrical. The drone is nearly always tuned 2 octs. below the chanter keynote. If there are 2 drones, they are tuned in octs. or 5ths; 3 drones are post-medieval and now are found only in the British Isles, tuned in octs. and 5ths. We distinguish 2 principal groups of bagpipes, classifying them according to the bore and reed of their chanter: **1.** with cylindrical bore and single reed. This type is distributed in Asia, N. Africa, and Europe E. of Germany and Italy; **2.** with wide conical bore and double reed. This type is found in W. Europe (including Italy). The Brit. *small-pipe is an exception to this rule, as it has a cylindrical chanter. Generally speaking, the melodic compass does not exceed 9 tones, as the chanter is not overblown. Some chanters do overblow: the bellows-blown Irish bagpipe, for instance, can be made to overblow the oct. by squeezing the bag and pumping a little faster. With the exception of the *zampogna and *musette, drones have single reeds.

The origin of the bagpipe is still obscure, but probably lies in the Near East, where reeds were (and still are) not held between the player's lips, but taken entirely into the mouth. He continues to breathe while playing, so that the sound proceeds uninterruptedly. Later the reed is protected by a gourd or horn that serves simultaneously as air reservoir (the *hornpipe), and in its final stage the gourd or horn is replaced by a flexible bag of skin with a blowpipe. Primitive bagpipes with horn bells still exist in the Near East. The relationship of *bladder pipe to bagpipe, if any, has not yet been clarified. The bagpipe was known to the Romans in the first c. A.C. and possibly earlier, coming from Arabo-Persian lands. It may have continued in existence, but we lose all knowledge of it in Europe until the 9th c., when it is referred to as *chorus in the epistle to Dardanus by Pseudo-Jerome. John Cotton (11–12th c.) uses the Lat. word *musa* for bagpipe, and in the 12th c. the Fr. word *muse* comes into use. "Bagpipe" is first recorded in Chaucer's writings. The first bagpipes are depicted with 2 pipes: a blowpipe and a chanter. The drone is mentioned in Fr. literature in the first half of the 13th c. A separate drone is shown in the 14th c., but double pipes were in use before then, one pipe being a melody, the other a drone pipe. Double pipes still exist in France and in the Balkans. Double drones are shown in the *Cantigas de Santa María* (14th c.). A second, independent drone appears in the early 15th c. Bellows were first adopted by the Irish *union pipes, *ca.* 1588, and about 25 years later the French transformed their penetrating outdoor pipes into the bellows-blown *musette. From the 19th c. on, the bagpipe has shown signs of becoming obs. on the European Continent.

We have seen that there exist distinct Eastern and Western types of bagpipe. Whether our Western instrs. were derived from antiquity is not known, nor do we know whether the older ones were of independent Celtic origin; the younger ones are regarded as Oriental. Sachs pointed out that in India today there exist bagpipes with only drone pipes and others with either melody *or* drone pipe, that our source material from the 9th c. to the 14th c. shows only a melody pipe, and also that the drone is a med. addition, although droning is not a late med. Western form of polyphony. It was in Europe that the separation of chanter and drone pipes took place. Our long Western drones are the result of the greater Western compass, causing the organ point to be put down an oct. so as not to interfere with the melody. The bagpipe is distributed in Asia, N. Africa, and Europe, primarily as a shepherd's instr. See also: ascaules, askaulos, aski, bajānā sruti, balcsuegala, benilleux, biniou, Bock, boudego, bousine, Brian Boru, cabreta, cabrette, çanpolla, charanbel, chevrette, chevrie, chiboni, chobreto, chorus, chwibenigl a chod, cimpoi, cinfonía, cornamusa, cornemuse, diplye, duda, Dudelsack, Dudey, dudka, duduk, dudy, dutka, gadlje, gaida,

gaita, gajda, gajde, gajdy, gayda, ghaida, graile, great pipe, grosser Bock, half long pipe, Highland pipe, Hümmelchen, Irish organ, karabe, karamouza, koza, koziol, kozol, loure, Lowland pipe, mandoura, manxa borrega, mashak, mechawa, meshin, mezonad, mišnice, mješnica, musa, muse, musette, nāgabaddha, odrecillo, ormfa, ouire, parakapzuk, pibole, pilai, piobmala, piob mor, piva, polnischer Bock, roga, rouchalo, sac de gemecs, Sackpfeife, sacomuse, sampogna, Schäferpfeife, shabur, shapar, shkewa, shuttle pipe, shyabur, small pipe, sruti upāngi, stviri, suomu duda, surdelina, šutka, šutky, swegelbalc, tibia utricularis, torupill, tsampouna, tulum, tulum duduyi, tulumi, turlure, uillean pipes, union pipes, uter, utricularium, volynka, vunija, war pipe, zampogna, zampoña, zapp, zūkra, zurna (13, 14, 35, 151, 169, 180).

Baguettes entrechoquées, Fr.: concussion sticks.

Bahiri, 1. in ancient India a species of drum; **2.** syn. of gong beri (121).

Bahortsañ [*bahor,* center], a large palace drum of Burma (176).

Bahya, see: bāya.

Baint, see: bīnt.

Bajah, syn. of tuila.

Bajānā sruti, syn. of sruti upāngi.

Bajang kerek, a very small *musical bow of Java which is held in the mouth, the string being set in vibration by the player's breath. Used only in connection with certain secret rituals (121).

Bajidor, name given to the jedor in the Sundanese districts of Java (121).

Bajo de uña (Sp.), a very large guitar with short neck and 8 strings. Total length *ca.* 125 cm. (50 in.), body 75 cm. (30 in.) (57).

Bajón, 1. Sp.: curtal; **2.** organ stop at 16′ pitch, found on Sp. organs (W. Hill in 179A, Vol. 14).

Bajoncillo [dim. of *bajón*]; **1.** treble bajón of Spain, formerly played in churches together with the chirimía and bajón; **2.** organ stop of Spain, imitating the curtal, at 8′ pitch, rarely also at 4′ (57, 198).

Bajón torlote, instr. listed in a Sp. inventory of the late 16th c. and described as a large wooden chirimía; probably a low-pitched curtal or a bass crumhorn. *Cf.* torloroto.

Bajú, *hourglass drum made in Cuba for export only, imitative of an Afro-Cuban drum (152).

Bąk (pron. bonk), var. of buk.

Baka-baka, "tuning fork" idiophone of Ternate, Indonesia, corresponding to the genggong sakai (122).

Bakilo, *slit drum of the SW. Malagasy Republic.

Bakora, *marine-shell trumpet with lateral mouthpiece, of the Diégo-Suarez district of the Malagasy Republic. *Cf.* bakura (171).

Bakunansa, obs. 2-headed Afro-Cuban drum with nailed heads, only one of which is played. Conical in shape, it is made of a palm trunk, with 2 round holes, opposite each other, to let the drum "breathe." *Ca.* 50 cm. (20 in.) high (152).

Bakura, *marine-shell trumpet of ancient India, mentioned in the Rig-Veda. Later called shanka (170).

Bal, gourd trumpet of the Ingessana of Dar-Fur, Sudan, played in sets of 6 tuned to $c^0 c^0 f^0 g^0 b\flat^0 c^1$. Also called lal (H. Hilke: *"Die Ingessana,"* in: *Zeitschrift für Ethnologie,* Vol. 84, *Heft 2*).

Bala, generic name of the xylophone in Mali and Guinea. *Cf.* balafo (42).

Balában (Turk.), **1.** kettledrum of Turkey. *Cf.* baraban, belebän, darabána, taraban; **2.** cylindrical reedpipe of Turkey, with single reed, known from the 15th c. to the 17th. Also called näy-i balában (89 Farmer, 176).

Balafo, xylophone of the W. Sudan and of the Banda and Nduka of the Congo, with gourd resonators. Each gourd is pierced with a small hole covered with a spider's-egg membrane—a mirliton device. Laborde described the balafo in 1780. Actually balafo or balafon is the

European term for *bala. Fo* or *fon* means to speak; by extension, to play an instr. Balafo thus means to play a bala (19, 42).

Balafon, see: balafo.

Balag [Sum. *bal,* beat], drum of ancient Babylon (170).

Balag-di, the same as balag.

Balaggu, Akk. equivalent of balag.

Balah, *slit drum of the Sarakole of W. Africa, made from a hollowed tree trunk and beaten with 2 rubber-headed sticks. Identical with the kiringi of the Soso (132).

Balak, marimba (xylophone) of the Mandingo and Sarakole of W. Africa (176).

Balalaika, pop. Russ. chordophone of the guitar family, an 18th-c. descendant of the *dombrā, characterized by a triangular body, now made in 6 different sizes. The balalaika has a flat back, slightly arched belly, narrow neck bearing 4 movable frets, and 3 strings, usually of gut but sometimes of steel. Originally it had but 2 strings, the third being added in the course of the 18th c. The *Almanach de Gotha* of 1772 still mentions 2 strings. Tunings are as follows: piccolo $b^0 e^1 a^1$; prime $e^1 e^1 a^1$; second $a^0 a^0 d^1$; alto $e^0 e^0 a^0$; bass $E^0 A^0 d^0$; contrabass $E^1 A^1 D^0$; the prime is the most commonly encountered. *Cf.* cellalika (38, 176, 204).

Balangi, xylophone of Sierra Leone, with gourd resonators, each pierced with a small hole covered with spider's-egg membrane—a mirliton device. Its 15 or 16 slabs are beaten with rubber-headed sticks. *Cf.* balingi (176).

Balanyi, idiochord *raft zither of Dahomey, made of 10 bamboo sticks, each having one string (141).

Bālasarasvati, N. Indian equivalent of the mayurī.

Balc(h)suegala [OHGer. *balg,* bellows + *swegel*], OHGer.: bagpipe.

Baldoire, var. of baudoire.

Baldosa [Lat. *baudosa*], OSp.: pandoura. The word is first mentioned by

Juan Ruiz in the 14th c. and remained in use through the 15th c., also occurring as baudosa. *Cf.* baudoire.

Balimbo [*birimbao*], name of the Jew's-harp in Port. Guinea.

Baling, syn. of berbaling (18).

Balingi, xylophone of the Balika of the Congo, with 8 slabs of hardwood, usually *pterocarpus,* laid across 2 banana-tree trunks. No resonators (31).

Ballad horn (Sp.: *tromba de vocal*), **1.** valved brass instr. invented by one óf the English Distin family *ca.* 1870, with conical bore terminating in a bell, made in circular form with bell pointing forward or upward. The bore is wider and the bell narrower than those of the *Primhorn; otherwise the 2 are virtually identical. It is pitched in B♭ in the U.S., C in England, and is furnished with 3 piston valves; a tenor instr. intended for amateurs. Also called voice horn, vocal horn; **2.** in the U.S. a name of the mellophone (89 Baines).

Balu, *musical bow of the Aïmeri of the Congo, with tuning loop but without resonator (128).

Bambola, syn. of bamboula.

Bamboli, sansa of the Momvu of the Congo (19).

Bamboo pipe, a simple *whistle flute of bamboo, with 6 front fingerholes and a rear thumbhole, designed by Margaret James (of England) in 1926 for cheapness and for ease of making and playing, widely taught to children in Britain. The treble in d² is the type instr., but several other sizes are made for ensemble playing. *Cf.* shepherd's pipe.

Bamboula, Afro-Amer. drum of the W. Indies, made of a hollowed tree trunk with single laced head and played with bare hands. Also called bambola (152).

Bambulá, obs. Afro-Cuban drum with single head and open bottom, formerly played with bare hands; 90–120 cm. (3–4 ft.) high, 20–23 cm. (8–9 in.) in diam. Also called babulá (152).

Bambus, name given to the khais by various travelers (116).

Bāmsī, Beng. and Hindust. equivalent of vāmsī.

Bāmyā, small indoor kettledrum of India, with body of clay, wood, or copper. The head is stretched over a hoop and laced in W or Y pattern with leather thongs, tensed with wedge bracings. Occasionally a permanent black tuning paste is applied to the head (see: mridanga), in which case it is close to the edge, not in the center of the head. This drum is distributed all over the subcontinent and is played exclusively as a partner of the tabla. Called bānyā in Bengal, bāya in N. and C. India (173, 179).

Bana, chordophone of the Vei of Liberia, with 7 strings (176).

Banchi, bamboo *whistle flute of the Land Dayak of Borneo, with 3 fingerholes, similar to the suling nyawa (176).

Banchi-banchi, syn. of lolowe.

Bancloche [OFr. *ban,* to proclaim + *cloche,* bell], OFr.: tower bell, storm bell of the guard tower, alarm bell. The word occurs from the 12th c. to the 14th, together with the var. bancloke.

Band, pl. **Bände,** obs. Ger. var. of Bund. a fret.

Bandair (Arab.), widespread name of the Arab. *frame drum, a large tambourine with snares. The term is first recorded in Moorish Spain in the 13th c. and gave rise to *pandero. Nowadays played extensively in N. Africa, where it reaches a sizable diam. The drum is circular and has a single head. See also: abendair, allun, bendere, bendīr, bendo, bennde, pandair (89, 170).

Bandalon, see: bandolón.

Bandar, see: bandair.

Bandaska, Czech *friction drum with cord (169).

Bandflöte, Ger.: ring flute.

Bandi [Engl.: band], double-headed *cylindrical drum of the Lower Congo, imitative of European band drums, with greater diam. than depth. It is played by the Kamba and other peoples, who carry it by a strap over the left shoulder and beat it with a drumstick (185).

Bandingba, *musical bow of the Azande, Mayogo of Danga, and Okonfongwe of the Congo, without tuning loop or resonator. The Mayogo of Danga also have it with tuning loop (128).

Bandingba-ga-sende (ground bow), *grouna bow of the Azande of the Congo (128).

Bandja, see: bania, banju, banjú.

Bandoer, obs. Ger.: pandora.

Bandola, syn. of bandurria. The expression is used frequently in Latin America.

Bandolim, Port.: mandolin (7).

Bandolín, Sp.: mandolin.

Bandolón [aug. of *bandola], **1.** a large bandurria with 6 courses of 3 strings of brass and steel, played with a plectrum; **2.** in Mexico the name is given to a similar instr. with 6 courses of 4 strings tuned $2 \times F\sharp^0$ and $2 \times f\sharp^0$, $4 \times b^0$, $4 \times e^0$, $4 \times a^0$, $4 \times d^1$, $4 \times g^1$ (57).

Bandoneon [inventor's name], a large square concertina, invented by Heinrich Band of Krefeld in the 1840's, still pop. in Argentine tango bands. Some models have single action, others double (15 Howard, 176).

Bandoniphone, accordion played automatically by means of a perforated disc, with a frame 22½ by 23 cm. (8¾ by 9 in.). Presumably a stencil name (178).

Bandora, bandore, var. of pandora (Samuel Pepys, in 1662: ". . . with a bandore for a bass.").

Bandoura, 1. archlute of the Ukraine, with 2 pegboxes, an oval body, and 12 strings tuned $G^0 c^0 d^0 g^0 a^0 d^1/ g^1 a^1 b^1 c\sharp^2 d^2 e^2$ (38); **2.** a lute-like instr. of the Ukraine, with very short neck, circular body, and some 30 strings, all open, with 8 attached to tuning pins on the neck, the others to tuning pins inserted around the edge of the body. Played with a plectrum (15, 70).

Bandura, see: bandoura.

Bandürchen, Ger.: pandurina (159).

Bandurilla [dim. of *bandurria] Sp.: small bandurria.

Bandurion, word said to be derived

from *bandore,* but more likely from *bandurria.* It occurs in Gascoigne's *Jocasta* (1566).

Bandurka, 1. syn. of luk muzycyny; **2.** dim. of bandoura.

Bandurria [Gk. *pandoura], a flat-bodied plucked chordophone of med. and modern Spain, mentioned by Juan Ruiz in the early 14th c. (as mandurria) and described by Juan Bermudo in 1555 as having the shape of a rabel. In *his* day it usually had 3 strings (against 4 for the guitar and 6 for the vihuela, as he points out), which were tuned to fundamental, 4th, and oct., or to fundamental, 5th, and oct. Bermudo mentions other sizes, with 4 and even 5 strings, and says that they were usually played with frets, but sometimes without. By the mid-18th c. the bandurria had acquired 5 pairs of strings, tuned in 4ths: $c\sharp^1 f\sharp^1 b^1 e^2 a^2$. A sixth pair has since been added, tuned to $g\sharp^0$. The modern instr. has a wooden body shaped like that of a deeper cittern, much smaller than a guitar, with central soundhole, a very short neck, and 12–14 fixed frets. The strings pass from a frontal string fastener to a large, elongated, flat pegdisc with rear pegs. It is played with a plectrum; 55–58 cm. (22–23 in.) long. Often called bandola in Latin America; known as mandurria in the Balearic Islands. *Cf.* bandolón, bandurilla, mandurria (24, 127, 132, 178).

Bandziurka, syn. of luk muzycyny.

Bandzunge, Ger.: ribbon reed.

Banga, a name formerly given to the banjo in England (89).

Banga-banga (Kikongo), scraper of the Lower Congo, made of a bamboo palm segment into which a large number of notches have been cut. These are scraped with a flat hardwood stick; 50–100 cm. (20–40 in.) long (185).

Banger, name by which, according to Thomas Jefferson (in *Notes on Virginia*), the Negroes called their banjos, which they brought with them from Africa.

Bangi, name given by the Mabudu of Bafwaga, Congo, to the kweningba (31).

Bangio, It.: banjo.

Bangkula (Bare'e), *pellet bells of Celebes, more or less globular, made of metal and each containing a small piece of metal or a pebble (112).

Bāngyā, see: bānyā.

Bania, lute-like instr. of Senegal, with piriform body. *Cf.* banjo (176).

Banjanga, name of the manja among the Bwaka of the Congo (31).

Banjar, 18th-c. term for the banjo, used, *i.a.*, by Thomas Jefferson.

Banjo (It.: *bangio*), plucked chordo-phone of African Negro origin, intro-duced to the New World by slaves, popu-larized in 19th-c. U.S., whence it was exported to Europe, Cuba, etc.; an instr. primarily used in music hall and jazz. Thomas Jefferson called it a "banjar" and wrote (in *Notes on Virginia*) that Negro slaves brought it with them from Africa and that they called it "banger." The banjo has a body like a tambourine, a parchment membrane stretched over a circular frame, with an open bottom, a bridge, and a long neck. On earlier speci-mens the neck is a detachable cylindrical stick without frets; on later ones the neck is shorter and provided with a finger-board and raised metal frets. Originally there were 4 gut strings; since, banjos have been made with 5, 6, 7, or 9 metal strings, those having more than 5 long strings being called *English guitar banjo. Banjos are played with a plectrum or with bare fingers ("finger-style banjos"). In the latter instance it has 5 gut strings, the 4 usual plus a drone chanterelle called "thumb string," which is half as long as the other strings and is placed next to the lowest string, secured by a peg in-serted halfway up the neck. The chan-terelle is said to have been added by Joe Sweeny in 1837. This type of banjo is tuned $g^1 c^0 d^0 b^0 d^1$. The chanterelle is not fitted to plectrum-played instrs. ("plec-trum banjos"). Nowadays both types have wooden resonators at the back and

their membranes are stretched by a number of screws fitting into the frame. Tunings are subject to *scordatura*, but a normal tuning might be $(g^1) c^0 g^0 b^0 d^1$ or $(g^1) G^0 d^0 g^0 b^0 d^1$. Banjo orchestras also make use of tenor, bass, and contrabass banjos, banjolin, banjo-mandolin, banjo-rine, and zither-banjo. See also: Ameri-can banjo, banga, bania, Banjogeige, banjo-harp, banjo-ukulele, banjo zither, banju, banjú, banjulele, banshaw, hew-gag (89, 132, 151).

Banjogeige (Ger.: banjo fiddle), a 19th-c. attempt to combine a banjo body with the neck, scroll, and strings of a vio-lin (176).

Banjo-harp, 18-string zither in harp form, of 19th-c. American invention, with a double-headed drum set in the lower portion of the body to act as reso-nator, and 5–7 buttons at the left for changes of pitch (149).

Banjolin, banjo with 4 single strings and a neck shorter than usual (89).

Banjo-mandolin, mandolin with a banjo head (*i.e.*, membrane) and dou-ble strings.

Banjorine, banjo with short neck, tuned a 4th higher than the ordinary banjo.

Banjo-ukulele, banjo with a ukulele fin-gerboard.

Banjo zither, instr. invented by C. L. Steffen of Stettin in 1879, having a small, banjo-like round body with F holes and a long neck. Not to be confused with the zither banjo (22).

Banju, board zither of the Azande and Idio of the NE. Congo (19).

Banjú, the Afro-Cuban banjo, with 4 strings, introduced from the U.S. (152).

Banjulele, a simplified banjo tuned like a ukulele (15).

Bankiya, drum of the Mbelo and Okongo of the Congo, made of *bopako* or *boshongo* wood, with antelope-skin heads, played with bare hands. As a war drum it is carried in the rear guard and played with drumsticks to produce greater volume of sound. Also called bonkendja (30).

Ban ko, a small Chin. bossless gong with a low rim (176).

Bankora, var. of bakora.

Banku, a S. Indian name of the karnā.

Bānkula, see: bangkula.

Ban ñac, see: cai ban ñac.

Bansarī, Hindi: flute. *Cf.* bansurī (176).

Banshaw, an 18th-c. appellation of the banjo.

Banshi, *cross flute of the Garo of Assam, made of bamboo with 3 finger-holes near the lower end. *Ca.* 46 cm. (18 in.) long (172).

Bansi, bangsi, 1. Sans.: flute (176); **2.** clarinet of Flores, Indonesia, identical with the pupui (173); **3.** *whistle flute of Sumatra, of bamboo, with 6 or 7 finger-holes (122); **4.** in Batavia, Java, syn. of suling (*cross flute); **5.** cross flute of Sangi, Indonesia, mouth-blown, identical with the vāmsī (203).

Bansing, var. of bansi, 4.

Bansuli [Sans. *bangsurī*], bamboo *whistle flute of Java, with 7 front finger-holes and 1 rear fingerhole, of Indian origin. *Cf.* vansali (176).

Bansurī (Sans.), half-stopped *whistle flute of the Punjab, with 4–6 fingerholes. Also called halur, husor, solor (68, 173).

Bant, see: bīnt.

Bānyā, Beng. equivalent of bāmyā.

Banza, guitar-like instr. of the Dominican Republic, Haiti, and the other Antilles, made of a half gourd, with skin belly and 4 strings (152).

Banzie, stick zither of the Azande of the Congo (128).

Banzu, board zither of the Mangbetu and Boa of the Congo, with bark resonator (128).

Bapili, board zither of the peoples of the Ituri Forest, Congo (103).

Bapsillus [Lat. *batillus*], Lat.: clapper of a bell (188).

Baraban [Turk. *balāban*], Bulg., Russ., Ruth., Serb.: drum. Roquefort

(in 1808) describes it as a "copper bassin, a kind of kettledrum on which one strikes in order to announce something." *Cf.* darabána, taraban.

Barabanca [Russ. *baraban*], Rom.: drum.

Barabit, pl. of barbat.

Baradundu [*bara,* calabash + *dundu,* drum], calabash drum in Dyoula, a Sudanic language (93).

Barātaka (Beng.), a large *marine-shell trumpet of Bengal, made of cowrie shell (132).

Baratyu [*bara,* calabash + *tyu,* drum], calabash drum in Mandingo, a Sudanic language (93).

Barbat, pl. **barabit** (Arab., Pers.) [corr. of Gk. *barbiton*], **1.** chordophone in use *ca.* 600 by Byzantine singing girls, identified in a 10th-c. Arab. encyclopedia as a Pers. lute. Ibn-Sina (Avicenna) described it as a lute in the 11th c., at which time it was unfretted (170); **2.** Arab.: tambourine (98).

Barbata (Lat.: bearded), see: vox barbata.

Barbiton, barbitos, a variety of lyra of ancient Greece, concerning which we know little more than that it was tuned an oct. lower than the pektis and was played with a plectrum. As mention is made of the low pitch, we may infer that it was a form of lyra with strings longer than usual. From the late 6th c. B.C. to the mid-5th c. B.C. an elongated form of lyra appears on vases, with delicately incurved arms, and some writers now associate this form with the barbiton. With the Roman poets it became a generic term for stringed instrs. In modern times the word has been used to denote the archlute; *"doulz barbitons"* are mentioned in 1533 (21, 170, 204).

Barbud, see: barbat.

Bardone, It.: bourdon (organ stop).

Barduen, Bardun, Bardura (Ger.), corrs. of bourdon (organ stop) (133).

Bare, *vessel rattle of Japan, consisting of a hollow bronze ring in which rattling objects are enclosed. A dancer's instr. (178).

Barem, Borem (Ger.), organ stop of stopped cylindrical flue pipes of narrow scale, a form of lieblich Gedackt. To Praetorius it was a syn. of Bordun, Gedackt. It occurs at 16′, 8′, and, exceptionally, also at 4′ pitches (133, 159, 198).

Bargialera [*bargir,* to cry], **1.** *ribbon reed of Romansh Switzerland, made of a piece of wooden tile with 2 stretched grass blades, held horizontally between the player's lips. The sound produced resembles the crying of a small child. Called Rebhüppi in Canton Aargau; **2.** syn. of bec de grive (102).

Bāri, a large variety of nāgasuram— the expert's instr. (179).

Barikendikendi, *musical bow of the Amadi of the Congo, with tuning loop but without resonator (128).

Barimbo [Sp. *birimbao*], bamboo Jew's-harp of the Philippine Islands, generally over 30 cm. (1 ft.) long. Also called kulang (176).

Baritone (Fr.: *baryton en si♭, corbasse ténor;* Ger.: *Barytonhorn;* Sp.: *barítono*), **1.** brass wind instr. similar in all respects to the euphonium except that it has a narrower bore (with concomitant change of tone quality) and only 3 valves. A pop. band instr. Also called B♭ baritone. The instr. called baritone in England is a tenor horn in the U.S.; **2.** organ stop, see: vox humana (89, 170).

Barítono, Sp.: baritone.

Barlum, bull-roarer of Finschhafen, New Guinea (176).

Baronstange, Ger.: column (of a harp).

Baroxyton [Gk. *barus,* low + *oxytonos,* high], a valved bugle with a very wide bore, invented in 1848 by Vaclav F. Červeny of Königgrätz (Hradec Králové), built in helicon, tuba, and bassoon forms and pitched in B♭, F, or E♭. The B♭ instr., of baritone range, has a compass of 3½ octs., D¹–a¹, and is called Tenorbass or Primbass in Ger. In the

U.S. it is known as B♭ bass or bass in B♭, in France as the basse en si♭ (25, 176).

Bärpfeife, Bärpipe (Ger.), equivalent of the baerpijp (133).

Barre, Fr.: barring; bass-bar; jackrail; capotasto; string fastener.

Barre d'harmonie, Fr.: bass-bar.

Barrel, 1. (Fr.: *cylindre;* Ger.: *Walze*) the pinned, rotating cylinder of a carillon, barrel organ, dumb organist, etc.; **2.** the barrel-shaped joint of a clarinet, next to the mouthpiece; **3.** the axle on which the key of a woodwind instr. turns.

Barrel and finger organ, *barrel organ furnished with a keyboard for manual playing (89).

Barrel drum (Fr.: *tambour en tonneau;* Ger.: *Fasstrommel*), drum in which the diam. is larger in the middle than at the ends and the outline of the body is curved (100).

Barrel organ (Fr.: *orgue à cylindre, orgue à manivelle, orgue de Barbarie;* Ger.: *Drehorgel, Leierkasten, Leierorgel, Walzenorgel;* It.: *organino a cilindro, organo portatile*), mechanical portable organ descended not from the *portative organ but from the miniature *bird organ, of which it is merely an enlargement, possibly of It. invention and dating from the turn of the 17th c. to the 18th c. (see: orgue de Barbarie). Essentially it consists of 2 or more ranks of organ pipes in an enclosed cabinet above a bellows, the pipes being controlled by a pinned or stapled horizontal cylinder rotated by a hand crank or some other automatic device. In order to save space the bass pipes are stopped, and in at least one type (the Wiener Werkl) reed pipes are also employed to that end. The compass was rarely chromatic: tunes pinned on the barrels were all transposed so as to require few tonalities, the precise number depending on the size of the instr. Flat tonalities were not used. Elaborate barrel organs made for drawing rooms were, however, furnished with barrels pinned with secular music requiring complete compasses, and these of course had the required range. The barrels were of wood, mounted on a metal spindle attached to a board, and could be slid into the position required for the playing of a given piece. Each tune required one revolution of the barrel, and several pieces were pinned side by side. Extra barrels were kept in a storage space provided in the cabinet. Up to the middle of the 19th c. many poorer churches and chapels in England had barrel organs in lieu of organs, and at least one Engl. builder, J. W. Walker, built barrel organs with an organ manual. Such instrs. were known as "barrel and finger organs." In the early 19th c. Gavioli, an It. maker in Paris, made portable barrel organs, the earliest of which had perforated cardboard strips, folding bookwise, instead of barrels. Such instrs. could be mounted on small carts and wheeled about by mendicant street "musicians"—the familiar "organ grinders." This type of instr. was called "street organ." More refined cabinetwork and often a larger compass were required for drawing-room models, as more complicated pieces, such as ouvertures, would be expected of them. The development of the *orchestrion prevented them from assuming undue dimensions. See also: bird organ, dumb organist, flaşnetă, harmoniflûte, Leierkasten, Leierorgel, organino, organo a cilindro, organo portatile, orgue d'Allemagne, orgue de Barbarie, pantophone, pierement, realejo, street organ, suona-tutto, Wiener Werkl, Wimmerorgel (37, 43, 89, 197).

Barrel piano (Fr.: *piano à cylindre;* Ger.: *Drehklavier;* It.: *pianoforte a cilindro*), mechanical upright piano devoid of its keyboard, with pinned cylinders set in motion by a hand crank—a product of the 19th c. that lingered on into the 20th c. The treble section was reinforced by having 4 strings to a note; the hammers were leathered and the usual dampers were lacking. Barrel pianos mounted on little wheeled carts were played on the streets of England and Italy by mendicant street "musicians." Also called street piano; often misnamed hand organ, handle organ (37).

Bart (Ger.), see: Seitenbart, Streichbart.

Bartpfeife (Ger.: bearded pipe), any gedackt organ stop. The term occurs up to the mid-17th c. and is derived from the large beards of stopped pipes. *Cf.* vox barbata (133).

Barugumu, Swah.: antelope horn with a lateral mouthhole (176).

Baryaulos, modern Gk.: bassoon; also called baryphonos aulos (144).

Baryphone, organ stop of free reeds at 16' pitch, with trumpet bodies, formerly also used in orchestrions (198).

Baryphonos aulos, see: baryaulos.

Baryton, 1. (It. *viola di bordone*), bowed instr. of bass range which evolved at the end of the 17th c., similar to the bass viola da gamba, but with 16–40 additional wire strings that passed close to the belly and under the neck, so that several of them could be plucked by the left thumb. This plucking, combined with the extremely broad neck, made it a most difficult instr. to play. The bowed strings were usually tuned $A^0 d^0 f^0 a^0 d^1 f^1$, the sympathetic strings at semitone intervals from C^0 to $d\sharp^0$. (Majer in 1732 writes that the tuning was that of a gamba, $D^0 G^0 c^0 e^0 a^0 d^1$.) The fingerboard was fretted. James Talbot, *ca.* 1700, seems to be the first author to describe the new instr. He calls it "viol barytone," says that it is the same as the lyra viol but 2 tones lower in pitch, with wire basses for the thumb. Today the short-lived instr. is chiefly remembered as that for which Haydn composed 175 pieces for his patron, Prince Nicolas Esterhazy;

2. a cello-like instr. invented by F. Battachon in 1848; 3. a large tenor violin built in 1847 by Charles Henri of Paris (who Latinized his name to Carolus Henry), tuned an oct. below the violin, *i.e.*, $G^0 d^0 a^0 e^1$, and played in violin

position; **4.** Ger.: euphonium (26, 89 Hayes, 134, 144, 176).

Baryton aigu (Fr.: sharp baritone), althorn in E♭, built by Fontaine-Besson of Paris in the 1880's to the specifications of Sellenick and shown at the Paris 1889 Exposition (176).

Baryton B, Ger.: euphonium.

Baryton en si♭, Fr.: baritone.

Barytonhorn, Ger.: euphonium; baritone.

Baryton impérial, see: Kaiserbass.

Baryton-violon, a "new instrument" by this name was patented on Feb. 17, 1900, by Paroche of Paris (204).

Bar zither, zither having a bar-shaped string bearer, often described as or called a *stick zither.

Bas (Pol.: bass), syn. of luk muzycyny.

Basamkub, 5-stringed lyre of the Bisharin of Upper Egypt (144 Hickmann).

Bascatibia (Basque pipe), syn. of chistu.

Base, 1. obs. Engl.: bass; **2.** coll. for bass viola da gamba.

Base violin, corr. of bass violin.

Bas hautbois, 16th-c. Fr. for basse de hautbois.

Bashingili, drum of the Lake Bangweulu area of N. Rhodesia (30).

Basing-basing, small clarinet of S. Celebes (121).

Bass, 1. Engl.: syn. of violoncello; **2.** obs. Ger.: bass viola da gamba.

Bassanelli, a rare Renaissance organ stop of regal pipes, imitative of the bassanello. Andreas Werckmeister says that it was "almost unknown" in his day. Apart from the fact that it was at 8′ or 4′ pitch we have no details concerning it.

Bassanello, a soft-voiced double-reed woodwind of the Renaissance, with narrow cylindrical bore, 6 front fingerholes, and one open key for the little finger. The reed was carried on an S-shaped metal crook. The sound was muted by insertion of a perforated lid or cover at the lower end. First mention of the bassanello occurs in a Graz inventory of instrs. purchased between 1577 and 1590, where 1 bass, 3 tenors, 1 contralto, and 1 soprano are listed. Latest mention is that of Praetorius, who wrongly ascribes their invention to the Venetian composer Giovanni Bassano. In modern times their invention has been credited (*i.a.*, by Wallner) to the Bassani brothers, musicians and instr. makers at the Engl. court; Anthony Bassano played the sackbut there in 1581. Praetorius gives their compasses as: soprano d⁰–g¹, alto/tenor G⁰–c¹, bass C⁰–e⁰ or f⁰. Their lengths were roughly 80 cm. (32 in.), 115 cm. (45 in.), 162 cm. (64 in.). Few specimens are known to have survived, notably one in the Kunsthistorisches Museum of Vienna (89, 183).

Bassaune, corr. of Posaune.

Bassa viola (It.), short for bassa viola da gamba, the bass gamba. Johann Mattheson (*Orchester*, 1713) says that the bassa viola, the cello, and the viola da spalla are small "Bassgeigen," or bass fiddles. Eisel in 1738 copies this passage and adds that the instr., is very pop. among the French (67).

Bassbalken, Ger.: bass-bar.

Bass-bar (Fr.: *barre, barre d'harmonie;* Ger.: *Bassbalken;* It.: *catena*), a long, narrow piece of softwood usually glued to the underside of the belly of instrs. of the viol and violin families; in a few instrs. it is carved right out of the belly. It lies under the left foot of the bridge, running almost but not quite parallel with the grain of the belly. The ends are tapered. Nowadays a violin bass-bar measures *ca.* 28 cm. (11 in.) in length and is *ca.* 5 mm. wide. Its function is to stiffen the belly, distribute its vibrations, and create resistance to the pressure of the bridge. In former centuries the bass-bar had perhaps half the mass over the same length, that it does today.

Bass cittern, see: archcittern.

Bass clarinet (Fr.: *clarinette basse;* Ger.: *Bassklarinette;* It.: *clarinetto basso, clarone in B♭*), a large clarinet pitched an oct. lower than the ordinary clarinet, and outwardly resembling a narrow-bored saxophone, as bell and mouthpiece are bent back in order to bring the keys within the player's reach. Pitched in Bb, it is notated a 9th higher than it sounds. Its present form dates back to the model designed by Adolphe Sax, then in Brussels, presumably in 1838. By making an acceptable straight model he did away for good with the serpentine form of his predecessors. The only major change since then has been the application of the Boehm mechanism in the 20th c. Bass clarinets have been made at least since 1772, when Gilles Lot of Paris produced the *basse-tube. This was followed by the *Klarinettenbass of Carl August Grenser the Elder of Dresden in 1793, built in bassoon form. The *basse-guerrière of Dumas appeared in 1807, the *basse-orgue of Frédéric Sautermeister in 1812, and the *glicibarifono of P. Maino of Padua ca. 1835. Some earlier models were also pitched in C and A, but these are now obs.; generally they were made of wood, with upturned metal bells, the mouthpiece carried on a metal crook. Sax reversed the curve of the bell, making it downturned. Basses in F and Eb, an oct. below the *alto clarinet, are made in France as clarinettes contralto. See also: basse-guerrière, basse-orgue, basse-tube, clarinette contralto, glicibarifono, Klarinettenbass (89 Rendall, 126, 164, 170).

Bass drum (Fr.: *grosse caisse, tonnant;* Ger.: *grosse Trommel;* It.: *catuba, gran cassa, gran tamburo*), a large *cylindrical drum of indefinite pitch, with 2 heads lapped over hoops and rather shallow body, the diam. always being greater than the length. The bass drum is made in different sizes; for orchestral purposes a minimum diam. of 80 cm. (32 in.) is required, less for rhythm bands. Nowadays both an orchestral and a military instr., the bass drum is set or carried with its heads facing sideways and is played close to the rim with a single padded stick. The

shell is of brass, and tension of the heads is adjusted by thumbscrews. Two distinct instrs. have been called bass drum, namely 1. that just described, short and wide, known to the West until the 19th c. as Turkish drum—in Europe it can be traced to the late 14th c.—and 2. the long drum, with cylinder about twice the diameter. In the course of the 19th c. this was transformed until it came to resemble (l.): the shell was shortened and widened, and wood was replaced by brass (nowadays by laminated wood). Gluck was an early writer for the new instr. (1764), and Mozart scored for it in *Die Entführung aus dem Serail* (1782). See also: long drum (89, 151, 170).

Basse à clefs, Fr.: bass ophicleide.

Basse à pistons, Fr.: euphonium; baritone saxhorn.

Basse-contre (Fr.), **1.** short for basse-contre de viole; **2.** short for basse-contre de violon; **3.** for the organ stop see: contrabass.

Basse-contre de viole (Fr.), *double-bass viol; such an instr. is mentioned in a 1556 Parisian instr. maker's inventory (80 VII).

Basse-contre de violon (Fr.), a *"basse-contre de violon façon de Venise"* is listed in a 1570 Fr. inventory: a double bass (80 VII).

Basse-cor (Fr. bass-horn), an improved *bass–horn of Louis-Alexandre Frichot, approved by a commission of the Paris Conservatoire on Nov. 13, 1806, made of metal and bent into a V shape. Frichot then proceeded to improve the basse-cor and named the resulting instr. basse-trompette (170, 204).

Basse de chalumeau (Fr.), name given to some clarinet parts in the early 18th c. Not an instr. (89 Rendall).

Basse de cornet à bouquin (Fr.), see: cornone.

Basse de cromorne (Fr.), **1.** bass crumhorn; **2.** obs. term for bassoon. Sébastien de Brossard, Johann Philipp Eisel, and other writers use the word in this sense (67).

Basse de Flandre, Flem. folk instr., similar to the *bladder and string and the *Bumbass.

Basse de hautbois, Fr.: bass shawm.

Basse de musette (Ger. *Musettenbass*), obs. woodwind instr. with wide conical bore, terminating in a bell and played with a double reed, probably of Swiss origin, and named by Chouquet. Surviving specimens have 6 fingerholes, 4 open keys, and a low hole with swallowtailed key. The bore is wider than that of an oboe. *Ca.* 1.25 m. (50 in.) long. See also: courtaut (25, 89).

Basse des Italiens (Fr.), obs. Fr.: double bass. The *Encyclopédie méthodique* (1751) says that it was a minor 3rd lower than the basse de viole, its lowest tone being E¹ (the same as that of the contreviolon or grosse basse de violon).

Basse de viole (Fr.), **1.** bass viola da gamba; **2.** organ stop of flue pipes with préstant scale; Dom Bedos wrote (1766–78) that it was not "yet" common in France (20).

Basse de viole d'amour, obs. Fr.: viola bastarda with sympathetic strings.

Basse de violon (Fr.), one of many names given to the bowed instrs. of bass range on the European Continent in past centuries. Fr. writers identify it with the violoncello. Sébastien de Brossard (in 1703) describes it as being half the size and an oct. higher than the violone; the *Encyclopédie méthodique* says that it was tuned an oct. below the viola. Note: the Ger. Bassviolon is a different instr.

Basse d'harmonie (Fr.), **1.** generic Fr. term denoting wind instrs. of bass register; **2.** an improved ophicleide patented by Halary of Paris on Feb. 9, 1822; **3.** an improved ophicleide patented by Frédéric Sautermeister of Lyon in 1827, with 11 keys, of which 6 were open keys (89, 204).

Basse en si♭, Fr.: euphonium.

Basse gigantesque (Fr.), name given to the octobasse of Vuillaume.

Bassegue, OFr.: clapper (of a bell).

Basse-guerrière (Fr.), bass clarinet with 13 keys, built by Dumas of Paris in 1807. *Cf.* contrebasse guerrière (126, 170).

Basse impériale (Fr.), see: Kaiserbass.

Bassel, syn. of Bassete.

Basse-orgue (Fr.), *bass clarinet patented by Frédéric Sautermeister of Lyon on Aug. 12, 1812. It was built in bassoon shape with a cylindrical bore and had a compass of over 3 octs. (126, 164).

Basse si♭ (Fr.), the same as basse en si♭.

Bassete [dim. of *basso*], small *double bass; also called Basset, Bassl, Kammerbass. Leopold Mozart said that it formerly had 5 strings but in his day had 4. See also: basso da camera.

Basset horn (Fr.: *cor de basset;* Ger.: *Bassetthorn;* It.: *corno bassetto*), **1.** elongated clarinet pitched in F (rarely in E♭), originally also in G, probably invented by A. and M. Mayrhofer of Passau, Bavaria, *ca.* 1770. Made of wood, it has the same bore and mouthpiece as the A and B♭ clarinets. Historically, 3 types have existed: the earliest instrs. were sickle-shaped, like the *cor anglais (from which they probably received the name basset *horn*), with 2 *basset keys taking the compass down to F and G. They were made by splitting a block of wood, hollowing out the sections, gluing them together again, and covering them with leather. The so-called "box" (Ger. *Kasten*), an oblong piece of wood fitted at the lower end, contained 3 parallel lengths of bore connected top and bottom, to reduce the over-all length, and carried a wide, flaring metal bell. Its curved shape led to its occasionally being called Krummhorn (crumhorn) in Ger.-speaking countries. By 1782 a new form appeared: the angular basset horn. This instr. received a sharp bend instead of the old curve, because it was easier to make it out of 2 straight pieces of wood connected by a very short elbow joint, and the "box" now became a protective cube of wood or metal. Early in the 19th c. Heinrich Grenser of Dresden made changes that ultimately led to the present form: straight, with the reed carried on a curved *barrel (called crook if made of metal, as it usually is nowadays) and terminating in an upturned bell. In the first quarter of the 19th c. Anton and Johann Stadler of Vienna added 2 more basset keys, for F♯ and G♯, and by 1825 basset horns were being made with 14 keys. Except for the crook and the metal bell, the present-day instr. has the appearance of an orchestral clarinet. Its compass is F^0–f^3, notated a 5th higher. By 1774 the basset horn was known in Paris, by 1789 in London. Mozart wrote for it from 1780 on, using it in opera, chamber works, and the *Requiem*. It was still scored by Mendelssohn in 1833 (Op. 113, 114), but changes in orchestral writing and the increasing importance of valved horns caused the basset horn to fall into near-oblivion until Richard Strauss wrote for it in his *Elektra* (1909). See also: clara voce, contra-clarinette (14; 89 Rendall, 170);

2. organ stop of reed pipes with cylindrical resonators, first built by Lohelius of Prague in 1785, later also built temporarily as a free-reed stop. As *corno di bassetto, it was built as a flue stop.

Basset key, key added to certain woodwind instrs. in order to increase their bass range.

Basse-trompette (Fr.), improved *basse-cor of Louis-Alexandre Frichot, then of Lisieux, approved by the Paris Conservatoire in 1806 and patented by him in France on Dec. 31, 1810. The improvements consisted of better curving of the tube and the addition of 4 slides to bring the instr. into D for concert use, C♯ for church performances, and C for military bands, the fourth being a flat-pitch slide in C. The basse-trompette was made entirely of brass, with expanding bore, 6 fingerholes, and 4 keys, and ter-

minated in a bell. The total tube length is given as 7 ft. 7 in., reduced to 25 in. according to the patent (*ca.* 2.30 m. and 65 cm.). It could be played with either a serpent or a trumpet mouthpiece. With the former it had a compass of A^1–d^0, with the latter d^0–d^3, or a total of 4½ octs. Also known as trombe and so described by Choron (89 Morley-Pegge).

Bassett, 1. Engl. and Ger.: syn. of bassete, bassetto, Bassettl, etc.; **2.** Ger.: abbr. of Bassettbombard; *cf.* Bombard.

Bassettl, Austrian var. of Bassett, 1.

Bassetto (It.), **1.** small *double bass. Sébastien de Brossard (in 1703) says that it is like our *"quintes"* or our *"basses de violon,"* a remark reiterated by the *Encyclopédie méthodique* in 1791; see also: basso da camera; **2.** as an organ stop, Bassetto is a term applied in S. Germany to the Hohlflöte at 4′ pitch in the pedal (133).

Bassetto di mano (It.), see: Handbassl.

Basse-tube (Fr.), name of an early bass clarinet, perhaps the earliest, made by Gilles Lot of Paris, as announced by the *Avant-Coureur* of May 11, 1772. It was furnished with several keys and had a compass of 3½ octs. (164, 176).

Basseuphonium (Ger.), a short-lived form of the *bass-horn, made by Heinrich J. Haseneier of Koblenz *ca.* 1850. The instr. was of wood with a metal bell and had unusually large keys. *Ca.* 128 cm. (50½ in.) long (89 Morley-Pegge, 176).

Bass fiddle, coll. for double bass.

Bass flugelhorn, Brit. name of a bugle-shaped brass instr. of tenor range, pitched in C, similar to the euphonium (89 Baines).

Bassflügelhorn, an Austrian designation of the tenor horn (176).

Bass flute (Fr.: *basse de flûte, flûte basse;* Ger.: *Bassflöte;* It.: *flautone*), **1.** *cross flute pitched in c^0, an oct. below the ordinary, or concert, flute, and thus in reality a tenor. For bands it is also made in $d♭^0$ and $e♭^0$, all with coiled heads. Bass flutes have existed since

Agricola's day—he described them in 1528—but in modern form only since the mid-18th c. To reduce the length to manageable proportions, both ends were folded in. No really successful model was produced prior to the *albisifono of 1910; **2.** Engl. designation of the alto flute; **3.** for the organ stop see: flute bass (169, 170).

Bassgeige (Ger.), Praetorius (in 1618) and Halle (in 1764) define it as a violoncello, but then, as now, it designated a cello or a double bass indifferently. The term occurs in a Graz inventory of 1577: *"drei neue bassgeigen so man zwischen füeszen zu nemen pflegt"* (90, 159).

Bass guitar (Fr.: *guitare théorbée;* Ger.: *Bassgitarre;* Sp.: *guitarrón*), a large guitar with off-board strings, first appearing in the mid-17th c. (176).

Bass-horn, 1. (Fr.: *cor basse;* Ger.: *Basshorn;* It.: *corno basso*), woodwind instr. the invention of which was claimed by Louis-Alexandre Frichot; manufactured by George Astor in London by 1800, when Frichot brought out a tutor for it. Actually the bass-horn was a metal version of J. J. Regibo's wooden *Russian bassoon. Because it was made in England it became known on the Continent as "English bass-horn" or as *"serpent anglais."* The bass-horn is a variety of upright serpent in the shape of a bassoon, with the conical bore of the serpent, made usually of copper, terminating in a wide bell and played with a cup mouthpiece. This is inserted into a long S-crook that accounts for about one-third of the over-all length of some 2.25 m. (7½ ft.). Originally 6 fingerholes and 3 keys were provided, 1 for the left thumb and 1 for each little finger; 2 more were added later. The fingering was that of the serpent. The bass-horn became pop. in England and until about 1815 was played only there and perhaps in France. From then until *ca.* 1830 it was adopted in Brit. and Continental military bands. In addition to the standard model in C, it was also built in B♭, and for the Prussian infantry in E and F. By 1835 it had become displaced by the ophicleide. Compass C^0–g^1. Frichot improved his bass-horn and named the resulting instr. *basse-cor. In the 1840's several builders, including Vaclav Červeny, built baritones with valves and called them bass-horns. A contrabass-horn was built by J. B. Coeffet (fl. 1828–45);

2. obs. organ stop of reed pipes, similar to the horn, at 8′ pitch, in the pedal. See also: Basseuphonium, chromatic bass-horn (89 Morley-Pegge, 126, 132, 169, 198).

Bassin [Lat. *bacchinon* or Gael. *bacca,* basin], a Fr. word for drum, in use from the 13th c. to the 17th, particularly a small kettledrum carried on the saddle. *Cf.* bacin, bachin, bachas (53, 204).

Bass in B♭, a U.S. designation of the baroxyton.

Bassl, a small *double bass. The term was in use in S. Germany and Austria. Syn. of bassete, basso da camera.

Bass ocarina, organ stop invented in the 20th c. by John Compton, at 32′ pitch, consisting of *Compton cubes.

Basso da braccio (It.), bass viola da braccio.

Basso da camera (It.), a small *double bass, halfway in size between a violoncello and a double bass, a string bass in G^1, known historically under a variety of names, chiefly as Halbbass or violone, also as Bassel, bassete, Bassl, Bierbass, Kammerbass (169).

Basso da gamba (It.), bass viola da gamba.

Basso dei flauti (It.), in the 18th c. a bass recorder (176).

Basso di camera (It.), see: basso da camera.

Basso di viola (It.), bass viola da gamba.

Basson [It. *bassone*] (Fr.), **1.** bassoon. The term has been in use since 1613, when it denoted the curtal. To Mersenne (in 1636) it designated a curtal with bass extension to B♭^{1}. For the rest of the century the word was also in use in England; **2.** the bassoon stop (197).

Basson à fusée, Fr.: racket bassoon.

Basson à raquette, Fr.: racket bassoon.

Basson d'amour (Fr.), modern name for a 3-keyed bassoon with an "amore"-shaped bulb bell of brass. Surviving specimens all appear to be from the same workshop, possibly Swiss, as some are known to have served in churches of Canton Bern. They have a pirouette on the crook and are *ca.* 115 cm. (3 ft. 10 in.) high (89 Langwill).

Basson de hautbois (Fr.), an early term for the bassoon.

Bassone [aug. of *basso,* low], obs. It.: **1.** bassoon; **2.** any instr. of low pitch (197).

Bassonetto [dim. of **bassone*], It.: a rarely used syn. of fagottino.

Basson Forveille (Fr.), syn. of serpent Forveille.

Basson français (Fr.), organ stop of reed pipes found in Fr. organs (33).

Basson grosso (*sic*), contrabassoon made by Stanesby for Handel's *L'Allegro* and *Royal Fireworks Music* and now preserved in the National Museum, Dublin. It has 4 keys and a bass compass of B♭² and is 2.70 m. (9 ft.) tall. See also: bassono grosso (14).

Basson-hautbois (Fr.) (Ger. *Fagott-Oboe*), organ stop of reed pipes with narrow, funnel-shaped resonators, at 8′ pitch; on some organs it forms a bass to the hautbois, 2, or its equivalent (133).

Bassono (It.), name occasionally given to the bassoon by composers of the past, including J. S. Bach (1708 on) (89 Langwill).

Bassono grosso (It.), term occasionally used by Ger. composers for the contrabassoon (including J. S. Bach in the *St. John Passion*). See also: basson grosso (125).

Bassonore (Fr.) [*bass* + *sonore*], metal bassoon invented by Nicolas Winnen of Paris (d. *ca.* 1834) and patented by his son Jean in 1844. Intended for military bands, it had a wide bore, 13 keys, and a compass of B♭¹–d² (125, 204).

Basson quinte, Fr.: tenoroon.

Basson russe, Fr.: Russian bassoon.

Bassoon [It. *bassone*] (Fr.: *basson;* Ger.: *Fagott;* It.: *fagotto;* Sp.: *fagote*), **1.** a low-pitched woodwind instr. developed from the curtal in the mid-17th c., with conical bore, played with a double reed (but *cf.* dolcino). Whereas the curtal had a double channel bored up and down in one piece of wood, the bassoon is made of 4 separate joints: the butt, or double joint, which holds the wing joint (also called tenor joint); the bass joint (also called long joint), and a slightly flared bell joint—all made traditionally of maple or pearwood—with a curved metal crook carrying the double reed. These sections form a continuously expanding tube of some 2.60 m. (8½ ft.) including the crook, with a height of *ca.* 1.40 m. (4½ ft.). The bassoon is pitched in C, as was its predecessor, has fingerholes (drilled at about a 45-degree angle) and keys. Its compass is B♭¹–f² or a², notated as it sounds. The new instr. was at first called "French basson" in England, until the Engl. version was coined (earliest mention of "bassoon" was in 1706). At the same time it continued to be called curtal. In Ger.-speaking countries the terminology was just as confused, Dulzian and Fagott being interchangeable terms; and Basson also occurred. The composer Reinhard Keiser wrote in 1720 of the King of Denmark that he had eight *"solche Bassons und Bassonetten bey seiner Grenadier-Guarde"* (such Bassons and Bassonetts in his grenadier guards). The bombard continued in use side by side with the curtal until the mid-17th c., and by the 18th c. these 2 terms had become confused and "Fagott" was used to designate the earlier shawm. In 1732, Majer had to point out that Dulzian and Fagott were the same. In Italy the term *fagotto* had been in use from the mid-16th c., at first denoting the curtal. To the 2 keys of the curtal a third was added at the time of the instr.'s transformation into the bassoon (for B♭[1]). Mattheson, in 1713, gives its compass as C^0–f^1 or g^1, with occasional downward extension to B♭[1] or A[1]. By 1730 a fourth key had been added (for A♭[0]), and during most of the 18th c. the 4 keys were standard. Eisel, in 1738, depicts such an instr. Halle mentions 7 keys in 1764, a very early date, as by the end of the century no more than 6 were common. By 1827 it had 15 keys, increased to 17 by 1839. The first bassoon with all covered keys was designed by Charles-Joseph Sax of Brussels and was shown in 1825. Metal bassoons with covered holes were patented by him and his son, Adolphe, from 1842 on. In 1851, Adolphe Sax made a bassoon with 23 keys. A 29-key Boehm-type instrument was made by Triébert of Paris in 1855 and was exhibited there that year, and in London in 1862. From the early 19th c. on, 2 distinct schools of bassoon making developed—Fr. and Ger. —with Heckel playing a preponderant role in Germany, maintained until now, and Buffet in France. The Ger. model is played in America and is becoming increasingly favored in Europe outside of France. Although independent parts were not customarily written for the bassoon until the late 18th c., the instr. was used in orchestras much earlier. Quantz, for instance, requires a bassoon for a chamber orchestra of only 9 string instrs. Its function was that of a continuo instr. until later in the century, when it was given a staff of its own and an independent part. (Mozart's bassoon concerto dates from 1774.) In addition to the ordinary bassoon, a contrabassoon in C is in use today, the only one to have been retained of a number of different-sized bassoons formerly in use. Others, now obs., were the bassoon in D, a tone higher than the ordinary bassoon, the E♭ bassoon (Terzfagott in Ger.) a minor 3rd higher, the F bassoon and G bassoon—better known as tenoroons—and low-pitched instrs. such as the semicontrabassoon and subcontra-

bassoon. The Boehm-system bassoon, made by Triébert of Paris in 1855 and later, never caught on and was abandoned. See also: alto fagotto, bajón, basse de cromorne, basson, basson d'amour, bassonetto, bassono, bassono grosso, bassonore, Basspfeife, Chorist-Fagott, contrabassoon, curtal, dolcian, dolcino, Doppelfagott, Doppelkortholt, Dresdner Fagott, Dulzian, echo bassoon, Fagot, Fagott, fagottino, fagotto chorista, phagotum, Quartfagott, Quintfagott, racket bassoon, semicontrabassoon, subcontrabassoon, tenoroon (89 Langwill, 125);

2. organ stop of reed pipes, mentioned by Praetorius (as Fagott), at which time it had cylindrical resonators of medium scale. In Dom Bedos' day (1778) it was a *regal stop of large or narrow scale; still later it was made with conical resonators and formed the bass section of an oboe or clarinet stop. Found in the pedal at 16′ or 8′ pitch, rarely at 32′ or 4′ (20, 129, 133).

Bassoon serpent, syn. of Russian bassoon.

Bassoon stop (Fr.: *basson; jeu de basson;* Ger.: *Fagottzug;* It.: *pedale di fagotto*), harpsichord stop and piano stop found on some 18th-c. and early-19th-c. instrs., a "Turkish music" stop consisting of a strip of wood to which a roll of parchment was glued. This could be lowered onto the strings by means of a pedal. Usually it was applied only to the bass section, going up to c^1 at most (92).

Basso tuba, It.: bass tuba.

Basspfeife, Ger.: **1.** bass pipe; **2.** in the 18th c. a rare syn. of bassoon (90).

Basstromba (Ger.), wind instr. in E♭, designed by Wilhelm Wieprecht of Berlin; according to Adolphe Sax, it was identical to his saxhorn in low E♭. Basstrombas in D and G were used in Austrian and occasionally Prussian cavalry bands around 1827, but details of their construction are not known (176).

Basstrompete (Ger.), false designation

of a B♭ bass Cornet-Instrument of Vaclav Červeny (25).

Bass tuba, organ stop of overblowing
reed pipes, also called helicon; a tuba stop
at 16′ pitch. For the orchestral instr. see:
tuba (133).

Bass viol, bass viola da gamba.

Bass violin, 17th-c. term for the violoncello. John Playford (in 1660) and
James Talbot (*ca.* 1700) give its tuning
as B♭^{1} F^0 c^0 g^0, a tone below our modern tuning. Adriano Banchieri (in 1609)
had a bass violino da braccio tuned
G^0 d^0 a^0 e^1, or an oct. below the violin,
in reality a tenor violin.

Bassviolon (Ger.), according to Mattheson and Eisel, the same as a violone
(the Fr. basse de viole is a different
instr.).

Basszink (Ger.), see: cornone.

Basulī, syn. of vāmsī.

Basune [Lat. **buccina*], OFr. var. of
buisine.

Basviool, Du.: violoncello.

Bata, 1. drum of the Nago of Dahomey; 2. *conical drum of the Yoruba of
Nigeria, with 2 laced heads. *Cf.* batá-
kotó (103).

Batá, double-headed Afro-Cuban drum
with laced heads, used in Yoruba liturgy.
Made in various forms—conical and cylindrical. Often one head has a belt of
pellet bells and bells attached to it. See
also: okónkolo (152).

Batá-cotó, obs. drum of the Nago Negroes of Brazil, made of an elongated
calabash, with a single head (7).

Batá-kotó, obs. *cylindrical drum of
the Kukumi or Yoruba of Cuba, with a
single head (152).

Batallum, Lat.: clapper (of a bell).

Batē, drum of the Timne of Sierra
Leone, with wooden body and single head
(176).

Batel [Lat. **batallum*], Fr. for bell
clapper from the 14th c. to the 16th (82).

Bathyphone (Ger. *Bathyphon*), *contrabass clarinet first built by Eduard
Skorra of Berlin in 1839 to the design
of Wilhelm Wieprecht, later built by C.

Kruspe of Erfurt. Pitched in C, 2 octs.
below the ordinary clarinet, the bathyphone had 2 parallel tubes of maple or
brass united in a butt joint, an upturned
metal bell, and S-crook. It looked rather
like a Russian bassoon and had a compass E^1–c^1, its lowest tones being weak.
A surviving specimen in Copenhagen has
17 keys. The bathyphone served as a military instr. and is now obs. (164, 169).

Batillus, Lat.: clapper (of a bell).

Batiwtiw, bamboo "buzzers" of the
Hanunoo of the Philippine Islands (103).

Bâton de rythme, Fr.: stamping tube.

Bâton frappé, Fr.: percussion stick.

Batsi, see: bachi.

Batsu, metal cymbals of Japan, with
large central boss. *Ca.* 30 cm. (1 ft.) in
diam. Equivalent of the Chin. po and Korean tong pal. Also called hatsu (176).

Batta, a spherical calabash drum of the
Hausa (93).

Battachio, It.: clapper (of a bell).

Battaglio, var. of battachio.

Battal, a large obs. Turk. nāy (76).

Battant, Fr.: clapper (of a bell).

Batyphone, see: bathyphone.

Baudoire, baudoise [Lat. *baudosa*],
OFr.: pandoura. The term is mentioned
in Fr. literature from *ca.* 1150 to the 13th
c. *Cf.* baldosa.

Baudosa, Lat. equiv. of baldosa.

Bauernflöte (Ger.: peasant flute), organ stop that originated in the late Renaissance and assumed many forms. Adlung describes it as a small Gedackt at
2′, 1½′, and 1′ pitches; it was also a
wide-scaled flute of open cylindrical
pipes, in Germany at 2′ or 1′ pitch, in
Holland as Baarpijp at 8′ or 4′ pitch; it
occurred furthermore as a half-stopped
Rohrflöte and as a reed stop with short
resonators (3, 133).

Bauernleier, obs. Ger.: hurdy-gurdy.

Baushi, flute of N. India (103).

Bava, *barrel drum of Alor Island,
Indonesia, used to accompany dances
(173).

Bavariazither (Ger.), original name of
the Elegiezither.

Bawa, *musical bow of the Aïmeri of the Congo, without loop or resonator (128).

Bawwāqe, pl. **bawāwīq,** Arab.: trumpet (176).

Baxoncillo, see: bajoncillo.

Baya, stick zither of the Teke of Kasai, the Congo (185).

Bāya, N. and C. Indian name of the bāmyā.

Bayan, chromatic accordion of Russia, still pop. (38).

Baylama, syn. of tanbura, 1.

Bayohabao, var. of mayohuacan (152).

Bāz, abbr. of tabli bāz.

Baza, xylophone of the Gobu of the Congo, similar to the kalanba (31).

Bazara, *stamping tube of the Washambala of Kenya, consisting of a thin bamboo tube with longitudinal slits, stamped rhythmically against the ground during dances and also struck with a stick (111).

Bazombe, musical bow of Katanga, the Congo, similar to the nxonxoro (149).

Bazoo, syn. of kazoo.

Bazuin [Lat. *buccina* via OFr. *buisine*], **1.** ODu.: trombone; **2.** organ stop of reed pipes at 32′ or 16′ pitch, equivalent of the Ger. Posaune (133).

Bazuna [Lat. *buccina*], wooden trumpet of the Kashubian of Pol. Pomerania, with conical bore; 1.80–2.10 m. (6–7 ft.) long. See also: ligawka (89).

B♭ baritone, see: baritone.

B♭ bass, U.S. designation of the baroxyton.

BB♭ bass, contrabass tuba.

B♭–C clairon (Ger. *B–C Clairon*), *duplex instrument by F. Hirschberg of Breslau, shown at the Vienna Exposition of 1873—a combined flugelhorn in B♭ and cornet in C (176).

Beabobo, *marine-shell trumpet of the Tuléar district of the Malagasy Republic, with lateral mouthpiece, used for ritual purposes. Also called maromena (171).

Beaked flute (Fr.: *flûte à bec;* Ger.: *Schnabelflöte*), any *vertical flute with

its upper end shaped into a beak to facilitate blowing. Note: the Fr. and Ger. equivalent terms also denote specifically the recorder.

Beard, cylinder of wood or metal affixed under the ears of narrow-scaled flue organ pipes like a fender, to assist speech (101).

Beating reed (Fr.: *anche battante;* Ger.: *Aufschlagzunge;* It.: *ancia battante*), a reed that beats against a frame. See: single reed. Reeds of organ pipes were beating reeds until the advent of the *free reed in Europe in the late 18th c.

Bebaling, var. of berbaling.

Bec de grive (Fr. thrush beak), *double reed of Fr. Switzerland, made of fine tubes of birch, hazel, or other twigs; sometimes these are affixed to a short wooden tube. Called bargialera in Romansh (102).

Bechertrommel, Ger.: goblet drum.

Becken, Ger.: cymbals. The word is first recorded in 1732. Up to the early 20th c. Cinellen was a commoner term.

Bedon (belly), obs. Fr.: drum. The word was in use from the 13th c. to the 17th. In the early 15th c. it designated a kettledrum. Cotgrave (in 1611) translates it as "tabret"; Trichet (*ca.* 1640) describes it as a cylindrical drum with laced heads (82, 190, 197).

Bedon de Biscaye, a small Fr. tambourine with jingles, sounded by rubbing the membrane with one's thumb, according to Mersenne (70, 140).

Bedon de Suisse, obs. Fr. term for a snare drum.

Bedug, a large barrel-shaped drum of C. Java, with 2 nailed heads, suspended from a frame and struck with a beater. Also called teteg (121).

Beffroi [MHGer. *bercvrit,* watchtower] (Fr.), originally a watchtower where the watch was kept with an alarm bell; since the 15th c. the alarm bell itself (197).

Begenna, see: bagana.

Beh, shepherd's flute of Nepal, with 7 fingerholes (176).

Bēhālā, small *spike fiddle of Bengal, with clay body, skin belly, and bamboo neck. Its 2 gut strings are bowed with a short horsehair bow (173).

Beiaard [U.], Flem.: carillon, particularly the larger type of carillon that the French call carillon de Flandres (160).

Belangi, var. of balangi.

Belapella, painted wooden, zoomorphic rattle, filled with pebbles, of the Vancouver Indians (176).

Belebān, trumpet of the Kurds. *Cf.* balāban (176).

Belière [*?belle*], Fr.: **1.** bell worn by the bellwether; **2.** the ring by which a bell is suspended (197).

Bell [OEngl. *belle*] (Fr.: *cloche;* Ger.: *Glocke;* It., Sp.: *campana*), **1.** hollow body of wood or metal, either provided with an inside clapper or struck from the outside with a hammer. Those of wood are considered to be older than those of metal. Bells differ from (hollow) gongs in that their vibrations issue from the sound bow (close to the rim), while the vertex is dead; whereas in gongs the vibrations issue from the center, the rim being dead. The bell is known to all peoples. Its origin has not yet been fully determined, but we know that its earliest uses were magical and ritual, not musical: bells served as amulets, hung on animals to protect them from evil spirits; they were placed at doors to protect the home; were sounded at places of worship to purify them, not to call the worshipers; were suspended from the necks of sacrificial animals; were sewn on priests' garments for their protection, and were used as fertility charms. To this day doorbells of New Ireland and parts of Africa do not announce visitors; they protect the occupants.

Bells have been made in a number of forms: an excavated cast bronze bell of Assyria, dating from the 8th c. or 9th c. B.C. is beehive-shaped; those of the Far East, ancient Egypt, and Ireland were originally quadrangular in cross-section; ancient Peru had wooden bells of rectangular form, as have Estonia, Burma, and parts of the Malay Archipelago today. The clapperless bell of Asia was originally square. The shallow, bowl-shaped, or hemispheric *cymbala of med. Europe have the same form as the Far Eastern *resting bell, both being struck from the outside with a hammer. This form has existed in Europe since *ca.* 1300, first as a clock bell, now as an electric bell; but it must be considered of Asiatic origin. The European clapper bell was beehive-shaped at first, but around 1200 its waist changed from a convex to a concave shape, resulting in the campaniform bell. Not all bells are cast: bent and soldered sheet-metal bells are by far the oldest form in Europe, as they were in use in antiquity for herd animals: the cowbell is a descendant of the bell hung on sacrificial animals for magico-ritual purposes. In postclassical Europe, use of cattle bells is authenticated in Nonsberg, S. Tirol, as early as 397. Prehistoric bells have been found in Iceland, and cast bells were known in China in the second millennium B.C.; a bronze Assyrian clapper bell in beehive form, ornamented with reliefs, is preserved in the Berlin Museum; some 80 bronze hand bells were excavated at Nimrud (destroyed 612 B.C.). Numerous bronze bells were also found in Egypt, both resting bells and quadrangular hand bells; in Hellenistic times they were also made of gold and silver, occasionally in pottery. Roman bells of bronze and of iron are fairly common and have been found in many parts of the Roman Empire.

In the 6th c. church bells were mentioned in Scotland, and during the same century they spread south to Gaul and Italy (see: campana, signum, also cloca). Bede mentioned church bells in Britain (680). But the ancient art of casting bells had been lost and was not rediscovered until the 8th or 9th c.—in Britain not until the 10th—and as bellmaking was primarily a church art it was confined at first to monks. In early med. times sets of bells were made either by increasing the amount of metal toward the bass—in which case the bells grew longer—or by increasing it toward the treble. In the latter case they were all of the same size but of different thicknesses: the thicker the wall of a bell, the higher its pitch. Theophilus, a monk now assumed to have lived *ca.* 1100, gives formulas for raising and lowering the pitch of a bell. From his and other early treatises we know that monochord ratios were employed in calculating the sizes of bells, and that these calculations did not work. The large number of variant formulas offered gives some idea of the scope of the med. bellmaker's difficulty. Despite such factors the size of bells increased after the 11th c., but it was not until the 14th c. that really large bells could be founded. By 1372 Goulain could write that there existed 6 kinds of bells in churches: *"tentans, tymbres, noles, nolettes, eschelettes et cloches."* In the second half of the 14th c. bells in towers were mechanized with weight-driven clocks. Up to then the hours were sounded by men who were armed with hammers and went into the tower at regular intervals. With the improvement of casting methods, bigger and bigger bells came to be made, until in 1733–34 the *"Tsar Kolokol"* (Emperor Bell) of Moscow was cast, largest known bell, *ca.* 5¾ m. (19 ft.) high with a diam. of *ca.* 6¾ m. (22½ ft.) and a weight of some 180 tons.

Although bells were historically made of wood or metal, other materials have been used: animal horn, glass, porcelain, for instance. Cast bells are made of an alloy termed bell metal, which is composed of about 78 per cent copper, about 22 per cent tin, with small amounts of other materials. A bell consists of shoulder, waist, sound bow, and rim. Cast bells have greater carrying power than uncast ones. Those in towers are arranged either so that they may be swung or so that they remain stationary ("hung dead"). In Catholic churches bells are traditionally

swung, with the clapper striking. The Engl. custom of change-ringing on the principle of permutation was introduced in the early 18th c., at which time half-wheels were employed and the bells were not raised so high as they are now. The term "ringing" implies that a bell is swung. The tone of a stationary bell is at its best if it is struck on the inside by a clapper, rather than by an exterior hammer. Both modes of playing a stationary bell, *i.e.,* pulling the clapper by a rope or striking the outside with a hammer, are called "clocking" a bell. The process of "chiming" consists in swinging the bell just far enough for the clapper to strike the sound bow, whereas in "ringing" the clapper is made to hit with full force.

In the orchestra, bells became so unwieldy that they were replaced by *tubular bells or other metallophones. Bell tone is composed of harmonic and nonharmonic partials. Lord Rayleigh was first to study it in 1890 (*Philosophical Magazine*), and our knowledge of the subject is still so incomplete that virtually no 2 acousticians are in agreement on it. It now appears that the *strike note of campaniform bells may be nonexistent per se, but is manufactured by the ear; and the so-called "five-point system" of bell harmonics (the heard tone, often misnamed fundamental; the oct. below it; minor 3rd above it; 5th above it, and oct. above it) is currently said to be more theoretical than factual. See also: bell chime, carillon, cymbala, resting bell, strike-note, tubular bells, and: abanangbweli, abivadongbwali, adja, aeolian bell, agau, agōgo, agogō, alambre, angong, anzel, apolo, aporo, appeau, arol, arran, arrancadera, bancloche, belière, bell wheel, bilbilla, bimpombu, binza, bulunba, cai chuong chua, cai chuong de chung, cai chuong gang, cai mo ña chua, camel bells, campa, campaínha, campana, campane, campenole, carroccio, cascabel, cascavelle, cencerro, chak, chilin, chilincha, chilindrín, chilimera, chincha, chinchasko, ch'ing, chingongo,

Chlepfe, Chlöpfe, choca, chueca, chung, cloc, cloca, cloche, clochette, clog, clopot, cloque, cloquette, clugge, cianciana, ciric belle, clag, clarain, clare, clarine, corrigiuncula, cowbell, cymbale, cymbalum, dandin, danno, darā, daule, den sho, dibu, dingdingti, dobachi, double bell, dril-bu, dunba, echelle, echelette, ekón, elonja, eltzabor, enkanika, eschile, eskilla, esquerlòtis, esquilla, esudsu, ezkilats, fale, gā, gale, gan, gangana, gangarria, gankogui, gara, garbish, gare, gegrumbungan, genta, ghant, ghantā, ghantikā, ghanghara, ginnu, Gleppe, glocca, Glocke, Glogg, Glogga, gobo, gonga, gonguē, grunong, gulunba, han sho, hilezkilak, hin, hyang ryong, ikelengue, irna, jānk, jaras, joare, juljul, kampan, kansilemba, kell, kello, kembone, keretok, khalok, khlopki, khonglong, kili, kin, kinkini, 1, kinkoto, kipkurkur, kiskilla, kitsika, kizugo, klentong, klocka, klok, klokje, klokka, klotak, klukka, kolokol, kolotok, konron, ko sho, kpanlingān, krapp, kunda, kutorka, küzkuilü, kyēdi, ling, ling tang, longa, lo to ling tang, lubembe, mage ling, ma ling, marawat, matraco, mbombu, mbonga, metale, mjedenica, mmanga, motbel, mpovila za londe, munkunku, muta, namalanga, nāqūs, ndingi, negpwapwo, ngonga, ngongila, ngunga, nkola, nola, nole, nolette, nolula, notolo, ogán, o-gane, ongola, pa'amon, pamigán, panpalina, pellet bell, pitorka, pivora, plumbe, po chung, puchero, pumpiang, pworu, resting bell, sain, saint, sampuegn, san, scella, schella, Schelle, scilla, segundilla, sein, seny, sguilla, shin gane, shun, signulum, signum, sin, sineta, sing, sino, sint, skella, skellat, skellie, skellilinum, sonnaille, sonneau, sonnette, sumle, sun, Swiss bells, taku, talancă, tantan, t'e chung, tedoc, tentant, thak, thuk chong, timbre, 1, tinniolum, tinternel, tintinele, tintinnabulum, tintinnus, tintinullum, to, tocsin, tonabulum, toquassen, toxin, trinklen, truc, tymbris, umudende, Viktoriaglocke, vizugo, wana, wei-shun, xin-

cherri, zangak, zanj, zeinu, zeng, zenk, Zimbel, zinzerri, zumba;

2. (Fr.: *pavillon;* Ger.: *Schallstück, Stürtze;* It.: *padiglione*), flared or bulbous terminal of most wind instrs., playing an important role in determining the timbre; **3.** inverted cone surmounting certain organ pipes (79, 89, 155, 160, 168, 169, 170, 198).

Bellarmonic [bell + *armonica*], metallophone designed by Francis Hopkinson of Philadelphia in 1787 (an improvement of Franklin's armonica [see: glass harmonica]), with metal instead of glass bowls (144, 169).

Bell chime, a set of bells tuned to various pitches, by extension also a set of *tubular bells. The difference between chime and *carillon is merely one of compass, any set of more than 1½- or 2-oct. compass being considered a carillon. Bell chimes are Bronze Age counterparts of neolithic *lithophones, according to Sachs, and are not confined to Europe: ancient China had sets of bells struck on the inside by a clapper or from the outside with a hammer. The European bell chime appears in the 9th c. as *cymbala (pl. of cymbalum). A number of small bells, bowl-shaped from the 9th c. to the 12th c., later campaniform, are arranged according to pitch, and are suspended from a frame or horizontal rod, and are struck on the outside by a hammer. This type of chime is frequently depicted from the 11th c. to the 15th, with the number of bells varying from 4 to 15. The tuning of these bells presented great difficulties (see: bell). The 13th-c. *Cantigas de Santa María* shows 7 bells in a frame with long clappers (or attachments to the clappers?) pulled by a seated musician. In the same century mechanized chimes appear, and in the 14th c. a new form appears in the Low Countries: large chimes for church and other towers, at first trodden by foot, later combined with a manual or pedalboard and driven by means of clockwork actuating a pinned cylinder. Hammers struck the outside of the bells.

The hours could be announced mechanically and chorales also played. A variety with far smaller bells was connected to the organ keyboard and later incorporated as a stop or half stop (*not* the *Zimbelstern, which is a survival of the bell wheel). The modern chime, consisting of metal tubes, is struck with a mallet, generally has 1½-oct. compass, c²–f³, and is notated an octave lower. See also: carillon, cymbala, ko chung, orugŏru, pien chung, pyon chong, saptaghantikā, tubular bell (E. Buhle: *"Das Glockenspiel . . ."* in: *Festschrift . . . von Liliencron,* 1910; 89, 169).

Bell cittern, Engl.: hamburger Cithrinchen.

Bell clapper, see: clapper.

Bell clarionet, clarinet organ stop with resonators surmounted by a "bell" (133).

Bell diapason, see: flûte à pavillon.

Belle, MLGer.: small bell (197).

Bellesonorereal, keyboard instr. of secret construction, invented by Johann Christian Jürgensen of Silesia in the last quarter of the 18th c., said to have produced the sound of a harpsichord, clavecin royal, fortbien, and other instrs. Also called bellsonore (27, 176).

Bell gamba (Ger.: *Glockengambe*), obs. organ stop of the gamba family, the pipes being surmounted by a "bell," at 16′, 8′, and 4′ pitches. Not identical with the cone gamba (131, 186).

Bell harp, *box zither invented by John Simcock of Bath in the early 18th c., consisting of a box with campaniform profile strung with 14–24 (usually 16) courses of 3 or 4 strings. Tuning pins were inserted at the top. The strings were plucked with a plectrum worn on each thumb. According to William T'ansur, writing in 1767, the instr. was kept swinging while played. Strings for the right thumb were tuned d¹ d² e² f♯² g² a² b² c♯³ d³ and for the left e¹ f♯¹ g¹ a¹ b¹ c² c♯² (79, 89 Galpin).

Bell lyre (Ger.: *Stahlspiel, Lyra;* It.: *strumento d'acciaio*), a portable glockenspiel in lyre form, designed for the use

of marching bands. A series of tuned metal bars is fixed at each end to a lyre-shaped frame. The player holds it by a handle and strikes the bars with a small metal beater. Because of its shape it is also called lyra. Other names are lyra glockenspiel, metal harmonica (89, 151).

Belloneon, free-reed automatophone built by Johann Gottlieb Kaufmann, of Dresden, and his son Friedrich, in 1805, a forerunner of their famous automatic *trumpeter; 24 free metal reeds and a drum terminated in simulated trumpets and kettledrums, housed in a mahogany case and sounded by means of a pinned cylinder (37, 176).

Bellows [OEngl. *blastbaelig,* blow bag] (Fr.: *soufflet;* Ger.: *Blasebalg;* It.: *mantici;* Sp.: *fuelle*), organ bellows are known to have existed in the E. Roman Empire in the 4th c. and are possibly older. In the West they appear as trodden bellows in NE. France by the second third of the 9th c. (Stuttgart psalter), or as smithy bellows. Rectangular bellows came into use in the 15th c. Until the early 19th c. the bellows of all large organs were trodden. Bagpipe bellows appear in the 16th c. (62, 185A).

Bellsonore, syn. of bellesonorereal.

Bell wheel (Fr.: *roue à clochettes;* Ger.: *Glockenrad*), a series of small bells set around the edge of a wheel, known from med. times on. See also: cymbala, horologium, rotllo, roue flamande, Zimbelstern.

Beluwat [*bulu,* bamboo], bamboo *vertical flute of the Batak of Sumatra, also played as a *nose flute (203).

Bemastocc, bemalstocc [*beme* + *stocc,* wood], OEngl.: wooden trumpet.

Bembé, Afro-Cuban drum of confused typology: generally single-headed, nearly cylindrical, or barrel-shaped, with nailed head, set up on end and played with drumsticks; formerly made of a tree trunk. A double-headed variety also exists. Up to 1.60 m. (5 ft. 3 in.) high (152).

Beme (OEngl.), med. trumpet, mentioned in OEngl. and MEngl. literature. The word was glossed *ca.* 800 as *concha,* and dies out around 1500. The word also occurs as *byme.* See also: glēo-bēam, trumpe (89, 180).

Bemola, name given in the Malagasy Republic to local imitations of European violins and viols (171).

Bemu nggri-nggo, idiochord bamboo *tube zither of Flores, Indonesia (119).

Ben, see: bīnt.

Bendair, see: bandair.

Bendé, small gong of C. and E. Java, with central boss, suspended vertically and used chiefly as a signal instr. Often confused with the gong beri (121).

Bendere [Arab. *bandair*], calabash drum in Siti, an African language (93).

Bendīr, Moroccan name of the bandair (93).

Bendo [Arab. *bandair*], calabash drum in Nafana, an African language (93).

Bendrong, stamping trough of Java, consisting of a long, hollow tree trunk resting on 2 rollers so that resonance should not be impeded—actually a rice trough. Women stamp or beat in or on it at eclipses of sun or moon, on moonlit nights, and in the Sunda districts also at circumcision feasts. Also called gejongan, genrong, kotekan (89 Kunst).

Bendukuku, *musical bow of the Amanga, Andebogo, Andekuju, Adoi, Andoni, Andragbo, Obvango, and Tenza of the Congo; it has a gourd resonator that is not attached to the bow (128).

Bengāla, Sudanese lute with oval body, skin belly, and wide, flat neck, often carved, with 2 pairs of strings. *Ca.* 48 cm. (19 in.) long (132).

Bengalu, *cross flute of the Nzakara of the Union of Central African Republics, with 2 fingerholes (42).

Benilleux, benilloux, (phonetic) var. of biniou in Rennes, France (197).

Benn-crot (pointed *crot*), name occasionally given to the ancient Irish timpan (79).

Bennde [Arab. *bandair*], Dyoula (Sudanic language): large drum (93).

Bent, see: bīnt.

Benta, *musical bow of W. India, held between the player's teeth and tapped with a short stick (17).

Bentside (Ger.: *Hohlwand*), the curved, long side of a piano, harpsichord, or wing-shaped spinet.

Bentwa [Ewe *beta*], *musical bow of the Twi of Ashanti, W. Africa, with 1 or 2 strings (93).

Be-orla, syn. of dakado (119).

Berbaling, 1. *bull-roarer of Malay, now very rare, formerly used for scaring elephants away from plantations; **2.** *aeolian pipe of Malay, with one end stopped and the other beveled, attached to a windmill-like device. Also called baling (18).

Berde (Serb.) [Gk. *barytonon*], **1.** Croatian contrabass tanbura with 4 strings tuned $G^1 G^0 D^0 d^0$; **2.** Serb.: bass pipe (34, 176).

Bergzither, a 19th-c. Ger. name of the cittern; not to be confused with Gebirgszither (169).

Beri, see: gong beri.

Berimbao, Port.: Jew's-harp. See also: birimbao, marimbau.

Berimbao de barriga, syn. of urucungo (7).

Berliner Pumpen, Berliner Pumpventil, an improved short piston valve of large diam., devised in 1835 by C. W. Moritz of Berlin. Also called Bombenventil (25).

Berra-boi, bull-roarer of Brazil (7).

Berri, small barrel-shaped drum of Ceylon, with 2 heads, played with bare hands. *Cf.* gong beri (176).

Berrigodea, a long drum of the Sinhalese of Ceylon, played with bare hands (176).

Bersag horn [It. *Bersaglieri*], valved bugle with a single piston valve that lowers the tone a 4th, allegedly first used in the Bersaglieri corps of the It. army, and played in sets of 4: soprano, alto, tenor, and baryton or bass, all of which are pitched in B♭. During the First World

War it became pop. because it was so easy to play. It is still in use in France and in Spain (89).

Bertz, Basque folk zither, a *tambourin à cordes played with the one-hand flute (56).

Beta, word meaning *musical bow in Ewe (a Sudanic language) (93).

Bettlerleier (beggar's drone), Ger.: hurdy-gurdy.

B♭ euphonium, see: euphonium.

Beure hevehe (gourd *hevehe*), syn. of hevehe.

Bēyālā, see: bēhālā.

Bhairi, var. of gong beri.

Bhajana-sruti, see: bajānā sruti.

Bharata-vīnā (Sans., Beng.: Indian *vīnā*), modern combination of a rudra vīnā and a kachapi vīnā, with body of a half calabash, membrane belly, 5 rib-fastened metal strings tuned $f^1 c^1 c^1 f^1 c^0$, and both frontal and lateral pegs. *Ca.* 110 cm. (43 in.) long (173).

Bhavarkatū (Sans.), drum of India, played in funeral processions (176).

Bhaya dindina (Sans.), battle drum (176).

Bher, Hindust.: tūrya.

Bhēri (Sans., Hindi, Beng.), **1.** a large nāgārā of India, formerly used in battle; **2.** see: gong beri (179).

Bhuri, Tel.: tūrya.

Bia, an elongated drum of the Bwaka of the Congo, with 2 heads, chiefly cylindrical. In many cases the lacing forms a network over the body (30).

Bibelregal, Ger.: Bible regal.

Bibi, corr. of Fr. *bébé* (baby): pop. name of the low upright piano of Bord of Paris, called pianette in England (89).

Bibita, drum of the Congo people, long and narrow, with a laced head (30).

Bible clavichord, a small fretted clavichord at 4′ pitch in form of a large book, presumably inspired by the *Bible regal.

Bible regal (Ger.: *Bibelregal*), modern name of a regal in form of a book, allegedly first made by the Nürnberg organ builder Georg Voll (d. 1565). This form of regal was made from the mid-16th c.

to the 18th c. Also called book regal (2).

Bicitrabīn, vīnā of N. India, without frets. It corresponds to the gotuvādyam of S. India, where it is also called vichitra vīnā (144).

Biciŭ, pl. **bice** (Rom.: whip), *whirled friction drum of Romania (169).

Bideru, *slit drum of the Galla of NE. Africa, made of a hollowed tree trunk and used for signaling purposes (176).

Bierbass (Ger.: beer bass), pop. name of the Halbbass.

Bifaria [Lat. *bifariam,* twofold], organ stop composed of 2 ranks of pipes of the same name and pitch. Before the baroque era only diapasons were so disposed, but later the arrangement was carried over to other stops, chiefly strings. Bifaria is also a stop of large-scaled open metal flue pipes at 8′ or 4′ pitch with 2 mouths, one cut up a little higher than the other, causing a slight beat. The name has been confused with *piffaro. The stop is also called bifara, tibia bifaris, etc. (12, 133).

Biffara, see: bifaria.

Biglo, term for trumpet in Gā (a Sudanic language), assumed to be the local pron. of "bugle" (93).

Bignou, see: biniou.

Bigophone, bigotphone, mirliton invented by Bigot, a Fr. toymaker, in 1883, made of zinc, often in form of orchestral brass instrs., with a hole in the wall of the tube covered with tissue paper (127, 169).

Bigopp, cog rattle of St. Gall, Switzerland (169).

Bigu, small *bull-roarer of the Torres Strait area (176).

Bihuela, see: vihuela.

Bijuga cither [Lat. *bi + jugatus,* yoked], Engl. term coined by Carl Engel (of the S. Kensington Museum), presumably an adaptation of Mersenne's *cithara bijuga, the theorbo.

Bikife, *musical bow of the Andekelao of the Congo, with a gourd resonator not attached to the bow (128).

Bikuara, pl. of ekuara.

Bikunda, pl. of kunda.

Bikut, W. Borneo name of the bumbun (173).

Bilbilla, bell of the Somali and Galla of E. Africa (176).

Bili, drum of the Logo of the Congo, identical with the bia. Played alternately with the larimva. *Ca.* 80 cm. (32 in.) long (30).

Bilo, Russ.: semanterion (176).

Biludi (Kikongo), wooden trumpet of the Bwende of the Congo, with lateral blowhole, held vertically, and played in ensembles of other instrs. It is 1–1½ m. (40–60 in.) long. *Cf.* ludi (185).

Bimbonifono, vertical trombone invented by Giovacchino Bimboni of Florence in 1850, pitched in F, with a 4-oct. compass. Pitch was changed by means of 7 tubes controlled by keys; 5 of the tubes lowered the tone by a whole tone, 2 by a semitone (176).

Bimpombu, small campaniform metal bells of the Lower Congo region, suspended on a cord and played during dances (185).

Bīn (Hindi, Hindust., Mar., Punj.), *tube zither of N. India, equivalent to the vīnā of S. India, made of a bamboo tube with 19 or more chromatic frets, connected to 2 large gourd resonators, 1 of which rests against the player's left shoulder during performance. Of the 7 metal strings 3 are off-board drones tuned to the keynote. The bīn is tuned either $A^0 a^0 a^1/c\#^0 e^0 A^0 d^0$ or $c^2 c^1 c^2/c^0 g^0 c^1 f^1$. Played with bare fingers or a plectrum. *Ca.* 1 m. (40 in.) long (46, 170).

Bina, Beng.: bīn.

Binco, name of the pandero in Galicia, Spain.

Bindere [Arab. *bandair*], in Nafana (an African language) a calabash drum (93).

Bindi, bindu, bindula, bindwa (Kikongo), a small, high-pitched mbindu (185).

Bingi, see: bingy.

Bingo, trumpet of the Sakaraha and Betioky districts of the Malagasy Repub-

lic, made of narrow-bore bamboo, cane, or papaya wood, with a bell of cattle horn. Introduced after the arrival of the French (171).

Bingy, *cylindrical drum of the Majunga region of the Malagasy Republic, with 2 oxhide heads; 60–70 cm. (24–28 in.) high (171).

Biniou, small, mouth-blown bagpipe of Brittany, with a sheepskin bag, conical, wide-bore chanter *ca.* 15 cm. (6 in.) long, provided with 7 front fingerholes and a double reed. Its scale is B♭ major. The single bass drone is *ca.* 38 cm. (15 in.) long, with cylindrical bore, and terminates in a wide bell. It has a single beating reed. The biniou was always played together with the *bombarde, which sounded an oct. lower, *i.e.,* in oct. unison. The true biniou disappeared during the 1930's, to be gradually replaced by the larger Scot. bagpipe retuned to the B♭ scale. *Cf.* benilleux (13, 89, 132).

Bin-jogi (Punj.), *double clarinet of Lahore, India, equivalent to the tiktirī, with 8 fingerholes on the melody pipe (144).

Bin-sasara, serpentine rattle of Japan, used in Shinto and folk music, made of wooden discs strung together (135).

Bīn-sitār (Beng.), *stick zither of Bengal, a composite bīn and sitār, built like a bīn but strung like a sitār (173).

Bīnt, generic name of harps in ancient Egypt, possibly related to the bīn of N. India. *Cf.* tebuni.

Binza, clapperless iron bell of the Wumbu of Gabon, campaniform and *ca.* 50 cm. (20 in.) high (185).

Bion, *marine-shell trumpet of horse-herders of the Camargue, France (132, 176).

Bipanchi, Beng. equivalent of the vipanchi vīnā.

Birbyne, idioglott clarinet of Lithuania, with cylindrical tube and 3 front fingerholes set in indentations. The upper end is closed by a stopper. The entire length of the reed is taken into the player's mouth. *Ca.* 15 cm. (6 in.) long (174).

Bird call, wooden pipe used for attracting birds one wished to catch (Cotgrave in 1611). For the modern bird call see: bird whistle. See also: botet, courcaillet, reclain, reclamo.

Bird flageolet (Ger.: *Vogelpfeife*), small flageolet formerly used for training birds to sing.

Bird organ (Fr.: *serinette;* Ger.: *Vogelorgel*), miniature *barrel organ devised for the somewhat incongruous task of teaching birds to sing. In existence since the late 17th c., the bird organ is a mechanized portative organ with a few flue pipes, usually a single stop at 2′ pitch, but larger models also had 4′ and even 8′ pipes. Laborde in 1780 describes the *serinette as an "orgue de Barbarie" or barrel organ used for training finches to sing, with 2 bellows and a wind chest (the pallets opened by depressing the keys), 13 pipes, and a cylinder pinned with 12 tunes worked by a hand crank. The barrel was shifted to obtain different tunes. It is from this kind of instr. that the later barrel organ developed. Joseph Engramelle's *Tonotechnie* of 1775 contains detailed instructions for "notating" serinette cylinders. In the 18th c. a different type of bird organ came into being: inventors then attempted to imitate the warbling of birds. Very small metal pipes were placed in the bottom of real cages containing artificial birds. By the mid-century another principle was employed: that of the *bird warble; P. Jacquet-Droz produced such an instr. *ca.* 1752; it gave an excellent imitation of trills and warbles. To the first type of organ (teaching instr.) belong the bouvrette, perroquette, pionne, serinette, turlutaine; to the second type belongs the merline (37, 124, 169).

Bird warble, simple wooden *piston flute imitating the warbling of a bird.

Bird whistle, in modern rhythm bands a series of short metal whistles, drummer's accessories, including bobwhite, canary, quail, warbler, woodchuck, etc. See also: safīr-i bulbul.

Birimbao [U.], Sp., Port.: Jew's-harp. The word seems to have come into use in the 19th c. Ortiz suggests that it may derive from the Bantu root *imba,* meaning song (152).

Biripfeife, largest of the Austrian Schwegels, still being manufactured, and difficult of speech; 43 cm. (17 in.) long (117).

Bisak beton, metallophone of the Dayak of Borneo, with 7 metal bars set on a rectangular resonator (173).

Bischero, It.: tuning peg.

Biseau, Fr.: languid, block (of organ pipes).

Bisernica, tanbura of Croatia (144).

Bisha, word that occurs in a 14th-c. Pers. ms. meaning pipe (170).

Bīsha-i mushta (Pers.), Pers. name for the Chin. sheng (75 II).

Bishnica, double hornpipe of N. Albania, of wood, with 5 fingerholes on the right pipe and 1 on the left. Each is fitted with a single reed (13).

Bishur, Mongolian name of the oboe (170).

Bissex (Lat.: twice six), guitar invented by Van Heck of Paris and built by Jean-Henri Naderman in 1773, with 2 groups of 6 strings. One group of strings passed over a fretted fingerboard; the others were off-board strings. The neck carried 20 frets; 3½-oct. compass (124, 176).

Bit, see: tuning bit.

Bita, syn. of nabita, 1, among the Mangbele of the C. Sudan (30).

Biti (Kikongo), a name of the sansa among the Congo people (185).

Bitu-uvu, *cross flute of the Fiji Islands, made of a bamboo internode, stopped at both ends. The tube is pierced with 7 holes: a blowhole near each end; 3 holes around the circumference of the center, and a hole between these and each blowhole, at, respectively, the first and third quarters of the tube's length. Judging by its similarity to the fango-fango, it was probably also played as a nose flute. *Cf.* mbitu-uvu (132).

Biucola [Engl. bugle], name given to the flicorno in Neapolitan bands.

Biwa, 1. flat lute of Japan, equivalent to the Chin. *p'i p'a, introduced from China ca. 935 A.C., but subsequently modified, an attribute of the goddess Benten. The size of the piriform body varies considerably and is made of either a hollowed block of wood or more often, 2 pieces of wood. The wood belly is pierced, as a rule, by 2 small, crescent-shaped soundholes. The upper portion of the short neck is thrown back at a 180-degree angle and carries the lateral conoid pegs. The number of strings and of frets is variable, but 4 silk strings are standard. If it has 1 or 2 more, they duplicate the pitch of the lowest 2. The melody is nearly always played on the top string. As the instr. developed, the frets became increasingly higher. Originally the biwa was played in guitar position (the performer sitting cross-legged), but an upright playing position was developed during the Meiji period. See also: bugaku biwa, chikuzen b., gaku b., heike b., moso b., satsuma b. (135, 157);

2. term used by the Kalmuk to designate the *dörwen chikhe khuur (69).

Biwabon, Jap.: panpipes (176).

Biwa no koto, a name of the koto in old Jap. music treatises (144).

Biya, see: bia.

Bladder and string, bowed *stick zither, a folk instr. of England that became obs. in the early 19th c. Like its Continental counterparts, it consisted of a stick held under tension by a string attached to both ends. An inflated pig's bladder, acting as resonator, was inserted at one end between stick and string. The string was then played with a round horsehair bow. Hogarth's burlesque of *The Beggar's Opera* shows a cello-sized bladder and string. Since the 17th c., if not before, similar instrs. have existed in France, Iceland, Italy, Poland, and Spain. Philip Hainhofer, in 1629, called it a new instr., but this is most unlikely. The bladder and string is also called drone. See

also: basse de Flandre, bumba, Bumbass, luk muzycyny, optopka, rabel, smyk, turututela (89, 174).

Bladder pipe (Fr.: *vèze;* Ger.: *Platerspiel*), med. woodwind instr., forerunner of the crumhorn; it first appears in the 13th c. and has survived in Brittany and Sicily—albeit as a toy—in Poland as a shepherd's instr., and among the Chuvash of the U.S.S.R. and the Turks in Europe. In the rest of Europe it became obs. during the Renaissance, last recorded on an etching by Wolfgang Kilian dated 1612. Fundamentally the bladder pipe is a simple form of bagpipe in which the bag is replaced by an elastic animal bladder and a stiffener, inserted between a short blowpipe and the main tube. Air is pumped in by the blowpipe and sounds the reed, which is inserted in the top of the pipe. No description of the med. bladder pipe has reached us; only pictures. These show 2 types of tube: 1 straight or very slightly curved, almost or quite cylindrical, the other frankly conical and with upturned end. This second variety was to be transformed into the crumhorn during the course of the 15th c. Both forms are depicted in the 13th-c. *Cantigas de Santa María:* the straight form shown apparently has a short drone parallel with the chanter. Martin Gerbert reproduces a drawing of one from the same century, called *chorus. Bladder pipes are frequently depicted during the 16th c. Sachs was of the opinion that they originated in the East and might possibly be derived from the *tiktirī of India or from some similar instr. The modern instrs. of Brittany and Sicily are made by fixing a mouthpiece and small chanter to an ordinary balloon, and are sold at fairs, etc. But those of Poland have a wooden pipe with 6 front fingerholes, curved horn bell, and single reed held in a sheep's bladder. See also: Blaterpfeife (14, 36, 114, 169).

Blasebalg, Ger.: bellows.

Blasspaltrohr, Ger.: slit tube.

Blaterpfeife, obs. Ger. term for bladder pipe, now called Platerspiel. The word occurs in literary sources from the 13th c. on (117, 169).

Blechinstrumente, Ger.: brass instrs.; usually abbr. to Blech.

Blikan, scaphoid lute of the Dayak of Borneo, over 1 m. (40 in.) long, with 2 strings, originally of rattan, now generally of metal. These are plucked with the fingernails. The blikan has a slender, hollow body, a wooden belly, and a head that is usually sculptured; it is often but not always fretted (173).

Block, 1. (Fr.: *biseau;* Ger.: *Nuss, Kern;* It.: *anima*), in wooden organ flue pipes, that part which corresponds to the languid of metal pipes; in organ reed pipes, that part which separates tube or resonator from the *boot (101); **2.** (Fr.: *tasseau;* Ger.: *Klötzchen;* It.: *zocchetto*), block of wood inserted at the corners, neck, and button in certain European bowed instrs. to strengthen the body and provide a gluing surface; **3.** a fipple.

Blockflöte (Ger.) [*Block,* fipple], **1.** recorder; **2.** organ stop of conical metal flue pipes at 4′ or 2′ pitch, with wide scale, or of stopped pipes at 8′ or 4′ pitch. Adlung described it as similar to the Rohrflöte, occasionally stopped, at 16′, 8′, 4′, 2′ pitches (3, 133).

Blockwerk (Ger.), the pipework of a Gothic organ before the invention of registers, later broken up to form a rank of fundamentals with a *Vordersatz and a *Hintersatz, *i.e.,* (mixture) pipes in front and behind it. Assuming an 8′ pipe as fundamental, the pipes of a Blockwerk, sounded simultaneously, would have been (front to back, on one key) 1′, 1⅓′, 2′, 2⅔′, 4′, **8′**, 4′, 2⅔′, 2′, 1⅓′, 1′. Aliquots were built up in this fashion on each key (161).

Boali, see: poari.

Board zither (Fr.: *cithare sur planche;* Ger.: *Brettzither*), zither in which the strings are stretched over a board, with or without resonator. It is distinguished from the long zither in being absolutely flat, whereas the latter has a vaulted sur-

face. Size and number of strings are variable. See also: akidi, akimbi, alungu, banju, banzu, bapili, bwanzi, chelempung, dingba, dorungu, ekidi, epigoneion, gwanzu, ihango, kachapi, 3, kayoma, kinanda, 4, kpai, kungu, malongu, namukenge, ndara, ngbandje, ŝanzu, sipa na pili, siter, unanga.

Bobre, 1. *musical bow of the Malagasy Republic, with tuning loop and resonator attached to the end of the bow; **2.** musical bow of Mozambique, with a round stick for a bow and a gourd resonator held against the player's body. *Ca.* 2 m. (80 in.) long (17).

Boca de peix (Cat.: fish mouth), wind instr. of Catalonia, with a fish-shaped aperture instead of a bell (57).

Bocal, Fr.: S-shaped crook.

Bocchino, It.: mouthpiece.

Bocina [Lat. *buccina*], OSp.: horn.

Bock (Ger.: he-goat) [translation of Pol. *koza*], **1.** mouth-blown bagpipe depicted by Praetorius, with a chanter compass of 9 tones, B^0–c^1 and a bass drone tuned to C^0. Both chanter and drone terminate in horn bells. The pitch was probably an oct. higher than Praetorius indicates. Also called polnischer Bock. *Cf.* grosser Bock; **2.** obs. tremulant organ stop of the Rückpositif, also called Bocktremulant, tremblant à vent perdu (133, 159, 169).

Bocu, syn. of bokú.

Bode melochord, monophonic *electrophonic instr. of the electronic type, designed by Harald Bode, primarily for purposes of tone-analysis. It employs electron tube oscillators as basic tone generators. The characteristics of the tone are controlled by 2 manuals, each of which represents an independent monophonic playing range (58, 60).

Bodongo, ground bow of the Boa of the Congo (128).

Bogen, Ger.: bow.

Bogenflügel (Ger.), a gut-strung *bowed keyboard instr. invented by Johann Hohlfeld of Berlin in 1753. Sound was produced by pushing the strings against a continuous horsehair bow by means of small hooks controlled from the keyboard. Both C. P. E. Bach and Friedrich Wilhelm Marpurg voiced their approbation (27, 149).

Bogengitarre, Ger.: bowed guitar.

Bogenhammerklavier (Ger.), keyboard instr. built by Johann Carl Greiner of Wetzlar in 1779; it combined an ordinary piano with a bowed keyboard instr. (176).

Bogenharfe, Ger.: **1.** *arched harp; **2.** term used erroneously by some writers for Harfenbogen (harp bow).

Bogenklaviatur, Ger.: concave keyboard.

Bogenklavier, Ger.: bowed keyboard instr.

Bogenlaute, Ger.: pluriarc.

Bogenzither, Ger.: bowed zither.

Bogir, slit drum of New Guinea, used for signaling purposes (176).

Bogonga, *musical bow of the Ngombe of the Congo, without tuning loop or resonator. Also called igonga (128).

Bohrung, Ger.: bore.

Bois-crolant (Fr.) [OFr. *croler,* to shake], 16th-c. expression for a leper's clapper (204).

Boisi, Khanda: vāmsī.

Boisine, var. of buisine.

Boîte à musique, Fr.: music box.

Boîte expressive, Fr.: swell box.

Bokio, *footed drum of the Ekota and Bakutu of the Congo, with head of antelope, snake, or crocodile skin tied with a liana. *Ca.* 80 cm. (32 in.) high. Also called bonkeli (30).

Bokú, Afro-Cuban drum of Oriente Province, in form of a slender, truncated cone, with single, nailed head. Played with bare hands (152).

Bolange, xylophone of the Susu and Koranko of Sierra Leone, with 20 graduated slabs set on a low frame, each provided with a small, globular gourd resonator. A hole cut in the wall of the gourd is covered by a spider's-egg-deposi-

tory membrane—a mirliton device. The player wears bracelet rattles: iron suspension rattles in *kemanak form, with small metal rings at either end, attached to a band of leather (Collection of the Commonwealth Institute, London).

Boletón, idiochord *tube zither of the Philippine Islands, made of bamboo from which 3 strings are cut close together. A bridge with 3 notches is wedged beneath them. It is 50–60 cm. (20–24 in.) long (176).

Bolima, pluriarc of the Ngando of the Congo (128).

Bolin-gozo, Basque name of the dulzaina (56).

Bolon, *harp lute of the Fula of Sierra Leone, with a large spherical resonator of gourd, a belly of animal skin with the hair left on, and an arched neck that pierces the resonator and projects as a stub at the far end. A bridge bored with holes, through which 3 strings pass, rises perpendicular to the belly. These are fastened to the neck by tuning rings. The neck is surmounted by a large copper plaque hung with metal rings and pellet bells. Chauvet reports that such an instr. is also played in Guinea (Collection of the Commonwealth Institute, London).

Bom, see: cai bom.

Bomba [Sp. *bombo*], **1.** single-headed Afro-Brazilian and Afro-Puerto Rican drum, nearly cylindrical; **2.** in Santiago de Cuba generic term for Negro drums; **3.** in Argentina syn. of caja (152).

Bombard [Fr. *bombarde*] (Ger.: *Bombard*), the lower-pitched members of the shawm family developed between the 14th and 16th c., elongated versions of the shawm, very slender, with narrow and slightly conical bore ending in a flare and played with a double reed. The Engl. term was first used in 1393 (Gower) and but infrequently thereafter, the term "tenor shawm" being preferred (see below). In Germany the word had become corrupted to "Bombhardt" by

Virdung's day (writing in 1511) and was further corrupted to "Pommer" by that of Praetorius (in 1618). The soprano members of the family, distinguishable to the eye by their lack of *fontanelle, were just called "shawm." Bombards had 6 front fingerholes in 2 groups of 3, and 1 key with a fontanelle slipped over the tube for its protection; some sizes had 3 or 4 extension keys as well. The bombard first appears in Fr. miniatures of the 13th c., is then mentioned in It. and Sp. sources, later in Fr. ones, and finally in Engl. and Ger. ones. By the 16th c. the shawm had developed into a whole family, of which Praetorius lists 7 sizes:

	Lowest Tone	Length	
		cm.	in.
Klein Schalmey (sopranino shawm)	b^1	ca. 50	(20)
Discant Schalmey (soprano shawm)	d^1	60	(24)
Klein Altpommer (alto bombard; called tenor shawm in England)	g^0	75	(30)
Nicolo	c^0	90	(36)
Bassett or Tenor Pommer	G^0	130	(52)
Basspommer	C^0	180	(72)
Gross-Basspommer (great bass, called contrebasse in France)	F^1	290	(116)

The great bass was also made as a Quart bass in G^1, measuring about 275 cm. (108 in.). The larger sizes, from the tenor down, were played without a *pirouette but with a metal crook on which the reed was carried. Praetorius also shows a separate Bassett-Nicolo with *reed cap and a rear thumbhole lacking on his other shawms. The alto and tenor instrs. were either made with 1 open key or furnished with *basset keys that took the compass down a 4th. The 4-keyed Nicolo was presumably identical with the basset or tenor Pommer. Most of these sizes were short-lived, as the unwieldy basses were gradually abandoned in favor of the more manageable *curtals. In 1590 *"un double bas haultbois autrement apelé bombarde"* (a double bass hautbois otherwise called bombard) was to be placed

in a belfry, but by 1636 Mersenne knew only 3 sizes, the *dessus, taille,* and *basse.* The first of these corresponded to the Discant Schalmey of Praetorius, the second to his Klein Altpommer, and the last to his Bassett. A surviving great bass in the National Museum of Prague has a tube length of 2.72 m. (*ca.* 9 ft.), 5 keys, and a compass E^1–b^0. The same collection contains a 4-keyed bass with a tube length of 1.32 m. (52 in.) and a compass A^1–e^0; 2 tenors or Nicolos, with single key and a tube length of 1.08 m. (42½ in.) and a compass c$\sharp^0$–g^1; and an alto with one key and a tube length of 75 cm. (30 in.), compass e^0–b^1. (These compasses are of course given in modern pitches.) The frontispiece to Praetorius' *Theatrum instrumentorum* shows a large bombard being played while the end of its tube is held up by a second person. However, it was also played with the bell resting on the floor. In Germany the larger sizes were occasionally called "Brummer." *Cf.* Schalmei (35, 36, 89 Baines, 159, 170, 180).

Bombarda [Lat. *bombus,* to drone, buzz], It., Sp.: bombard.

Bombarde (Fr.) [Lat. *bombus,* to drone, buzz], **1.** Fr. equivalent of bombard. The word is taken over from an artillery piece of the same name and first appears in the sense of a musical instr. in 1342 (*Le Livre des mestiers*). In 1376 *"grosses bombardes"* were designated as new, and in 1453 we hear of a *"chalemie appelée bombarde"* (a shawm called bombard), in 1590 of *"un double bas haultbois autrement apelé bombarde"* (a double-bass hautbois otherwise called bombard) (35, 82, 89); **2.** folk shawm of Brittany, still extant, always played together with the biniou. It has a wide bore, detachable bell, measures *ca.* 30 cm. (12 in.), and always plays an octave below the biniou (14, 89); **3.** organ stop of reed pipes of the trumpet class, much used in France. It occurs at 32′, 16′, or 8′ pitch; Dom Bedos described it as having conical resonators (3, 20, 63).

Bombarde organ, organ manual and

the pipework it controls, appearing in France in the early 18th c. (63).

Bombardino, 1. Sp.: euphonium; **2.** It.: alto bombard; **3.** It.: tenor or baritone flicorno.

Bombardo, It.: bombard.

Bombardon, 1. the bass bombard; **2.** name given by Johann Riedl of Vienna to his 12-keyed bass ophicleide, invented *ca.* 1820; **3.** name given to the 3- or 4-valve bass tuba after C. W. Moritz's patent for a 5-valve tuba was circumvented, shortly after 1835; **4.** 32′ or 16′ bombarde organ stop in the pedal (12).

Bombardone, It.: bass bombard.

Bombare (Fr.), var. of bombarde (82).

Bombenventil, syn. of Berliner Pumpen.

Bombionko, drum of the Azande of the Congo, in form of a truncated barrel, with 2 laced heads. The lacing forms a network over the whole body. *Ca.* 60 cm. (2 ft.) high (30).

Bombo [Lat. *bombus,* to drone, buzz], **1.** Cat., Port., Sp.: bass drum; **2.** in Cuba the snare drum, particularly that of military bands (152); **3.** *musical bow of the Aïmeri, Andekaka, Andekote, Andemanza, Andile, Atalo, Daba, Kilima, Mari, and Obvango of the Congo, without ·tuning loop or resonator; **4.** musical bow of the Momvu Aïmeri and Kilima of the Congo, with tuning loop but no resonator. See also bomba, bombú (128).

Bombú [Sp. *bombo*], Afro-Cuban drum of Matanzas Province, Cuba, with single head lapped over a hoop and laced to pegs, generally of trunco-conical shape. *Ca.* 30 cm. (12 in.) high, 20 cm. (8 in.) in diam. (152).

Bomhart, 16th-c. corr. of bombard.

Bomo, *percussion beam of the Eshira, Iveïa, and Vili of the Congo Republic; a horizontally suspended beam is struck with wooden sticks (185).

Bompete, pluriarc of the Bonkanda-Moma of the Congo (128).

Bonaccordo, var. of buonaccordo.

Bonang, *gong chime of Java, formed of a number of bossed gongs with wide rims, placed open side down on a wooden frame, isolated on taut strings. The gongs are often called "bonang kettles." Sometimes earthenware resonators are placed underneath them. Nowadays a bonang usually consists of 2 rows of 7 gongs, but in *sléndro* music twice 5 or 6 may be used. In *pélog* the compass is always 2 uncompleted octs.; the sléndro bonang with twice 6 gongs has a closed 2-oct. compass. The player sits at the long side of the instr. and strikes the gongs on their bosses with 2 padded sticks, often playing in octaves. The higher-pitched gongs have wider rims and are regarded as male, the lower-pitched ones female. The pitch can be raised by filing away from the boss, or lowered by filing away from the upper rim. Older instrs. have 4 small holes in the rim, as do those of Farther India—they were mounted differently—and also have peaked bosses. Bonang gongs were formerly cast in molds, but today they are heated and forged. The bonang forms part of the *gamelan* orchestra. It is also met with in Ambon, Bali, Banda, parts of Borneo, Farther India, W. Flores, Lombok, Madura, Muna, Sumatra (121). See also: babarangan, brekuk, chelempung, duwabelas, gembyang, gom-gom, gong sembilan, kangsi, kepyak, kolenang, kromong, monggang, rentang, reyong, rinchik, setukat, talemon, talimpuen, trompong.

Bonang barung, 2-row bonang of Java, of intermediary pitch; its lowest oct. is at the same pitch as the highest of the bonang panembung; its highest at that of the lowest oct. of the bonang panerus (121).

Bonang kettle, name sometimes given to the gong of a bonang.

Bonang panembung, the lowest-pitched of the double-row bonangs of Java. Its highest oct. is at the same pitch as the lowest one of the bonang barung (121).

Bonang panerus, the highest-pitched of the double-row bonangs of Java; its lowest oct. is at the same pitch as the highest oct. of the bonang barung. See also: rinchik, setukat (121).

Bonda, 1. *cylindrical drum of the Ngbandi of the Congo, with single head laced to the bottom; **2.** *footed drum of the Gombe of the Congo, with head laced to carved monoxylous knobs; a dancing drum. *Ca.* 125 cm. (49 in.) long (30).

Bondin [OFr. *bondir,* to resound], OFr.: horn. The word occurs in the 13th c. (197, 204).

Bondofo, side-blown antelope horn of the W. African Mandingo (42).

Bondundu, drum of the Nkundo of the Congo, with a slight taper and a laced head. The lower conical portion is not hollowed out. *Ca.* 1½ m. (6 ft.) high (30).

Bondung, a long drum of Burma (176).

Bones, European clappers, originally made of ox rib—whence the name—then of flat hardwood sticks. The player holds a pair in each hand; one "bone" is held between thumb and index finger, a second between index and middle fingers. They are clicked together by flicking the wrist. Known since med. times, when jongleurs brought them from ancient Rome, they are still played as a child's toy in England.

Bongele, *stick zither of the Ngandu of the Congo (128).

Bongengu, *musical bow of the Ntomba of the Congo, without tuning loop or resonator (128).

Bonggang, syn. of monggang.

Bonginda, drum of the Topoke of Stanleyville district, Congo, with a cylindrical body set on a conical base and one nailed head. *Ca.* 30 cm. (12 in.) high (30).

Bongo, Cuban term for a variety of small Afro-Cuban drums comprising at least 4 distinct types. One such has been adopted by Western rhythm bands: it consists of 2 small conical or cylindrical drums of the same height but of different diams., joined together horizontally. The single heads are nailed or have spring fasteners, representing tunable and nontunable versions. The shell is made of thick hardwood. Bongo drums are played with bare hands (152).

Bongo-bongo, *musical bow of the Andemanza, Andemeri, Andingbili, Azo, and Daka of the Congo, with tuning loop, but without resonator (128).

Bongoga, *musical bow of the Bokote, Bosaka, Injolo, and Kutu of the Congo, without tuning loop or resonator (128).

Bongogo, *musical bow of the Mbole and Oli of the Congo, without tuning loop or resonator (128).

Bongolo, barrel-shaped drum of the Bangandu of the Congo (30).

Bongwabi, drum of the Abangba of the Congo, identical with the ndima (30).

Bonkeli, syn. of bokio.

Bonkendja, 1. drum of the Ekonda and Nkundo of the Congo, similar to the ndungu; **2.** syn. of bankiya (30).

Bonkenge, *pot drum of the Baloie of the Congo; the rattan lacings form a network over the body (30).

Bonnet chinois, Fr.: Jingling Johnnie.

Bonto, bamboo trumpet of NE. Celebes, introduced from Ambon, consisting of a tube *ca.* 65 cm. (25 in.) long partly inserted into a larger bamboo tube as thick as a man's arm and closed at the bottom. Changes of pitch are obtained by moving the second, larger tube back and forth. The bonto is also found on Saparua and Nuslaut, E. of Ambon (112).

Book harmonium, a very small harmonium in shape of a large book; a 19th-c. version of the Bible regal.

Book regal, syn. of Bible regal.

Boot (Fr.: *pied;* Ger.: *Stiefel*), the socket in which the block of an organ reed pipe is set, corresponding to the foot of a flue pipe.

Boquilla, Sp.: mouthpiece; mouth of an organ pipe; staple; crook.

Bordellotto, 7-stringed It. cittern , its 4 courses being tuned $g^1 a^1 f\sharp^1 b^1$ (Cerretto Scipione: *Della prattica musica,* 1601).

Border pipe, a name of the Northumbrian *small-pipe.

Bordón, Cuban *percussion stick, consisting of a long, flexible stick surmounted by a *maruga (gourd rattle), tapped on the ground during Catholic processions. *Cf.* bourdon (152).

Bordone, It.: **1.** drone; **2.** bourdon organ stop.

Bordun, Ger.: **1.** drone; **2.** bourdon organ stop.

Bordunal . . . , see: Portunal (but Bordunalflöte is a var. of Bordunflöte).

Bordunflöte (Ger.), organ stop of stopped cylindrical pipes of soft intonation, at 16′, 8′, or 4′ pitch (133).

Bordunsaite, Ger.: drone string; offboard string.

Bore (Fr.: *perce;* Ger.: *Bohrung*), **1.** the internal diam. of a tube; **2.** the foot hole of an organ pipe.

Borem, var. of Barem.

Botet (Cat.) [*bota,* barrel], decoy whistle to attract quail and partridge, used by hunters in Catalonia. A skin bag or small bladder is attached to a cane or wooden whistle flute in the manner of old automobile horns. Its Cast. equivalent is called reclamo (57, 165).

Botijito, clay *whistling pot of Murcia, Spain, that imitates the warbling of birds (152).

Botijuela [Sp. *botija,* earthenware jug], 19th-c. Sp. earthenware oil jar, used as an Afro-Cuban *percussion pot and wind instr. It is played 3 ways: 1) a flat beater is shaped to fit the mouth and is tapped rapidly and successively against it, the air pressure creating vibration. The performer's hand can also act as a beater; 2) a hole is made in the wide part of the jar to serve as a blowhole. The jar is held horizontally, its open mouth being stopped more or less by the player's right hand, thus regulating the pitch; 3) outside of Cuba it has also been played by blowing across the mouth, there being no lateral hole. Also called bunga (152).

Botuto, 1. ancient clay trumpet of the Indians of Guiana, S. America, with 2 or 3 bosses, played chiefly during mourning or death dances. Over 1 m. (40 in.) long (176); **2.** sacred *marine-shell trumpet of the Orinoco Indians (152); **3.** occasional name of the *fotuto (152).

Botutu, syn. of pututu.

Botuturu, drum of the Mbelo and Okongo of Lake Leopold II area, the Congo, of *bopako* or *boshongo* wood, with antelope-skin head, played with bare hands (30).

Botzina, [Lat. *buccina*], Cat.: trumpet (197).

Bouché, Fr.: stopped.

Boudego, New Prov.: a cornemuse of the Aude Department, France (35).

Bouke (MHGer.), Ger. kettledrum and *cylindrical drum of the 13th and 14th c. *Cf.* Pauke (169).

Bourdon (Fr.) [Lat. *burdones,* pilgrim staves], **1.** in France the bourdon was an attribute of pilgrims throughout the Middle Ages and up to modern times, and particularly the attribute of St. Jacques: a *"bâton à pomme",* the pilgrim's staff. The staff itself was straight, the *"pomme,"* or knob, constituting the "bourdon" proper. In England, among Henry VIII's instrs., *pilgrim staves are listed as "pipes" or "flutes." This does not solve the problem of their organological identity, but the prototype permits us to look for a slender tube, preferably with a knob. The term *bourdon* occurs in Fr. literature in a musical sense from the 13th c. on, and from the beginning of that century bourdon, or drone, pipes appear on miniatures. These are tall bass organ pipes, narrow-scaled (as all pipes at that period were of the same diam.), disposed at bass or treble end or even at both ends of organs. When it became the practice to stop, *i.e.,* to close, pipes in order to lower their pitch by an octave, thereby saving space and materials, the word "bourdon" was applied by analogy to the stopped pipes. Thus by the late Middle Ages the word became syn, with "stopped." As the name of an organ register, "bourdon" already appears in the

15th c. (at Delft). From their function as drones, the open strings of certain stringed instrs. also became known as bourdons. Jerome of Moravia in the 13th c. uses the term "bordunas" for the drone strings of the viella; it is also the old name for the drone strings of the organistrum. Later the name passed to the lowest string of plucked stringed instrs., also to the off-board strings of the larger lutes, to sympathetic strings. Again from the 13th c. on, the word designates the drone pipe of a bagpipe, by extension occasionally the instr. itself. As time passed the association with low pitches was such as to cause a very heavy bell to be termed a bourdon. Sachs also reports a *whirled friction drum of France by that name. None of this sheds light on the pilgrim staves, of course. Mersenne (in 1636) referred to *"de grands bourdons semblables à ceux des pélérins de Sainct Jacques"* and to those which the pilgrims to St. Jacques at Compostella (Santiago de Compostella) used in order to while away the time. Furetière, at the end of the 17th c., speaks of the courtaud and says that some people made large pilgrim staves (*"de grands bourdons de Pelerins"*) out of them. A bourdon stop of the organ at St. Étienne, Troyes, of 1551, was said to sound like the singing of pilgrims who go to St. Jacques. At any rate, the instr. seems to have been called bourdon because it resembled the staff, not because it was made from one. See also: bordón, burden, burdones, gardon (35, 79, 82, 133, 140, 169);

2. organ stop of stopped pipes which corresponds to the stopped diapason, the Ger. Gedackt, the Lat. vox obtusa, although it is of a slightly wider scale than the Gedackt. Bourdon is also the generic term for stopped registers. Bourdon pipes of Amer. and Engl. organs are almost always made of wood, rarely of metal (12).

Bourdon bass, bourdon organ stop at 16′ pitch in the pedal.

Bourdon d'écho, organ stop of narrow-scaled stopped cylindrical flue pipes of very soft tone (12, 133).

Bourdon doux (Fr.), organ stop of softly intoned stopped flue pipes, similar to the lieblich Gedackt (12).

Bourdon flute, see: Bordunflöte.

Bourdon subbass, bourdon organ stop at 32′ pitch, in the pedal. Also called subbourdon.

Bousine [Lat. *buccina*], **1.** var. of buisine; **2.** in the Orne region of Normandy, a cornemuse (197).

Bout [MEngl. *bought,* to bend] (Fr.: *échancrure;* Ger.: *Bügel*), the outward-curved top and bottom sections of violins, viols, etc., forming the upper and lower bouts, and the inward-curved center section, forming the center bout.

Bouvrette (Fr.) [Fr. *bouvreuil,* bullfinch], small *bird organ for teaching finches to sing.

Bouzine, var. of buisine.

Bow (Fr.: *archet;* Ger.: *Bogen;* It., Sp.: *arco*), one of the oldest musical implements of man, reaching back to the Stone Age. We find that the *musical bow was first plucked by the fingers or tapped with a small stick, then rubbed, and subsequently bowed with a second bow. However, it is the bow as an accessory to chordophones that concerns us here. Primitive bows everywhere assume the form of a flexible stick of wood or a tube (bamboo) held under tension by a string. Three fundamental shapes can be discerned: when the stick is evenly curved, we call it a round bow; it can also be formed by having the curve only at one end—the point; or the stick may be straight in the center and curved at both ends. A primitive *frog is formed by taking a stick that has the stub of a branch left on it. On curved bows the string may be fastened by knotting and placing it in a cleft at the point, or winding it around the stick at the handle end, where it is either knotted or placed in a notch. The earliest definite knowledge we have of the bow as an accessory rather than as an instr. is derived from Al Farabi, an Arab. author who died in 950—evidence points to C. Asia, possibly Khwarizm, as its place of origin —and from 10th-c. miniatures (see: fiddle). Sp. miniatures of the 10th c. also depict large viol-type instrs. being played with very large bows; two types are portrayed on the Sp. miniatures: the earliest, or round, bow, held in the center, a Moorish bow; and the bow curved at one end and held by the other. This second bow is shorter and has a branch stub on the concave side of the proximal end to which the hair is attached. The end itself becomes a handle. This form has survived until today as the *gusle bow, whereas the round bow disappeared in Europe by the 14th c. An interesting passage in the *Chronicum picturatum brunsuicense* occurs in an entry for the year 1203. It reads in part *"In dussem Jahre . . . sat de Parner des Mitwerkens in den Pingxsten und veddelte synen Buren to dem Danse, da quam ein Donreschlach unde schloch dem Parner synen Arm aff mit dem Veddelbogen . . ."* (in this year . . . the parson fiddled on Wednesday of Whitsuntide for his peasants to dance, and a clap of thunder came and cut off his arm with the fiddle bow). The frog starts to appear in the 15th c. By the 17th c. it is completely formed and no longer connected to the stick. In the second quarter of that c. the violin bow loses much of its convexity and by the mid-c. is almost straight. The *crémaillère* of the second half of the c. is a serrated section that holds the frog; it is replaced by a screw *ca.* 1700, at which time the stick runs practically parallel to the hair. According to tradition, Corelli improved the bow so that the hair was at the same distance from the stick at both ends, and Tartini lengthened it, but these attributions are questionable. François Tourte (1747–1835) has been credited with creating the modern bow by giving it its slightly concave curve, determining the best distance from stick to hair, lightening the head, standardizing the length (violin bow 75 cm., viola 74 cm.,

cello 72 cm.), arranging the hair in ribbon form by flattening it with a ferrule, and providing a metal screw for the frog. Actually, metal screws go back further than L. Tourte, and it is probable that François Tourte did no more than bring the art of bow making to a high degree of perfection; L. Tourte has traditionally been called "Tourte *père*," fàther of François, but at this writing (1962), his relationship to François, if any, has not been established; L. Tourte has, however, left us straight bows in mid-17th-c. style as well as later style concave ones, and transformation of the bow is deemed more likely to have been his work than that of François.

The thinner the stick of a modern bow, the sharper its concave curve. The free hair of a modern violin bow is 65 cm. in length; that of the viola is the same, but the stick is heavier. The cello bow has 61 cm. of free hair. Double basses sport 2 different kinds of bow, the so-called "French" bow, an enlarged violin bow, and the "Simandl" bow, with a far higher frog; the French bow is used by players who bow palm down, the Simandl by those who bow palm up. (The Simandl is modeled on the Dragonetti bow.) Both forms have 53 cm. of free hair. In the 19th c. Jean-Baptiste Vuillaume experimented with further improvements, combining frog with stick and making bows of metal.

In most primitive bows the hair is loose and is tightened by the player's fingers. This was also the case with the early European bow (the jouhikantele continued to be so played until the 19th c.) and a measure of control was exercised until well after the invention of the *crémaillère*. Since the first half of the 17th c. brazilwood has been used for the making of bows, along with a number of other woods. Trichet, *ca.* 1640, mentions bows of brazil, ebony, and "other woods," and bows of *"indianisch"* wood (brazilwood? Pernambuco?) are mentioned in Austria a little later (2 bows of *"cana d'India"* were owned by the Verona Academia Filarmonica in 1562). Pernambuco has been the preferred material of many makers for over 2 centuries, although a number of different woods remain in common use, such as ironwood, snakewood, campèche, etc. In 18th-c. Italy snakewood was more expensive than Pernambuco; the latter was also called *vanin* in It. (9, 89, 154, personal communication of Rembert Wurlitzer).

Bowed guitar (Fr.: *guitare à archet;* Ger.: *Bogengitarre;* It.: *chitarra coll'arco*), guitar invented in 1826 and played with a bow. It had *FF instead of a central soundhole and was said to have the timbre of the cor anglais. See also: arpeggione (176).

Bowed harp (Swed. *Stråkharpa*), term coined by Otto Anderssen for the ancient Nordic lyre played with a bow; it survived until this century. A 12th-c. stone carving at Trondhjem Cathedral, Norway, is the oldest record we possess of one. According to Anderssen, the bowed harp followed a general stream of Northern culture that flowed from west to east. The bowed harp had an almost rectangular body hollowed out of a single block of wood or made of thin slats, with either a flat or a curved back, 2–4 strings inserted from the rear, bridge, and tailpiece. The upper portion of the instr. had 1 or 2 handholes. If 2, they were separated by a wooden centerpiece. Arms extended from the sides and were connected at the top by a crossbar. The instr. rested on its player's left knee, tilted slightly upward, its lower end resting on the inside of his right knee. Its upper end was held in the left hand by passing the fingers through the soundhole from the back. The strings were stopped either by the player's nails or by the upper surface of his fingers, *i.e.,* laterally, while the other hand bowed. Two-string varieties had a melody string and a drone string; those with 3 strings had 2 outer melody strings and a central

drone string. Harps with 2 handholes were played by moving the hand from one to the other during performance. Conclusive information regarding the tuning is not available. The looseness of the bow hair and flatness of the bridge caused the drone always to sound when the melody strings were played, lending great fullness to the tone. See also: eestikannel, jouhikantele, kannel, stråkharpa, talharpa, wibukannel (9).

Bowed instruments were known to Europe from the first third of the 10th c. on. They were preceded, at least in Asia, by chordophones rubbed by friction sticks. Among the Chinese, bowed chordophones were at first folk instrs., and the high cultures of the East have always given pride of place to the plucked, rather than to the bowed, instrs. In medieval Islam they were considered imperfect because of their weak tone and unattractive sound, perhaps an indication of difficulties encountered in obtaining the greater tension needed for bowing. All bowed chordophones of C. Asia are played in a-gamba position, with one string stopped and the others sounding as a continuous drone; among several peoples, this results to our day in organum at the fourth.

Bowed keyboard instrument (Fr.: *clavecin à archet, piano à archet;* Ger.: *Bogenklavier, Streichklavier;* It.: *cembalo da arco*), a hurdy-gurdy wheel applied to a wing-shaped keyboard instr., where it controls the motion of a continuous, rosined band. The movement of the keys either raises the strings to the rotating band or guides the moving band to the strings; both principles were used. Such instrs. originated in an attempt to create a keyboard instr. of sustained tone capable of gradated dynamics, one with *"piano e forte,"* and, owing to the string tone produced as a result of these efforts, bowed keyboard instrs. became convenient substitutes for the "chest" of chamber music instrs. Leonardo da Vinci was the first to design a bowed keyboard instr. (*ca.* 1490; see: viola organista) and Hans Haiden was, as far as we know, the first person to have built one successfully (see: Geigenwerk). He was followed and imitated from the late 16th c. to the early 20th c. Galilei's reference (in 1581) to a gut-strung harpsichord bowed by means of a treadle is to one of Haiden's Geigenwerke. See also: arched viol, Bogenflügel, Bogenhammerklavier, celestinette, clavecin-vielle, clavichordium, Clavier-Gamba, claviola, clavioline, épinette à archet, épinette à orchestre, Geigenwerk, Harmonica, Harmonichord, lyrichord, nail piano, orchestrine, organo-diapazo, orpheon, 1, piano-viole, piano-violon, plectro-euphone, Polyplectron, sostinente piano, violicembalo, vis-pianoforte, xenorphica.

Bowed lyre, see: lyre; bowed harp.

Bowed mandolin (Ger.: *Streichmandoline*), bowed mandolins were made in the U.S. in the 19th c.; they had flat backs, crescent-shaped soundholes, and 4 pairs of metal strings (176).

Bowed melodion (Ger.: *Streichmelodion*), *bowed zither, also called Breitoline.

Bowed zither (Ger.: *Streichzither*), a heart-shaped zither played with a bow, invented by Johann Petzmayer of Munich in 1823, with a fretted central fingerboard, originally 3 metal strings tuned $a^1 d^1 g^0$, and a fourth string added later, whereupon the instr. was usually tuned like a violin. Larger sizes were tuned like a viola or even a cello. For the bowed zither in viol form see: Breitoline. See also: bowed melodion, pentaphone, solophone (22, 176).

Bow harp, a translation of the Ger. word *Bogenharfe;* the instr. is now generally termed arched harp.

Bowl drum, a very shallow kettledrum.

Bowl lyre (Fr.: *lyre sur coque;* Ger.: *Schalenleier*), lyre having a natural or hollowed-out bowl for a resonator and a membrane belly: the lyra of ancient Greece and of modern Africa. Some African bowl lyres are still made of a tortoise carapace, as were those of ancient Greece. Its home in modern times is Ethiopia, and it has hardly advanced beyond the sphere of influence of that country (100, 195).

Bow lute (Ger. *Bogenlaute*), see: pluriarc.

Box lyre (Fr.: *lyre sur caisse;* Ger.: *Kastenleier*), lyre having a built-up wooden box for resonator and wooden soundboard, such as the *kithara of ancient Greece. In modern times it has not survived outside Ethiopia. Those of ancient Ur, Sumer, Babylon, and Egypt, as well as those of Ethiopia today, tend to an asymmetrical design with arms of unequal length set at different angles (100, 195).

Box valve (Fr.: *piston à boîte carrée;* Ger.: *Büchsenventil*), name given to the early rectangular valve of Heinrich Stölzel and Friedrich Blühmel, invented in or by 1815.

Box zither (Fr.: *cithare sur caisse;* Ger.: *Kastenzither*), zither having a built-up string bearer of slats.

Bozuk, a medium-sized saz of Anatolia, with 8 strings (89).

Brač, a plucked tanbura of Croatia (144).

Bragna, *marine-shell trumpet of Sicily, to the tip of which a mouthpiece is attached (89).

Brahmatālam, cymbals of India, larger than the jalra, used in temple services. Also called brihattālam (179).

Bramadera [Sp. *bramar,* to groan], Sp. **1.** horn used by shepherds to frighten animals away from vineyards; **2.** bull-roarer, now a child's toy.

Bratsche [It. *braccio,* arm], Ger.: viola.

Braù (bull), friction drum of Aveyron, S. France, with friction cord (132).

Brchak (Serb.), rattle of Yugoslavia. *Cf.* Britsche, Pritsche (176).

Breitoline [inventor's name], *bowed zither of irregular viol shape, invented in

1856 by Leopold Breit of Brno, Moravia. Originally it had 5 strings, later 4, tuned as the violin. The fingerboard was fretted. When played, it was held on the lap (149).

Brekuk, word occurring in 902 A.C., believed to denote the bonang (121).

Brelka, divergent *double pipes of Russia, terminating in large bells of horn or coiled bark, with idioglott reeds protected by a reed cap. The pipes are of unequal length and are played with one hand holding each pipe. In the early 20th c., V. V. Andreef of St. Petersburg fitted single pipes with keys and incorporated them into his balalaika orchestra. In this form the brelka had a compass f^1–e^2 or f^2 and was notated a 4th lower (14).

Brettgeige, Ger.: mute violin.

Brettzither, Ger.: board zither.

Brian Boru, modern Irish *war pipe, a mouth-blown bagpipe, developed by Henry Starck of London *ca.* 1900–10, with 3 drones in 1 stock. The tenor drone sounds an oct. below the chanter keynote (Bb), the bass drone an oct. lower still, and the baritone a 5th between them (14, 89).

Briazalo, 11th-c. Russ. word for kettledrum (25).

Bridge (Fr.: *chevalet;* Ger.: *Steg;* It.: *ponticello*), **1.** on bowed instrs. and those plucked instrs. having rib-fastened strings, the bridge is a removable piece of hardwood set under the strings and maintained in position by their tension. Nut and bridge determine the speaking length (the scale) of a string. The function of a bridge, however, is not to determine the scale, but to transmit the strings' vibrations to the belly. Tradition, pitch, and the thickness of the strings have determined the bridge's position on European violins. Nowadays this is between the cross-strokes of the *FF; formerly it was lower, as may be seen in the iconography of past centuries. (The earlier C holes varied considerably in position and did not become standardized until the 17th c.) The height of a bridge is determined by the desired space between fingerboard and strings, and the degree of its arching by that of the fingerboard. On bowed instrs. the arching permits the strings to be bowed individually, as on the violin, or several to be bowed together, as on the viol. Bridges are usually made of spotted maple, and though nowadays they are turned out in factories, it is still necessary to finish and fit each bridge carefully to its particular instr.; if the feet are not curved to follow the arching of the belly exactly, the instr. will not sound. In form the violin bridge is virtually unchanged since the early 18th c.; the top is about half as thick as the bottom, but the actual size and weight vary with each instr. to be fitted. A most interesting form of bridge is that of the now obsolete *crwth, and some surviving folk instrs. that have retained their med. form. Here the feet are of uneven length; the longer one passes through a hole in the belly and rests against the back of the instr., taking the pressure from the strings and acting as a soundpost. One foot of the trumpet marine's bridge is suspended slightly above the belly; when played, the strings' vibrations cause this foot to "tremble" or rattle against the belly. Sometimes this rattling is increased by placing a small metal plaque under the foot (see also: hurdy-gurdy in this connection);

2. the bridge of a keyboard instr. fulfills the same function as that of other stringed instrs., namely, that of transmitting the strings' vibrations to the belly. Here also, height and weight are critical in relationship to thickness of the strings and of the soundboard. On pianos, increases in both height and width have paralleled changes in stringing and scale over the past 1½ centuries. On all keyboard instrs. the shape of the bridge emerges ultimately as a result of the instr's. scale, though this is less true of early straight and V-shaped bridges than of later curved ones. It has been customary to refer to the nut (a term taken over from *lutherie*) as a "second bridge," "wrestplank bridge," etc., but this practice is now being abandoned;

3. the bridge of an organ flue pipe is a cylindrical piece of metal or wood placed horizontally in front of the mouth for voicing purposes. Also called roller bridge or harmonic bridge.

Brihattālam, syn. of Brahmatālam.

Brimbale [OFr. *brimbaler*, to oscillate], OFr.: pellet bell, jingle; the bells tied to horses' harness (204; Cotgrave).

British harp lute, an improved *harp lute, patented by Edward Light of London in 1816. His patent covered a series of finger keys that he called "ditals" (as opposed to pedals), with which the strings were stopped, thus raising their pitch by a semitone. In 1819 he renamed it *dital harp.

British lyre, lyre fitted with a keyboard and hammer action, patented by William Jackson in 1784. The hammers had 2 heads, 1 of wood, the other of leather-covered wood; both could be used together, or each separately (92).

Britsche (MHGer.), **1.** clapper depicted by Virdung in 1511, of 3 spoon-shaped lengths of wood hinged together, the outer 2 being clicked against the central one; **2.** obs. Ger.: pegdisc (194).

Brofwe-awe [Turk. *būrū*], trumpet in Agni (a Sudanic language) (93).

Brommtopp (LGer.), N. Ger. *friction drum. See also: Brummtopf (169).

B'ru [Turk. *būrū*], trumpet in Dyoula (a Sudanic language) (93).

Brumbice, syn. of drumelca.

Brumle, Czech: Jew's-harp (176).

Brummeisen (Ger.: drone iron), Ger.: Jew's-harp; the word has been in use since the 17th c. (169).

Brummer, Ger.: **1.** drone; **2.** occasional name of the bombard because of its reedy tone quality (89 Langwill).

Brummkreisel, Ger.: humming top.

Brummtopf (Ger.: drone pot), Ger. *friction drum with friction cord (169).

Brunda, Yugo. *friction drum, consisting of an earthenware pot, with a friction stick that is pushed up and down (89).

Bsura, see: bzura.

B♭ tenor, syn. of tenor horn (in England, a baritone).

Bu, *marine-shell trumpet of the W. Torres Strait (144).

Bubanj, Yugo. drum of great antiquity, made of a hollowed block of wood. The 2 heads are lapped over hoops, and an optional snare is provided. Nowadays the bubanj is very rare; in Macedonia it has died out completely and is replaced by the *tupan. See also: buben (89).

Bubbolo [It. *bubbolare*, to tremble], It.: pellet bell.

Buben, pl. **bubni, 1.** Russ. kettledrum; the term was in use during the 13th and 14th c.; **2.** Russ. tambourine formerly used in military bands (25, 169).

Bubu, see: imbubu.

Buccin, see: buccine, 2.

Buccina (Lat.) [U.], **1.** signal horn of Roman antiquity, used by the army and as a pastoral instr. The term denoted both an animal horn and the metal form used by the army. By late classical times it came to denote the: **2.** a large circular metal horn of ancient Rome, *ca.* 3 m. (10 ft.) long. See also: bucium, cornu; **3.** a straight trumpet of med. Europe. See: buccine, buse, busette, buzina; **4.** organ stop, the name given by It. builders to a reed stop equivalent to the posaune (12, 89, 176).

Buccine (Fr.) [Lat. *buccina*], **1.** horn of med. Europe, of horn or wood, a signal instr. later imitated in metal. In 1372 it was defined as *"une petite trompe de corne ou de boys ou d'arain"* (a little *trompe* of horn or wood or bronze). *Cf.* buisine; **2.** in the early 19th c. the old term was revived by Belgian instr. makers and used for a fanciful trombone with upturned bell terminating in a serpent's head. It had a short existence in European military bands and was also known as trombone buccin à tête de serpent (89, 176, 204).

Bucén, Sp.: horn.

Buchaïü (bull), Rom. *friction drum made of a watering can, the bottom of which has been replaced by a piece of leather. The friction cord is of horsehair and the instr. is said to emit a noise similar to a bull's roar. *Cf.* buhai.

Bûche [Lat. *busca,* log], folk zither of France, with 5 or more strings stretched over a slender rectangular box, with fixed frets fitted to the left long side. Two strings are for melody, the others for accompaniment (drones), tuned $g^1 g^1/g^1 g^1 c^0$. They are plucked with a plectrum while the player's left hand holds a small stick taut against the melody strings, thus sounding them in unison. If they are to be played in 3rds, they are stopped by the player's index and middle fingers; other intervals are stopped accordingly. Also known as épinette des Vosges. See: tambourin à cordes. See also: bûche de Flandres, chat'han, humle, Hummel, langleik, Noordsche balk, Scheitholt.

Bûche de Flandres, folk zither of Flanders, with 5–8 strings, similar to the bûche.

Büchel [*Bürke,* birch], name of the Bürkel in Canton Glarus, Switzerland (187).

Buc horne [buck], horn of 16th-c. England.

Büchsenventil, Ger.: box valve.

Bucina, see: buccina.

Bucium [Lat. **buccina*], Rom. alphorn used as a signal instr. by shepherds, made in different forms: straight, hooked, or S-shaped, 1½–3 m. (5–10 ft.) long. The bucium is made of 2 hollowed sections of wood, glued together and bound with cherry bark, played with a wooden mouthpiece. In the W. Carpathians only women and girls play it. See also: tulnic (5, 132).

Bucum-bumba, syn. of urucungo (7).

Budbudika, see: budubuduke.

Buddipotte, friction drum of E. Jutland, with friction stick (169).

Budu [Turk. **būrū*], name of the būrū in Malinke (Sudanic) dialect (93).

Budubuduke, a miniature dāmaru of

India, played by gypsies and jugglers (179).

Bufacanyes [Cat. *bufar,* blow + *canye, cane*], Cat.: panpipes.

Buff leather (Fr.: *peau de bufle*), not buffalo leather, despite its name, but oxhide or other skin that has undergone a certain oiling process, rather similar to that which produces chamois. Pascal Taskin seems to have been first to make use of it for plectra in his harpsichords. The *Encyclopédie méthodique* gives details of the manufacturing process. See: buff stop, clavecin à peau de bufle.

Buff stop, 1. on a harpsichord, the same as *harp stop, 1; **2.** on the piano, a stop invented by John Geib in 1786, similar to the harp stop, 1, except that the buff leather presses against one string of each pair from below and in the treble section only, to facilitate tuning; **3.** a piano stop, invented by Robert Wornum in 1811, whereby pieces of buff leather damp one of each pair of unison strings (92).

Bugaku biwa, biwa of the Jap. court orchestra. It was renamed bugaku biwa when the old music of China was performed as accompaniment to bugaku dances. The bugaku biwa is the largest and most massive of the biwas, *ca.* 1 m. (40 in.) long, with 4 silk strings and 3–5 high frets. Its tuning is variable (157).

Bugari, *vertical flute of the Kotar from the Nilgiri Hills of S. India, made of cane, with 5 or 6 fingerholes. *Cf.* bughri (173).

Bugariya, medium-sized tanbura of Croatia, with long neck and elongated body, smaller than the sharqī, tuned B^0 $d^0 g^0 g^0$. See: tanbura, 2 (89, 176).

Bügel, Ger.: **1.** bout; **2.** abbr. of Stimmbügel.

Bügelhorn [Fr. *bugle* + Ger. *Horn*], Ger. term coined at the end of the 19th c. to denote both the natural and the valved bugle.

Bughri, bamboo trumpet with buffalo

horn of the Toda of Nilgiri Hills, S. India. *Cf.* bugari (103).

Bugle, (med. instr., Fr.: *bugle;* Ger.: *Hiefhorn, Hifthorn;* brass instr., Fr.: *clairon;* Ger.: *Signalhorn, Bügelhorn;* valved instr., Fr.: *bugle;* Ger.: *Saxhorn, Bügelhorn*), the OFr. word *bugle* is derived from the Lat. *buculus,* meaning "bullock," via OFr. *busgle;* it was borrowed by the English in the 13th c., only to be borrowed back by the French in 1814. In OFr. *bugle,* in the sense of an instr., is an abbr. of *cor bugler,* the horn of a bugle or wild bullock, which served as a hunter's signal instr. In later med. times its use was not restricted to hunting; it became a signal instr. of tower watchmen and shepherds and the soldiery; *"3 cornua de bugle"* are mentioned in 1322, and an Engl. will of 1378 reads in part: *"lego . . . cornu meum magnum de bugle, ornatum cum auro . . ."* (I bequeath . . . my large bugle horn, ornamented with gold . . .) In post-med. times it retained its shape, even though made of metal (brass, copper, silver): that of a short, curved, wide-bore horn. In the last quarter of the 18th c. it was bent into a semicircle and became a military instr. under the name of bugle horn. In the early 19th c. its shape was again changed: the tubing was lengthened, and it was coiled trumpet-fashion, the instr. being pitched in C or B♭. Its compass then was c^1–g^2, and from a military signal instr. it was transformed into a military band instr. This brass instr. became known in France as *clairon,* in Germany as *Signalhorn.* Shortly after it had assumed a coiled form, keys were applied to it (see: keyed bugle), but it has continued its existence as a keyless and valveless instr. to this day, having now a continuous wide conical bore, and is played with a cup mouthpiece. The tones obtainable on a C bugle are: c^0 c^1 g^1 c^2 e^2 g^2 b♭^{2} c^3. When valves were first introduced, they were fitted on instrs. of soprano range: the bugle and the *post horn.* Much experimenting ensued until

finally Adolphe Sax narrowed the bugle's bore and developed it into a homogeneous family that he named *saxhorn. In modern Fr. bugle denotes the saxhorn; in Engl., the (natural) bugle. See also: Antilopenhorn, contre-clairon, Halbmond, herebyme.

Bugle à clefs, Fr.: keyed bugle.

Bugle alto, Fr.: althorn; alto saxhorn.

Bugle à pistons, Fr.: flugelhorn.

Bugle baryton, the same as bugle ténor.

Bugle basse, a Fr. name of the tenor horn.

Bugle horn [*bugle], *ca.* 1300 the word is a syn. of bugle. In the last quarter of the 18th c. the name was given to the bugle bent into semicircular form.

Bugle omnitonique (Fr.), saxhorn fitted with Chaussier's transposition device, permitting it to be played in all tonalities (176).

Bugleral [*bugle], bugle of med. France. The word occurs in the 13th c.

Bugleret, the same as cor bugleret.

Bugle soprano, Fr.: soprano saxhorn; soprano flugelhorn.

Bugle ténor, Fr.: tenor horn; tenor saxhorn.

Bugosip, Hung.: bassoon.

Buguri, see: bughri.

Buhai, *friction drum of Moldavia and Wallachia, Romania, with friction cord of horsehair, rubbed with wetted hands. It accompanies the flute for "New Year wishes." See also: buchaĭŭ (5).

Buinne, Celtic: horn (79).

Buisine (OFr.) [Lat. *buccina], OFr. term for larger horns and trumpets, first recorded in the *Chanson de Roland* (1100–20) and frequently mentioned thereafter. Until the late 12th c. it was a long horn, slightly curved, used as a martial signal instr. By the 13th c. it was supplanted by a straight, long Saracen trumpet to which the name *buisine* was transferred. This had a tapering tube some 1.20–2.10 m. (4–7 ft.) long, made of several sections, the joints being covered by ornamental bosses, and terminating in a wide bell. This instr. was generally played in pairs, its use being both domestic and military. According to literary sources, it was made of brass, copper, or silver. The word died out in the 16th c. Rabelais was among the last to use it. *Cf.* bousine, buccine, busenne, busine (35, 89 Baines, 170, 204).

Buk, *friction drum of NW. Poland, used only at Christmas time. The top and bottom of a small barrel are removed and a sheepskin is stretched over one aperture. A horsehair friction cord is passed through a small hole in the skin and is rubbed with moistened fingers. Also called bąk (89).

Bukal, Bohemian *friction drum, consisting of a jar partly filled with water and covered with leather. A horsehair cord is passed through a hole in the leather and pulled up and down. Also called bukatsh (38).

Bukari, *bull-roarer of the Elema people of Papua (201).

Bukatsh, syn. of bukal.

Bukkehorn (goat horn), primitive fingerhole horn of Norway made of a goat's horn with 3–5 fingerholes but no mouthpiece. Also called prillarhorn (79, 176).

Būl ahank, syn. of sūpurga (76).

Bulgaría, syn. of tanbura, 1.

Bull fiddle, coll. term for double bass.

Büllhäfen, Austrian *friction drum, made of a clay pot with a pig's bladder or thin leather membrane, and a friction cord, formerly in use during *Fasching* (carnival) (117).

Bull-roarer (Fr.: *planchette ronflante, rhombe;* Ger.: *Schwirrholz;* It.: *rombo sonore;* Sp.: *palo zumbador*), aerophone consisting of a rhomboid piece of wood, frequently carved, attached to a string passed through a small hole pierced at one end, and whirled through the air. The string is held in the player's hand or is attached to a stick, thereby forming a whip. The smaller the piece of wood, the faster it whirls and the higher the pitch of the sound it produces. While being whirled it turns on its own axis, and the resultant noise is likened to the howling, roaring, or thundering of animals or spirits—chiefly the latter. Since prehistoric times it has been a symbol of fertility and has been used in initiation rites, where it represents the voice of ancestors. Women are not permitted to see it. The bull-roarer's area of distribution is paleolithic Europe, ancient Greece, C. Asia, Indonesia, Africa, the Americas, Australia, and the S. Seas. In modern Europe it exists as a toy. In Australia, Africa, C. Brazil, Melanesia, S. and E. New Guinea it still serves magical functions. Also called thunder stick, whizzer. See also: adya oro, aidye, barlum, berbaling, berra-boi, beure hevehe, bigu, bramadera, bukari, burubush, burumamaramu, churinga jucla, cicala, czurynga, ebero, ereg-ereg, firringila, frullo, goinggoing, hevehe, hevoa, hohoang, hurava, kaiavuru, kekinchiran, kgabududu, koheoheo, kowaliwali, lapuni, luvuvu, mam ma lie, matahu, matapu, me galo, meromero, moriuncar, mudji, ngwingwingwe, nodivu, noli-noli, odeguiliguili, o-e-o-e, oro, palo roncador, palo zumbador, papan, rhombe, rhombos, rombo sonore, ruba, seburuburu, sevuruvuru, snorrebot, tarabilla, tibura, tiparu, tshivhilivhi, tundum, wanes, wer-wer, wilmurra, yelo, yokeli, yumeru, zumba, zumbador, zumbidor, zurrumbera (123, 168, 170).

Bul me jock, "spirit" drum of the Acholi of Uganda, with single nailed head (195).

Bulo lae-lae (Mac.), a bamboo (bulu) lae-lae.

Bulo paseya-seya, bulo siya-seya [*bulu,* bamboo], syn. of siya-siya.

Bulowok, *bird whistle of the Kayan of Borneo, without fingerholes, frequently beaked (173).

Bul tyang'apena (drum of canes), *percussion sticks of the Lango of Uganda, used by boys as practice drums. A piece of cane is broken into 3 sections, still attached to each other, the outer 2 being bent to form a U. These are inserted into the ground, and the center portion, which forms a bridge, is beaten with 2 sticks (195).

Bulu, 1. [Turk. **būrū*], name of the būrū in Mende (a Sudanic language) (93); **2.** *arched harp of Senegambia, with 10 strings and long pegs (176).

Bulu decot [*bulu,* bamboo], name given to the bumbun (pigeon decoy whistle) by the Malayans of Thailand.

Bulunba, Basque cattle bell; the bellwether's bell (176).

Bulu pārinda, a large composite *Aeolian pipe of SE. Asia, hung in a treetop. A bamboo tube up to 10 m. (11 yds.) long has a longitudinal slit and several cross-slits made in it; found in Bali, Borneo, Java, Malaya. *Cf.* bulu ribut (148).

Bulu ribut, a composite *Aeolian pipe of the Orang Besiri and Orang Mentera of Malaya, actually an Aeolian "organ": a number of stopped bamboo pipes up to 8 m. (26½ ft.) in length are furnished with slits of different lengths and breadths and suspended in the highest possible treetop. It can be turned into the breeze or away from it. *Cf.* bulu pārinda (173).

Buluwat, see: beluwat.

Bumba, obs. Icelandic version of the *bladder and string: pellet bells and cymbals were attached to a pole, as were 2 inflated ox bladders, over each of which a string was stretched. This was rubbed with a wooden pick and was said to produce a sound like a drum roll. It was in use up to the 17th c. See also: bumbass (176).

Bumbard, see: bombard.

Bumbass [Lat. *bombus,* to drone, buzz, via OFr. *bombace*], Ger. and Austrian folk instr., a *stick zither similar to the Engl. *bladder and string. It seems to have had 3 strings originally and as such was described by Philip Hainhofer in 1629 (he called it a new invention). Subsequently it had a single string passed over an inflated pig bladder or ox bladder, and was bowed with a notched stick, thus producing a noise like a drum roll. After becoming a mendicant's instr. it

was revived in modern times as a carnival instr. (now manufactured in Markneukirchen) provided with additional jingles, pellet bells, and cymbals. The lower end of the stick was struck rhythmically against the ground and "bowed" with quick strokes. The older form is still played occasionally in the Austrian Alps (117, 176).

Bumba-um, syn. of bum-bum.

Bumbo, Port. var. of zabumba, 1.

Bumbuli, drum of the Babemba of the Congo, held between the knees when played (30).

Bum-bum, 1. *musical bow of the Lenca Indians of Honduras, with tuning loop toward the end of the bow, attached to a small gourd. Frequently a larger half-gourd is inverted on the gourd and the lower end of the bow rests on it. *Cf.* wurumbumba (17); **2.** carved *hourglass drum of Finschhafen, New Guinea, of wood with glued heads (178).

Bumbun, *pigeon whistle of the Borneo Sea Dayak, made of 2 bamboo tubes. The first, very wide, is some 50 cm. (29 in.) long and closed at the top; the bottom is cut to form a spur. A hole is cut in the upper wall and air is driven in by a second, narrow tube over 2 m. (6½ ft.) long, inserted at an angle into the hole. The pipe is devoid of fingerholes. See also: bikut, bulu decot, dakut (18, 173).

Bumbung, syn. of gumbeng.

Bumumbu, *footed drum of the Washambala of Tanganyika, its head the skin of goat, dwarf antelope, or buck. A magician's instr., *ca.* 37 cm. (14½ in.) high (111).

Buncácan, "tuning fork" idiophone of the Philippine Islands, identical with the genggong sakai (176).

Bund, Ger.: fret.

Bundfrei, Ger.: unfretted.

Bung, *conical drum of Burma, with 2 laced heads, only the larger of which is played. Tuning paste is applied to its center. See also: saeng (176).

Bunga, syn. of botijuela.

Bungas, drum of ancient Latvia (89).

Bunge, MHGer.: **1.** kettledrum; **2.**

*cylindrical drum. The term was in use from the 13th c. to the 16th (169).

Bungkuk, instr. mentioned in Hindu-Javanese literature from 943 A.C. on, believed to denote the kenong (121).

Buni, see: tebuni.

Bunu [Turk. *būrū*], name of the būrū, 2, in Bambara (a Sudanic language) (93).

Bunun-giogu, *nose flute of the Semang of the Malay Peninsula, with 2–8 fingerholes, usually 4 (203).

Buonaccordo, 16th- and 17th-c. It. term for the clavichord. The hitherto unidentified buonaccordo is listed among the keyboard instrs. of his day by Vincenzo Galilei in 1581, but without description. He does, however, say that a "piccolo buonaccordo" was used by organists as a practice instr. and in another passage mentions it in reference to learning to play the organ and harpsichord. Such remarks are typical and fairly frequent occurrences in the literature of the clavichord. Furthermore, the name itself —and still more clearly that of its variant, bonaccordo—points to "monocordo" as the probable origin. In the early 17th c. G. B. Doni also refers to the buonaccordo. Thereafter the word is used in a historical sense only, 19th-c. lexicons usually defining it as a small It. spinet.

Būq, pl. **būqāt** or **abwāq** [?Gk. *bukane* or ?Lat. *buccina*], generic term for horns and trumpets of the Arabs and Persians, and specific term for one with a conical bore. Originally a *natural horn, the būq was subsequently made of metal. By the 10th c. one form had reached very considerable proportions— up to 1.80 m. (6 ft.) in length—and was in use in Islamic armies. According to Farmer, a far shorter form was converted into a shawm in the same century by the Andalusian Caliph Al-Hakam II, by the simple expedient of inserting a double reed at the narrow end and providing it with fingerholes. The Spaniards adopted this form as *albogón, the Basques called it alboquea or alboka; 14th-c. writers still mention the būq (73, 89 Farmer, 144).

Būq zamri (also abbr. to būq), an Islamic shawm. *Cf.* zamr (147 Farmer).

Bürchel, var. of Bürkel.

Burden, obs. word for the drone of a bagpipe. See: bourdon.

Burdones, med. Lat.: *pilgrim staves; by extension, the long bass pipes of an organ. *Cf.* bourdon (176).

Bürghū, |var. transliteraton of būrū.|

Burgmote horn, a curveu metal horn *ca.* 90 cm. (36 in.) long, used in med. Britain for announcing the assembly of the burgh motes (79).

Buri, 1. Mongolian straight trumpet, made of copper, sometimes decorated with gold or silver, used only in lamaist rituals. As it attains a length of *ca.* 4.80 m. (16 ft.), its bell must be rested on the ground or supported; **2.** trumpet of India, taken over from Mongolia.

Būrī, syn. of būru.

Burifē, signal horn of the Mande and Susu of W. Africa, made of wood or ivory (176).

Bürkel [*Bürke*, birch], small alphorn of the Prätigau Valley of Switzerland, with a slight curve, wound with birch bark; 60–100 cm. (2–3 ft.) long (187).

Burloir, wooden folk trumpet of the Bourbonnais, France, without a mouthpiece, shaped like a megaphone (136).

Buro, horn of Ghana, made of animal horn (176).

Bur-rting, temple gong or bronze disc of Tibet, suspended by a cord and struck with a wooden mallet. Possibly the same as the k'ar-rnga (89 Picken).

Buru [*būrū*], side-blown wooden horn of the W. African Mandingo, rarely also made of ivory, *ca.* 60 cm. (2 ft.) long (42).

Būrū (Turk.), **1.** obs. trumpet of the Turks and Turkomans, known in the 17th c. and introduced into Negro Africa from N. Africa; **2.** horn of the Sudanese Bambara and of the Vai (25, 76, 93).

Buruburu, small *cylindrical drum of the W. Torres Strait, with single head, played with bare hands (176).

Burubush, bull-roarer of the Korana Hottentots of S. Africa (116).

Buruga, a S. Indian name of the karnā.

Burumamaramu, bull-roarer of the Fly River area of New Guinea (176).

Burumbúmba [*buru,* talk], syn. of sambi, 2.

Būrūsī, horn of Turkey (144).

Busaun [MHGer. **busîne*], MHGer.: trombone. Of the several variants of this word, Martin Luther decided on *Posaune, which became HGer. (88).

Buse [Lat. **buccina*], OFr.: trumpet (197).

Busel [dim. of **buse*], OFr.: pipe; by extension, flute. Froissard used the term *ca.* 1400; it became obs. after the early 16th c. (85, 204).

Busenne, var. of buisine.

Busette [dim. of **buse*], OFr.: a small pipe (197).

Bushuki, see: buzuki.

Busîne (MHGer.) [Fr. **buisine*], a large straight trumpet of med. Germany, the name becoming transformed to busune at the end of the Middle Ages. *Cf.* buisine (170).

Busoi, *musical bow of the Borneo Tanjong, placed on a wood-covered resonator of clay or metal. The string is tapped with a small stick. It has no tuning loop (17).

Bussophone [inventor's name], instr. of unknown identity, patented by Busson of Paris on Nov. 18, 1873, probably with free reeds. *Cf.* accordéon-orgue, flûtina-polka (204).

Busûne, see: busîne.

But sheau, free-reed pipe of bamboo, of the Palaung of Shan State, Burma, with 6 front fingerholes and a rear thumbhole. A free reed of metal is set in a hole cut in the wall, and the instr. has a calabash air reservoir (172).

Butsina, syn. of karakoru (176).

Butt (Fr.: *culasse;* Ger.: *Stiefelstück*), **1.** bottom joint of a bassoon, containing a U-shaped bore, into which the wing and long joints are fitted; **2.** the knee-shaped piece of wood into which a hammer shank is fitted.

Buttori, deer-hoof rattle of the E. Bororó of the Mato Grosso (105).

Butyu, horn of the S. African Bomvana, made of oxhorn, with lateral blowhole, yielding but one tone (116).

Buye, see: fuye.

Buyong, *marine-shell trumpet of the Borneo Malays, made from the *Cassis tuberosum* with a blowhole pierced in the tip (176).

Buyung, see: goōng buyung.

Buzain, var. of bazuin.

Buze (OFr.), see: buse.

Buzina [Lat. **buccina*], Port.: horn; hunting horn.

Buzine, see: busîne.

Buzuk [Turk. *buzurk,* large], Alb. tanbūr, with piriform body, fretted fingerboard, and 3 pairs of metal strings (176).

Buzuki [Turk. *buzurk*], chordophone of modern Greece, closely related to the tanbūr, with long, thin neck, piriform body, mixed frontal and lateral tuning pegs, rib fastener, and a low bridge. The neck is fretted. The stringing consists of 2 courses, each of 3 metal strings. *Cf.* buzuk (91).

Bwanzi, *board zither of the Bogoro-Basire of the Congo, with bark resonator (128).

Bwebalabala, panpipes of Leper Island, New Hebrides, with 6 or 7 bamboo pipes; 7–18 cm. (3–7 in.) long (176).

Byakushi, wooden clappers of Japan, made of thin slats of bamboo, formerly of hardwood (157).

Byme, var. of beme.

Byo, double-headed drum of Burma, with laced heads (176).

Byong, syn. of klinting.

Byo-tsongsang, drum of Burma (176).

Byrgy, decoy horn of the Kanchin of Siberia, made of sections of hollowed wood bound together with birch bark. It imitates the sound of a doe and is used by hunters to decoy the stag (176).

Bzura, kobza of the Crimean Tatars (176).

C

C . . . , see also: ch . . .

Ç . . . , see: sh . . . ; s . . .

Cabaca, adaptation of the Afro-Brazilian cabaça for Western rhythm bands: a synthetic gourd covered with a network of beads threaded on gut.

Cabaça (Port.: gourd), syn. of piano de cuia (7).

Cabinet d'orgue, Fr.: chamber organ.

Cabinet piano, upright piano invented by William Southwell of Dublin in 1807 and improved by him in 1821. It was large and cumbersome, 1.80–2 m. (6–6½ ft.) high, with the tuning pins at the top of the soundboard and a large, open front panel covered with cloth. Despite its size it remained pop. until the mid-c., when smaller uprights came to be preferred (92, 149).

Cabreta [Lat. *capra,* goat], med. Lat.: bagpipe.

Cabrette [Lat. *capra,* goat], the cornemuse of rural Auvergne, France, named for its goatskin bag. *Cf.* chevrette (13).

Caccarella, Neapolitan *friction drum, made of a tin pot covered with a bladder and furnished with a friction stick some 75 cm. (30 in.) long (16).

Cacciapensieri (It.: chase the thoughts), var.' of scacciapensieri, in use from the 17th c. on.

Cai, in Vietnamese, a prefix to names of all inanimate objects; it is not the equivalent of our "a" or "the" (132).

Cai ban ñac, clapper of Vietnam, made of 3 slabs of lacquered wood hinged together at one end, the longer, central one assuming the form of a dragon. A number of pellet bells are attached to the outer slabs; used in religious ceremonies only (132, 173).

Cai bon, barrel-shaped drum of Vietnam, with 2 heads of buffalo skin. Tuning paste is applied to the center of one head, which then yields 2 sounds, usually B and F. Played with bare hands; 36–38 cm. (14–15 in.) long, 13–15 cm. (5–6 in.) in diam. The cai bon corresponds to the tapone of Thailand, taphon of Laos, mādalā of India, samphor of Cambodia (65, 176).

Cai cañ, gong of Vietnam, with large boss, suspended by a wooden handle from a frame (173).

Cai cap ke, concave castanets of Vietnam, made of ironwood, 3½ cm. (1½ in.) thick and some 20 cm. (8 in.) long. A pair is held in one hand and clicked together (132).

Cai chak, hardwood clappers of Vietnam, used by dancers to accompany their songs (132, 173).

Cai cheng, gong of Vietnam made in various sizes, 44–80 cm. (17–31½ in.) in diam., with central boss and turned rim. It serves at religious and military functions. A smaller, rimless gong is also known as cai cheng (132, 173).

Cai chum chua, temple cymbals of Vietnam, made of copper, with central boss (176).

Cai chuong chua (*chuong,* bell; *chua,* temple), temple bell of Vietnam, made of bronze with ornaments in relief (132).

Cai chuong de chung, *resting bell of Vietnam of copper or bronze, set on a cushion. Its edge is struck with a wooden stick. A ritual instr. (132).

Cai chuong gang, temple bell of Vietnam, cup shaped, *ca.* 12 cm. (5 in.) high and 10 cm. (4 in.) in diam. *Gang* is the name of the alloy of which it is made (132).

Cai cong, copper gong of Vietnam with turned rim—actually a small cai cheng (132).

Cai dan bao (*dan,* lute: *bao,* gourd), an evolved ground bow of Vietnam, sometimes called a one-string harp. A flexible rod is placed upright on a rectangular resonator; a wire string is attached to the top of the rod and its other end tied to the resonator. The string is plucked with a plectrum, and its pitch regulated by flexing the rod. Played by women and blind persons (170).

Cai dan day, long-necked lute of Vietnam, with rectangular hardwood body *ca.* 1 m. (40 in.) long, with 8 frets, 3 strings tuned $G^0 d^0 a^0$, and a compass G^0–e^2. A soundhole *ca.* 10 cm. (4 in.) wide is cut in the back. The cai dan day is an accompaniment instr. of singers. Total length *ca.* 130 cm. (51 in.) (176).

Cai dan ña tro (*dan,* lute; *ña tro,* singer), lute of Vietnam, with trapezoid body, the back of which is slightly larger than the belly, so that the ribs slant. The neck, *ca.* 116 cm. (45½ in.) long, carries 12 wooden frets. Its 3 strings are secured to lateral pegs and a frontal string fastener. A soundhole is cut in the back (132).

Cai dan nguyet (*dan,* lute; *nguyet,* moon), flat lute of Vietnam, with circular body and medium-long neck, of Chin. origin. Its 2 pairs of strings are tuned a 5th apart. The neck carries 8 frets. A vibrating metal tongue is affixed inside the body. Its compass is G^0–a^1. It corresponds to the yüeh ch'in of China and the cha pei toch of Cambodia (132).

Cai dan thap luc (*dan,* lute; *thap luc,* sixteen), zither of Vietnam, with vaulted surface and flat bottom, symbolic of heaven and earth, furnished with 16 metal strings stretched from a frontal string fastener over movable ivory bridges to ivory tuning pegs and played with a plectrum; 3 soundholes are cut in the back. Similar to the ch'in of China and

the koto of Japan. Also called cai dan trañ. Its compass is f^0–f^3 (91, 173).

Cai dan ti, flat lute of Vietnam, with piriform body and 4 silk strings tuned $G^0 c\#^0 e b^0 g^0$. The neck carries 9 or 10 frets. A vibrating metal tongue is affixed inside the body. Equivalent to the p'i p'a of China (173).

Cai dan trañ, syn. of cai dan thap luc.

Cai ken (*ken,* pipe), shawm of Vietnam, with an arched profile and devoid of bell. The tube consists of 2 pieces of hollowed wood glued together, with 7 or 8 fingerholes (132, 173).

Cai ken doi (*ken,* pipe; *doi,* double), double reedpipe of Vietnam, made of 2 cai ken mot of identical length and fingerhole disposition, glued together with resin. Both reeds are taken into the player's mouth. The sounds yielded are not in complete unison but produce strong beats (132, 144).

Cai ken loa, 1. shawm of Vietnam similar to the sona, with wooden body, brass bell, and 8 fingerholes, used chiefly during funeral ceremonies (132); **2.** *marine-shell trumpet of Vietnam (144).

Cai ken mot (*ken,* pipe; *mot,* single), reedpipe of Vietnam, a cylindrical tube of cane with 7 fingerholes and a thumbhole, all of oval shape. According to Mahillon, the reed is double, made of a chrysalis hull; according to Hickmann, the reed is single (132, 144).

Cai khang, *musical stone of Vietnam, a disc of irregular form, suspended from a gallows-shaped frame; often as large as 1 m. (40 in.) in diam. and 10 cm. (4 in.) thick (173).

Cai ma la, gong of Vietnam, with turned rim and a depressed center (173).

Cai mo, *slit drum of Vietnam, made from a block of camphorwood and usually given the shape of a fish, frog, fruit, or even pellet bell, hollowed through a slit and provided with a handle. Struck with a stick, it serves to announce the hours of the night and is also a temple and orchestral instr. Better specimens are lacquered (173).

Cai mo ca (*ca,* fish), cai mo in fish form, used in Buddhist rituals (132).

Cai mo ña chua (*ña,* house; *chua,* temple), bell of Vietnam, of red-lacquered wood, almond-shaped, with a gilded handle, used in Buddhist rituals (121, 132).

Cai nao but [Arab. *naubat*], cymbals of Vietnam, with central boss and turned rim, made in different sizes. The largest, some 50 cm. (20 in.) in diam., are primarily theater instrs., but are also used in religious festivities. The medium-sized ones are *ca.* 14 cm. (5½ in.) in diam. and are made of thin sheet copper; the smallest measure 5 cm. (2 in.) across. *Cf.* nabat, naubat, nobut (173).

Cai nhac, *pellet bell of Vietnam, made of 2 concave metal shells, suspended from horses' collars and also used as an orchestral instr. (132).

Cai ñi, *spike fiddle of Vietnam, with ivory body, 4-sided neck and 2 silk strings tuned a 5th apart, secured by large rear pegs. The nut consists of a cord loop that passes over the strings and holds them taut against the neck. The bottom is open. A bow is permanently inserted between the 2 strings, 1 being touched from above when played, the other from below. It corresponds to the t'i ch'in of China, so-i of Laos, sa dueng of Thailand, and amrita of India (47, 132, 173).

Cainorfica, It.: xenorphica.

Cai ong dich (*dich,* tube), *cross flute of Vietnam, similar to the *ti of China, with an extra hole above the 7 fingerholes, closed by a goldbeater's skin —a mirliton device. *Ca.* 55 cm. (22 in.) long (173).

Cai sao (*sao,* singing bird), *whistle flute of Vietnam, with an extra hole above the fingerholes, closed by a goldbeater's skin—a mirliton device (173).

Cai siñ, *percussion stick of Vietnamese mendicants, held between the toes and struck with 2 hardwood sticks. *Ca.* 15 cm. (6 in.) long (173).

Caisse [Lat. *capsa,* box], Fr.: originally the wooden shell of a drum; by ex-

tension the drum itself. *Cf.* grosse caisse, quesse.

Caisse à timbre, Fr.: snare drum.

Caisse claire, Fr.: snare drum.

Caisse roulante, Fr.: tenor drum.

Caisse sourde, syn. of caisse roulante.

Cai tam (*tam,* three), * long lute of Vietnam that has 3 silk strings. Top and bottom of the body are covered with snakeskin; a sliding *capotasto permits changes of pitch. The instr. is undoubtedly of Chin. origin and corresponds to the san hsien (132, 173).

Cai than la, small gong of Vietnam, of copper with turned rim; it serves in both orchestra and Taoist rituals (132, 173).

Cai thieu cañ, *gong chime of Vietnam, composed of small tuned gongs suspended in an upright frame—a derivation of the yün lo of China. *Cf.* cang-chen (173).

Cai tiu, a small *resting bell of Vietnam, in form of a copper or bronze cup. It rests in the hand, open side up, and is struck with a small stick. *Ca.* 10 cm. (4 in.) in diam. (132).

Cai trong (*trong,* drum), a large *barrel drum of Vietnam, with 2 heads of buffalo skin and lacquered body, suspended horizontally and struck with a large stick. It corresponds to the thôn of Thailand. It is 50–80 cm. (20–32 in.) long, 40–50 cm. (16–20 in.) in diam. (173).

Cai trong boc, drum of Vietnam, with hemispherical body and single, nailed head, made in numerous sizes; an orchestral instr. played with a stick (132).

Cai trong cai (*cai,* great), *barrel drum of Vietnam, with red and gold lacquered body and 2 nailed heads. It serves as a signal instr. in religious and civilian life. *Ca.* 48 cm. (19 in.) high, 36 cm. (14 in.) in diam. (132).

Cai trong com (*com,* boiled rice), a small *barrel drum of Vietnam, suspended from the player's neck by a cord. Its 2 nailed heads are played with the fingers, and both have tuning paste of boiled rice applied to the center (132).

Cai trong con (*con,* child), child's drum of Vietnam, similar to the cai trong tien co but unlacquered. It stands *ca.* 7½ cm. (3 in.) high (132).

Cai trong giang, a small drum of the mendicant monks of Vietnam, conical, open at the larger end; the head of the smaller is glued. Variations of pitch are obtained by striking the head in the center or close to the rim. *Ca.* 19 cm. (7½ in.) high (173).

Cai trong khan, a small *barrel drum of Vietnam, with 2 nailed heads, lacquered body, and a handle (173).

Cai trong kuan, ground zither of Vietnam (173).

Cai trong mañ (*mañ,* thin), syn. of cai trong met.

Cai trong met, *frame drum of Vietnam, struck with 2 small sticks. The inner diam. is *ca.* 21 cm. (8 in.) (132).

Cai trong quan, see: cai trong kuan.

Cai trong tien co (*tien,* small; *co,* neck), drum of Vietnam, with lacquered body, 2 heads, and a handle by which it is held while beaten with a stick (132).

Cai trong va, drum of Vietnam, with a single, nailed head (132).

Cai tu loa, *marine-shell trumpet of Vietnam that serves as a signal instr. in rural areas (132).

Caixa, Port.: a (military) drum.

Caixa clara, Port.: snare drum.

Caixa de rufo, Port.: tenor drum.

Cai xiñ tien (*xiñ,* clapper; *tien,* cash), scraped clapper of Vietnam, made of 2 hardwood slabs 27 cm. (10½ in.) long; one of these ends in 2 points, to each of which 3 cash (small coins) are attached; the other terminates in one point, also garnished with cash. Held in the right hand, the clappers are clicked together and the cash jingle; at the same time the clappers are scraped with a notched stick held in the player's left hand (132).

Caja [Lat. *capsa,* box], **1.** Sp.: drum; **2.** name given by the S. American Chipaya Indians to their tambourine. Although round ones are encountered, the square form is common, its 2 heads being laced in zigzags. The name, but not the instr., is Sp. (104).

Caja peñarandina (Sp.: drum of Peñaranda), *cylindrical drum of Spain, with 1 thin and 2 thick snares; it accompanies the dulzaina. *Ca.* 35 cm. (14 in.) high, 65–70 cm. (25–27 in.) in diam. (57).

Cajita china (Sp.: small Chinese box), percussion instr. of Cuba: a wooden block, shaped like a brick, that has a slit running lengthwise from one narrow end to the other; the block is drummed on. It is frequently constructed in 2 parts, as a box with glued-on lid. *Cf.* Chinese block, nbogoi, popó (152).

Cajón (aug. of Sp. *caja,* box), Afro-Cuban substitute for a drum: a wooden box with apertures on the side is beaten with bare hands (152).

Cakot, gourd rattle of the Papago Indians of Arizona (51).

Calamaula, same as calamella.

Calamela [Lat. *calamus*], OProv.: shawm.

Calamella [Gk. *kalamaulos*], med. Lat.: shawm, pipe (61).

Calamellus [dim. of *calamus*], Lat.: shawm.

Calamus (Lat.) [Gk. *kalamos*], **1.** in ancient Rome a reed, reedpipe, a syn. of tibia; in late antiquity an organ pipe; **2.** in the Middle Ages a shawm.

Calandrone [It.: *calandro,* lark], folk oboe of It. shepherds and peasants, mentioned by Buonanni and Laborde. Two keys cover holes bored on opposite sides of the tube to enlarge the compass upward (36, 39, 124, 176).

Calascione, see: colascione.

Calasciontino, see: colasciontino.

Calcatorium, Lat.: pedalboard. Paulus Paulirinus used the expression *ca.* 1460.

Calderarpa [maker's name], claviharp made by L. Caldara of Turin and Racca of Bologna *ca.* 1890. It was unlike older models in that the strings were not plucked, but were struck by small, cloth-covered bars, the lowest ones even by hammers. The harp shape was preserved; compass 6 octs., F¹–f⁴ (176).

Caledonica, see: alto fagotto.

Calichon [Ger. corr. of Fr. *cola-chon*], a small early-18th-c. version of the colascione, of which Majer said (in 1732) that it was like a lute and had 5 strings tuned as a viola da gamba; Eisel (in 1738) gives it 6 strings, however, tuned D G C E A D (67, 134).

Calliope (muse of epic poetry), William of Malmesbury's dream come true: a real steam-driven organ (*cf.* hydraulos) invented, not by the Alexandrine Ktesibios, but by the American A. S. Denny in the 19th c. A row of pipes was connected to a steam boiler; pressure from the boiler was controlled by valves either from a keyboard or by a pinned cylinder. The calliope first appeared in the U.S. in 1856 and caused a sensation. It had been designed to attract people to fairs, showboats, etc., from great distances: if it could not be heard from Jerusalem to the Mount of Olives, it could at least reach a public 12 miles distant. For the organ stop, see: Kalliope.

Calliophone [*Calliope + *phone,* sound], a variety of Calliope operated by air pressure, according to Webster's New International Dictionary, 2nd Edition.

Callissoncino, corr. of colasciontino.

Cambreh, see: kambreh.

Camel bells, a tuned set of clapper bells used in modern percussion. *Cf.* cowbell.

Campa, 1. in Portugal, a church bell; **2.** in Brazil, abbr. of campaínha (7).

Campaínha [Lat. *campana*], Port.: **1.** small bell; **2.** obs. term for Jingling Johnnie.

Campana, 1. It., Lat., Port., Sp.: bell. For a long time campana was thought to be derived from the Campania district of Italy; this etym. was given by Abbot Cumenaeus Albus *ca.* 660 A.C. Now, however, Sachs's etym. is accepted. He derived the word from the Gk. *kampto,* to bend, *kampoulos,* bent, a characteristic of the bell as opposed to the flat *semanterion. The word has been in use since the

early 6th c.; **2.** syn. of Glockenspiel, 2, an organ stop.

Campane [Lat. *campana*], obs. Fr.: bell. From the 13th c. to the 16th campane denoted both a very small bell, such as that attached to a falcon, and a tower bell (204).

Campanella [It.: dim. of *campana*], It.: small bell.

Campanelle, obs. Fr.: small bell.

Campanelli, organ stop, syn. of Glockenspiel, 2.

Campanette, It.: Glockenspiel.

Campanillas chinas (Chinese bells), Cuban adaptation of the Jingling Johnnie, with small bells, pellet bells, and metal plaques (152).

Campassi, 2 bass and 2 tenor "campassi" are mentioned in an Austrian inventory of 1596 (the local pronunciation of "gambas"?).

Campenole [Lat. *campana + dim. -ola*], obs. Fr.: small bell. The word was in use during the 13th and 14th c. (204).

Campignole, var. of campenole.

Cañ, see: cai cañ.

Canale [Arab. *qānūn*], med. Ger. name of the psaltery.

Canarí, Afro-Haitian *percussion pot corresponding to the zin-li (152).

Canda bemba, drum of Lake Bangweulu area, Africa, held against the chest when played (30).

Candele, obs. spelling of kantele (9).

Canemelle [Lat. *calamus*], 14th-c. var. of chalemele.

Cang-chen, gong chime of Tibet. *Cf.* cai thieu cañ (89 Picken).

Cangueca, trumpet of ancient Brazil, made of human bones (176).

Cannale [Arab. *qānūn*], var. of canale.

Canne-basson, Fr.: walking-stick bassoon.

Canne-clarinette, Fr.: walking-stick clarinet.

Canne-flûte, Fr.: walking-stick flute.

Canne-flûte à bec, Fr.: czakan.

Canne-hautbois, Fr.: walking-stick oboe.

Canne-pochette, Fr.: walking-stick violin.

Canne-trompette, Fr.: walking-stick trumpet.

Canno, var. of caño.

Caño [Arab. *qānūn], med. Sp. name of the psaltery.

Caño entero, med. Sp. name for the larger form of psaltery, in contradistinction to the medio caño.

Canon [Arab. *qānūn], med. Fr. and Lat. name of the psaltery.

Canone, med. It. name of the psaltery.

Canon harmonicus [Gk. *kanón harmonikos], Lat.: the monochord.

Çanpolla [Gk. *symphonia], obs. Sp.: bagpipe.

Cansar, scraper of Luanda, Angola (185).

Cantino, It.: chanterelle.

Cantophone, a Fr. patent was granted to Le Jeune on Feb. 1, 1882, for an instr. of this name, apparently a mirliton (204).

Canuto (Sp.: internode), simple wooden tubes of Cuba, played in sets 52–115 cm. (20–45 in.) long. Introduced by the Haitian population, which calls them vaccin(es) (152).

Canzá, var. of ganzá.

Capador (Sp.: gelder), panpipes of Colombia, by means of which the gelder announces his arrival. Cf. capapuercas, castrapuercas.

Capapuercas [Sp.: capar, geld + puercas, pigs], according to Covarrubias (in 1611), a Sp. panpipe composed of 5–6 pipes. Cf. capador, castrapuercas.

Capistrum, Lat.: phorbeia.

Cap ke, see: cai cap ke.

Capodaster, Ger.: capotasto.

Capodastro, Engl.: capotasto.

Capotasto (It. chief fret) (Fr.: barre), **1.** *nut; **2.** a movable nut in form of a wooden bar or metal band tied or clipped to the fingerboard of certain plucked instrs., thereby shortening the speaking length of the strings. Its great advantage is that it permits the same fingering in any tonality. A number of old

instrs.–citterns especially–have holes bored through fingerboard and neck for the accommodation of a capotasto; **3.** a metal pressure bar that acts as a nut in the treble section of pianos, exerting downward pressure on the strings, invented by Antoine Bord of Paris in 1843. The word was used by G. B. Doni in 1640 (*Annotazioni*) and has since become corrupted to capodasto, capodastro, Capotaster, etc. Also written "capo tasto."

Capus [Turk. *qūpūz], obs. var. of cobza.

Caquelcultrun, drum of the Araucano Indians of S. America, made from a hollow log of wood, with 2 heads. Cf. cultrun (105).

Cara (Sp.: face), organ stop of 16′ diapason pipes, found in Sp. organs (A. G. Hill, in 179A, Vol. 14).

Caracacha, notched bamboo *scraper of the Guato and Mura Indians of Brazil (171, 176).

Caracaxá, in Brazil a name applied to the: **1.** ganzá; **2.** reco-reco; **3.** maraca (7).

Caracola, Sp.: *marine-shell trumpet.

Caramba, syn. of arpa-ché.

Carambano, syn. of carángano.

Caramillo [Lat. *calamus], Sp.: shawm. The word is recorded from the 14th c. on. See also: zampoña, 2.

Carángano, *stick zither of Bolivia, Colombia, Argentina, Mexico, and Venezuela, with straight stick, single string, and tuning peg. The string is fixed in a cleft of the wood. Ca. 90 cm. (3 ft.) long. Also called carambano (103, 137, 152).

Carbassola [carbassa, fruit of the carbassera], scraper of Catalonia, similar to the peixet but made of a small gourd (57).

Carcan [Prov. *cascavelo], regional Fr.: large pellet bell, formerly suspended from horses' necks (197).

Careignon, OFr.: carillon.

Carenon, OFr.: carillon.

Cariglione, It.: carillon.

Carillon (Fr.) (Fr.: clochettes; Ger.:

Glockenspiel; It.: *cariglione;* Sp.: *carillón*), **1.** a set of tuned bells hung dead, *i.e.,* stationary, in a tower and played from a keyboard, or automatically by clockwork or by electrically controlled pneumatic mechanism. The difference between a carillon and a *bell chime is merely one of compass, any set of more than 1½ to 2 octs. being considered a carillon. This at least is the sense of the word in Engl. In Fr. the word formerly denoted any set of tuned bells, regardless of their number, hung dead and sounded by means of clockwork; nowadays (in Fr.) it means a tune, not the instr. that plays it. The etym. of the word *carillon,* which does not appear in the Fr. language until 1345, is not altogether satisfactory: *carillon* is said to derive from *quadrilionem* or *quaternis,* either of which would point to a set originally composed of 4 bells. Small chimes of 4 bells are indeed depicted in med. mss., but well before the 14th c.

The carillon is a development of the *cymbala, 2, or early bell chime, made possible by the gradual perfecting of casting methods. In the 13th c. chimes were mechanized by connecting the bells to the town clock, with a cogwheel causing exterior hammers to strike the bells in a given sequence and at given times. In the Low ·Countries and N. France a more elaborate system prevailed: the bells were suspended from a frame in a tower and their hammers were released by iron pegs set in a large, rotating cylinder, weight-driven, permitting a whole tune to be played automatically. Bells were provided with up to 6 hammers to ensure repetition, and the old wooden barrels were replaced with larger metal ones. *Ca.* 1500 a keyboard was added to the carillons in and around Antwerp (one is mentioned in Audenarde in 1510), and manual playing was then made possible by disconnecting the carillon from its barrel and connecting the hammers to the keyboard by wires and rollers in an arrangement rather similar to an organ action. With increasing compasses, the deeper-pitched bells with their heavy hammers could no longer be played by hand, and so a pedalboard was added. The earliest pedalboard seems to have been in Mechelen in 1583. A carillon keyboard is laid out like a piano keyboard, with 2 rows of "keys," wooden cylinders 2 cm. (¾ in.) in diam. The pedalboard, usually of 1½ octs., is connected to the manual by pulldowns. Although even today most carillon towers are to be found in the Low Countries, the carillon spread to other countries in the 16th and 17th c. From the 16th c. on, small carillons for indoor use were also made. The 19th c. brought improvements in hammer release by employing spring triggers, later followed by electric and electrophonic carillons. See also: beiaard, bell chime, careignon, carenon, carillon de Flandre, clockspele, codophone, cymbala, hosanna, quarregnon (160, 169, 197);

2. organ stop consisting of: a) real bells; b) metal bars; c) tubular bells; d) a 2- or 3-rank mixture stop of high-pitched flue pipes, frequently used by Abbé Vogler (also called Glockenton); e) a conventional carillon played from the organ;

3. Fr.: Glockenspiel.

Carillón, Sp.: carillon.

Carillon à musique, the earliest name of the music box (43).

Carillon de Flandre (Fr.), a large carillon, called beiaard in Flem. (160).

Carimba [*marimba*], **1.** *musical bow of the Mosquito Indians of C. America, with tuning loop and gourd resonator, tapped with a short stick; **2.** musical bow of El Salvador Indians, with tuning loop attached to the gourd resonator. *Ca.* 150 cm. (5 ft.) long; **3.** name of the quijango (musical bow) among the Nahuatl Indians of Nicaragua; **4.** xylophone of the Congo people of Angola, with fixed slabs and gourd resonators (17, 105, 185).

Carmel [Lat. *calamus*], Prov.: shawm (176).

Carnyx, long, hooked bronze trumpet

of the ancient Celts, a martial instr., with straight tube ending in a bent-back bell that characteristically assumed the form of an animal's head with open mouth. The carnyx was played with a lead mouthpiece. Descriptions and many representations have come down to us from antiquity. Except for the design of its bell, it resembles the lituus. The only surviving specimen, now lost, measured 76 cm. (30 in.). Prototype of the carnyx was a wooden tube with animal horn affixed to its end, combining cylindrical with conical bore. Its relationship, if any, to the lituus has not yet been clarified. On a silver dish found at Gundestrup in Jutland, carnyx players are shown holding their instrs. upright with the bells well above their heads. This implies a curve at the mouthpiece end or a laterally inserted mouthpiece, lacking on other representations (21, 89, 170).

Carquavel [Prov. *cascavelo*], OFr.: pellet bell.

Carraca, Sp.: cog rattle (57).

Carrasca (Sp.: evergreen oak), Afro-Cuban scraper, consisting of a notched stick that is scraped (152).

Carrasquiña [dim. of *carrasca*], xylophone of Andalusia, consisting of a series of graduated wooden slabs strung on a cord. Cf. ginebras (152).

Carrau, Cat.: carraca.

Carrilhão, Port.: carillon.

Carroccio, It. bell cart, containing a large bell suspended from a frame; it served as a signal instr. in It. armies up to the 17th c. Sachs was of the opinion that it had been in use before 1000 A.C. (176).

Cart, corr. of quarte (de nazard) (186).

Cartel, *music box first produced in Geneva in 1820, larger than any of its forerunners, *i.e.*, than the snuffbox, watch, or jewel-box models (43).

Cartonium [Fr. *carton*, cardboard], mechanical free-reed instr. invented by Joseph-Antoine Testé of Nantes and patented July 16, 1861, and again in 1864.

The free reeds worked on the suction principle, and thus the cartonium is one of the earliest *American organs. A surviving specimen in the Brussels Conservatoire museum is in form of a small harmonium with the reeds disposed on rectangular boxes containing an air reservoir. A strip of perforated cardboard moved between 2 rubber-coated rollers controlled by a hand crank (37, 132).

Cascabel [Lat. *cacabellus*, pan, kettle], Sp.: small bell, pellet bell; bell hung on animals' necks. Cf. kaskabeleta, kaskabilo.

Cascabeles, the Sp. equivalent of the Zimbelstern, in use up to the 19th c., made of a set of harness bells attached to a paddle wheel (A. G. Hill in 179A, Vol. 14, 170).

Cascagnette [Lat. *castanea*, chestnut], MFr.: castanet, made of wood or ivory (197).

Cascaveaux [Lat. *cacabellus*, pan, kettle], Prov.: in the 17th c. a dancer's jingle or pellet bells; also clappers similar to castanets (197).

Cascavel [Lat. *cacabellus*, pan, kettle], 1. Port.: small bell, pellet bell; 2. Sp.: var. of cascabel.

Cascavell, *stick rattle of Catalonia, made of a number of pellet bells attached to a stick that is either shaken by hand or struck with a short stick (57).

Cascavelle (Fr.) [Prov. *cascavelo*], a small bell. The word occurs in this sense from the 14th c. to the 16th. In the 17th c. the word was also applied to clappers. Trichet, *ca.* 1640, says "*cascavelles dictes autrement castaignettes*" (otherwise called castanets) (190).

Cascavellus, med. Lat.: pellet bell. The term is recorded from the 13th c. on (61).

Cascavelo, Prov.: small bell.

Cassa, It.: snare drum.

Cassa rullante, It.: tenor drum.

Cassi-flûte [inventor's name], instr. containing flue pipes for which a Fr. patent was granted Sept. 15, 1857, to Cassi-Meloni. Cf. Meloni-cor (204).

Cassuto, scraper of the Ambundu of Angola, consisting of a piece of hollow wood *ca.* 90 cm. (3 ft.) long, covered with a notched board and scraped with a stick. Played together with the quilando (185).

Castagnette [Lat. *castanea*, chestnut], Fr.: castanet. The word has been in use since 1606 (197).

Castagnolo, Prov.: castanet.

Castanet [Sp. *castañeta* from *castaña*, chestnut] (Fr.: *castagnette;* Ger.: *Kastagnette;* It.: *castagnetta*), shallow, hollow, rounded clappers, made of wood, known to ancient Egypt and still played today in Andalusia, the Balearic Islands, and S. Italy. Its prototype was a bivalve shell. Castanets of ancient Egypt either were shaped like a small boot, with the tapering foot serving as handle, or were very similar to the modern Sp. ones but less flat. They were also known to Greece and are mentioned in late Greco-Roman literature as krotalon, krembalon, or krouma—a dancer's instr. Sachs assumed an Asiatic origin for the castanet and suggested that the chestnut-shaped ones might originally have been Phoenician. Spain, like S. Italy, was a Phoenician colony and already a center of dancing in antiquity. Castanets remained in use in Spain throughout the Middle Ages; they are depicted in the *Cantigas de Santa María* of the 13th c. and in earlier mss., later to become a national instr. Apparently they traveled no farther until they moved N. with the sarabande in the late 16th c., but even then they did not gain a real foothold outside of S. Italy. The Engl. word castanet is not recorded until 1670.

Castanets are played in pairs, 2 half shells, as it were, being joined by a cord. The player holds a pair in each hand, passing the cord around thumb and one finger. Today, as in the past, castanets are chiefly used by dancers, clicked rhythmically or sounded in a long roll. Good castanets are extraordinarily resonant. Nowadays they are made of grenadilla, walnut, chestnut, box, or other wood. For modern orchestral and rhythm-band use, 1 or 2 single castanets, or a pair, are attached to a long handle; they may be of bakelite or wood. Castanets without handles are known in the trade as "finger type" castanets. Sp. names for the instr. are: castañetas, castañuelas, pulgaretes, pulgarillas, tejoletas. See also: arxalu-ak, cai cap ke, cascagnette, castanholas, chahārpāra, champara, chapa, chipla, distinette, kasik, kayamba, krisket, kwa da ban tse, lamako, qarāqib, scattagnetti, tarreña (44, 89, 169, 170, 197).

Castañeta, Sp.: castanet.

Castanholas, Port.: castanets (used in pl. form only).

Castañuela, Sp.: castanet.

Castrapuercas [Sp. *castrar,* geld + *puercas,* pigs], panpipes of Colombia, by means of which the gelder announces his arrival. See: capador, capapuercas, sanaporcs, sanatrujes.

Castrera, the same as castrapuercas.

Castruera, the same as castrapuercas.

Catá, *percussion tube of E. Cuba, consisting of a trunk of mahogany or other hardwood, open at both ends, laid horizontally on a stand, and beaten with 2 sticks. Modern ones are considerably smaller than older ones. Also called hueco (hollow). *Cf.* gua-gua (152).

Catena, It.: bass-bar.

Catuba, It.: bass drum.

Cavaco, chordophone of Portugal, a hybrid of guitar and mandolin, with 4–6 strings of gut, silk, or metal, and a fretted neck. The 4-stringed variety is tuned $d^1 g^1 b^1 d^2$ or $d^1 g^1 b^1 e^2$; 6-stringed ones are tuned to the guitar. See also: cavaquinho (89, 170).

Caval [Turk. *qawūl*], *end-blown flute of the Balkans (and Turkey), with cylindrical bore and a regionally variable number of fingerholes. Specifically, it is played in Albania and Bulgaria; in Dobruja, Moldavia, Oltenia, and Walachia of Romania; and in Yugo. Macedonia. Until recently it was also played, under the name of ny, by the Ruffai dervishes of

Macedonia. As 2 cavals are generally played together, by different players, they are usually made in pairs. Softwood is employed for their manufacture, the upper end being beveled to form a sharp edge. The whole instr. is then oiled or buttered. Tone production is extremely difficult, but little wind is required and a long phrase can be played on one breath. Rom. cavals have 5 front fingerholes, those of Yugoslavia 7 front holes and 1 rear hole as well as 4 lower vents. The Yugo. instrs. are stopped with 2 joints of the fingers. The fourth finger is never lifted (*cf.* gusle playing technique). When playing in duet, called *dvojice,* one performer plays a drone, or both play at unison, with one flute embroidering the melody of the other. A rustic instr., it is played by shepherds and peasants. Yugo. specimens are 72–79 cm. (28–31 in.) long with a bore of 15–16 mm.; elsewhere they attain a length of up to 90 cm. (3 ft.). *Cf.* qawūl (5, 33).

Cavalche, a name of the caval in Bulgaria.

Cavalry cornet, cornet made in the second half of the 19th c., with the bell pointing upward for greater convenience of playing by mounted bands (89 Baines).

Cavaquinho [dim. of **cavaco*], Port.: small cavaco with 4 single strings. Also called machete (7).

Caviglia, It.: tuning pin.

Cavonto, tanbūr of modern Greece, with flat back, rose, elongated neck with metal frets, and 3 pairs of steel strings held by T-shaped pegs (176).

Caxixi, Afro-Brazilian rattle made of a bell-shaped wickerwork basket, flat gourd bottom, and wickerwork handle, filled with dried seeds. Also called mucaxixi (7).

CC, Fr. and It. designation of the center bouts of instrs. of the violin and viol families.

Cécilium, free-reed instr. built by Arthur Quentin de Gromard in 1861, in form of a cello or lute, actually an imitation of the melophone. Made in 3 sizes: soprano with compass A^0-e^4, tenor C^0-e^3, contrabass E^1-b^1 (132).

Cécilium-flûte, cécilium with organ pipes and a keyboard, patented by Roger of Bordeaux on June 28, 1887.

Cedra, OSp.: cittern.

Ceirnin, an obs. portable Irish harp.

Celesta (Fr. *célesta*), **1.** keyboard metallophone in form of a small upright piano, invented by Auguste Mustel of Paris and patented on June 15, 1886, a successor to the *clavi-lame, with steel bars suspended over box-shaped wooden resonators and struck by piano hammers. The bars are equipped with dampers controlled by a pedal. Originally made with a 4-oct. compass from c^1, notated an oct. lower, now made with a 5-oct. compass and provided with an additional soft pedal. An orchestral instr.; **2.** harmonium stop. Mustel and Schiedmayer incorporated the celesta into the harmonium, giving it a manual of its own (89, 151, 169).

Celeste song bells, glockenspiel with tempered-aluminum bars, added resonator, vibrato, and damper pedal, invented by John Deagan *ca.* 1920 (B. Edgerley: *From the Hunter's Bow*).

Celestina, organ stop of wooden flue pipes invented by William Hill of London in the 19th c., at 4′ pitch (176, 186).

Celestina stop (Ger.: *Cölestin*), a number of 18th-c. keyboard instr. stops are known by this name: **1.** stop patented by Adam, and D., and J. Walker of London, covering the principle of sustained tone by a hand-worked bow, similar to a violin bow, held in the player's hand; **2.** stop patented by Samuel Gillespie of London in 1774, having an action with "heads of tanned leather, buff leather, kid leather, cloth and wool"; **3.** rosin-coated "endless fillet" acting as a bow on metal rods of a keyboard instr. patented by Charles Claggett in 1788; **4.** pianoforte stop of the late 18th c. consisting of strips of buff leather which could be intercalated between hammers and strings. Not to be confused with Cölestine (27, 176; A. J. Hipkins: *History of the Piano*).

Celestina-viol, organ stop, a viole d'orchestre at 4' pitch.

Celestinette, *bowed keyboard instr. of Adam Walker, 1772, better known as celestina.

Celimela, Lat.: shawm.

Cellalika, a triangular plucked chordophone, with 2 strings, of the Kamchadal of NE. Siberia. *Cf.* balalaika (176).

Cello, abbr. of violoncello.

Cellone [aug. of It. *cello*], a large violoncello made by Alfred Stelzer of Dresden *ca.* 1890, tuned a 4th lower than the cello, *viz.*, $G^1 D^0 A^0 e^0$, designed to provide the double-bass part in chamber music (89, 176).

Cello-Streichzither, *bowed zither invented by E. Salomon of Aachen, tuned $E^0 d^0 a^0 e^1$ (176).

Cembal d'amour, see: Cimbal d'amour.

Cembaletto ottavino, It.: 4' harpsichord (the term was used by Cristofori).

Cembalo [Lat. *cymbalum], It.: **1.** obs. term for cymbal; **2.** tambourine; see: cembalo loreto; **3.** harpsichord, abbr. of clavicembalo; **4.** piano stop; see: cembalo stop. The Gk. word *kymbalon* denoted a percussion instr.: the cymbal, as did its Lat. derivative, the *cymbalum*. The Gk. *tympanon* was also a percussion instr.: a frame drum. These 2 words, phonetically so similar, were confused in the Middle Ages, possibly as a result of incorporating cymbal-shaped metal jingles—*kymbala*—(in modern Fr. *cymbalettes*) into the frame of the tympanon. The confusion resulted in transferral to the cymbalum of the traditions attached to the tympanon. Furthermore, both terms became associated with the percussive stringed instr. called dulcimer in Engl. (the *cimbalom* of Hungary, *Cymbal* of the Alps, *cymbali* of Russia, etc., the *tympanon* of France, *tímpano* of Spain). Identification of the tympanon as a stringed instr. goes back to the 10th c., if not earlier (see tympanon, 2, and timpan). A similar stringed instr., with added keyboard, becomes a clavicymbolum, or keyed cymbolum, by 1404, is called clavizimbel, then clavicembalum by 1429, the latter term leading to the It. *clavicembalo*. This word, in use today, is generally abbr. to *cembalo* and means harpsichord. At the same time the word *cymbalum,* or, rather, its derived It. form, *cembalo,* continued to represent the old E. Mediterranean *frame drum (tympanon), originally an attribute of Astarte and played traditionally by women. As a frame drum, the cembalo still exists in Italy; writers such as Boccaccio and Zarlino used the word in this sense. The latter wrote on p. 312 of his *Sopplimenti* (1588) that "here in Venice" the instr. with parchment head, pellet bells, and jingles is called cembalo. And its ancient function in the hands of women is not forgotten, for in his index to the same work is mentioned *"cembalo, instrumento da donne."* In the next century Praetorius and, after him, Schütz refer to stringed keyboard instrs. as *"Instrument vors Frauenzimmer"* or even merely as *"Frauenzimmer,"* a term that at the time lacked the pejorative connotation it has today, perhaps best rendered as "gentlewoman." It is unlikely that they took their cue from Zarlino's index; rather, their "source" was surely the old tradition: women, having played the cembalo for so long (Miriam the prophetess, sister of Aaron, took a timbrel in her hand . . .), continued to play the clavicembalo. See also: virginal.

Cembalo angelico (It.: angelic harpsichord), harpsichord "invented" at Rome *ca.* 1778, in which quill plectra were replaced by velvet-covered leather ones (176).

Cembalo a penna (It.: quilled harpsichord), name given to the harpsichord in Italy after the invention of the piano, to distinguish it from the latter.

Cembalo da arco, It.: *bowed keyboard instrument.

Cembalo loreto, It. frame drum, circular, with single head and metal jingles (89 suppl.).

Cembalon, see: cimbalom.

Cembalone [aug. of *cembalo], It.: large harpsichord.

Cembalo omnicordo (or *omnisono*), syn. of Proteus.

Cembalo regio, It.: clavecin royal.

Cembalo stop, name of a piano stop intended to imitate the sound of a harpsichord by means of leather or cloth tongues tipped with brass or other hard material interposed between hammer and strings. This stop first appeared on a Silbermann piano formerly at Potsdam and was in use in England and Germany. Also called harpsichord stop (92).

Cembalo verticale, It.: clavicytherium.

Cembas, OProv.: cymbals (197).

Cemmanello, corr. of cennamella.

Cencerro [Arab. *jul-jul], Sp.: cowbell; bellwether's bell. See also: cianciana, cincerria, xincherri, zinzerri (57).

Cennamella [Lat. *calamellus*], It.: shawm. *Cf.* ciaramella.

Cércol [Lat. *circulus*], hoop of Catalonia, with metal jingles; actually a tambourine without a membrane. *Cf.* chalchal (57).

Cervelas, cervelat [It. *cervellato*], Fr.: racket.

Cetarissima [*cetera], archcittern invented by the Venetian composer Simon Balsamino in 1594, with 7 courses of metal strings tuned $A^0 d^0 g^0 c^1 e^1 g^1 c^2$, and 19 frets on the neck; played with a plectrum and the thumb (80 VI).

Cetera, It.: cittern.

Cetera tedesca (It.: German cittern), according to the anon. *Kurtzgefasstes musikalisches Lexicon,* of 1737, a Ger. 10-stringed lute with somewhat flat body and scalloped profile. But *cf.* deutsche Guitarre.

Cetra, occasional name of the *English guitar (79).

Cetula, Tinctoris' (*ca.* 1490) name for the citole, which he describes as having 4 metal strings and frets, and as being of It. invention.

Četvorka, a quadruple flute of Yugoslavia; neither this nor the trojnice has become a folk instr. (33).

Cevara, obs. *whistle flute of Yugoslavia that existed in E. Serbia up to World War I. It had a rear duct, cylindrical bore, and fingerholes like those of the Yugo. caval; 70–85 cm. (27½–33½ in.) long (33).

Ch . . . , see also: tch . . .

Chachá, 1. E. Cuban syn. of erikunde; **2.** Afro-Cuban gourd rattle, covered with a network of small percussion objects. Also played in Haiti (152).

Cha chiao, a modern Chin. trumpet, with upturned bell, made in different sizes and played with a very shallow mouthpiece; used in wedding processions. It is a variety of the siao t'ung kyo (89, 132, 142).

Chachra, syn. of khat tālī.

Chaghāna (Pers., Turk.), Turk. *percussion stick that was adopted by European military bands as Jingling Johnnie. According to Farmer, the word *chaghāna* was known in the 13th c., when it denoted the crotal. As a percussion stick, it was surmounted by a crescent and other symbols, from which bells, jingles, and generally 2 horsehair tails were suspended. Sachs pointed to a parallel among Chou dynasty (1122–255 B.C.) conductors, whose custom it was to signal the start of the music by lifting a dance wand ornamented with sun, star, and 2 white oxtails. In Turkey the crescent became its distinguishing feature and the chaghāna a symbol of dignity. See also: vargan (75 II, 169, 170).

Chahārpāra, obs. Pers. castanets of wood, possibly identical with the p'o pan of China (75 II).

Chahārtāra, see: chartār.

Chai . . . , see: cai . . .

Chaing vaing, *drum chime of Burma, composed of 16–24 drums, graduated in size and suspended in a low, circular frame. The drums are of wood, barrelshaped, with 2 laced heads. They stand 12–40 cm. (5–16 in.) high and are played with bare hands.

Chair organ (Fr.: *positif de dos;* Ger.: *Rückpositiv;* Lat.: *tergale positivum*), a small organ situated at the back of the organist's seat, its pipework being controlled from the lowest manual of the *great organ (called choir manual). In modern times the term has been corrupted to *choir* organ. The chair organ originated in the early 15th c.: Troyes had one by 1433. Henri Arnaut of Zwolle, ca. 1440, describes that of Dijon, which had 195 pipes. See also: organ.

Chak, 1. bell of Korea, occasionally used to accompany dances; **2.** see: cai chak (66).

Chakhe (alligator), wooden *tube zither of Thailand, carved in form of a crocodile. It corresponds to the mi gyaun of Burma. Also called garatē. *Cf.* takhe (173).

Cha kiao, see: cha chiao.

Chalam, see: halam.

Chalang, see: chalung.

Chalapata, syn. of gabi (56).

Chalcedon, Ger. corr. of colascione (169).

Chal-chal, percussion instr. of the Tamil of Ceylon, consisting of a metal frame with 4 pairs of jingles, actually a tambourine without a membrane, held by a metal handle soldered to the frame. *Cf.* cércol (141).

Chalemele [Lat. *calamus*], OFr.: shawm. The word is recorded in Fr. literature from the 12th c. to the 16th (204).

Chalemie [Lat. *calamus*], **1.** OFr.: shawm. In this sense the word was in use from the 14th c. to the 17th, though the word *hautbois* was in general use after 1500. By the mid-17th c. it denoted 2 different instrs.: the shawm, or *"dessus de hautbois,"* and also: **2.** the cornemuse of shepherds. According to Trichet (ca. 1640), this was a musette chanter separated from the musette, its double reed protected by a little box, *i.e.,* a reed cap, pierced with 2 holes. Mersenne confuses the issue by defining the chalemie as a cornemuse with 2 drones. *Cf.* chalumeau.

Chalempung, see: chelempung.

Chalil, see: hālil.

Chalintu, *notched flute of Batavia and S. Banten, Java, with 5 fingerholes (121).

Chellemelle [Lat. *calamus*], OFr.: shawm (61).

Chalmeye, var. Engl. spelling of shalmeye.

Chalpāra [Pers. *chārpāra*, four pieces], **1.** Turk.: cymbals; **2.** clappers of med. Persia. *Cf.* chārpāra (76, 147 Farmer).

Chalumeau (Fr.) [Lat. *calamellus*], name given to several woodwind instrs. and to an organ stop, often confused with *chalemie: **1.** chalumeau was formerly a term for any rustic reedpipe. It survives in this sense in Fr.-speaking Switzerland, where it denotes a shepherd's reedpipe, and in a generic sense any primitive musical tube; **2.** it was also the (double-reed) chanter of a bagpipe, detached and blown as a separate instr. (*cf.* chalemie, pibole). Mersenne uses the word in this sense and does not know of the single-reed instr.; **3.** it was further a short cylindrical instr. with wide bore, 7 fingerholes, played with a single reed, having a compass f^1–a^2, apparently a folk instr., in contrast to: **4.** an improved model made of boxwood, with 7 fingerholes, rear thumbhole, 2 brass keys, and a compass f^1–a^2 or even c^3, according to Majer (in 1732). This instr., also played with a single reed, was made in various sizes. With the appearance of parts written specially for it, its name gradually changed to clarinet. Transformation of the chalumeau into the clarinet ca. 1700 is credited to Johann Christoff Denner of Nürnberg. The old word continued in use for the new instr., however, until the end of the 1760's (the scores of Gluck's *Orfeo ed Euridice* and *Alceste,* 1764 and 1769, had parts for the chalumeau; later editions call them clarinet). See also: chalemie, clarinet, mock trumpet; **5.** an instr. similar to 3, terminating in a slight flare, with 6 fingerholes, 1 key, of present-day Ger. manufacture; **6.** name of the lowest register of the clarinet (80 XIV, Hunt; 102, 134, 164) **7.** organ stop of reed pipes with cylindrical resonators. As *jeu de chalumeaux*, it occurs in Dijon in the 13th c. and is the oldest known reed stop. Since, it has been built in a number of forms, sometimes surmounted by a bell, at 16', 8', or 4' pitch. Not identical with the Schalmei stop (3, 129, 133).

Chalumeau eunuque (Fr.), 17th-c. syn. of mirliton, flûte eunuque.

Chalung, tubular chime of W. Java, consisting of 12, 14, or 16 graduated bamboo tubes closed by a node at the bottom, with the top cut back about half the length so as to form a tongue. The tubes are strung together like a ladder and suspended by the smaller end from the wall of a house or from a tree; played with 2 padded beaters (121).

Chalybssonans [Lat. *chalybs,* steel + *sonans,* sounding], an imitation of Ernst Friedrich Chladni's euphone, but with steel bars instead of glass bars, built by Johann Christian Dietz, Sr., before 1806 (169).

Chamada do carnaval (Port. carnival call), Port. wind instr. used by Estremadura shepherds between Christmas and carnival, made from an oxhorn with a beating reed inserted in the narrow end. A lateral hole is pierced halfway down the tube (132).

Chamade (Fr.) [Lat. *clamare,* to call], a row of organ pipes is said to lie *en chamade* when they project horizontally from the organ case. Only reed pipes are so disposed, chiefly in Spain, where the practice dates back to the 17th c., but some larger Fr. organs include such a stop.

Chamber flute-orum, double *cross flute invented by David Hatton of Dunfermline, Scotland, in 1823. One of the tubes is a melody pipe, the other a drone. The fingering is conventional, but the wind is supplied by bellows (126, 176).

Chamber organ (Fr.: *cabinet d'orgue;* Ger.: *Kammerorgel*), *positive organ of the baroque and the 18th c., usually built in form of a large cupboard, with

single manual and a varying number of stops. These are often divided to permit execution on one manual of music written for 2.

Champara [Turk. **chalpāra*], Rom.: castanet, cymbal.

Champare [Turk. **chalpāra*], Pers. equivalent of the champareta.

Champareta [Turk. **chalpāra*], miniature cymbals of Yugoslavia *ca.* 6 cm. (2½ in.) in diam., hung with tassels. Encountered in Bosnia and Herzegovina (89).

Champari [Turk. **chalpāra*], Bulg. equivalent of the champareta.

Chanang, medium-sized gong of the Dayak of Borneo and the Achinese of Sumatra, with central boss. Often richly ornamented (173).

Chanang triëng, idiochord bamboo *tube zither of the Achin and Gayo regions of Sumatra, with 3 strings (119).

Chanan naga (snake gong), gong of the Dayak of Borneo, with a polygonal outline, ornamented with snake and geometrical designs, made of copper alloy (173).

Chanbar (Pers.), round *frame drum of ancient Persia. See also: gambar (75 II).

Chandrapirai, *frame drum of S. India, restricted to temples. A piece of parchment is stretched over an iron hoop that has one side indented, and is fastened by a handle to a person's forehead. Played with a stick. *Cf.* sūryapirai (179).

Chang (Pers., Pahl.: bent), **1.** *angular harp of pre-Islamic Persia, with tapering resonator and a variable number of strings: 13–40 are mentioned. The strings were plucked by both hands. It was introduced in pre-Islamic times into Arabia, where the name became modified to *jank; **2.** in the 18th c. the name chang was given to a dulcimer or psaltery, usually with 6 strings; **3.** Jew's-harp of the Kirghiz; **4.** syn. of murchang, the Jew's-harp of India (89 Farmer, 170).

Changa (Hindust.), the arched harp of ancient India (173).

Chang go, Korean *hourglass drum, with a lacquered body and with 2 heads stretched over hoops. One head is played with the bare hand, the other with a stick. It corresponds to the Chin. chang ku and the Jap. o-tsuzumi. *Ca.* 66 cm. (26 in.) long, 45 cm. (18 in.) in diam. (66, 176).

Changiri, bossless gong of Japan, struck with an ivory hammer (176).

Chang ku (Chin.: long drum), *hourglass drum of China, with 2 snakeskin heads lapped over metal hoops, laced, with central tension ligature. The central portion of the drum is a length of bamboo. It corresponds to the chang go of Korea and the o-tsuzumi of Japan (132, 142).

Chang kun, clay *percussion pot of Korea that is struck with a bamboo switch. *Ca.* 24 cm. (9½ in.) high, 36 cm. (14 in.) in upper diam. (66).

Ch'ang ti, syn. of ti (89).

Chang-tu, see: rnga-ch'un.

Changu, Kan. equivalent of murchang.

Changuion, free-reed organ patented Dec. 1, 1846, by Changuion, an organ builder of Lyon (204).

Changuoro, Afro-Cuban pellet bells and clapper bells affixed in clusters to a drum. Also called ichaoró (152).

Chank, see: chang.

Chan ku, barrel-shaped war drum of China, similar to the t'ang ku, about twice as wide as it is high. Also used in processions (142).

Chankun, *percussion pot of Korea; an earthenware pot struck with a bamboo switch (170).

Chanrara (Quechua), **1.** rattle of ancient Peru made of copper or silver jingles; **2.** rattle of the S. American highland Indians, made of sea snails (80 XII, 105).

Chantang balung, 1. usual name of the Javanese kepyak, 2; **2.** possibly also the former name of the chelepita, 3 (121).

Chanter [Fr. *chanteur,* singer] (Fr.:

chalumeau; Ger.: *Spielpfeife*), the melody pipe of a bagpipe. *Cf.* grall.

Chanterelle [Fr. *chanter,* to sing] (Fr.) (Ger.: *Sangsaite;* It.: *cantino*), the highest string of any chordophone having a neck. In France today the term is applied only to the E string of the violin, although the word has been in use there in the wider sense since the second quarter of the 16th c. (85, 127).

Chanteur, see: piano chanteur.

Chanuri, *spike fiddle of Tiflis, Georgia, U.S.S.R., with small gourd body, glued membrane belly, long spike, and 3 metal strings held by lateral pegs. *Ca.* 90 cm. (3 ft.) long (141).

Ch'ao, sheng of 19 pipes (89).

Chap, large cymbals of Thailand, with central boss and turned rim. Also called charp (173).

Chapa, 1. Sp.: castanet; Nebrija's translation of crotalum (1495); **2.** small cymbals of Japan, used in *kabuki* (135).

Chapara [Turk. *chalpāra*], cymbals of Korea, rarely used. *Ca.* 20 cm. (8 in.) in diam. (66, 170).

Chape, Fr.: upper-board.

Chapeau chinois, Fr.: Jingling Johnnie.

Cha pei, pop. long-necked lute of Cambodia, with flat, almost square body, elongated, narrow neck, and 2 strings held by lateral pegs. Larger than the cha pei toch (47).

Cha pei thom, flat, long-necked lute of Cambodia, with heart-shaped body and extremely long, slender neck terminating in an elegant curve; 4 strings. Similar to the ka-chapi of Thailand. Often 1.50 m. (5 ft.) long or more (46, 173).

Cha pei toch, flat lute of Cambodia, identical with the cai dan nguyet of Vietnam. At present it is being displaced by guitar or banjo. It corresponds to the yüeh ch'in of China (47, 173).

Cha-pen, see: ch'ung tu.

Chapey . . . , see: cha pei.

Chaping buyuk, name of the kowangan in Solo (an Indonesian language) (121).

Chaplachaul [*chapler,* to beat, strike], OProv.: cymbals. A 15th-c. term.

Chaplachoire [*chapler*, to beat, strike], Fr.: small cymbals (132).

Chara, scraper of the Washambala of Tanganyika, a notched stick combined with a resonator. Also called kwacha (176).

Charamel [Lat. *calamus*, via dim. *calamellus*], Basque and Gasc.: reedpipe, shawm. *Cf.* ciaramella.

Charamela [as *charamel*], **1.** OSp.: shawm; the chirimía. The term occurs in the 14th c.; **2.** Port.: shawm, folk oboe, made in 3 sizes: bastarda, media, charamelinha.

Charamelinha [dim. of *charamela*], a Port. charamela pitched a 5th higher than the ordinary charamela.

Charamita, var. of charamela.

Charanbel, a Basque bagpipe.

Charango, a small guitar of S. America, made of an armadillo shell dried in a mold to give it the desired shape, with 5 single or double strings, rib or belly fastened, and flat pegdisc with rear pegs. Tuning: $g^1 c^2 e^2$ (and e^1) $a^1 e^1$. Distributed in NW. Argentina, in Bolivia, and Peru. Not a native instr. *Cf.* charranga (192).

Charb lek (small cymbals), small cymbals of Thailand and Cambodia, some 13–15 cm. (5–6 in.) in diam. (46, 65).

Charb yai, cymbals of Thailand and Cambodia, some 24–26 cm. (9½–10½ in.) in diam. (46, 65).

Charga, sitar of Kashmir, with gourd body, wooden soundboard, 14 movable frets, and 6 metal strings; these are attached to 3 frontal and 3 lateral tuning pegs (176).

Charka, bamboo oboe of the Colla Indians of Bolivia (89).

Charkhi (Hindust., Punj.), *cog rattle of India, a child's toy. See also: girugate (173).

Charmeù [Lat. *calamus*], Prov.: shawm (176).

Charp, var. of chap.

Chārpāra (Pers.), syn. of chalpāra, 2.

Charranga, guitar of Guatemala. *Cf.* charango.

Charrasca, scraper of Venezuela, made of a bull's horn (15 Wachsmann).

Chartār (Pers.: four strings), long lute of Persia with 4 strings, otherwise similar to the dutār. In the 17th c. it was known in Turkey as chārtār, but is now obs. both there and in Persia. Among the Uzbek it is still extant and has 5 strings (76).

Charumbela, var. of charamela.

Charumera [Sp. *charamela*], conical shawm of Japan, made of wood or metal, with 7 front fingerholes and a rear thumbhole, introduced to Japan by Iberian priests and traders in the 16th c. (157).

Chashtār, see: shashtār.

Chata, Afro-Cuban drum, with single, nailed head, played with 2 sticks. 15–20 cm. (6–8 in.) high, 60 cm. (2 ft.) in diam. (152).

Chat'han, *box zither of the Kachinz of Siberia, related to the bûche, with each end terminating in a volute. Of the 7 metal strings 1 is a melody string; it has sheep-bone frets. *Ca.* 150 cm. (5 ft.) long, 15 cm. (6 in.) wide (149, 169).

Chaunter, var. of chanter.

Chayna, woodwind instr. of ancient Mexico, probably an oboe (176).

Chazozeroth, see: hatzozroth.

Chebuzga, *whistle flute of the Kalmuck, made of wood, bound with bast, covered with a transparent membrane, and provided with 3 fingerholes. Also called sebizga (176).

Chechempres, name of the kechicher in W. Java (121).

Cheh oc mazcab, pellet bells of Mayan dancers (144).

Chekeré [Yoruba: *shekere*], syn. of agbé (152).

Chekker (Fr.: *eschiquier;* Sp.: *escaque, exaquier;* Lat.: *escacherium*), unidentified stringed keyboard instr. of the 14th to 16th c., described as being like an organ but sounded by strings, and first mentioned in 1360, when Edward III of England gave one made by a certain Jehan Perrot to John of France. Machault called it the *"eschaqueil d'Angle-terre."* His contemporary Eustache Des-champs also mentioned it. In 1385 the Burgundian court purchased one made in Tournay: *"un instrument nommé es-chiquier"* was to be placed in the chapel. A few years later John I of Aragon wrote to Philip the Bold of Burgundy for an *exaquier,* described as an *"isturment semblans d'orguens qui sona ab cordes"* (instr. resembling the organ but sounded by strings), as well as for an organist capable of playing *"los petits orguens,"* presumably portatives. The exchange of letters indicates that chekkers were played by organists. In 1404 Eberhart Cersne lists the *Schachtbrett* in his *Minne Regel* (*Rules of the Minnesänger*). Since the romance forms of the word denote a chessboard, it is likely that *Schachtbrett* is the Ger. equivalent of "chekker." An interesting entry occurs in the *Archives nationales* (KK 70) for 1488, when the purchase of an *"eschiquier ou mani-cordion"* (*i.e.,* clavichord) is mentioned. In 1507 Molinet mentions *"bons echi-quiers"* (*chanson sur la journée de Guin-gate*), and in 1511 the Duke of Lorraine purchases an instr. *"faisant eschiquier, orgues, espinette et flustes."* As late as 1577, Antonius de Arena refers to it (as *escacherium*) in a list of keyboard instrs. Attempts at identification have been nu-merous: Galpin compared it to the *dulce melos and derived the word "chekker" from its checking action; Farmer pointed to an Arab. *al-shaqira mentioned by a 13th-c. author—an unlikely derivation; Hickmann suggested a stringed instr. akin to the *portative organ; and Sachs pointed to the possibility of its having been a small upright harpsichord. Such instrs. were known by the mid-15th c. The association with a chessboard may refer to black and white key buttons, but these were already in existence at the time the chekker originated. A spinet-regal in form of a chessboard, dated 1587, is preserved in the Kunsthistorisches Museum of Vienna, but there exists no reason for as-sociating it with the chekker. The puzzle remains unsolved. A list of early refer-ences is to be found in André Pirro's *Les Clavecinistes* (53, 82, 89).

Cheko, panpipes of the Ticuna Indians of W. Brazil (105).

Chelempung, 1. bonang of C. Sumatra, also called talemon or talimpuen, consist-ing of 5–7 roughly made gongs in a row, or occasionally in 2 rows of 5 each; **2.** a large, trapezoid *board zither of E. Java, usually made of teakwood, set on 4 legs, of which the 2 rear ones are higher than the front ones, so that the instr. slopes downward toward the player; 13 pairs of strings are stretched between hitch pins at the near (player's) end; the tuning pins, at the far end, are set in a curious S-shaped pin block: this is not an integral part of the instr., but rests on 2 small wooden blocks attached to the belly. A bridge is placed on the bias across the soundboard. A soundhole is cut in the bottom. Nowadays the chelempung is plucked with the thumbnails, but formerly it was played with a plectrum. Altogether the modern form shows European influ-ence; on an 1820 drawing it looks far closer to the Chin. zither. *Cf.* kachapi, 3 (121).

Chelepita, 1. the Solo (Indonesian) name for the gambang gangsa; **2.** an E. Java name for the kemanak; **3.** clapper of Bali that has recently become obs., made of 4 oval slabs of wood. See also: chantang balung, 2 (121).

Chelumpungan, Solo (Indonesian) for the kowangan (121).

Cheluring, *musical cups of Java, of considerable antiquity; they are already found on the Borobudur reliefs, of *ca.* 800 A.C., where they are depicted as ac-companying dancers and are sounded by being touched together. Later the chelur-ing consisted of a number of bronze cups nailed down side by side on a wooden frame and played with a small iron rod. The number of the cups varies; if there are only a couple, they serve as a rhythm instr., but if there are 7, as is frequently the case, the cheluring becomes a melody instr. It is but rarely encountered now. See also: churing (121).

Chelys (Gk.: tortoise), **1.** Gk. name for the ancient lyra; **2.** writers from med. times to the 17th c. have used the word to denote a lute or viol, even a violin.

Chempung, gong of C. Sumatra that rests on a bed of banana leaves (144).

Chemtyi, *cross flute of the Ao-Naga of Assam, closed at both ends and provided with one fingerhole (172).

Cheng, 1. Chin. zither, smaller than the shē or the ch'in but similar, with individual movable bridges, usually 14 strings but sometimes fewer, said to have been invented in the 3rd c. B.C. It is still played on festive occasions. *Cf.* fu ch'in, yatag. It corresponds to the sō no koto of Japan; **2.** shallow, basin-shaped gong of China that corresponds to the ching, 2, of Korea; **3.** see: cai cheng (89, 170).

Cheng-cheng, Balinese name of the largest kechicher (cymbal) (121).

Chengkung, name of the ketuk in Indramayu and Cheribon, W. Java (121).

Chengu, Khanda equivalent of tambattam.

Chen ku, see: chan ku.

Chente, Solo (Indonesian) name of the saron panerus (121).

Chepkong, lyre of Kenya (120).

Cheplanget, *friction drum of the Nandi of E. Kenya, made of a water jar covered with a membrane; the friction stick is rubbed with wet hands; used only at female circumcision rites (176).

Cherewata, *spike fiddle of Ethiopia, with a diamond-shaped body, goatskin belly, and single horsehair string. It serves as both a solo and ensemble instr. and is played by men only. In Shoa Province it is known as asmari (45).

Chermak, small Kirghiz lute with either: 2 strings made from 1 length of gut, rear tuning pegs, and 8 movable frets; or 3 strings, lateral tuning pegs, and no frets. See also: dumburak (176).

Cherubine minor, a combination piano, harpsichord, organ, and glass harmonica,

patented by Henry Whitaker on March 19, 1859.

Chevalet, Fr.: bridge.

Cheville, Fr.: tuning pin, tuning peg.

Cheviller, Fr.: pegbox.

Chevrette (Fr.: kid), bagpipe of France, its name being derived from the skin of which the bag was made, mentioned in Fr. literature from the 13th c. to the early 15th. Jean de Brie said in 1379: *"musette d'Almaigne ou autre musette qu'on appelle chevrette"* (bagpipe of Germany or other bagpipe that one calls chevrette). *Cf.* cabrette. Also called chevrie (35, 82).

Chevrie, var. of chevrette.

Chi, cross flute of Japan, of bamboo with 7 fingerholes (157).

Ch'iang ti, cross flute of China, a ti of Tatar (Ch'iang) origin (75 II, 142).

Chiave, It.: key (of wind instrs.).

Chiboni (pron. tsh . . .), name of the tulum in Adzhar, U.S.S.R., where it has a serrated cow-horn bell (13).

Chicahuaztli, 1. ceremonial rattle of the ancient Aztecs and Mayas, made of a hollow staff, several feet long, that was filled with seeds. When moved or shaken it made a sound like rain (105). This instr. is still in use among the Cora and Huichole Indians of N. America, beautifully adorned (137); **2.** scraper of Mexico, made of a long piece of notched bone. *Cf.* omichicahuaztli (127).

Chicauaztli, see: chicahuaztli.

Chicharra (Andalusian: cricket), *friction drum of Spain, similar to the zambomba but with a friction cord in lieu of a stick. The sound is said to resemble the chirping of crickets (16).

Chichikone, gourd rattle of the Missisauga Indians of Canada (176).

Chi-chu, zither of China, rather like the cheng; the left hand stops the strings while the right strikes them with a bamboo rule (142).

Chicotén, folk zither of Aragon, a *tambourin à cordes, with 6 coarse-gut strings that are struck with a stick. The fingerboard is fretted. It is usually played together with a one-hand flute. In the Basque country it is called tambourin. *Cf.* salterio (57, 165).

Chien ku, former name of the ying ku (176).

Chien pan, clappers of China, made of 2 bamboo strips *ca.* 75 cm. (30 in.) long, held in the left hand and clicked together. They can also be of hardwood, in which case they are only *ca.* 30 cm. (12 in.) long; played together with the yü ku, principally by blind men (142).

Chifla, folk flageolet of the Asturias (57).

Chifonie [Gk. **symphonia*], var. of the OFr. word *symphonie,* in use from the 12th c. to the 15th to designate the hurdy-gurdy. By Deschamps's day (1380) it had already become a mendicant's instr. (*"aveugle chifonie aura"*). It was later called vielle, although the old name lingered on (Laborde still used it in 1780) (124).

Chigwana, see: tshigwana.

Ch'ih, *cross flute of China of considerable antiquity—in Sachs's opinion the oldest known. Originally a stopped pipe with central blowhole, in med. times it had 3–5 fingerholes distributed on each side of the blowhole, but not in line with it. The modern instr. is an open cylindrical pipe of lacquered bamboo, 45 cm. (18 in.) long, with 5 front fingerholes and a rear thumbhole, not in line with the blowhole. Mahillon's experiments with reconstructions led him to believe that the ch'ih originated as a pitch standard. See also: kia chung ch'ih (132, 170).

Chikārā (Beng., Hindust.), a bowed string instr. of N. India and E. Bengal, in rebab form, cut out of a single block of wood, having a long neck and fixed frets, membrane belly, and a large pegbox. In addition to 3 melody strings of gut or horsehair, it has 3–9 sympathetic strings, 5 being the most common number. The melody strings are tuned $g^1 c^1 g^0$; the sympathetic strings: $g^1 a^1 b^1 c^2 d^2 e^2 f^2$. Total length *ca.* 55 cm. (21½ in.) (91, 173).

Chiku no koto (Jap.: bamboo koto), a 13-stringed koto, struck with a short bamboo stick (157).

Chikuzen biwa, smallest biwa of Japan, commonly made with 4 strings, occasionally 5, each type having 5 frets; played with a thick, broad plectrum and held sideways like a samisen. The name is derived from the *chikuzen* style of music performed upon it. *Ca.* 80 cm. (31 in.) long (135).

Chil-chil, 1. *marine-shell trumpet of Ecuador, made of a giant conch. Also known as quipa. See also: quepa (89); **2.** *frame drum of the Peruvian Incas (70).

Chilibitu, Basque: whistle flute.

Chilimera, a number of bells or pellet bells suspended from an animal's neck in the Basque country.

Chilin, Basque: bell.

Chilincha, chilinda, Basque: small bell. *Cf.* chincha.

Chilindrín, in Costa Rica a small bell or pellet bell.

Chilitli, clay whistle of ancient C. America, usually with 1 fingerhole, sometimes molded into the shapes of flowers or animals. Also known as cohuilotl (170, 176).

Chilla, Sp. decoy whistle that imitates the cry of foxes, rabbits, hares. *Cf.* xilla (57).

Chillar, Cast. equivalent of the chistu.

Chilmandi, *frame drum of Turkestan, with goatskin membrane, made in several sizes. It is held in both hands, and the skin is drummed upon with the fingers of both hands while accompanying songs and dances. In Samarkand and Bokhara it is known by the Pers. name of da'ira (176).

Chi lo, gong of China, used in Buddhist rites (1).

Chimbe, MEngl.: chime.

Chime, see: bell chime, drum chime, gong chime, tubular bells, yen ma. For stone chime see: lithophone.

Chime bells, see: bell chime, carillon, clokarde, cymbala.

Chimney flute, see: Rohrflöte (organ stop).

Chim'umugizi, drum of Ruanda, a symbol of royalty (30).

Chimvale [Lat. *cymbalum*], Rom.: cymbals. *Cf.* kimvalu.

Ch'in, classical * long zither of China. It appears on a later Han dynasty (25–220 A.C.) relief in Szechwan and is considered the oldest string instr. of China. Seven strings (originally there may have been only 5) are stretched over a long, narrow, slightly convex, hollow board and are fastened (without tuning pins) on the underside after passing over a bridge and through holes in the soundboard. Six strings are played as open strings, tuned in 4ths and 5ths, to provide accompaniment to the single melody string. Instead of frets, 13 small ivory or mother-of-pearl discs are inlaid in the soundboard under the melody string to indicate stopping positions. All strings are of equal length, but their thicknesses are of Pythagorean proportions, being composed of 48-54-64-72-81-96-108 strands of silk, producing the ratios 9:8 (204 cents) and 27:32 (294 cents). The scale is pentatonic without semitones. When played, the ch'in is set horizontally on the ground or across the player's knees, a table, etc. The right hand plucks the strings while the left stops the melody string, gliding from one position to another and often playing harmonics by not depressing the string entirely. Plectra are not used, as more subtle control can be exercised by the bare fingers. To the Chin. intellectual the ch'in is perhaps even more important as a symbol of culture than as a musical instr. Historically its music has been his domain. The ch'in corresponds to the komunko or kum of Korea, the koto or kin of Japan (136, 170, 177).

Chi na, small sona, *ca.* 25–28 cm. (10–11 in.) long (142).

China sampan, name given the yüeh ch'in in Batavia (121).

Chincha, Basque: **1.** herd animal bell;

2. small clapper bell; **3.** pellet bell. *Cf.* chilincha. Also called joare, panpalina (56).

Chinchasko, chinchilín, var. of chincha.

Chin chi chi, circular brass gong of Jap. mendicant priests (176).

Chin daul, war kettledrum of Turkestan, with metal body (176).

Chinditi, xylophone of the Loango area of Angola (176).

Chinesco, Sp.: Jingling Johnnie.

Chinese block, percussion instr. of Western rhythm bands, presumably adapted from the Cuban *cajita china. A block of wood shaped like a brick has slots cut in it and is struck with a stick. Also called Chinese temple block. *Cf.* Korean temple block, wood block.

Chinese crash cymbals, crash cymbals of Chin. manufacture, used in Western rhythm bands.

Chinese crescent, Chinese pavilion, see: Jingling Johnnie.

Chinese temple block, see: Chinese block.

Chinfonia [*symphonia*], OSp.: symphonia.

Ching, 1. small, bowl-shaped cymbals of Thailand and Cambodia, thick and heavy, with large boss and small rim, about 5½–6 cm. (2¼ in.) in diam. They set the tempo in ensemble playing. *Cf.* sing (65); **2.** gong of Korea, bossless and with turned rim, that corresponds to the Chin. cheng, 2. 36–40 cm. (14–16 in.) in diam. Also called gwangmagi (66).

Ch'ing, 1. *musical stone of China, of great antiquity, confined to Confucian temples. The best ones are made of nephrite. They are cut into an L-shape, 30–60 cm. (1–2 ft.) long and suspended from a frame; **2.** syn. of shun (resting bell) (1).

Chingongo, double bell of bronze or iron of the Bavili of Loango, Angola, made of 2 flattened single bells connected by a single handle; chiefly a symbol of dignity, but also used in fetish ceremonies (176).

Chingraq (Arab.), *pellet bell of 16th-c. Turkey, attached to frame drums or suspended from animals' necks (76).

Chingufo, see: shinguvo.

Ch'in Han p'i p'a, p'i p'a with 4 strings and 4 frets. *Cf.* ch'in p'i p'a (142).

Chiniloi, *nose flute of the Senoi of the Malay Peninsula. The nostril not used for playing is stopped up (203).

Chin-kabai, *goblet drum of the Palaung of Cambodia, with conoid body on a long stem. The membrane is attached by V lacings. *Ca.* 120 cm. (48 in.) high. *Cf.* chu-che (172).

Ch'in kang t'ui, a small, 3-stringed *p'i p'a with 10 frets and a total length of *ca.* 66 cm. (26 in.) (142).

Chin ko, Korean drum similar to the *kon ko but of smaller diam., with nailed heads. It corresponds to the Chin. *tsin ku and the Jap. *da daiko. *Ca.* 95 cm. (37½ in.) in diam. (66).

Chin ku, brass gong of China, with turned rim and central boss. *Ca.* 35 cm. (14 in.) in diam. (142).

Ch'in p'i p'a, *p'i p'a that first appeared in the 5th c., associated with the Ch'in dynasty of China. Considered as the earliest ovoid lute, it was originally played with a plectrum, later plucked with the fingers. *Cf.* ch'in Han p'i p'a (80 VIII).

Chinsete, *footed drum of the Bemba of the Congo, with lizard-skin head, held under the left arm and played with both hands (30).

Chiocciola, It.: scroll.

Chioccolo, It.: a decoy pipe for birds.

Chipendani, see: tshipendani.

Chipla, castanets of India, made of 2 pieces of hardwood *ca.* 15 cm. (6 in.) long, flat on one side and rounded on the other, S-shaped. Metal jingles are attached in lateral slits and pellet bells are suspended from both ends. A brass ring is attached to the center of each castanet, for passing the fingers through (179).

Chiponi, see: chiboni.

Chirimaya [Sp. *chirimía], *double pipe of the Guajiquero Indians of Hon-

duras, with common mouthpiece (176).

Chirimía, [Lat. *calamus via OSp. charamela], shawm of Spain. The word appears *ca.* 1600 and today denotes a folk shawm made in 2 sizes: tiple and tenora, both played with a pirouette and short, triangular reeds with a wide opening. *Cf.* gralla, gralla seca, xeremia, xirimia (14).

Chirimigo [Sp. *chirimía], oboe-like instr. of the Lacandón of the N. American Pacific coast (176).

Chirimilla, 15th-c. Cat.: chirimía.

Chirisuya, name of the chirimía in Peru. *Migo* means "mine" and *suya* means "his" or "hers"; humor or folk etym.? (80 XIII).

Chiro, var. of chirula.

Chirola, chirolo, var. of chirula.

Chirribika [*rabel], Basque: a rustic violin (57).

Chirrín, Basque: a form of chirribika.

Chiru, panpipes of the Empera-Chocó Indians of Panama and Colombia (105).

Chirula [U.], Basque galoubet with slightly conical bore, 2 front fingerholes, and a rear thumbhole, played with the left hand, the right being engaged in striking a Basque *tanborín (drum). Also called chiro, chirola, chirolo, chiula, churula, xiula. See also: chistu.

Chisanchi, sansa of the Baluba of the Congo (103).

Chistu, chistua, Basque galoubet, similar to the flaviol of Catalonia, usually made of ebony with silver rings; simpler ones of boxwood are also found. The conical tube has a cylindrical bore and is provided with 2 front fingerholes and a rear thumbhole. In the Soule district it measures 32 cm. (12½ in.), elsewhere 43 cm. (17 in.). The common chistu is pitched in G. There also exists a bass, called silbote. The chistu is held in the left hand and is accompanied by a small drum called tanborín, suspended from the (chistu) player's left arm. Also called bascatibia, silbo; chillar in Cast. See also: chirula (14, 57, 89).

Chitara, Rom.: guitar. In rural areas

it is played with only 2 or 3 strings (5).

Chitarra, It.: guitar.

Chitarra a pianoforte, It.: keyed guitar.

Chitarra battente (Fr.: *guitare en bateau*), an It. form of guitar with characteristically deep body and highly arched back with rounded edges and slight waist. The belly is bent to form a slope just below the bridge. A large central soundhole is covered with a rose. The strings are rib-fastened, pass over a fingerboard with fixed metal frets to a flat pegdisc with rear pegs. Normally there are 5 courses of metal strings, tuned $d^1 g^1 c^2 e^2 a^2$. On older instrs. these are generally bichord, whereas in later specimens 3 strings to a course are usual. The chitarra battente is played with a plectrum and measures 85–100 cm. (33–40 in.), with ribs up to 18 cm. (7 in.) high. Also called chitarra mandola, guitare à dos bombé, guitare capucine, guitare toscane, guitarra battente.

Chitarra coll'arco, It.: bowed guitar.

Chitarra d'amore, syn. of arpeggione.

Chitarra latina, see: guitarra latina.

Chitarra-lira, It.: lyre-guitar.

Chitarra mandola, syn. of chitarra battente.

Chitarra-salterio, a hybrid guitar and psaltery, formerly built in Italy, with 6 pairs of strings stretched over a guitar fingerboard, and a rose in the guitar body; a psaltery was attached to one side of the latter, with 29 pairs of brass strings and 3 further roses. *Ca.* 87 cm, (34 in.) long (176).

Chitarra saracenica, see: guitarra morisca.

Chitarrino [dim. of **chitarra*], a small guitar pitched a 3rd higher than the ordinary guitar. According to Valdrighi, the term occurred in 1445. Called Terzgitarre in Ger. According to O. Bachmann (*Handbuch des Geigenbaues*, 1835), it served for teaching children the guitar.

Chitarrone [aug. of **chitarra*], **1.** literally "large guitar," the word nowadays denotes a bass guitar. Historically, however, it has designated an *archlute. The word *citarone* occurs in a Mantua document as early as 1524, but we cannot be sure of what it stands for. The chitarrone as we know it appears in detail·in a portrait of Lady Mary Sidney (d. 1586), as a tall instr. with straight pegbox set on a long neck, surmounted by a second straight pegbox for off-board strings. The body is that of a small lute, the long, broad neck is fretted, the number of strings variable. Banchieri (in 1609) gives their tuning as $G^1 A^1 Bb^1$ $C^0 D^0 Eb^0 F^0 G^0 c^0 f^0 a^0 d^1 g^1$, the top string being marked *"come piace"* (as you like it). Praetorius states that the chitarrone was also called Roman theorbo, and gives it six stopped and eight open strings, tuned $F^1 G^1 A^1 B^1$ $C^0 D^0 E^0 F^0 / G^0 c^0 d^0 f^0 g^0 a^0$. It was strung with steel and brass wire. The chitarrone was up to 2 m. (6½ ft.) long. Also called arcichitarra;

2. an 8-course mandola is known in Naples as chitarrone (159, 169).

Chiterna, It.: gittern.

Chitike, Kan. equivalent of karatāli (173).

Chitikelu, Tel. equivalent of karatāli (173).

Chitiringo, see: tshitiringo.

Chitkul, cymbals of the Muria of Bastar, India, made of brass, often attached in pairs by chains of cowries; played preponderantly by women (68).

Chiufolo, var. of zuffolo in Umbria, Italy.

Chiula, syn. of chirula.

Chivhana, see: tshivhana.

Chiyeyek, name of the kechicher in Grobogan, Java (121).

Chizambi, *musical bow of the Venda of S. Africa, similar to the nxonxoro but smaller. A resonator made of a globular fruit shell filled with seeds or pebbles is impaled upon the stick (116).

Chlefeli, bones of Switzerland (102).

Chlepfe, syn. of Gleppe.

Chloie, see: khloi.

Chlöpfe, syn. of Gleppe.

Chnouē, metal trumpet of ancient Egypt, with wide bell, played with a conical mouthpiece. First depicted in 1415 B.C. in the hands of soldiers, it also served ritual purposes and was sacred to Osiris. Chnouē may be the Gk. pronunciation of the Egyptian word shnb or šneb. Ca. 60 cm. (2 ft.) long (147, 170).

Cho, *mouth organ of Korea, similar to the Chin. sheng, with 13 bamboo pipes furnished with free reeds (66).

Choa ko, *barrel drum of Korea that has been in use for over 2000 years, with nailed heads, suspended in a frame. It corresponds to the Chin. tsu ku. Ca. 30 cm. (12 in.) long, 56 cm. (22 in.) in diam. (66).

Chobreto, regional Fr.: bagpipe.

Choca [Lat. *clocca], Gal., Port.: bell, cowbell.

Chocalho, Port.: rattle (7).

Choco, Sp. *bladder pipe, composed of a spherical skin bag, a mouth tube, and a tube pierced with fingerholes. Nowadays it serves as a child's toy (57, 165).

Chocolo, percussion instr. of Latin American origin found in Western rhythm bands, consisting of a cylinder of bamboo, hardwood, or metal which is tapped.

Chofar, Fr.: shofar.

Choir organ, 1. organ that accompanies the choir; 2. corr. of *chair organ. See: organ.

Choke cymbals, pair of cymbals attached to an upright metal rod so as to lie horizontally. The lower one is fixed, the upper one mobile. By means of a pedal that lowers the upper cymbal, the 2 are "choked." They serve in rhythm bands. See also: crash cymbal.

Cho ko, Korean drum played together with the *no ko (66).

Chol ko, Korean drum with a diam. of some 45 cm. (18 in.) (66).

Chong tu, see: ch'ung tu.

Chontang, bamboo xylophone of E.

Java, similar to the angklung, with 5 tubes placed on a wooden frame (121).

Chor, a beaked *globular flute of E Turkestan, with 2 fingerholes; a child's toy (176).

Chor . . . (Ger.), as a prefix to names of Ger. organ stops, Chor . . . denotes one of choir pitch (Chorton), as opposed to one at chamber pitch (Kammerton).

Choral . . . , as a prefix to names of Ger. organ stops, Choral . . . denotes "strong intonation"; stops so labeled were used for the playing of chorales (3).

Choral bass, 1. a rare organ stop of open flue pipes in the pedal, at 4' or 2' pitch; 2. at Einsiedeln monastery, Switzerland, a 3-rank mixture (176, 186).

Choraleon, instr. similar to the aeolomelodicon, patented by Fidelis Brunner of Warsaw in 1825. Apparently more powerful than the aeolo-melodicon, it was designed to accompany choirs in smaller churches, hence its name (89).

Chordarmia, *upright piano of soft tone, invented 1886 by W. Marshall and built by W. J. Thomas of London. It had a violin soundboard (176).

Chordaulion [Gk. chorde, string + aulos, pipe], mechanical organ invented by Johann Gottlieb Kaufmann of Dresden and his son Friedrich in 1815, with open and stopped pipes that could imitate string and wind instrs., controlled by pinned cylinders. The sound could be modified dynamically without any change of pitch simply by increasing or decreasing the wind pressure. In 1830 one was shipped to Havana, Cuba, and, according to a contemporary description, it stood about 10 ft. high, contained 10 cylinders that played 34 pieces, and was actuated by a flat lead weight raised by a hand crank, without the assistance of clockwork. A remarkably developed early orchestrion. For a later model see: symphonium (37, 176).

Chorde, Gk.: string.

Chord flute (Fr.: flûte d'accord; Ger.: Akkordflöte), any *double flute that permits the simultaneous playing of 2 tones at different pitches (in contradistinction to those having a melody pipe and a drone pipe, for instance).

Chordophone [Gk. *chorde,* string + *phone,* sound], musical instr. having strings as tone-producing elements, the pitch of the instr. being dependent on the strings. The oldest forms of chordophone are idiochord: a narrow strip of a cane segment is loosened by 2 longitudinal incisions, then raised and held taut by a very small piece of wood inserted under it at each end. Such instrs. are found in the Malagasy Republic, the Malay Archipelago, and W. Africa (169).

Chord organ, *electrophonic organ provided with a series of chord buttons that, when depressed, generate a chord to accompany any note played on the conventional organ keyboard. Chord organs are designed to permit persons of little musical ability to play polyphonic music. *Cf.* harmonista (59)

Chord zither (Fr.: *cithare d'amateur;* Ger.: *Akkordzither*), name given to 2 kinds of modern folk zithers: **1.** that which has a series of chord bars, such as the autoharp, etc.; **2.** that which has its strings arranged in chordal groups. This latter type is usually rectangular and sometimes bowed; others are almost harp-shaped, with pillar (149).

Choriphone [Gk. *choros,* choir + *phone,* sound], church harmonium designed to accompany choirs, patented by Dumont on Feb. 4, 1887, and exhibited by Dumont & Lelièvre of Paris in 1889. It contained a special pedal to give the illusion of a bowed double bass (176, 204).

Choriste, Fr.: pitch pipe. The term occurs in 1765. *Cf.* corista (204).

Chorist-Fagott, Ger. equivalent of the double curtal (fagotto chorista in It.), precursor of the bassoon. Praetorius gives its compass as C^0-f^1; Lodovico Zacconi (in 1592) as C^0-b^1 (159).

Chorist-Laute, Ger.: the alto lute.

Chorma(a)ss, obs. Ger. term denoting: **1.** 8′ pitch; **2.** any organ stop at 8′ pitch.

Chormorne, see: cormorne.

Ch'örna, *cylindrical drum of Tibet, carried upright by means of a meter-long (40 in.) handle and struck with a curved stick. *Ca.* 20–25 cm. (8–10 in.) high, 60 cm. (2 ft.) in diam. (176).

Chorobenite, instr. of unknown nature mentioned by Eustache Deschamps (d. 1407) (176).

Choron, OFr., **1.** horn; **2.** chorus. The term occurs from the 12th c. on (170).

Choros, var. of chorus.

Chorstimme, Chorstymme, term occurring in 15th-c. Ger. organ literature, believed to denote the Prinzipal and Hintersatz (167).

Chorus (Lat.), name given to 3 instrs. of med. Europe: **1.** the 9th-c. epistle to Dardanus by Pseudo-Jerome defines the chorus as a simple skin with 2 brazen pipes, a blowpipe, and a melody pipe—a primitive bagpipe, the earliest mention of such an instr. in postclassical Europe;

2. all known mss. with illustrations of the instrs. listed in the epistle in question (with one exception) also depict the chorus as a stringed instr. with 4 strings; as such it is mentioned in literary sources from the mid-9th c. on. By the 11th c. it is described as a wooden instr. with 4 strings, possibly a confusion with the crwth (in the 15th-c. *Promptuarium parvulorum* it is identified as such); in the 12th c. Giraldus Cambrensis writes that the chorus was in general use in Scotland and Wales, thereby giving rise to the belief that the bagpipe was then played in those countries, whereas he was evidently referring to the crwth. Aimeri de Peyrac in the 14th c. describes the chorus as having 2 pairs of strings tuned a 4th apart;

3. again in the 14th c. Gerson describes the chorus as a *tambourin à cordes with 2 strings. In the 17th c. Praetorius rather surprisingly talks of the *"chorus seu tympanischiza"* (the *trumpet marine) with 4 strings (Hammerstein, R.: *"Instrumenta Hieronymi,"* in: *Archiv f.*

Musikwissenschaft, XVI, 1959; 159, 169, 170).

Chosen, samisen of Japan, with very long neck. Total length *ca.* 110 cm. (3½ ft.) (157).

Chotonka, *whistle flute of the Kiowa Indians of N. and S. Dakota, U.S., used by them when courting; provided with 6 fingerholes (Galpin, F. W., in: *Proceedings of the Music Association,* XXI).

Chouette (owl), cylindrical *beaked flute patented by Jarrein of Marseille on Aug. 9, 1877, imitating the cry of an owl (204).

Chromamètre [Gk. *chroma,* color + meter], vertical monochord invented by Roller & Blanchet of Paris in 1827, for the tuning of pianos. The string was struck by a hammer placed inside the soundbox (204).

Chromatic bass-horn (Ger.: *chromatisches Basshorn*), an improved bass-horn made by Johann Heinrich Gottlieb Streitwolf of Göttingen, Germany, in 1820. The outer form of the bass-horn (wood with metal bell) was retained, but the bore was changed, as were fingerholes and keywork, the last consisting of 2 open keys close to the bell and 8 closed keys. The compass Bb^0-g^1 could be taken down to G^0 or F^0 (132, 169).

Chromatic drum, a syn. of machine drum.

Chromatic harp (Fr.: *harpe chromatique;* Ger.: *chromatische Harfe*), harp having a string for each semitone. This may be accomplished by providing several rows of parallel strings, as is the case with the *double harp of Mersenne, etc., by a single row of equidistant strings (18 to 19th c.), or by 2 rows of crossing strings. Jean-Henri Pape of Paris took out a patent on May 17, 1845, for a chromatic harp designed to eliminate pedals. It had 2 rows of strings crossing at half their length, one row corresponding to the natural keys, the other to the accidental keys of a keyboard. Lyon of Paris and Lyon and Healy of Chicago subsequently made similar but improved

models with a compass C^1-g^4. Pleyel Wolff & Cie. of Paris took out a patent in 1894 for a chromatic harp with a metal frame; the strings, which ran from right to left, corresponded to the natural keys of a keyboard. Pleyel's chromatic harp had a compass of 76 strings and stood nearly 2 m. (6½ ft.) high. See also: double harp, harpe-luth.

Chromatic horn (Fr.: *cor chromatique;* Ger.: *chromatisches Horn;* It.: *corno cromatico*), French horn provided with valves, a valved horn.

Chromatic trumpet (Fr.: *trompette chromatique;* Ger.: *chromatische Trompete;* It.: *tromba cromatica*), trumpet provided with keys or valves.

Chromatic trumpet and French horn, the prototype of *duplex instrs.: a double trumpet or French horn patented by Charles Claggett of London on Aug. 15, 1788, consisting of 2 trumpets (or French horns), one in Eb, the other in D, played with a common mouthpiece that could be switched from the tube of one to that of the other instantly by means of a pin projecting from a little box below the mouthpiece (89 Morley-Pegge).

Chromatine, an improved accordion of G. Mirwald of Söllitz, Bavaria, *ca.* 1891, with a chromatic compass of 4 octs. and a register for changing the tone quality (176).

Chrotta, Lat. equivalent of cruit.

Chu, wooden percussion instr. of China, mentioned as early as *ca.* 1100 B.C. and formerly known as k'iang. The chu is a square box with walls sloping outward so that the top is larger than the bottom. Its sides are struck on the inside by a wooden mallet that reaches in through a round hole cut in one of the walls. The exterior is decorated with painted flowers, animals, etc.; used in Confucian ceremonies. The shape of the chu is that of a grain measure, its size *ca.* 60 cm. by 60 cm. (2 ft. by 2 ft.). See also: chuk (89, 132, 142).

Ch'uan ling, rattle of Chin. itinerant physicians, consisting of a hollow metal ring filled with pellets, whirled rapidly on a stick (142).

Chubchiq (Pers.), free-reed *mouth organ of Persia, adapted from the Chin. *sheng. Ibn Ghaibi (d. 1435) described it as the "mūsīqār" (panpipes) of China; it was not known as chubchiq until Mogul times. *Cf.* mushtaq sini (75 II, 147 Farmer).

Chu-che, *goblet drum of the Palaung of Cambodia, with conoid body. The membrane is attached by V lacings. *Ca.* 90 cm. (35 in.) high. *Cf.* chin-kabai (172).

Chueca [Lat. *clocca*], Asturian: bell.

Chuen, Chin. polychord of the first c. B.C., used for tuning bell chimes. It consisted of a wooden soundboard 9 ft. long over which 13 strings were stretched; 12 of these were open strings, the 13th, or center, string was laid over a calibrated scale (177).

Chufa, Sp.: shepherd's flute; cross flute (176).

Chūgūr (Turk., Pers.), Near Eastern lute with piriform body. In Turkey it has 6 strings and a fretted neck; in Persia a shorter neck and larger body (76).

Ch'ui pien, rustic wind instr. of China, made of a spirally rolled leaf and played by shepherds and children. In the 14th c. it was considered "modern" (142).

Chuk, idiophone of Korea, similar to the Chin. *chu. The trough-shaped body is some 75 cm. (30 in.) high and is sounded with a phallic-shaped pestle passed through an aperture in the lid. The walls slope outward (66).

Chu ko ku, bronze kettledrum of China (176).

Chul, flute of the Mayas of C. America (144).

Chullo-chullo (Quechua), rattle of Bolivia (89).

Chulubita, Basque folk flageolet made by children in springtime (56, 57).

Chülüila, syn. of chirola.

Chum chua, see: cai chum chua.

Chung, generic term in China for bells struck from the outside with disconnected hammers, in contradistinction to the ling. See: ko chung, pien chung, po chung, shun, t'e chung.

Ch'ung, hemispheric cymbal of Cambodia, with central boss (173).

Chunga, musical bow of Cuba, without resonator (152).

Chung ko, kettledrum of Korea, *ca.* 75 cm. (30 in.) in diam. (66).

Ch'ung tu, 1. originally a *stamping tube of China, made of a bamboo segment split several times for part of its length and stamped against the ground. *Cf.* tok; **2.** former clappers of China, made of 12 narrow bamboo strips *ca.* 30 cm. (12 in.) long, tied together at one end by a leather strap so as to fan out slightly at their free ends. They were played by temple singers, who held them in one hand and struck them against the palm of the other hand. Now replaced by the shu pan (142, 170).

Ch'un kuan, bamboo clarinet of China, with 6 fingerholes; the only Chin. instr. with a single beating reed. Nowadays it is a child's toy. Also called la pa. See also: tui hsiao (142).

Chuong chua, see: cai chuong chua.

Chuong de chung, see: cai chuong de chung.

Chuong gang, see: cai chuong gang.

Chup en parri, nose flute of Ponape, Micronesia. *Cf.* kash (203).

Churamantalam, Tamil equivalent of satatantri vīnā.

Churing, believed to be an early name of the cheluring (121).

Churinga, bull-roarer of the Aranda of Australia, taboo to women and children. Made of a stone or wood slab, usually flat, varying from a few inches to several feet in length, incised with designs (G. P. Murdock: *Our Primitive Contemporaries,* 1934).

Churlika, Bosnian *whistle flute, with 6 fingerholes (176).

Churu, rattle of S. American highland Indians, made of metal jingles (105).

Churula, var. of chirula.

Churumbela, OSp.: chirimía.

Ch'u tse p'i p'a, the 5-stringed p'i p'a, introduced into China ca. 500 A.C.

Chwibenigl a chod (pipe and bag), Welsh: bagpipe. The term is recorded in the 14th c. (153).

Chyfonie, see: chifonie.

Chyintat, a long *cylindrical drum of the Kachin of Shan State, Burma, having 2 heads with V lacings connected to a central cover; suspended horizontally; 170 cm. (5 ft. 7 in.) long, ca. 30 cm. (12 in.) in diam. (172).

Cialamello, corr. of ciaramella.

Cianciana [Arab. *jul-jul*], Sicilian: cowbell. See also: cencerro, cincerria, zinzerri.

Ciarameddari, Calabrese dial.: zampogna.

Ciaramella (It.) [Lat. *calamellus,* dim. of *calamus*], folk oboe of the Abruzzi, Italy, with conical bore ending in a short, flared bell, 7 front fingerholes, occasionally a rear thumbhole, and several vents in the bell; played without a pirouette, the reed being tied to a staple, and accompanied by a zampogna. Ca. 30 cm. (12 in.) long. Also called cornamusina, piffaro, Abruzzi oboe. Cf. charamel (13, 14, 132).

Cicala (It.: cricket), bull-roarer of Italy (152).

Cici'gwan, *rattle drum of the N. American Chippewa Indians, played in sets of 4. The small wooden body is covered with a hide membrane, sewed on, and contains pebbles. It is pierced by a handle and serves ceremonial uses (49).

Cicuta (Lat.: hemlock), Lat.: pipe; by extension, an organ pipe.

Ciembalo, OSp.: cymbal.

Cieramel, OSp. var. of chirimía.

Cilindro, It.: valve.

Cilindro rotativo, It.: rotary valve.

Cimbal, 1. 15th-c. var. of cymbala (188); **2.** name of the dulcimer in Ger.-speaking countries, obs. now except in the Austrian Alps and Appenzell, Switzerland. Majer in the 18th c. used the expression as syn. of Hackbrett, the more

common Ger. term (*"Cimbal heisset sonst auch Hackbrett"*). Most frequently encountered size of extant instrs. is one with trichord stringing and a compass C^0-c^3 (117, 134, 187).

Cimbala, see: cymbala.

Cimbal d'amour, name given by Gottfried Silbermann of Freiberg, Saxony, to a polygonal clavichord he invented in 1721; it became known as cembal d'amour or as clavecin d'amore (*sic*). The instr. was first depicted in the *Sammlung von Natur- und Medicin-, Kunst- und Literaturgeschichten,* Breslau, in 1723 (reproduced in Ernst Flade: *Gottfried Silbermann,* 1953). As with the 17th-c. muselaer its tangents hit the strings at one half of their speaking length, necessitating strings twice as long as those of ordinary clavichords, and a nut and soundboard to each side of the tangent. The center of each string rested on a padded rail from which it was raised by the action of the tangent, *i.e.,* the strings were damped as soon as the key was released. No specimen has survived.

Cimbale, OFr.: cymbal.

Cimbaletto [dim. of *cimbalo*], It.: tambourine. Around 1600 the It. term for a tambourine with jingles was *"cimbaletto con sonaglie alla spagnuola."* Cf. cembalo (169).

Cimbalillo [dim. of *címbalo*], Sp.: a small cymbal. The word has been used in this sense since the 16th c.

Cimbalino, 16th-c. syn. of cimbaletto.

Cimbalo, It.: **1.** cymbal; **2.** syn. of cembalo, 2 (tambourine); **3.** Serb.: dulcimer.

Címbalo, Sp.: cymbal.

Cimbalom [Gk. *kymbalon*], dulcimer of the Hung. gypsies, the basis of their orchestra. In the second half of the last century the cimbalom was modernized by Schunda of Budapest; it is now a shallow trapezoid box resting on 4 legs, with 2 bridges and 35 courses of metal strings, of which the lowest 16 are trichord and are spun; the upper courses

have 4 or even 5 strings to a note. Some
strings pass over both bridges, others over
1 only, and some are not divided by a
bridge at all, but sound their entire
length. Damper pedals are often provided. Its compass is E⁰–e⁵. *Cf.* cimbal,
ţambal (149, 170).

Címbalos, Sp.: bell chime.

Cimbalum, var. of cymbalum.

Cimbasso, a narrow-bore It. contrabass tuba in B♭ (89 Baines).

Cimbel, see: cimbal, cymbal, zimbel.

Cimble, var. of cimbale.

Cimpoi, cimponi (pron.: tsh . . .)
[Gk. *symphonia*], mouth-blown bagpipe of Romania, with double chanter
terminating in a large wooden bell and
furnished with 2 single reeds. The right
pipe has 5 fingerholes, the left 1. The
right pipe is stopped. The bass drone has
a cylindrical bore made in 3 joints, and
sounds 2 octs. below the chanters. Its
over-all length is reduced by bending it
back on itself. The cimpoi is encountered
in Slavonia, Voivodina, Banat, and Oltenia (13).

Cincerria, var. of zinzerri.

Cinellen, Ger., see: cinelli.

Cinelli, It.: cymbals. Up to the early
20th c. the Germans used the word form
"Cinellen."

Cinfonía [Gk. *symphonia*], **1.** OSp.:
symphonia (hurdy-gurdy); **2.** obs. Sp.:
bagpipe.

Cinquiè(s)me, obs. Fr.: viola; syn. of
the term quinte de violon.

Cinsete, drum of Lake Bangweulu area,
Africa, with an aperture at the base covered by a thin membrane—a mirliton device. *Ca.* 50 cm. (20 in.) high (30).

Ciocca-ciocca, clappers of Sicily, made
of 3 pieces of flat wood tied together,
with a handle in the center.

Ciombal [Lat. *cymbalum*], Irish:
cymbal, bell.

Cioro, *panpipes of the Peruvian Amazon region, with 3 tubes (103).

Ciric belle [OEngl. ciric, church],
OEngl.: church bell.

Cirulón, cane *cross flute of Estremadura, Spain (57).

Cister [Fr. *cistre*], Ger.: cittern.

Cistertheorbe, Ger.: archcittern.

Cistole, see: citole.

Cistre [Lat. *cithara*], Fr.: cittern.

Cistre à clavier, Fr.: keyed cittern.

Cistre portuguais, Fr. name of the
guitarra, 2.

Cistre-théorbe, cistre-théorbé, Fr.:
archcittern.

Cistrum, Mersenne's Lat. for cittern.

Citara, obs. It.: cittern (190).

Cítara, Sp.: cittern (1481: *"citharas
sive guitarras"*). Covarrubias (in 1611)
translated the term as *lira da gamba;* it
is also used for zither.

Citarino [dim. of *citara*], It.: a very
small 17th-c. cittern of Engl. origin, with
half-open back. Also called englisches
Cithrinchen, englisches Zitterlein, citharino (169).

Citarone [aug. of *citara*], a large
chordophone, possibly a *chitarrone, first
mentioned in Mantua in 1524. The word
does not occur after the 17th c. (169).

Citarruni, in Sicilian dialect a 3-
stringed double bass (169).

Cithar, var. of cithara. A cithar is mentioned in the late-12th-c. chronicle of
Svend Aagesen together with fiol and
trumma (9).

Cithara (Lat.) [Gk. *kithara*], **1.** the
kithara. Around 500 A.C., Clovis, King
of the Franks (d. 511) requested his
brother-in-law Theodoric, King of the
Ostrogoths in Italy, to send him a *citha-
roede* (cithara player). This is probably
the latest mention of the cithara as a
contemporaneous instr.; **2.** in med. times
the cruit (rotta), described in the epistle
to Dardanus by Pseudo-Jerome (9th c.)
as having a body in the shape of the Gk.
letter Δ *i.e.*, triangular, and 24 strings. In
the 8th c., Cuthbert had mentioned the
cithara that "we" call rotta, and in the
7th c. Isidore of Seville had written of a
*"cithara barbarica in modum deltae lit-
erae";* **3.** in late med. and post-med. times
the word designated a variety of instrs.,

sometimes serving as a generic term for stringed instrs. Paulus Paulirinus *ca.* 1460 describes it as a 5-course cittern with gut strings, always geminated, 9 frets, and a soundhole (*cf.* citara). To Glarean and other 16th-c. writers cithara denoted a harp. See also: cythara.

Cithara bichordos, Mersenne's Lat. for colascione.

Cithara bijuga, Mersenne's Lat. for theorbo. *Cf.* bijuga cither.

Cithara germanica, Lat.: cittern (176).

Cithara hispanica, Mersenne's Lat. for guitar.

Cithara trijuga, Mersenne's Lat. for cittern.

Cithare, Fr. equivalent of cithara. In modern times it means zither.

Cithare à cadre, Fr.: frame zither.

Cithare anglaise, Fr.: English citra.

Cithare d'amateur, Fr.: chord zither.

Cithare en radeau, Fr.: raft zither.

Cithare en terre, Fr.: ground zither.

Cithare-harmonium, a combination of harmonium and string instr., patented by Neumayer & Hessling on July 4, 1899. *Cf.* Harmonium-Zither (204).

Cithare sur bâton, Fr.: stick zither.

Cithare sur planche, Fr.: board zither.

Cithare sur tuyau, Fr.: tube zither.

Citharino, var. of citarino. Georg Falck, writing in 1688, says that it is also called Citharinchen.

Cither, 1. obs. Engl. form of the word zither; **2.** Ger.: cittern.

Cithern, Engl. var. of cittern, first recorded in 1566.

Cither viol, syn. of sultana.

Cithrinchen, see: englisches Cithrinchen, hamburger Cithrinchen.

Citole (OFr.) [?Lat. **cithara* or *cistella,* box], name of an important med. stringed instr., precursor of the cittern. The word occurs in Fr. literature from *ca.* 1200 on (*Roman du renard*), in Engl. literature from *ca.* 1310 (*King Alisaundre*). By 1292 there were 4 *citoleurs i.e.,* makers of stringed instrs., in Paris. Tinctoris, *ca.* 1490, says that the citole was invented by the Italians, had a flat

body, 4 brass or steel strings, was fretted, and that the strings were plucked with a quill. The piriform body seems to have been all of a piece with the short neck; frontal pegs were inserted into a flat pegdisc, the strings being attached to a frontal string fastener. The word citole disappears after the early 16th c., at which period the instr. becomes transformed into the cittern. Sachs was of the opinion that its origin was to be found in the early fiddle, the flat pegdisc and frontal pegs being indicative of a bowed instr. However, the string fastener of the citole was not exchanged for a bridge until after it had become a cittern. See also: cetula (82, 89 Galpin, 180).

Citra, occasional name of the English guitar (79).

Citre, 1. Fr.: cittern; **2.** name by which the zither was formerly known in Slovenia; now obs. there (144).

Citter, obs. Ger.: cittern.

Cittern (Fr.: *cistre;* Ger.: *Cister;* It.: *cetera*), successor to the citole, the cittern evolved at the end of the 15th c. and remained a pop. instr. until displaced by the guitar in the 19th c. The frontal string holder of the citole was exchanged for a rib fastener and bridge; the flat pegdisc became a pegbox with lateral pegs. The transformed instr. had a piriform body, flat back that tapered toward the neck, rather short neck with 12 or more fixed metal frets, a central soundhole covered with a rose, and a variable number of strings. The pegbox was often sickle-shaped. The quill plectrum of the citole was abandoned and the cittern was finger-plucked. Its compass was over 2 octs., and it was written for in lute tablature. The mid-16th c. *Mulliner Virginal Book* contains pieces for it, and in 1565 Adrien LeRoy published a cittern tutor. During the 16th c. a combination of frontal and lateral tuning pegs prevailed; Praetorius still depicts one such along with others having lateral pegs exclusively. By the end of the c. different sizes were being made, as we learn from an Ambras inventory of 1596 that mentions tenor and bass instrs. Two years later we hear of an It. archcittern bearing the very apt name of *cetarissima. But the transformation was not completed until well after 1600: the frontal pegs were inserted into a continuation of the neck, which by its form announced the later sickle shape. During the 16th and 17th c. the number of courses varied from 4 to 12, according to size, 4 being considered standard in Praetorius' day. These could be tuned according to Fr. fashion ($a^0 g^0 d^1 e^1$) or to the It. ($b^0 g^0 d^1 e^1$). The number of tunings for the cittern was almost legion, perhaps the commonest one for the 5-course instr. being $d^0 b^0 g^0 d^1 e^1$ or $F^0 e^0 c^0 g^0 a^0$. In addition to those with 4 and 5 courses, Praetorius lists larger ones with 6 courses, tuned a 4th lower, and a still larger one of 12 courses. Furetière (in 1690) mentions one with 9 courses. Need for an increasingly deeper compass resulted in It. and Fr. makers' creating an archcittern with 2 pegboxes and gut strings, rather like a theorbo (in England often referred to in modern times as *bijuga cither), with 5–7 melody strings and 6 or 7 drone strings. By the 17th c. the cittern had become a barbershop instr., apparently on an international level: in England it was placed at the disposal of patrons wishing to while away time, while Trichet in France (*ca.* 1640) informs us that it was played by barbers themselves. Praetorius bitingly characterizes it as an *"illiberale, sutoribus et sartoribus usitatem instrumentum."* By the mid-18th c. the cittern had lost much of its former elegance: the body was of the same depth throughout, rather than tapered toward the neck as theretofore, and the pairs of strings were gradually replaced by single strings of gut instead of the traditional wire, a result of the ascending influence of the guitar. Many 18th- and 19th-c. specimens have holes drilled in their fingerboards for the attaching of a *capotasto. Koch, in his *Lexikon* of 1802, writes that capotasti

made the instr. far easier to play than the guitar, as the fingering remained the same in all keys. Around 1800 a new variety, called deutsche Guitarre, appeared in Germany, with 7 single strings and open soundhole: again, concessions to the guitar. By 1740 the *English guitar, an offshoot of the cittern, had come into existence in an attempt to compete with the guitar, but by the end of the 19th c. the cittern had died out everywhere except for a few mountain "pockets" in Germany, where it lives on under the names of *Thüringer Zither or Harzzither. See also: archcittern, Bergzither, bijuga cither, cetarissima, cister, Cistertheorbe, cistole, cistre, citara, citarino, cithara germanica, citole, deutsche Guitarre, englisches Cithrinchen, English guitar, guitare allemande, guitare anglaise, hamburger Cithrinchen, keyed guitar, penorcon, sister, Spanish cittern, syron, terzina, Thüringer Zither, Waldzither (78, 80 Dart, 89 Dart, 144, 159, 170).

Ciufolo, var. of zuffolo.

Ciufolo pastorale, obs. It.: panpipes (39).

Ciumpoi (pron. tsh . . .), var. of cimpoi (13).

Čivink, syn. of pisk.

Claasagh, Manx: harp (176).

Clacke [Fr. *claque*], MEngl.: rattle. *Cf.* claquette.

Clackers, MEngl.: clappers.

Clack idiophone, see: cricri.

Clag, Gael.: bell.

Clair-accord, a misreading of claviaccord.

Clairon (Fr.), **1.** word used in France from the early 14th c. on to denote a trumpet, and especially a high-pitched one. As such, it is often found listed together with trumpets. The difference between clairon and ordinary trumpet is brought out clearly by Nicot in 1606: *"le clairon est la trompette qui a le tuyau plus estroit . . . le clairon, anciennement, ainsi qu'en usent encore les Moresques et les Portuguais qui le tiennent d'eux, servoit comme d'un dessus à plu-*

sieurs trompètes sonnans en taille et basse contre" (the clairon is a trumpet with a narrower tube . . . the clairon served formerly, as it still does among the Moors and the Portuguese who got it from them, as a treble to several trumpets sounding the tenor and double bass). Laborde in 1780 still uses the word in this sense. *Cf.* clareta;
2. in modern Fr.: bugle; **3.** (Ger.: *Klarinc*) organ stop of reed pipes at 4' pitch, the oct. stop of the *trompette, with medium-wide, inverted conical resonators. It occurs occasionally at 2' pitch, when it corresponds to the Engl. clarion stop, the top oct. of which was usually made of open flue pipes because the treble reeds did not stay in tune. According to Adlung, it was also called clarino (3, 20, 82, 99, 124, 133).

Clairon à clefs, Fr.: keyed bugle.

Clairon-chasseur (Fr.), coiled bugle invented by François Millereau of Paris in 1883 for the use of Fr. military (chasseur) bands (176).

Clairon chromatique, Fr.: keyed bugle.

Clairon chromatique basse, Fr.: bass ophicleide (176).

Clairon harmonique (Fr.), *trompette harmonique organ stop at 4' pitch (133).

Clairon métallique (Fr.), brass clarinet submitted by Halary (Jean-Hilaire Asté) to the Académie des Beaux-Arts in 1817, and exhibited by him in 1823 (126).

Clairon-trompette (Fr.), a patent was granted on May 9, 1873, to Arsène-Zoé Lecomte & Cie. of Paris, apparently for a valved bugle in B♭, which could be lowered to E♭ by a valve and was intended for military bands (204).

Clairseach (Irish Gael.), see: Irish harp.

Clamor avium, see: nightingale.

Clapet [MFr. *claper,* to clap], **1.** OFr.: *cog rattle or clapper that announced the services during Easter week; **2.** in the 15th and 16th c. a bell clapper (85, 204).

Clapper, 1. (Fr.: *cliquet, cliquette;* Ger.: *Klapper;* Sp.: *tarreña*), *concussion idiophone of worldwide distribution,

a substitute for hand clapping or body slapping. Two or more sticks, plaques, troughs, or vessels are struck together; they may be made of wood, bone, ivory, nutshells, marine shells, etc. They may be composed of several pieces, or 2 or more may be hinged together at one end; or 2 may be hinged to a larger, central piece. Specimens have been found from prehistoric times on: Egyptian necropolises have yielded 3 different, elongated forms, straight-, rectangular-, and boomerang-shaped. All 3 coexisted. The oldest datable ones depicted are those of Sumer. The oldest surviving specimen is from *ca.* 3200 B.C. Those of ancient Egypt represent a pair of hands, either straight or curved, or hands and forearms, as well as other forms, made of wood and ivory. In Europe clappers were used in former times, *i.a.,* by lepers, who were obliged to sound them to warn people of their approach. See also: aldaba, amatambo, bois-crolant, bones, Britsche, byakushi, cai ban ñac, cai chak, cai xiñ tien, cascaveaux, cascavelle, chachra, chalpāra, chantang balung, chārpāra, chelepita, chien pan, chitike, chitikelu, Chlefeli, ch'ung tu, ciocca-ciocca, clackers, clapet, clicket, cliquet, crepitaculum, crotal, crotalum, cucchiare di legno, danda suthra, dapla, elibo, etimoika, haku han, hyōshige, kalaka, karatāli, kartāl, kartali, kaskabeleta, kepyak, 2, khat tālī, kisketa, Klaffe, Klapper, knicky-knackers, kolatka, krap fuong, krap puang, krembalon, krouma, kroupalon, kroupezion, marapo, mbizi, moulinet, okpelé, okuelé, olezkilla, p'ai pan, pak, pan, p'o pan, sang, scabellum, shaku byoshi, shu pan, shuqaifat, slapstick, sok yet, spagane, tablettes, tablilla, tarabast, tarreña, thandanda, tingšak, tokere, torotok, va let kyong, yotsu dake, zeng;

2. (Fr.: *battant;* Ger.: *Klöppel;* It.: *battachio;* Sp.: *badajo*), tongue of a bell, made of metal or wood (96, 144 Hickmann, 170).

Claquebois, Fr.: xylophone.

Claquette [Fr. *claquer,* to clap], **1. obs.**

Fr.: rattle; 2. a military idiophone of the 19th c. that imitated the snapping of whips.

Clarabella, name of 2 different organ stops: 1. of open conical flue pipes of wide scale, invented by J. C. Bishop of London ca. 1840; the pipes had a high cutup, went down only to c^1 or c^0, and were at 8' or 4' pitch. Also called claribel, claribel flute; 2. an open, medium-scaled conical *dulzian stop is occasionally called Clarabella in Germany (133, 176, 186).

Clarain, 13th- and 14th-c. var. of clarine (82).

Claramella, 14th-c. var. of charamela.

Clara voce, name given to the *basset horn in England at the turn of the 18th–19th c. (89 Rendall).

Clare [Lat. *clarus,* clear], OFr.: bell attached to the necks of animals, specially those in pasturage. The term is recorded from the 14th c. on.

Clareta [Lat. *clarus,* clear], trumpet depicted by Virdung (in 1511), that later became the clarin trumpet, intended for playing high harmonics. *Cf.* clairon (170, 194).

Clariana, clariona, organ stop of open flue pipes at 8' pitch (198).

Claribel(la), syn. of clarabella.

Claribel flute, syn. of clarabella.

Clarichord, claricord, obs. var. of clavichord.

Claricon, obs. var. of clavichord.

Clarin, 1. OFr. var. of clairon, recorded in Fr. literature from the 14th c. on; 2. New Prov. equivalent of clarine. See also: clarin trumpet.

Clarín (Sp.), wooden trumpet of Mexico and Peru. See also: acocotl, trutruka.

Clarine [dim. of *clare*], a small clare (bell). Also called clarain.

Clarinet (Fr.: *clarinette;* Ger.: *Klarinette;* It.: *clarinetto*), 1. organologists and ethnomusicologists consider as a clarinet any reedpipe with a mouthed single beating reed; Sachs defined it in this wider sense as a tube closed at the upper end, with a nearby blowhole covered by a

beating reed. Such instrs. were already known to ancient Egypt, where the blowhole was made by cutting a 3-sided oblique slit into the cane, thereby forming a tongue, *i.e.,* an idioglott reed. Their origin is unknown. When the clarinet first appears in higher civilizations, it is in form of a *double clarinet. The ancient Egyptian pipes, if we may judge by the manner of present-day performance throughout the East, were played by mouthing the reed while the player continued to breathe through his nose, thus creating a continuous sound. Modification of timbre and dynamics is not possible with this playing technique. Idioglott clarinets are played in modern Egypt and also in Asia. From the East they reached Sardinia (*launeddas), the Basque country (*alboka), Wales (*pibcorn), and the Balkans by water routes, Russia (*brelka), Poland (*duda), and Lithuania (*birbyne) overland. As the clarinet's bore is cylindrical, the instr. has the characteristics of a stopped pipe, sounding an oct. lower than an open pipe, with concomitant stress of the uneven harmonics; thus it overblows the 12th, not the oct. On the European clarinet this necessitates keywork more complicated than that on the flute or oboe, as there is a wider gap to bridge between fundamental and 12th.· It also requires a different fingering.

The European clarinet is a transformation or improvement of the *chalumeau, owing, according to Doppelmayr, to Johann Christoff Denner of Nürnberg (d. in the first years of the 18th c.). Denner made a chalumeau with an a^1 key and a rear b^1 key and gave it a separate mouthpiece. Either he or his son and successor developed the bell, transformed the b^1 key into a bb^1 key, placing it higher so as to overblow the 12th, thereby adding the higher clarinet register to the extant chalumeau register. Early clarinets had cylindrical bores and were played with 15-mm.-wide reeds placed against the upper lip. Mouthpiece and barrel were of one piece, the body joint had 6 fingerholes and was separated from the foot joint, which was pierced with twin holes and fitted with a long key. The instr. was pitched in C. (The pitch of old clarinets cannot be ascertained by length alone, because the bore varies considerably.) The 2-keyed model was made up to the mid-18th c. or later, long after the third key had been added. Maier in 1732 gives it a compass f^0–a^2 or higher. First mention of the word *clarinet* found so far occurs in 1716, when Roger advertised *"airs à deux clarinettes ou deux chalumeaux."* The old name continued in use for another half c. at least, side by side with the new one. Chalumeau parts were scored for from 1704 on in operas written for the Vienna court (see: Van der Meer in 80 XV); the Paris and Vienna editions of Gluck's *Orfeo* and *Alceste*, published in 1764 and 1769, still contained chalumeau parts; these became clarinet parts in later editions. The earliest known illustration of the clarinet appears in the *Encyclopédie méthodique* of 1767, in which a 2-piece instr. is depicted: its cylindrical body has no bell, is provided with 8 fingerholes and a detachable mouthpiece. By the 1730's the word *clarinette* was coming into common use, although the *Encyclopédie* of 1767 calls it a *"sorte de hautbois"* (a kind of oboe). By 1753 it was played in Paris; by the 1760's some orchestras had specialized players for the new instr. and parts for the clarinet were beginning to appear in orchestral scores. The need for playing in different tonalities caused the body to be divided into 3 parts so that interchangeable joints (called *corps de rechange or *pièces de rechange* in Fr.) might be used. Around the mid-c. a fourth and fifth key were added for $f\sharp^2/c\sharp^2$ and $g\sharp^2/d\sharp^2$. This development of the key system may be responsible for the extraordinary spurt of popularity the clarinet started to enjoy in the late 1750's, when it competed with the well-established oboe and for a time even

threatened to displace it (in military bands it actually succeeded in doing so, little by little). For a short while the clarinet was played, not with, but in lieu of, the oboe. It then was being made of boxwood or fruitwood, usually pearwood. The mouthpiece was narrower and the reed shorter than that now in use; next to this came a piriform barrel; this was followed by the upper, or left-hand, joint, with 4 holes and 2 keys; the right-hand joint had 3 holes; the lower joint 1 hole and 3 keys; the bell joint was sometimes made of 1 piece with the lower joint. By 1790 a sixth key was added for $c\sharp^0/g\sharp^0$.

Clarinets at different pitches were developed during the 18th c.: one in B♭ for the flat keys, others in A, B, and D for the sharp ones. These were intended to spare the player from having to finger remote tonalities. Around 1800 the 5-keyed instr. was still a favorite, although its chalumeau register was poor. At that time alterations were made to the bore, and 6 or 7 new keys were added by Iwan Müller and Merklin; the E♭ and high F clarinets were introduced, and greater use was made of the B♭, as the clarinet remained prominent in military bands. In 1839 a ring key mechanism was applied by Louis-Auguste Buffet (Buffet *jeune*). In 1843 Boehm-system clarinets were produced, making it theoretically possible to play all parts on one instr. The *omnitonic clarinet was another attempt in this direction. Because of its somewhat shrill tone the C clarinet was discarded; the sopranino in F was also abandoned. Instead, the B♭ and E♭ came to the fore. A very rare oct. instr. in high B♭ was created; together with a high A♭ clarinet it exists in Italy, the 2 being called *settimino and *sestino, respectively. Nowadays the ordinary clarinet is that in B♭; the A clarinet, also in use, has the same bore, mouthpiece, and barrel as the B♭ clarinet. Flat parts are written for the B♭, sharp ones for the A clarinet. In Italy and Spain the A also has been abolished and everything is played on a B♭ clarinet.

Tonal positions	Name	Pitch	Compass
Octave	Piccolo clarinet	B	d^1–bb^3
		Ab	c^1–bb^3
Sopranino	Sopranino clarinet	F	a^0–bb^3
		Eb	g^0–bb^3
		D	$f\#^0$–a^3
Soprano	Soprano clarinet	C	e^0–g^3
		Bb	d^0–f^3
		A	$c\#^0$–e^3
Alto	Alto clarinet	F	A^0–c^3
		Eb	G^0–bb^2
Tenor	Bass clarinet	C	Eb^0–g^2
		Bb	Db^0–f^2
		A	C^0–e^2
Bass	Contrabasset horn	F	A^1–c^2
		Eb	G^1–bb^1
Contrabass	Contrabass clarinet	Bb	A^2–f^1
		A	Ab^2–e^1

The C clarinet is currently being revived in Ger.-speaking countries. The Boehm system is in use except in Austria, Germany, Holland, and the U.S.S.R. In rhythm bands the clarinet is played with the reed uppermost (as was the early clarinet); elsewhere with the reed down. The clarinet is treated as a transposing instr., notated in relation to the (defunct) C clarinet. The lowest oct. of any clarinet is known as its chalumeau register; this is followed by a half oct. of intermediate register; the clarinet register starts with the overblown 12th and continues up for an oct., with the same fingering as the chalumeau register, and a further oct. can be obtained by the extreme register. See also: alto clarinet, bass clarinet, clarinette-contralto, clarinette d'amour, clarinette multiphonique, combination clarinet, contrabass clarinet, double clarinet, omnitonic clarinet, piccolo clarinet, quartino, sestino, settimino, Sextklarinette, soprano clarinet, subcontrabass clarinet, tenor clarinet, walking-stick clarinet (14, 41, 164, 170);

2. organ stop of reed pipes with wide cylindrical resonators, derived from the Fr. *chalumeau, at 16' or 8' pitch. Sometimes labeled orchestral clarinet (101, 129).

Clarinet flute, organ stop of half-stopped flue pipes, usually of wood, at 8' pitch, of soft intonation; it corresponds to the Nachthorn. Also called clarionet flute (133, 186).

Clarinette basse, Fr.: bass clarinet.

Clarinette-bourdon (Fr.), *contrabass clarinet built by Adolphe Sax *ca.* 1840, in Bb, an oct. below the *bass clarinet, a close successor to the *bathyphone. Both attempts at creating a true contrabass were unsuccessful (164).

Clarinette contralto (Fr.), Fr. *bass clarinet pitched in F or Eb, an oct. below the alto clarinet. *Cf.* contrabasset horn (169).

Clarinette contrebasse, Fr.: contrabass clarinet.

Clarinette d'amour (Fr.) (It.: *clarinetto d'amore*), a large clarinet made with either straight or angular body of comparatively small bore, ending in an *amore,* or bulb-shaped, bell and sometimes provided with a curved metal crook to carry the mouthpiece. Generally it is pitched in G, but occasionally in Ab or F, a 4th, 3rd, or 5th, respectively, below the ordinary clarinet. It appeared in continental Europe in the late 18th c. and was made from then until about 1820. As there is no literature for this instr., one assumes it to have been a solo instr.

Heckel of Biebrich has now revived it (14, 132, 164).

Clarinette multiphonique (Fr.), a *combination clarinet invented by Frédéric Triébert of Paris, patented Dec. 24, 1847; it could be crooked to C, B♭, or A (176, 204).

Clarinette omnitonique (Fr.), see: omnitonic clarinet.

Clarinette-pédale (Fr.), *contrabass clarinet invented *ca.* 1890 and patented 1891 by Fontaine Besson of Paris, who produced a military and an orchestral model, the bore being mainly cylindrical (164).

Clarinette système omnitonique (Fr.), see: omnitonic clarinet.

Clarinetto a doppia tonalità (It.), *combination clarinet in C, B♭, A, of Maino and Orsi of Milan, 1887, with wide bore and 3 slides (176).

Clarinetto contrabasso, It.: contrabass clarinet.

Clarinetto d'amore (It.), see: clarinette d'amour.

Clarinetto sestino, see: sestino.

Clarino (It.) [Lat. *clarus,* clear], **1.** a *clarin trumpet; **2.** the upper register of an ordinary (*i.e.,* principal) trumpet, in which the partials lie close enough together to permit the playing of a scale; **3.** in 18th- and early-19th-c. scores a trumpet; **4.** name given to the clarinet in 18th-c. Italy; **5.** the clarin register of a clarinet; **6.** organ stop identical with the clairon.

Clarinophon, organ stop invented by Hopferwieser of Graz, Austria, consisting of 2 ranks of flue pipes at the same pitch but of different families (principal and gamba), sounded simultaneously, at 8′ pitch (131, 133).

Clarino transpositore (It.), a short-lived *combination clarinet of Agostino Rampone of Milan, 1901, in B♭ and A, with separate tone holes for each key (176).

Clarin trumpet (Fr.: *clairon;* Ger.: *Clarintrompete;* It.: *Clarino*), *natural trumpet of a bore slightly narrower than

that of the principal trumpet, played with a flat, broad mouthpiece to facilitate the producing of high partials. See also: clairon, clarin, clarín, clarino.

Clario, med. Lat.: trumpet (176).

Clarion [OFr. **clairon*], **1.** *clarin trumpet. The term is first recorded in Engl. literature in 1325 and was still in use in the 16th c., when it denoted a "wound" trumpet; **2.** Engl. name of the *clairon organ stop.

Clariona, automatic free-reed instr. in which a crank simultaneously operated the bellows and a strip of perforated cardboard. Also called orguinette.

Clarionet, obs. form of clarinet.

Clarion mixture, mixture organ stop of 3 ranks of reed pipes at 4′, 2⅔′, and 2′ pitches on heavy pressure, designed by Walker in the 19th c., now obs. (133, 198).

Clarioun, var. of clarion.

Claro [Lat. *clarus,* clear], med. Lat.: trumpet, particularly a shorter form of trumpet (79).

Claron, 1. OFr.: var. of clairon; **2.** Sp.: clarin trumpet.

Clarone, 1. med. Lat.: trumpet; the equivalent of tuba or clairon; **2.** It.: name applied to the early clarinet; **3.** It.: basset horn; **4.** It.: bass clarinet (164, 176).

Clarone in B♭, It.: bass clarinet.

Clarsach, clarsech (Scot. Gael.), the Scot. harp, identical with the Irish harp (89).

Clash-pan, syn. of cymbals (79).

Classica, var. of classicum (61).

Classicum, med. Lat.: trumpet; glossed as *buisine* in the 14th c. (61, 82).

Classique [Lat. *classica*], OFr.: trumpet. The term occurs from the 13th c. to the 16th (204).

Clavaeoline (Ger.: *Klaväoline*), **1.** a perfected aeoline invented by Carl Schmidt of Pressburg (Bratislava) in 1826; **2.** free-reed organ stop imitative of the above, invented by organ builder Beyer of Naumburg in 1830, at 8′ pitch. Not to be confused with clavioline (131, 176).

Clave, 1. Sp.: generic term for stringed keyboard instrs.; specific term for the harpsichord; **2.** *concussion stick of Cuba. See: claves.

Clavecímbano, obs. Sp.: harpsichord.

Clavecin [Lat. *clavicymbalum*], Fr.: harpsichord. The word was first used by Cotgrave in 1611, but see clavecinon.

Clavecin à archet, Fr.: bowed keyboard instr.

Clavecin acoustique (Fr.), keyboard instr. invented by De Virbès of Paris in 1771 and performed upon before the Dauphine that year. It could imitate 14–18 orchestral instrs. but had no hammers, pipes, or pedal. See also: clavecin harmonieux et céleste (27, 204).

Clavecin à grand ravalement (Fr.) [Fr.: *ravaler*, to make lower], 18th-c. Fr. term denoting a harpsichord with a manual compass of 5 octs., F^1–f^3.

Clavecin à maillets, early Fr. name for the piano; the name given by Jean Marius in 1716 to his different models. See: piano.

Clavecin à maillets et à sautereaux (Fr.: harpsichord with hammers and jacks), piano-harpsichord of Jean Marius of Paris, designed by 1716. See: piano.

Clavecin à marteaux, an early Fr. name for the piano.

Clavecin à peau de bufle (Fr.: buff-leather harpsichord), harpsichord furnished with plectra of *buff leather, apparently an "invention" of Pascal Taskin of Paris in 1768. His claim has been challenged in modern times on the grounds that leather had been used for plectra earlier. See 179A, XII and XIII, for the organological battle. Taskin first used it in a harpsichord with 3 rows of jacks; in instrs. with 4 rows of jacks only the back row was fitted with plectra of *bufle,* the remainder being quilled. According to Brenet, Oesterlein of Berlin also used it for plectra in 1773, as did Érard in 1776 (33).

Clavecin à ravalement (Fr.) [Fr.: *ravaler,* to make lower], 18th-c. term denoting a harpsichord with an enlarged compass of more than the former standard 4 octs. but less than 5 octs. See also: clavecin à grand ravalement.

Clavecin brisé [Fr.: *briser,* to fold], portable folding harpsichord invented by Jean Marius of Paris, for which he received a 20-year privilege in 1700. Designed for travel purposes, it was made in 3 sections hinged together so as to fold over each other most compactly. Several specimens have survived. Marius seems to have been singularly attracted to things that fold: he also invented folding tents and folding umbrellas remarkably like the beach umbrellas of today.

Clavecin d'amore, name sometimes given to the *cimbal d'amour.

Clavecin électrique (Fr.), not a harpsichord, but a series of bowl-shaped bells suspended in a vertical frame, controlled from a keyboard, and sounded by means of static electricity, the invention of Jean-Baptiste de Laborde in 1759. For each tone there were 2 unison bells with a clapper between them, somewhat like our electric bells (83, 124).

Clavecin harmonieux et céleste (Fr.), keyboard instr. invented in 1777 by De Virbès of Paris, presumably an improved version of his *clavecin acoustique. Although it had no hammers, pipes, or pedals, it could imitate orchestral instrs. (27, 204).

Clavecin harmonique, see: orchestrine.

Clavecin-luth, Fr.: lute harpsichord.

Clavecin mécanique (Fr.), a combination *piano-harpsichord of Sébastien Érard of Paris, built in the 1770's. Each instr. could be played separately or they could be combined (176).

Clavecinon, early-16th-c. Fr. term for harpsichord (27).

Clavecin organisé, Fr.: claviorganum.

Clavecin parfait accord (Fr.), *enharmonic harpsichord with 21 keys to the oct., built by Jacques Goermans of Paris in 1781 (27, 204).

Clavecin royal, 1. square piano built by Johann Gottlob Wagner of Dresden in 1774, with 6 variations of tone of which 4 were controlled by knee levers, and a 5-oct. compass, F^1–f^3. Co-inventor was Johann Gottlob's younger brother, Christian Salomon Wagner. Its tone resembled that of a harpsichord; **2.** a similar instr. with 12 variations of tone, built in the late 18th c. by Johann Christian Jürgensen of Silesia (27, 92).

Clavecin vertical, Fr.: clavicytherium.

Clavecin-vielle (Fr.), *bowed keyboard instr. built by Cuisinié of Paris in 1708 on the principle of the *hurdygurdy. A revolving wheel was actuated by a pedal, leaving both hands free to play (176).

Clavecin-viole, Fr.: Geigenwerk.

Clavemusicum omnitonum (Lat.), name of the only preserved *enharmonic harpsichord of the early baroque, built by Vito Trasuntino of Venice, dated 1606, and preserved in the Museo Civico of Bologna. The harpsichord has 31 tones to the oct. and a 4-oct. compass. Its single manual consists of natural keys like those of any harpsichord, the accidental keys being as wide as the natural ones and split into 4 sections of alternating black front and white rear sections, with added shorter and narrower keys placed between the E and F, B and C keys. The clavemusicum is said to have been built to the design of Nicolo Vicentino (d. 1572). See also: clavicymbalum universale (64).

Claves (Sp.) [Lat.: *clavis,* key], Cuban *concussion sticks adopted by Western rhythm bands. The claves consist of 2 short cylindrical hardwood sticks, preferably made of cocabola, one of which is held in the cupped left hand while it is struck with the other stick; 20–25 cm. (8–10 in.) long.

Clavessin, obs. var. of clavecin.

Clavi-accord (Fr.), a compact portable harmonium invented by Ludovico Gavioli of Paris by 1855, when it was patented in England (he also took out or renewed a Fr. patent in 1861). Upon being depressed, the keys actuated the bellows (176, 204).

Clavi-arpa (Sp.), *keyed harp said to have been invented by Juan Hidalgo, 17th-c. Sp. composer and harpist. *Cf.* clavi-harp, clavi-lyra (89).

Claviarum, med. Lat.: keyboard (176).

Claviatur-Contrafagott (Ger.), contrabassoon designed by Carl Wilhelm Moritz of Berlin in 1845, with a small keyboard of 15 keys, similar to those of a piano. It was patented on Oct. 24, 1856, a year after his death. No specimen has survived (89 Langwill).

Clavicembalo, It. and modern Ger.: harpsichord, usually abbr. to cembalo. The word first occurs in a Modena document of 1461, when Sesto Tantini requests payment for a clavicembalo. See also: clavicimbalum (Valdrighi: *Musurgiana*).

Clavicembalo col piano e forte (It.: harpsichord with soft and loud), early It. name of the piano. Bartolommeo Cristofori called his pianos *"gravicembali con pian e forte."*

Clavicembalo verticale, It.: clavicytherium.

Clavicembalum (Lat.), see: clavicimbalum.

Clavichord [Lat. *clavis,* key + Gk. *chorde,* string] (Fr.: *clavicorde;* Ger.: *Klavichord;* It.: *clavicordio*), stringed keyboard instr. in form of a rectangular box, with keyboard set in the long side and strings, usually 2 per note, running diagonally from the hitch pins on the player's left over a bridge at his right, to be secured by tuning pins at the extreme right. The action is one of greatest simplicity: a brass blade called tangent is set upright upon the rear portion of each key; when a key is depressed, the tangent strikes the string from below and, as there is no form of *escapement whatever, remains in contact with it until the key is released. The tangent acts as nut at the same time, determining the string's speaking length. The short section of string between tangent and hitch pin is muted by a strip of felt or similar material so that the sound is damped as soon as the tangent leaves the string. Historically, clavichords were first "fretted" (Fr.: *lié;* Ger.: *gebunden*), later "unfretted" (Fr.: *libre;* Ger.: *bundfrei*). In the older, fretted form, more than one key acted on a given pair of strings, their several tangents producing tones of different pitches. Although there was no standardization in these matters, the middle section of the compass had 2 or 3 keys to a string, the treble 2, 3, or 4 keys to a string. The bass octave was always left unfretted. Of the keys thus fretted together only one could be sounded at a time (the highest one in pitch); their tangents were spaced so as to sound a semitone apart. Since this arrangement was not feasible with straight keys of equal size, some keys were made in curved form and the rear portion of the treble keys was made increasingly narrower, permitting the tangents to lie closer together. The back end of each key was provided with a short, projecting blade that guided the key up and down in a saw-cut slot in the rear wall of the clavichord and that also prevented sideways motion. The position of these slots (collectively called *Rechen,* rake, in Ger.) was carefully worked out by monochord ratios, their emplacement determining that of each tangent.

In the later, unfretted form each key acted on a separate string. Some instrs., however, continued to be built with the top 3, 4, or 5 keys fretted, as a space-saving device. The lack of standardization in fretting has already been mentioned; despite this, one system is encountered frequently enough to form a definite pattern. In this the keys are fretted together in pairs except for the D's and A's, which remain unfretted. These unfretted D's and A's have led to various interpretations in the past, usually implying a nonexistent relationship to the Dorian and Hypodorian modes. Actually, once it is decided to pair a key together with its accidental, 2 natural keys must of necessity remain unfretted, as there are 7 of them per oct., but only 5 accidental keys. Early

It. theorists and tuning tutors generally considered the latter as 3 sharps and 2 flats (C♯, F♯, G♯, E♭, B♭). And if C and C♯, F and F♯, G and G♯, E♭ and E, B♭ and B are fretted together, then there is no key with which D and A can be paired, and the following layout results: C/C♯, D, E♭/E, F/F♯, G/G♯, A, B♭/B. This pattern is found on It. clavichords of the 16th c. and on later Ger. and Swed. ones. Praetorius reports in 1618 that 30 years earlier an It. clavichord with unfretted D's and A's in all octs. was sent to Meissen in Saxony, apparently a novelty in Germany then. If, however, the E♭ were considered as D♯ (as it was, *i.a.,* by Virdung), and the B♭ as A♯, then a different fretting pattern would result: C/C♯, D/D♯, E, F/F♯, G/G♯, A/A♯, B, and this is in effect the pattern adopted by Iberian clavichord makers. Most fretted clavichords had a *short octave in the bass. Owing to the saving of space and materials made possible by fretting and the short oct., it was possible to provide a cheap and eminently portable instr. with a compass of 4 octs. and measuring only some 110 by 30 cm. (43 by 12 in.).

The clavichord is the oldest of our surviving stringed keyboard instrs. Its early history is not entirely clarified: confusion results from the fact that, having evolved from the monochord, it continued to be called by that name after it had acquired an identity of its own. The present state of research suggests that literary references to monochords as musical instrs. occurring prior to the 14th c. denote a plucked, single-string monochord, and that the clavichord descended from it at the end of that c. Johannes de Muris (in 1323) is said to have described a 19-string "monochord" with a 2½-oct. compass; this, as Walter Nef has pointed out (in Source 80, Vol. IV) is a misinterpretation: the author is describing the theoretical division of a single string into 19 parts. Elsewhere he refers to an instr. with 4 strings, but we cannot tell whether reference is to the *"instrumentum Mercurii tetrachordum"* or to a 4-stringed polychord. The strings of the oldest type of clavichord were all of the same length, diam., and pitch. Such instrs. coexisted for a time with the clavichord as we know it today, in which the strings are of different length, diam., and pitch (Virdung in 1511 still portrays the older type). Ramis de Pareja in 1482 describes both types and calls both "monochord." Perhaps this coexistence explains the occurrence of the words *clavicordium* and *monocordium* listed together in Eberhart Cersne's *Minne Regel* (*Rules of the Minnesinger*) of 1404—earliest mention of the word clavichord. But the old terminology lingers yet awhile: the "monochord" of Georgius Anselmi (in 1434) for instance was a clavichord with 8 unison strings. The first representations of the instr. are found in an It. painting of 1433 (according to Valentin Denis in Source 80, Vol. II), in the treatise of Henri Arnaut of Zwolle of *ca.* 1440, which depicts a fretted clavichord with 9 pairs of strings and 37 keys, having a compass B^0–b^2 (an average of 4 semitones per course), and in the *Weimar Wunderbuch* of the same period, in which a rough drawing shows an instr. with projecting keyboard, soundhole with rose, and all strings of the same length. Some 20 years later the clavichord had assumed a highly developed form: Paulus Paulirinus, writing *ca.* 1460, speaks of its geminated strings and also of its pedalboard; thus equipped, it became a practice instr. for organists. Virdung refers to the use of brass strings for the bass and steel ones for the treble. He also mentions the optional addition of a third string to each course; later, in the 17th c., a third string, at 4′ pitch, was occasionally added in the bass. His instrs. had a compass of 38 keys. In 1512 Cocleus confirms the use of both brass and iron strings. The earliest preserved clavichord, an It. one by Domenico of Pesaro dated 1543, now housed in the

instr. collection of Leipzig University, is a 6-sided instr. of cypress with a 4-oct. compass (short oct.), C^0–c^3, and 22 pairs of strings. Instead of the customary V- or S-shaped bridge it has 3 independent straight bridges; the keyboard projects and the whole instr. is housed in an outer case from which it was removed for performance—a feature it shares with other It. stringed keyboard instrs. of the period. Exactly the same type of instr. is depicted by Praetorius, who calls it a clavichord with It. scale. He depicts 3 clavichords; in all 3 the damper listing is replaced by a damper board fitted over the short ends of the strings to the rear of the tangents; this lends a little more resistance to the touch and facilitates the replacement of strings. The clavichord shown by Mersenne (in 1636) is already unfretted except for the 5 top keys. For the remainder of the c. small fretted clavichords continued to be made, while the better instrs. were larger and partly unfretted. In the second half of the 17th c. the 2 lowest accidental keys were often split in order to lengthen the short oct.: the rear portion of the D key sounded F♯, and that of the E key sounded G♯. The first completely unfretted instrs. appear to have been made in the early 18th c. (a clavichord made by Weidner in 1697, which has somehow acquired the reputation of being the earliest unfretted clavichord, proves on examination to be thoroughly fretted). During the 17th c. the compass was in most instances 4 octs. with bass short oct.; the tuning pins were placed along the treble wall in a straight line, but with the larger number of pins required by the increased number of strings of the unfretted instrs., the tuning pins were laid out in form of an obtuse angle, 4 abreast. Until approximately the mid-18th c. the lower limit of the compass was C^0, thereafter F^1, usually reaching up to f^3. Toward the mid-c. it became customary to furnish clavichords with separate stands and in the last quarter of the c. screw-in legs became standard. During the entire 18th c. small, inexpensive fretted instrs. continued to be made alongside the large unfretted ones with a 5-oct. compass (in some cases up to 6 octs.). The *Empfindsamkeit* of the 18th c. brought about a great revival of clavichord playing in Germany, where the instr. had never died out. In rural areas it continued in use there until at least the end of the first quarter of the 19th c. Thus one is surprised to find that Gustav Schilling, in his *Universal Lexikon der Tonkunst* of 1835, has so far forgotten the nature of the clavichord that he talks of quilling it. A characteristic of the clavichord's playing technique is the *Bebung*, or *vibrato*, whereby a note can be graced or a tone sustained: this is accomplished by rapidly alternating the pressure applied by the finger to a key without releasing the latter. The increase in pressure on an instr. that is not too heavily strung will affect the tension and thus the pitch of a string. Praetorius even suggested taking advantage of this feature to modify the temperament of the (unequally tempered) 3rds by pressure on the keys.

After the clavichord had come into existence, the term "monochord" became changed in some countries to *manicorde, manicordion*, etc. (literally: hand stringer). In England, where it seems to have been but little played (the collection of Henry VIII contained 32 "virginals" and 2 clavichords), it was called by both names, clavichord and monochord, and numerous variants thereof, from the late 15th c. to the middle of the 18th c. Judging by the total lack of recorded Brit. makers, it appears that clavichords there were imported ones. In France the word *manicordion* denoted the clavichord from its early days until the end of the 17th c. In 1611, Cotgrave translates the word into English as "an old-fashioned claricord." *Sourdine* and *épinette sourde* were other Fr. terms; they refer to the small tone. In 1740 Grassineau asserts, as do several other writers, that the tiny volume of sound was due to the strings' being covered with pieces of cloth for the purpose of muting the sound. In 1692 a factory of organs and *manicords* existed on Rue St. Julien des Ménéstriers, Paris, according to the *Livre des adresses;* and in 1723 "*manichordion*" was the name of the finest brass wire known in France, then in use for "manicords", spinets, harpsichords, and other instrs. At the end of the c. Milchmeyer reported in *Die wahre Art, das Pianoforte zu spielen* (1798) that there were no clavichords in France or England. Germany produced clavichords uninterruptedly until the 19th c.; in the 17th and 18th c. they were occasionally referred to as **Instrument* and from 1741 on as **Clavier*. The keyboards of Ger. instrs. are recessed. To judge by the rarity of surviving specimens, Italy did not produce many clavichords after the 16th c., although they continued to serve as practice instrs. for organists (see: buonaccordo). The same remark holds true for the Low Countries, where they were probably replaced by Antwerp virginals from the mid-16th c. on. Netherlandish clavichords were exported to the Iberian peninsula and Germany during the 16th c. In Portugal and Spain the words *monocordio* and *manicordio* denoted the clavichord until the mid-17th c. and the word *clavicordio* was used as a generic term for stringed keyboard instrs. After *ca.* 1650 the 2 former words were dropped, *clavicordio* retaining its earlier sense. The word *clave* was also used in a generic sense. In Portugal *clavicordio* denoted the clavichord after the mid-17th c.; sometimes the word *cravo*, which normally designated the harpsichord, was also used for clavichord. Iberian instrs. remained fretted in the 18th c. and were in use up to the early 19th c.; they often had but one string per note; the keyboards were recessed. Scandinavian instrs. were patterned on the Ger. model and also remained in use up to the early 19th c.

Although standard clavichords are built at 8′ pitch, small instrs. were occasionally built at 4′ pitch. See also: Bible clavichord, buonaccordo, cimbal d'amour, épinette muette, épinette sourde, fretted, Instrument, dulce melos, pedal clavichord, sordine, sourdine (82, Iberian instrs.: S. Kastner in: *Acta musicologica*, 1952; M. Scholz, Basel: personal communication).

Clavichordium (Lat.), bowed harpsichord invented by Le Gay of Paris in 1763, with 122 gut strings of which half (presumably 1 string for a compass of 5 octs., or 61 strings) were played from an ordinary keyboard by leather-plectra jacks in conventional fashion, the others being controlled from a second keyboard by a continuous horsehair bow that produced *"les fortes et les pianos"* (204).

Clavicimbalum, Lat. word designating quilled keyboard instrs. in their early days. Earliest form of the word so far known is Eberhart Cersne's *clavicymbolum* of 1404. A vocabulary of 1429 glosses *"clavicimbel, clavicembalum, instrumentum musicum."* In Zwickau payment was made in 1438 to a *"spilman der da slug uff dem klavizimbel."* In France *"un instrument a jouer nommé clavycimbale"* is mentioned in 1447; the term appears logically as *"clavier cymbolon,"* also in France, in 1485, and as *"clave chimbolon"* in 1498. The It. word form is *clavicembalo, which was taken over into modern Ger. The treatise by Henri Arnaut of Zwolle, *ca.* 1440, is partly devoted to the clavicimbalum, instr. identified by him as a harpsichord. Some 20 years later Paulus Paulirinus likens its shape to that of the psaltery. Generally, the 15th c. seems to have reserved the word for the harpsichord-shaped instr. but the early 16th c. uses it more indiscriminately. In the Leckingfield proverbs of Henry VII's day it probably meant *claviorganum, as pipes are mentioned. Virdung and Scaliger use it to denote a rectangular instr.; Mersenne, in the classical sense of *clavi* + *cymbala,* to designate a carillon with key-

board and a keyed xylophone. The etym. is discussed under cembalo (79, 82, 197, W. Salmen: *Der fahrende Musiker im europäischen Mittelalter,* 1960).

Clavicor (Fr.: *keyed horn) (It. *clavicorno*), valved brass instr. invented by Danays of Paris and made by A. G. Guichard, also of Paris, and patented there in 1837 and again on Sept. 22, 1838. Built in alto and tenor sizes, pitched in E♭ and B♭, and designed to replace the alto *ophicleide, the clavicor was actually a narrow-bore althorn or tenor horn, depending on the pitch. It was adopted by military bands in France and also in Italy, where it was called *clavicorno* (15 Morley-Pegge, 89 Baines, 126).

Clavicorde, Fr.: clavichord.

Clavicorde organisé, Fr.: *organized clavichord.

Clavicordio, 1. It.: clavichord; **2.** Port. and Sp.: generic term for stringed keyboard instrs. from early times on. In Portugal it has specifically denoted the clavichord since the mid-17th c. (S. Kastner in *Acta musicologica*, 1952).

Clavicordium (Lat.), early form of the word *clavichord,* so written by Eberhart Cersne in 1404 and in Fr. literature from 1515 on. Mersenne translates the word as *clavecin* (harpsichord) (140, 197).

Clavicorno, It.: clavicor.

Clavicylinder (Ger.: *Klavizylinder*), an improved euphone invented by Ernst Friedrich Chladni in 1799 and given its definite form in 1814: a friction bar instr. in shape of a square piano, controlled by a keyboard; C-shaped metal bars of graduated lengths were attached horizontally to the rear of the keys and pressed, by motion of the key, against a wet glass cylinder that was rotated by a treadle worked by the right foot. Compass C^0–f^3, later G^1–a^3. See also: hymnerophone (115, 132, 178).

Clavicymbalum (Lat.), **1.** see: clavicimbalum; **2.** Mersenne's name for the keyed xylophone.

Clavicymbalum universale (Lat.), *enharmonic harpsichord seen and described by Praetorius; it was then the property of Carl Luython of Prague, but built some 30 years earlier. It had a 4-oct. compass with 19 tones to the oct. and a total of 77 keys. All accidental keys were split and extra ones were inserted between the E and F, B and C keys. Furthermore, the keyboard could be shifted 7 times. Compass C^0–c^3 (159).

Clavicytherium (Lat.) [*clavis*, key + *cithara*, harp] (Fr.: *clavecin vertical;* Ger.: *Klavizytherium;* It.: *cembalo verticale*), upright harpsichord with action more complicated than that of the ordinary harpsichord, for the jacks do not fall back by their own weight but have to be pulled back. As clavicytheria saved a considerable amount of space, they became fairly popular in the 18th c., until they were replaced at the end of that c. by the upright piano. Laborde wrote in 1780 that they were made to accommodate dwellers in small apartments. The instr. existed before its name, which is first mentioned by Virdung (1511). Paulus Paulirinus, *ca.* 1460, lists the *–nnportile (initial letter lacking), an upright harpsichord combined with a positive organ. A late-15th-c. sculpture in the Kefermarkt parish church, Austria, shows a small upright harpsichord being played in portative organ position. The name clavicytherium seems to have been applied to the larger, nonportable version. The word occurs infrequently until the 17th c. Mersenne calls it a new instr. "in use in Italy," and it seems to have been little used in other countries before its revival in the 18th c. However, Praetorius depicts one with a characteristically Ger. rounded tail (*cf.* harpsichord).

Clavicythern, syn. of clavicytherium.

Clavier [Lat.: *clavis,* key], **1.** Fr.: keyboard; **2.** Ger.: obs. spelling of Klavier.

Clavier de pédales, Fr.: pedalboard.

Clavier-Gambe, 1. *bowed keyboard instr. built by Johann Georg Gleichmann of Ilmenau in 1709, according to Walther, but probably not before 1725. An imitation of the Geigenwerk, it had an oval body under which a large wheel was placed; this actuated several smaller wheels situated inside the body. Gleichmann had repaired Haiden's Geigenwerk No. 22 in 1722; **2.** a similar instr. of Nils Söderström for which a privilege was granted in 1765, also an imitation of the Geigenwerk; **3.** generic name for gutstrung, bowed keyboard instrs. of 18th-c. Germany. Walther and Majer (both in 1732) reported that they were coming into use again (149).

Claviers transpositeurs, Fr.: transposing keyboards.

Clavi-flûte (Fr.), **1.** a small keyboard instr. patented by Ludovico Gavioli of Paris on April 2, 1860; it could be played automatically or manually; **2.** a small positive organ invented by L. Duvivier of Nevers and patented by Simon of Paris on Oct. 25, 1862 (176, 204).

Clavi-harp (Fr.: *clavi-harpe;* Ger.: *Klavierharfe*), *keyed harp invented by Johann Christian Dietz, Sr., of Paris in 1813, patented Feb. 18, 1814, and made by him, his son Johann Christian, Jr., and his grandson Christian of Brussels. The silk-covered metal strings were controlled from a keyboard by an ingenious system of mechanical plectra that gently plucked the strings with a sideswiping motion. It had a 6-oct. compass, F^1–f^4; height 2.15 m. (*ca.* 7 ft.). See also: calderarpa, claviarpa, clavi-lyra, keyed harp (91, 132).

Clavi-lame (Fr.: keyed bar), keyboard instr. invented by Papelard in 1848, with metal tongues, a successor to his *claviola, 2. The tone was said to be soft and less brilliant than that of a piano. A forerunner of the celesta (176, 204).

Clavi-lyra, 1. keyboard instr. invented by Johann Christian Dietz, Sr., of Emmerich and Paris, with mechanically plucked metal strings, intended to imitate guitar tone. A precursor of his clavi-harp; **2.** *keyed harp invented by John Bateman of London, who took out a patent on Dec. 9, 1813. The strings were plucked by leather-covered tangents. The following year Bateman published "A

Description of the Clavi-lyra . . ." See also; clavi-arpa, clavi-harp, keycd harp (115, 176).

Clavi-mandore, see: Klavi-Mandor.

Claviola, 1. *bowed keyboard instr. in shape of an upright piano, invented by John Isaac Hawkins of Bordertown, N.J., in 1802, with metal strings sounded by a continuous bow. By depressing the keys the corresponding strings were raised and pressed against the bow. Its 25 strings had a compass g^0–b^2 (the top 4 keys lacked strings of their own and acted on those of the lower oct., producing flageolet tones). The instr. was shown in London in 1813 (92, 176); **2.** keyboard instr. invented by Papelard of Paris and patented on July 11, 1847. The sound was produced by 2 metal bars for each tone, tuned an oct. apart. They rested horizontally and were fixed at one end. A year later it was succeeded by the *clavi-lame. Compass c^0–c^4 (132, 169); **3.** instr. apparently similar to 2 (above), invented by George Crawford of London, patented May 22, 1862, and called pianoforte by its inventor (132).

Clavioline, monophonic, imitative *electrophonic instr. of the electronic type, similar in appearance to the *Solovox: a small panel keyboard attached to the keyboard of a conventional piano, with separate amplifier and speaker. The electronically generated tone provides string, flute, and reed organ registers. Not to be confused with the clavaeoline (60).

Claviorganum [Lat.: *clavis*, key + *organum*] (Fr.: *clavecin organisé;* Ger.: *Orgelklavier;* It.: *claviorgáno;* Sp.: *llaviórgano*), historically the term has specifically designated the combination of harpsichord and organ, but has also been applied in a larger sense to other stringed keyboard instrs. combined with an organ. The earliest form of claviorganum so far known is probably also the most complicated one: that of an upright harpsichord combined with a positive organ, described by Paulus Paulirinus of Prague

ca. 1460. The next reference comes from Spain, where in 1480 *"dos clabiórganos"* were in the possession of Don Sancho de Paredes at the Sp. court. In 1511, Alessandro of Modena built for the Duke of Modena an *"organo cum el clavazimbano."* These early claviorgana may have been 2 separate instrs. without coupling device; some texts refer to the organ part as the claviorganum, as does for instance a Sp. inventory from the time of Philip II: *"clavicordio* [*i.e.,* harpsichord] *y llaviórgano todo junto en una pieza."* A pedalboard is mentioned in a Sp. inventory of this period also. Several claviorgana were listed among Henry VIII's instrs. (1547). The earliest extant specimen is that of the Anglo-Flem. maker Theeuwes dated 1579, a harpsichord set above organ pipes and bellows, now preserved in the Victoria and Albert Museum, London; there is also a surviving spinet-regal by Bidermann dating from 1587. This latter combination was far rarer, and there is no reason to assume that the *épinette organisée* of writers such as Rabelais (16th c.) or Trichet (17th c.) refers to it rather than to the harpsichord-organ, as the Fr. used the term *épinette* to designate the harpsichord. A Dresden inventory of 1593 lists 2 combinations of *"Instrument"* and organ, and 2 of clavichord and organ; an Este inventory of 1612 mentions 5 *"organi grandi, detti claviorgani,"* suggesting that in Italy the term may have been used to indicate some other form of organ, probably the chamber organ. Later in the c. Eugen Casparini built several claviorgana of cypress, remarkable for their organ sections (see: organ). In 1667, Samuel Pepys saw a claviorganum and considered the organ "but a bauble, with a virginal joining to it." A 3-rank instr. of 1685 by Bortolotti is preserved in the Brussels Conservatoire museum. Claviorgana continued to be built throughout the 18th c. Dom Bedos describes one of 3 manuals, 2 for a harpsichord with 8' and 4' strings, coupled to a 4-register organ. Crang of England and Johann Andreas Stein of Augsburg were among those to build them. After the piano had succeeded the harpsichord, builders continued combining the newer instr. with the organ, and when the reed organ had successfully displaced the chamber organ, the original pipes and plucked strings were replaced by reed and struck strings. See also: instromento pian e forte, organized clavichord, piano-harmonium, piano-organ (95, 154, Valdrighi: *Musurgiana*; E. van der Straeten: *La Musique aux Pays-Bas*, Vol. VII, 1885).

Claviphone, 1. a small harmonium patented in France by Le Toulat in 1847; **2.** a small harmonium invented by Dumont & Lelièvre of Paris and shown at the Paris Exposition of 1889. The bellows were actuated by depressing the keys (176, 204).

Clavis, Lat.: key (of keyboard instrs.).

Clavi-timbres, metallophone controlled by a keyboard and hammers, with cylindrical resonators for each tone, now produced by the Société Mustel (formed in 1922). An earlier patent was taken out in France by Chomel on Aug. 24, 1900 (144, 204).

Clavi-tromba, an improved trombone patented in 1855 by Gustave Auguste Besson of Paris (204).

Clavi-tube, a modified *keyed bugle invented by Halary (Jean Hilaire Asté) of Paris in 1817 and patented by him in 1821, with a notched tuning sliuc and 7 keys for putting it in A♭, F, E♭, D, C, B♭, A (25, 126, 132).

Clavitympanum, obs. term for xylophone.

Clear flute, organ stop of open wooden flue pipes at 4′ pitch, invented by Kirtland & Jardine of Manchester, England. The mouths are inverted and placed in the narrow side of the pipes (186).

Clef, Fr.: key (of a wind instr.); in 14th-c. Fr. also a tuning peg.

Clicket [Fr. *cliquet*], obs.: clappers.

Clie, see: glîe.

Cliquet, cliquette (Fr.) [*cliquer*, to make a noise], Fr. term for clapper, in use from the 14th c. It formerly designated the clappers by which lepers announced their presence. Trichet, *ca.* 1640, says that they consisted of 3 pieces of wood, a long one and 2 shorter ones either played like "bones" or attached at one end. Nowadays we understand a handle clapper by this term, with 2 shorter pieces of wood hinged to a longer, central one provided with a handle (96, 190, 204).

Cloc, Irish: bell.

Cloca, clocca, Lat.: bell. The word is first recorded *ca.* 690 and is now believed to be of Irish origin, distributed on the Continent by early missionaries. The Lat. form of the word gave rise in turn to *cloche, Glocke, klok,* etc., but remained unchanged in OProv. and Cat. (169).

Cloch, clych, Kym.: bell.

Cloche [Lat. **clocca*], Fr.: bell. The word is first recorded in the 11th c. and denotes in general a campaniform bell with clapper (197).

Cloche éolienne, Fr.: aeolian bell.

Clochette [dim. of **cloche*], Fr.: a small bell. The word is first recorded in the 12th c. (204).

Clochettes, Fr.: carillon (organ stop).

Cloche tubulaire, Fr.: tubular bell.

Clockspele, name of the keyboard carillon in the Low Countries *ca.* 1600 (169).

Clog, Irish: bell.

Clokarde [Lat. **clocca*], chime bells. The word came into use around 1400 (79).

Clopot, Rom.: bell (5).

Cloque [Lat. **clocca*], OFr.: bell; a bell that sounded the hours (82).

Cloquette [dim. of **cloque*], small cloque.

Clugge [Lat. **clocca*], OEngl.: bell.

Clutsam keyboard, an experimental keyboard invented by the Australian pianist George Clutsam, patented July 21, 1907, and first exhibited at Leipzig in 1909, with keys radiating in crescent form. See also: concave keyboard (89, 178).

Coach horn (Ger.: *Kutschhorn*), obs. Engl. horn consisting of a straight conical tube of copper with silver mountings, wide bore, ending in a funnel-shaped bell without flare, and played with a cup mouthpiece. Traditionally it was made of one piece, but in the later 19th c. a telescoping variety was introduced, made of 2 sections. The size should not exceed 36 in. (91 cm.), but it has been made 46 in. (117 cm.) long, as this length is easier to sound. It yields $c^1 g^1 c^2 e^2 g^2$. See also: post horn, tandem horn (150).

Cobo, syn. of guamo.

Coboro, barrel-shaped drum of Tigrai, Ethiopia, made from a hollowed log where timber is available. The heads are of different diam. and are laced. Smaller instrs. are sometimes made of empty cans. The coboro is played in horizontal position with bare hands, the larger head facing to the right (45).

Cobsa, see: cobza, kobza.

Cobuz, obs. form of cobza. *Cf.* kobus.

Cobza [Turk. **qūbūz*], lute of Romania, with mandolin-shaped body, very short neck, many small soundholes forming patterns on the belly, and 5–12 strings. A typical tuning is: $d^0 d^1/a^0 a^1/d^0 d^0/g^0 g^1 g^1$. The cobza is played with bare fingers or with a plectrum. In the older Rom. literature it is called cobuz, copus, capus, cabuz. The musical amateur Felix Platter of Basel (d. 1614) had one in his instr. collection. See also: kobza, koza (5, 205).

Cochlos, *marine-shell trumpet of ancient Greece, mentioned by Euripides and still in use as a signal instr. on the Gk. islands, where it is blown through a hole cut in the tip (199).

Cococello, chordophone consisting of a coconut body and membrane belly, with a long neck and single string, concocted by Professor Adalbert Niemeyer of Munich in the early 20th c. (176).

Cocoloctli, small beaked *whistle flute of ancient Mexico, made of bone or baked clay, usually with 4 fingerholes. Those of clay terminate in a false bell. *Cf.* cuiraxezaqua, tlapiztalli, zozoloctli (170).

Cocowa, "percussion bell" of the Baoule of the Ivory Coast Republic (103).

Codophone, a series of tubular bells played from a keyboard, invented *ca.* 1890 (169).

Coelestina, see: Cölestine.

Coelestinette, see: celestinette.

Coelophone, automatophone with perforated cardboard discs, invented by Claude Gavioli in the 19th c. (204).

Coelophone-orchestre, instr. of unknown construction exhibited in Paris in 1900 by J. Thibouville-Lamy (204).

Cog rattle (Fr.: *crécerelle;* Ger.: *Schnarre, Knarre*), *scraped idiophone consisting of a cogwheel with axle serving as handle and a tongue fixed to the frame. When it is whirled, the tongue strikes the cogs of the wheel one after the other. Cog rattles are found in Europe and in Asia. In Europe they served in monasteries of the Orthodox Church and in Catholic churches during Easter week, replacing the bells, and in some areas still fulfill that function. Formerly also in use by night watchmen. In Buonanni's day they were already reduced to the status of a toy (100, 169).

Cohuilotl, syn. of chilitli.

Colachon, Fr.: colascione.

Colascione (It.) [U.] (Fr.: *colachon*), European offshoot of the Eastern long-necked lute, played in Italy in the 16th and 17th c.; it penetrated to France and Germany in the early 18th c. The colascione has a small body and disproportionately long neck with up to 24 movable frets and 2–6 gut or metal strings. Mersenne relates that its belly was sometimes made half of wood and half of parchment, a typically Eastern arrangement. It took on the lateral tuning pegs and frontal string fastener of the European lute. Its normal complement of strings was 2 or 3, tuned to (E^0) A^0 d^0, according to Mersenne. Mattheson writes of its use as a *continuo* instr. in Germany. By the mid-18th c. it was becoming obs. outside Italy and today is played only in Sicily. *Ca.* 2 m. (6½ ft.) long. See also: calichon, chalcedon, cithara bichordos, colasciontino (136, 169, 170).

Colasciontino [dim. of **colascione*], a small colascione, formerly in use in Naples, *ca.* 96 cm. (38 in.) long. Also called mezzo colascione (176).

Cölestin, Ger.: celestina stop.

Cölestine, a combination organ and *glass harmonica with 3 manuals, invented by Zink of Hesse-Homburg. The upper manual acted on a glass harmonica, the second on the organ, and the lower on a secret device for imitating various instrs. Not to be confused with the celestina (176).

Colison, 1. *glass harmonica or glass chime invented by Martin Kratschvil in the early 19th c.; **2.** chordophone invented by Maslowski of Poznan in 1804, in form of an upright piano with a 4-oct. compass. Instead of keys it had a number of wooden bars that were stroked by the player's fingers, thereby setting the strings in vibration. Its inventor took it to Berlin in 1805, but it did not become popular (38, 176).

Collone, unidentified woodwind instr. of the late Renaissance, listed in several Ger. inventories of the period. In the 1570's we hear that it was made by turning, and there is mention of the cutting of mouthpieces. A consort listed in a Stuttgart inventory of 1589 seems to have been made by a reed-instr. maker (114).

Colo, var. spelling of koh'lo.

Colomaula, med. Lat. var. of calamella (61).

Colonna, It.: column (of a harp).

Colonne, Fr.: column (of a harp).

Column (Fr.: *colonne;* Ger.: *Baronstange;* It.: *colonna*), the upright post of a *frame harp, also called pillar or forepillar. In modern European pedal harps this is hollow to permit the pedal action to pass through it, and straight for the

same reason. See also: frame harp, harp.

Combination clarinet (Ger.: *Kombinationsklarinette*), clarinet that unites several pitches in the same body, made during the 19th and early 20th c. in an attempt to furnish the orchestral clarinetist with a single instr. (without *pièces de rechange). The first in a series of complicated models was that of Jacques-François Simiot of Lyon, *ca.* 1827. His was in B♭ with a separate upper joint in A and an extendable bell. In 1847 Frédéric Triébert of Paris patented his *clarinette multiphonique; in 1862 Auger Buffet *jeune* introduced a metal combination clarinet. His successors included Maino and Orsi with their *clarinetto a doppia tonalità of 1887. As late as 1901, Agostino Rampone introduced a short-lived *clarino transpositore (89 Rendall, 176).

Compensation mixture (Ger.: *Kompensationsmixtur*), late-19th-c. mixture organ stops designed to "compensate" the weakness of the treble in relation to the stronger (pedal) bass. The earliest such mixture was the "discant mixture," invented by Tauscher in 1778 but probably never built: starting on f^0, it was to increase on every note. Instead the *progressio harmonica was built (133).

Compensation valve (Fr.: *piston compensateur;* Ger.: *Kompensationsventil*), mechanism for automatically correcting the faulty intonation of valved wind instrs. Numerous devices were patented from 1850 on.

Componium, Engl., Fr.: Komponium.

Compton cube, an invention of organ builder John Compton, whereby 2 cubes built on the ocarina principle, furnished with several holes, can be made to sound all the tones of an octave and thus replace an octave's worth of organ pipes. *Cf.* bass ocarina.

Concave keyboard (Ger.: *Bogenklaviatur*), keyboard in crescent form, devised to permit the player to maintain the same hand position throughout the compass of the keyboard and first applied in 1824 by

Georg Staufer and Max Heidinger of Vienna. Various systems were subsequently patented, including the *Clutsam keyboard (89, 176).

Concert alto, see: concert horn, 2.

Concert flute (Ger.: *Konzertflöte*), **1.** the *cross flute in C; **2.** Engl. 18th-c. term for flute (*vs.* recorder); **3.** a modern organ stop of flue pipes at 8′ or 4′ pitch, originally but no longer identical with the Wienerflöte (198).

Concert horn, 1. in the U.S. another name of the mellophone; **2.** in Europe "concert horn" or "concert alto" is another term for Primhorn.

Concertina (Ger.: *Konzertina*), *free-reed instr. built on the principle of the accordion, invented by Charles Wheatstone of London and patented by him on June 19, 1829. Two hexagonal heads, each furnished with a keyboard and a handle, are connected by expandable bellows. The treble concertina has 2 reeds per tone, operating both on pressure and on vacuum, and a 4-oct. compass, g^0–g^4. Larger models have likewise a 4-oct. compass but only one reed per tone, working on pressure. The concertina is also falsely designated as melophone. See also: aeola, bandoneon. *Cf.* accordion (89, 176).

Conch-shell trumpet, see: marine-shell trumpet.

Concordia, a variety of the physharmonica, invented in England by 1834 (204).

Concussion idiophone (Fr.: *idiophone par entrechoc;* Ger.: *Gegenschlagidiophon*), 2 or more sonorous, complementary objects are struck together, such as sticks, clappers, castanets, cymbals (100).

Concussion sticks (Fr.: *baguettes entrechoquées;* Ger.: *Gegenschlagstäbe*), a form of *concussion idiophone distributed in ancient Egypt, modern Africa, Asia, America, S. Seas (168).

Concussion vessels (Ger.: *Gegenschlaggefässe*), a form of *concussion idiophone composed of hollow objects, such as castanets (100).

Condi, arched harp of the Abandya of the Congo (19).

Cone flute, conical *end-blown flute.

Cone gamba, Engl. organ stop similar to the Spitzflöte, of inverted conical open flue pipes. Not identical with the *bell gamba (198).

Cone gedackt, organ stop invented by Robert Hope-Jones (d. 1914), made of stopped pipes at 8′ pitch with solid stoppers into which inverted cones are fitted from g^1 up (198).

Cong, see: cai cong.

Conga, Afro-Cuban drum (the word also means dance, song, etc.) played in conga music. All varieties are elongated but assume a number of different shapes. A common feature was the single nailed head, but 2-headed congas have now been created. *Cf.* congo, konga (152).

Congo, generic name for Afro-Cuban drums that originated in the Congo. Some are also called *ngoma or engombo in Cuba. Barrel-shaped and cylindrical versions with single heads, made of a number of narrow strips of wood, are now pop. in Western rhythm bands. They are set upright (89, 152).

Congoerá, a notched scraper of the Guaraní Indians of S. America (152).

Conguinho, a small tin rattle of Brazil, used by dancers of the *moçambique* in Santa Isabel (São Paulo) (7).

Conical drum (Fr.: *tambour en cône;* Ger.: *Kegeltrommel, Konustrommel*), drum with considerably different terminal diameters (100).

Conoclyte, organ stop of early-19th-c. invention, of free reeds with *gemshorn-shaped bodies (198).

Conque-trompette, Fr.: marine-shell trumpet.

Console (Fr.: *console;* Ger.: *Spieltisch*), **1.** that portion of an organ which contains the keyboards and stop handles and at which the organist sits; **2.** Fr.: the neck of a harp.

Consonnante (Fr.), according to Furetière (in 1690), a harpsichord-harp combination invented by Abbé Du Mont, having the body of a large harpsichord, placed upright on a pedestal, with strings on both sides of the soundboard, played harp-fashion. Presumably a large arpanetta (78).

Consort viol, a large bass viola da gamba, used in 17th-c. England for consort playing, with strings having a speaking length of *ca.* 71 cm. (28 in.). See also: division viol (94).

Contra, 1. as a prefix to names of instrs., contra denotes that they are at 16′ pitch; **2.** abbr. for contrabassoon; **3.** the lowest rows of pipes in an organ, collectively; **4.** as a prefix to names of organ stops, contra denotes a stop one oct. lower than that named (133).

Contrabaixo, Port.: double bass.

Contrabass (Ger.; also: *Kontrabass*), organ stop made: **1.** as a low-pitched (16′) Prinzipal; **2.** as a Gedackt. Adlung says that it was a 32′ Gedackt and as such identical with the *subbass, 2, stop; **3.** as a wide-scaled stop of open cylindrical flue pipes with string tone; **4.** syn. of double bass (3, 133).

Contrabass clarinet (Fr.: *clarinette contrebasse;* Ger.: *Kontrabassklarinette;* It.: *contraclarone, clarinetto contrabasso*), clarinet at 16′ pitch, either in C or in B♭, 2 octs. below the ordinary clarinet. Attempts to create such an instr. date from the early 19th c., but were not successful until Fontaine Besson of Paris produced their model *ca.* 1890 (patented 1891). Since then various other satisfactory models have been made, either of wood or of metal, usually with conical bore, 3 U-bends, and terminating in an upturned bell. Smaller instrs., pitched in F or E♭, were made by Adolphe Sax, Streitwolf, and others. Selmer of Paris has recently brought out a wooden model in E♭; Fr. models at this tonal position are called clarinette contralto, Ger. ones, Kontrabassethorn. Contrabasses were generally made of metal, Fr. ones being fitted with the Boehm mechanism. Most of the manufacture took place in the early 19th c. in response to the need for new mili-

tary contrabass instrs. The compass of the B♭ or C instr. is A¹/B♭¹–f¹. Total length 2.70 m. (*ca.* 9 ft.). See also: bathyphone, clarinette-bourdon, clarinette-pédale, contrabasset horn, contrebasse guerrière (89 Rendall, 164, 170).

Contrabasset horn (Ger.: *Kontrabassethorn*), *contrabass clarinet in F, pitched an oct. below the *basset horn, first made by Johann Heinrich Gottlieb Streitwolf of Göttingen in 1829. His model was shaped like a bassoon and fitted with 19 keys, including 4 "basset" keys. Its lowest tone was F¹, notated C⁰. Various models in F and E♭ appeared subsequently. *Cf.* clarinette contralto (89 Rendall, 176).

Contrabasso, 1. It.: double bass; **2.** for the organ stop see: violon, 4.

Contrabasso da ancia, It.: contrabass *sarrusophone.

Contrabasso da gamba, see: violone.

Contrabassoon (Fr.: *contre-basson;* Ger.: *Kontrafagott;* It.: *contrafagotto, fagottone*), bassoon pitched an oct. below the ordinary bassoon, nowadays usually made of metal; it took its present form in the 19th c. The bore is slightly conical and the tube bent back on itself several times in order to reduce the over-all length and bring the keys within convenient playing position. The air column of a modern instr. is about 4.80 m. (16 ft.) long, and its chromatic compass is from C¹ (sometimes A2) to f⁰ or even c¹, notated an oct. higher. The contrabassoon descending to C¹ is provided with a wooden bell rim; an inverted metal rim can be slipped over this to take the compass down to B♭² and an even larger one will give A². All fingerholes are covered with keys so as to bring them within reach of the fingers. The presence of 2 oct.-keys causes a playing technique slightly different from that of the bassoon. Lower-than-ordinary bassoons have existed ever since the late 16th c. Zacconi (in 1592) is the first to mention them. He is followed by Praetorius, who describes bassoons that are pitched a 4th and a 5th below the ordinary ones and

that he calls *Doppelfagott; he also relates that Hans Schreiber was constructing one with C^1 as its lowest tone—the
earliest mention of a true contrabassoon.
In 1626 one is mentioned in an inventory
of the Barfüsser Church of Frankfurt am
Main, possibly that of Schreiber. Despite
the great difficulties in making such large
instrs. without recourse to modern tools
and keywork, efforts continued: Talbot,
ca. 1700, mentions a pedal or double bassoon in "FFF." During the 18th c. large
bassoons are called for in orchestral
scores, i.a., by Bach and Handel. By 1807
the Vienna court orchestra had a contra-
bassoonist on its payroll. The need for a
contrabass instr. in military bands of the
early 19th c. forced makers to take up
old experiments, and a number of new
instrs. resulted. Advent of the saxhorn
spelled their doom, and they continued a
restricted life in the orchestra. In 1855,
Johann Stehle of Vienna produced bass
contrabassoons 1.65 m. (5½ ft.) high
with 15 covered holes and a 2-oct. compass. Other models were made with up to
20 keys. By 1880 J. A. Heckel had
brought out a contra in modern form,
and in 1898 he extended its compass to
A^2. Manufacture in France did not start
until the second half of the 19th c., and
makers there still prefer wood as the material. See also: basson grosso, bassono,
bassono grosso, Claviatur-Contrafagott,
contrabassophone, contrebasse à anche,
Doppelfagott, Fagotcontra, fagotto dop-
pïo, Mullerphone, Tritonikon (89 Langwill, 151).

Contrabassophone (Ger.: *Kontrabas-
sophon*), a form of contrabassoon invented by Heinrich J. Haseneier of Co-
blenz in 1849, with very wide conical
bore, made of wood, 1.42 m. (4 ft. 8 in.)
high. The tube, some 5 m. (16 ft.) in
length, was bent back on itself 4 times
and terminated in a crook carrying a
large double reed. Pitched an oct. below
the bassoon, it had an extreme compass
of 3 octs., C^1–c^1 (89 Rendall, 126,
176).

Contrabass trombone, made sporadically ever since the early 17th c. Praetorius writes of one made by Hans
Schreiber "four years ago," pitched an
oct. below the tenor, in B♭, with E♭^{1} as
its lowest tone. The 19th c. in particular
showed a renewed interest in these low-
pitched trombones. In 1816 Gottfried
Weber proposed a double slide, which
was adopted. Halary (Jean Hilaire Asté)
of Paris made one in F, ca., 1830 with
double slide; Moritz of Berlin made one
for Wagner in the 1860's in B♭, the commonest size. The double slide was moved
by a single stay and reduced the shift to
half the movement otherwise necessary
(89 Baines, 170).

Contra-clarinette, an 18th-c. Fr. name
of the *basset horn (89 Rendall).

Contraclarone, It.: contrabass clarinet.

Contrafagott, obs. spelling of Kontrafagott.

Contrafagotto, 1. It.: contrabassoon;
2. *fagotto organ stop at 16′ pitch.

Contrahorn (Ger.: *Kontrahorn*), alto
*saxhorn built by J. and A. Lamferhoff
of Essen in 1845 (126, 158).

Contralto, a large viola designed by
Jean-Baptiste Vuillaume of Paris ca.
1855, with high ribs and lower bouts considerably wider than usual. It measured
67½ cm. (26¼ in.) and had the compass
of the ordinary viola (Chouquet).

Contralto bugle, 1. in the U.S. an althorn or alto saxhorn; **2.** in England the
soprano saxhorn in E♭ (89).

Contra-serpent, or contrabass serpent;
see: serpent.

Contraviola Paganini, an oversized viola "invented" by Nicolò Paganini in
1834, allegedly to imitate the human
voice (191, 204).

Contra-violin, an oversized violin of
Herbert Newbold of Jersey, Channel Islands, 1917, intended for the playing of
second-violin parts in chamber music, according to Percy Scholes (*Oxford Companion to Music*).

Contraviolon, 1. obs. Ger. term for the
double bass; **2.** a large violone, also

called *grosse Bassgeige, Bassviolon*, in the 18th c. In the Fr. translation of Quantz it is called *grande basse de violon*, the tuning being given as $E^1 A^1 D^0 G^0$, that of our double bass. Eisel in 1738 describes it as a double bass with 4 strings, sometimes tuned an oct. below the violoncello, *i.e.*, $C^1 G^1 D^0 A^0$, sometimes in 4ths, and says that the Italians call it *violone grosso* (67, Koch: *Lexikon*, 1802).

Contrebasse, Fr.: double bass.

Contrebasse à anche (Fr.) (It.: *controbasso ad ancia*), Tritonikon built by Charles Mahillon of Brussels in 1868, almost identical to that of Vaclav F. Červeny except that its lowest tone was D^1, whereas Červeny's went down to Bb^2. Since then it has been built by other makers intent on providing a satisfactory metal contrabassoon for military bands. It continued to be made in tuba form with 17 keys, of which 2 were oct. keys —all closed except for the first. The tone holes were so large they required no further venting, and thus only one key needed opening for any given note, resulting in a piano-like fingering. See also: Klaviaturkontrafagott (89 Langwill, 176).

Contrebasse à clavier, 3-stringed *double bass, with a detachable piano keyboard of 35–38 keys, invented by L. Duvivier of Nevers and patented by him on Nov. 10, 1892. Earlier patents had already been granted for applying keyboards to stringed instrs., however (176).

Contrebasse à pistons, Fr.: bass tuba; bass or contrabass saxhorn.

Contrebasse de hautbois, bass oboe made in France from the 18th c. on, pitched in F, an oct. below the *taille des hautbois. The *Almanach musical* of 1781 mentions one, built by Lice, that was played for 6 months at the Paris Opéra and cost 100 livres (176, 204).

Contrebasse d'harmonie, generic Fr. term denoting wind instrs. of contrabass register.

Contrebasse guerrière, *contrabass clarinet built by Dumas of Paris in 1808,

pitched 2 octs. below the ordinary clarinet and having a larger number of keys. See also: basse-guerrière.

Contre-basson, Fr.: contrabassoon.

Contre-clairon, bass bugle invented by Hostié of Paris in 1791 (176, 204).

Contre-éclisse, Fr.: lining.

Contreviolon, Fr.: syn. of grosse basse de violon.

Controbasso ad ancia, It.: contrebasse à anche.

Controfascia, It.: lining.

Controviolino, tenor violin made by Valentino de Zorzi of Florence in 1908, tuned $G^0 d^0 a^0 e^1$, an oct. below the violin (26).

Copendoff [*Coppel + *doeff], another name of the Rauschpfeife organ stop (133).

Coperto, It.: stopped.

Copólogo, Sp.: *musical glasses.

Copophone, according to Stainer & Barrett's dictionary of 1888, a name under which *musical glasses were revived (113).

Coppel, Coppelflöte (Ger.), originally an organ stop of open principal pipes, but the earlier sense was lost and Coppel came to mean *Gedackt*. More recently it has been built as a half-stopped register of conical pipes at 16′, 8′, or 4′ pitch. Coppel also stood formerly for a 2- or 3-rank mixture. Also called Copula, Coppelprinzipal (131, 133).

Copula, see: Coppel.

Cor [Lat. *cornu], **1.** Fr.: horn. The term has been in continuous use since the early 12th c. OFr. vars. are *corn, corne* (204); **2.** flute of Mongolia that corresponds to the Chin. hsiao (1).

Cora, musical bow of Argentina. *Cf.* gora (152).

Cor a clefs, Fr.: keyed bugle.

Coradoiz (OFr.) or **cor à doigts,** fingerhole horn, a precursor of the cornett. The term occurs from the 13th c. to the 15th (*"Ces cors c'on sonne as dois"* are mentioned in the 13th-c. *Sone de Nausay*) (35).

Cor à l'anglaise, name given in France

to horns furnished with a tuning slide in addition to crooks, in the late 18th c. and early 19th. Thus Laborde in 1780 defines it as a *cor de chasse* with *coulisses* (slides). Not to be confused with the cor anglais (89 Morley-Pegge, 124).

Cor allemand (Fr.: German horn), obs. Fr.: French horn.

Cor alto, a valved brass instr. built by Couesnon et Cie. of Paris in the 1890's to the specifications of Ligner: a cross between a French horn and an alto cornet, in F or E♭, pitched an oct. higher than the French horn, with half its tube length. In appearance it was similar to the French horn, but had 3 or 4 valves worked by the right hand. It is still made for school and amateur bands and is known in England as the tenor cor. Its bore is conical throughout (89 Baines).

Cor à main, Fr.: hand horn.

Cor anglais [U., not *cor anglé*] (Fr.) (Ger.: *englisches Horn;* It.: *corno inglese*), **1.** neither a horn nor English, but an oboe pitched in F, a 5th below the ordinary oboe. Nowadays built in straight form, terminating with a bulb bell having a relatively small opening, and with keywork and fingering system of the oboe. The double reed is carried on a bent metal crook. Around 1760 the term *corno inglese* started appearing in Viennese scores; the term has been matched with preserved late-18th-c. instrs., mostly of Viennese or It. make, similar in appearance to what we believe to be specimens of the *oboe da caccia, but with narrower bore and different bells. These putative *corni inglesi* are of wood, with slightly conical bore, either curved to a near semicircle or angled; both forms are covered with leather. Halle, writing in 1764, describes *"englische Waldhörner"* of wood, which were bent into a curve. The relationship of these instrs. to the *corno da caccia, if any, is still not clarified. The latter may well be the immediate ancestor of the cor anglais. The present-day straight form (*cor anglais moderne) was created by the Fr. maker Henri Brod

in 1839; he simply called it an *hautbois alto.* It did not immediately displace the older forms, but coexisted with them—at least in Italy—for about half a c. Compass from e⁰ (e♭⁰) to a² (b♭²); *ca.* 1 m. (40 in.) long; treated as a transposing instr. and notated a 5th higher than it sounds. Formerly also called quinte de hautbois. See also: cor de chasse anglais (14, 90, 151);

2. organ stop of reed pipes, similar to a wide-scaled shawm, with free reeds and inverted conical resonators surmounted by a double bell, at 8' and 4' pitches (133, 198).

Cor anglais moderne (Fr.), see: cor anglais, 1.

Cor à pistons, Fr.: valve horn.

Cor basse, Fr.: bass horn (204).

Cor-basse ténor, Fr.: baritone, 1.

Cor bouquin, var. of cornet à bouquin.

Cor bugler [OFr. *busgle,* from Lat. *buculus*], med. Fr. bugle. The word occurs from the early 12th c. on. *Cf.* bugle horn, bugleral.

Cor bugleret, dim. of cor bugler.

Cor chromatique, Fr.: chromatic horn; valve horn.

Cor crochu (Fr.: hooked horn), OFr. designation of the (newly) S-shaped trumpet; recorded *ca.* 1300 as *cor croçu* (79).

Corda, It., Port.: string.

Cor d'araine, see: arain(e), 1.

Corde, Fr.: string.

Cor de basset, Fr.: basset horn.

Cor de chamois, Fr.: gemshorn.

Cor de chasse, Fr.: hunting horn.

Cor de chasse anglais, early (1782) expression for the *cor anglais in France (79).

Cor de Kent, Fr.: Kent horn.

Cor de nuit, see: Nachthorn.

Cor de pin (Fr.: pine horn), wooden signal horn of med. France, first recorded in the mid-12th c. (35).

Cor des Alpes, Fr.: alphorn.

Cor d'harmonie, 1. Fr.: French horn; **2.** organ stop invented by the Fr. builder Charles Martin (133).

Cordier, Fr.: tailpiece.

Cordiera, It.: tailpiece.

Cor d'invention, Fr.: Inventionshorn.

Cor d'olifant, see: olifant; oliphant.

Cordone, obs. It.: syn. of bordone.

Cor euphonique, Fr.: euphonic serpentcleide.

Corista, It.: tuning fork; pitch pipe. *Cf.* choriste.

Cormorne, corr. of cromorne. See also: Krummhorn, 2.

Corn [Lat. *cornu*], OFr., Prov., Rätoromansch, Rom., Welsh: horn.

Cornaboux [OFr. *corn*, horn + *bouc*, he-goat], Fr. var. of cornet à bouquin. The term was used by Rabelais and was translated by Cotgrave (in 1611) as "cornett."

Cornadouelle, rustic horn of Fr. shepherds, made of spirally rolled bark in the springtime only. *Cf.* corniard (204).

Cornaldo, see: kort Instrument.

Cornamuda, OSp.: crumhorn.

Cornamuda tuerta, Sp.: crumhorn (Pietro Cerone's translation of Zacconi's *"cornamuto torto"*).

Cornamusa (It., med. Lat.), **1.** mouth-blown bagpipe of the Abruzzi, Italy, with double chanter having conical bores and fitted with double reeds, and 2 drones with cylindrical bore, also fitted with double reeds; **2.** obs. bagpipe of Catalonia; **3.** elusive family of Renaissance reed-cap instrs., described but not depicted by Praetorius, and mentioned in It. accounts of musical performances in the second half of the 16th c. Praetorius describes them as being straight, stopped, with several vents, and made in 5 sizes: soprano b^0–c^2, alto d^0–e^1, tenor c^0–d^1 and $B\flat^0$–c^1, bass F^0–g^0. Whether his *"Cornamusen"* are identical with the *"cornamusa"* of the It. writers is a moot point. Massimo Trojano lists them together with dolzainas, which they must have resembled closely (13, 14, 159, 176).

Cornamusina (It.), syn. of ciaramella.

Cornamuto torto, obs. It.: crumhorn. Zacconi used the term in 1592.

Corne, OFr. var. of cor.

Cornemuse (Fr.) [med. Lat. *cornamusa*], **1.** generic Fr. term for bagpipe, depicted in France from the 13th c. on, but it does not appear in Fr. literature before the 14th c. The word was also taken over into MEngl., first used by Chaucer. In France the bagpipe occurs in both mouth-blown and bellows-blown form. Characteristic of both is a flat, rectangular chanter stock bored with 2 channels, for the chanter and for a small drone to its left. The chanter has a conical bore, 7 front fingerholes, and a rear thumbhole, fitted with a double reed; the drone has a single reed and cylindrical bore. A longer, bass drone is attached to a separate stock, pitched an oct. below the chanter keynote. This type is found in the Berry and Nivernais, and up to a c. ago was also found in Normandy. In the Auvergne, where it is also called *cabrette*, from the material of which the bag is made, it is bellows-blown and lacks a bass drone. A third type exists in the Landes; here chanter and drone are bored in parallel channels out of a single piece of wood— in appearance a double chanter. The right (chanter) pipe has 6 front fingerholes and a rear thumbhole; the left (drone) pipe has no holes. Both pipes measure *ca.* 19 cm. (7½ in.) and are fitted with single reeds. The Landes bagpipe is mouth-blown. In the Cantal region the bagpipe is played together with the hurdy-gurdy for the *bourrée*. See also: boudego, sacomuse (13, 35, 180, 190);

2. *musette chanter separated from its musette, also called chalemie.

Cornemuse de Poitou (Fr.), bagpipe that Mersenne described as differing from the ordinary bagpipe (cornemuse) only in that it had 1 drone instead of 2. Its chanter was at unison with the *hautbois de Poitou, with which it was played in duet (114, 140).

Cornet (Fr.: *cornet, cornet à pistons, piston;* Ger.: *Kornett, Ventilkornett;* It.: *cornetta, pistone;* Sp.: *cornetín*), **1.** valved brass instr. of medium conical bore, played with a cup mouthpiece, usually built in trumpet form, formerly also in helicon form. The cornet is a descendant of the old coiled *post horn; at the beginning of the 19th c. this was provided with crooks and a tuning slide, and around 1825 it was fitted with 2 valves by Halary (Jean Hilaire Asté) of Paris. The old instr. with crooks was thereupon called *cornet ordinaire* or *cornet simple*, to distinguish it from the valved cornet called *cornet d'harmonie*, later *cornet à pistons*. In England the early valved instr. was known as *cornopean*. The new valved instr. was prompt of speech and quickly became pop., chiefly in wind and military bands, but also in the orchestra (Rossini: *Guillaume Tell*, 1829). In appearance it became increasingly like a wide, stumpy trumpet, as builders modified their patterns, making the bore partly cylindrical and widening it in order to improve the tone quality, which remained a subject of criticism for years to come. The cornet was made primarily as a soprano in B♭ or A—in England in C—and as an alto in E♭; for military bands there was also a sopranino in E♭ and an oct. cornet in A, in high C, and in B♭, the last-mentioned first made by Vaclav Červeny of Königgrätz (Hradec Králové) in 1862. The compass of the B♭ soprano is e^0–b♭^{2}, notated a second higher. The true cornet has been built down to tenor range, and includes the *althorn and the *tenor horn. For larger instrs. bearing the name of cornet see: Cornet-Instrumente. The alto was made from *ca.* 1830 on and introduced by Wieprecht into the Prussian army bands in 1833; it was made both in trumpet and tuba shape and has merged its identity with that of the althorn. In 1829 Étienne-François Périnet added the third valve. The true cornet was not built in tonal positions lower than tenor because the bore would have been too narrow for the pitch required. The It. althorn and tenor horn are still built with a true cornet bore. See also: cavalry cornet, Cornet-Instrumente, echo cornet;

2. OFr.: syn. of *cor*, a horn; in the sense of a rustic horn, used from the 13th c. to the 16th; **3.** Fr.: *post horn; **4.** mixture organ stop, often of 5 ranks, composed of the fundamental and first 4 harmonics, known by the early 16th c. presumably the first cornets lacked the tierce, which was to become their characteristic feature. The classical cornet was developed in France, sometimes with a doubling of the fundamental and first harmonic. In the late 17th c. and in the 18th c. virtually every organ in France had a cornet in the pedal. See also: mounted cornet (63, 133, 156).

Corneta, Sp.: cornett.

Cornet à bouquin [Fr. *bouc*, he-goat], Fr.: cornett. The term does not occur before the 16th c. (35).

Cornet à cylindres, Fr.: cornet (with rotary valves).

Corneta muta, Sp.: mute cornett.

Cornet à pistons (Fr.), **1.** cornet (with piston valves); **2.** organ stop of reed pipes at 8′ pitch, of the horn class (131).

Corneta tuerta, Sp.: curved cornett.

Cornetbass, organ stop of reed pipes at 8′ pitch, also at 4′, 2′, or 1′ (2).

Cornet-coulisse (Fr.: cornet slide), cornet provided with a slide, patented by Courtois of Paris on Aug. 20, 1838 (204).

Cornet courbe, Fr.: curved cornet.

Cornet-Cousin, cornet of Jean-Léon Cousin of Lyon, patented on Dec. 17, 1873, with 5 descending valves for lowering the pitch by 1, ½, 1½, 2½, and 2 tones (126, 176).

Cornet d'écho (Fr.) (Ger.: *Echokornett;* It.: *cornetto in ecco*), organ stop first mentioned in Como in 1650 and later known to Dom Bedos as a solo register. Its echo character was obtained by placing the pipes in a closed box. Gottfried Silbermann introduced it to Germany, but it was rarely built there. The pipes are similar to those of the cornet de récit, but sometimes of narrower scale (20, 133).

Cornet de poste, Fr.: post horn.

Cornet de récit (Fr.), solo *cornet organ stop found in Fr. organs (133).

Cornet de Rette, cornet patented in 1856 by Pierre-Jean Derette, a Belgian army bandmaster, and made by Courtois & Derette of Paris. In addition to the usual 3 valves it had a fourth, which lowered the pitch by 2 tones, and a fifth, which lowered it by the interval of a 4th (126, 176).

Cornet d'harmonie (Fr.), the oldest Fr. name of the valved cornet, corresponding to the Engl. cornopean (176).

Cornet droit, Fr.: straight cornett.

Cornetín, Sp.: cornet.

Cornet-Instrumente, a group of valved brass instrs. patented by Vaclav Červeny of Königgrätz (Hradec Králové) in 1876, built in circular form and ranging from sopranino in Eb to contrabass in Bb[1]. They were narrow-bore bugles played with a cup mouthpiece and are not identical with the cornet. They were adopted by Austrian and Ger. military bands. See also: Basstrompete (25, 176).

Cornet omnitonique (Fr.), **1.** *duplex cornet-bugle invented in 1855 by J. Chrétien Roth of Strasbourg, with changes in tube length effected by a spring; **2.** cornet with Chaussier's transposition mechanism (developed in 1889), permitting it to be played in any key (176, 204).

Cornet ordinaire (Fr.), name given in France to the *post horn with crooks and tuning slide after the invention of the *cornet à pistons, to differentiate it from the latter. The cornet ordinaire was built in C and had Bb and Ab crooks. It was also called cornet simple (89 Baines).

Cornet sarrazinois, the same as cor sarrazinois.

Cornett [OFr. *cornette,* dim. of Lat. *cornu,* horn] (Fr.: *cornet à bouquin;* Ger.: *Zink;* It.: *cornetto;* Sp.: *corneta*), obs. wind instr. derived from an animal horn, pierced with fingerholes and played with a cup mouthpiece. Its correct Engl. name, "cornet" (first mentioned *ca.* 1400 in the *Morte d'Arthure*), having been bestowed on a modern brass instr., the word is nowadays customarily written "cornett." Two kinds of cornetts existed:

straight and curved, and the *straight cornetts were subdivided into those played, like the *curved cornett, with a detachable mouthpiece, and those rarer ones known as *mute cornetts, with mouthpiece turned inside the top of the instr. The curved variety, being covered with black leather, was also known in continental Europe as "black cornett," the straight variety in contradistinction as "white cornett" from the light color of the boxwood of which it was made. To quote Praetorius, all these cornetts yielded 15 tones naturally, a^0–a^2, and some players even reached e^3 and occasionally g^3; in the low range g^0 and f^0 could be obtained by falset tones, *i.e.,* by slackening the lips.

The ancestor of the curved cornett appears in med. miniatures from the 10th c. on as a horn pierced with a few fingerholes, very similar to an instr. still made by shepherds in Europe (see: horn). By the 12th c. it had already acquired its characteristic octagonal exterior. From the 13th c. to the 15th, the *coradoiz is recorded, a Fr. fingerhole horn. In common with the straight cornett, the curved version ultimately had 6 front fingerholes and usually a rear thumbhole; its cup mouthpiece was of ivory, bone, horn, metal, or even wood. The curved model was made from a log of wood split lengthwise; a conical bore was then hollowed out of the sections, which were then glued back together and bound tightly in black leather. The straight cornetts were turned and bored on a lathe. The ordinary cornett had the same compass as the violin of its day, g^0–a^2 or higher; other sizes included the *cornettino, a smaller version, the *cornone, a larger one; in the 16th and 17th c. these were pitched, respectively, a 5th above and a 5th below the ordinary cornett. In addition, cornetts pitched a tone or so below the type instr. were made (*hautecontre de cornet à bouquin; Altzink*), and 2 *contrebasses de cornet à bouquin* survive, one with octagonal exterior and

4 extension keys, preserved in the Paris Conservatoire museum, another, in Hamburg, with 2 keys. The heyday of the cornett was the c. from 1550 to 1650. Jacques Cellier enumerated 5 sizes in 1585: *dessus, hautecontre, taille, sacqueboute, pédale*. Trichet, *ca.* 1640, writes of the cornett as being much in vogue "now" in both church and secular music; that the ordinary ones were curved but that sometimes another sort was made, which was straight and of a single piece of wood, and that the cornett was used more in vocal than other music because its range enabled it to soar higher than voices, "*paroissant comme une lumière brillante . . .*" (appearing as a brilliant light). Whoever has heard a cornett in concerted music will surely agree with him. Although the provision of fingerholes in a lip-vibrated instr. greatly taxed the player's ability, the cornett proved most pop. from the late 15th c. on, when it assumed its final form, since it was capable of being played very softly and, as Baines has put it, could play a scale beginning on any note as *ut*–a very great advantage before the days of equal temperament. Also it was an excellent substitute for the forbidden trumpet, forbidden by the guild rules, that is, as well as for the unsatisfactory soprano trombone. It replaced these 2 in tower music and town bands, and it is in these capacities that it lingered on in Germany through the 18th c. and in a few cases even well into the 19th. Bach and Gluck are the most prominent late writers for the instr., Bach having scored for it in 11 of his cantatas. Gluck scored for "*trombone soprano o cornetto*" in his *Orfeo ed Euridice*, thereby leading Berlioz to believe that the soprano trombone had formerly been called cornetto. The Ger. word *Zink*, employed without qualification in the 18th and 19th c., always refers to the curved cornett. It is probable that the straight versions did not outlive the 17th c. See also: fingerhole horn, Quartzink (14, 70, 169, 170, 180, 190).

Cornetta, It.: cornet in B♭ and A.
Cornetta a chiavi, It.: keyed bugle.
Cornetta da postiglione, It.: post horn.
Cornettin [dim. of *cornet], mixture organ stop of 5 ranks, with pure 3rd and 7th, *e.g.*: $g^1 b^1 c^2 e^2 g^2$ (131).
Cornettino (It.), **1.** small cornett of the 16th c. to the 18th. In the 16th and 17th c. it was pitched a 5th higher than the ordinary cornett, with a compass e^1-e^3; in the 18th c. only a 4th higher, from d^1-d^3, the same as that of the 18th-c. flute. This lower version was equivalent to the Ger. Quartzink. The oldest surviving cornettino so far known is dated 1518. Trichet, *ca.* 1640, gives its length as 1½ ft. (89 Baines, 169, 190); **2.** Zink organ stop at 2′ pitch; also a 2- or 3-rank mixture. Also called Klein Cornett (131).
Cornetto, It.: cornett.
Cornetto curvo, It.: curved cornett.
Cornetto dritto, It.: straight cornett.
Cornetto in ecco, see: cornet d'écho.
Cornetto muto, It.: mute cornett.
Cornetto torto, syn. of corno torto.
Corniard, "*corniarz*" occurs once in 12th-c. Fr. literature. Today in Montbéliard patois it denotes a shepherd's trumpet of bark. *Cf.* cornadouelle (35).
Cornichet [dim. of *cor], OFr.: small hunting horn. The term is recorded from *ca.* 1360 to 1603 (197).
Cornicyll, another name of the pibcorn (79).
Corno [Lat. *cornu], **1.** It.: horn; **2.** organ stop, see: horn.
Corno a macchina, It.: valve horn.
Corno bassetto, It.: basset horn.
Corno basso, It.: bass-horn.
Corno cromatico, 1. It.: chromatic horn; **2.** horn in F of J. Keil of Prague, with 2 valves, having a (notated) compass c^0-c^3 (176).
Corno da caccia, It.: hunting horn.
Corno da tirarsi, Bach calls for a "*tromba o corno da tirarsi*" in his Cantata No. 46, and elsewhere for "*corno da tirarsi.*" A mystery so far. Sachs has suggested that the tromba and corno in

question may be the same instr., so named to avoid the necessity of dealing with the trumpeters' guild (170).

Corno delli Alpi, It.: alphorn.

Corno di bassetto, 1. pop. name of the *corno bassetto; **2.** organ stop of open flue pipes of inverted conical form, but see also: basset horn, 2 (133).

Corno dolce, organ stop of open conical flue pipes of the dulzian type, at 16' or 8' pitch; also a stop of reed pipes of the horn class (133).

Corno flute, 1. organ stop invented by Herbert Norman of Norwich, of open metal flue pipes with inverted languids; **2.** organ stop of reed pipes with wooden resonators, at 8' pitch, invented by William Hill (99, 133, 186).

Corno inglese, It.: cor anglais.

Cornon (Ger.: *Kornon*), **1.** wide-bore Fr. horn, invented by Vaclav F. Červeny of Königgrätz (Hradec Králové) in 1846, played with a funnel-shaped mouthpiece and intended for use in military bands. In 1846 he brought out a bass in F; in 1872 he produced a whole family of cornons: Eb alto, Bb tenor, Eb bass, and Bb contrabass, built in forms of tuba, helicon, ellipse and semiellipse; **2.** instr. developed by Fontaine Besson of Paris in 1880, patented in 1890 under the name of cornophone.

Cornone (It.) (Fr.: *basse de cornet à bouquin;* Ger.: *Basszink, grosser Quartzink, Grosszink*), a large *curved cornett in shape of an obtuse S, pitched in d⁰, a 5th below the ordinary cornett, usually supplied with a key for the little finger which yielded c⁰ when closed, with a compass of c⁰–d². Its main period of activity was from 1550 to 1650, but in Germany it lingered on until the 18th c., when its pitch was only a 4th below the type instr. (*cf.* cornettino). Majer in 1732 could still write that it was held at one or the other side of the player's mouth, depending upon the condition of his teeth, but that it could also be held straight, placed in the middle. (The iconography from the 16th c. on shows

cornetts being played out of a corner of the player's mouth.) The cornone is called tenor cornett in England. It was 95–105 cm. (37–41 in.) long (89 Baines, 134, 170).

Corno par force, term once used by J. S. Bach for the Parforcehorn (144).

Cornopean [Lat. *cornu,* horn + Engl. pean, song of praise], **1.** name by which the early 2-valved, narrow-bore cornet was known in England up to the middle of the 19th c. The term corresponds to the Fr. *cornet d'harmonie.* At that time it was made in a range of soprano in C to tenor in C; **2.** organ stop of reed pipes invented by William Hill, with slightly conical resonators, at 8' pitch (131, 186).

Cornophone, family of valved brass instrs. developed by Fontaine Besson of Paris under the name of *cornons,* but patented by him in 1890 as cornophones. They were characterized by a wide conical bore, a flared bell tilted back, tubing coiled in a rectangle, and were played with a funnel-shaped mouthpiece. Members of this short-lived family were: soprano in Bb, compass e⁰–bb²; alto in F and Eb, compass A⁰/B⁰–eb²/f²; tenor in C or Bb, compass E⁰/F♯⁰–bb¹/c²; bass in C or Bb, compass Eb⁰/F⁰–bb¹/c²; contrabass in F or Eb, compass A¹/B¹–eb¹/f¹. All were notated from f♯⁰ to c³ (176).

Corno storto (It.: bent horn), It.: crumhorn.

Corno torto (It.), see: curved cornett.

Cornotragone, Austrian brass instr. of alto register in existence in 1849, with rotating bell, played with a cup mouthpiece. Sachs suggested that the name might more properly be *cornodragone* (dragoon's horn) (176).

Corno ventile, It.: valve horn.

Cornpipe, var. of hornpipe.

Cornu (Lat.: horn), **1.** circular trumpet of ancient Rome, a military and circus instr., of Etruscan origin, with narrow conical bore and slender bell, in form of a letter G. Two specimens excavated at Pompeii are 3.33 m. (11 ft.)

long, are pitched in G, and have detachable mouthpieces (average length of mouthpiece 17 cm.) that are wide and shallow. A wooden bar set across the diam. served to strengthen the instr. structurally and furnished a handhold; one end rested on the player's left shoulder, while the other was held by his left hand, with bell forward. His right hand held the mouthpiece to his mouth. For its revival in the 18th c. see: tuba curva (21, 89, 170); **2.** med. Lat.: cornett.

Cornu alpinus, Lat.: alphorn. The term was used by Tacitus (161).

Cornuielle [Lat.: *cornu* + dim. *elle*], small horn of med. France (204).

Cornul, Rom.: horn (5).

Cornu organicum, Lat.: Hornwerk (161).

Cornuto, It.: cornett (176).

Cor-oboe, organ stop of open wooden flue pipes at 8′ or 4′ pitch, of 19th-c. invention. Not to be confused with the oboe horn (186).

Cor omnitonique, Fr.: omnitonic horn.

Coron [Lat.: *cornu*], OFr.: horn (197).

Corpo di ricambio, It.: corps de rechange.

Corps de rechange (Fr.) (It.: *corpo di ricambio*), **1.** a tuning bit; **2.** an interchangeable joint or extra middle joint of certain 18th-c. woodwinds, to accommodate different pitches.

Corrigiuncula [Lat.: *corrigo,* to correct], disciplinary bell of med. monasteries (61).

Cor russe, Fr.: Russian horn.

Cor saradinois, corr. of cor sarrazinois.

Cor sarrazinois (OFr.), or *cornet sarrazinois,* a short, straight metal trumpet, possibly identical with the nafir. The term is used up to the late 14th c., usually for a martial instr. Its use as a pastoral instr. also is vouched for in the following passage of 1360: *"2 bergiers dont l'un joue d'une fleute de saus et l'autre d'un cornet sarrazinois"* (2 shepherds one of whom plays a willow flute

and the other a *cornet sarrazinois*) (82).

Cor saxomnitonique, the name that Charles-Joseph Sax of Brussels (father of Adolphe Sax) gave to his *omnitonic horn in 1824.

Cor-solo, an improved Inventionshorn made by Joseph Raoux of Paris *ca.* 1776 and said by Wilhelm Schneider to have been designed by Carl Thürschmidt, a Bohemian virtuoso then living in Paris. It was intended for solo concert work and had only 5 crooks: G F E Eb D (89 Morley-Pegge, 184).

Cortali, 16th-c. It.: rackets. The word appears in several late-16th-c. Austrian inventories (Graz, 1577: *"Rogetten oder Cortali genannt . . ."*) (89, 114).

Corthol, see: curtal.

Cort Instrument, see: Kort Instrument.

Cor transpositeur (Fr.: transposing horn), an imitation of the *omnitonic horn, invented by Gautrot of Paris and patented in 1855. Earlier, in 1849, it had been awarded a silver medal (204).

Cor-tuba (Fr.), wind instr. invented by Gustave-Auguste Besson of Paris (126).

Cos-dung, Tibetan trumpet, possibly identical with the rag-dung (89).

Cosmophone, spherical musical box patented in France by L'Épée on Sept. 28, 1886 (204).

Coštimaje, panpipes of Slov. shepherds, made of 6 cane pipes of different lengths, in raft form, arranged in 2 sets of 3 between small slats of wood. The pipes are tuned with wax and resin. *Cf.* trstenke (144).

Côte, Fr.: rib (of a lute, etc.).

Cottage organ, 19th-c. term for *American organs built in form of cottage pianos.

Cottage piano, small upright piano, vertically strung originally called harmonic piano, made by Robert Wornum in 1813 and improved in 1828, at which time it was only 117 cm. (3 ft. 10 in.) high. The name was subsequently extended to low uprights of other makers also (92).

Coulisse, Fr.: slide.

Coulisse d'accord, Fr.: tuning slide.

Coupler [Lat.: *copula*] (Fr.: *accouplement;* Ger.: *Koppel, Kopplung;* It.: *accopiamento*), device whereby 2 or more keyboards can be played together, or whereby 2 or more strings or pipes are made to sound simultaneously when only one key is depressed.

Courcaillet [Fr. *caille,* quail], quail decoy whistle of France from the 14th c. to the 17th. *Cf.* quagliere, Wachtelpfeife (204).

Courne, 14th-c. Fr. var. of cor.

Courtaut (Fr.) [OFr., a short bombard or cannon], obs. Fr. woodwind instr. described by Mersenne (in 1636) and Trichet (*ca.* 1640), of which the latter says that it differed from the *basson* by being made of a single piece of wood with 2 channels, a little thicker than a doublebass recorder, with double reed covered by a box (*i.e.,* reed cap); both Trichet and Praetorius state that it served as a bass to musettes. Apparently the courtaut could be played either with a reed cap or with the reed mounted on a short crook. Its double channel had a cylindrical bore and was provided with 6 front fingerholes. It was a stopped pipe, and the air escaped by a lateral vent near the top. A feature of the courtaut was the *tétines,* 2 groups of 3 short tubes projecting obliquely from the wall of the tube, of which only one group was used, the other being closed by wax, as the groups were duplications for left- or right-handed players. Although the courtaut is not identical with the Engl. *curtal (which has a conical bore), some contemporary Engl. writers used the Fr. word to designate the Engl. instr., a most confusing practice. The courtaut is similar to, but not identical with, the *Kortholt and the *sordone. Mersenne likened its appearance to a thick walking stick. No specimen is known to have survived. *Cf.* bourdon, curtal, Kortholt, Kort Instrument, tarot (89 Langwill, 140, 190).

Cowbell (Fr.: *sonnaille;* Ger.: *Schelle,*

Kuhschelle), **1.** clapper bell that is not cast but bent and soldered, in certain areas made of wood. The metal variety assumes 2 main forms: a) the height is greater than the diam.; b) the diam. is greater than the height. The word cowbell has come to denote form rather than function; as an indication of function it is a misnomer, as "cowbells" are also suspended from the necks of other herd animals, and in some areas cow owners hang cast, campaniform bells on their prize stock. Cowbells are still used in the Alps, Auvergne, and Pyrenees; **2.** a clapperless square metal bell 11–19 cm. (4½–7½ in.) long, introduced into Western rhythm bands as a drummer's accessory (169).

Cow horn (Ger.: *Stierhorn*) **1.** a primitive horn of antiquity and the early Middle Ages, *ca.* 1 m. (3 ft.) long; **2.** a set of 3 straight brass tubes with conical bore, made (chiefly) for Wagner's *Ring des Nibelungen* (89).

Coyolli, small pellet bell or jingle of the ancient Aztecs, made of copper or gold (105).

Cracaxá, var. spelling of caracaxá (7).

Crap . . . , see: Krap . . .

Crapaud (Fr.: toad), Charles Gounod's name for the *baby grand piano, by which it is now familiarly known.

Crash cymbal, metal cymbal suspended by a cord and "crashed" with a drumstick.

Cravo, Port.: harpsichord; occasionally also: clavichord.

Crécelle, Fr.: cog rattle.

Crécerelle (Fr.: kestrel), Fr.: cog rattle (169).

Crembalum, 1. see: krembalon; **2.** in the 17th and 18th c., Lat.: Jew's-harp (169).

Cremona, corr. of cromorne, an organ stop. In England it was already known by this name in Hawkins' time. He refers to it in his *History,* II, p. 245. The cremona was a reed stop at 8' and 4' pitches (99).

Crepitaculum (Lat.), plain clappers of ancient Rome (144); med. Lat., a rattle.

Crescendo, 1. *pyramid piano by Hofrat Bauer of Berlin *ca.* 1780, with a device for transposing by shifting the keyboard, a 5-oct. compass, and 3 pedals for controlling the dynamics. See also: royal crescendo; **2.** a combined piano-harpsichord by Pehr Lindholm of Stockholm, in 1781, with 5 variations of tone (176).

Crescent, see: Jingling Johnnie.

Cresselle, OFr. form of crécelle.

Cribrum (Lat.: sieve), Lat.: guide (of keyboard instrs.).

Cricri, plucked idiophone with a lamella carved in the surface of a nut, fruit shell, or other spherical matter that serves as a resonator. The lamella so formed is plucked by the thumb. Also called clack idiophone (77, 100).

Cri de la belle-mère (Fr.: mother-in-law's scream), *whirled friction drum of France (16).

Crincrin [onom.], coll. Fr.: a bad violin. Molière uses the expression in his *Fâcheux*, 1661 (204).

Croix sonore (Fr.: sonorous cross), monophonic *electrophonic instr. invented by Nicolai Obukoff, Russ. composer, in Paris *ca.* 1934, in the symbolic form of a cross mounted on a sphere. The principle is that of the Theremin.

Crometta, It.: crook.

Cromorne, 1. Fr.: crumhorn. The word was used up to *ca.* 1650, then superseded by *tournebout;* **2.** organ stop of reed pipes with short cylindrical resonators at 8′ pitch. In Britain the term is sometimes erroneously applied to the clarinet stop. For the Ger. equivalent see: Krummhorn, 2 (89 Baines).

Crook (Fr.: *allonge, bocal, cuivrette, ton de rechange;* Ger.: *Stimmbogen, Krummbügel, Ess, S-Rohr;* It.: *ritorto, pompa, crometta*), **1.** an S-shaped tube that carries the mouthpiece of a bassoon, etc., or other removable tube carrying a reed; **2.** detachable piece of tubing applied to a brass instr. in order to change

its pitch, introduced *ca.* 1718. See also: Einsatzbogen, Setzstück, shank.

Crook harp, see: hook harp.

Crosse, Fr.: scroll.

Cross flute, term coined by the late Canon Galpin to denote the transverse, or side-blown, flute. The principle is the same as that of the vertical, or end-blown, flute: the player directs wind against a sharp edge, but here it is that of a lateral hole, which in primitive flutes is placed in the middle, in more developed ones close to the end. Cross flutes may be open or stopped and occur up to 6 m. (20 ft.) in length. Stopped cross flutes are found in America, Asia, S. Seas; open ones on every continent. In Europe they are met with from the early Middle Ages on (possibly earlier in Etruscan civilization). The cross flute is first recorded in the 9th c. B.C. in China, but it may be older and of C. Asian origin. For details of the European instr. see: flute (144, 168).

Crot, crott, OIrish syn. of cruit. The word occurs in the 8th c. (170, 185A).

Crotal [Gk.: *krotalon*] (Fr.: *crotale;* Ger.: *Gabelbecken*), a pair of small metal cymbals attached to a hinged fork or forked sticks, used in ancient Egypt, Greece, and Rome and apparently also in the early Middle Ages, as well as in present-day Burma. *Cf.* crotalum, cymbala, krotalon (169).

Crotala, pl. of crotalum.

Crotale, Fr.: crotal.

Crotalon, see: krotalon.

Crotalum, pl. crotala [Gk. *krotalon*], clappers of ancient Rome, made of wood, metal, horn, even clay or shells, often depicted in the hands of dancers. *Cf.* krotalon (176).

Crotta, var. of crot.

Crouma, see: krouma.

Croupezion, see: kroupezion.

Crouth, OFr. and 14th-c. Engl.: crwth (153).

Crowd, MEngl.: crwth.

Cruit (Irish), also known as crot(t), in continental Europe as rota, rote, rotta, rotte, chrotta, hruozza, etc.; a med. instr. mentioned in literary sources from the 7th c. to the 14th and identified by a capital of the Moissac cloister near Toulouse dating from 1085–1115, where a triangular psaltery is represented, inscribed *"Eman cum rotta."* The instr. has about 30 strings and the tuning arrangement is on top; the form is that of the Gr. letter delta inverted: ▽ , the horizontal side uppermost. Similar instrs. appear on contemporary sculpture and pictorial material and seem to imply the presence of a soundboard. *Ca.* 600 Venantius Fortunatus wrote *". . . chrotta Britanna canat,"* referring to Britons or Bretons, virtually identical at that time. Sachs sifted the literary and pictorial evidence and showed that the cruit was not a lyre, as had been supposed; he took it to be an early harp. It now seems, however, that the triangular cruit coexisted for a while with the (triangular) harp. The cruit was also known as *cithara in the early Middle Ages. Judging by pictorial sources the number of strings varied considerably, and this is confirmed in literary sources. See also: cithara, hruozza (170, 185A).

Crumhorn [OEngl. crump, crooked + horn] (Fr.: *cromorne, tournebout;* Ger.: *Krummhorn;* It.: *storto, piva torto;* Sp.: · *orlo*), reed-cap woodwind instr. of the 16th and 17th c., usually made of boxwood, with narrow cylindrical tube and bore, terminating in a hooked end like the letter J, and provided with 6 front fingerholes and a rear thumbhole. The double reed is set on a staple and enclosed in a reed cap or perforated box that protects it and also serves as a wind chamber. As the crumhorn does not overblow, its compass is limited to 9 tones. The fingering is that of the recorder. The Ger. word *Krummhorn* is first recorded as an organ stop in 1489 at Dresden, and last mentioned by Schein in 1617. But the instr. lived on longer in France, better known in the 17th c. as *tournebout.* Mersenne said

that it had reached France from England. His contemporary, Trichet, relates that the reed cap was put on the instr. only after one had finished playing, the earliest information we have concerning the remodeling that the crumhorn underwent in France, where it was transformed into an outdoor instr. with wider bore and leather-covered tube, and reed carried on a crook. In this form the crumhorn gained admittance to the band of the Grande Écurie after the mid-c.

The crumhorn is descended from a form of med. *bladder pipe. Virdung (in 1511) shows 4 sizes, as does Agricola in 1528 (but he describes 3 sizes only). Praetorius lists a sopranino (*"exilent"*), lowest note c^1, soprano on g^0, alto on c^0, tenor on G^0, bass on C^0, great-bass on F^1. A set of 6 boxwood instrs., once the property of Alfonso II d'Este (d. 1597), preserved in the Brussels Conservatoire museum, consists of a soprano on g^0 with a speaking length of 47 cm. (18½ in.) including the reed, 3 tenors on c^0, 70 cm. (27½ in.) long, a bass on F^0, 100 cm. (39 in.) long, and a great-bass on C^0, 117 cm. (46 in.) long. Bass and great-bass had an extension system for lowering the pitch a 4th. The National Museum of Prague houses an extended great-bass with a tube length of 1.57 cm. (5 ft. 2 in.) standing 110 cm. (43 in.) high, compass G^1–d^0, with 2 keys and 2 slides. A "long straight basset to the crumhorns" mentioned in a 1613 Cassel inventory has been identified by Baines as the *Nicolo of Praetorius, a straight, slender reed-cap shawm with bell instead of the hooked end.

For the organ stop of this name see: Krummhorn. See also: stortino (36, 89 Baines, 114, 170, 190).

Cruth, OEngl.: crwth (185A).

Crwth, pl. **crythau** (Kym.), bowed lyre of ancient Wales that survived the Middle Ages and did not quite disappear until the early 19th c.; called "crouth" in 14th-c. England and later "crowd." In the Middle Ages it was also known by the

Lat. name of *chorus.* An Engl. 11th-c. ms. describes the chorus as a wooden instr. with 4 strings; Aimeri de Peyrac in the 14th c. tells us that it had 2 pairs of strings tuned a 4th apart. Up to this point it lacked a fingerboard and was plucked. *Ca.* 1300 it was transformed into a bowed instr.; a seal dated 1316 shows a crwth with fingerboard, bridge, and tailpiece. The earliest surviving specimens are from the 18th c. They have an oblong body with flat belly and back, straight sides continuing in arms joined at the top by a yoke; the large square hole resulting at the upper end was divided into 2 holes by a central fingerboard; 2 circular soundholes were cut into the belly. Of the 6 strings 4 were on-board, 2 off-board; all were secured by rear pegs inserted in the yoke. A characteristic feature of the crwth was its flat bridge with a foot 7 cm. (2¾ in.) long that passed through a soundhole and rested against the back (similar to that of some gadulkas), thus serving simultaneously as soundpost. The bridge was set obliquely and had a flat top. Only the treble string was stopped; the others served as drones. Galpin relates that the off-board strings were plucked by the player's bow-hand thumb, or bowed (touching the drones with thumb or bow was part of a med. fiddler's technique). Late tunings, dating from 1794 and 1814, are given as $g^0 g^1/ c^2 c^1, d^1 d^2$ and $a^0 a^1/e^1 e^2, b^1 b^2$. At that time it was held almost in violin position, probably under the influence of the more modern instr. Both were about the same size. By the late 18th c. the crwth was very rare indeed (*cf.* John Hawkins, *History* . . . , 1776) and shortly thereafter became extinct. Today the word is used in Wales to denote any stringed instr. Palsgrave in 1530 glossed crwth as rebec; in 1537 John Hogan was reprimanded for "singing lewd ballads with a crowd or fyddyll" (J. Payne Collier's ed. of Shakespeare). In 1949 a 12th-c. crwth-like instr. was excavated

at Gdańsk (Danzig). See also: chorus (9, 79, 153).

Crwth trithant (Welsh), the 3-stringed rebec of Wales, now also called crwth (79).

Crystallophone [Gk. *crystallos,* glass] (Fr.: *crystallophone;* Ger.: *Krystallophon*), a series of tuned, graduated glass bars, cups, bowls, etc., played with hammers, beaters, or the performer's fingers, either directly or by intermediary of a keyboard. In the 19th c. their chief use was as toys. See: fortepiano à cordes de verre, glasschord, glass harmonica, glass harp, musical glasses, p'ung kyong, Spirafina, sticcado pastorale (169).

Crystalphonicon, a (trade?) name of *musical glasses in existence *ca.* 1870 (113).

Cuatro (Sp.: four), **1.** guitar of Puerto Rico, with 5 courses of strings, 4 pairs and a single *chanterelle, played with a plectrum; **2.** a small guitar of Venezuela, with 4 strings. *Cf.* quinto (103, 176).

Cucchiare di legno (It.: wooden spoon), It. folk clappers, according to Buonanni (39).

Cuckoo (Fr.: *sifflet coucou;* Ger.: *Kuckuckspfeife*), **1.** a small pipe with a single fingerhole, yielding 2 tones, usually a major 3rd apart, imitating the call of the cuckoo. Used occasionally as an orchestral instr. and now incorporated as a drummer's accessory into Western rhythm bands; **2.** auxiliary organ stop of the baroque, consisting of 2 pipes, imitating the call of the cuckoo. Now obs. (3, 176).

Cuculus, Lat.: cuckoo, 2.

Cuerda, Sp.: string.

Cuerna, cuerno, Sp.: horn.

Cuíca, *friction drum of Brazil, with friction stick rubbed with wetted hands or a damp cloth. Also called puíca. See also: adufo (7).

Cuiraxezaqua, Tarascan word for the cocoloctli.

Cuivrette, Fr.: crook.

Culasse, Fr.: butt.

Cultrun, rattle drum of the Araucano

Indians of S. America, made of a round wooden platter—or occasionally a half calabash—with horseskin head, containing pebbles that rattle when the drum is struck. It is played with a drumstick; 40–45 cm. (16–18 in.) in diam., 16 cm. (6½ in.) high. Also called rali cultrun. *Cf.* caquelcultrun (105).

Cumbé, a square *frame drum of Guinea. *Cf.* gumbé (152).

Cupa-cupa, *friction drum of Apulia, Italy, played with a friction stick (169).

Cup mouthpiece (Fr.: *embouchure;* Ger.: *Kesselmundstück*), made of wood, horn, or ivory, commonly of metal, this type of mouthpiece has existed since prehistoric times and serves to support the player's lips. In Europe it is circular, in Africa oval. Detachable cup mouthpieces seem to have been first used by the Etruscans. *Cf.* lituus.

Cura saz, smallest of the Anatolian saz, with 3 strings (89).

Čurlik, čurlika (Serb.: trill), Dalmatian *whistle flute related to the Bosnian *svirala, richly carved, with fingerholes a finger's breadth apart. Often 50 cm. (20 in.) long (34).

Curtal, obs. Engl. woodwind instr., precursor of the bassoon, equivalent during the 16th and 17th c. of the Fr. *basson* or *fagot,* the Ger. *Dulzian* or *Fagott,* the It. *fagotto* and the Sp. *bajón* (but not identical with the courtaut, from which it derived its name, nor with the cognate Kortholt). The word was in use from the 16th c. to the mid-18th. Usually the curtal was made of a single block of wood with 2 parallel conical channels bored up and down it, connected at the lower end, but occasionally it was made of 2 sections hollowed out and glued together and then covered with leather. A short, slightly flared bell was set on top, and it was played with a double reed mounted on a short crook (Mersenne says that the reed was sometimes attached to a staple). It is briefly recorded in an Engl. inventory of 1574, and a Graz inventory of 1577 lists a bass, 2 tenor,

and a soprano *dolzoni,* also a chest of 2 bass, 2 tenor, and 1 soprano *alte schlechte fagati* (old plain *fagati*), but details are lacking until Praetorius describes and depicts it for us. From him we learn that the so-called single curtal was a tenor and the double curtal a bass instr., the latter corresponding to the Ger. *Chorist-Fagott,* the type instr. He gives the single curtal a compass of G^0–f^1, the double curtal that of C^0–d^1. All told there were 6 sizes in existence by his time: soprano, some 38 cm. (15 in.) high, compass g^0–c^2; alto 46 cm. (18 in.), compass c^0–f^1; tenor 68 cm. (2 ft. 3 in.), compass G^0–f^1; bass, or *Chorist-Fagott* 1 m. (39 in.), compass C^0–d^1, *Quartfagott* compass G^1–f^0, *Quintfagott ca.* 145 cm. (4 ft. 9 in.), compass F^1–eb^0. Tenor and Chorist were made both open and stopped, *i.e.,* covered with a perforated lid that muffled the tone. Stopped instrs. had no bell. The fashion of making gedackt specimens persisted into the 18th c., as we know from a surviving example of Denner's, now in the Leipzig University (formerly Heyer) collection. The double curtal, or Chorist-Fagott, called fagotto chorista in Italy, was the most important size and is the only one mentioned by Zacconi. It derives its name from its unison pitch with the 8′ of choir-pitched organs. It had 6 front fingerholes and 1 key for F, plus 2 rear thumbholes and 1 rear key giving E, D, and C. The high-pitched models seem to have been used only in Germany, Austria, and Spain (*cf.* bajoncillo). Of the sizes in existence in 1600 only the double curtal has survived, namely as our bassoon. In 1636 Mersenne used the term *basson,* but reference is still to the curtal, albeit a different type, with the bell lengthened to obtain a downward range to Bb^1. Baines has suggested this may have been in order to match the compass of Louis XIII's cellos, tuned a tone lower than normal. Sometime in the mid-17th c. the one-piece curtal was transformed in France into a separately jointed instr., the bassoon. The new instr. was scored for by Lully in 1674, but the name curtal continued in use for the new instr. until the early 18th c. (14, 89 Langwill, 169).

Curved cornett (Fr.: *cornet courbe;* Ger.: *krummer Zink;* It.: *corno torto, cornetto curvo;* Sp.: *corneta tuerta*), cornett in form of an obtuse S, as opposed to the *straight cornett, made of a section of wood split lengthwise, hollowed out, and glued together, with conical bore and octagonal exterior, covered with black leather and hence also known as the "black cornett." A Bohemian 16th-c. illustration shows a curved cornett with trunco-conical bell, an unusual feature; It. *cornetti* occasionally terminated in form of an animal's head with open mouth (36, 89 Baines).

Cuspida, see: Spitzflöte.

Cutín, *slit drum of the Chorti Indians of Guatemala (152).

Cutup (Ger.: *Aufschnitt*), in an organ pipe the distance between the edge of the lower lip and that of the upper lip, *i.e.,* the height of the mouth. The mouth is made purposely low for the voicer to "cut up" to the proper height (101).

Cylinder lyre, a small, hand-cranked instr. with pinned cylinder, patented in the 18th c. by H. P. Møller of Copenhagen, in form of a classical lyre, also furnished with a keyboard (27).

Cylinder quint, *quint organ stop of cylindrical pipes, as opposed to one of conical pipes (198).

Cylindre, Fr.: barrel; rotary valve.

Cylindre à rotation, Fr.: rotary valve.

Cylindrical drum (Fr.: *tambour en cylindre;* Ger.: *Röhrentrommel, Walzentrommel*), drum having the same diam. in the middle as at the ends. Those of Europe have 2 heads, laced or tightened by screws, only one of which is struck, the other being provided with a snare. Known long before the kettledrum, the cylindrical drum was spread among the barbarians by the joculators of ancient Rome. Isidore of Seville called it *sym-*

phonia. In 16th-c. Europe cylindrical drums were 50–70 cm. (20–28 in.) high and 50–55 cm. (20–22 in.) wide generally, although some were far larger; 7 small holes were disposed in a circle or rosette pattern. After the Thirty Years' War only one hole was retained; by the 18th c. height and width were about equal, *ca.* 40–45 cm. (16–18 in.), and the wooden shell was replaced by metal: the military *snare drum was thus created (100, 169).

Cymbal, see: cimbal, cymbals.

Cymbala (pl. of *cymbalum*) [Gk. **kymbalon*], **1.** cymbals of late Roman culture. The word itself is a Vulgate Latinization of the Gk. *kymbala,* used in the Septuagint to translate the Heb. word **selslīm*. Cassiodore and Isidore use it in this sense. The Roman cymbals were metal plates with concave centers and turned rims. During the Carolingian period they are illustrated attached to forked sticks (see: crotal); sometime before 1000 A.C. the meaning of the word changed to denote: **2.** set of tuned bells, bowl-shaped, arranged in a tuned series of 8 or 9 to the oct. (with synemmenon) suspended from a frame and struck on the outside with hammers: a bell chime. See: bell chime, crotal, cymbalum (E. Buhle: *Das Glockenspiel . . .* in: *Festschrift . . . von Liliencron,* 1910); **3.** med. Lat.: harpsichords. The term was used, *i.a.* by Francisco Salinas (*De musica,* 1577) in analogy to the word form *organa,* as in the expression *"organa et cymbala."*

Cymbale, Fr.: **1.** cymbal; **2.** obs. term for triangle; Richelet so defines it in 1680; **3.** obs. term for small bell. In this sense the word has been in use since *ca.* 1280; **4.** mixture organ stop that corresponds to the acuta. Originally composed of 8', 5⅓', and 4', by the time of Dom Bedos it had 9 ranks of octs. and quints, and together with the *fourniture formed the *plein-jeu. *Cf.* Zimbel (20, 133, 166, 197).

Cymbalettes, 1. obs. Prov.: cymbals,

made of bronze or steel, also called palets (23); **2.** Fr.: jingles of a tambourine (70).

Cymbali, Russ.: dulcimer (169).

Cymbalki, Pol.: dulcimer (169).

Cymbalon, see: kymbalon.

Cymbals [Lat. *cymbala*] (Fr.: *cymbales;* Ger.: *Becken;* It.: *cinelli, piatti*), **1.** vessel clappers of Asiatic origin, usually of indeterminate pitch (owing to the production of inharmonic partials), traditionally a ritual rather than a martial instr. that does not appear in primitive cultures. In ancient Assyria a form is depicted that does not occur elsewhere: funnel-shaped, with the necks of the funnels serving as handles, held horizontally and struck with a vertical movement. Otherwise, in the ancient and modern East, from Israel to Java, 2 forms have been in use: a) a broad-rimmed, small-bossed version held in horizontal position and struck vertically; and, b) a narrow-rimmed, large-bossed one held in vertical position and struck horizontally with a vigorous motion. Cymbals were in use in Israel by *ca.* 1100 B.C., but do not appear in Egypt until approximately 800 B.C.; there they had large central bosses and flat rims (but see also: crotal). In Europe cymbals appear intermittently from the 13th c. on, although they had been imported earlier; they are depicted in the *Cantigas de Santa María, ca.* 1270. Their orchestral début did not occur until the late 17th c. (N. A. Strungk's opera *Esther,* 1680); they were then forgotten and reintroduced in the Turk. music of the 18th c. Cymbals were new to Burney in 1770 (he called the cymbal *crotalo*) and did not gain a permanent position in the European orchestra until the late 18th c.

European cymbals have nearly always been imported from China or Turkey, although some were made in Italy. Their exact composition has traditionally been a carefully guarded secret, but the alloy consists roughly of 8 parts of copper to 2 parts of tin. Those from China have bent rims and central bosses, are made of thin metal, 35–55 cm. (14–22 in.) in diam., and are cheaper than the Turk. ones. The latter are thicker, heavier to hold, flatter, nowadays made in different sizes, and are said to be tonally superior. The modern orchestra demands heavy cymbals at least 35 cm. (14 in.) in diam.; those employed in rhythm bands are lighter. Cymbals are struck together with a brushing motion, as clashing them together directly might cause them to crack. For *piano* playing one cymbal may be touched lightly with the edge of the other. Chin. cymbals are generally played singly, struck with a beater. Cymbals clashed by means of a pedal, known as "foot cymbals," are used in light orchestras and rhythm bands; **2.** in the past the triangle has been termed cymbal, by Mersenne, for instance; **3.** 19th-c. piano stop consisting of 2 or 3 thin strips of brass brought down against the bass strings (15 Blades, 89, 92, 169, 170). See also: acetabula, albogue, batsu, brahmatālam, brihattālam, cai chum chua, cai nao but, chalpāra, champara, champare, champareta, champari, chap, chapa, chapara, chaplachaul, chaplachoire, charb lek, charb yai, chechempres, cheng-cheng, chimvale, Chinese crash cymbals, ching, chitkul, chiyeyek, choke cymbals, ch'ung, cimbalillo, cimbalo, clash-pan, crash cymbal, crotal, cymbala, cymbalettes, ding sha, dobyoshi, engkuk, finger cymbals, gini, gubar, hi hat, hsing erh, jalra, jhānjha, ka könshau, kakva, kanching, kas, ka shakuriau, katral, kayitalama, kechicher, kemong, kenchek, kencher, kimvalu, ku'ūs, kymbali, lang kwang, mahāmandirā, mandirā, manjira, metziltāyīm, musāfiq, nao, nengilsi, nihoihagi, nuqaisāt, nyo, palets, p'eng chung, po, richik, rivet cymbal, rojeh, rol-mo, saffaqātān, sajjāt, salāsil, sanj, sanūj, selslīm, siao po, sil, sil-sil, sil-snyau, sing, sinj, sizzle cymbal, slasal, sock cymbals, sunūj, tāla, talam, tālyika, than kvin, tin-tin-sags, togha, tong pal,

Tschinellen, t'ung po, ya gvin, zil, zile, zymbel.

Cymbalum, pl. **cymbala** (med. Lat.) [Gk. **kymbalon*], early med. word for a small, bowl-shaped bell, as opposed to the larger campana, used from the 9th c. on. In pl. form the word denotes a *bell chime. Paulus Paulirinus, writing *ca.* 1460, still refers to it as a *nola parva* (small bell). *Cf.* bell chime, cymbala, horologium, Zimbelstern.

Cymbalum orale (mouth bell), Lat.: Jew's-harp; a med. term.

Cymbasso, see: cimbasso.

Cymbelstern, see: Zimbelstern.

Cymphan, Engl. 16th-c. var. of symphony (79).

Cyphoine, OFr. var. of symphonie.

Cythara, var. spelling of cithara. A *cythara anglica*, med. harp, depicted in a 12th-c. ms. was published by Martin Gerbert (*De Cantu et musica sacra*); the instr. was triangular and had 12 strings; a *cythara teutonica* depicted in the same ms. represents a med. lyre.

Cytole, see: citole.

Czakan [Hung. *csakany*] (Fr.: *canne-flûte à bec;* Ger.: *Stockflöte*), recorder in form of a walking stick, a Hung. instr. probably of Bohemian origin, much in vogue in the 1820's. First mentioned in the *Wiener Zeitung* of Oct. 1, 1808, it is said to have been invented by a musician named Anton Heberle. The czakan not only resembles but was also used as a walking stick. Two small holes were bored in the knob to serve as blowhole. The tube was of inverted conical form, fitted with 6 front fingerholes and a rear thumbhole. It was made in A♭ with a compass a♭^{1}–d♭^{4}, or in B♭. A tutor by Krämer appeared in 1830, another in 1855 (89, 176, 184).

Czakanflöte, organ stop of overblowing flue pipes at 8′ pitch, found in the manual of the Marienorgel at Lübeck, also in Bremen ⊣(1850 by F. Schulze) (133, 176).

Czurynga, *bull-roarer of Poland, now a child's toy, made of a narrow board fastened to the lash of a whip and whirled; 15–60 cm. (6–24 in.) long (89).

D

Daarē [Pers. *da'ira*], frame drum of Bulgaria (89).

Daba, cylindrical drum of the Malagasy Republic, with 2 heads (171).

Dabbūs (Arab., Pers.), dervish's rattle consisting of a stick to which chains and pellet bells are attached, *ca.* 70 cm. (28 in.) long. *Cf.* dara, 2 (75 II, 176).

Dabdaba (Arab.), a small drum of the N. African Berber, also called dardaba (75 II).

Da daiko, the great drum of Japan, used in *gagaku* and on rare occasions also in *bugaku*. The slightly barrel-shaped body is some 1½ m. (5 ft.) long, with heads projecting beyond the body, their diam. being *ca.* 180 cm. (6 ft.). The heads are stretched on hoops and laced. The da daiko rests on a stand or is suspended in a frame and struck with 2 heavy lacquered beaters, always in left-right sequence. It corresponds to the Chin. tsin ku and the Korean chin ko (135, 157).

Daera, see: dāira.

Daf (Pers., Turk.), single-membrane *frame drum of Persia and Turkey, with jingles, corresponding to the Arab. *duff and the *tambattam of S. India (76, 173).

Dafli [Pers. *daf*], pop. Hindust.: frame drum (173).

Dafri [Pers. *daf*], Punj.: frame drum (173).

Dahare [Pers. *da'ira*], frame drum of Caucasia.

Dai byoshi (Jap. great time beater), barrel-shaped drum of Japan, with 2 heads mounted on hoops and laced to each other, and central tension ligature. Primarily a Shinto instr., it is played with 2 beaters. *Ca.* 46 cm. (18 in.) long, 47 cm. (18½ in.) in diam. of heads (135, 157).

Daiko (Jap. great drum), generic term for barrel-shaped drums in Japan, also an abbr. for *tsuri daiko. See also: asobi daiko, da daiko, den den daiko, gaku daiko, geza daiko, jin daiko, ko daiko, ni daiko, ninai daiko, o-daiko, shime daiko, tsuri daiko, uchiwa daiko, uta daiko.

Da'ira (Pers.: circle), in pre-Islamic Arabia da'ira was the generic name of round drums; subsequently it became the (round) tambourine of Islam, including Moslem Spain, with jingles and pellet bells attached to its frame. In modern times it is the Arab., Turk., Serb., and Alb. tambourine, devoid of jingles and pellet bells; it is also another name of the Samarkand *chilmandi. See also: chilmandi, daare, dahare, dāira, daire, dariya (76, 147, 170).

Dāira (Hindi) [Pers. *da'ira*], single-headed circular or octagonal *frame drum of India. The membrane is either nailed or glued and the drum is played with the bare hand (170).

Daire [Pers. *da'ira*], Yugo. frame drum with flat metal jingles (89).

Dairea [Pers. *da'ira*], Rom.: tambourine.

Dai shoko, large shoko of Japan, now very rare, used for accompanying the *da daiko. *Ca.* 35 cm. (14 in.) in diam. (157).

Dāk, a large variety of the dhol (138).

Dakado, idiochord *tube zither of E. Timor, made of bamboo. Also called beorla (119).

Daki, *frame drum of Orissa and of the Muria of Bastar, India, made of a

goatskin stretched over a ring 38 cm.
(15 in.) in diam. It hangs suspended from
the player's neck and is struck with 2
slender sticks (68).

Dakut, decoy *pigeon whistle of S. and
C. Celebes, similar to the bumbun. Also
called dikut (122).

Dalinzi, drum of the Bahavu of Ruanda, given to future chiefs (30).

Dama, barrel-shaped wooden drum of
the Garo of Assam, with 2 cowskin heads,
tensed with V-lacings. *Ca.* 1 m. (40 in.)
long (172).

Damāma (Pers.), kettledrum of ancient Persia (75 II).

Damāmā (Sans.), the largest kettledrum of India, of Pers. origin. The body
is of clay, the membrane is stretched by
Y-shaped thongs and a central belt. Also
called mahānāgarā, nahabat, naubat (170,
173).

Damarinpfeiffe (Ger.), corr. of Tämerlinpfeife.

Dāmaru (Beng., Sans., Hindi), drum
of India, similar to the udukkai but in
addition it has a cord wound around its
waist, with knotted ends that strike against
the heads when the drum is shaken. The
dāmaru is sacred, being an attribute of
Siva, but now it is in the hands of mendicants all over India. *Cf.* budubuduke,
damru, dauru, davandai (68, 179).

Damārum, a pair of rounded, conoid
drums of India, almost in form of kettledrums, used in temple processions. The
body is wooden, the head laced; played
with 2 sticks, one curved, the other
straight (179).

Damba, stringed instr. of the Vogul
(NE. Urals), U.S.S.R. *Cf.* dombrā (9).

Dambras, Lith.: Jew's-harp. *Cf.* dom-
bra, 4.

Dame, var. of dan (77).

Dami, a Sundanese name of the dermenan (121).

Damper (Fr.: *étouffoir;* Ger.: *Dämpfer;*
It.: *sordino*), device for muting the sound
of certain instrs.

Dämpfer, Ger.: damper, mute.

Dampha (Beng.), octagonal *frame

drum of the mendicant monks of Bengal,
with nailed head. *Ca.* 60 cm. (2 ft.) in
diam. (132, 173).

Dāmphu, octagonal *frame drum of
Nepal (138).

Damru, 1. Hindust. equivalent of dāmaru; **2.** syn. of hulki māndri (68).

Damyadamyan, the ancient Hindu-
Javanese name of the dermenan (121).

Dan, slit drum of the Admiralty Islands (77).

Danafil, Port. var. of añafil.

Danang, heterochord bamboo *tube
zither of the Nicobar Islands, with a
single string. *Ca.* 1 m. (40 in.) long
(173).

Danbal, var. writing of dunbal.

Dan bao, see: cai dan bao.

Danboliñ, 1. var. of tanborín; **2.** var.
of danbore (56).

Danbore [Pers. *tabir*], Basque: drum.
Also called danboliñ, gatamore, gathanbore, katambore, katamore. *Cf.* atambor
(56).

Danbur, see: tanbur.

Danda suthra (Punj.), clappers of
Punjabi mendicant priests; 25–45 cm.
(10–18 in.) long (173).

Dan day, see: cai dan day.

Dandin (OFr.), a small bell of 14th-
and 15th-c. France, attached to the necks
of animals (82, 204).

Dangamut [*garamut*], slit drum of
New Hanover, Melanesia (176).

Danki, bronze *kettle gong of the
Abor of the N. confines of Farther India,
the edges of the head being rounded,
and provided with 8 small handles (172).

Dan ña tro, see: cai dan ña tro.

Dan nguyet, see: cai dan nguyet.

Danno, wooden bell of Cambodia,
with several clappers (172).

Dan thap luc, see: cai dan thap luc.

Dan ti, see: cai dan ti.

Dan trañ, see: cai dan trañ.

Daola-daola, slit drum of N. Nias, Indonesia (176).

Dapla, clappers of the Mundari of
Chota Nagpur, India, clicked together by
means of a handle (173).

Dara (Beng.), **1.** [Pers. *da'ira*], round *frame drum of N. India; **2.** stick rattle of Kashmiri fakirs, made of a hooked metal bar on which a number of metal rings are strung. *Cf.* dabbūs (173, 176).

Darā (Pers.), Arab. clapper bell hung on the necks of elephants and camels (76).

Darabána [Turk.: *balāban*], Rom.: drum. *Cf.* balāban, baraban, taraban.

Darabuka, pl. **darbukat** (Arab.), goblet-shaped drum of the Arab world, made of clay or wood, with single, glued head, 2 snares, and usually painted. It is played with both hands, the fingers of the right hand forcefully tapping the center of the head, while those of the left play gently close to the rim. *Cf.* darbuka, tarabonka, tunbūk (11, 144 Chottin).

Darbaka, see: darabuka.

Darbuk [Arab. *darabuka*], drum of Yugo. Macedonia, in form of a clay pot, with single head, played with the finger tips of both hands. It is found only among the Turk. and gypsy population (89).

Darbuka [Arab. *darabuka*], **1.** *frame drum of N. Africa; **2.** clay kettledrum of Turkey; **3.** var. writing of darabuka (75 I, 89).

Darbukat, pl. of darabuka.

Dardaba, see: dabdaba.

Darhama, percussion gourd of Mauritanian women, similar to the humbaldú, used for accompaniment of their songs (193).

Dariya, pl. **dariyaluna** [Pers. *da'ira*], frame drum of Afghanistan.

Darkun, a large *musical bow of the Bhuiyar of Mirzapur, India, made of bamboo tapered toward the ends, with a string of twisted bark. A number of notches are cut along its surface. One end of the bow is rested on a basket placed on the ground, the other on the ground proper. The bow is scraped, causing the basket to reverberate. The Korwas play it with a bamboo switch. *Ca.* 2 m. (6½ ft.) long (17).

Darubiri, turnip-shaped Jew's-harp of

New Guinea, made of wood or bamboo, *ca.* 15 cm. (6 in.) long. Also called kalinguang (176).

Darvyra, *end-blown flute of (modern) Greece, made of cane, with 6 front fingerholes and sometimes an additional venthole (132).

Dāsari thappattai, see: thappattai.

Dastan, pl. **dasatin,** Pers.: fret. See also: 'atab (75 II).

Daul, see: dawūl.

Daula-daula, see: daola-daola.

Daulbas [Turk. *dawūl*], small kettledrum of the Serbian and Bosnian areas of Yugoslavia (176).

Daule, 1. a modern bell of Ethiopia, also called dawal; **2.** [Turk. *dawūl*], a large drum of Albania (144, 176).

Daúli [Turk. *dawūl*], drum of modern Greece, played like the tupan, *i.e.*, with a drumstick in the right hand and a switch in the left, in the Turk. manner (144).

Dauru, pop. Hindust.: dāmaru.

Dauwala [*tabla*], *hourglass drum with zigzag lacings, of chieftains of former Candy (Ceylon) (176).

Davandai (Tamil), a large dāmaru played with a stick. A temple instr. (179).

Davane, Kan.: davandai.

David's harp (Ger.: *Davidsharfe*), Ger. 18th-c. name for the ordinary harp without pedals, to distinguish it from the arpanetta or Spitzharfe. Thus Halle, writing in 1764, says that harps are either *"Spitzharfen"* or *"Davidsharfen."* Eisel in 1738 uses the term in the same sense (67, 90).

Davul, see: dawūl.

Dawal, syn. of daule, 1.

Dāwud, next to largest of the modern Turk. nāys (76).

Dawūl (Turk.), formerly a drum of the Turk. Janissaries, with 2 heads, one of which was struck with a drumstick, the other with a switch. Nowadays it is a bass drum that usually accompanies the zurna, and is played in the Balkans as well as in Turkey. The word corresponds to the Arab. tabl. *Cf.* duhul (76, 89).

Dayra, see: da'ira.

Dayuray, a very small drum of Mindanao, Philippine Islands, with a coconut or bamboo body (176).

Dbang-dung, a small copper trumpet or horn of Tibet, at least 60 cm. (2 ft.) long (89 Picken).

Deadar, var. of deiadar.

Dea-Violina, automatic violin by L. Hupfeld of Leipzig (37).

Debbūs, see: dabbūs.

Debdeba, see: dabdaba.

Deblek, syn. of dumbelek in S. Turkey, where it assumes the form of a clay goblet drum with glued head, very similar to if not identical with the darabuka. Also called deblet, debuldek, delbek, dirimbekki, dümbek.

Deblet, debuldek, var. of deblek.

Décacorde (Fr.), 1. the 10-stringed psaltery of late med. Fr. literature (53); 2. see: guitare décacorde.

Decima (It.), see: tierce (organ stop).

Decimanona (It.), see: nineteenth (organ stop).

Decimaquinta (It.), see: fifteenth (organ stop).

Dedeco, panpipes of the Philippine Islands (176).

Def, see: deff.

Deff [Arab. *duff*], *frame drum with jingles of the Alb. population of Yugoslavia, played only by women. *Cf.* duff, tof (89).

Degangande [*ganga*], drum in the Gurma (Sudanic) languages. See also: ganga (93).

Degemma, percussion gourd of the Toucouleur of Senegal, similar to the humbaldú (152).

Degongo, var. of digongo.

Degung, *gong chime of W. Java, composed of 6 rather small gongs having central bosses and turned rims, suspended in a frame (121).

Dehol, see: duhul.

Deiadar [*adar*, horn], Basque signal horn. See also: adar.

Delbek, var. of deblek.

Demāme, see: damāma.

Demen(an), var. of dermenan.

Demi-canon (Fr.: half *canon*) [Arab. *qānūn*], 14th-c. form of micanon.

Demi-doussaine, OFr.: a small douçaine.

Demi-lune, see: trompette demi-lune.

Dempling, name of the gambang gangsa in W. Java. Also called kedempling (121).

Demung, Javanese saron. Of the 4 1-oct. sarons it is the second lowest, and stands an oct. below the saron barung (121).

Demung gantung, single-oct. gender of Java, pitched an oct. above the *slentem gantung and found only in *gamelan klenengan* (121).

Demung jemblung, idiophone of Java, consisting of 5 bamboo tubes tied together and suspended in a frame and struck. They are found in the *jemblung* ensemble (121).

Denaka, short *cylindrical drum of the Malagasy Republic (171).

Denbāl, see: danbal.

Dende, 1. *musical bow of the Thonga of S. Africa, similar to the uhadi, with string looped to the bow; 2. musical bow of the Venda of S. Africa, similar to the above, but both sections of the string (divided by the loop) are stroked with a feather, the pitch being altered by pressure at the middle of the string. Also called tshikala. *Cf.* nkoka, sekgapa, tshitendje, tshitendole, umakweyana (116).

Den den daiko, fan-shaped *frame drum of Jap. mendicant priests of the Buddhist Hokke sect, with single membrane and a handle, struck with a stick. *Ca.* 37 cm. (14½ in.) wide (176).

Denis d'or, stringed keyboard instr. built *ca.* 1730 by Procop Diviss, a Moravian preacher of Znaim, with 790 strings and 130 variations of tone. The instr. was capable of imitating nearly all wind and stringed instrs., also of giving the performer an electric shock whenever its inventor so desired. Only one specimen was built. It measured *ca.* 1½ m. by 90 cm. (5 by 3 ft.) and could be tuned in three quarters of an hour. Also called goldner Dionys, orchestrion, 1 (27, 176).

Den sho, clapperless bell of Jap. Buddhist temples, struck on the outside by a hammer. Also called han sho (135).

Derbūka, see: darabuka.

Deren, Santali: sringa.

Dermenan, idioglott rice-straw pipe of Java, with a node at the top and upcut reed just below it. It may or may not have 2 or 3 fingerholes and/or a bell of spirally twisted coconut leaf (121).

Dero, panpipes of the S. American Paressi Indians (105).

Dessauerbratsche [inventor's name + *Bratsche,* viola], viola with violin scale, invented by H. Dessauer of Linz in 1901, to enable violinists to play the viola without change in fingering (176).

Dessus, Fr.: **1.** treble; **2.** abbr. for dessus de violon.

Dessus de viole, Fr.: soprano viola da gamba.

Dessus de violon, obs. Fr. term for violin (Mersenne gives it the same tuning as our violin).

Dettoi, syn. of trompetica china (152).

Deutsche Guitarre (Ger.: German guitar), a variety of cittern that appeared in Germany *ca.* 1780, originally with 4, later with 7 single strings tuned $G^0 e^0 f^0 g^0 c^1 e^1 g^1$, notated in violin clef an oct. higher, with one soundhole. Used for the accompaniment of songs (Koch: *Lexikon,* 1802).

Deutsche Mechanik, see: German action.

Deutsche Schalmei, Ger. name of a very slender shawm made in Germany and the Low Countries, in use from *ca.* 1680 to 1720. Made in soprano and tenor sizes, the former being *ca.* 60 cm. (2 ft.) long, lowest tone c^1. Each had an extremely narrow bore, terminated in a long, flaring bell, and was provided with a fontanelle. On the soprano this was nonfunctional, as it only covered a venthole, but the tenor had a key. Museum specimens have survived (14, 89 Baines).

Devil's fiddle, *stick zither of the pres-ent-day U.S., consisting of a rigid stick with a single string attached under tension to its ends. This passes over a circular frame provided with a parchment head and snares. The stick is surmounted by 2 brass cymbals. Similar to the Bumbass. *Cf.* bladder and string.

Deze, sansa of Rhodesia and of the Lemba of Bavandaland, S. Africa, consisting of a rectangular board, hollowed, to which 21 thin iron tongues, spatulate at one end, are fixed. These are bent into a double curve and held by 2 bridges. When played the deze is held inside a large calabash resonator that has jingles attached to it. Also called mbila in Rhodesia (116).

Dezem (tenth), mutation organ stop sounding a 10th higher than the key played. *Cf.* tenth (3).

Dge-glie, a large *cross flute of Tibet (89 Picken).

Dhak, dhakkā (Beng., Sans.), drum of N. India, almost cylindrical in shape, with 2 laced heads, both of which are played with drumsticks. It was formerly a martial instr.; its use nowadays is confined to religious festivals (132).

Dhapla [Pers. *daf*], syn. of dafli.

Dhenka, *stick zither of the Madras area, India, similar to the kinnari, with 2 coconut resonators and cowrie-shell frets. A mendicant's instr. (138).

Dhol (Hindi, Pashto) [Pers. *duhul*], **1.** a small barrel-shaped drum of India, sacred to the Chamar of S. Uttar Pradesh, played chiefly by women. Its 2 heads are laced with leather thongs. The drum is suspended horizontally from the player's neck, but only its left head is struck, by a drumstick. *Ca.* 33–60 cm. (13–24 in.) high; **2.** among the Muria of Bastar, India, the dhol is slightly conical, has 2 cowhide heads, of which only one is played. This is stretched over a hoop and laced to the other membrane. Played with a single stick. *Cf.* dāk, dhola, dhōlaka (68, 89, 173).

Dhola, Sans. and Beng. equivalent of dhol.

Dhōlaka (Sans.) [Pers. *duhul], barrel-shaped drum of India, found all over the subcontinent, with body hollowed out of a single block of wood. Its 2 heads have the same diam. and are tensed by lacings passed through a small metal ring, rendering wedges unnecessary (173, 179).

Dholi, double-headed *cylindrical drum of Tiflis, U.S.S.R., with laced heads stretched over metal hoops. *Ca.* 30 cm. (1 ft.) high, 35 cm. (14 in.) in diam. (141, 178).

Dholki (dim. of *dhōlaka), a small dhōlaka (173).

Dholuk, a large variety of the dhol of India (138).

Dhudka, S-shaped trumpet of India, with slightly conoid bore, ending in a flare, with 3 ornamental bosses concealing the joints. The dhudka is held upright with bell high above the player, facing forward. (*Encyclopédie française,* Paris 1937–).

Dhurki, friction drum of Orissa, India (173).

Dhusir, *spike fiddle of the Muria of Bastar, India, with body of a half coconut, lizard-skin belly, bamboo handle, and 2 horsehair strings attached to lateral pegs; held against the shoulder like a European instr. and played with a bamboo bow (68).

Diable des bois (Fr.: forest devil), Fr. *whirled friction drum with whirling stick.

Diable skrzype (devil's fiddle), obs. Pol. folk stringed instr. in use among the Kurpians and Mazovians up to the 1860's, with square wooden body, straight sides, cylindrical neck, and single string. The neck was surmounted by a knob to which the string was attached. The string could be tightened by turning the knob, and was either plucked with bare fingers or struck with a stick (89).

Diapason (Gk.), **1.** Fr.: pitch pipe; tuning fork; scale; **2.** organ stop of cylindrical metal flue pipes of wide scale at 8′ pitch, the foundation of Amer. and Brit. organs, equivalent to the Fr. montre and Ger. Prinzipal. When it occurs at 4′ pitch in the manual, it is called *octave. The diapason is nonimitative in tone and has been in existence since the 16th c. See also: open diapason, stopped diapason (129).

Diapason à bouche, Fr.: pitch pipe.

Diapason phonon, organ stop of flue pipes invented by Robert Hope-Jones (d. 1914), a large-scaled modified diapason with leathered lips (129).

Diaphone, organ stop of reed pipes introduced 1888 by Blackett & Howden of Newcastle, one of many attempts at replacing the metal tongue by some other arrangement: instead of a tongue it had a leather valve that beat against the wood. This was further developed by Robert Hope-Jones in 1893. It was built at 32′, 16′, and 8′ pitches (101, 133).

Diaphonic piano, see: piano diaphonique.

Diben, var. of ibi in Adele and Animere (Sudanic languages) (93).

Diblă, Rom.: fiddle.

Dibu, pl. **madibu, 1.** generic name for wooden bells among the Bembe, Bwende, and Sundi of the Lower Congo, patterned on the shape of the borassus fruit. The smaller ones are *ca.* 10 cm. (4 in.) high and are attached to dogs during the hunt. Larger and more ornate ones serve ritual purposes; these are 15–30 cm. (6–12 in.) high. Some have more than one clapper. The Bembe have a large dibu, with 5 clappers, that is considered male; a smaller one, with 3 clappers, is considered female. Metal clappers are also in use. Also called nkembi; **2.** small bell of the Ladi of the Lower Congo, made of dried fruit husk, with a wooden clapper (185).

Dibwa, var. of dibu.

Dichela, leg rattles of the S. African Pedi, made of long strings of cocoons containing pebbles and sewn in pairs to a long fiber cord. A completed cord is about 1½ m. (6 ft.) long. Worn by women only (116).

Didilavy, *musical bow of the Malagasy Republic, with tuning loop attached to a gourd resonator. The latter is placed near the end of the bow. It is pressed against the player's stomach and the string is tapped with a stick (17).

Didimbadimba, equivalent of the mbila, 1, among the Baluba of the Congo (31).

Didjeridoo, straight trumpet of NW. Australia, made of a tree trunk, 120–150 cm. (4–5 ft.) long, with wax mouthpiece or rim covered with resin, the end often being inserted into a tin-can resonator.

Diga, drum of the Akare of the Congo, made of clay, in form of an inverted beehive. The membrane, of resin, is attached to the body by 8 wooden protuberances (30).

Digiticor, wooden horn with metal bell and crook, made by Boileau of Paris in 1819. He made other instrs., including a wooden trumpet with metal bell and mouthpiece (132).

Digongo [*ganga], Akasele (a Sudanic language): drum. See also: ganga (93).

Digulka, syn. of gadulka.

Dikanmbo, stamping tube of Loango, Angola (185).

Dikomana, kettledrum of several Sotho and Chwana tribes of NW. Transvaal, made of solid timber, provided with handles; 18–46 cm. (7–18 in.) in diam. (116).

Dikubila, *hourglass drum of the Balunda of the Congo, with 2 nailed heads and carved body. A hole is pierced in the drum and covered with a thin membrane —a mirliton device (30).

Dikut, var. of dakut.

Dilruba [*rubāb], an esrar of N. India and Afghanistan, having lateral tuning pegs only, sometimes made with a square or trapezoid body (144, 168).

Dima, syn. of ndima.

Dimba, 1. name given to the *madimba xylophone by the Luishia of the Congo (31); **2.** a name of the sansa in the Lower Congo (185).

Dimplipito, small clay kettledrum of Georgia, U.S.S.R., with laced head and flat bottom in which there is a small hole; it may also have an open bottom. Always played in pairs, 2 drums being connected together by leather thongs. They differ in diam. but are of the same height. In Tbilis (Tiflis) they are also known as nagara. *Ca.* 20 cm. (8 in.) high, 15 and 21 cm. (6 and 8¼ in.) in diam. (132, 141, 178).

Dinbik (Kurd.), Kurd. equivalent of tunbūk.

Dindima (Sans., Beng.), *frame drum of India, similar to the khanjanī (132, 138).

Dindo, drum of the Gombe of the Congo, in form of a truncated barrel, with 2 laced heads. The lacing forms a network that covers the entire body. *Ca.* 60 cm. (2 ft.) high. *Cf.* dundu (30).

Dindo moana, drum of the Gombe of the Congo, smaller than the dindo, with a palm nut in the body (30).

Ding, *piston flute of the Papuans of New Guinea, up to 2 m. (6½ ft.) long, without fingerholes. The pitch is modified by adjusting the piston; used at circumcision rites (176, 178).

Dingba, 1. *musical bow of the Amaza and Andebogo of the Congo, without loop or resonator; **2.** musical bow of the Andovi and Obvango of the Congo, with tuning loop but without resonator; **3.** *board zither of the Mangbetu of the Congo, without resonator (128).

Dingdingti, square wooden buffalo bell of the Gaunto-Haren of Shan State, Burma, with 3 wooden clappers suspended on a wire (172).

Dingi golm, a long mengagl minge (202).

Dinglye, idiochord *tube zither of the Moi Kao of Cambodia, with 6 to 8 strings (119).

Ding sha, small cymbals of Tibetan lamas, about 5 cm. (2 in.) in diam., identical with the mandirā of India (176).

Dingwinti [Kikongo: *kwinta,* to roar like a leopard], *friction drum of the

Bwende and Sundi of the Lower Congo, with nailed membrane and friction stick, strap, or cord. Said to sound like the roar of a leopard, it was formerly used only for ritual purposes but nowadays serves increasingly for secular ones; 40–100 cm. (16–40 in.) long. Also called: kingulu-ngulu, kinkwinta, mwan'angulu, ngulu (185).

Dinni, a shallow kettledrum of the Sivaite mendicant monks in Mysore, S. India (176).

Dintara, bowed string instr. of the E. Bengal Khassiya, with 4 strings, similar to the chikārā (176).

Din tenkhin, bamboo *stamping tube of Malaya, used in pairs. The largest ones are called fathers; the medium-sized ones, mothers; the smallest—the children —are no longer in use. The tubes are stamped against the ground or a log of wood.

Dipela, xylophone of the S. African Bakwelo and Balubedu, very similar to the mbila, 2, of the Venda (116).

Diple, see: diplye.

Diplice, dipličice [dims. of *diplye], a small diplye.

Diplo-kithara (Gk.: double kithara), instr. invented ca. 1800 by Edward Light of London, similar to the arpanetta, with 23 wire strings on either side of a sound-board; those on the right side were for the melody, those on the left, for accompaniment (79, 176).

Diplye, 1. a group of *double pipes of Albania and Yugoslavia, some of which are hornpipes, others bagpipes, and yet others are merely double chanters without bell or bag. In all cases the 2 chanters are made of a single piece of wood with dual bores. Some have equal finger-holes, others unequal, in a number of different arrangements. Primarily a Croatian instr., it occurs also in Bosnia as a single pipe without a bag (14, 89, 144); **2.** among the shepherds of Albania and the Lake Scutari region of Montenegro, the diplye is a double hornpipe made of 2 pieces of cane tied together, with 2 equal

fingerholes. Both tubes end in a common cowhorn bell with down-cut reeds usually left open at the upper end. Some specimens lack the horn bell. The player takes both reeds into his mouth and closes the open end with his tongue; he continues to breathe while playing, thus producing a continuous sound. The pipes are tuned so as to bring the second lowest tone of both into unison while the others are tuned slightly apart, producing beats; **3.** in Herzegovina and nowadays rarely in Bosnia the diplye is a bagpipe, either mouth- or bellows-blown; the double-bore chanter has 6 pairs of fingerholes and is furnished with single reeds; **4.** in Dalmatia the same instr. is known as mješnica (34).

Dirimbekki, var. of deblek.

Discant mixture, see: compensation mixture.

Disc buzzer (Ger.: *Schwirrscheibe, Surrscheibe*), a thin wooden disc with 2 holes in the center through which a string is passed. The player holds both ends of the string and twists them and then pulls them apart; the string then twists itself up again and hums while being so rotated. Disc buzzers occur in Europe as toys, otherwise in Africa, Asia, N. and S. America, and the S. Seas. See also: aḅalla, disco zumbador, flügere, gurrufio, poka-kaa, roncador, runche, sona-cigales, uvuru (77, 168).

Disco zumbador, Sp.: disc buzzer (152).

Discus (Lat.), percussion disc of an-cient Rome, of Asiatic origin, made of metal and suspended by a cord, often with a metal clapper attached by an iron chain, and used as a signal instr. (48).

Dishi, drum of the Newar of Nepal, similar to the dholuk (176).

Diskantgeige (Ger.), early-17th-c. name of the violin in Germany. See also: Diskantvioline, treble violin.

Diskant Prinzipal, see: Prinzipal Dis-kant.

Diskant-Tuba, name by which the soprano *flugelhorn is known in Germany (25).

Diskantvioline, Ger. expression in use *ca.* 1700 for the violin. *Cf.* Diskantgeige, treble violin.

Disposition, term employed to indicate the number and kind of: **1.** organ stops; **2.** harpsichord registers.

Disque sonore, Fr.: percussion plaque.

Distinette, imitation castanets of metal invented by Henry John Distin of London and patented on Feb. 23, 1876. They were pop. both in France and in Britain (89, 132).

Dital harp, name given by Edward Light of London to an improved version of his *British harp lute in 1819. The ditals of his invention were finger keys that stopped the strings and raised the pitch by a semitone. The number of strings was augmented to 19 or more, playable with both hands. They were tuned eb^0–bb^2 or higher, to eb^3. Like the other Light instrs., the dital harp was tuned in Eb and notated a 6th higher, in C (89, 204).

Ditanaklasis, a very low vertical piano invented by Matthias Müller of Vienna in 1800, originally designed for 2 performers, with 2 keyboards facing each other, low enough for the players to see one another. Some models were made with a single keyboard. The Ditanaklasis was built down to the floor instead of resting on a stand, as other pianos of the period, thus becoming the prototype of the modern upright piano. Its bichord stringing was perpendicular. It had a 5-oct. compass, F^1–f^3 (92, 176).

Diti, a name of the sansa in the Lower Congo (185).

Ditumba, pl. **matumba, 1.** footed *goblet drum of the Basanga of the Congo, with nailed head and carved body, provided with a mirliton membrane; **2.** goblet drum of the Bena-Lulua of Kasai, the Congo; **3.** drum of the Baluba-Shankadi, used during dances and initiation ceremonies (30).

Ditumba dya ngenge, bowl-shaped

drum of the Baluba-Shankadi of the Congo, made of *mulela* wood, provided with a mirliton membrane, used during initiations of girls. Also called ndanga (30).

Divinare, Ger. corr. of flûte d'ivoire (organ stop), via flaut devoir (133).

Division viol, a small bass viola da gamba used in 17th-c. England for playing divisions, *i.e.,* for solo work, slightly smaller than a *consort viol and with narrower waist, but at the same pitch. Speaking length of its strings was 63½–66 cm. (25–26 in.) (94).

Diyānai, a double nãy (75 I).

Dj . . . , see: j . . .

Do, slit drum of Siar and Bilia, Oceania (77).

Doal-doal bulo, idiochord *tube zither made of bamboo of the Toba Batak of N. Sumatra, with 4–6 strings (119, 149).

Dob, Hung.: drum. *Cf.* toba.

Dobachi, *resting bell of Jap. temples, set on a cushion and struck with a mallet (157).

Do bat, drum of Burma (103).

Doblado (Sp.: of small or medium size), Pietro Cerone's translation of the doppioni, mentioned by Zacconi.

Dobon, slit drum of the Nor-Papuans (77).

Dobyoshi (Jap.: copper time beater), cymbals of Japan, made of brass with turned rims, used by dancers (157).

Docke, Ger.: jack.

Dodaku, tubular metal trumpet of Japan, originally made of wood, so long that its end must be supported during performance. In lieu of a bell it has a long, wide cylinder of wood, iron, or brass into which the main tube slides telescopically when at rest. The mouthpiece is shallow with a broad rim. Played in pairs at funeral processions. It corresponds to the *ta t'ung kyo of China (157, 170).

Doeff, a *principal organ stop of the Low Countries (2).

Dog-dog, conical drum of W. Java, called reog in E. Java, in shape of a flowerpot, with a nailed head. The membrane is struck with either the bare hand or a stick. Made in various sizes from *ca.* 24 cm. (9½ in.) to 80 cm. (32 in.) (121).

Dohol, see: duhul.

Doifflöte, a syn. of Doppelflöte (organ stop).

Doka, rattle of Farafangana, S. coast of the Malagasy Republic, made of a bamboo segment containing seeds. See also: faray, voamaintilany (171).

Doko, small brass or copper gong of Japan, introduced from S. China, suspended in a frame. Dokos are usually arranged in a set of 3 (157).

Dokri [*do,* spirit + *kri,* drum], 2-headed fetish drum in Agni, a Sudanic language (93).

Dōlak, see: dhōlaka.

Dolçaina, var. of dulzaina.

Dolcan, organ stop, syn. of dolce.

Dolce, dolze, organ stop of flue pipes, open, invertedly conical, of narrow scale, at 8′, 4′, 2′, or 1′ pitch, introduced into Brit. organs by Snetzler in 1741. Nowadays it is built as a form of the obs. Schwegel and is also known as dulciana and dolcissimo. See also: Dulzflöte, Dulzian (131, 133).

Dolce campana, piano stop consisting of a series of weights applied to the bridge or soundboard, muffling the tone, marketed in the mid-19th c. as an attachment by Boardman and Gray of Albany, N.Y.

Dolce suono, obs. It.: dolcian (159).

Dolcian (It.: *dolcino*), Engl. translation of the Ger. word *Dulzian.* For the precursor of the bassoon see: curtal. See also: dulcian (organ stop).

Dolciano, organ stop found in Ger. organs, of open wooden flue pipes at 8′ pitch; not identical with the Dulzian (131).

Dolciato, organ stop of flue pipes at 4′ pitch, between the dolce and dulciana (131).

Dolcimela [Lat. *dulce melos*], It.: dulcimer. Zarlino still used the term (*Sopplimenti,* 1588).

Dolcino (It.), **1.** small bassoon in B♭

at 4′ pitch, played in military bands, with a single reed; in use up to the early 19th c.; **2.** It.: dolcian (89).

Dolcissimo, dolzissimo (It.), organ stop of open metal flue pipes, conical and narrow-scaled, at 16′ or 8′ pitch, also known as dolce or dolze (133, 198).

Doli, see: dholi.

Doli-doli, xylophone of Nias, with 3 or 4 slabs, played by women who sit with their legs stretched over a pit in the ground, with the slabs laid across their legs. The pit acts as resonator (122, 173).

Dolla (Khanda), syn. of nāgārā in E. India (173).

Dolzaina [Lat. *dulcis,* sweet], obs. woodwind instr. of the Renaissance, mentioned in S. Ger. inventories and by It. writers such as Massimo Trojano (1569) and Zacconi (1592) but not by Praetorius. Zacconi informs us that the keyless dolzaina had a compass of a 9th, c^0–d^1 and that with 2 keys it ascended to f^1. This information agrees with Praetorius' description of the *"Cornamuse,"* a double-reed instr. with reed cap and single cylindrical bore. From his table—Praetorius does not depict the instr.—we conclude that there existed 5 sizes, all with the compass of a 9th. The dolzaina is presumably identical with the Fr. douçaine, Sp. dulzaina, and Engl. dulceuse, clearly a Romance instr. It must have been widely known in France at least, for an organ stop named variously doucines or douchaine existed by the early 16th c. Following Kinsky's study of reed-cap instrs., several writers have identified dolzaina with cornamusa. That the 2 cannot be identical is clear from Trojano's lists of instrs. played in performance in 1568, when both dolzaina and cornamusa participated in several ensembles; unless of course the *"Cornamusen"* of Praetorius were not the same as the *"cornamuse"* of the It. writers.

Dolzan, var. of Dulzian (organ stop).

Dolzflöte, see: Dulzflöte.

Dolzian, see: Dulzian.

Dolziana, organ stop identical with the dulcian.

Dolzone [Lat. *dulcis,* sweet], 16th-c. var. of Dulzian. *Cf.* curtal.

Dombara, see: dombrā.

Dombrā [**tanbur*], **1.** plucked stringed instr. of the U.S.S.R., a forerunner of the balalaika and still closely akin to it, already known in the 16th c., when it existed with 3 strings. Today the dombrā is a lute-like instr. with round body, long neck, and 3 metal strings, made in 6 sizes. The strings are tuned a 4th apart; it is played with a plectrum; **2.** among the Kirghiz the dombrā has an oval body, 6 frets, pegdisc, and 2 strings held by rear pegs, and is played with bare fingers; **3.** among the Kazak and the Volga Kalmuk and in Mongolia it has a triangular body, long, narrow neck, 2 strings, and movable frets. *Cf.* damba; **4.** Russ.: Jew's-harp (38, 69, 144, 170).

Domo, arched harp of the Bari of the Congo (128).

Domrā, see: dombrā.

Domu, arched harp of the Mangbele of the Congo (128).

Donbek, var. writing of tunbūk.

Dongeldongel, idiochord *musical bow of the Trans-Fly area of New Guinea, usually made of sago palm leaf rib, with central bridge. Held between the player's lips (not his teeth), the string is tapped with a stick by one hand while being plucked with the other (77).

Dono, Ashanti: hourglass drum (93).

Dön trañ, see: cai dan trañ.

Doppel . . . , see also: double . . .

Doppelfagott, Praetorius' term for the Quartfagott and the Quintfagott, curtals pitched a 4th and 5th respectively below the ordinary curtal. The It. equivalent was the fagotto doppio (159).

Doppelflöte (Ger.) (Fr.: *flûte double;* It.: *flauto doppio*), organ stop of stopped wooden flue pipes having 2 mouths, 1 opposite the other. Praetorius ascribes its invention to Esaias Compenius, who called the new stop duifflöte. Usually built at 8′ pitch. Also called Plattflöte. *Cf.* Grossflöte (3, 133, 159).

Doppelkegelregal (Ger.: double cone regal), organ stop of regal pipes surmounted by a double cone. Pop. in 17th-c. Germany (133).

Doppelkonustrommel, Ger.: double conical drum.

Doppelkortholt, Praetorius' term for the double curtal or Chorist-Fagott (not the double Kortholt) (159).

Doppelpedalharfe, Ger.: double-action harp.

Doppelrohrblatt, Ger.: double reed.

Doppione (Sp.: *doblado*), a mystery woodwind of the It. Renaissance, mentioned by Zacconi (1592), who lists 3 sizes, with compasses c^1–d^2, c^0–d^1, C^0–d^0. Praetorius stated that he had never seen the instr. As the doppione had a compass of a 9th, it was probably furnished with a double reed and wind cap and had a cylindrical bore (80 VI, 114).

Dora, small brass gong of Japan, with central boss, suspended by a cord and struck with a hammer (135).

Dorje, *stick rattle of Buddhist Mongolia and Tibet, terminating in a ring on which smaller metal rings are strung. It corresponds to the khakkhara. Also called vajra (1).

Dorremi [do re mi], small Cuban panpipes with 3 pipes, sounding do, re, mi (152).

Dorungu, *board zither of the Anderimba Pygmies of the Congo, with resonator (128).

Dörwen chikhe khuur (four-eared *khuur*), bowed instr. of the Sunit Mongols. The body is usually circular, sometimes octagonal, the belly commonly of hide. The stick handle holds 4 rear pegs. Two pairs of silk strings tuned a 5th apart pass through a small metal loop or a cord tied to the handle. This can be moved by the player to change the pitch. The instr. is held on the player's left thigh and is stopped by the end or middle joints of his finger, or from underneath by a nail. The bow passes between the strings so that 2 are always sounded together. Larger than the Chin. *su hu but otherwise identical. Called biwa by the Kalmuk. *Cf.* khorae (69).

Dory, 2-headed *cylindrical drum of the Sakalava of the Malagasy Republic, used for ritual purposes only. It may not be touched by women. *Ca.* 60 cm. (2 ft.) in diam. See also: anakidory (171).

Dō shō (Jap.: cave flute), obs. flute of Japan, equivalent of the Chin. tung hsiao, *ca.* 60 cm. (2 ft.) long (135, 157).

Dotara [Pers. **dutār,* two strings], plucked stringed instr. of N. India (103).

Double . . . (Engl., Fr.) (Ger.: *doppel*), **1.** as a prefix to names of organ stops, double denotes a stop that is an oct. lower than named, *e.g.,* double principal 16'; see also: dupla; **2.** as prefix to names of Renaissance and baroque instrs., double denotes one with a compass descending below Γ ut (gamma ut). Playford, in the introduction to his *Skill of Music,* informs us that notes below "gam-ut" are called double notes, and as late as 1740 Grassineau writes of the harpsichord that "the notes . . . below the bass stave are called Double." (They were written FF, EE, DD, etc., in Britain, pron. "double F," etc.) On the Continent the term usually indicated an instr. of 16' pitch; **3.** 2 instrs., such as double pipes, double bells, etc.

Double-action harp (Fr.: *harpe à double mouvement;* Ger.: *Doppelpedalharfe;* It.: *arpa con doppio movimento*), modern harp with 7 pedals, each provided with half and whole hitches to raise the tone by 1 and by 2 semitones respectively. For details see: harp.

Double banked, said of a harpsichord having 2 manuals.

Double bas haultbois, Fr.: contrabass shawm.

Double bass (Fr.: *contrebasse;* Ger.: *Kontrabass;* It.: *contrabasso*), bowed stringed instr. of contrabass range. As played today, it has 4 strings, tuned E^1 $A^1 D^0 G^0$, and is notated an oct. higher than it sounds. As the double bass was

never standardized either as to size or to pattern, precise measurements are impossible; the instr. now in use in the orchestra may perhaps be said to have an over-all length of 180–200 cm. (6–6½ ft.), a body length averaging 112 cm. (44 in.), and a speaking string length of 107–08 cm. (42–42½ in.). Disparities are still such, however, that Ger. *luthiers* talk of full, three-quarter, and half-size double basses; part of this trouble stems from the fact that *violoni are still played and are counted as double basses.

Contrabass stringed instrs. are known to have existed since the mid-16th c. (Sp. miniatures of the 10th c. depict outsize viol-type instrs. already, but these disappear until the Renaissance): a *viola di contrabasso* was played in an ensemble in Ferrara in 1529; a *basse-contre de viole* is listed in a Parisian maker's inventory of 1556, a *double basse contre de viole* among the effects of a deceased Parisian maker in 1557, and a *basse-contre de violon façon de Venise* in a 1570 inventory; a *sottobasso di viola* was played in a Florence *intermedio* of 1565. Whether the double bass was originally designed as a member of the *da braccio* or of the *da gamba* family is a matter of dispute, but early references and iconography seem to place it among the *da gamba* group. Its earliest representations (Veronese: *Marriage at Cana,* 1563; Jost Amman: *Turnirbuch,* 1566) show a fretted neck with 4 strings, gamba-type flat back, and C-holes are visible in the *Turnirbuch.* Some early It. instrs. have arched backs, but later instrs. were often made with gamba-type backs, making the instrs. considerably easier to handle. We have no information concerning their tuning until the second half of the 18th c., when it was the same as that in use today. The later Ger. models tended structurally more toward the gamba, with short, fretted neck, characteristic sloped shoulders, and flat back bent at the shoulder level to reduce body depth, high ribs, back, and belly that did not project beyond the ribs, sometimes with rounded corners, and with 5 strings tuned $D^1 E^1 A^1 D^0 G^0$. Occasionally a sixth string was added. This type of bass continued to be played in Germany until the mid-18th c., sometimes with its neck fretted. Quantz recommended the use of a 4-stringed double bass in preference to the smaller violone with 5 or 6 strings; Leopold Mozart in 1756 spoke of both 4- and 5-stringed double basses. In 1687 Daniel Speer mentioned a 3-stringed double bass, tuned $G^1 C^0 F^0$, and a 4-stringed one tuned as today, and from then on we hear much of the 3-stringed instr., which came to be used in Italy and England as well as in Ger.-speaking countries. Schubart, writing *ca.* 1785, comments on its being in common use for orchestral work, but adds that for solo work a 4- or 5-stringed instr. was indispensable. The 3-stringed basses lasted longest in Italy and England —up to the end of the 19th c. in some instances. They were tuned $G^1 D^0 A^0$ in England, $A^1 D^0 G^0$ or $G^1 D^0 G^0$, in Italy. Most of the double basses built prior to the mid-19th c. were originally intended for 3 strings, and in some parts of Europe the 3-stringed version lives on as a folk instr. When the 4-stringed It. version was taken up again in the 19th c., it was first tuned $D^1 G^1 D^0 G^0$, the 2 lowest strings subsequently being raised by one tone. But in the 19th c. the need was felt for a downward extension of the compass to C^1; this was effected at first by restoring the fifth string (now retuned to C^1) and later in the c. by the newly invented "C-string attachment," which carries the E^1 string to the top of the head and provides for mechanical stopping of the semitones down to C^1 if so desired; alternately, it depresses the string onto the nut for normal E^1-string use. The metal pegs with cog tuning devices, a great convenience in so large an instr., were in use by Praetorius' day but later were forgotten, to be reinvented in the late 18th c. by Carl Ludwig Bachman of Berlin. Giant double basses, actually sub-contrabasses, have been made sporadically since the early 17th c. Praetorius is the first author to describe one; he says that it was a recent introduction and depicts an instr. similar to his double bass but *ca.* 225 cm. (90 in.) high, with a body length of about 140 cm. (55 in.). A 17th-c. It. giant in violin form but with flat back is preserved in the Victoria and Albert Museum, London; it stands 247 cm. (8 ft.) high and has a body length of 173 cm. (68 in.). The 19th c. saw a 7-stringed instr., mechanically bowed, produced in Vienna in 1829; Jean-Baptiste Vuillaume of Paris left 2 *octobasses; and in 1889 John Geyer in the U.S. made a monster 4½ m. (15 ft.) high. Such instrs. were created in an attempt to provide the orchestra with a stringed instr. of 32′ pitch. For double bass viol see: viola da gamba, violone. See also: citarruni, contrebasse à clavier, grosse basse de violon, grosse Bassgeige, grosser Bass, octobasse, violone (15, 41, 80 VII, 169, 170).

Double bass . . . , see also: contrabass . . .

Double bass viol, see: viola da gamba, violone.

Double bell, 2 single, clapperless bells connected by a common handle, usually made of metal but occasionally of wood. The handle may be bent, in which case the bells lie side by side, or straight, in which case they are shaped like a dumbbell. They differ either in length or diam., and always in pitch. Found in Negro Africa, from where they were introduced into the New World (170).

Double clarinet (Fr.: *clarinette double;* Ger.: *Doppelklarinette*), oldest known form of clarinet, portrayed on reliefs that date back to 2700 B.C. of the Old Kingdom of Egypt. Both Sachs and Schaeffner found that pairs of parallel pipes occurring in antiquity were clarinets, pairs of divergent pipes, shawms (*i.e.,* single- and double-reed instrs. respectively), and this conclusion is now generally accepted. Double clarinets are played nowadays all over the Islamic East. They consist of 2 pieces of cane glued and tied together, with equidistant equal fingerholes. They are also played in India, where one pipe is a drone and the reeds are usually enclosed in a gourd wind chamber. The double clarinet occurs today in Europe, Africa, and Asia, the older forms being those with equal holes and the same number of holes on each pipe (63 Schaeffner, 168, 177).

Double conical drum (Fr.: *tambour en double cône;* Ger.: *Doppelkonustrommel*), drum having its largest diam. in the center, tapering toward both ends, with rectilinear body (100).

Double curtal, see: curtal.

Double dulciana, organ stop invented *ca.* 1828 by J. C. Bishop of London, with open metal flue pipes at 16′ pitch (176).

Double English horn, organ stop invented by Robert Hope-Jones (d. 1914), with metal flue pipes of inverted conical shape surmounted by large bells (198).

Double escapement, see: escapement.

Double euphonium, euphonium furnished with 2 tubes and bells, to enable the production of 2 tones of different tone quality at the same pitch, consequently a *duplex instr. Played with a single mouthpiece.

Double expression (Fr.: *expression double*), harmonium stop invented by Victor Mustel of Paris in 1854, a divided *expression stop worked by knee levers (176).

Double flageolet (Fr.: *flageolet double;* Ger.: *Doppelflageolet*), double whistle flute, pop. in past centuries, made either of 2 separate pipes or of 2 bores pierced in a single block of wood, mentioned from the 13th c. on (as *flajos doubliers* in Fr. literature) and often depicted during the Middle Ages. Samuel Pepys wrote in 1668 of *"two pipes of the same note,* fastened together, so I can play on one and then echo it upon the other."* In the early 19th c. William Bainbridge took out several patents for a dou-

ble flageolet called *English flageolet. See also: triple flageolet, double flute (35).

Double flute (Fr.: *flûte double;* Ger.: *Doppelflöte*), term that designates: **1.** parallel connected double pipes, usually with a duct, found in Europe, America, Asia, S. Seas; **2.** double vertical flutes similar to those of the African Yaunde; **3.** double *cross flutes of bamboo, either stopped at both ends by nodes and divided internally into 2 chambers by another node, with a blowhole at each side of the central node and fingerholes near the ends, or with single blowhole in the center and open ends, one or both of which are closed by the player's fingers. See also: chord flute, double flageolet, double pipes, dvogrle, dvoyanki, dvoykinye, dvoynice (168).

Double grand piano, grand piano intended for 2 performers, patented by Pirsson of New York in 1850; the players faced each other from opposite ends, with single string-plate for both instrs. "the short string of one being in line with the long strings of the other," according to the patent. *Cf.* vis-à-vis (92).

Double harp (Ger.: *Doppelharfe;* It.: *arpa doppia;* Lat.: *harpa gemina*), earliest known *chromatic harp, in existence during the 16th and 17th c., with 2 rows of gut strings, the second being for accidentals. Vincenzo Galilei ascribed its invention to the Irish; Monteverdi called for one in his *Orfeo* (1607), and Praetorius depicted a cumbersome "great double harp."

Double horn (Ger.: *Doppelhorn*), horn in B♭ and F, produced in the late 19th c., a *duplex instr. with 2 sets of valve crooks operated by a thumb valve that adds or subtracts a length of tubing. (It adds for the F horn, subtracts for the shorter, B♭ horn.) See also: chromatic trumpet and French horn (25, 176).

Double melodia, melodia organ stop at 16′ pitch (131).

Double organ, 1. in the 16th c., an organ with manual compass extending below Γ ut (see: double, 2); **2.** in the 17th

c. a 2-manual organ or, according to Matthew Locke (*Melotheia*, 1673), the "chaire and greate organ."

Double percussion piano, see: piano à double percussion.

Double pipes, the common form of pipe during antiquity and the early Middle Ages. The earliest extant specimens are from Ur and date from *ca.* 2700 B.C., now preserved in the University Museum at Philadelphia. They are some 30 cm. (12 in.) long and made of silver. Toward the middle of the second millennium B.C. double pipes were introduced into Egypt. Specimens with unequal holes have been found in Egyptian tombs (4 holes in 1 pipe, 3 in the other). The divergent pipes, which Sachs and Schaeffner identified as *double-reed pipes, were the most frequently employed in the Mediterranean area and appear to have preceded the parallel pipes, which are identified with *single-reed pipes. All the classical Gk. auloi were divergent double-reed pipes, the single *aulos coming into use only in postclassical times. With the end of antiquity the double-reed pipe gives way to single-reed parallel pipes. These were adopted by Arab. culture, under whose aegis they spread as far as the Far East. In med. times double pipes continued to be played in Europe: a pair of cranebone parallel pipes was excavated in 1933 from an Avar grave in Hungary, dating from the 7th or 8th c., with 5 holes in the right pipe and 2 in the left. So far these are the earliest known extant parallel pipes. Double pipes resembling Gk. auloi appear in art works of the 9th and 10th c. but may be mere imitations of antiquity. In many countries double pipes survived the Middle Ages in form of folk instrs., sometimes with horn bell, sometimes with a bag, sometimes with both, but also as plain parallel pipes. Divergent pipes have become extinct. Double whistles of clay, often in form of human figures, have been found in Mexico, dating back to archaic culture. These yield the interval of a second (89 Baines, 127, 168, 182).

Double piston valve, syn. of Vienna valve.

Double recorder, several double recorders dating from the 16th c. have been preserved, one in All Souls College, Oxford, with 2 connecting pipes, 1 shorter than the other, having 2 whistle heads that terminate in a common blowhole; both have 4 front fingerholes, but not in equal positions, those of the longer pipe being lower. Another is in the Landesmuseum of Zürich; here the holes, 14 in all, are paired so that 2 can be stopped by 1 finger. Similar instrs. are played today in E. Europe as folk instrs.

Double reed (Fr.: *anche double;* Ger.: *Doppelrohrblatt;* It.: *ancia doppia*), reed made from 2 blades of cane (*Arundo donax*) or other material. In its early form a double reed was made of cornstalk, rush, etc., flattened at one end. Double reeds of antiquity were pinched flat and clamped to hold the tip in shape; they had long necks and were inserted directly into the pipe. Short reeds mounted on metal staples do not occur until postclassical times. The pinched type of reed is still in use in the Orient. The later form of double reed has been traced back to the 16th c. but may be older; it consists of a long strip of cane bent double and is unknown outside the West. The double reed associated with a conical tube was probably introduced to Europe by the Moors and is still characteristic of W. Asian wind instrs. In antiquity it was associated with a cylindrical tube (14, 89 Galpin).

Double slide, 2 parallel slides, such as those of a trombone, connected and moved together by a single stay. Each shift necessitates only half the distance that would be required with a single slide.

Double touch, device for increasing the tone of a harmonium by depressing the keys more firmly, invented before 1855 by August L. Tamplin of England and applied to the *Mustel organ (176).

Double trumpet, see: chromatic trumpet and French horn.

Doublette, Fr.: *fifteenth (organ stop); also a mixture organ stop of either 2 ranks (2⅔' and 2') or 3 ranks (with 4' added), rarely of 4 ranks. As a mixture, it corresponds to the Quarte (133).

Double virginal (Fr.: *épinette double*), virginal at 8' pitch with a smaller, removable one at 4' pitch set in a recess between soundboard and bottom, usually to the left of the (8') keyboard. Such instrs. were made in the Low Countries, chiefly in Antwerp, in the 16th and 17th c. When played, the smaller instr. was withdrawn from its recess and placed on top of the 8' virginal, from which the jack rail had previously been removed; a diagonal slot was cut across the bottom of the 4' instr. so that the jacks of the 8' instr. actuated the 4' virginal's keys. Trichet, *ca.* 1640, mentions this manner of playing the 2 together—a simple and most efficient form of coupler—which was forgotten shortly after he wrote. For a triple virginal see: virginal.

Doublophone, *duplex instr. of Fontaine Besson of Paris, 1890; it combined a 3-valved baritone with a valved tenor trombone, each having separate tubing. In appearance it was a baritone with a second bell set at an angle (176).

Douçaine (Fr.) [Lat. *dulcis,* sweet], **1.** woodwind instr. mentioned in Fr. literature from the late 13th c. to the mid-16th, presumably identical with the dulcina of Tinctoris, the It. dolzaina, and the Sp. dulzaina, thought to have been a cylindrically bored reed-cap instr. played with a double reed; **2.** for the organ stop of this name see: douchaine. See also: demi-doussaine, dolzaina, douchaine, doucine, doussaine, dulceuse, dulcina (35).

Doucemelle (Fr.), see: doulcemelle.

Doucet, Engl. 14th- and 15th-c. term for the recorder, first used by Chaucer. See also: doucette.

Doucette, var. of the word "doucet," which occurs in 15th-c. Engl. literature.

Douchaine, 1. var. of douçaine; **2.** organ stop that existed at Rouen in 1515, as doucines at Tours in 1550 (82, 167).

Doucine, 1. var. of douçaine; **2.** organ stop, see: douchaine.

Doul, see: dholi.

Doulcemelle, doulcemer [Lat. *dulce melos*], 15th-c. and early-16th-c. Fr.: dulcimer. Various forms of the word occur in Fr. literature of the period: *doulz de mer* in 1449; *doulcemelle, doucemelle,* and *doulcemer* are in use chiefly in the 15th c.; *doulce-mère* is recorded in 1506 (53, 82, 106).

Doussaine (Fr.), 16th-c. form of the word *douçaine.*

Döwel (to sound), musical stone of Ethiopia, used as a substitute for church bells, suspended from a tree or frame outside the church door and struck like a gong. Frequently it occurs as a chime of 2, 3, or 4 stones. A small döwel is known as katchel (45).

Drahtgeige, Ger.: nail violin.

Drahtharfe, Ger.: syn. of Spitzharfe.

Draw stop (Fr.: *registre;* Ger.: *Registerzug;* It.: *registro*), device for bringing on a stop of organ pipes or row of harpsichord jacks.

Drehklavier (Ger.), in a wider sense any barrel-actuated keyboard instr.; in the narrower sense a *barrel piano. Although the word literally means cranked keyboard, it is applied to instrs. devoid of a keyboard.

Drehleier, Ger.: hurdy-gurdy.

Drehorgel (Ger.), in a wider sense any hand-cranked organ; in the narrower sense a *barrel organ.

Drehscheiben, Ger.: fork action (of a harp).

Drehventil, Ger.: rotary valve.

Dreiviertelgeige, Ger.: three-quarter-size fiddle.

Dresdner Fagott, name sometimes given to the bassoon in Germany in the late 18th c., because of the excellence of its Dresden makers (89 Langwill).

Dretsa, syn. of sódina.

Dril-bu, Tibetan hand bell, campaniform, with clapper and handle, derived from the Indian *ghantā. It serves in temple orchestras (89 Picken).

Drimba, Rom.: Jew's-harp (5).

Drom, early form of drum.

Drombla, Bulg.: Jew's-harp (176).

Drombulye, Jew's-harp of Yugoslavia, now a child's toy (89).

Dromla [Ger. *Trommel*], Pol.: Jew's-harp. The word goes back to the mid-17th c. or earlier (176).

Dromslade, var. of drumslade.

Drone (Fr.: *bourdon;* Ger.: *Bordun;* It.: *bordone*), **1.** pipe or string that sounds a continuous tone. Drone pipes reach back to antiquity, when double pipes consisted of a right-hand drone pipe and left-hand melody pipe. The holes not required were stopped up with wax, just as they are today. Drone strings were common in the Middle Ages (organistrum, early bowed chordophones). Both drone pipes and strings are today more common in Eastern Europe and Asia than in the West. **2.** another name of the *bladder and string.

Drum (Fr.: *tambour;* Ger.: *Trommel;* It.: *tamburo*), membranophone with a body that is either tubular (cylindrical, conical, barrel-shaped, etc.) or vessel-shaped (kettledrum) or that consists of a frame (tambourine, etc.) and is sounded by percussion, being struck by the player's bare hands or by beaters. Drums may have 1 or 2 heads, and these may be glued, nailed, or laced to the body. The body of tubular and vessel drums is also called *shell*, which acts as a resonator. A very elementary form of membranophone has been reported by Kirby from S. Africa, where the edge of a large hide is grasped and held taut by several players while they beat it. In one form or another, drums are known all over the world (with the exception of a few primitive peoples); their age is unknown, but we can follow them back to about 3000 B.C. In many areas they serve less as rhythm instrs. than as sacred or ritual objects endowed with magical power, sometimes becoming a status symbol. This is par-

ticularly true of the kettledrum. In Africa the extramusical function of drums is such that in many regions they may be said to participate actively in daily life, at religious and civil ceremonies, at the hunt, in transmitting messages, etc.

European antiquity knew no drum other than the Semitic *frame drum used in Greece and Rome (tympanon). During the Middle Ages drums were introduced from W. Asia; they were struck with sticks and served above all as timekeeping devices with little metrical development. The Engl. word *drum* does not occur before the 16th c., when it was applied to the snare drums of the Swiss drummers and fifers. See also: barrel drum, bass drum, bowl drum, conical drum, cylindrical drum, daiko, double conical drum, footed drum, frame drum, friction drum, goblet drum, gong drum, ground drum, hourglass drum, kettledrum, ku, machine drum, pedal drum, plucked drum, pot drum, rattle drum, sand drum, side drum, slit drum, steel drum, tabor, "talking drum," tambourin, tambourine, tsuzumi, water gourd (79, 170, 177).

Drum chime, set of drums. See: chaing vaing, pat waing, saeng, saing waing.

Drumelca, Slov. Jew's-harp, also called brumbice (144).

Drum gong, former designation of the kettle gong.

Drumla, var. of dromla.

Drum pedal (Ger.: *Trommel*), auxiliary organ stop consisting of a pedal that when depressed admitted air to the 2 lowest pipes, creating the effect of a roll of drums. See also: Sumber (198).

Drumscheit, var. of Trumscheit.

Drumslade [Du.: *trommelslag,* drumbeat], originally the word meant drummer in England, but during the 16th c. and first half of the 17th c. it indicated the drum (180).

Drunka, syn. of tanbura, 1.

Druri dana, "tuning fork" idiophone of Nias that corresponds to the rere (122).

Dsanadsel, see: tsanatsel.

Du, Burmese: gong (176).

Dū ahank, obs. Turk. wind instr., not further identified (76).

Dub (Sum.), drum of ancient Babylon that appears in the third millennium B.C. According to Galpin, it was an *hourglass drum, also found in the Indus Valley and China; according to Sachs, it was a *frame drum. See also: tibbū, timbuttu (89 Galpin, 177).

Duba [Hung. *dob], double-headed *cylindrical drum of Romania, beaten with a knobbed stick; 12 cm. (4½ in.) high, 20–25 cm. (8–10 in.) in diam. *Cf.* toba (5).

Dubbūs, see: dabbūs.

Duct flute (Ger.: *Kernspaltflöte*), flute in which the air stream is directed through a narrow duct against the sharp edge of a lateral aperture. Ducts can be internal or external, terminal or central. Internal ducts are situated inside the tube and may be formed by a natural node, a block of wood, or of resin. External ducts are often formed by a ringlike sleeve (ring flute) tied around the wall of the tube. In flutes with terminal ducts the player blows directly into the duct; in those with central ducts he blows into a hollow tube that acts as wind chamber as far as the duct; the block is then a blob of resin; such flutes rarely have fingerholes; they are found in America, Asia, and the S. Seas. Duct flutes are frequently made with beaked mouthpieces to facilitate the embouchure; they are found in Algeria, America, Asia, Europe, the S. Seas (100, 168).

Duda, pl. **dudy** [Turk. *duduk], bellows-blown bagpipe of Hungary, Poland, the Ukraine, and Yugoslavia, with kidskin bag, hair outside, a double chanter set in a stock carved to resemble a goat's head, and a bass drone. The left chanter pipe has 6 front fingerholes and a rear thumbhole, the right pipe 1 fingerhole, both being provided with idioglott single beating reeds of cane. The right chanter

terminates in a wooden foot joint. The bass drone is of metal (13, 89).

Dudei, var. of dudey.

Dudelsack [Pol. *dudlič*, from *dudy], S. Ger. and Austrian: bagpipe. The common Ger. word for bagpipe is *Sackpfeife.* The term Dudelsack does not occur before the late 17th c. (117, 169).

Düderli, mirliton of Uri, Switzerland (102).

Dudey [Pol. *dudy,* from Turk. *duduk], 17th-c. Ger. bagpipe, described by Praetorius as being similar to the Hümmelchen but with an additional, small drone pitched an oct. above the lower drone. The word appears first in the 17th c. and becomes *Dudelsack* by the end of the c. (159).

Dudi, syn. of edaka.

Dudka, 1. *whistle flute of Russia, of turned wood, with 6 front fingerholes; *ca.* 60 cm. (2 ft.) long; 2. Pol.: small bagpipe (176).

Duduk (Turk.) [Pers. *tutak], 1. Turk.: pipe, *whistle flute; 2. whistle flute of SW. Bosnia, made of maple or pearwood, with cylindrical bore, a flare at the mouthpiece, and 6 equidistant fingerholes. The top fingerhole is not uncovered, as the instr. is held by forefinger and thumb: because of its wide mouthpiece it cannot be held by the performer's lips. The duduk is played chiefly by Mohammedans, who hum a deep drone while they accompany dances. It is 24–40 cm. (9½–16 in.) long (34); 3. whistle flute of E. and S. Serbia, with rear duct, both duct and blowhole being on the side opposite the fingerholes. The tube is conical with cylindrical bore and has 6 fingerholes. In S. Serbia it is 50 cm. (20 in.) long or less, in N. and C. Serbia up to 1 m. (40 in.) long. The top fingerhole is bored at one half the total length of the tube. Longer instrs. have so narrow a bore that the fundamental oct. will not speak at all unless the player's lower lip is used as a *beard. In W. Serbia the duduk is known as frula or as svirala

(34); **4.** bagpipe of Dagestan, U.S.S.R. *Cf.* dyudyuk (103).

Duduki [Turk. *duduk], conical oboe of Georgia, U.S.S.R., with *pirouette, 8 front fingerholes, and a rear thumbhole, identical with the Arab. zamr (178).

Dudy [Turk. *duduk], **1.** Czech bellows-blown bagpipe with goatskin bag, hair outside, a single chanter, a conical pipe with cylindrical bore, its stock carved to resemble a goat's head, 7 front fingerholes, and a rear thumbhole. The chanter terminates in a cow-horn bell and is furnished with a single beating reed. The bass drone is in 2 joints, the first of which is bored with 3 channels to reduce its over-all length. It has a single beating reed, sounds 2 octs. below the chanter keynote, and terminates in a large horn bell. The Moravian dudy, also called gajdy, varies slightly in that it usually has 6 front fingerholes and a thumbhole; **2.** pl. of duda (13).

Duetton, *duplex instr. invented by J. J. Chediwa of Odessa in 1887, usually consisting of a cornet and a tenor trombone with common mouthpiece, built in form of a classical lyre, with both bells turned upward (126, 156).

Duff, pl. **dufuf** (Arab.), **1.** generic Arab. term for a *frame drum; **2.** in particular a square or octagonal tambourine with 2 membranes and snares; **3.** in Algeria a square tambourine with 2 membranes, and with jingles and snares; **4.** in Albania and Turkey, a tambourine. See also: adufe, daf, deff, tof.

Dugdugi, *friction drum of S. India, made of a dish-shaped clay pot covered with a membrane and having a friction stick. *Cf.* gubgubi (16).

Duggi, drum of N. India (103).

Duhul (Pers.), barrel-shaped drum of Persia, with 2 laced heads. The word corresponds to the Arab. *tabl.* See also: dawūl, dhōlaka (75 II, 147, 176).

Duifflöte, see: Doppelflöte.

Dukrah, kettledrum of Afghanistan (176).

Duku, wedge-shaped, zoomorphic *slit drum of the Mandja of the Congo (19).

Dukulu (Kikongo), small, 2-headed *cylindrical drum of the Congo; the lacings form a W or network pattern (185).

Dulcan, see: dolcan.

Dulcema, OSp.: dulcimer. The term was employed in the 14th c. See also: dulce melos.

Dulce melos, stringed instr. of the 15th c. which assumed 2 forms, a simpler one as *dulcimer, a more complicated one as a keyboard instr. Our knowledge of both forms is due almost entirely to Henri Arnaut of Zwolle, who wrote *ca.* 1440, and to Paulus Paulirinus, writing some 20 years later. Arnaut says that the simplest form of dulce melos is that played *cum baculo,* with a stick; Paulirinus says that it is provided with *ligniculo aut penna,* a small stick or quill. The keyboard version is perhaps best described as an ingenious cross between fretted *clavichord and *Tangentenflügel. Arnaut writes of it as having a rectangular case and a chromatic compass B^0–a^2, with 35 keys. The strings were stretched over 2 bridges placed between 2 nuts at distances calculated to produce the ratios 1:2:4, the lowest segment of each string (between nut and first bridge) giving its fundamental, the central segment (between bridges), its oct., the top segment (between second bridge and top nut), its superoctave. As a single string could thus sound 3 tones, depending on the key depressed, only 12 pairs of strings were needed for 35 keys. The keys were not straight, but fanned out like those of a fretted clavichord. As far as one can determine, the action consisted of lead-weighted jacks that rested on the rear portion of each key; a brass plectrum or tangent projected from the upper end. When a key was depressed, the jack jumped against the string. The design of a key shows a narrow tongue projecting from its rear, presumably meant to ride in a groove, the closed upper part of which may have acted as a check. Paulirinus describes the dulce melos as a hollow oblong box strung with metal strings —his favorite instr. A *dulcemel para tañer* (keyboard-type dulce melos) listed in a 1503 inventory belonged to Queen Isabella the Catholic. See also: dulsacordis.

Dulcet, oct. dulciana stop.

Dulceuse [Lat. *dulcis,* sweet], "short instruments called dulceuses" are listed in the inventory of Henry VIII's instrs. (in 1547), an Engl. occurrence of the dolzaina, douçaine, etc.

Dulcian (Ger.: *Dulzian*), **1.** organ stop of funnel-shaped open flue pipes of medium scale. According to Praetorius, it was invented by Nicolaus Maass, in imitation of the Dulzian. Adlung characterizes it as penetrating in tone. Usually at 8′ pitch, it occurred also at 4′ pitch; **2.** organ stop of reed pipes which first appears *ca.* 1500, usually at 16′ pitch, rarely 32′ or 4′. Numerous variants of the word occur: dolzan, dulcan, dolcan, etc. Also called fagotto; **3.** 19th-c. Engl. translation of the Ger. word *Dulzian* (3, 159).

Dulciana (Ger.: *Dulziana*), organ stop of 18th-c. origin, of small-scaled slightly conical pipes, open, of metal. Snetzler introduced it into Engl. organs in 1754. From the mid-19th c. on it assumed the form of a medium-scaled cylindrical register at 16′, 8′, or 4′ pitch. The octave dulciana is called dulcet.

Dulciana flute (Ger.: *Dulzianflöte*), organ stop of open metal flue pipes, small-scaled, of inverted conical shape (133).

Dulcian bass (Ger.: *Dulzianbass*), **1.** organ stop of reed pipes in the pedal, at 16′ or 8′ pitch; **2.** 16′ dulciana in the pedal (176).

Dulcimer [Lat. **dulce melos*] (Fr.: *tympanon;* Ger.: *Hackbrett*), a zither, differentiated from the psaltery by its playing technique: instead of being plucked it is struck with curved beaters, padded sticks, etc. The modern European instr. consists of a shallow, trapezoid box resonator, strung with a variable number of metal strings—2–5 to a course— with tuning pins running along the right diagonal side and with one or more bridges, which divide the strings in a ratio of 2:3, the portion of the string lying on one side of the bridge being a 5th higher in pitch than the other. In order to provide space for the beaters, the strings are led alternately over and under the bridge(s), or rather, through cutouts provided for this purpose. The bridges are not glued to the soundboard, but are placed freely, as their position is of critical importance, and are held in place by the pressure of the strings.

The struck zither is probably of Near Eastern origin and was introduced to Europe by the Arabs, first to Spain, where it was known by the second half of the 12th c., subsequently to the Balkans. Much later, about 1800, it traveled to the Far East, from either Europe or Turkey. The med. dulcimer seems to have been known to 14th-c. Spain as *dulcema* and was described *ca.* 1440 in Burgundy as *dulce melos* and during the same c. as *doucemelle* in France; the Engl. word *dulcimer* first occurs *ca.* 1475. During the 15th c. it was also often called *tympanon,* as it is in France today. Dulcimers are mentioned in Swiss records of 1447, Cleves 1477, Augsburg 1512. It. writers refer to the *salterio tedesco* (German psaltery), or to *stromento di porco,* equivalent to the Ger.: *Schweinskopf.* By the 16th c. the instr. had fallen into disrepute; Luscinius in 1536 remarks that the dulcimer *"instrumentum ignoble est."* Despite such adverse opinions it continued in existence: Praetorius described it as having 12 pairs of strings, Mersenne, 13 pairs, and a little later, in 1662, Samuel Pepys heard it played. At the end of the c. Pantaleon Hebenstreit transformed it into a far larger and louder instr. named Pantaleon, and thereby created a new vogue for the instr. During the 18th c. and well into the 19th the dulcimer was accepted by polite society, but from the delicate and highly ornate object of the 18th c. it became a rather coarse piece of 4-legged furniture in the early 19th c. and was completely displaced by the piano toward the mid-19th c. Details of construction varied throughout its history, a compass of 2–3 octs. being common. Although now dead as an "art" instr., the dulcimer lives on as a folk instr. in parts of Europe, notably in Hungary and Romania (cimbalom), Greece (santouri), Czechoslovakia, and the Alps (Cimbal, Hackbrett), although it is now dying out in the Alps. Most of these folk dulcimers are suspended from the player's neck by a strap or are set on the seated player's knees. For the U.S. folk zither called dulcimer see: Appalachian dulcimer (117, 149, 169, 180).

Dulcina [Lat. *dulcis,* sweet], woodwind instr. described only by Tinctoris (*ca.* 1490), who remarks that it was a kind of tibia with 7 fingerholes and 1 thumbhole and had a limited compass. It is thought to be identical with the Fr. douçaine, It. dolzaina, Sp. dulzaina. *Cf.* dolzaina (14).

Dulcitone, *tuning-fork piano with graduated metal tuning forks in lieu of strings, struck by hammers. A label on a specimen in the Claudius Collection in Copenhagen states that the patentees and sole makers were Thos. Machell & Sons of Glasgow. *Cf.* typophone (89).

Dulsacordis [Lat. *dulcis,* sweet + *chorda,* string], unidentified instr. mentioned 1450 by Holland (Howlat); possibly the dulce melos.

Dulzain, see: dulzian (organ stop).

Dulzaina [Lat. *dulcis,* sweet], **1.** woodwind instr. of Spain, mentioned in OSp. literature, when it was the equivalent of the Fr. douçaine and It. dolzaina, and still played today, albeit as a modified folk instr. Pietro Cerone (in 1613) echoes Zacconi (in 1592) when he says that the keyless version had a compass of a 9th, c^0–d^1, or, with 2 keys, of an 11th. As its name indicates, the tone was soft. Today it has been transformed into a loud-voiced shawm, played out of doors,

with broad double reed mounted on a wide metal staple and played without a *pirouette (despite its reputed Moorish origin). The conical bore terminates in a bell. Made of wood or metal with 7 front fingerholes, it has either no keys or, occasionally, simple keywork. The dulzaina is always accompanied by a drum (*cf.* caja peñarandina), measures some 40 cm. (16 in.), including staple, and is *not* identical with the *cobla* shawm. Its Basque name is bolin-gozo. Sometimes it is called gayta. In the past it was often spelled dolçaina (14, 35, 57, 80 VI); **2.** var. of dolzaina.

Dulzaina peñarandina, the dulzaina of Peñaranda, played as a substitute for the gaita (hornpipe), which is tuned identically. It has 7 fingerholes and is 30 cm. (12 in.) long (57).

Dulzflöte (Ger.) (Fr.: *flute traversière à bec*), **1.** cross-blown recorder of the Renaissance. Praetorius shows a cylindrical instr.; **2.** organ stop made in several forms: a) as open cylindrical flue stop of very narrow scale, also known as flauta dulcis; b) of overblowing, narrow-scaled, open cylindrical pipes, from 8′ to 2′ pitch; c) the name was also given to an overblowing cylindrical Gedackt of narrow scale. The stop is also known as flauto amabile, flauto amoroso, flauto dolce, tibia dulcis.

Dulzian [Lat. *dulcis,* sweet], **1.** Ger. equivalent of curtal, so named because its tone was sweeter than that of the contemporary bombard. The term becomes obs. by the mid-18th c. Also called dolzoni. Not to be confused with the dulzaina; **2.** organ stop of inverted conical flue pipes at 8′ pitch, identical with the dolce, dulcian (3, 101).

Dulziana (Ger.), see: dulciana.

Dulzianbass, see: dulcian bass.

Dulzianflöte (Ger.), see: dulciana flute.

Duma, syn. of dunda (30).

Dumba, *musical bow of the Balese of the Congo, without resonator (128).

Dumbalak (Pahl.), equivalent of dunbalāk (75 II).

Dümbek, syn. of deblek.

Dumbelek (Turk.), **1.** small kettledrum of Turkey, always played in pairs, equivalent of the naqqāra. Called deblek in S. Turkey; **2.** in the past, generic name for drums in Turkey, made of either earthenware or other material (76, 89).

Dumbing, bamboo Jew's-harp of New Guinea (176).

Dumb organist, obs. 19th-c. device set on the manual of an organ for depressing the keys mechanically. The boxlike container housed a pinned barrel actuated by a hand crank. It operated on the same principle as the *barrel organ, but was of course devoid of pipework and blowing mechanism. The appropriate keys were depressed by a series of levers. *Cf.* pianista.

Dumb piano (Ger.: *stummes Klavier*), practice keyboard. *Cf.* Virgil practice clavier.

Dumburak, name of the chermak among the Tadjik of Tadzikistan, U.S.S.R. (176).

Dumo, 1. *arched harp of the Mangbetu of the Congo; **2.** pluriarc of the Mangbetu (19, 42).

Dumri, zither of the Muria of Bastar, India, made of a thick board over which brass strings are fixed, and a large gourd resonator. It is held in one hand while the other plucks the strings (68).

Dumtek [?Turk. *dumbelek*], kettledrums of Afghanistan (120).

Dūnāy (Pers.), double clarinet of Islam, known to the Turanian peoples as kūshnāy. See also: nāy (75 II, 89).

Dunba, Basque: **1.** a large cowbell; **2.** bass drum (56).

Dunbak (Pers.), var. of tunbūk (74).

Dunbal (Pers.), 2-headed *cylindrical drum of Persia, played with bare hands; known already in the 17th c. (75 II).

Dunbalāk [dim. of *dunbal*], in ancient Persia probably a small *cylindrical drum (75 II).

Dunda, *pointed flute of Sokoto Province, Nigeria. Also called duma (123).

Dunde, *stick zither of the Bare'e-

speaking peoples of Celebes, with short, flattened bar, one end of which terminates in a carved head holding the single, lateral tuning peg. The bar is connected at its middle to a half gourd or coconut resonator by a bamboo fork that also acts as bridge to the single string. Also called sosanru, tutalo (112, 173).

Dundu [*dundubhi*], **1.** generic name for drum among the Mandingo-speaking peoples of Africa; **2.** in Bolom, Kiki, Limba, and Timne (Sudanic languages) any drum with a skin head (93); **3.** drum of the Gombi of the Congo, similar to the bia; the same people have a footed drum of this name (30).

Dundubhi (Sans., Pali), a thundering war drum of ancient India, made of wood with cowskin heads, mentioned in the *Atharva-Veda.* In modern times a large variety of nāgārā with a metal body, formerly used in battle; played with 2 curved sticks (138, 179).

Dundufa [*dundu*], 2-headed *cylindrical drum of the Sudanese Hausa, belonging principally to butchers and fish vendors (93).

Dunduha [*dundu*], var. of dundufa in Sokoto (a Sudanic language) (93).

Dundun, 1. the largest *hourglass drum of the Yoruba of Nigeria (93); **2.** drum of the Yoruba of Cuba, now apparently obs. (152).

Dung, 1. Tibetan word meaning trumpet; **2.** syn. of dung-dkar.

Dung chen, straight trumpet of Tibet, made of red copper, occasionally decorated with gold or silver. The conical tube is so long it must be rested on the ground or supported when played; used at lamaist rituals. It is 1½–2½ m. (5–8½ ft.) long (170, 176).

Dung-dkar, *marine-shell trumpet of Tibet, made from the *Xancus pyrum,* which is found only in India, where the dung-dkar originates. End-blown, with metal mouthpiece and brass or silver mountings, it is used as a signal instr., *ca.* 23 cm. (9 in.) long (89 Picken).

Dungga wo'o, idiochord bamboo *tube

zither of W. Sumba Island, Indonesia (119).

Dungo, obs. Afro-Cuban drum made of a hollowed tree trunk. Also called ndungo. *Cf.* dungu (152).

Dungu, 1. drum of the Badia, Basakata, and Nkundu of the Congo, similar to the ndungu of the Ekonde; **2.** drum of the Bakongo, very slender, with single head, *ca.* 3½ m. (12 ft.) long; **3.** var. of ndungu (30).

Dunsi-koni [*dunsu,* hunter], *harp lute of Upper Guinea, similar to the koni-mesin (42).

Duo-Art, device incorporated into a conventional piano for automatic playing, formerly made by the Aeolian Piano Co. and worked by an electric motor. It was very pop. in the 1920's. For a list of similar devices see: pianola.

Duodecima (It.: twelfth), organ stop of flue pipes at 2⅔′ pitch, which corresponds to the *twelfth.

Duolon, perfected *nail violin built by the Duolon Co. of Vienna and first shown 1912. It had no sympathetic strings but was provided with tuning devices (169).

Duophone, brass wind instr. with a removable bell, invented by Bezuchet of Paris in 1890 (204).

Dupla (Lat.: double), a now obs. prefix to names of organ stops; as such, dupla meant double the size, or an oct. lower, *e.g.,* dupla sesquialtera, which is an oct. lower than sesquialtera. The Engl. and Fr. equivalents are "double" and "*double*" (133).

Duplex coupler piano, see: Emanuel Moór piano.

Duplex instruments (It.: *gemelli,* twins), brass instrs. that can either produce 2 different tone qualities at the same pitch, being provided with 2 separate bells for this purpose, or play in 2 different tonalities without change of mouthpiece. Or, to put it differently, a combination of 2 dissimilar instrs. at the same pitch, or of 2 similar ones at different pitches. Prototype of the first variety

is Charles Claggett's *chromatic trumpet and French horn of 1788. Experiments designed to produce an instr. of the second type did not get under way until the mid-19th c. or cease until its end. See also: B♭–C clairon, chromatic trumpet and French horn, cornet omnitonique, double euphonium, double horn, doublophone, duetton, Harmonietrompete, lyrophone (176).

Duraij, see: durraij.

Durbatudu, horn of E. India, made of brass or cowhorn (144).

Durchschlagende Zunge, Ger.: free reed.

Durdavets, rattle of Bulgaria (89).

Duri, Jew's-harp of N. Nias, Indonesia, similar to the rinding (176).

Durraij, a small, vase-shaped, single-headed drum of med. Islam and of the Maghrib today (89 Farmer, 146).

Duruitoarea, Rom.: cog rattle (5).

Dusanbass, obs. organ stop in the pedal at 16′ pitch (159).

Dutār (Pers.: two strings), long-necked lute of Persia, with small piriform body, wooden belly, 15 movable frets on the round neck, and 2 strings. These may be of silk or metal. They are secured by T-shaped tuning pegs inserted sometimes from the front, sometimes from the side, and sometimes from both front and side. The shape of the dutār remains that of the ancient Babylonian and Egyptian lute. The poet Hafiz mentioned it in the 14th c. and it is still a favorite in Persia and Turkestan. Played with a tortoise-shell plectrum. *Cf.* chartār, panchtār, setār, shashtār (76, 132, 170).

Dutka [Turk. *duduk*], mouth-blown bagpipe of Romania, similar to the gayda, with whole-skin bag, conical chanter with 6 fingerholes, and single drone (13).

Duwabelas, bonang of Ambon, with 12 bonang kettles arranged in 4 rows of 3 each. Also called gong duwabelas (121).

Duzan, stringed instr. of modern Albania, of the lute family (76).

Dvităra (Beng.: two strings), 2-stringed version of the yaktăra (173).

Dvogrle [*dva*, two + *grlo*, throat], *double flute of Herzegovina, similar to the dvoynice of Bosnia, with almost parallel bores. The tubes are connected for most of the length, a narrow slot separating their lower portions only. The bores end in a common mouthpiece with 2 ducts. The left pipe always has 4 fingerholes, the right pipe 3. The dvogrle is held at the side of the mouth so that the left pipe receives more wind than does the right; it is played in parallel seconds with the same fingering for both hands, or played in unison and often embroidered. Also called svirale (34).

Dvoyačky (Slovakian), generic name for *double-pipe folk instrs. in Slovakia, many of which are homemade (89).

Dvoyanki, *double flute of Bulgaria (89).

Dvoyka, syn. of dvoynice in Croatia (144).

Dvoykinye, syn. of dvoynice in Croatia and Slavonia only (34).

Dvoynice [Serb. *dva*, two], *double flute of Yugoslavia which assumes different forms, all being made from a single block of wood. **1.** Bosnian: the bores of this instr. are not parallel, but run into each other. The pipes are separated at their lower end for about a third of their length. The right pipe has 4 fingerholes, the left 3. It is held on the left side of the player's mouth so that the right side receives more wind than does the left. When accompanying dances the player sometimes hums a drone. The lowest right hole is never closed, but acts as a vent. Both pipes are played with symmetrical fingerings, thus producing a series of parallel 2nds, but some players have developed the playing technique further and use their hands independently; 30–40 cm. (12–16 in.) long; **2.** C. Serbian: these instrs. are considerably rarer than the Bosnian ones and of similar construction; **3.** Dalmatian: built in rounded rather than flat form, with 4

right and 3 left equidistant fingerholes. The lowest right-hand hole is never stopped. The player holds his instr. straight, both pipes receiving the same amount of wind; **4.** Croatian and Slav.: the number of fingerholes depends upon the size of the instr. Those over 30 cm. (12 in.) in length have 5 right holes and 4 left; those of 20–30 cm. (8–12 in.) have 4 and 3 holes, respectively; those under 20 cm. (8 in.) are children's instrs. and have 3 and 2 holes, respectively. This form of dvoynice is played in parallel 3rds. The lower right hole is not stopped; sometimes both lowest holes and the second right-hand hole are not stopped. The right-hand pipe always has the upper voice. Also called dvoykinye, vidulice; **5.** Serbian: in this variety the right pipe has 6 fingerholes, the left none, merely a lateral vent that is carefully tuned to the second hole of the right pipe, which is a drone. Primary use of the dvoynice is by shepherds (34).

Dyadiko, *slit drum of the Uitoto and Bora Indians of S. America. A flat gutter is cut out of a slender tree trunk that is set on 2 logs over a pit. Its ends are sculptured, one in shape of a woman's breast, the other in shape of a lizard's head. Men dance and stamp on it (32, 105).

Dyanga, *vessel rattle of the Baholoholo of the Congo and N. Rhodesia, made of a long-necked calabash filled with seeds, pebbles, etc., or made of 3 or 4 dried fruit husks containing seeds and strung on a stick (42).

Dyedye, * bar zither of the Baholoholo of the Congo and N. Rhodesia, identical to the seze (19, 42).

Dynamophone, 1. free-reed instr. patented in France by Vaclav Nohohradsky on Jan. 28, 1893; **2.** syn. of telharmonium (204).

Dynaphone, monophonic *electrophonic instr. of the electronic type, invented by René Bertrand in 1938 (37).

Dynatone, *electrophonic piano made by the Ansley Radio Corp. of N.Y., of the electroacoustical type with conventionally generated tone and electrostatic pickup (W. Meyer-Eppler: *Elektrische Klangerzeugung*. Bonn, 1949).

Dynda, dyndy, Czech equivalent of Klarfiedel.

Dyophone, a combination harmonium and piano (40).

Dyphone, double lute described by Thomas Mace, who called it a "new" instr. It had 1 body with 2 necks going in opposite directions, and only 1 was played, the strings of the second being sympathetic (180).

Dyudyuk [Turk. *duduk*], whistle flute of Bulgaria (89).

Dzamara, pastoral, *end-blown flute of modern Greece (144).

Dzendze, bar zither of the Budu of the Congo. *Cf.* nzenze, seze, zeze (128).

Dzhio, *end-blown flute of the Venda of S. Africa, conical, very short, made of either a solid piece of wood burned out or 2 pieces of wood hollowed out and bound together with bark or gut. *Ca.* 12 cm. (5 in.) long (116).

Dzigulitsa, syn. of gadulka.

E♭ alto, see: althorn.

E♭ alto horn, see: althorn.

Eapamale, panpipes of the Uaikena Indians of S. America (105).

Ears (Fr.: *oreilles;* Ger.: *Seitenbart*), ears of an organ pipe are projections on each side of the mouth, placed at right angles to it. Their function is to assist speech and to a lesser extent to influence pitch. If they are bent inward, the pitch rises, if outward, it drops. Ears were already known to Praetorius (129).

E♭ bass, bass tuba.

Ebero, bull-roarer of Port Essington, N. Australia (176).

Ebubu, see: imbubu.

Ebumi, *globular flute of the Congo people, made from the dried hollow berries of the *ebumi* tree, with large blowhole on top and 2 fingerholes. The ebumi is capable of a chromatic scale of 19 "distinct and clear" tones c^1–f^2, although the Kikongo themselves are unaware of this compass. See also: kigwara (185).

Ebundi, syn. of kigwara (195).

Echancrure, Fr.: bout.

Échappement, Fr.: escapement.

Echeion (Gk.), possibly a flat gong of ancient Greece, or a percussion plaque. We know that at their death rituals the Greeks played an instr. of metal that continued to sound long after it had been struck (the same practice exists in SE. Asia); Jaap Kunst was of the opinion that this might have been the echeion (121, 144 Kunst).

Echelle [?OHGer. *scella;* not Lat. *scala*], med. Fr.: bell. The term is recorded from the 12th c. on, both for a tower bell and for a small collar bell (53, 204).

Echelette [dim. of *echelle*], 1. med. Fr.: bell. From the mid-12th c. to the 14th c. the term designated bells of different sizes; during the latter part of this period it was applied more particularly to a hand bell; 2. from the 17th c. on, a form of xylophone consisting of a variable number of graduated wooden slabs strung vertically on a rope according to size, rather like a ladder and struck with a beater. *Cf.* ginebras.

Échiquier, Fr.: chekker.

Echo . . . , as a prefix to names of organ stops, echo denotes a softer variety of the stop named, *e.g.*, echo gamba. Synonyms are: human, lieblich, still, zart (133).

Echobass (Ger.), organ stop, a subbass 16′ on very low pressure (133).

Echo bassoon (Ger.: *Echofagott*), instr. invented in Naples *ca.* 1830, said to have imitated the human voice, and doleful sounds particularly, for which reason it was used in mourning music. By 1835 it had not become known outside Naples (Schilling, *Universal Lexikon der Tonkunst,* II, 1835).

Echo cornet, 1. cornet made during the latter part of the 19th c. and early 20th c. with a nondetachable mute controlled by a piston valve; 2. for the organ stop see: cornet d'écho. Not to be confused with Echokornett (89).

Echofagott, Ger.: echo bassoon.

Echo flugelhorn, flugelhorn made during the latter part of the 19th c. and early 20th c. with a nondetachable mute controlled by a valve.

Echoklavier, square piano built by Johann Georg Schenk of Weimar in 1800 with forte and piano pedals and a tremulant likened to the *unda maris (176).

Echokornett (Ger.), see: cornet d'écho.

Echo mixture, syn. of harmonia aetherea.

Echo organ (Ger. *Echowerk*), a division of the organ, having its pipework enclosed in a box. In Fr. organs it contains chiefly the *cornet d'écho.

Echowerk, Ger.: echo organ.

Éclisse, Fr.: rib (of a violin, etc.).

Ecoc, conical *end-blown flute of the Lango of Uganda, made of animal horn terminating in a point, with a cup-shaped embouchure cut in the upper end and a small hole pierced in the lower end. The upper portion is encased in a skin. The ecoc is suspended from its owner's neck (195).

Edaka, *hourglass drum of India, made of metal. One head is beaten with a drumstick, the other by the player's bare hand. *Ca.* 30 cm. (12 in.) long. Also called dudi (176).

Eddenge, stopped *end-blown flute of the Ganda of Uganda, with one fingerhole, used as a signal instr. (195).

Eddik le bodon (to play in the nose), nose flute of Truk, Micronesia (203).

Edibu, var. of dibu.

Ediokeko, heteroglott Jew's-harp made of metal, of Enggano Island (S. Sumatra) (173).

Edjwa, drum of the Basangele of the Congo, conical, with monoxylous flared base and single head. The head is laced to a leather band nailed to the body. *Ca.* 50 cm. (20 in.) long (30).

Edungu, lyre of the Samia of Uganda, with 8 strings (195).

Ee-neng, syn. of enne.

Eestikannel, *bowed harp of Swed. Estonia, similar to the talharpa but with built-up body having sides, back, and soundboard. The sides are prolonged to form arms united at the top by a horizontal yoke. It had 4 strings tuned in 5ths and was laid across the player's lap during performance. Up to the first quarter of this c. the eestikannel was still to be found on Dagö (Khiuma) Island, Estonia, but is now obs. It represented the old Swed.-Estonian tradition. *Ca.* 52 cm. (20½ in.) long (9).

Effet d'orage, see: orage.

Eggwara, 1. end-blown trumpet of the Ganda of Uganda, made from a conical, slightly curved, tubular gourd, the mouthpiece being merely the natural scar at the end where the gourd was attached to its stalk. A gourd bell is attached to the other end and the entire instr. is covered with cowskin. Also called akawunde, kawunde; **2.** side-blown trumpet of the Soga of Uganda, made from a slightly conical gourd covered with cowskin. A small hole is pierced in the tip. Also called ekkondere, kondere; **3.** mirliton of the Lango of Uganda, made from an elongated gourd (195).

Ego, bottle-shaped Jew's-harp of Flores, Indonesia, made of bamboo (173).

Egoboli, musical bow of Uganda, with gourd resonator and tuning loop (195).

Ehecacozcatl, *marine-shell trumpet of pre-Columbian Toltec culture, made from half a *Strombus giga,* suspended from priests' necks (137).

E♭ horn, see: althorn.

Einfaches Rohrblatt, Ger.: single reed.

Einsaiter, Ger.: monochord.

Einsatzbogen (Ger.), crook inserted by a double slide into a brass instr., as, for instance, into the Inventionshorn. Also called Einschaltbogen.

Einschaltbogen, syn. of Einsatzbogen.

Eisenvioline, Ger.: nail violin.

Ejin, see: njin.

Ejwa, see: edjwa.

Ēka tantrikā, Sans. and Beng. equivalent of yaktāra.

Ēkatāra, Beng. equivalent of yaktāra.

Ekende, 9-tongued sansa of the Bangala of the Congo (42, 176).

Ekidi, *board zither of the Bari of the Congo, without resonator (128).

Ekidongo, ekidongoli, *arched harp of

the Nyoro of Uganda, with narrow, oval body and 8 strings (195).

Ekihako, syn. of kinanga, 1 (195).

Ekinimba, *notched flute of the Kiga of Uganda, *ca.* 90 cm. (36 in.) long, with 2 fingerholes (195).

Ekiro, rattle of Japan, made of pellet bells, used in certain *kabuki* dances (135).

Ekitulege, *ground bow of the Toro and Konjo of Uganda, used as a child's toy (195).

Ekitulenge, *musical bow of the Konjo of Uganda, made from a piece of split bamboo, with a half-gourd resonator near the center. The opening of the gourd is placed over the player's mouth or across his mouth and cheek. His left thumb and forefinger stop the string while his right hand strokes it with a broad piece of grass (195).

Ekkalam, Tamil: ranasringa.

Ekkondere, syn. of eggwara, 2, trumpet of the Soga of Uganda. *Cf.* makondere (195).

Ekón, Afro-Cuban bell made of sheet metal soldered along the side and provided with a handle. The bell is often campaniform and is struck with a short stick, but it may assume a variety of forms. Generally it is held upright in the left hand. Double ekóns also exist. Also called ogán, oggán, kpanlingán, pamigán. See also: elonja, ngongui (152).

Ekonde, pl. of akonde.

Ekorro, var. of kora.

Ekpe (pron. ekue), friction drum of SE. Nigeria (152).

Ektār (one string), *spike lute of C. and S. India today, formerly a * ground bow with open, bucket-like body having a membrane bottom, from the side of which rose a bamboo stick that acted as string bearer. A single string was attached to the center of the membrane, passed through the cavity of the body to be wound around a tuning peg inserted at the top of the string bearer. Nowadays the ektār is made of a round stick, usually bamboo, *ca.* 120 cm. (4 ft.) long,

one end of which passes through a gourd resonator and projects from it, the long end carrying a single tuning peg. The string passes from tuning peg over a bridge and is attached to the spike. A piece of silk or woolen thread is placed between bridge and string to increase the "richness" of the tone. The gourd has a wooden bottom but was formerly of skin or parchment. The string is plucked by the player's forefinger. The ektār serves as a drone for mendicant monks. Also called tungtungi. *Cf.* yak (16, 138, 179).

Ekuara, pl. **bikuara,** *concussion sticks of the Fang of Gabon, a rhythm instr. of dancers (176).

Ekue [*ekpe*], Afro-Cuban *friction drum, usually in form of a footed drum, with membrane laced to a central belt and played with a friction stick. Also called tanse (152).

Ekuku, drum of the Doko of the Congo, beaten with a stick to call the people to war or to celebrate the death of a notable person (30).

Ekulu, drum of the Batetela of the Congo (30).

Elbow melodeon, another name of the lap organ.

Ele [Lat. *ala,* wing], med. Fr. psaltery. See also: ala, ala bohemica.

Electric guitar, *electrophonic instr. consisting of a conventional guitar of which the sound is electrically amplified through a speaker. Generally the tone can be modified by electrical controls. Some models are devoid of the usual body.

Electrochord, *electrophonic piano of the electroacoustical type, patented by Oscar Vierling of Berlin in 1933 and built by Förster of Löbau, in which the tone is conventionally generated. The strings are provided with a series of pickup plates; their characteristics, including attack and decay, may be modified and are transmitted by loud-speaker (59, 60, 144).

Electronde, *electrophonic instr. invented by Leo Taubmann in 1933.

Electronic carillon, see: electrophonic carillon.

Electronic instrument, the term is used here in its narrower sense, *i.e.,* that pertaining to instrs. having their tone generated by electron tubes. See: electrophonic instrs., of which they form a category.

Electronic monochord, a development of the Trautonium by Trautwein, with 2 monophonic tone generators in one cabinet. Continuous variation of frequency is possible.

Electronic piano, see: electrophonic piano.

Electronium (Ger.: *Elektronium*), monophonic *electrophonic instr. made by Hohner of Trossingen, mounted in an accordion case.

Electrophonic carillon, as a result of applied electronics, carillons since the 1930's are usually composed of *tubular bells, generally of constant diam., played from a keyboard; the acoustically generated tone is picked up, amplified, and fed into a system of loud-speakers in the tower. Most electrophonic carillons are so arranged that they can be used both as organ chimes and for tower music (155).

Electrophonic chimes, syn. of electrophonic carillon.

Electrophonic instruments are those having electron tubes, gas tubes, or transistors. The difference between conventional-mechanical and electrophonic instrs. is that the tones of the latter are transmitted through electrical circuits ending in transducers. According to their system of tone generation, they may be classified as follows: 1) electromechanical, 2) electroacoustical, 3) electronic. The first category includes those instrs. with electrostatic, electromagnetic, or photoelectric tone generators, such as the telharmonium and a number of electrophonic organs. The second category consists of conventional instrs. with acoustical tone production, the tone being converted into electrical vibrations and then amplified; their tones may or may not have their characteristics modified.

This category includes electrophonic pianos, amplified guitars, reeds, etc. The third category comprises instrs. with electron-tube tone generators, as for instance the Theremin, Trautonium, and certain electrophonic organs. Furthermore, electrophonic instrs. can be divided into imitative and nonimitative, monophonic (*i.e.,* capable of producing only one tone at a time), and polyphonic. Among those which are imitative we must count most of the organs (the Hammond organ being an exception), the clavioline, electrophonic carillons, the Solovox, etc. Nonimitative are the Theremin, ondes Martenot, Trautonium, etc. Such instrs. as the electrochord and the music synthesizer are both imitative and nonimitative. The creation of nonimitative tones is of course nothing new: it has been done by mutation stops of conventional organs for centuries. Monophonic instrs. include the Solovox, as its name implies, the Bode melochord, etc.; and polyphonic instrs., the Novachord, all organs, etc. See also: Bode melochord, chord organ, clavioline, croix sonore, dynamophone, dynaphone, dynatone, electric guitar, electrochord, electronde, Electronium, emicor, Everett orgatron, Hammond organ, hellertion, Lowery organo, melodium, Mixturtrautonium, music synthesizer, neo-Bechstein piano, Novachord, ondes Martenot, Partiturophon, piano-harp, pianotron, Rangertone, Solovox, Sphärophon, superpiano, telharmonium, Theremin, Trautonium, valvonium, variachord, vivitone, Wurlitzer electronic piano.

Electrophonic organs, a class of *electrophonic instrs. that are furnished with an organ console and that usually imitate the tone of the conventional pipe organ. They have been produced both experimentally and commercially since *ca.* 1930. As variants of electronic circuits are patentable, it follows that no 2 makers use identical means of tone generation, timbre construction, or other tonal characteristics. A partial list of such organs follows: A.W.B. organ, Allen organ,

Baldwin organ, Compton electrone, Conn organ, Conn sonata (forerunner of the Conn organ), Constant Martin organ, Coupleux and Givelet organ, Everett orgatron, Goodell and Swedien organ, Hammond organ, Hardy-Goldthwaite organ, Hugoniot organ, Kinsman organ, Lichtton Orgel, Lincoln organ, Magnetton, Midgley-Walker organ, Minshall organ, Organova, orgues des ondes, Photona, Polychord III, radio-synthetic organ, Rangertone, Robb wave organ, Schober organ, Spilman et Toulon organ, Thomas organ, Tournier organ, WCAU organ, Welte organ, Wurlitzer organ. See also: chord organ.

Electrophonic piano, *electrophonic instr. with acoustical tone generation; this is usually produced by hammers striking the strings of a conventional piano, but in some models it is generated by hammers striking metal reeds (percussion reeds). See also: choralcelo, dynatone, electrochord, electronic piano, neo-Bechstein piano, pianotron, super-piano, variachord, Wurlitzer.

Electrophonic timpani, chromatic electrophonic timpani were invented by B. F. Miessner and consist of 13 short strings stretched over a rectangular frame, tuned to the semitones of an oct. They are struck with timpani beaters and the resulting vibrations are picked up and electrostatically amplified.

Electropneumatic action, organ action patented in 1864 after much preliminary experimental work had been done by a number of people working independently. In this action the wind-chest pallet is opened by the armature of an intermediate electromagnet (89, 170).

Elegiezither (Ger.), concert zither built by G. Tiefenbrunner of Munich to the design of Franz Stahl in 1850, and called Bavariazither by its maker. It differed from the ordinary zither in having a wider fingerboard, a longer body with less curve, and an open string length of 50–58 cm. (20–23 in.). The tuning was up to a 4th lower, i.e., $G^0 d^0 a^0 e^1$. Not

to be confused with the Zitherelegie. *Cf.* Aliquodium (22, 176).

Elektrochord, see: electrochord.

Elem, *musical bow of the Pangwe and Fang of W. Africa, the string of which is held between the player's teeth (19).

Elembe, 1. drum of the Ababua of the Congo, identical with the ndima; **2.** drum of the Basoko of the Congo, with 2 laced heads; **3.** a large drum of the Bangelima of the Congo (30).

Elemú, small Afro-Cuban drum, hourglass-shaped, played with both hands (152).

Elet, *whistle flute of Batavia and S. Banten, Java, with 4–6 fingerholes (121).

Elibo, wooden clapper of Fernando Po Island, W. Africa (176).

Elicon, It.: helicon.

Elingingile, *musical bow of the Ndo of the Congo, with gourd resonator that is not attached to the bow (128).

Ellag (Sum.), unidentified instr. of ancient Babylon, probably a primitive wooden horn, equivalent to the Akk. pukku. Authorities are divided in dating the instr.'s first appearance, one placing it in the third millennium B.C., another in the second (89 Galpin, 147).

Elodikon [*aeolodicon], free-reed keyboard instr. built by Heinrich Baltzer, a watchmaker in Frankfurt on the Oder, by 1840, with a 6-oct. compass, $F^1–f^4$ (176).

Eloña, see: elonja.

Elonja, bell of Ecuador and "Central Africa" which corresponds to the ekón. Also spelled eloña (152).

Eltzabor [*eltze,* pot], **1.** Basque *friction drum made of an earthenware pot covered by a membrane, through the center of which a friction stick is inserted. Also called eltzagor, eltze-gogor, elzütsü, thipinütsü; **2.** Basque alarm bell.

Eltzagor, var. of eltzabor.

Eltze-gogor, var. of eltzabor.

Elú, name of the ilú in N. Brazil (7).

El-'ud or **al-'ud,** see: 'ud.

Elymos, see: auloi elymoi.

Elzütsü, var. of eltzabor.

Ema, generic term for drum in Edo, a Sudanic language (93).

Emaba [*ema* + *aba,* anklet], drum made of a calabash, with a rattle appended to it, in Edo, a Kwa (Sudanic) language (93).

Emanuel Moór piano, 2-manual piano devised by Emanuel Moór (d. 1931), the Hung. composer. Owing to an oct. coupling mechanism, the upper keyboard sounds an oct. higher than the lower. Each keyboard can be played separately, or both can be played together. Also called duplex coupler piano (89).

Embaire, xylophone of C. Soga, Uganda, with 15 or 16 slabs loosely placed on 2 banana stems and separated by sticks; owned by men of importance (195).

Embilita, *whistle flute of the Galla of Ethiopia, with 7 front fingerholes in 2 groups, 1 of 4, the other of 3; or with 2, 3, or 5 fingerholes. Ownership is restricted to the higher dignitaries (144).

Emboliclave, brass instr. similar to the baritone, invented by J. B. Coeffet of Chaumont-en-Vexin, Oise, with a special valve mechanism, intended as a substitute for the bass ophicleide. He obtained a patent on Feb. 19, 1844 (126, 176).

Embouchure [Fr. *bouche,* mouth], Fr.: **1.** mouthpiece of a brass instr.; **2.** blowhole of a flute; **3.** lip technique of a wind-instr. player. In Engl. the word is used in senses 2 and 3.

Embuchi, ivory horn of the Congo, with lateral blowhole, first mentioned by Girolamo Merollo in 1682, when it belonged only to royalty. Today it is an instr. of the Basonga, who pierce the blowhole close to the tip (132, 185).

Emicor, monophonic, imitative *electrophonic instr. of the electronic type, built in the U.S. in 1930 by N. Langer and J. Halmágyi in form of a small square piano with 2-oct. keyboard. Characteristics of the tone can be modified to imitate the sound of several instrs. (W. Meyer-Eppler: *Elektrische Klangerzeugung,* Bonn, 1949).

Empete, drum similar to the bondundu, known to the Ekota, Mbole, Bosaka, Gombe, and Bakutu of the Congo (30).

Empet-empetan, dermenan of W. Java, with a bell of coconut leaf (121).

Empila, footed *cylindrical drum of the Baloie of the Congo, with nailed head. *Ca.* 80 cm. (32 in.) high (30).

Enanga, 1. *arched harp of the Ganda of Uganda, with circular or oval body and 8 strings; **2.** word used by the Ganda for any European keyboard or stringed instr.; **3.** word used all over Uganda to denote the *trough zither; **4.** *trough zither of the Bahaya of Bukoba district, Tanganyika, played by men only, often by professional players in the chief's palace. Also called okuterananga; **5.** *arched harp of the Bambula of the Congo; **6.** *musical bow of the Baziba of the Congo (19, 108, 195).

Enclume, Fr.: anvil.

Endara, a very rare xylophone of the Konjo of Uganda, with 16 to 18, exceptionally 9, wooden slabs of graduated sizes, 35–90 cm. (14–36 in.) long, laid across 2 banana stems resting on notched banana tree trunks. The slabs are slightly convex; played by 5 men, each with 2 sticks. The name is also known to the N. Sogo, Nyoro, Gwere, and Alur of Uganda. Among the Baswaga and Ndo of the Congo the name is given to the kweningba. *Cf.* ndara (30, 195).

End-blown flute, flute in which the player's breath is directed against the sharp edge of the open upper end. End-blown flutes may be open or stopped, with or without fingerholes. Our earliest record of such a flute is on a prehistoric slate of the fourth millennium B.C. from Hieraconpolis. In historic times we encounter it in Sumer *ca.* 2600 B.C. as a shepherd's instr. Also called rim-blown flute. *Cf.* notched flute, vertical flute (100, 170).

Endere, *notched flute of the Ganda of Uganda, made of reed, bamboo, or wood, with 4 burned-in fingerholes. The endere is made in 5 sizes and is played in ensembles. Also called nyamulere (195).

Endiga, xylophone of the Ruli and Nyala of Uganda, with 16 or 17 slabs loosely placed on 2 banana stems, separated by small sticks. One or 2 of the slabs have bosses. Only men of some importance own them (195).

Endingidi, *spike fiddle of Uganda, introduced ca. 1907, with open cylindrical body pierced by the handle, which projects 1–2 cm. It has a skin belly pegged to the body; a single string held by a frontal or lateral peg; a bridge but no nut. A saddle is formed by a bulge in the belly. When played it is held against the performer's waist, the neck pointing away from him (195).

Endingindo, see: endingidi.

Endong-akum, see: mban-akum.

Endongo, see: ndongo.

Endumba, drum of the Doka of the Congo, played with a stick (30).

Engalabi, *cylindrical drum of the Ganda of Uganda, with single nailed head, beaten with both hands (195).

Engboma, footed *cylindrical drum of the Budja of the Congo, with nailed head (30).

Engkuk, small cymbal of Java, inseparable from its twin, the kemong. They have rims like a gong and differ in one respect only: the engkuk is tuned to *barang* and the kemong to *nem* (121).

Engkurai, see: enkerurai.

Englische Doppelflöte, Ger.: English flageolet.

Englische Mechanik (Ger.: English action), piano action not identical with the *English action but, in its earlier form, to the *Stossmechanik. In this type of action the hammer is hinged to a block behind the keys and points toward the player. The earlier form has no escapement. With added single escapement the action is known in Ger.-speaking countries as Englische Mechanik. The earliest *square piano (1742) has this form of action (92).

Englisches Cithrinchen, a small 17th-c.

cittern, identical with the citarino, characterized by a half-open back. Also called englisches Zitterlein (169).

Englisches Horn, see: cor anglais.

Englisches Violett, see: English violet.

Englisches Waldhorn, Ger. 18th-c. term for the cor anglais (90).

Englisches Zitterlein, syn. of englisches Cithrinchen.

English action, piano action developed by Americus Backers in England, probably in 1772, from that of Bartolommeo Cristofori and Gottfried Silbermann, in which the hammer is not connected with the key, as in the Vienna action, but pivoted to a hammer rail. The hammer points away from the player. A jack inserted in the key provides (single) escapement. This type of action was adopted by Broadwood later in the c. and became the preferred action of Brit. makers. *Cf.* German action, Vienna action. Not the same as englische Mechanik (92, 176).

English bass-horn, see: bass-horn.

English citra (Fr.: *cithare anglaise*), var. of the Spanish guitar, invented by Angelo Benedetto Ventura of London *ca.* 1851 (204).

English flageolet (Ger.: *englische Doppelflöte*), name given to the early-19th-c. flageolets made by William Bainbridge of London from 1803 on, and patented in 1803, 1807, 1810, 1819. Bainbridge produced: **1.** single flageolets similar in form to the Fr. flageolet, with sponge chamber, 6 front fingerholes, and a rear thumbhole (sometimes a seventh fingerhole for c♯¹), in D major; **2.** *double flageolets, with single mouthpiece, sponge chamber, the left pipe with 7 fingerholes and a thumbhole, the right pipe with 4 fingerholes. These were usually played in parallel 3rds or, by overblowing the right pipe, in 6ths. The left pipe could also be played alone by silencing the other pipe. Both bores were pierced in a single block of wood; **3.** *triple flageolets, with single mouthpiece, also made from a single block of wood. The fingering of these instrs. was the same as that of the recorder. Also called English flute (89, 178).

English flute, name applied to the early-19th-c. flageolets by their Brit. makers. *Cf.* English flageolet (79).

English guitar, the It. form of cittern introduced *ca.* 1750 into England, where it became extremely pop. and was known as English guitar, cetra, or citra. Although it was similar in appearance to the cittern, the body was deeper, the fixed frets fewer, the neck terminated in a sickle head or in a flat, fan-shaped tuning device with machine screws, and the tuning was changed. Its 6 courses consisted of 2 single metal strings and 4 pairs of metal strings tuned $c^0 e^0 g^0 c^1 e^1 g^1$. Some makers added piano-like keys and hammers and called this variety a *keyed guitar. In the early 19th c. it was displaced by the Spanish guitar (89, 169).

English guitar banjo, obs. banjo with 6, 7, or 9 strings, formerly played in Britain (89).

English horn, see: cor anglais.

English violet (Ger.: *englisches Violett*), according to Leopold Mozart, the only difference between an English violet and a *viola d'amore was that the violet had 14 sympathetic strings tuned differently from the (7 melody and 7 sympathetic) strings of the amore. Unknown in England, the name is probably reminiscent of the early Engl. use of sympathetic strings on bowed instrs. See also: viola all'inglese, violet, violetta.

Engoma, see: ngoma.

Engono, see: ingombe.

Enharmonic harpsichord, harpsichord built from the mid-16th c. on in an attempt to re-create the 3 genera (diatonic, chromatic, and enharmonic) of classical Greece. In practice the term denotes any harpsichord having more than 12 keys and strings to an oct. and includes late specimens constructed for acoustical experimentation. Instrs. having keyboards furnished with the fairly common *split keys of the period are not included, however. Nicola Vicentino describes an enharmonic harpsichord in his *L'Antica musica* of 1555 and superintended the making of 2 such instrs. Zarlino, the great theorist of the same c., had one built by Domenico of Pesaro, in which all keys were split. These 2 authors created considerable interest in the construction of such instrs. Bottrigari in his *Desiderio* of 1594 devoted much space to the revival of the Gk. genera and referred to Vicentino's instr. In 1606 Vito Trasuntino built the *clavemusicum omnitonum; by 1618 Fabio Colonna had designed his *linceo,* also called *sambuca lincea or *pentecontachordon; at the same time Praetorius described the *clavicymbalum universale, made *ca.* 1590. Mersenne furnished diagrams of keyboards arranged for enharmonic tunings; *ca.* 1630 Giovanni Pietro Polizzino made an enharmonic harpsichord with 2 sets of strings, 1 for the Phrygian, the other for the Dorian and Hypolydian tonalities; Francisco Nigetti designed the *proteus *ca.* 1650; Galeazzo Sabbatini, Giovanni Battista Doni, and others designed similar instrs. during the course of the 17th c. One gathers from Athanasius Kircher that they were of fairly frequent occurrence in 17th-c. Italy. In the 18th c. Kirkman built one (*ca.* 1757) for Robert Smith, with a single set of strings, and Jacques Goermans of Paris made his *clavecin parfait accord as late as 1781. Only one specimen has come down to us, the *clavemusicum omnitonum of Vito Trasuntino. The multiplicity of strings required for even a few octaves' worth of microtones rendered tuning extremely difficult: enharmonic harpsichords served for theoretical demonstrations rather than musical purposes. The number and disposition of keyboards varied from model to model, as did the number of tones into which the oct. was divided. In Italy the instrs. were known as *arcicembali.* See also: clavecin parfait accord, clavemusicum omnitonum, clavicymbalum universale, pentecontachordon, proteus, sambuca lincea (27, 64, 89 Harding).

Enharmonic organ (It.: *arciorgano*), organ having more than 12 semitones, keys, and pipes to the octave. Nicolo Vicentino devised one before 1561, with a single register of 126 pipes, a portable model on which all 3 of the ancient Gk. genera could be played. See also: enharmonic harpsichord (*Journal of Music Theory*, April 1961).

Enharmonic piano, piano having more than 12 keys and strings to the oct. Roller & Blanchet of Paris built one by 1886 for Bottée de Toulmon and Vincent, with 2 keyboards and a 2-oct. compass. See also: telio-chordon (204).

Enharmonium, name bestowed by Hans von Bülow on various enharmonic instrs., including Shohe Tanaka's experimental harmonium of 1889; this had been built by Johann Kewitsch of Berlin, could be tuned to pure intervals, and had 20 keys to the oct.; also to Bosanquet's harmonium with 53 microtones to the oct. Helmholtz had one built by J. and P. Schiedmayer with 2 manuals. All these instrs. were used for demonstrating principles of tuning, not for musical purposes (64).

Enkanika, Afro-Cuban square clapper bells of wood or metal. Several are attached to a belt and worn during certain rites (152).

Enkerbap, *spike fiddle of the Sea Dayak of Borneo, with coconut body, lizard-skin belly tied on with rattan, and 2·or 3 strings (176).

Enkerurai, free-reed mouth organ of the Dayak of Borneo, similar to the sheng. It has a calabash wind chest with curved neck, and bamboo pipes arranged in circular form (173).

Enmorache, var. of morache, 1.

Ennanga, see: enanga.

Enne, bowed instr. of the Seri Indians of Tiburón Island, Sonora, Mexico, with a board or box body and single string; played with a round bow. A long lateral tuning peg penetrates a primitive, wide pegbox. *Ca.* 44 cm. (17 in.) long (137).

Enneachordon (Gk.: nine strings), stringed instr. of antiquity, believed to have been a 9-stringed kithara with rounded base. It was played in Hellenistic Egypt (144).

Ensansi, syn. of kindembo (152).

Ensegu, rattle of the Ganda of Uganda, consisting of a flat, box-like container filled with dried seeds. The box is made of thin canes laced together in raft form. The player holds it in his upturned palms, which provide a shaking motion, while his thumbs beat a rhythm against the box. It is 30–40 cm. (12–16 in.) long. *Cf.* akakyenkye, musesegeto (195).

Ensutu, Jew's-harp of the Sea Dayak of Borneo, made of metal (173).

Entaala, 1. xylophone of the Ganda of Uganda, with 12 wooden slabs laid on a frame of 2 banana tree trunks and separated from each other by thin, upright sticks. Nowadays called amadinda; **2.** xylophone of the Gwere of Uganda, with 6 slabs supplemented by a drum, placed on 2 banana stems and separated by sticks. The drum is treated as though it is another slab. At present the instr. is being replaced by tuned drums. Also called miruli. The slabs are *ca.* 50 cm. (20 in.) long (195).

Entara, a name of the xylophone in Nyoro and among the Ruli of Uganda (195).

Entongoli, arched harp of the Jopadhola of Uganda, with 8 strings (195).

Entuning, idiochord *tube zither of W. Borneo, with 3 strings (119).

Enzebe, percussion beam of the Konjo of Uganda, played together with the kinanga, 1 (195).

Enzenze, * bar zither of the Konjo of Uganda, with flattened bar, 3 frets, a gourd resonator, and 2 or 3 strings, of which 1 is stretched over the frets. The resonator is tilted upward during performance. *Cf.* njenjo, nzenze, nzeze, sese, zenze (195).

Enzenzya, var. of enzenze (195).

Enzonga, see: nzonga.

Eol . . . , see: aeol . . .

Éoli-Courtier, a perfected accordion with a 6-oct. compass, by Courtier of Paris, who was granted a patent on Sept. 2, 1844 (176, 204).

Eoli-melodicon, see: aeolo-melodicon.

Eoline, Fr.: aeoline.

Eolodicon, see: aeolidicon.

Epankal, pl. of apānkal.

Epigoneion [Gk. *epi,* upon + *gony,* knee], 40-stringed instr. of ancient Greece, held on the player's knees, possibly a board zither (170).

Épinette [It. *spinetta*], **1.** Fr.: spinet. Historically the word has been used with the same freedom as the Engl. word *virginal,* frequently to denote a harpsichord; **2.** Laborde says (in 1780) that it was formerly a name of the Jew's-harp. *Cf.* cymbalum orale, épinette des Vosges.

Épinette à archet, *bowed keyboard instr. built in 1745 by Renaud of Orléans, later in Paris. *Cf.* épinette à orchestre (156, 158).

Épinette à orchestre, *bowed keyboard instr. built *ca.* 1750 in Paris, according to Pontécoulant (158).

Épinette des Vosges (Fr.: spinet of the Vosges Mountains), syn. of bûche.

Épinette double, Fr.: *double virginal. However, Furetière in 1690 says that it is a spinet with 2 rows of strings, and the term has also been applied to a 2-manual harpsichord (78).

Épinette expressive (Fr.), spinet of Jean-Antoine Berger of Grenoble, France, submitted to the Paris Académie des Sciences in 1762. See also: pneumacorde (27, 204).

Épinette muette (Fr.: mute spinet), a name formerly given to the clavichord in France, *i.a.* by Mersenne, in 1636, because of its soft tone.

Épinette organisée (Fr.), a Fr. term for claviorganum. Rabelais used it in the mid-16th c. and Trichet a c. later (190, 204).

Épinette sourde (Fr.: mute spinet), a name formerly given to the clavichord in France.

Eraqye, see: 'iraqiya.

Erato harp, improved *Prince of Wales harp with damping mechanism (79).

Erbab [Arab. *rabāb*], syn. of rebab.

Erbabi [Arab. *rabāb*], name of the rabāb on Sula Besi and Buru Islands, Indonesia (173).

Erdbogen, Ger.: ground bow.

Erdtrommel, Ger.: ground drum.

Erdzither, Ger.: ground zither.

Ereg-ereg, syn. of wer-wer (121).

Erh hsien, *spike fiddle of China, a hu ch'in with hexagonal body of wood, belly and back of *t'ung* wood, otherwise similar to the erh hu (89, 142).

Erh hu, *spike fiddle of China, a hu ch'in with small hexagonal body of wood, snakeskin belly, 2 strings looped to the handle and tuned a 5th apart, and a tubular neck that pierces the belly. A very pop. instr. The bow passes between the strings, thus causing them to sound simultaneously (170).

Erikunde, Afro-Cuban wickerwork rattle in form of 2 beehives connected by a common handle, the bottoms formed by a flat piece of gourd, and containing small hard objects. This variety is called chachá in E. Cuba, also called maraca de canasta. Another variety is a multiple metal rattle, made of truncated cones joined at the widest part (152).

Erke, see: erque.

Erkencho, hornpipe found in Bolivia, Paraguay, N. Argentina, and S. Brazil, consisting of a clarinet inserted into a bell of horn. It is devoid of fingerholes and is played with one hand while the other strikes a drum (192).

Erque, *side-blown trumpet of N. Argentina, Bolivia, and Peru, straight, made of wood with a curved bell, 3–6 m. (10–20 ft.) long and similar to the trutruka (192).

Eruma, stopped *end-blown flute of the Amba of Uganda, the upper end being deeply cupped by making 2 oblique cuts in the rim; no fingerholes. Occasionally decorated with tufts of raffia or hair; made and played in sets of 8 or more. *Cf.* oseke (195).

Erus, unidentified instr. of ancient Israel, thought to have been a frame drum.

Erzähler (Ger.: narrator), organ stop of open conical flue pipes at 8' pitch of the gemshorn type, invented by E. M. Skinner in 1904 (186).

Erzcister, Ger.: archcittern.

Erzlaute, Ger.: archlute.

Esambori, pl. of asambori.

Esandju, pluriarc of the Mongo of the Congo (128).

Escacherium, Lat.: chekker.

Escapement (Fr.: *échappement;* Ger.: *Auslösung;* It.: *scappamento*), the component parts of a piano action which permit repetition of. a key by causing the hammer to rebound after striking the string. A single escapement, in form of the *linguetta mobile,* or jack, was already present in the action of Bartolommeo Cristofori. Double escapement, in use today, is the invention of Sébastien Érard of Paris, in 1822. It enables the hammer to strike the string any number of times without falling back all the way, *i.e.,* without completely releasing the key.

Escaque, OSp.: chekker.

Eschaquier, see: chekker.

Eschelette, var. of echelette.

Eschequier, see: chekker.

Eschile, Fr. 16th-c. var. of echelle.

Esembe, drum of the Ababua of the Congo, identical with the ndima (30).

Eshirtu (Ass.), horizontal harp of ancient Babylon, with 10 strings; it first appears in the second millennium B.C. (89 Galpin).

Esikulu, kettledrum of the São Salvador region of Angola, made in 2 sizes, the smaller being called *ntuta* and the larger *nkonzo a mpanzu.* They are played, together with trumpets, at funerals and public festivities. *Cf.* sikulu (185).

Eskilaño [dim. of **ezkila*]. Basque: a small eskilla.

Eskilla [med. Lat. **squilla*], Basque: large clapper bell (56).

Espinette (Fr.), obs. form of épinette, recorded from the 15th c. on (53).

Esquela, **esqueleta** [med. Lat. **squilla*], OProv.: bell.

Esquerlòtis [med. Lat. **squilla*], obs. Prov.: bell wheel (23).

Esquilla [med. Lat. **squilla*], Sp.: small clapper bell; cowbell, bell of convents, schools, etc. *Cf.* eskilla, esquille, ezkila.

Esquille, var. of eschile.

Esraj, see: esrar.

Esrar, bowed broad-necked lute of N. India, a cross between a sitar and a sārangī, with waisted body, skin belly, 16 movable frets on the neck, 4 or 5 melody strings held by frontal tuning pegs, and 10–15 sympathetic strings held by lateral pegs that pierce one side of the neck for its entire length. The strings are of wire. See also: bālasarasvati, dilruba, mayurī, mīnā sārangī, sur vāhara, taus, tāyus (170, 173).

Ess (Ger.: S), Ger.: an S-shaped crook.

Estive [Lat. *stipes,* pole, stick (source 197)], instr. frequently mentioned in med. Fr. literature and believed to have been a form of bagpipe. However, *"muses"* and *"estives"* are sometimes mentioned together, which speaks against such identification. In 1235 and again in 1280 the term *estives de Cornouailles* is encountered, which Chaucer translated as "hornpipe of Cornwall." A 13th-c. glossary renders it as *tibia,* the generic term for pipes without bags. Generally the word occurs in pl. form, as for example in *"estives ab votz pivas"* (estives with piping tone). *Cf.* stive (35, 89 Baines, 204).

Esudsu, clapperless bronze temple bell of Japan (178).

Etabule, pl. of atabule.

Etama, pl. of atama.

E♭ tenor horn, name of the althorn in Britain.

Etherophone, see: aetherophone.

Etimoika, bone clappers of Easter Island (77).

Etouffoir, Fr.: damper.

E-tsuzumi, syn. of o-tsuzumi.

Etumba, *goblet drum of the Basonge of the Congo, with nailed head (30).

Eturma, pl. of aturma.

Etuto, see: tutu.

Eufonio, It.: euphonium. Also called flicorno basso.

Eumatia, probably a misreading of eumélia.

Eumélia (Gk.: harmonious song), set of improved *musical glasses in which the pitch was adjusted by water, devised by Tait *ca.* 1827 (204).

Eunuch flute (Fr.: *flûte-eunuque*), mirliton described by Mersenne (in 1636) as having one open, bell-like end, the other being closed by a membrane protected by a removable cap. The player spoke or sang into an aperture close to the membrane. Nowadays the instr. is made only as a toy. See also: onion flute (89, 140).

Euphone (Ger.: *Euphon*), 1. friction bar instr. invented by Ernst Friedrich Chladni of Halle in 1790, composed of a series of tuned glass cylinders about as thick as a pen, rubbed lengthwise by the player's wet fingers. Compass c^0–f^3. In 1792 Chladni built a modified version and continued his experiments until, in 1799, he produced its successor, the *clavi-cylinder. Several imitations of the euphone were made. See also: chalybssonans, clavicylinder;

2. organ stop of reed pipes built as a clarinet stop or a horn stop; also built with free reeds (132, 133, 169, 170).

Euphonia [Gk. *eu*, good + *phone*, sound], 1. friction bar instr. invented in 1812 by Louis Klatte of Erfurt, with brass bars rotated against a brass cone; an imitation of the clavicylinder; 2. organ stop of reed pipes, identical with the clarinet type of euphone stop (133, 176).

Euphonicon, 1. a combination piano and harp invented by Beale of Cramer, Addington & Beale, of London, patented

July 7, 1841, with 7-oct. compass and triple soundboard, of the clavi-harp type; 2. name given to the euphonion; 3. upright piano patented 1841 by Dr. John Steward. The patent mentions a tape action (89 Harding, 176, 204).

Euphonic serpentcleide (Fr.: *cor euphonique*), contrabass serpent in C, with 11 keys, invented by James Jordan of Liverpool *ca.* 1850 and shown in London in 1851. See also: serpentcleide (89, 125).

Euphonion, an early name of the euphonium.

Euphonium (Fr.: *basse à pistons, basse en si♭;* Ger.: *Baryton, Baryton B, Barytonhorn;* It.: *flicorno basso;* Sp.: *bombardino*), 1. valved bugle of baritone range, said to have been invented by Sommer of Weimar in 1843, with wide conical bore, 4 or 5 valves, built in helicon, tuba, or trumpet form and pitched in C or B♭. It differs from the baritone by its wider bore and consequent different timbre. In view of the lack of standardization in brass instr. terminology it is also classified as a tuba or a saxhorn. Originally the instr. was also known as euphonion; at that time it had 3 valves, was pitched in C, B♭, or A, and had a comparatively narrow bore. In this form it replaced the bassoon in Ger. and Russ. military bands in the mid-c. and was also admitted to Austrian wind bands. Today it has a 3-oct. compass B♭^{1}/C^0 to b♭^{1}/c^2 and is notated a 9th (or oct.) higher than it sounds. See also: double euphonium;

2. *tuning-fork piano invented by A. Appunn of Hanau and patented Oct. 20, 1885. See also: sommerophone (25, 89, 170, 176).

Euphotine, keyboard instr. invented by Emily Pettit and patented in England on Nov. 4, 1852, with a series of tuning forks controlled by a keyboard and bellows (176, 204).

Everett orgatron, *electrophonic organ with tone acoustically generated by wind-blown reeds, and electrostatic pickup.

Evongi, *globular flute of the Congo people, made of a round seed capsule, about the size of an egg, of the *evongi* tree (185).

E'wiu, syn. of poretu (203).

Exabeba, var. of axabeba.

Exaquier, OSp.: chekker.

Excelsior Manopan, see: manopan.

Exilent, Praetorius' designation of sopranino instrs.

Expression, reed organ stop: **1.** in the orgue expressif of Gabriel Joseph Grenié, expression was obtained by compressing air in the reservoir by means of a treadle; **2.** in the harmoniums of the 1840's expression in form of crescendo and decrescendo was obtained by a valve that communicated variable pressure directly to the reeds without intermediary of an air reservoir. It was con-trolled by a treadle. This form of expression was the invention of Victor Mustel of Paris, 1843. Probably the most pop. of all harmonium stops, it was applied to both pressure and suction types of instr. See also: double expression, orgue expressif (132).

Expression double (Fr.), see: double expression.

Expressionsharmonium, Ger. term for a harmonium furnished with an expression stop.

Expressionsorgel, Ger.: orgue expressif.

Eyābi, pl. of ayābi.

Ezkila [med. Lat. *squilla*], Basque: church bell, campaniform bell; syn. of zeinu.

Ezkilats [*ezkila*], Basque: the smallest tower bell (56).

Fa'ali, slit drum of Samoa, used as a signal instr. (176).

Fa'ali laiti, see: pulotu.

Faberton (Lat.: *tonus faber*), name of a 16th-c. organ stop of unknown identity, mentioned in a 1544 Freiburg organ contract and in a ms. of *ca.* 1557 at Einsiedeln Monastery. The word may be a corr. of *faux-bourdon,* or derived from the Lat. *faber* (smith) and the Ger. *Ton* (tone). Mahrenholz believes it to have been a 2-rank mixture stop. Later both Eugen Casparini (d. 1706) and his son Orazio built a stop by this name, with It. principal or wide conical scale, at 2′ or 1′ pitch. Also called Glöckleinton (131, 133).

Fabiol, var. of flaviol.

. . . fach, Ger.: rank (of organ pipes).

Fadno, primitive oboe of the Lapps, possibly taken over from neighboring peoples (144).

Fagot [It. *fagotto*], Engl., Fr., and Ger.: curtal; syn. in 16th-c. France of *basson,* in Germany of *Dulzian.* The term was also used *ca.* 1700 in England (*i.a.,* by Talbot). In Germany the word becomes *Fagott* (bassoon). A chest of *alte schlechte fagati* (old plain *fagati*) is mentioned in a Graz inventory of 1577.

Fagotcontra, 17th-c. Ger. for Kontrafagott (contrabassoon).

Fagote, Sp.: curtal, dolcian, bassoon. Bermudo uses the term (1555). *Cf.* bajón (125).

Fagote-corista, Sp. equivalent of the double curtal. The term was used by Pietro Cerone (in 1613), inspired by Zacconi's fagotto chorista.

Fagott [It.: *fagotto*], **1.** Ger.: bassoon; also the curtal; **2.** syn. of bassoon (organ stop).

Fagottgeige (Ger.: bassoon fiddle) (It.: *viola di fagotto*), small violoncello of the 18th c., held on the arm like a viola, but with tuning ($C^0 G^0 d^0 a^0$) and compass of the ordinary cello. It was slightly larger than a viola and had spun strings. Leopold Mozart said that it was sometimes called Handbassl. The name is said to be derived from the bassoon-like quality of the spun strings. It was probably identical with the viola da spalla, although Welcker von Gontershausen identifies it with the viola di bordone.

Fagottino [dim. of **fagotto*] (It.), obs. treble bassoon. The term is applied to those of the 17th c., properly speaking curtals, pitched in g^0 (compass g^0–c^2) or pitched in c^0 an oct. above the ordinary curtal (compass c^0–f^2). Later the name came to be applied to any bassoon of higher than ordinary pitch. Also called bassonetto (89 Langwill).

Fagotto, 1. It. term for bassoon and its predecessor, the curtal. The word is first recorded in 1565 in a tutor for the phagotum, where each pillar of the instr. was called a *"fagoto"* (89 Langwill); **2.** syn. of bassoon (organ stop); **3.** syn. of dulcian (organ stop) (3).

Fagot-Oboe (Ger.), see: basson-hautbois.

Fagotto chorista, It. equivalent of the double curtal (Chorist-Fagott in Ger.). Zacconi (in 1592) gives its compass as C^0–b^1, slightly larger than that of Praetorius (C^0–f^1).

Fagotto doppio, It. equivalent of the Doppelfagott, a quart or quint bassoon.

Fagottone, It.: contrabassoon.

Fagotto octavo, the fagottino.

Fagotto quarto, see: Quartfagott.

Fagottserpent, Ger.: Russian bassoon.

Fagottzug, Ger.: bassoon stop.

Fajfarica, see: fayfarica.

Fakurst, fakürt, Hung. alphorn made of a log of wood, split, hollowed, and glued together, bound with bark or willow shoots; 50–250 cm. (20–100 in.) long (70).

Fala, *cross flute of the Aymara Indians of Bolivia, made of cane, with 6 fingerholes (70).

Falahuita, a small fala.

Fale, Basque: cowbell (56).

Fandir, according to Sachs, fandir is the Ossetic etymon for names of the fiddle, related to *pandur*. Bottle-shaped fiddles named panduri or fandur are still in use in the Caucasus and neighboring regions (170).

Fandur, bottle-shaped fiddle of the Caucasus (170).

Fanfami, wooden trumpet of the W. African Hausa. *Cf.* pampame (170).

Fanfarentrompete, see: herald's trumpet.

Fanfóni, Prov. equivalent of zanfoña. *Cf.* founfóni (44).

Fang hiang, metallophone of China, an imitation of the older lithophone *pien ch'ing, introduced in the 7th c., probably by the Turks; 16 metal slabs *ca.* 20 cm. (8 in.) long are suspended in 2 rows in an upright frame. It corresponds to the pang hiang of Korea (142, 170).

Fango-fango, *nose flute of the Fiji Islands, Futuna, Rotuma, Samoa, Tokelau, Tonga, Uvea, Viti (Polynesia), made of a bamboo internode closed at both ends. A blowhole is pierced close to each end; the fingerholes, usually 4, are placed around the circumference in the middle of the instr. and another is placed between these and each blowhole. Some specimens have fingerholes on the same plane as the blowhole, and a rear thumbhole. *Cf.* bitu-uvu (8, 77, 176).

Fan harp (Ger.: *Fanharfe*), a name given by some writers to the harp zither of the W. African Fan people.

Farai, *percussion beam of the Betsimisaraka of the Malagasy Republic; it corresponds to the *tsikaretika (171).

Farara, primitive reedpipe of the Malagasy Republic, made of leaves or bark (171).

Farara hazu, slit drum of the Malagasy Republic (171).

Faray, 1. rattle of the Diégo-Suarez area of the Malagasy Republic, which corresponds to the doka; **2.** bamboo scraper of the same country (171).

Farpa, OSp.: harp.

Fascia, pl. **fasce,** It.: ribs (of violins, etc.).

Fasstrommel, Ger.: barrel drum.

Faustfagott, Ger.: racket bassoon.

Faux-sommier, Fr.: rack board.

Fayfarica, syn. of stranka (34).

F-bass, a bass tuba.

Fedel, Nordic var. of Fiedel, fiddle.

Federsaitenpianoforte (Ger.: spring string piano), piano invented *ca.* 1840 by Wilhelm Schwab, a Budapest instr. maker, with steel strings bent into serpentine form, thus permitting a far shorter scale. One of its alleged advantages was that it remained in tune almost indefinitely (176).

Feku, *pointed flute of the Atoni of C. Timor (123).

Fela, Nor.: violin, fiddle.

Feldflöte, syn. of Feldpfeife (organ stop).

Feldpfeife (Ger.: field pipe), **1.** 17th-c. syn. of Schweizerpfeife; **2.** organ stop of open, narrow-scaled flue pipes of wood or metal, at 4′, 2′, or 1′ pitch, also called Feldflöte in the 18th c. (2, 159).

Feldtrommet (obs. Ger.: field trumpet), organ stop of reed pipes of the trumpet class at 16′ pitch.

Feldtrompete (Ger.: field trumpet), **1.** obs. term for a military trumpet or a principal trumpet (*vs.* a clarin trumpet) played by the field trumpeter; **2.** organ stop, syn. of Feldtrommet (144, 176).

Feldtrummet, early form of Feldtrompete.

Fele, in mod. Nor. a violin (9).

Fellahi, lute of Turkey, with octagonal body of wood, skin belly, long, straight neck, and 4 strings. *Ca.* 80 cm. (32 in.) long (168, 170).

Fendir, see: fandir.

Feng cheng, aeolian *musical bow of China, consisting of a bamboo bow tied to the end of a paper kite. *Cf.* yao p'ien (142).

Feng huang hsiao (Chin.: phoenix flute), full name of the hsiao (142).

Feng ling, *aeolian bells of China, with straps attached to their clappers, which are like horizontal crosses, and a thin plate of brass, shaped like a fishtail, dangles from them. The bells are suspended from the corners of houses or pagoda roofs and are sounded by the wind (142).

Fere, name of the flute in Yoruba, a Sudanic language (93).

Fernflöte (Ger.: distant flute), organ stop of small-scaled conical flue pipes, capped, of soft intonation, at 8' or 4' pitch (131).

Fernhorn (Ger.: distant horn), Engl. organ stop of small-scaled open metal flue pipes (198).

Ferreñas (Sp.: of iron), also called ferraña; an idiophone of Galicia, Spain, consisting of a hoop with jingles, actually a tambourine without a membrane (57).

Ferrule, a small ring that holds flat the hair of violin, etc., bows.

Ferryphone, wind instr. patented on June 15, 1857 by Ferry, who is probably identical with Armand Ferry of Mirecourt, patentee of a cornet valve in Britain on March 15, 1858 (126, 204).

Festel, var. of frestel.

Feðilo, Samoyede name for drum which Sachs believed cognate to *fendir (9, 169).

Feyle, obs. Nor.: fela (violin) (9).

FF, the F-shaped soundholes of violins, etc.

Fiddle [the etym. suggested by Sachs is a W. Asiatic one: the Ossetic *fandir. Related and derived words are: feandir, feðilo, fidil, pandur; ONordic: fiðlu; OEngl.: fiðele, fithele; OHGer.: fidula; MHGer.: videle, fidel; OFr.: fideille; MFr.: vielle, vièle, viole; Ger.: Fiedel; It.: viola; Sp.: vihuela; Nor.: fele; Swed., Icelandic: fidla; med. Lat.: fidella, vigella, vitula, vidula, vialla, viella], **1.** generic name for a bowed instr. having a neck; **2.** from the 17th c. on, familiar name for the violin; **3.** the fiddle was a stringed instr. of med. Europe whose early history is still not satisfactorily clarified. In the early Middle Ages it was often plucked, and Nordic epics prior to 1200 speak of a *fiðlu-sloetti,* a fiddle striker (*cf.* the Ger. *Lautenschläger*); thereafter the word *draga,* to draw (*ergo,* a bow), was used. *Viola* and *vihuela* have also designated non-bowed instrs. Despite the large body of pictorial and sculptural evidence showing the fiddle in all of its development, a precise description is difficult, as virtually no 2 instrs. are identical: size, shape, and playing technique vary from one to the other. But they have one feature in common: a flat pegdisc with front or rear pegs, and as this distinguishes them from the rebec and Geige, it is now customary to designate as a fiddle any med. bowed instr. of Europe having a pegdisc. The earliest evidence of bowed instrs. in Europe (discounting the highly ambiguous Utrecht psalter) is found in the 10th c.: a fiddle held at the shoulder is depicted in the St. Gall codex 21 (reproduced in 185A), and a man-high instr. is depicted in a Sp. ms., played with a round bow. The Sp. instr. is shaped like a bottle with a cork, as Sachs has aptly put it; fiddles of this shape are being played in the Caucasus today. A second form, with piriform body, called *lira, is first mentioned in a Pers. literary source of the 9th c., in which it is described as having 5 strings, and by Otfried von Weissenburg in the same c. This form was adopted in the Byzantine Empire, from where it reached Europe. In the Near East today it is called *kāmanja rūmī, or Greek fiddle, and in the Balkans it has retained its old name of lira. Its later development in 16th-c. Italy became known as the *lira da braccio. Its Byzantine origin was still vaguely remembered in Europe in the 15th c.: Tinctoris could write in 1484 that the viol was said to have been invented in Greece. The lira type of instr. is also depicted in the 10th- or 11th-c. Sp. mss. The body bulges slightly and tapers toward the pegdisc, there being no proper neck. In the 12th c., 2 Ger. mss. depict bowed instrs. of oval shape termed "*lyra.*" In the same c. a curious fiddle appears: its body is in form of the figure 8; it modifies this shape constantly, popping up periodically until it disappears for good in the 16th c. By the 13th c. the fiddle had reached its final form—with developed neck and flat body. The bulging-body type lasts longest in Spain, as does the Oriental style of playing it while held on the lap. All these instrs. had been carved out of a single block of wood, but by the 12th c. they appear as built-up instrs. with separate ribs. The early fiddle had 3, 4, or 5 strings (the 3 strings were retained by the lira); 5 appeared by the 11th c. but had already been mentioned in the 10th; they were to become the classical number of European fiddles. Elias Salomon mentions 5 strings in 1274, and a little earlier, *ca.* 1250, Jerome of Moravia gave the first details of their tuning: $D^0 \Gamma G^0$ $d^0 d^0$, but for secular music $D^0 \Gamma G^0 d^0 g^0$ was preferred; a third tuning is given, but unfortunately the text is corrupt here. The D^0 of the first 2 tunings was an off-board drone plucked with the thumb; the other strings were those retained by the lira, one of which was duplicated at the unison or oct. The compass was from Γ to a^0 (relative pitch). In 1372 Corbichon, in his *Propriétaire des choses,* describes the function of the center string as being that from which the others were

tuned *(". . . la moyenne corde de la vielle ou de la guisterne qui accorde les autres.")* From the 12th c. on the fiddle is occasionally depicted with a waist to facilitate bowing, yet unwaisted models continue up to the 15th c. Early fiddles were played in the Oriental position, *i.e.,* held vertically and bowed with the palm up; other instrs. were held in the lap, in front of the body, on the left shoulder, across the upper body, etc. (82, 170).

Fidel, MHGer.: fiddle.

Fidicula (Lat.), a stringed instr. mentioned by Cicero, who states (*De natura deorum,* Lib. 2) that it was made of plane-tree wood (*platanus*).

Fidil, early Irish form of the word *fiddle,* meaning little bent rod, which Grattan Flood believed to indicate a bow. The word certainly stands for an early Irish bowed instr. (9).

Fidla, 1. instr. of ancient Norway and Sweden, mentioned in the sagas as having been plucked; **2.** Icelandic bowed instr., with elongated, trapezoid body (almost like that of a Scheitholt), with 2 or 4 horsehair strings, obs. by the 18th c. (89, 144).

Fidula, OHGer.: fiddle. The word is first recorded *ca.* 868 in the *Liber evangeliorum* of the monk Otfried von Weissenstein. Later the word becomes equivalent of the Ger. *Geige. See also: polnische Geige (168).

Fiedel, Ger.: fiddle.

Fieould, panpipes of the Hautes-Pyrénées, France, made of a single block of wood in which a variable number of tubes, 8–14, are cut. An instr. of local goatherds and of the pig gelders of Provence (70, 132, 136).

Fife (Fr.: *fifre;* Ger.: *Querpfeife;* It.: *fiffaro;* Sp.: *pífano*), a small transverse flute with narrow, cylindrical bore, made of a single piece of wood (modern versions in metal and plastic exist also), historically keyless but with an E♭ key added to some modern specimens, and provided with 6 fingerholes. Fifes and drums have been associated with foot troops from the 15th c. on, when the Swiss became mercenary soldiers and introduced the instrs. to much of W. Europe. By 1507 the fife was known in France as a military instr., and by 1510, according to Farmer, in England. Praetorius calls it *Schweizerpfeife*—the Swiss fife—and gives its compass as g^1–c^3, also as d^1–a^2, and its length as 2 ft. Trichet, *ca.* 1640, describes it as a short, narrow form of cross flute, louder and *plus vif* of speech, having the compass of a 15th and pop. as a military instr. The older instr. was usually pitched in G, but since the late 18th c. either in C, with a d^2–d^4 compass, or in B♭. Professional fifers seem to have carried both. In the 19th c. it was remodeled, given a conical bore and little-finger hole for E♭, with or without a key, and this model coexisted with the older one. Today the fife is considered to be in A♭ and is *ca.* 39 cm. (15½ in.) long. See also: flute (89, 151, 170).

Fiffaro [Ger. *phife*], It.: fife, cross flute; the term goes back to the 16th c.

Fifre (Fr.) [Ger. *phife*], Fr.: fife. The word does not occur before 1507, when it appears as a military instr. played with a drum. In 1588 Thoinan Arbeau writes: ". . . *nous appelons le fifre une petite flutte traverse à six trouz de laquelle usent les Allemands et les Suysses . . .*" (we call a fife a small cross flute with 6 holes used by the Germans and the Swiss) (35).

Fifre allemand, another name of the flûte allemande organ stop.

Fifteenth (Fr.: *doublette;* Ger.: *Superoktave;* It.: *decimaquinta;* Sp.: *quincena*), organ stop sounding 2 octs. higher than its fundamental; a 2′ diapason.

Fifth, see: quint (organ stop).

Figella, med. Lat.: fiddle, viola.

Figle, Port., Sp.: ophicleide.

Filet, Fr.: purfling.

Filetto, It.: purfling.

Filjan saz (Pers.), musical bowls similar to our *musical glasses, tuned by pouring water into them, mentioned in

the 15th c. and still in use in 17th-c. Turkey (76).

Fillagori, syn. of muralī.

Filomela, see: philomela.

Fingerboard (Fr.: *touche;* Ger.: *Griffbrett;* It.: *tastiera;* Sp.: *mastil*), board attached to the upper surface of the neck of certain stringed instrs. against which the strings are pressed by the performer's fingers. The earliest reliable record of one appears on a mural painting in a Theban tomb of the 15th c. B.C., where a lutanist is depicted playing a W. Asiatic type of lute with 9 frets on a neck (177).

Finger cymbals, a form of cymbal used chiefly by dancers, either thimble-shaped, or shaped as miniature cymbals with central bosses, worn on thumb and finger, known since antiquity and still played in the Nr. East today. Small ancient Egyptian cymbals of 5–8 cm. (2–3 in.) in diam. have been excavated; they probably were finger cymbals. Such cymbals have definite pitch, and dancers often prefer a pair tuned a semitone apart (170).

Fingerhole horn, horn with fingerholes; see: cornett, horn; see also: aza rag, bukkehorn, coradoiz, mangval, prillarhorn, rhyton, rozhok, soittotorvi, sokusarv, vallhorn.

Fiol, Nordic: fiddle.

Fipla, var. of fidla. The word occurs in Nordic sagas.

Fipple (Ger.: *Kern*), the plug or block of certain duct flutes; it contains the flue and mouthpiece, the latter often cut back to form a beak (151).

Fipple flute (Fr.: *flute à bloc;* Ger.: *Blockflöte*), flute sounded by a fipple and a flue (also called duct or windway). A hole is cut in the wall of the flute below the fipple, its sharp edge being known as the lip. The player's breath is directed by the flue against the lip. Flageolets and recorders are examples of fipple flutes. The Ger. word *Blockflöte* has come to denote specifically the recorder. Also called whistle flute.

Firisai, rattle of the Uitoto Indians of Colombia, made of the dried fruits of a liana strung on a band and worn by dancers below their right knee. Sometimes they are attached to a staff that is then stamped (32).

Firringila, Basque: bull-roarer; now a child's toy (56).

Fisarmonica [*physharmonica*], It.: piano accordion.

Fiscorno, Sp.: flugelhorn. The word corresponds to the It. flicorno (154).

Fistola [Lat. *fistula*], name given to the panpipes in Campania (89).

Fistola pani [Lat. *fistula* + Pan], name given to the panpipes in Lombardy (132).

Fistula, Lat.: pipe.

Fistula angelica (Lat.), a 16th- and 17th-c. name of the recorder (89).

Fistula germanica (Lat.), a 16th- and 17th-c. name of the cross flute (89).

Fistula helvetica (Lat.), a 16th- and 17th-c. name of the Schweizerpfeife (176).

Fistula largior (Lat.), a wide-scaled flageolet organ stop (133).

Fistula maxima (Lat.), the wind trunk of early med. organs.

Fistula militaris, Lat.: fife, Schweizerpfeife.

Fistula minima (Lat.), a small-scaled flageolet organ stop (133).

Fistula organica, Lat.: organ pipe.

Fistula pani, Lat.: panpipes; *cf.* fistola pani.

Fistula pastoralis, Lat.: shawm; shepherd's pipe.

Fistula rurestris, Lat.: the Bauernflöte organ stop.

Fistula vulgaris, Lat.: recorder.

Fistule, OFr.: pipe. The term occurs from the 14th c. on.

Fithele, OEngl.: fiddle. The word occurs from the early 13th c. on (180).

Flabellum, Lat.: bellows (61).

Flabiol, var. of flaviol.

Flachflöte (Ger.), organ stop that evolved at the end of the 16th c. from the Spitzflöte, with narrow-scaled open conical pipes and wide mouths, at 8′, 4′, and 2′ pitches. Also called Flachpfeife (133).

Flagel [OFr. *flageol*], med. Engl. and Fr.: flageolet.

Flageol [Lat. *flabeolum*, flute, an assumed etymon], OFr.: flageolet, the pipe of the *pipe and tabor ensemble. The word occurs from *ca.* 1180 to the mid-17th c., at which time it was a *beaked flute, sometimes played in pairs. See: flageolet (197, 204).

Flageolet [see: flageol], **1.** med. Fr. name of an end-blown *whistle flute of Asiatic origin; it reached the West in the 11th c. The term is recorded from the 13th c. on (the word *flageol* earlier). Although it was commonly made of wood or cane, we hear in 1383 of *"un flageolet de cuivre ouvré et paint que Mgr. donna au roy"* (a copper flageolet decorated and painted which my lord gave the king). Around 1581 the Sieur de Juvigny of Paris constructed a straight flute with narrow, contracting bore and a beak, 4 front fingerholes, and 2 rear thumbholes, called *flageolet,* and the word has been applied to this type of instr. ever since. Trichet, *ca.* 1640, says that it was shorter than the flute (meaning of course the recorder). Samuel Pepys mentions it frequently in his diary (1667, 1668) shortly before it was superseded in England by the recorder. Majer, in 1732, describes it as a flute used for teaching canaries to sing, made of ivory, boxwood, or other wood, with a compass d^1–a^2 or higher. Its most important role in the 18th c. was, however, as orchestral precursor to the piccolo flute, being scored for as flautino or flauto piccolo by such composers as Handel (*Rinaldo,* 1711), Gluck, and Mozart. About 1750 the beak was replaced by a slender ivory mouthpiece connected to a chamber; this enclosed a small sponge for the absorption of moisture from the player's breath. This instr. was later known as French flageolet to distinguish it from the English flageolet produced in England since the first quarter of the 19th c. The latter differed from the Fr. model in that it had the same fingerhole arrangement as the recorder (6 front fingerholes and 1 thumbhole). During the 19th c. the (French) flageolet acquired up to 6 keys, although keyless models continued to be made. Its compass was g^2-a^4, notated a 12th lower. Both the flageolet and the English flageolet were also made as *double flageolets with a common mouthpiece in the 19th c.; the English flageolet was also made as a *triple flageolet. See also: larigot, quadrille flageolet;

2. organ stop of flue pipes at 2' and 1' pitches, of Fr. origin, first recorded in Rouen in 1515. Adlung equated it with the Schwegel stop (3, 63 Schaeffner, 133, 134, 170, 190).

Flageoletgeige (Ger.), instr. of the violin family furnished with a device for mechanically "fingering" flageolet tones, invented by H. Dessauer of Linz, *ca.* 1912 (176).

Flageot, 13th-c. var. of flageol.

Flahute [Lat. *flauta*], OFr.: flute. This, together with var. spellings, was the name given to the pipe of the *pipe and tabor ensemble.

Flahutet, pop. name of the galoubet in Provence and the Comtat Venaissin today. Made of bone, boxwood, or olive-wood, with 3 fingerholes and generally pitched in B♭. *Ca.* 25 cm. (10 in.) long (23).

Flaiol, OFr.: var. of flageol.

Flajo, OFr.: var. of flageol.

Flankenwirbel, Ger.: lateral (tuning) pegs.

Flaschenett(chen), 18th-c. Ger. corr. of flageolet (90).

Flaşnetă [Ger. *Flaschenett*], Rom.: barrel organ (5).

Flatsche (birch bark ribbon), **1.** in Styria a trumpet or short S-shaped alphorn; **2.** in Carinthia a mirliton made of bark (117, 169).

Flat trumpet, an early form of *slide trumpet in use in England in the 1690's, with a slide in the loop nearest the player.

A single specimen, dated 1691, survives. The name is probably derived from the instr.'s ability to play in "flat," *i.e.,* minor, keys. Henry Purcell scored for it, and James Talbot, *ca.* 1700, described it, after which it disappears. A similar instr. reappears in 1798 as *slide trumpet (15 Monk, 80).

Flat twenty-first, mutation organ stop sounding a minor 7th above the *fifteenth, at 4⁴⁄₇', 2²⁄₇', or 1¹⁄₇' pitch, introduced by Jackson of Liverpool in 1847 (198).

Flauste, var. of flaüte.

Flauta, OCat., Lat., Port., Prov., Rom., Sp.: flute.

Flauta armonica, Sp.: flûte harmonique.

Flauta de pico, Sp.: recorder, flageolet.

Flautado, Sp.: flue pipework of the organ.

Flautado principal, Sp. organ stop equivalent of the diapason (198).

Flautado violón, Sp. organ stop equivalent of the Geigen Prinzipal.

Flauta dulcis, name of the Dulzflöte *ca.* 1700.

Flauta Euskaria (Sp.: Basque flute), Sp. organ stop of flue pipes at 8' pitch.

Flaut devoir, Ger. corr. of flûte d'ivoire (an organ stop); it led to the further corr. "divinare" (133).

Flaüte, OFr.: recorder. The term is recorded from the 12th c. on.

Flautele [dim. of *flaüte*], OFr., Prov.: a small recorder, a tabor pipe. The term was in use from *ca.* 1230 on (204).

Flaut hemiol, obs. organ stop of flue pipes at 8' pitch, despite its name (176).

Flautilla, Cast. equivalent of flaviol.

Flautín, Sp.: a piccolo flute.

Flautino [dim. of *flauto*] (It.), **1.** a small flute, either flageolet or recorder, not identical with the piccolo flute. In 18th-c. scores it denotes a small recorder or flageolet; **2.** organ stop, syn. of flute, Waldflöte (41, 101).

Flautino alla vigesima seconda (It.: flautino at the twenty-second), flautino with a fundamental of c³; the name is derived from organ terminology, where the 22nd is a 1′ stop. Monteverdi scores for one in his *Orfeo* (1607) (176).

Flauto, It.: flute (up to the 18th c. the word meant recorder, not cross flute).

Flauto a camino, It.: Rohrflöte (organ stop).

Flauto alemano, obs. It. designation of the cross flute.

Flauto amabile, see: Dulzflöte.

Flauto amoroso, see: Dulzflöte.

Flauto cuspido, see: Spitzflöte.

Flauto d'amore, It.: flûte d'amour.

Flauto di Pan, It.: **1.** panpipes; **2.** organ stop of metal flue pipes at 2′ or 1′ pitch. *Cf.* Pandean flute (198).

Flauto di voce (It.: voice flute), mirliton patented by Malcolm McGregor of London in 1810, an alto flute with large hole in the second body joint, covered by a thin membrane (25).

Flauto dolce (It.), **1.** recorder; **2.** another name of the dolce organ stop.

Flauto doppio (It.), see: Doppelflöte.

Flauto dritto, It.: recorder.

Flauto major, organ stop composed of principal pipes at 16′ pitch, usually of wood, in recent times also built at 8′ pitch. Also called major flute, tibia major.

Flauto minor, organ stop of flute pipes in octave, *i.e.,* 4′, position (133).

Flautone [aug. of *flauto*] (It.), **1.** It.: bass flute; **2.** organ stop of cylindrical flue pipes of narrow scale, an echo stop at 16′ pitch (133).

Flautophone, a small pipe organ with flue pipes, invented by Maurice Baduel of Paris and patented Apr. 26, 1876, with stopped metal pipes and key buttons, and a compass of 2 octs. and a 3rd. The wind chest was fed not by bellows but by a flexible tube that the player blew into (91, 132, 176).

Flauto piccolo (It.), **1.** piccolo flute; the term is rarely used now; instead it is usually called *ottavino* in Italy. In 18th-c. scores flauto piccolo generally designated a flageolet; **2.** organ stop of flue pipes at 2′ pitch.

Flauto tedesco (It.: German flute), organ stop of open flue pipes at 8′ and 4′ pitches, resembling the Hohlflöte.

Flauto traverso, 1. It.: *cross flute; an 18th-c. designation of the flute, to distinguish it from the flauto, or recorder; **2.** organ stop of cylindrical or conical flue pipes at 8′ or 4′ pitch, either of wood or metal, made in various designs and scales (129).

Flauto verticale, It.: vertical flute.

Flavel [Lat. *flabellum,* bellows], OFr.: wind instr. mentioned infrequently in the 13th and 14th c. The *Roman de la rose* (*ca.* 1280) uses the expression *"flavel de Cornouailles,"* possibly a bagpipe or bladder pipe (197, 204).

Flaviol (Cat., Prov.), a small flageolet of the Pyrenees that assumes 2 forms: **1.** in Andorra and the Fr. Pyrenees it is a one-hand pipe, some 16 cm. (6 in.) long, devoid of keys, with 1 fingerhole, played together with a small drum (tamborí), a *pipe and tabor combination that has remained in use since the 13th c.; **2.** in Catalonia and Roussillon it forms part of the sardana *cobla.* Made of ivory, with 3 front fingerholes and 2 ventholes, a rear thumbhole and 2 rear vents, plus 3 closed keys. Compass g²–g⁴. 24 cm. (9½ in.) long. In Cast. it is called flautilla; in the Basque country it lives on as chistu. Also called fabiol, flabiol, fluviol (14, 57, 127, 132).

Flegel [OFr. *flageol*], MEngl.: flute, flagel. The word is recorded from the early 14th c. (169).

Flegil [OFr. *flageol*], MHGer.: flute, flageolet. The word was used by Eberhart Cersne in 1404 (176).

Flestel, OProv.: frestel.

Fletna, Czech.: flute.

Flicorno [Ger. *Flügelhorn*], It.: flugelhorn. See also: biucolo, bombardino, eufonio, genis, helicon, pelittone.

Flicorno basso, It.: euphonium; also called eufonio.

Flicorno contralto, It. brass instr. that corresponds to the althorn and is identical with the genis.

Flicorno contrabasso (It.), bass tuba in F, also called helicon or pelittone.

Flicorno soprano, It.: flugelhorn.

Flicorno tenore, It. brass instr. very similar to the tenor horn but with a different bore; pitched in B♭ (89 Baines).

Flieg, obs. S. Ger. pop. term for keyboard instr.

Fliscorno contralto, Sp. brass instr. that corresponds to the althorn and flugelhorn.

Flödel, Ger.: purfling.

Flöduse, Ger. corr. of flûte douce.

Flogera, pastoral end-blown flute of modern Greece (144).

Floite [OFr. *flahute*], MHGer.: flute.

Flosszither, Ger.: raft zither.

Flöte [OFr. *flahute* via MHGer. *floite*], Ger.: **1.** flute; **2.** in organs of the 15th c. the equivalent of principal pipes, especially when used in pl. form; later it denoted flue pipework in general; **3.** a class of organ stops, see: flute, 3 (3, 167).

Flöte harmonica, another name of the harmonica organ stop (133).

Flötenbass, 1. obs. Ger.: bass flute; **2.** Ger.: flute bass (organ stop).

Flötenprinzipal (Ger.), organ stop of open wooden flue pipes of principal scale, with narrow mouths. Since the 16th c. they have also been built of metal. Also called Flotenprinzipal, suavial (133).

Flötenuhr, Ger.: musical clock.

Flötenwerk, Ger.: **1.** flue pipework; **2.** small organ having flue pipes only, called *organo di legno* in 16th- and 17th-c. Italy; **3.** in 15th-c. organs the Prinzipal and Hintersatz jointly. See also: flute, 2 and 3 (167).

Flötgedackt (Ger.), gedackt, *i.e.,* stopped, flue pipe organ stop.

Flötuse, var. of Flöduse.

Floute [OFr. *flaute*], MEngl.: flute. The term was first used by Chaucer.

Flue (Fr.: *lumière;* Ger.: *Kernspalte*), the windway or duct of organ *flue pipes or *duct flutes.

Flue pipe (Fr.: *tuyau à bouche;* Ger.: *Labialpfeife, Lippenpfeife*), organ pipe having a flue or windway between the edge of the languid and lower lip if it is a metal pipe; or, if it is of wood, a flue between the top edge of the cap and the *block. Flue pipes may be open, stopped, or half-stopped, and may be made of metal or wood. Metal pipes are usually round, wooden ones square. Other materials have been used exceptionally (101).

Fluer [U.], Rom. rustic *whistle flute with 6 front fingerholes, made of wood (132).

Flue work (Ger.: *Flötenwerk*), or flue pipework; the collective flue pipes of an organ.

Flugel, common name of the flugelhorn.

Flügel (Ger.: wing), **1.** Ger. term that formerly designated the harpsichord—an abbr. of *Kielflügel,* quilled Flügel—and later the grand piano—an abbr. of *Hammerflügel,* from the wing shape of these instrs.; **2.** Ger.: wing of a bassoon.

Flügelgitarre, instr. invented by Johann Roth of Nürnberg in 1882 (176).

Flügelharfe, Ger.: arpanetta.

Flugelhorn [horn of the *Flügelmeister*] (Fr.: *bugle à pistons;* Ger.: *Flügelhorn;* It.: *flicorno*), **1.** formerly the name of a small, valveless signal horn or bugle used in the hunt by the *Flügelmeister.* See also: parforce horn (88); **2.** valved bugle first made in Austria between 1820 and 1830, with wide conical bore and medium-sized bell, played with a cup mouthpiece, and built in trumpet, helicon, or tuba form. Makers increasingly narrowed the bore until the flugelhorn came to resemble the cornet, but the bell remains slightly larger. Formerly built with 3 or 4 valves, nowadays with 3 only, it is made in sopranino (E♭ and F), soprano (B♭ and C), and alto (E♭) sizes, the B♭ soprano being the most pop. The flugelhorn has the same compass and notation as the cornet and is still in use in military and wind bands. Also called Bügelhorn. See also: bass flugelhorn, Bassflügelhorn, echo flugelhorn (89 Baines).

Flügere, disc buzzer of Balgach, Switzerland (102).

Fluit, Du.: flute.

Flute [OFr. *flahute* from Lat. **flauta*] (Fr.: *flûte;* Ger.: *Flöte;* It.: *flauto;* Sp.: *flauta*), a woodwind instr. known since prehistoric times and distributed among practically all peoples, the flute is classified according to form, playing technique, or blowing device. Flutes are usually tubular but also occur in globular form (*globular flute); the former are said to be end-blown, rim-blown, or vertical if the upper orifice is used as a blowhole; the edge of this orifice may be notched, in which case we speak of a *notched flute; if the blowhole is cut laterally in the wall, the flute is said to be side-blown and called *cross flute or *transverse flute; if the air stream is directed by a duct to the sharp edge of a lateral aperture, we speak of *duct flutes; if the flute is very short, of *whistles. Duct flutes containing a *fipple are also known as *fipple flutes or *whistle flutes. We also distinguish between *beaked, *cone, *piston, *pointed, and *ring flutes. Several end-blown flutes of different pitches combined into a single instr. form *panpipes. The lower end of a flute may be open or stopped; an open pipe overblows the oct.; a stopped pipe the 12th. Flutes are usually but not always provided with fingerholes; on primitive types these are equidistant. Actually, with minor deviations, all fingerholes up to the 19th c. were equidistant. The end-blown flute is of greater antiquity than the side-blown variety. Flutes have been made of bone, bamboo, dried fruit shells, wood, clay, ivory, metal, crystal, plastic, etc. Among primitive flutes many are of bone, and those of bird bone are believed to be the oldest. Generally these are devoid of fingerholes and often yield only one tone—a signal whistle rather than a musical instr. —whereas mammalian bones are often provided with fingerholes, 4 or more being most common, and are considered to be of later origin. According to Sachs,

the duct flute with fipple preceded both the plain, end-blown flute and the cross flute; and holeless flutes preceded those with fingerholes. Other writers believe that the stopped, end-blown flute came first. Tone production is effected by blowing ·the fundamental or by blowing the harmonics (overblowing). The pitch may be varied by stopping an open flute with the flat of the hand or the knee, by modifying the tube's length through use of fingerholes, by blowing from each end those flutes having a lateral hole in the middle, by lengthening the tube with the hollowed fist, etc. Flutes are closely connected with magic belief and are still in use in many parts of the world in magico-religious ceremonies. As phallic symbols they are associated with fertility and rebirth, hence often encountered in ancient tombs, where they served as life charms.

The earliest evidence we have of wind instrs. is the prehistoric reindeer phalanges found in Europe and N. America, pierced on one surface, and animal bones found pierced with a blowhole and several round fingerholes. Vertical flutes are also recorded on a prehistoric slate of the fourth millennium B.C. from Hierakonpolis and, in historic times, *ca.* 2600 B.C. in Sumer, where they occur as shepherds' flutes. They are also found in Egypt, dating from the Middle Kingdom on. Cross flutes are depicted in the 9th c. B.C. in China, possibly earlier, and in India from the 1st or 2nd c. A.C. as art instrs., the vertical duct flute being a shepherd's instr. there. Many early or primitive flutes have a bore too narrow to sound the fundamental, and the lowest tone of an open tube is thus an oct. above the fundamental; if the player blows harder, he produces a tone a 5th higher; harder still, the double oct., and so forth. On wider-bored instrs. the fundamental is sounded, and the first overblown tone is an oct. higher. In order to play melodies it thus becomes necessary to create artificial means for bridging so large a gap, and 6 fingerholes provide the solution. But this number is not found prior to Hellenistic times, fewer than 6 having been in use until then. It is interesting to note that the Jap. and Middle Eastern pitch tone is d¹, and that this pitch is derived from the lowest tone of the vertical flute, that of Japan sounding 292 cps. Standard pitch in China under the Chou dynasty (1122–255 B.C.) was that of a flute cut exactly one Chin. foot (*yo*) long (229.9 mm.); according to Sachs, it sounded the note *huang chung*, or f♯⁰, and was probably identical to the Gk. mese.

The classical flute of W. Europe is the cross flute. It was first depicted there in a 12th-c. ms., the *Hortus deliciarum* of Herrad von Landsberg, in which it is called swegel, after being introduced from the East via Byzantium and the Slav. countries. The vertical flute was also known by then (see: flageol). In the later Middle Ages the cross flute was chiefly a military instr. in Switzerland and Germany, whence it spread to other countries, becoming known as the flûte allemande, flauta alemana, or Schweizerpfeife. Played with a cylindrical drum, the fife, a shorter version of the cross flute, formed fife-and-drum ensembles, which have been in use since the end of the Crusades in certain areas. Virdung in 1511 still knew of only the military fife, but by 1528 Agricola describes a family of flutes: a bass in C, a tenor in G, and a soprano in D, the last of these being the forerunner of our concert flute. Here it is perhaps well to recall that with all 6 fingerholes closed the flute sounded d¹. By successively opening them a diatonic D-major scale was produced. The chromatic notes had to be obtained by cross-fingering assisted by a flexible embouchure until such a time as extra holes were pierced and covered with keys. Thus the flute was said to be a D flute. After the addition of the C foot, the lowest tone became c¹; this, plus the fact that the type instr. (our "flute") was never treated as a *transposing instr., caused it later to become known as a C flute. Flutes of other sizes are treated as

transposing instrs., the transposition being calculated from C (except in Engl. flute bands, in which the type instr. is considered to be still in D, its 6-finger tone).

The bore in the 16th c. was cylindrical, and smaller-sized flutes were made of a single section. Thus they could not be tuned, and this may account for the large number of flutes enumerated in Renaissance inventories. Basses were made in 2 sections, however. Boxwood was and remained the favorite wood, although glass flutes were included in the inventory of Henry VIII's instrs. in 1547 (crystal flutes were also made in the 19th c.). Praetorius lists 3 sizes: a bass in g⁰, 90–100 cm. (36–40 in.) long; a tenor in d¹, *ca.* 70 cm. (27½ in.) long, which he says was also used as a soprano; and a soprano in a¹, *ca.* 45 cm. (18 in.) long. Mersenne's flute (1636) still has the cylindrical bore. But the old soprano could no longer meet musical demands and the single-joint flute was gradually transformed in France. First it was made of 3 joints (head, middle joint, and foot joint), then *ca.* 1660 an additional hole was bored and covered with a key for d♯¹. Around 1680, probably owing to the efforts of the Hotteterres—the most important family of Fr. woodwind makers and players—the bores of middle and foot joints were made conical, tapering toward the foot, while that of the head joint remained cylindrical. Ornamented with ivory bands, this "new" flute remained in use for over a c. From about 1720 on the middle joint was divided into 2 separate sections, each with 3 fingerholes. The upper of these sections, served by the left hand, was interchangeable with 3 or more *corps de rechange* of slightly different lengths, for tuning purposes. (Halle, writing in 1764, says that some flutes had 6 such joints.) In 1717 J. S. Bach first wrote for the *flauto traverso,* the one-keyed flute; up to then he had scored only for the recorder. For much of the 18th c. the latter is scored as *flauto,* the cross flute specifically as *flauto traverso,* German flute, *traver-*

sière, etc. Quantz's great work, his *Versuch einer Anweisung die Flöte Traversière zu Spielen,* appeared in 1752. He knew the cork stopper already and claimed for himself invention of the tuning slide (the metal tuning slide was patented in 1785 by Richard Potter of London). Poor cross-fingerings were responsible for the flute's becoming the first woodwind instr. to be supplied with additional chromatic keys: by 1760 London makers had added 3 closed keys to the 1 already in existence, for f^1, $g\sharp^1$, $b\flat^1$, thereby creating the 4-keyed flute. The foot joint, previously neglected, was frequently given 2 keys, for c^1 and $c\sharp^1$, by London makers at this time, resulting in the 6-keyed flute. Once the c^2 and duplicate long key (f^1) had been added at the end of the century, the final development of the pre-Boehm flute was reached. In 1831, Theobald Boehm, a flute maker of Munich, heard the Engl. virtuoso Charles Nicholson play in London on a flute of very powerful tone which had some larger than normal holes. Boehm realized that in order to match it he would have to redesign completely his conservative, small-holed flute. This he proceeded to do, after much experimenting, by incorporating large holes systematically throughout the instr., placing them as closely as possible to the acoustically correct positions, changing the closed keys into open ones and controlling them with rings. (Rings had been invented in 1808 by the Rev. Frederick Nolan.) This revolutionary instr. was first produced in 1832. After years of further experimentation Boehm decided to change the inverted-conical bore to a cylindrical one, since the greater volume of air would produce a fuller and clearer tone, and to redesign the head, to which he gave a parabolic curve. The still-larger fingerholes necessitated replacing the rings with padded finger plates. This cylindrical model was introduced in 1847 and is still played today. Boehm's earlier instrs. were of metal, his later ones of wood. Today metal flutes are played in America, but wooden ones are still the rule rather than the exception in Europe. It must be mentioned that in creating the modern cylindrical flute Boehm had also changed the instr.'s timbre. Today's flute has a compass c^1–c^4 or higher, a length of 67 cm. (26½ in.), and 13 tone holes (14, 15, 89, 144, 169, 170; Megaw: "Penny Whistles and Prehistory," in *Antiquity,* March 1960); see also: alto flute, bass flute, Quartflöte, tierce flute;

Modern flute family

Piccolo flute	$d\flat^2$ (band)
Piccolo flute	c^2 (orchestra)
Fife	$a\flat^1$
Tierce flute	f^1 (in F historically; now considered in E♭)
	$d\flat^1$ (band)
Concert flute	c^1
Flûte d'amour	a^0 (obs.)
	$a\flat^0$ (band)
Alto flute	g^0
	$e\flat^0$ (band)
	$d\flat^0$ (band)
Bass flute	c^0

2. in 15th-c. organs the name given to flue pipework; when this was split into 2 groups, the narrow pipes were called principals (a word originally denoting pitch); see: Flötenwerk; **3.** a class of organ flue pipes known since *ca.* 1500, formerly made of metal, now chiefly of wood. The stop occurs nowadays at 32', 16', 8', 4', 2', or 1' pitch, or as a mutation stop. Historically the pipes have been either open or stopped. Modern flute tone is produced either by causing pipes with low mouths to overblow, or by boring 1 or 2 small holes about halfway up the pipes (see also: flûte harmonique), or by boring a hole in the stopper, or by building wide-scaled pipes with wide mouths. They have also been designed with double mouths (59, 62, 133).

Flûte à bandeau, Fr.: ring flute.

Flûte à bec (Fr.), **1.** recorder; in a larger sense a *beaked flute; **2.** organ stop of stopped wooden flue pipes at 8' or 4' pitch (2).

Flûte à bloc, Fr.: fipple flute.

Flûte à cheminée (Fr.: chimney flute), Fr. organ stop equivalent to the Rohrflöte.

Flûte à coulisse, Fr.: piston flute.

Flûte à encoche, Fr.: notched flute.

Flûte à fuseau, Fr.: Spitzflöte.

Flûte allemande (Fr.: German flute), **1.** the *cross flute. As *flûte d'Alemaine,* it is recorded in 1514; as *flûte allemande* from 1702 on (204); **2.** organ stop of flue pipes which has been built in a number of forms over the centuries; originally a flute stop, as its name indicates, it was made as a wide-scaled, overblowing cylindrical stop of open pipes, also as a nonoverblowing, narrow-scaled cylindrical stop. In the late 18th c. and early 19th c. it was transformed into a string stop, with overblowing open conical pipes. In old Fr. organs it occurred as a half-stopped register—equivalent to the Rohrgedackt—of medium scale, cylindrical. Mersenne describes it as a half-stopped, narrow cylindrical stop with long and wide chimney. See also: fifre allemand (133).

Flûte à l'oignon, Fr.: onion flute.

Flûte à neuf trous (Fr.: nine-holed flute), obs. Fr.: the recorder, so called because it had 6 fingerholes, a duplicate lower hole, and a rear thumbhole, 9 in all. The expression dates from the 16th c. (35).

Flûte à pavillon (Fr.), in Engl. called bell diapason, organ stop of cylindrical or inverted conical open flue pipes of medium scale, surmounted by a bell, invented by Pierre-Alexandre Ducroquet of Paris *ca.* 1850 (133).

Flûte à registre, according to Quantz, an 18th-c. *cross flute fitted with a foot joint in 2 sections that could be pulled out for tuning purposes, depending upon the length of the middle joint in use (89).

Flûte à six trous (Fr.: six-holed flute), obs. Fr.: the *cross flute, so called because of its 6 fingerholes. Trichet, *ca.* 1640, uses the term.

Flûte à trois trous (Fr.: three-holed flute), obs. Fr.: galoubet or pibole.

Flûteau, obs. Fr.: a small larigot or flageolet. Thoinan Arbeau, in **1588,** writes of the *"fluttot nommé arigot,"* which had a variable number of fingerholes, depending upon its size, the best having 4 front and 2 rear ones. *Cf.* larigot (204).

Flute bass (Ger.: *Flötenbass*), organ stop of flue pipes, usually stopped, at 8′ pitch in the pedal. Made of wood or metal and having flute tone (12, 101).

Flûte basse, Fr.: bass flute. Also called basse de flûte.

Flûte Behaigne or **flûte de Behaigne,** unidentified flute mentioned in a 1349 regulation pertaining to *ménéstriers. Flauteurs de Behaigne* are mentioned in *Cléomades* (13th c.); Machault (d. 1377) refers to a *"flûte brehaigne,"* and one var. of the word reads *"Bretaigne."* Some modern writers have interpreted the word as "Bohemian" (35).

Flûte bouchée harmonique (Fr.), organ stop of stopped flue pipes of wood, overblown, of late-19th-c. invention. Similar to the Zauberflöte (186).

Flûte brehaigne, see: flûte Behaigne.

Flûte conique (Fr.), **1.** *cone flute; **2.** organ stop of metal flue pipes of inverted conical shape and powerful tone (198).

Flûte couverte, organ stop invented by Conacher of Huddersfield and first introduced in 1894, similar to the *flûte à cheminée but of wider scale, at 8′ pitch. Furnished with chimneys from c^1 up (198).

Flûte creuse, Fr.: Hohlflöte.

Flûte d'accord, Fr.: chord flute.

Flûte d'Alemagne, flûte d'Allemagne, obs. var. of flûte allemande.

Flûte d'amour (Fr.) (It.: *flauto d'amore*), **1.** 18th-c. flute in A, a 3rd below the ordinary flute, nearly extinct now, although it has since been made on occasion with the Boehm system. *Ca.* 78 cm. (31 in.) long (14); **2.** organ stop similar to the Dulzflöte.

Flûte d'Angleterre, a 17th-c. name of the recorder.

Flûte de Pan, Fr.: panpipes. Furetière in 1690 defined it as a *sifflet de chauderonnier (tinker's whistle) (78).

Flûte diatonique (Fr.), improved *cross flute of William Gordon of London, in 1834, with keys and large, open fingerholes for $d^0 e^0 f\#^0 a^0 b^0$. See also: flute (176).

Flûte d'ivoire (Fr.: ivory flute), obs. Fr. organ stop of wide-scaled, open cylindrical flue pipes, corresponding to the tibia aperta or Offenflöte, said to have been made of ivory. In Ger. workshops the name was corr. to flaut devoir and, finally, divinare (133).

Flûte double, see: Doppelflöte.

Flûte douce, 1. 17th-c. Fr.: recorder; **2.** organ stop of open conical flue pipes, a narrow-scaled echo stop (133).

Flûte droite, Fr.: vertical flute.

Flûte éolienne, Fr.: aeolian flute.

Flûte eunuque, Fr.: eunuch flute.

Flûte fondamentale (Fr.), Engl. organ stop, a variety of Hohlflöte at 8' pitch (198).

Flûte harmonique (Ger.: *Harmonieflöte*), organ stop of wide-scaled, open cylindrical *harmonic pipes, invented by Aristide Cavaillé-Coll of Paris, at 8' or 4' pitch (133).

Flûte nasale, Fr.: nose flute.

Flûte octaviante (Fr.), organ stop found in Fr. organs, a narrow-scaled *harmonic flute at 4' pitch (131).

Flutéole [Fr. *flûte* + Gk. *Aeolus*, god of wind], flute with conical bore and blowhole of a particular shape, invented by Coste of Paris in 1847 (158).

Flûte ouverte, Fr.: Offenflöte.

Flûte pastorale (Fr.), organ stop of stopped cylindrical flue pipes, usually at 4' pitch, and of narrow scale. It corresponds to the Zartflöte.

Flûte polycalame, Fr.: flute of 2 or more pipes. (The term *flûte monocalame,* for a single flute, is nowadays also in use.)

Flûtet (Fr.), pipe of the *pipe and

tabor ensemble; Fr. name of the Prov. galoubet. Laborde (in 1780) describes it as having 3 holes (124).

Flûte tierce, Fr.: tierce flute.

Flûte traversière (Fr.), **1.** the *cross flute. As *fluste traversaine,* the term has been in force from the 13th c. on. In the 14th c. Machault differentiates between this and the ordinary (vertical) flute; **2.** organ stop found in Fr. organs: a narrow-scaled *harmonic flute at 8' pitch (35, 131).

Flûte traversière à bec, Fr.: Dulzflöte.

Flutina, see: music box.

Flûtina (Fr.), a small accordion with a keyboard on each head, patented by Wender of Paris on Dec. 8, 1842 (204).

Flûtina-polka, accordion with 2 ranks of reeds, patented by Busson of Paris on Apr. 15, 1851 (204).

Flûtophone, var. of flautophone.

Flutophone, modern plastic end-blown "woodwind," with beak mouthpiece, 7 front fingerholes, terminating in a flared bell; compass c^2–d^3.

Flûtot, see: flûteau.

Fluttuan, organ stop of open flue pipes of beechwood, designed by Abbé Vogler; it sounded like a French horn; a manual stop at 16' pitch from c^1 up (133, 176).

Fluviol, var. of flaviol.

Fodrahi, tall *goblet drum of S. Nias, with laced head. The lacings form a network that covers the body (122).

Foekepot, Du. or Flem. friction drum.

Foi mere, an indirectly blown *bass flute of W. Flores Island, with cylindrical tube and 6 equidistant fingerholes (122).

Fol [Lat. **follis*], OFr. and Gal.: bellows.

Folle [Lat. **follis*], Port.: bellows (197).

Follis, Lat.: bellows.

Fololitsy, syn. of sódina.

Fon, abbr. of simfon (organistrum). The term was used by Jon Arason, Icelandic bishop (d. 1550), who said that it had both strings and keys (9).

Fond d'orgue (Fr.), syn. of jeu de fond.

Fondrahi, see: fodrahi.

Fong hsiao, syn. of p'ai hsiao.

Fong sheng, a large variety of sheng.

Fonola, an automatic piano with pneumatic mechanism, similar to the pianola, made by M. Welte & Sons of Freiburg from 1904 on. For a list of player devices see: pianola; not to be confused with Phonola (37).

Fontanelle (Fr.), a perforated cover in shape of a little box or barrel; it was slipped over the keywork of some med. and Renaissance wind instrs. in order to protect the keys, and generally was pierced with a number of small holes.

Fontomfrom, a *"talking drum" of Ashanti (162).

Foot (Fr.: *pied;* Ger.: *Fuss;* It.: *piede;* Sp.: *pie*), **1.** the lowest joint of certain woodwind instrs.; **2.** the lowest part of an organ pipe; **3.** a unit of length and hence of pitch, as the pitch of a pipe depends upon its length. In organ building this is expressed in terms of, and in relationship to, an organ pipe 8′ long from the foot up (*i.e.*, not counting the foot), sounded by a C key. A stopped pipe sounds an oct. lower than does an open one, and its pitch is usually indicated in terms of pitch, not pipe length, as with open pipes; *e.g.*, an 8′ Gedackt is a pipe 4′ in length but is said to speak at 8′. The pitch of reed pipes is also indicated by pitch and not by length. When the lowest manual key on continental European organs was F (chiefly during the 17th c.), pitch lengths were expressed in terms of a 6′ or 12′ pipe. Quint stops, nowadays said to be at 5⅓′ pitch, were historically considered as being at 6′ pitch.

Foot cymbals, cymbals clashed by means of a pedal. See: choke, cymbals, hi hat.

Footed drum (Fr.: *tambour sur pied*), drum having its lower end carved to form a socle or feet (170).

Footed harp (Fr.: *harpe à support;* Ger.: *Stützharfe*), harp of the New Kingdom of ancient Egypt; it rested partly on a slanting leg and partly against the player's knees (170).

Force, la (Fr.: strength), pedal register of organ pipes built by Josef Gabler in the Benedictine church of Weingarten, Württemberg, a Hornwerk emphasizing the lowest pedal tone, C. A stop of the same name is also to be found in Ravensburg, where it is said to be a 5- or 6-rank mixture (131, 161).

Fork action (Fr.: *système à fourchettes;* Ger.: *Drehscheiben*), harp action invented by Sébastien Érard in 1794, still in use today. It has the advantage of not displacing the strings laterally, as did earlier actions. See: harp.

Fortbien [It. *forte piano;* pun or Ger. pronunciation?], Ger. 18th-c. term for square piano.

Forté-campano [*forte,* loud + *campano,* bell], metallophone imitating the sound of bells, patented in 1825 by François-Marie Lemoine, a Parisian clockmaker and mechanic (176, 204).

Fortepiano (It.: loud soft), expression used in the 18th c. to distinguish those keyboard instrs. with hammer action from those with jack action—actually an abbr. of gravicembalo col forte e piano.

Fortepiano à cordes de verre (Fr.: fortepiano with glass strings), name given by Beyer of Paris to his crystallophone, *ca.* 1785, which Benjamin Franklin christened glasschord (169).

Fortepianoclavier, a combination piano-harpsichord invented in 1794 by Elias Schlegel of Altenburg (176).

Forte stop (Ger.: *Fortezug*), stop applied to pianos, consisting of a device to raise the dampers. In the 18th c. it was often divided so that treble and bass could be controlled separately (92).

Fotuto, 1. syn. of putoto; **2.** an Afro-Cuban marine-shell trumpet; **3.** Cuban horn made of a cattle horn (152).

Fotzhobel (Ger.: mouth plane), **1.** in Styria coll. for mouth organ; **2.** in Bavaria panpipes (176).

Foundation stops (Fr.: *jeux de fond;* Ger.: *Grundstimmen*), the flue pipework of an organ without mixture or mutation stops.

Founfóni, Prov. equivalent of zanfoña. *Cf.* fanfóni (44).

Fourniture (Fr.), mixture organ stop composed of octaves and quints, found in Fr. organs in which, together with the cymbale, it forms the plein-jeu.

Fowa, leg rattle of the Thonga of S. Africa, made of a root placed in a palm-leaf basketry box and tied around the legs of convalescent persons (116).

Frame drum (Fr.: *tambour sur cadre;* Ger.: *Rahmentrommel*), drum with a diam. as great or greater than the depth of its body; it may have 1 or 2 heads, be round or have corners, be large or small. Some varieties are fitted with handles. Frame drums were known to ancient Sumer, where they assumed great proportions, and are still played in many parts of the world today, in Europe chiefly as the tambourine. Also found in Africa, America, Asia (100).

Frame harp (Fr.: *harpe à cadre;* Ger.: *Rahmenharfe*), harp composed of 3 sections: resonator; neck or harmonic curve; and column or pillar, also called fore-pillar. The column takes the tension of the strings, consequently frame harps are able to withstand far greater tension than are other types. Non-European countries (except Siberia) do not know the frame harp (170).

Frame rattle (Ger.: *Rahmenrassel*), rattle consisting of objects attached to a carrier against which they strike (100).

Frame zither (Fr.: *cithare à cadre;* Ger.: *Rahmenzither*), zither having strings attached across an open frame (100).

Franklin harmonica, see: glass harmonica.

Frauenzimmer (Ger.: gentlewoman), 17th-c. Ger. term for plucked keyboard instrs. For origin of the term see: cembalo.

Free reed (Fr.: *anche libre;* Ger.: *durchschlagende Zunge;* It.: *ancia libera*), metal or cane tongue that vibrates through a closely fitting frame, moving freely at one end and held down at the other. Length and thickness determine its pitch. Such reeds can be tuned by filing close to the free end to raise the pitch, or close to the fixed end to lower it. Known for millennia in Asia, where free-reed pipes are still in use singly or combined (as in mouth organs), it was not introduced to Europe until the late 18th c. A sheng sent from China was examined in St. Petersburg by the physicist Kratzenstein of Copenhagen, who suggested its use to the organ builder Kirschnik, who incorporated free reeds into his piano-organs. It was left to that great innovator Abbé Vogler to introduce them into the organ. He did so in Darmstadt in 1792. After 1800 experimentation was intensified, resulting from 1810 on in a series of free-reed keyboard instrs. (117, 169, 170).

Frein harmonique (Fr.) (Ger.: *Streichbart*), metal *beard attached to a spring and fixed to an organ pipe, invented by Charles Lemaire of Paris and introduced by Gavioli in the 19th c. (198).

French basson, 17th-c. Engl. name of the bassoon (14).

French flageolet, name sometimes given to the flageolet to distinguish it from the *English flageolets of Bainbridge.

French horn, 1. Engl. name of the circular coiled horn, first recorded in 1681. See: horn; **2.** organ stop invented by John Compton of Nottingham in the 20th c., a reed stop with long resonators surmounted by a bell, on heavy pressure. The name is also given to the horn organ stop in the U.S. and Britain (133, 198).

French lute, an Engl. 17th-c. appellation of the theorbo-lute.

French trompe, an early name of the French horn.

Frestel, frestele [Lat. *fistella,* small tube] (OFr.), small panpipes of med.

France, a rustic instr., mentioned from the mid-12th c. on. Cotgrave (in 1611) calls it a kind of whistle that the sow-gelders of France usually carry about them. *Cf.* capapuercas.

Fret [Fr. *frette,* ring, band] (Fr.: *ton;* Ger.: *Bund;* It.: *tasto, ligatura;* Sp.: *traste*), divisions of the fingerboard, neck, or belly of a string instr., indicating the points at which the strings are to be stopped. Frets may be movable (of gut, etc.) or fixed (metal, ivory). In Western antiquity they consisted of tied loops. The home of frets is Asia, whence they reached Egypt in the 15th c. B.C. In Europe they do not occur until the 14th c., at which time they were probably introduced by the Arabs (177).

Freteau, fretiau, var. of frestel.

Fretel [OFr. **frestel*], Engl. form of *fretel,* mentioned in 15th-c. literature (180).

Fretted (Fr.: *lié;* Ger.: *gebunden*), said of a clavichord having more than one key to a course of strings. The Engl. word is also applied to instrs. having frets on their necks.

Friction drum (Fr.: *tambour à friction;* Ger.: *Reibtrommel;* Sp.: *tambor de fricción*), membranophone sounded by friction. This can be accomplished by rubbing the drumhead with a piece of hide, as is sometimes done in Africa, or by means of a stick or cord fixed to the head. In its simplest form, the European friction drum consists of a wooden bucket or a clay pot with the top open and the bottom closed by a membrane. A small hole is pierced in the center of the membrane and a wooden stick inserted. This is either pulled up and down or rubbed with wet fingers, in each case causing the membrane to vibrate. In some instances the stick is replaced by one or more cords. Mersenne is the first writer to have mentioned the friction drum; he believed it to be a non-European instr. Buonanni (in 1722) describes it as being used during the grape harvest in Italy. Carol singers of Bohemia still play it,

holding it between their knees and stroking the horsehair cord with wet fingers; it is also used at carnival time in Naples. The friction drum is distributed in W. and C. Europe, N. and S. America, India and Japan. There exists also a *whirled friction drum. See also: adufo, akunde, bandaska, braù, Brommtopp, Brummtopf, brunda, buchaĭŭ, buddipotte, buhai, buk, bukal, büllhäfen, caccarella, cheplanget, chicharra, cuíca, cupa-cupa, dhurki, dingwinti, dugdugi, ekpe, ekue, eltzabor, Foekepot, Fubbdöpp, fungador, furuco, girgiri, gubgubi, gudalo, guffepotte, ha ma, hukelpott, hüldopp, ingungu, jackdaw, juco, kalumpemba, kinfuíti, kingulungulu, kinkwinta, kipuita, kongo-longo nkueko, koy na bala, lukombe, manfula, maroto, mēgha, menghi, morupa, moshupiane, muanza, mutisánguisi, mwan'angulu, mwandu, najoroto, namalua, ngetundo, ngulu, omelé, pignato, puíca, puita, ranita, Rommelpot, Rummelpot, Rummeltopf, sanbomba, simbomba, socador, tambor-onça, tambue, wokkepot, wupu-wupu, ximbomba, zabumba, zambomba (16, 38, 176).

Frog [Ger.: *Frosch*] (Fr.: *hausse;* Ger.: *Frosch;* It.: *tallone*), that part of a bow which serves to tighten the hair, nowadays made of ebony, ivory, etc., attached to the lower end of the bow by means of a metal screw. Called nut in England.

Frosch, Ger.: frog.

Frula (Serb.), **1.** generic name for flute in Yugoslavia; **2.** syn. of stranka; **3.** syn. in W. Serbia of duduk; **4.** Serb. *cross flute in D, with 6 fingerholes (34).

Frullo, frullone, bull-roarer in Italy (152).

Fuá, simple Afro-Cuban chordophone. A string is tied to the horizontal branch of a tree, the other end being fixed to a log. The log is placed in front of the seated performer's chair and held taut by having his feet placed on it. The string is plucked (152).

Fubbdöpp (Rhenish dialect), N. Ger. friction drum (169).

Fu ch'in, a variety of the cheng, 1, found in Kiangsu, China (176).

Fučkec, primitive wooden pipe of Slovenia (144).

Fuelle, Sp.: bellows.

Fugara [*fujara*], organ stop of narrow, open cylindrical flue pipes at 8', 4', 2', or 1' pitch; it originated *ca.* 1600 and became obs. by 1800. In older organs it was also spelled Vogara (131, 133).

Fujara, *whistle flute of the Detva region of Slovakia, with cylindrical tube, tuned to the mixolydian mode. A shepherd's instr. *ca.* 1 m. (40 in.) long, held vertically, with a projecting mouthpiece placed at some distance from the upper end so as to bring the fingerholes within the player's reach (38, 89).

Fujarka, *whistle flute of Poland, with 6–8 fingerholes (89).

Fukulu, drum of the Batambwe of the Congo, in form of a truncated barrel, with a nailed head and carved body. Formerly a war drum, it is now used by professional dancers, who hold it against the chest, and used secretly by sorcerers. *Ca.* 30 cm. (12 in.) high (30).

Fuli, Mandingo name of the tuni, 1.

Füllflöte, organ stop of wide-scaled, cylindrical stopped pipes, at 8' pitch (133).

Füllquinte, Füllflöte at 5⅓' pitch.

Fulu, free-reed *mouth organ of the Muhsö (Lahu) people of Shan State, Burma, similar to the sheng, with 5 cane pipes furnished with metal free reeds. The pipes are inserted in a calabash that serves as wind chest, its neck as blowpipe (172).

Fumabata ngoma, syn. of yuka (152).

Fumbo, elongated *cylindrical drum of the Jopadhola of Uganda, with single nailed head. *Ca.* 1 m. (40 in.) high (195).

Fundamentalbrett, Ger.: table (of an organ).

Fungador (snorter), name of the *cuíca friction drum in Maranhão and Pará, Brazil, also called socador (7).

Furi, stopped *end-blown flute of the Republic of Niger, with 3 fingerholes (176).

Furin (wind bell), *aeolian bell of Japan, with wide clapper, suspended from temple roofs (157).

Furi tsuzumi (Jap.: shaking tsuzumi), *rattle drum of Japan, consisting of 2 very small drums with 5 or 6 pellet bells, attached to the end of a stick 50 cm. (20 in.) long. The drums are *ca.* 10 cm. (4 in.) long, 7 cm. (3 in.) in diam.; used in processions. It is equivalent to the Korean to-ko (157).

Fürst Pless-Horn, see: Prince Pless horn.

Furuco, *friction drum of Venezuela, made of a barrel over which a piece of leather is stretched. The leather is perforated in the center to admit the friction stick, which is pulled up and down (16).

Fuss, Ger.: foot.

Fusuna . . . , see: phusana . . .

Futaku, *aeolian bell of Japan, equivalent to the pangul of Korea (66).

Fututo, 1. syn. of putoto; **2.** syn. of fotuto, 2 and 3 (152).

Fuye, generic term for flute in Japan. See: amma-no-fuye, azuma-fuye, kagura fuye, koma fuye, shino fuye, sho no fuye, tama fuye, yamato fuye, yoko fuye (157).

G

Ga, rattle of Ubangi, Africa, made of 5 dried strychnos shells containing seeds, strung on a handle; a dancer's instr. (132).

Gä, free-reed horn of the Karen of Shan State, Burma, made of a curved buffalo horn provided with a free reed of cane (172).

Gã, syn. of agogó (6).

Gabbus [Turk. *qūbūz*], the name of the gambus in Zanzibar, E. Africa. See also: gabus (169).

Gabelbecken, Ger.: crotal.

Gabelharfe, Ger.: Kru harp.

Gabi, Basque: a large *cog rattle that replaces bells during Easter week (56).

Gabuki, chordophone of India, similar to the ānanda laharī. The string is held taut in the left hand, the resonator under the right arm, and the string is plucked with the right hand. It is used by mendicants and generally accompanied by a drum (138).

Gabus, *musical bow of the Korana Hottentots of S. Africa, held between the player's lips. The string is plucked by the right forefinger. By varying the size of the oral cavity, the harmonics are reinforced, although the pitch proper is not changed. *Ca.* 75 cm. (30 in.) long (116).

Gabusifono, a variety of soprano, tenor, and bass trombones made by Giuseppe Gabusi of Bologna in 1880 (126).

Gada, Kan. equivalent of the gātha (173).

Gādar, Marvari: tūrya.

Gadlje, syn. of gajde, 1.

Gadulka [OSlav. *gudu,* to drone], bowed chordophone of Bulgaria, a folk instr. corresponding to the (Gk.) lira, with piriform body continuing in a short neck that tapers to a pegdisc, wooden belly, strings held by rear pegs and a tailpiece, lacking both nut and fingerboard. The body and neck are made from a single piece of hollowed-out wood; this can be maple, sycamore, locust, mulberry, walnut, elder, or fruitwood. The soundholes are usually semicircular, exceptionally round or rectangular. The bridge is flat. A soundpost is propped against the upper part of the bass side of the bridge and passes through the soundhole, to rest against the back. The number of strings varies: throughout Bulgaria, but particularly in Dobrudja, three are common, tuned $a^1 a^0 e^1$, with a compass of but a 10th (the center string is a drone), or $a^1 e^1 d^1$, a tuning preferred by gypsies; here the third string is usually a drone (d^1); the so-called Thracian tuning is $a^1 e^1 a^1$, all melody strings. Four-stringed gadulkas are derived from those having three strings; instrs. with 2 or 5 strings are also known, as are specimens with sympathetic strings. Formerly the strings were stopped by the player's fingernails, nowadays by sideways pressure of the fingers. The gadulka is held in vertical position, resting on the seated player's knee, or against the belt of a standing player, but in the Ikhtiman district of W. Bulgaria players now hold their instrs. horizontally against the chest. In Thrace, the Balkans, and W. Bulgaria the instrs. measure 50–55 cm. (19½–21½ in.) long and 18–22 cm. (7–8½ in.) wide; in Dobrudja they are 40–45 cm. (16–17½ in.) long, 13–15 cm. (5–6 in.) wide. Although not mentioned in literary sources prior to the 16th c., the gadulka is considerably older, apparently existing under the name of gusla, as it is occasionally still called nowadays. Widespread in Bulgaria, it serves as solo and as accompanying instr. Also called g'ola, gusla, kemenche, kemene, tsigulka; rarely digulka, dzigulitsa, gunilka, viola. See also: gudok, gusla, guslice, lirica, smyk (80 XVI, 89).

Gadza, *vessel rattle of the Malagasy Republic, made of a shallow basketry box containing seeds (176).

Gafa, antelope horn of the Galla of E. Africa, played during dances. Identical with the ges of the Somali (176).

Gagambangam, xylophone said still to exist in W. Java, having the appearance of a gambang cut in half—a transitional form (121).

Gagöka, cylindrical *end-blown flute of the Uitoto Indians of Colombia, open at both ends. A block of resin is placed in the center and a hole is cut in the wall opposite it. A piece of bark partly closes this hole, forming a duct. The exterior is bound with strips of bark. Ca. 110 cm. (43 in.) long (32).

Gah-gah, percussion gourd of the W. African *griots* and Moors, a large, hollow calabash with an orifice on top, held in both hands and stamped against the ground (152).

Gaida [Turk. *ghaida*], **1.** bagpipe of Bulgaria and Macedonia, mouth-blown, with sheepskin bag. The single cylindrical chanter terminates in a small, angular cow-horn bell, has 7 front fingerholes, a rear thumbhole, and a single beating reed. Its bass drone is horn-mounted and pitched 2 octs. below the chanter's keynote. Some Macedonian specimens have in addition a small treble drone pitched a 12th or 2 octs. above the bass drone. This type is sometimes called the "Bulgarian" bagpipe. In Bulgaria these small drones can be either cylindrical or conical and are furnished with single reeds (13); **2.** Pol. and Ruth. bagpipe (169).

Gait [Frankish *wahten*], OFr.: watch-

man's pipe (14th c.) or horn (15th c.), equivalent to the Engl. *wait. Also written guaite.

Gaita [OGal. from Gothic *gaits*, goat, or Arab. *ghaita*], generic Sp. term for pipes and specifically: **1.** bagpipe of Spain; Trichet mentions it *ca.* 1640. See: gaita asturiana, gaita gallega, gaita zamorana; **2.** double-reed instrs. In this sense it is defined as a shawm in both Portugal and Spain; **3.** hornpipe of Spain; see: gaita extremeña, gaita madrileña, gaita salamanquina; **4.** in Portugal the word denotes panpipes; see: gaita de capador; **5.** in Brazil it designates a small bamboo or metal flute, also called *pife; **6.** in S. Brazil an accordion used by Gauchos, also called sanfona. *Cf.* gayta, zampoña, 1 (7, 44).

Gaita asturiana, the gaita of the Asturias, Spain, identical with the gaita gallega (13).

Gaita de capador (gelder's *gaita*), Port. panpipes played by gelders to announce their arrival in villages.

Gaita de foles (bellows *gaita*), Port.: bagpipe. Also called gaita galega.

Gaita de odre (bag *gaita*), Sp.: bagpipe.

Gaita extremeña (*gaita* of Estremadura), hornpipe of Spain with cylindrical bore, 3 fingerholes, and a deerhorn bell at both ends of the pipe. 42–54 cm. (16½–17½ in.) long.

Gaita gallega (*gaita* of Galicia), bagpipe of Spain, generally mouth-blown but occasionally furnished with bellows. The chanter is 30 cm. (12 in.) long, has 7 front fingerholes and a rear thumbhole, a low rear hole that is never stopped, a projecting bell with 2 ventholes, and a double reed. The drone is 70 cm. (28 in.) long, with cylindrical bore, single reed, and 2 tuning slides (13).

Gaita grilera, bagpipe of Galicia, Spain, tuned in D, with single drone (57).

Gaita madrileña, hornpipe of the Sierra of Madrid, with cylindrical pipe of figwood having a cylindrical bore, and provided with 3 front fingerholes and a rear thumbhole. It has a mouth horn and a cow-horn bell. The single reed is also protected by a section of horn. The scale is pentatonic (13; *Anuario musical*, 1956).

Gaita redonda, bagpipe of Galicia, Spain, tuned to C (57).

Gaita roncadora (drone *gaita*), syn. of gaita tumbal.

Gaita salamanquina (*gaita* of Salamanca), hornpipe of Salamanca, Spain, with 3 fingerholes (57).

Gaita tumbal [*tumba,* obs. Andalusian dance], bagpipe of Galicia, Spain, a variety of the gaita gallega, with 2 drones, each cylindrical and furnished with a single reed. Tuned to B♭. Also called gaita roncadora (57).

Gaita zamorana (*gaita* of Zamora), **1.** bagpipe of Zamora, Spain, with 2 drones; **2.** instr. mentioned twice in Cervantes' *Don Quijote* (1605) as a hurdy-gurdy and (on the basis of this?) said to be an obs. Cast. hurdy-gurdy. Pedrell states that it is unknown as such in Zamora (154).

Gait-horne, 16th-c. var. of goat-horn: "ane pipe maid of ane gait horne" (*The Complaynt of Scotlande,* 1549). This quotation is often cited as the earliest literary reference to the *gemshorn (Oxford English Dictionary).

Gajda [Turk. *ghaida*], bagpipe of Slovakia (89).

Gajde [Turk. *ghaida*], **1.** Serb. bagpipe with 2 chanters, a bass drone, horn bell, and single reeds; **2.** Slov. and Croatian bagpipe with double chanter and drone; in Slovenia the chanter terminates in a removable bell (34, 144).

Gajdy [Turk. *ghaida*], the bagpipe of Moravia (89).

Gaku biwa, 4-stringed biwa of Japan, played in *gagaku* music. The strings are pressed down against the frets—4 in number—not between them, as with the heike biwa. It is played with a plectrum. *Ca.* 90 cm. (3 ft.) long (135, 144).

Gaku daiko, *frame drum of Japan,

with 2 nailed heads, played with 2 sticks in *kabuki* music. *Ca.* 50 cm. (20 in.) in diam. (135).

Gaku no tsuzumi, tsuzumi with laced head, used in *gagaku* music (176).

Gaku sō, sō no koto of Japan used in *gagaku* music, an unaltered version of the Chin. *cheng mentioned in the 756 inventory of Todai-ji Temple, Nara. It has 13 strings, is *ca.* 2 m. (6½ ft.) long, max. width 25 cm. (10 in.). Also called sō, shin sō (144).

Gala, Gujarati: ranasringa.

Galamutu [*garamut], name of the garamut on St. Matthias Islands, Bismarck Archipelago (77).

Galandronome [Galender + Gk. *nomos,* law], military bassoon in B♭ invented *ca.* 1853 by Galender of Paris, with tall, wide flared bell and 19 keys (89 Langwill).

Gale, Basque: cowbell (56).

Galinquang, bamboo Jew's-harp of New Guinea, elongated and pointed. A minute piece of wood is sometimes affixed to the tip to increase and deepen the tone (176).

Galischan, Ger. corr. of colascione.

Galoubet (Fr., Prov.) [OProv. *galaubiar,* to play superbly], Prov. pipe of the *pipe and tabor ensemble, made of wood, usually boxwood, with 2 front fingerholes and a rear thumbhole. The bore is cylindrical and very narrow, so that fundamentals are not used, although it is possible to sound them. The galoubet is pitched in d², its lowest used tone (the second harmonic) is d³. As Thoinan Arbeau already pointed out in 1588, it overblows the 5th very easily, hence the fingerholes have to fill in only the interval of a 5th. The player holds his instr. in the left hand, with thumb, index, and middle fingers covering the 3 holes. Prior to the 18th c., when galoubet became a Fr. word, it was known as *flûte à trois trous* or *flûtet* outside Provence. *Ca.* 30 cm. (12 in.) long. *Cf.* flahutet, jombarde (14, 132).

Gamakha's, *musical bow of the Berg-

Dama of S. Africa, made of solid wood with a string of twisted leather. One end of the bow is placed on a block of wood that acts as resonator, the upper end being held in position by player's chin. The string is plucked with his right hand, while his left modifies the pitch by changing the bow's tension. Often a second person taps the string with a thin rod (116).

Gamba (It.), **1.** Engl., Ger.: abbr. of viola da gamba; **2.** generic name of a family of organ stops with string tone, first built by Esaias Compenius in Bückeburg in 1615. They consist of cylindrical flue pipes of small scale at 8′ or 4′ pitch, nowadays mostly bearded and slotted, with low mouths (63, 129).

Gambang gangsa, multi-oct. saron of Java, now obsolescent, with 14–15 bars, generally without bosses. It represents an older period when the 3 other sarons did not exist as separate instrs. Also called gambang selukat. If the bars are bossed, it may be called pantu. See also: chelepita, dempling (121).

Gambang kayu, trough xylophone of Java, composed of 16–21 graduated slabs of bamboo, teak, or other wood, laid on small cushions placed in a carved wooden trough and secured by pins. Some small, 1-oct. instrs. have bamboo slabs, but usually the compass extends from just over 3 to over 4 octs. Exchange slabs for the different tunings are kept inside the trough. The higher the pitch, the rounder the slabs become, until the treble ones are virtually rods. It is played with mushroom-shaped beaters held loosely between forefinger and thumb (121).

Gambang selukat, syn. of gambang gansa (121).

Gambar (Pahl.), same as the Pers. chanbar.

Gambareh, name of the Kru harp among the Sarakole of W. Africa (16).

Gambe, Fr., Ger.: gamba.

Gambenbass (Ger.), organ stop, a rarely encountered 16′ pedal stop of string tone.

Gambenwerk, generic 18th-c. Ger. name for bowed keyboard instrs.

Gamber, viola-shaped humle of S. Jutland (176).

Gambette, organ stop; a gamba at 4′ pitch (101).

Gambili, syn. of kumbili.

Gambus [Turk. *qūbūz*], lute of W. Borneo, N. Celebes, and W. Java, of Islamic origin, usually bowed, a descendant of the qūbūz, with elongated, piriform body, the lower half of its belly being made of parchment, the upper of wood, lateral pegs in a sickle-shaped pegbox, and 3 or 6 strings. In W. Java the belly is entirely of parchment, and in addition to 3 pairs of silk strings it has a low seventh string of metal. In the archipelago some instrs. are found with all-wood bellies. The gambus is identical with the kabosa of the Malagasy Republic (112, 121, 173).

Gamelan, orchestra of Indonesia, composed chiefly of percussion instrs.

Gamen-wudu, var. of gomen-wudu.

Gamti, syn. of kolamut.

Gan, syn. of agogó in Bahía (7).

Ganang, Cham: slit drum (176).

Ganbo, stamping tube of Haiti.

Ganda-ganda, small kettledrum of Bonerate Island (near Flores Island), with coconut body and rattan head (173).

Gandang (drum), single-headed drum of the Borneo Dayak. See also: gendang (112).

Gandang bavoi (Dayak: pig drum), idiochord *tube zither of Borneo that is struck (176).

Gane, Jap.: gong, bell.

Ganga (Hausa), name for drum in the Benue-Cross languages; also in Tunisia among the Guang and Hausa, where it is cylindrical; in Morocco, where it is a kettledrum; among the Yoruba, where it is an hourglass drum. The Hausa carry theirs on the left shoulder. See also: aganga, agonga, agongo, degangande, digongo, gangan, gangano, gangatan, gengaun, ligangale, oganga, uganga (93).

Gangan, hourglass drum of the Yoruba of Nigeria (103).

Gangana, iron bell of the Dogon of Mali (103).

Gangano [*ganga], Mossi (a Sudanic language): drum (93).

Gangarria, Cuban word for a large bell of draft animals (152).

Gangatan [*ganga], cylindrical or conoid drum of the Tuareg, N. Africa, made of wood or clay, with 1 or 2 heads, struck with an oxhide thong or a beater called *ekotar.* Used in wartime and on social occasions. Also called al-tubel. See also: ganga (176).

Ganggereng, bamboo *stamping tube of the Borneo Dayak, with dried fruit seeds inserted that rattle when the stick is stamped against the ground during dances. *Ca.* 220–230 cm. (7 ft. 2 in.–7 ft. 6 in.) long (176).

Gang'sa, gong of the Igorot of Bonton, Philippine Islands. *Cf.* gambang gangsa (176).

Gangsingan, humming top of C. Java, also called panggalen (121).

Gangurih, trumpet of the Kalmuk, made of the armbone of a slain enemy (176).

Ganjur, an older name of the kempul, still used sporadically (121).

Gank, see: jank.

Gankogui, *double bell of the Ewe of Ghana, clapperless, made of beaten iron. Elongated, almost cylindrical in form, the 2 bells are welded at the top so as to produce a tine by which they are held. The pitch varies from instr. to instr. A rhythm instr. (109).

Ganza, *musical bow of the Bonda of Lower Guinea, with tuning loop. The string is tapped with a small stick while stopped with the left thumbnail (17).

Ganzá, 1. rattle of Brazil consisting of a closed cylinder of tin plate. Called xeque in Amazonia and the NE. provinces, amalé in Bahía; **2.** syn. of reco-reco (7).

Ganze Orgel (Ger.: whole organ), obs. Ger. term for an organ having as its foundation a register of 16' pitch. The expression was not used after the mid-18th c. See also: halbe Orgel, viertel Orgel (90).

Ganzinstrument (Ger.: whole instr.), term coined by Karl von Schafhäutl in 1854 to designate those brass instrs. which have a bore wide enough to permit the fundamental to speak. In such instrs. the fundamental (also called pedal tone) is at the same pitch as a pipe of the same length. See also: Halbinstrument (25, 176).

Gara, leg bells of Kenya (120).

Garabato, syn. of lungória (152).

Garadap, *spike fiddle of the Dayak of Borneo, with body of coconut or calabash, the bottom pierced with soundholes, a thin wooden or fishskin belly sealed on with wax, a footed bridge and 1 or 2 strings of cane or of copper wire; played with a cane bow with one end serving as handle and rattan "hair." The fiddle is held between the player's toes (176).

Garamo, syn. of ngilamo (77).

Garamudu, name of the garamut on the Duke of York Island (77).

Garamut, *slit drum of the Duke of York Island, New Ireland, and, together with the following vars., of an area in the Pacific that includes the Bismarck Archipelago: angremut, dangamut, galamutu, garamudu, geramo, gerom, karamut, kolamut, naramut, ngaramut, ngilamo, qaramut, tarremut (77).

Garanktum, xylophone of the Batak of Sumatra (176).

Garantong, name of the tawak in S. Borneo (173).

Garatē, syn. of chakhe.

Garáwung, *cylindrical drum of the Black Carib of C. America, made of a single block of wood with deerskin head; played with bare hands; 50–75 cm. (20–30 in.) high, 30–50 cm. (12–20 in.) in diam. (105).

Garbish, Serb. cattle bell made of sheet iron (176).

Gardon [*bourdon], folk cello. of the Komitate Czík (Siebenbürgen), Hungary, like a violoncello, formerly handmade by the peasantry out of a single block of wood. Older specimens have a very short neck, elongated body, very long tailpiece. Some modern ones have cello-shaped bodies, but the usual form is that of a large med. fiddle, either with sound slits or FF. The 3 or 4 strings are secured by lateral pegs in a conventional pegbox. All are tuned to d⁰. They are not bowed, but are struck with a stick, and immediately after being struck one string is plucked by hand. If the player is seated, he holds the gardon horizontally across his lap; if standing, he holds it obliquely in one hand, with the soundholes on a level with his waist. It serves as a rhythm instr. to accompany the mozsika. Nowadays most of the players are gypsies (54).

Gare, Basque: herd animal bell (56).

Gare-bulunba, Basque: herd animal bell (56).

Gargara, instr. of ancient India mentioned in the Rig-Veda. Presumed to have been a horizontal *arched harp. See also: gharghara, karkarī (170).

Gar gross (Ger.: very great), a prefix to names of organ stops, indicating 32′ pitch.

Garinding, see: grinding.

Gar klein (Ger.: very small), a prefix to names of organ stops, indicating 1′ pitch.

Gar klein Geiglein, Praetorius' term for the kit. His had 3 strings tuned in 5ths, a¹ e² b² or a tone lower.

Garland, the rim of a brass instr.'s bell, made of a double thickness of metal and often engraved.

Garmon, see: karmon.

Garmonica [Ger. *Harmonika*], Russ.: accordion. *Cf.* karmon.

Garmoshka [dim. of *garmonica*], familiar name of the garmonica.

Garmut, see: garamut.

Garneta, clarinet of Macedonia (144).

Garras, end-blown stopped pipe of the Kalahari Bushmen, SW. Africa, made of a duiker or springbok horn (116).

Garude, syn. of kladdi.

Gasa-bin, a large *slit drum of the Baia of Cameroun (42).

Gasba, see: qasaba.

Gāshiqlar (Turk.: spoon), see: lozhky.

Gatambore, gatenbore, gatamore, vars. of danbore (56).

Gātha (Sans., Mar.), *pot drum of India, large, spherical, made of clay, with narrow aperture covered with parchment. The pots are specially made for this purpose, and lend rhythmic accompaniment to stringed instrs. The wrists, fingers, and fingernails are used in playing, but it is the pot and not the parchment that is drummed on. See also: gada, koda, kumbhavādya (179).

Gathanbore, syn. of gatambore.

Gau adar, Basque horn, blown to frighten away wild animals at night (56). See also: abilosen adar.

Gawāq, *whistle flute of NW. Africa, made of cane, rough and very short (170).

Gawu-kha's, bowed *bar zither of the S. African Bushmen, borrowed from the Chwana and similar to the tsijolo. The pitch is changed by stopping the string (116).

Gayda [Turk. *ghaida*], bagpipe of Bulgaria, mouth-blown, with sheepskin bag. A cowhorn forms the chanter stock; wooden stocks for drone and blowpipe are inserted into the forelegs. The chanter is conical with single reed, 6 fingerholes, and a rear thumbhole. The drone is 43 cm. (17 in.) long and has 2 tuning slides furnished with single reeds. The term is also used in Greece (89, 144).

Gayta, syn. of dulzaina.

Gaza, 1. drum of the Abandja of the Congo, in form of a truncated barrel with 2 heads, only 1 of which is played. Their lacings cover the entire body. It is played with a stick held in the right hand, while the left either strikes the membrane or is placed on the membrane to modify the pitch. *Cf.* ndima; **2.** largest drum of the Azande of the Congo, with single head; played with bare hands. *Cf.* lari, ndima (30, 132).

Gbere, syn. of oliko (195).

Gbingbe, name of the kweningba in the Pakabete, Egenza, and Buja languages of the Congo (31).

Gebirgszither (Ger.: mountain zither), Ger. name of the standard modern zither, rectangular, with tuning pins paralleling an S-shaped side, 29 frets, and a variable number of strings; 5 melody strings and 24 or 37 open strings are common. Not to be confused with the Bergzither (169).

Gebrochene Tasten, Ger.: split keys.

Gebunden, Ger.: fretted.

Gedackt, Ger.: stopped (said of pipes). In the organ a Gedackt corresponds to the stopped diapason, the Fr. bourdon, the Lat. vox obtusa.

Gedämpftregal (Ger.: muted regal), regal organ stop of soft intonation. Gedämpft is synonymous with sanft (gentle) (2).

Gede, see: gong gedē.

Gedo, *musical bow of the Bakongo Pygmies of the Congo, with a rattan string, without tuning loop or resonator; 80–130 cm. (32–51 in.) long (128).

Gedombak, wooden *goblet drum of Malaya, with snakeskin membrane and zigzag lacing of split cane. *Ca.* 23 cm. (9 in.) high. It corresponds to the thōn of Thailand and the skor of Cambodia. Also called gedu (18).

Gedu, syn. of gedombak.

Gefäss . . . , Ger.: vessel . . .

Gefässflöte, Ger.: globular flute.

Gega, Pol., OSlavic, Serb. equivalent of Geige.

Gege, chordophone of Serbia, with a single string (144).

Gegenschlaggefässe, Ger.: concussion vessels.

Gegenschlagidiophon, Ger.: concussion idiophone.

Gegenschlagstäbe, Ger.: concussion sticks.

Gegrumbungan, large wooden buffalo bell of the Malayans (173).

Gehong, single-headed *frame drum

of the Bukar Dayak of Borneo, with bamboo frame and monkey-skin membrane laced by rattan thongs to a rattan belt (176).

Geige [MHGer. **gîge**], Ger.: nowadays a familiar name for the violin in the same sense that "fiddle" designates a violin in Engl. From late med. times to the baroque, Geige denoted a rebec or a bowed instr. with lateral tuning pegs. The terms kleine Geige and Grossgeige were used to designate the viola da braccio and the viola da gamba, respectively. See also: gîge, gigle, gigue, Grossgeige, kleine Geige, polnische Geige, violin.

Geigen(d) . . . , a prefix to names of certain organ stops. When used in conjunction with a flue pipe stop, it implies narrower diam., string tone, increased upper partials; in conjunction with a reed pipe stop it implies strong upper partial formation, weak fundamental, short resonators. *Cf.* singend . . . (133).

Geigen-Clavicymbel, syn. of Geigenwerk.

Geigen diapason, see: violin diapason.

Geigenlyra, obs. Ger.: lira da braccio.

Geigen Prinzipal, see: violin diapason.

Geigenregal, organ stop of regal pipes, also called Geigendregal, Jungfernregal, now obs. It occurred at 8' or 4' pitch. So called because when played together with an 8' quintadena it sounded like a "Geige" (3).

Geigenwerk (Ger.) (Fr.: *clavecinviole*), *bowed keyboard instr. invented by Hans Haiden of Nürnberg *ca.* 1570 and perfected by him *ca.* 1600, the first successful instr. of its nature. Haiden's first instrs. had a continuous band acting as a bow, and gut strings; later his perfected version (he called it the *instrumentum reformatum*) had 5 or 6 parchment-covered steel wheels instead of the continuous band, and the gut strings, which did not hold their tuning, were replaced with brass and steel. Band or wheels were set in motion by a treadle; dynamics were controlled by touch: the harder the key was depressed, the harder the string was pressed against the moving band, and the louder the tone. Haiden's surviving (incomplete?) salesbooks contain entries covering 23 Geigenwerke, of which 19 were sold, 4 given away. The first was made in 1575 for August of Saxony, who gave it to Albrecht of Bavaria at the latter's request; it was sent to Munich, where Vincenzo Galilei saw and later described it. In 1599 Haiden presented one to Maximilian I of Bavaria. The fourth was sold to Heinrich Julius of Braunschweig-Lüneburg, who spent much time at the Prague court; in 1604 Michael Praetorius became his court Kapellmeister and saw it there, also to describe it later. No. 8 was bought by Christoph Fugger. No. 22 was repaired in 1722 by Gleichmann of Ilmenau, maker of the Clavier-Gambe, an imitation of the Geigenwerk. No. 23 was presented to Haiden's son, David, who later sold it to "Don Medicce" of Florence, *i.e.*, Ferdinand II (d. 1670). Ultimately it came into the possession of his grandson, Ferdinand (d. 1713), whose instr. collection was under the care of Cristofori, and is listed in the inventory of Ferdinand's instrs. which Cristofori drew up in 1716. What influence—if any—this instr., with its piano and forte, exercised on the inventor of the pianoforte will probably never be known. An imitation of the Geigenwerk by the Spaniard Raimundo Truchador, dated 1625, is preserved in the Brussels Conservatoire museum. It has a compass of 4 octs. with bass short oct., C^0–c^3, with 45 gut strings. These are sounded by means of 4 vertical revolving wheels; that for the bass strings makes 1 revolution to 2½ revolutions of the treble wheel. About ⅓ of each wheel projects above soundboard level; their 1-cm.-wide rims are covered with a band of cloth forming a perpetual bow. The top of the pin block and bridge undulate to conform to the level of the strings. Two wooden members, likewise undulating, reach from treble to bass, set between nut and wheels; attached to these are metal rods con-

nected to the rear of each key, by means of which the strings are pushed down in a forklike grip against the cloth band of the wheels (132, Kinsky: *Zeitschrift für Musikwissenschaft*, VI, 1923/24).

Gejjam, syn. of salangai (179).

Gejongan, syn. of bendrong (121).

Gekkin [Jap. *getsu,* moon], "moonshaped" lute of Japan, with flat, circular body of wood, short, fretted neck, no soundhole, frontal string holder, and lateral pegs for 2 pairs of strings tuned a 5th apart. A metal tongue is affixed to the interior of the body. The 9 or 10 frets of the neck decrease in height progessively. It has a 2-oct. compass. Both name and instr. are derived from the Chin. moon lute, the yueh ch'in (157, 170).

Gekko [Jap. *getsu,* moon], moon drum of Japan, with wooden shell and 2 heads (176).

Geliti, name of the sansa in the Lower Congo (185).

Gembri, syn. of the 2-stringed gunībrī.

Gembyang, syn. of setukat.

Gembyung, name of the terbang in W. Java (121).

Gemelli, It.: duplex instr.

Gemischte Stimme, Ger.: mixture stop.

Gempret, an ancient Hindu-Javanese name of the Javanese selompret (121).

Gemshorn (Ger.: chamois horn), **1.** early form of recorder, made of a chamois horn with a fipple inserted at the wide end and apparently 3–6 front fingerholes. Virdung (in 1511) also shows a rear thumbhole. Agricola also depicts the instr., but in his last edition, of 1545, it is suppressed. A specimen found by Sachs in a Berlin arsenal has 6 fingerholes, a vent at the tip and measures *ca.* 33 cm. (13 in.). During the 15th c. it must have been a fairly common instr., as there existed an organ stop of that name. See also: gait-horne;

2. organ stop, called *cor de chamois* in Fr., known already to Arnold Schlick (in 1511), at 8', 4', or 2' pitch, of short, wide-scaled, conical flue pipes of metal. If the stop is of wood, the pipes are given pyramid form. Adlung knew it at 16′, 8′, 4′, 2′, and 1′ pitches, and in recent times it has also been made at 32′ pitch. Sometimes the metal Gemshorn is called alphorn (2, 89 Baines, 131, 133, 169, 194).

Gemsquint, Gemshorn organ stop at 5⅓′, 2⅔′, or 1⅓′ pitch; Adlung says that it was sometimes called *Nasat* (*cf.* nazard). Also called Quintgemshorn (2).

Genbri, see: gunbrī.

Gendang (Mal.), *barrel drum with rattan lacings, found throughout the SE. Asian archipelago (173).

Gendang batak, 1. idiochord *tube zither of the Malayans; **2.** *ground zither of the Malayans, formed by a cord, 2 m. (6½ ft.) long, pegged to the ground over a pit; the pit is covered with a palm leaf that carries a bridge. Both cord and palm leaf are struck with small sticks (18, 119, 176).

Gendang bavoi, idiochord *tube zither of the Dayak of SE. Borneo, with 2 or 3 strings (176).

Gendang bulu (*bulu,* bamboo), heterochord *tube zither of the Batak of Sumatra, with 3 fiber strings stretched over a bamboo tube (176).

Gendang-gendang, idiochord *tube zither of N. Sumatra, with 1 or 2 strings. *Cf.* gettun-gettun (173).

Gendang mara, gendang of the Dayak of Borneo, with 2 heads, 60–75 cm. (2–2½ ft.) long. The upper head has a diam. larger than that of the lower; always played in pairs with drumsticks (176).

Gendang naubat, a naubat of Malaya.

Gendang panjang, large *barrel drum of Bangka, Indonesia, with 2 laced heads (176).

Gendang pendek, drum of Bangka, Indonesia, with wooden body and single laced head (176).

Gendang prang, war drum of W. Borneo, with slightly conical body, 2 parchment heads, rattan zigzag lacings, set horizontally on 2 pieces of wood and played with bare hands. *Ca.* 50 cm. (20 in.) high (176).

Gendang rebāna, see: rebāna.

Gendang toto, *cylindrical drum of the Dayak of Borneo, with single head, the other extremity being left open. The head is laced and is tensed by wooden cylinders inserted under the lacings. Beaten with rattan sticks or with bare hands (176).

Gender, metallophone of Java and Bali, with thin bronze bars suspended on cords in a carved wooden frame, usually above tubular resonators. These are of bamboo in most instances, but in newer instrs. they may be of metal or glass; they are half-stopped so that the whole instr. can be built lower, enabling the player to squat on the ground. The resonators are tuned in unison with their respective bars. The bars are fine-tuned in the same manner as the sarons. Genders are made in single- and multi-oct.-compass versions. Those with single oct. have 6 or 7 bars, multi-oct. ones 11–13 bars, except that the earlier ones had only 10. They are played with mushroom-shaped beaters held loosely between forefinger and middle finger. Gender-type instrs., not always with resonators, existed in the archipelago as early as 1157. They are to be found in Madura, Lombok, and in Borneo around Banjermasin. The fact that tone sequences of many African marimbas and balafos are identical to those of the Indonesian genders, as to both pitch and intervals, suggests migration of the Indonesian instrs. to Africa, and from there to C. America. This hypothesis was put forward by the late Jaap Kunst. For the different genders see the entries below, and also: demung gantung, kliningan, slentem gantung (118, 121).

Gender barung, multi-oct. gender of Java, pitched an oct. below the gender panerus (121).

Gender panembung, the Jogya name of the slentem gantung (121).

Gender panerus, multi-oct. gender of Java, pitched an oct. above the gender barung (121).

Gender wayang, 10-keyed gender of

Bali (J. Kunst: *Music of Bali*, London, 1949).

Gendong, syn. of bendrong (121).

Gengaun [**ganga*], Grussi (a Sudanic language) for a long drum (93).

Genggong, Jew's-harp of the Malay Peninsula and Bali, heteroglott, made of bamboo. *Ca.* 11 cm. (4 in.) long (18, 103).

Genggong sakai (Jew's-harp of the Sakai people), percussion instr. of the Malay Peninsula, made of bamboo in shape of a tuning fork or clothespin. A bamboo segment is split between 2 nodes so as to form 2 prongs and a handle; 2 holes are pierced in the handle, and by stopping these the pitch can be varied. The instr. is slapped against the player's wrist or thigh. It originated in Yunnan, S. China, and reached the peninsula via the Philippine Islands. Also found nowadays in Banggai, Celebes, Nias, Philippine Islands, Sangihe, Sarawak, Sula Islands, Talaud, Ternate. *Ca.* 38 cm. (15 in.) long. See also: baka-baka, buncácan, ore-ore, re-re, ta uto (18, 112, 173).

Genis, genis corno, It. brass instr. identical with the flicorno contralto; it corresponds to the althorn.

Genjur, an older name of the kempul, still used sporadically (121).

Gen kin, see: ichi gen kin, ni gen kin, san gen kin, shi chi gen kin.

Genkwan, flat lute of Japan and Mongolia, with octagonal body, long neck, and 4 strings tuned in pairs, $c^1 c^1$ and $g^1 g^1$, with a compass c^1–e^3. The body lacks soundholes, but a small metal tongue is attached to its interior and rattles when the instr. is played. Of Chin. origin, it corresponds to the shuang ch'in. *Ca.* 90 cm. (3 ft.) long, 25 cm. (10 cm.) in diam. Also called shi gen (157, 170).

Genouillère, Fr.: knee lever.

Gensle, 1. see: gęsle; **2.** syn. of gensliki.

Gensliki (Pol., dim. of *gensle*), bowed folk instr. of Pol. mountain regions, with body in form of a double cone joined at

the largest part, without waist or ribs, otherwise similar to the violin. Its 4 strings are tuned in 5ths (89).

Genta, 1. generic name of metal bells in Java; **2.** the ancient Hindu-Javanese name for bell; **3.** cattle bell of C. and E. Java; **4.** syn. of klinting (121).

Gentong, see: gong gentong.

Gentorag, syn. of klinting (121).

Gerader Zink, Ger.: straight cornett.

Geramo [**garamut*], large *slit drum of Rumba, Manam Island, and of the Hansa volcano area of New Guinea. See also: garamut, gerom (176).

German action (Ger.: *deutsche Mechanik*), piano action invented by Johann Andreas Stein of Augsburg in the mid-18th c., developed from the Prellmechanik. Stein transferred the fixed Prelleiste into an escapement by replacing it with a series of hinged and sprung members, one for each hammer. The "Kapsel" was retained. This action was used both for square and grand pianos. The hammers point toward the player. The name is also applied to the Prellmechanik (92).

German flute, 1. Engl. 18th-c. name of the *cross flute; **2.** organ stop introduced by Snetzler in 1754 at King's Lynn; it was a harmonic stopped register of cylindrical, small-scaled pipes at 8' pitch. Later it was built as a harmonic Gedackt (133).

German guitar, see: deutsche guitarre.

Gerom [**garamut*], slit drum of Jabim and Bukawa, New Guinea. See also: garamut, geramo, gram (176).

Gerremut, see: garamut.

Ges, antelope horn of the Somali of E. Africa, identical with the gafa (176).

Gesba, a misreading of qasaba.

Gęsle (pron. ganshla); **1.** Pol.: gusle; **2.** in recent years the word has been applied to various stringed instrs. associated with Poland, both ancient and modern.

Geśle, Russ. equivalent of gęsle.

Geso-geso, *spike fiddle of Celebes, with coconut or gourd body, belly of palm leaves, neck often carved (the more elaborate ones are those of C. and S. Celebes), with single string (112).

Getary, Engl. 14th-c. form of the word guitar (180).

Getron, var. of gittern.

Gettun-gettun, idiochord *tube zither of Sumatra and neighboring islands, with 1 or 2 strings. *Cf.* gendang-gendang (173).

Geudumba, vase-shaped drum of W. Sumatra (122).

Geure, syn. of gievre (144).

Gewgaw [?Ger. *Geige*], Scot. and N. Engl. dialect for Jew's-harp, first recorded in that sense in the latter part of the 18th c. In the *Promptuarium parvulorum* (*ca.* 1440) it appears as a translation of cala-maula (Oxford English Dictionary).

Geza daiko, syn. of uta daiko.

Gezarke, Nubian name of the kissar (176).

Ghāba, an old Arab. name for the flute (144).

Ghachaka [Pers. *ghizhak*], bowed instr. of Afghanistan (176).

Ghadam, Mal. equivalent of ghāta.

Ghaida (Turk.), bagpipe of Turkey, mouth-blown, with whole skin bag, a 7-holed chanter, and single drone, similar to the gayda of Bulgaria (89).

Ghaita (Arab.), reedpipe of Islam that has been played since the Middle Ages. According to Farmer (Encyclopaedia of Islam), it originally assumed 2 forms, 1 with cylindrical bore and single reed, the other with conical bore and double reed. The latter version became typical in N. Africa, where it is still the most important woodwind; indeed, in the Maghrib it is used in connection with the pilgrimage. By the 13th c. the instr. (but not necessarily the name) is known to have reached Spain, where, provided with a bell, it became a hornpipe, or, if an air reservoir in form of a bag was added, a bagpipe. In its European dispersal, probably owing to gypsies, it assumed all these forms. See also: algaita, algaitaru, algeta, aligeta, gaida, gaita, gajda, gajde, gajdy, ghaida, gheta, ghita, rheita (89, 93, 147).

Ghan, Hindi, Hindust.: gong (176).

Ghana, generic name for idiophones on the Indian subcontinent (147).

Ghanghurū, see: ghunghura.

Ghant, Hindi: ghantā.

Ghantā (Sans., Pali, Beng., Punj., Mar.), temple hand bell of India, of considerable antiquity, made of bronze, the highly decorated handle being surmounted by the figure of a divinity. The bell is small, campaniform, and has a thick clapper; used in Hindu rituals (132, 170).

Ghantikā, dim. of ghantā (176).

Gharghara, Sans.: bell. *Cf.* gargara (176).

Ghari (Sans., Beng.), thick, circular *percussion plaque of bronze, found in temples of India, suspended from a cord and struck with a wooden mallet; 20–30 cm. (8–12 in.) in diam., ½ cm. thick (132, 173).

Gharī, Hindi, Hindust.: equivalent of ghari (170).

Ghariyal, Hindi equivalent of ghari.

Gharthabe, according to Farmer, a faulty reading of 'artaba.

Ghāta, *percussion pot of India; the mouth of a large pottery jar is pressed against the player's stomach while it is struck alternately by both his wrists (170).

Ghatam, var. of ghāta.

Ghatamu, Tel. equivalent of gātha (173).

Ghentā, shepherd's horn of Ethiopia, made of cow horn; a small qand (Villoteau, 1823, quoted in 176).

Gheta [Arab. *ghaita*], cylindrical clarinet of Egypt, with metal bell and 6 or 7 fingerholes, possibly influenced by the European clarinet (144).

Ghichak (Arab.), unidentified instr. of Arab culture, possibly a spike fiddle with 2 strings. *Cf.* ghizhak (75 II).

Ghirbāl, frame drum of Egypt. *Cf.* girbāl (89).

Ghironda [It. *girare,* to turn], It.: hurdy-gurdy.

Ghita [Arab. *ghaita*], shawm of the N. African Berbers (89).

Ghiterna, guiterna, Lat.: gittern. Tinctoris uses both words (ca. 1490).

Ghittern, var. of gittern.

Ghizhak (Pers., Turk.), a large kāmanja, with 8 additional sympathetic strings, known in the 15th c. Cf. ghachaka, ghichak, ghordjek, ha erh cha ko (89).

Ghordjek, *spike fiddle of Pamir, C. Asia, very like the kāmanja but with 3 strings. Cf. ghizhak (91).

Ghūghā (Arab.), bowed stringed instr. of Algeria and Morocco, with bowl-shaped body, skin belly, and single string secured by a tuning ring (72, 170).

Ghunda, small Pers. signal trumpet of metal (176).

Ghunghunā, Hindi, Hindust.: pellet bell (176).

Ghunghura (Beng.), ghanghurū (Sans.), rattle anklets made of clusters of pellet bells and worn by male and female dancers of India (173).

Ghutru (Tel.), *goblet drum of the E. coast of India, made of clay, with cylindrical foot, zigzag lacings, and open bottom (173).

Gievre, obs. *frame drum of Lapland, a shaman's instr. with reindeer membrane, struck with a small beater of reindeer horn. Also called geure. Cf. goabdes (144).

Giga [MHGer. *gîge], It. and Sp. equivalent of gigue.

Gîge [OHGer. gîgen, to sway], MHGer. word in use from the 12th c. on, ancestor of the words Geige and gigue. In late med. writings Gîge and Fiedel are mentioned together frequently as separate but closely related instrs. and must be identified as rebec and fiddle. See also: Geige, gigue, rebec.

Gigelira, gigelyra, It.: xylophone (89, 176).

Gigid (Sum.: long cane), believed to have been a long vertical flute of ancient Babylon, possibly the same as the tigi. It corresponds to the Akk. malīlu (147, 170).

Gigje, in modern Nor. a violin (9).

Giglaros (Gk.), syn. of gingras.

Gigle (OFr., dim. of *gigue), a small gigue. The word occurs in OFr. literature of the 12th and 13th c.

Gigue (OFr.) [MHGer. *gîge], bowed instr. of med. France, mentioned from the mid-12th c. to the late 14th. In the 12th c. it is mentioned together with the viele, but never with the rebec, and is assumed to have been identical with the latter. Sachs was first to suggest this identification (53, 82, 169).

Gihumurizo, largest drum of Ruanda. It accompanies the king on his journeys. Also called nyampundu (30).

Gihyan, fiddle of W. Java, of Chin. origin, with half-coconut body, long, slender neck, wooden belly, rear sound-holes, 2 rear pegs. The bow hair passes between the 2 strings so that they are always sounded together. Also called rebab batok besar (121).

Gili, drum of the Bwaka-Mabo of Ubangi, Africa (30).

Gimbeh, *goblet drum of the Fula of Sierra Leone, with laced head and several cord belts. Five sticks ca. 40 cm. (16 in.) long are thrust into the top belting and project above the drum; each terminates in a rectangle of sheet metal pierced all around by small metal rings that rattle when the drum is played. See also: gimbi (Collection of the Commonwealth Institute, London).

Gimbi, Mandingo name of the gimbeh (Collection of the Commonwealth Institute, London).

Gin dai (Jap.: great kin), koto of Japan, identical with the shi chi gen kin except that it has 13 strings (157).

Gindi, Kan. equivalent of kamsya.

Ginebras, Sp. xylophone consisting of a graduated series of wooden slabs, strung on a cord in ladder fashion, the smallest at the top. The word is first recorded in the sense of a musical instr. in 1628. Called pianito in Cuba. Cf. carrasquiña, echelette (44, 152).

Ginēra, late Egyptian or Coptic form of the word *knr (lyre) (170).

Gingala, idiochord *tube zither of SE.

Europe, particularly the Balkan region, nowadays a toy. Made from a piece of cane (*Arundo donax*) 15–30 cm. (6–12 in.) long, with 2 strings on the same bridge. The gingala always occurs in pairs, one instr. acting as a bow (149, 176).

Ginger, bowl lyre of the Ingessana of Dar-Fung, Sudan, with 5 strings (176).

Ginggung, see: genggong.

Gingiru, harp lute of the Dogon of Mali (103).

Ginglaros (Gk.), syn. of gingras.

Gingras (Gk.), high-pitched aulos of Phoenicia and Greece, of Egyptian origin, used in mourning the dead (176).

Gingrina (Lat.), **1.** Lat. name of the gingras; **2.** med. name of the shawm; **3.** organ stop of reed pipes, in existence *ca.* 1600.

Ginguvo, see: shinguvo.

Gini, small, bossed cymbal of Orissa, India (176).

Ginkale, Alb.: shawm (176).

Ginnu, iron bell of the Dogon of Mali (103).

Giorgi flute, keyless flute patented by Carlo Tomaso Giorgi of Florence on March 24, 1896, made of ebonite; 11 large fingerholes, for as many semitones, rendered cross-fingering unnecessary. The embouchure was placed at the end of the bore in a special short head joint. Pitched in d^1, the flute was supplied with $c\sharp^1$, c^1, and b^0 joints. The spacing of the fingerholes demanded very large hands, and possibly because of this a model with 15 square, flat keys was introduced, also with vertical embouchure. A model with 3 keys and 10 open holes also exists (126, 132).

Giraffe piano (Fr.: *piano giraffe;* Ger.: *Giraffenflügel*), a form of *upright grand piano with straight bass side, the treble side usually curving over to form a scroll at the tail, made from *ca.* 1798 to 1850, generally with hanging *German action. Earlier models reached to the ground in order to provide maximum string length. From about 1830 smaller models were made that stood on 4 legs and were strung

obliquely; these usually had standing German action. Wachtel and Bleyel of Vienna claimed the giraffe piano as their invention (92).

Giramo [*garamut*], name of the *gerom on the Maclay coast of New Guinea. Also called onge (77).

Girbāl (Arab.: sieve), *frame drum of Islam, now obs., that was large, circular, and provided with snares. It was known to Moorish Spain and was mentioned by Al-Shalahi in the early 14th c. *Cf.* ghirbāl (170).

Girellina [It. *girare*, to turn], It.: pellet bell (169).

Girgila, Basque: pellet bell.

Girgiri, *friction drum of S. India, made of a dish-shaped clay pot covered with a membrane and provided with a friction stick (16).

Girift, generic name of a family of small flutes of Turkey, made in different sizes, with 7 front fingerholes and a rear thumbhole (76).

Gironda, var. of ghironda.

Girugate, Kan. name of the charkhi (173).

Gisaba rwanda, drum of Ruanda, Africa (30).

Gi-sal (Sum.), gourd horn of ancient Babylon; it first appears in the third millennium B.C. Equivalent to the Akk. gizallu (89 Galpin).

Giš-ban, Sum. name of the *angular harp (84).

Gishikiso, drum of the Warundi of Ruanda-Urundi, Africa. Also called nkiranwa (30).

Gis-zag-sal, see: zag-sal.

Gitarre, Ger.: guitar. The word is first recorded in 1615, spelled guitarre (169).

Gitarrenharfe, Ger.: the *harp guitar and its successor instrs.; also any 19th-c. instr. combining the guitar and the harp. Also called Harfengitarre.

Git-git, 3-stringed fiddle of the Hanunoo of the Philippine Islands (103).

Gittern [OFr. *guiterne*], together with its Continental equivalents and vars., gittern is a generic term by which the *guitarra latina, the *guitarra morisca, and their offspring were known outside Spain, the word itself corresponding to *guitarra.* By the time Tinctoris wrote (late 15th c.), "gittern" and "guitar" were already syn. According to contemporary descriptions, we can differentiate between 2 main types: 1. one with flat back and belly, slight waist, a short, fretted neck at first carved out of the same block of wood as the 4-cornered body, usually with 4 strings, and played with a plectrum. Sometimes body and neck were divided by a handhole. Early illustrations show many variations of this type, most having lateral pegs; they are assumed to derive from the *guitarra latina and thrived until the 17th c. Four "gitterons" "caulled Spanish vialles" are listed in an inventory of Henry VIII's instrs. in 1547, without further description. In England and France the 4 strings gave way to 3 pairs of strings and a chanterelle, all of gut, tuned $d^0 g^0 b^0 e^1$, with the strings of the 3 lower choirs doubling at the octave. Music was written for this instr. (in tablature) from *ca.* 1550 to the 1650's. In Germany, where it was known by its Fr. or Engl. name, it generally had 5 single strings, sometimes 4 double strings. Praetorius gives their tūning as $c^0 f^0 a^0 d^1$ or $f^0 b^0 d^1$ g^1. These tunings are closely related to those of the second type of gittern: 2. small lute with vaulted back (see: guiterne, Quinterna, quinterne), derived from the *guitarra morisca, and already described in the 14th c. as being *"bossue dessoulz,"* i.e., as having a humped back. Tinctoris *ca.* 1480 attributes its invention to Spain. From the 12th c. on this form was known in France—as it was elsewhere later on—as the *mandola. The gittern must not be confused with the *cittern. See also: getron, ghiterna, ghittern, guitar, guiterne (79, 159, 169).

Gizallu (Akk.), Akk. equivalent to the Sum. gi-sal.

Glasharfe, Ger.: glass harp.

Glasharmonika, Ger.: glass harmonica.

Glasschord, crystallophone called *fortepiano à cordes de verre* by its maker, Beyer of Paris, and named glasschord by Benjamin Franklin in or by 1785. The *Journal de Paris* of Nov. 18 of that year reports its having been approved by the Académie des Sciences. A series of glass bars was laid horizontally on thick cloth strips and struck from above by small wooden, cloth-covered hammers controlled from a keyboard. Dampers were lacking. Compass 3 octs., c^0-c^3 (169, 204).

Glass harmonica (Fr.: *harmonica de Franklin;* Ger.: *Glasharmonika*), a series of tuned glass bowls pierced in the center, strung vertically in close position on a wire spindle, and rotated by means of a treadle; the glasses were suspended above a trough partly filled with water. The player touched the rotating wet rims with the fingers of both hands. The glass harmonica came into existence in 1761, when Benjamin Franklin transformed the *musical glasses into a new instr. that he called "Armonica." Attempts made to attach a keyboard to it were not successful until 1784 (a glass harmonica played from a keyboard is known as a *keyed harmonica). After an initial period of popularity both types were driven out by the harmonium in the 19th c. Mozart wrote several works for the glass harmonica. The initial compass of 2 octs. g^0-g^2 was increased to c^0-c^4. See also: bellarmonic, colison, harmonicon, instrument de Parnasse, keyed harmonica (113, 169).

Glass harp (Fr.: *harpe de verre;* Ger.: *Glasharfe;* It.: *arpa di vetro*), a 20th-c. version of *musical glasses made by Bruno Hoffmann, consisting of 46 glass bowls with short stems. Compass 3½–4 octs., g^0-c^4 or d^0-c^4 (144).

Glasspiel, Ger.: musical glasses.

Glegni, pellet bells of the Baoule of the Ivory Coast Republic (103).

Glēo, OEngl., MEngl.: musical instr. The word was used from *ca.* 1000 through the 15th c., rarely later, and also meant music, playing, or any form of entertainment.

Glēo-bēam (OEngl.), word in use up to the 13th c., glossed as *musicum lignum, harpa, tympanum,* and said to denote the med. harp. Beowulf used the expression. "Glēo" has been translated as "glee," and Otto Anderssen surmised the term to be related to the harp of Finn. folk songs, an instr. called "joy." However, the word *harpa* denoted chiefly the (bowed) lyre in N. Europe, not the harp. Furthermore, *nares-jux* also means "music wood" in Ostyak, the instr. in question being a lyre (180, 189).

Gleppe, square cowbell of Alemannic Switzerland, made of copper or sheet iron. Also called Chlepfe, Chlöpfe.

Glicibarifono, early *bass clarinet designed by Catterino Catterini of Padua and built by P. Maino, also of Padua, *ca.* 1835. Made of a single block of wood with 2 parallel bores, and a brass bell, 24 brass keys, and a crook. Pitched in C. A short-lived instr. because it could not compete against Sax's *bass clarinet. *Ca.* 58 cm. (23 in.) high (132, 164, 170).

Glîe (MHGer.) [MEngl. glie, glēo], unidentified instr. mentioned in med. Ger. literature. *Cf.* glēo-bēam (189).

Gligbēam, syn. of glēo-bēam.

Gling-bu, *whistle flute of Tibet, made of wood, with 7 or more equidistant fingerholes and a rear thumbhole. Occasionally 2 or 3 are tied together to form a double or triple pipe. A secular and pastoral instr. 38–40 cm. (15–16 in.) long (89 Picken, 176).

Globular flute (Ger.: *Gefässflöte*), flute with a body that is not tubular but vessel-shaped, made of a gourd, coconut, clay, porcelain, etc., in which the air stream is directed against the sharp edge of a round blowhole. Globular flutes were known to prehistoric China, ancient Egypt, pre-Columbian America, Bronze Age Europe (Hungary), and are found in modern Europe, W. Africa, and the S. Seas. As might be expected with so wide an area of distribution, the instr.

has assumed numerous forms, from the simple ovoid *hsüans of China to the *whistling pots of S. America and the different zoomorphic forms encountered in many regions today. In instrs. provided with fingerholes the pitch rises as the number of open holes increases; expressed differently, it is the number of fingerholes closed, and not the order in which they are closed, that controls the pitch; and the larger the air chamber, the lower the fundamental pitch (59, 168, 169).

Glocca, var. of clocca.

Glocke [Lat. *clocca*], Ger.: bell; specifically a clapper bell, originally in contradistinction to the Zimbel, which had no clapper. Nowadays the word implies a cast bell, as opposed to the uncast Schelle.

Glockenakkord, syn. of Akkord (133).

Glockengambe, Ger.: bell gamba (organ stop).

Glockenrad, Ger.: bell wheel.

Glockenspiel (Ger., Engl.) (Fr.: *carillon;* It.: *campanette*), **1.** metallophone consisting of a series of tuned steel bars arranged in 2 rows, as are the keys of a piano, and played with 2 knobbed beaters. The glockenspiel is probably an offshoot of the military *bell lyre and has been used in the orchestra since the latter part of the 18th c., more recently also in rhythm bands. The bars are flat rectangles of different lengths, 2½ cm. (1 in.) wide. Their usual compass is 2½ oct., G–C, in high or low pitches (g^1–c^4, g^2–c^5), both notated as g^0–c^3. In 1935 William F. Ludwig of Chicago added resonators to the glockenspiel. Some instrs. are furnished with a small keyboard having metal hammers that strike the bars from beneath. See also: bell lyre, celeste song bells, metal harmonica, metallino (89);

2. the organ stop of this name consists of tuned metal plaques or bars struck by hammers actuated by manual or pedalboard, at 8', 4', 2', 1' pitches; it has existed since the early 18th c., but nowadays the celesta is preferred (133);

3. in earlier times Glockenspiel (Ger.) denoted a set of small bells, as its name indicates. *Cf.* cymbala.

Glockenton (Ger.), mixture organ stop, identical with carillon, 2d.

Glockentriangel (Ger.: bell triangle), triangle built by Vaclav Červeny of Königgrätz (Hradec Králové) in 1877, in form of an inverted V, made of a 4-sided metal bar. It gave a bell-like tone when struck with a wooden hammer, and sounded like a triangle when played with a triangle stick (176).

Glöckleinton (Ger.), organ stop of wide-scaled flue pipes at 2′ pitch, identical with the *Faberton (2, 131).

Glogg [med. Lat. *glogga*], Swiss dialect: bell, church bell, cowbell of bell metal.

Glogga, med. Lat.: bell. *Cf.* clocca.

Glycleide, brass instr. of tenor range built in tuba form by Vaclav Červeny of Königgrätz (Hradec Králové) in 1846. Pitched in B♭, it could also be put into A (176).

Gnbri, see: gunbrī.

Go, drum of the Abandya, Azande, and Basire of the Congo, in truncated barrel form, with single head laced to a piece of hide covering the lower end. The lacings form a network that covers the body. Playing technique is that of the gaza (30, 132).

Goabdes, obs. *frame drum of Lapland, formerly used for ritual purposes. *Cf.* gievre (176).

Goaramba, *musical bow of El Salvador, C. America, similar to the uhadi (149).

Goare, var. of joare.

Goarna, Rom.: bugle (5).

Goasspfeiff [Ger. *Geiss,* goat], smallest of the modern Austrian Alpine *Schwegel, with cylindrical bore. 33 cm. (13 in.) long (117).

Goat-horn, see: gait-horne.

Gobais [*gabai,* to sing], flute of the Somali of E. Africa (176).

Go beto, idiochord bamboo *tube zither of Ende, Indonesia. Also called riang wulu baba (119).

Gobi-gobi, idiochord *tube zither of S. Nias, made of bamboo (119).

Goblet drum (Fr.: *tambour en goblet;* Ger.: *Bechertrommel*), drum in which the main section of the body is gobletshaped or cylindrical and set upon a slender stem (168).

Gobo, 1. bell of the Washambala of Kenya, made from the seeds of the *Borassus aethiop* palm, with 2 clappers. During the hunt it is tied around dogs' legs, occasionally also attached to sheep (111); **2.** syn. of urucungo (7).

Goboi, Russ.: oboe.

Goč, a name of the tupan in Macedonia and S. Serbia (11).

Goddang, wooden *goblet drum of Flores Island, with parallel lacings of rattan (173).

Godumbas, *goblet drum of the Achin of Sumatra (176).

Godye, name of the ghūghā among the Sudanic Agni (93).

Goga dhol, wooden kettledrum of the Muria of Bastar, India, with cowhide skin; its lacings form a network over the body. It is slung around the player's shoulders and beaten with a single stick. *Ca.* 35 cm. (14 in.) high, 43 cm. (17 in.) in diam. (68).

Goge, pl. **goguna,** name of the ghūghā among the Hausa (93).

Go gekkin, syn. of gekkin.

Gogeru, pl. **gegeji** [*ghūghā*], fiddle of the Fulbe of Cameroun Republic, with gourd body, leather belly, lateral soundhole, neck carrying 1–3 strings; no bridge. If there are 3 strings, 2 are long and 1 is short (176).

Going-going, bull-roarer of the S. African Bushmen (116).

Gok, gong of the Miau of Vietnam (103).

Go kin (Jap.: five-stringed kin), 5-stringed koto of Japan, with body tapering slightly to the lower end. The strings are secured to tuning pegs on the body and are tuned with a wooden key. One movable bridge and one fixed. Plucked with bare fingers (157, 170).

G'ola, syn. of gadulka.

Goldner Dionys, see: Denis d'or.

Gol-gol, see: jul-jul.

Golom, var. of gerom.

Goly, stringed instr. of the Baoule of the Ivory Coast Republic, with single string (103).

Goma, 1. var. of ngoma; **2.** *cylindrical drum of the Malagasy Republic, with single head (171).

Gombi, *stick zither of the Azande and Makere of the Congo (128).

Gomen-wudu (glee wood), OEngl.: a musical instr. See: glēo-bēam.

Gom-gom, 1. colonists' name for the *bonang (121); **2.** Kolbe's name (1704) for the gora.

Go-mukka (Sans., Beng.), *marineshell trumpet of Bengal, made from the *go-mukka* shell (132).

Gondang, W. Java equivalent of the bendrong (121).

Gondang bulu (*bulu,* bamboo), idiochord bamboo *tube zither of the Toba Batak of N. Sumatra (119).

Gondra hao (bamboo drum), idiochord bamboo *tube zither of N. Nias (119).

Gong (Javanese), circular *percussion plaque of bronze made in various sizes, having definite or indefinite pitch, usually with a turned-down rim, either flat or with central boss. The gong is distinguished from the bell in that it has a dead rim and vibrations issuing from the center, whereas a bell is most resonant close to the rim and is dead at the vertex. Gongs are struck in the center with a beater. They are made of hammered metal, the alloy varying somewhat, but containing roughly 70% copper, 30% tin, and added impurities. The oldest form of gong was apparently flat (see: kettle gong) and, according to Sachs, may be a descendant of the *frame drum. Earliest mention of the gong is in 6th-c. China, but Chin. tradition ascribes its introduction to "barbarians," *i.e.,* aliens, farther W. Its origin is usually sought in SE. Asia, but Kunst believed the E.

Mediterranean to have been its source (see: echeion). From China the gong spread to SE. Asia, reaching Java by the 9th c., then traveling W. through Asia to Africa and Europe. Gongs of the archipelago are still bossed; those of India are flat. The *gong chime is still the outstanding instr. of SE. Asian orchestras. First W. mention of the word *gong* was in England in 1590, but use of the instr. is not recorded in Europe until 1791, when it was played at Mirabeau's funeral (Gossec's *Funeral March*). Since then it has gained acceptance in the orchestra as an instr. of indefinite pitch. Orchestral gongs are at least 90 cm. (3 ft.) in diam.; 3 types are in use: Burmese, with a turned rim of 10–12 cm. (4–5 in.) in height, of thick metal; Chin., with smaller rim and of thinner metal; Turk., made of cymbal metal. See: gong chime, kettle gong, rock gong. See also: agung, atari gane, atoke, babandi, ban ko, bendē, berri, bur-rting, cai cañ, cai cheng, cai cong, cai ma la, cai than la, chanang, chanan naga, changiri, chempung, cheng, chin chi chi, ching, chin ku, dai shoko, doko, dora, du, gang'sa, ganjur, garantong, genjur, ghan, gindi, gok, gong ageng, etc., goōng, gwangmagi, hitotsu gane, hontsuri gane, hsüan tse, hyang pal, jin gane, kamsala, kamsara, kamsya, kāngsara, kāngshi, k'ar-rnga, katiwul, kemong, 2, kempli, kempul, kempur, kenong penontang, khong . . . , kin, 3, kromong, 2, kye-nong, ling tse, lo, matsumushi, mong, nārī mong, ngong, ni shoko, pahawang, pao chün chih, peddaganta, penganak, penontong, rang, sha lo, shoko, sō ban, suri gane, tamtam, tang lo, tang tse, tawak, tien erh, t'i tang, t'ong ku, t'ong tyen, tsuri gane, t'ung lo, wani guchi, yin ch'ing (89, 121, 144, 169, 170).

Gonga, 1. double bell of iron, of the Mobenga of the Congo (19); **2.** drum of Fezzan, Libya, and of the Tebu of the E. Sahara, with 2 heads, one of which is played with a stick, the other with bare hands (176).

Gong ageng (High Javanese), largest gong of C. and E. Java, with central boss and turned rim. It has definite but very low pitch and is beaten on the boss with a mallet or the player's fist. In ancient Javanese literature it was referred to as "gong." The normal diam. is 60–70 cm. (24–28 in.), but it is found with a diam. of up to 1 m. (40 in.). Called gong gedē in Low Javanese (121).

Gong angang-angang, name of the gong kemodong in Banyumas, Java (121).

Gong bass drum, see: gong drum.

Gong beri, small gong of Java, often bossless, specially in W. Java, where it also lacks a rim. Originally the gong beri was a drum, but the name was transferred. As a drum, it had been exclusively a war and signal instr.; as a gong it never entered the *gamelan but retained its martial character. Often confused with the bendē. *Cf.* berri. Also called bahiri (121).

Gong bumbung, syn. of gumbang (121).

Gong chime (Fr.: *carillon de gongs;* Ger.: *Gongspiel*), set of graduated gongs —the outstanding instr. of SE. Asian orchestras. The gongs are arranged on a low, horizontal frame or bed, with each gong resting boss upward on crossed cords. The frame is generally circular or semicircular. See also: babarangan, bonang, cai thieu cañ, cang chen, degung, gong hui, jengglong, khong ñai, khong noï, khong thom, khong toch, khong vong lek, khong vong yai, kolintang, kromo, kye vaing, maung saing, mong, tatabuan, yün lo (170).

Gong drum, name given to a type of bass drum with single head and very short shell, too short for the drum to be stood up, in fact; for this reason it is suspended by straps from a frame. The gong drum was introduced in the mid-19th c. for theater use, as it took up little space. It was known by 1859. Also called gong bass drum (89, 169).

Gong duwabelas, see: duwabelas.

Gong gedē, Low Javanese name of the gong ageng (121).

Gong gentong, name of the gong kemodong in Kebumen, Java (121).

Gong guchi, name of the gong kemodong in Panarukan and Banduwasa, Java. Also called gong pangang (121).

Gong hui, gong chime of Thailand, consisting of 3, 5, or 7 gongs suspended vertically in a frame and played with padded sticks; 28–52 cm. (11–21 in.) in diam. (65).

Gongina, bamboo Jew's-harp of the Garo of Assam, elongated and narrow. *Ca.* 13 cm. (5 in.) long (172).

Gong jemblok, name of the gong kemodong in E. Java (121).

Gong jun, name of the gong kemodong in E. Java (121).

Gong kemada, Jogya name of the gong kemodong (121).

Gong kemodong, gong of Java that because of its cheapness often serves as a substitute for the gong ageng. In C. and E. Java it consists of 2 large bronze or even iron bars with bosses (beating knobs), suspended on cords over a hollow frame. Two earthenware pots are frequently set in the frame to act as resonators. In W. Java it consists of a single bar. The pitch is between that of the gong ageng and the gong suwukan. *Cf.* gong angang-angang, gong gentong, gong guchi, gong jemblok, gong jun, gong kemada, goōng buyung (121).

Gongo, Sp.: gong.

Gong pangang, syn. of gong guchi.

Gong sembilan, *bonang of Banda, Moluccas, with 9 kettles in 3 rows of 3 (121).

Gong siyem, syn. of gong suwukan; name originally given only to cast gongs suwukan, not forged ones. The meaning of the word *siyem* is unknown (121).

Gongspiel, Ger.: gong chime.

Gong suwukan [*suwuk,* ritardando], gong of C. Java similar to the gong ageng but smaller. Its pitch is between 2 and 2½ octs. higher and clearly definable. Like the gong ageng, it has a central boss and turned rim and is suspended in a frame. Its name derives from its formerly having been struck at the end of a piece, after a ritardando. Also called gong siyem (121).

Gongué, 1. name of the single agogó (bell) in Recife, Brazil; **2.** in the N. provinces of Brazil a small drum (6, 7).

Gonongo, crescent-shaped iron *pellet bell of the Washambala of Kenya, containing iron pellets and attached by leather thongs to a wooden handle (111).

Gonra, idiochord *tube zither of Nias, with 1 or 2 strings, 54–76 cm. (21–30 in.) long (149, 173).

Goŏng, name of the gong in W. Java (121).

Goŏng buyung, W. Java name of the gong kemodong (121).

Goŏng leutik (small gong), a W. Java name of the kempul (121).

Gopichand, var. name of gopi yantra (138).

Gopi yantra (Sans., Beng.), a widely distributed form of the *ānanda laharī in N. India, with cylindrical bucket having a membrane bottom. A flat bamboo segment is split for most of its length and 2 prongs are attached to the sides of the bucket, the upper end of the segment projecting like a handle. This end carries a tuning peg to which a single metal string is attached, the other end being affixed to the center of the membrane. Pitch is varied by exercising more or less pressure on the bamboo prongs. The string is plucked. Also called gopichand, nandin (132, 138).

Gora, *musical bow of the Cape and Korana Hottentots of S. Africa, from whom it has passed to the Bushmen, Chwana, Sotho of Basutoland, Xhosa, and Zulu, first described in 1686. The string passes through a hole pierced in a flattened ostrich quill tied to the end of the bow. The player takes the quill between his lips, but without touching it with them, and sets both quill and string into vibration by inhaling and exhaling sharply, producing the fifth to ninth harmonics by modifying the force of his breath and shape of his oral cavity. Ca. 110 cm. (3½ ft.) long. Cf. gom-gom, hã, koali, kwadi, lesiba, makwindi, ugwala, ugwali (116).

Gordang, *cylindrical drum of Sumatra, similar to the ogung but twice as high (173).

Gore, *end-blown flute of Opa, Leper Island, New Hebrides, made of bamboo, with 3 front fingerholes and a rear thumbhole. 56–76 cm. (22–30 in.) long. Cf. kaur, kora (176).

Gorr, drum of the Miau of Vietnam (103).

Gorra, see: gora.

Gorteh, syn. of kladdi.

Gorzia, *stick rattle of Val d'Anniviers, Switzerland, consisting of a shepherd's wand ca. 1 m. (40 in.) long, with metal rings strung at the top (102).

Gosba, misreading of qasaba.

Goslice, 1. syn. of orglice, 1; **2.** var. of guslice.

Gotuvādyam, vīnā of S. India, very similar to the Sarasvati vīnā, but unfretted. The strings are stopped by a wooden cylinder ca. 5 cm. (2 in.) long, 2½ cm. (1 in.) in diam., or by a piece of crystal, held in the left hand, that glides over the melody strings. In addition to these there are 7 sympathetic strings that pass over a small bridge of their own, lying underneath the main bridge. It corresponds to the N. Indian bicitrabīn. Also called mahānātaka vīnā (144, 179).

Goukha's, 1. *musical bow of the Damara of S. Africa, made of solid wood, with a tuning loop near the center of the bow, the player's mouth acting as resonator. Plucked with a plectrum or bare fingers; **2.** pluriarc of the Berg-Dama of S. Africa, with 5 bows (116).

Goura, see: gora.

Gourd bow, *musical bow with gourd resonator.

Gousla, see: gusla.

Gowangan, Jogya: kowangan (121).

Gragé, scraper of Haiti that corresponds to the Afro-Cuban guayo (152).

Graile [Lat. *gracilis*, slender], **1.** Fr.: late 11th c. on, a small horn of metal (*graile menu*). In the 16th c. the term seems to denote the upper register of a trumpet; **2.** Languedoc: oboe; **3.** Cat.: bagpipe. See also: grall (82, 197, 204).

Grall, Cat.: chanter of a bagpipe (57).

Gralla (Cat.: jackdaw), shawm of Catalonia, equivalent to the Sp. chirimía, made of wood with a metal *pirouette, 6 fingerholes, and a rear thumbhole. Pitched in F. *Ca.* 37 cm. (14½ in.) long (57, 132).

Gralla seca, keyless gralla (57).

Gram [*garamut*], name of the gerom on the Maclay coast of New Guinea (77).

Granboe, Afro-Haitian *percussion tube consisting of a large bamboo internode. The upper aperture is opened and closed by player's left hand while the right hand strikes it with a small stick (152).

Gran cassa, It.: bass drum.

Grand (Fr.), **1.** as a prefix to names of organ stops, grand denotes a pitch one oct. lower than that named; **2.** (Engl.), coll. for *grand piano.

Grand accord, *transposing piano devised by William E. Newton in 1866 (149).

Grand cornet (Fr.), the widest-scaled cornet organ stop of the *great organ (133).

Grande basse de violon, obs. Fr.: double bass. See also: violone.

Grand hautbois, late-17th-c. Fr. term for the oboe *players* of the "*douze grands hautbois du Roi.*" Not to be confused with *great hoboy.

Grand jeu (Fr.), the tutti on a harmonium. Not to be confused with the *plein-jeu.*

Grand orgue, Fr.: great organ.

Grand piano (Fr.: *piano à queue;* Ger.: *Flügel;* It.: *pianoforte a coda;* Sp.: *piano de cola;* Port.: *piano de cauda*), piano built in harpsichord shape, *i.e.,* a horizontal instr. with a *bentside and

strings running parallel to the individual keys.

Gran tamburo, It.: bass drum.

Grantang, *sliding rattle of Bali, similar to the *angklung, 2, but of superior finish (121).

Grave mixture, mixture organ stop composed of 2 ranks of pipes, as opposed to the *sharp mixture. *Cf.* acute mixture (198).

Gravicembalo (It.), corr. of clavicembalo.

Gravicembalo col piano e forte, the name given by Cristofori to his pianos.

Gravicordo (It.), corr. of clavicordio.

Gravissima (Lat.: lowest), organ stop, a resultant bass at 64′ pitch derived from a 32′ stop sounded with its quint 21⅓′. *Cf.* acoustic bass (186).

Gravitone, syn. of acoustic bass.

Gravures, Fr.: grooves (of an organ).

Great hoboy, Engl. late-17th-c. name for the *shawm, to distinguish it from the new oboe. Not to be confused with *grand hautbois.

Great organ (Fr.: *grand orgue;* Ger.: *Hauptwerk*), **1.** formerly a large organ, as opposed to a *chair organ or auxiliary small organ of a church. The great organ appears in Bonn, Bruges, Exeter, Prague, Strassburg in the 13th c., in France in the 14th c.; **2.** the main section of an organ and its pipes, controlled from the second manual from the bottom (62).

Great pipe, syn. of Highland pipe.

Great quint, in Brit. organ building a quint 10⅔′. The Ger. Grossquinte usually indicates quint 5⅓′ (131, 133).

Grefelle, *cog rattle of Fr. Switzerland (102).

Grêle [Lat. *gracilis*, slender], MFr. and new Fr.: graile, 1.

Grelot [U.], Fr.: *pellet bell. The term is recorded from the 14th c. on (204).

Griffbrett, Ger.: fingerboard.

Griffbrettsaite, Ger.: onboard string; stopped string, as opposed to open string.

Griffklapper, Ger.: handle clapper.

Grillet, obs. syn. of grelot.

Grinding, see: rinding.

Grob . . . , Ger.: obs. equivalent of *gross . . .* (organ stops).

Grobfiedel, alto *klarfiedel of Iglau (Jihlava), Moravia, with 3 strings tuned g⁰ d¹ a¹. Only double stops are played on it, as its function is to fill in the middle voices (117).

Gronde, obs. Fr.: Jew's-harp (78).

Grooves (Fr.: *gravures;* Ger.: *Kanzellen*), in an organ, divisions in the upper section of the wind chest; they conduct the wind to the individual pipes. Formed of thin walls on both sides, they are closed at the bottom by pallets.

Gros, grosse (Fr.), in the organ, equivalent of *gross . . .*

Grosbois (Fr.: low wood), obs. Fr. term for the low-pitched shawms, as opposed to the *hautbois, or higher-pitched ones. *Gros,* literally "thick," has the same sense here as in organ terminology.

Gros nazard, *nazard organ stop at 5⅓' pitch (20).

Gross . . . (Ger.), as a prefix to names of organ stops, gross denotes a pitch of one oct. lower than the stop named, generally 16' pitch.

Grossbass . . . , Ger.: contrabass . . .

Gross-Basspommer, Ger.: contrabass shawm.

Grosse basse de violon, obs. Fr.: double bass, pitched either C¹ G¹ D⁰ A⁰ or E¹ A¹ D⁰ G⁰. See also violone, basse des Italiens.

Grosse Bassgeige, obs. Ger.: double bass, violone. Praetorius mentions one tuned F¹ C⁰ G⁰ d⁰ a⁰; Mattheson (in 1713) equates it with the violone.

Grosse caisse, Fr.: bass drum.

Grosse Geige, see: Grossgeige.

Grosser Bass, obs. Ger.: double bass, violone. Leopold Mozart says that there exist many sizes of the instr. but only one tuning, namely, an oct. below the violoncello. The large models had 5 strings rather than 4. *Cf.* violone.

Grosser Bock (Ger.: great he-goat), Ger. bagpipe described by Praetorius as having a drone pitched a 4th lower than that of the *Bock, *i.e.,* on G¹, but similar in other respects. The pitch may have been an oct. higher than he indicates (89, 159).

Grosser Quartzink (Ger.), see: cornone.

Grosse Trommel, Ger.: bass drum.

Grossflöte (Ger.), powerful organ stop of the flute class, at 16' or 8' pitch, sometimes built as a *Doppelflöte (198).

Grossgeige, Ger. Renaissance term for the viola da gamba, in contradistinction to the kleine Geige. An Ambras inventory of 1596 lists bass, tenor, discant, and small discant *"viole de gamba, grossgeigen genannt."* See also: Geige, kleine Geige (183).

Grossmixtur (Ger.), mixture organ stop descended from the *Hintersatz. Nowadays it contains 6–12 ranks of large pipes with consequent low tonal position. See: Hintersatz (133).

Grossquinte (Ger.), organ stop of 10⅔' or 5⅓' pitch. Not identical with the Brit. *great quint.

Grosszink (Ger.), see: cornone.

Grosszymbel, see: Zimbelscharf.

Ground bow (Fr.: *arc-en-terre;* Ger.: *Erdbogen*), primitive form of bow found only in Africa now, although encountered in neolithic excavations on several continents. It consists of a flexible stick set in the ground, with a cord attached to its upper end. The lower end of the cord is tied to the bark cover of a nearby pit, which serves as resonator; the cover of the pit is weighted down with earth or stones, and often a gourd or pot is placed in the pit to augment the sound. The string is plucked with right thumb and forefinger, while the left hand stops it. A portable version exists in Uganda, made of a log into which a stick is fixed at one end, with a gourd holding the string at the other end. The string of a ground bow can also be struck with a small stick. See also: awunene, babakungbu, babakungu, bandingba-ga-sende, bodongo, ekitulege, igbombo, ikpwokpwo, itikili, itumbilongonda, itumbolongonda, jigi-jigi, kiturege, kungunangu; malaba, maloba, musokolome, papakungbu, sekitulege, tingotalango, titimotiti, tum, tumbandera, zuzu (170, 195).

Ground drum (Fr.: *tambour en terre;* Ger.: *Erdtrommel;* Sp.: *tambor terrero*), membrane attached to several poles stuck in the ground and beaten as a drum. *Cf.* ingqongqo.

Ground harp, the same as a ground bow.

Ground zither (Fr.: *cithare en terre;* Ger.: *Erdzither*), chordophone with a string stretched horizontally between 2 upright posts, over a bark-covered pit; a second string runs from the center of the first one to the bark cover, which is weighted down with a stone. The horizontal string is then struck with small sticks. Distributed in Asia and E. Africa, and also found in neolithic excavations on several continents. See also: amponga, amponga fantrotrarana, amponga-tany, cai trong kuan, gendang batak, 2, kakalari, kikilo, kudrekene, kudrenene, kudru-gu, kuze-gene, pitikilangy, tiduran, tindi de kileru, tsipakilangay (168, 170).

Grundstimmen, Ger.: foundation stops.

Grunong, cowbell of the Malayans of Brunei, N. Borneo, made of brass, almost spherical, the aperture being a mere slit, with spherical brass clapper (176).

Grzechotka, Pol.: clapper.

Gu, syn. of gä.

Guacharaca, scraper of Colombia and Venezuela, equivalent to the carrasca of Cuba (89, 152).

Guache, rattle of Colombia, similar to the alfandoque.

Gua-gua, Afro-Cuban *percussion tube, a variety of *catá, but longer and narrower, with patches of metal from gasoline cans affixed to the top. The metal patches are struck with 2 sticks (152).

Gualamban, Jew's-harp of the Toba Indians of S. America (105).

Gualambo, *musical bow of the Caingua Indians of Brazil and Paraguay, without resonator. The player hums while

striking the string with a small stick. *Ca.* 1.80 m. (6 ft.) long (105, 152).

Guamo, *marine-shell trumpet of Cuba, and in Bayamo, Cuba, also an oxhorn. Formerly war instrs. of the Antilles, today they serve as signal instrs. Cuban Indians suspend them from their roofs. Also called cobo (152).

Guayo, Afro-Cuban scraper made from a gourd with a natural handle, notched along one surface and scraped with a stick or a 3-pronged plectrum. 30–50 cm. (12–20 in.) long. It corresponds to the gragé of Haiti (152).

Gubar, ancient bossless cymbal of Java (121).

Gubgubi, friction drum of N. India. *Cf.* dugdugi (103).

Gubo, heterochord *musical bow of the S. African Amazulu, usually with gourd resonator and tuning loop (17, 100).

Gubu, name of the kaligo xylophone among the Angoni of Nyasaland (31).

Gubuolukhulu, syn. of ugubo (116).

Gucha, small horn of Prätigau, Switzerland. Not an alphorn (187).

Guchi, see: gong guchi.

Gudalo, *friction drum of Slovenia, with friction stick. Up to World War I it served as a bass to the mouth organ. Also called muga (144).

Gudok [OSlav. *gudu,* to drone], obs. bowed chordophone of Russia, of the rebec type, a folk instr. with piriform body and three strings tuned to fundamental, 5th, and 12th; the highest string was a melody string, the others served as drones; all were sounded simultaneously. It was held upright on the knees, exceptionally also against the chest. It was played from med. times to the late 18th c. The gudok corresponds to the gadulka of Bulgaria. *Cf.* gadulka, smyk (80 XVI, 176).

Gudu-gudu, kettledrum of the Yoruba of Nigeria (103).

Gudú-gudú, single-headed Afro-Cuban drum of which there are 3 varieties: a) open bottom, head stretched over a hoop;

b) open bottom and nailed head; c) closed bottom and nailed head (152).

Gue, obs. bowed instr. of the Shetland Islands, with 2 horsehair strings, said to have been in use prior to the introduction of violins, when the islands were still under Nor. rule. Otto Anderssen suggests that it may have been a *bowed harp. The *Destruction of Troy, ca.* 1390, mentions a *que,* which is not further identified but might be a syn. of *gue* (9, 180).

Guë-guë, *arará drum of Cuba in tronco-conical form, with single head stretched over a hoop and laced to large pegs projecting from the body. The drum is set on a tripod frame (152).

Guenbri, see: gunbrī.

Guet, var. of gait.

Guffepotte, *friction drum of E. Jutland, with friction stick (169).

Guggu, wedge-shaped, zoomorphic *slit drum of the Azande of the Congo (19).

Gughe, Algerian *spike fiddle with membrane belly and single horsehair string attached to a tuning ring (132).

Gugu, see: guggu.

Guide (Fr.: *mortaise;* Ger.: *Sieb;* Lat.: *cribrum*), also called lower guide. In keyboard instrs. having jacks the perforated frame set under the *slides to keep the jacks in place.

Gui dounou, *water gourd of the Malinke of the Republic of Guinea, consisting of a floating calabash struck with 2 beaters (103).

Guimbarda [Fr. *guimbarde*], Sp.: Jew's-harp.

Guimbarde [U.], Fr.: *Jew's-harp. The word has been used in this sense only since the mid-18th c. Earlier Fr. terms are gronde, rebube, trompe (82).

Guinterne, OFr. var. of guiterne. See: gittern.

Guïra, guïro, scraper of Brazil, Cuba, and Mexico, made from the oval *guïra* gourd. Notches are cut in the exterior and scraped with a stick. The gourd is held by its natural handle. Now adopted by Western rhythm bands (89, 103, 132).

Guïro de jobá, syn. of jícara de jobá (152).

Guiso, Port.: pellet bell (176).

Guisterne, OFr.: gittern.

Guitar [Gk. *kithara* via Arab. *qitāra* and OFr. *guiterne*] (Fr.: *guitare;* Ger.: *Gitarre;* It.: *chitarra;* Sp.: *guitarra*), plucked *chordophone with built-up, characteristically incurved ribs forming a waist. Prototypes of the guitar are believed to be represented by 4 specimens of a wooden instr. with built-up body, sharp incurve of the ribs, and long, narrow neck bearing signs of having had 3 or 4 strings and frets, excavated in Egypt and assigned to a period between the 4th and 8th c. A.C. Such instrs. might have been introduced to Spain by the Arabs, it is argued. Guitars occurring outside med. Egypt and Europe are not considered autochthonous. Until more is known about the early Egyptian instrs., our guitar must be considered a descendant of the *guitarra latina of 13th-c. Spain, known during the early period of its existence as *gittern. The guitar is a plucked chordophone with built-up ribs, gently waisted body, fretted neck, flat pegdisc, rear tuning pegs, frontal string holder, and large, circular soundhole, traditionally played with bare fingers, although nowadays it is often metal-strung for playing with a plectrum. Form and stringing have been modified over the centuries: the modern instr. of standard size has 6 strings tuned $E^0 A^0 d^0 g^0 b^0 e^1$, either with 3 of gut or nylon and 3 of metal-spun silk, or all of metal, with fixed metal frets on a fingerboard that runs down to the open soundhole and is some 90 cm. (3 ft.) long. Transposition is made possible by a *capotasto; notation is an oct. higher than the actual sound. Other sizes have been built, such as the *bass guitar, and a contrabass was built by Monzino of Milan in 1890, with 4 strings, an almost viol-shaped body furnished with a spike, *ca.* 2 m. (6½ ft.) tall. The modern guitar of Spain is made in a whole family of sizes: guitarra (the type instr.), *guitarra tenor, *guitarra requinto, *guitarró, *guitarillo or *tiple.

Guitars are already mentioned in 14th-c. inventories, some with carved heads, even of ivory. In the next c. a *magister de sona guitarra* is mentioned in Spain in 1429, and Tinctoris, toward the end of the c., informs us that it was called *viola* in Italy and *vihuela* in Spain. For several c. the instr. continued to be known indifferently as guitar or gittern (1547/48: *la vieille guiterre qu'on souloit nommer guisterne* [the old guitar one used to call gittern]), and the older term did not die out until the 17th c. By the mid-16th c. the instr. had become pop. in Spain, Italy, and France. Indeed, the anonymous author of a Fr. treatise on playing lutes and gitterns, published in 1556, could state that for the past 12 or 15 years "everybody" plays the guiterne and the lute is practically out of use. The earlier guitar had a far narrower and deeper body than ours has today, with a less pronounced waist and with a long, narrow neck terminating in a flat rectangular pegdisc with rear pegs for 4 courses of strings: 3 pairs and a chanterelle—a slender and elegant instr. Adrien LeRoy, writing in the mid-16th c., confirms its having 4 courses of strings tuned to the intervals of a 4th, a major 3rd, and a 4th. This is the tuning that Bermudo, LeRoy's Sp. contemporary (1555), referred to as the "new" tuning, and that corresponded to that of the 4 inner strings of lute and vihuela. The "old" tuning differed solely in that the fourth (lowest) course was one tone lower. Old and new tunings had been mentioned by Mudarra in his *Tres libros de musica* of 1546. Bermudo also reports having seen 5-course guitars; addition of the fifth (lowest) course is generally attributed to Vicente Espinel of Madrid (1550–1624) in the second half of the 16th c. As he was a guitarist, perhaps he popularized rather than invented it. Most common tuning of the 4-course guitar was $c^0 f^0 a^0 d^1$ (add G^0 and g^1 and you have the contemporary

lute and vihuela tuning). Praetorius in 1618 also gives a tuning of $f^0 b^0 d^1 g^1$. From the time the fifth course was adopted, the instr. became known outside of Spain as the Spanish guitar; it gained a prompt foothold in Italy and from there spread to the rest of Europe. The new course was tuned a 4th below the c^0 strings, *i.e.*, G^0. According to Trichet, *ca.* 1640, who still knew the old term, gittern, the guitar was played a great deal in France and Italy, but even more so in Spain; he comments that the depth between flat top and bottom was from 3 to 4 fingers, the neck a mere 3 fingers wide with 8 frets, the soundhole covered by a rose; he also mentions 5 courses of strings, geminated except for the chanterelle, and the fact that guitars could also be built with vaulted backs (see: chitarra battente). Shortly after he wrote, the chanterelle was also duplicated, and this stringing was maintained until about the middle of the 18th c., but the pitch was raised by a tone sometime during the 17th c., to $A^0 d^0 g^0 b^0 e^1$. Espinel made use of both high and low tunings, but since Ribayez (in 1677) the higher pitch prevailed. In Spain the guitar had been an instr. of the people, in contrast to the aristocratic vihuela. According to Praetorius, in Italy it was in the hands of charlatans and *saltimbanchi,* but by the late 17th c. it had been transformed into an object of fashion, especially in France, where it is said to have been introduced by It. actors in Paris. Makers such as Stradivari and Tielke did not hesitate to build such instrs., sometimes lavishly ornamented. By the mid-18th c. the guitar had become an amateur's instr., and the stringing was consequently made simpler: the 5 pairs of strings made way for 6 single strings, tuned $E^0 A^0 d^0 g^0 b^0 e^1$, as they are today. In the 19th c. wooden tuning pegs were replaced by metal screws, the lower bouts were considerably widened, and the rose disappeared. Today it is still heard as a pop. instr. and has been revived as a classical one, chiefly by the efforts of Sp. players. Guitar music has traditionally been written in tablature. See also: Akkordgitarre, Apollo guitar, arpeggione, arpi-guitare, bajo de uña, bass guitar, bissex, bowed guitar, charango, charranga, chitara, chitarra, chitarra battente, chitarrino, chitarrone, cithara hispanica, cuatro, English citra, getary, gittern, guitare, guitarion, guiterne, harpo-lyre, Hawaiian guitar, iguana, jarana, jaranita, kaitara, keyed guitar, kitarra, kronchong, ligina, lyroharpe, machada, machete, métallicorde à archet, morache, octavilla, pléniphone, quinto, rajão, ramkie, requinta, tenore, tiape, timple, tre, tres, triplo, ttinya, ukulele, venturina, viola d'arame, viola francesa, violão, Zupfgeige (24, 82, 89, 132, 144 Hickmann, 169).

Guitare, Fr.: guitar.

Guitare à clavier, Fr.: keyed guitar.

Guitare à dos bombé, Fr.: chitarra battente.

Guitare à l'archet, Fr.: bowed guitar.

Guitare allemande, a Fr. term for the cittern.

Guitare anglaise, a Fr. term for cittern.

Guitare-basson (Fr.), guitar with snares to imitate the sound of a bassoon, patented by L. G. Warnecke of Nancy on Feb. 24, 1826 (176, 204).

Guitare capucine, obs. Fr.: chitarra battente (obs. term).

Guitare-cithare (Fr.), guitar with offboard strings, invented by Menzenhauer & Schmidt in the late 19th c. (204).

Guitare d'amour, syn. of arpeggione.

Guitare décacorde (Fr.: ten-stringed guitar), 10-stringed guitar with wider than usual neck and large pegbox. 5 strings run over the fretted fingerboard; the other 5 are drones (132).

Guitare en bateau, Fr.: chitarra battente.

Guitare-harpe, the name under which Edward Light's *harp lute was imported into France.

Guitare Laprévote, guitar with circular body, pegbox, and slightly arched back, invented by Etienne Laprévote of Paris *ca.* 1844 (176).

Guitare latine (Fr.), mentioned in Fr. literature from the 14th c. on. *Cf.* guitarra latina.

Guitare-luth, Fr.: lute guitar.

Guitare-lyre (Fr.), lyre-shaped guitar with 6–9 strings, patented by Mougnet of Lyon on Apr. 13, 1811. *Cf.* lyreguitar (204).

Guitare moresque, mentioned in Fr. literature from 1349 on. See: guitarra morisca (176).

Guitare multichorde, guitar patented by Louis Charpentier and Munchs of Paris on Nov. 5, 1832, with 25 strings. To the 6 strings of an ordinary guitar 19 harp strings were added, giving the instr. a 4-oct. compass (204).

Guitare théorbée, Fr.: bass guitar.

Guitare toscane, Fr.: chitarra battente.

Guitarillo, smallest of the Sp. guitars, with 5 gut strings tuned $a^1 d^2 g^1 c^2 e^2$. Also called tiple (176).

Guitarion, guitar that could be plucked or bowed indifferently, patented by Franck of Paris on Feb. 28, 1831 (158).

Guitar-lyra-zither, see: chord zither, 2.

Guitarra (Port., Sp.), **1.** Sp.: guitar; usually with 6 strings tuned $E^0 A^0 d^0 g^0 b^0 e^1$, the bass of a family comprising *guitarra tenor, *guitarra requinto, *guitarró, guitarillo; **2.** Port.: instr. similar to the Sp. *bandurria but with a far longer neck (the Port. instr. resembling the guitar is called *violão). Generally it is provided with 6 pairs of strings tuned $c^1 e^1 g^1 c^2 e^2 g^2$. Often used for accompanying *fados,* together with a violão, in which case it is tuned $d^1 a^1 b^1 e^2 a^2 b^2$. In Spain this instr. is known as the *guitarra portuguesa,* in France as the *cistre portuguais* (7, 89).

Guitarra battente, see: chitarra battente.

Guitarra de cinco órdenes (Sp. five-course guitar), syn. of guitarra española.

Guitarra española (Sp.), the 5-stringed guitar of 16th- and 17th-c. Spain, also called guitarra de cinco órdenes.

Guitarra latina (Sp.), on the basis of illustrations of the 13th-c. *Cantigas de Santa María,* Sachs concluded that this was a plucked instr. with ribs, waisted body, fretted neck, and probably 4 strings. His conclusions are still accepted. Kastner, in his *Danse des morts,* quotes a 1349 source listing a *joueur de la guiterre latine* and a *joueur de guiterne moresche* then in the employ of the Duke of Normandy. Juan Ruiz, in the 14th c., also mentions both kinds of guitarra (169).

Guitarra morisca (Sp.), on the basis of illustrations in the 13th-c. *Cantigas de Santa María,* Sachs concluded that this was a plucked instr. similar to the E. *tanbūr, with oval body, vaulted back, numerous small soundholes in the belly, large, round pegdisc, introduced into Spain by the Moors. Other forms with lateral pegs are also met with in pictorial sources. Juan Ruiz mentioned the instr. a c. later. Also called guitarra saracenica and mentioned as such by Johannes de Grocheo *ca.* 1300 (169).

Guitarra portuguesa, Sp. name of the guitarra, 1.

Guitarra requinto (Sp.: quint guitar), small Sp. guitar tuned $B^0 e^0 a^0 d^1 f\sharp^1 b^1$, *i.e.,* a 5th higher than the guitarra, notated an oct. higher (176).

Guitarra saracenica, see: guitarra morisca.

Guitarra tenor, Sp. tenor guitar tuned $(G^0) c^0 f^0 b\flat^0 d^1 g^1$, a 3rd above the bass.

Guitarre, 1. OFr. var. of guiterne; 2. obs. Ger. spelling of Gitarre.

Guitarró, Cat., Sp.: small guitarra with 4 or 5 strings, larger than the guitarillo (165).

Guitarrón [Sp., aug. of *guitarra*], 1. in Spain a *bass guitar; 2. in Chile a guitar with 24 strings.

Guitar stop, name occasionally given in the past to the *harp stop, 1 (27).

Guitar violoncello, syn. of arpeggione.

Guitar-zither, see: chord zither, 2.

Guiterne, Fr.: gittern. The term was in use from the 13th c. on.

Guiterre, var. of guiterne.

Guitharfe [contraction of Ger. *Guitarre + Harfe*], a combination guitar and harp invented by the Viennese mathematician Joseph Petzval and built in 1862 by J. Scherzer of Vienna. It was provided with 2 fingerboards, 1 for 6 melody strings, the other for 6 bass strings (176).

Guke, side-blown horn of the Lugbara of Uganda, made of animal horn, used by men and boys in their dances (195).

Gukon-grute, *globular flute of the Canella Indians of C. Maranhão, Brazil, with blowhole and 2 fingerholes (176).

Gul-gul, Madurese name of the kentongan (121).

Gül-gül, see: jul-jul.

Gulieng, bamboo *whistle flute of Borneo, with 3 fingerholes (176).

Gullāl, frame drum of Algeria. *Cf.* quwāl (75 I).

Gulunba, Basque: 1. large cowbell; 2. bass drum (56).

Gulung-gulung, rattle of Borneo rice planters, made of 7 bamboo or hardwood tubes of different lengths, containing very small pieces of wood provided with antler points. The rattle is played by 7 men. Known as tugal in W. Borneo, tongkat krutak in N. Borneo (132).

Gulutindi, syn. of kilingila.

Gumbang, wind instr. of C. Java of the flute class, consisting of a very stout bamboo segment closed at the bottom by a node, open at the top. The player blows into a much thinner tube, open at both ends, while holding its lower end inside the wide tube. Sometimes the large tube is replaced by an elongated calabash. Said to yield 3 tones: fundamental, 5th, and oct. Also called gong bumbung. *Cf.* serbung (121).

Gumbé, square *frame drum of Jamaica, of African origin, with nailed parchment head; it stands on 4 wooden legs and looks like a low table. The same drum exists in Cuba, where, however, it has no name. *Cf.* cumbé (152).

Gumbeng, idiochord *tube zither of Java, made of bamboo, the node being pierced at one end. A single string is detached from the surface and raised over 1 or 2 small nuts. Sometimes a vibrating, spoon-shaped bridge is inserted about halfway along the string. Also called bumbung. *Cf.* guntang (121).

Gumongo, see: komunko.

Gumra, *goblet drum of the Khanda of the E. coast of India, made of clay, with snakeskin head on the narrower end (173).

Gunbrī [Sudanic corr. of *gunāwī* or *gināwī*, of the Negroes], degenerated form of the ancient Egyptian lute, it survives primarily as an instr. of the Negroes of Morocco, Senegal, and Gambia, described in the 18th c. as *kitāra kināwa*, the Negro guitar. It is larger than the gunībrī, and its heavy body is rectangular or scaphoid, covered with a skin belly that may be glued, nailed, or laced on. The neck is a plain cylinder, sometimes terminating in a scroll or fork. Its lower end penetrates the body immediately under the belly, acting as a bass bar and reaching as far as the soundhole. Most instrs. have 3 strings, but specimens with 2 or 4 strings also exist. They are tuned by means of leather tuning rings. The gunbrī is plucked, usually with bare fingers. In N. Africa, chiefly Morocco, gunbrīs are made in many sizes, all characterized by a tortoise-carapace body, a neck, and generally also tuning pegs. Among the Shlūh the carapace is often replaced by a tin bowl; in towns it assumes an elongated pear shape. N. gunbrīs are smaller than their S. counterparts (75 I, 144 Chottin, 170).

Gunda, side-blown horn of the Washambala of Tanganyika, made of kudu or *kurungu* horn, partly covered with skin. Used as a war horn and at civic festivities (111).

Gundi, harp of N. Cameroun (103).

Gunga, syn. of urucungo (7).

Gunge, pluriarc of the Bahuana of the Congo (19).

Gunguma, a drum of the Galla of E. Africa (144).

Gunībrī [dim. of *gunbrī*], small gunbrī, reduced in size and adopted as a very pop. instr. by Arabs and Moors, known since the 7th c. The body is of wood, coconut, tortoise shell, gourd, or even metal, and assumes an ovoid, piriform, or hemispheric shape. The neck is longer in relation to the body than that of the gunbrī; here again it penetrates the body. The belly is of skin, punctured by several soundholes. Two strings are the most common number, tuned a 5th apart in most instances; 3 are less frequent. The strings are held by lateral pegs that penetrate the neck; occasionally they are given a pegbox of their own (75 I, 170).

Gunilka, syn. of gadulka.

Čunk, see: jank.

Gunta, see: ghantā.

Guntang, 1. name of the gumbeng (tube zither) in 14th c. documents; **2.** name of the gumbeng in Bali today (121).

Gupek, 2-headed drum of Bali (103).

Gura, see: gora.

Guro awal, friction gourd of the Acoli of Uganda. The rims of 2 hemispheric gourds are rubbed against a stone or wooden board by 2 girls, each holding 1 gourd; 2 different tones are produced (195).

Gurrufio, disc buzzer of Venezuela (152).

Guru, *musical bow of the Logo of the Congo, with tuning loop but no resonator (128).

Gurugú, *arará drum of Jovellanos, Cuba, in shape of a truncated cone (152).

Guruma [*garamut], name of the gerom in Astrolabe Bay, New Guinea (77).

Gusla [OSlav. *gusti*, to drone], **1.** bowed chordophone of Bulgaria, mentioned in literary sources from the 10th c. on. It corresponds to the gusle of Yugoslavia; 75–80 cm. (29½–31½ in.) long; **2.** syn. of gadulka. See also: husla, gusle, guslice (80 XVI).

Gusle [OSlav. *gusti*, to drone], bowed chordophone of Yugoslavia, made of a single block of maple, with ovoid body carved like a ladle, and single string of twisted horsehair secured by an elongated rear peg set in the neck, holding the string clear (there is no nut). Several small soundholes are pierced in the skin belly, and often a soundhole is cut in the back. Three types of gusle are distinguished: 1) Serbian, with bowl-shaped body; 2) Bosnian, more elaborate, with carved, piriform body and a bridge set higher than on Serbian instrs. The Bosnian is also deeper and lacks soundholes in the belly; 3) the Herzegovinian or Montenegrin type, which is the largest, has a heart-shaped, ornamented body and a high bridge.

The string is stopped by the player's index, middle, and little fingers, the weak fourth finger never being used. These fingers touch the string from the side with lateral pressure, in the absence of a fingerboard; formerly the fingers were held straight; nowadays they are held curved. The bow in use is an early, curved type, the stick still serving as handle. Some gusles may have a second string, which is then tuned a 2nd below the first. The performer plays while seated, holding the gusle on his lap, and accompanies himself while singing epic songs. Thus the pitch is dependent on that of the singer's voice. It is 63–75 cm. (25–30 in.) long, 10–13 cm. (4–5 in.) deep (Walter Wünsch: *Geigentechnik der südslavischen Guslaren*, 1934; 9, 89).

Gusli, [OSlav. *gusti*, to drone] formerly a generic Russ. term for stringed instrs., the word is now reserved for a triangular psaltery with incurved sides, descended from the med. triangular psaltery or, rather, a petrifact thereof, resembling instrs. depicted in Russ. mss. from the 14th c. on. Nowadays it is a folk instr. of the Cheremiss of the Volga area, also of the Chuvash and Votyak. The body is a shallow box strung with a variable number of strings. Among the Cheremiss it has 23 to 28 gut strings.

Elsewhere the number may vary from 12 to 36 and be of metal or gut, all of the same diam. but of different lengths. In addition to the typically triangular form it is also made as a trapezium or rectangle. In the 1880's W. W. Andreyev modernized the gusli and even attempted to combine it with a keyboard. Since then it has been made in a number of sizes, the longest strings being *ca.* 1 m. (40 in.). The seated player lays it horizontally across his lap and plucks the strings with bare fingers (9, 132, 149, 176).

Guslice [OSlav. *gusti*, to drone], Yugo. instr. corresponding to the gadulka, with rebec-shaped body, wooden belly, semicircular soundholes, and three horsehair strings. The rear pegs are set in a flat *pegdisc; it lacks both nut and fingerboard. The strings are tuned (relatively) $f^1 c^1 g^1$ with the center string acting as drone; all three are touched simultaneously by the bow. Formerly they were stopped by the player's fingernails, nowadays by sideways pressure of the fingers. The guslice is a Balkan form of the (Gk.) lira. *Ca.* 38 cm. (15 in.) long. See also: gusla, lirica (15, 89).

Guwak, see: juwāq.

Guzla, guzle, see: gusla, gusle.

Gwale, musical bow of S. Africa, played by boys (17).

Gwan'bal, syn. of mushits (30).

Gwangmagi, syn. of ching, 2 (66).

Gwaningba, syn. of ninga (128).

Gwanzu, *board zither of the Ababua of the Congo (19).

Gwara me akuta, straight side-blown trumpet of the Lango of Uganda, made of 2 sections of hollowed wood covered with black leather, with narrow, almost cylindrical bore. A small hole is pierced in the tip. *Ca.* 75 cm. (30 in.) long (195).

Gyo, scraper of Japan, of Chin. origin, in form of a wooden tiger with notched back; it is scraped with a bamboo switch. It corresponds to the yü of China, the ö of Korea (173).

Gythren, var. of gittern.

Hã, the gora of the Bushmen of S. Africa (116).

Haarr gie (Nor.: hair fiddle), Nor. instr. mentioned in the 17th c.; it probably corresponded to the talharpa (9).

Hackbrett (Ger.: chopping board), Ger.: dulcimer. The word is recorded since 1477.

Hade, *musical bow of several Bantu tribes of S. Africa, with one heterochord string and gourd resonator but no tuning loop (17, 100).

Ha erh cha ko, Chin. name of the ghizhak (75 II).

Hafen (S. Ger.: pot), scraped pot of 16th- and 17th-c. Germany (169).

Hahel, nose *ring flute of the Nicobar Islands (203).

Hahi, side-blown trumpet of the Canella Indians of C. Maranhão, Brazil, made of a cylindrical cane tube with an oxhorn fastened to one end (176).

Haiau, heterochord *tube zither of Malaya, with 3 or 4 rattan strings (173).

Hai kom, see: he kum.

Hai lo, end-blown *marine-shell trumpet of China, possibly of Indian origin. The player's hand is inserted into its natural opening. It serves both as Buddhist ceremonial instr. and as a signal instr. Also called lo tse. It corresponds to the sora of Korea and hora of Japan (1, 89, 170).

Haitari, Finn.: accordion. See also: hanuri (89).

Hakenharfe, Ger.: hook harp.

Haku han, wooden clappers of Japan. They correspond to the p'o pan of China and the pak of Korea (157).

Halam, lute of the Wolof of Gambia, with scaphoid body, membrane belly, handle that penetrates the body and acts as a bass bar, and 4 or 5 strings attached to the handle by tuning rings. *Ca.* 80 cm. (32 in.) long. *Cf.* kambreh (103, 141).

Halbbass (Ger.: half bass), Ger. equivalent of the basso da camera, a small double bass.

Halbe Orgel (Ger.: half organ), obs. Ger. term for an organ having as its foundation a register of 8′ pitch. The expression was not in use after the mid-18th c. *Cf.* ganze Orgel, viertel Orgel (90).

Halbgeige, Ger.: violino piccolo. Also called Quartgeige, according to Leopold Mozart.

Halbinstrument, term coined by Karl von Schafhäutl in 1854 to designate brass instrs. with a bore too narrow to permit the fundamental (pedal tone) to speak. In such instrs. the second harmonic is the lowest tone. See also: Ganzinstrument (25, 176).

Halbkontrafagott, Ger.: semicontrabassoon.

Halbmond (Ger.: half moon), **1.** Ger.: Jingling Johnnie; **2.** semicircular army bugle in crescent form of the 18th c. and early 19th c. *Cf.* huchet (176).

Halbprinzipal, organ stop of Prinzipal pipes at 4′ pitch, *i.e.,* having half the length of the Prinzipal (133).

Half bass, see: Halbbass.

Half long pipe, bellows-blown bagpipe of Northumberland, recently revived, similar to the *Lowland pipe except that it has 3 drones tuned a⁰ (tenor), e⁰ (baritone), A⁰ (bass) (13, 89).

Half-tube zither, see: tube zither.

Halhallatu, Akk. equivalent of shem.

Hālil [Heb. *hālal* pierced], double pipes of the biblical era of ancient Israel, made of cane, wood or metal. Translated by the Septuagint as *aulos,* they may have been double-reed instrs. In their early form they were cylindrical, becoming conical in the 2nd c. Always played as divergent pipes and used in the second Temple, although primarily a secular instr. See also: halhallatu (89 Baines, 170).

Halilu, Akk. equivalent of nā.

Hals, Ger.: neck.

Halur, syn. of bansurī (68).

Ha ma, *friction drum of China in form of a clay frog with a hollow body. The bottom is covered with a piece of strong paper. A single horsehair passes through a hole in the paper and is rubbed with wet fingers (142).

Hamaton, *automatophone by Cornelius van Oeckelen of Breda (d. 1865) (176).

Hamburger Cithrinchen, small *cittern with campaniform silhouette and 5 pairs of strings; it originated in Hamburg during the last quarter of the 17th c. Mattheson's concise definition (in *Orchester,* 1713), *"Cithrinchen alias Huhr-laute,"* implies greater popularity than most modern writers have accorded it. Called bell cittern in Engl.

Hami, *hourglass drum of the Huon Gulf area of New Guinea, identical with the oñ (28).

Hammer (Fr.: *maillet;* Ger.: *Hammer;* It.: *martello;* Sp.: *macillo*), characteristic component of a piano action, composed nowadays of hammer head, heel, shank, and butt, screwed to a hammer rail. Originally covered with leather, first felted by Henri Pape of Paris in 1826.

Hammerclavier, Ger. equivalent of pianoforte. The expression was coined during the early 19th c. in reaction to the use of foreign words in the Ger. language. In 1817 Beethoven wrote to his publisher, Steiner, instructing him to use the word *Hammerclavier* instead of *pianoforte* in all his works having a Ger. title. Nowadays the word is spelled Hammerklavier and is used only in a historical sense (169).

Hammerflügel, obs. Ger.: grand piano.

Hammerklavier, see: Hammerclavier.

Hammond organ, *electrophonic organ made by the Hammond Organ Co., with electronic tone generation. Its 2 manuals have a 5-oct. compass.

Han, large percussion board of Buddhist monasteries in Japan, of wood, beaten with a small mallet. *Cf.* semanterion (135).

Handäoline (Ger.), original name of the accordion; named by its inventor, Friedrich Buschmann of Berlin, 1822 (176).

Handbassl, according to Leopold Mozart, an instr. of the violin family slightly larger than the Fagottgeige, but smaller than a cello; an instr. used for bass parts, occasionally even known as Fagottgeige. Possibly identical with the violoncello alto. It is referred to as *bassetto di mano* in It.

Handharmonika (Ger.), name given to the accordion by makers who infringed Cyril Demian's privilege rights by copying his Akkordion. The word is still in use in certain Ger.-speaking areas (117).

Hand horn (Fr.: *cor à main*), natural French horn played with hand in bell.

Handja, xylophone of the Fan of W. Africa, with bamboo frame. The calabash resonators have a small hole pierced on one side, covered with a spider-egg membrane—a mirliton device. The performer sits and holds the handja between his knees (42).

Handle clapper (Fr.: *cliquet;* Ger.: *Griffklapper*), any clapper provided with a handle.

Handle organ, syn. of barrel organ.

Hand organ, 1. syn. of barrel piano; 2. in the U.S. the name of the barrel organ.

Handorgel, coll. Ger.: accordion.

Hango, see: hunga.

Han koto (Jap.: half koto), small, obs. koto of Japan, made for traveling.

Hano, *globular flute of Hawaii, made from a small piriform gourd, with 3 holes, also played as a nose flute. Also called kio-kio (176).

Han sho, syn. of den sho (135).

Hanuri, Finn.: accordion. See also: haitari (89).

Hao, *la pa of Shantung, China (176).

Hao talla, straight trumpet of the Naga of Assam, made of 11 bamboo sections that telescope into one another, terminating in a bell of animal horn. Played without a mouthpiece. *Ca.* 2 m. (6½ ft.) long (172).

Hao t'ung, pop. name of the t'ung kyo (89).

Hapa'i, name of the rabāb in the Achin region of Sumatra (178).

Hapetan [Sans. *kachapa*], syn. of kachapi among the Batak of Sumatra (173).

Happu, Jap. drum of considerable age, in form of a ni-daiko, filled with rice powder, with 2 laced heads and shallow, cylindrical body. Suspended in an ornate circular frame and played with 2 drumsticks. Now obs. (157).

Hardablis, var. of hardulis.

Hardanger fele (Nor.: Hardanger fiddle); Nor. folk violin with 4 melody strings and 4 sympathetic strings, smaller than the ordinary violin—only some 60 cm. (24 in.) long—with short neck, flatter bridge, and more highly arched belly. The melody strings are tuned A D A E, the sympathetic ones D E F♯ A. According to tradition, the Hardanger fele was invented by a schoolteacher of Hardanger, *ca.* 1670, but was improved to its present condition by Isak Nielsen Botner (d. *ca.* 1780) (91).

Hardingfela, see: Hardanger fele.

Hardulis [Gk. *hydraulos*], Heb.: organ. *Cf.* hirdolis.

Harfa, Czech: harp.

Harfe [OHGer. *harfa*], Ger.: harp.

Harfenbogen, Ger.: harp bow.

Harfenett [It. *arpanetta*], Ger.: arpanetta.

Harfenett d'amour, mechanical arpanetta controlled by a cylinder, of 18th-c. invention; 27 pairs of strings were tuned G^0–e^8; 27 sympathetic strings were stretched on the same side of the soundboard, 19 on the opposite side (37).

Harfengitarre, syn. of Gitarrenharfe.

Harfenklavier, Ger.: keyed harp.

Harfenlaute, Ger.: *harp lute or its successor instrs.

Harfenprinzipal (Ger.), organ stop of Prinzipal pipes in echo form, of narrow scale. Also called Salizional-Oktave, Salizional-Prinzipal, singend Prinzipal (133).

Harfenregal, obs. organ stop of short, cylindrical regal pipes at 8' pitch (133).

Harfenzither, Ger.: harp zither.

Harfenzug, Ger.: harp stop, 2.

Harib, see: rgya-glin.

Harigot, var. of larigot.

Harmomélo, tall upright piano, precursor of the *cabinet piano, patented on Sept. 19, 1806, by Pfeiffer & Cie. of Paris, with strings reaching to the ground, trichord, with 4 stops (harp, bassoon, una corda, forte) and a 6-oct. compass. *Ca.* 2 m. (6½ ft.) high (92).

Harmonette, automatophone with perforated paper discs, made in the second half of the 19th c. by the Automatic Organ Co. of Boston (204).

Harmonia aetherea, mixture organ stop, usually composed of 3 ranks of pipes of principal scale. Also known as echo mixture, mixtura aetherea (131, 133).

Harmonic . . . (Fr., Ger.: *Harmonie . . .*), as a prefix to names of organ stops, harmonic indicates that the pipes are constructed so as to overblow the second harmonic, *i.e.,* the oct. if the pipes are open ones, the 12th if they are stopped. This is accomplished by drilling a hole halfway up the body of an open pipe, or ⅔ to ⅗ up the body of a stopped pipe. Sorge described the same principle in 1773, with overblow hole at ⅗ of the pipe length; it was forgotten and reinvented by Aristide Cavaillé-Coll in the 19th c. (129).

Harmonica (Ger.: *Harmonika*), **1.** Du., Fr.: glass harmonica; **2.** see: mouth organ; **3.** Engl. name of the piano stop more generally known as *una corda; **4.** *bowed keyboard instr. invented by organ builder H. Schmidt of Rostock *ca.* 1782. Its continuous bow was worked by a treadle. Its compass was F¹–f⁸ (149); **5.** organ stop of open flue pipes, cylindrical, very narrow, usually of metal, at 8′ pitch and on occasion at 16′ pitch; also, the name of a free-reed organ stop. *Cf.* harmonica flute (133).

Harmonica à bouche, Fr.: mouth organ.

Harmonica à clavier, Fr.: keyed harmonica.

Harmonica de bois, Fr.: xylophone.

Harmonica de Franklin, Fr.: glass harmonica.

Harmonica flute (Ger.: *Harmonikaflöte*), another name of the harmonica organ stop with very narrow flue pipes, at 8′ or 4′ pitch, found in British and Ger. organs (131).

Harmonica-Jaulin, a perfected typotone presumably invented by Jaulin of Paris.

Harmonic bass, syn. of acoustic bass (organ stop).

Harmonic canon (Lat.: *regula harmonica*), the monochord.

Harmonic curve, name given to the curved neck of frame harps, so called because its shape, like that of a piano bridge, is the result of the *scale of its strings.

Harmonicello, bowed instr. similar to the Baryton, built by Johann Carl Bischoff of Dessau in 1794. It had 5 gut melody strings and 10 metal sympathetic strings; the latter could also be played pizzicato (176, Welcker v. Gontershausen, 1855).

Harmonic flute, see: flûte harmonique.

Harmonic gedackt, see: German flute (organ stop).

Harmonichord, bowed keyboard instr.

in form of a *giraffe piano, invented *ca.* 1810 by Friedrich Kaufmann of Dresden, in an attempt to solve, by application of the *clavicylinder principle, the problems inherent in bowed keyboard instrs. A rosin-coated cylinder was worked by foot, and the strings were pressed against it by means of wooden bars. Weber wrote an *Adagio and Rondo* for it in 1811. Not to be confused with harmonicorde (37, 89, 169).

Harmonicon (Ger.: *Harmonikon*), **1.** name sometimes given to the *musical glasses; **2.** name sometimes given to the *glass harmonica; **3.** a later name of the *vis-à-vis; **4.** a combination of a glass harmonica with keyboard and of 4 stops of organ pipes, built by the Bremen Kapellmeister Wilhelm Christian Müller, *ca.* 1795. The 2 manuals permitted the instrs. to be played separately or together.

Harmonicor, free-reed instr. in form of a horn, with 27 piston valves arranged in keyboard fashion, patented by Jaulin of Paris on Dec. 31, 1861. The instr. had a compass of 2 octs. and is said to have sounded like an oboe. When made in trumpet form, it was called harmonitrompe.

Harmonicorde (Fr.), harmonium of Alexandre-François Debain of Paris, 1851. Not to be confused with the harmonichord (176).

Harmonic piano, the original name of Wornum's *cottage piano (92).

Harmonics, modern mixture organ stop, composed of octaves, 5ths, 3rds, and 7ths (186).

Harmonic swell, piano stop patented by F. W. Collard of London in 1821, consisting of the provision of a second bridge to permit the afterlengths of the strings to vibrate sympathetically with the speaking lengths. A system of dampers for this section was also provided (92).

Harmonie . . . (Fr., Ger.), syn. of harmonic; it also denotes an organ stop voiced for combinational use (198).

Harmoniebass, obs. Ger. term for wind instrs. of bass register.

Harmonie d'Orphée, Fr.: Orpheusharmonie.

Harmonieflöte, see: flûte harmonique.

Harmoniekontrabass, improved bass ophicleide built by Griessling & Schlott of Berlin in 1833, with a compass A^1–c^2 (176).

Harmonieorgel (Ger.), harmonium patented ca. 1892 by Johann Kewitsch, with key fronts slightly lower than the backs, the front portions being tuned one syntonic comma higher than the rear portions, so that pure 3rds could be played (178).

Harmonietrompete (Ger.), **1.** early-19th-c. *duplex instrument, a combination trumpet and French horn in which the tones could be stopped in horn fashion (Hermann Eichborn). Cf. chromatic trumpet and French horn; **2.** organ stop, see: trompette harmonique.

Harmoniflûte, 1. a variety of *piano accordion, first built by Bouton of Paris in 1852. It could be set on a stand, and the bellows worked by a treadle, or it could be held in the lap. Usual compass f^0–f^3; **2.** *barrel organ built from 1853 on (169, 178).

Harmoni-harpe (Fr.), zither laid horizontally on a table but played in harp fashion, patented Feb. 18, 1864, by Papelard of Paris (204).

Harmonika, Ger.: harmonica.

Harmonikon, Ger.: harmonicon.

Harmonino, a small harmonium intended to be placed upon a piano and played with it. First shown at the 1851 London Exhibition (204).

Harmoniphon, 1. a small physharmonica designed to replace the cor anglais, patented on Aug. 19, 1836, by Paris, Lecrosnier & Tremblai of Dijon. Its 2-oct. compass of reeds was actuated either by bellows or by a flexible mouth tube. Valves were opened by depressing the keys. Compass c^1–d^3; **2.** a similar instr., mouth-blown, was made in the 1850's in Berlin for Capt. J. Dresky, to replace the missing oboists of his officers' club orchestra. Not to be confused with harmoniphone (132, 204).

Harmoniphon-cor-anglais, an improved Harmoniphon made by the same makers ca. 1839 (204).

Harmoniphone, 1. automatic organ patented July 22, 1887, by Deroudel & Rocacher of Paris, worked by means of perforated paper discs; **2.** instr. of unknown construction patented by Soualle of Paris on Feb. 6, 1859. Not to be confused with Harmoniphon (204).

Harmoniphrase, chord harmonium of Dumont & Lelièvre of Paris, exhibited by them in 1889 (176).

Harmonique (Fr.), see: harmonic . . .

Harmonista, harmonium accessory invented 1873 by V. Gevaert of Ghent to enable persons unable to play a keyboard instr. to accompany plain chant. The device, in form of a rectangular box, was set on the keyboard. It contained 26 buttons; when depressed, each sounded a chord, the upper tone of which was that of the plain chant. Cf. chord organ (132).

Harmoniton, harmonium patented in France in 1892 by Müller & Kebelac (204).

Harmonitrompe, see: harmonicor.

Harmonium, *free-reed keyboard instr. using wind under pressure supplied by compression bellows (as opposed to the *American organ, which uses wind supplied by suction bellows), invented by Alexandre-François Debain of Paris in 1840. After the introduction of the *free reed to Europe from China, a series of experiments got under way, resulting in a whole series of new instrs., starting with Gabriel-Joseph Grenié's *orgue expressif in 1810 and culminating in the harmonium, first keyboard instr. to be furnished with several registers of free reeds. Debain patented his instr. on Aug. 9, 1840, under the name of harmonium, thus forcing his competitors to resort to other designations. The harmonium consists of a series of tuned free reeds actuated by pressure wind and controlled by a keyboard. The wind supply is provided by 2 pedal-operated bellows connected to a wind chest. The reeds are mounted in brass frames on top of the wind chest. Each key communicates with a valve that controls the wind supply. Standard models were made with 4 registers, all divided, and a compass of 4 or 5 octs. from C^0. In 1843 Debain added the *expression, permitting crescendo and diminuendo. Later the *double expression was also applied to the harmonium. Mechanical harmoniums were also built. They could be played either from the keyboard or by means of pinned cylinders, perforated cardboard strips or metal discs. Both as a substitute for the organ in small churches and as a home instr. the harmonium was enormously pop. for close to a century. Some models were fitted with *transposing keyboards, which shifted sideways, permitting transposition of any interval while playing the keys called for by the score. For precursor instrs. see: aeoline, aeolodicon, aeolo-melodicon, aérophone, organino, 4, Organo-Violine, orgue expressif, physharmonica. See also: angélophone, book harmonium, choriphone, cithare-harmonium, claviaccord, claviphone, double touch, enharmonium, expression, harmonicorde, Harmonieorgel, harmonino, harmoniphrase, harmoniton, harmonium-célesta, Harmonium-Zither, Luftdruckharmonium, marmotine, médiophone, melodina, mélodi-orgue, melodium, mélophilon, melophone-zither, métaphone, musique perforée, Mustel organ, orchestrelle, orchestrion, 6, orchestrium, organophone, orgue excelsior, orphéa, orphéi, pianon, trylodeon, viola a cembalo, violo-clave (127, 151, 170).

Harmonium-célesta, a combination harmonium and celesta of late-19th-c. Fr. invention (204).

Harmoniumklavier, Ger.: piano-harmonium.

Harmonium-Zither, a combination harmonium and zither, invented 1902 by M. L. Buschnigg of Leipzig. Perhaps identical with the cithare-harmonium (176).

Harp [OEngl. *hearpe*] (Fr.: *harpe;* Ger.: *Harfe;* It., Sp.: *arpa*), 1. chordophone with strings running in a plane perpendicular to the resonator, consisting of a resonator, or body, and a neck, between which a series of parallel strings are stretched vertically or diagonally. In addition, the Western harp has a pillar, or column, that connects body and neck, taking the strain of the strings' tension. This form is known as frame harp. Some, but not all, harps of European antiquity had pillars; outside Europe the frame harp was also known to ancient and med. Syria and is found in Siberia today. Columnless, or open, harps are classified as *arched harps or *angular harps; this classification is now held to be too rigid, as it does not allow for intermediate types. Many investigators hold the harp to be a development of the polychord *musical bow, but this point is still debated. Harps are played in primitive and developed cultures alike. For their size primitive harps are low in pitch, as they can take but little tension. Their resonators are of many shapes: elongated, ovoid, round, etc., and they often have membrane bellies. Tuning is by means of movable tuning pegs or by tuning rings, but ancient Egypt and Java used pegs best designated as tuning knobs, as they were wedged into the neck from the rear and glued fast: they did not turn, but prevented the strings from slipping. Many modern exotic harps are tuned by bast or cloth tuning rings, knotted to the strings of which they form prolongations, and turned around the neck several times; they can be moved slightly to tighten or relax the string. This system was also in use from ancient Sumer to India.

Harps of antiquity are represented from about 3000 B.C. on (Sumer). In Mesopotamia both arched and angular harps were known and occurred in horizontal and vertical forms. Horizontal harps are held with their strings lying in horizontal position, the resonator away from the player; vertical harps are held with the strings in vertical position and the resonator placed against the player's chest. Vertical harps were plucked with the fingers of both hands, whereas horizontal ones were played with a long, slender plectrum or stick held in the right hand; the left hand appears to have acted as a damper. Sumer knew only the arched harp; it was succeeded *ca.* 2000 B.C. by the angular harp. Sumerian arched harps were held with the resonator uppermost, whereas those of Egypt were held with the resonator below. The arched harp of Egypt is now considered to be descended from that of Sumer; it was held in vertical position, usually placed on the ground, and played by a kneeling performer (but see: shoulder harp). In the New Kingdom these harps grew to 1 or even 2 m. (3 or 6½ ft.) in height, with 19 strings, and were played by standing musicians. The angular harps of Egypt seem to have originated in the Near East and were also played in vertical position only. They were composed of a narrow, one-piece body having a round stick for a neck. The resonator was held against the seated player's body, the neck resting on his lap. A number of both angular and vertical harps of ancient Egypt have come down to us. The harp was known to ancient Greece but played a very minor role there. It is represented in continental Greece on a bowl of 750-700 B.C. as a frame harp, after which both angular and arched versions appear, albeit rarely. In Persia 3 types of harp are depicted on Sassanid reliefs at Taq-i Bustan, *ca.* 600 A.C.: the horizontal angular harp makes its last appearance here; the vertical angular harp is shown, also to disappear thereafter; and the arched vertical harp is represented for the first time in this area. This instr., a classical one of Persia from then on, was introduced to Arabia before the advent of Islam and spread to the Arab-speaking world.

Earliest evidence of the harp in post-classical Europe is the small, fragmentary instr. recovered from the Sutton Hoo burial ship of the 7th c., formerly identified as a harp, is now considered to have been a lyre. However, reliefs on stone crosses in Ireland dating from the 9th to the 11th c. are now conceded to represent harps (rather than lyres): the instrs. show pillars and are held as harps. The 9th-c. Utrecht psalter also depicts harps. In a 12th-c. ms. the drawing of a harp is identified as "cythara anglica." A 13th-c. *chanson de geste* mentions "*et d'Ingleterre i out des harpors.*" All these were angular harps with tuning pegs inserted in the neck at the top of the instr. and a pillar connecting neck and body, thus forming a triangle. Med. harps had metal strings and were tuned with a tuning key, sometimes called plectrum. Guillaume de Machault (14th c.) mentions a harp with 25 strings, but size and stringing were of course not standardized. Glarean, in 1547, depicts a beautiful harp, described as being 5 ft. high, with 24 strings and a compass F^0–a^0. Both hands were used in playing early harps; later the instr. was held by one hand and played with the other. By the mid-15th c. the squat harp with outcurving pillar of the later Middle Ages gave way to the slender Gothic harp, its almost straight pillar indicating an increase in tension. It appears to be carved out of one piece of wood, whereas the modern harp is distinctly in 3 sections. From the late Middle Ages on the harp remained virtually unchanged until the 18th c., except for the greater number of strings. Tuning was diatonic, and the problem of providing accidentals was tackled in different ways: the *double harp of the 16th and 17th c., with its 2 rows of strings, was one answer; the *Welsh triple harp of the 17th c., with its 3 rows, another answer. In the late 17th c. the *hook harp was invented, allegedly in the Tirol (documentation is lacking), with hooks set in the neck; when the strings were pressed against them, the pitch was raised by a semitone. Invention of the important pedal mechanism has been credited to several people: in 1720 Hochbrucker of Donauwörth and J. P. Vetter of Nürnberg produced a hook harp in which 5 pedals (C D F G A) were connected to the hooks by wires passing through the hollow pillar. When the F pedal was depressed, all the F's were raised by a semitone, etc. Subsequently the number of pedals was increased to 7. The harp was tuned to E♭ and could be played in 8 major and 5 minor keys. This type of action is known as "single action"; Naderman, the well-known Paris maker, used it for his harps. By 1752 the Parisian harp maker Cousineau, with his son, had improved the pedals, done away with the hooks that pulled the strings out of tune, and substituted for them small metal crutches (*"béquilles"*). In 1780 they doubled the number of pedals (to 14) to increase the pitch by a semitone, and tuned the harp in C♭, as it still is today. It could then be played in 15 keys. In 1792 Sébastien Érard of Paris, then in London, patented his improved single-action harp, doing away with the crutches and using instead metal forks (*fourchettes*), rotating brass discs with 2 projecting studs that gripped the string. In 1810 he patented his double-action Greek model harp, with elaborate scrollwork, reduced the number of pedals to 7, provided each with a half hitch and a whole hitch for raising the pitch by a semitone and a tone, respectively, and added a second fork for each string. These efforts had necessitated straightening the pillar in order to accommodate the pedal action. His nephew Pierre Érard further modified the harp in 1836 by spacing the strings farther apart and changing the column from Greek to Gothic. Today the pedals for D C B are placed to the player's left, those for E F G A to his right. A short-lived attempt was made to provide a damper pedal, and some older instrs. are still found with an eighth pedal placed to the right of the D pedal. Compass of the modern harp varies: the big concert model has 6½ octs., C^1–g^4, with 46 strings, and is *ca.* 175 cm. (5 ft. 8 in.) high. As already stated, it is tuned to C♭. In performance it is tilted back against the performer's right shoulder. The strings are plucked with thumbs and 3 fingers of each hand, and the right hand plays chiefly the higher-pitched strings; 19th-c. efforts to abolish the pedals resulted in the *chromatic harp, now forgotten. See: aeolian harp, angular harp, arched harp, chromatic harp, double harp, double-action harp, footed harp, frame harp, hook harp, Irish harp, keyed harp, Kru harp, shoulder harp. See also: adeudeu, adungu, akalumbe, apānkal, ardin, bīnt, bulu, cai dan bao, ceirnin, chang, changa, claasagh, clairseach, clarsach, column, condi, consonnante, cythara, domo, domu, dumo, ekidongo, ekihako, enanga, entongoli, eshirtu, fork action, gambareh, giš-ban, gundi, harpe d'harmonie, harpe ditale, harpe harmonico-forté, harpinella, harp lute, jank, Kafir harp, kalung, kimasa, kinanga, kiotang, komba, kondu, kugo, kundi, k'ung hu, lebed, lonfembe, loterokuma, luth des maîtres chanteurs, maringa, m'bagga, nanga, nebel, nedomu, neduma, ngombi, ngomo, nja, nkundi, ocht-tedach, ombi, opuk agoya, ore, orodo, otongoli, pa, para, salbāq, shiragi koto, shotang, shu k'ung hu, telein, télen, telyn, tilpanu, tsaung, tum, Welsh triple harp, zag-sal, zakkal, Zitherelegie, Zupfgeige (15, 133, 144, 169, 170);

2. Renaissance organ stop composed of regal pipes; a "harpe" is mentioned in Troyes in 1551.

Harpa, 1. believed to have been a generic name for stringed instrs. in ONorse; **2.** Lat., Port., Swed.: harp; **3.** Swed. name for the talharpa, jouhikantele, and bowed lyres; **4.** *tube zither of modern Mexico, with single string attached to a tuning peg.

Harp aeoline, organ stop, syn. of aeoline, 2.

Harpa gemina, Lat.: double harp.

Harpanetta, see: arpanetta.

Harpa-phone, vibraharp without propellers (89).

Harp bow (Ger.: *Harfenbogen*), idiochord *musical bow with several strings that pass over a notched stick or bridge, nowadays usually called harp zither (100).

Harp d'amour, see: harfenett d'amour.

Harpe, Dan., Fr.: harp.

Harpe à cadre, Fr.: frame harp.

Harpe à clavier, Fr.: keyed harp.

Harpe à crochets, Fr.: hook harp.

Harpe à double mouvement, Fr.: double-action harp.

Harpe angulaire, Fr.: angular harp.

Harpe à pédales, Fr.: pedal harp.

Harpe arquée, Fr.: arched harp.

Harpe à support, Fr.: footed harp.

Harpe chromatique, Fr.: chromatic harp.

Harpe-cithare, Fr.: harp zither.

Harpe d'Eole, Fr.: aeolian harp.

Harpe de verre, Fr.: glass harp.

Harpe d'harmonie, harp patented by Thory of Paris on Nov. 7, 1815, with copper strings and a specially built resonator. It was 2 m. (6½ ft.) high. Later it was furnished with a keyboard (158, 204).

Harpe ditale, small harp built by J. Pfeiffer of Paris *ca.* 1830, with flat resonator and 7 keys for raising the pitch of the strings. Tuned in E♭ with a compass eb^0–e^3. Although the name is reminiscent of the *dital harp, Pfeiffer's instr. was based on the *harpinella (176).

Harpe éolienne, 1. Fr.: aeolian harp; **2.** harmonium stop invented by Victor Mustel of Paris, consisting of 2 rows of free reeds tuned very slightly apart, thus causing beats (89).

Harpe epaulée, Fr.: shoulder harp.

Harpe fourchue, Fr.: Kru harp.

Harpe-guitare (Fr.), **1.** term applied to the *bow lute, now generally called

pluriarc, both in Fr. and Engl.; **2.** the *harp guitar and its successor instrs.

Harpe harmonico-forté, harp patented by Keyser de l'Isle in Paris on June 9, 1809, with 7 bichord bass strings of brass in addition to the regular harp strings. The extra strings were struck by hammers controlled by pedals (204).

Harpe-luth (Fr.), *chromatic harp built by Pleyel, Lyon & Cie. of Paris, with wire strings and a compass A^1–$g\#^3$ (176).

Harpfe, MHGer.: harp.

Harp guitar (Fr.: *guitare-harpe;* Ger.: *Gitarrenharfe*), **1.** stringed instr. invented by Edward Light of London in 1798, intended to replace the guitar. Neck and head were those of a guitar, but the body formed a triangle. Its 8 strings were tuned in E♭: $Ab^0 Bb^0 eb^0 gb^0 eb^1 g^1 bb^1$, notated a 6th higher, in C, f^0–g^2. For Light's improved version see: harp lute guitar; **2.** harp guitar furnished with a keyboard and 7 pedals, invented by Carl Müller of Bavaria in 1836, according to Pontécoulant (89, 158, 204).

Harpichordum, med. Lat.: arpicordo.

Harpinella, a small harp in lyra form, built in 1818 by Marstrand of Copenhagen, bichord, with 7 finger keys for changes of pitch. Tuned in E♭ with a compass C^0–g^3. *Ca.* 75 cm. (30 in.) high. See also: dital harp, harpe ditale.

Harp lute (Fr.: *harpe-luth;* Ger.: *Harfenlaute*), **1.** chordophone in which the plane of the strings is at right angles to the belly; the strings pass over a notched, vertical bridge. Found only in W. Africa. See also: bolon, dunsi-koni, gingiru, kasso, khalam, konimesin, kora, kunting, o'rdu, sanku, sarong, seron; **2.** instr. invented by Edward Light of London in the first years of the 19th c., successor to his *harp lute guitar. The new instr. was characterized by a greater number of strings, usually 11 or 12, of gut, the off-board strings running from a harp-shaped neck supported by a pillar. As were all of Light's instrs., this was tuned E♭ B♭^{0} e♭^{0} f^0 g^0 a♭^{0} b♭^{0} c^1 d^1 e♭^{1} f^1

$g^1 b\flat^1 (e\flat^2)$ and was notated a 6th higher, in C. For its successor instr. see *British harp lute. See also: guitare-harpe, Regency harp lute; 3. Praetorius depicted a "newly invented" instr. that he called a lute, but it was played like a harp, having a lute body and some 2 dozen strings stretched between a frontal string fastener and the pegbox of a laterally bent, lute-like neck (89, 100, 159, 170).

Harp lute guitar (Fr.: *guitare-harpe*), an improved *harp guitar, introduced by Edward Light of London *ca.* 1800. Its neck and head were like a guitar with a double pegbox. In addition to the stopped strings of the harp guitar it had 4 off-board strings. It was tuned $B\flat^0 e\flat^0 f^0 g^0/$ $a\flat^0 b\flat^0 c^1 d^1 e\flat^1 g^1 b\flat^1$, and was notated a 6th higher, in C. For Light's successor instr. see: harp lute. On Oct. 6, 1825, a London music teacher, Mordaunt Levien, took out a Fr. *brevet d'importation* (import license) for the harp lute guitar under the name of *guitare-harpe*. He is said to have also improved the instr. by adding 3 thumb ditals (89, 176, 204).

Harpo-lyre, guitar in form of a lyra, invented by Jean-François Salomon of Besançon in 1827 and patented March 19, 1829. A guitar body was combined with 3 fretted necks bearing a total of 21 strings; the middle neck carried 6 strings tuned like those of a guitar ($E^0 A^0 d^0$ $g^0 b^0 e^1$); the left, or chromatic, neck carried 7 spun strings tuned $A^0 B\flat^0$ $c^0 d\flat^0 d^0 e^0$; and the right, or diatonic, neck carried 8 gut strings tuned $c^1 d^1$ $e^1 f^1 g^1 a^1 b^1 c^2$ (132, 204).

Harppu, 1. Finn.: harp; **2.** name also given to the jouhikantele.

Harpsichord [med. Lat.: *harpichordum*] (Fr.: *clavecin;* Ger.: *Kielflügel, Cembalo;* It.: *cembalo, clavicembalo*), stringed keyboard instr. in shape of an elongated wing, in which the strings are plucked and run from front to back of the instr., parallel to the individual keys. The keyboard occupies the short front side; the long bass side, to the player's left, is known as the spine, the short treble side as the cheekpiece, the long curved section adjoining it is called the bentside, and the diagonal wall at the far end, the tail. Directly behind the visible portion of the keys comes the name-board, which reaches from spine to cheekpiece; behind this lies the wrest plank, or pin block, in which the tuning pins are inserted and which bears the nut(s). To its rear is a gap for the slides, which hold the jacks, after which comes the soundboard, or belly, the front edge of which rests on the belly rail. The soundboard bears the curved bridge(s). The action of a harpsichord, which is also that of the *spinet and *virginal, consists of jacks provided with plectra. Jacks are flat pieces of hardwood, usually fruit-wood, set upright on the rear end of each key. A deep slot is cut in its upper end to provide space for a wooden tongue that pivots on a pin. A plectrum of quill, leather or other material is inserted in a slit or hole cut in the tongue's upper portion. A smaller saw cut in the top of the jack, parallel to the large slot, holds a piece of thick cloth, nowadays felt, that constitutes a damper. Such are the elements of the traditional action. When the key is at rest, the top of the plectrum is about 1 mm. below the string; when it is depressed, the plectrum flexes and plucks the string in passing upward; when the key is released, the string is by-passed as soon as the plectrum touches it by an escaping movement of the pivoted tongue; the tongue is then returned to its normal position by a spring. Modern instrs. are additionally provided with end screws set in the bottom of the jack to regulate its height, *i.e.,* the vertical relationship of plectrum to string, and a voicing screw is set in the upper portion to regulate the angle of the tongue, or the critical horizontal relationship between plectrum and string. The damping system also often varies on modern instrs. Jacks are maintained in an upright position by movable upper slides and an immobile lower guide (on many It. instrs. the 2 are combined into 1 element). The slide is a long, narrow strip of wood perforated with as many holes as there are jacks to a row, and is placed between soundboard and pin block, on the same level. The lower guide, normally invisible because of its position beneath the slides, is a boxlike affair of wood, honeycombed with holes for all jacks of the instr. The jacks are prevented from being thrown clear of the instr. during performance by a cover, called the jack rail, placed close above them. This is padded with thick cloth, and its height is so regulated as to serve simultaneously as a check for the keys: when the top of the jack hits the jack rail, the key cannot be depressed further. As almost without exception harpsichords have more than one set of strings and row of jacks, provision is made for placing the jacks in a plucking, or "on," position, and a silent, or "off," position, so that they may be combined or not at the player's will, usually accomplished by shifting the slides (some It. harpsichords form an exception to this rule; see below). On many 16th- and 17th-c. instrs. the slides pierced the cheekpiece and projected a few inches beyond, within reach of the player's right hand; on 18th-c. instrs. registration was effected by hand stops, knee levers, or registration pedals connected with the slides. Harpsichords are normally provided with 2, 3, or 4 rows of jacks (in the 18th c. as many as 6 rows occur), and 2, 3, or 4 sets of strings (in the 18th c. exceptionally 5). The basic set of strings was at 8′ pitch, also called unison pitch (Ger.: äqual), expressions taken over from organ terminology. Often these were supplemented by a set of shorter strings at 4′ pitch, also called octave register (Fr. 18th-c. term: petit jeu; Ger. Spinettzug or Kornettzug); in 18th-c. Germany a longer set, at 16′ pitch, was occasionally added. Instrs. with only 4′ strings were made from the 16th to the 18th c.

(called cembaletto ottavino in It.). Harpsichords have been built with 1, 2, and exceptionally 3 manuals; 2-manual instrs. generally had a coupler permitting the jacks of the upper keyboard to be played also from the lower, thus adding to the tutti. This was usually accomplished by pushing in the upper manual about 1 cm.; alternately the lower manual was pulled out that amount. Engl. harpsichords were not provided with couplers; instead the upper-manual jacks were "dog-legged" so that they could rest indifferently on the keys of either manual. There never was any standardization of size, disposition, or decoration, although the national schools of harpsichord making have their own pronounced characteristics.

Like the history of most other prepiano keyboard instrs., that of the harpsichord is not yet fully known. Organ keyboards and drawn iron wire preceded the emergence of stringed keyboard instrs. in the 14th c. But as at that time iron wire could be drawn only to short lengths, the earliest stringed keyboard instrs. must of necessity have been short and comparatively high-pitched. Whether or not the long (harpsichord) form preceded the square (spinet) form is still unknown. Both represent adaptations of a keyboard to a psaltery, as is evidenced not only by the nomenclature (see: cembalo) but also by the ornamental *roses that appear from the earliest depictions on. In 1404 Eberhart Cersne enumerated among the instrs. of his day a clavicymbolum, the earliest known name of the harpsichord, commonly spelled clavicimbalum (q.v. for early references). This word seems to have designated specifically the harpsichord during the 15th c., but Virdung and Scaliger in the 16th c. confuse the terminology by using it to denote a square instr. The name indicates a mechanized psaltery, a cimbal with claves. The earliest reproductions so far known are those of the Weimar Wunderbuch and of Henri Arnaut of Zwolle's treatise, both dating from ca. 1440. Arnaut gives a drawing to scale of the clavicimbalum, also a description and drawings of no fewer than 4 actions. None of these resembles our present harpsichord action as described above. His Latin is difficult and the illustrations are not clear, but it seems that in 3 of the actions the action parts were not set freely on the keys, but rather were attached in a groove that ran the breadth of the instr., and apparently furnished with metal plectra. In the fourth action the jacks appear to have been thrown against the strings somewhat as they are in the *Tangentenflügel. Quill plectra were also known to Arnaut, as elsewhere in the ms. he mentions a monochord with quills. With the freedom offered by a combination of different types of action and different forms of case, it is not surprising that precision of terminology was slow to develop. Arnaut writes typically that with a given action one can make a *clavicimbalum* or a *clavichordium* or a *dulce melos*. Or again, ". . . *posset fieri quod clavichordium sonaret ut clavicembalum*" (it can be made that the clavichord sounds like a harpsichord). Arnaut knew already of harpsichords with 2 sets of strings, but these were arranged one above the other and both were plucked by the same jack. *Ca.* 1460 Paulus Paulirinus described a combination quill-plucked upright harpsichord and portative organ. In 1461 Sesto Tantini of Modena requests payment for a *clavicembalo.* The complicated Lat. word had appeared in a number of vernacular forms from 1429 on (see: clavicembalum). In fact the instr. was so familiar by the end of the c. that an inventory of 1503 records 2 "old" *clavecímbanos* that had belonged to Isabella the Catholic of Spain. In 1514 a harpsichord with 2 "registers" was built for Pope Leo V, and as the instr. took much of its terminology from the organ, 2 "registers" at that time probably meant 2 rows of jacks plucking 2 (horizontally arranged)

sets of strings. This at any rate is the disposition of the earliest preserved harpsichord, made by Jerome of Pesaro in 1521 and housed in the Victoria and Albert Museum, London. A 4' stop occurs from 1538 on, and 3 registers were known by the 1570's. The "ii payer of virginalls in one coffer with iiii stoppes," listed in 1530 among the Privy Purse expenses of Henry VIII, were assumed by A. J. Hipkins to have been a 2-manual harpsichord, but this assumption is more than questionable, as no reference is made of a 2-manual harpsichord until late in the c. The Innsbruck court bought a Venetian "double" harpsichord in 1580; a *Symphonei* with 4 stops was among the Brandenburg court instrs. in 1582, and the earliest surviving 2-manual harpsichords date from 1590. A Dresden inventory of 1593 enumerates 3 "Instruments" with 2 keyboards. The "ii payer" of Henry VIII probably referred to 2 separate instruments contained in 1 case; the British acquired at an early date the habit of referring to their keyboard instrs. in the dual, and the terms "a pair of organs" and "a pair of virginals" were common. Until the introduction of the word *harpsichord,* in use from 1607 on, harpsichords were known in Britain as virginals, and even later in the 17th c. the phrase "harpsicon or virginal" is frequently encountered. Samuel Pepys is one of the earliest writers to employ specific terms, although he does not do so consistently; in the entry for April 4, 1668, of his diary he mentions virginal, spinet, and harpsichord. Before the word *clavecin* was in use (from 1611 on), the French called their harpsichord an *épinette,* or spinet, and this usage lingered on for a good c. Thus D'Anglebert, who in 1664 had become harpsichordist to Louis XIV, received in addition to his salary the sum of 270 livres *"pour la nourriture de son porte-épinette"* (for food for his spinet-bearer).

During the 16th c. the harpsichord appears primarily as an adjunct to the organ and a practice instr. for organists. As a secular instr. it was restricted in its use to lighter entertainment: writers such as Diruta make it plain that performance of serious music on quilled instrs. was considered bad form and as affecting the dignity of the organ. In its role as *continuo* instr. in the 17th c. it was still governed by organists, and in its use as a solo instr. its outstanding performers and composers during the *grand siècle* were organists. Only in the 18th c. did it manage to free itself from this link, and schools of solo-harpsichord building flourished in England, France, and Germany. The earlier schools, those of Italy and the Low Countries, barely survived the 17th c.

Of the different schools of harpsichord building, that of Italy is the oldest. The typical It. instr. had a single manual; up to the 18th c. both case and soundboard, unadorned except for decorative moldings or ivory studs, were made of very thin cypress. Fioravanti writes in 1564 that wood used for making them must have been dried for several years and should be as old as possible so that it will not swell in the humidity. The short treble scale of It. instrs. results in a sharp incurve of the bentside. Manual compass was commonly 4 oct., C^0–c^3, with short oct., and the disposition was 2 sets of strings at 8′ pitch. A 4′ register was rarely added. It. instrs. were placed in a separate outer case with lid and stand, from which they were withdrawn for performance; cases were often handsomely painted or provided with ornamental sculpture. From *ca.* 1700 on the frail instr. was built directly into its outer housing; compass and disposition remained unchanged. On many It. harpsichords made prior to the 18th c. the slides are fixed and cannot be moved. Registration on such instrs. was effected by very slightly pulling out the keyboard, thereby disengaging the back row of jacks, according to Trichet. The other great school of harpsichord making was

centered at Antwerp, in the Low Countries, where quantities of not only harpsichords but also smaller keyboard instrs. were turned out from the early 16th c. on. The Flem. instrs. were of more robust construction than their It. counterparts: the casework was of considerably thicker softwood, the soundboards of pine or spruce, decorated with paintings. Case and lid were either painted or decorated with printed paper on which Lat. mottoes were often applied. The makers were members of the guild of St. Luke, which required them to sign their instruments by some prominent device, the most usual one being a pewterware "rose" bearing the maker's initials, inserted into the soundhole. From a letter by Duarte to Constantijn Huygens in the mid-17th c. we learn that at that time Antwerp makers completed their instrs. even to the stringing before sending them *nud,* as it was called in Fr., to the workshop of a painter to receive their ornamentation, which was governed by the taste of the owner and of the times. Compass of Flem. 16th-c. instrs. was 4 octs., C^0–c^3, with short oct., increased in the 17th c. to 4½ octs. The Antwerp school is remembered today chiefly for its most illustrious members, the Ruckers dynasty, who worked there for a c. from the last quarter of the 16th c. on. The beauty of their tone was such that long after their musical usefulness had been impaired, the instr. would be rebuilt and reornamented to conform to prevailing fashion. The large majority (nearly ⅘) of the surviving harpsichords by members of this family, made between 1590 and 1640, have 2 manuals. According to Quirin van Blankenburg and the evidence of surviving instrs. in Belgium, Britain, and Germany, these originally transposed by half an oct. (see: transposing keyboards), in keeping with differences of pitch of contemporary organs. Each manual disposed of an 8′ stop and a 4′ stop; needless to say, the manuals could not be coupled. In the middle of the 17th c. and probably owing to the efforts of Jean Couchet, nephew of Johannes Ruckers, the manuals were brought into unison, only one of the two 4′ stops being retained; this was actuated from the lower keyboard, which became the *forte* manual, the upper manual never controlling more than one 8′ stop. The Ruckers tradition exercised a strong influence on the Engl. and Fr. schools of building in the 18th c., and their instrs. remained prized objects in France until the Revolution: of 23 harpsichords kept in the king's library at Versailles in 1780, no fewer than 11 were by members of the Ruckers family.

Fr. instrs. of the 15th and 16th c. seem to have been inspired by It. models. Although the names of various Fr. builders have come down to us, extremely few instrs. have survived, and our slender knowledge of Fr. instrs. prior to the 18th c. is derived chiefly from literary sources. Mersenne (in 1636) depicts instrs. of the It. type and, still much under the influence of the organ, also mentions obviously experimental models, which he calls *eudisharmoste*, with 4 registers at 8′, 6′, 4′, and 2′ pitches. Trichet, *ca.* 1640, speaks of 2- and 3-manual harpsichords with 7 or 8 *jeux;* here again one suspects experimental models. Fr. harpsichord making came into its own in the 18th c., when an important school developed, headed by the Blanchet family and their pupil Pascal Taskin of Theux, in the Low Countries, based on the Ruckers tradition, and with the Ruckers scale. A specialty of these particular makers was the *mise à *ravalement* and rebuilding of Ruckers and other older instrs. Taskin applied knee levers to some of the instrs. he rebuilt, and introduced a very ingenious machine or composition stop. In 1768 he introduced plectra of *buff leather, which gave a softer tone than quill or ordinary leather. The *peau de bufle,* as it was called, created quite a sensation in Paris. But to no avail; it was an ill-omened time for harpsichords, the year that the world's first piano recital took place, with Johann Christian

Bach playing a square piano by Johann Christoph Zumpe in London. Nonetheless, there were still 19 harpsichord makers working in Paris alone in 1788, together with 16 pianoforte makers, according to the *Calendrier Musical Universel* for that year.

The school of Brit. harpsichord making is linked directly to Antwerp by Tabel. This maker had learned his trade there from the Ruckers descendants and became the teacher of Jacob Kirkman and Burkat Shudi, who were leading Engl. builders whose output falls mainly within the second half of the 18th c. Engl. harpsichords of this period are far more standardized than Continental models. They are characterized by a compass F^1–f^3, a larger scale than the Flem., casework of walnut or mahogany, some with *Venetian swell (after 1769), some 2-manual instrs. with machine stop (1750 on), and all 2-manual instrs. with *lute stop.

Extant Ger. instrs. are extremely rare, even those of the 18th c. A characteristic feature found on many of them is the rounded tail resulting from a double curve in the bentside (this is already present on a *clavicytherium depicted by Praetorius). Another is the addition of a set of strings at 16′ pitch on larger instrs., typically with a soundboard of their own. Handel had a 16′ one on his (now lost) Shudi harpsichord.

The revival of harpsichord building originated in France in 1888 with Érard and Pleyel, to be followed by Arnold Dolmetsch of England in 1896, and by numerous other makers in the Old World and New World since. From the onset 2 different conceptions of the modern instr. were manifest: one aimed at producing an instr. that would withstand the rigors of climate and modern transportation (alas, where is the *porte-épinette* of D'Anglebert?) and that would have a tone powerful enough to be heard in modern concert halls; the other, to reproduce the instrs. of a specific school of the past. A number of builders have since attempted a compromise between these 2 directions. Registration is effected on modern harpsichords by pedals instead of hand stops, with some exceptions.

Mechanical harpsichords were known by Henry VIII's time. The inventory of his instrs. (1547) included a "virginal that goethe with a whele without playing upon." The keys of such instrs. were depressed by the studs of a revolving barrel actuated by clockwork. Mersenne describes this type of action. See also: cembaletto ottavino, cembalo angelico, clavichordium, enharmonic harpsichord, Ibachord, lute harpsichord, pedal harpsichord, piano-harpsichord, and the following harpsichord stops: bassoon, buff, guitar, harp, Lautenzug, lute, telyn, 2.

Harpsichord stop, syn. of cembalo stop (92).

Harpsicon, corr. of harpsichord.

Harp stop, 1. on harpsichords (Fr.: *registre de luth;* Ger.: *Lautenzug*) a series of pieces of buff leather, felt, etc., mounted on a slide, placed alongside the nut, that can be pushed up against a set of strings, muting them and giving a pizzicato effect. Also known as buff stop, guitar stop; **2.** on Ger. pianos (Ger.: *Harfenzug*) a strip of wood to which a fringe of wool or silk was attached formerly and that could be interposed between strings and hammers; **3.** in Engl. pianos (known as "the harp") a device for interposing strips of leather between hammer and one string of each course. The hammers were shifted so as to strike only one string (27, 92).

Harp-theorbo, *harp lute guitar of Edward Light of London, *ca.* 1800, with a double neck (176).

Harp Ventura, chromatic *harp lute patented by Angelo Benedetto Ventura of London on Feb. 21, 1828, with a crescent-shaped cutout of the body to facilitate stopping high notes, and a hollow neck containing a device for raising the pitch of the strings by a semitone. Also called Ventura guitar (89, 176).

Harp zither (Fr.: *harpe-cithare;*

pseudo-arc; Ger.: *Harfenzither*), **1.** idiochord *musical bow with several strings held by a vertical bridge. Found in W. Africa among the Fan, Bule, Muri, Ossieba, Senufo, Teke, Yaunde, Yola. Called harp bow or Fan harp by some writers. See: mvet, nguomi, nkraton, okiribongo; **2.** name given to a 19th-c. European zither in harp form, with short pillar and usually 5 melody strings. The lower portion of the body may be circular or semicircular, with a straight side parallel to the melody strings (128).

Harzzither (Ger.: zither of the Harz Mountains), syn. of Thüringer Zither.

Hasosra, see: hatzozroth.

Hatong, bamboo panpipes of W. Java, usually played in pairs, 1 having 2 or 3 large pipes, the other 10–14 small ones (121).

Hatong manuk, short bamboo *whistle flute or *ring flute of W. Java, used as a bird whistle (121).

Hatranatra, slit drum of the SW. Malagasy Republic (171).

Hatsu, syn. of batsu.

Hatuntaqui, slit drum of the Cara Indians of Otavalo, Ecuador, used as a signal instr. Nowadays abbr. to tontaqui (105).

Hatun-tinya, syn. of huancar.

Hatzozroth (Heb., pl. of *hazozrah*), straight trumpets of biblical Israel, made of silver, ending in a bell, and always played in pairs. At a very early period they became the insignia of priests and served both as ritual and signal instrs. They corresponded to the *salpinx and the *tuba. *Ca.* 90 cm. (3 ft.) long (89, 170).

Hauptwerk, Ger.: great organ.

Hausse, Fr.: frog. Also called talon.

Hautbois (Fr.: high wood), **1.** Fr.: shawm, oboe. The term has been in use since the late 15th c. for the higher-pitched shawms, as opposed to the lower-pitched grosbois. The word was also used in England, where it is first recorded in 1561 (as howeboies); **2.** organ stop of reed pipes of small scale, at 16' or 8' pitch, with bodies of normal length (62, 79).

Hautbois baryton (Fr.), oboe in C, an oct. below the ordinary oboe, built by Triébert of Paris ca. 1825 for oboist Vogt, with a bulb-shaped, upturned foot joint. Also built by Henri Brod (14, 25).

Hautbois d'amour (Fr.), see: oboe d'amore.

Hautbois de chasse (Fr.), see: oboe da caccia.

Hautbois de forêt (Fr.), see: oboe da caccia.

Hautbois de Poitou, Renaissance reedcap shawm of France. It had a conical bore, 6 single fingerholes, 1 double fingerhole, and a rear thumbhole. Our only source for data is Mersenne, who lists 3 sizes: *dessus* in D, *taille* in G, and *basse* (in G?), the last doubled back on itself like a bassoon and furnished with an open key protected by a *fontanelle. Together with the *cornemuse de Poitou these instrs. formed a consort that was represented in the Grande Écurie du Roi of Louis XIV for a while. Its Ger. equivalent, which became obs. earlier, was the *Rauschpfeife (114, 176).

Hautbois pastoral, name given by Paul Évette and Ernest Schaeffer of Paris, ca. 1885, to their oboe in high G or A♭ (126, 176).

Hautboy, obs. Engl. form of hautbois.

Haute-contre (Fr.), **1.** any alto instr.; **2.** baroque name of a small viola of ca. 64 cm. (25¼ in.) long, notated in alto clef. According to Mersenne, it was second in size of the 24 *violons du Roi,* but third in size (out of 5) of the stringed instrs. of an "ordinary musician." Daniel Merck (in 1695) equates it with the viola, violetta, or soprano viol. The tuning was that of the viola (26, 94, 170).

Haute-contre de violon, see: hautecontre, 2; the *Encyclopédie méthodique* of 1751 identifies it with the *quinte and the *taille.

Havirare, panpipes of the Camayura Indians of Brazil (105).

Hawaiian guitar, guitar with metal strings raised on a steel nut so high that they cannot be stopped against the fingerboard; instead, they are stopped by the pressure of a steel bar held in the player's hand and made to slide along the strings, thus giving a characteristic wavering or glissando effect. It is laid flat across the performer's knees. Also called steel guitar (59, 151).

Hayllaquepa, *marine-shell trumpet of ancient Peru. See also: quepa (80, XII).

Hazolahi, 2-headed cylindrical or conical drum of the Malagasy Republic, always played in pairs. Also called manandria (172).

Hazozrah, sing. of hatzozroth.

Hearpe [ONorse: *harpa*], OEngl.: harp.

Hearpe-naegel, OEngl.: plectrum; literally: harp nail.

Heckelclarina (Ger.: *Heckelklarina*), woodwind instr. similar to the saxophone, devised by the firm of Wilhelm Heckel in Biebrich in 1890 to play the part of the shepherd's pipe in Wagner's *Tristan und Isolde.* A soprano instr. in E♭, played with a single reed, with a compass of a^0–$c\sharp^3$ notated a tone higher, in theory at least, as it is questionable whether the instr. was ever actually built. See also: Heckel-piccoloclarina, Tristanschalmei (89, 176).

Heckelphonclarinet, a wooden saxophone with wide conical bore and compass d^0–c^3, made by W. Heckel of Biebrich in 1907 (89, 176).

Heckelphone, woodwind instr. invented by the firm of W. Heckel of Biebrich in 1904, with conical bore, played with a double reed, pitched in C at baritone range, and often referred to as a baritone oboe, which it is not, having a far wider bore than that instr. Built in straight form, of maple, it terminates in a bulb bell. The double reed is carried on a short, wide crook. The body is in 3 sections and measures ca. 120 cm. (4 ft.). Compass A^0–g^2. In addition to the baritone, there exist 2 less successful sopraninos: the Terz-Heckelphone in E♭ with a compass d¹–g³, notated a 3rd lower, and a piccolo in F with compass e¹–a³, notated a 4th lower.

Heckel-piccoloclarina (Ger.: *Heckelpikkoloklarina*), sopranino *Heckelclarina in E♭ with a compass d¹–a³, notated a 3rd lower (176).

Hedeiaphone, organ stop invented by Robert Hope-Jones (d. 1914). In lieu of pipes it consisted of metal plaques made to vibrate by alternating currents of air (198).

Heerhorn, see: Herhorn.

Heerpauke (Ger.: army drum), **1.** obs. Ger.: kettledrum. The word is recorded from the early 16th c. on (88); **2.** organ stop consisting of a few low-pitched flue pipes in the pedal, sounded simultaneously. *Cf.* Sumber, Hersumber (167).

Heertrommel, organ stop, the same as Sumber or Heerpauke (133).

Hehei, heheiba, panpipes of the Cubeo Indians of the Upper Amazon (105).

Heike biwa, biwa of Japan, smaller than the gaku biwa, with 4 strings and 5 raised frets. The strings are stopped between the frets, not against them, as on the gaku biwa (135).

He kum, fiddle of Korea that corresponds to the erh hsien of China. Also called kekum (66).

Helicon [Gk. *helikos*, coiled] (Fr.: *hélicon;* Ger.: *Helikon;* It.: *helicon, elicon*), **1.** large bass tuba built in circular form for convenience in carrying, first used in Russia (by 1845), according to Wilhelm Wieprecht. In 1849 Ignaz Stowasser of Vienna started making helicons to Wieprecht's specifications, for military band use. The bell rested on the player's left shoulder, the tube passing under his right arm. Higher-pitched instrs. were occasionally built in this shape also, but it was the bass and contrabass that became pop. in Europe and the U.S. Helicons have been built in F or E♭, C or B♭; **2.** organ stop, see: bass tuba, 3.

Hélicon trombone, see: trombone da tracolla.

Helicor, var. of helicon.

Helikon, Ger.: helicon.

Helikonposaune (Ger.), contrabass trombone built by A. Richard Weller of Markneukirchen, 1898, in helicon form with slide mechanism. Compass F¹–f¹ (176).

Hellebylle [N. Ger.: *hellen,* to sound + *bellen,* to strike], early form of Hillebille (169).

Hellertion [inventors' names], monophonic electrophonic instr. of the electronic type, both imitative and nonimitative, invented by B. Helberger and P. Lertes of Leipzig in 1930, with a stretched metal band forming a "manual" (*Bandmanual*) controlled by the pressure of a finger. Later other "manuals" were added, so that several monophonic bands could be played by both hands (W. Meyer-Eppler: *Elektrische Klangerzeugung,* Bonn, 1949).

Hellflöte (Ger.), organ stop of open flue pipes, a narrow cylindrical flute stop, the same as Hellpfeife (133).

Hellhorn [inventor's name], brass *baritone made by Ferdinand Hell of Vienna *ca.* 1843 (126, 176).

Hellpfeife, syn. of Hellflöte. The prefix *hell* means "clear" and denotes tone color.

Helmzither (Ger.: helmet zither), see: Salzburg zither.

Hemat-hāllilīm, bag of (or for) pipes of the ancient Hebrews, not a bagpipe (170).

Heng chok, *cross flute of Korea, cylindrical, with 3 or 4 front fingerholes and 1 or 2 thumbholes. Another aperture between blowhole and fingerholes is covered with a thin membrane—a *mirliton device (66).

Heng ti, name of the ti in Shantung Province, China (142).

Henhel, var. of hahel.

Heptacorde, name given by Raoul to his 7-stringed bass gamba at the surprisingly late date of 1828 (158).

Heptagonon (Gk.: seven-sided), unidentified instr. of ancient Greece (144).

Herald's trumpet (Ger.: *Fanfarentrompete, Heroldstrompete*), **1.** name given in modern times to a med. straight trumpet of the type illustrated in the 13th c. *Cantigas de Santa María;* **2.** 20th-c. trumpet in form of a natural trumpet, either valveless or with 2 or 3 piston valves. See also: Aïda trumpet.

Heraphone, musical box of the late 19th c. (38).

Heravoa [Arab. *ar-rabāb*], onestringed fiddle of the Malagasy Republic (171).

Herebyme [OEngl. *heres*, army + *byme*, trumpet], med. Engl. bugle.

Hērēroka, *panpipes of the Yahuna Indians of S. America (105).

Herhorn (MHGer.), med. horn of metal, slightly curved, *ca.* 5 ft. long, a signal instr. played with the bell turned upward. *Cf.* Wic-horn (161).

Herkulesphone, a family of brass horns created 1888 by J. J. Chediwa of Odessa, for Russ. military bands, with very wide bore: E♭ cornet, 2 B♭ cornets, 2 althorns, tenor horn, baritone, E♭ bombardon, B♭ bombardon (176).

Hermione, *automatophone patented by Calba of Malzeville on Aug. 3, 1899, with perforated paper discs (204).

Herpfe, MHGer.: harp.

Herrach, Cat.: cog rattle (132).

Hersumber, Hersumper [MHGer. *Her*, army + *sumber*, grain measure], 14–15th-c. Ger. military drum. See also: Sumber (169).

Hetupue, panpipes of the Coto Indians of Peru and Ecuador, with 10 pipes (105).

Hevehe, bull-roarer of the Elema people of Papua. Also called beure hevehe (201).

Hevoa, bull-roarer of the Elema people of Papua. Also called hevoa bobobobo (201).

Hewgag (19th-c. U.S.) [?gewgaw], **1.** single-string banjo with a short keyboard on the fingerboard, invented 1884

(Sachs in *Zeitschrift für Instrumentenbau,* V); **2.** mirliton composed of a tube with a parchment-covered hole, a child's toy, first mentioned 1858 (Oxford English Dictionary).

Hi, porcelain percussion cup of Japan (157).

Hiang te, syn. of sona.

Hibernicon, contrabass and tenor woodwind instr. closely resembling Frichot's *bass-horn, invented by Rev. Joseph Rogerson Cotter of Castlemagner, County Cork, patented 1823. The contrabass had a conical tube 5 m. (16½ ft.) long, terminating in a bell, with 8 keys, pitched in D. No specimen has survived (89 Morley-Pegge).

Hibiligizo, small drum of the Bashi of Ruanda, used primarily for dancing (139).

Hichiriki, short cylindrical oboe of Japan of W. Asiatic origin, with conical bore, known in Japan since the 8th c. Formerly made of hardwood, bone, or horn, nowadays usually of bamboo lacquered on the inside and bound with cherry or wisteria bark, with 7 front fingerholes and 2 rear thumbholes. The thick double reed is maintained in shape by a keeper ring of cane. The hichiriki does not overblow the oct. Both reed and fingering are reminiscent of the later *monaulos as found in Egypt. Employed in *gagaku* music. 18 cm. (7 in.) long (89 Baines, 135, 157).

Hiefhorn (Ger.) [*Hief*, sound of a hunter's horn], med. Ger. bugle that maintained itself as a hunting horn up to modern times. It was made in 3 sizes: Rüderhorn, the largest; Mittelhorn, medium-sized (*cf.* moienel); and Zink. Later the word was changed to *Hifthorn. Ordinarily of horn, it was also made of metal and even ivory (88, 144, 169).

Hierochord, single-string hurdy-gurdy invented in 1824 by A. Schmidt, a singing teacher, of Greifswald, Germany, for accompanying singers in school and church (169).

Hifthorn, later name of the Hiefhorn.

Both instr. and name are still in use (161).

High hat, choke cymbals used in rhythm bands.

Highland pipe, mouth-blown bagpipe of Scotland, the oldest extant specimen of which dates from 1409. This has a long blowpipe, conical chanter with 8 holes, and 2 tenor drones set in 1 stock. Around 1700 a third (bass) drone was added. Nowadays the bag is of sheepskin, with 5 stocks. The chanter has a conical bore, 7 front fingerholes, and a rear thumbhole, is furnished with a double reed, and has a compass of g^1-a^2. The 3 drones spread out fanwise: the 2 tenors are 38 cm. (15 in.) long, tuned to a^0; the bass is twice as long and is tuned an oct. lower. In the past, however, drones were occasionally tuned a 5th apart. Highland pipes are made in 3 sizes, the smallest of which are chamber pipes. Also called Great pipe (13, 89).

Hi hat, the same as high hat.

Hikile, syn. of khakkhara (1).

Hilezkilak [*ezkila*], Basque: funeral bell (56).

Hillebille, N. Ger. percussion board, 80 by 20 cm. (32 by 8 in.) in size, struck with 2 mallets. Formerly known as Hellebylle, it was introduced to Brunswick from the Erzgebirge and used as a signal instr. Today it serves only during carnival (169).

Hin, bronze bell of Shan State, Burma, with a wooden clapper. It hangs from a horseshoe-shaped frame placed on the backs of pack animals (172).

Hintersatz (Ger.), in med. organs those pipes which stood behind the front pipes (Vordersatz or préstant). During the Renaissance this developed into a mixture—the Grossmixtur of Schlick's age—of pipes at higher pitches than those of the front pipes. As Grossmixtur, the pipes were wide-scaled principals, nonrepeating, composed of octs. and quints, later also with tierces. Praetorius gives the disposition of a 42–44 rank mixture of this nature, containing pipes at 16′,

8′, 5⅓′, 4′, 2⅔′, 2′, 1⅓′, 1′, ⅔′ pitches. A c. earlier Schlick had compared its sound to the screaming of pigs. Also called Locatz (133).

Hiohkat, scraper of the Papago Indians of the W. U.S., consisting of a pair of sticks, one of which is curved and notched, the other smooth. Sometimes the end of the notched stick is set upon an upturned basket, which then acts as resonator. It is 45–60 cm. (18–24 in.) long (51).

Hirdolis, hirdulis [Gk. *hydraulos*], syn. of magrepha. The word occurs in Talmudic commentaries (170).

Hirschruf (Ger.: deer call), small conical tube, usually of horn but also of wood or marine snail, with which hunters imitate the cry of a deer. Played with a cup mouthpiece. *Ca.* 30 cm. (12 in.) long (88, 132).

Hirtibüchel [Ger. *Hirt,* shepherd + *Büchel*], Swiss goatherd's horn with which he announces his arrival in the village.

Hitotsu gane, small gong of Japan set on a tripod, similar to the atari gane but struck on its outside surface. Often used in Buddhist music, also at festivals (135).

Hitoyogiri, *end-blown flute of Japan, actually a shorter, thinner version of the shaku-hachi, and made of bamboo except for the upper rim, which is of wood. It first appeared in the Muromachi period (1534–1615), played by mendicant priests. By the 19th c. it had become very rare, and attempts are currently under way to revive it. 53 cm. (21 in.) long (135, 157).

Hitsu no koto, obs. Jap. koto of great antiquity, said to have originally possessed 50 strings, subsequently reduced to 23 or even fewer. It measured 2.45 m. (8 ft.) in length and was 53 cm. (21 in.) wide. *Cf.* sho hitsu no koto (149, 157).

Hne, a large oboe of Burma, with a flaring metal bell affixed to the wooden tube, a large wooden *pirouette, 7 front fingerholes, and a rear thumbhole; 3-oct. compass. Also called kaya (172).

Ho, a small sheng of China, with 13 pipes. Also called ho sheng (89).

Hoboy [*hautbois*], in 16th-c. England a shawm; in the 18th c. it designated the oboe.

Hochet [*hocher*, to shake], Fr.: rattle, jingle. The word has been in use since the 14th c. (53).

Hochette [dim. of *hochet*], OFr.: small rattle; baby's rattle.

Hoepelspel (Du.: hoop game), see: roue flamande.

Hog fiddle, Afro-Bahaman name for a bamboo scraper (152).

Hohlflöte (Ger.) [*Holefluyte*], **1.** see: Holefluyte; **2.** (Engl.: hohlflute) organ stop of open flue pipes, usually of wood, cylindrical, and of wide scale. Formerly it occurred in the manual from 8'–1' pitches and in the pedal at 16', nowadays almost always at 8' in the manual, occasionally at 4'. The Fr. equivalent is called *flûte creuse*. Also called Hohlpfeife (133).

Hohlflute, Engl.: Hohlflöte.

Hohlpfeife, syn. of Hohlflöte, 2.

Hohlquinte, Hohlflöte organ stop of 5⅓', 2⅔', or 1⅓' pitch. Also called Quintflöte (131).

Hohlschelle, organ stop of half-stopped cylindrical flue pipes of narrow scale, now obs. Also the name formerly given to the stopped Quintadena (133).

Hohoang, bull-roarer of Tasikmalaya, Java, made of coconut leaf. See also kekinchiran (121).

Hokeo, syn. of pa-ipu (176).

Hokioko, nose-blown *globular flute of Hawaii, made of a calabash, with 2 or 3 fingerholes usually disposed in a straight row or a triangle. Also called ipu (calabash) hokioko (77).

Hokum, hunting horn of the Muria of Bastar, India, originally of buffalo horn but nowadays often of brass. Curved, embossed, and hung with ornaments, it corresponds to the sringa of the north, the kombu of the south (68).

Ho kyo, a fragmentary lithophone of 9 stones preserved in the Shōsoin of Japan, probably the remains of a 16-stone lithophone suspended vertically in a frame (70).

Holefluyte [Ger. *?Holunter*, elder tree], believed to have been a small flageolet of med. Germany, played together with a Sumber. Also called Holpfeife. *Cf.* Hohlflöte, Holler (144).

Holler, Holre [Ger. *?Holunter*, elder tree], syn. of Holefluyte. The term is recorded from the 13th c. on.

Hölzernes Gelächter [S. Ger. *Klächel*, stick], **1.** obs. S. Ger. and Austrian term for xylophone. In the Austrian Alps the term lingered on until the mid-19th c., when it was exchanged for *xylophone;* **2.** obs. organ stop of unknown composition. In 1506 it was called a "new" stop in Speyer. Schlick mentioned it in 1511; it occurred in several early-16th-c. organs of which that at Bern (built in 1517) seems to have been the latest; **3.** modern organ stop of flue pipes (117, 133, 167).

Holzfiedel, obs. Ger.: xylophone.

Holzflöte (Ger.: wooden flute), organ stop of open wooden flue pipes of Prinzipal scale at 8' or 4' pitch (133).

Holzharmonika, Ger.: xylophone.

Holzprinzipal (Ger.), organ stop, a syn. of Holzflöte (133).

Holztrommel, until recently, Ger.: slit drum.

Holztrompete, 1. Ger.: wooden trumpet; **2.** coll. for alphorn; **3.** instr. built for Wagner's *Tristan und Isolde,* with cylindrical or conical tube of wood, the bell of a *cor anglais,* one valve; played with a cup mouthpiece (176).

Holz- und Strohinstrument (Ger.: wood and straw instr.), Ger. 19th-c. term for xylophone (117).

Hom, trumpet of the C. American Maya (144).

Hommel [Du.: *hommelen,* to drone], syn. of noordsche balk.

Hong, straight metal trumpet of Nepal,

made of brass, with wide conical bore (176).

H'onoroate, *musical bow of the Chama Indians of the Upper Amazon, made of a small, flat cane and a string of cotton. One end is held in the player's mouth while the string is struck by a small bow of palm (105).

Hontsuri gane, temple gong of Japan, also used in *gagaku* and as a signal instr. It is struck with a large, padded beater (135).

Hook harp (Fr.: *harpe à crochets;* Ger.: *Hakenharfe;* It.: *arpa a nottolini, arpa ad uncinetti*), diatonic harp with a series of hooks set in the neck to permit raising the pitch of the strings by a semi-tone, allegedly invented in the Tirol (documentation on this point is lacking) in the second half of the 17th c. But while turning the hooks the player temporarily lost the use of one of his hands. This inconvenience was remedied *ca.* 1720 by the invention of a pedal mechanism controlling hooks that pressed against the strings, but this had the disadvantage of displacing the hooked strings from the plane of the others and the system ultimately gave way to the *béquilles* of Cousineau. On some hook harps only the Fs and Cs could be modified in pitch; in other models all the strings were affected. See: harp.

Hool, see: jul.

Hoo'r, see: hummer.

Hoorn, Du.: horn.

Hopper, in certain piano actions the jack, or escapement lever.

Hora, end-blown *marine-shell trumpet of Japan, used by Buddhist priests and also as a signal instr. by boatmen. It corresponds to the hai lo of China and the sora of Korea (170).

Horanewa, painted oboe of Ceylon (173).

Hörböggen, corr. of Hörpauke.

Horesemoi, signal trumpet of the Warrau Indians of S. America, made of a bamboo stump. *Cf.* matabo (105).

Horn (Fr.: *cor;* Ger.: *Horn;* It.:

corno; Sp.: *trompa*), 1. lip-vibrated wind instr. originally made of animal horn or tusk, later imitated in wood or metal (a trumpet, on the other hand, was originally made of a length of straight bamboo or wood). As Sachs pointed out, in Europe horns are more conical than cylindrical and trumpets more cylindrical than conical, but this does not hold true elsewhere. In ancient Egypt, for instance, trumpets had conical bores throughout. Conicity can therefore not be a criterion of classification, nor can length: the elongated lur belongs to the horns, and some ancient Egyptian trumpets are but *ca.* 60 cm. (2 ft.) long. As to curvature, the European natural trumpet is curved, whereas the straight cornett is unquestionably a fingerhole horn. Some writers solve this problem of definition by classifying all horns as trumpets, using the latter term in its larger sense of lip-vibrated aerophone. In this dictionary instrs. known or assumed to be descended from horn or tusk prototypes are called *horn* and those lip-vibrated instrs. derived from other materials, including marine shells, are called *trumpets*.

Primitive horns served magical ends rather than musical purposes, as they still do in some areas of Africa, where they are spoken or shouted into at the wide end; in other parts of Africa they are treated like clapperless bells and become percussion instrs. This use has been extended to certain Afro-Cuban horns. Horns played as wind instrs. are either end-blown or side-blown, the latter form being characteristic of Africa and S. America. Ivory horns, for instance, are side-blown in Africa but were end-blown in Europe after their introduction here in the 10th c. from Byzantium. In Africa and Europe they were considered as royal regalia. Some horns were also pierced with fingerholes: about 700 A.C. a short animal horn clearly pierced with fingerholes is depicted on a Persian silver dish. Similar instrs. are in use today by shepherds in Estonia, Finland, Norway,

Sweden, Yugoslavia, and remote areas of the Iberian Peninsula, as well as among the Bongo of the Sudan. Fingerhole horns also appear in European miniatures from the 10th c. on; imitated later in wood or ivory, the form is refined until it emerges as the *cornett.

Horns are mentioned in Mesopotamia ca. 2000 B.C. and are depicted there ca. 1250 B.C. In Egypt we hear of a gift of 40 horns to Amenophis IV ca. 1400 B.C., 17 of which are expressly called oxhorns. All were covered with gold and some were incrusted with precious stones. Horns were also known to ancient Israel; the *shofar, an instr. of magic rituals and religious function, is the only horn to have come down to us in the form it bore in antiquity. The *rhyton of classical Greece was made both with and without fingerholes.

Whereas primitive horns are often sounded without mouthpieces, the more developed varieties are played with a cup-shaped, later a funnel-shaped, mouthpiece that originally was not detachable. The early med. horn of Europe, as used by hunters and watchmen and for military purposes, was a signal instr. of horn —often that of a bugle—or its imitation in wood or metal. Mention has already been made of the princely ivory horn in use from the 11th c. on; as they were of elephant tusk, they became known as *oliphants. In 1227 we hear of "4 cornua de ebore quedam [sic] sunt cum argento" (4 ivory horns, some with silver). Many elaborately decorated horns are listed in Fr. 14th-c. inventories. In 1420 a "gran cor qui se met en 2 pieces" is mentioned, unfortunately without details as to what the 2 pieces consisted of. Instrs. of this period were still horn-shaped or semicircular and of varying lengths. As a signal instr. used during the hunt, the horn was known as cor de chasse, trompe de chasse, and Jägerhorn or Jäger Trommet. In a 1502 edition of Virgil there is a woodcut by the Strassburg humanist Sebastian Brant, showing a hooplike horn

with 3 or 4 coils, hung around the player's neck, the bell projecting outward from his left shoulder. We do not hear of a hooplike horn again until ca. 1680, and there are good reasons for believing that the woodcut (reproduced in Source 144, article: "Horn") did not represent a horn at all, but rather a trumpet; see: trompeta bastarda. Nine years after it appeared, Virdung published his Musica getutscht in the same town that Brant had studied in; he knows only the old curved signal horn, and a wide-bore helical horn, terminating in a bell, which he calls Jägerhorn. Such an instr., made ca. 1575, is preserved in the Dresden Historical Museum and measures some 16½ cm. (6½ in.) across the coils with a tube length of ca. 165 cm. (5½ ft.). In 1606 Nicot writes that "the hunter's horn is not the brass trompe that we use today, but is a horn of ivory or horn" (le cor du veneur n'est pas la trompe d'airain . . .); as the term trompe was later applied to the hooplike horn, this phrase may be indicative of the horn's development, it being now generally agreed that the helical instr. became transformed in France into the wide circular instr. we know as the orchestral "French" horn. During the 17th c. the number of coils was reduced, ca. 1660 to 2½, ca. 1680 to 1½, with a diam. of 45 cm. (18 in.), and a tube length of ca. 210 cm. (7 ft.). The mouthpiece end of the tubing was made cylindrical, the bell was widened, and a funnel-shaped mouthpiece came to replace the old cupped one. From 1680 to 1682 the Bohemian Count von Spork made the grand tour, in the course of which he encountered the hooplike horn, or trompe. He took several instrs. back with him and laid the foundation of the Bohemian school of horn playing as a result. The oldest preserved trompe is dated 1689; it has but one coil and is housed in the Leipzig University instrument collection. But whereas in France the instr. remained a hunting horn until the mid-18th c., in

Germany it entered the orchestra. In 1705 a far larger model with double the tube length of the former instr. was introduced in France. That year Reinhard Keiser's opera *Octavia* was produced in Hamburg, and it contained parts for horns scored as *cornes de chasse*. Mattheson, in 1713, relates that the horn was employed in church, chamber, and theater. Such early orchestral horns were mere *trompes de chasse* built in different keys, but from 1718 on *crooks came into use. The tube could then be lengthened as required by inserting one terminal crook into another. In 1732 Majer writes of the horn as being easier to play than the trumpet and usually pitched in F, a 5th below the latter, but recently also made in C, an oct. lower. By 1748 La Pouplinière had imported both horns and horn players from Germany for his Paris orchestra, and the horn thence became known as the *"nouveau cor de chasse allemand"* (the new German hunting horn). At about the same time the "hand in bell," or handstopping, playing technique was being developed, owing to the efforts of the Bohemian school of players, who were first to recognize the potentialities of the horn's lower register. The new technique was formalized by Anton Joseph Hampel, a Dresden hornist; it consisted in partly stopping the bell with the hand and thereby changing the pitch a semitone to a whole tone or more. The horn so played was called *hand horn. Partly closing the bell in this fashion modified the tone quality and gave the horn the muffled sound it has now. But it was not found convenient to play terminally crooked horns in this manner, and Hampel subsequently (by 1753) designed the *Inventionshorn, with central crooks, an improved version of which became known as *cor-solo. Prior to the introduction of hand stopping, horns were held with the bell up in the air, projecting over the player's head. Keyed horns, representing the earliest attempt at making

horns chromatic, were invented by the Bohemian hornist Kolbel and appeared *ca.* 1770, but enjoyed a *succès d'estime* only; they were known as *taille d'amour* in France and *Amorschall in Ger. By 1776 the tuning slide had been invented and the earliest *duplex horn followed shortly thereafter: in 1788 Charles Claggett of London inaugurated a long series of such instrs. with his *chromatic trumpet and *French horn. The next attempt at chromaticism was the *omnitonic horn, which appeared *ca.* 1815, a horn with an extra length of tubing built into the body proper, obviating the need for detachable crooks. Very shortly thereafter the *valve was invented and adapted to the horn; at first 2 valves, since the 1830's 3, were fitted. As the right hand was used for stopping, the valves were disposed for use by the player's left hand, and this practice obtains today. (Other valved instrs. are right-handed.) At the end of the c. the *double horn in F and B♭ appeared, now widely used in symphony orchestras. The single horn in (high) B♭ is also in common use and has in fact largely superseded the classical horn in F; in Germany a horn in high F is coming into use. Most horns played nowadays are provided with 3 valves that lower the pitch by a tone, a semitone, and 3 semitones, respectively. In France the third valve is ascending: it raises the pitch by a tone. Rotary valves are by far the most common nowadays, although in some areas piston valves are in use. In the U.S. a 5-valve horn is also played: it has a muting valve and a *Quartventil. As to bore, the Fr. prefer a narrower bore, the Germans a wider one. See also: abu qurun, achromatic horn, adar, adarturanta, ajjub burusi, akbele, akofe, aluut, amokoderi, Amorschall, ampondokaka, andulón, anjombo, apunga, arain, asokoben, aturma, awe, ayābi, aza rag, azkonadar, barugumu, bondin, bondofo, bramadera, buccina, bucén, buc horne, bugle, bugle horn, bugleral, buinne, buisine, būq, būr-

247 HORNPIPE

ghū, Burgmote horn, burifē, buro, būrū,
būrūsī, butsina, buzina, byrgy, choron,
coach horn, cor, cor à l'anglaise, cor de
pin, corn, cornadouelle, cornet, cornichet,
corno, cornon, cornuielle, coron, cor
saxomnitonique, cor-solo, cor transpositeur, courne, cowhorn, cuerna, deiadar,
digiticor, durbatudu, embuchi, fingerhole
horn, gä, gafa, gau-adar, ges, ghentā, gi-
sal, gizallu, graile, grêle, gu, gucha, guke,
gunda, hokum, Her-horn, Herkulesphone,
Hiefhorn, Hirtibüchel, huanco, iholere,
ikondo, Inventionshorn, isambu, isigodhlo, javata, jjembe, jobel, jubal, kabilles-
adar, kafo, karakoru, katakyi, katso, kengere, 2, keras, keren, khara, kidiyo, kofen,
kwai, kwatha, langlju, lepapata, lubr,
luik, lur, mairu-adar, mangval, mbana,
mbema, m'bia, Meloni-cor, mfuhlulu,
Mittelhorn, moienel, monzo, mpalampala, mpandala, mpundshi, mpungi,
mushereko, mvumvuni, nafīr, nakamunsale, nambongo, narasringa, nembongo,
nya won, obute, ohiva, oliphant, olukula,
opi, oukpwe, pandapanda, Parforce horn,
phalaphala, Prince Pless horn, pualtem-
puch, puch, pukin sarvi, qanā, radius
French horn, riedehorn, riethoorn, rog,
rongo, Rüderhorn, Russian horn, rwa-
dung, šabbur, saddu, sarpa, Schallhorn,
shaing, shipalapala, shofar, si-im, sing,
singa, soittotorvi, soku-sarv, Stockhorn,
tandrokaka, tarro, tasīnfak, tat, Thurnerhorn, thuthaurn, tori, tromp, trompa,
trompe, trompe de chasse, trompe de
Lorraine, trompe Dufouilloux, trompe
Maricaux, trompetine, troumpeto de San
Jean, truŏhorn, tshihoho, tube, Tudelhorn, tülök, tuohitorvi, ture angwa, turullo, tuta, upondo, valtorna, vizgunok,
wic-horn, zink, 2 (25, 89 Morley-Pegge,
169, 170);

2. organ stop of reed pipes, surmounted by a funnel, introduced by
the Engl. builder R. Bridge in 1730,
usually called French horn in Engl. and
Amer. organs. At 16′, 8′, or 4′ pitch.
Also called corno, Waldhorn (133).

Hornbass, organ stop of open cylindrical flue pipes of very wide scale at 2′

pitch in the pedal. Also called Hornbäss-
lein, Hörnlein (133).

Horn diapason (Ger. *Hornprinzipal*),
organ stop of open cylindrical flue pipes
with slightly smaller than diapason scale,
usually at 8′ pitch (129).

Hörnli, early-16th-c. organ stop of unidentified structure (167).

Hornpipe, in its simplest form the
hornpipe is a reedpipe with single reed,
terminating in an upturned bell of cow-
horn (prototype of later bells). A hornpipe may also consist of 2 parallel pipes
tied together, with either 2 independent
bells or 1 common bell. When it is played,
each finger covers both pipes; or, again,
the reeds may not be mouthed directly,
but may be enclosed in another horn
(mouth horn), which protects the reeds,
or in a gourd. Many Eastern species
have gourd-enclosed reeds. In some areas
the pipe is covered with skin and provided with a mouthpipe, thus becoming
transformed into a bagpipe, but whether
or not there is a bag, the instr. is still
called hornpipe. The hornpipe is distributed, primarily as a pastoral instr.,
from Spain and the Maghrib to the Urals
and India; the double hornpipe (nowadays) from Morocco to Arabia and
Mesopotamia; with the exception of the
instrs. of Morocco, these are all provided
with bags. The hornpipe of antiquity disappeared in the 6th c. A.C., to reappear
in the West in the 10th c., and during
the Middle Ages most or all of Europe
knew it. The mouth horn first appears
depicted in the 13th c. *Cantigas de Santa
María,* as does the hornpipe with bag.
Chaucer was the first writer to mention
the word "hornpipe." The Celtic instr.
survived in Britain until the 18th c., that
of the Basque country until *ca.* 1900. The
Basque and Yugoslav species had unequal pipes, *i.e.,* pipes with an unequal
number of fingerholes on the 2 tubes.
For details see: alboka, bishnica, cornicyll, diplye, erkencho, gaita, hu kya,
jaleika, lavikko, nud'i, pepa, pibcorn,
pilli, pipinë, stock and horn, swegelhorn,

zāmar, zinburruna, zummare (13, 14, 180).

Hornprinzipal, Ger. equivalent of horn diapason.

Hornwerk (med. Lat.: *cornu organicum*), in the Austrian territory of Gothic and Renaissance times, a number of organ flue pipes set on a chest of their own in a tower, all of which sounded simultaneously and continuously as long as the bellows supplied wind. They announced the hours and served to summon the faithful to worship. By the Renaissance such simple "calls" were no longer satisfying and the Hornwerk was connected to a pinned barrel that interpolated tunes between the "calls." The pipework of a Hornwerk was simply a note of the old *Blockwerk organ containing only triads, the fundamental being usually F or C; thus it sounded a continuous triad. In Gothic times the compass was 4'–¼', later extended downward. Three Hornwerke survive: the Salzburg *"Stier"* (bull), dating from the early 16th c., and the remains of those of Heiligenkreuz and Rein. Also called Orgelhorn (161).

Horologium (Lat.), in med. Europe a number of small campaniform bells with clappers, attached to the rim of a large wheel that was made to revolve, sometimes by rope and crank, sometimes by clockwork. The term is recorded already in the 10th c., when the horologium was used on feast days. Subsequently such wheels were used in the churches of Europe, often attached to the front of the organ. These were later to become known as bell wheel, in France as roue à clochettes, in Ger.-speaking areas as Zimbelstern. Also called nolarum circulis, rota campanarum, rota tintinnabulis. See also: rotllo, roue flamande, roue à clochettes, routelle, Zimbelstern (61, 169, 188).

Hörpauke, Hörpaugge, obs. var. of Heerpauke.

Hosanna, small carillon patented by Sève in France on Feb. 4, 1898 (204).

Ho sheng, see: ho.

Hourglass drum (Fr.: *tambour en sablier;* Ger.: *Sanduhrtrommel*), drum in form of an hourglass, with diam. smaller in the middle than at each end, distributed in Asia, E. Africa, Melanesia (176).

Hpa si, see: ka si.

Hruozza, OHGer.: cruit. Glossed in the 10th c. as sambuca (185A).

Hsiang ch'ih, *percussion stick of China made of redwood, struck with a short stick. In N. China it preceded the coffin at funerals. *Ca.* 60 cm. (2 ft.) long (142).

Hsiang pan, *percussion plaque of China, made of thick brass and struck with a long stick (142).

Hsiao, 1. *end-blown flute of China, in use since the 12th or 11th c. B.C., formerly made of copper, marble, etc., but nowadays of bamboo, its upper end closed by a natural node in which a notch is cut, thus leaving a narrow flue, with 5 front fingerholes and a rear thumbhole; a Confucian instr. that *ca.* 700 B.C. was a *yüeh, in med. times a *yo and a *ti. The modern instr. is called *tung hsiao. Its full name is feng huang hsiao. See also: cor, 2, fong hsiao; **2.** see: siao (170).

Hsiao ku, small *frame drum of China, with single, nailed head of cowskin. Played with a knobbed withy. *Ca.* 5 cm. (2 in.) high, 8 cm. (3 in.) in diam. (142).

Hsiao tse, syn. of ko ling.

Hsien tse, syn. of san hsien.

Hsing erh, Chin. cymbals. In N. China they are almost hemispheric in shape (142).

Hsing lung sheng, Chin. term for organ, first introduced from the West during the reign of Kublai Khan (1260–94) (75 II).

Hsüan, ovoid *globular flute of China, known since the Shang period (mid-second millennium B.C.). Originally of bone, later of clay or porcelain. The earliest ones had 2 or 3 holes, by the 11th c. 8 holes, later usually 6 or 7. Today there is a blowhole on top of the red-lacquered body, with 4–6 fingerholes. The hsüan serves in Confucian rites. It corresponds to the hun of Korea (89, 132, 170).

Hsüan tse, gong of China, with central boss, used by mendicants in Shantung Province. Identical with the pao chün chih (142).

Hsun, see: shun.

Hsü pan, percussion board of China, suspended by a cord and used both as a curfew and to summon monks to meetings in monasteries. *Ca.* 75 by 46 cm. (30 by 18 in.) in size (142).

Hu, bamboo *nose flute of Pak, Admiralty Islands, Melanesia, with blowhole in the septum. *Ca.* 20 cm. (8 in.) long (203).

Hua chiao, obs. wind instr. of China, probably a double-reed instr. (142).

Huada, name of the *maraca (rattle) among the Araucano Indians of Chile (192).

Hua ku, barrel drum of China with 2 nailed heads, suspended by copper rings. It serves in Confucian temples, but also in theaters, and is carried, hung from the performer's right shoulder, by strolling bands of players. Some specimens have wire jingles inside that rattle when the drum is played. Made in varying sizes, often 25 cm. (10 in.) long. Formerly known as ya ku or yao ku (132, 142).

Hua mei chiao tse, bird whistle of China made of bamboo, used for imitating the call of the *hua mei* (thrush). 4 cm. (1½ in.) long (142).

Huancar (Quichua), **1.** generic name for drums of ancient Peru, shallow, cylindrical or square, with heads of human, llama, or deerskin either nailed or sewn on (170); **2.** *frame drum of modern Argentine made in several sizes (192); **3.** large kettledrum of present-day Peruvian Indians (89).

Huancar tinya, small huancar (105).

Huanco, horn of Bolivian Indians (89).

Huang chung, bamboo flute of China with 6 fingerholes, known since pre-Christian times. Originally it was a standard of pitch and formed the basis for standards of length and hollow measures (144, 177).

Huang la pa, a large *la pa of Tibetan lamas (176).

Huang teh, syn. of ta t'ung kyo.

Huanka, see: huancar.

Huan t'u, split idiophone of itinerant barbers of China, made of metal. *Ca.* 33 cm. (13 in.) long (142).

Huare, *slit drum of the Uitoto Indians of Colombia, with walls of different thicknesses, thus yielding 2 tones. Made in pairs of male and female and struck with rubber-headed wooden beaters while in horizontal position. Used only as a signal instr. (32).

Huayra-puhura, panpipes of ancient and modern S. America, in ancient times either made of cane or having bores hollowed out of a mass of wood or clay, stone or metal. One old surviving specimen has 2 corresponding rows of 7 pipes each, of which 1 row is stopped and consequently sounds an oct. below the other row; another, made from a block of soapstone, has 8 pipes of which 4 have a lateral hole; when stopped the pitch is lowered by a semitone, so that, all told, 12 tones can be played. The modern instr. is in use among the Quechua Indians of Peru. It has 2 corresponding rows of 8 pipes each, the front row being open, the rear row stopped. The longer pipes are on the right-hand side (8, 170).

Huchet [OFr. *huchier,* to call loudly], **1.** 15th-c. Fr. hunting horn made of a semicircular animal horn; **2.** its 17th-c. imitation, usually made of 2 sections of hollowed wood, bound with leather, but also made of copper. *Cf.* Halbmond (78, 82, 132).

Hu chia, obs. pastoral reedpipe of China, made of a spirally twisted rush or of wood, without fingerholes (142).

Hu ch'in, generic name for *spike fiddles in China, instrs. possibly of C. Asian origin. The body is a small cylinder or hexagon of bamboo, wood, or coconut, the lower end being left open, the upper covered with a lizardskin or snake-skin belly. The handle pierces the body; there is no fingerboard. Its 2 strings are usually tuned a 5th apart. Played with a small bow that passes between the strings and is not removable from the instr. Called sze hu hsien in Peking, it corresponds to the sa dueng of Thailand and the kei kin of Japan. See also: erh hsien, erh hu, hu hu, hui hu, su hu, ta hu ch'in, tan ch'in, t'i ch'in (170).

Hueco (Sp.: hollow), syn. of catá (152).

Huehuetl (old-old), generic term for drums of pre-Columbian C. America, still in use today for a wooden, footed drum. The ancient huehuetl was of wood, in the Mayan culture also of clay; it lacked lacings and was played with bare hands, whereas today it is played with sticks. In modern times it has assumed the form of a single-headed, footed drum, usually with 3 feet, made in various sizes, none of very large dimensions. Two distinct sounds are produced: that obtained by striking the center of the head is a 5th apart from the tone yielded by striking its side. See also: panhue-huetl, tlapanhuehuetl (137, 170).

Hu hu, *hu ch'in with coconut body, wooden soundboard, lateral pegs (142).

Hui, see: gong hui.

Hui hu, *hu ch'in with cylindrical wooden body, snakeskin belly, rear pegs, and strings looped to the handle, and a body diam. of 5 cm. (2 in.) (170).

Huilacapiztali, zoomorphic *globular flute of the Aztec, made of clay, with 2–5 fingerholes. It imitates the song of the turtledove (137, 144).

Hukelpott (LGer.), N. Ger. *friction drum (169).

Hu k'in, see: hu ch'in.

Hu kya, obs. hornpipe of China, according to Courant, of C. Asian origin, with slender horn and 3 fingerholes (13).

Hula kalaau, *percussion sticks of Hawaii. A 90-cm. (35-in.) stick is held by its middle and struck with a shorter one (77).

Hüldopp, Westphalian *friction drum (169).

Hu le, syn. of ta hu le (4).

Huli-huli, scraper of the Carajá Indians of Brazil made of a tortoise carapace (176).

Hulima, gourd rattle of the Cocopa Indians of the W. U.S., with hardwood handle (52).

Hulki māndri, parrang (hourglass drum) made of a hollowed block of wood with lizardskin heads stretched over bamboo hoops and tied by a cord. Very small specimens have a stick or stone tied to a central belt so as to strike against the heads when the drum is shaken, like a dāmaru, of which it is a variant. Also called damru, ojha parra. *Ca.* 28 cm. (11 in.) long (68).

Hülze glechter, Schlick's spelling of *hölzernes Gelächter (1511).

Human . . . as a prefix to names of Ger. organ stops, human is syn. with echo . . . (133).

Humangedackt, older name of the lieblich Gedackt organ stop (133).

Humbaldú, percussion gourd of the Futa women of Senegal. A dried, cucumber-shaped gourd, open at both ends, is held by the player's left hand while she alternately opens and closes the upper aperture. The lower end is opened and closed by being placed on and removed from her thigh. The sound is sufficient for the accompanying of songs. See also: darhama, degemma (152).

Humle, folk zither of Denmark that assumes a number of shapes, usually that of a rectangular box, ending in a violin-like pegbox, with fretted soundboard; similar to the *bûche.* The number of strings is variable, 10 being common, 4 of which are melody strings. The 3 pairs of drones are tuned to tonic and dominant. The instr. is played with a plectrum. The name is sometimes also given to the långspel. The humle corresponds to the langleik of Norway. *Ca.* 70 cm. (28 in.) long (91, 149).

Hummel (bumble bee), **1.** obs. Du.

folk zither that became extinct by the mid-19th c., similar to the humle; **2.** Ger. name of the above instr. as well as for the humle and långspel.

Hümmelchen [dim. of *Hummel*], **1.** 17th-c. bagpipe described by Praetorius as having a chanter with a compass c^2–c^3 and 2 drones on 1 stock sounding f^1 and c^2; **2.** obs. auxiliary organ stop consisting of 1 or several pipes, usually reed pipes, as f^1 and c^2 or g^1 and c^2. Esaias Compenius built 1 of 6 pipes in the Frederiksborg organ, Denmark (133).

Hummer, obs. Engl. *whirled friction drum, known in Coventry up to the 19th c. and later called hoo'r. It consisted of a paper box and a thread by which it was whirled (16).

Humming top (Fr.: *toupie bourdonnante;* Ger.: *Brummkreisel;* Sp.: *trompo silbador*), top containing reeds that hum when the top spins, usually a child's toy. Found on all continents, but in Africa only among the E. African Warundi (168).

Hum-strum [Engl.: hum + strum], Engl. folk instr., a survival of the rebec, with rebec-like body and 4 wire strings that pass over a large bridge made of a tin can or similar material. In Dorsetshire it was still to be found in the early 19th c. Now obs. (79, 94).

Hun, 1. *globular flute of Korea, made of clay, with 6 holes. It corresponds to the Chin. hsüan. 9 cm. (3½ in.) high (66); **2.** syn. of hunpi.

Hunga, *musical bow of Angola, with gourd resonator that is held against the player's stomach. The string is held between finger and thumb and tapped with a small stick. *Cf.* hungo (17).

Hungo, *musical bow of the Malenge of S. Africa, with tuning loop and resonator, the latter pressed against the player's chest in performance (17).

Hunpi, Afro-Brazilian drum of Bahía. Also called hun.

Hun pu sze [Turk. *qūbūz*], plucked chordophone of China, an adaptation of the qūbūz, with piriform body, belly half

of wood and half of snakeskin, 3 or 4 lateral pegs all on the same side of the elongated neck (4, 75 II).

Hunting horn (Fr.: *cor de chasse, trompe de chasse;* Ger.: *Jagdhorn;* It.: *corno da caccia*), valveless horn that has been made in many shapes. See: horn.

Hu po, Moule's reading of *hun pu sze, according to Farmer (75 II, 142).

Hurava (west), bull-roarer of Orokolo, Papua (201).

Hurdy-gurdy [U.], mechanically bowed chordophone known since med. times, when it was called *organistrum, and which we first hear of in a short treatise by Odo of Cluny (d. 942) entitled *Quomodo organistrum construatur* (*How an Organistrum Should Be Constructed*), which deals with monochord string divisions to determine the emplacement of the organistrum's key rods. From the 12th c. it is also depicted. At first it appears with a cumbersome, fiddle-shaped body and 3 strings, all of which were sounded simultaneously. Its characteristic feature was and still is the hand-cranked, rosined wooden wheel at the lower end of the body which sets the strings in vibration. These pass over the vertex of the wheel, through a boxlike device containing the rear portion of the key rods, and are attached by frontal or rear pegs to a short and deep pegbox. As the instr. was some 1.50–1.80 m. (5–6 ft.) long, it was placed across the laps of 2 performers: one worked the wheel, the other the key rods. In Odo's day these numbered 8, with a compass of a diatonic oct. from C with B♭. The key rods were rotating levers with a flat, perpendicular piece attached at the back, acting, when the rod was turned, as individual bridges.

The origins of both instr. and its name are unknown. As the related *nyckelharpa also had an incurved waist in its early form, it has been suggested that both may originally have been bowed prior to the attachment of a wheel. Despite its form we cannot derive it from the fiddle because we cannot show the existence of fiddles before that of the organistrum. From the 12th c. on we can follow its development fairly closely: At that time its outer (drone) strings were tuned an oct. apart and the center string (melody) a 4th or 5th below the highest drone: a perfect instr. for playing or accompanying organum, as the key rods stopped all strings at the same time. Up to the 13th c. it served in church and monastic school; during the 13th c. it appears to have lost its position there, possibly in favor of the organ. It became considerably smaller, and the system of key rods was changed to nonrotating push levers that stopped the strings from the side and fell back of their own volition, provided the instr. was held in a slightly tilted position, as it has been ever since. Gradually it became first a pop. and then a folk instr. The word organistrum fell into disuse in the 14th c., and from the 12th to the 16th c. it was known as *symphonia*, in France as *symphonie, chifonie, armonie*, and the word *vielle* was also applied to it in the 15th c., when the instr. became restricted to *musica irregularis*. Both Mersenne and Trichet in the 17th c. speak of it as a beggar's instr., as had Deschamps before them (*aveugle chifonie aura*); its name by then had once more changed: to *vièle à roue* in France, *Leier* in German-speaking countries. The Engl. term *hurdy-gurdy* did not appear until the 18th c. In the early 16th c. the instr. had 4 strings, according to Virdung, in the 17th c. 4 or 5. In the 18th c. it enjoyed an upsurge of popularity in France, where it was refined and given 6 strings, with a melody compass of 2 octs. Of the 6 strings 2 were melody strings called *chanterelles. These passed over the vertex of the wheel, through the key-slider box, over a nut, and into the pegbox, where they were secured by frontal pegs. The drones were known as *gros bourdon, bourdon, mouche*, and *trompette*. The last was so named because it was sometimes provided with a mobile drumming bridge, similar to that of the *trumpet marine,

with one foot longer than the other, called *trompillon* or *coup de poignet*. The trompette was set drumming by running an auxiliary string from a special tuning peg inserted in the tailpiece to the *trompette*, and by attaching it to the latter behind the bridge. *Trompette* and *mouche* were situated behind the key-slider box, the 2 *bourdons* in front of it. Both chanterelles were tuned to g^1; if the tuning were to be in C, the *trompette* was tuned to c^1, the *mouche* to g^0, the *petit bourdon* to c^0, and the *grand bourdon* was suppressed by hitching it to a peg provided for this purpose. If the tuning were to be in G, the *trompette* was tuned to d^1, the *mouche* to g^1, the *petit bourdon* was suppressed, the *grand bourdon* tuned to G^0. Some instrs. had additional sympathetic wire strings on the right side. These were tuned $c^1 e^1 g^1 a^1$ for the so-called *vielle en guitare* tuning, $c^0 c^1 d^0 d^1 g^0 g^1$ for the *vielle en luth* tuning. Some models had a special device for raising the pitch of the *trompette* from c^1 to d^1 without retuning it: a special peg pressed the string against the edge of a fixed nut placed so as to shorten it by $\frac{1}{10}$ of its length. The hurdy-gurdy of that period was made in guitar, lute, or fiddle form. In the course of the 18th c. a number of old guitars and lutes were rebuilt into *vièles à roue*, and toward the end of the c. they started to be built with a miniature organ in the body; this form was called *viel(l)e organisée* (see: organized hurdy-gurdy). It was held on the lap with its 1 or 2 rows of slider keys pointing away from the player, the wheel at his left, and tilted slightly to permit the slider keys to fall back freely. Ambulant musicians carried their instr. suspended from the neck by a band. Its great popularity in France was cut short by the Fr. Revolution; when it was revived in the 19th c., it was as the instr. of street musicians. In that role it may occasionally still be heard. In the Austrian Alps it was played up to *ca*. 1900, often as a beggar's instr. In Russia it was known as *rilya and also became a mendicant's instr. See also: fanfóni, fon, founfóni, gaita zamorana, ghironda, hierochord, instrument truand, Leier, lira rustica, lira tedesca, lyra mendicorum, organized hurdy-gurdy, rilya, sambuca rotata, sanfonha, sanforgna, sinfonia, vièle à roue, vielle, vielle d'amour, viola da orbo, viola de rueda, zanfoña (25, 89 Galpin, 117, 132, 169, 206).

Huruk (Hindi), very pop. *dāmaru of India, with V-lacings and tension ligature, 20–30 cm. (8–10 in.) high. Called huruka in Bengal (176).

Huruka, Beng. name of the huruk.

Huryluth [inventor's name], flat-backed mandolin invented in 1900 by Louis Hury of Paris and exhibited there that year (191, 204).

Husapi [Sans. *kachapi*], syn. of the kachapi lute among the Batak of Sumatra (173).

Husla, Wendish fiddle of med. shape with short neck and fingerboard, rosette and sound slits, long tailpiece, flat peg-disc with rear pegs and 3 strings tuned $d^1 a^1 e^2$. According to Kinsky, it was still in use by the Wends of Niederlausitz, Prussia, in the first half of the 19th c. *Cf.* gusla (25, 91).

Husor, syn. of bansurī (68).

Hustrum, see: hum-strum.

Hu ti, ch'iang ti with 4 or 5 fingerholes, played by shepherds (89, 142).

Hüxtüla, syn. of chirola.

Hvon kem, see: hyon kum.

Hyang pal, Korean gong used in pop. music (66).

Hyang p'i p'a, Korean p'i p'a played with a plectrum or with bare fingers, *ca.* 98 cm. (39 in.) long (68).

Hyang ryong, small bell of Korea, played during dances (66).

Hydraulicon (Gk.), abbr. of *hydraulicon organon;* an obs. term used in Engl. literary sources for the hydraulos.

Hydraulis (Gk.), syn. of hydraulos.

Hydraulos (Gk., Lat.) [Gk. *hydor,* water + *aulos,* pipe], (Fr.: *orgue hydraulique;* Ger.: *Wasserorgel*), early type of organ that differed from the so-called

"pneumatic" organ only in its wind supply and its size. The wind supply consisted of 2 essentials: pumps and a reservoir. The latter was a large hexagonal container half filled with water; it formed the lower section of the hydraulos. Inside it was a bucket-like object of metal called *pnigeus,* placed open side down on feet; a connection led from the *pnigeus* to the wind chest above, a small, boxlike affair called *arcula.* Air from 1, or more often 2, hand-worked pumps passed to the wind chest. As the pressure of the air in the wind chest was raised by the pumping, water was driven from the *pnigeus* into the container. If the pressure in the wind chest dropped, owing to a slowing of the pumping or to the flow of air into the pipes, the displaced water flowed back from the container and the level in the *pnigeus* rose, thereby compressing the air above it, restoring the pressure in the wind chest. Thus the reservoir acted to keep the air pressure continuous and steady, as the presence of the water assured pressure between pumping strokes. The water level of the *pnigeus* remained more or less constant while the instr. was in use, in much the same way that the bag of a bagpipe remains inflated while the pipe is being played. The later, purely pneumatic organs had no need for the large reservoir, and when it was discarded the organ was transformed from a cumbersome, nonportable instr. to a portative small enough to be held in the lap.

Invention of the hydraulos is attributed to Ktesibios of Alexandria (3rd c. B.C.). Unfortunately his description of it has not come down to us. The hydraulos is of course too complicated an instr. to have been the creation of a single individual, and his part in its development is unknown. The earliest extant description of the hydraulos is that of Heron of Alexandria (*Pneumatika*), said by some historians to have been written *ca.* 120 B.C., by others *ca.* 100 A.C.; it is followed by that of Vitruvius Pollio (*De Architectura*) written in the first c. A.C. The instr.

of Heron had only 1 row of pipes; that of Vitruvius could have 4, 5, or even 8 rows, possibly for playing in different tonalities. The Anonymous Bellermann (first or second c. A.C.) informs us that the hydraulos could be played in 6 *tropoi*, or tonalities: Hyperlydian, Hyperiastian, Lydian, Phrygian, Hypolydian, and Hypophrygian, which tonalities required up to 1 sharp and 3 flats in our notation (Dorian tonalities would have required 4–6 flats). The precise nature of the hydraulos was greatly clarified by the discovery in Carthage in 1885 of a clay model measuring some 18 cm. (7 in.) in height, dating from the second c. A.C. and now preserved in the St. Louis Museum of Carthage. This shows 3 ranks of pipes; the organist is seated at a raised seat, and if the broken upper portion of his body were intact, the head would project above the pipes, as it does on numerous contemporary representations. This model had a compass of 19 keys and would have been about 3 m. (10 ft.) high. A similar model is housed in the National Museum of Copenhagen. According to Vitruvius, the wind chest was grooved longitudinally (*i.e.*, from bass to treble) and the grooves could be opened by tuning gears, equivalent to a system of registers. In size the hydraulos seems to have varied from about 2–3 m. (7–10 ft.) in height and 1–1½ m. (40–60 in.) in width. From the second c. A.C. bellows were in use. Philo, writing in the 2nd or 3rd c. A.C. relates that bellows forced the air into a bronze container (the *pnigeus*) placed in water; as described in his *Pneumatika*, these were collapsible cylindrical bellows. More important is the statement of Julius Pollux in the 2nd c. A.C. that the hydraulos, in appearance a *syrinx, was filled with air in its lower portion, either by means of bellows if it was small, or by "compressed water [*hydati* . . . *anathlibomeno*] which drives out the air." This passage was known to med. writers and, being no longer understood, was mistranslated.

Thus the 12th-c. chronicler William of Malmesbury speaks of hot water (*"organa hydraulica, ubi mirum in modum aquae calefactae violentia ventus emergens implet concavitatem barbiti . . ."*), forcing air into the wind chest, giving rise to the idea that the ancient hydraulos was powered by steam; as *aqua calefacta* was involved, the *"ventus"* (air) logically became "steam." This idea, current in the 18th c., has unfortunately been revived in the mid-20th despite the efforts of Galpin and others to demonstrate the true nature of the instr.

A late writer, Claudian, informs us at the end of the 4th c. A.C. that the hydraulos' action was effortless. The hydraulos was mentioned by writers up to the end of the 5th c. despite the fact that the purely pneumatic organ had already been introduced (Pollux had also mentioned the latter); it is evident that this was first known by the name of the older instr. The hydraulos was well distributed in the Roman world from Gaul to Africa; it was used at private banquets (Cicero), in the emperor's palace (Nero was not only a player but also an improver of the hydraulos), at public performances in amphitheaters, etc.; it is represented on mosaics, medallions, sarcophagi, statuettes. After the 5th c. mention of the hydraulos does not occur again before the 9th c. According to Eginhard, Georgius Venetus built an organ in 826 or 828 in Aix la Chapelle for Louis le Débonnaire; it was called hydraulos (*"organum quod Graece hydraulica vocatur"*); that this was in effect a water organ seems most improbable. It is true that the Utrecht psalter dating from later in the same c. contains representations of hydraulic organs, but these are inspired by antiquity and of misunderstood nature, illustrative of the word *organa* in the psalms presumably, as they chiefly portray double organs. A writer named Muristus, known in Arab. in the 9th c., describes a one-pipe hydraulos, complete with huge water reservoir, but with wind supplied by collapsible bellows rather than pumps, and writes that the hydraulos was originally used for warlike purposes, as a signal or noisemaking instr. Other Arab. authors of the c. also mention the hydraulos, sometimes called *"urghan rumi"* (Gk. organ). See also: magrepha; for details of pipework see: organ.

Hydrodaktulopsycharmonica, the hard way of saying "*musical glasses." A Gk. monstrosity excavated by Percy Scholes (Oxford Companion to Music): a London *Times* reader (1932) reported having heard a performance on this instr. in his youth.

Hydrophone, a pipe with its head immersed in water, yielding a birdlike warble, patented by Montenat of St. Denis on March 23, 1865 (despite the fact that this type of pipe had been in the public domain since the early 16th c.) (204).

Hymnerophone [Gk. *hymnos,* song], clavicylinder invented in 1814 by P. Riffelsen of Copenhagen, a friction bar instr. with a series of lead forks controlled by a keyboard. They were brought into contact with brass discs attached to a rotating cylinder (176).

Hyon cha, obsolescent long-necked lute of Korea, with 3 strings. It corresponds to the *san hsien of China and the *samisen of Japan (66).

Hyon kum, *board zither of Korea, a very pop. instr., usually with 6 strings, rarely with 4, of which 3 pass over the raised, fixed frets. *Cf.* ch'in, koto (66).

Hyōshige, clappers of Japan, consisting of solid rectangular blocks of hardwood, struck either together or against a wooden board. Used in *kabuki* and also by fire watchers (135).

Iambyke, unidentified instr. of ancient Greece (144).

Iamut [*garamut], syn. of kolamut.

Iba, sistrum of ancient Egypt, generally made of metal but also of wood or clay, in form of a closed horseshoe with a handle. Wires were strung across the frame and jingled as they slid back and forth. During the Old and Middle Kingdoms metal discs were added to the wires to augment the sound. These were discontinued in the New Kingdom. Also called sehem. See also: sesheshet (147, 170).

Ibachord, harpsichord manufactured by the firm of Ibach of Barmen from 1902 on, originally with 1 8′ register and felt-covered jacks that pushed up against the strings. Subsequently the action was changed to normal harpsichord action (115).

Ibeka, sansa of the Bakele of Gabon, with gourd resonator and 6 wooden or cane lamellae (42).

Ibi, generic term for drum in Akpafu (a Sudanic language) (93).

Ibigumbiri, *musical bow of the Campa Indians of E. Peru, ca. 48 cm. (18 in.) long (105).

Ibindiren, pl. of abendair.

Ichaoró, syn. of changuoro (152).

Ichi gen kin (Jap.: one-stringed kin), single-stringed koto of Japan, said to have been invented at Suma in 901 A.C. The string is stopped by the left hand at positions marked off by small, circular insets in the board, and plucked with a plectrum. Made of kiri wood or bamboo, ca. 110 cm. (43 in.) long and 11 cm. (4¼ in.) wide (157).

Ichi no tsuzumi, small *tsuzumi, 35 cm.

(14 in.) long with a diam. of 20 cm. (8 in.). Also called ikko (157).

Ichy'umwe, drum of Ruanda, a symbol of royalty (30).

Icibitiku, drum of the Lala of Nigeria (109).

Icilongo, 1. hooked trumpet of the S. African Zulu, virtually the only end-blown instr. of S. Africa. It consists of a bamboo tube 60–120 cm. (2–4 ft.) long with a diam. of 2½ cm. (1 in.); the lower end is fitted into a curved oxhorn and the upper clipped off at a right angle. It yields several harmonics. Kirby considers it to be of probable European inspiration; **2.** name given by the Zulu to any European brass instr. (116).

Icitali, long-necked tanbura of modern Greece with 2 strings. Also called kitelis (76).

Icombi, cylindrical trumpet found in the vicinity of Buluceke, Uganda, with a gourd affixed to the tube; a hole is cut into the apex of the gourd (195).

Ida, *hourglass drum of the Sudanese Edo, introduced by the Yoruba, with whom it is a royal perquisite (93).

Idai surungu parai, syn. of udukkai (179).

'Idān, pl. of 'ud.

Idiophone, any instr. that yields a sound by its own substance, being stiff and elastic enough to vibrate without requiring a stretched membrane or strings. See: concussion idiophone, percussion idiophone, plucked idiophone, shaken idiophone, struck idiophone (100).

Idiophone par entrechoc, Fr.: concussion idiophone.

Idiophone par percussion, Fr.: percussion idiophone.

Idiophone par pincement, Fr.: plucked idiophone, linguaphone.

Idiophone par secouement, Fr.: shaken idiophone.

Idje, drum of the Balendu of the Congo, identical with the idzdzai. Also called idzibile (30).

Idrablis, Heb.: hydraulos.

Idudu egu, *percussion pot of the Ibo of Nigeria, beaten with a palm-leaf beater and played by women only. It corresponds to the zin-li. Also called udu. *Cf.* kuku (152).

Idzdzai, drum of the Bahema of the Congo, in form of a truncated barrel, with cowskin or elephant-ear head. Played during dances and also used as a signal instr. Also called kibili. *Cf.* idje (30).

Idzibile, syn. of idje (30).

Igangat, pl. of aganga.

Igbin, *footed drum of the Yoruba of Nigeria (103).

Igbombo, *ground bow of the Nepoko Pygmies of the Congo. A rattan string is attached at one end to a flexible vertical stick, at the other to a piece of bark laid over a nearby pit and tied down. The performer plucks the strings with his left hand while beating the bark with a drumstick, to the accompaniment of a companion's singing (30, 128).

Igemfe, pl. **amagemfe, 1.** *notched flute of the Zulu of S. Africa, made of 2 cane segments of different diams. The thinner one is inserted in the thicker, thus prolonging it. The flute can be stopped by the player's finger, in which case it sounds a 4th lower. Always used in pairs, antiphonally, the 2 being tuned a semitone apart, the higher-pitched considered female, the lower, male; **2.** *cross flute of the Zulu, similar to the tshitiringo except that it is usually open at the lower end (116).

Igonga, syn. of bogonga (128).

Iguana, Mexican guitar with 5 pairs of strings tuned $a^0 d^1 g^1 c^2 f^2$. Total length *ca.* 84 cm. (33 in.) (132).

Iguí-égun [Yoruba *iqui*, stick + *egun*,

spirit of the dead], syn. of págugu (152).

Ihango, rectangular *board zither of the Mbuti of the Congo with 6 or 7 strings. The board is convex, and a single length of string is wound back and forth along it. *Ca.* 38 cm. (15 in.) long (149).

Ihara, *percussion tube of Tahiti, made of a section of bamboo cut just beyond 2 nodes. It is placed horizontally on the ground and struck with 2 sticks (8).

Iholere, side-blown horn of the Bashi of Ruanda, usually of antelope horn, occasionally of ivory. Both ends are open. A blowhole is cut some 5–8 cm. from the tip. The length varies from 25–35 cm. (10–14 in.). It accompanies social dances and songs. Also called mushereko (139).

Ije, see: idje.

Ika, side-blown trumpet of the Bororo Indians of C. Brazil, made of an upper section and a thicker bell joint, both cylindrical, bound with bark (176).

Ikelengue, bell of Sp. Guinea (152).

Ikimbe, *sansa of the Ngundi of the Congo (19).

Ikisandasanda, end-blown *notched flute of the Rundi of Urundi, Africa, with 3 fingerholes near the lower end (176).

Ikko, syn. of ichi no tsuzumi (157).

Ikoka, *musical bow of the Lokalo of the Congo, without tuning loop or resonator (128).

Ikokolo, 1. percussion trough of the Gishu of Uganda, consisting of a short beam hollowed out on one side, shallow, *ca.* 90 cm. (3 ft.) long, played with the opening turned downward with 2 drumsticks; **2.** percussion pot of the Gishu of Uganda, who beat its mouth with the palm of the hand (195).

Ikondo, pl. **ikondis,** large horn of the Nandi of E. Africa, made of a kudu horn.

Ikoro [name of a spirit], wooden drum of the Sudanese Ibo, often from 2.40–3.60 m. (8–12 ft.) in length, kept in a special hut near the chief's palace (93).

Ikpwokpwo, syn. of papakungbu.

Ikú-achán, syn. of pachán.

Ikulu (big), master drum of the Lala of N. Rhodesia (109).

Ikur ngon, signal drum of the Badzing of the Congo, held under the arm (30).

Ikuru, vertical *slit drum of Calabar, Nigeria, with a vertical slit. Very similar to the Afro-Cuban *tambor mumbomba. It is up to 3½ m. (12 ft.) high (152).

Ikuta koto, modern koto of Japan, descended from the sō no koto, played almost exclusively in the western part of the country, of beautiful workmanship, furnished with 13 strings. Played with an ivory or tortoise-shell plectrum (tsume). *Ca.* 1.80 m. (6 ft.) long, 25 cm. (10 in.) wide, 7½ cm. (3 in.) high (149, 157).

Ilimba, xylophone of the Balamba of the Congo, with calabash resonators (31).

Ilo-ilo-goto, name of the dermenan in Tegal, Java (121).

Ilongo, 1. *goblet drum of the Nkundo of the Congo, with nailed head, *ca.* 75 cm. (30 in.) high; **2.** *pot drum of the Bolia, Ekonde, Nkundo, and Ibeke-y-Onkusa of the Congo, made of clay, with membrane often of *pambi* antelope with rattan lacings. *Ca.* 25 cm. (10 in.) high (30).

Ilonma, *cross flute of the Garo of Assam, made of bamboo with 3 fingerholes near the lower end. *Ca.* 70 cm. (28 in.) long (172).

Ilú, *barrel drum of Pernambuco, Brazil, with 2 heads, played with sticks. In the 1920's and now again the name has also been applied to the large atabaques. See also: elú (7).

Imangu, a large 2-headed drum of the Balamba of the Congo, beaten with drumsticks; used as a war drum and also sounded at the death of a man. Too heavy to be transported, it remains in the village. The heads are laced. *Cf.* mangu (30).

Imbalanyi, percussion board of the Gishu of Uganda, beaten with drumsticks close to its ends (195).

Imbande, a small conical *notched flute of the Zulu of S. Africa, made of a bird's leg bone. No fingerholes. *Ca.* 10 cm. (4 in.) long (116).

Imbila, xylophone of the Matabele of the Transvaal, taken over from the Karanga of S. Rhodesia. *Cf.* ilimba, mbila (176).

Imbingi, idioglott clarinet of the Garo of Assam, of bamboo with 3 square fingerholes toward the lower end (172).

Imbubu, unidentified instr. of ancient Babylon, first mentioned in a text of *ca.* 800 B.C. The word corresponds to the Heb. and Syriac *abuba and may have denoted a conical double-reed instr. Also called bubu. See also: malîlu (89 Galpin).

Imele, pluriarc of Oli of the Congo (128).

Imiguza, rattle of the Xhosa of S. Africa, made of dried gourds and fastened to the dancer's waist (116).

Impai, name given to the safé in Lonvia, Borneo.

Impempe, 1. *end-blown flute of the Zulu and Xhosa of S. Africa, made of river reed, stopped at the bottom by a node. Nowadays made with a fipple; **2.** stopped *whistle flute of the Zulu, an imitation of the European recorder; **3.** syn. of the ixilongo of the Xhosa (116).

Imperial bass, see: Kaiserbass.

Imperial euphonium, see: Kaiserbaryton.

Imperial grand horizontal piano, grand piano patented by Robert Wornum of London by 1838, with strings running underneath the soundboard (92).

Imperial helicon, see: Kaiserhelikon.

Imperial ottavino, harp lute built by Angelo Benedetto Ventura of London in the mid-19th c., with rotary rings for shortening the strings. Apart from the rings it was identical to Edward Light's harp lute (178, 204).

Imperial tenor, see: Kaisertenor.

Impuruza, *conical drum of the Bahutu of the Congo with laced head. See also: ishako (30).

Imvingo, syn. of inkohlisa (116).

Inanga, 1. *trough zither of Ruanda and Urundi, similar to the lulanga; **2.** fiddle of the Murumvya of the Congo, with single string. *Cf.* enanga, nanga (128).

Inauina, *humming top of the Carajá Indians of Brazil (168).

Incudine, It.: anvil.

Indandala, small drum of the Ila of the Zambezi River area (176).

Indingidi, fiddle of the Rundi of Urundi, with cylindrical or semispherical body and single string (128).

Indip, *cylindrical drum of the Badzing of the Congo, with laced head (30).

Ingoma, var. of ngoma.

Ingomba, var. of ngoma.

Ingombe [*ngoma*], name of a large, single-headed drum used in voodoo rites in Pernambuco, Brazil. Vars. of the word—ingono, engono, ingomba—are used in the NE. and N. provinces to denote cylindrical drums with laced heads as well as barrel drums with nailed heads (7).

Ingondjo, drum of the Bombesa of the Congo, identical with the lilenga (30).

Ingono, see: ingombe.

Ingqongqo, *ground drum of the S. African Bantu, now found only among the Xhosa of the Transvaal and vicinity, and also known to the Tembu. A dried oxskin or bullock skin is stretched between poles stuck in the ground, the hide being some 90–120 cm. (3–4 ft.) above the ground. Another variety has small loops of hide fastened at intervals around the skin; these are held by the player's left hand while the right strikes the surface with a stick (116).

Ingungu, *friction drum of the Zulu of S. Africa, now rare, made from a spherical beer pot, covered by a trimmed goatskin laced with leather thongs and played with a friction stick with wet fingers (116, 185).

Injua, rattle of the Ila of N. Rhodesia, made of a tin can suspended on a stick, filled with pebbles or dried seeds. Used as a signal instr. Also called njua (176).

Inkinge, *musical bow of the Pondo and Xhosa of S. Africa, similar to the lugube, made of river reed with a hair string and played with a plectrum by women and girls, also by young herdboys (116).

Inkohlisa, 1. *musical bow of the Zulu of S. Africa, with gourd resonator and tuning loop. Also called imvingo; **2.** syn. of ugubo (116).

Insimbi, *linguaphone of the Zambezi Kafir, similar to the *sansa, with metal tongues attached to a wooden board (132).

Instromento . . . , see also: stromento . . . ; strumento . . .

Instromento di Laurento, syn. of instromento di porco.

Instromento di penna, It.: quilled keyboard instr.

Instromento di porco, It. name for the psaltery or dulcimer that is triangular with incurved sides. *Cf.* Schweinskopf.

Instromento omnisono, see: strumento omnisono.

Instromento pian e forte (It.: soft and loud instr.), mentioned in the late 16th c., this may have designated a *claviorganum, but is more likely to have been a harpsichord with several registers that could be played singly (pian) or together (forte). In 1598 Ippolito Cricca *alias* Paliarino, maker of organs and stringed keyboard instrs., writes concerning an *"instromento pian e forte con l'organo di sotto";* in December of the same year he writes concerning the need of materials *"per far tastadura per lo Instromento Pian e Forte che si fa di nuovo,"* and a year later he mentions *"l'instromento da sonare piani e forte piccollo."* An *Instromento Piano e forte* is also mentioned in an undated Este inventory of the 16th c. (Valdrighi, *Nomocheliurgraphia,* and *Musurgiana;* 170).

Instrument (Ger.), in 17th- and 18th-c. Germany a rectangular form of keyboard instr., *i.e.,* a clavichord, spinet, or virginal.

Instrument de Parnasse (Fr.), *glass harmonica built by the Bohemian virtuoso Grassa in Paris, 1796, with a pedalboard for the left foot (the right being engaged in working a treadle) (115).

Instrument truand, obs. Fr. name of

the hurdy-gurdy. The term was no longer in use when Laborde wrote (in 1780) (124).

Intambula [?Port. *tambor*], primitive *pot drum of the S. African Swazi, made of a clay pot over which a goatskin is stretched but not tied; it is held by an assistant while 1 or 2 persons play it simultaneously with sticks. Used for exorcising spirits (116).

Inventionshorn (Ger.) (Fr.: *cor d'invention*) [Lat. *in* + *ventus*], Fr. horn furnished with "inventions," first built by Johann Werner of Dresden *ca.* 1754 to the specifications of hornist Anton Joseph Hampel. Hampel is best remembered as originator of the hand-in-bell playing technique; this manner of playing was difficult, if not impossible, as long as terminal crooks were compounded and the length of the instr. constantly changed. The "inventions" were crooks, not placed next to the mouthpiece as previously, but inserted in the center of the horn between the circular windings. The coils were cut into and bent so as to form slides over which one of a series of U-shaped crooks was fitted. The crooks were of different lengths and served simultaneously as tuning slide, making it possible to put the horn into any pitch desired without adding to its length. See also: cor-solo (89 Morley-Pegge).

Inventionstrompete (Ger.), trumpet fitted with the mechanism of an *Inventionshorn, invented *ca.* 1780 jointly by Michel Wöggel of Karlsruhe and Johann Andreas Stein of Augsburg.

Inzina, var. of nzira.

Ipiano, syn. of utiyane.

Ipili, *globular flute of the Wasongola of the Congo, made from a gourd pierced with 2 holes (42).

Ippaki-ni, deer call of the Ainu of Japan, made of a piece of skin stretched over a flat piece of wood that has a hole drilled in it. The skin functions as a retreating reed when the hole is blown into (Galpin, F. W., in *Proceedings of the Music Association,* 21st session).

Ipopa, great drum of the Ila of N. Rhodesia, played in pairs. Only men may play it (176).

Ipu hokioko, var. of hokioko.

Ipu hula (*ipu,* calabash), stamping vessel of Hawaii made from a double calabash, *i.e.,* one that has been restricted around its middle during growth, one end of which is stamped against the ground (8).

Iqliq, obs. *spike fiddle of Turkestan and Arabia, with 2, 3, or 4 strings. Also known in Turkey by the 15th c. if not earlier. Similar to a small kamānja, it is now replaced in Turkey by the rabāb (76).

'Iraqiya [Iraq], foreshortened Arab. shawm with cylindrical tube and bore and domelike head, played with a very wide reed, 8–9 cm. (3–3½ in.) long and 3–4 cm. (1¼–1½ in.) wide, 7 front fingerholes and 2 rear thumbholes. Played chiefly in Egypt; 18–23 cm. (7–9 in.) long (132).

Irish harp, believed to have evolved in the 11th c., the Irish harp is characterized by the outward curve of its pillar and by having brass strings. Among several ancient instrs. preserved is the so-called "Brian Boru" harp, now thought to date from the 14th c. and housed at Trinity College, Dublin. Its resonator is cut from a block of willow, the pillar is of oak. Later instrs. were made with 30–50 brass strings traditionally plucked with long fingernails. In the late 18th c. the tradition of Irish-harp playing died out; a revival was promptly attempted, led by harpmaker John Egan, of Dublin, who by 1820 produced a portable, gut-strung harp that stood some 90 cm. (3 ft.) high and had a 3-oct. compass. To make it competitive with the pedal harp, he placed 7 finger levers on the inner curve of the pillar. When these were depressed, the pitch was raised by a semitone. Today the Irish harp lives on in a simplified version of the Egan harp, with hooks replacing the mechanism. Called clairsearch in

Irish Gaelic. See also: ceirnin, ocht-tedach (15 Birch).

Irish organ, name sometimes applied to the Union pipes.

Irna, clapper bell of the Muria of Bastar, India, made of brass. Tied to the buttocks of dancers, together with some *muyang (68).

Irriliku, *nose flute of the Motu of SE. New Guinea, with 2 fingerholes, also played as a conventional flute. 50–60 cm. (20–24 in.) long (203).

Isambu, horn of the Baziba of Lake Victoria, E. Africa, with lateral blowhole, made of a gourd or animal horn (176).

Isankuni, *musical bow of the Pondo of S. Africa. The stick is thrust into the open end of a gallon can that acts as resonator. A single string is attached to the bottom of the can and secured to the tip of the bow. Held with the resonator down, it is bowed with a curved bow (116).

Isanzi, pl. **bisanzi,** name of the sansa among the Teke and other tribes of W. Africa (185).

Iselwa, rattle of N. Zululand, probably borrowed from the Thonga; similar to the njele (116).

Ishako, *conical drum of the Bahutu of the Congo, identical with the impuruza (30).

Isigodhlo, side-blown horn of the Xhosa of S. Africa, made of oxhorn, formerly of antelope horn (116).

Isigubu, *cylindrical drum of S. Africa, with 2 laced heads, played with padded drumsticks. An imitation of the European bass drum (116).

Isikehlekehle, bowed *tube zither of the Swazi of S. Africa, which corresponds to the tsijolo of the Venda (116).

Isikunjane, rattle of the Xhosa of S.

Africa, consisting of a small can containing pebbles, etc., attached to the dancer's legs below the knees (116).

Isiqomqomana, *musical bow of the Zulu of S. Africa; it corresponds to the isitontola (116).

Isiqwemqwemana, syn. of inkohlisa.

Isis, see: Ysis.

Isitontola, *musical bow of the Swazi of S. Africa, with tuning loop (116).

Isquitra, *globular flute of E. Turkestan, made of baked clay, with blowhole and 2 fingerholes (183).

Istromento . . . , see also: instromento . . . , stromento . . . , strumento . . .

Istromento d'acciajo (It.: steel instr.), see: strumento d'acciaio.

Itag, syn. of yatag (69).

Itikili, *ground bow of the Lugbara of Uganda, used as a child's toy (195).

Itulasi, drum of Samoa (77).

Itumbilongonda, *ground bow of the Bokote of the Congo (128).

Itumbolongonda, 1. *ground bow of the Beloko of the Congo; **2.** *musical bow of the Nkundo of the Congo, without loop or resonator (128).

Ivenge, syn. of umtshingo.

Ixilongo, 1. var. of icilongo; **2.** end-blown flute of the Xhosa of S. Africa, identical with the umtshingo (116).

Iyamaombe, 2-headed drum of the Balamba of the Congo, used in initiation rites (30).

Iyupana, *panpipes of the Tebas Indians (105).

Iyup-iyup, name of the *dermenan in the Alas district of W. Java (121).

Izeze, fiddle of the Rundi of Urundi, with single string (128).

Izkila, see: ezkila.

Jack (Fr.: *sautereau;* Ger.: *Docke, Springer;* It.: *saltarello*), **1.** in plucked keyboard instrs. the slip of wood that constitutes the action. Inserted in a *slide, it rests on the rear of a key; **2.** in pianos it is an intermediary member of the action which assists the escapement; it is also known as sticker.

Jackdaw, name of a *friction drum, with friction cord, found in Lincolnshire, England (16).

Jādaghara, war drum of Bengal (176).

Jaga, var. of njaga.

Jagajampa (Sans.), name given to the naguar in Bengal (173).

Jagd-Hautbois, 18th-c. Ger.: oboe da caccia.

Jagdhorn, Ger.: hunting horn.

Jägerhorn, obs. Ger.: hunting horn.

Jäger Trommet, depicted by Praetorius as a close-coiled horn with 4 windings, almost cylindrical. See: horn.

Jalājil, pl. of jul-jul.

Jalatharangini, see: jaltarang.

Jaleika, double hornpipe of the U.S.S.R., with idioglott reeds and parallel tubes, attached together, the lower ends of which are inserted into a common bell of horn, occasionally of bark. The left pipe is generally provided with 6 fingerholes, and the right pipe with 3, the holes of both pipes being stopped by one hand. In Smolensk each pipe has 5 fingerholes. Also made as a single pipe with 4 to 6 fingerholes (132, 136).

Jalousieschweller, Ger.: Venetian swell.

Jalra, cymbals of India, smaller than the jhānjha, made of brass or bell metal, flat with central boss (179).

Jaltarang (Hindust., Mar., Punj.: water waves), musical cups of India, made of porcelain or clay with a compass of 2–3 octs. Each cup has a different pitch when empty. Now rare, it is usually comprised of 18 bowl-shaped cups arranged in semicircle in front of the player, with the lowest-pitched to the left. The cups are partly filled with water and are played with 2 very slender bamboo sticks having cork or felt tips. The water serves to: a) modify the pitch; b) sustain the tone; c) permit the playing of *gamakas* (embellishments) by bringing the stick into contact with the water surface. *Cf.* kastratrang (179).

Jamisen, original form of the samisen, the long-necked lute of Japan, first introduced from China *ca.* 1400 into the Ryukyu Islands. The body is made from an oval block of hardwood 15 cm. (6 in.) long, 12½ cm. (5 in.) wide, with 7 cm. (2¾ in.) depth, in which a hole 5 cm. (2 in.) in diam. is cut. Top and bottom were covered with snakeskin, but as this did not stand up to the Jap. *bachi technique, it was replaced by catskin. The slender neck terminates in a reversed pegbox with 3 lateral pegs. The strings are rib-fastened and pass over a small wooden bridge (135, 157).

Janil, *nose flute of Satowal, Micronesia, made of mangrove root or bamboo (203).

Jānja, see: jhānjha.

Janj khanjani, see: jhanjh khanjani.

Jank, pl. **junuk** (Arab.) [Pers. *chang*], *angular harp introduced to Arabia from Persia in pre-Islamic times; it subsequently spread to other countries. In Egypt it was still in use in the 15th c.; in Turkey it was frequently mentioned by

15th-c. poets and was in use there until the late 17th c. See also: chang (76, 170).

Jänk (Turk.), bell of Turkey, E. Turkestan, and of the Cheremiss of the Upper Volga (76, 176).

Jank 'ajami (Arab.: Pers. harp), harp of Egypt (89 Farmer).

Jank misri (Arab.: Egyptian harp), harp of Egypt, with 2 sets of strings separated by a wooden soundboard; it has existed since the 15th c. Cf. arpanetta (89 Farmer).

Janko keyboard (Ger.: *Janko-Klaviatur*), keyboard invented by Paul von Janko in 1882, originally built by R. W. Kurka of Vienna and introduced to the public in 1886. Its object was to give equal value to all tonalities by the disposition of the keys, to reduce the oct. span and to open up new possibilities of fingering. The Janko keyboard had an oct. span of 13 cm. as opposed to the 18½-cm. standard keyboard. Its keys were arranged in 6 terraced rows, sloping slightly to the front. Each key lever actuated 3 key "fronts," 1 behind the other, thus permitting each note to be played from 3 different positions. The 6 parallel rows were arranged in whole-tone sequence: front row C D E F♯ G♯ B♭ C; second row C♯ E♭ F G A B C♯; the third and fifth rows merely repeated the first, the fourth and sixth rows repeated the second row. Natural keys were white, accidentals black. The following pattern was repeated 3 times:

BLACK		WHITE			BLACK	
C♯	E♭	F	G	A	B	C♯ etc.
C	D	E	F♯	G♯	B♭	C etc.
WHITE		BLACK			WHITE	

Jarami, a Sundanese name of the dermenan (121).

Jarana, a small Mexican guitar.

Jaranita [dim. of *jarana*], small Mexican guitar with 5 pairs of strings (192).

Jaras, pl. **ajras** (Arab.), bell of Islam, conoid or square, with clapper, hung around the necks of elephants and camels (76).

Jarupei, small bamboo flute of SE. Borneo, with 3 fingerholes (176).

Jatag, jataga, see: yatag.

Jaumin, *hourglass drum of the Kate of New Guinea, similar to the oñ (28).

Javata, horn of the Washambala of Tanganyika, made of animal horn, side-blown. The large end is covered with skin. Used as a signal instr. and also to frighten wild animals from plantations at night (111).

Jawbone, jawbone of a horse, mule, or donkey used as a scraper in Louisiana and the Carolinas. See also: quijada (152).

Jaw's-harp, see: Jew's-harp.

Jayadhakka, Hindi: large drum (176).

Jayaghantā, Hindi: large bell (176).

Jayasringa, syn. of ranasringa (176).

Jazzo-flûte, Fr.: Swannee whistle.

Jedina, *whistle flute of N. Croatia and Slavonia, made like the *stranka and of the same materials, differing only in that the jedina has a whistle head instead of a blowhole. To lend color to the tone, players use a special technique when performing for dances: they hum a deep bourdon while playing. See: svirala (34).

Jedor, large drum of Java, slightly conoid, with one nailed head at the larger end, set on a stand resembling a campstool. See also: bajidor (121).

Jejaok, small, pointed Jew's-harp of the Mentawai Islands, Indonesia (176).

Jejilava, *musical bow of the Malagasy Republic (171).

Jejy (Swah.), *stick zither of the Malagasy Republic (171).

Jemblok, see: gong jemblok.

Jeme, drum of the Balesa-Basa of the Congo, with laced head. Played with bare hands to accompany dances (30).

Jengglong, W. Java gong chime composed of 6 or 7 bonang-shaped gongs lying on a frame (121).

Jeremia, see: xeremia.

Jericho trombone (Ger.: *Jerichoposaune*), trombone with exceptionally loud tone invented by Ignaz Stowasser of Vienna *ca.* 1873 (176).

Jerupai, shawm of Borneo, with free tongue (120).

Jester's flute (Ger.: *Narrenflöte*), *whistle flute with a globular center that could be filled with soot or other material (176).

Jeu, Fr.: set, chime, rank of pipes, register of harpsichord.

Jeu à anche, Fr.: organ stop of reed pipes.

Jeu à bouche, Fr.: organ stop of flue pipes.

Jeu à reprise, Fr.: repeating stop.

Jeu céleste, Fr.: the piano stop of a piano.

Jeu composé, Fr.: mixture stop.

Jeu d'acier (Fr.), organ stop of Abbé Vogler's invention, a 3⅕' carillon stop believed to have been composed of 3 ranks (3⅕', 2⅔', 2') (133).

Jeu de basson, Fr.: bassoon stop.

Jeu de chalumeau, organ stop of reed pipes with cylindrical resonators, first recorded in Dijon in the 13th c. Later called *chalumeau (133).

Jeu de clochettes, Fr.: **1.** carillon organ stop; **2.** Glockenspiel. Also called clochettes.

Jeu de fond, Fr.: foundation stop (of an organ). Also called jeu d'octave, fond d'orgue.

Jeu de harpe, syn. of jeu de luth.

Jeu de luth, Fr. piano stop that corresponds to the lute, or sordino, stop. Also called jeu de harpe (92).

Jeu de timbres, Fr.: chime, bell chime.

Jeu d'octave, syn. of jeu de fond.

Jeux de fond, see: jeu de fond.

Jew's-harp [U.] (Fr.: *guimbarde;* Ger.: *Maultrommel;* It.: *scacciapensieri*), expression in use from 1595 on (preceded by Jew's trump[e]) to denote an instr. consisting of a frame of wood or metal, in clothespin or horseshoe form, to which one end of a flexible lamella is attached, its other end remaining free. The narrow end of the frame is held loosely between the teeth so that the lamella can swing freely and is plucked with a finger, causing it to vibrate in the player's mouth, which thereby becomes a resonator. Depending on the position of tongue, lips, and cheeks, one or another harmonic can be emphasized. The harmonic series is that of the trumpet (hence its trumpet-associated names in many languages); the first to third harmonics do not speak at all, the fourth to tenth speak clearly. In order to play certain melodies it is necessary to have a second instr. tuned a 4th lower to complete the scale. Tuning is done by applying wax or sealing wax to the end of the lamella. The oldest forms of Jew's-harp are found in SE. Asia: elongated, like an oversize clothespin, made of bamboo, with idioglott lamella set in vibration by a series of jerks from a cord attached to its end. Transitional types occur on Formosa and on Engaño, Philippine Islands, where heteroglott tongues of metal are used, plucked directly by the finger without intermediary cord. Then follows a tuning-fork-shaped instr., and finally one of horseshoe form. Throughout Asia as well as in med. Europe the broad end of the lamella of this horseshoe variety projected beyond the frame. The European Jew's-harp came from Asia and is first seen *ca.* 1350 on a sculpture of Exeter Cathedral; a Jew's-harp was found in the excavation of Tannenberg Castle, Hessen, which was destroyed in 1399. By the time Virdung wrote (1511), it formed part of the *musica irregularis*. This did not prevent Hans Burgkmair from including one in his engravings of the *Triumph of Maximilian* (1515) (Emperor Maximilian I had a court jester who played it). A c. later Praetorius mentions it as *crembalum* and *Brummeisen*. About 1800 the Jew's-harp temporarily became a virtuoso instr. in Europe; several instrs. were even connected together to form one (see: Aura). In the Austrian Alps it was played up to the late 19th c. In Molln, Upper Austria, there had been a guild of Jew's-harp makers since 1679.

By 1818 this had a membership of 33 masters and 14 apprentices who turned out an annual production of some two and a half million pieces, all by hand. By 1935, long after it had been officially declared dead in Europe (having been succeeded by the mouth organ), 10 masters and their families still produced annually an estimated one and a half million pieces, iron-made. A similar enterprise existed near Riva on Lake Garda (then Austrian). Its output was exported overseas via Genoa and Livorno (Leghorn). Jew's-harps are distributed in Europe, Asia, and the S. Seas; they are unknown to Africa and to the American Indians. See also: ab-a-fu, aghiz tanburasi, aman-khuur, anoin, aping, Aura, balimbo, barimbo, berimbao, birimbao, brumbice, brumle, Brummeisen, cacciapensieri, chang, changu, crembalum, cymbalum orale, dambras, darubiri, dombrã, drimba, drombla, drombulye, dromla, drumelca, dumbing, ediokeko, ego, ensutu, galinquang, genggong, gewgaw, gongina, gronde, gualamban, guimbarda, guimbarde, jejaok, Jew's trump(e), juring, kach-tehendor, kalinguang, ka-mien, kamuti, k'api, kareng, karinding, kinaban, koma, koms, ku ch'in, kukau, kulang, kutsi biwa, lokanga vava, mago, marimbao, Maultrommel, mazin, mondtrom, morshingu, mosugitarra, muchanga, mukkuri, munchang, Mundharmonika, mungiga, munharpa, munnharpe, murchang, mursing, musugitarra, mynn harpa, namarue, neve, ngab, ngannalarruni, niau-kani, nvatt, pampa, pau, pingoru, pio poyo, pipo, pirutu, pyē, rabube, rbairbe, rebube, rinda, rinding, rinding besi, roria, rudien sulu, sanfornia, scacciapensieri, shong nong, sinfonia, sinfoyna, spassapensieri, stobung, su pill, tanguri, tawaya, temürkhuur, teruding, titapu, tong, trimmi, trombula, trompa, trompa de Paris, trompa gallega, trompa goajira, trompa inglesa, trompe de Béarn, trompe de Berne, trompe-laquais, tronpa, trump, Trumpel, Twangl, ukeke, unkin, utete,

vargan, vazang, viabò, vivo, yangong, yangroi, yheku (117, 169, 170, Piffl, M.: *"Die Musik im alten Tirol,"* in *Meraner Kurzeitung,* No. 29, 1911/12).

Jew's trump(e), obs. expression for Jew's-harp, first recorded in 1545 and in use until the late 18th c. (Oxford English Dictionary).

Jhãnjha (Sans., Beng., Hindi, Hindust., Mar., Punj.), the "clashing" cymbals of India, which go back to pre-Islamic times. Made of thin bronze with a wide, flat rim and central boss, connected pairwise by a cord (170).

Jhanjhana (Sans., Beng.), *vessel rattle of India, made of metal, wood, clay, or basketwork, containing pellets or dried seeds. The form is an imitation of the calabash, presumably the material of which it was originally made (173).

Jhanjh khanjani, see: khanjani.

Jhãrídhap, piriform clay drum of Bengal, with single head (176).

Jícara de agua (Sp.: water calabash), *water gourd of Mexico, played by the Yaqui and the Maya of Sonora, said to be of pre-Columbian origin (137).

Jícara de jobá (Sp.: calabash of the jobo fruit), Cuban *water gourd consisting of a hemispheric half gourd placed open side down in a bowl of water and played with 2 sticks. Also made with 2 half gourds. Its chief use is at funeral rites of the African population. Also called guïro de jobá (152).

Jicarita [Sp., dim. of *jícara,* calabash], Cuban percussion instr. shaped like a short, deep spoon, made of wood and played in pairs by being struck rhythmically against the ground or a table. *Ca.* 5 cm. (2 in.) in diam. (152).

Jicotea (Sp.: mud turtle), Afro-Cuban rattle and scraper consisting of a turtle carapace impaled on a stick and filled with pebbles. *Cf.* ayotl (152).

Jidor, var. of jedor.

Jigi-jigi, *ground bow of the Alur of Uganda, used as a child's toy (195).

Jimba, 1. sansa of the Aruwimi area of the Congo, with hollowed-out wooden resonator, a soundboard held down by clasps, and 5 brass tongues (176); **2.** name given to the madimba by the Bachioko of the Congo (31).

Jimpai, syn. of safé.

Jinã, Arabic *panpipes having 7 or more pipes (176).

Jin daiko, *barrel drum of Japan, with 2 nailed heads, *ca.* 35 cm. (14 in.) high, with the same diam. (178).

Jin gane, bronze gong of Japan, formerly a war instr., now used in temples (176).

Jinge, *stick zither of the Gombe of Busu-Djoana, the Congo (128).

Jingling Johnnie [Johnnie, corr. of *chaghāna], *percussion stick surmounted by a crescent and an ornament shaped like a Chin. hat, from which bells and jingles and usually 2 horsehair tails —1 red and 1 white—are suspended, adopted by European military bands from the Turks, hence also known as Turkish crescent. Europe knew of it by the 16th c.; a Pressburg inventory of 1527 lists a "Turkish bush of horsehair on a chime . . ." Brit. military bands adopted it in the late 18th c., Ger. ones in the 19th. The British discarded it after the Crimean War of 1856, but it survives in Germany, albeit in slightly altered form, with lyre-shaped frame. See also: campanillas chinas, chaghāna, klinting, vargan (89 Farmer, 98).

Jingivi, syn. of pūngī.

Jitag, syn. of yatag.

Jjembe, Ganda: horn (195).

Jo, see: gyo.

Joare, Basque: small bell; syn. of chincha, panpalina.

Joare kuxkula, Basque: cowbell.

Jobel, ram's-horn mentioned in ancient Jewish sources. *Cf.* jubal (144).

Jojo, drum of the Fulbe of Senegal.

Jombarde (Fr.), coll. name of the galoubet (124).

Jomo, drum of the Modjombo of Dongo, the Congo, played with a mongondo during dances (30).

Jongka, bar zither of Sumba, Sunda Island, with single string and coconut resonator (149).

Joraghai (Beng.), see: yoraghayi.

Joucoujou, Haïtian equivalent of the yucuyu (152).

Jouhikannel, var. of jouhikantele (9).

Jouhikantele (horsehair *kantele), *bowed harp of Finland, a lyre that in the 18th c. still had 3 horsehair strings tuned a 5th and 4th apart, in later times tuned in 5ths. During the latter part of the 19th c. the number of strings was increased to 5, and it seems that the increase caused the bow to be abandoned and the strings to be plucked. In many instances further strings were added, and 1 specimen with a total of 16 is recorded. Originally the strings were fastened by a horizontal pin, without bridge or nut. Pegs were inserted from the rear. The jouhikantele is thought to have reached Finland from Sweden. Preserved older specimens vary in size from 40–83 cm. (16–32½ in.) in length, 9–19 cm. (3½–7½ in.) in width, with a handhole 10–12 cm. (4–5 in.) long and 4–5 cm. (1½–2 in.) wide (9, 89).

Jouhikas, var. of jouhikantele (9).

Jouhikko, syn. of jouhikantele (9).

Jourou, see: juru.

Jousi, Finn.: bow (9).

Jubal, according to modern research, another name for the shofar of the ancient Hebrews. *Cf.* jobel (144).

Jubalflöte, organ stop of open flue pipes with double mouths, at 16′, 8′, 4′, or 2′ pitch (131).

Juco, Nicaraguan *friction drum with friction cord (152).

Juk jang go, bamboo *stamping tube of Korea (130).

Jul, *musical bow of the Maya of Yucatán, Mexico, without resonator, but with a wooden stick inserted between bow and string, acting as tension regulator. The player's mouth acts as resonator while the string is tapped with a small stick. *Ca.* 60 cm. (2 ft.) long (17, 105).

Jula, obs. organ stop of conical flue

pipes, usually at 5⅓' pitch, also at 8' or 4' (2).

Jul-jul, pl. **jalājil** (Arab.), **1.** Saracen bell; **2.** spherical pellet bell of Arab. culture (74).

Jun, see: gong jun.

Jungfernregal, softly intoned organ stop of regal pipes at 8' or 4' pitch, syn. of Geigenregal (3).

Jungga au, idiochord bamboo *tube zither of E. Sumba Island, Indonesia (119).

Jura (Turk.: treble), small zurna of Albania, also called surla (11).

Jura zurnā (Turk.: treble *zurnā), zurnā of the Kurds and of modern Egypt (76, 89).

Juring, Jew's-harp of bamboo, of Lampong, Sumatra (176).

Juru, stringed instr. of the Baoule of the Ivory Coast Republic, with 5 strings (103).

Jurusian, idiochord *tube zither of the Aru Island, Indonesia, with 2 strings. Also called mariri (119, 149).

Jututo, syn. of putoto.

Juwāq (Arab.), *whistle flute of the Maghrib, formerly also of the Sp. Moors, with 5 to 6 front fingerholes, sometimes also with a rear thumbhole (75 I).

Juzale, double clarinet of the Kurds of Iraq (103).

Jyabisen, primitive shamisen of the Amami Islands (120).

K

K . . . , see also: c . . .

Ka, 1. drum found in Cuba, the Fr.-speaking Antilles, Haiti, New Orleans, and the Virgin Islands, made from a commercial barrel with single, nailed head and open bottom (152); **2.** side-blown trumpet of the Dogon of Mali (103).

Kāapolo, tubular rattle of the Cuna Indians of Panama (105).

Ka'ara, *slit drum of the Cook Islands, with hourglass- or 8-shaped slit, beaten with 2 sticks (77).

Kabacha, straight metal trumpet of Nepal, without a bell (173).

Kabar (Arab.), single-headed drum of Islam, first mentioned in the 9th c., glossed as *chorus in the 10th c., and identified with the *asaf by Al-Shalahi in 1301 (75 II).

Kabaro (Amh.), **1.** great drum of Ethiopia, similar to the tabl turki, a shallow *cylindrical drum with 2 heads; **2.** name given to the nagarit by the Galla (176).

Kabarome, 1. *musical bow of the Mbuti Pygmies of Amba, Uganda, with tuning loop but no resonator. The middle of the bow is taken between the player's teeth. Both sections of the string are plucked with a short grass plectrum, and the string is stopped with the fingers of the left hand; **2.** *sansa of the same people, with 9 or 10 rattan lamellae mounted on a piece of bark (195).

Kåbdes, obs. bowl-shaped drum of Lapland, a shamanist instr. that had a reindeer membrane and was struck with a reindeer bone beater (144).

Kabek, bowed stringed instr. of E. Anatolia (89).

Kabilles-adar, syn. of gau adar (56).

Kabirizi, sacred drum of Urundi, Africa.

Kabiry, double-reed instr. of the Malagasy Republic, *ca.* 40 cm. (16 in.) long (171).

Kabisli, *cross flute of the Khasi of Assam, with 6 equidistant fingerholes near the lower end. *Ca.* 44 cm. (17 in.) long (172).

Kabosa, kabosy [Turk. *qūpūz], short lute of the Malagasy Republic, with 3 or 4 pairs of strings and lateral pegs, carried to the island by Islamic immigration. Identical with the gambus of Celebes (170, 171).

Kabosi, bowed lute of the Maronene of SE. Celebes and of the Butong of Borneo, with single string. Known elsewhere as gabbus, gambus, kabosa (173).

Ka-chapi [*kachapi], flat lute of Thailand similar to the *cha pei thom of Cambodia, with 3 or 4 strings and 12 frets on the long, slender neck. Lateral pegs. The neck terminates in a reversed arch (46, 132).

Kachapi [Sans. *kachapa cedrela,* the *Cedrela toona* tree], the word *kachapi* means tortoise in Beng., Mal. and Sans., giving rise to the belief that these instrs. were originally made of tortoise carapace, but Sachs's etym., given above, is now generally accepted; **1.** lute of the Batak of Sumatra, with oval wooden body terminating at the lower end in a clawlike extension, a carved head on the neck, and 2 fiber strings. Some specimens have angular bodies and 5 flat frets. See also: asopi; **2.** scaphoid lute of E. and S. Celebes and Sumba Island, with slender body, small lateral pegs, and 1 or 2 fiber strings. Some specimens have metal bellies. *Cf.* kachaping; **3.** *board zither of the Sunda district of W. Java; it corresponds to the E. Java chelempung, 2, with large rectangular body, 6–18 strings with tuning pegs inserted laterally through the walls of the body, open bottom, and one fixed bridge as well as a movable one. The strings are plucked with finger and thumb. Nowadays a more modern variety, called siter, is made in less elegant form, more like the European zither and with only a slit in the bottom (121, 173).

Kachaping [*kachapi], scaphoid lute of S. Celebes, identical with the kachapi, 2 (173).

Kachapī vīnā [*kachapi], vīnā of Bengal, of the sitār type, with a large gourd body, wooden soundboard, fretted neck that is long, flat, and wide, and both frontal and lateral pegs. The 6 strings are tuned c³ c² g⁰ c¹ c¹ f¹ (relative tuning) and are rib-fastened (138, 173).

Kācha vīnā [*kachapi], modern lute of India of the sitār type, the body being made of a half gourd and the belly of wood, with a long neck terminating in a volute and a glass fingerboard, also a second, shorter neck and a fingerboard running parallel to the first neck; 6 melody strings and 11 sympathetic strings (132, 170).

Kach-tehendor, metal Jew's-harp of the Muria of Bastar, India, made of locally smelted iron, of elongated shape. *Ca.* 9½ cm. (3¾ in.) long (68).

Kachvā, a form of sitār, with 2 melody strings, tuned a 3rd apart, and 2 higher drone strings (176).

Kadia m'buji, *hourglass drum of the Bena-Lulua of Kasai, the Congo, with 2 nailed heads and carved body, and provided with a mirliton membrane (30).

Kaduar, *slit drum of the Humboldt Bay area of New Guinea (77).

Ka duitara [Sans. *dvitāra,* two strings], lute of the Khasi of Assam, with wooden, spade-shaped body and glued parchment belly. Four strings pass from rib fastener over a wooden bridge to lateral pegs inserted in a square pegbox. The instr. is either plucked with a plectrum or bowed (172).

Ka ea-ea, syn. of pu tatara.

Ka eke-eke, syn. of ohe ke eke.

Kaengere, see: kangere.

Kaffir piano, name given by Europeans to the *sansa. Buonanni, in 1722, wrote of the sansa as *marimba dei Cafri* (39, 109).

Kafir harp, *arched harp played in the Hindu Kush of Afghanistan, with 4 or 5 strings. The neck pierces the resonator's membrane belly and reappears to form the string holder, pierced with holes through which the strings are knotted. The Kafir harp has been likened to a harp of ancient Gandhara, in whose cultural sphere Afghanistan lies (15 Wachsmann).

Kafo, pl. **kafoni,** small horn of the Hausa and Fulbe of W. Africa (144).

Kafoa, name of the dermenan in Donggo, E. Sumbawa, Indonesia (121).

Kagan, smallest *barrel drum of the Ewe of Ghana. Similar, except for its size, to the atsimevu. The performer plays seated, holding the drum between his knees and striking it with 2 sticks. *Ca.* 56 cm. (22 in.) long (109).

Kagura . . . (Jap.: god music), as a prefix, kagura is a generic term for instrs. used in Shinto music in Japan.

Kagura fuye, cylindrical *cross flute of Japan, used in Shinto music, with 6 equidistant fingerholes, giving a scale of D E F♯ G A C; 40–55 cm. (16–22 in.) long (144).

Kagura sutsu, *percussion stick of Japan, consisting of a lacquered wooden stick to which a number of pellet bells and metal rings are attached. *Ca.* 30 cm. (12 in.) long (176).

Kaha, straight metal trumpet of Nepal, with a wide-rimmed, flat mouthpiece (173).

Kāhalam, Mal.: ranasringa.

Kahara, var. of ka'ara.

Kahel, syn. of hahel.

Kāhuis, *percussion stick of the Choroti Indians of the S. American Chaco, 2–3 m. (6½–10 ft.) long, of wood or bamboo. Rattling hoofs are attached to the top. The staff is stamped rhythmically during adolescence rites for girls (105).

Kaiamba, bamboo rattle of the Malagasy Republic. *Cf.* kajamba (171).

Kaiavuru, generic name for bullroarers among the Elema people of Papua (201).

Kai hui, end-blown stopped pipe of the buffalo herders of Timor, conical with wide collar at the top, made of a single section, with one very small fingerhole. A signal instr. (173).

Kaiko, obs. form of the kakko of Japan, but wider and shorter, that was played in processions with the fingers of the right hand. The head, painted white, had a diam. of 35 cm. (14 in.) (157).

Kairata vīnā (vīnā of the Kairata people), *stick zither of Bengal, with gourd resonator, 4–7 very high movable frets, and 3 or 4 metal strings attached to lateral pegs (149, 173).

Kais, misreading of 'air.

Kaiserbaryton (Ger.) (Fr.: *baryton impérial*), wide-bore, completely conical *baritone (brass instr.) of Vaclav Červeny of Königgrätz (Hradec Králové), 1882, made in elliptical or tuba form, pitched in C or B♭, with 4 rotary or piston valves and a compass D^0–d^2. Called imperial euphonium in Engl.

Kaiserbass (Ger.) (Fr.: *basse impériale*), bombardon (brass instr.) of Vaclav F. Červeny of Königgrätz (Hradec Králové), 1883, similar to his Kaiserbaryton; made in tuba or helicon form, pitched in F or E♭, C or B♭, with 3 or 4 valves and a bell having a diam. of up to 55 cm. (22 in.). Called imperial bass in Engl.

Kaiserhelikon (Ger.), large *helicon in C or B♭ with 3 or 4 valves, made by Vaclav F. Červeny in the 19th c.

Kaisertenor (Ger.) (Fr.: *ténor impérial*), *tenor horn made by Vaclav F. Červeny in 1885, similar to his Kaiserbaryton, in elliptical form, pitched in C or B♭, with 4 rotary or piston valves. Called imperial tenor in Engl. (176).

Kaisertuba, syn. of Kaiserbass.

Kaitara (Arab.) [Gk. *kithara], in Moorish Spain the name of the European guitar. The word was in use from the 10th c. on. Outside Spain it was applied to an Arab. stringed instr., later to become a lute. *Cf.* qītāra (75 II, 147 Farmer).

Kaithār, see: kaitara.

K'ai ti, small sona of Peking; a syn. of chi na (142).

Kajamba, rattle of the Wabondei of Tanganyika. *Cf.* kaiamba (111).

Kajirei, rattle of Japan, consisting of 3 hollow metal rings attached to a handle (176).

Kakaki, 1. large horn adopted by the Sunghai of W. Sudan *ca.* 1500, according to Farmer. Probably identical with: **2.** straight metal trumpet of the Sudanese Hausa, *ca.* 1.80 m. (6 ft.) long, made in 3 sections that can be taken apart to facilitate transportation. A signal instr. blown only on important occasions. It has been taken over by the Yoruba. *Cf.* kakati, katakyi (72, 93).

Kakalam, Tamil: ranasringa.

Kakalari, *ground zither of the Logo of the Congo (128).

Kakanika-kanika, equivalent of the *rondro in the Majunga region of the Malagasy Republic (171).

Kakara, syn. of pu tatara.

Kakati [*kȧkaki*], long bronze trumpet of the Sudanic Nupe (93).

Kakeeke, 1. obs. bamboo flute of Hawaii; **2.** *percussion tube of Hawaii, made of bamboo (8).

Kakhara, *percussion stick with jingles, used by mendicant monks of Java, of great antiquity. Some specimens are believed to date back to *ca.* 1000 (121).

Kakko, small *barrel drum of Japan, with 2 projecting deerskin heads mounted on hoops and laced to each other. Both heads are played, always with drumsticks. Used in *gagaku* and *bugaku* music. Of Turkestan origin. *Ca.* 30 cm. (12 in.) long. *Cf.* kaiko, o-kakko (135, 157).

Ka könshau, bronze cymbals of the Khasi of Assam (172).

Kakonti, "tuning fork" idiophone of the Sula Islands, identical with the *re-re (112).

Kakosh, fiddle of the Holo of the Congo, with 3 strings (128).

Ka ksin, *barrel drum of the Khasi of Assam, made of wood, with 2 heads and Y-lacings (172).

Kaku koto (Jap.: square koto), ancient koto of Japan, now obs. It had 25 strings and was *ca.* 60 cm. (2 ft.) long (148, 157).

Kakulumbumba, *musical bow of the Lunda of Dilolo (Angola and the Congo), with gourd resonator and tuning loop (128).

Kakva, cymbals of the Garo of Assam (173).

Kalah, small *slit drum of Malaya and Thailand, of bamboo, with single, longitudinal slit, used as a signal instr. (18).

Kalaka (Basque), **1.** Basque clappers made of 3 pieces of wood *ca.* 25 cm. (10 in.) long and 10 cm. (4 in.) wide, the center one with a handle, all 3 tied together with a piece of wire. Used instead of a bell during Easter week at Catholic services. Also called olezkilla; **2.** var. of carraca (56).

Kalam, Tamil: ranasringa.

Kalama [Arab. *qalam* from Gk. *kalamos*], oboe of N. India, of bamboo or cane, with 7 equidistant fingerholes. *Ca.* 23 cm. (9 in.) long without reed (132, 173).

Kalanba, xylophone of the Togbo and Mono of the Congo, with 10 hardwood slabs all the same length but of different thicknesses, and calabash resonators. A small lateral hole bored near the tip of the resonators is covered with a thin membrane, a *mirliton device. Also called karangba (31).

Kalangu, 1. var. of kalungu; **2.** *pluriarc of Africa (100).

Kalangual, pl. **kalanguje** [Arab. *kūbā*], *hourglass drum of the Fulbe of W. Africa (93).

Kalangwa, xylophone of the Ngbandi of the Congo, with 5 slabs of hardwood of the same length but of different thick-

nesses, and calabash resonators. A small lateral hole bored near the tip of the resonators is covered with thin animal membrane, a *mirliton device (31).

Kalembete, fiddle of the Holo of the Congo, with 2 or 3 strings (128).

Kaligo, *musical bow of the Chinyanja of Nyasaland, with resonator made of a half gourd. See also: gubu (*Journal of the Royal Anthropological Institute,* 1907).

Kalimba, syn. of sansa.

Kalinga, 1. drum of the Bahavu of the Congo, made from the hollowed trunk of the *muvusangoma* tree. A new one is made for the enthroning of each *mwami* (great chief). The head of the deceased chief is inserted inside the new drum, which is then closed with the skin of a bull from the sacred herd. Each kalinga is interred with the *mwami* to whom it belongs. It is never sounded, but in exceptional circumstances may be brought out from the hut in which it remains hidden; **2.** royal drum of Ruanda (30).

Kalinguang, syn. of darubiri (176).

Kalirangwe, *musical bow of the Nyanja of Lake Nyasa area, with calabash resonators (176).

Kal ko, a very large *hourglass drum of Korea, up to 90 cm. (3 ft.) in length. *Cf.* tho ko (170).

Kalliope (muse of epic poetry), organ stop of stopped flue pipes of extremely wide scale, invented by Robert Hope-Jones (d. 1914), at 8' or 4' pitch. *Cf.* calliope (198).

Kallist-organon [Gk. *kallistos,* best + *organon,* instr.], keyboard instr. similar to the *physharmonica, patented by Silvestre of Mirecourt on Apr. 23, 1830 (204).

Kalophone, Boehm flute made by Wilhelm Heckel of Biebrich *ca.* 1900, incorporating some of the Heckel characteristics (176).

Kalove, *musical bow of Florida Island (Solomon Islands), with 2 heterochord strings but neither tuning loop nor resonator. The performer takes the curved bow into his mouth and strikes both strings with a plectrum held in the right hand, while keeping one string permanently stopped (77).

Kalumba, pl. **tulumbu,** *musical bow of the Ila of N. Rhodesia, with resonator (105).

Kalumpemba, *friction drum of Cuba, of African origin (152).

Kalung, arched harp of the Mbum of C. Africa (19).

Kalungu [Arab. *kūbā*], *hourglass drum of the W. African Hausa. Originally part of the royal regalia, it is now an instr. of professional drummers. Also called kalangu (93).

Kalur, *end-blown flute of the Copi of Uganda, conical, made of a gourd, with stopped lower end, and one fingerhole. *Ca.* 9 cm. (3½ in.) long. *Cf.* kilu, kiluka (195).

Kalutang, percussion sticks of the Hanunoo of the Philippine Islands (103).

Kalwaking, brass or iron *pellet bells of the Muria of Bastar, India, worn as anklets by dancers (68).

Kalyalya, fiddle of the Umda and Tshokwe of the Congo, with 3 strings (128).

Kam, *hourglass drum of Tami Island, New Guinea, that corresponds to the oñ (28).

Kamān, Pers.: formerly a generic term for bowed instrs., now a bow (75 I).

Kamānja (Pers.) [dim. of *kamān*, bow], *spike fiddle of Persia that first appeared *ca.* 900. According to Farmer, it is not mentioned in Pahl. or early Pers. texts. By the time it appeared in Persia, it was already known in Egypt and the Sind; subsequently it spread throughout the Arab.-speaking world, as far afield as India and Celebes. See also: kāmanja, kemence, kyamancha (89 Farmer, 144 Chottin).

Kāmanja, pl. **kuamenj** (Arab.) [*kamānja*], Arab. *spike fiddle of Pers. origin, with small round or heart-shaped body, often of coconut, a long neck, long metal spike, and 2 or 4 strings, generally 2 tuned a 4th apart and secured by lateral

pegs. Still played with a primitive bow. Today the kāmanja is played in the Near East but is extinct in the Maghrib. In Egypt its body is a half coconut and its belly is of fishskin. Nowadays the word *kāmanja* means viola or violin in most of N. Africa, where these instrs. are played held vertically on the seated player's knee (144 Chottin, 147 Farmer).

Kāmanja a'gūz (Arab.: old fiddle), *spike fiddle of Egypt, with very small body of coconut pierced by a round handle to form a long spike on which the instr. rests when played. The belly is of skin. Two or occasionally 3 strings of hair, held in lateral pegs, are tuned $a^0 e^0$. *Cf.* kāmanja farkh, kāmanja taqti, sitāra (170).

Kāmanja farkh (Arab.), small kāmanja with 2 strings tuned $e^1 b^0$ (170).

Kāmanja rūmī (Arab.: Greek *kāmanja*), name of the lira in the Near East, introduced from the Byzantine Empire in the Middle Ages. The body is piriform, tapering to a pegdisc with 3 rear pegs. The 3 gut strings are tuned 4-1-5, the central string being a drone. The outer strings are played in harmonics with the fingernails (170).

Kāmanja sogair (Arab.), syn. of kāmanja farkh (170).

Kāmanja taqti (Arab.), kāmanja a'gūz with trapezoid body, membrane belly and bottom, and 3 strings. *Ca.* 1 m. (40 in.) long (176).

Kambaua, *musical bow of the Kandoshi Indians of Ecuador and Peru, held like the tomangu, the string being plucked with bare fingers (105).

Kambi, pluriarc of the Nkundo of the Congo (128).

Kambili, syn. of kumbili.

Kambreh [*gunībrī*], small lute of Niger, Senegal, and Sierra Leone, with scaphoid body, skin belly tied on with leather thongs, cylindrical neck that often terminates in a long metal leaf and pierces the body immediately below the belly, acting as bass bar, and 2–4 horsehair strings attached by tuning rings; it is played with a plectrum. *Ca.* 50 cm. (20 in.) long. *Cf.* halam, pomsa (75 I, 93, 173).

Kami (fish), secret *stamping tube of the Iatmul of the Sepik River area of New Guinea. Used in initiation rites, it is dashed against the bottom of a pit (77).

Ka mien, Jew's-harp of the Khasi of Assam, bottle-shaped, of bamboo (173).

Kammer . . . , as a prefix to names of organ stops, Kammer denotes a stop tuned to *Kammerton* (chamber pitch). *Cf.* Musik . . . , Musizier . . .

Kammerbass, see: basso da camera.

Kammu, *end-blown flute of the Cuna and Ashlushlay Indians of Panama, made of a bamboo tube *ca.* 70 cm. (28 in.) long, with 2 fingerholes. The performer often holds a rattle in one hand while playing the kammu (105).

Kammu-purru, panpipes of the Cuna Indians of Panama, made of cane. The pipes are wound with black and white thread for most of their length (105).

Kampan [see: campana], OSlav.: bell.

Kampi, Finn.: clapper of a bell.

Kampolongo, syn. of kangere.

Kamsala, Mar. equivalent of the Sans. kamsya.

Kamsara, Beng. equivalent of the Sans. kamsya.

Kamsatālo, Pali equivalent of the Sans. kamsya.

Kamsya (Sans.), generic name of gongs in India (170).

Kamuti, Jew's-harp of the Manegre of the Upper Amur River, of brass (176).

Ka nākrā [Arab. *naqqāra*], wooden kettledrum of the Khasi of Assam, with V-lacings (172).

Kanala [Arab. *qānūn*], psaltery of Livonia. *Cf.* kannel (176).

Kanango, smallest *hourglass drum of the Yoruba of Nigeria (93, 103).

Kāncha bīnā (Beng.), *sitār with gutter-shaped neck covered by a glass fingerboard and with a second, parchment-covered body set inside the main body, with 11 sympathetic brass strings (173).

Kanching (Mac.), brass cymbals of the Malay Archipelago, used by priests to dispel evil spirits (112).

Kanda, large drum of the Balunda of the Congo, with 2 nailed heads, kept in the hut of the king-apparent (30).

Kandara, *hourglass drum of the Marind-Anim of W. New Guinea, with glued head and large square handle.

Kandiri-kandiri, *musical bow of the Balese of the Congo, with tuning loop but no resonator (128).

Kandiroē, *musical bow of the Kashibo Indians of the Upper Amazon. The bow is held in the hand and its string plucked with right index finger and thumb (105).

Kandla, Livonian name of the kantele (149).

Kane, see: gane.

Kanga, 1. side-blown trumpet of the Alur of Uganda, short, covered with cowhide, and having a prominent embouchure. A set of these forms part of the sultan's regalia; **2.** end-blown trumpet of the Logo of the Congo (195).

Kan'gan, *musical bow of the S. African coastal Bantu tribes, borrowed from the Bushmen, with single string and tuning loop. The player's mouth acts as resonator (116).

Kang dung (bone trumpet), Tibetan trumpet made of a human bone, or having a middle section of bone, and a copper bell and mouthpiece. A ritual instr. *Cf.* kang tung (176).

Kangere, *globular flute of the Warega of the Congo, made of a gourd, with blowhole and one fingerhole (42, 152).

Kang ku, *goblet drum of China, with 2 nailed heads of which only the wider is played; it is suspended in a stand by 4 metal rings and beaten with 2 sticks (4).

Kang ling bu, Tibetan pipe made from a human thigh bone, nowadays often of metal (176).

Kangoma [*ngoma], small drum of the Batshoko of the Congo, played by children; it is made of a hollow wooden cylinder with a skin tied around one end (30).

Kāngsara, temple gong of Bengal of *ca.* 25 cm. (10 in.) in diam. *Cf.* kāngshi (132).

Kāngshi (Beng., Hindi, Hindust.), gong of India, with turned rim, played together with the dhol; 15–17 cm. (6–7 in.) in diam. (144, 176).

Kangsi, name by which the bonang of Java was known *ca.* 1000 (121).

Kang t'u, conical trumpet of China, made of bronze or brass, in 2 telescoping sections and played in pairs. 3 m. (10 ft.) long. Also called ta wang (142).

Kang tung (Chin.: bone trumpet), conical trumpet of N. China, made of copper with brass mounts, terminating in a dragon's head. A temple instr. *Cf.* kang dung (89, 142).

Kani, *frame zither of the Kru of Liberia, with 7 fiber strings strung across a triangular wooden frame having a calabash resonator. Also known as Kru harp. *Cf.* gambareh, oba (176).

Kanjeri, Tel. equivalent of khanjanī.

Kanjiri, Mar. equivalent of khanjanī.

Kankles, Lith. psaltery, closely related to the kantele, made in different sizes, the larger ones being strung with gut, the smaller with wire. 5 strings (9, 174).

Kanklys, syn. of kankles.

Kankobele, pl. **tunkobele,** sansa of the Ila of N. Rhodesia, with calabash resonator (176).

Kannār (Pahl.), stringed instr. of the Sassanid age. *Cf.* kinnōr (75 II).

Kannel, Estonian psaltery that corresponds to the kantele but is bowed, with a rectangular body and 4 strings tuned in 5ths. Also known as rootsikandel (9).

Kanon, OHGer.: med. name of the qānūn.

Kanón (Gk.), **1.** monochord used by the ancient Greeks.

Kanonaki [Arab. *qānūn], the qānūn of modern Greece (144).

Kansambi, sansa of the Warega of the Congo, with gourd resonator held against the performer's body (19, 42).

Kansara, see: kāngsara.

Kanshingiri, drum of the Babemba of the Congo, a woman's drum used during female puberty rites. The drum is laid flat on the ground, straddled by the performer, who beats it with her hands (30).

Kansi, see: kangsi.

Kansilemba, hand bell of the Warega of the Congo (19).

Kansya, see: kamsya.

Kantele, national instr. of Finland, already mentioned in the Kalevala and still in use today. The kantele is a psaltery of irregular trapezoid shape with 2 long sides that almost meet at the bottom and with a diagonal upper side. The tuning pegs are inserted along the diagonal side. Originally the kantele was furnished with 5 horsehair strings and tuned to the scale of G A Bb C D, but with time the number of strings increased; today the number is variable, and they are now of metal. The instr. is held horizontally and plucked with bare fingers. Called soittu in Karelia. See also: jouhikantele, kankles (9, 91, 149).

Kantom, syn. of pagang.

Kanun, 1. double *tube zither of Kitchern, Java, made of 2 bamboo tubes joined together. Each has one brass string, under which a soundhole is pierced. Both are provided with a tuning peg. *Ca.* 44 cm. (17 in.) long; **2.** see: qānūn (141).

Kanuna [Arab. *qānūn], syn. of satatantri vīnā.

Kanutitsunanikoya, *musical bow of the S. American Omagua Indians. The end of the bow is taken into the player's mouth and the string is struck (105).

Kanzabu (Akk.), syn. of kitmu.

Kanzelle, Ger.: groove.

Kao, ancient Chin. war drum. *Cf.* ku, 2 (170).

Kao-kao, small drum of Java, with 2 painted heads, of Chinese origin (132).

Kao tari, ancient *samisen of the Ryukyu Islands, Japan, with circular body, snakeskin belly and 3 strings (157).

K'api, Jew's-harp of Tibet, of bamboo

with a bamboo sheath, made by non-Tibetans of the SE. part of the country in 3 sizes, all of which are played simultaneously. Held in the player's left hand, they are plucked with fingers of the right hand (176).

Kāra, Sudanese instr. similar to the gunībrī, with piriform body, leather belly, cylindrical neck, and 2 gut strings (132).

Kārā, small drum of Bengal of truncoconical form with 2 laced heads, suspended from the player's neck and played with sticks (176).

Karabe, bagpipe of Serbia (144).

Karadisamela, kettledrum of S. India, a temple instr. (176).

Karakoru, signal horn of the Baré boatsmen of NW. Brazil (176).

Karamouza [It. *cornamusa*], **1.** shawm of Gk. gypsies and shepherds; **2.** bagpipe of modern Greece (132).

Karamuntse, shawm of Albania.

Karamut [*garamut*], *slit drum of the Duke of York Island, Bismarck Archipelago. See: garamut (176).

Karan, Sum. equivalent of labbanātu (89 Galpin).

Karana (Sans., Beng.) [Pers. *qarna*], straight trumpet of India, made of copper, brass, or bronze, with conical bore except for a short cylindrical section below the mouthpiece. An instr. of the priestly castes and of princes. Probably of W. Asian origin. See also: karnā (169).

Karangba, var. of kalanba.

Karaning, Mandingo name of the ngenge (Collection of the Commonwealth Institute, London).

Karāqib, see: qarāqib.

Karatāli (Sans., Beng.), wooden clappers of India, circular, with a short handle. One is held in each hand and they are clicked together. An instr. of fakirs and mendicants in some regions; in others it is provided with a cluster of pellet bells and serves as rhythm instr. *Cf.* chitike, chitikelu, kartāl, kartali, khat tālī (46, 173, 179).

Karatsaka, *percussion beam of the Majunga region of the Malagasy Re-public. It corresponds to the tsikaretika (172).

Karatu, *goblet drum of Celebes temples, made of wood, with laced head. The lacings are tightened with wedges held by strips of rattan. The karatu is set on the ground during performance. It is 50–75 cm. (20–30 in.) high (112).

Karchilambu, syn. of silambu.

Kareng, karinding made of bamboo (121).

Karinding, W. Java name of the rinding, with forked tongue and bamboo tube resonator (121).

Karinga, var. of kalinga.

Kariso, *panpipes of the Tukano Indians of the Guianas (105).

Karkarī (Sans.), unidentified instr. of ancient India, mentioned in the Atharva-Veda (170).

Karmon, accordion of the Cheremiss of the U.S.S.R., also called muzekan. *Cf.* garmonica (146).

Karnā (Hindi, Tamil) [Pers. *qarna*], straight ceremonial trumpet of India, made of metal. Also called banku, in S. India buruga. See also: karana.

Karnay, see: karranay.

Karnyx, see: carnyx.

Karraka, Basque equivalent of the Sp. carraca (56).

Karranay [dim. of karnā], obs. curved trumpet of Turkey, known in the 15th c. According to a 17th-c. Turk. author, it sounded like the braying of an ass (*khar*) (76).

K'ar-rnga [Tibetan *r'ar ba,* bronze + *rnga,* drum], generic name for gongs in Tibet, ranging from large temple gongs to the small silver hand gong with deep rim and no boss (89 Picken).

Kartāl, Hindust., Mar., Punj. equivalent of karatāli.

Kartali, Beng. equivalent of karatāli (138).

Karyenda, sacred drum of Urundi, Africa (30).

Kas, kāsa, pl. **kāsāt, 1.** finger cymbals of Islam; **2.** large bowl-shaped cymbals of Islam, made of bronze (132, 147).

Kasa, a name of the tupan among E. Albanians (11).

Kasambongan, syn. of katambong.

Kasanga, name of the sansa in Lourenço Marques Bay area, E. Africa (176).

Kasapi [*kachapi*], **1.** syn. of kachapi, 2; **2.** syn. of safé.

Kāsāt, pl. of kas or kāsa.

Kasayi, sansa of the Bashi and other peoples of Ruanda and the Congo, with wooden base to which a gourd resonator is attached, and 9 lamellae on the right side, 8 on the left. These are made of metal. Their common (relative) tuning is: left $c^1 c^2 bb^1 d^1 d^2 ab^1 eb^2$, right $g^0 g^1 g^2 f^0 f^1 f^2 bb^1$. The base is held by the player's fingers while the lamellae are plucked with both thumbs. Cf. likembe (103, 139).

Kash, 1. generic name for flutes in Ponape, Micronesia; **2.** specific name of a *nose flute of Ponape, made of mangrove root or bamboo, with 3 fingerholes, or with 3 fingerholes and a rear thumbhole, or without fingerholes; formerly also made with 6 fingerholes. Said to be used together with a drum for accompanying dances. See also: ang en tsuma, chup en parri, parri chup en ro (203).

Ka shakuriau, syn. of ka könshau.

Kashakwe, drum of the Warundi of the Congo (30).

Kashane, *musical bow of the Balubedu of S. Africa, with a single string looped to the bow (116).

Kashila, 2-headed drum of the Balamba of the Congo, cylindrical, suspended from the player's neck by a cord and struck on both heads with bare hands. It forms part of a chief's escort. It is 80–90 cm. (32–36 in.) long (30).

Ka si (Burmese: frog drum), bronze *kettle gong of the Karen of Shan State, Burma, with 4 pairs of small ornamental frogs on the plate. Also called kaun chet (138).

Kasik, castanets of Turkey (120).

Kaskabeleta [Sp. *cascabel*], Basque children's clappers made of split corn stems (56).

Kaskabilo [Sp. *cascabel*], Basque: pellet bell (56).

Kasso, *harp lute of Gambia, with 22 strings, similar in other respects to the bolon. The strings pass over a notched bridge in 2 nearly vertical rows.

Kastagnetten, Ger.: castanets.

Kastenleier, Ger.: box lyre.

Kastratrang, *musical cups of India, consisting of a variable number of cups (without water), played either by rubbing the rims with wetted fingers or by striking them with small sticks. Cf. jaltarang.

Katakyi [*kakaki*], long ivory horn of Ghana, insigne of royalty (93).

Katambong, conical wooden *goblet drum of Borneo, with rattan lacings. Also called kasambongan. Cf. gatambore, katambore (173).

Katambore, Basque: tambourine; var. of danbore.

Katamore, syn. of katambore.

Katana, vessel rattle of the Hopi Indians of NE. Arizona, made of a gourd filled with seeds and pierced by a handle (132).

Ka tanmuri, *whistle flute of the Khasi of Assam, made of bamboo. The lower end is half stopped, a natural node being pierced. It has 7 equidistant front fingerholes (172).

Katchel, small döwel (45).

Katiboke, slit drum of the SW. part of the Malagasy Republic (171).

Katiwul, a W. Java name of the kempul.

Katjapi, see: kachapi.

Katral (Akk.), small cymbals of ancient Babylon (89 Galpin).

Katso, syn. of karakoru (176).

Kattivadiyam, Tamil equivalent of gātha (173).

Katumba ka vidye, small *goblet drum of the Baluba-Shankadi of the Congo, with nailed head. A lateral hole is covered with a thin membrane, a *mirliton device (30).

Katumbi, *cylindrical drum of the Bena-Lulua of Kasai, the Congo, with flared base and single nailed head. *Ca.* 40 cm. (16 in.) long (30).

Katungu, *musical bow of the Wasongola of the Congo, played by women (19, 42).

Katyayana vīnā, syn. of satatantri vīnā.

Kaun chet, syn. of ka si.

Kaur, 1. end-blown *notched flute of New Britain, Bismarck Archipelago, stopped, with 2 oval fingerholes burned in close to the lower end. *Ca.* 38 cm. (15 in.) long; **2.** stopped *panpipes of New Ireland, Bismarck Archipelago, of bamboo. *Cf.* gore, khor (176).

Kauss, *spike fiddle of Turkestan, shaped like a large ladle; body, neck, and spike are carved out of one block of wood; it has 2 strings (173).

Kaval, see: caval, qawūl.

Kavalche, see: cavalche.

Kawo, free-reed double pipe of the Kwanhai-Palaun of Shan State, Burma, consisting of a cylindrical melody pipe with 7 front fingerholes and a rear thumbhole, and a drone pipe without fingerholes. Both pipes are of bamboo, furnished with metal free reeds, and terminate in a calabash that acts as air reservoir (172).

Kawunde, syn. of eggwara, 1 (195).

Kaya, syn. of hne (173).

Kaya kin, syn. of shiragi koto (144).

Kaya kum, *board zither of Korea, rectangular, with convex upper surface, movable bridges, and 12 strings attached to the underside. *Ca.* 150 cm. (5 ft.) long (66).

Kayamba, castanets of Kenya (120).

Kayanda, 1. the ordinary drum of the Ba Ila of Rhodesia; **2.** drum of the Balamba of the Congo, and of the Bayeke, who borrowed it from them; also known to the Basanga. A dance drum (30).

Kayitalama, bronze cymbals of Ceylon, thick and perfectly flat, with slight center boss. *Ca.* 12 cm. (5 in.) in diam. (141).

Kayoma, *board zither of the Amba of

Uganda, with single rattan string laced from end to end (195).

Kayum, small clay drum of the Lacandón Indians of C. America, a direct descendant of the ancient Mayan drum, made in different sizes and shapes. The head is laced to a hoop of liana and braced with wedges (137).

Kazoo (Engl., U.S.), mirliton made to resemble a flute, consisting of a tube, usually of boxwood, with a membrane covering a lateral hole and devoid of fingerholes. Also called bazoo.

Kebero, name of the coboro drum in S. Ethiopia (45).

Kebluk, a somewhat heavier type of *ketuk of Indramayu and Cheribon, W. Java (121).

Kechapi [*kachapi*], **1.** idiochord *tube zither of the Gayo of Sumatra; **2.** see: kachapi (119).

Kecher, var. of kechicher (121).

Kechicher, bronze cymbals of Java, made in 3 sizes. One of a pair is fixed to a carved wooden frame while the other is clashed against it. Their use is restricted to a few *gamelans,* except in E. Java, where they are more frequently encountered. See also: chechempres, chiyeyek (121).

Kechrek, rattle of Java, consisting of 2 or more small rectangular iron slabs, of equal or unequal lengths, loosely tied together. They imitate battle noises in theatrical performances and are used by itinerant tinkers. They are played with the performer's toes. Also called kepyak (121).

Kechruk, syn. of angklung (121).

Kedempling, syn. of dempling (121).

Kedondolo, *musical bow of the Bakwelo of S. Africa, with single string looped to the bow (116).

Kegellade (Ger.), organ wind chest, a transformation of the spring chest by Eberhard Walcker of Ludwigsburg, 1842.

Kegeltrommel, Ger.: *conical drum.

Kei, *metallophone of Jap. Buddhist temples, consisting of bronze plaques of different sizes and irregular shape, suspended by cords from an ornate frame. Sometimes the plaques are gilded. Struck with a wooden mallet (135, 157).

Kei kin, *spike fiddle of Japan, with 4 strings; it corresponds to the *hu ch'in of China. The bamboo body has a diam. of 10 cm. (4 in.), the neck is 70 cm. (27½ in.) long, the open strings 27 cm. (10½ in.) long. They are tuned in pairs, a 5th apart, occasionally a 4th apart. The bow, 71 cm. (28 in.) long, is entwined in the strings so that they cannot be sounded separately. *Cf.* ko kun, tei kin (157).

Keirnine, see: ceirnin.

Kekechrek, name of the kechrek in W. Java (121).

Kekinchiran, *bull-roarer of Tasik-malaya, Java, made of materials other than bamboo. See also: hohoang (121).

Kekreng, scraper of the Muria of Bastar, India, made of a bamboo or iron pole some 1.50 m. (5 ft.) long; the lower end is notched, the upper end ornamented with a bunch of feathers. The notched portion is scraped with a stick (68).

Kekum, syn. of he kum (66).

Kele, 1. *slit drum of the Mende of Sierra Leone, cylindrical, with 3 longitudinal slits. *Ca.* 60 cm. (2 ft.) long; **2.** drum of the Nago of Dahomey; **3.** *cross flute of the Dogon of Mali (Collection of the Commonwealth Institute, London; 103).

Kelen, Kpelle (a Sudanese language) for a canoe made of a hollowed-out tree trunk, turned upside down and beaten upon to accompany dance or song, and thus also denoting a drum (93).

Kelenton, metallophone of C. Sumatra, with 6 slabs of different sizes (173).

Keliningan, var. of kliningan (121).

Kell, Estonian: bell (169).

Kelleli, old saucepan covered with a skin and strung up as a lute, played by the Tedas of Tibesti region, Sahara. Only men may play it (193).

Kello, Finn.: bell (169).

Kelontong, see: klontong.

Keluri, one of the Dayak terms for mouth organ. See also: kladdi (121).

Kemada, see: gong kemada.

Kemae, scraper of Indians of the Peruvian Amazon area, made of a turtle carapace (103).

Kemanak, *concussion idiophone of Bali and Java, now obsolescent. It consists of a pair of bronze or iron objects that Kunst aptly described as having the form of a banana on its stalk, opened lengthwise on its convex side, with the pulp taken out. The 2 are attached by a cord. In Cheribon and E. Java they are struck together so that the back of 1 strikes the slit side of the other. Elsewhere they are played by 2 persons, each holding 1 instr. and striking it with a beater. Both absolute and relative pitch vary with each set. The kemanak is a rhythm instr., recorded in E. Java from the 12th c. on, used in the hieratic dances of *bedayas* (court dancers of noble birth). The same instr. is found among the Fang of W. Africa, where it also accompanies religious dances. There the 2 instrs. are of slightly different sizes. More surprising still is the fact that a pair of kemanaks appears in a prehistoric rock drawing in SW. Africa, believed—after radiocarbon tests—to be over 3000 years old. Kunst has suggested a common cradle in the E. Mediterranean. *Cf.* chelepita, kenawak, kende, kete, kolendang, nawek, tewek (121, 123).

Kemanjeh, see: kāmanja.

Kembang delima (pomegranate blossom), syn. of klinting (121).

Kembone [see: *campana*], Alb.: bell.

Kemence, kēmenchē [*kāmanja], bowed instr. of Macedonia and Anatolia, with 3 metal strings (110).

Kemenche, syn. of gadulka.

Kemene, syn. of gadulka.

Kemer, misreading of kabar.

Kemin, *marine-shell trumpet of India (144).

Kemkem, Coptic: drum (C. Sachs, in: *Zeitschrift für Musikwissenschaft,* I).

Kemodong, see: gong kemodong.

Kemong, 1. small cymbal of Java. See

engkuk for description; **2.** gong of Bali (121, 144).

Kempli, gong of Bali (144).

Kempul, gong of C. and E. Java, with central boss and deep rim, suspended in a frame. Pitched about an oct. higher than the gong suwukan and an oct. lower than the kenong. *Ca.* 50 cm. (20 in.) in diam. Known in W. Java as katiwul, weleri, or goōng leutik (121).

Kempur, Balinese gong with central boss, suspended from an ornate frame (J. Kunst: *The Music of Bali*, London, 1949).

Kempyang (bright-sounding), **1.** in Java a unit of 2 small kettle gongs with central boss, mounted on a frame and played simultaneously; **2.** name given to a small terbang in W. Java (121).

Kempyang slendro, kettle gong of Java, shaped like a bonang gong, placed horizontally and tuned to *barang*. It replaces the engkuk and kemong in the Jogya *kepatihan* (121).

Ken, see: khen, cai ken.

Kenadi, idiochord bamboo *tube zither of Alor, Indonesia (119).

Kena'na'wr, name that appears to have been given *ca.* 1200 B.C. in Egypt to the kithara in use there (147 Farmer).

Kenawak, name of the kemanak in E. Java (121).

Kenchek, Balinese name of the medium-sized kechicher (121).

Kencher, name of the kechicher in E. Java (121).

Kendang, trunco-conical drum of W. Java, with laced heads (121).

Kendang awi, *stamping tube of Tasikmalaya, W. Java, made of a bamboo internode stopped at one end and open at the other. Two instrs. of different size are played together (121).

Kendang chiblon, *barrel drum of Java, with heads of different diam., otherwise similar to the kendang gending (121).

Kendang gending, drum of C. Java, either barrel-shaped with heads of unequal diam., or conoid, the older form. The

heads are stretched over rattan hoops and laced in Y pattern. The drum is held horizontally and played with bare hands; exceptionally, with a stick. Nowadays the heads are rarely tuned (121).

Kendang jemblung, *percussion tube of Java, consisting of a bamboo segment *ca.* 90 cm. (3 ft.) long, with a node just above the center, open at both ends and planed down lengthwise on one surface. This surface is beaten on both sides of the node. As the node is not in the middle, the sounds yielded are a 5th apart. Several such tubes may be suspended from a stand in *jemblung* ensembles (121).

Kendang leutik, name of the ketipung in W. Java (121).

Kende, instr. of the Kissi of W. Africa, similar in shape, function, and playing technique to the kemanak (123, quoting Schaeffner).

Ken doi, see: cai ken doi.

Kengere, 1. *cylindrical drum of the Madi of Uganda, with single nailed head, always played by a woman, with bare hands; **2.** royal drum of the Alur of Uganda, of *bonda* wood with lizardskin membrane; **3.** horn of the Warundi of the Congo, made of cowhorn (30, 42, 195).

Ken loa, see: cai ken loa.

Ken mot, see: cai ken mot.

Kenong, high-pitched kettle gong of Java, with central boss, set on crossed cords over a wooden box, and forming part of a *gamelan*. The kenong is considered male, being smaller and higher-pitched than the kenong japan. See also: brekuk, bungkuk (121).

Kenong japan, a large, rather flat kenong, pitched an oct. below the ordinary kenong and found only in areas of Java under Jogya influence. Said to have been named for a regent of Japan who introduced it. The kenong japan is considered female, being larger and lower-pitched than the kenong (121).

Kenong penontong, syn. of penontong.

Kenong playon, kenong tuned to *nem;* it performs a rhythmic function (121).

Kenong ringgitan, a High Javanese name of the kenong wayangan (121).

Kenong wayangan, kenong tuned to *nem;* it performs a rhythmic function (121).

Kent bugle, see: keyed bugle.

Kent horn (Fr.: *cor de Kent*), see: keyed bugle.

Kentongan, *slit drum of Java and Celebes, made from a hollowed-out tree trunk or large bamboo section, closed at both ends, with a horizontal slit 90–180 cm. (3–6 ft.) long. Often carved to resemble a human being or animal, it terminates in a handle from which it is suspended vertically or, if very large, horizontally. Smaller ones of bamboo are struck while held in the player's hand. A signal instr. Also called titir in Java. See also: gul-gul, kohkol, kukulan gantang, kul-kul, tonggong (112, 121).

Kentung-kentung, slit drum of Malaya (176).

Keplek, a combination of several small bamboo slit drums of W. Java (121).

Keprak, horizontal slit drum of Java, played with a wooden mallet. It accompanies dances (121).

Kepyak, 1. an ensemble of 3 bonang kettles of Cheribon, W. Java, 2 of which are at unison; **2.** quadruple clapper of Java, made of buffalo bones: an ancient tantric instr.; **3.** syn. of kechrek (121).

Keranting, heterochord *tube zither of the Orang Temiar of Malaya, with up to 20 strings and palm-leaf resonator (173).

Kerar, lyre of Ethiopia, a descendant of the Gk. lyra. Symmetrical, with rectangular or round body and membrane belly, wooden arms and crossbar. Strings are attached to the crossbar by tuning rings. Villoteau gave its tuning as $d^2 g^1 a^1 b^1 e^2$. The stringing is bichord, one string of each pair being tuned to the oct. of the other. Played with a plectrum or with bare fingers. See also: timbo (89 Baines, 144).

Keras, curved horn of ancient and modern Greece. *Cf.* keren, rhyton.

Keraulophone [Gk. *keraulis,* horn

player + *phone,* sound], organ stop of open cylindrical metal flue pipes of narrow scale, invented by Gray and Davison in 1843, at 8' pitch. Rarely built in the 20th c., if at all. Its characteristic tone was produced by a small hole bored in the pipe's body, close to the top, or by a sliding cap (99, 129).

Kerbflöte, Ger.: *notched flute.

Keren (Heb.: animal horn), generic name for horns among the ancient Hebrews, including the shofar. Made of ox-horn or ram's-horn, they emitted a few tones only and were used as signal or alarm instrs. in biblical times. The word corresponds to the Pers. and Arab. qarna. *Cf.* keras (84).

Kereteta, slit drum of Mangareva Island, SE. Pacific (77).

Keretok, herd-animal bell of Thailand, made from the seed of the *tah* or sugar palm, with the lower end cut off so as to provide a wide aperture, and a palmwood clapper. *Ca.* 6 cm. (2½ in.) high (18).

Keretok-krebau, wooden buffalo bell of the Malay Peninsula, flat, of rectangular shape, furnished with a wooden clapper (18).

Keri-keri, hourglass drum of the Yoruba of Nigeria (103).

Kerilong, cross flute of Benkulen, Sumatra, with 6 fingerholes (176).

Keriten, ankle rattle of the S. African Qung Bushmen, made from the ear of a springbok and containing *kerri* berries or other substances. Worn by male dancers (116).

Kern (Ger.), **1.** languid of a flue organ pipe; **2.** block of a reed organ pipe; **3.** fipple of a duct flute.

Kernspalte, Ger.: flue, duct, windway.

Kernspaltflöte, Ger.: duct flute.

Kero, small *barrel drum of Japan, with nailed heads, originally a Chin. signal instr., now a rhythm instr. in orchestras. The leader suspends it from his neck and beats it with a stick. *Ca.* 15 cm. (6 in.) long, 17 cm. (6½ in.) in diam. (157).

Keronaru, lute of the Fula of Sierra

Leone, with scaphoid body, skin belly, and a handle that pierces the body as far as a large soundhole, at which point it carries a wooden string fastener. The 6 strings are held by tuning rings. See also: konding (Collection of the Commonwealth Institute, London).

Kerophone, organ stop with free reeds, broad tongues, no pipes, at 8' pitch (198).

Kesan, misreading of kirān (75 II).

Kesarat, misreading of kinnāra (75 II).

Kesba(te), see: qasaba.

Kesselgong, Ger.: kettle gong.

Kesselmundstück, Ger.: cup mouthpiece.

Kesseltrommel, obs. Ger.: kettledrum.

Kete, 1. *notched flute of Ghana, made of cane with 4 fingerholes close to the lower end. A hole is pierced near the upper end and is closed by a thin membrane, a mirliton device (141); **2.** an E. Java name of the kemanak (121).

Keteng-keteng, idiochord bamboo *tube zither of the Karo Batak of N. Sumatra (119).

Ketipluk, Balinese name of the klontong (121).

Ketipung, drum of Java, either barrel-shaped with heads of uneven diam., or slightly conical. The heads are of sheepskin or deerskin, laced with rattan, and are played either with bare hands or with sticks. The ketipung is also played together with the kendang gending. It corresponds to the marvas of Sumatra. Also called penuntung (121, 132).

Ketjapi, see: kechapi.

Ketobong, drum of Borneo, similar to the ketipung but with only one head (176).

Ketsü (Angami), straight trumpet of the Naga of Assam, narrow and slightly conical, made of a tree root closed at the wider end but with a semicircular hole cut nearby. *Ca.* 2 m. (6½ ft.) long (172).

Kettledrum (Fr.: *timbale;* Ger.: *Pauke;* It.: *timpano*), membranophone with a vessel-shaped body that acts as resonator and as distributor of vibrations, of definite pitch. Very shallow specimens are called bowl drums. The kettledrum cannot lay claim to great antiquity, as the earliest record of its existence is a Pers. relief of *ca.* 600 A.C., on which a bowl drum is represented, struck with 1 or perhaps 2 sticks. The larger type does not appear until the 12th c., when it is found in Mesopotamian miniatures. From the evidence of early representations Sachs concluded that kettledrums were originally a primitive form of pottery drum, and even today oriental kettledrums are more frequently made of clay than of metal; their heads are secured by lacings. Two types of kettledrums are encountered, a small and a large. Both were propagated by and with Islam, westward to Europe, southwest to Africa, east to the Indian subcontinent, and even farther. Kettledrums from India to Africa are associated with royal trumpets and indeed became emblems of royalty, just as they were in Renaissance Europe. Another feature they have in common is that they are invariably played in pairs. Throughout the Orient a player has 2 kettledrums tuned a 4th or 5th apart; in Africa royal drums are always beaten with sticks, although other kettledrums played in pop. performances may be beaten with bare hands; here also they are kept in pairs: even when they form part of a larger set, they are tied together pairwise.

The first type of kettledrum to reach Europe was the small one. According to the chronicler Jean de Joinville (in 1309), the kettledrum was unknown to Europeans until Damietta was taken by Crusaders in 1249. In 1281 it is recorded as *naguarre* (from the Arab. *naqqāra*), an early form of the Fr. word *nacaire,* which became *naker* in Engl. The large form was known in Hungary by the mid-15th c., if not earlier, and was introduced from there to W. Europe: in 1457 the envoys of King Ladislas of Hungary to France were accompanied by "drums like great kettles, carried on horseback." By the turn of the 16th c. the large type appeared in Germany as the *Heerpauke. Following the Hungarian fashion (taken over from the Arabs) of carrying a kettledrum slung on either side of the saddle, European noblemen kept mounted drummers to support their trumpeters. Virdung, in 1511, says that the copper kettledrums recently introduced were called *tympana*. He depicts a surprisingly modern form of the instr., with hoops and screws. These 2 items distinguish the Western from the Eastern kettledrum, but screws are not generally met with until the end of the 16th c. Thoinan Arbeau, in 1589, still speaks of the *tambour des Perses* (Pers.: drum), and gives it a diam. of some 75 cm. (2½ ft.). This would be about the size of the very deep-bodied drums drawn by Leonardo da Vinci (d. 1519) as studies for automatic kettledrums. After a c. and a half of courtly and military existence, kettledrums also entered the church and opera, along with the trumpet, tuned a 4th apart to the keynote and (lower) dominant of the trumpets. Until the middle of the 19th c. they were notated, as were the trumpets, in C, and were hence called C and G kettledrums. Halle writes in 1764 that the diam. of the G kettledrum was 9 in. ("*Zoll*") and that of the C drum, 8 in. The smaller kettledrum was placed to the left of the larger one. Modern instrs. consist of a hemispherical bowl made of copper or brass, called *shell*, with a head of calfskin which can be adjusted as to tension, as the modern orchestra requires many changes of pitch, and is played with 2 padded sticks. Two types of drum are in use: hand-tuned kettledrums and *machine drums. On both types the head is stretched over a hoop known as *flesh hoop*. That of the hand-tuned drum is wooden, and a metal counterhoop is fitted over it. This type of drum is provided with a number of handles that tighten the head by engaging 14–16 threaded screws, and it was to ob-

viate the necessity for turning so many screws that the machine drum was invented; in its improved form, the latter becomes a *pedal drum. Nowadays 2 drums, pitched in F and B♭ with diams. of 75 cm. (30 in.) and 58 cm. (23 in.), are standard orchestral equipment. The F drum can be tuned to any tone from F⁰ to c⁰, and the B♭ drum from B♭⁰ to f⁰, so that between them they span an oct. The larger drum is usually placed to the left, but the old cavalry drum disposition of Halle's day is still occasionally met with (15 Blades, 89, 90, 151, 170). See also: amata, ampongalava, ampongavilany, anacaire, anaka, angūahuasi, angūarai, atabale, balāban, bāmyā, bānyā, baraban, barabanca, bassin, bāya, bedon, bhēri, bouke, briazalo, buben, bunge, chin daul, chu ko ku, chung ko, damāma, damāmā, darbuka, daulbas, dikomana, dimplipito, dinni, dolla, dukrah, dumbelek, dumtek, dundubhi, esikulu, ganda-ganda, ganga, goga dhol, gudu-gudu, huancar, kabaro, 2, ka nākrā, karadisamela, khoradek, kociel, kundri, kurga, kūrka, kuwargā, lda-man, litavri, mahānāgārā, mahorathuk, mi'zaf, mu ko, nabat, nacaire, nacara, nacchera, nacorne, nagara, nāgārā, nagarit, nāghārā, naguarre, na ka la, naker, nakri, nal, naqāra, naqqāra, naqqārya, naquaire, na'ra, naubat, ndembo, negarit, nobut, nuqairāt, pa la man, Pauke, pim-pim, poukhan, qasa', qudūm, romanca, sahib nahabat, sutri nahabat, taballo, tabaq, tabbāl, tabl . . . , tabli bāz, talambasi, tambari, tambor, tambora, tambour, tambour de Perse, tambula, tambura, tamburo, tamukku, tarshā, tās, tāsā, tembelic, tikārā, timbale, timbalou, timpan, timpani, tiumbelek, tobol, tolombas, trampes, tubaile, tulumbaz, tumbelechiŭ, turam, turburi, tymbalon, tympana, tympane, tympanum, Votivtimpani, wainkya, wask-trumm.

Kettle gong (Fr.: *tambour de bronze;* Ger.: *Kesselgong*), bronze gong of SE. Asia of great antiquity, with curved rims so deep that they form a wall. The surface is flat, often ornamented with concentric circles and small cast figures of frogs. Kettle gongs are suspended by handles, so that the striking surface hangs vertically, and are struck with beaters. Formerly called metal drum or drum gong. See also: chengkung, danki, ka si, kaun chet, kebluk, kempyang, 1, kenong, kenong japan, kenong playon, kenong ringgitan, kenong wayangan, ketuk, ran.

Ketuk, a small *kettle gong of Java, with central boss, flatter and less brilliant of tone than the kenong. Mounted on crossed cords over an elaborately carved wooden box, occasionally with a calabash placed underneath it to act as resonator, or an earthenware resonator. Both the *pelog gamelan* and the *slendro gamelan* contain one ketuk. See also: kebluk (121).

Ketuk kintel, Jogya name for a ketuk tuned to *gulu* (121).

Ketuk kungkang, Jogya name for a ketuk tuned to *barang* (121).

Key, 1. (Fr.: *touche;* Ger.: *Taste;* It.: *tasto;* Sp.: *tecla;* Lat.: *clavis, palmula*), successor to the early med. *slider key, the key is a balanced lever pivoted on a balance rail. Button-like keys appear on organs of the 13th c., shaped like either the letter T or a typewriter key; when depressed they opened a pallet. These types were replaced by domino-shaped keys that became elongated until they assumed their present proportions. Full chromaticism and increase of compass in the 14th c. required the keys to be ordered in 2 rows, 1 exclusively reserved for accidentals. Today our natural keys are covered with ivory or plastic; the accidentals are black. In the 18th c. this color pattern was reversed. The standard octave span on modern pianos and organs is 18½ cm. (7¼ in.). See also: keyboard;

2. (Fr.: *clef;* Ger.: *Klappe;* It.: *chiave;* Sp.: *llave*), sprung lever on a wind instr., terminating in a padded cup or plate, by means of which the player's fingers open and close a vent. An open key leaves the hole open when the key is at rest, a closed

key leaves it closed when at rest. Open keys are considerably older than closed keys, being first recorded in 1413.

Keyboard (Fr.: *clavier;* Ger.: *Klaviatur;* It.: *tastiera;* Sp.: *teclado*), the keyboard as we know it has existed since the 13th c. and was fully chromatic by the early 15th c. The organ illustrated in the Bible of Etienne Harding, now dated between 1098 and 1109, has letters of the alphabet marked on the keys, as follows: C D E F G a b ♮, *i.e.,* showing both B natural and B flat. (Odo of Cluny, in his 10th-c. *De fistulis,* gives C D E F G a b c and suggests making the low C, the first pipe, "as long as you like"). Keyboards with B♭ as the only "black" keys are referred to by Praetorius in a historical sense, and it is interesting to note that on the keyboards of 4 late-14th-c. Swedish organs both B♮ and B♭ appear as "white" keys, a perfectly logical arrangement, as B♭ was an integral part of the hexachord system. Manual compasses were increased earlier in Spain and Italy than in other countries, presumably because they lacked an independent pedal organ. The compass of stringed keyboard instrs. expanded N. of the Alps in advance of that of the organ, as the former had no built-in 16′ or 2′ stops to draw upon. The med. organ compass of 2 octs. lasted until the late 12th c. In the 13th and 14th c. it was increased to 3 octs., but was not completely chromatic until *ca.* 1400. Arnaut of Zwolle, *ca.* 1440, shows a compass of B^0–f^2 with 31 keys. The organ of Ste.-Marie-de-la-Mer in 1425 had 35 keys, but many organs of the period had fewer. From 1490 to the mid-16th c. the lowest key was usually F. In the 16th c. a 4-oct. compass was common; it was increased to 4½ octs. in the 17th c. From the 16th to the 18th c., It. harpsichords maintained a 4-oct. compass with relatively few exceptions, while the contemporary spinets had one of 4½ octs. (C^0–c^3 and C^0–f^3, respectively, with short oct.); Flemish stringed instrs. terminated in the bass on C up to the time of the *ravalement; Engl. instrs. commonly on G (up to Kirkman), following British organ-building practice. A 5-oct. compass was reached on harpsichords *ca.* 1700, and the first pianos were also of this compass. By the end of the 18th c. some pianos had already attained 6 octs. (F^1–f^4), which increased rapidly to 6½ octs. in the 19th c. (C^1–f^4); Broadwood reached this compass by 1811. Today pianos have a compass of 7 octs. and a minor 3rd, from A^2 in the bass, and organs a compass of 5 octs. The standard oct. span of present-day organs and pianos is 16½ cm. (6½ in.). *Cf.* organ, ravalement, short octave, split keys. See also: Clutsam keyboard, concave keyboard, Janko keyboard, Olbrichklaviatur, transposing keyboards.

Keyed bugle (Fr.: *clairon chromatique, clairon à clefs, bugle à clefs;* Ger.: *Klappenhorn* [originally: *Klappenflügelhorn*]; It.: *cornetta a chiavi*), bugle to which Joseph Halliday, an Irish bandmaster stationed in Dublin, applied 5 keys in order to bridge the gap in the natural scale and for which he was granted a patent on May 5, 1810. Soon thereafter a sixth key was added in England, and later up to 4 more were added on the Continent. With the exception of the lowest all were closed keys. Also known as Kent horn or Kent bugle, in honor of the Duke of Kent, it was introduced under his patronage into British military bands as Royal Kent bugle. In England it was built in C with a crook for B♭, elsewhere in B♭, at soprano range. In 1817 Halary (Jean-Hilaire Asté) of Paris created a whole family of keyed bugles, the baritone member of which he called *ophicleide. Despite the disadvantages inherent in its side holes, the instr. retained its popularity until after the mid-c., when it was displaced by the valved cornet. See also: clavi-lame, quinticlave (73, 80 IX, 89).

Keyed cittern (Fr.: *cistre à clavier;* Ger.: *Tastencister*), another name of the *keyed guitar (actually a cittern).

Keyed guitar (Fr.: *guitare à clavier;* Ger.: *Tastengitarre;* It.: *chitarra a pianoforte*), an improved *English guitar, patented by Christian Clauss on Oct. 2, 1783, and again by John Goldsworth in 1785. The improvements took the form of plucking or striking devices; in the former a number of buttons placed on the right side of the body controlled levers that plucked the strings; in the latter a detachable box was affixed to the body, with 6 keys and piano hammers that struck the strings. In both cases the object was to do away with finger plucking. Identical with the keyed cittern. Formerly called pianoforte guitar (79, 89 Galpin).

Keyed harmonica (Fr.: *harmonica à clavier;* Ger.: *Tastenharmonika;* It.: *armonica a cembalo*), *glass harmonica furnished with a keyboard. Early attempts at attaching a keyboard to the instr., made from 1769 on, were unsuccessful. An experimental model was first produced in 1782, but models with keyboards were not marketed until 1784. Hessel of St. Petersburg supplied them a year later, and in 1798 Carl Röllig improved them. Additional improvements were made in the 19th c., when the compass was also enlarged (113, 115, 170).

Keyed harp (Fr.: *harpe à clavier;* Ger.: *Harfenklavier*), *frame harp controlled by a keyboard. The earliest mention of such an instr. is that of Mersenne, who refers to It. instrs. of this nature, and a *clavi-arpa is said to have been invented in Spain by Juan Hidalgo in the 17th c. Gerber reports that an organist named Johann Kurtz built one in 1681; he calls it a newly invented instr. Jean-Antoine Berger (d. 1777) of Grenoble also constructed one. The *clavi-lyra and *clavi-harp appeared in the early 19th c. Similar instrs. were built up to the last decade of the 19th c. In appearance they resemble large frame harps with the pillar to the left and neck to the right, projecting above a shallow upright-piano case (no soundboard). The strings are of gut or metal, spun with silk, and are sounded by a plucking mechanism controlled from an ordinary piano keyboard. See also: clavi-arpa, clavi-harp, clavi-lyra.

Keyed horn, horn provided with keys. Attempts at creating such an instr. were made in the 1760's but failed. See: Amorschall, taille d'amour.

Keyed monochord (Fr.: *monocorde à clavier;* Ger.: *Tastenmonochord*), invented by J. Pousset of Pierre, Meurthe-et-Moselle, in 1883, and patented in 1886, the keyed monochord consisted of a large rectangular box furnished with a projecting keyboard and terminating in a small ovoid body set on folding legs, having one metal string. The usual compass was 29 notes. Pousset made 3 varieties: 1) with a movable bridge; 2) with keys spaced unevenly, corresponding to monochord string divisions; 3) with equally spaced, piano-like keys. They were produced in a whole range of sizes, the smallest being called monocorde-étude, chiefly a publicity item, also used as a toy; monocorde-fifre; monocorde-soprano; monocorde-alto; monocorde-baryton; monocorde-basse, and, finally, monocorde-contrebasse. Pousset's object was to replace the harmonium in the accompaniment of church singing (149, 191).

Keyed psalmodicon (Fr.: *psalmodicon à clavier;* Ger.: *Tastenpsalmodikon*), psalmodicon of Sweden and Finland, furnished with a keyboard and usually having 2 strings and 24 keys (149).

Keyed trumpet (Fr.: *trompette à clefs;* Ger.: *Klappentrompete;* It.: *tromba a chiavi*), trumpet fitted with keys, first devised by the Vienna court trumpeter Anton Weidinger and made by Joseph Felix Riedl of Vienna in 1801. Shaped like a natural trumpet, the new version was fitted with 4 closed keys, later with 6. Gioacchino Rossini introduced it in his *Guillaume Tell* (1829), and it became pop. in Austrian and It. military bands

during the first half of the 19th c. The brevity of its success was probably caused by the muffled tone produced by the side holes and soft pads. A bass trumpet with 6 keys was built in 1845 by Piatet and Benoit of Lyon (89 Baines, 126).

Keyed xylophone (Fr.: *xylophone à clavier;* Ger.: *Tastenxylophon*), see: xylophone.

Kgabududu, bull-roarer of the S. African Pedi (116).

Khais, *pot drum of the Hottentot of S. Africa, made of a jar or pot of willow wood, with a goatskin membrane tied over the aperture, and struck with the flat of the hand. Played by women only, to accompany songs. Called bambus by various travelers (116).

Khakhānī, an old Turk. name for the kūs, which the Turks took to be of Chin. origin (75 II).

Khakkhara (Sans.), old Buddhist *stick rattle still in use in Turkestan and E. Asia, with metal rings strung at the upper end. Also called dorje, hikile (148).

Khalam, harp lute of the Wolof of Senegal and Gambia (42).

Khalok, cowbell of Burma (176).

Khang, see: cai khang.

Khanh-da, musical stone of ancient Cambodia (47).

Khanjani (Sans., Beng.), small *frame drum of India, used by mendicant monks and also in concerts: Conical wooden frame with curved profile and single glued head. Jingles and pellet bells may be attached; 20–23 cm. (8–9 in.) in diam., 8–10 cm. (3–4 in.) high (173, 179).

Khanjri, Hindi equivalent of khanjani.

Khara, horn of Burma (176).

Kharraka, Basque: cog rattle. *Cf.* carraca (56).

Kharunhāmon-lim, marine-shell trumpet of Burma (144).

Kha's (hunting bow), *musical bow of the Korana Hottentot of S. Africa, made of solid wood, with a string of twisted leather and played with a beater (116).

Khat tālī (Sans., Beng.), square metal clappers of N. India, held pairwise like castanets; 15–20 cm. (6–8 in.) long. Also called chachra. Cf. karatāli (132, 173).

Khen, free-reed *mouth organ of Laos, made in 3 sizes, 1–3 m. (40 in.–10 ft.) long, with 6, 14, or 16 bamboo pipes of identical diam. disposed in 2 rows and held together in a wind chamber of wood or ivory which they pierce and from which they project underneath. The reeds are usually of silver. See also: kyen, sheng (46, *Zeitschrift für vergleichende Musikwissenschaft,* II, 1934).

Khil, name of the khil-khuur in Khalka Mongolia (69).

Khil-khuur (in the written language: *kili kugur*), Mongolian *spike fiddle with trapezoid body tapering upward, membrane belly, slender neck, 2 thick horsehair strings, lateral pegs, and a pegbox often carved in shape of a horse's head. Soundholes, usually circular, are cut in the back, which, like the belly, is of hide. Among some tribes the body is circular. The strings are attached to the stubby projection of the spike and are tuned a 5th apart; their pitch can be raised somewhat by inserting a knife under the bridge. This type of instr. is found elsewhere only in N. Africa and occasionally in China. Cf. ta hu ch'in (69).

Khloi, *cross flute of Cambodia, of bamboo with ivory tips and 7 fingerholes. The scale produced is $c^2 d^2 e^2 f\sharp^2 g^2 a^2 b^2$; the compass extends upward to eb^3. See also: khlui (176).

Khlopki, large copper goat bell of Bulgaria (89).

Khlui, generic term for pipes in Thailand, including stopped flutes, with or without free reeds. The pipes are made of bamboo, wood, or ivory and have cylindrical form and bore. In some instances a side hole is added above the fingerholes, covered by goldbeater's skin on the mirliton principle. Others are cylindrical cross flutes with a free reed of metal set in the blowhole, with 7 front fingerholes of which the lowest is never stopped; others again have 6 fingerholes. See also: khloi (132, 173).

Khobun, Burmese: drum (176).

Khol (clay-ey), drum of India, made of clay, in form of 2 truncated cones joined at their largest part, having heads of different diams. held by leather thongs in zigzag lacings, with tension wedges. Such an instr. is already depicted on the stupa of Borobudur in Java, dating from *ca.* 800. Played with bare hands. Cf. mridanga (170).

Khong, Thai: gong (144).

Khong hui, set of 3 gongs of Cambodia, of different sizes (47).

Khong khu, gong of Thailand (144).

Khong lek, see: khong vong lek.

Khong long, Burmese: great bell (176).

Khong malo, gong of Thailand (176).

Khong mong, bronze gong of Thailand, suspended from a tripod (176).

Khong ñai, gong chime of Laos, equivalent to the khong vong yai (46).

Khong noï, Laos equivalent of the khong vong lek (47).

Khong rao, gong of Thailand (144).

Khong that, drum of Laos, identical with the skor thom of Cambodia (47).

Khong thom, high-pitched gong chime of Cambodia, corresponding to the khong vong lek (47, 173).

Khong toch, low-pitched gong chime of Cambodia, corresponding to the khong vong yai (47, 173).

Khong vong lek, gong chime of Thailand, similar to the khong vong yai but of higher pitch, consisting of 18 gongs (the lowest 2 of which are never used: $b^1 c\sharp^2$) with diams. 9–13 cm. (3½–5 in.) and a (played) compass of d^2–e^4 (65).

Khong vong yai, gong chime of Thailand, of 16 tuned gongs with central boss and turned rim, arranged in a low circular frame, with the lowest-pitched gong to the player's left, the highest to his right. The player sits in the center of the frame with the gongs around him. Their diams. vary from 12–16 cm. (4¾–6¼ in.). The gongs have a compass d^1–e^3 and are struck with 2 beaters (65).

Khong yai (great drum), see: khong vong yai.

Khor, *notched flute of Aurora Island, New Hebrides, made of bamboo. The lower end is stopped by a node. *Cf.* gore, kaur (176).

Khoradak, small Indian kettledrum of clay, of ancient Pers. origin. It is oval, with laced head, and is always played in pairs and with bare hands. The lower-pitched is on the player's left, the higher on his right (132).

Khorae, the *dörwen chikhe khuur of the Khorchin Mongols (69).

Khram, *conical drum of the Garo of Assam, with 2 heads stretched by V-lacings. *Ca.* 84 cm. (33 in.) long (172).

Khudra katyayana vīnā (Beng.), see: kshudrā katyayana vīnā.

Khui, Laos equivalent of khlui (47).

Khullāl (Arab.), *goblet drum of the Berbers and of Moorish Spain, mentioned in the 13th c. (89 Farmer).

Khumbgwe, stopped vertical flute of the Venda of S. Africa, consisting of a small, globular *strychnos* shell fitted onto a length of cane. The latter has 3 finger-holes at its lower end, which is stopped. A hole at the top of the shell serves as blowhole, the player's breath being directed across it. *Cf.* ombiwe (116).

Khum-mubra, marine-shell trumpet of Persia (144)..

Khur, name of the khil-khuur among the Buriat Mongols and Khorchin Mongols (69).

Khut mandri, conical 2-headed mandri of wood or clay, with cowhide membranes held by zigzag lacings. *Ca.* 75 cm. (30 in.) long (68).

Khuuchir, the dörwen chikhe khuur of the Khalka Mongols and Buriat Mongols (69).

Khuur, the dörwen chikhe khuur of the Khalka Mongols (69).

Ki, bamboo *whistle flute of the Marquesas Islands, with or without finger-holes, possibly of European origin, as this type does not occur elsewhere in Oceania (77).

Kia chung ch'ih, ch'ih pitched in g^1 (176).

K'iang, see: chu.

K'iang ti, see: ch'iang ti.

Kiatso dim-bava, *ribbon reed of the Betsileo of the Malagasy Republic (171).

Kiatsódy, syn. of sódina.

Kibanda, sansa of the Babunda, Bakwese, and Bapende of the Congo, with cane lamellae. The Bapende hollow out their lamellae and fill them with seeds, causing them to rattle when played. *Cf.* kimbanda (42).

Kibbi, conical drum of the Bongo of the NE. Congo (19).

Kibili, syn. of idzdzai.

Kibiti, a W. African name for the sansa (185).

Kibitiko, drum of the Basanga, adopted by the Bayeke of the Congo (30).

Kibudikidi, small *slit drum of São Salvador region of Angola, and of the Bwende of the Lower Congo area, often scaphoid or crescent-shaped (185).

Kibukandet, lyre of Kenya (120).

Kibuku (Kikongo), syn. of dukulu (185).

Kibulu kinteta, *cylindrical drum of the Bakongo of the Congo, used for accompanying dances (30).

Kidete, *notched flute of the Congo, made of cane with 4 fingerholes near the lower end. Sometimes the performer hums a drone while playing (139).

Kidi, 1. single-headed vertical drum of the Ewe of Ghana, barrel-shaped and encircled with iron hoops. The bottom is closed. It has the same type of head as the *atsimevu and is wetted in the same manner. It sounds about a 5th higher. The player sits on the ground with the drum in front of him and beats it with 2 sticks. *Ca.* 28 cm. (11 in.) long (109); **2.** drum played by (low-caste) smiths of Egidi, Zazawa, in the Sahara. Tuning paste of goat brains and soot from cooking pots is applied (193).

Kidideka, bamboo *concussion sticks of the Malagasy Republic (171).

Kidimba, name given to the madimba by the Baluga of the Congo (31).

Kidimbadimba, var. of didimbadimba.

Kidiyo, end-blown cowhorn of the Amba of Uganda. The name is also applied to their side-blown ivory horns (195).

Kidrar, syn. of kirar.

Kidrigo, syn. of kilingila.

Kielflügel (Ger.: quilled wing), Ger.: harpsichord. Nowadays the word *cembalo* is used almost exclusively.

Kien pan, see: chien pan.

Kigwara, kigwari, *globular flute of the Gishu, Gwere, and Nyole of Uganda, made of dry *oncoba* fruits or the tip of a gourd, with blowhole and 2 fingerholes. Also called ebumi, ebundi (195).

Kijonga, musical bow of Costa Rica, with half-gourd resonator (149).

Kikasa, drum of the Baluba of the Congo, adopted by the Basanga, played at war dances and at the enthroning of chiefs. Also called tshikasa (30).

Kikilo, ground zither of the Dongo of the Congo. Also called tsitsilo (128).

Ki kohe puru, nose flute of the Marquesas, Polynesia. See also: ko'e (203).

Kikomfi, cylindrical *slit drum of the Manyema of the Congo, with dumbbell-shaped slit (19).

Kikongwe, very short, wide-bore *cylindrical flute of the Washambala of Kenya, made of a stalk of the castor-oil plant, closed at the bottom by a node, or of *kilapinde* stalk, 6–8 cm. (2½–3 in.) long. See also: wikongwe (111).

Kikóri, syn. of kindembo (152).

Kilando, slit drum of the Congo, made of a large, bottle-shaped gourd (176).

Kilangay, slit drum of the SW. area of the Malagasy Republic (176).

Kili, wooden bell of the Azande of the Congo, flat, of ovoid shape, with 3 clappers, surmounted by a carved woman's head. It functions as a symbol of the chief's dignity and also forms part of the dance orchestra. In Medje (language) it is known as negpwapwo (132).

Kiliba, wooden rattle of the Wasongola of the Congo, carved out of a root and filled with pebbles and seeds (42).

Kilibongo, *musical bow of the Azo and Andemaderi of the Congo, without resonator or tuning loop (128).

Kili kugur, see: khil-khuur.

Kilingbindiri, *musical bow of the Dongo of the Congo, with gourd resonator not attached to the bow (128).

Kilingila, *musical bow of the Logo of the Congo, with gourd resonator not attached to the bow. Also called gulutindi (128).

Kilu, name of the kalur among the Acoli of Uganda (195).

Kiluka, name of the kalur among the Alur of Uganda (195).

Kim, *mouth organ of Burma (103).

Ki-ma, name of a Tibetan stringed instr. that occurs in literary sources only (89 Picken).

Kimasa, *arched harp of the Soga of Uganda, now extremely rare, with carved wooden body and 8 strings. Occasionally it assumes a footed form (195).

Kimbanda, sansa of the Bahuana, Bakwese, Bambala, and Batetela of the Congo. *Cf.* kibanda (19).

Kimbandu, *goblet drum of the Bayaka of the Congo, with nailed head, used in male initiation rites; 50–100 cm. (20–40 in.) long (30).

Kimbolo, *percussion beam of the Majunga region of the Malagasy Republic; it corresponds to the tsikaretika (171).

Kimbumba, obs. Afro-Cuban *ground drum, also called kumbandera (152).

Kimchek, see: kamänja.

Kimvalu [Lat. *cymbalum*], Slav.: cymbals. *Cf.* chimvale.

Kimwanyewanye, fiddle of E. Africa, similar to the tad (173).

Kin, 1. bronze *resting bell of Japan, made in a variety of sizes and attaining several feet in diam. They serve in Buddhist rites, set on a cushion and struck with a stick. Also called uchinarashi (135); **2.** dancing rattle of the Berg-

Dama of S. Africa, consisting of long strings of cocoons filled with pebbles, hard seeds, etc., twined around the lower part of male dancers' legs. Also called namen (116); **3.** gong of China (89); **4.** syn. of koto. *Cf.* ch'in.

Ki na, small sona (176).

Kinaban, Jew's-harp of the Hanunoo of the Philippine Islands (103).

Kinanda, 1. stringed instr. of Mombasa and Zanzibar, with wooden body, skin belly, and hollow neck, probably derived from an Indian instr. such as a kinnarī vīnā (116); **2.** *stick zither of Moliro, the Congo, with 7 strings and a gourd resonator (132); **3.** *trough zither of Tanganyika and Uganda; it corresponds to the lulanga (139); **4.** *board zither of the Komo of the Congo, without resonator (128).

Kinanga, 1. *arched harp of the Konjo of Uganda, with 8 strings of twisted raffia. Also called ekihako. *Cf.* enzebe; **2.** *musical bow of Ziba, S. Uganda, that corresponds to the adungu, 1 (195).

Kinchir, name of the kendang awi in the Bandung district of W. Java (121).

Kindembo, Afro-Cuban name of the *maraca de muñeca (Sp.: wrist maraca). Also called kikóri (152).

Kinditi kia nsi, largest sansa of the Bembe of the Congo, with rectangular resonator and lamellae of palm strips (185).

Kinditi kiantele kia mbasa, smallest sansa of the Bembe of the Congo, without resonator. Played while walking (185).

Kindja, rattle of the Nzakara of the Union of Central African Republics, made of a cluster of fruit-shell *pellet bells, worn by dancers on their arms and legs (42).

Kindri, drum of the Logo of the Congo, mainly cylindrical, with single head laced to a skin that covers the lower end. Also called lari. *Ca.* 125 cm. (50 in.) high (30).

Kindu, lyre of the Logo of the Congo (19).

Kinera, unidentified instr. of ancient Greece. *Cf.* kinnōr, kinyra.

Kinfuíti, Afro-Cuban *friction drum, with friction taking place inside the resonator. The drum consists of a short barrel, 60–80 cm. (24–32 in.) long with a membrane bottom to which a friction cord or stick is fitted in such a manner that it can be rubbed in the body of the drum. Also called manfula. See also: puita (152).

King, *bar zither of the Punjab, with single metal string, 7 raised frets, and 2 large gourd resonators (173).

Kingira, *stick zither of India, with gourd resonator, described by Arab. authors Al Jahiz (d. 868) and Al-Masudi (d. 956) as having one string stretched over a gourd. Possibly an adaptation of the vīnā, it was pop. in Persia in the 14th c. and was still played there in the 17th c. (75 II).

Kingoma kya nkisi, small portable drum of the Lower Congo, with 2 laced heads, carried under the arm (185).

Kingulu-ngulu, syn. of dingwinti.

Kingwa ndikila, idiochord *stick zither of the Bembe of the Congo, made of a raffia palm frond from which a strip of bark is detached and stretched over 2 small bridges. Ligatures applied at both ends prevent it from tearing. One player taps it with 2 sticks while another places and laterally moves over the string a tin can filled with seeds. Also found among the Yaunde and Pahouin of W. Africa (185).

Kinkini, 1. Sans.: small bell (176); **2.** syn. of salangai (179).

Kinkoto, clapperless bell of the Diki-Diki of the Congo, made of sheet metal, of near-conical form. Used for ritual purposes only (185).

Kinkwinta, syn. of dingwinti.

Kinnara, 1. name of a *stick zither in Hindu and old Javanese literature. Such an instr., with single string and gourd resonator held against the body, is found on the reliefs at Borobudur (*ca.* 800). *Cf.* kinnōr, kinnāra, kinyra (118); **2.** Tel.: kinnari.

Kinnāra, pl. **kinnarat** [Heb. *kinnōr*], ancient Arab. name for the lyre (170).

Kinnari (Sans., Mal., Tamil), bamboo *stick zither of S. India, of great antiquity, with 2 or 3 metal strings, 12 raised frets, and 3 gourd resonators. The strings are stretched one above the other over a high, notched bridge, and attached to very long lateral and frontal pegs. The lower end of the stick terminates in a carved head. The large central gourd is flanked by 2 smaller ones. Nowadays the kinnari is played only by members of lower castes (173, 179).

Kinnarī vīnā, modified kachapī vīnā of N. India, with ostrich egg or wooden body and 5 to 7 strings. Not connected with the kinnari stick zither (132, 170, 173).

Kin no koto, early Jap. name of the kin, introduced from China in the 5th c. and played without plectrum or frets (144).

Kinnōr [U.] (Heb.), **1.** generic name for stringed instrs. among the ancient Hebrews; **2.** trapezoid lyre of the ancient Hebrews, played in biblical times. The Vulgate (*ca.* 400) translates it as *kithara,* the Septuagint as *kinyra, psalterion.* It was the "harp" of King David, related to the knr, both a Temple and a secular instr. Made of wood and strung with sheep-gut strings, it was played with a plectrum when accompanying dances, otherwise with bare fingers. Ancient reproductions show 3 to 12 strings. Flavius Josephus (b. 37 A.C.) reports it as played with a plectrum and having 10 strings (5 courses of 2 strings?). In late representations the kinnōr closely resembles the classical kithara. See also: kannār, kinnāra, kinyra, knr, lyre (84, 170).

Kinteta, *cylindrical drum of the Bakongo of the Congo, used for accompanying dances (185).

Kinura, organ stop of small-scaled reed pipes surmounted by a hood-like lid, at 8' pitch, built by Robert Hope-Jones (d. 1914) (198).

Kinyra, word that occurs in the Septuagint for kinnōr.

Kio-kio, syn. of hano.

Kiondo, cylindrical *slit drum of the Baholoholo of the Congo, with dumbbell-shaped slit (19).

Kiotang, syn. of shotang.

Kipkurkur, Nandi: bell (176).

Kipokan, pl. **kipokandin,** lyre of the Nandi of Kenya (176).

Kipuita, see: puita, 1.

Kiragutse, royal drum of Ruanda (30).

Kirān (Arab.), pre-Islamic lute of the Arabian Peninsula, still known in the early 14th c. (75 I, II).

Kirar, name of the kerar in Shoa Province, Ethiopia. Also called kidrar. *Cf.* kinnōr (45).

Kiringi, *slit drum of the Soso of Sierra Leone, made of a hollowed tree trunk and beaten with 2 rubber-headed sticks. Identical with the balah of the Sarakolle (132).

Kiri-pill, Estonian: reedpipe.

Kirisen, 3-stringed samisen of Japan, with square body, parchment belly, played with a plectrum. *Cf.* taisen (157).

Kirrika, Basque: *cog rattle. *Cf.* carraca, kharraka (56).

Kirr-kishi, scraper of the Baiga of Arwar, Balaghat district, India. A wooden rod with carved notches is scraped with a bamboo switch (68).

Kisachi, sansa of the Basonge of the Congo. *Cf.* kisanchi, kisansi (19).

Kisanchi, sansa of the Dembo and Mahungo of the Congo (19).

Kisandasanda, var. of ikisandasanda.

Kisansi, sansa of the Baluba-Hemba of the Congo (19).

Kisirka, Nubian name of the kissar (176).

Kisketa, Basque: clapper (56).

Kiskilla [Lat. *squilla*], Basque: **1.** small eskilla; **2.** *pellet bell (56).

Kisli, see: gusli.

Kissanga, Afro-Cuban pluriarc. *Cf.* kissumba (152).

Kissar [Gk. *kithara*], *bowl lyre of E. Africa, a survival of the ancient Gk. lyra, still found in Ethiopia, Sudan, and Uganda. The body is shallow, of wood, covered with a sheepskin membrane laced to the back of the body. The strings —variable in number—are attached to the yoke by tuning rings. See also: gezarke (89 Baines).

Kissumba, syn. of wambi. *Cf.* kissanga.

Kit (Fr.: *poche, pochette;* Ger.: *Taschengeige;* It.: *sordino;* Lat.: *linterculus*), obs. tiny fiddle, last survivor of the med. rebec. It appeared in the 16th c. and established itself as a dancing master's fiddle, housed in its master's pocket. Mersenne explains its Fr. name (meaning *pocket*) from this use. Trichet, *ca.* 1640, describes it as made of 2 pieces of wood glued together, 1 for the bottom, sides, neck, and head, the other for the soundboard. Praetorius calls it a *gar klein Geiglein* and gives the tuning of its 3 strings as $a^1 e^2 b^2$ or a tone lower ($g^1 d^2 a^2$). The word "kit" is first recorded as a musical instr. in the second decade of the 16th c., but its identity at that time is unknown; possibly it denoted the rebec then. In France it came into vogue in the first half of the 17th c. and did not disappear until the 18th. During the 2 c. of its existence it was made in a number of shapes: round, scaphoid, as a miniature violin or viola da gamba (the last 2 are later forms), often of beautiful workmanship. The kit has 3 or 4 strings, a length of 38–50 cm. (15–20 in.), and is played with a bow 38–45 cm. (15–18 in.) long. The common tuning was $c^1 g^1 d^2$. Also called Sackgeige, sourdine, Spitzgeige, Stockgeige, Tanzmeistergeige (89 Heron Allen, 94, 159, 190).

Kitara, see: qītāra.

Kitāra kināwa, see: gunbrī.

Kitarra, Basque: guitar (56).

Kitelis, syn. of icitali.

Kithara (Gk.), national instr. of ancient Greece, a box lyre, with square, flat wooden box resonator, 2 thick, hollow arms connected at the top by a crossbar, and a variable number of gut strings of equal length, originally 3, increased to 11 by the 5th c. B.C., and played with a plectrum. A heavy, rather cumbersome instr., it was held upright when played, in contrast to the tilted lyra, its weight partly supported by being rested against the player's body. Many of the kitharas depicted are held by a broad band passed over the player's shoulder, or by a narrower one leading from one of the yoke arms over his left wrist. Generally the strings were secured to the crossbar by leather tuning rings, but in later times systems are described for tightening all strings simultaneously by slightly raising the yoke. The kithara is distinguished from the lyra by material and shape: a square resonator of wood identifies the instr. as a kithara (the lyra was rounded). In preclassical times the kithara was an instr. of bards, who accompanied their epic songs on it; by classical times it had become the instr. of professional players, the *kitharoedes.* Lyres very similar in shape were known earlier in Mesopotamia, but we do not know their name. A few early Gk. writers remembered the kithara's Asiatic origin, but this was forgotten, and the instr. came to be considered as an autochthonous national instr. We find the kithara depicted from the 7th c. B.C. on, chiefly on vases; in the 6th c. it achieved its final form. We can follow it pictorially through Hellenistic to Roman times, when the resonator changes shape and becomes overcrowded with ornamentation. For tuning see: lyre (21, 175).

Kitharis, a Homeric term, probably designating the Gk. lyra, as a bulging form is mentioned (170).

Kitimplik, W. Java term for a very small terbang (121).

Kitingbi, *musical bow of the Watsa-Gombari region of the Congo, played by the Balese, Mangbetu, Mdo, and Dongo, who press the bow against an inverted half gourd, clay pot, etc. (128).

Kitingi, *musical bow of the Mamvu of

the Congo, with gourd resonator not attached to the bow (128).

Kitmu (Akk.), wind instr. of ancient Babylon, a pipe with single reed covered by a cap; it appears in the first millennium. Also known as kanzabu (89 Galpin).

Kitsarakara, pair of rattles of the Bembe of the Congo and other peoples, joined by a cord, made of spherical *oncoba* gourd or other fruits, filled with seeds, pebbles, etc. Worn by women and girls, but by boys only among the Bembe (185).

Kitsatsa, a decadent form of the masaka, a rattle of the Kamba of Loudima region of the Congo Republic, made of a tin can that has holes bored in it and contains pebbles. Sometimes a wooden handle is affixed (185).

Kitsika, bell of the Bembe of the Congo, made of the fruit shell of the *kitsika* tree, with a hardwood clapper. Worn by women during rites for the protection of a newborn child (185).

Kitsódy, syn. of sódina.

Kitumba, syn. of umukunto.

Kiturege, *ground bow of the Bahaya of Tanganyika, a child's toy (108).

Kivudi-vudi (Kikongo), a wooden trumpet *ca.* 50 cm. (20 in.) long, found in the Manianga region of the Congo, sometimes ornamented with geometric designs. Also called vudi-vudi (185).

Kiyamba, rattle of Zanzibar, E. Africa, made of sections of hollow cane *ca.* 30 cm. (1 ft.) long, connected raftwise and filled with pebbles, seeds, etc. (176).

Kizanzi, see: kisansi.

Kizugo, wooden *double bell of the Washambala of Kenya, East Africa, of hourglass shape, made from a single piece of wood hollowed out at both ends and provided with 3 iron clappers. Pellet bells are strung at its waist. Used by magicians to drive demons away (111).

Klächel, Klächl, Ger.: bell clapper. *Cf.* Klöppel (88).

Kladdi, free-reed *mouth organ of the Dayak of Borneo, consisting of 6 or 8 bamboo pipes in bundle form, inserted into a small gourd that serves as wind chamber. Its natural neck serves as blowpipe. The reeds are fitted into a hole cut for this purpose at the lower end of each pipe. Also called garude, gorteh, keluri (173).

Klaffe, MHGer.: clapper; the instr. of lepers in the Middle Ages (189).

Klangboden, Ger.: soundboard (rare).

Klappe, Ger.: key (of wind instr.).

Klappenflügelhorn, the oldest Ger. name of the keyed bugle.

Klappenhorn, Ger.: keyed bugle.

Klappentrompete, Ger.: keyed trumpet.

Klapper, Ger.: clapper.

Klarfiedel, treble member of a family of bowed instrs. made in Jihlava (Iglau), Moravia, since the 16th c. if not far earlier. The family consists of Klarfiedel, an alto called *Grobfiedel, and a bass, the *Plâschprment. Their shape is similar to that of the med. fiddle. Back, ribs, and pegdisc are carved out of a single block of maple, the belly being of fir with rectangular soundholes. The pegdisc is flat, with pegs inserted from the rear. The bridge is cut like a comb. The body is unvarnished and no bass bar is used. Its 4 strings are tuned like those of a violin. Some specimens are shaped like rectangular boxes with a slight taper at the waist in lieu of center bouts. Bows are made of beechwood, with black horsehair. In quartet playing the second Klarfiedel is named Sekundfiedel; structurally they are identical. Called dynda, dyndy, in Czech (86, 117).

Klarflöte, organ stop identical with the Hellflöte or Offenflöte (133).

Klarine (Ger.), see: clairon, 3.

Klarinette, Ger.: clarinet.

Klarinettenbass (Ger.), *bass clarinet designed 1793 by Carl August Grenser the Elder of Dresden, the first of a series of such instrs. to be built in bassoon shape. It had a 4-oct. compass, its lowest tone being B^1, and 9 keys (164).

Klater, Flem.: rattle (132).

Klaväoline, Ger.: clavaeoline.

Klaviatur, Ger.: keyboard.

Klaviaturharmonika (Ger.), syn. of Tastenharmonika.

Klaviaturkontrafagott, see: Claviatur-Contrafagott.

Klaviatur-Sphärophon, see: Sphärophon.

Klaviaturzither, zither built in 1903 by Johannes Rehbock of Duisburg, with a keyboard. Compass of D^0–a^2 (176).

Klavichord, Ger.: clavichord.

Klavidon, keyboard instr. invented 1806 by Sauer of Prague, with small compass and dulcimer-like tone (176).

Klavier (Ger.) [Fr. *clavier*], Fr. word taken over into MHGer. since Virdung (in 1511) in its original sense of keyboard, and since 1677 to denote any stringed keyboard instr.; during most of the 18th c. (recorded 1711 on) specifically denoting the clavichord. During the 19th c. the word became almost syn. with square piano but was also used for upright piano, in contradistinction to the grand form then known as Fortepiano or Flügel. Today the word applies chiefly to the upright piano. The term is most ambiguous, and often only the context will determine which instr. is meant. As a prefix, it denotes any instr. furnished with a keyboard. Until the early 20th c. the word was spelled Clavier.

Klaviergamba, see: Clavier-Gambe.

Klavierharfe, Ger.: keyed harp. See also: clavi-harp.

Klavi-Mandor, keyboard instr. of unknown construction, built by Johann Andreas Mahr of Wiesbaden, from 1788 on (83).

Klavizimbel [Lat. *clavicimbalum*], obs. Ger.: harpsichord.

Klavizylinder, see: Clavicylinder.

Klavizytherium, Ger.: clavicytherium.

Kledi, see: kladdi.

Klein . . . (Ger.: small), **1.** as a prefix to names of organ stops, klein denotes a pitch one oct. higher than that of the stop named, *e.g.*, Kleingedackt 4′; **2.** as a prefix to names of instrs., it denotes soprano or sopranino range.

Kleine Bassgeige, Eisel (in 1738) says it is the same as a violoncello (67).

Kleine Geige, 1. Ger. 16th- and 17th-c. equivalent of the It. word *violetta;* **2.** Virdung (in 1511) and Agricola (in 1528, 1545) depict rebecs under this name; they show 3 strings and split-level bellies. Later, kleine Geige comes to denote viole da braccio, as for instance in an Ambras inventory of 1596, in which Grossgeigen or viole da gamba are also mentioned. See also: Geige, Grossgeige.

Kleines Kornett, Ger.: sopranino saxhorn.

Kleine Trommel, Ger.: snare drum.

Kleinzink, syn. of Quartzink.

Klenengan, var. of kliningan (121).

Klentong, oval cattle bell of Java, made of bronze (176).

Klepalce (OSlav.), small semanterion. *Cf.* klepalo (176).

Klepalo (Bulg., Serb., Russ.), the semanterion of Bulgaria, Russia, and Yugoslavia. In Bulgaria it is becoming obs. In some Orthodox monasteries of Yugoslavia it is still to be found in the form of a large wooden board hung on a chain and struck with a mallet. See also: klopotac, klopótiz (89, 176).

Klepavka, Czech: semanterion.

Klepetalo, small klepalo.

Klepsiambos, unidentified instr. of ancient Greece.

Kleron, 18th-c. Ger.: clairon, 3.

Klimperküle, *stick rattle of N. Ger. horseherds in form of a crook to which iron rings were attached (173).

Kliningan, name of the gender in W. Java (121).

Klinkik, wind instr. of Nootka Islanders, Vancouver, made of 2 pieces of hollowed wood tied together like a duckbill. One end is flattened and acts as a double reed when the opposite end is blown into (176).

Klinting, *Jingling Johnnie of Java, consisting of a pole from which a number of small bells are suspended at different levels, attached to cross members or a wheel. The klinting forms part of the archaic *gamelan kodok ngorek*. Also called byong, genta, gentorag, kembang delima (121).

Klintingan, Javanese: pellet bell (121).

Kloboto, syn. of klodzie.

Klocka, Swed.: bell.

Klocktrumma (bell drum), Swed.: tambourine to which small bells are affixed.

Klodzie, *barrel drum of the Ewe of Ghana, with single head and open bottom, played during special dances, when it is hooked to a forked stand. Also called kloboto (109).

Kloïe, see: khloi.

Klok [Lat. *clocca*], Du.: bell.

Klokje, dim. of klok.

Klokka [Lat. *clocca*], Nor.: bell.

Klokke, Dan.: bell.

Klokkenspel, Du.: carillon (160).

Klokó, *arará drum of Cuba, cylindrical, almost as wide as it is high, with single head fitted on a hoop, laced to pegs protuding from the body. Played vertically with 2 sticks (152).

Klong, Thai: drum.

Klong khek (foreign drum), Thai *barrel drum of Mal. origin (173).

Klong tad, *barrel drum of Thailand, resembling the Javanese bedug. Only 1 of the 2 nailed heads is played, tightened with tuning paste; the drum is propped up so that the lower head can vibrate freely. Loud tones are produced with bamboo sticks; padded sticks are used for soft tones. Played in pairs or sets of 3. *Ca.* 60 cm. (2 ft.) high, 45 cm. (18 in.) in diam. (65, 121).

Klontong, miniature *barrel drum of Java, with 2 snakeskin heads, affixed to a handle. Balls of wax are attached to the drum by cords and strike against the heads when the drum is swung. Of Chin. origin, it is used only by the Chin. population of Java. In Bali it appears under the name of ketipluk. An ancient bronze klontong, 14 cm. (6 in.) long, has been excavated. Ancient instrs. were either cylindrical or conoid. *Cf.* dāmaru, 2 (121).

Klopotac, Serb. percussion board. *Cf.* klepalo (176).

Klopótiz, Slov. percussion board (176).

Klöppel, Ger.: bell clapper. *Cf.* Klächel.

Klotak, klotang, Javanese names for bells made of wood (121).

Klötzchen, Ger.: block (of violins, etc.).

Klowa, percussion sticks of the Canella Indians of C. Maranhão, Brazil (176).

Klū, bamboo *whistle flute of the Padaung of Shan State, Burma, with 4 front fingerholes and a rear thumbhole. *Ca.* 47 cm. (18½ in.) long (172).

Klui, see: khlui.

Klukka [Lat. *clocca*], ONordic: bell.

Klung kung, idiochord *tube zither of Bali, with single string. The tube is closed by nodes at the ends. A round or square hole is cut near the middle and covered with a flat piece of wood that is drummed upon with a beater (149).

Klurai, var. of keluri.

Knarre, Ger.: cog rattle.

Knaverharpa, obs. Swed. instr. believed to have been identical with the nyckelharpa, as keys were sometimes called *knavrar*. The term occurred in the 18th c. and the instr. is known to have been in use in the late 17th c., possibly in the 16th (9).

Knee lever (Fr.: *genouillère;* Ger.: *Kniehebel*), registration levers moved by the player's knee, found on certain 18th- and 19th-c. keyboard instrs. Jean-Antoine Berger of Grenoble built by 1765 a harpsichord fitted with a knee lever, Virbès in 1766 a harpsichord with 2 knee levers, Pascal Taskin used them by 1773 if not earlier; Johann Andreas Stein and contemporary builders adapted them to their grand pianos. Later in the 19th c. they continued in use on harmoniums.

Knicky-knackers, Engl. 17th-c. term for clappers or bones (79).

Kniegeige, obs. Ger.: viola da gamba.

Kniehebel, Ger.: knee lever.

Knnr, see: knr.

Knopfregal (Ger.: knob regal), syn. of Apfelregal.

Knot, 17th-c. Engl.: rose.

Knr, lyre of ancient Egypt that appears

in the New Kingdom and disappears in Alexandrian times, of W. Asian origin. Asymmetrical until *ca.* 1000 B.C., it is depicted held either horizontally or vertically. See: lyre. See also: ginēra, kinnāra, kinnōr, kinyra (170).

Ko, Korean: drum. See: chin ko, choa ko, cho ko, chol ko, chung ko, kon ko, kyo pang ko, no ko, sak ko, ung ko.

Koa, ceremonial *cross flute of the Kamaon region of NE. New Guinea, closely connected with male initiation rites and always played in pairs. Every family owns a pair. Koas are made in 2 varieties: one has no fingerholes, the pitch being modified by lip tension and by stopping the lower end by hand; the other has 1 fingerhole and is stopped. This second variety is often decorated with a carved wooden head tied on the upper end. The koa is also found among the Iatmul of the Sepik area (202).

Koala, var. of koali.

Koali, pl. **likoali,** name of the gora among the Sotho of Transvaal, S. Africa. Also called koala (116).

Koanapa, percussion stick of the Indians of the Peruvian Amazon area (103).

Koauau, obs. *end-blown flute of the Maori of New Zealand, made of wood or human bone, open at both ends, and provided with 1–6 fingerholes, the usual number being 3. These are arranged so that 2 lie close together, the third farther away. The koauau was made in a variety of sizes, shapes, and bores, and was played both orally and as a nose flute. Older ones are said to have been mouth-blown only. Many specimens are short, up to 20 cm. (8 in.) in length, with very wide conical bore. According to Wolf, the nose-blown specimens were cylindrical. When played as a nose flute, the koauau was provided with an extra-large hole for the nostril, situated just below the upper end, according to Andersen. Fingerholes of nose-blown flutes are usually smaller than those of mouth-blown ones (8, 77, 203).

Kōbe, Kotar: syn. of ranasringa, sringa.

Koboz [Turk. **qūbūz*], short-necked lute, of Near Eastern origin, that spread to Europe via Byzantium. A Gk. tract of *ca.* 800 A.C. mentions a *kobuz* or *pandurion* with 7 frets and 3, 4, or 5 strings. In Europe the instr. is still played in Hungary, Latvia, Poland, Romania, Ukraine; also in Arabia and by the Kirghiz, with minor modifications of form and name. See also: cobza, kobus, kobza, qabūs, qūbūz (38, 169).

Kobus [Turk. **qūbūz*], MHGer. term occurring in literary sources (176).

Kobuz, see: koboz.

Kobyz [Turk. **qūbūz*], a primitive form of sarangi, played by the Kirghiz and Tatar of Turkestan (170).

Kobza [Turk. **qūbūz*], **1.** Pol. and Russ. lute of Near Eastern origin. See: koboz; **2.** syn. of rilya; **3.** name erroneously given to the koza; **4.** see: cobza.

Ko ch'ing, *musical stone of China, suspended in a frame. It assumes a variety of forms: that of a fish, a heart, etc. (1).

Ko chung, obs. *bell chime of China, formerly used in Confucian rites. It was pitched an oct. higher than the *pien chung and consisted of 12–24 bells. *Cf.* chung (176).

Kociel, kociol [Lat. *catillus*, kettle], Pol.: kettledrum (176).

Koda, Kan. equivalent of the gātha (173).

Ko daiko, small daiko used in processions and in *kagura*, beaten with 2 sticks. *Ca.* 66 cm. (26 in.) long, 56 cm. (22 in.) in diam. (157).

Kodili, stick zither of Norfolk and Solomon Islands, made of bamboo, without resonator.

Ko'e, *nose flute of Hawaii, Cook Islands, Mangareva, and New Zealand. Also called kofe. See also: ki kohe puru (77).

Ko erh nai [Arab. *qānūn*], Chin. name of the qānūn, which was introduced from W. Asia (75 II).

Kofe, 1. syn. of ko'e; **2.** *nose flute of Niue, Polynesia (203).

Kofen [*kon*, horn + *fe*, to blow], horn in Gã (a Sudanic language) made of animal horn. See also: akofe (93).

Kohe, var. of ko'e (77).

Koheoheo, syn. of o-e-o-e.

Kohkles, Latvian equivalent of the kankles. Also called kuakle or kuokle.

Kohkol, Sundanese name of the kentongan (121).

Koh'lo, *musical bow of the Tehuelche Indians of Patagonia, with horsehair string. One end of the bow is held between the player's teeth, while the string is "bowed" with a long condor bone. *Ca.* 30 cm. (12 in.) long (17, 105).

Kojo, conical drum of the Kabba-Sara of the Congo (19).

Ko kin, *spike fiddle of Japan that corresponds to the Chin. erh hsien and resembles the kei kin. The belly is of skin, and the bottom is open; its 2 strings are tuned a 5th or 4th apart (157).

Kokkara, scraper of the Pulayar, Vedar, and Kuruvar sorcerers of S. India, made of a piece of metal bent into a tube, with serrated edges (68).

Kokles, see: kohkles.

Koko, 1. side-blown whistle of the Dendi of the Congo, with 2 fingerholes (42); **2.** name of the *slit drum in the Lower Congo; that of the Sundi is often 2 m. (6½ ft.) long (185).

Kokolo, pluriarc of the Lessa of the Congo (19).

Kokondi, syn. of tuba pondi.

Kokpworo, syn. of okporo.

Ko kun, *spike fiddle of Japan, of Korean origin, more ornate but otherwise identical with the kei kin (157).

Kokyu, bowed chordophone of Japan, similar in shape to the samisen, with square body, very long neck, parchment belly and back, made in various sizes, the average being 70 cm. (27 in.) long. The kokyu has 2, 3, or 4 strings. The 2 highest ones of the 4-stringed version are tuned in unison. Normally the strings are tuned in 4ths, or a 5th and a 4th apart. When the performer plays seated, a spike

is used. The kokyu bow is very long (114 cm., or 45 in.); its loose hair is pulled taut by a ring held by the player's little finger, the bow itself being held like a pair of chopsticks (135, 157).

Kolamut, the name of the garamut on New Ireland, Tabar, and Tanga, Bismarck Archipelago. Also called gamti (77).

Kolanter, name of the ketipung in W. Java (121).

Kolatka, Pol.: clapper, beater.

Kolenang, name usually given the bonang in W. Java (121).

Kolendang, W. Java name of the kemanak (121).

Kolilo, slit drum of Pukapuka and Manihiki, Cook Islands. Also called koriro (77).

Ko ling, *pigeon whistle of China, an aeolian pipe tied to the tails of birds to protect them from birds of prey while in flight. The whistles are tubular or globular, the latter type being made of dried fruit husks or gourds with the top cut off and replaced by a whistle, the tubular ones of bamboo. Sometimes they occur as multiple whistles, made up of as many as 15 pipes in 3 rows. Their chief use is in Peking, where as many as 40 varieties have been known. Also called hsiao tse, ko tse (132, 142).

Kolintang, gong chime of the Alfuro of Celebes, similar to the bonang (173).

Kol-kola, small slit drum of the Kisser of Malaya (173).

Kolla, drum of the Tedas of Tibesti region, Sahara, with 2 heads, only 1 of which is played. Used by men only, to accompany women's dances (193).

Kollone, see: Collone.

Kolokocho, obs. dancer's rattle of the Washambala of Kenya, made of seeds of the *Entada scandens* strung together (111).

Kolokol [Lat. *clocca*], Russ.: bell.

Kolong-kolong, tube zither of W. Flores, with 4 to 6 idiochord strings (149).

Kolongwe, double-headed drum of the Bena Kalundwe of the Congo (30).

Kolotok, wooden cattle bell of W. Java (121).

Koma, Jew's-harp of the Washambala of Kenya, made of *bali* wood, now a child's toy (111).

Koma fuye (Jap.: Korean flute), *cross flute of Japan, of Korean origin, of thin bamboo with 6 equidistant finger-holes, smallest of the *gagaku* flutes. It replaces the azuma fuye. *Ca.* 37 cm. (14½ in.) long (135, 157).

Komba, arched harp of the Budu of the Congo (128).

Kombinationsklarinette, Ger.: combination clarinet.

Kom boat, mouth organ of the Moi of Vietnam (103).

Kombu, S. India equivalent of the sringa (179).

Kommu, Tel. equivalent of kombu.

Kompensationsmixtur, Ger.: compensation mixture.

Kompensationsventil, Ger.: compensation valve.

Komponium (Engl., Fr.: *componium*), a remarkable instr. invented by Dietrich Nikolaus Winkel of Amsterdam, built in 1821, now preserved in the Brussels Conservatoire museum. It comprises: 1) an orchestrion with pinned cylinders, 5 stops of organ pipes on 1 chest and 3 on another, a triangle, and a drum; 2) an automatic composing machine that can compose variations on a given theme, by means of rotating cylinders that alternate 2 bars of silence with 2 bars of sound, adjusted so that one plays while the other is silent, despite continuous rotary motion. The cylinders are pinned with the original theme on the extreme left, followed by pins for 7 successive variations on this theme, thus totaling 8 tunes. Owing to the alternation of the cylinders, 2 bars of any one of the 8 tunes of *one* cylinder can be followed by *one* of the 8 variations of the following 2 bars of the other cylinder. For details of the mechanism see 132, Vol. 1.

Koms, 1. tanbūr of the Kachinz of Siberia, with wooden body, leather belly, and 2 horsehair strings tuned a 5th apart; **2.** iron Jew's-harp with steel tongue, also of the Kachinz (176).

Kömsöl, Korean instr. that corresponds to the p'i p'a of China (176).

Komunko, *long zither of Korea that corresponds to the ch'in of China and is furnished with 6 strings. Also called kum. *Ca.* 140 cm. (55 in.) long. See also: sul, te chang (66, 148).

Kondele, *notched flute of the Kisiba and Uyamtura of E. Africa, with 4 finger-holes. *Ca.* 35 cm. (14 in.) long (203).

Kondere, syn. of eggwara, 2. *Cf.* makondere.

Konding, Mandingo name of the Keronaru.

Kondu, arched harp of the Azande of the Congo (128).

Konene, mirliton of the Madi of Uganda, made of an elongated gourd (195).

Kong, see: gong, khong.

Konga, drum of the Bolia of Lake Leopold II area, the Congo. *Cf.* conga (30).

Kongkeh, *spike fiddle of the Ao-Naga of Assam. The body is a bamboo cylinder with a node forming the bottom; the snakeskin belly is tied on with bast, and the single string of plant fiber is tied directly to the handle (173).

Kongo, *musical bow of the Ashira (Ogowe) of the Congo Republic. The string is taken into the player's mouth; his right hand taps it with a stick while his left hand stops it (176).

Kongo-Guitarre, term formerly used by some Ger. writers for the pluriarc.

Kongo-longo nkueko, obs. Afro-Cuban *friction drum (152).

Königshorn [inventor's name], wind instr. invented by König in 1855 and built by A. Courtois of Paris; it was a cross between an althorn and a French horn in F, furnished with 3 valves (176).

Konimesin, harp lute of Upper Guinea, with either a spherical body of gourd or an elongated one of wood, and 4 strings (42).

Konkeh, see: kongkeh.

Kon ko, large *barrel drum of Korea,

equivalent of the Jap. o-daiko. *Ca.* 1.50 m. (5 ft.) high. *Cf.* chin ko (66).

Konkon, 1. primitive xylophone of the Orang Belende and Orang Mentera of Malaya. Four slabs, pointed at one end, are placed across the stretched legs of 2 performers who sit on the ground facing each other. *Cf.* krotong; **2.** *musical bow of the Cheremiss (146, 176).

Konron, wooden bell with several clappers, of the Kachin of Shan State, Burma, and Assam (173).

Konsonanzpianino (Ger.), upright piano with sympathetic strings on the reverse side of the soundboard, invented in 1877 by Friedrich Hölling of Zeitz (176).

Kontra (Ger.), see: contra.

Kontrabass (Ger.), **1.** double bass; **2.** see: contrabass.

Kontrafagott, Ger.: contrabassoon.

Kontrahorn, see: contrahorn.

Kontraserpent, Ger.: contrabass serpent.

Kontrastbombardon (Ger.), brass instr. of exceptionally low pitch, built by A. Barth of Munich in 1840, of unknown construction (176).

Konustrommel, Ger.: conical drum.

Konzerthorn (Ger.), see: concert horn.

Konzertina, Ger.: concertina.

Köpflinregal, obs. organ stop of regal pipes at 4′ pitch, identical with Kopf- or Knopf- or Apfelregal (159).

Kopfregal, see: Apfelregal.

K'o-pong, syn. of sgra-snyau.

Koppel (Ger.), **1.** Ger.: coupler. Also called Kopplung; **2.** see: Coppel, Coppelflöte.

Kora, 1. *harp lute of the Mandingo and Wolof of Senegal, with 16 strings, also of the Malinke of the Guinea Republic (where it is called seron), similar to the bolon, with spherical resonator, skin belly, perpendicular bridge. Also called ekorro; **2.** var. of gora (42, 103).

Korean temple block, hollow wooden block struck with a mallet, used in sets of 5 in Western rhythm bands. Also called wood block. *Cf.* Chinese block.

Korei, *stick rattle of Japan, consisting

of iron jingles strung on an iron frame attached to a handle (178).

Koriro, syn. of kolilo.

Kornai [Pers. *qarna*], straight trumpet of Turkestan, made of brass, slightly conical, with a slender bell. Played in pairs. *Ca.* 75 cm. (2½ ft.) long (176).

Kornett, Ger.: cornet.

Kornettbass, see: Spitz (organ stop).

Kornon, see: cornon.

Kornophone, Ger.: cornophone.

Koro, percussion board of the Dogon of Mali (103).

Kortholt (short wood), obs. woodwind instr. depicted by Praetorius. His drawing shows a straight gedackt instr. with cylindrical 2-channel bore, played with a double reed, differing apparently from the bass sordone only by being played with a reed cap. (The compass of the bass sordone is given as $B\flat^1$–$b\flat^0$.) It was identical with the Kort Instrument, or Kurzpfeife, but not with the curtal (which had a conical bore), and similar to, but not identical with, the courtaut (114, 159).

Kort Instrument (Ger.: short instrument), syn. of Kortholt, mentioned twice by Praetorius. A Cleve inventory of 1610 lists *"zwei Cort Instrumenten genannt racketten oder Cornaldo"* (2 Kort Instruments called rankets or cornaldo) (200).

Kōshnāy, see: kūshnāy.

Ko sho, clapperless, beehive-shaped bell of Japan, suspended in a frame. *Ca.* 11 cm. (4½ in.) high (178).

Kotekan, syn. of bendrong (121).

Kotly, pl. of kociol.

Koto, *long zither of Japan, also known as kin, derived from the shē of China and long considered the national instr. of Japan. Originally the term denoted any horizontally plucked instr.; later it was used specifically for the long zither with slightly convex board and flat bottom, with 13 silk strings passing over as many individual movable bridges. Formerly reserved for classical Chinese music, it is now admitted as a household instr., played by women. The 13 strings have a compass of 2 octs. from f#⁰, the intervals varying with the scale in use. The koto is placed horizontally on the ground, a table, etc., and played with 3 plectra, worn on the right thumb, index finger, and middle finger. The left hand damps the strings and presses them down behind the bridges when necessary, in order to raise their pitch by a half tone or whole tone. See also: akikiri koto, ame no nori koto, azuma koto, biwa no koto, chiku no koto, gaku sō, gin dai, go kin, han koto, hitsu no koto, ichi gen kin, ikuta koto, kaku koto, kaya kin, kin no koto, kudara koto, ni gen kin, ni kin, roku kin, sage koto, san gen kin, shi chi gen kin, shin sō, shiragi koto, sho hitsu no koto, sō no koto, suga koto, suma koto, taki koto, tsukushi sō, tsuma koto, wagon, ya koto, yakumo koto, yamada koto, yamato koto, yan kin, yo kin, zoku sō (89 Picken, 157).

Ko tse, syn. of ko ling.

Kotso, single-headed *hourglass drum of the Hausa of the Sudan (176).

Ko tsuzumi (Jap.: small tsuzumi), *hourglass drum of Japan, with body of zelkova wood, carved and lacquered, and 2 removable heads of horsehide stretched over iron hoops and laced. The drum is held by its lacings when played, and the pitch may thus be varied. The ko tsuzumi forms part of the *noh* orchestra, in which it is played with beaters. 25–30 cm. (10–12 in.) high. Also called oto tsuzumi (135, 157).

Kou . . . , see: ku . . .

Koumpouzi [Turk. *qūbūz*], bass lute of modern Greece, of Turk. origin (89 Farmer).

Kowaliwali, see: o-e-o-e.

Kowangan, a most curious combination of chordophone and idiophone of Java, now very rare: a number of bamboo leaves are laid over one another, overlapping like fish scales, to form a matting. This is kept in position by fiber strings and, on the inside, by small bamboo laths. Large pieces are formed in this manner, 4 of which are united to constitute a sort of portable tent. Not only does it protect its owner in case of rain, but the fiber strings are plucked. Two flat bamboo sticks are wedged between lathwork and leaves and they also are plucked. See also: gowangan (121).

Koy na bala (village leopard), *friction drum of the Bapende of the Congo, with a palm leaf rib passed through the membrane, rubbed with a handful of dried grass or leaves. Played during secret society initiation rites and at the death of members of these societies. *Cf.* lukombe, 5 (42).

Koza (Pol.: goat), bagpipe of Poland, also found in W. Russia from Vilna to White Russia. Bellows-blown, it has a goatskin bag, as its name implies, a chanter bored with 7 or 8 fingerholes and terminating in an upturned bell of horn or metal. The single drone is bent at a 90° angle and also ends in an upturned horn or metal bell. Traditionally the koza is in E♭. Some chanters can be overblown and the compass extended to 2½ octs. Also called koziol (13, 89).

Koziol (Pol.: he-goat), syn. of koza.

Koziol slubny (Pol.: wedding he-goat), bagpipe of Poland, slightly smaller than the koziol, a ritual instr. of wedding celebrations (89).

Kozol (goat), large bagpipe of the Wends, bellows-blown, with goatskin bag, a chanter with 9 front fingerholes and a rear thumbhole, and single drone (13, 176).

Kpai, board zither of the Mamvu and Balese of the Congo, with resonator (128).

Kpandu, percussion instr. of the Baoule of the Ivory Coast Republic, consisting of a hollow iron cylinder, split lengthwise, affixed to a handle, reminiscent of the sistrum. Played with a metal rod (176).

Kpanlingán, syn. of ekón (152).

Kpedimba, kpeninga, syn. of kweningba.

Kpwokolo, *musical bow of the Balese of the Congo, without resonator or tuning loop (128).

Kpworo, *conical drum of the Banza of the Congo, with 2 laced heads, played in pairs by the same performer, suspended from a pole thrust in the ground. It corresponds to the ta ngo and is played at dances and when death occurs. *Ca.* 88 cm. (35 in.) long (30).

Kragen, Ger.: the neck of a lute.

Kralu, wooden *goblet drum of Celebes, of conoid shape, with parallel rattan lacings (173).

Kram, drum of the Garo of Assam, used for ritual purposes, nearly 1 m. (40 in.) long (173).

Kranti, idiochord bamboo *tube zither of the Mantra of the Malay Peninsula (119).

Kraobi, rattle of the Carajá Indians of Brazil, made of a monkey's skull (176).

Krap fuong, clappers of Cambodia, consisting of 2 pieces of rectangular hardwood of different sizes (176).

Krapp, wooden bell of Estonia, with several clappers (172).

Krap puang, clappers of Thailand, consisting of 6 pieces of wood: 2 thick outside slabs with turned-up ends, and 4 thin flat inside ones, all threaded together at one end (173).

Krar, var. of kerar.

Kraton, see: Nkraton.

Kratzzither (Ger.: scratch zither), Ger. name for the older rectangular folk zither (176).

Krebelle, rustic stopped *end-blown flute of the Aar region of Switzerland, filed thin at the upper end (102).

Krembalon, pl. **krembala,** ancient Gk. clappers, identical with krouma, krotalon.

Krena, *notched flute of the Quechua Indians of Bolivia, made of bamboo, with 6 fingerholes: 4 front, 1 rear, and 1 lateral (132).

Kre-nong, see: kye-nong.

Krewaing, krewong, see: kye vaing.

Kri, Agni (a Sudanese language) word for drum (93).

Krilaët, *frame drum of the Greenland Eskimo up to 1 m. (40 in.) in diam.,

with a head of whale-liver membrane fastened in a slit in the frame. Generally it is held by its handle in the player's left hand and beaten on the frame (not on the membrane) with a wooden beater (91, 144).

K'rims-dung, judgment trumpet of Tibet, used in courts of justice (89 Picken).

Krisket, Basque: castanet.

Kritsa-kritsa, rattle of the Tuléar region of the Malagasy Republic, made of a bamboo segment containing seeds.

Krob, idiochord *tube zither in Sakai (a language of the Malay Peninsula) (119).

Kromo, lithophone or *gong chime of the Sea Dayak of Borneo (173).

Kromong, 1. name of the bonang in Banten, W. Java; **2.** gong of S. Sumatra, laid on a bed of banana leaves (121, 144).

Kronchong, 5-string guitar of W. Java, small and narrow, of Port. origin (121).

Krong, bamboo drum of Thailand (176).

Krotalon, pl. **krotala,** clappers of ancient Greece, made in various forms, chiefly of wood and in shape of boots joined together at one end. As they were used in pairs, they are generally referred to by the plural form of the word. Homer and Sappho already mentioned them (199).

Kroto, *whistle flute of the Land Dayak of Borneo, with 5 front fingerholes and a duct on the side opposite them, bound with rattan (176).

Krotong, primitive xylophone of the Land Dayak of Borneo, with slabs either placed across the player's knees or laid on a softwood log. *Cf.* konkon (173).

Krouma, clappers of ancient Greece, syn. of krembalon, krotalon.

Kroupalon, clapper of ancient Greece, made of wood, attached like a sandal to the player's right foot; a conductor's "baton" rather than a musical instr., as it served to beat time. First recorded pictorially in the 3rd c. B.C. Also called kroupezion (144, 170).

Kroupezion, syn. of kroupalon.

Kru harp (Fr.: *harpe fourchue,* Ger.:
Gabelharfe), *frame zither of the Kru of
Liberia, with strings in a triangular
wooden frame over a calabash resonator.
The Toma of the Republic of Guinea also
play the Kru harp. See also: kani, oba,
toa (100, 103).

Krumba, idiochord *tube zither of
Nias, drummed upon and plucked simultaneously (173).

Krummbogen, Krummbügel, Ger.:
crook (of brass instrs.).

Krummer Zink, Ger.: curved cornett.

Krummhorn, Ger.: **1.** crumhorn; **2.** organ stop of reed pipes, probably the oldest Ger. reed stop, recorded in Dresden
in 1489, with narrow, cylindrical resonators, at 16', 8', 4', or 2' pitch. After the
instr. was discarded, the nature of the organ stop was misunderstood; Adlung, for
instance, found "nothing crooked" about
it. *Cormorne,* a later corr. of the Fr. term
cromorne, was translated into Ger. as
Sanfthorn. Cf. cromorne, 2 (3, 133).

Krummhornregal, obs. organ stop of
regal organ pipes at 8' pitch, made with
both narrow and wide resonators. The
older form, which disappeared *ca.* 1600,
gave way to covered resonators, perforated to permit the sound to issue (133).

Krupalon, see: kroupalon.

Krystallophon, Ger.: crystallophone.

Kshudrā katyayana vīnā, small satatantri vīnā of Bengal, with calabash body,
almost circular soundboard, and 18 steel
strings (173).

Ku, 1. generic term for drums in China,
and specifically for a drum of ancient
China mentioned in the Shih King (1135
B.C.), still in use today, with one head
secured by copper nails. See: chang ku,
chan ku, chien ku, chu ko ku, hsiao ku,
hua ku, kang ku, man t'u ku, pa fang
ku, pang ku, pan t'ang ku, shu ku, su ku,
t'ang ku, tien ku, t'ong ku, ya ku, yao ku,
ying ku; **2.** lute of Japan, with flat, circular body, 4 strings, and 9 frets on a
short neck. Similar to the genkwan and

richly ornamented with gold lacquerwork
(91, 157).

Kuakle, syn. of kohkles.

Kuamenj, pl. of kāmanja.

Kuan, 1. obs. *notched flute of China,
one of the earliest of Far Eastern wind
instrs., mentioned *ca.* 1100 B.C. in a Chin.
poem. Devoid of fingerholes, it served as
a pitch pipe, being tuned to one of the 12
lü (pitch standards); 12 kuans formed a
*p'ai hsiao; **2.** short oboe of China, with
cylindrical bore, 7 equidistant front fingerholes, and 1 or 2 rear thumbholes,
played with a double reed, 7–8 cm. (2¾–
3⅛ in.) long, kept in shape by a cane
keeper ring. The kuan does not overblow
the oct. Baines has pointed to its kinship,
both in reed and in fingering, to the
*monaulos. Its chief use is at weddings
and funerals. It corresponds to the hichiriki of Japan and the p'iri of Korea; 19–
28 cm. (7½–11 in.) long (89 Baines,
114).

Kuan tse, 1. syn. of kuan, 2; **2.** modern 12-pipe sheng (89).

Kūbā (Arab.), *hourglass drum of
med. Islam; the term goes back to the
9th c. Among the Arabs today it is known
as tabl mukhannath. See also: kalangual,
kalungu, lunga (93, 147 Farmer).

Kubar, *marine-shell trumpet of Geel-
vink Bay, New Guinea, with lateral blowhole (132).

Ku ch'in, Jew's-harp of N. China (unknown in S. China), where it appears in
horseshoe form, of metal, with idioglott
tongue pointed at the end (142, 170).

Kuchiru, gourd rattle of the Tariana
of NW. Brazil, also called kuteru, kutsiru (176).

Kuckuckspfeife, Ger.: cuckoo.

Kudam, see: kutam.

Kudara koto (Jap.: koto from Kudara
in Korea), syn. of kugo (144).

Kudlung, bamboo zither of the Hanunoo of the Philippine Islands (103).

Kudre, *conical drum of the Mombutu
and Momvu of the Congo, with 2 laced
heads. *Ca.* 40 cm. (16 in.) long (30).

Kudrekene, *ground zither of the

Watsa-Gombari region of the Congo (128).

Kudrenene, *ground zither of the Daka, Andowi, Azo, Andéu, Andekote, and Andekaka of the Congo (128).

Kudru-gu, *ground zither of the Kilima and Andemanza of the Congo (128).

Kudu, lyre of the Mundo of the Congo (128).

Kudungba, 1. *musical bow of the Amate, Adoi, Amanga, and Andekuju of the Congo, without resonator or tuning loop; **2.** musical bow of the Amaza, Adoi, Amanga, Andebogo, Andekuju, and Atalo, with tuning loop but no resonator (128).

Kudyapi [?kachapi], lute of the Hanunoo of the Philippine Islands (103).

Kuelé, syn. of okuelé, 2.

Kugelregal (Ger.), syn. of Apfelregal.

Kugo, vertical *angular harp of ancient Japan, with 23 strings, played with both hands, in use up to the Heian period (9th to 12th c.). It disappeared in that era as a result of musical reforms then undertaken, in the course of which a number of instrs. were eliminated. It corresponded to the k'ung hu and has been identified with the old Sassanid harp introduced through E. Turkestan, China, and Korea. Also called koto, tatekoto (66, 144).

Kuhschelle, Ger.: cowbell.

Kūītra, see: kuwītra.

Kuitzialflöte, see: Kützialflöte.

Kujamba, rattle of the Washambala of Tanganyika, made of a number of cane segments or rushes, tied raftwise and held in position by 3 transverse sticks. The shorter ends are filled with peas and shaken rhythmically during dances (111).

Kukau, a name of the Jew's-harp among the Maori of New Zealand (8).

Kukem [kem, to beat], Coptic: drum.

Kuku, *percussion pot of the Niger River delta Carabali, identical with the idudu egu (152).

Kukulan gantang, a Hindu-Javanese name of the kentongan (121).

Kulang, syn. of barimbo (176).

Kule paganeg, friction idiophone of Kapsu, New Ireland. For description see: nunut (77).

Kulepa ganeg, see: kule paganeg.

Kul-kul, modern Balinese—and probably also ancient Hindu-Javanese—name of the kentongan (121).

Kultrun, see: cultrun.

Kum, syn. of komunko (66).

Kumbandera, syn. of kimbumba (152).

Kumbhavādya, Kan. equivalent of gātha (173).

Kumbili, *musical bow of the Lobo, Andedema, and Timogia of the Congo, with gourd resonator not attached to the bow. Also called gambili, kambili (128).

Kumpuzi, see: koumpouzi.

Kumurere, *notched flute of the Gishu of Uganda, made of wood or bamboo, with 2 fingerholes (195).

Kunda, pl. **bikunda,** *double bell of the Lower Congo, used by the Bwende, Sundi, Yombe, and other peoples, made of wood in hourglass shape. The kunda is hewn out of a block of wood and has from 1 to 3 clappers for each bell. Its principal uses are ritual, but it serves also as a signal instr. (185).

Kundi, 1. *arched harp of the Azande, Barambo, Boyele, Bogoru-Basire, Gunda, Mbanja, and Nzakara of the Congo, with belly of monkeyskin, 5 strings secured by lateral pegs, and a neck often terminating in a carved head. Cf. nkundi; **2.** xylophone of the Kabba of the Congo (10, 128).

Kundri, kundur, kundurka, syn. of turburi (68).

Kundye, fiddle of the Soso of the Republic of Guinea, with half-gourd body, membrane belly, and single horsehair string. Cf. ngime (176).

Kune tsuzumi, percussion instr. of Japan, introduced from S. China, consisting of a wooden ring beaten with a stick (157).

K'ung cheng, double *humming top of China, consisting of 2 *ti ko tse mounted on a wooden stick (142).

K'ung hu [Pers. chang], vertical *angular harp of China, a development of the Sassanid chang introduced from E. Turkestan *ca.* 400 A.C., with 21–25 strings; it became obs. *ca.* 1000 A.C. and corresponded to the Jap. kugo. Also called pe k'ung hu, shu k'ung hu (89, 142, 170).

Kung long, stamping trough of Thailand (121).

Kungu, board zither of the Warega of the Congo (19).

Kunguleme, musical bow of the Baluba-Hemba of the Congo (19).

Kungunangu, ground bow of the Mondo of Faradje, the Congo (128).

Kunkulkawe, double *musical bow of the Araucano Indians of S. America, consisting of 2 interlocked bows, the string of one being scraped over that of the other. It serves to induce trances and magical or religious exaltation. Also called Quicahue (137).

Kunting, *harp lute of the Mandingo of W. Africa, with 3 strings passing over a notched bridge (176).

Kuokle, syn. of kohkles.

Kupu, *musical bow of the Babembe of N. Rhodesia and adjacent Congo (19).

Kurai, *vertical flute of the Bashkir of the U.S.S.R., conical, tapering to the lower end, with 4 front fingerholes and a rear thumbhole. The player hums a drone while he plays; 60–70 cm. (24–28 in.) long (176).

Kural, double flute of India, both mouth-blown and nose-blown (203).

Kurbel-Sphärophon, see: Sphärophon.

Kurga, a very large kettledrum, almost as tall as a man, introduced into the Arab world by the Moguls and always played in pairs. The med. equivalent of the tabl al kabir, sometimes transported on a chariot (74).

Kürka, Mogul name of the kurga, played in India and Persia, always in pairs (75 II).

Kurna, panpipes of the Camayura Indians of Brazil (105).

Kurtar, see: karatāli.

Kurze Oktave, Ger.: short octave.

Kurzpfeife (Ger.: short pipe), syn. of Kortholt (159).

Kūs, pl. **kūsāt,** large Arabian drum, first mentioned in the 10th c. See also: khakhānī (170).

Kūsāt, pl. of kūs.

Kūshnāy, *double clarinet of the Sart of Turkestan. *Cf.* dūnāy.

Kuskulu [*ezkila*], Basque: pellet bell (56).

Kuta, Kan. equivalent of gātha (173).

Kutam (pot drum), chordophone of the W. coast of India, played by the Pulluvam of Malabar, a tribe of serpent worshipers. A clay pot is closed with vellum; a string is attached to the center of the vellum, passed through a small hole in the bottom of the pot, and fastened to a metal cup (originally to a half gourd). This in turn is affixed to one end of a wooden plank, to keep the string under tension. The pot itself, lying on its side, rests at the other end of the plank, its mouth facing away from the cup. The string is struck with a small stick, the pot acting as resonator. *Cf.* plucked drum. Also called Pulluvam kutam (179).

Kuteru, syn. of kuchiru (176).

Kutorka, syn. of pitorka (68).

Kutschhorn, Ger.: coach horn.

Kutsi biwa, Jap.: Jew's-harp (176).

Kutsiru, syn. of kuchiru.

Kützialflöte, obs. organ stop of open, cylindrical pipes. Syn. of Bauernflöte (133).

Ku'ūs, bowl-shaped cymbals of ancient Islam (147 Farmer).

Kuwaitara [dim. of *kaitara*], syn. of kuwītra.

Kuwargā, var. of kurga (147 Farmer).

Kuwītra (Arab., dim. of *kaitara*) [*kithara*], vulgar name of a small, unfretted, long-necked lute of the Maghrib, with 4 pairs of gut strings; a small kaitara, played with a quill plectrum. *Ca.* 70 cm. (28 in.) long, 35 cm. (14 in.) wide (75 II, 144 Chottin).

Kuze-gene, ground zither of the Balese, Atolo, and Andimbi of the Congo (128).

Küzkuilü, Basque: small bell; cowbell.

Kwacha, syn. of chara.

Kwa da ban tse, castanets of China (176).

Kwadi, name of the gora in Mochudi district, S. Bechuanaland (116).

Kwagasho, see: nkwagasho.

Kwai, free-reed horn of the Padaung of Shan State, Burma, made of curved buffalo horn, open at both ends and with a free reed attached to it by wax (172).

Kwakwa, syn. of sakala.

Kwan, see: kuan.

Kwanga, var. of makwanga (185).

Kwangu, var. of mukwanga.

Kwatha, horn of the S. African Venda, made of kudu or gemsbok horn, with lateral blowhole. The name is also occasionally given to a horn made from the sable antelope (116).

Kwendibe, *musical bow of the Aimeri of the Congo, with gourd resonator not attached to the bow (128).

Kwengwe, name given by the Nbandi of the Congo to the kweningba (31).

Kweningba, xylophone of the Azande of the Congo, without resonators, and with a variable number of slabs. These are of hardwood, usually *pterocarpus,* laid over 2 trunks of banana tree. Wedges are driven between the slabs to keep them in position. They are played with rubber-padded sticks. The Azande have var. names for this instr.: kpedimba, kpeninga, paningba, pendibe. See also: bangi, endara, gbingbe, kwengwe, linz, mozungu (31).

Kwenxo, *percussion idiophone of the Yuman Indians of the Western U.S., consisting of an ordinary household basket turned upside down and used as a drum. Played with drumsticks or with the palms of both hands (52).

Kwidi, mirliton of the Tsangi of the Lower Congo, made of a bamboo tube. A rectangular hole is cut in the wall and covered with a piece of cellophane. A child's toy (185).

Kwitra, see: kuwītra.

Kwororo, slender drum of the Banza of the Congo, almost cylindrical, with laced head. Also called pakwulo (30).

Kya, *stamping tube of the Akamba of Kenya and Tanganyika, formerly called muvungu (130).

Kyamancha [Pers. *kamānja], Armenian fiddle having the appearance of a very small banjo. *Cf.* kamānja (89).

Kyēdi, Buddhist bell of Burma (103).

Kyen, free-reed *mouth organ of the Karen of Shan State, Burma, with 10 cane pipes of different lengths, inserted into a long-necked gourd and each provided with a metal reed. The gourd serves as wind chamber, its neck as blowhole. See also khen, sheng (172).

Kye-nong, Burmese: small gong (170).

Kye tsi, bronze *percussion plaque of Burma, of irregular shape, roughly triangular, suspended from a cord and struck with a small mallet (172, 178).

Kye vaing, *gong chime of Burma, composed of 16–18 graduated gongs, suspended horizontally in a low, circular frame and struck with leather-padded beaters. The player sits in the center of the frame. See also: bonang, khong vong lek (172, 173).

Kymato-Geige [Gk. *kyma,* wave], experimental violin with undulating belly, built by Moritz Gläsel of Markneukirchen (176).

Kymbali [Gk. *kymbalon], Finn.: cymbals (176).

Kymbalon, pl. **kymbala,** cymbals of ancient Greece, of W. Asiatic origin. As 2 were clashed together, the plural form of the word is usually employed. The Gk. cymbals were about the size of a plate, had a central boss and flat rim; they were generally connected pairwise by a strap or a chain. *Cf.* cymbala (170, 199).

Kyo kei, *percussion plaque of Japan, a circular bronze disc suspended in a circular wooden frame (178).

Kyo pang ko, drum of Korea, played by 2 musicians or dancers (66).

L

Laala, *stick rattle of the Fula of Sierra Leone, made of a V-shaped piece of wood with discs of gourd strung on a prong. See also: wansamba (Collection of the Commonwealth Institute, London).

La'au, obs. percussion instr. of Hawaii, believed to have been identical with the pakuru. Made of kanuila wood, it was formerly played during hula dances (8).

La-bak, modern Pers.: flute (98).

Labbanātu (Akk.), straight trumpet of ancient Babylon; it first appeared in the first millennium B.C. See also: karan (89 Galpin).

Labial . . . , as prefix to Ger. names of organ stops, labial denotes a register of flue pipes.

Labium, Lat., Du., Ger.: the lips of an organ flue pipe.

Labu, free-reed *mouth organ of Celebes, similar to the khen (47).

La ch'in, bowed *long zither of N. China, with hollow wooden body in shape of a truncated cone, with a convex surface, and 10 pairs of silk strings. These are attached to iron pegs at one end and threaded through small holes pierced through 10 very high individual bridges. The tuning is pentatonic without semitones. The la ch'in is held in semiupright position, 2 small holes at the base serving as fingerholds. It corresponds to the *a chang of Korea. Ca. 65 cm. (26 in.) long. The bow is almost as long as the instr.

Lade, coll. Ger. for Windlade.

Lae-lae, *percussion stick of S. Celebes priests, consisting of a long bamboo pole struck with 2 short bamboo switches. The pole is up to 2 m. (6½ ft.) long. Cf. siya-siya (112).

Lag-na, *frame drum of Tibetan lamas, set on a vertical pole and beaten with a sickle-shaped stick. 90–150 cm. (3–4 ft.) in diam. (89 Picken).

Laguni, *percussion plaque of Celebes, of irregular shape, beaten with an ebony stick. Used for driving devils away (112).

Lai waghē, name of the dermenan on Nias; also that of a similar instr. provided with a double reed (121).

Lakado, idiochord *tube zither of Timor, with strings lying very close together (173).

Laka do'o, *tube zither of E. Flores Island with 3 idiochord strings (119).

Laku, *globular flute of the Carajá Indians of Brazil, made of a calabash, and having several fingerholes. Also called volavuk adjulona (176).

Lal, syn. of bal.

Lalango, *musical bow of the Apagibeti of Dundusana, the Congo, with resonator not attached to the bow (128).

Lali, *slit drum of Tonga (New Hebrides), Futuna, Uvéa (Loyalty Islands) (77).

Lalipok, *percussion tube of the Land Dayak of Borneo, made of several connecting bamboo sections with thinned walls. One end is left open and is struck against a hard object (176).

Lalis, slit drum of the Fiji Islands, used for signaling (176).

Lamako, castanets of the Malagasy Republic, made of ox jawbones (171).

Lamba, large drum of the Wolof of Senegal, with closed bottom (176).

Lame musicale, Fr.: musical saw.

Lamiré, Port.: tuning fork. Also called alamiré.

Lanat . . . , Laos equivalent of ranat . . . (103).

Langflöte, Ger.: vertical flute.

Långharpa, obs. string instr. of Sweden, unidentified so far but thought to have been similar to the Nor. langleik. It is known to have been in use in the late 17th c. and is said by Hüphers to have been in use in the 16th c. (9).

Langhörpu, syn. of langleik (149).

Lang kwang, cymbals of Burma (176).

Langleik (long instrument), ancient folk zither of Norway, known since the mid-16th c. and still played. It has a slender rectangular body of the Scheitholt type, with fixed frets placed along the left (long) side, and 4–14 steel strings of which 1 or more are melody strings, the remainder being drones. All are secured to lateral pegs. They are stopped by 3 fingers of the left hand and plucked with a plectrum. Specimens with 8 strings have 1 melody string tuned to G and 7 drones tuned $c^0 c^1 g^1 c^2 c^2 e^2 g^2$. Hortense Panum gives the tuning of a 7-stringed langleik as $a^0 a^0/a^0 a^0 e^1 e^1 e^2$ or $c\sharp^2$. The highest strings have individual bridges. Occasionally called langspil (15 Baines, 91).

Langlju, wooden horn of Estonian Swedes (176).

Langoro, langorao, *cylindrical drum of the Malagasy Republic, with 2 heads stretched on hoops and laced. Probably an imitation of the European military drum (171).

Längs . . . , Ger.: end-blown.

Långspel, *bowed zither of Sweden; it corresponds to the langspil of Iceland. Sometimes called humle (149).

Langspil, *bowed zither of Iceland, with slender rectangular body of the Scheitholt type, fretted along one long side. It has no bridge. One melody string and 1 or 2 drone strings are secured to the pegbox by lateral pegs. The drones are tuned to tonic and dominant of the melody string. The name langspil is occasionally given in Norway to the langleik (91).

Languette, Fr.: languid.

Languid (Fr.: *biseau, languette;* Ger.: *Kern, Pfeifenkern;* It.: *lingua*), plate of metal fixed horizontally to the upper extremity of the foot of metal flue organ pipes, with beveled front edge. The block of a wooden pipe is sometimes called languid.

Lantoy, nose flute of the Batak of Palawan (203).

Lantuy, flute of the Hanunoo of the Philippine Islands (103).

La pa [Mongolian *rapal*], **1.** pop. name of the siao t'ung kyo. *Cf.* huang la pa; **2.** syn. of ch'un kuan.

La pa pu, Chin. name of the rubāb (75 II).

Lap organ, portable free-reed organ made in the U.S. from 1825 to the mid-19th c., in form of a deep rectangular box. The name is derived from its being held across the lap; 37 ivory buttons are arranged like piano keys on the upper surface. When depressed they open valves admitting air to the reeds. The left hand works double bellows divided diagonally into 2 chambers, the lower (left) being a feeder, the upper a wind chest. Dynamics are made possible by shutter sliders placed on the upper surface. The earlier lap organ was called elbow melodeon. Subsequently it was known also as rocking melodeon, from the motion of the bellows, or as teeter (25).

Lapuni, bull-roarer of Sicily (152).

Lari, 1. drum of the Mangbetu of the Congo, identical with the gaza, 2; **2.** syn. of kindri (30).

Larigot [*arigot*] (Fr.), **1.** word first recorded in 1403 and used until the early 17th c. for a flageolet, originally made of a sheep's thigh bone. Thoinan Arbeau wrote in 1588 that it had a varying number of holes, according to its size, the best having 4 frontal holes and 2 rear. Cotgrave in 1611 translated the word as recorder. In the 16th c. it became part of military music; **2.** mutation organ stop of open metal flue pipes, an oct. above the nasard, or a 5th above the doublette, found in Fr. organs (*i.e.*, at 2⅔' or 1⅓' pitch). It corresponds to the *nineteenth. Also built as an It. principal, preponderantly at 1⅓', also as a stop corresponding to the Spillflöte (20, 133).

Larimva, drum of the Logo of the Congo, identical with the bia. Always played alternately with the bili. *Ca.* 64 cm. (25 in.) long (30).

Latowe, nose flute of Celebes (203).

Láud [Arab. *el-*'ūd], Sp.: lute.

Laudis, Lat.: lute.

Lauka, friction idiophone of Lelet, New Ireland, also called livika. For description see: nunut (77).

Launeddas [U.], triple pipe of Sardinia, divergent, of different lengths, provided with single reeds. Two pipes are melody pipes, the third, center pipe, is a long drone attached to the left pipe by wire struts or a cord. The pipes are of cane, that on the right being the shortest. The right melody pipe is called mancosa, and has 5 front holes, of which one is a vent; the left pipe is called mancosedda and has 6 holes; the drone is called tumba. All 3 reeds are mouthed. The launeddas is thought to be of Phoenician origin; a similar instr. is portrayed in the 13th-c. *Cantigas de Santa María* (89 Baines, 132).

Lauré, iron *percussion plaque of the Baoule chiefs of the Ivory Coast Republic, shaped like a horseshoe. The pitch varies according to where it is held. Struck with a special wooden hammer, beautifully carved. *Ca.* 20 cm. (8 in.) long (42).

Laut, Prov.: lute.

Lauta (Turk.), small modern unfretted lute of Algeria, Egypt, Iraq, Morocco, Syria, Tunisia, and Turkey. *Cf.* lauto, lutar (75 II).

Laute, Ger.: lute.

Lautengitarre, Ger.: lute guitar.

Lautenklavier, Ger.: lute harpsichord.

Lautenklavizimbel, Ger.: lute harpsichord.

Lautenwerk, Ger.: lute harpsichord.

Lautenzug (Ger.: lute stop), Ger.

name of a harpsichord stop, equivalent to the harp stop; on the piano, equivalent to lute stop and to the British sordin, or mute, stop (92).

Lauto, lauton, lute of modern Greece, with 4 pairs of gut strings tuned in 5ths, like our viola ($c^0 g^0 d^1 a^1$), and fretted, in contrast to the Gk. uti, which is tuned in 4ths and unfretted. *Cf.* lauta (144).

Lavikko, syn. of pilli.

Laya vamshi, *notched flute of Bengal, with 7 fingerholes (173).

Laye, Fr.: wind chest.

Lda-man, large kettledrum of Tibet, made of copper with laced membrane of hide. Always played in pairs; used in secular and lama bands (89 Picken).

Lebed (swan), Russ. name of the torop-jux (169).

Lechaka, reed *piston flute of the Bechuana of S. Africa, without fingerholes. The movable stopper permits changes of pitch (176).

Legawka, var. of ligawka.

Legnofono, name given to the xylophone made by Lasina of Rome in 1882 (176).

Legwegwe, globular basketwork rattle with a handle, found in an area between the Aruwimi and Bomu rivers of the Congo. Used by dancers and as a child's toy (132).

Leier [OHGer. *lira*], from the 17th c. on, Ger. for hurdy-gurdy.

Leierkasten, N. Ger.: barrel organ.

Leierorgel, Ger.: barrel organ.

Lekhitlane, *end-blown flute of the Sotho of Basutoland, S. Africa, made of the horn of the female blesbok. The blesbok has now disappeared from that area and the flute is becoming rare. It is blown at the wide end, with a minute hole pierced through the tip, thus converting it to an open pipe that can be stopped by the player's finger (116).

Lekolilo, *end-blown flute of the Sotho of Basutoland, S. Africa, identical with the umtshingo and mokoreie (116).

Lekope, 1. *musical bow of the Sotho of Transvaal, S. Africa, similar to the lugube but with a small twig serving as bridge under one end of the string. It is finger-plucked. That of the Sotho of Basutoland is plectrum-plucked. It is played by women and girls only; **2.** musical bow of the Pedi and Sotho of Transvaal, with tuning loop. One section of the string is plucked with the left hand, the other by a plectrum held in the right hand. It is played only by males (116).

Lelēo, reedpipe of NE. Celebes, similar to the pu pai, made in 3 sizes; also called lolodio (112).

Lemana, bamboo flute of the Galla of E. Africa (176).

Lengope, *musical bow of the Chwana of S. Africa, identical with the lugube (116).

Lengueta, Sp.: reed.

Lengwane, *notched flute of the Bakgatla and Pedi of S. Africa, made of a leg bone of goat or sheep, the lower end being stopped. Often ornamented with bands of leather or gut. A boy's instr. played with a vibrato achieved by the throat muscles (116).

Lepakusu, syn. of nemurambi (19).

Lepapata, side-blown horn of the Chwana of S. Africa, made of the horn of sable antelope or kudu (116).

Lēra, idioglott clarinet of Morocco (144).

Leri, elongated *cylindrical drum of the Logo of the Congo, terminating in a short conical section, with heads of different sizes; 125–275 cm. (4–9 ft.) long (30).

Leriyo, generic term for drums used by the Kakwa of Uganda (195).

Lero viol, obs. spelling of lyra viol.

Lesiba, the gora of the S. African Chwana.

Lethlakanoka, reedpipe of the Bakgatla of S. Africa, identical with the naka ya lethlaka, 1. It is played by boys only, and with less elaborate technique (116).

Letlot, bamboo *slit drum of the Kai Islands, Indonesia, with single slit. *Ca.* 40 cm. (16 in.) long (119).

Leu, med. Fr. lute.

Lēut, syn. of lolob.

Leutik, see: goōng leutik.

Leuto, OIt.: lute.

Levier pneumatique, Fr.: pneumatic lever.

Levigrave régulateur, dumb keyboard of A. Dumas *fils* and Colin of Nîmes (176).

Libellion, music box with perforated cardboard discs, patented in France on Aug. 12, 1891, by Thost & Richter of Rudolstadt (204).

Libi, var. of ibi in Bowili (a Sudanic language) (93).

Libitshi, var. of limbitji.

Libu, var. of dibu.

Lichaka, cane *piston flute of the Bechuana of S. Africa, used as a signal instr. (10).

Liduku, *raft zither of the Gishu of Uganda, made of several idiochord single-string zithers of millet stalk cut off at the nodes. It is held in the player's open palms and plucked in an upward motion by the index fingers. Tuning is apparently possible by cutting narrow strips for high tones and broad for low tones (195).

Lié (tied), Fr.: fretted. The term is applied to clavichords only.

Liebes . . . , Germanization of the It. *d'amore, e.g.,* Liebesoboe.

Liebesgeige, precious 18th-c. Ger. term for viola d'amore.

Lieblich . . . (Ger.), as a prefix to names of organ stops, lieblich is syn. of echo (133).

Lieblich Gedackt (Ger.), an exception to the previous remark; lieblich Gedackt implies conical construction, as opposed to the usual cylindrical Gedackt of Praetorius' day. In modern organ building it is a narrow-scaled, high-mouthed Gedackt of wood or metal at 8' or 4' pitch. *Cf.* bourdon doux (129, 133).

Lieblich geschallt (Ger.), small-scaled, soft lieblich Gedackt organ stop invented by Robert Hope-Jones (d. 1914) (198).

Liederzither, syn. of Elegiezither.

Lien hua lo, rattle of N. China, made of bamboo slips threaded together with cash (obs. small Chin. coins), held in the right hand and shaken while a pair of castanets is held in the left (142).

Lifogo, *cylindrical drum of the To-poke of Stanleyville district, the Congo, with single head nailed with dowels (30).

Ligangale [*ganga*], Tobote (a Su-danic language) for drum. *Cf.* ganga (93).

Ligatik, nose flute of Hok, Micronesia, made of mangrove root or bamboo (203).

Ligatura, Lat.: fret.

Ligawka, wind instr. of Poland, similar to the bazuna and alphorn, with conical wooden tube, either straight or curved, played with a funnel-shaped mouthpiece; 120–150 cm. (4–5 ft.) long (89).

Ligina, small guitar of Brazil, with 6 pairs of wire strings. Also called viola (6).

Lignum sacrum (Lat.: holy wood), church Lat.: semanterion.

Ligo, xylophone of the Mbwaka of the Congo.

Ligoshu, rattle of the S. African Swazi, similar to the njele, borrowed from the Thonga (116).

Ligubu, *musical bow of the Swazi of S. Africa, with half-gourd resonator, played like the uhadi (116).

Lijerica, the lira of Croatia, found only on the S. coast and used for accompany-ing folk dances. Its 3 strings are tuned a 2nd and a 4th apart (144).

Likembe, generic term for the sansa in the E. Congo, Ruanda, Urundi, and parts of Uganda, the resonator of which is an integral part of the instr. For tuning see: kasayi (139).

Lik haanga, long, side-blown trumpet of Kavirondo, Kenya, made from a wooden tube and a cow horn (195).

Likoali, pl. of Koali.

Lilemo, drum of the Topoke of the Congo (30).

Lilenga, *cylindrical drum of the Lalia of Ngolu, Tshuapa district, the Congo,

with single head nailed with dowels. *Cf.* ingondjo, limbitji (30).

Lilimba, xylophone of the Baluba-Hemba of the Congo (19).

Lilis (Sum.), see: lilissu.

Lilissu (Akk.), drum of ancient Baby-lon that first appears in the second mil-lennium B.C., called lilis in Sum. Goblet-shaped, made of metal, with membrane head, it was *ca.* 1 m. (40 in.) high (89 Galpin, 170).

Limba, 1. Rom.: bell clapper; **2.** [Tibetan *gling-bu*], *cross flute of Mon-golia with 12 holes; it corresponds to the ti tse of China. One of the holes is a blowhole, another a mirliton, 6 are equi-distant fingerholes, and 4 are vents; **3.** side-blown wooden trumpet of the Madi of Uganda, very rare, in form of a hu-man figure. The tip is carved to resemble a head, and the blowhole is placed at the naval. *Ca.* 60 cm. (2 ft.) long (69, 195).

Limbitji, 1. drum of the Bombesa of the Congo, identical with the lilenga; **2.** drum of the Bangandu, played during women's dances (30).

Limbombe, *cylindrical drum of the Mobango of the Congo, made of *Ricino-dendron africanum* wood, with nailed head of antelope skin or elephant ear (30).

Limele, pluriarc of the Saka of the Congo (128).

Limonaire, syn. of orchestrophone.

Linardion, a combination piano-har-monium, patented in France by Buschek on March 6, 1889 (204).

Lincea, see: pentecontachordon.

Ling, generic word in Chin. for bells struck by a clapper from the inside, in contradistinction to chung (170).

Lingile, drum of the Bombesa of the Congo, identical with the lilenga (30).

Lingita, name of the ndundu among the Gombe of the Congo. Tuning paste is applied to the lizardskin or elephant-ear membrane. It is struck by the chief or one of the notables (30).

Lingongo, *musical bow of the Ngando

of the Congo, without resonator or tuning loop (128).

Lings-dung (hunt + trumpet), Tibetan hunting bugle (89 Picken).

Ling tang, generic term for bell in China, but specifically one of cast iron used by itinerant oil vendors (142).

Ling tse, gong of N. China, smaller than the tang lo, suspended by 3 or 4 cords in a wire circle affixed to a wooden handle. One or 2 beads are appended in such a manner as to hit the gong when it is twirled (142).

Lingua, Lat.: languid, reed.

Linguaphone, plucked idiophone.

Lining (Fr.: *contre-éclisse;* Ger.: *Reifchen;* It.: *controfascia*), in violins and certain other European stringed instrs. strips of wood glued to top and bottom of the ribs to create gluing surfaces for belly and back. Originally a term of *lutherie,* it has been taken over—in Engl. at least—by keyboard-instr. makers.

Linterculus (Lat.) [dim. of *linter,* small boat or trough], Lat.: kit (39, 140).

Linz, linzi, name given by the Balendu and Bahema of the Congo to the kweningba (31).

Lippenpfeife, Ger.: flue pipe.

Lipombo, *musical bow of the Boa of the Congo, without resonator or tuning loop (128).

Lira [Gk. *lyra*], **1.** bowed instr. of modern Greece, also of Bulgaria and Dalmatia, characterized by its piriform body, wooden belly, pegdisc with rear pegs and 3 strings. The body tapers toward the pegdisc without distinct neck. The lira is played in vertical position, resting on the player's knees, the strings being stopped laterally by the player's fingernails, thus obviating the need for a fingerboard. The Cretan lira is tuned $g^0 d^1 a^1$, the Dodecanese lira either is tuned $c^1 g^0 d^1$, the center string being a drone, or it is provided with 4 strings for the so-called "Turkish" tuning, $G^0 d^0 a^0 e^2$. Gk. refugees from Pontus brought with them to Greece a different, Cau-

casian form of lira, with narrow, elongated body, straight sides, sound slits, and 3 strings tuned $d^0 g^0 c^1$. The Dalmatian variety, called also vialo, has a central drone and is tuned $d^2 a^1 e^2$.

The lira is in all probability the same instr. that med. Europe acquired from Byzantium and called *fiddle, and that the Near East still calls *kāmanja rūmī (Greek fiddle). Ibn Khurdādhbih (d. *ca.* 912), speaking of Byzantine instrs., said that the *lura* of the *rumi* (*i.e.,* Greeks) was made of wood, resembled the *rebab* of the Arabs, but had 5 strings—the classical number of European fiddle strings. An 11th-c. glossary equates *rabāb* with *lira;* some 12th-c. illustrations of fiddles are entitled *lira;* the word is taken over into OHGer. and becomes syn. with fiddle from the 12th c. on. See also: guslice, lijerica, vialo;

2. name given to the hurdy-gurdy in late med. times. Virdung (in 1511) designates it as *lyra;* today it is the pop. name of the hurdy-gurdy in Sweden; in Russia *lira* is a syn. of rilya; in Romania the term has now become obs.; **3.** recorder of the Maghrib; **4.** stopped reedpipe of Morocco, furnished with a retreating reed; **5.** abbr. for lira da braccio or lira da gamba. See also: lyra (5, 33, 168, 189).

Lira barberina, see: lyra barberina.

Lira da braccio (It.) [Gk. *lyra*], bowed chordophone of the It. Renaissance; it evolved in the late 15th c. and is now generally assumed to be a development of the med. fiddle. It coexisted with the *viola da braccio, with which it was confused and by which it was ultimately replaced. Vasari in 1564 speaks of the *lira ovvero viola* and Galilei in 1581 mentions the "viola da braccio that was called lira not many years ago" (*viola da braccio detta da non molti anni indietro lira*). Lire da braccio were made in 2 sizes, the smaller being about 70–75 cm. (27½–29½ in.) long, the larger, called also *lirone da braccio, *ca.* 80–90 cm. (31½–36 in.) long. Both were characterized by a gentle waist, flat pegdisc with front pegs, wide fingerboard, 2 off-board and 5 on-board strings that passed over a somewhat flat bridge. Earlier instrs. had C holes, later ones FF. The smaller model is generally depicted held against the left shoulder; the larger model is held lower. Giovanni Lanfranco (in 1533) indicated its tuning (small model) as $d^0 d^1/g^0 g^1 d^1 a^1 e^2$. Both he and Bottrigari (in 1594) state that the instr. was not fretted, but Praetorius, latest author to mention it, represents it with frets and gives its tuning as $d^0 d^1/g^0 g^1 d^1 a^1 d^2$. Paintings up to ca. 1600 bear out the It. writers on the subject of frets. The off-board strings, too far removed for stopping, were drones; the string or even the 2 strings next to them were stopped by the performer's thumb. Except for the drones and the doubled oct., Lanfranco's tuning is that of a violin, but as the lira da braccio was larger than our viola, these tunings must be interpreted as indicating relative pitch. A *Geigenlyra* with 7 strings, mentioned in a Cassel inventory of 1613, would seem to indicate a rare transalpine appearance of the lira da braccio. Also called lira di sette corde, lira moderna (55b, 94, 144).

Lira da gamba (It.), bass *lira da braccio little known outside Italy and France; it evolved in the mid-16th c. and fell into disuse in France by the mid-17th c. and in Italy by the end of the c. Earliest mention of the lira da gamba seems to occur in a Graz inventory of 1577: *"ain gar grosse geigen, haist man lira de camba."* In shape it was similar to a viola da gamba but with wider neck and fingerboard, flat bridge to facilitate chordal playing, pegdisc with rear pegs, often a circular soundhole covered by a rose in addition to the regular soundholes, usually 2 off-board drones and 9–14 apt melody strings, for which various tunings are given. The neck was fretted. Unlike those of the lira da braccio, its center bouts were well defined. Body length was ca. 62–65 cm. (24½–25½ in.), speaking length of strings 63½–68½ cm. (25–27

in.), total length 107–112 cm. (42–44 in.). Scipione Cerreto in 1601 gives its tuning as $G^0 g^0/c^0 c^1 g^0 d^1 a^0 e^1 b^0 f\sharp^1 c\sharp^1$, Praetorius in 1618 as $G\flat^0 d\flat^0/A\flat^0 e\flat^0 B\flat^0 f^0 c^0 g^0 d^0 a^0 e^0 f\sharp^0 c\sharp^0$. Maugars still heard it played in Rome in 1639, but by the time Mersenne and Kircher wrote, it had exchanged its pegdisc for a pegbox with lateral pegs. Richelet in 1680 states that the "lyre" had 13 melody strings and 2 drone strings, a wider fingerboard, but was in other respects the same as the viola da gamba. Also called accordo, arciviolata lira, lira grande, lirone da gamba, lirone perfetto, lyra perfecta (55a, 94, 115, 144, 183).

Lira di sette corde (seven-stringed lira), syn. of lira da braccio.

Lira grande, syn. of lira da gamba.

Lira moderna, a name given to the lira da braccio to distinguish it from the lyra of antiquity.

Lira organizzata, It.: *organized hurdy-gurdy. The name is also misapplied to the hurdy-gurdy (without pipework).

Lira rustica, It.: hurdy-gurdy.

Lira tedesca, It.: hurdy-gurdy.

Lire, 1. MHGer.: lyra; hurdy-gurdy; **2.** pop. Dan.: hurdy-gurdy (149).

Lirica, syn. of guslice.

Lirone, syn. of lira da gamba.

Lirone da braccio, a large form of the lira da braccio, the tuning of which is unknown. Its body length was 52–60 cm. (20½–23½ in.), total length 80–92 cm. (31½–36 in.).

Lirone da gamba, syn. of lira da gamba.

Lirone perfetto, syn. of lira da gamba.

Litavri [Arab. *al-*tabl*], obs. Russ. cavalry kettledrum of silver or copper; it made its appearance in the 16th c. (25).

Litenda, drum of the Mobango of the Congo, similar to the limbombe (30).

Lithokymbalon, lithophone of alabaster, made by Franz Weber of Vienna in 1837 (169).

Lithomo, pl. of thomo.

Lithophone [Gk. *lithos,* stone + *phone,* sound], set of percussion bars or plaques made of stone and capable of vibration. Lithophones occur in 2 forms: 1) oblong bars like those of a xylophone are suspended horizontally; 2) vertically suspended plaques. Existence of the bar type was not discovered until 1949, when a prehistoric lithophone was found in Vietnam. Since then 2 more have been brought to light, also in Vietnam, the largest of which is preserved in the Musée de l'Homme, Paris. This has 10 bars 65–100 cm. (26–40 in.) in length and yields a pentatonic scale of unequal intervals. The plaque type usually consists of 16 tuned stones suspended vertically in a frame, and is found in the Middle East, the Far East, and Samoa. See also: kromo, lithokymbalon, musical stone, phyen kyung, pien ch'ing, pyon kyong, rock harmonicon (70, 170).

Liti [abbr. of **lituus*], up to 1820 or so the name of the alphorn in Unterwalden, Switzerland (187).

Litolotolo, pl. of setolotolo.

Litumba, drum of the Lake Bangweulu area, Africa, similar to the cinsete except that the aperture is on the side and not at the base (30).

Litungu, 1. lyre of the Logoli of E. Africa; **2.** syn. of liduku (195).

Lituus, hooked bronze trumpet of the Etruscans, taken over from them by the Romans, whom it served as a cavalry instr. Prototype of the lituus was an animal horn attached to one end of a straight wooden tube. The lituus consisted of a slender tube with cylindrical bore, terminating in an upturned bell, forming a letter J. Later Etruscan litui are indistinguishable from those of Rome, but earlier Etruscan ones have a bell sharply bent back connected to the main tube by a strut, which assumes various forms. Litui are always represented in pairs. The mouthpieces of the Etruscan instrs. were removable: 2 litui are represented on the Tomba dei Rilievi near Cerveteri, one of which has a mouthpiece of a color (red) different from that of the tube (yellow). Mouthpieces of the Roman instrs., however, were not detachable. A later Etruscan specimen, preserved in the Vatican, varies from Roman models only by its greater length (it measures 1.60 cm. [63 in.]). Mahillon examined it and found it to be pitched in G (2 Roman cornua found in Pompeii are also in G, but pitched an oct. lower than the Vatican lituus). Other surviving Roman instrs. are identical with later Etruscan ones except that they are shorter. One specimen, found intact in the Rhine near Düsseldorf, is pitched in A. Although the Roman lituus is frequently mentioned in literature, it is rarely depicted or referred to in military accounts. Fortunately a number of archaeological finds have been made. The word *lituus* continued in use in postclassical times, usually in the sense of crumhorn or cornett, but in the 18th c. it denoted a brass instr. So, for instance, in a 1706 inventory of Osseg monastery in Bohemia, where *"litui vulgo Waldhörner . . . in G"* are enumerated. Bach's Cantata No. 118 (*O Jesu Christ*) calls for 2 litui, probably tenor trumpets in B♭. The term remained in use until the second half of the 18th c. (21, 89 Baines, 170).

Lituus alpinus (Lat.), an early name of the alphorn. *Cf.* liti (187).

Liuto [Arab. *el-*'ūd*], It.: lute.

Liuto attiorbato, tiorbato, It.: theorbo-lute.

Liuto moderno, name occasionally given to a mandola with 5 pairs of strings, tuned c^0 g^0 d^1 a^1 e^2.

Livika, see: lauka.

Lizarden, see: lyzarden.

Llamasencka, *notched flute of Indians of the Jujuy and Chaco regions of Argentina, made of cane, nearly always with 3 fingerholes; 15–30 cm. (6–12 in.) long (192).

Llave [Lat. *clavis*, key], Sp.: key (of a wind instr.).

Llaviórgano, llaviórganum, Sp.: claviorganum.

Lo, gong of Buddhist China, still used in temples. Flat, with shallow rim, struck with a copper beater; *ca.* 24–60 cm. (9½ in.–2 ft.) in diam. (178).

Locatz, Ger. 16th-c. expression for the Hintersatz, used by Schlick and his contemporaries.

Locust, obs. *whirled friction drum of the U.S., sold in Philadelphia, in the early 19th c. It consisted of a tin or cardboard cylinder with a thread and is said to have sounded like a locust (16).

Log drum, syn. of slit drum.

Logo, var. of longo.

Lohāti, syn. of nissan (66).

Lohenga, warrior's drum of the Batatela of the Congo, played with bare hands. Formerly, fingers of dead enemies were placed inside and their hands were suspended from the exterior (30).

Lojki, see: lozhky.

Lokanga, bowed instr. of the Malagasy Republic, imitative of the European violin, with neck fitted to a calabash body (42, 171).

Lokanga vava, Jew's-harp of the Merina of the Malagasy Republic, made of metal, shaped like the European instr. (171).

Lokango voatavo, *stick zither of the Malagasy Republic, similar to the seze (171).

Lokanko, slit drum of the Babiso of Lake Bangweulu, Africa (185).

Lokilo, drum of the Basengele of the Congo, similar to the ndungu. With the Bolia it is cylindrical with one head, a small aperture near the base, and is used chiefly as a war drum (30).

Lokiro, drum of the Nkundo of the Congo, similar to the ndungu (30).

Lökkelje [prob. *nökkel gige,* keyed fiddle], Nor. equivalent of the nyckelharpa; it occurred sporadically in Søndre Helgeland (9, 69).

Lokole, cylindrical *slit drum of the Bussira and Wangata of the Congo, with dumbbell-shaped slit; also of the Baganzi, Balolo, and Bangala of the Congo, with 2 communicating rectangular slits. Also called nkole-nkole (19, 42, 176).

Lokombe, 1. *slit drum of the Wason-

gola of the Congo, cuneiform, zoomorphic; **2.** pluriarc of the Konda of the Congo (19, 128).

Loku, gourd trumpet of the Šavaje (?Shavante) of Brazil (176).

Lolkin, straight cylindrical trumpet of the Araucano Indians of S. America, with very narrow bore, terminating in a gourd bell. Pop. among young people as a solo instr., also played in puberty initiation rites, and on Good Fridays, when it is blown from a tower. *Ca.* 1.50 m. (5 ft.) long (137).

Lolo, rattle of the E. Torres Strait; it corresponds to the padatrong (176).

Lolob, slit drum of the Admiralty Islands (176).

Lolodio, syn. of lelēo (112).

Lolowe, name of the tulali among the Toradja of Celebes. Also called tujali, banchi-banchi (112).

Lona, var. of lunga (93).

Lonfembe, arched harp of the Wangata of the Congo River area (19).

Longa, pl. **lomgam, 1.** clapperless double bell of Loango, Angola, and adjacent Congo area. The bells are struck alternately with a stick; **2.** great drum of the Akasele of Togoland (176).

Long drum, Engl. 18th-c. name of a bass drum.

Longo, slit drum of Samoa and Niue, beaten with a stick. Also called logo (77).

Longombe, pluriarc of the Bakatola, Bondengo, Eso, Lia, and Nkundo of the Congo (128).

Longombi, pluriarc of the Bai, Lia, Mongo, and Oli of the Congo (128).

Long zither, or vaulted zither, a rectangular zither intermediate between a half-tube zither and a board zither, such as the koto, shē, etc. (170).

Lontana, musical bow of the Babembe of N. Rhodesia and the Congo (19).

Lo pan, syn. of t'i tang (176).

Loterokuma, arched harp of the Acoli of Uganda, with 5 or 7 strings (195).

Lo to ling tang, N. China camel bell with oval aperture and wooden clapper (142).

Lotong, idiochord *tube zither made of bamboo, of Kanowit, Sarawak. Also called tutung (119).

Lo tse, syn. of hai lo.

Loure [Lat. *lura,* leather bag], bagpipe of France, particularly of Normandy, of the 16th and 17th c. By the late 17th c. the term was obs. (35, 197).

Lourette, small loure of 17th-c. France.

Loutna, Czech: lute.

Louvre, Trichet's name of the loure (*ca.* 1640).

Louvrette, Trichet's term for a small loure (190).

Lowery organo, polyphonic, imitative *electrophonic instr. of the electronic type, made by the Lowery Organ Co., Chicago. The tone is generated by electron tube oscillators. In appearance it is a small control panel clipped to the keyboard of a conventional piano, with a separate cabinet for tubes and speaker. Three different tone qualities are provided: principal, horn, and string tones (58, 60).

Lowland pipe, Scottish bagpipe, bellows-blown, played seated, with 2 tenor and 1 bass drones on the same stock. Chanter and drones are somewhat smaller than those of the Highland pipe. Another form of Lowland pipe, introduced in the mid-18th c., was a hybrid Irish Union pipe. It had a chanter of the Union pipe pattern, with added removable foot joint, and 2 drones and a regulator in one stock. The ordinary form was tuned $A^0 a^0 a^0$. Both forms are now obs. (13, 89).

Lozhky (Russ.: spoon) [translation of Turk. *gāshiqlar*], Russ. idiophone adopted from the Turks in the 18th c. In its original form, brass or copper clappers, sometimes with pellet bells added; later a rattle-clapper of cavalry bands. As such it consisted of 2 V-shaped metal cylinders connected by a yoke, forming a lyre, armed with pellet bells and jingles, always used in pairs, 2 being clashed together and shaken (132, 169).

Lozki, see: lozhky.

Lubembe, lubembo, iron *double bell of the Lunda, Basonge, and Baluba-Hemba of the Congo. Also called rubembe (19).

Lubr, med. Nordic horn (197).

Luc, obs. Fr.: lute.

Ludaya [*mudaya,* tree], *cross flute of the Gishu herders of Uganda, made from the tip of a lobelia, slightly conical, tapering toward the lower end (195).

Ludi (Kikongo), **1.** autochthonous wooden trumpet of the Sundi of Nganda of the Lower Congo, partly covered with elephant skin. According to Laman, it serves to frighten away elephants. It is 45–60 cm. (1½–2 ft.) long; **2.** the name is also given to a larger instr. found in the same area, with square lateral blowhole, held vertically and surmounted by a sculptured head. It is 90–150 cm. (3–5 ft.) long. *Cf.* biludi (185).

Ludo (Lat.: to play), device for playing instrs. mechanically, invented by J. Carpentier and patented on May 18, 1900, employing perforated paper strips. Contained in a box 40 by 20 by 25 cm. (16 by 8 by 10 in.). See also: mélographe, mélotrope (204).

Lue, panpipes of the Trio Indians of the Guianas (105).

Luftdruckharmonium, Ger. term for the pressure harmonium, in contradistinction to the suction, or *American, harmonium.

Lugoma, 1. drum of the chief of the Bashi of Ruanda, sometimes over 1.50 m. (5 ft.) high; **2.** large hand drum of the Ambunda of Angola (139, 176).

Lugube, *musical bow of the Venda of S. Africa, played by girls and young women. It corresponds to the gabus, but is only 46–60 cm. (1½–2 ft.) long. The lugube is held in the mouth, like the gabus, with the oral cavity modifying the harmonics; the string is plucked with the right index finger and stopped with the left hand to produce 3 tones (116).

Lugumba, *conical drum of the Kongo people of Africa, played during dances (30, 185).

Luhenga, small *goblet drum of the Bajok and Batetela of the Congo, with short stem and nailed head. Rubber tuning paste is applied to the center of the membrane. That of the Bajok has a hole pierced in one side, covered with a thin vesicle, a *mirliton device. Played with bare hands (42).

Luik, Estonian shepherd's horn, made of wood, ca. 2 m. (6½ ft.) long. The name is also given to a horn made of goat horn (176).

Luk, Pol., Serb.: bow.

Lukembi, sansa of the peoples of the Ituri Forest, Congo (103).

Lukeme [Alur, *lukembe*], name by which the sansa is known to the Acoli of Uganda (195).

Luk muzycyny (Pol.: musical bow), the *bladder and string of Poland, a surviving folk instr. of considerable age. A highly arched wooden slat is held under tension by 2 or 3 strings affixed to its ends, and a small vesicle is inserted between strings and wood at the lower end, acting as resonator. Played with a bow. Also called bandurka or bandziurka, bas, optopka, smyk (89).

Lukombe, 1. pluriarc of the Teke and Lali of the Lower Congo, also of the Kwango River area, with 5 bows. The under side of the resonator is open. The instr. is held horizontally, with the resonator pressed against the player's stomach, and is usually played with a bamboo plectrum attached to the player's right forefinger. The strings are stopped with both hands (185); **2.** 8-stringed pluriarc of the Bakuba of the Congo (10); **3.** pluriarc of the Jia, Lia, Ipangu, Mgando, Ntomba, Sakata, Sogo-Meno, Sengele, Titu, Tumba, Yaelima of the Congo (128); **4.** *cylindrical drum of the Wasongola of the Congo, with single nailed head, over 1 m. (40 in.) high (30); **5.** *friction drum of the Bambala and Bashongo of the Congo, identical with the koy na bala (42).

Lukonde, pluriarc of the Bakuba of the Kasai River area of the Congo, with open back, 8 strings, and resonator terminating in a point at the upper end (10, 19).

Lukumbi, syn. of alindi.

Lulanga, *trough zither of the Bashi of Lake Kivu area, Congo, and of the Fuliri, made of wood, with 8 strings of fiber or cow tendon spaced about 2 cm. (¾ in.) apart. The instr. is laid horizontally on the player's knees and the strings are brushed rather than plucked. The scale corresponds to an ascending pattern of C E G A♭ B♭ C D♭ E♭. It is 75–90 cm. (30–36 in.) long (128, 139).

Lulimba, sansa of the Wayao of N. Mozambique and adjacent areas (176).

Lumbamba (Kikongo), a small double-headed *cylindrical drum of the Kongo people, with heads laced with *mbamba* (rattan) (185).

Lumière, Fr.: mouth; flue (of a pipe).

Lumždze, double whistle flute of Lithuania (169).

Lunanga, name given by the Bahavu of Ruanda to the lulanga (139).

Lunat, friction idiophone of New Ireland. For description see: nunut (77).

Lunga [Arab. *kūbā*], word that designates a drum in several Sudanic languages. In Mossi and Akasele it means a large drum; in Agni, Dyoula, and Huela, an hourglass drum (93).

Lung ching ti, obs. cross flute of China, with 8 fingerholes (142).

Lung ku (Chin.: dragon drum), drum of China, mounted on a stand or tripod and ornamented with dragons. Cf. ryong ko (75 II).

Lungo ndolo, cylindrical drum of the Kongo people, played during dances (30, 185).

Lungória, *percussion stick of Cuba, a hooked stick beaten rhythmically against the floor. Also called garabato (152).

Lung ti (Chin.: dragon flute), *ti formerly used in Confucian and state services, with both ends ornamented with carvings in form of a dragon's head and tail (142).

Lungunga, musical bow of the Bembe of the Congo, without resonator (185).

Lungungu, musical bow of the Sonde of Kibombo (Feshi), Lower Congo, with gourd resonator and tuning loop (128).

Lunko, pluriarc of the Bali of the Congo (19).

Lunuot, friction idiophone of Fesoa, Laraibine, Nayama, Tabar, Mandine (all in New Ireland). For description see: nunut (77).

Lunyege, rattle of the Bashi of Ruanda, consisting of a hollowed fruit containing hard seeds, suspended by a cord from the 2 ends of a forked stick; 70–80 cm. (28–32 in.) long (139).

Luoü (Angami), double *cross flute of the Naga of Assam, made of a bamboo segment *ca.* 90 cm. (3 ft.) long, with central node and 2 terminal nodes. Two stopped flutes are thus created, a 5th apart in pitch. They are devoid of fingerholes (172).

Lupondo, *goblet drum of the Basonge, Baluba, and Batatela of the Congo, with nailed head (30).

Lur, pl. lurer (Dan.) [ONordic *luðr,* horn], **1.** N. European horn of the Bronze Age, found chiefly in Denmark but also in Sweden, on the W. coast of Norway, and in N. Germany, with entirely conical bore and terminating not in a bell but in a flat ornamental disc. So far close to 3 dozen specimens have been found, all made of bronze; currently they are said to date from *ca.* 1100 to 500 B.C. Lurer were first excavated in Denmark in 1797, at which time the name *lur* was applied to them. Apparently they were always made in pairs; their form is that of an S-shaped curve, the second part of which is twisted in a plane at right angles to that of the first part, and the 2 lurer forming a pair are twisted in opposite directions. From their length and form Sachs concluded that mammoth tusk was probably the material of which they were originally made: this would explain their pairwise appearance and their curvature toward one another. As lurer found in pairs are at the same pitch, it is thought

that they were used antiphonally; their absolute pitch varies considerably, but those examined have yielded up to 12 tones. A notable feature of the lur is its nondetachable cup mouthpiece, similar to that of a modern tenor trombone, with a diam. of 2½–3 cm. (*ca.* 1 in.) and a depth of 1.6–3 cm. (*ca.* ½–1 in.). From these data it will be clear that the lur is often found in an excellent state of preservation. This is due above all to its discovery on moors, often the sites of sacrifices to the ancient deities. Contemporary rock drawings, chiefly those along the S. coast of Sweden, confirm their use as cult instrs. Where lurer are shown in pairs they curve away from each other. Extant lurer measure 1.51–2.38 m. (*ca.* 5–8 ft.); **2.** wooden alphorn of Scandinavia, made of hollowed sections of wood, glued together and bound with birch bark. Formerly used by shepherds to frighten away wolves. The conical tube has a length of *ca.* 1.25 m. (4 ft.). It is played without a mouthpiece (21, 89, 169).

Luru, end-blown trumpet of the Lugbara of Uganda, consisting of a bottle-shaped gourd covered with hide. It is used occasionally in place of their side-blown horn guke (195).

Lusengo, horn of the Warundi of Africa, made from a cow horn and used as a signal instr. It yields 2 tones (42).

Lusese, stick zither of the Luntu of the Congo (128).

Lusinga, pluriarc of the Congo, with square, rectangular, or rounded resonator, 4 or 5 bows, and a small bridge. The strings are plucked with bare fingers or a plectrum. See also: nsambi (185).

Lusuba, musical bow of the Baluba-Hemba of the Congo (19).

Lusukia, sansa of the Wasongola of the Congo (19).

Lut, OFr.: lute.

Lutar, lute of the N. African Berbers, with 3 strings tuned $f^0 c^1 g^1$. *Cf.* lauta (89 Farmer).

Lute [Arab. *el-*'*ūd*] (Fr.: *luth;* Ger.: *Laute;* It.: *lauto;* Sp.: *láud*), organological term for a chordophone having a neck that serves as string bearer and as handle, with the plane of the strings running parallel to the soundboard or belly. We distinguish between bowed lutes (as, for instance, the violin) and plucked lutes; also between short-necked and longed-necked lutes. In the former the neck is usually shorter than the body, its prototype being a wooden body tapering to form neck and fingerboard, whereas in the latter, the neck is longer than the body, its prototype being a stick attached to a bulging fruit shell. A *spike lute is one whose handle passes diametrically through the body.

The home of the lute, according to Sachs, is probably to be found in the vicinity of the Caucasus. The instr. first appears in Mesopotamia *ca.* 2000 B.C., with small ovoid body and long fretted neck; sometimes 2 strings played with a plectrum are visible. It reached Egypt *ca.* 1500 B.C. and seems to have been played there only by women. The body of the Egyptian lute was oval or almond-shaped, made of wood, with membrane belly and long fretted neck. The handle penetrated the whole length of the body but didn't project at the bottom. The strings were fastened to the lower end of the handle and emerged through a hole cut in the belly, to be secured by tuning rings at the upper end of the handle. Generally 2 strings, occasionally 3, are shown. Here also the lute was played with a plectrum. This type of lute survives in NW. Africa today (see: gunbrī and gunībrī). The lute of the Greeks, and of the Romans to whom they bequeathed it, was similar to those described; the body remained small; in late classical times it was sometimes spade-shaped, with 3 strings, the long neck wider than on earlier forms and fretted. It was rare both in Greece and in Rome.

The short-necked lute is first encountered on Pers. clay figurines of the 8th c. B.C. It then disappears, to turn up on Gandhara art works some 8 centuries later, with piriform body, short neck, lateral pegs, and frontal string holder, all characteristics of the Near Eastern, Far Eastern, and European lutes. Recent research suggests that the short-necked lute may have been known to China as early as the 2nd c. A.C. It appears there on 6th-c. sculptures, on Jap. ones a c. later. The short-necked lute of the Islamic Near East was characterized by a bent-back pegbox, lateral pegs, rib fastener, and membrane belly. It followed Islam to the S. and E., and westward to Europe, where it is encountered from the 10th c. on. Short-necked lutes with frontal string fastener also appear on Sassanid art objects. A frontal string fastener implies a wooden belly rather than one of membrane, and these lutes are so depicted.

The earliest lute-type instrs. depicted in med. Europe are of both the long- and short-necked varieties, with pegdisc and pegbox, indicative of different routes of arrival. The classical lute was introduced by the Arabs in the 13th c. It is mentioned in France as *leu ca.* 1270 and in Engl. literature from *ca.* 1395 on. In 1396 the Duke of Orleans had a *joueur de viele et de lus* in his employ. Early iconography shows a rounded body, short neck, bent-back pegbox with lateral pegs, frontal fastener, 4 strings; like the Arab lute, it was unfretted and played with a plectrum. In or by the early 15th c. a fifth string was added to the treble. The 15th c. also saw the appearance of frets, 4 at first, later increased to 7, 8, or 10. Tinctoris, writing toward the end of the c., said that the lute had 5 and sometimes 6 strings, and that these might be geminated, 1 string of each course being tuned to the oct. of the other in order to obtain greater volume. The lute of his day was plucked with either a plectrum or bare fingers. The relative tuning of the 5-stringed lute was $c^0 f^0 a^0 d^1 g^1$. Many 16th-c. authors give instructions for tuning the lute, and almost invariably for tuning the highest string, the chanterelle, as high as it will go; as neither sizes of lute nor thicknesses of strings were standardized, this is understandable. The lute spread quickly throughout Europe; lute players appear in Hungary in 1427. Although it was not a pop. instr. in Spain, where the vihuela was preferred, an inventory of the instrs. of Queen Isabella the Catholic of 1503 lists 6 lutes. In 1507 the first lute music was printed (by Spinaccino); in 1509 a luter was employed at the court of Henry VIII, and in 1511 the first book devoted to musical instrs. (Virdung's *Musica getutscht*) contains instructions for the lute and depicts one with 6 courses and 7 frets: the golden age of the lute has started. In its final and classical form, assumed by 1500, the lute had a large piriform body with flat wooden top and bulging body composed of a varying number of very thin, narrow ribs (some authors considered 9 or 11 as the best number, although as many as 40 or so were used). A Fugger inventory of 1566 (published by A. Sandberger in *Denkmäler der Tonkunst* in Bayern, V, 1904) enumerates lutes made of a variety of materials: ebony, ivory, whalebone, of gray, black, and red *canna d'India*, cypress, brazilwood, yellow and red maple, sycamore, yew, and oak. But the best woods, according to Trichet (*ca.* 1640), were maple or sycamore (*érable*), yew, plum, cherry, or ebony. Ivory and ebony were often considered tonally inferior. Trichet also mentioned that old lutes with dried wood were preferable to new ones. The string holder was attached to the belly below a central circular soundhole covered by a rose. The neck, with its 7–10 frets, accounted for *ca.* ⅓ of the open string length; width of the fingerboard varied from 6 to 10 cm. (2½ to 4 in.); the pegbox was set at a 90-degree angle to the neck and contained lateral pegs. Later instrs. often had a special attachment for the chanterelle, placed next to the nut. A sixth string was added in the bass by 1500. Bermudo in 1555 calls the lute a *vihuela de Flandres* and gives its tuning as $G^0 c^0 f^0 a^0 d^1 g^1$, which was also that of the vihuela. By the end of the c. a seventh string was sometimes added to the bass. Adriano Banchieri in 1609 gives the tuning of a 7-course lute as $F^0 G^0 c^0 f^0 a^0 d^1 g^1$, but the low string could also be tuned a 4th or 5th below the second string. He also gives the tuning of a *leuto grosso,* or bass lute, as $C^0 D^0 G^0 c^0 e^0 a^0 d^1$. His tunings are interesting in as much as they are no longer relative but absolute: they correspond to the pitch of his organ. The bass lute of Praetorius had 9 strings tuned $C^0 D^0 F^0 G^0 c^0 f^0 a^0 d^1 g^1$. In addition, there existed a treble lute, pitched one tone higher than the alto, or common, lute. The alto remained the type instr. and was known in Ger.-speaking countries as *Chorist-Laute, or gemeine Altlaute.* The continued addition of bass strings, supplied to meet the demands of *continuo* players, made a second neck necessary: the *archlute came into existence and the decadence of the true lute set in. Whereas previously the bass strings had been stopped, those of the archlutes were open strings; Praetorius mentioned the *theorbo-lute as a new instr. Thomas Mace's oft-quoted book on the lute is, ironically enough, concerned with the archlute rather than with the true lute: he describes a theorbo-lute with 8 courses on the lower pegbox and 4 on the upper, known in England as the French lute. The basic lute tuning given above (G^0–g^1) was known as the "old tuning" (*viel accord*), and by the early 17th c., if not before, it no longer corresponded to musical requirements, in view of the ever-increasing number of strings. In 1600 Francisque published pieces for a lute *à cordes avalées,* tuned $B\flat^1 E\flat^0 F^0 G^0 B\flat^0 f^0 b\flat^0 d^1 g^1$. Other new tunings of the 17th c. include the "sharp tuning" ($G^0 c^0 f^0 a^0 c^1 e^1$); the "flat tuning" ($B^0 e^0 a^0 c^1 e^1 g^1$); the *"accord nouveau"* ($A^0 d^0 f^0 a^0 d^1 f^1$). The last continued in use in Germany in the 18th c., after the lute had been abandoned in other European countries. A more robust build and the use of spun strings made it possible to confine all strings to one pegbox. Baron in 1727 gives the tuning of an 11-course lute as $C^0 D^0 E^0 F^0 G^0 A^0 d^0 f^0 a^0 d^1 f^1$, all strings being of the same length. Lute music is written in tablature, a system of notation in which symbols (letters or numbers, or both) are substituted for notes (24, 89 Prynne, 145, 154, 170, 180, 190, A. Banchieri).

Lute guitar (Fr.: *guitare-luth;* Ger.: *Lautengitarre*), 19th-c. hybrid guitar with lute body (often, alas, that of an old one); it originated in Italy *ca.* 1850. Some specimens were fitted with 6 single strings, others with 5 pairs of strings (132, 169).

Lute harpsichord (Fr.: *clavecin-luth;* Ger.: *Lautenklavier, Lautenwerk;* It.: *violicembalo*), gut-strung harpsichord built intermittently from the early 16th c. on; Virdung is first to mention it in 1511. Eugen Casparini, the organ builder (1623–1706), made *"theorbische und auf Lauten Art bezogene Instrumente"* ([keyboard] instrs. strung like theorbos and lutes), according to his son Orazio. Orazio also mentioned that his father saw lute harpsichords in Venice. De Chales had suggested in 1674 that harpsichords be strung with gut rather than metal. In the 18th c. lute harpsichords were made by Johann Christoph Fleischer in 1718 (see: Theorbenflügel); one by Longfellow of Cambridge, dated 1720, is still in existence; Adlung informs us that Hildebrand made one for J. S. Bach *ca.* 1740; others were built by J. N. Bach, Friderici of Gera, J. G. Gleichmann. See also: clavichordium.

Lute stop, 1. on harpsichords (Ger.: *Nasalzug*) a set of strings plucked close to the nut by setting a slide in a gap cut diagonally across the wrest plank. The resulting tone is more or less nasal, depending on the plucking point, hence its Ger. name. The lute stop appears to date from the 18th c. Quirin van Blankenburg, writing in 1739, claimed to have invented it in 1708. Up to the mid-c. it was used sparingly, but became standard equipment on the 2-manual instrs. of the Engl. school. Tabel's surviving harpsichord of 1721 was already fitted with a lute stop. Also called cut-through stop; **2.** on pianos (Fr.: *jeu de luth, jeu de harpe;* Ger.: *Lautenzug*) a strip of cloth or leather-covered wood which could be pressed against the strings close to the nut, from either above or below. Patented by John Broadwood in 1783 under the name of "sordin," it developed into the *mute stop.

Luth, Fr.: lute.

Luth des maîtres chanteurs, a small, cross-strung *chromatic harp with a compass of c^0–g^3, built by Pleyel & Cie. of Paris since *ca.* 1900 for performances of *Die Meistersinger von Nürnberg* (176).

Luthéal, piano attachment that allegedly makes the piano sound like a Hungarian cimbalom. Maurice Ravel wrote a version of his *Tzigane* for violin and luthéal (*Revue musicale*, 1924/25).

Luth-orgue (Fr.), portable reed organ with a 4-oct. compass, patented by Dupland of Paris on July 10, 1860. See also: orphéa (204).

Luth théorbé, Fr.: theorbo-lute.

Lutina, Lat.: mandora; small lute; quinterne (61).

Luveve, 1. stopped *end-blown flute of the Swazi of S. Africa, made of the horn of duiker bok or springbok; it serves as a whistle for calling dogs; **2.** conical end-blown flute of the Swazi, made of wood in imitation of horn, with conical bore tapering to the lower end and blown across the wide end. Covered with an ox-tail skin, it is suspended from its owner's neck and used as a signal instr. (116).

Luvuvu, syn. of tshivhilivhi (116).

Luz, OFr.: lute.

Lydian pipes, syn. of tibiae serranae.

Lyra (Gk.), **1.** stringed instr. of ancient Greece, a *bowl lyre with tortoise-shell resonator (or its imitation in wood), skin belly, and 2 curved arms, originally animal horns, projecting from the bowl and connected at the top by a crossbar. A variable number of gut strings of equal length were secured to the yoke by tuning rings, and attached at the lower end of the resonator, passing over a bridge that raised them off the belly. Earliest representations of the lyra are found on vases of the geometric period (roughly 1200–800 B.C.). According to one Gk. tradition, the lyra came from Thrace and would thus be an autochthonous instr. Sachs, however, ascribed its origin to the Syrian rounded lyre. Of simpler construction than the *kithara, the lyra is said to have sounded at lower pitch. It was the instr. of amateurs, as opposed to the professionally played kithara, and did not live to Roman times. Some lyras are depicted as held by a band passed from one yoke arm over the player's left wrist. Lyras were often held in a tilted position, whereas the heavier kithara was always held upright. For its tuning see: lyre. See also: chelys;

2. syn. of glockenspiel organ stop; 3. alternate spelling of lira; 4. Tinctoris' (15th c.) name for the lute; 5. see: bell lyre; 6. Swed.: barrel organ.

Lyra barberina, triple lyre in form of a tripod, invented in the early 17th c. by G. B. Doni and dedicated by him to his patron, Cardinal Barberini, later Pope Urban VIII. The 3 sets of strings laced between the legs were tuned to the Dorian, Phrygian, and Lydian modes. Also called amphichord.

Lyrachord, 1. piano with a striking point of half the strings' speaking length, invented by the Rev. Joseph Rogerson Cotter of County Cork between 1840 and 1865; **2.** electric piano of the New York Lyrachord Co., 1912 (89, 176).

Lyra da braccio, see: lira da braccio.

Lyra da gamba, see: lira da gamba.

Lyraflügel, Ger.: lyra piano.

Lyragitarre, Ger.: lyre-guitar.

Lyra glockenspiel, syn. of bell lyre.

Lyra mendicorum (beggar's lyre), Lat.: hurdy-gurdy.

Lyra moderna, see: lira moderna.

Lyra perfecta, syn. of lirone perfetto, the lira da gamba.

Lyra piano (Ger.: Lyraflügel), *upright grand piano in form of a classical lyre, with symmetrically arched sides and Engl. action. The strings of the lyre were imitated by ornamental gilt rods. Said to have been invented by J. C. Schleip of Berlin ca. 1824, the lyra piano was also patented by Eulriot in 1834; another, by Hund & Son, was exhibited in London in 1851 (92).

Lyra viol, 1. a small bass viola da gamba, pop. in 17th-c. England and known as viola bastarda on the Continent (for description see: viola bastarda). It was one inch "shorter in body and neck" than the *division viol, also an inch narrower at the top of the belly and an inch narrower at the bottom, according to James Talbot (ca. 1700), and was tuned on the principle of the *lira da braccio, i.e., in mixed 4ths and 5ths to facilitate chordal playing, from which characteristic it probably derives its names. (The term lyra viol, said to occur in an Ambras inventory of 1596, is a misreading of "mer [mehr] viole." The lyra viol had a body length of 71 cm. (28 in.), a neck of just over 28 cm. (11 in.)—again, according to Talbot; average speaking length of the strings was 61 cm. (24 in.). Music for the instr. was always written in tablature, as a number of different tunings were in use, the required one being indicated at the beginning of each piece of music. Some of these tunings were: $C^0 F^0 c^0 f^0 a^0 d^1$; $A^1 E^0 A^0 e^0 a^0 d^1$; Praetorius gives $A^1 D^0 G^0 d^0 a^0 d^1$ or $C^0 G^0 c^0 e^0 a^0 d^1$; Playford's *harpway sharp* tuning was $D^0 G^0 d^0 g^0 b^0 d^1$; his *harpway flat:* $D^0 G^0 d^0 g^0 b\flat^0 d^1$; his *high harpway sharp:* $D^0 A^0 d^0 f\sharp^0 a^0 d^1$; his *high harpway flat:* $D^0 A^0 d^0 f^0 a^0 d^1$; Talbot's *sharp tuning* was: $E^0 A^0 c\sharp^0 e^0 a^0 c\sharp^1$; his *flat tuning:* $E^0 A^0 c^0 e^0 a^0 c^1$. The reason generally given for such numerous tunings is that it permits an increase in the variety of chords easily available; however, it is more likely that the object was to produce maximum sympathetic resonance of the open strings by having them tuned to the triad of the key in which a piece was to be played. Toward the end of the lyra viol's life Thomas Mace wrote (in 1676) that in consort playing it would stand as a second treble and that it could also be used for divisions;

2. *ca.* 1600 Daniel Farrant invented a lyra viol with sympathetic metal strings "conveyed through a hollow passage made in the neck of the viol," as Playford wrote, tuned in unison to the bowed strings. Such instrs., apparently confined to England, were short-lived; Playford could write in 1661 that, although he had seen many, "time and disuse" had set them aside. The central soundhole would have favored the resonance of the sympathetic strings (Talbot in 80, 94).

Lyra rustica, see: lira rustica.

Lyra-zither, see: chord zither, 2.

Lyre [Gk. *lyra*], **1.** chordophone with strings attached to a yoke that lies in the same plane as the resonator, and consists of 2 arms and a crossbar. Lyres are divided into *bowl lyres and *box lyres. The first variety is exemplified by the Gk. *lyra, the second by the *kithara. Box lyres can be traced back to *ca.* 2800 B.C., when they first appear on Sumerian art works. Eight specimens have been excavated at the royal cemetery of Ur, 3 of which, preserved in the Baghdad Museum, the British Museum, and the University Museum of Philadelphia, measure 106, 116, and 120 cm. (*ca.* 42, 45½, and 47 in.). Sumerian lyres are invariably portrayed in vertical position, even when carried. They were asymmetrical, the yoke consisting of 2 straight divergent arms, one longer than the other, connected by a crossbar. The front of the resonator was usually adorned with the sculptured figure of a bull or of a bull's head, placed at the joint of resonator and arm—either the shorter or the longer of the 2—and this arm was then held away from the player. The strings, 9–11 are visible on some representations, were

fastened in a bunch on the lower front of the resonator at the side opposite the carving. They were tied around the crossbar, tightened by wooden wedges, and plucked with the bare fingers of both hands. Babylonian lyres are already smaller: a relief of *ca.* 1700 B.C. in the Berlin Museum shows one played in horizontal position, with the crossbar held away from the body; its arms are gracefully curved. The Sumerian type of asymmetric lyre, with oblique yoke holding strings of slightly unequal length, is representative of the lyre of Assyria, Phoenicia, and Asia Minor generally. In Egypt the lyre appears *ca.* 2000 B.C., also as an asymmetric box lyre with divergent arms and oblique crossbar, tuning rings, and string fastener on the front of the resonator. Its arms were either straight, as on the Sumerian lyre, or curved, with pronounced asymmetry. It was played with a long plectrum held in the right hand, all strings being plucked together, while the left-hand fingers fanned out to silence the unwanted ones. As a rule it was held horizontally with the crossbar away from the player. After 1000 B.C. a smaller, symmetrical lyre came to Egypt from Asia, with parallel arms, held upright. The lyre was also known to the ancient Hebrews, trapezoid with 3–12 strings of different thicknesses of sheep gut. In the days of Flavius Josephus (b. 37 A.C.) it had 10 strings. Recent investigation suggests that it may not have been tuned pentatonically, but diatonically with microtones. This instr. is perhaps best known as the "harp" of King David. The classical lyres of Greece were attributes of Apollo. The phorminx and the kitharis, mentioned in the *Iliad* (*ca.* 9th c. B.C.), are believed to designate the kithara and the lyra.

These 2 instrs., national instrs. of Greece, were strung alike, with 3 or 4 strings in the 9th c. B.C., 5 in the 8th c., 6 and 7 in the 7th c., 8 in the 6th c., 9, 10, 11, or 12 in the 5th c. B.C., with a 2-oct. compass. Sachs has shown that the tuning of Gk. lyres was pentatonic without semitones, E G A B D (but not necessarily in that order), any extra string(s) duplicating those notes at higher or lower pitches. The F, C, and other needed notes were obtained by stopping the next lower string to raise its pitch by the requisite amount (see: Sachs, C.: *"Die griechische Instrumentalnotenschrift,"* in *Zeitschrift für Musikwissenschaft*, VI, 1923). Rome took over the kithara from the Greeks, but not the lyra.

Representations of lyres dating from the Hallstadt period (8th c. to 5th c. B.C.) have been found in excavated material at Sopron (Ödenburg), Hungary, and at Klein-Glein, Styria, Austria.

In postclassical Europe the lyre appeared at an early date and in a number of forms, thus giving rise to many interesting if unconfirmed theories. Prior to 1000 it had reached an area encompassing Britain, France, Germany, Scandinavia, Finland, and Estonia. Up to then all these lyres were plucked; in the 7th and 8th c. they had parallel sides and the strings were plucked with the player's right hand, his left hand stopping them from the back, as in antiquity. A waisted type appears from the 9th c. on, depicted with the left hand holding the lyre at its top. Parallel sides occur again in the 12th c., now on bowed instrs., and the left hand is seen reaching through the strings to stop them; this type is still played in Finland and Estonia. Waisted bowed instrs. occur from the 11th c. on, the top of the lyre usually being held by the player's left hand, but on some Fr. mss. the strings are stopped by reaching through with the left hand. The earliest of these types are quite possibly descended from the classical lyres, either directly or indirectly, but there are fundamental differences between antique and med. instrs.: in med. instrs. the arms and usually also the crossbar are made of the same block of wood as the body, and the tuning rings and wooden pegs are replaced by frontal or rear tuning pegs.

Two lyres dating from the 6th or 7th c. A.C. have been found at Oberflacht, Württemberg. One measures 80.5 cm. (*ca.* 32 in.), with a max. width of 20.5 cm. (*ca.* 8 in.), and is made of hollowed-out oak 1 cm. thick, the crossbar having been made separately. The aperture between parallel arms, body, and crossbar is an elongated V. A Frankish lyre of the early 8th c., formerly in Cologne, was destroyed during World War II. Its resonator, arms, and yoke were made of a single piece of wood. Both instrs. had 6 strings. Another, believed to date from the 12th c., was excavated in 1949 at Gdańsk (Danzig); it had 5 strings, a nut, rear pegs, and a large round handhole (no fingerboard). The plucked lyre did not survive the Middle Ages in Europe; the bowed lyre survived only in Wales (see: crwth) and in Finland and Estonia, where it is played today. Plucked lyres are still played in Asia and E. Africa, in Asia by the Ostyak and Vogul of Siberia. Both lyra and kithara passed from Greece to Alexandrian Egypt, where they underwent modification of form, and as a result both box lyre and bowl lyre are known in NE. Africa today. Both are played in Ethiopia and among the Sebei, a Nilo-Hamitic people to the south; other areas of Africa in which the lyre exists know only the bowl lyre (the Upper Nile, a region N. and E. of Lake Victoria, and the Nile-Congo watershed). African lyres are equipped with tuning rings and in Ethiopia wooden wedges are inserted as on the lyres of ancient Sumer. Resonators of these bowl lyres consist sometimes of a tortoise carapace, as with the Gk. lyra, but are often of wood with skin bellies. Lyres of the Congo are invariably symmetrical. See also: al-gar, amphichord, bagana, barbiton, basamkub, bowed harp, British lyre, chelys, chepkong, cythara (teutonica), edungu, ginger, kena'na'wr, kerar, kibukandet, kidrar, kindu, kinnāra, kinnōr, kipokan, kirar, kisirka, kissar, kithara, knr, krar, kudu, litungu, lyra barberina, masonquo, nares-jux, ndongo,

nzira, odi, qatros, rababa, rapapa, sabitu, sangkultap, simsimijah, tam, tanbur, thum, timbo, tohmu, tom, tum (15 Wachsmann, 21, 89 Folk music Poland; 128, 170; 185A O. Seewald: *"Die Lyrendarstellungen* . . . *,* in *Festschrift Alfred Orel,* 1960);
2. syn. of bell lyre; **3.** see also: lira, lyra.

Lyre anacréontique (Fr.), original name of the lyre-guitar.

Lyre d'Apollon, Fr.: Apollo lyre.

Lyre-guitar (Fr.: *lyre-guitare;* Ger.: *Lyragitarre;* It.: *chitarra-lira*), **1.** guitar of late-18th-c. Fr. invention, in form of a modified kithara, with a central fingerboard, usually 6 but occasionally 9 strings, fretted, and with a guitar-type string holder. The 6-stringed variety was tuned $E^0 A^0 d^0 g^0 b^0 e^1$. Despite the elegance of its form it was unwieldy to play, but this did not prevent it from enjoying considerable popularity all over Europe during the first 3 decades of the 19th c. Occasionally it was also built in bass size with 2 additional, open strings. In France it was at first known as *lyre anacréontique;* in England it also became known as Apollo lyre;
2. guitar invented *ca.* 1800 by Charpentier & Münchs, with 25 strings and a compass of 4 octs. (89, 204).

Lyre organisée, lyre-guitar with keyboard and 15 strings, patented by Led'huy of Coucy-le-Château on Nov. 21, 1806 (176, 204).

Lyre sur caisse, Fr.: box lyre.

Lyre sur coque, Fr.: bowl lyre.

Lyric harp, *chromatic harp of C. J. Hentrichs of Philadelphia, 1908, with 88 strings (176).

Lyrichord, *bowed keyboard instr. patented by Roger Plenius, a London harpsichord maker, on Dec. 30, 1741, with

rotating wheels worked by clockwork, and both gut and metal strings. An illustration of it appeared in the Aug. 1755 issue of the *General Magazine of Arts and Sciences.* The lid was divided into 2 sections, one of which could be opened or closed by a pedal, thus providing a swell. In 1745 Plenius added his *Welsh harp stop, controlled by a pedal. No specimen has survived. *Cf.* Geigenwerk (27, 89 Hipkins).

Lyro-harpe, name given to a guitar with 2 necks and 19 strings, with a compass of over 4 octs., invented in 1837 in Berlin (176).

Lyrophoinix, unidentified instr. of ancient Greece, probably a chordophone (21, 176).

Lyrophone, valved *duplex instr. invented by J. J. Chediwa of Odessa, in 1887, with 2 tubes of the same length but with different bores. A fourth valve controlled the air admission to one or the other tube. The narrow-bore tube was used for solo and piano passages, the wide-bore tube for tutti and forte passages (126, 154, 176).

Lyro-pianoforte, keyboard instr. built by Robert Thomas Worton and patented in England on Nov. 16, 1861, with combination jack-and-hammer action. A device similar to a harpsichord jack was affixed to each hammer, and the instr. could be played as either a piano or a harpsichord. See also: vis-pianoforte (176).

Lyro-vis-pianoforte, a combination of *lyro-pianoforte and *vis-pianoforte, patented by Robert Thomas Worton on Nov. 16, 1861 (176).

Lyzarden, wind instr. mentioned in various 16th- and 17th-c. Engl. documents, and tentatively identified by Galpin as a tenor or bass cornett (89 Galpin).

Ma, 1. stopped *end-blown flute of the Karen of Shan State, Burma, of bamboo, devoid of fingerholes; **2.** panpipes of the Karen in raft or bundle form, with 4 stopped pipes (172).

Ma', see: mat.

Ma'azif, pl. of mi'zaf.

Machada, syn. of machete.

Machete, 4-stringed guitar of Portugal, identical with the cavaquinho. Port. sailors are said to have introduced it to the Hawaiian Islands, where it was transformed into the *ukulele.

Machine drum (Ger.: *Maschinenpauke*), kettledrum with some mechanical device for turning all tuning screws simultaneously. Three systems are in use: **1.** *pedal drums; **2.** drums tuned with a single handle; **3.** drums that rotate on a stand. Machine drums in America are either pedal or rotary type. A device that acted on all tuning screws at once was invented in 1812 by Gerhard Cramer of Munich, and in 1821 J. C. N. Stumpff of Amsterdam devised a system for turning the drum itself, rather than the screws. Pedal drums are more recent. Also called chromatic drum (89, 170).

Machine stop, hand stop or knee lever found on some Fr., but chiefly on Engl., harpsichords of the 18th c.; it controls more than one row of jacks simultaneously.

Macillo, Sp.: hammer.

Macungo, syn. of urucungo (7).

Mādalā (Sans., Beng.), *barrel drum of India, made of clay, with laced heads. A modern form is also made of wood. *Cf.* tapone (173).

Maddala, Pali equivalent of the mādalā (173).

Madera y paja (wood and straw), Sp.: xylophone (98).

Madibu, pl. of dibu.

Madilan, bowed chordophone invented in 1883 by Mirzā Ghulām Husain of Teheran. *Cf.* tarab angiz (89 Farmer).

Madimba, African xylophone with a variable number of hardwood slabs, usually made of *pterocarpus,* and gourd resonators pierced laterally with a small hole that is covered with a thin animal membrane—a mirliton device. The slabs are fixed to a framework and isolated by means of fiber padding. The name madimba is used by the Baluba of Kamina, Dibaya, and Mwanza, the Bakuba of Lusambo, the Bayeke of Nguba, the Bena-Kanioka of Mutombo-Mukulu, and the Bena-Lulua of Luluabourg. *Cf.* dimba, jimba, kidimba, madiumba, malimba, midimba (30).

Madinda, var. of amadinda.

Madiumba, xylophone of the São Salvador region of Angola, with 9 slabs and gourd resonators (185).

Mādlā, Mar. equivalent of mādalā (173).

Mafowa, leg rattles of the S. African Thonga, made of fruits and cocoons mounted on strips of skin and wound around the performer's legs (116).

Magada (Gk.), **1.** the fixed semicircular wooden nut at one end or both ends of a monochord; it is also referred to as hemipherium (*sic*); **2.** the movable bridge of a monochord; **3.** any kind of bridge. Also called magas.

Magadis (Gk.), unidentified chordophone of ancient Greece, the same as pectis, according to some authors. The poet Sopatros, contemporary of Alexander the Great, called it *dichordos*, 2-stringed, from which it has been inferred that it might have been bichord, with strings pitched an oct. apart. Anacreon mentions 10 strings (pairs?). Aristoxenos adds that it was played without plectra. It was possibly a small harp of W. Asiatic origin, known to Greece by the 6th c. B.C. (89).

Magas, Gk.: bridge. In med. times it also meant monochord.

Mag-dung [*dmag*, army + *dung*, trumpet], Tibetan bugle of Western origin (89 Picken).

Mage ling, small bell of Cambodia (176).

Mago, Jew's-harp of the Lisha of Shan State, Burma, of bamboo, forming a slender rectangle. Sachs describes a set of 3 that sound the fundamental, 5th, and major 7th, tuned with wax (172).

Magondo, xylophone of the Mondjembo and the Bongo of the Congo (19).

Magonga, pl. of ngonga.

Magrepha, small, bellows-blown organ of the ancient Hebrews, used as a signal instr. by priests during the last period of the Temple. One of its functions was to convoke the priests. Talmudic tractates describe it as being an *amma* (about 50 cm., or 20 in.) high, and as wide, with 10 times 10 pipes, possibly a symbolic figure. The word *magrepha* means rake in Heb., and the instr. was probably named for its shape. See also: hirdolis, hydraulos (84, 170).

Magri sumpi, *double pipe of the Kachin of Shan State, Burma, with free reeds. The cylindrical pipes are of cane, each provided with a metal reed. The melody pipe has 5 front fingerholes and 2 rear thumbholes; the drone pipe is narrower and devoid of fingerholes (172).

Magudi (Tamil), S. India equivalent of the tiktirī. Sometimes it is nose-blown, and then it is called nāsa jantra (179).

Magyaun, see: mi gyaun.

Mahāmandirā (Sans., Beng.), large mandirā *ca.* 8 cm. (3 in.) in diam. (132).

Mahānāgārā [Pers. *naqqāra*] (Hindi), largest kettledrum of India, a syn. of damāmā. See also naubat.

Mahānātaka vīnā, syn. of gotuvādyam (179).

Mahati vīnā (great *vīnā*), classical vīnā of N. India, usually just called "vīnā." The mahati vīnā represents the acme of *stick zither development, with round stick neck from which 2 large gourds are suspended; it has 4 or 5 melody strings of metal, 1 or 2 drone strings, and 20–24 movable frets. Nowadays it is rare. The drone strings are shorter (and higher-pitched) than the melody strings and are secured by lateral tuning pegs inserted in the stick neck. The very high frets are held in position by wax and can be moved according to the requirements of the tuning. The vīnā is held with the upper (peg end) gourd resting against the player's left shoulder, and the strings are plucked with a ring plectrum or with bare fingers. It is a solo instr. with very complicated finger technique. The S. India equivalent is called naradiya vīnā. *Ca.* 125 cm. (4 ft.) long. *Cf.* ranjanī vīnā (149, 170, 173).

Mahea, ankle rattle worn by dancers in the Menabe district of the Malagasy Republic. It is also a gourd rattle there (171).

Mahorathuk, kettledrum of Thailand, with copper shell (176).

Mahuri (Odiya), small oboe of S. India, *ca.* 25 cm. (10 in.) long (173).

Mai, *end-blown flute of Opa, Leper Island, New Hebrides, of bamboo, with 2 fingerholes (171).

Maillet, Fr.: hammer.

Mailloche, Fr., drumstick with a padded end (127).

Mailloche double (Fr.), see: tampon.

Mairu-adar, Basque: Moorish horn.

Maiso, panpipes of the S. American Chipaya Indians, comprising 2 pipes tied together. Both are stopped. *Ca.* 10 and 12 cm. (4 and 5 in.) long (104).

Mait, see: mat.

Maitai talla, straight trumpet of the Naga of Assam, made of bamboo with a bell of gourd and a wooden mouthpiece. *Ca.* 110 cm. (43 in.) long (172).

Majimba, var. of madimba, a xylophone of the Baluba of Museka and of Kayumba, the Congo (31).

Major, when used as a prefix or suffix to names of organ pipes, major denotes 16′ pitch, or in some cases 8′ pitch.

Major bass, organ stop of diapason pipes, either open or stopped, at 16′ or 32′ pitch (133).

Major flute, see: flauto major.

Makaji, xylophone of the Baluba of the Congo, with 9 slabs (103).

Makasa, rattle of the Soalala district of the Malagasy Republic (171).

Makata, set of 9 *percussion sticks of peoples of the Ituri Forest, the Congo (103).

Makkow, dancing rattle of the Batlaping of S. Africa, similar to the mathlo (116).

Makondere, side-blown trumpet of the Tutsi of Ruanda-Urundi. *Cf.* ekkondere, kondere (103).

Makuku, clay whistle of the Palikur Indians of the mouth of the Amazon (105).

Makuta, Afro-Cuban drum of Congo origin, with single head, usually nailed, of barrel or cylindrical shape, tied with bands of iron. Played with bare hands (152).

Makwanga, panpipes of the Yombe of the Lower Congo, with 4 stopped pipes having beveled embouchures, tied in 2 pairs, with raffia ligatures. The longer pipe of each pair is considered the husband, the shorter, the wife. Specimens with 6 and 8 pipes are also known and occur in raft form. Those with 6 pipes are 18–30 cm. (7–12 in.) long, those with 8 pipes 11–18 cm. (4–7 in.) long. Also called kwanga, mavonda (185).

Makwindi, name given to the gora in Swaziland (116).

Ma la, see: cai ma la.

Malaba, maloba, *ground bow of the Gishu of Uganda, used as a child's toy (195).

Malaka, see: maraca.

Malakat, side-blown trumpet of Ethiopia, made of a long bamboo tube with bell of copper or of an elongated gourd, covered entirely with skin. The bell is attached to the tube by means of a length of curved horn, so that it is perpendicular to the tube. The malakat was described by Laborde in 1780. Also called meleketa (124, 132, 144).

Mali calaf, syn. of mali caval.

Mali caval (small *caval*), *end-blown flute of S. Montenegro, without mouthpiece, now becoming obs. It occurs in different parts of Yugoslav Macedonia as mali calaf, sviralja, sviraljka (not to be confused with svirala). Formerly a homemade instr. of wood, it is now manufactured of iron or brass tubing. Those made of wood, of walnut or beech, are cylindrical, *ca.* 40 cm. (16 in.) long, with 6 equidistant fingerholes. Those of metal are conical. The playing technique is that of the Eastern shawm: constant, uninterrupted breathing, the breath being drawn in by the nose while the mouth serves as wind chamber; the player's cheeks are not blown out, but his tongue functions somewhat as does the piston of an air pump by its back-and-forth motions. The holes are stopped by the middle joints of the player's fingers. The mali caval is an instr. of peasants and shepherds (34).

Malīlu, Akk. equivalent of the Sum. gigid; possibly the same as the imbubu (89 Galpin).

Malimba [*madimba*], **1.** xylophone of the Bapende and Bambana of the Congo, with 17 slabs and gourd resonators with mirliton devices (see: madimba). The slabs are strung on 2 cords; **2.** xylophone of the Bango-Bango of the Congo, without resonators; a form of manja; **3.** African horn similar to the marimbula (31, 152).

Ma ling (Chin.: horse bell), hemispheric brass bell of N. China, with iron clapper, attached to the collar of beasts of burden. In Peking it often has a double clapper. *Cf.* tu ling (142).

Maliphone, music box of the late 19th c. (38).

Malluch, a zummāra of the Dinka of Sudan, with 6 fingerholes (176).

Malongu, *board zither of the Balese of the Congo, with resonator (128).

Malume, xylophone of the Luba of the Congo (103).

Mamapu, percussion instr. of Samoa; a number of bamboo panpipes, up to 120 cm. (4 ft.) long, are tied by their open ends to the inside of a basket, which is struck (176).

Mambisa, Afro-Cuban drum, with single nailed head, slightly conical, played with 2 sticks. *Ca.* 100 cm. (40 in.) high (152).

Mam ma lie, bull-roarer of Australia (176).

Man, bamboo panpipes of the Padaung of Shan State, Burma, made of 20 pipes in raft form, closed by an internal node (172).

Manandria, syn. of hazolahi (172).

Manche, Fr.: neck.

Mandal, Punj., Hindi equivalent of the mādalā (173).

Mandar, sacred drum of the Kharvār of S. Uttar Pradesh, India (173).

Mandileh, ankle rattles worn by boys of Multan, Punjab (176).

Mandirā (Sans., Beng.), small, heavy tinkling cymbals of India, with central boss and sloping rim or no rim at all; in the latter case they are hemispheric. *Ca.* 4 cm. (1½ in.) in diam. Called manjira in Hindi and Hindust. See also: ding sha (170).

Mandobass, modern double-bass mandolin.

Mandocello, bass mandolin (204).

Mandoire, obs. var. of mandore.

Mandola, syn. of mandora.

Mandolin [dim. of It. *mandola*] (Brit., Fr.: *mandoline;* Ger.: *Mandoline;* It.: *mandolino*), plucked chordophone of early-18th-c. origin, today played chiefly in Italy as a melody instr. often accompanied by a guitar, elsewhere in mandolin bands. The instr. we call "mandolin"

without further qualification is actually the Neapolitan mandolin (see: mandolino napolitano), with piriform body very deeply vaulted at the lower end, made of narrow ribs, with fretted neck, open circular or oblong soundhole, 4 pairs of steel strings tuned $g^0 d^1 a^1 e^2$, a flat rectangular pegdisc set at an obtuse angle, rear pegs, a low bridge glued to the belly (at which point the belly is bent), and rib fastening. It is played with a plectrum and measures about 60 cm. (2 ft.) in length. In our c. the mandolin has been developed into a family: the instr. just described serves as soprano, a mandora as alto and tenor, the mandocello as bass, and the mandobass as contrabass member. Since Sachs drew attention (in Source 169) to a painting by Fra Angelico (first half of the 15th c.), showing a "mandolin" closely resembling an instr. to be seen on Pers. miniatures, it has been assumed that the mandolin was a Near Eastern instr. introduced through SE. Europe (*cf.* the cobsa of Romania). In the 18th c. it was made in different towns of Italy with varying stringing and consequent structural modifications. See: mandolino fiorentino, etc. A bass instr. of the same period, now obs., was called mandolone or arcimandola. The mandolino milanese is not a mandolin except in name: it is the 18th-c. name for the 17th-c. *pandurina. Compositions for the mandolin start around 1700; a c. later the instr. was almost forgotten and was not taken up again until the late 19th c. (151, 169).

Mandoline-lute, instr. invented by Angelo Benedetto Ventura of London, in shape of a lute, otherwise like a mandolin. The invention took place by 1851. See also: harp Ventura (204).

Mandoline Michelin, see: mandolineviolon.

Mandoline-violon, instr. invented by Michelin of Angers and patented on Aug. 16, 1897, in shape of a mandolin when seen full face, but having the profile of a violin, with 8 strings. Also called mandoline Michelin (204).

Mandolino fiorentino (It.), mandolin with body smaller than that of the *mandolino napolitano, and with a longer neck. Its 5 pairs of strings were tuned $d^1 g^1 c^2 e^2 a^2$, like the chitarra battente (169).

Mandolino genovese (It.), mandolin similar to the Neapolitan mandolin (see: mandolino napolitano) but with wider neck to carry 5 pairs of strings tuned $g^0 c^1 e^1 a^1 d^2$ or 6 pairs tuned $g^0 b^0 e^1 a^1 d^2 g^2$ (176).

Mandolino milanese (It.), 18th-c. name of the pandurina, which in the 17th c. had 6 pairs of strings, in the 18th, 6 single strings of gut, plucked with bare fingers. Despite its name this instr. is a form of mandola, not a mandolin. The usual tuning was $g^0 b^0 e^1 a^1 d^2 e^2$ or $g^0 b^0 e^1 a^1 d^2 g^2$.

Mandolino napolitano (It.), the classical mandolin of the 18th c., for which, *i.a.*, Beethoven wrote; it is still played today. Described under: mandolin.

Mandolino padovano (It.), 18th-c. mandolin with 5 courses of strings (169).

Mandolino romano (It.), mandolin with 4 courses of strings (169).

Mandolino senese (It.), mandolin with either 4 or 6 single strings (169).

Mandolino siciliano (It.), mandolin similar to the Neapolitan mandolin, but with 4 single strings (169).

Mandolin-Zitter (Ger.), zither with a bottle-shaped profile, built by J. Haslwanter of Munich in the second half of the 19th c. (176).

Mandoliole, alto mandolin invented *ca.* 1900 by P. G. B. Maldura of Rome (191, 204).

Mandoloncello, It.: tenor mandolin.

Mandolone (It.) [aug. of *mandola*], bass mandolin of the 18th c., with 7 or 8 pairs of metal strings (except for the chanterelle, which was single), tuned $F^0 (G^0) A^0 d^0 g^0 b^0 e^1 a^1$. Apart from its size and stringing it was similar in all respects to the Neapolitan mandolin. It was

90–100 cm. (36–40 in.) long. Also called arcimandola (169).

Mandora [Gk. **pandoura*] (Fr.: *mandore;* It.: *mandola;* Sp.: *mandora;* Lat.: *testudo minor*), name of a small variety of lute, distinguished from the classical instr. by its sickle-shaped pegbox, which in the Renaissance was often set at an obtuse angle, at other times upright, and by a narrower neck. The word is recorded in Fr. literature from the 12th c. to the 14th (chiefly as *mandoire*) and reappears in the 16th c.; in Prov. literature it occurs from 1235 on. Pictorially it is recorded for the remainder of the Middle Ages. Originally the mandora was a form of *guitarra morisca, and was also known as *gittern and as *mandola; these at least are its principal synonyms. A Ger. source identifies it as a *Quinterne* as late as the 16th c. In its earliest form it had 4 or perhaps 5 strings; the pegbox was a mere continuation of the neck, and the instr. was played with a plectrum. By the 16th c. it was plucked with bare fingers. In 1585 Adrien LeRoy wrote a tutor for it that unfortunately has not come down to us and that is known only through Trichet's reference. Trichet wrote (*ca.* 1640) that originally the mandora had had no frets but had since acquired 9; that formerly 4 single strings had been common but that in his day some players added a fifth or a sixth string, even geminating them, with the strings of a pair being tuned to fundamental and oct., and that a mandora so strung was known as a *mandore luthée;* finally he confirms that the only difference between lute and mandora was in the latter's smaller size and different number of strings, those of the mandora being tuned to the intervals 4-4-5. He gives its length as 1½ ft. Mersenne in 1636 depicted an instr. with almost almond-shaped body, pegbox reversed like that of a lute, and 4 single strings tuned $c^1 g^1 c^2 g^2$. From about the mid-16th c. the lute tuning of $c^1 f^1 a^1 d^2$ was also in use. Praetorius in 1618 gives 2 tunings for the 5-course mandora: $c^0 g^0$

$c^1 g^1 c^2$ and $c^0 f^0 c^1 f^1 c^2$. Music for the 5-course mandola was written from the early 17th c., and this stringing appears to have been preferred in France. Praetorius is our earliest source of information concerning an offspring of the mandora: he described a smaller form, called pandurina, with a very narrow, almost almond-shaped body, a wide neck, and a sickle-shaped pegbox. The further development of these instrs. is not clear: the pandurina turns up in the 18th c. under the name of *mandolino milanese, thus creating much confusion with the true mandolin. In the course of the 17th and 18th c. 6- and 8-course mandoras made their appearance, yet Furetière in 1690 could still write of the 4-course instr. with chanterelle plucked by the right-hand index finger, wearing a plectrum, while the other courses were plucked by the thumb. Johann Georg Albrechtsberger a c. later (1790) describes the mandora as a small lute with 8 pairs of gut strings tuned $C^0 D^0 E^0 A^0 d^0$ $g^0 b^0 e^1$ (this should probably read an oct. higher), the lowest 4 of which could be retuned according to the requirements of the piece to be played. Other tunings are given, as for instance $d^0 g^0 c^1 f^1 a^1 d^2$ and $A^0 d^0 g^0 c^1 f^1 a^1 d^2 f^2$. The 5-course It. mandola, tuned $c^0 g^0 d^1 a^1 e^1$, was sometimes called a *liuto moderno;* a larger version, with 8 courses, was known in Naples as *chitarrone;* on the other hand, a modern tenor mandolin is known as mandora. By the early 19th c. the mandora had been abandoned. Surviving specimens measure 40–65 cm. (16–25½ in.) (53, 78, 89 Prynne, 169).

Mandore, Fr.: mandora. *Cf.* almadurie.

Mandore luthée (Fr.: luted mandora), mandora strung with geminated strings, those of a course being tuned to fundamental and oct. Mersenne gives the name to a mandora with more than the customary 4 strings. See also: mandora.

Mandoretta, syn. of pandurina.

Mandorone, syn. of mandolone.

Mandoura, bagpipe of Crete, mouth-blown, with kidskin bag and double chanter of 2 cane pipes. Each pipe has 5 fingerholes directly opposite those of the other pipe, and a single reed (13).

Mandri, drum of the Muria of Bastar, India; it exists in 2 forms: **1.** hourglass-shaped, called hulki māndri; **2.** mridanga-shaped, called khut māndri. Formerly of wood, they are now increasingly made of clay, as bowls or clay drums can be readily purchased. Used chiefly at weddings (68).

Mandura, OProv.: mandora.

Mandürchen, Mandurinchen, Ger.: pandurina.

Manduria, var. of mandurria.

Mandurina, syn. of pandurina.

Mandurria, early form of the word *bandurria,* mentioned in the 14th c.

Manfula, syn. of kinfuíti (152).

Manga, see: mmanga.

Mango, Sp.: neck.

Mangu, drum of the Bazimba of the Congo in form of a truncated barrel, with 2 laced heads. *Cf.* imangu (30).

Manguare, *slit drum of the Bora Indians of the Upper Amazon, suspended from a frame, with walls 1¼–10 cm. (½–4 in.) thick. Used both as a signal and as a musical instr. (105).

Mangval, antelope horn of the Bongo of the Congo and SW. Sudan, with 3 fingerholes (176).

Manico, It.: neck (of a chordophone).

Manicorde (OFr., OProv.), a corr. of monochord, the term is first recorded in the *Roman de Flamenca* (1235), when it probably designated a monochord. It continues to be mentioned on the Continent until the late 15th c., when the word *manicordion comes into use. During the 15th c. the sense is invariably that of clavichord. In England the word occurs as late as 1680 (15 Dart, 53).

Manicordio, Port., Sp.: syn. of monocordio.

Manicordion (Fr.), corr. of *monochord. The term appeared *ca.* 1470 and replaced the older *manicorde; it remained in use until the **mid-16th c. and**

designated the clavichord. A Fr. inventory of 1556 mentions a *manicordion double* 3½ ft. long (53, 80 VII).

Maniura, unidentified instr. mentioned in Basque literature of the 17th c. (56).

Manja, xylophone of the Ngbandi and the Sango of the Congo, with 10–13 slabs of hardwood, usually *pterocarpus*. They lie on a frame, isolated by padding of fiber, bark, cloth, etc., and are played with rubber-padded sticks. See also: banjanga malimba, manjanga, manza, menza (31).

Manjaira, *end-blown flute of Syria, of bamboo, with 6 fingerholes in 2 groups (176).

Manjanga, name of the manja among the Manja of the Congo (31).

Manjira, Hindi and Hindust. equivalent of mandirā.

Manopan, hand-cranked free-reed instr. patented on Jan. 11, 1888, by C. F. Pietschmann et Fils, with perforated cardboard strips. The Berlin instr. collection contains one called Excelsior Manopan, which has 4 bellows and a comb (178, 204).

Mansu (Akk.), circular tambourine of ancient Babylon; it first appeared in the third millennium B.C. Also transcribed as mazu. *Cf.* meze (89).

Mansūr, medium-sized modern nāy. *Cf.* qīz, shāh (76).

Mantici, It.: bellows.

Mantsakota, wind instr. of the Venda of S. Africa, similar to the sitlanjani but made of wood and serving ritual purposes only (116).

Mantshomane, *frame drum of the Thonga of S. Africa, associated with witchcraft. The goatskin or buckskin head is laced to the underside, where the lacings form a grip for the hand. Played with a stick. Also called ubhababa (116).

Man t'u ku, S. Chin. drum similar to the pang ku, used on the stage (142).

Manual [Lat. *manus,* hand] (Fr.: *clavier;* Ger.: *Manual*), a keyboard for the hands, as opposed to a pedalboard.

Manuel, var. of moienel.

Manxa borrega [*manxa,* bellows +

borrega, lamb], one of several Cat. names for the bagpipe, used in the 16th c., now obs. (57, 165).

Manyinyi, straight wooden trumpet of the Bongo of the SW. Sudan (176).

Manza, 1. syn. of manja; **2.** name given to the kweningba by the Sango of the Congo; **3.** xylophone of the Azande, Basire, and Abandja of the Congo, with 5–10 slabs of hardwood, all of the same length but of different thicknesses, and gourd resonators. The latter are suspended from a board pierced like an organ pipe rack (31).

Manzu, var. of mazu.

Mapa, idiochord *half-tube zither of Flores Island, of bamboo, with 3–9 strings (149).

Maqrūn, double reedpipe of the Maghrib. *Cf.* mijwiz (75 I).

Mār (Pahl.), oboe of ancient Persia (75 II).

Marābba, see: murabba.

Maraca, 1. gourd rattle, originally of the S. American Indians, piriform, with a natural handle, filled with dried seeds or pebbles; or an imitation thereof in wood, clay, bakelite, etc., filled with beads, shot, or other material, widely distributed in C. and S. America. In Brazil it is formed of 2 truncated cones soldered at the wide part; in Pernambuco it is also known as xere or adja. In Cuba the maraca is made of *guïra,* an oval gourd. Twin or even multiple maracas occur there, some shaped like dumbbells, others cruciform. The word itself is thought to be of pre-Columbian Araucano origin. Western rhythm bands have adopted the gourd-shaped variety for use when playing Latin-American dances; **2.** bone flute of Venezuelan Indians.

Among the numerous Amer. vars. of the word are: maracá, malaka, matraca, mbaraca (7, 105, 152, G. Friederici: *Amerikanisches Wörterbuch,* Hamburg, 1960).

Maraca de canasta (Sp.: wickerwork maraca), syn. of erikunde (152).

Maraca de muñeca (Sp.: wrist maraca), spherical maraca tied to the player's wrist by a strap, usually worn by a drummer or dancer (152).

Maradika, idiochord bamboo *tube zither of Sula Island, Indonesia (119).

Marapo, *bones of the Chwana of S. Africa, made of rib bones and probably of European origin (116).

Marawat, church bell of Ethiopia of fairly recent introduction (144).

Marbab [*rabāb], *spike fiddle of Gorong Island, Indonesia (112).

Marche, obs. Fr.: key (of a keyboard).

Marddala (Sans., Beng.), var. of mādalā (173).

Mare, side-blown wooden trumpet of the Lugbara of Uganda, cylindrical, with a spherical gourd, bearing the blowhole, attached to one end. Its function is to underline the beats of the drum (195).

Marientrompete, obs. Ger.: trumpet marine.

Marimba [?Bantu *imba,* song], **1.** xylophone of Africa, recorded in the Congo from the 17th c. on and still played there and in Angola by a number of peoples, including the Azande, Babunda, and Baluba. Each slab is provided with a gourd resonator. See also: madimba; **2.** in certain regions of the Congo River the name is applied to the sansa, as for example by the Bangalo. Buonanni in 1722 called the sansa *marimba de Cafri;* **3.** introduced to America possibly in pre-Columbian times (105) or by the slave trade (176), the xylophone of this name spread through C. and S. America. By now it has disappeared from Peru as well as Brazil, in which country it was still in use in the 19th c. In S. America it is now known only in Ecuador, and there to only the Cayapa and Colorado Indians. The Colorados believe their instr. to have come from Guatemala (oral communication from Colorado chief to author). In C. America it remains a pop. instr., specially in Nicaragua, Guatemala, Cuba, and Mexico. In Cuba, in addition to the traditional form, it is also made of metal. The Mexican marimba is also called

zapotecano; it assumes the large rectangular form of a frame on legs, 150–80 cm. (5–6 ft.) long, with a 5-oct. compass. Under each slab hangs an elongated oblong resonator of cedarwood with a mirliton device in the bottom. Four persons, each provided with 2 sticks, play it together; **4.** the name of a combination musical bow and scraper of the Busintana of N. Colombia, of African origin. One side of the bow is notched. The palm-fiber string is held between the player's lips, his mouth forming a resonator. The bow is scraped by a stick while a second stick bows the string; **5.** in Brazil marimba is also the syn. of the urucungo (musical bow); **6.** in Europe and N. America, the marimba is a large xylophone with resonators and a 4-oct. compass, C^0–c^3, made in the U.S. since *ca.* 1910 (7, 42, 105, 151, 170, 185).

Marimba-ché, syn. of arpa-ché.

Marimba gongs, a modern metallophone, actually a marimba (xylophone) with metal instead of wooden bars, fitted with resonators, similar to the glockenspiel (89).

Marimbao [Port. *berimbao*], name of the Jew's-harp in Brazil (7).

Marimbaphone, metallophone, marimba (xylophone) with metal bars, made by J. C. Deagan, Inc., of Chicago. Also called steel marimba.

Marimbula [*marimba*], **1.** Afro-Cuban sansa with a variable number of short lamellae on a large resonator provided with a soundhole, usually rectangular but also circular or scaphoid. *Ca.* 44 cm. (17 in.) long. See also: quisanche; **2.** according to Ortiz, a horn of Africa. *Cf.* malimba, 3 (152).

Marine-shell trumpet (Fr.: *conque-trompette;* Ger.: *Muschelhorn;* Sp.: *caracola*), marine shell, often a conch, blown as a trumpet. Originally used as a voice distorter, it has served as a signal instr. since ancient times. It may be end-blown, in which case a hole is pierced at the tip, or side-blown, in which case one is pierced in the *spira.* The end-blown form is the older of the 2, side-blown shells not having been used until the end of the pre-Christian era. In some regions a mouthpiece is fitted to the tip, in others the shell is carved or otherwise ornamented with metal bands, semiprecious stones, etc. Distribution of the marine-shell trumpet is world-wide. Also called conch-shell trumpet, a misnomer, as many trumpets in this category are not made of conch. See also: akora, ananta vijaya, anjombona, ankárana, ankóra, antsiva, antsiva láhy, antsiva váry, arrain-beharri, atecocolli, atvur, bakora, bakura, barátaka, beabobo, botuto, bragna, buyong, cai ken loa, cai tu loa, caracola, chil-chil, cobo, cochlos, dung-dkar, ehecacozcatl, fotuto, go-mukka, guamo, hai lo, hayllaquepa, hora, ka ea-ea, kakara, kemin, kharunhãmon-lim, khum-muhra, kubar, lo tse, maromena, maromogny, milarchy, mir sang, ndavni, ntuantuangi, phusana ochulu, poti-poti, pu hau re roa, puhoho, pühuri, pu moana, pupakapaka, pu tara, pu tatara, putoto, queng, quepa, quipa, quiquiztli, rapakai, sankh, sanko, shanka, sora, su-ghosha, tahur, tau, taule, taure, tawi, tawul, tecciztli, tepuzquiquiztli, ugun (168).

Marine trumpet, see: trumpet marine.

Maringa, 1. *arched harp of the Azande of the Congo; **2.** sansa of the same people (42, 128).

Marionetta, Tinctoris (ca. 1490) says that this is another word for *rebec. It occurs occasionally in Fr. literature, mentioned as a stringed instr. (53).

Mariouneto, N. Prov.: toy whistle (53).

Mariri, syn. of jurusian (149).

Marmotine [Fr. marmot, small child], a small harmonium intended for children, patented by Debras in France in 1859 (204).

Maromena, syn. of beabobo.

Maromogny, ritual *marine-shell trumpet of the Maintirano region of the Malagasy Republic, with lateral mouthpiece (171).

Maroto, *friction drum of the Mamvu and Mambutu of Uele district, the Congo,

consisting of a cylinder of sticks or arrows over which a skin is stretched. The player holds fresh grass in his hands while rubbing the friction cord. Women are not permitted to see it, under penalty of stillbirth. It accompanies ritual dances. Also called najoroto (132).

Marovany, syn. of valiha.

Marszalka, obs. folk instr. of Poland, made of a small, forked branch with a ribbon and metal jingles. Formerly used at wedding celebrations (89).

Marszelnik, syn. of marszalka.

Martello, It.: hammer.

Martelo, Port.: hammer.

Martenot waves, see: ondes Martenot.

Martinophone, improved clarinet of Martin frères of Paris, patented on July 8, 1898 (204).

Martintrompete, see: Schalmei, 2.

Maruga, Afro-Cuban *vessel rattle made in a variety of shapes, often consisting of a gourd filled with hard objects. Cf. bordón (152).

Marvas, small drum of Sumatra, with 2 laced heads. It corresponds to the ketipung of Java (122).

Maryna, largest of the Pol. bowed folk instrs., a bass with a body having straight sides and sound slits, a spike, 3 lateral pegs, surmounted by metal jingles strung on a wire. The 3 strings are tuned in 4ths. During performance the maryna is tapped against the floor by its spike, causing the jingles to rattle. Nearly 2 m. (6½ ft.) long (89).

Masacalla, maraca of Argentina, made of maté gourd (152).

Masaka, *vessel rattle of Upper Sankuru, the Congo, made of split rattan in basket form, with a handle of twisted fiber and calabash bottom; filled with palm husks or nut husks. Cf. kitsatsa (185).

Masaké, *footed drum of the Bangala of the Congo, with head of antelope skin held by wooden pegs. Ca. 70 cm. (28 in.) high (42).

Masamba (Lesbian woman), Cuban Creole corr. of maraca (152).

Maschinenpauke, Ger.: machine drum.

Maseke, footed *cylindrical drum of the Bangala and Banza of the Congo, with nailed head (30).

Mashak (Hindust.: skin bag), mouth-blown bagpipe of N. India, played either melodically or as a drone. Its single chanter has up to 7 fingerholes that are plugged as required, and a single reed. At present it is being supplanted by the Highland bagpipe. Its S. India equivalent is the sruti upāngi. Cf. nāgabaddha (13).

Mashroqītā [Heb. *sharaq,* to whistle], wind instr. of Babylon and ancient Israel of the biblical era, considered to have been a double oboe or panpipes. See also: sharqoqitha (170).

Mashūra (Arab.: enchanted), *double clarinet of modern Egypt, smaller than the zummāra, with 4 fingerholes on each pipe and downcut reeds. Also, a double clarinet of ancient Syria (89 Farmer, 96).

Masonquo, *bowl lyre of Ethiopia, with circular, hollow body, leather belly, and symmetrical arms united at the top by a crossbar. The 6 strings are stretched over a bridge and secured by tuning rings. The left hand stops the strings as required, while the right hand plucks all 6 strings at once. Said in Ethiopia to have been the harp of King David. Called kirar or kidrar in Shoa Province (45).

Massaneqo, bowed instr. of Ethiopia, a degeneration of the rabāba, with square body, stick neck, single string attached to a rear peg long enough to raise it off the neck (144).

Massunda, *musical bow of the Rongo of the Lower Congo, similar to the nxonxoro. It serves simultaneously as scraper (185).

Mástil, Sp.: fingerboard.

Mat, generic term in ancient Egypt for flutes and reed instrs., also transcribed as ma', mait, met. The flutes were of cane or metal, 90–100 cm. (3 ft.) long, ca. 1¼ cm. wide, with 2–6 fingerholes at the lower end, end-blown, without mouthpiece. Flutes dating from the Middle Kingdom have been excavated, with wide

bores, fingerholes spaced far apart. The oboes were shorter, ca. 60 cm. (2 ft.) long, of cane, with a slightly narrower bore than that of the flutes, and were always played in pairs. The left pipe was a drone, the right, a melody pipe. The number of fingerholes was variable (144 Hickmann, 170).

Matabo, signal trumpet of the Caribs of Moruca and the upper Pomeroon River, British Guiana; it corresponds to the horesemoi (105).

Matahu, bull-roarer of the Nahuqua Indians of C. Brazil (176).

Matalam, Tamil equivalent of mādalā (173).

Matali, *frame drum of Uganda, of Arabic origin, with single head of sheepskin or goatskin (195).

Matapu, bull-roarer of the Mehinaku Indians of C. Brazil (176).

Mathlo, leg rattles of the S. African Chwana, worn by male dancers, made of moth cocoons containing small pebbles, etc., strung on long cords (116).

Mathotse, rattle of the Thebaina district of N. Transvaal, similar to the njele (116).

Matraca [vulg. Arab. *matrāqa,* hammer] (Sp., Port.), **1.** large *cog rattle of up to 2 m. (6½ ft.) in diam., with hammers that hit against wooden boards when the wheel is rotated, formerly used in Port., Sp., and Mexican churches during Easter week to call worshipers to prayer. In the Philippine Islands the matraca is used to frighten off locusts from fields under cultivation. The word *matraca* has been used since 1570; in 1591 Percivale defined it as a "rattle or toy for a child"; **2.** var. of maraca. See also: matraqueta (44).

Matraco, Sp.: large cattle bell.

Matraqueta [dim. of *matraca*], rattle consisting of a wooden board with a handle to which 4 small mallets are attached. When shaken, they strike against the board. The matraqueta served as a semanterion in Spain (132).

Matsumushi, small hitotsu gane (135).

Mattauphone, *musical glasses devised by Joseph Mattau, a Brussels dancing master, in or by 1855. Mattau became a virtuoso on the instr. It consisted of 38 graduated, tuned glasses set in a rectangular box and played with moistened fingers. The tuning was adjusted by varying the amount of water (132, 169).

Matumba, pl. of ditumba.

Matungo, syn. of urucungo.

Matutu, obs. funeral drum of the Bakongo of the Congo (30).

Maultrommel, Ger.: Jew's-harp. The word is first recorded in the 1582 translation of Rabelais's *Gargantua* (117).

Maultrumpe, 17th-c. Ger.: Jew's-harp (117).

Maung saing, gong chime of Burma, consisting of 12 gongs suspended in frames (103).

Maussil, syn. of argūl as-sogaija (144).

Mausul (Arab.: joined), obs. *double pipe of Egypt, first mentioned in the 13th c. (89 Farmer).

Mavonda (Kikongo), syn. of makwanga (185).

Mawahellis, half-tube zither of California Indians, with single string attached to a tuning peg (17).

Māwāloti, syn. of nissan (68).

Mawu, mawuwi, *musical bow of the Yokut Indians of N. America. The player's mouth acts as a resonator (105).

May-horn, syn. of whithorn.

Mayohuacan, slit drum of the Antillean Indians, also called bayohabao (152).

Mayurī (Sans.: peacock), **1.** esrar of S. India, with a very elegant resonator in the shape of a peacock. Its body and neck are painted; the bird's long tail forms the neck of the instr. During performance the neck is held against the player's shoulder while the peacock's legs remain on the ground, a table, etc. Like the esrar, the mayurī is bowed. Its N. India name is bālasarasvati. Also called peacock sitar; **2.** a mayurī is mentioned in India ca. 500 A.C., but it was probably not the same instr. (170, 179).

Mazāmīr, pl. of mizmār.

Mazanki, small bowed chordophone of Poland, with violin-like body but having sloping shoulders, very elongated FF, highly arched back, shallow ribs, 3 strings tuned in 5ths and held by lateral pegs (89).

Mazhar [*?mizhar*], *frame drum of Egypt and Turkey, furnished with jingles but no snares; circular, ca. 45 cm. (18 in.) in diam. (98, 170).

Mazin, Jew's-harp of the Naga of Assam, of bamboo, in form of an elongated rectangle, ca. 10 cm. (4 in.) long (172).

Mazoko, syn. of nzau.

Mazu, see: mansu.

Mbabi, drum of the Abangba of the Congo (30).

M'bagga, arched harp of the Bobango of the Congo, terminating in a sculptured head (42).

Mbamba nsia, antelope-horn whistle of the Bembe of the Congo, ca. 11 cm. (7 in.) long (185).

Mbambi (Kikongo), whistle of the Congo people, made of the horn of the gazelle, *nsia,* or *nsuma.* The word also designates wooden whistles or flutes (185).

Mbana, side-blown horn of the Mangbetu of the Congo, made of marsh antelope horn. Also called mbema (19).

Mban-akum, mirliton of the Fang of W. Africa, made of a wooden box. Also called endong-akum (176).

Mbande, var. of imbande.

Mbandu, Kikongo: small drum.

Mbanju, psaltery of the Aruwimi River area of Africa (176).

Mbaraca, name of the maraca among the Guaraní Indians of S. America (152).

Mbasa, 1. *vertical flute of the São Salvador region of Angola, with conical bore. Devoid of fingerholes, it yields only one tone and is used in the hunt; **2.** xylophone of the Banziri of the Congo (19, 185).

Mbe'i, 1. *cross flute of New Guinea, always played in pairs of unequal size.

The longer one is considered male, the shorter one, female; **2.** single-headed drum of the Fan of W. Africa, with wedge tensioning (77, 176).

Mbema, syn. of mbana.

M'bia, large horn of the Banda of Africa, hollowed out of a tree trunk or large branch, and used during *ganza* dances. Also called uzo (42).

Mbichi, name given by the Bangala of the Congo to the sansa (42).

Mbila, 1. simple xylophone of the Basonge of the Congo, with single hardwood slab mounted over a calabash and played with a rubber-padded stick. *Cf.* didimbadimba (31); **2.** xylophone of the Venda and Tshopi of S. Africa. The Tshopi instr. is the smaller and is frequently carried suspended from the player's neck. The larger one, of the Venda, has an average of 22 slabs and is set on the ground. The mbila has resonator gourds with spider-web membrane covering a small hole bored in each one, a mirliton device. The slabs are of different sizes and are arranged in a frame. That of the Tshopi is also called muhambi; **3.** syn. of deze in Rhodesia; **4.** xylophone of the Karanga of Ethiopia; *cf.* ambira. See also: imbila (116).

Mbili, Mendi (a Mandingo language): wooden drum (93).

'Mbilta, *end-blown flute of Ethiopia, made of metal, without fingerholes. It is played in sets of 3, at dances, sometimes accompanied by drums and the cherewata. In the southern part of the country they are frequently made of wood (45).

Mbindu, double-headed drum of the Lower Congo, similar to the tutila but narrower. Used chiefly for accompanying dances. *Cf.* bindi (185).

Mbira, name of the sansa among all Bantu-speaking peoples (108).

Mbiri [*mbili*], syn. of mbili in Gband and Mendi (Sudanic languages) (93).

Mbitu-uvu, syn. of bitu-uvu.

Mbizi, wooden clapper of the Zaramo of E. Tanganyika (176).

Mbobila, a W. African name of the sansa (185).

Mbombu, large bell of the Bobati of C. Africa, without clapper but with a handle, and struck with a wooden stick. Primarily a symbol of power, it also serves as signal and domestic instr. *Ca.* 60 cm. (2 ft.) high. Also called pivora (132).

Mbonda, 1. syn. of ta ngo among the Ngbandi of the Congo; **2.** large drum of the Mbole, Bosaka, Gombe, and Bahutu of the Congo. Among the Gombe it is a dance drum with a nailed head (30).

Mbonga, metal bell soldered along the sides, distributed throughout Equatorial Africa (19).

Mbott, *mouth organ of Cambodia, with bamboo pipes containing free reeds, placed in a small gourd that acts as a wind chamber, its curved neck as a blowpipe. See also: sheng (173).

Mbrunau, nose flute of the Admiralty Islands, Melanesia (203).

Mbudikidi, medium-sized slit drum of W. Africa (185).

Mbugi, pellet-bell anklet rattle of the Washambala of Kenya, made of iron and containing iron pellets. A number of these, up to 2½ cm. (1 in.) in size, are strung on a strip of goat leather and are worn by male dancers. Also used for ritual purposes at death ceremonies (111).

Mbuki, small drum of Balunda and Batshoko sorcerers of the Congo. *Ca.* 30 cm. (12 in.) high (30).

Mbutu, 1. mushroom-shaped drum of the Ganda of Uganda, with nailed head; **2.** sansa of the Efik of Nigeria, with cane lamellae, about 30 cm. (12 in.) long and 15 cm. (6 in.) wide (42; Charles Partridge, *Cross River Natives,* London, 1905).

Me, syn. of mi.

Mechanical . . . , see name of instr. in question. See also: automatophone.

Mechawa, bellows-blown bagpipes of the Wend (13, 169).

Media ala (Lat.: half wing), defined

as a semitriangular psaltery by Paulus Paulirinus (*ca.* 1460), held horizontally, the same as medius canon, a half psaltery; probably half a symmetrical trapezoid with incurved sides.

Medicinale [Lat. *medius,* half + ***canon**], med. Fr., Ger., Lat. for a small, *i.e.,* half, psaltery.

Medilen, see: madilan.

Medio caño [Arab. ***qānūn**], med. Sp. name of a small, *i.e.,* half, psaltery. *Cf.* caño, meo canno.

Médiophone, upright harmonium made by Dumont & Lelièvre in 1889 (204).

Medius canon [Arab. ***qānūn**], med. Lat. name of the small, *i.e.,* half, psaltery. *Cf.* canon.

Medzang, xylophone of the Pahouin and Bakele of Gabon, with 7 slabs resting on a bamboo frame, each slab with a bamboo resonator. See also: menzan, menzi (42).

Meerflaut, Meereswelle, Ger.: unda maris.

Me galo, bull-roarer of the Apinayé Indians of Brazil (105).

Megalopente [Gk. *megalo,* great + *pente,* five], large ***quint** organ stop at 10⅔' pitch (198).

Megalophone, ***acoustic** bass organ stop at 32' pitch (198).

Megan me bongo, idiochord ***musical** bow of the Fan of W. Africa, now a child's toy (176).

Mēgha, ***friction** drum of Benares, India, consisting of a small kettledrum with membrane and friction cord, now a child's toy (173).

Megyung, see: mi gyaun.

Meião, ***cylindrical** drum of Brazil, made of a hollowed-out tree trunk. The single head is secured by large wooden dowels. *Ca.* 70 cm. (28 in.) high (6).

Mekku-pukku (Akk.), see: pukku.

Meleketa, syn. of malakat.

Melkharmonika [U.], friction bar instr. of unknown 19th-c. authorship, consisting of a number of wooden or metal bars inserted upright in a base and tuned to the scale of C major. The bars, 8–18

in number, are rubbed with rosined gloves (91, 178).

Mellohorn, syn. of mellophone.

Mellophone, brass instr. designed as a substitute for the ***French** horn in marching bands, an althorn in circular form having the appearance of a French horn, pitched in E♭ and F, and generally made right-handed. Also known as ballad horn, concert horn, mellohorn. Called tenor cor in England. Not to be confused with melophone.

Melochord, see: Bode melochord.

Mélocor, ***music** box patented by Monterrubio of Paris in 1879 (204).

Melodeon, 1. an early name of the ***American** organ, particularly for those models having a horizontal case on legs (rather than the vertical, harmonium type). Not to be confused with melodion; **2.** see: rocking melodion.

Melodia, organ stop of wide-scaled wooden flue pipes of soft intonation, at 8' or 4' pitch, found chiefly in early-20th-c. American and British organs. At 16' pitch it is known as ***double melodia** (131).

Melodic . . . , prefix to names of organ stops indicating that they speak on a melody attachment. This silences all notes played except the highest one (198).

Melodica, 1. 20th-c. successor to the Psallmelodikon, manufactured by Hohner of Trossingen. A ***mouth** organ with a rectangular body held like a recorder, encasing free reeds and terminating in a detachable, beaked plastic mouthpiece. The upper surface carries 2 octs. of push keys disposed like piano keys, the diatonic keys being played with the right hand, the chromatic with the left. Made from 1959 on in soprano and alto sizes, with a 2-oct. compass; **2.** organ stop identical with the melodia. Not to be confused with Melodika.

Melodichord, not a musical instr. but a device to facilitate reading psalmodicon notation.

Melodicon, see: Melodikon.

Melodicon with drums, piano with

chromatically tuned tambourines, patented by Nunns & Fischer of New York in 1847. The keys were connected by rods to a second set of hammers under the piano which struck the drums. Piano and drums sounded simultaneously (92).
Melodic symphonium, see: symphonium mélodique.
Melodika, 1. pipe organ in form of a small grand-piano case, some 3½ ft. long, invented by Johann Andreas Stein of Augsburg in 1772, intended for melody playing only. It has a single stop of flue pipes and a compass g^0–c^4. When it was set on a piano, the performer could play the bass on the piano with his left hand. The pipes were arranged horizontally. A feature of the Melodika was the volume control obtained by means of touch; **2.** aeoline invented by Wilhelm Vollmer & Son of Berlin in 1820 (27, 184).
Melodikon, *friction bar "piano" invented *ca.* 1800 by P. Riffelsen of Copenhagen. By depressing a key the corresponding tuning fork was brought in contact with a rotating steel cone. Its lowest tone was c^0 (176).
Melodina, harmonium invented by J.-L.-N. Fourneaux, *jeune,* and Lazard, music teacher, of Paris, and patented on Mar. 26, 1855 (204).
Melodion, friction-bar keyboard instr. invented by Johann Christian Dietz, Sr., then of Emmerich, in 1805, similar to the Melodikon—an imitation of Chladny's euphone. It had curved metal bars sounded by contact with a rotating metal cylinder. Compass F^1–c^4. *Ca.* 120 by 60 cm. (4 by 2 ft.). Not to be confused with melodeon (169).
Mélodi-orgue, small harmonium with improved bellows, patented in France on Apr. 10, 1860. An Engl. patent was taken out by William Edward Gedge on Mar. 14, 1861 (204).
Melodium, 1. very small portable harmonium made from 1844 on; **2.** an early name of the *American organ; **3.** monophonic *electrophonic instr. of the electronic type, developed by H. Bod and

O. Vierling of Berlin *ca.* 1940, controlled from a keyboard (W. Meyer-Eppler, *Elektrische Klangerzeugung,* Bonn, 1949).
Melodium-organ, see: orgue-mélodium.
Mélodore, *alto clarinet made by Coste of Paris in 1847, with upturned brass bell (126, 204).
Melody saxophone, U.S. designation of the tenor saxophone in C.
Mélographe, device invented by J. Carpentier in the late 19th c. for recording music on perforated paper strips by electromagnetic means. See also: ludo, mélotrope (37).
Meloni-cor, horn devised by Meloni, an It. pianist, patented in France on Oct. 14, 1853 (204).
Mélophilon [Gk. *melos,* song + *philein,* to love], harmonium with special bellows, patented by Piron of Paris on Aug. 31, 1846 (158).
Melophone, 1. false designation of the accordion; **2.** organ stop of cylindrical metal flue pipes of diapason scale at 8' or 4' pitch (133).
Mélophone, free-reed instr. invented by Lecler, a Parisian clockmaker, by 1837, in form of a large guitar or hurdy-gurdy. Bellows, housed in the body, were worked by pulling and pushing a metal handle called *archet* with the right hand. The broad neck was fitted with 7 or 8 rows of 12 button keys that were depressed by the player's left hand. It has the usual compass of B^0–e^4. In 1842 Lecler sold his inventor's rights to Pellerin and Brown of Paris. *Ca.* 80 cm. (32 in.) long. See also: melodic symphonium. Not to be confused with the mellophone (115, 132).
Melophone-zither, a combination of zither and harmonium invented by Burger of Budapest *ca.* 1900 (204).
Mélophonorgue, accordion patented by J.-B. Leterme of Paris on Oct. 23, 1854, with a tremolo register consisting of 2 ranks of reeds tuned slightly apart (204).
Melopiano, 1. piano invented by Caldara & Brossi of Turin in 1873, with a special device for sustaining sound by

means of quick repetition of small hammers; **2.** a similar instr., marketed by Henri Herz of Paris, the hammers being controlled by clockwork. *Cf.* armonipiano (149, 176).

Mélotétraphone [Gk. *melos*, song + *tetra*, four + *phone*, sound], a piano keyboard and mechanism adapted to a violoncello or viola, patented by Edmond de Vlaminck and Limonier on Dec. 12, 1892. The idea was subsequently revived by Egide Dansaert and Victor Mazel of Brussels, the instr. proper being called violoncelle-piano, alto-piano, and somewhat resembling a large *keyed monochord (149, 191).

Mélotrope, crank-driven device invented by J. Carpentier, patented Oct. 31, 1884, and later, for automatically playing a piano by means of perforated cardboard strips—a precursor of the pianola. For a list of similar devices see: pianola (132).

Membranophone [Gk. *membrana*, skin], instr. in which sound is produced by vibration of a stretched membrane, brought about by striking, friction, or sound waves (as in drum, friction drum, mirliton).

Memet, *double clarinet of ancient Egypt, first recorded *ca.* 2700 B.C. *Cf.* mat, zummāra (144 Hickmann).

Mena'anim (Heb.), rattle of ancient Israel, probably a form of sistrum. It served both secular and liturgical needs in biblical times (89, 170).

Mendzan, see: menzan.

Mengagl minge, bamboo *cross flute of Kurugu, NE. New Guinea, with burned-in blowhole and unadorned tube. Short specimens are called dingi golm, long ones, nerrembarre. Always played antiphonally in pairs, by men only. See also: dingi golm (202).

Menghi (frog), syn. of tavalaika.

Menschenstimme, a Ger. name of the vox humana (organ stop).

Mensur, Ger.: scale; bore.

Menuel, var. of moienel.

Menuier (Fr.), **1.** var. of moienel; **2.**

the word also occurs as an adjective in connection with cor, graile, etc., meaning of medium size.

Menza, 1. syn. of manja; **2.** xylophone of the African Dendi (42).

Menzan, xylophone of the Fang of W. Africa, usually with 10 slabs. See also: medzang, menzi (19).

Menzi, xylophone of the Abandja of the Congo. See also: medzang, menzan (19).

Meo canno [Arab. *qānūn*], med. Sp. name of a small, *i.e.,* half, psaltery. *Cf.* caño, medio caño.

Merdap [Arab. *rabāb*], name of the rabāb among the Batak of Sumatra (173).

Merline [Fr. *merle*, blackbird], *bird organ larger than a serinette, imitating the sound of blackbirds (37).

Merlotina [Fr. *mirliton*], Czech: mirliton.

Mero-mero, bull-roarer of W. Australia (176).

Meropa, pl. of moropa.

Meshin, a Ukrainian name of the bagpipe.

Mesi (Sum.), see: meze.

Mesigit, *barrel drum of S. Celebes, with single, laced head. Max. diam. 40 cm. (16 in.) (112).

Mesiltayim, see: metziltāyīm.

Mesnika, see: mišnice; mješnica.

Messingregal (Ger.: brass regal), obs. organ stop of regal pipes, with brass resonators.

Met, see: mat.

Metagofano, piano attachment invented by Abbé Gregorio Trentino of Venice in 1824, for sustaining piano tone, operated by a pedal (92).

Metal drum, a name formerly given to the kettle gong.

Metale, Basque: cowbell.

Metal harmonica, another name of the bell lyre.

Métallicorde à archet (Fr.: bowed metallicorde), large bowed guitar with metal strings patented by Aloysio in

France on June 28, 1873, said to have sounded like a violin (191, 204).

Metallino, glockenspiel with keyboard, invented by O. Major of Dresden, having a 3-oct. compass (176).

Metallophone (Ger.: *Stahlspiel, Stabspiel*), percussion instr. having a series of tuned metal bars, rather like a xylophone except for the material of which they are composed. In China such instrs. were known in the 7th c. A.C., in Indonesia by 900 A.C. In Europe they were first used as practice instrs. by carillon players until, in the 18th c., they became instrs. in their own right. (Sébastien de Brossard in 1703 refers to the carillon as being composed of pieces of metal.) Mustel's celesta and the tubular chimes are developments of the metallophone. See also: aluminophone, bellarmonic, bisak beton, celesta, chalybssonans, chelepita, 1, clavi-timbres, dempling, demung, demung gantung, fang hiang, forté-campano, gambang gangsa, gender, gender barung, gender panembung, gender panerus, gender wayang, glockenspiel, gong kemodong, istromento d'acciajo, kei, kelenton, kliningan, marimba gongs, marimbaphone, pang hiang, ranat lek, ranat thong ek, ranat thong thum, roneat dec, salundi, salunding wesi, saptaghantikā, saron, saron barung, etc.; saz-i alwah-i fūlad, slentem gandul, slentem gantung, staafspiel, Stabspiel, vibraharp, vibraphone (169).

Metal xylophone, name occasionally misapplied to various metallophones.

Métaphone, device patented by Victor Mustel and his sons, of Paris, on May 28, 1878, designed to soften the tone of the harmonium by means of a sliding leather shutter (89, 204).

Métraphone, tuning device with free reeds of Fourneaux of Paris (176).

Metziltāyīm [Heb. *salāl*, clash], ritual cymbals of ancient Israel, used in the Temple. Their use is recorded from *ca.* 1100 B.C. to *ca.* 400 B.C. Possibly they are identical with the selslīm (170).

Metzkanon [Arab. *qānūn*] (OHGer.),

med. Ger. name of the small, *i.e.,* half, psaltery. *Cf.* canale.

Mey [*nāy*], woodwind instr. of Erzerum and environs, Turkey (89).

Meydan saz, largest of the Anatolian saz, with 3 courses of strings (89).

Meze, Sum. equivalent of mansu. Also transcribed as mesi.

Mezonad, mouth-blown bagpipe of Tunis, with double chanter, each tube being pierced with 5 fingerholes, furnished with a single reed, and terminating in a horn bell. A snake charmer's instr. (141).

Mezzo canone [Arab. *qānūn*], med. It. name of the small, *i.e.,* half, psaltery. *Cf.* canone.

Mezzo colascione, the same as colasciontino.

Mfengwane, occasional name of the impempe, 2 (116).

Mfie-mfie, *end-blown flute of the Kinkenge region of Manianga, the Congo, used as hunting and signal instr. It yields 2 tones (185).

Mfuhlulu, term sometimes used by the Venda of S. Africa to designate horns similar to the tshihoho (116).

Mfukulu, var. of fukulu (30).

Mi, slit drum of the middle Sepik area, New Guinea. Also called me, miaba (77).

Miaba, syn. of mi.

Micanon [Arab. *qānūn*], med. Fr. name of a small, *i.e.,* half, psaltery. The term is recorded in Fr. literature from *ca.* 1275 to 1370. *Cf.* demi-canon.

Michaudière, bass drum patented by Michaud of Grenoble on Apr. 29, 1889 (204).

Midé, *cylindrical drum of the Ojibway Indians of N. America, wooden, with 2 heads of rawhide stretched while wet. Frequently water is poured into the bottom of the drum (105).

Midimba [*madimba*], xylophone of the Balunda and Kapansa of the Congo, identical with the madimba (31).

Mi gyaun (crocodile), wooden *tube zither of Burma and Assam, carved to represent a crocodile, with its tail serving as pegbox. The instr. is lacquered and

set on a lacquered stand; 3 metal strings
are held by lateral pegs; they pass over
8–11 raised, movable frets placed on the
flat belly. The player's left hand depresses
the strings while the right hand plucks
them with a plectrum. *Ca.* 110 cm. (43
in.) long. Also called mingas, patola. *Cf.*
chakhe, takhe (138, 172).

Mih, syn. of mišnice.

Mijwiz, double reedpipe of Israel and
Syria, equivalent of the maqrūn of the
Maghrib (75 I).

Mikropan, portable organ of Georg
Christian Knecht of Tübingen, 1803.
Knecht was a pupil of Abbé Vogler
(176).

Milacor, portable organ of Abbé La-
roque, *ca.* 1878 (204).

Milarchy, side-blown *marine-shell
trumpet of the Maintirano region of the
Malagasy Republic. *Cf.* maromogny
(171).

Militärtrommel, Ger.: snare drum.

Mina, drum of Venezuela (103).

Mīnā sārangī (Beng.: fish sārangī),
esrar of N. India, with fish-shaped body.
Ca. 125 cm. (50 in.) long (168).

Mingas, syn. of mi gyaun.

Minīm [pl. of *men*, hair], generic name
of stringed instrs. among the Hebrews of
biblical times (89).

Minkanda, var. of mukanda.

Minor . . . , prefix to names of organ
stops denoting 4′ pitch (133).

Min teki, *end-blown flute of Japan,
with 6 fingerholes. *Cf.* teki (176).

Mirdang, Hindust. equivalent of mridanga (173).

Mi re ut, obs. It.: short octave.

Mirliton (Fr.), an instrumental auxiliary rather than a musical instr., the
mirliton is a membranophone that modifies the sound of a voice or of an instr.
This is accomplished by directing the
voice against its membrane, and thereby
setting it in vibration, or by holding the
membrane against the throat, or by directing the vibrating air column from a
sounded instr. against it. In each case the
membrane's vibrations amplify and color

the tone with a buzzing nasal timbre.
The membrane may be free (free mirliton) as in the familiar comb covered
with tissue paper (depicted by Buonanni
in 1722), or may be affixed to an aperture in a tube or vessel (tube or vessel
mirlitons). It may be of parchment,
paper, onionskin, spider's-egg membrane,
or other material. Tube mirlitons have
been known in Europe since the 16th c.,
often made to resemble shawms, flutes,
etc., usually with parchment or onionskin
membranes. By the 19th c. the mirliton
had become a mere toy and is still occasionally met with as such. In India the
*nyastaranga represents a different form
of tube mirliton: its membrane is placed
against the throat chords of a humming
performer and thereby set in vibration.
This principle has been used by the recording industry in the U.S. in recent
times. In different parts of Asia flutes
are sometimes made with a lateral hole
covered by a membrane. In Africa a
number of xylophones have a spider's-
egg tissue glued over an aperture in the
resonators. See also: abeng, akasitori,
bazoo, bigophone, cantophone, chalumeau eunuque, Düderli, eggwara, eunuch
flute, Flatsche, flauto di voce, hewgag,
kazoo, konene, mban-akum, merlotina,
nyastaranga, onion flute, Strählorgeli,
varinette, zazah (168).

Mir sang, pl. **sanguna,** *marine-shell
trumpet of Persia and Afghanistan (176).

Miruli, syn. of entaala 2.

Misfaqa, singular of musāfiq.

Mišnice, mouth-blown bagpipe of Croatia, with double chanter but without
drone, actually a diplye with a bag. See
also: gajde, mješnica (89, 144).

Mita'v, *cylindrical drum of the Me-
nominee Indians of N. America, made of
a block of hollowed wood, narrowing toward the top, with permanent rawhide
bottom and with a head secured by an
iron hoop. Water is poured into the drum
before use. *Ca.* 40 cm. (16 in.) high
(105).

Mithqāl [*mūsīqāl*], Turk. name of the mūsīqāl (147 Farmer).

Mitig'wakik (wooden kettle), *cylindrical drum of the Chippewa Indians of the U.S., used in ceremonies of their Midiwirvin society, made of a hollowed log of basswood *ca.* 40 cm. (16 in.) long, with single head of tanned deerskin stretched over a hoop. A thin wooden disc forms the bottom. Part of the way up the cylinder a hole is drilled and stopped with a wooden plug. A few inches of water are poured into the drum through this hole, allegedly causing it to be heard at great distances while not seeming loud close by. Played with a curved stick. *Cf.* mita'v (49).

Mitote, musical bow of the Cora of Mexico, with gourd resonator.

Mittelhorn (Ger.), medium-sized Hiefhorn, equivalent to the Fr. moienel.

Mittenwald zither, Ger. folk zither with a circular projection on each side of the lower end of the body, but retaining frets and fingerboard. Several vars. of this shape exist. The Mittenwald zither originated in the 1830's and was presumably created or made in Mittenwald, Bavaria.

Miurabi, according to Farmer, a word erroneously used to designate an early Arab. instr. (75 II).

Mixtur [Lat. *mixtura*] (Ger.), see: mixture stop.

Mixtura aetherea, see: harmonia aetherea.

Mixture stop (Fr.: *jeu composé;* Ger.: *Mixtur, gemischte Stimme*), compound organ stop having more than one pipe to a key, the fundamental plus one or more of its harmonics, controlled by one drawstop. The tonal position of a mixture stop is indicated by the length in feet of the biggest pipe on the C⁰ key. In describing a mixture it is usual to indicate the number of ranks (133).

Mixturtrautonium, *electrophonic instr. of the electroacoustical type, derived from the Trautonium and developed by Oskar Sala of Berlin. The tone is generated

from a spun gut string and is controlled by 2 keyboards.

Mi'zaf, pl. **ma'azif** (Arab.), Arab. instr. mentioned in literary sources from the 8th to 10th c. as a chordophone. Nowadays it designates a kettledrum. *Cf.* mizhar (98, 147 Farmer).

Mizhar (Arab.), instr. of the pre-Islamic and Islamic Near East, glossed in the 10th c. as tympanum and considered to have been a frame drum, preserved under the modern name of mazhar (75 II, 170).

Mizmār, pl. **mazāmīr** (Arab.), classical Arab. name of the shawm, corresponding to the Pers. surnā (170).

Mizmār al-muthannā, Arab.: double mizmār (75 I).

Mizmār al-muzawwaj, Arab.: double mizmār (75 I).

Mizmār dūduyī, obs. panpipes of the Turks (76).

Mizungu, pl. of mzungu.

Mjedenica, Yugo. campaniform cattle bell, made of brass (176).

Mješnica [*mijeh,* bellows], mouthblown bagpipe of Dalmatia, with double chanter furnished with a single reed. The left pipe has 6 fingerholes, the right pipe 2 or 3. In a larger sense the word is used as a syn. of diplye. See also: mišnice (34, 132).

Mjolo, crescent-shaped *pellet bells of the Washambala of Tanganyika, of iron or copper, made into bracelets and anklets (111).

Mkinda, *cylindrical drum of the Washambala of Tanganyika, made of roughhewn wood, up to 1 m. (40 in.) long, with 2 heads stretched over hoops and held by V-lacings. It is suspended from the player's neck and beaten with both hands when it accompanies dances, but for ritual playing it is held in the lap (111).

Mmanga, elongated herd-animal bell of the Washambala of Tanganyika, made of one long piece of metal, bent back on itself, the sides not being closed, and furnished with a single clapper (111).

Mna'anim, see: mena'anim.

Mo, see: cai mo.

Mo ca, see: cai mo ca.

Mochanga, see: muchanga.

Mock trumpet, early Engl. name for the chalumeau, 4, or early clarinet. The earliest tutor for the mock trumpet was printed in London in 1698. Not a *trumpet marine, as formerly believed. See: Dart, in 80, VI.

Modeku, sansa of the Azande of the Congo (132).

Modimba, zoomorphic, cuneiform slit drum of the Basonge of the Congo (19).

Modjoko, footed drum of the Gombe of the Congo, similar to the bonda, 2 (30).

Mohea, mouhaia, gourd rattle of the Malagasy Republic (171).

Mohori (Khandra), small oboe of S. India with 7 fingerholes. Ca. 25 cm. (10 in.) long (173).

Moienel, manuel, menuel, or **menuier,** term used from the 12th to the 14th c. in France to designate a medium-sized hunting horn. It corresponded to the Ger. Mittelhorn.

Mokita, 1. *footed drum of the Mongo of the Congo, cylindrical, with nailed head and large monoxylous handle. Ca. 60 cm. (2 ft.) long; **2.** the chief's drum of the Doko of the Congo, inherited from his father or predecessor; formerly a war drum among the Gombe (30).

Mokkin, xylophone of Japan, with 13–16 slabs laid over a trough, played with 2 small wooden mallets. A rhythm rather than a melody instr. Used chiefly in *kabuki* music (135, 157).

Mo ko, Korean equivalent of the Jap. mo kugyo and Chin. mu yü, in shape of a fish, struck with a knobbed stick; 1–2 m. (40–80 in.) long. See: mu yü for details (66).

Mokoreie, *end-blown flute of the Bangwaketse of Kanye, Bechuanaland, made of cane; equivalent of the lekolilo (116).

Mok that, hollow gong of Korea, made of wood, in form of a flat bell, struck

with sticks. Played in temples and by mendicant priests (66).

Mo kugyo (Jap.: wooden fish), ritual *slit drum of Buddhist Japan, formerly shaped like a fish with its tail in its mouth, nowadays like a bird. Equivalent of the Chin. mu yü and Korean mo ko. See: mu yü (157).

Molli-pill, Estonian: monochord.

Molo, sansa of the Mbum of the Congo, of Hausa origin (19).

Molossos, instr. of ancient Greece, so far unidentified (144).

Mombye, cylindrical *footed drum of the Bateke of Mbe, the Congo, painted and carved, its goatskin head being secured by wooden pegs (30).

Mo ña chua, see: cai mo ña chua.

Monacorde, see: monochord.

Monaulos, (Gk.), late type of aulos played in Ptolemaic Egypt, a single pipe fingered with both hands and provided with fingerholes similar to those of double pipes, *i.e.,* twice 4 fingerholes and 2 rear thumbholes. Surviving specimens have 2 groups of 4 fingerholes separated by 1 thumbhole, the other being below the top fingerhole (14).

Mondo, name given to the slit drum from São Salvador, Angola, to Lake Tanganyika (185).

Mondtrom (mouth trump), Du.: Jew's-harp.

Moneche, var. of morache, 1.

Mong, 1. medium-sized gong of Thailand, with central boss, of indefinite pitch. Suspended from a tripod stand and struck with padded beaters. Ca. 35 cm. (14 in.) in diam.; **2.** *gong chime of Shan State, Burma, composed of 6 gongs with small center bosses and turned rims. Diams. are 11–48 cm. (4–19 in.) (65, 172).

Mongele, stick zither of the Saka of the Congo (128).

Mongenda, double drum of the Bosaka of the Congo, made of either 2 drums tied together or a single block of wood (30).

Monggang, bonang of E. Java with a

1-oct. compass, composed of a single row of very large bonang kettles. They are left unpolished and thus have a very dark tone color. Also called bonggang (121).

Mongondo, *slit drum of the Modjombo of Donga, the Congo, played together with a jomo during dances (30).

Mongungu, 1. *cylindrical drum of the Bakumu of Stanleyville district, the Congo, with single head nailed with wooden dowels; **2.** cylindrical *slit drum of the Bapopoie of the Congo, with simple longitudinal slit (19, 30).

Monicordis, obs. var. of monochord, denoting the clavichord.

Monkela, drum of the Balesa-Basakata of the Congo, reserved for the use of members of the reigning clan and used only under solemn circumstances (30).

Monkita, drum of the Balesa-Basakata of the Congo, with laced head. Only local chiefs are permitted to possess one (30).

Monochord [Gk. *monos,* single + *chorde,* string] (Fr.: *monocorde;* Ger.: *Monochord, Einsaiter;* It.: *monocordo*), device first used in antiquity for the measuring and theoretical demonstration of musical intervals, later a musical instr. in its own right, finally an organ tuner's and piano tuner's adjunct. In its earliest form the monochord was an elongated rectangular box with a single string stretched across the calibrated upper surface. Used in Greece as a theoretical and testing device since the 6th c. B.C. and possibly earlier, it became known to med. musicians and theorists through the writings of Boethius (*ca.* 500 A.C.), and treatises on monochord ratios began to appear in the 10th c. From numerous depictions it is clear that a movable bridge was added, of the same height as the 2 semicircular nuts placed at each end. The bridge could be shifted to any position desired, the string being held down firmly against the top of the bridge by one hand while the other plucked it, usually with a plectrum (in practice it is very difficult to get a clear tone by this means). This then was the instr. used to demonstrate mathematical divisions of the scale and as an adjunct in the teaching of solmization. From being a piece of musical equipment the monochord became a musical instr.; this transformation was at first purely one of function, not of structure, and took place by the late 11th c. Pictorial and literary evidence points to the single-string apparatus (without keys) having been used as a plucked musical instr. at that time. Wace's *Roman de Brut* (12th c.) enumerates "symphonies, psalterions, monachordes," and Guiraut de Calanson (13th c.) lists the *"manicorda una corda"* among other instrs. The polychord "monochords" mentioned by med. theorists fall into 2 groups: 1) monochords with a few strings—Johannes de Muris appears to have suggested four in the 14th c. (but see: clavichord); 2) clavichords with strings all of the same length, still called by the older name. The former would have continued to serve for demonstrations of intervals and chords. As a musical instr., the monochord lived on into the 15th c.: it is so mentioned in the *Echecs amoureux, ca.* 1375, for example, and in 1404 Eberhard Cersne lists it in an enumeration of the instrs. of his day (he mentions the clavichord separately), and Paulus Paulirinus describes it (*ca.* 1460) as a musical instr. with one gut string stretched over a hollow body and plucked *cum penna aut ligno,* with quill or stick. In the 16th c. the term is often applied to the *trumpet marine. But the role in which it lived longest was that of organ tuner's accessory. The organ literature of the baroque contains many detailed references to it: on arriving at the church the tuner, accompanied by an apprentice who carried the monochord, would proceed to tune the monochord to a trumpet brought along for that purpose (a fixed-pitch instr.), and then to tune the organ to the monochord. Whatever its deficiencies may have been, the 18th c. still held it to be vastly superior to the human ear for tuning purposes, and monochords were still manufactured in Paris as a tuner's tools in the 1820's (see: chromamètre). Also called: harmonic canon, regula harmonica. See also: chuen.

Monocorde, Fr.: **1.** monochord; **2.** clavichord. See also: manicorde, manicordion.

Monocorde à clavier, Fr.: keyed monochord.

Monocordio, Port., Sp.: clavichord.

Monocordo, It.: monochord.

Montre [Lat. *monstrare,* to show] (Fr.), the front, or show, pipes of the classical Fr. organ, cylindrical flue pipes of 32', 16', or 8' pitch. At 4' pitch the stop is called préstant. The montre corresponds to the principal elsewhere (62).

Mon yi (Chin.: wooden fish), syn. of mu yü.

Monzo, side-blown horn of the Wasongola and the Tofoke of the Congo, made of buffalo horn (42).

Moorish guitar, see: guitarra morisca.

Moór piano, see: Emanuel Moór piano.

Moose call, single-reed wind instr. of the Chippewa Indians of N. America, consisting of a short wooden tube separable into 2 sections. A pointed reed of thin bone or horn, less often of birch bark, is affixed to the inside of the instr.

Mora, name of the sānāyī among the Muria of Bastar, India (68).

Morache [Sp. *morisca,* Moorish], **1.** OFr. term for the guitarra morisca; **2.** scraper of the Ute Indians of the U.S., consisting of a notched stick placed on a resonator and scraped with a stick of wood or bone. The resonator was formerly a basket set on the ground, now it is a piece of zinc. The same instr. is used by the Pima Indians as a rhythmical accompaniment to ceremonial songs, and plays a very important part in their rain ceremonies. The Sp. name has become established by usage (50).

Morengy, drum of the Malagasy Republic, played during the morengy dances (172).

Morenne, Fr. 14th-c. syn. of sonnette, a small pellet bell (85).

Mörenpäuklein (Moor's drum), Praetorius' name for the tambourine. Note the implied reference to Spain in *cimbaletto.*

Morin khuur (horse's head), see: khilkhuur.

Moriuncar, *bull-roarer of Australia, elliptic in form, 25–48 cm. (10–19 in.) long. Cf. churinga jucla (176).

Morka, xylophone of the Sidamo of Ethiopia, with 6 or 7 slabs separated by wooden pegs. An instr. of field watchmen, played to help kill time (A. E. Jensen: *Im Lande des Gada,* Stuttgart, 1936).

Moropa, pl. **meropa, 1.** *conical drum of the Pedi of S. Africa, hollowed out of a block of wood, with 2 monoxylous handles and an open bottom. The membrane is stretched by pegs. It is played with bare hands by women; **2.** clay drum of the Sotho of Basutoland, with laced head. Cf. morupa (116).

Morothloane, ankle rattle of the Sotho of Basutoland. Pieces of goatskin are sewn into little bags containing a few pebbles that are then tied to leather bands and fastened to dancers' ankles (116).

Morshingu, Tamil equivalent of murchang (173).

Mortaise, Fr.: guide, lower guide.

Morupa, *friction drum of the Marutse and Masupia of Barotseland, N. Rhodesia, with a friction stick that is rubbed with a piece of wet baobab. Cf. moropa (116).

Moshug, var. of mashak.

Moshupiane, *friction drum of the Pedi of S. Africa, played in secret by old women. Made of wood, it is shaped like a bowl, being built of staves like a barrel, and has a goatskin membrane. The head is rubbed with a bundle of cornstalks (116). It is played by women during the initiation rites of young girls (185).

Moska, syn. of nāgasuram.

Moso biwa (Jap.: blind-priest biwa), small biwa of Japan that originated in Kyoto, with 5 very high frets and 4 strings (135).

Mossundro, cylindrical drum of the Malagasy Republic (171).

Mosu-gitarra (lip guitar), Basque: Jew's-harp. Also called musu-gitarra.

Motbel, OEngl.: bell for calling an assembly together.

Mothlatsa, flute of the Bakgatla of S. Africa, equivalent to the naka ya phatola (116).

Moti, drum of Sissano, New Guinea, equivalent to the oñ (28).

Motoa, stopped *end-blown flute of the Sotho doctors of S. Africa, made of a bird bone, only a few inches long (116).

Mots, clarinet of C. Celebes and Timor, equivalent of the pupui (173).

Moulinet [dim. of moulin, mill], Fr. 16th-c. term for a clapper in church towers, used during Easter week. The term is derived from the shape of its windmill-like wings fitted around an axle and struck by hammers as they turned (169).

Mountain zither, a name of the *Appalachian dulcimer.

Mounted cornet, organ stop formerly built in Britain, consisting of a *cornet, 4, mounted on a soundboard of its own a few ft. above the great organ, in order to save space and facilitate tuning (99).

Mouth bow, musical bow in which the player's mouth acts as a resonator.

Mouth harp, U.S. term for mouth organ.

Mouth organ (Fr.: harmonica à bouche; Ger.: Mundharmonika; It.: armonica a bocca), the modern Western mouth organ is a small *free-reed instr. consisting of a grooved rectangular metal box on which free reeds are mounted, played by moving it back and forth in front of the player's mouth while breathing into it. The grooves lead from the reeds to apertures along one of the long sides. The player breathes into these, the wind supplied being either pressure or suction, depending on whether he in-

hales or exhales. Each groove leads to 2 reeds of the same pitch, one of which operates on pressure, the other on suction wind. Size and compass are not standardized. The scale is a diatonic one, and occasionally several instrs. may be combined to permit changes of tonality.

The principle of the free-reed mouth organ reached Europe from Asia in the late 18th c., and mouth organs were first made in the early 19th c. Many claims for its invention have been made. In 1821 Friedrich Buschmann of Berlin made an instr. for experimental purposes only, with 15 steel tongues blown through channels. During that year and the next he took out patents for early forms of mouth organs (see: Aura); in 1829 the manufacture of mouth organs started in Vienna. In the same year Charles Wheatstone of London patented his *symphonium, with single blowhole and key buttons. Later in the c. the slider stop was added, whereby the instr. could be switched to a second set of reeds tuned a semitone above the first. Hohner of Trossingen, Germany, has made mouth organs since 1857, and recently introduced the *Melodica, with single blowhole and piano-like keys.

The home of the mouth organ is Asia —Laos, according to Sachs, S. China, according to Norlind. It is recorded in China from 1100 B.C. on; it appears on the Borobudur temple carvings of ca. 800 A.C., and reached Persia in the 6th or 7th c. Eastern mouth organs consist of a number of pipes made of bamboo or other material, each provided with a free reed of metal or thin cane, arranged in the bowl of a gourd that serves as wind chamber, its natural neck as blowpipe; in more advanced types the gourd is replaced by a lacquered container. The reed responds to both pressure and suction wind, so that the player inhales and exhales while playing. The number of pipes varies considerably, some organs having but a couple, the classical *sheng having 17. For details see: Aura, ch'ao, cho, chubchiq, enkerurai, fong sheng, Fotzhobel, fulu, gorteh, ho, keluri, khen, kim, kladdi, kom boat, kuan tse, kyen, labu, mbott, mouth harp, Mundäoline, Mundharmonika, mushtaq sini, muzicuta, orglice, phan, phen, saing, sheng, sho, symphonium, Xylophon-Mundharmonika (15 Howarth, 117, 118, 151).

Mouthpiece (Fr.: *embouchure;* Ger.: *Mundstück;* It.: *bocchino;* Sp.: *boquilla*), that portion of a wind instr. that touches the player's mouth or is taken into it. See also: cup mouthpiece.

Mozsika [Lat. *musica*], rustic fiddle of the peasants and gypsies of Komitate Czík (Siebenbürgen), Hungary, with 4 strings tuned in 5ths (some specimens have a fifth drone string). Most players use only 3 fingers in stopping the strings. Another peculiarity of the playing technique is that the first position is not used at all. The peasants make their own instrs., but the gypsies buy theirs from a factory. The mozsika is played together with the *gardon (54).

Mozungu, name given by the Makere of the Congo to the kweningba (31).

Mpalampala, 1. var. of phalaphala; **2.** side-blown horn of the Swazi of S. Africa, made of kudu horn. *Cf.* shipalapala, upondo (116).

Mpandala, wooden horn of the Basonga of the Congo, side-blown, made in imitation of an ivory horn. The bell is wound with fiber (176).

Mpats'ibihugu, royal drum of Uganda (30).

Mpempe, var. of impempe.

Mpetshanga, syn. of mushits.

Mpolomono, side-blown trumpet of the Bembe of the Congo, made from a tree root or hollowed branch, with a square or rectangular embouchure. *Ca.* 90 cm. (3 ft.) long (185).

Mpovila za londe, small clapper bell made of the fruit husk of the *Borassus flabelliformis,* found in the Lower Congo. Also called ndingi (185).

Mpundshi [Kikongo *mpungi,* elephant tusk], ivory horn of Loango, Angola (185).

Mpungi (Kikongo), term used by the Bakongo people to designate horns in general, whether of wood, ivory, or antelope horn. Originally it must have designated the ivory horn only (185).

Mpungui [*mpungi*], obs. wind instr. of Cuba, probably a whistle, according to Ortiz (152).

Mridanga (Sans., Beng., Kan.) [Sans. *mrd,* clay], the classical drum of S. India, of elongated barrel shape with heads of different diams. Essentially the same as the *khol, from which it differs only in having a wooden body, despite its name. The shell is hollowed out of a block of wood; both heads are fastened to hoops and tightened by leather thongs laced from end to end. The heads are tuned by tension wedges and the application of tuning paste. The right head receives a permanent application of black tuning paste made of manganese dust, boiled rice, and tamarind juice, or of iron filings and boiled rice. A different paste is temporarily applied to the left head before playing, so as to tune it to the oct. below the right head. This paste is scraped off after performance. Generally the diam. of the left head is 1½ times that of the right. The mridanga is played with wrists and finger tips. The word goes back to *ca.* 400 B.C. *Cf.* khol, pakhawaj (179).

Msiltayim, see: metziltāyīm.

Msomari, oboe of the Washambala of Tanganyika, of foreign inspiration, made as either a conical or a cylindrical tube of wood, with 6 or 7 equidistant fingerholes, joined with resin to a calabash bell or a flared wooden bell. It is played with a wooden pirouette, metal staple, and double reed made of a folded leaf (111).

Mtangala, *musical bow of the Nyanja of N. Rhodesia, played by women only (176).

Mtorilo, syn. of mululi.

Muana, cylindrical drum of the Bakongo people, played during dances (185).

Muanza, *friction drum of the Wanika of E. Africa, made from a hollowed tree trunk, with friction thong rubbed with coconut fiber. *Ca.* 180 cm. (6 ft.) long (16).

Mubango, *percussion beam of the Ganda of Uganda, consisting of a beam some 175–200 cm. (70–78 in.) long, beaten with drumsticks close to its ends (195).

Mucaxixi, syn. of caxixi.

Muchanga, Beng. equivalent of murchang.

Mudidi, *goblet drum of the Bena-Lulua of Kasai, the Congo, with extremely short stem and nailed head. Some specimens have a small hole covered with a thin membrane, a mirliton device (30).

Mudji, bull-roarer of S. Australia, used during puberty rites (176).

Muérgano [Lat. *organum*], vulg. Sp. from the Golden Age to the 18th c.: musical instr. See also: uérgano (44).

Muga, syn. of gudalo.

Mughni [Pers. *mugnī*], broad-necked lute of Georgia, U.S.S.R. (170).

Mugnī (Pers.), obs. chordophone of Persia, described in a 14th-c. musical ms. (*Kanz al tufah*) as a combined rubāb-qānūn-nuzha, *i.e.*, a zither in lute form. It had a long, bulging body, flat, wide neck, and 39 open strings arranged as on the qānūn, passing over a diagonally placed bridge (170).

Muhambi, syn. of mbila, 2, among the Tshopi of S. Africa (116).

Mujegereza, rattle of the Bashi of Ruanda, made of hollowed-out dried fruits as large as an apple and containing hard seeds; 3 or 4 are impaled on a stick (139).

Mukaja, frame drum of Bengal (176).

Mukanda, 1. drum of the Babemba of the Congo, with 2 laced heads, played with sticks; 90–180 cm. (3–6 ft.) long; **2.** drum of Lake Bangweulu region, played during dances. *Ca.* 50 cm. (20 in.) long (30).

Mukavina, small nāgasuram of S. India, with very broad reed. Formerly used in dance music, it has now been replaced by the clarinet. It plays to the drone accompaniment of the sruti upāngi. *Ca.* 25 cm. (10 in.) long (179).

Mukko, rare *half-tube zither of the Ainu of Japan, with 5 strings, plucked with bare fingers. The mukko and mukkuri are the only musical instrs. that the Ainu possess; 130 cm. (51 in.) long (176).

Mukkuri, idioglott Jew's-harp of the Ainu of Japan, made of wood or bamboo, with a pointed tongue. Played by women only. *Ca.* 12 cm. (5 in.) long (135).

Mu ko, kettledrum of Korea that rests on a frame and is played by 2–4 persons. About 25 cm. (10 in.) high with a diam. of *ca.* 75 cm. (30 in.) (66).

Mukoko, name of the slit drum in the Lower Congo (185).

Mukonzi, 1. *slit drum of the Bembe of the Congo, played with 2 sticks. *Ca.* 90 cm. (3 ft.) long; **2.** drum of the Sundi of the Congo, almost cylindrical, with single nailed head. *Ca.* 160 cm. (5 ft. 4 in.) long (185).

Mukumbi, scraper of the Bwende of the Lower Congo, consisting of a wooden resonator similar to a slit drum, with one extremity carved to represent a head. A notched stick is laid on a piece of animal skin over the slit. This instr. was formerly also found among the Kuni. *Cf.* nkumbi, 2. *Ca.* 80 cm. (32 in.) long (185).

Mukupele, drum of the Balunda and Minungo of the Congo, equivalent to the mukupila (30).

Mukupila, *hourglass drum of the Bambala, Basuku, and Batshoko of the Congo, with 2 nailed heads, ornately carved and provided with monoxylous handles. A small lateral hole is drilled and covered by a thin membrane—a mirliton device; 40–50 cm. (16–20 in.) high. *Cf.* mukupele (30).

Mukwanga, calabash rattle of the Bakongo, Bembe and neighboring peoples of Africa, with natural neck serving as a handle, filled with seeds of *Canna indica,* used for magical and ritual functions. Also called kwangu, nkwanga (185).

Mulimba, cuneiform *slit drum of the Baluba-Hemba of the Congo, also called nkumoi (19).

Mulizi, *notched flute of the Bashi of Ruanda, made of cane, with 2 fingerholes near the lower end burned out with a heated stick, and a U- or V-shaped notch burned into the rim. A compass of 3 octs. is obtainable, with 7 tones to the oct. It is played by cattle herders who sing while they play. 60–90 cm. (2–3 ft.) long. Also called shwegu (139).

Mullerphone, a contrabass clarinet invented by Louis Muller of Lyon and patented on March 3, 1855, with bassoon-shaped parallel tubes, a metal bell, and cylindroconical bore. The pitch was an oct. below that of the bassoon. No surviving specimen is known (89 Langwill, 169, 204).

Multiflûte, recorder that could also be played as a cross flute or flageolet, patented in France on Nov. 7, 1896, by Ullmann. It had 3 interchangeable mouthpieces and was ca. 20 cm. (8 in.) long without mouthpiece (176, 204).

Mululi, 1. flute of the Washambala of Kenya, made of a cylindrical open tube, with 2–6 fingerholes close to the lower end. Used by cattle herders who make it of a stalk and throw it away shortly after use. Ca. 30 cm. (12 in.) long; **2.** a more durable cross flute, usually of bamboo, with 5 equidistant fingerholes close to the lower end, often ornamented with burned-in designs. Both flutes are called mtorilo in regions where there are many Wapare (111).

Mulungú, obs. frame drum of the Negroes of Alagoas, Brazil (7).

Mumbeta, mumbeto, small ndungu (185).

Mumbiki wa ngoma, *goblet drum of the Bapende of Kasai, Congo, with nailed head and short stem. Ca. 50 cm. (20 in.) high (30).

Mumboma, see: tambor mumbomba.

Munchang, Punj. and Kashmiri equivalent of murchang (173).

Mundamba, syn. of nlambula.

Mundäoline, an early name of the mouth organ.

Mundharmonika, 1. Ger.: mouth organ; **2.** since 1792 (Jean Paul), Ger.: Jew's-harp (117).

Mundstück, Ger.: mouthpiece.

Mungiga, Swed.: Jew's-harp.

Mungubire, *cylindrical drum of the Wavira of the Congo, with 2 heads of bulu skin (a lizard) (30).

Mungungi, drum of the Bambala and Basuku of the Congo, played during dances (30).

Mungwin, syn. of mushits.

Munharpa, Swed.: Jew's-harp.

Munkambu, munkandu, munsaku (Kikongo), small ndungu. Also called nkandu.

Munkoko, name for the slit drum in the Lower Congo (185).

Munkunku, clapperless bell of the Sundi of the Lower Congo, tulip-shaped, made of 2 pieces of metal soldered together; 90–100 cm. (36–40 in.) high (185).

Munkwaka, scraper of the Bembe and Dondo of the Congo, consisting of a notched stick that is scraped (185).

Munnharpe, Nor.: Jew's-harp.

Munsenkele, *barrel drum of the Basonge of the Congo, on a monoxylous stand, with nailed head and carved body (30).

Munsiasi, munsasi, small nsembu of the Bembe of the Congo (185).

Munswangala (Kikongo), together with several vars., name of a very long ndungu (185).

Muntshintshi, *footed drum of the Thonga of S. Africa, of hollowed-out wood, with head of the hide of buffalo, ox, or antelope, or elephant-ear skin. Possibly borrowed from the Venda. Cf. shikolombane (116).

Mupimpi, drum of the Wasongola of the Congo, with single nailed head (30).

Mupunpi, drum of the Wasongola of the Congo, now obsolescent, of a hollowed-out tree trunk, with open bottom and laced and pegged head of antelope skin. Played with sticks or bare hands (42).

Murabba (Arab.: square), bowed

chordophone of the Arabs, mentioned by Niebuhr in 1774, with rectangular body, skin belly and back, and single horsehair string. Presumably a form of rabāb that has now died out (75).

Muralī (Sans., Beng.), *cross flute of India, made of cane, with 3–5 fingerholes, also played as a nose flute. Also called fillagori. See also: murli, zangskar (173, 203).

Murchang (Hindi: mouth harp), circular Jew's-harp of India, of iron with thin metal tongue that projects at both ends. Its curled tip is plucked with the player's right hand. Also called chang (harp). Cf. changu, mochanga, munchang, muchanga, mursing (173, 179).

Murli, Baluchistan name of the muralī, with 6 fingerholes; 35 cm. (14 in.) long (178).

Mursing, syn. of murchang (179).

Murumbu, *conical drum of the Venda, Pedi, Chwana, and Sotho of Basutoland, with single oxhide head, laced, and large handle. The bottom is left open. It is played by women who tap it with the palms or fingers while standing and holding the drum between their legs. Ca. 60 cm. (2 ft.) high (116).

Musa [?Gk. *moúsa*], Lat.: bagpipe.

Musāfiq (Arab.) [pl. of *misfaqa*], obs. designation of small cymbals of med. Islam. Cf. shuqaifāt (75 II).

Muscal [Turk. *mūsīqāl*], panpipes of Romania, syn. of nai (132).

Muschelhorn, Ger.: *marine-shell trumpet.

Muse [Lat. *musa*, bagpipe], OFr.: bagpipe. The word was in use from the 12th to the 17th c. Cf. cornemuse, musette (190).

Muselaer, 17th-c. virginal of the Low Countries, with jacks that plucked the strings at one half of their speaking length, according to Klaas Douwes.

Musenkele, drum of the Basanga of the Congo, with membrane covered by a thin layer of rubber. Played at funeral dances (30).

Musesegeto, rattle of the Konjo of Uganda, identical with the ensegu (195).

Musette [Fr.: dim. of *musa*], **1.** bagpipe of France, mentioned in Fr. literature from the 13th c. on, but without description. Judging from a phrase in Jean de Brie (1379): ". . . *musette d'Almaigne ou autre musette qu'on appelle chevrette . . .*" (musette of Germany or other musette that one calls chevrette), it seems to have been a generic term for small bagpipes. In 1501, 3 "musettes" were among the members of Philippe le Beau's chapel and accompanied him on his travels. We have no knowledge of its construction before the 17th c., when the musette appears full-blown as a very small and delicate bellows-blown instr., with exquisitely made ivory pipes and elaborately ornamented silk- or velvet-covered bag trimmed with lace, and matching bellows. In the early 17th c. it had a narrow cylindrical chanter, ca. 19 cm. (7½ in.) long, devoid of keys, played with a double reed, and a stubby, *racket-like drone. By the time Mersenne wrote (1636) the chanter had acquired several keys. At mid-c. Jean Hotteterre added a second chanter with 6 closed keys, placed in the same stock as the first and lying parallel with it. These were known as the *grand chalumeau* and *petit chalumeau*. The compass of the *grand chalumeau* was f^1–a^2, extended upward by the *petit chalumeau* to d^3. The drone arrangement was a cylindrical block of ivory some 15 cm. (6 in.) long and 4 cm. (1½ in.) wide, resembling a racket, with parallel bores pierced longitudinally, interconnected in pairs, and emerging in the outer wall. The exterior was grooved to hold wooden or ivory sliders called *layettes* for tuning the drones. The drones were tuned to C and G in octs. and fitted with double reeds. Furetière (in 1690) commented that the only difference between cornemuse and musette lay in its drones, the musette having 4 on 1 cylinder. Because of the convenience afforded by its bellows, and the compact size of the drones, the musette remained in the hands of nobility, courtiers, and musicians for nearly 2 centuries and did not become extinct until the latter part of the 18th c. A number of compositions were written for it, and in 1672 Borjon wrote the only known musette tutor (13, 14, 35, 78, 82);

2. musette chanter of the 18th c., played without its bagpipe. In such cases the reed was covered by a wooden reed cap to protect it. This was the instr. from which the *bal musette* took its name, as participation of a musette (now replaced by an accordion) was mandatory. During the 19th c. the reed cap was dispensed with, thus transforming the chanter into a small oboe in G (a 5th above the ordinary oboe), marketed as a toy, sometimes with 4, 5, or 6 keys;

3. organ stop found in Fr. organs of the 17th and 18th c., composed of reed pipes with conical resonators, tonally similar to the crumhorn. In England the musette stop is built as a crumhorn at 16′, 8′, or 4′ pitch (20, 133; Gachard, ed., *Collection de voyages des souverains des Pays-Bas*, Vol. I, 1876).

Musettenbass, Ger.: basse de musette.

Mushag, see: moshug.

Mushekera, trumpet of the Wanande of the Congo (30).

Mushereko, syn. of iholere.

Mushits, drum of the Babunda of the Congo, with laced head. Also called gwan'bal, mpetshanga (30).

Mushtaq sini (Pers.: Chinese mushtaq), free-reed *mouth organ of Sassanid Persia, introduced from China and known by the 6th c. Its form, as it appears on a silver vessel of the period, is very similar to the Chinese model. *Cf.* chubchiq (21, 147 Farmer).

Musical bow (Fr.: *arc musical, arc sonore;* Ger.: *Musikbogen;* It.: *arco sonoro;* Sp.: *arco musical*), primitive chordophone shaped like a shooting bow. Opinion is still divided as to its origin. Sachs pointed to what appear to be the earliest forms of musical bow; they are

3 m. (10 ft.) long, sometimes idiochord, and useless for shooting. Others, including Kirby, have derived the musical bow from the shooting bow. Montandon believed in a reversal of this procedure. Fusion of function has obviously occurred in many areas at different times: Kirby observed the daily use by Bushmen of their shooting bows as musical bows; the root of the word meaning "war" in Sudanic languages is *ta;* it is also the root of the word for musical bow in both Sudanic and Bantu languages. The age of the musical bow is also unknown; what appears to be our first record is a wall painting in Les Trois Frères cave of SW. France, dated *ca.* 15,000 B.C., where an object believed to represent a musical bow is being played in a religious ceremony.

Musical bows consist of a flexible wooden stick held under tension by a string stretched between its 2 ends. We distinguish between 4 varieties of bow: 1) bow without resonator of any kind, such as is still played in Assam; 2) bow with separate resonator; here the bow is placed horizontally on a detached vessel such as a half gourd, pot, vase, etc.; 3) bow with attached resonator made of a gourd, tin can, etc. This type is also called *gourd bow. The gourd is truncated and the open end often pressed against the player's body; 4) bow with the player's mouth acting as resonator, also known as *mouth bow. Here either the stick is held against the player's teeth, with the string outside his mouth, or the string vibrates freely inside the oral cavity with the stick outside. Bows vary in size from some 45 cm. (1½ ft.) to 3 m. (10 ft.) and may be held horizontally or vertically. The string is set in vibration by being tapped with a small stick, or by plucking it or stroking it with a plectrum. Shorter bows are more highly curved than longer ones, some being bent until they are almost semicircular. The wood of the bow is usually round, but sometimes flat; it can have notches cut in it and be scraped with a stick while the string is being tapped (this type is found only in Loango, N. Congo, and S. Africa). The string can be divided into 2 sections by tying it close to the wood by means of a tuning loop, and the sections so formed can be of equal or unequal length (in the latter event they are of different pitches). Bows with 2 or more strings are also encountered. Finally, several bows may be stuck in the ground and played together. The *pluriarc appears to be a combination of several bows with a common resonator. Pitch is varied on musical bows by stopping the string with either a small stick or the player's thumb and index finger; by touching it very lightly flageolet tones are produced. In mouth bows the harmonics are augmented by changing the size of the oral cavity, with the fundamental serving as a drone. A special variety of musical bow, sounded by air, is the *gora (see also: aeolian bow). Widely distributed as it is, the musical bow appears in mythology or saga in different parts of the world and plays an important part in religious and magical rites. It is found in America from Patagonia to California (many investigators believe it to have been imported from Africa), C. and S. Africa, Asia, S. Seas, and formerly in Europe (Holland, Italy, Lithuania, E. Prussia); today the Polish *bladder and string is called musical bow (see: Luk muzycyny) (93, 137, 144 Kirby, 168, 170). See also: adingili, adungu, aeolian bow, andobu, arpa-ché, bagili, bajang kerek, balu, bandingba, barikendikendi, bawa, bazombe, bendukudu, benta, bentwa, berimbao de barriga, beta, bikife, bobre, bogonga, bombo, bongengu, bongo-bongo, bongoga, bongogo, bucumbumba, bumba-um, bum-bum, burumbumba, busoi, caramba, carimba, chizambi, chunga, cora, darkun, dende, didilavy, dingba, dongeldongel, dumba, egoboli, ekitulenge, elem, elingingile, enanga, feng cheng, gabus, gamakha's, ganza, gedo, goaramba, gora, goukha's, gourd bow, gualambo, gubo, gubuolukhulu, gulutindi, gunga, guru, gwale, gwaningba, hade, h'onoroate, hunga, hungo, ibigumbiri, igonga, ikoka, imvingo, inkinge, inkohlisa, ipiano, isankuni, isiqwemqwemana, isiqomqomana, isitontola, itikili, itumbolongonda, jejilava, jul, kabarome, kakulumbumba, kaligo, kalirangwe, kalove, kalumba, kambaua, kambili, kandiri-kandiri, kandiroē, kan'gan, kanutitsunanikoya, kashane, katungu, kedondolo, kha's, kidrigo, kijonga, kilibongo, kilingbindiri, kilingila, kinanga, kitingbi, kitingi, koali, kodili, koh'lo, kongo, konkon, kpwokolo, kudungba, kumbili, kunguleme, kunkulkawe, kupu, kwadi, kwendibe, lalango, lekope, lengope, lesiba, liguba, lingongo, lipombo, lontana, lugube, lungunga, lungungu, lusuba, macungo, makwindi, marimba, marimbaché, massunda, matungo, mawu, megan me bongo, mitote, mouth bow, mtangala, mutanda, mutungo, narimba-ché, ndaludali, ndimga, ndono, ngumbo, ngungu, ngwosto, ninga, nkango, nkoka, nkungu, nokukwane, nsadi, nxonxoro, omudage, omugoboli, outa, pagolo, pango, paruntzi, paštše, penda, pināka, pingoru, pitjol cumui, quicahue, quijango, quinquecahue, recumbo, régale de bois, régale de percussion, sambi, samuius, segwana, sekgapa, setolotolo, sundaren, teiboro, thomo, timbirimba, titapu, to, tolotolo, tomangu, tomo, trompa, trumpa, tshigwana, tshipendani, tshitendje, tshitendole, turumba, tusese, uele, ugubo, ugwala, ugwali, uhadi, ukeke, ukeke-laau, umakweyana, umcunga, umqangala, umqunge, umrube, undemoū, urucungo, uta, utete, utiyane, villukottu, vuhudendung, wánamigi, wedsa, wurumbumba, yóeri, zambi, zampoña, zedzilava.

Musical clock (Ger.: *Flötenuhr*), timepiece with a small, built-in automatic organ, its pinned cylinder rotated by clockwork, of late-18th-c. invention. It succeeded a larger instr. known from the 16th c. on, the clockwork organ, which usually had 2 ranks of pipes, a stopped 4' and an open 2'. Both types were replaced by the *music box in the 19th c. (37).

Musical cups, a set of graduated cups of porcelain, metal, or other material, struck with small sticks. Distributed in Asia, W. Africa, and in 7th-c. Turkestan. See also: cheluring, hi, jaltarang, kastratrang, saz-i kāsāt, sing, 3, ye gwin (121).

Musical glasses (Fr.: *verrillon;* Ger.: *Glasspiel;* Sp.: *copólogo*), a set of glasses, tuned by pouring different quantities of water into them and struck with small sticks or rubbed around the rim with wetted fingers. We hear of them in the Near East and in Europe in the 15th c., but metal or earthenware bowls struck with sticks are portrayed in a Gk. ms. of the 4th c. A.C., and our musical glasses may be derived from them. In the late 15th c. Franchino Gafuri shows a set of 6 drinking glasses marked with ratio numbers for determining mathematically the intervals of the musical scale. A *Glasswerk* of unidentified nature is listed in an Ambras inventory of instruments dated 1596. In 1677 a Brit. author describes a "gay wine music" made by rubbing the rims of wineglasses with wet fingers. Usually called by the Fr. term *verrillon* in former centuries, they were mentioned under this name by Walther in his dictionary of 1732. From about 1740 on they became extremely pop., chiefly in Britain. On Apr. 23, 1746, Gluck played in the Haymarket Theatre, London, "a concerto on twenty-six drinking glasses filled with spring water." Later this type of glass was played with sticks rather than with the fingers. In 1761 Benjamin Franklin transformed the musical glasses into the *glass harmonica, but the older form continued in use well into the 19th c., generally in form of graduated glasses with stems, inserted upright in a wooden frame. See also: copophone, crystalphonicon, eumélia, filjan saz, hydrodaktulopsycharmonica, Mattauphone, seraphim, tusūt (113, 169, 170).

Musical saw (Fr.: *lame musicale*), handsaw played as a musical instr., one end being held between the player's knees while the other is grasped and flexed by his left hand. The edge is bowed with a violin or cello bow. The pitch is varied by changing the arc of the saw (89).

Musical stone, slab of sonorous stone struck with a heavy beater. Greatly valued in Asia, musical stones have also been found in places as far apart as Venezuela and Samoa (tuned stone in Samoa). In some Christian churches of Ethiopia and Chios they are used instead of bells. The largest stones are found suspended in Vietnamese temples, where they reach several ft. in size and a thickness of *ca.* 10 cm. (4 in.). In China musical stones are cut in L shape, with an obtuse angle. In antiquity they were used there on all formal occasions but are now confined to Confucian temples. The *rock gong, as it has been called, is yet another form of musical stone. A set of several tuned stones is called lithophone or stone chime; a single stone is also called phonolith. See also: cai khang, ch'ing, döwel, katchel, khanh-da, ko ch'ing, t'e ch'ing, thuk kyong (170).

Music box (Fr.: *boîte à musique;* Ger.: *Spieldose*), automatic linguaphone consisting essentially of a comb of tuned metal teeth, their free ends pointed, and a pinned barrel actuated by clockwork, all contained in a box. The deeper the pitch required, the deeper the tooth was cut. Successors to the *musical clock, the first music boxes were made *ca.* 1770 in Switzerland, with a comb of from 15 to 25 teeth worked by a watch spring. They were called *carillon à musique.* Credit for producing the first music boxes has been accorded several makers, but the underlying idea is unknown, unless the comb mechanism was inspired by the African *sansa. Early models were far smaller than the boxes we know; they were contained in pocket watches, then placed in snuffboxes, later housed in rectangular wooden boxes. Prior to 1810 the movements were made of steel pins set in both sides of a brass disc *ca.* 3 cm.

(1¼ in.) in diam., with the teeth fanning out on either side of the disc. *Ca.* 1780 David Lecoultre is said to have replaced the disc with a brass cylinder, but cylinders are known to have existed in the decade 1770–80. From about 1820 on the combs were cut from steel sheets, which permitted greater elaboration— previously they had been combined of separate lamellae. Barrels were also developed, until up to 10 tunes could be played on one. From the mid-19th c. on "improvements" were added in form of drums, bells, etc., in an attempt to vary the rather monotonous sound, and even a "flutina," or row of air-actuated free reeds, was incorporated. For a c. from 1810 on, music boxes were extremely pop. household instrs., but the advent of the phonograph caused them to be put aside. Nowadays they are still made, but as curios rather than as musical instruments. See also: ariston, carillon à musique, cartel, cosmophone, heraphone, libellion, maliphone, mélocor, musical clock, orchestral organette, organophone, Polyphon, regina, stella, symphonium (37, 43, 151).

Musicier . . . , see: musizier . . .

Music synthesizer, polyphonic *electrophonic instrument of the electronic type, built by Radio Corporation of America in 1951, when it was designed primarily for tone-analysis purposes. Tuning forks are used as primary tone sources for electron tube oscillators. All characteristics of each tone are controlled by a punched code on a paper roll. Thus the synthesizer produces only stored signals and consequently must be regarded as an addition to musical automata. The tones produced are both imitative and nonimitative.

Musik . . . , as prefix to names of organ stop, Musik is synonymous with Kammer . . .

Musikbogen, Ger.: musical bow.

Musikstab, Ger. term for European folk *stick zithers such as the bladder and string, Bumbass, etc. (169).

Mūsīqāl, mūsīqār (Arab., Pers., Turk.), classical term for the panpipes of Islam; it corresponds to the shu'aibīya of Egypt (147 Farmer).

Musique perforée (Fr.), small automatic harmonium played by means of perforated cards, a forerunner of the *cartonium, patented by Martin de Corteuil of Paris in 1852 and shown at the Paris Exposition of 1855. See also: antiphonel, orgue magique (132).

Musizier . . . , syn. of Musik . . .

Musokolome, ground bow of the Soga of Uganda, used as a child's toy (195).

Musompola, drum of the Baluba-Shankadi of the Congo, used by the secret Bambbudye sect during its initiation rites (30).

Mussamba, Brazilian word for maraca (152).

Mustahsin, large modern Turk. nāy (76).

Mustak, Pahl.: equivalent of mushtaq.

Mustel organ, harmonium incorporating improvements devised by Victor Mustel of Paris, notably his *double expression (patented in 1854).

Musu-gitarra, var. of mosu-gitarra.

Muta, Lat.: muted monastic bell (61).

Mutanda, *musical bow of the Bangango of the Congo, with gourd resonator and tuning loop (42).

Mutation stop, organ stop in which the depressed key controls a tone other than its own, *e.g.,* when c^0 is depressed, g^1 sounds. Mutation stops are never played alone, but always in combination with foundations. If the 12th above a given key is sounded, the stop is called a quint; if the 17th (*e.g.,* e^2 when c^0 is depressed), it is called a tierce. The proper size of the largest quint is ⅓ that of its foundation stop (*e.g.,* 10⅔' from a 32' foundation, 5⅓' from a 16', etc.); that of the largest tierce is ⅕ of its foundation stop. Quint stops are older than tierces (99, 133).

Mute (Fr.: *sourdine;* Ger.: *Dämpfer;* It.: *sordino*), device applied to certain musical instrs. in order to soften their tone. Drums have traditionally been muted by covering the membrane with cloth. Trumpet mutes were mentioned by Vasari in the mid-16th c., and muted trumpets were scored for by Monteverdi in his *Orfeo* (1607). Trumpet mutes were made of hollow wood, carefully turned; both Praetorius and Mersenne describe them and Mersenne depicts one. Trichet (*ca.* 1640) said that they must be made thin enough to give a little and adjust to the bell into which they are inserted. According to most early writers on the subject, insertion of a mute raised the pitch and the trumpet had to be played with a corresponding crook to lower it again, but Cotgrave in 1611 translates *sourdine* as "a pipe or tenon put in the mouth of a trumpet to make it low." Altenburg, writing in 1795, says that it gave the trumpet an oboe-like timbre. Trumpet mutes were transferred to the horn and even to the trombone and tuba. *Corni sordinati* are mentioned in the early 18th c. Later in the c. leather-covered metal or cardboard mutes were used for the horn, and muting by hand was also practiced. Nowadays cardboard horn mutes, which do not affect the pitch, are in use. Trombone mutes are also of cardboard, shaped like small megaphones, and likewise do not affect the pitch. Tuba mutes are not standardized, but assume a variety of shapes, usually being homemade. Oboes were muted in the first half of the 18th c., when the instr. achieved prominence in military bands: paper, cotton, or other material was stuffed into the bell; a piriform wooden mute of the 18th c., *ca.* 7½ cm. (3 in.) long, was sometimes inserted into the bell; it did not affect the pitch, but veiled the tone. Bassoons are occasionally muted; sometimes by stuffing a handkerchief into the bell or by inserting a cloth-covered metal cylinder. Clarinets were muted in the 18th c. (Tuerlinckx of Malines sold 23 clarinets with *sourdines* to a military band in 1785). Among the chordophones, members of the violin family are muted; violins were already

muted in Lully's opera *Armide et Renaud,* of 1686. A violin mute is a comblike affair clamped onto the bridge, made of wood or metal, ivory or plastic. *Cf.* muta (15 Morley-Pegge, 89 Baines, 190).

Mute cornett (Ger.: *stiller Zink;* It.: *cornetto muto;* Sp.: *corneta muta*), straight cornett, with mouthpiece turned in the tube of the instr. itself. The mouthpiece is conical and merges with the bore without sharpness; its upper diam. is *ca.* 13 mm., its depth 9 mm. Praetorius says that the tone quality of the mute cornett was gentle, soft, and sweet (14).

Muted viol, see: viole sourdine (organ stop).

Mute stop, obs. piano stop developed from the *lute stop and found on some British pianos of the past. It consists of a thin strip of leather-covered wood shaped to lie along the bridge and hinged to the case. It could be lowered onto the strings and raised again by means of a pedal. In 1783 Broadwood patented it as the "sordin" (92).

Mute violin (Fr.: *violon sourdine;* Ger.: *Brettgeige, stumme Violine*), practice violin. Leopold Mozart describes it as 4 strings stretched over a curved board. A normal fingerboard is provided. The board itself may assume a number of shapes, but it never forms part of a resonator.

Muthallath, triangle of modern Egypt (98).

Mutingo, Pali equivalent of mridanga (173).

Mutisánguisi, Afro-Cuban friction drum (152).

Mutoto, *goblet drum of the Balunda of Africa, with nailed head, carved body, and short stem (30).

Mutshakatha, leg rattle of Bavandaland, S. Africa, made of small, globular fruit shells containing stones, and threaded on sticks. These are attached to pads of cloth and tied to dancers' legs. *Cf.* thuzo (116).

Mutumbi, drum of the Baholoholo of

the Congo, with single nailed head (30).

Mutumbwe, 1. *goblet drum of the Basanga of the Congo, with nailed head. The base is partly closed by an inserted calabash section; **2.** drum of the Baluba-Shankadi that accompanies their great drums (30).

Mutungo, syn. of urucungo (7).

Muvungu, obs. name of the kya (130).

Muwannaj, chordophone of ancient Persia, mentioned in the 9th c. as having 7 strings, but not described further (75 I).

Muwattar, lute of the Arabian Peninsula of pre-Islamic times (75 I).

Muyang, small *pellet bells of the Muria of Bastar, India, tied to dancers' buttocks, usually together with 2 or 3 *irna (68).

Mu yü (Chin.: wooden fish), ritual *slit drum of China, carved out of a block of camphorwood, formerly in form of a fish with a small ball in its interior, nowadays more like a human head. The exterior is lacquered. The mu yü is either placed on a cushion or suspended and is struck with a heavy stick. Both Taoist and Buddhist priests use it at services when collecting alms and to mark time when reciting prayers. It corresponds to the mo kugyo of Japan, the mo ko of Korea. Up to 30 cm. (12 in.) in diam. See also: ao yü, cai mo ca, yü pang (142, 170).

Muzekan, syn. of karmon.

Muzicuta, Rom.: mouth organ (5).

Muzumbi, a simple form of sansa encountered in Kasai, the Congo, consisting of a single free tongue made of split raffia and held in the mouth. The oral cavity acts as resonator (185).

Muzungu, see: mzungu.

Mvet, idiochord *harp zither of the Fan of W. Africa, made of a stalk of raffia palm 1–1.80 m. (3–4½ ft.) long, from the surface of which a number of strings are detached, usually 3 or 4, rarely 5. These are raised on a central bridge that projects vertically and is notched to hold the strings one above the other. One or 2 calabash resonators are attached to the string bearer. It is played by men only. The mvet is also known as Fan harp (185).

Mveul, pluriarc of the Pahouin of Gabon Republic, with 4 strings (42).

Mvöt, see: mvet.

Mvumvuni, obs. *side-blown horn of the Bembe of the Lower Congo, made of antelope horn. Formerly in use both as a signal and a ritual instr.; 40–55 cm. (16–22 in.) long (185).

Mwakasa, *vessel rattle of the Lower Congo, made of dried cylindrical or flat pods of acacia fruit, etc. It is of magical and religious significance (185).

Mwan'angulu (Kikongo), syn. of dingwinti.

Mwandu, friction drum of the Ila of N. Rhodesia, with friction stick (176).

Mwanzi, whistle of the Azande of the Congo, used for calling dogs when hunting. Conical, stopped, often ending in a piriform ornament, and with 2 ducts facing each other (132).

Mwemvo, *end-blown flute of the Lower Congo, without fingerholes. It yields 2 tones (185).

Mwimba, drum of Lake Bangweulu, N. Rhodesia, carried under the arm and played while walking (30).

Mynn harpa, Jew's-harp of Swed. Estonians (176).

Mzungu, pl. **mizungu,** *stamping tube of the Wapare of Usambara, Tanganyika, made of bamboo, with one open end. The other is closed by a node pierced to admit a wooden cylinder, said to act as resonator. The main tube is 1.30–2 m. (52 in.–6½ ft.) long, the cylinder *ca.* 60 cm. (2 ft.) long, 5 cm. (2 in.) in diam. These are held in pairs by dancers, one in each hand, and stamped on the ground with full force (111, 130).

N

Nā (Sum.), reedpipe of ancient Babylon, equivalent to the Akk. halilu (89).

Nabat, pl. **nabati** [Arab. *naubat*], very large kettledrum of Russia (25).

Nabiba, conical drum of the Mombutu of the Congo, with 2 laced heads (30).

Nabita, 1. slender *conical drum of the Mangbele and Makere of the Congo, with 2 laced heads. Also called tshembe; **2.** large, double-headed, bowl-shaped drum of the Mangbele, with laced heads; **3.** drum of the Mangbetu and Momvu of the Congo (30).

Nabla (Gk., Aram.) [Heb. *nebel*], chordophone of ancient Greece, identified as a harp of foreign origin: Gk. writers refer to the "Phoenician nabla." The Byzantine Suidas, writing probably in the 10th c., says that it is identical with the psalterion, *i.e.*, a plucked instr. (89, 170, 199).

Nablium, Lat. name of the nabla.

Nacaire (Fr.) [Arab. *naqqāra*], Fr. word for the Eastern kettledrum, which Europeans first got to know during the Crusades, when Damietta was taken in 1249. Spelled "naguarre," it is recorded in 1281. The chronicler Jean de Joinville was first to use the new spelling in 1309, when he described the noise of the Saracen drums. The nacaire was about 30 cm. (12 in.) in diam. See also: anacaire, naker, naqqāra, naquaire (53, 85, 169).

Nacara [Arab. *naqqāra*], Sp. name of the Near Eastern kettledrum, which reached Spain by 1300.

Nacchera [Arab. *naqqāra*], It. name of the Near Eastern kettledrum, naqqāra; Marco Polo used the spelling *naccar*.

Naccherone [aug. of It. *nacchera*], It.

equivalent of nacaire. The term was first used in 1303 (53).

Nachsatz, 1. Ger. equivalent of nazard; **2.** syn. of Hintersatz.

Nachthorn (Ger.: night horn) (Fr.: *cor de nuit;* It.: *pastorita*), organ stop of open cylindrical flue pipes of very wide scale, of Dutch origin, historically at 8′, 4′, 2′, or 1′ pitch. Nowadays it corresponds to the clarinet flute. In the past it occurred in several forms (2, 131).

Nachtigall, Nachtigallenzug, see: nightingale.

Näckharpa, word used in C. European sources to designate the nyckelharpa (149).

Nacorne [Arab. *naqqāra*], Engl. 15th-c. var. of naker.

Nādesvara vīnā (Sans., Beng.), modern bowed chordophone of India, with body, pegbox, and scroll of the European violin, fretted fingerboard, 7 strings affixed to frontal and lateral pegs. Also played with a metal plectrum (132, 173).

Nadjoroto, see: najoroto.

Nafa, *slit drum of Samoa, now obs., according to some authors. *Cf.* naffa, nawa (77).

Nafari [Arab. *nafīr*], small straight trumpet of India (176).

Naffa, *slit drum of the Tonga Islands, 90–120 cm. (3–4 ft.) long, with a slit 7½ cm. (3 in.) wide, beaten with 2 hardwood sticks. *Cf.* nafa, nawa (8).

Nafil, OProv. var. of añafil.

Nafīr, pl. **anfur** (Arab., Pers.), straight trumpet of Arab. culture, known by this name since the 11th c. Made of metal with a cylindrical bore, it had no bell originally but acquired one at an early date. It was played in med. times by

Arabs, Persians, Moors; the Spaniards adopted it as the añafil and also called it trompeta morisca; the Crusaders certainly knew it: it was probably the instr. that they termed *cor sarrazinois and that they subsequently transformed into their *buisine. It is still played in parts of N. Africa and the Balkans. That of Morocco, still with cylindrical tube and bell, is strikingly similar to the trumpets of Tut Ankh Amon; it is 1.30–1.50 cm. (4¼–5 ft.) long and yields only one tone. In modern Turkey the nafīr is a cow horn (89 Farmer, 170; H. Hickmann: *La Trompette dans l'Égypte ancienne,* Cairo, 1946).

Nāgabaddha, mouth-blown bagpipe of N. India. The chanter is furnished with a single reed. Sometimes there is a second pipe, which then acts as a drone; in other words, the instr. is played as either a melody instr. *or* a drone instr. *Cf.* mashak.

Nāgaphani, syn. of tūrya (176).

Nagara [Arab. *naqqāra*], syn. of dimplipito in Tiflis, Georgia, U.S.S.R.

Nāgārā [Arab. *naqqāra*], large kettledrum of India, of Near Eastern origin, with hemispheric body. In Bengal it is made of clay, with a laced head attached in zigzag pattern to 2 leather belts. Elsewhere the shell is of copper, brass, or sheet iron, and the head is either laced to the belts or stretched over a hoop and laced to the underside of the drum. A temple instr., it is also used in outdoor ceremonies, when it is placed on a 2-wheeled carriage or on the back of a decorated elephant. See also: bhēri, dolla, dundubhi (173, 179).

Nagarit [Arab. *naqqāra*], kettledrum of Ethiopia, always played in pairs. For centuries they have been symbols of power: those belonging to princes have silver shells, those of high officials are of copper, those of lesser persons are of wood with a membrane of white gemsbok. The Galla and Somali have taken over the nagarit, and among them it is also a symbol of power. Until the Ethiopian

war Emperor Haile Selassie had a band of 400 nagarits. Despite its secular origin the instr. has now found its way into the church (45, 144).

Nāgasaram, see: nāgasuram.

Nāgasuram [Tamil, Mal., *nāga,* snake + *surnā*], large *shawm of S. India, with conical bore terminating in a metal bell, 7 equidistant fingerholes, and 5 tuning holes, played together with the drone shawm *ottu. Half tones and quarter tones are not produced by fingering, but are controlled by the player's breathing. Compass 2½ octs.; 60 or 75 cm. (2 or 2½ ft.) long, depending on whether the smaller version, called timiri, or the larger, called bāri, is played. It corresponds to the sānāyī of N. India. See also: bāri, moska, mukavina, nāgesar, nagsar, nāyanam, pāmbunāgasuram, timiri (173, 179).

Nāgasvaram, see: nāgasuram.

Nāgbin [*nāga,* snake], copper trumpet of Nepal, in serpentine shape, terminating in a bell formed to resemble the mouth of a snake (173).

Nagelgeige, Ger.: nail violin.

Nagelharmonika, Ger.: nail violin.

Nagelklavier, Ger.: nail piano.

Nāgesar, Hindust. equivalent of nāgasuram.

Nāghārā, Turk. equivalent of naqqāra.

Nagra [Arab. *naqqāra*], clay drum of the Garo of Assam, used for ritual purposes (173).

Nagsar, Mar. equivalent of nāgasuram.

Nag's head swell, crescendo pedal invented in 1712 by Abraham Jordan, London organ builder; it opened a door of the *echo organ (170).

Naguar [Arab. *naqqāra*], *cylindrical drum of S. India, with 2 heads stretched by zigzag lacings. See also: jagajampa, pāni (173).

Naguarre [Arab. *naqqāra*] (Fr.), earliest form of the word nacaire.

Nahabat, syn. of damāmā. See also: sahib nahabat, sutri nahabat (173).

Nai [Pers. *nāy*], stopped panpipes of Romania, in raft form, now becoming rare. Two centuries or so ago they were composed of 7 or 8 pipes, now they have up to 23. The pitch is varied by the tilt at which the pipes are held. The tuning is to a major scale, that of D or G. Also called muscal.

Nail fiddle, see: nail violin.

Nail harmonica, see: nail violin.

Nail piano (Ger.: *Nagelklavier*), a transformation of the *nail violin by a teacher named Träger of Bernberg, Saxony, in 1791, into a continuously bowed instr. controlled by a keyboard. 4 rows of iron nails were set horizontally into an oblong block of wood. The bow, a belt of resin-coated linen, was rotated by means of a treadle (89, 176).

Nail violin (Fr.: *violon de fer;* Ger.: *Nagelgeige;* It.: *violino di ferro*), bowed friction idiophone invented by Johann Wilde of St. Petersburg *ca.* 1740, consisting of a circular, flat wooden resonator with a set of nails or iron pins driven into its sides. The nails were tuned by driving them more or less deeply into the wood (the shorter the nail, the higher its pitch). Originally the instr. had 12, 18, or 24 nails. It was held in the left hand by a handhole underneath and bowed with a violin bow. The number of nails increased until 37 became the usual number. *Ca.* 1780 Senal of Bohemia added 15 sympathetic strings and made the new model known by concertizing with it; he called it violino harmonico or Violino-Harmonika. Manufacture of the nail violin was carried on almost exclusively in Germany and Sweden. By the mid-19th c., if not before, it was obs. See also: Aliquot-Streichflöte, duolon, Eisenvioline, Nagelharmonika, Nagelklavier, nail fiddle, nail harmonica, nail piano, semiluna, spikharmonika, spikharpa, Stiftgeige, Stiftharmonika, violino harmonico, violon de fer (83, 89, 170).

Naiu, var. of nai.

Najoroto, 1. drum of the Makere of the Congo, in form of a truncated barrel, with laced heads; **2.** syn. of maroto (30, 132).

Naka, 1. stopped, end-blown pipe of the S. African Chwana doctors. Made of bone, it is suspended from its owner's neck and yields a single tone; **2.** syn. of pala (116).

Na ka la [Turk. *nāghārā*], Chin. equivalent of the nāghārā (75 II).

Nakamunsale, *side-blown horn of the Ganda of Uganda, forming part of a set (195).

Naka ya lethlaka, 1. reedpipe of the Pedi of Steelport Valley, Transvaal, played by boys. The pipe is stopped by a natural node. The boys make it from Oct. to Dec., when the cane starts ripening, and whistle a tune while sounding the pipe's only tone. *Ca.* 8 cm. (3 in.) long. *Cf.* lethlakanoka; **2.** cross flute of the Pedi that corresponds to the tshitiringo (116).

Naka ya makoditsane, syn. of naka ya phatola (116).

Naka ya phatola, conical stopped flute of the Pedi, Bakgatla, and Venda of S. Africa, made of hardwood split down the center and hollowed out, encased in buckskin applied when wet and then bound with wire. A small hole is drilled in the tip, thus converting it to an open pipe that may be stopped by the player's finger. A feather is kept inside the flute. It is very difficult to play and is carried by warriors. See also: mothlatsa (116).

Naka ya sefako, *end-blown flute of the S. African Pedi doctors, made of impala horn encased in leather and blown at the wide end. A small fingerhole is drilled at the wide tip. The flute is suspended from its owner's neck. A feather is kept in it (116).

Naker [Fr. *nacaire*] (Fr.: *nacaire;* It.: *nacchera;* Sp.: *nacara*), MEngl. name of the Near Eastern kettledrum *naqqāra. The word is recorded in Engl. literature from 1352 to 1440, when it disappears until revived by Sir Walter Scott in *Ivanhoe,* 1819. See: nacorne, naqqāra (180).

Nakkara, see: nagara, naqqāra.

Nakotiba, wooden goblet drum of NE.

Timor, with parallel lacings of rattan (173).

Nakri [Arab. *naqqāra*], **1.** formerly a small kettledrum of Russia; the term was employed in the 15th c. A larger model was called nabat; **2.** formerly a kettledrum of Yugoslavia (25, 89).

Nal (Hindust.), **1.** kettledrum of India; **2.** pipe of India (176).

Nal-nari, conical oboe of India, of the sona type (176).

Namalanga, iron handbell of the Bapopoie of the Congo (19).

Namalua, *friction drum of the Mashuku-Lumbwe of Barotseland, N. Rhodesia. The cylindrical body is ornamented and covered with a membrane held with pegs through which a friction stick passes (16).

Namarue, Bare'e: Jew's-harp (176).

Nambongo, side-blown ivory horn of the Mangbetu of the Congo (19).

Namen, syn. of kin, 1.

Namukenge, *board zither of the Bapopoie of the Congo (19).

Nandin, syn. of gopi yantra (138).

Nanduni, lute of Travancore, India, made of a single piece of wood, with elongated body, wooden belly, narrow neck, 2 lateral pegs, and 7 raised, fixed wooden frets, all placed at the lower end of the neck. The upper third of the neck is not fretted and thus the first fret sounds a 5th above the open string (173).

Nanga, Nubian arched harp with 5 or more strings. *Cf.* enanga, inanga (89, 141).

Nanga ya danga, stopped *end-blown flute of the S. African Venda doctors, made of a vulture's wing bone (116).

Nanga ya davhi, flute of the Venda of S. Africa which corresponds to the naka ya phatola but is sometimes made of a single piece of wood (116).

Nanga ya ntsa, stopped *end-blown flute of duikerbok or springbok horn of the S. African Venda, used for calling dogs (116).

Nao, small po, *ca.* 20 cm. (8 in.) in diam.

Nao but, see: cai nao but.

Nao chin chieh, rattle of China, consisting of 4 or 5 iron plates loosely attached to 2 cords at the end of a bamboo or wooden stick. Used by knife grinders to announce their presence (142).

Naos sistrum, see: sesheshet.

Na pal, trumpet of Korea, similar to the la pa (66).

Napura, *vessel rattle of India, consisting of a hollow copper ring in which pellets are enclosed, worn as an anklet. See also: nūpura (132).

Naqāra [Arab. *naqqāra*], small clay kettledrum, pot-bellied, played by children in the Punjab (173).

Naqqāra (Arab.), small kettledrum of med. and modern Islam, made of metal or wood, the head laced with cords, always played in pairs. At first in use in N. Africa, Turkey, Egypt, and Syria, often carried in front of the rider on horse or camel and beaten with 2 sticks. From that area it spread to Europe via the Mediterranean and the Balkans in the 13th c. (see: nacaire) and to India by the trade routes. The nomenclature of Eastern drums is very confused: in Pers., Arab., and Kurdish today, naqqāra denotes a small kettledrum, usually with copper body, rarely of wood, but similar names in other languages stand for quite different types of drum. See also: anacaire, anacaria, anaka, dumbelek, mahānāgārā, nacaire, nacara, nacchera, naccherone, nacorne, nāgārā, nagarit, nāghārā, nagra, naguar, naguarre, naker, nakri, naqāra, naqqārya, naquaire, na'ra, nuqairāt, tabl al markab (89 Farmer, 170, 173).

Naqqārya, kettledrum of the modern Near East, played in pairs, 2 being carried on donkey or camel back with the lower-pitched of the 2 to the player's right. They are large, flat kettles of metal, played with 2 sticks (170).

Naqrazān, syn. of naqqārya.

Naquaire [Arab. *naqqāra*], early Fr. spelling of *nacaire; also an Engl. 16th-c. var. of *naker.

Nāqūs, hemispheric, clapperless bell on a metal handle, struck with metal rods; it serves as a liturgical percussion instr. of the Copts and is used as a gong by Christians in Arab.-speaking lands. *Cf.* nuqaisāt (74, 144).

Na'ra [Arab. *naqqāra*], name given by the gypsies of Turkey to the naqqāra (76).

Naradiya vīnā (*vīnā invented by Narada), S. Indian syn. of mahati vīnā (138).

Naramut, name of the garamut on Gazelle Island, New Britain (77).

Naras-jux, see: nares-jux.

Narasringa, copper horn of Nepal. *Cf.* sringa (176, Tagore).

Narasta-jux, var. of nares-jux.

Nares-jux (Ostyak, musical wood) [Sum. *nar*, musician], lyre of the Ostyak of NW. Siberia, called *sangkultap among the Vogul, who also play it—the only surviving lyre in Asia. The rectangular body is made of a single block of hollowed wood, the back is almost flat, the soundboard is of spruce. The body comes to a point at the bottom and a hole is pierced laterally through this point; a string that acts as string holder is passed through it. The crossbar at the upper end is mortised into short arms resulting from a V-shaped cut into the body; 5 gut strings tuned diatonically pass over a flat-topped bridge and are secured to wooden or bone tuning pins. Inside the body are pebbles that rattle when the instr. is played. The nares-jux is held in the player's lap, the strings being plucked with bare fingers, although sometimes the nails of the right hand are scratched across the strings. Both hands are used in playing: the melody is played by the left hand while the right accompanies on the 2 highest strings. Of 6 specimens preserved in the National Museum at Helsinki, the lengths are 92–125 cm. (36–49 in.), the widths 8–23 cm. (7–9 in.), and the depths 4½–7½ cm. (1¾–3 in.). Also called pannang-jux. See also: glēo-bēam (9, 170).

Naresyuk, see: nares-jux.

Narimba-ché, syn. of arpa-ché.

Nārī mong [nārī, clock], gong of Burma with which the hours are announced (176).

Narrenflöte, Ger.: jester's flute.

Narsringa, Hindi equivalent of ranasringa.

Nāsa jantra, name of the magudi when blown by the nose (179).

Nasalzug, modern Ger.: lute stop.

Nasard [Lat. *nasus*, nose] (Fr.), 1. woodwind instr. known through literary references only, as for instance: *nazards gros, moiens nazards, petits nazards, petits cornetz, saqueboutes* (Gironde archives, 1519); 2. for the organ stop see: nazard (85).

Nasardo, It., Sp.: nazard (organ stop).

Nasardos, Sp.: mixture organ stop. The term was in use by the 16th c. (133).

Nasarē, globular flute of the S. American Chaco population.

Nasat (Ger.), see: nazard.

Nasatflöte, syn. of nazard.

Nasenflöte, Ger.: nose flute.

Nason, obs. var. of nazard. The word has also been found in some old Engl. organs, where it denoted a stopped flute at 4' pitch (99).

Natural horn, horn without keys or valves; a valveless French horn.

Natural trumpet, trumpet without keys or valves.

Naubat (Arab.), a very large kettle-drum; syn. of damāmā. See also: gendang naubat, mahānāgārā, nabat (173).

Nauksvebon, name given in Burma to a set of 4 small conical 2-headed drums. They form part of a Pwe orchestra (176).

Nawa, slit drum of Uvéa, Tonga, Niue, and Pukapuka Islands, S. Pacific. *Cf.* nafa, naffa (77).

Nawek, name of the kemanak in E. Java (121).

Nāy, pl. nāyāt (Pahl., Pers., Turk.), in the course of its history the nāy has come to be many things in many places. In early times it seems to have been a generic term for woodwinds and, together with surnāy, a specific term for the shawm. From about the 9th c. on it replaced the smaller Arab. *qasaba; in the 15th c. it appears as a shawm. Nowadays it is: **1.** long *end-blown flute of the Near East, in use from Egypt to Persia (it corresponds to the qasaba of the Maghrib), the only wind instr. played in Arabian art music. Made of cane, it lacks an embouchure, has 5 or 6 fingerholes disposed in 2 groups. Some specimens have a rear hole to facilitate overblowing; 60–70 cm. (24–28 in.) long; **2.** generic term for flute in Turkey; **3.** shawm of the Punjab; **4.** *cross flute of Turkestan and Kashmir; **5.** syn. of vāmsī; **6.** panpipes of Romania (see: nai). See also: battal, būl ahank, dāwul, diyānai, dūnāy, kūshnāy, mansūr, mustahsin, pīsha, qīz, shāh, sūpurga, zarbasnay, and the different nāy entries (89 Farmer, 98, 170).

Nāyanam, Tamil syn. of nāgasuram.

Nāy-i aswad, a 15th-c. name of the nāy siyāh (89 Farmer).

Nāy-i balāban, see: balāban, 2.

Nāy-i narm, Pers.: recorder (89 Farmer).

Nāy-i safid (white nāy), Pers. flute (147 Farmer).

Nāy jiraf, the shortest Egyptian nāy, ca. 50 cm. (20 in.) long (89).

Nāy labek, syn. of sūt.

Nāy shāh, the largest Egyptian nāy, ca. 75 cm. (30 in.) long (89).

Nāy siyāh (black nāy), Pers. equivalent of the zamr. Also called zamr siyāh nāy (89 Farmer).

Nāy tunbūr, 2-stringed tunbūr of Islam, played with a plectrum. The strings are tuned a 4th apart (147 Farmer).

Nāy zunāmī, the nāy as improved in the early 9th c. by Zunam. The term survived in W. Islamic countries as *zulami (75 I).

Nazard (Fr.) [Lat. nasus, nose], **1.** for the woodwind instr. see: nasard; **2.** (Ger.: Nasat; It., Sp.: nasardo), organ stop imitative of nazard, 1, consisting originally of open cylindrical flue pipes of very wide scale, at oct. pitches. Later

it became a mutation stop at 2⅔' or 1⅓' pitch, made of conical pipes, either stopped or half-stopped. Dom Bedos knew it as a stopped or half-stopped register in the lower positions, and as a conical open stop in the higher ones. At 5⅓' pitch it is known as gros nazard.

Nbogoi, syn. of cajita china (152).

Nchabagome, drum of Ruanda, Africa, struck to announce the condemnation of the guilty (30).

Ncwa, syn. of nsegu (195).

Ndaludali, *musical bow of the Zaramo of E. Tanganyika, with gourd resonator (10).

Ndamutsu, drum of Ruanda, Africa, sounded when the king appears (30).

Ndandala, var. of indandala.

Ndandi, syn. of sansa.

Ndanga, syn. of ditumba dya ngenge.

Ndara, 1. xylophone of the Alur of Uganda, kept by the Sultan of Alur only. It has 8 slabs laid on bundles of grass pegged to the ground, all mounted over a pit. Cf. endara; **2.** *board zither of the Andekobe of the Congo, with resonator (128, 195).

Ndavni, end-blown *marine-shell trumpet of Viti Levu, Fiji Islands, with one fingerhole bored at the center of the shell. This is alternately stopped and opened by the player's finger, thus changing the pitch.

Ndembo, kettledrum with nailed head of the Mayombe of the Congo, and the Vili of Loango, Angola, made in different sizes. The round base is massive, the head is of antelope skin, the body is sculptured. An instr. of the great chiefs, it serves ritual purposes only (185).

Ndenda, drum of the Wolof of Senegal (176).

Ndere, see: endere.

Ndibu, ndibi, var. of dibu.

Ndidi, *cylindrical drum of the Sundi of the Lower Congo, with laced head, often over 1 m. (40 in.) high (185).

Ndima, drum of the Abarambo of the Congo, identical with the gaza. Also called dima. See also: elembe, 1 (30).

Ndimga, pl. **zindimga,** *musical bow of the Vakaranga tribe of the Shona, S. Rhodesia, with gourd resonator (176).

Ndingi, 1. syn. of mpovila za londe; **2.** wooden cowbell of the Lower Congo. The word also designates the fruit of the *Brassus flabelliformis* in the Lower Congo (185).

Ndingidi, see: endingidi.

Ndj . . . , see: nj . . .

Ndona, pluriarc of the Pangwe of W. Africa (19).

Ndongo, 1. bowl lyre of the Ganda and Soga of Uganda, with 8 strings tuned $b^0 e^0 g^0 c^0 d^0 e^1 d^1 c^1$; the body is of calabash or tortoise carapace. Also called ntongoli; **2.** pluriarc of the Fan of W. Africa (42, 176, 195).

Ndono, musical bow of the Wanyamwezi of Tanganyika (176).

Nduma, 1. *conical drum of the Langbase of the Congo, with 2 laced heads. Made of *kopworo* wood; **2.** *cylindrical drum of the Banziri; **3.** drum of the Mono of the Congo, in which a pebble is enclosed. Formerly the finger of a slain enemy was enclosed (30).

Ndundu, drum of the Bapote and Gombe of the Congo, in form of a truncated barrel, with laced heads. It is played in a vertical position. Often a pebble or other hard object is enclosed (30).

Ndungo, syn. of dungo.

Ndungu, 1. single-headed drum of the Dunde of the Lower Congo, made of the fruit of the baobab tree, with laced head; 38 cm. (15 in.) high; **2.** single-headed drum of the Ekonde of the Congo, the upper portion being cylindrical, the lower tapering. The bottom part is not hollowed out. *Ca.* 50 cm. (20 in.) high (30, 185).

N'dweie, drum of the Balesa-Basakata of the Congo, with laced head; a signal instr. sounded in case of alarm. It is kept suspended near the chief's hut. Also used as a war drum (30).

Neapolitan mandolin, see: mandolin.

Nebel, pl. **nbalim** (Heb.: skin, wine bag), vertical *angular harp of the ancient Hebrews, an instr. of the Levites in biblical times, with a variable number of gut strings, possibly of Egyptian origin. Flavius Josephus (b. 37 A.C.) knew it with 12 strings; the Psalms seem to indicate 10. It is now thought to have assumed the form of the Gk. letter delta inverted: ∇. (84, 97).

Nebel 'asor [*'asor,* ten] (Heb.), 10-stringed nebel.

Nebuguwu, drum of the Malele of the Congo; it accompanies the chief on his travels or lends rhythm to dances (30).

Neck (Fr.: *manche;* Ger.: *Hals;* It.: *manico;* Sp.: *mango*), section of certain chordophones by which they are held, sometimes called handle. The neck of a harp is more properly called harmonic curve (*console* in Fr.).

Nedomu, arched harp of the Mangbetu of the Congo. *Cf.* neduma (128).

Neduku, syn. of nendime.

Neduma, arched harp of the Meje of the Congo. *Cf.* nedomu (128).

Nedunguzhal, rustic flute of S. India, cylindrical, pierced with a few fingerholes (179).

Nefer, said to have been an instr. of ancient Egypt.

Negarit, Amh.: nagarit (45).

Negpwapwo, name of the kili in Medje (language) (132).

Nembongo, ivory horn of the Mangbetu of the Congo, with lateral blowhole. The tip of the tusk is pierced and the pitch is changed by alternately opening and stopping the resulting hole (132).

Nemurambi, zoomorphic *slit drum of the Mangbetu of the Congo, with dorsal slit. Also called lepakusu (19).

Nendime, bowl-shaped drum of the Abarambo of the Congo, with 2 laced heads. Also called neduku (30).

Nengilsi, hemispherical cymbals of the Garo of Assam (173).

Nengoniki, stick zither of the Makere of the Congo (128).

Néo-alto (Fr.: new alto), valved brass instr. of the 1840's, presumably identical with the néocor.

Neo-Bechstein piano, *electrophonic

piano of the electroacoustical type, invented by Oskar Vierling of Berlin in 1928, in which the tone is conventionally generated by very small hammers, is amplified and transmitted through loudspeakers.

Néocor (Fr.: new horn), valved alto cornet with *corps de rechange, made by Goudot *jeune* of Paris *ca.* 1842. See also: néo-alto (156).

Nerrembarre, short mengagl minge.

Neusfluit, Du.: nose flute.

Neu Tschang (Ger.: new sheng), brass instr. with free reeds, invented by Reichstein in the early 19th c., inspired by the Chin. sheng. A metal cylinder, closed at the bottom, was provided with a mouthpiece, 16 keys, and 2 rows of metal free reeds set in the walls. It is said to have had a compass g^0–g^3. See also: Psallmelodikon (178, 184).

Neve, *Jew's-harp of Santa Isabel, Solomon Islands, made of bamboo (176).

Nevel, see: nebel.

Newphonion, valved brass instr. made by a member of the Distin family *ca.* 1863, when it was mentioned in the *Revue musicale* (204).

Ngab, Jew's-harp of the King, a people of New Ireland (176).

Ngala, sansa of the Bahaya of Tanganyika, of wood with iron lamellae, played in sets of 4 (108).

Ngalabi, see: engalabi.

Ngalir, trumpet of the Wolof of Senegal (176).

Ngannalarruni, Jew's-harp of Sicily (176).

Ngarabi, drum of the Baziba of Lake Victoria, Africa, of a hollowed-out tree trunk, with single lizardskin head. It is played with bare hands. *Ca.* 1.50 m. (5 ft.) long (176).

Ngaramut, name of the garamut on New Ireland, Tabar, Tonga (77).

Ngbandje, board zither of the Mbuja of the Congo, with bark resonator (128).

Ngenge, *spike fiddle of the Fula of Sierra Leone, the body being made of a truncated gourd, with lizardskin belly,

movable cylindrical bridge, and single string of hair. Played with a hair bow. The string is held by a tuning ring and the round handle is surmounted by a rectangle of sheet metal pierced with jingles all the way around the edges. See also: karaning (Collection of the Commonwealth Institute, London).

Ngetundo (lion), **1.** *friction drum of the Nandi of Kenya, with goatskin membrane, used at circumcision rites; **2.** bullroarer of the Nandi, made of an oval piece of wood fastened to a string of goatskin, also used at circumcision ceremonies (176).

Nggonggri, syn. of santo (119).

Ngilamo, name of the garamut in the Talasea and Lakonai areas of W. New Britain. Also called garamo (77).

Ngime, fiddle of the Mandingo and Sarakole of W. Africa, identical with the kundye of the Soso (132).

Ngina [U.], not a chordophone of ancient Israel, but probably a melodic pattern (170).

Ngkratong, see: nkraton.

N'go, drum of the Ngbandi of the Congo, identical with the leri except that it is shorter (30).

Ngoma, word meaning drum, musical instr., dance, in Bantu languages. Ngomangoma is the local appellation of the *Ricinodendron africanus* (tree).

Ngomba, var. of ngoma.

Ngombi, arched harp of the Bwaka of the Congo (19).

Ngomfi, 1. pluriarc of the Lower Congo; **2.** lute of the Bembe of the Lower Congo, of recent origin and possibly of European inspiration. The neck and body are of one piece, the belly is nailed, its 5 strings are plucked with the thumbs like a sansa. Held in both hands when played (185).

Ngomo, 1. *arched harp of the Fang of Gabon Republic; **2.** footed *cylindrical drum of the Bosaka of Tshuapa district, the Congo, with single nailed head (30).

Ngong, Burmese: gong (176).

Ngonga, pl. **magonga,** small metal or

wooden bell of the Teke of Kasai, the Congo. A metal bell of this name is worn by women in the Lower Congo or tied to pigs to enable them to be located easily (176, 185).

Ngonge, war drum of the Batetela of the Congo, beaten loudly with a stick during battle. Victims' severed fingers were inserted into the cavity by an aperture in the bottom which was then closed with resin; they rattled when the drum was shaken (30).

Ngongi, bell of the Bakongo, more or less conical, made of sheet metal bent into a double bell with vertical slit, united by a metal handle. A tulip-shaped bell of the Lower Congo is also so called; this is made of 2 pieces of iron soldered down the sides. Both varieties are struck with a stick (185).

Ngongila, *double bell of the Bwende of the Congo, conical, made of iron. *Ca.* 22 cm. (9 in.) high (185).

Ngongui, Sp. spelling of ngongi; syn. of ekón in Cuba (152).

Ngotad, gourd rattle of the Cayapó Indians of Brazil (176).

Ngulu, ngulu-ngulu, syn. of dingwinti.

Ngumbi, stick zither of the Azande of the Congo (128).

Ngumbo, syn. of ugubo.

Ngunda, *globular flute of the Kwili district and of the Yombe people of the Congo, made of clay or of a dried fruit the size of a billiard ball, with blowhole and 2–6 fingerholes (185).

Ngunga (Kikongo), generic name for cast metal bells among the Congo people (185).

Ngungu, 1. *slit drum of Mayombe, the Congo; **2.** *musical bow of Luanda, Angola, without resonator. The string is plucked, struck with a stick, or scraped. It also serves as a child's toy (185).

Nguomi, *harp zither of the Teke of Gabon Republic and the Congo, and of the Kukuya of Djambala of the Congo (185).

Nguru, *end-blown flute of the Maori of New Zealand, also played as a nose

flute, made of wood, stone, or whale tooth (ivory). It presents the appearance of an ornate sea cucumber, being only 9–12½ cm. (3½–5 in.) long, with a diam. of 3 cm. (1¼ in.). The tube is conical with tapering bore, is carved, and terminates in a short, upturned neck bearing the blowhole. The number of fingerholes varies but is usually 3–2 front holes and 1 rear. This type of flute is played nowadays only in New Zealand, but prehistoric specimens, though longer, have been found in Peru (8).

Ngwalala, stopped *vertical flute of the Sundi of the Congo, with slightly conical bore, devoid of fingerholes. The flute is partly or completely covered with *mbala* (civet) tail to prevent splitting. It yields one tone only. *Ca.* 23 cm. (9 in.) long. *Cf.* nsembu (185).

Ngwana, conical drum of the Congo people; it accompanies dances (185).

Ngwen, pluriarc of the Yan of the Congo (128).

Ngwinda (Kikongo), drum and dance of the Congo people (185).

Ngwingwingwe, *bull-roarer of the Congo people of São Salvador, Angola, made of bamboo or wood, used as a toy (185).

Ngwombi, pluriarc of the Teke of the Congo (128).

Ngwomi, stick zither of the Kikuyu of Kenya (185).

Ngwomo, pluriarc of the Mbama, Mbau, Ndasa, and Wumbu of Gabon (185).

Ngwosto, *musical bow of the Mbum of the Congo, with gourd resonator and tuning loop (128).

Nhac, see: cai nhac.

Ñi, see: cai ñi.

Niau-kani, heteroglott Jew's-harp of Hawaii, made of wood with tongue of turtle shell, bamboo, or other material (8, 77).

Nibiles, side-blown trumpet of Ethiopia (144).

Ni chin, see: ni kin.

Nicolo, Renaissance bombard described

by Praetorius as a bassett with one key, but depicted by him with reed cap and 4 keys. Possibly made both ways. See: bombard, reed-cap shawm.

Ni daiko, *barrel drum of Japan, with 2 heads stretched over projecting hoops and laced. The heads and body are painted. *Ca.* 38 cm. (15 in.) long, 78 cm. (31 in.) in diam. (157).

Ni gen kin (two-stringed kin), 2-stringed koto of Japan, with highly arched board of wood, or of a bamboo half tube with wooden bottom, actually an *ichi gen kin with 2 strings. The points at which the melody string is to be stopped are marked by small discs inlaid in the soundboard. Both strings are tuned to f#⁰ (148, 157, 178).

Nightingale, auxiliary organ stop consisting of several high-pitched pipes imitating the twittering of birds. Either the pipes were set in a pan half filled with water, the wind being introduced from below the water level, or up to 8 open pipes were set on a small chest, with their tops bent over and placed in a pan containing water or thin oil. The earliest nightingale stop recorded is that in Zürich in 1507. That of St. Étienne, Troyes, 1551, included the figure of a nightingale that beat its wings when the stop was played. Other names are: Amsel, avicinum, clamor avium, don, garritus avium, merula, Nachtigall, Nachtigallenschlag, Nachtigallenzug, philomela, rossignol, Vögel, Vogelgeschrei, Vogelsang (133).

Nihoihagi, bronze cymbals of Japan, with central boss and slightly turned rims, used in Buddhist temples. *Ca.* 35 cm. (14 in.) in diam. (132).

Ni kin, circular koto of Japan, with a body 38 cm. (15 in.) in diam. and 5 cm. (2 in.) thick, and 6 strings attached to pegs and stretched over 2 bridges. A metal tongue placed inside the body rattles against the side. The ni kin represents a stage in the evolution of the gekkin from the koto (157).

Ninai daiko, daiko of *gagaku* (court music); it is also carried in processions (135).

Nineteenth (Fr.: *larigot;* Ger.: *Superquinte;* It.: *decimanona*), mutation organ stop of open metal flue pipes, a 5th above the *fifteenth, at 2⅔' or 1⅓' pitch. Renatus Harris introduced it into Brit. organs in 1670.

Ninga, *musical bow of the Azande of the Congo, without resonator or tuning loop. Also called gwaningba (128).

Ni no tsuzumi, tsuzumi of Japan, mentioned only in ancient records (157).

Nira, var. of lira, 3.

Nisen, bowed chordophone of Japan, of Korean origin, more ornate than the kokin but otherwise nearly identical with it (157).

Ni shoko, small gilt shoko of Japan, in an elaborate frame, carried on a pole during processions, when it accompanies the *ni daiko; 20 cm. (8 in.) in diam. (157).

Nissan, large, single-headed drum of the Muria of Bastar, India, played with 2 sticks. Sometimes called lohāti or māwāloti (68).

Nja, arched harp of the Werre of the Nigerian plateau (19).

Njaga, xylophone of the Gbea-Manja of the Congo (19).

Njavata, var. of javata.

Njele, rattle of the S. African Thonga, made of an oval calabash about 15 cm. (6 in.) long, with a hole, burned in top and bottom, through which a stick 30 cm. (12 in.) long is thrust to serve as a handle. Pebbles are put inside the calabash, and side holes are burned in to increase the volume (116).

Njembo, pluriarc of the Bateke of the Congo (19).

Njenjo, *stick zither of Lake Tumba region of the Congo, similar to the nzenze (139).

Njin, cross flute of the Fan of Gabon, with one fingerhole (176).

Njua, var. of injua.

Nkaku, var. of nkoka.

Nkandu, syn. of munkambu.

Nkango, musical bow of the Tikar of Cameroun. *Cf.* nkungu (19).

Nkembi, syn. of dibu.

Nkenke, small side-blown trumpet of the Bwende of the Lower Congo, made of a branch or root of a tree (185).

Nkiranwa, syn. of gishikiso.

Nkoka, *musical bow of the Thonga of S. Africa, identical with the dende, 2; it is played by men only (116).

Nkoko, *slit drum of the Vili of the Lower Congo, scaphoid, up to 2 m. (6½ ft.) long (185).

Nkola, wooden dog bell of the Fang of W. Africa (176).

Nkole-nkole, syn. of lokole.

Nkongolo, *end-blown flute of the Bomvana of S. Africa, which corresponds to the umtshingo (116).

Nkonjo, drum of the Mpongwe of the Congo Republic, with 2 laced heads (176).

Nkonko, small *slit drum of the Vili, Yombe, and other peoples of W. Africa, used by secret societies where it serves as a rhythm and dance instr. Often provided with a sculptured, monoxylous handle. Struck with a small stick; 20–25 cm. (8–10 in.) long. The name is also applied to a long slit drum of the Bwende, Sundi, and Yombe, *ca.* 1.80 m. (6 ft.) long (185).

Nkonzi, Kikongo equivalent of nkonko.

Nkraton, *harp zither of the Sea Dayak of Borneo, consisting of a wooden box set over a pit, with 2 notched bridges in the center, 2 notched nuts at the extremities, and 4 strings (144, 173).

Nku, slit drum of the Fang of W. Africa (176).

Nkuimbi, see: nkwimbi.

Nkumbi, 1. ancient drum of the Congo people, now obs. It was cylindrical with antelope-skin heads; 2. scraper of the São Salvador area of Angola, consisting of a notched stick laid on a pad resting on the back of a resonator carved to resemble an antelope. Scraped with 1 or 2 sticks. It has ritual functions only. *Cf.* mukumbi (185).

Nkumoi, syn. of mulimba (19).

Nkundi, *arched harp of the Azande and Bari of the Congo, identical with the kundi, 1 (128).

Nkungu, *musical bow of Angola, with fiber string, tuning loop, and gourd resonator. The player holds it vertically in his left hand, with the gourd resting on his left hip, and strikes the string with a small stick. *Cf.* nkango (17, 185).

Nkwagasho, obs. scraper of the Washambala of Tanganyika, consisting of 2 slender notched sticks of hardwood attached to a narrow board; it is scraped with a stick during dances (111).

Nkwaka, scraper of the Sundi of the Musana area of Lower Congo, consisting of a notched stick (185).

Nkwanga, syn. of mukwanga.

Nkwimbi, scraper of Loango, Angola; a notched piece of wood, slightly arched, is scraped with a stick (176, 185).

Nlambula, andungu *ca.* 3 m. (10 ft.) long, sometimes set in a carved wooden stand. Also called mundamba (185).

N'lapa, vertical *cylindrical drum of the Malagasy Republic, with single nailed head (172).

–nnportile (initial letter lacking), Paulus Paulirinus, writing *ca.* 1460, describes this as a combination of an upright harpsichord, in front, and a positive organ, in the back, in shape of a *media ala (*i.e.,* semitriangular), both played from the same keyboard.

No, shawm of Thailand, identical with the sona (176).

Nobut [Arab. *naubat*], the largest kettledrum of India. *Cf.* cai nao but, nabat, naubat (176).

Nodivu, bull-roarer of the Kafir of S. Africa (176).

Nofre, see: nefer.

Nō kan, *cross flute of Japan, made of bamboo, similar to the riū teki, with 7 front fingerholes, lacquered red on the inside, black on the outside. Over-all length 34 cm. (13½ in.), bore length 29 cm. (11½ in.). As its name indicates, it is a *nō* instr. (135).

No ko, drum of Korea, played together with the cho ko, which is smaller (66).

Nokukwane, *musical bow of the Chwana of S. Africa, with a vesicle resonator (116).

Nola [?Lat. *campanola*], med. Lat.: bell; first recorded in the 4th c. (169).

Nolarum circulis, see: horologium.

Nole [Lat. *nola*], OFr.: bell. The term was in use until the 14th c.

Nolette, dim. of nole.

Noli-noli, bull-roarer of the Carajá Indians of Brazil, affixed to a pole (176).

Nolipiru, slit drum of the Tariana of Brazil (176).

Nolula [dim. of *nola*], Lat.: small bell; bell placed on a horologium in med. times (61, 82).

Nonnengeige, Ger.: nun's fiddle.

Noordsche balk (Du., Flem.), folk zither of the Low Countries, described by Klaas Douwes in 1699 as having 3 or 4 strings and diatonic frets; it is plucked with a plectrum or bowed. It corresponded to the bûche, épinette des Vosges, Scheitholt, etc.–a rectangular box zither. Also called hommel (132).

Noqairāt, see: nuqairāt.

Northumbrian pipes, see: half long pipe, shuttle pipe, small-pipe, war pipe.

Nose flute (Fr.: *flûte nasale;* Ger.: *Nasenflöte*), flute blown with nasal rather than oral breath. Nose flutes are very often also played as mouth flutes; this is true of certain instrs. of Africa, America, India, Indonesia, New Guinea, New Caledonia, New Zealand. Any form of flute may be played as a nose flute: globular and tubular flutes, cross flutes, end-blown flutes, open and stopped flutes; their only common feature is their mode of playing. Nose flutes are distributed on all continents (in Europe they occur only in Macedonia), but are found chiefly in Melanesia and Polynesia, where they are used for ritual and medicoritual purposes, also as instrs. of courtship and in field-fertilizing ceremonies. In this area particularly they seem to form a link in the chain of many fertility traditions connected with the nose,

as nasal breath is held to contain the soul. Some cross flutes intended for nasal playing have a blowhole conveniently placed close to the end. Since only one nostril is used in playing, the other is either plugged or closed by the player's hand, the fingers of the same hand being used to stop the fingerholes. See also: abeng, ang en tsuma, angun, anim, bituuvu, bunun-giogu, chiniloi, chup en parri, eddik le bodon, e'wiu, fango-fango, hahel, hano, hokioko, hu, ipu hokioko, irriliku, janil, kahel, kash, ki kohe puru, koauau, ko'e, kofe, kural, lantoy, latowe, ligatik, mbrunau, muralī, nāsa jantra, nguru, ohe hano ihu, parri chup enro, pinkui, ponitu, poretu, pu-a, pu heko heku, pu iho, pututue, rankoan, salet, sangoi, sangona, sigu nihu, silingut, suling, suling idong, surune, telali, thith, tsihali, tsimbi, tsula ya noko, tungali, turali, ulili, vivo (168, 203).

Notched flute (Fr.: *flûte à encoche;* Ger.: *Kerbflöte*), *end-blown flute in which the player's breath is directed against a small notch cut in the upper edge of the instr., usually beveled to facilitate speech. The opening is partly closed by the lower lip of the player, thereby replacing the fipple. It is found in Africa, America, Asia, S. Seas (168, 170).

Notiru, panpipes of the Ikito Indians of Peru, with 10 pipes (105).

Notolo, wooden dog bell of the Bapopoie of the Congo (19).

Notstok (note stick), Swed. pop. name of the psalmodicon (149).

Novachord, polyphonic, imitative *electrophonic instr. of the electronic type, in form of a large square piano with a 6-oct. keyboard.

Nsadi, *musical bow of the Ladi of Boko, Congo Republic, without resonator; a child's toy (185).

Nsakala, var. of sakala.

Nsambi, 1. pluriarc of the Ndembo secret society of São Salvador, Angola, with 4 bows, tuned (left to right) A♭ F E♭ C. The strings are not stopped but are plucked with a plectrum. The shape of the resonator varies. *Cf.* lusinga; **2.** 5-

stringed lute of the Congo area; it corresponds to the ngomfi, 2 (185).

Nsansi, 1. name of the sansa in the Lower Congo; **2.** *vessel rattle of the Lower Congo, made of dried fruits of the *Oncoba spinosa* impaled on a stick that serves as a handle. It is carried on long poles by candidates in puberty rites (185).

Nsatong, xylophone of the Tikar of Cameroun (19).

Nsegu, conical *end-blown flute of the Nyoro, Toro, and Nkole of Uganda, closely connected with the royal courts there. Made of 2 hollowed sections of wood, bound tightly by a skin cover and played from the wide end. Also called ncwa (195).

Nseke, rattle of the Ganda of Uganda, made of small hollow twigs filled with seeds and bound in raft form. It is played during dances (42).

Nsembu, stopped *vertical flute of the Bembe and Bongo of Sibiti district, Congo Republic, of wood with conical bore, devoid of fingerholes, partly covered with a monkey's tail to prevent splitting. It yields one tone only. *Ca.* 28 cm. (11 in.) long without cover. *Cf.* ngwalala (185).

Nsengu, conical flute of the Amba and Konjo of Uganda, made of wood, tapering to a point, with a cupped mouthpiece cut into the upper end. The bottom tip is cut off and the extremity is pierced with a very small hole (195).

Nsiba, 1. wooden trumpet of the Bembe of the Lower Congo, identical with the ludi, played in instrumental ensembles; **2.** whistle of the Congo people, made of *nsia* antelope horn or of ivory; **3.** end-blown wooden flute of the Congo people, stopped, with conical bore, no fingerholes, often partly covered with monkey skin to prevent splitting and used during the hunt. Some specimens have a lateral vent (185).

Nsimbi (iron), name given to the sansa in the Zambezi River area of Africa (176).

Ntamba (Kikongo), side-blown wooden

trumpet of the Bwende of the Lower Congo, made of a branch or root. The lower end is open or closed; if open, the player closes it with his hand to change the pitch; if closed, it may be carved (185).

Ntambwe, see: tambue.

Ntandu, *cylindrical drum of the Congo people, with single nailed head of antelope skin (30).

Ntara, see: entara.

Ntimbo, royal *goblet drum of the Nyoro and Toro of Uganda, with nailed head of water-lizard skin. It is carried under the arm suspended from a leather band and is beaten with both hands. *Ca.* 50 cm. (20 in.) high (195).

Ntongoli, syn. of ndongo.

Ntshinda, drum of the Ekota and Bahutu of the Congo (30).

Ntuantuangi, *marine-shell trumpet of the Poso Toradja of Celebes, made of a triton shell, with lateral blowhole. Used as a signal instr. and also to summon the wind spirits at sea in the event of a calm (112).

Ntubu, pl. **sintubu,** percussion gourd of the Vili of the Lower Congo, made of a baobab fruit, open at both sides. It is struck against the thigh or hit with the flat of the palm (185).

Ntumpani, chief *talking drum of the Ashanti of Ghana, played in pairs; barrel-shaped, on a cylindrical base, with single head stretched over a hoop and laced to pegs projecting from the body. The membrane, of elephant ear, is beaten with drum sticks. *Cf.* atukpani, atumpani (162).

Ntuta, *cylindrical drum of the Congo people, with single head of antelope skin, nailed; it is used during dances; 1–2 m. (40–80 in.) long (30, 185).

Nud'i, double hornpipe of the Mordvin of the U.S.S.R., consisting of 2 cane pipes tied together, with idioglott upcut reeds and a common cow-horn bell. The left pipe has 6 fingerholes, the right pipe 3 as a rule, but the combination of 5 holes in the left pipe and 3 holes in the right also occurs (13).

Nugarit, see: nagarit.

Nulolematan, panpipes of the Yameo Indians of Brazil and Peru (105).

Nungneng, idiochord bamboo *tube zither of the Toba Batak of N. Sumatra (119).

Nungungu, tubular *slit drum of the Bapopoie and Mangbetu of the Congo (19).

Nunib, stopped end-blown pipe of the Berg-Dama of S. Africa, made of the upper portion of a springbok horn and used as a hunter's whistle (116).

Nun's fiddle (Ger.: *Nonnengeige*), a name of the *trumpet marine, said to have been played in convents as a substitute for the trumpet. There is but meager record of its ever having been put to such use.

Nunumata, panpipes of the Yagua Indians of S. America, with 10 pipes (105).

Nunut, friction idiophone of New Ireland, made of a large block of wood, up to 2 m. (6½ ft.) long and 60 cm. (2 ft.) in diam., with 3 crosscuts of graduated depth chiseled out so as to form an upper surface of 4 giant teeth. The player rubs its surface with rosined hands, producing 4 tones. See also: alaunut, kule paganeg, lauka, livika, lunat, lunuot (77).

Nūpura, Sans. and Beng. equivalent of napura.

Nuqairāt (pl.) [Arab. *naqqāra*], small kettledrums of Syria and N. African Berbers, made of clay or metal (89, 144).

Nuqaisāt [dim. of *nāqūs*], *finger cymbals of the N. African Berbers (89).

Nura, unidentified instr. mentioned by Al-Shaqandi (d. 1231) as being made in Seville (75 I).

Nürnbergisches Geigenwerk, see: Geigenwerk.

Nuss, Ger.: block (of organ pipes).

Nut, 1. (Fr.: *sillet;* Ger.: *Sattel;* It.: *capotasto*), on stringed instrs. having a neck, a raised ridge of ebony, ivory, etc., glued to the upper end of the neck. It

raises the strings over the fingerboard and determines one end of their speaking length. The term has been taken over from *lutherie* and applied to stringed keyboard instrs. also; **2.** Brit. term for frog.

Nutu-pill, syn. of kiri-pill.

Nuzha (Pers.), zither of ancient Persia, described in a 14th-c. treatise (*Kanz al tufah*) as being twice the size of a *qānūn, with 108 strings, in courses of 3, of which 81 strings were full length; 27 were half-length treble strings stretched between the longer ones. It was played horizontally (75 I, 170).

Nvatt, metal Jew's-harp of the Bönon of Cambodia, needle-shaped, of a copper alloy (173).

Nxonxoro, *musical bow of the Qung Bushmen of S. Africa; it also serves as a scraper. A thin bow is bent into a semicircle and kept under tension by a fiber cord *ca.* 50 cm. (20 in.) long. The bow is notched and is scraped with a stick while the string is taken into the player's mouth, the bow being held in the crook of his arm (116).

Ny, see: caval.

Nyampundu, syn. of gihumurizo.

Nyamulere, 1. among the Ganda of Uganda, syn. of endere; **2.** among the Madi, Lango, and Acoli of Uganda the word designates a *notched flute also; **3.** flute of the Congo (103, 195).

Nyastaranga (Beng.: throat trumpet), mirliton of NW. India, in shape of a small brass trumpet. Below the shallow cup mouthpiece is an aperture covered with a thin membrane (rice paper, etc.) leading to the main tube. A pair of these trumpets is placed against the vibrating throat chords of a humming performer. The sound is transferred to the membrane and the cavity of the tube reinforces it. Also called throat trumpet (89).

Nya won (Angami), horn of the Naga of Assam, made of a curved buffalo horn (172).

Nyckelfiol, syn. of nyckelharpa.

Nyckelgiga, term erroneously said to have been used in Swed. sagas, but certainly used in the 18th c., when it presumably designated the nyckelharpa (9).

Nyckelharpa (Swed.: keyed *harpa*), *keyed fiddle of Sweden, depicted since the late 15th c., equivalent to the N. Ger. Schlüsselfiedel, which it has outlived to the present. The body is shaped like an elongated figure 8, the neck merges with the slider box as in an organistrum, and terminates in a flat pegdisc holding rear pegs. The strings are stopped by sliders similar to those of the organistrum, but they are bowed. Early specimens have incurved waists. The flat bridge permits all bowed strings to be played simultaneously. A 16th-c. example has 3 strings, of which 1 appears to have been a melody string, the other 2 drones, and 9 sliders giving a scale of $d^1 e^1 f^1 g^1 a^1 b\flat^1$ $c^2 d^2 e^2 f^2$ if the open string is considered to be d^1. The nyckelharpa attained the height of its popularity in the 17th c. Up to *ca.* 1800 it had 2 or 3 strings and a single row of sliders. Later examples had 4 or 5 strings of which the 3 lowest were drones, often tuned $c^0 g^0 c^1$, while the melody string was tuned to a^1; it also had acquired an additional row of sliders. Subsequently 11 sympathetic strings were added. Total numbers of strings and sliders, as well as the tunings, are variable factors, and even 2 melody strings (of gut) are met with. The nyckelharpa was held horizontally with a slight tilt (as was the organistrum) to keep the sliders free of the strings, its lower end nestled in the crook of the player's right elbow; the left hand worked the sliders while the right hand bowed. Nowadays the instr. is suspended from its player's neck by a leather band. Also called nyckelfiol. See also: knaverharpa, lökkelje, nackharpa (9, 91, 132).

Nyi n'go, drum of the Ngbandi of the Congo, conical, with 2 laced heads. *Ca.* 1 m. (40 in.) long (30).

Nyo, small cymbals of Korea, used in folk music. They correspond to the Chin. nao. *Ca.* 33 cm. (13 in.) in diam. (66).

Nzangwa, nzanza, W. African name of the sansa (185).

Nzau, basketwork rattle of the Kuta of the Lower Congo, used for accompanying dances during circumcision rites. Also called mazoko (185).

Nzegh akom, conical flute of the Congo, of horn, blown across the wide end (144).

Nzenze, *bar zither of the Bashi of Ruanda and the Bali of Batama of the Congo, with a wooden bar 75–100 cm. (30–40 in.) long, 4 cm. (1½ in.) wide, 3 frets, 2 strings, of which 1 passes over the frets, and a gourd resonator. The unfretted string is raised on a movable bridge of varying position. The nzenze is held with the resonator facing up. The right hand plays the melody string, the drone being played with the thumb. The melody string yields a scale of approximately $E\flat F G A$. *Cf.* enzenze, njenjo, seze, zenze (128, 139).

Nzeze, bar zither of the Ngombe of the Congo, and of Ubangi (128).

Nzira, *box lyre of Ethiopia, with rectangular body like that of the bagana, 3 strings, and a crossbar that rises in the center; the strings are attached at its highest point (Villoteau, 1823, in 176).

Nzobo, *pellet bell of the Azande of the Congo, made of sheet iron and worn by dancers as bracelets (132).

Nzoko, 1. funeral drum of the Congo people; **2.** *cylindrical drum of the Lower Congo, with single nailed head, made of *kingela* wood, 1–2 m. (40–80 in.) long (30, 185).

Nzolo, small *pellet bell of the Basiri of the Congo, made of sheet iron, attached to the upper end of a bagili (musical bow) (132).

Nzonga, small metal *pellet bell that magicians of the Fang of W. Africa tie to their hands or feet (176).

Nzundu, *concussion idiophone of the Congo people, consisting of nails struck against one another. *Ca.* 20 cm. (8 in.) long (185).

O

Ō, scraper of Korea, in form of a wooden tiger with 27 notches cut in its back, scraped with a segment of split bamboo. Its use is restricted to Confucian temples. It corresponds to the yü of China, the gyo of Japan (66).

Oba, name of the kani in Sierra Leone (176).

Oberwerk, on Ger. organs the manual above the Hauptwerk (Great) and that section of the organ it controls.

Oblique piano, diagonally strung *cottage piano, first made by Robert Wornum of London, patented by him in 1811; the object in stringing diagonally being to obtain as great a string length as possible.

Oboe [It. pron. of Fr. *hautbois*] (Fr.: *hautbois;* Ger.: *Oboe;* It.: *oboe*), in ethnomusicology oboe designates any woodwind instr. played with a mouthed double reed. For precursors of the European oboe see: shawm.

The European oboe is a woodwind instr. of slightly conical bore, played with a double reed; it evolved from the *shawm in the 17th c. and was probably invented and first played in 1657 by Jean Hotteterre and Michel Philidor at the Fr. court. In England it was known as "hautbois," "hoboy," or "French hoboy" until *ca.* 1770; its Ger. and It. name (pron. o-bo-eh) is merely a phonetic reduction of *hautbois*—a clear indication of its Fr. provenance. Unlike the old shawm, the new oboe was made in 3 sections, the tenon-and-socket system of making joints having become known earlier in the c. Also, its bore was narrower and the bell smaller than that of the older instr.; the pirouette was abolished, the reed cut narrower and mounted on a staple. The swallow-tailed open C key was transferred from the shawm and a closed E♭ key was added, duplicated for left- or right-handed players. The pitch was a tone below that of the soprano shawm, with c^1 as its lowest tone, and it had a compass of 2 octs. The new instr. met with immediate acceptance and was firmly established by the beginning of the 18th c., when virtually every European band and orchestra had its pair of oboes. James Talbot, writing *ca.* 1700, distinguishes between the "English" hautbois, a shawm, and the "French" hautbois, which he says was not 40 years old; he gives its compass as c^1–c^3. Thus oboe and shawm continued to coexist for a time. In the first half of the 18th c. keys were added for G♯ and A♯, and the duplicate E♭ key was discontinued around the mid-c., but during the next 50 years no major changes took place. By 1800 the instr. was no longer scored for in pairs, but was given solo parts. Development in the 19th c. progressed along uneven lines: although Ger. makers may have built 4-key oboes in the late 18th c., 2-key instrs. were still being made around 1820, and 4-key ones did not become common before *ca.* 1830. The speaker, or oct., key was added at about that time. While the 2-key oboe was still being played, 6 more keys were added to newer models, with a long-shank open key placed on the bell, giving b^0, making a total of 10 keys. These, together with 3 extra levers suggested by Sellner, produced "Sellner's 13-keyed oboe," built by Koch of Vienna. Ger. and Austrian models of today are little changed from this model. In 1825 Sellner fitted a tuning slide to the top of the oboe. Early in the 19th c. the Fr. school of oboe making started to develop, leading to the complete reform of the instr. in the hands of Parisian makers such as Henri Brod and the Triéberts. Keywork and the bore itself were revised, the silhouette was changed; pillars for the keys were screwed directly into the walls of the tube. In 1844 a Boehm oboe was produced by Buffet of Paris, but met with a very limited success. There are still structural differences between Fr. and Ger. models, perhaps the most notable of which is the bore, that of the Ger. instr. being wider. The Fr. model is the more widely accepted of the 2, and is currently gaining a following in Germany. Compass of the modern orchestral oboe is B^0–f^3. Oboes are, or have been, made in the following sizes: sopranino in E♭, soprano in D, C (the orchestral instr.), and B♭, mezzo-soprano in A, alto in F, baritone in C, bass in F. The alto is called tenor oboe in Britain; the baritone is called basset there. See also: contrebasse de hautbois, cor anglais, oboe basso, taille des hautbois (25, 41, 89).

Oboe basso (It.), a name of the oboe in A. Not the same as the oboe d'amore, but an oboe of mezzo-soprano range (25).

Oboe da caccia (It.: oboe of the hunt), 18th-c. woodwind instr. concerning which little is known. The term itself seems to be an Italianization of the Ger. *"Jagd-Hautbois,"* of which Zedler's *Universal-Lexicon* (1735) writes that it was used during the hunt, and in the mornings and evenings to play for the chief master of the hunt. Strangely enough, the instr. is not mentioned in the literature of the hunt. The terms *Wald-Hautbois, hautbois de chasse, hautbois de forêt* presumably apply to the same instr. Two *hautbois de forêt*, furnished with 3 *corps de rechange each, are enumerated in a 1780 inventory of instrs. kept in Louis XVI's library at Versailles, but detailed descriptions are lacking. Today it is generally assumed that the oboi da caccia were alto

oboes in F, built in shape of a curved hunting horn. Several such instrs. survive in museums, dating from the early 18th c. Oboi da caccia were in use from *ca.* 1720 to *ca.* 1760 and were scored for, *i.a.*, by J. S. Bach (14, 15, 169).

Oboe d'amore (It.) (Fr.: *hautbois d'amour*), oboe in A, a minor 3rd lower than the ordinary oboe, with a bulbous foot joint that modifies its timbre slightly. Keywork and fingering of the modern instr. are those of the oboe. Majer in 1732 and Eisel in 1738 state that the oboe d'amore had been known since *ca.* 1720; its compass is given as a^0–e^2 or higher; it had keys for b♭ and c¹. Older Ger. instrs. had the bulb bell, older Fr. ones an oboe bell. As far as we know, Georg Telemann was first to score for it (*Sieg der Schönheit*, 1722); Bach first wrote for it a year later. After the mid-c. it fell into oblivion until Victor Mahillon reconstructed it in Brussels in 1874 for Bach performances (his model had an oboe bell). A decade or so later Fr. and Engl. makers started making models with the bulb bell and full key mechanism. The oboe d'amore is treated as a transposing instr. *Ca.* 65 cm. (25½ in.) long (14, 134, 169).

Oboe flute, organ stop of open wooden flue pipes at 4' pitch, invented by William Hill of London (d. 1871).

Oboe horn, organ stop invented by Robert Hope-Jones (d. 1914), composed of large-scale reed pipes. Not to be confused with the cor-oboe (101, 198).

Obtusa, see: vox obtusa.

Obulere (little flutes), panpipes of the Sogo of Uganda, made of stopped pipes of bamboo or other material tied in raft form. The number of pipes varies from 8 to 13 (excepting 11), in 1 row. They are played together with a drum in an ensemble of 6, divided into 3 pairs (195).

Obute, side-blown horn of the Acoli of Uganda, made of animal horn, used as a signal instr. (195).

Obwoshe, bowed chordophone of the Bahaya of Tanganyika, with single horsehair string, skin belly, and a horn resonator. Played by men only (108).

Ocarina (It.: goose-like) (Fr.: *ocarina;* Ger.: *Okarina*), **1.** globular flute devised by Giuseppe Donati of Budrio, Italy, *ca.* 1860, made of clay or porcelain in oblong form, with whistle head, 8 fingerholes, and 2 thumbholes, a transformation of the old It. carnival whistle. Since Donati's day the instr. has been made in sizes ranging from soprano to bass and supplied with a tuning piston for ensemble playing, similar to that of a piston flute. *Ca.* 1½-oct. compass. *Cf.* potato, sweet potato; **2.** a modern organ stop, imitative of the above, consisting of metal flue pipes at 4′ pitch (14, 151, 170).

Ocht-tedach, a name of the Irish harp.

Octave, 1. in American and British organs a 4′ diapason in the manual or 8′ diapason in the pedal; **2.** in Continental organs a *principal organ stop one oct. higher than the fundamental; **3.** occasional name of the 4′ register of a harpsichord.

Octave . . . , 1. as prefix to names of organ stops, octave denotes a stop one oct. higher than that named, *e.g.,* octave bassoon; **2.** as a prefix to names of instrs., syn. of piccolo . . .

Octave courte, Fr.: short octave.

Octave quint, occasional name of the twelfth (organ stop) (101).

Octave viol, viole d'orchestre organ stop at 4′ pitch (129).

Octavilla, name given in Valencia Province, Spain, to a guitar with 6 pairs of metal strings (57).

Octavin (Fr. dim. of *octave*), **1.** Fr. organ stop of open metal flue pipes at 2′ pitch; **2.** see: Oktavin.

Octavina, anglicized version of the It. *ottavina. Grassineau already used the term in 1740.

Octavine, Fr. form of the word *ottavina. Sébastien de Brossard used it in 1703.

Octavin harmonique, organ stop invented by Aristide Cavaillé-Coll; a *harmonic flute at 2′ pitch. *Cf.* flûte harmonique (176).

Octobasse, name of a giant *double bass built by Jean-Baptiste Vuillaume of Paris in 1849; it stood 4 m. (13 ft.) high. Its 3 strings were tuned $C^1 G^1 C^0$; they were stopped by levers worked by 7 pedals, and the bow was supported by devices like oarlocks. In 1851 an improved model was brought out. Two specimens survive, one in the collection of the Paris Conservatoire, another in Moscow. Also called basse gigantesque.

O-daiko, elaborately ornamented *barrel drum of Japan, of Chinese origin, with 2 nailed heads. A temple instr., it also forms part of the *kagura* orchestra. Usually it rests on a stand, but it is provided with 2 iron rings by which it can be carried horizontally in processions. It is played with sticks, both on the heads and on the rim. *Ca.* 85 cm. (34 in.) long; diam. of heads *ca.* 75 cm. (29 in.) (135, 157).

Odeguiliguili, bull-roarer of the Ibo of Nigeria (152).

Odeophone [Gk. *odeon,* music theater + *phone,* sound], improved *clavicylinder invented by Vandenburg of Vienna *ca.* 1818. The only model was later sold to London (169, 204).

Odestrophédon, free-reed keyboard instr. patented on Feb. 7, 1842, by Reverchon and Merlavaud of St. Étienne, Loire (176, 204).

Odi, 1. lyre of the Kakwa of Uganda, also called rababa; **2.** lyre of the Madi and Lugbara of Uganda; that of the Madi has 4 or 5 strings, that of the Lugbara, 5 strings (195).

Odrecillo [Lat. *uter,* bag + dim. *cillo*], OSp.: small bagpipe.

O-e-o-e, obs. bull-roarer of Hawaii. According to Stewart Culin (*Hawaiian Games, 1899*), it was also called kowaliwali or koheoheo.

Oeriphone, instr. similar to the aeoline, invented by Johann Christian Dietz in 1828 (158).

Off-board strings, open strings that do

not pass over a fingerboard, in contrast to *onboard strings, which do.

Offenbass (Ger.: open bass), Ger. organ stop of wide-scale open flue pipes, usually of wood, in the pedal (133).

Offenflöte (Ger.) (Fr.: *flûte ouverte;* Lat.: *tibia aperta*), organ stop of open cylindrical flue pipes, wide-scaled, usually at 4′ pitch, so named to distinguish them from the stopped flutes of earlier organs (101, 133).

Oficleide, It.: ophicleide.

Ogán, syn. of ekón. In Haiti it is used in voodoo rites (152).

O gane, large bell of Japan, hung in a separate bell tower of Buddhist temple compounds and struck horizontally with a stout pole resembling a battering ram (135).

Oganga [*ganga*], Yaskwa and Kamuku (Sudanic languages): drum (93).

Oggán, var. of ogán.

Ogidan, drum of the Nago of Dahomey (103).

Ogo buru, side-blown trumpet of the Dogon of Mali (103).

Ogre, OFr. var. of orgue (organ); the term occurred from the 13th to the mid-16th c., chiefly in Normandy and Brittany (197).

Ogudú, single-headed Afro-Cuban drum, vertical, with head stretched over a hoop and laced to pegs projecting from the body. The bottom remains open (152).

Ogung, *cylindrical drum of Sumatra, with 2 heads and rattan lacings; 40–45 cm. (16–18 in.) high. *Cf.* gordang (173).

Ogung-ogung bulu, idiochord bamboo *tube zither of the Toba Batak of N. Sumatra (119).

Ohe hano ihu (Hawaiian: bamboo nose instr.), *nose flute of Polynesia, made of bamboo, *ca.* 2½ cm. (1 in.) in diam., and lengths 15–46 cm. (6–18 in.). Some specimens are stopped at both ends, others at one end or not at all. Some have a blowhole at one end, others at both ends, generally bored about 1 cm. from the end. They may have 1, 2, or 3 finger-holes, but 2 is the usual number, varying in their relative positions (8, 203).

Ohe ke eke, Hawaiian *stamping tube, made of bamboo, open at one end, the other end closed by a node. Sometimes 2 tubes are used by a player who holds one in each hand. Up to 120 cm. (4 ft.) long. Also called ka eke-eke (130).

O-hichiriki, large hichiriki.

Ohiva, obs. horn of the Herero of S. Africa, made of gemsbok horn and used for ceremonial purposes. Said to have been end-blown and to have yielded a single tone (116).

Ohotniche rogi (Russ.: hunting horn), see: Russian horn.

Ohsi, *goblet drum of Shan State, Burma, with head secured by V-lacings (172).

Ohyan, bowed chordophone of W. Java, of Chin. origin, with body made from a half coconut, long slender neck, wooden belly, rear soundholes, and 2 strings attached to rear pegs. The bow is not separable from the instr., but moves between the strings. Also called rebab batok kechil (121).

Ojha parra, syn. of hulki mãndri (68).

O-kakko, syn. of dai byoshi.

Okarina, Ger.: ocarina.

Okawa, syn. of o-tsuzumi.

Ok che, marble flute of Korea, equivalent of the Chin. yü ti (176).

O-kedo, drum of Japan used in *kabuki* and folk music, with 2 laced heads. It is played with sticks (135).

Okiribongo, *harp zither of the Koyo of Gabon Republic, similar to the mvet (185).

Okoco, rattle of the Acoli of Uganda, worn by men for the dance *oling*. It consists of a complete tortoise carapace from which a row of short iron chains is suspended. This is fixed to the dancer's upper arm by leather thongs (195).

Okonko, *percussion pot of a secret society of Guinea, consisting of a clay pot with side aperture added. The player holds his right hand over the top while his left hand opens and closes the lateral opening, thereby modifying the pitch (152).

Okónkolo, smallest of the Afro-Cuban *batá drums (152).

Okpelé (Yoruba), rare Afro-Cuban clapper, rather like a square handbell, made of wood. Wooden flaps are attached to the upper end of 2 sides; they clap when the instr. is shaken. Its Cuban name is okuelé (152).

Okporo, 1. drum of the Mono of the Congo, identical with the bia. Also called kokpworo (30); **2.** *conical drum of the Banda of the Congo, with laced head (19).

Oktavgeige, modern *tenor violin so named by its maker, the Mittenwald violin builder Johann Ritter. Body length 42 cm. (16½ in.); the strings are tuned G⁰ d⁰ a⁰ e¹ (26).

Oktavhorn, syn. of Primhorn.

Oktavin (Ger.), **1.** woodwind instr. said to have been invented by Julius Jehring of Adorf, but patented by Oskar Adler and Hermann Jordan of Markneukirchen in 1893 in Germany and in England. Rather similar to the saxophone, the Oktavin is made of rosewood, has a conical bore, terminates in an upturned metal bell, and is played with a single reed on a clarinet-like, beaked mouthpiece. The tube is furnished with 14 keys and 3 rings. It was originally made in C and B♭ with a compass of a⁰–f³ (g⁰– e♭³); 40 cm. (16 in.) long. A bass was also marketed, its lowest tone being G¹; **2.** name given by Vaclav Červeny of Königgrätz (Hradec Králové) to a small, straight, cornet-like instr. of his (89 Langwill, 176).

Oktavkornett, Ger.: octave saxhorn.

Oktavposaune, Ger.: contrabass trombone (159).

Oktawa, small Pol. folk fiddle, played by children (89).

Okuelé, 1. Cuban name of the okpelé; **2.** Afro-Cuban ritual drum, gobletshaped, with single nailed head, made in 3 sizes. The 2 smaller ones are played

with sticks, the largest with bare hands. Also called kuelé (152).

Okura-aulos, 20th-c. Jap. wind instr. invented by Okura Kishichiro, actually a keyed *shaku hachi designed to obtain a Western chromatic scale (135).

Okuterananga (beaten zither), syn. of enanga, 4 (108).

Okworo, 1. syn. of dundu; **2.** drum of the Togbo of the Congo. *Cf.* opporo (30).

Olbrichklaviatur, experimental keyboard of the Berlin pianist Emil Olbrich, 1890, with accidental keys 3 or 4 mm. less than standard height (176).

O le fa'a alii-la-iti, syn. of o le polotu.

Ole olean, a Sundanese name of the dermenan (121).

O le polotu, percussion board of Samoan and Tonga chiefs, used for accompanying solo songs. Also called o le fa'a alii-la-iti (77).

Olezkilla (Basque: wood + bell), syn. of kalaka, 1 (56).

Olifant (OFr.: *elephant*), Fr. abbr. of cor d'olifant, a horn of elephant tusk, frequently mentioned in Fr. literature from the 14th c. on. See: oliphant.

Oliko, conical, *end-blown flute of the Madi of Uganda, made of the tip of a gourd. It terminates in a point that is pierced with a small hole, the flute being blown at its wide end; 10 cm. (4 in.) long. Also called gbere (195).

Oli-oli, name of the dermenan in the Toba districts of W. Java (121).

Oliphant [OFr. *olifant*], Fr. abbr. of cor d'oliphant, a short, thick, heavy endblown horn of ivory that reached the West from Byzantium in the 10th and 11th c. and is first mentioned in Fr. literature in the early 12th c. Richly carved, oliphants became symbols of royalty in Europe. In later times they also served as highly prized and rare hunting horns (169, 170).

Olodero, *percussion beam of the Alur of Uganda, played together with the adungu to accompany dances (195).

Oloóke, sacred drum of the Iyesa Negro descendants in Cuba (152).

Olubeye, rattle of the Nyole of Uganda, made from 2 or more dry *oncoba* fruits threaded on a stick (195).

Olukula, see: amokoderi.

Olwet, trumpet of the Acoli of Uganda, with cylindrical tube; it assumes various forms, one being that of a hooked trumpet. Some specimens have a funnel-shaped mouthpiece (195).

Omakola, scraper played by women of the Cunene region of Angola, formed of a notched, arched stick mounted on 2 joined gourds (185).

Ombi, African *arched harp, found in Gabon and Guinea, with trough-like wooden body covered with skin, and 4–8 strings (10, 42, 91).

Ombiwe, *vertical flute of the Karanga of S. Africa, with 2 fingerholes. The player sings while playing. It corresponds to the khumbgwe (116).

Omelé, name of the cuíca friction drum in Rio de Janeiro (7).

Omichicahuaztli, *scraper of the Aztec, made of antler or bone, with a series of notches cut in one surface; in pre-Columbian times made of human bone. *Cf.* chicahuaztli (137, 144).

Omni-harmoni-orgue, small organ patented by Pointe in France on Aug. 8, 1882, with a second manual for harmonic accompaniment (204).

Omniton, improved ophicleide of Halary (Jean-Hilaire Asté) of Paris, in 1849 (126).

Omnitonic clarinet (Fr.: *clarinette omnitonique*), clarinet devised by Iwan Müller by 1812, pitched in B♭, which according to its author rendered the *corps de rechange unnecessary. Other makers put forth the same claim, including Buffet-Crampon and Blancou, who patented their model in 1845 (164, 204).

Omnitonic cornet, see: cornet omnitonique.

Omnitonic horn (Fr.: *cor omnitonique*), horn devised in the early 19th c. in an attempt to obviate the need for changing crooks. In the new instr. the different crooks (in Fr. *tons*) were incorporated in the horn proper and controlled by a graduated slide and dial or other means. As all the *tons* thus became part of the instr., it was called omnitonic. J. B. Dupont of Paris was the first to build omnitonic horns, in or about 1815. In 1818 he patented an improved design with a slide permitting 9 changes of tonality. This was followed in 1824 by the *cor saxomnitonique of Charles-Joseph Sax of Brussels, with one valve capable of connecting the ordinary horn tubing with the other, shorter or longer, crook tubes, and with a graduated slide. Numerous variants and improvements of the system were created in the course of the 19th c., of which that of Chaussier of Paris is probably the most important. His system was also applied to other instruments; it dates from 1889 and employs only 4 crooks, each with its own valve. Ultimately the omnitonic arrangement was abandoned, as the instrs. were too heavy and the manipulation too cumbersome (25, 80 II; 89 Morley-Pegge; 126, 132).

Omnitonic saxhorn, see: bugle omnitonique.

Omnitonic trombone (Fr.: *trombone omnitonique*), trombone provided with Chaussier's transposition device. For details see: omnitonic horn.

Omnitonic trumpet (Fr.: *trompette omnitonique*), trumpet provided with Chaussier's transposition device. See: omnitonic horn (176).

Om-om, 1. name of the dermenan among the Toradja of Indonesia; **2.** name of a similar instr., with a double reed (121).

Ompochawa, sansa of the Ashanti of W. Africa, with wooden lamellae (176).

Omudage, *musical bow of Ruanda, with tuning loop and gourd resonator. The latter is rested against the player's chest while the single string is tapped with a piece of grass or cane; 20–25 cm. (8–10 in.) long (195).

Omugoboli, 1. syn. of egoboli; **2.** the Konjo of Uganda say that they used to play a musical bow of this name (195).

Omukuri, *notched flute of the Kiga and Nkole of Uganda, with 4 fingerholes (195).

Omuleri, *whistle flute of the Bahaya of Tanganyika, made of horn, with 8 front fingerholes. Played by shepherds and boys (108).

Omvok, syn. of ongola.

Oñ, *hourglass drum of the Yabim and Bukana regions of New Guinea, with a single head of varan, glued, and a monoxylous handle; 50–75 cm. (20–30 in.) high. See also: amban, hami, kam, moti, oñum, wongang (28).

On-board strings, strings that are stopped against the fingerboard of a chordophone, as contrasted with *off-board strings.

Onda maris, see: unda maris.

Ondes Martenot, monophonic, nonimitative *electrophonic instr. of the electronic type, invented by Maurice Martenot of Neuilly-sur-Seine in 1928. The tone is generated by the heterodyne action between a fixed and a variable radio-frequency oscillator, the latter being controlled by: 1) a 7-oct.-compass keyboard, 2) relative proximity of the player's hand to a horizontally stretched cord. Also called ondes musicales.

Ondes musicales, see: ondes Martenot.

One goot, cane *whistle flute of the Papago Indians of Arizona, with 2 front fingerholes and a rear thumbhole. A dividing lamella is introduced into the tube in lieu of a fipple (132).

Ong dich, see: cai ong dich.

Onge, syn. of giramo.

Ongola, iron bell of the Fan of W. Africa, also called omvok (176).

Ongoma, obs. *cylindrical drum of the Herero of S. Africa, with 2 heads, 1 of which was beaten with 2 small sticks (116).

Onion flute (Fr.: *flûte à l'oignon*), another name of the *eunuch flute, so called because of its onionskin membrane.

Oñum, drum of the Kate of New Guinea, identical with the oñ (28).

Oobar, percussion instr. of Australia, made of a hollow log (103).

Opáteré, var. of akpateré (152).

Open diapason, organ stop of flue pipes, usually of metal with the lowest oct. of wood, a foundation stop at 8′ pitch in the manual or 16′ in the pedal. It corresponds roughly to the Ger. Prinzipal.

Ophibaryton [Gk. *ophis*, serpent], a Fr. variety of upright serpent, made in the first half of the 19th c. and characterized by a straight bell in form of a painted animal head (89 Morley-Pegge).

Ophicleide [Gk. *ophis*, serpent + *kleides*, key], **1.** (Fr.: *ophicléide, basse à clefs, basse d'harmonie, clairon chromatique basse;* Ger.: *Ophikleide;* It.: *oficleide;* Port., Sp.: *figle*), obs. family of large *keyed bugles, named and introduced by Halary (Jean-Hilaire Asté) of Paris in 1817. Halary tried to obtain a patent at that time, but was informed that his ophicleide was but a development of the *basse-guerrière, and the patent was withheld until March 24, 1921. The ophicleide was of metal with a U-shaped tube of wide conical bore ending in a slightly flared bell, played with a cup mouthpiece. Its very large tone holes were covered with 9–12 keys, 11 being the most common number; all were closed except the first (near the bell). Fingering and compass were variable (*cf.* *serpent), but a 3-oct. compass was considered normal. The original name of the ophicleide was *ophicléide ou serpent à clefs,* that of the alto member, *quintitube.* The following sizes were built: alto in A♭ (actually a soprano) with 9 keys; alto in F and E♭ (the former quinticlave); bass in C and B♭ (actually a baritone); and a contrabass in F and E♭ (actually a bass), dubbed *ophicléide monstre. Of these the B♭ bass was the most widely used. Numerous patents for improvements were taken out during the instr.'s relatively long life. It gained quick acceptance in military bands, wind bands, and even in the orchestra, but could not compete for long with the newer, valved instrs. Around the mid-c. it started being replaced by the tuba in the orchestra, but it maintained itself in bands in France until *ca.* 1880 and in Italy until the beginning of the 20th c. See also: basse d'harmonie, bombardon, clavi-tube, Harmoniekontrabass, omniton, ophicléide à piston, ophicléide monstre, quinticlave, tuba-Dupré; **2.** organ stop introduced by Pierre-Alexandre Ducroquet of Paris in 1855, of large-scale cylindrical reed pipes, at 16′ or 8′ in the manual, 32′ in the pedal.

Ophicléide à piston (Fr.: valve ophicleide), ophicleide to which A. G. Guichard, Sr., of Paris added 3 valves, patented in 1832. It was in E♭ and had slides for C and B♭. On June 14, 1836, he took out a 5-year patent for an ophicleide with single valve. This instr. was an early form of tuba in all but name (89 Morley-Pegge, 204).

Ophicléide monstre (Fr.), Fr. term for a contrabass ophicleide (actually a bass), made in 1821, pitched in F, with 11 keys and a compass E^1–c^1. 1.50 m. (5 ft.) high (89, 170).

Ophimonocléide (Gk.: one-keyed serpent), upright serpent with one open key, patented by J. B. Coeffet of Chaumont-en-Vexin, Oise, on May 2, 1828. It was provided with a slide for changing from opera pitch to church pitch, and terminated in a brass bell. One specimen survives (89 Morley-Pegge).

Opi, in Onitsa, a Kwa (Sudanic) language, a long calabash flute; in other Kwa languages it denotes a horn, either one made of cattle horn or an imitation thereof in wood (93).

Opporo, drum of the Togbo of the Congo, similar to the bia (30).

Oprekelj, obs. Slov. dulcimer used by village musicians until the 1870's, when it was gradually replaced by other instrs., chiefly the accordion. Also called šenterija (144).

Optopka, syn. of Luk muzycyny.

Opuk agoya, *arched harp of the Acoli of Uganda, with tortoise-shell body and 5 or 7 strings (195).

Orage (Fr.: thunderstorm), organ stop introduced in some large organs by Aristide Cavaillé-Coll of Paris, to imitate thunder; the lowest 32′ and 16′ pipes were brought to speak progressively. Also called effet d'orage (133).

Orchestra, automatic organ driven by clockwork, built by J. G. Strasser of St. Petersburg *ca.* 1801, imitative of an orchestra (176, 204).

Orchestral . . . , prefix to the name of organ stops, indicating that the particular stop is imitative of an orchestral instr., *e.g.,* orchestral clarinet.

Orchestral organette, *music box made by the British Organette and Music Manufacturing Co. of Blackburn, England, with 2 rows of free reeds, 2 hand-cranked bellows, and strips of perforated paper fed by the crank that actuated the bellows. The reeds worked on suction wind. All this was neatly contained in a box 37 cm. (14½ in.) long, 34 cm. (13½ in.) wide, and 15 cm. (6 in.) high. During the late 19th c. it was most pop. in England (132).

Orchestrelle, automatic harmonium made in the U.S. in the 1920's (196).

Orchestrina da camera, a series of small keyboard instrs. with free reeds actuated by bellows, patented by W. E. Evans of London on Oct. 29, 1862. They represented different orchestral instrs.: clarinet, flute, Fr. horn, bassoon, oboe, etc., had the same compass as these and imitated their tone. The clarinet and horn had shifting keyboards to facilitate transposition (89, 176).

Orchestrine, *bowed keyboard instr. built by J. C. Hübner and Pouleau in Moscow *ca.* 1801, and patented in France by Pouleau in 1805. It had a 5-oct. compass C^0–c^4. Also called clavecin harmonique.

Orchestrion [*orchestra*], automatophone imitating the orchestra, played by organ pipes controlled by perforated cards, pinned cylinders, or similar devices, of late-18th-c. invention. The idea, if not the name, is a good deal earlier: Athanasius Kircher in the 17th c. describes what was probably the first orchestrion. During its heyday in the 19th c., large orchestrions had up to 40 registers and 12 cylinders. Smaller but elaborately finished ones were supplied to private homes, with as many as 8 stops as well as cymbals, drums, triangle, etc., and a chromatic compass of over 5 octs. In 1887, Welte introduced paper rolls; prior to that all orchestrions were equipped with wooden cylinders. However, the cylinders could revolve 12 times while playing one tune, so that quite long pieces could be played. Instruments known as, or patented under the name of, orchestrion include the following: **1.** stringed keyboard instr., also called Denis d'or or goldner Dionys, invented *ca.* 1730 by Procop Diviss. See: Denis d'or for details; **2.** portable organ that could imitate an orchestra, built in Holland to the specifications of Abbé Vogler and first played in Amsterdam in 1789. Encased in a 9-ft. cube, it had 4 manuals of 63 keys each, a 39-key pedalboard, and crescendo and decrescendo devices for all registers. In 1796 he took it to Sweden; **3.** a combination *piano-organ invented by Thomas Anton Kunz of Prague in 1791 and built to his specifications by the Still brothers, also of Prague, between 1796 and 1798: Its shape was that of an oversize grand piano; its 2 manuals had a compass F^1–a^3. The piano rested on top of the organ section. Each instr. could be played separately if desired; **4.** grand piano by Hunn of Berlin, finished in 1812 by Scharrer, after Hunn's death, with several variations (or organ stops—it is not clear which) imitating orchestral instrs.; **5.** automatophone invented by Christian Heinrich Bauer and his nephew Johann Bauer of Vienna, in 1828, with 3 cylinders; **6.** harmonium patented by Fourneaux of Paris on Mar. 18, 1844;

7. automatic organ invented by Michael Welte, founder of the firm of Welte & Sons, in 1845; **8.** automatophone of Friedrich Theodor Kaufmann of Dresden, 1851; a technically perfected orchestrion containing, *i.a.,* several free-reed stops. See also: Apollonicon, chordaulion, psycho (37, 43, 176, 184, 196).

Orchestrium, improved harmonium of Mercklin, Schutze & Cie. of Brussels, *ca.* 1853 (204).

Orchestrophone, free-reed organ invented by the Limonaire brothers of Paris and exhibited there in 1900. It was hand-cranked and its reeds were controlled by perforated cards; drums, cymbals, etc., were played on the outside. As a former instr. of merry-go-rounds, it was in use at village fairs up to World War II (70, 204).

O'rdu, *harp lute of the Peuh of the Sudan (42).

Ore, *arched harp of the Madi (Aivu) of Uganda, with triangular body and 5 or 7 strings (197).

Orebi, panpipes of the Okaina Indians of the Upper Amazon (105).

Oreh, name of the arababu in Rumbia, SE. Celebes (112).

Oreilles, Fr.: ears.

Ore-ore, "tuning fork" idiophone of Butung, SE. Celebes, identical with the *genggong sakai.

Orf, a faulty reading of 'azf, according to Farmer.

Orgǎ, Rom.: organ.

Organ [Lat. *organum*] (Fr.: *orgue;* Ger.: *Orgel;* It.: *organo;* Sp.: *órgano*), the most complex of our musical instrs., a wind instr. consisting of pipework, wind supply system and action—usually in an enclosing case—and keyboards. Actually the large majority of today's organs are several separate organs, each with its own pipes, action, and keyboard, housed partly or completely in a common case. The earliest true organ was the water organ, or *hydraulos, invention of which is attributed to Ktesibios of Alexandria (3rd c. B.C.). Hitherto, the panpipes have been regarded as prototype of the organ, and evolution of the latter is presumed to have been from a mouth-blown to a mechanically blown set of tuned pipes. This theory was favored by Sachs's discovery of an Alexandrine figurine, of the first c. B.C., that apparently represented a seated player sounding panpipes, the long bass pipes of which were connected by a tube to a compressing bag held under his arm and to bellows worked by his foot; but the instr. has since been identified as an ordinary panpipe. The line of evolution may have been different: information available today points to a signal instr. rather than a musical one as the probable prototype. Recent research has shown that the *magrepha existed earlier than the developed form of hydraulos. Thus the organ may have evolved from a single, mechanically blown signal pipe to several (?simultaneously sounded) signal pipes inserted into a portable box (magrepha), and from there to a set of tuned—ergo, musical—pipes individually controlled and fed by a steady and continuous supply of wind.

The purely *pneumatic organ was first known by the name of hydraulos, as it was but a modification of this instr., and for a while the 2 coexisted. Thus it is often impossible to differentiate between them in early texts. Wind chest and pipework were identical, forming a unit that could be set upon a large base containing a cistern, etc. (a hydraulos), or upon a table and worked directly by bellows. The great advantage of the purely pneumatic organ was its portability; judging from the iconography, early organs were of *portative organ dimensions, whereas the hydraulos had been of *positive organ dimensions. Julius Pollux, believed to have lived in the 2nd c. A.C., mentions 2 kinds of organs: a large one, with air pump and water pressure; and a small one, with bellows. One gathers that both were well known in his day. In Rome the organ was known as *hydraulus* or *organum*. This word, however, was used in

the generic sense of musical instr. before it came to designate specifically the organ in postclassical Europe. Thus St. Augustine (d. 430) wrote: ". . . organa dicuntur omnia instrumenta musicorum. Non solum illud organum dicitur quod grande est et inflatur follibus, sed quicquid aptatur ad cantilenam . . ."

In 1932 the remains of an organ dated 228 A.C. were found in Aquincun, near Budapest, the most important contribution so far to our knowledge of ancient organs. Though it was badly damaged by fire, a number of metal parts survived. The wind chest was originally of wood covered with thin bronze; including the keyboard, it was 18 cm. (7 in.) high, 35 cm. (14 in.) long, 10 cm. (4 in.) wide, or, with projecting keyboard, 17 cm. (7 in.) wide. The biggest pipe measured ca. 45 cm. (18 in.). Unfortunately the wind supply system is totally lacking, so that we do not know whether the "hydra," as it is called in the dedicatory bronze plaque, was a hydraulos. The whole instr. was small enough to be set on a table or even held in the lap. The bronze lid of the wind chest was bored with 52 holes in 4 rows of 13 each, corresponding to 13 L-shaped keys and 4 longitudinal metal grooves in the chest. The keys, of wood covered with thin bronze, were ca. 1 cm. (⅜ in.) wide, and probably about 14 cm. (5½ in.) long; they were attached by their upper ends to metal sliders pierced with holes (corresponding to the grooves) thus forming a manner of *slider key that was returned by a metal spring. Of the 4 rows of pipes, 3 were stopped, 1 open, the last forming the back row. The front-row pipes were about half as long as those of the other rows. All were made of 82 per cent copper and 18 per cent zinc, were 0.5 mm. thick, cylindrical, with a soldered seam. Interestingly enough, the diam. was variable, all pipes being of a very narrow scale. Experiments with better-preserved ones showed that the third and eleventh pipes of the first row sounded an oct.

apart, and that the second row was apparently an oct. lower than the front. Construction of the pipes was of a method very different from ours: the lower end of the open pipes was cut off diagonally and a languid soldered to the shorter side, set obliquely; the top of the foot was pressed in, thus forming a windway of the same width as the pipe's diam.; a cut was effected in the upper part of the foot, enabling it to be bent at an angle to meet the diagonal of the pipe, and the 2 were then soldered. The top of each pipe was furnished with a tuning ring. Arrangement of the stopped pipes is equally interesting: each pipe contained, for almost its entire speaking length, a wooden stopper that must originally have been movable; the upper part of the foot was pressed in to form a semicircular slit to which a copper languid was soldered; a metal ring was placed around it and the pipe was inserted into the ring; the height of its mouth could thus be modified by shifting the ring. Walcker copied some of the pipes and reported that it was almost impossible to obtain the fundamental, but that they spoke promptly on very low pressure.

Our earliest unequivocal representation of the purely pneumatic organ is on a medallion fragment from Orange of the late 2nd c. or early 3rd c. A.C., followed by the small organ of the arch of Theodosius I (d. 395) at Constantinople, showing the wind trunk leading to bellows being trodden. Cassiodorus in the early 6th c. describes the organ in his commentary on Psalm 150, mentioning its wooden *linguae* or keys, its loud and soft *cantilena*, and its tower-like shape (*quasi turris*), clearly a reference to antiquity; from Aldhelm (d. 709) we hear of organs with gilded pipes, but we cannot be sure that he is not writing of symbols of the past. Every chronicler of the period recorded the arrival of the organ in France in 757 (*"organum in Francia venit"*), sent by Emperor Constantine Copronymus to King Pippin, an event possibly more important for its diplomatic implications than its musical value. The organ was erected at Compiègne. Charlemagne is said to have received in 812 a similar instr. from the Caliph of Baghdad, which was set up in Aix-la-Chapelle, but this is debatable. Jacques Handschin drew attention to the presence of an organ in the church of Cluain-Cremha, Ireland, in 814, so far our earliest knowledge of an organ in a church. Charlemagne's successor, Louis le Débonnaire, caused an organ to be built in 826 or 828 by the Venetian monk Georgius, which instr. was still called "hydraulos." In 872, Pope John VIII sent for the organ builder-organist of the Bishop of Freising in Bavaria (in the 16th c. both Zarlino and V. Galilei recall the tradition whereby organs were introduced to Europe from Greece via Hungary and Bavaria). The Utrecht Psalter dates from this time: it contains, *i.a.,* illustrations of double hydraulae, *i.e.,* of instrs. intended for 2 players, with 2 sets of pumps, 2 cisterns, 2 sets of pipes, obviously illustrative of the word *organa* of the Psalms, where it is of course used in the general sense of musical instr. (in another Psalter the passage *"in salicibus suspendimus organa nostra"* shows several miniature organs hung in the branches of a tree); the organs are surmounted by a large, nonfunctional frame, causing one to suspect that the illustrator had misunderstood Cassiodorus. The Utrecht Psalter is now generally conceded to have been greatly influenced by antiquity; at any rate, the hydraulae as depicted could never have worked. In the Eadwine Psalter, a c. later, the copyist added a third, meaningless cistern, showing that the function was by then no longer understood. But the term hydraulos was hard to kill: Sachs reports that the accounts of a German municipality in 1400 refer to the town organist as *"Hydraulier."*

The barbarian invasions had brought about a great retrogression in technology, the full extent of which becomes evident by comparing details of the Aquincum organ with the chapters on organ building in the *Schedula diversarum artium* of a monk named Theophilus, believed to have lived *ca.* 1100. From him we acquire the first insight into practical organ making in the Middle Ages. Theophilus goes to incredible trouble to make an airtight wind trunk, for instance. He takes the curved branch of a tree and drills a hole from both ends; the curve in the middle has to be burned out with a specially made tool consisting of an ovoid piece of metal affixed to a long rod. His organ has an unspecified number of cylindrical flue pipes, of copper and soldered down the seam. His wind chest, the *domus organaria,* is a *slider key chest, as is that of his approximate contemporary, the so-called Bern Anonymous (who refers to it as *capsa*). The chest was 2½ "feet" long; all pipes were of the same diam. Theophilus describes 2 types of action, one with wooden wind chest, the other with one of metal. In the former the chest was made of an upper and lower section, both grooved, those of the upper portion being closed by slider keys; these were inserted between the 2 sections and were pierced with but a single hole, with a thin board above them pierced with as many holes as there were pipes to a key. The second type was of copper, and its slider keys were pierced with as many holes as there were corresponding pipes, with the wind issuing from the lower part of the chest through an intermediary copper floor, through the aperture in the slider key (if this was pulled out), through another aperture in the leaden lid, into the foot of the pipe. Slider keys were pulled out by hand and returned by being pushed back. The organ of the Bern Anonymous had a compass of 15 keys, these being lettered A B C D E F G A B C D E F G H (*sic*), equidistant holes for the pipe feet, and 3 pipes to each key, sounding fundamental and oct. The author stated that certain organs had springs of horn to return the keys, which comment may be a reference to antiquity:

Heron had mentioned them in his description of the hydraulos. Zarlino described the wind chest of an ancient organ found at Grado, Italy, similar to that of the Bern Anonymous: it had equidistant holes for 2 rows of 15 pipes each, no registers, and round holes in the back for the introduction of bellows, "just like modern regals," as he commented; it measured 1 *braccio* in length, ¼ *braccio* in width. The organ illustrated in the Bible of Étienne Harding, now dated from betwéen 1098 and 1109, has the letters of the alphabet marked on the keys, as follows: C D E F G a b♮. An organ built *ca.* 980 at Winchester is described in a contemporary poem by the monk Wolstan. If we are to believe the author, it was a double organ requiring 2 players, each controlling his own keyboard. This consisted of 20 *linguae* and was marked with the letters of the alphabet; "twice six" as well as 14 bellows were worked by 70 men; each slider key had holes for 10 pipes, making a total of 400 pipes. The octs. are said to have consisted of *septem discrimina vocum* plus the "lyric semitone," presumably B♭. Furthermore, the organ is said to have made a deafening noise. One wonders how much of all this is fact and how much fiction (the far smaller and unquestionably softer organs of Theophilus were not to be built for at least another century). Many details lack the ring of contemporary realism: the 2 players with their individual keyboards and the "twice six" bellows, for instance, imply literal translation of the word *"organa"* again; the introduction into the poem of the mystical number 70 in connection with the bellows blowers, as well as the description of octs. consisting of *septem discrimina vocum*—the phrase is taken from Virgil—and a "lyric semitone" are probably no more than part of a med. littérateur's stock in trade; the alphabet marked on the keys is about the only convincing detail.

The relatively small, nonportable organs of the 10th to 17th c. were known as *positive organs, and for centuries they constituted the typical church organ. But they could not fill the new large cathedrals of the 13th and 14th c.; hence their compass was enlarged (see: keyboard), leading ultimately to their transformation into the *great organ, accomplished by the late 14th c. And with the invention of rollers and trackers in the same c. the organ was free to expand: organ builders were no longer forced to place the bass pipes to the left and the treble pipes to the right, in an unbroken line corresponding to that of the keys: they could now be arranged in V-shape, inverted V-shape, etc. But the larger number of pipes required their being placed on a bigger wind chest, and they also needed a greater supply of wind, so that extra and more powerful bellows were added; pipework and chest were raised above the level of the organist's head, and the instr. was from now on contained in a case. Wooden shutters protected the pipes from dust and damage (and were not totally abolished until the early 18th c.). The first great organs were built in the late 13th c.; by the 14th, it became necessary to add a second keyboard, as continued expansion made it impossible to add grooves, rollers, pipes, etc., to the chest indefinitely. Thus a small second manual was supplied for the low keys, as at first the compass extension was a downward one. This second manual was known as the tenor manual (later to become the pedal organ manual), its pipes being placed in towers, as a rule. Rouen had a second keyboard in 1386. A discant manual for treble pipes was sometimes added to counterbalance the now overpowering bass. In France this appears to have developed into the *positif de dos,* or *chair organ, which never assumed more than a few ranks of pipes there. In the Low Countries and Germany the development seems to have been slightly different, the chair organ, or *Rückpositiv,* not being considered an integral part of the organ. "An organ and a positive behind" was a common expression at the time, and it seems that the *Rückpositiv* originated from inclusion of a positive organ into the great organ. The pipes of the latter were enclosed in a separate case placed behind the organist, while the manuals of both instrs. were soon superposed. *Positifs de dos* are found as early as 1433 in Troyes, and by 1440 in Dijon (the latter described then by Henri Arnaut of Zwolle as having 195 pipes). Many churches had a second, smaller organ, or an organ and a positive. Basel Cathedral, for instance, had 2 organs and 3 positives for a while, and in 1473 employed an *organista cori* in addition to the regular organist. The organ at Hagenau in 1491 consisted of tenor, discant, and positive, as they were called, or pedal, manual, and chair organ, in our language. By 1429 Amiens Cathedral had 2500 pipes. Sweden possesses the remains of 4 organs from this period, one dated 1370, the others undated but made probably around 1400. All 4 have C as the lowest note, and, on all 4, B♭ appears as a "white" or natural key (as does of course the B♮). The case of the undated Norrlanda organ stands 2.60 m. (8 ft. 8 in.) high, and 1.27 m. (50 in.) wide. It has an 8-key pedalboard and 1 manual with 26 keys, roller action, 26 grooves in the wind chest, and holes for 141 pipes. The key width is 3 cm., length 6 cm., length of accidental keys, 2 cm. The Sundre organ, dated 1370, has one manual and pedalboard. The keys are lacking, but spaces are provided for 18 manual keys and 8 pedal keys. Spaces of the manual keys show that these must have been between 5 and 6½ cm. (2 and 2½ in.) wide. A roller action is also present.

The myth that the keys of old organs were so heavy they had to be depressed by full force of the clenched fist is based partly on Praetorius' statement to that effect, partly on such expressions as *pulsator organi, Orgelschläger,* and "organ beater." However, old Nordic epics refer to fiddlers as *fiðlu-sloetti* (fiddle strikers), in Renaissance Germany *Lautenschläger* (lute striker) was the accepted term for a lutanist, payment was made in Weimar in 1527 to a Hackbrettschläger (dulcimer beater) and to a Harpfenschläger, and the Roman poet Valerius Flaccus even spoke of a *pulsator citharae,* or kithara striker. None of these instrs. calls for a particularly heavy hand. The authority of Praetorius weighs heavily, but nothing in the vast amount of source material now available justifies such a statement. Several 15th- and 16th-c. contracts for renovation contain implied complaints about heavy actions, but present-day players of tracker action organs make the same comments. In his historical comments on the organ Praetorius is known to err occasionally; perhaps he too was influenced in this instance by the terminology. Zarlino reports as a curiosity the arrangement of an antique keyboard he saw in which the bass keys were so wide that the interval of a 5th could barely be spanned, but the remaining keys diminished increasingly in width toward the treble. Such a key disposition might be expected in an organ built before rollers were invented, yet having pipes of different diams. Praetorius saw keys 2½ Brunswick inches wide on an old organ at Minden, and said that on those of St. Egidius Church in Brunswick one could reach only a 5th in what was a normal oct. span.

Registers had been created by the mid-15th c. and, according to Dufourcq, may even have existed in large organs of the late 14th c. But the process of isolating every stop—or rather, of creating it by isolation—was a slow one, not completed in some areas until the early 16th c., possibly earlier in France and the Low Countries. Couplers were already known to Henri Arnaut, who wrote in Burgundy *ca.* 1440; and the *pedalboard, probably of Low Countries invention, was in existence in the 14th c. Invention of the roller and tracker system and of registers led to tremendous acceleration in the organ's growth. After the separation

of *principals (diapasons) from the *Blockwerk the organ was gradually provided with imitative solo stops in most countries. Organs in Italy and England were an exception, being satisfied for the most part with diapasons at different pitches, called *octave, *twelfth, *fifteenth, etc., and mixtures. After the Restoration (Pepys heard his first organ in 1660) an influx of foreign builders led to some modification of this pattern, but Brit. organs remained firmly anchored to their 8' diapasons and 4' principals, with few solo stops and no pedal (pedalboards were introduced in the 18th c.). In Italy also stops were known merely by their distance from the fundamental, *e.g.,* ottava, dodecima, etc., and the pedal was hung from the manual. Elsewhere stop indications were in pitch feet, and the rich *instrumentarium* of the Renaissance served as models for numerous oddly shaped pipes with new timbres, both *flue pipes and *reed pipes. The chair organ remained a 4' organ; the main body was generally at 8', or even at 16' pitch (*cf.* ganze Orgel). Until the 18th c. a preponderance of stops at higher pitches and of mixtures gave the organ a quality of great brightness and clarity, ideally suited for the playing of polyphonic music; in the 18th and 19th c. the organ was considerably toned down by excluding some of the more penetrating stops and the mixtures, and by altering the balance between higher- and lower-pitched stops in favor of the lower-pitched. The ideals of tonal character were changed. The *simplification system of Abbé Vogler, devised in the last decade of the 18th c., was in advance of the times and was a failure.

After the invention of the *pneumatic lever in the 19th c. no limits on size were imposed any longer, and organ history was no longer made in the church, but in concert and convention hall. The reaction to monster organs with up to 1000 stops on up to 100 in. pressure has fortunately now set in (spearheaded by Walcker's "Praetorius organ" of 1921). Modern organs are no more standardized than were their predecessors. The number and type of stop, number of manuals, even the type of action, vary from maker to maker and from church to church. Large organs nowadays often have 5 manuals with a 5-oct. compass, the lowest manual being for the choir (the former chair) organ, followed by great, swell, solo, and echo manuals, and a pedalboard. The traditional action, known as mechanical, or tracker, action, works in its simplest form as follows: when a key is depressed it lifts a *sticker on the rear of the key; the sticker raises the near end of a backfall that, being pivoted in the middle, causes the far end to fall, drawing down with it a tracker that pulls the *pallet open. Here backward motion is involved. In a *roller action the organ is divided into a C division (containing pipes for the C D E F♯ G♯ B♭ keys) and a C♯ division (containing pipes for the C♯ D♯ F G A B keys); here the sticker engages one arm of a roller, thereby rotating it and raising its other arm, which in turn lifts another sticker (establishing lateral motion); this communicates via a square with a tracker that pulls the pallet open. Here both backward and lateral motion are involved. (For more recent actions see: pneumatic lever, tubular-pneumatic action, electro-pneumatic action. For types of wind chest see: slider-key chest, slider chest, spring chest.) The wind supply is generated by fan blowers or motor-driven feeder bellows. Historically bellows were worked by a bellows blower (Ger.: *Kal-kant*) up to the 19th c., when a hydraulic engine was invented to do the job. This consisted of a cylinder with a piston actuated by water pressure, controlled by a valve and connected to the wind chest— a bigger and better *hydraulos (62, 63, 99, 151, 167, 170; Hennerberg in: *Bericht des dritten Kongress der I.M.G.*, 1909; Lajos Nagy: *Die Orgel von Aquincum*, 1933; Oscar Walcker: *Erinnerungen eines Orgelbauers*, 1948).

See: beard, bellows, Blockwerk, boot, Chormass, Chorstimme, console, electro-pneumatic action, fistula maxima, flue pipe, foot, foundation stops, fourniture, frein harmonique, grooves, Hintersatz, Kegellade, key, keyboard, languid, Locatz, mutation stop, nag's head swell, Oberwerk, pallet, pedal organ, phonomine, pneumatic lever, pipe, 3, positie, Postclaves, regal pipe, repeating stop, roller, roller action, roller board, slider, slider chest, slider key, soundboard, spring chest, sticker, swell, swell box, swell organ, table, tracker, tracker action, transmission, tubular-pneumatic action, Untersatz, upper board, Vordersatz, wind chest, wind gauge, wind trunk. See also: arciorgano, ardablis, arghanum, auto-harmonique-flûte, bible regal, bird organ, chair organ, chamber organ, choir organ, chord organ, clavi-flûte, 2, Cölestine, cottage organ, double organ, echo organ, flautophone, Flötenwerk, halbe Orgel, hardablis, hardulis, hirdolis, hsing lung sheng, hydraulos, idrablis, magrepha, Melodika, Mikropan, milacor, omni-harmoni-orgue, orchestra, orgă, organina, organola, organo-table, orgue Cabias, or-

Key	C^0	E^0	G^0	c^0	e^0	g^0	c^1	e^1	g^1	c^2
Interval		3rd	5th	8th	10th	12th	15th	17th	19th	22nd
Pitch feet from 8′	8	6⅖	5⅓	4	3⅕	2⅔	2	1⅗	1⅓	1
Pitch feet from 16′	16	12⅘	10⅔	8	6⅖	5⅓	4	3⅕	2⅔	2
Pitch feet from 4′	4	3⅕	2⅔	2	1⅗	1⅓	1	⅘	⅔	½

Key	e^2	g^2	c^3	e^3	g^3	c^4	e^4	g^4	c^5
Interval	24th	26th	29th	31st	33rd	36th	38th	40th	43rd
Pitch feet from 8′	⅘	⅔	½	⅖	⅓	¼	⅕	⅙	⅛
Pitch feet from 16′	1⅗	1⅓	1	⅘	⅔	½	⅖	⅓	¼
Pitch feet from 4′	⅖	⅓	¼	⅕	⅙	⅛			

gue de Barbarie, ourguéno, pneumatic organ, portative organ, positive organ, reed organ, symponia, triorganon, Viertelorgel.

Organa (Lat.), pl. of organum.

Organ-accordion, see: accordéonorgue.

Organette, see: orchestral organette.

Organetto (It.), **1.** street organ; **2.** street piano; **3.** hand-cranked upright piano (37).

Organina, hand-cranked organ made by the Automatic Organ Co. of Boston, England, in the last quarter of the 19th c., with perforated paper strips. It was distributed in France by J. Thibouville-Lamy (204).

Organine (Fr.), syn. of surdelina, according to Trichet (190).

Organino (It.), **1.** small pipe organ; **2.** small barrel organ, a bird organ; **3.** name applied in Lombardy to panpipes; **4.** a precursor of the harmonium, built by Alexandre-François Debain of Paris between 1834 and 1840, with 2 tones on each key pitched an oct. apart (89 Hipkins, 176).

Organino a cilindro, It.: barrel organ.

Organistrum [?Lat. *organae instrumentum*], see: hurdy-gurdy.

Organized clavichord (Fr.: *clavicorde organisé*), clavichord combined with one or more stops of organ pipes. Surviving specimens date from the latter half of the 18th c. See also: claviorganum.

Organized harpsichord, see: claviorganum.

Organized hurdy-gurdy (Fr.: *vielle organisée;* Ger.: *Orgelleier;* It.: *lira organizzata*), hurdy-gurdy with organ pipework and bellows housed in its body, made in France from the last quarter of the 18th c. on. The crank operates both wheel and bellows, and the valves controlling wind admission to the pipes are opened when the corresponding keys are depressed. The pipework consisted of 1 stop, sometimes 2, either or both of which can be drawn off. Made in several forms, most commonly in guitar shape (149, 176).

Organo, 1. It.: organ; **2.** see: Lowery organo.

Órgano, Sp.: organ. See also: muérgano, uérgano.

Organochordon, 1. a combination piano-pipe organ devised by Abbé Vogler and built in Stockholm by Rackwitz in 1798, in form of a square piano, with 3½ stops; **2.** *piano-harmonium built in the early 1890's by Gustav Adolf Buschmann of Hamburg, with 3 manuals and pedal, imitative of all orchestral instrs. (149, 158, 204).

Organo-diapazo, *bowed keyboard instr. made by Johann Christian Dietz, Sr., and exhibited in Paris in 1806. It is said to have taken up less space than an ordinary piano (176, 204).

Organo di legno (It.: organ of wood), It. 16th- and 17th-c. designation of a small flue pipe organ, as opposed to a regal organ. An organo di legno is recorded in Florence in 1589, and Monteverdi required 2 organi di legno for his *Orfeo* in 1607, as well as a regal. The Ger. equivalent of the term is Flötenwerk.

Organo-harmonica, improved seraphine invented by W. E. Evans of London, with free reeds of thin steel (89).

Organola, automatic organ built by Oscar Walcker of Ludwigsburg from 1901 on, intended for use in small churches and designed to be played with perforated paper rolls made by the Aeolian Co. (196).

Organo-lyricon, 2-manual *piano-harmonium devised by De St. Pern, a musical amateur, in 1810, with registers imitating wind instrs. (176, 204).

Organon, Gk.: tool, instr., musical instr.; finally, organ.

Organon trigonon enarmonion, Flavius Josephus' name for the Egyptian harp (170).

Organophone, 1. *music box patented 1856 by Soualle of Paris (158); **2.** improved harmonium shown by Claude Gavioli *jeune* at the Paris Exposition of 1900; **3.** a harmonium of this name, made by Alexandre-François Debain, is mentioned by Hipkins (89); see: organino, 4.

Organo-piano, a combined piano-orgue expressif with 2 manuals, shown at the 1834 Paris Exposition by Achille Muller. An instr. of the same name was shown by Rönisch at the London Exhibition of 1900 (149, 176, 204).

Organo portatile, It.: barrel organ (39).

Organo-table, small organ in form of a sewing box or table, of 4-oct. compass, patented in France by Fourneaux on May 23, 1857 (204).

Organo-Violine, free-reed keyboard instr. invented by Bernhard Eschenbach of Königshofen ca. 1814, with a 6-oct. compass.

Organ pipe, see: pipe, 2.

Organum [Gk. *organon*], Lat.: musical instr. During the Middle Ages the word denoted the organ.

Organum hydraulicum, Lat.: hydraulos.

Orgatron, see: Everett orgatron.

Orgel, Ger.: organ. See also: halbe Orgel, ganze Orgel.

Orgelhorn (Ger.), syn. of Hornwerk.

Orgelklavier, Ger.: piano-organ; claviorganum.

Orgelleier, Ger.: organized hurdygurdy.

Orglice, name of several Slov. instrs.: **1.** idiochord *tube zither made from a cornstalk, also called goslice, a child's toy; **2.** syn. of trstenke; **3.** mouth organ (144).

Orgue, Fr.: organ. See also: ogre.

Orgue à cent francs (Fr.: hundredfranc organ), the pop. and commercial name by which the *Alexandre organ was known (204).

Orgue à cylindre, Fr.: barrel organ.

Orgue Alexandre, see: Alexandre organ.

Orgue à manivelle, Fr.: barrel organ.

Orgue américain, Fr.: American organ.

Orgue à percussion, improved *orgue

expressif by Martin of Paris, 1852, with a clearer attack.

Orgue Cabias, simple organ invented 1834 by Cabias, with short keys, all identical in size (204).

Orgue d'Allemagne, Fr. term in use between 1797 and the mid-19th c. to designate the *barrel organ (197).

Orgue de Barbarie, Fr.: *barrel organ. Named after Giovanni Barberi of Modena, one of the first makers of barrel organs. The term was first used in 1702 (176, 197).

Orgue de coll (Cat.: neck organ), *portative organ of 15th-c. Spain.

Orgue excelsior (Fr.), improved harmonium invented by Gilbert de Sailly and R. de La Bastille of Paris in 1892 (204).

Orgue expressif (Fr.) (Ger.: *Expressionsorgel*), free-reed keyboard instr. invented by Gabriel-Joseph Grenié of Paris in 1810, the first keyboard instr. to be furnished exclusively with free reeds, and a forerunner of the harmonium. It had a single register, with a 5-oct. compass, F^1–f^3, and 4 bellows worked by 2 pedals. The "expression" was controlled by a stop establishing an intermediary connection between bellows and wind chest. After Debain had patented the word *harmonium,* other Fr. makers used the term orgue expressif for their harmoniums, so that orgue expressif became synonymous with harmonium for a time. Folding instrs. for travelers were made by Achille Muller of Paris ca. 1845. See also: expression, organ piano, orgue à percussion, orgue orphonium, orgue phonochromatique, phonéorgue, poïkilorgue, théorgue (132, 176).

Orgue hydraulique, Fr.: hydraulos.

Orgue magique, automatic organ invented by Martin de Corteuil of Paris and patented Aug. 24, 1863, played by means of perforated paper strips. See also: antiphonel, musique perforée (204).

Orgue-mélodium (Fr.), precursor of the *Alexandre organ; it was made by

Jacob Alexandre and his son in Paris *ca.* 1843 (204).

Orguen de coll (Sp.: neck organ), obs. Sp.: portative organ.

Orguen de peu (Sp.: foot organ), obs. Sp.: positive organ.

Orguene, orguine, OFr.: organ.

Orgue-orchestre, a hand-cranked *reed organ invented by Jean-Charles Ehrhart of Paris and patented Oct. 24, 1834, with 2 pinned cylinders and 6 stops (204).

Orgue-orphonium, a powerful *orgue expressif with 7 stops, patented by Gavioli *jeune* of Paris on Feb. 4, 1869 (204).

Orgue phonochromatique, improved *orgue expressif patented by Lorenzi of Paris on June 7, 1855 (204).

Orgue portatif, Fr.: portative organ.

Orgue positif, Fr.: positive organ.

Orgue-trompette, Fr.: trumpeter (automatic).

Orguinette, syn. of clariona.

Oricungo, var. of urucungo (152).

Orlo, 1. Sp.: crumhorn; first mentioned in Spain in 1559 as *orlos de Alemania;* **2.** organ stop found on Sp. organs, of narrow-scaled reed pipes at 8′ pitch. *Cf.* violeta (154).

Orloge (Fr.), probably the mechanized *bell chime of med. France. Mentioned in the *Roman de la Rose, ca.* 1300 (E. Buhle, *"Das Glockenspiel . . ."* in: *Festschrift . . . von Liliencron,* 1910).

Ormfa, name by which Paulus Paulirinus, *ca.* 1460, designates the bagpipe.

Oro, Afro-Cuban *bull-roarer, used at funeral rites of persons of Yoruba descent. It assumes different shapes, sometimes that of a fish (152).

Orodo, *arched harp of the Madi (Moyo) of Uganda, with 5 or 7 strings (195).

Orologium, see: horologium.

Orpharion [Orpheus + Arion], obs. stringed instr. identical with the pandora except that it was smaller (length *ca.* 1 m. [40 in.]) and was tuned like a lute— in other words, a substitute lute. Probably invented by John Rose, inventor of the pandora; an orpharion of his dated

1580 survives, though much restored. First mentioned in Engl. literature by Drayton in 1593, last in 1655 (89 Dart, 170, 180).

Orphéa [Orpheus], improved harmonium patented by Dupland of Paris on July 15, 1863 (204).

Orphéal [Orpheus], a combination piano, organ, and harmonium invented 1910 by Georges Cloetens of Brussels (176).

Orphéi [Orpheus], harmonium patented by Ligier in France on June 3, 1864, with bellows actuated by a hand crank (204).

Orpheon [Orpheus], **1.** *bowed keyboard instr. of the second half of the 18th c., with 4 gut strings and rotating wheel; **2.** organ stop imitative of the above, of metal flue pipes at 16′ pitch, similar to a Geigend Prinzipal (133, 176).

Orpheorion, var. of orpharion.

Orpheusharmonie (Fr.: *harmonie d'Orphée*), keyboard instr. of unknown construction, built by Leonhard Mältzel of Vienna, the younger brother of Johann Nepomuk Mältzel. It was completed in or by 1814 and had a 5-oct. compass (144, 176).

Orphica (Ger.: *Orphika*), small portable piano invented by Carl Leopold Röllig of Vienna in 1795, with one string per note, Vienna action, and a compass ranging from 2 to 4 octs. Built in shape of a harp lying on a box, it was intended for open-air performances and could be set on the player's lap or suspended from his neck by a band. The keys were about half standard width. Usual length of the instr. was 105 cm. (41 in.), but some were as much as 136 cm. (53½ in.) in length. Orphicas continued to be made until around 1830 (40, 149).

Orphion [Orpheus], unidentified instr. invented by Thomas Pilkington (b. 1625) (79).

Orugōru, chime of *resting bells used in Buddhist temples of Japan, also in *kabuki* music. The bells are inserted in a wooden board and played with 2 metal rods (135).

Oruto, lute of Kenya (120).

Oseke, flute of the Alur of Uganda, identical with the eruma. The term is also used by the Lugbara and Mali of Uganda (195).

Ossets [Cat. *os,* bone], Cat. friction idiophone made of a series of graduated bird bones strung by each end to a rope, like the steps of a ladder, and suspended from the player's neck. The left hand holds the lower loop of the cord while the right sounds the bones with a small ring (57).

Osun, Afro-Cuban ritual rattle consisting of a small metal vessel on a long metal stem, surmounted by the figure of a cock (152).

O-teki, syn. of riū-teki.

Otekra, bamboo *cross flute of the Garo of Assam, with 2 fingerholes (172).

Otongoli, *arched harp of the Gwere of Uganda, with 6 strings (195).

Oto tsuzumi (Jap.: shoulder *tsuzumi*), syn. of ko tsuzumi.

O-tsi, *goblet drum of Burma, with zigzag lacings (173).

O-tsuzumi (Jap.: large tsuzumi), large tsuzumi of cherry or quince wood, with heads usually of cowhide. It is held at the player's left hip and struck with 1–3 fingers of his right hand; used in nō music. *Ca.* 30 cm. (12 in.) long. Also called e-tsuzumi, okawa. It corresponds to the chang go of Korea and the chang ku of China (135, 157).

Ottavina [dim. of *ottava*], abbr. of spinetta ottavina, a spinet at octave (4′) pitch.

Ottavino (It.) [dim. of *ottavo,* eighth], **1.** piccolo flute; **2.** piccolo clarinet; **3.**

organ stop, a diapason at 2′ pitch; **4.** for the spinet see: ottavina.

Ottu, drone oboe of S. India that accompanies the nāgasuram. It resembles the latter but is slightly longer; 4 or 5 holes are pierced in the lower end; by closing these either partly or completely the *sruti* (keynote) of the ottu is brought to the desired pitch (179).

Oud, see: 'ūd, uti.

Ouïe, Fr.: soundhole.

Ouïre [Lat. **uter*], New Prov.: **1.** skin of a bagpipe; **2.** musette (bagpipe) (35).

Oukpwe, side-blown ivory horn of Upper Guinea (132, 185).

Ourguéno, Languedoc: organ (197).

Outa (hunting bow), *musical bow of the S. African Damara, converted into a musical instr. from a weapon by the addition of a tuning loop. The bow is held between player's teeth and is struck with a small stick, his mouth acting as resonator, his other hand stopping the string (17).

Outa otji humba, full name of the outa (116).

Ovambu guitar, name given to a pluri-arc of the S. African Damara, originally so called by C. J. Andersson in 1875 (116).

Ower-ower, syn. of wer-wer.

Oyualli, rattle of ancient Mexico, made of snail shells, worn as anklets or breast ornaments. The word also means pellet bell or jingle (105).

Ozi, drum of Burma (103).

Ozohahi, ankle rattle of the S. African Herero, made of cocoons filled with small stones, strung on strips of leather and tied around dancers' ankles. They are worn only by women (116).

Pa, *arched harp of the Chamba of Volta (19).

Pa'amon, small bells or *pellet bells of ancient Israel, sewn on garments of the high priests (170).

Pabellón [OFr. *paveillon*], Sp.: bell (of brass instrs.).

Pachán [Yoruba *okpa-achán*], Afro-Cuban *percussion stick made of a bunch of 9 twigs. Also called ikú-achán (152).

Pa chiao ku, syn. of pa fang ku.

Padang, see: pagang.

Padatrong, rattle of the W. Torres Strait, made of sticks bound together (176).

Padiglione, It.: bell (of brass instrs.).

Pa fang ku, *frame drum of China, an octagonal tambourine with wooden frame and glued snakeskin membrane, with brass jingles; 14–17 cm. (5½–6½ in.) diam. Also called pa chiao ku (178).

Pagang, idiochord *tube zither of the Long Kiput of Borneo. Also called kantom (119).

Pagie, Akk. equivalent of the sa-li-ne-lu.

Pagolo, polyheterochord *musical bow of New Britain, E. New Guinea, and New Ireland, with 2 strings and tuning loop, but no resonator. In New Britain it has been obs. since the 1880's, when it was supplanted by the Jew's-harp. In New Guinea it is played by women only (17, 141).

Pagon, panpipes of the Kashibo Indians of the Upper Amazon, with 3 pipes (105).

Págugu [Yoruba *okpa*, stick + *egungun*, spirits of the dead], Afro-Cuban *stamping tube, sometimes terminating in a carved head. It is used at funeral rites. The págugu is a symbolic substitution of the dead and must therefore be of the same length as the deceased person. Also called akpateré, ayíguí, iguí-égun (152).

Pahawang, syn. of babandi.

Pah pung, stamping tube of the Miau of Vietnam (103).

Pahu, 1. generic name for membrane drums in Polynesia. They are made of breadfruit tree wood or hollowed coconut palm, with laced sharkskin heads, usually of conical shape with a single head. The height is 30–90 cm. (1–3 ft.). Those of Hawaii were imported from the south some 6 centuries ago. Some specimens have elaborately carved pedestals or bases; on some S. Seas islands these reach a total of 2½ m. (8 ft.), 30 cm. (1 ft.) in diam. Formerly used in religious ceremonies, the drums are played with bare hands; **2.** *slit drum of the Maori of New Zealand, who have no membrane drums. The instrs. are suspended in the open from a simple frame on a raised platform, and used as signal instrs. Some specimens are shaped to resemble a canoe. The drum is struck with a wooden mallet. In some instances it consists of a living tree that is naturally hollow; it is then formed by cutting a long tongue out of the standing tree (8, 77).

Pahu vanana, single-headed drum of the Marquesas Islands, with laced head stretched over a hoop (176).

Pai ah, small bamboo shawm of Cambodia, with 6 front fingerholes (47).

P'ai hsiao, panpipes of China. In ancient times they were composed of 12 *kuans arranged in raft form, with the smallest pipe in the center and the others in 2 groups of male and female to each side. The actual number has varied in different epochs. Today the pipes are of cane, stopped, all of the same width, and number 16, their pitches corresponding to the 12 *lü* and the 4 grave *lü*. According to tradition the sounds are those of the phoenix. The p'ai hsiao is a Confucian ritual instr., tuned $a^0 b^0 c\sharp^1 d\sharp^1$ $f^1 g^1 a^1 b^1 a\sharp^1 g\sharp^1 f\sharp^1 e^1 d^1 c^1 b\flat^0 a\flat^0$. It corresponds to the Japanese sho no fuye. Also called fong hsiao (89, 142).

Pai k'ung hu, see: pe k'ung hu.

P'ai pan, clapper of China, made of 3 cuneiform pieces of wood connected by a cord and struck together by a flick of the wrist. The outer surfaces are slightly convex. It is played in the theater, at funerals, and by mendicants. Also called pan (142, 178).

Pa-ipu, *hourglass drum of Hawaii, made from 2 calabashes. Also called hokeo (176).

Pajupilli, rustic willow pipe of Finland. *Cf.* pilli (89).

Pak, wooden clappers of Korea, made of 6 pieces of hardwood, rarely of ivory, tied at one end by a silk cord. All are of the same length. The pak corresponds to the p'o pan of China and the haku han of Japan. *Ca.* 34 cm. (13 in.) long, 6 cm. (2½ in.) wide (66).

Pakhawaj (Sans.), the N. India name of the mridanga; however, the pakhawaj has smaller heads, tuned a 4th or 5th apart. The body is of clay (89, 179).

Pakhe dumbā, oboe of the Kachin of Shan State, Burma, with conical tube made of a single section of softwood, 4 front fingerholes and 2 rear (172).

Pakuda, stamping board of the Minkopie of the Andaman Islands, consisting of a curved board, pointed at one end and rounded at the other, with 2 holes like eyes close to the rounded end. *Ca.* 1½ m. (5 ft.) long (173).

Pakuru, obs. *concussion sticks of the Maori of New Zealand, played in different ways; 2 hardwood sticks, one 15 cm. (6 in.), the other *ca.* 36 cm. (14 in.) long, were struck together, the smaller

against the larger. The larger stick had one flat and one concave surface and was sometimes beautifully carved. It was held in the player's left hand, one end being placed between his teeth, flat side down. He then breathed the words of a song onto the wood while tapping it. Another method of playing consisted of 2 persons standing about 1.30 m. (4 ft.) apart, each holding one stick the length of a walking stick, which they threw to each other and caught; the sticks touched in mid-air, yielding a tone, while the players chanted (8).

Pakwulo, syn. of kwororo.

Pala, *end-blown flute of the Venda and Bakgatla of S. Africa, made of impala horn and used as a signal instr. It corresponds to the naka ya sefako. Also called naka (116).

Pa la man, Chin. name of the balāban (75 II).

Palets, syn. of cymbalettes.

Pallet (Fr.: *soupape;* Ger.: *Ventil;* It.: *valvula*), in an organ the hinged valve that controls the admission of air, particularly that from the wind chest to the pipes. *Cf.* pneumatic lever.

Palmula, Lat.: key (of a keyboard).

Palo, palo hueco (Sp.: pole, hollow pole), Sp.: **1.** occasional name of the yohuacán; **2.** syn. of yabó (152).

Palo roncador (Sp.: snoring stick), *bull-roarer of Colombia and Venezuela (152).

Palototan, small drum of Pegu, Lower Burma, to which little balls are attached so as to strike the membranes when the drum is shaken (176).

Palo zumbador, Sp.: bull-roarer.

Palsiphone [Gk. *palsis,* vibration + *phone,* sound], apparatus patented by Guerre & Martin of France on March 11, 1890, for setting strings of a piano, cello, etc., into vibration by electropneumatic means (204).

Palua, bamboo flute of the Batak of Sumatra, with 5 fingerholes (176).

Palwee, see: palweh.

Palweh, *ring flute of Burma, made of

cane, with a wax block or natural node forming the wind deflector. Also called pillui (14).

Pambai, *cylindrical drum of S. India, always played in pairs, the body being colored and decorated. The heads are stretched over projecting hoops and laced in Y pattern. Played with 2 sticks, 1 slightly curved, the other curved like a cow horn. *Ca.* 30 cm. (1 ft.) long (179).

Pāmbunāgasuram, Tamil syn. of nāgasuram.

Pamigán, single or double ekón (152).

Pampa, syn. of sinfoyna.

Pampame, long wooden trumpet of the Fulbe of W. Africa. *Cf.* fanfami (176).

Pan, syn. of p'ai pan. *Cf.* pang.

Panaba, see: pangaba.

Panaulon, *cross flute with a B♭ foot joint, built in 1813 by Langer of Vienna and improved by Wolfram of Vienna and J. L. Ickler of Bremen in 1825 (176).

Panchtār (Pers.: five-string), the long-necked lute of Persia and Turkestan, with 5 strings, similar to the dutār except for the number of strings (132).

Pandair [Sp. *pandero*], a Mozarabic tambourine mentioned in 12th-c. Sp. literature. *Cf.* bandair, pandero (44).

Pandapanda, Swah.: horn (144).

Pandean flute, organ stop of metal flue pipes at 8′ or 4′ pitch, a continuation of the higher *flauto di Pan, and similar to the Wiener Flöte (198).

Pandean pipe, see: panpipes.

Pandeiro, Port.: tambourine.

Panderete [Sp., dim. of *pandero*], **1.** Sp.: tambourine. The term was used by Juan Ruiz in the early 14th c.; **2.** Afro-Cuban *hourglass drum, played horizontally, resting on the player's knees (152).

Pandero [?Gk. *pandoura*], Sp. tambourine, round or square, often hung with jingles or pellet bells. Glossed as tympanum by Nebrija (in 1495). See also: bandair, binco, pandair, panderue.

Panderue, Basque: tambourine (56).

Pandir [Gk. *pandoura*], long-necked lute of Armenia. *Cf.* fandur (89).

Pandola, scraper of the S. It. Cam-

pagna, consisting of 2 sticks bowed with a saw-shaped wooden bow (169).

Pandora, obs. stringed instr. reputedly invented by the London viol maker John Rose in 1562. A continuo instr. of bass size, it had a flat belly and back, frontal string fastener, central rose, lateral tuning pegs, 15 fixed frets, and originally 6 pairs of metal strings. A characteristic feature of the pandora is its scalloped silhouette, usually composed of 3 lobes. Except for this outline and the string fastener, the pandora would be a bass *cittern. The name is first mentioned in Gascoigne's *Jocasta* of 1566, and occurs last in an inventory of the Berlin orchestra instrs. in 1667. Mersenne states that in his day it was scarcely in use any more. Trichet, *ca.* 1640, describes the oblique string fastener and nut, which gave greater speaking length to the lower strings, and the frets that slanted accordingly; of its 7 courses of metal strings the lowest were spun (*retortillé*), he reports. They were plucked with a plectrum. The increase from 6 to 7 courses of strings took place in the last decade of the 16th c., and the change from a straight to a slanting string fastener and nut also dates from that period. The tuning was $C^0 D^0 G^0 c^0 e^0 a^0$ or $G^1 C^0 D^0 G^0 c^0 e^0 a^0$; Praetorius gives $C^0 D^0 G^0 c^0 f^0 a^0 d^1$. The name pandora was also applied to the *orpharion, as well as to a variety of theorbo-lute, invented by Alessandro Piccinino of Bologna. The pandora measured 137–140 cm. (54–55 in.). Also called bandora, Bandoer (80 XIII, 140, 169, 170, 190).

Pandoura [?Sum. *pan tur,* small bow], long-necked lute of ancient Greece and Rome, similar to that of W. Asia and Egypt, with small body, in late classical times sometimes portrayed as spade-shaped, with fretted neck wider than that of earlier forms and devoid of tuning pegs. Pollux (in his *Onomastikon*) mentions its 3 strings, whence its Gk. name: trichordon. The pandoura was but rarely encountered in Greece and in Rome, but it lived on elsewhere as bandurria, tanbūr, tanbura, etc. (170).

Pandourion, instr. equated with the *koboz in a Gk. treatise of *ca.* 800, described as having 7 frets and 3, 4, or 5 strings (170).

Pandur [*pan tur*], Sum.: small bow; possibly the etymon of pandoura, tanbūr (170).

Pandura, see: pandoura.

Panduri, bottle-shaped fiddle of Georgia, U.S.S.R., with narrow, elongated body, pegdisc, and 3 strings tuned $d^0 g^0 c^1$; it is held vertically, lower end down. The shape is that of some early med. fiddles. Also called lira (170).

Pandurina, small mandora with very narrow, almond-shaped body, short and wide fretted neck, sickle-shaped pegbox, lateral pegs, central soundhole with rose, frontal string fastener, and gut strings. Praetorius described it as having 4 or 5 courses of strings. In the 18th c. the instr. appears under the name of *mandolino milanese, unchanged in form. Earlier syns. were Bandürchen, mandoretta, Mandöer, Mandurinchen, according to Praetorius.

Panflöte, organ stop. See: flauto di Pan.

Pang, 1. percussion instr. of China, consisting of a block of wood *ca.* 25 cm. (10 in.) long, shaped like a brick, with a series of deep slits running across it, thus forming vibrating teeth. Struck with a stick; **2.** *slit drum of China, used by night watchmen, made of a piece of bamboo 38–64 cm. (15–25 in.) long. Also called t'o (142).

Pangaba, classical drum of Bengal, conical, made of wood, with single head, wedge-braced.

Pangang, see: gong pangang.

Panggal awi, bamboo *humming top of W. Java (121).

Panggalen, syn. of gangsingan (121).

Pang hiang, metallophone of Korea, rarely used; it corresponds to the fang hiang of China. Its 2 rows of 8 plaques each rest horizontally in an elaborate frame, similar to those of the bell chimes and stone chimes. The plaques are about

18 cm. (7 in.) long and 5–6 cm. (2–2½ in.) wide. The instr. was introduced to Korea in the 12th c. (66).

Pang ku, drum of China, made of 6 wedges of wood held in place by a metal hoop, with single nailed head. The drum is small and flat, 15–25 cm. (6–10 in.) in diam., and is used in pop. orchestras and the theater (89, 142).

Pango, *musical bow of the Washambala of Kenya, with resonator (176).

Pangolo, var. of pagolo.

Pāngrā (Hindust.), syn. of pūngī.

Pang tse, 1. *percussion sticks of China, consisting of 2 redwood sticks of the same length, one half-round held in the hollow of the left hand and struck with the other (142); **2.** in W. Shantung the pang tse is a *slit drum with a handle on the underside (176).

Pang tse ti, flute (ti) of China, played together with the pang tse. The flute is *ca.* 30 cm. (12 in.) long in N. China, up to 45 cm. (17½ in.) elsewhere, has 6 fingerholes and an extra hole covered with a thin membrane, a mirliton device (142).

Pangul, *aeolian bell of Korea, with a clapper in form of a horizontal cross from which a brass fish is suspended to catch the breeze. It hangs from temple, pagoda, and palace eaves, also from private houses. Equivalent of the Jap. futaku (66).

Panharmonicon (Ger.: *Panharmonikon*), **1.** automatophone invented and built by Johann Nepomuk Mältzel of Vienna, completed in 1805. One of the earliest instrs. to contain free reeds, it was also furnished with wind and percussion instrs. and could imitate a whole orchestra, including the string section. It was actuated by pinned cylinders and bellows. Mältzel sold it in Paris and upon his return to Vienna built a second instr., an improved model. Beethoven's *Schlacht bei Vittoria* (*Wellington's Victory*), first performed in 1813, was written for the panharmonicon; **2.** automatophone similar to the above, made by Joseph Gurck of Vienna, 1810. The string sound was created by organ pipes (37, 144, 176).

Pan hu, rare *hu ch'in of China, similar to the erh hu but with a wooden belly (142).

Panhuehuetl, present-day drum of C. America, of pre-Columbian origin, formerly played by the Aztec. Today it is a *cylindrical drum with single head and carved body, ca. 1 m. (40 in.) high, played in vertical position. Cf. huehuetl (137).

Pāni, Kan. equivalent of the naguar (173).

Paningba, paningbwa, var. of kweningba.

Pan ku, see: pang ku.

Panmelodicon, friction bar instr. invented by Franz Leppich of Vienna in 1810, with rectangular metal bars controlled from a keyboard. It was an imitation of the *clavicylinder, and the bars were sounded by being pushed against a rotating metal cylinder (169).

Panna, trumpet of the Bororo Indians of Brazil, made of 3 or 4 gourds joined together with wax and perforated so as to form a tube (105).

Pannang-jux, syn. of nares-jux.

Panophone, piano patented in France on Aug. 8, 1894, by Bozza, with mechanism to sustain the sound (204).

Panorgue-piano, piano-organ of Jaulin of Paris, with the organ section underneath the piano (176).

Panpalina, Basque: small bell; syn. of chincha, joare.

Panpipes (Fr.: flûte de Pan, sifflet de Pan, flûte polycalame; Ger.: Pansflöte; It.: flauto di Pan, siringa), set of tuned tubes, usually stopped at the lower end and joined together to form a raft (raft pipes) or a bundle (bundle pipes). The tubes are devoid of fingerholes and are blown across the top. In the Far East they are often provided with notches. Commonly made of cane, they are also made of stone or metal, clay or wood, a whole set sometimes being carved out of a single block of stone or wood. Panpipes are found on all continents. In Europe all are stopped and are made in raft form. As *syrinx, the panpipes were known to ancient Greece, where they were played by shepherds; the usual number of tubes was 7, but as few as 3 and as many as 13 have been depicted. The Romans took their panpipes to the provinces: specimens in wood and in bronze have been found in France in the characteristic Gallo-Roman form of a rectangle with diagonal lower corner. In med. Europe we can trace panpipes back to the 11th c. See also: alumnaxkäki, antara, atala, biwabon, bufacanyes, bwebalabala, capador, capapuercas, castrapuercas, castrera, castruera, cheko, chiru, cioro, ciufolo pastorale, coštimaje, dedeco, dero, dorremi, eapamale, fieould, fistola, fistola pani, Fotzhobel, frestel, freteau, fretel, gaita, hatong, havirare, hehei, hērēroka, hetupue, huayra-puhura, iyupana, jinā, kammu-purru, kariso, kaur, 2, kurna, lue, maiso, makwanga, man, mavonda, mithqāl, mizmār dūduyī, muscal, mūsīqāl, nai, notiru, nulolematan, nunumata, obulere, orebi, organino, pagon, p'ai hsiao, peduba, pepe, perubali, peruliababaro, peruliro, phusa, piahanú, pirutu, piskulice, puepava, quarta, Rohrpfeife, rondador, ruliapa, sa fa fir, sa-it, sampoña, sanaporcs, sanatrujes, Satyrpfeife, seno, seringonási, serulo, seseri, sho no fuye, shu'aibīya sico, sifflet de chauderonnier, sifflet de Pan, sioulet cristedou, sipowanamige, siri, siringa, siroro, siru, sirumee, sisi, so, syringe, syrinx, täks, taliuma, talusuba, texboya, thilo, toriibakue, trstenke, tselo, tsula ya noko, tsungali, tule, tumpia-yot, ueobaba, ueopali, ueopama, urusa, urutsa, vatana, vatanatu, wezai, yupana, yuxpána, zampoña, zero, zuffolo pastorale (21, 170).

Pansflöte, Ger.: panpipes.

Pansymphonicon, a combined pianoharmonium of Peter Singer of Salzburg, 1839. Also called polyharmonion (176).

Pansymphonium, keyboard instr. invented by Robert Lechleitner of the

Lechtal, Tirol, by 1873, when it was shown at the Vienna World Exposition. Built in form of a large grand piano, it had registers for 2 different kinds of organ tone, 1 harmonium tone and 1 string tone. Only 1 model was produced.

Pantaleon [inventor's name], outsize dulcimer invented by Pantaleon Hebenstreit of Merseburg by 1697, made for him by Gottfried Silbermann, later by Hänel. Descriptions of the instr. vary considerably: some authors mention 2 soundboards, side by side, 1 for gut, the other for metal strings; Dr. Burney reports it as having had 186 strings and a length exceeding 9 ft.; another writer says that it was 5–8 ft. long and 2 ft. wide. The name Pantaleon (not Pantalon) was bestowed on it in 1705 by Louis XIV, before whom Hebenstreit performed. The fact that Dresden in 1719 employed a pantaleonist may give some idea of the vogue that the instr. enjoyed. Later its name was temporarily transferred to the square piano, particularly that with downstriking action (41, 92, 149).

Pan t'ang ku, *frame drum of China, with single head stretched over an iron hoop and played with thin bamboo sticks in funeral processions. Ca. 8 cm. (3 in.) high, 36 cm. (14 in.) in diam. (142).

Pantophone, *barrel organ invented by Masera, improved and patented by L'Épée in France in 1891. The barrels had movable pegs. In Italy it was known as suona-tutto (204).

Pantu, *gambang gangsa with bossed bars (121).

Pao chün chih, small brass gong of China, with central boss, circular, suspended from a horizontal bar; 10–15 cm. (4–6 in.) in diam. (142).

Papakungbu, *ground bow of the Andekelao Pygmies of the Congo. Also called ikpwokpwo (128).

Papan, oval bull-roarer of New Guinea (176).

Papanggalen, bamboo *humming top of W. Java (121).

Para, arched harp of Niger (144).

Paradon (Fr., Ger.), corr. of baryton.

Parakapzuk, bagpipe of Armenia, similar to the tulum, with horn bell and 5 holes on each of the 2 pipes, immediately opposite each other (13).

Parallele, Ger.: slider.

Pardessus de viole (Fr.), Fr. 5-stringed soprano *viola da gamba, tuned $g^0 c^1 e^1 a^1 d^2$, according to Jean Rousseau (1687). It was still played in Laborde's day (1780), and, according to him, it was held upright on the player's knees. See also: quinton (124).

Pardessus de viole d'amour, small-sized viola d'amore.

Paré, "tuning fork" idiophone of Kulavi, Celebes, identical with the re-re (112).

Paredon, see: paradon.

Parforcehorn, Ger. term for a natural horn with 1½ hoop-like coils used by hunters—the horn of the "*par force*" hunt with hounds. Possibly the origin of the flugelhorn, since the *Flügelmeister* was in charge of a *Flügel* (wing) of the hunt. See also: corno par force.

Parrai, 1. syn. of parrang; **2.** Tamil word meaning drum (68).

Parrang, *hourglass drum of the Muria of Bastar, India, made of clay with 2 cowhide heads with zigzag lacings. In some villages it is used as a substitute for the *māndri; 46–60 cm. (18–24 in.) long, with heads 23 cm. (9 in.) in diam. Also called parrai, parrayin, tori parra (68).

Parrayin, syn. of parrang.

Parri chup en ro, *nose flute of Ponape, Micronesia. Cf. kash (203).

Partition-Mustel, tuning device in form of a metallophone with keyboard, invented by Victor Mustel of Paris and patented Mar. 29, 1888, with 12 bronze bars tuned to the 12 equally tempered semitones of the octave, and furnished with sympathetically vibrating resonators (169).

Partiturophon, polyphonic *electrophonic instr. developed in 1935 by Jörg Mager from his Sphärophon.

Paruntzi, musical bow of Ecuador (89).

Pasedel, corr. of Bassettl.

Pastorita, see: Nachthorn.

Paštše, *mouth bow of the Maya of San Antonio, Brit. Honduras, tapped with a stick (105).

Pasu, *cylindrical drum of Tokelau, W. Polynesia, with sharkskin head (77).

Pat, patbo, small *cylindrical drum of Burma. *Cf.* pat waing (176).

Pataha, Sans.: drum (173).

Patala, see: pattala.

Pate, small *slit drum of Pukapuka, Ellice Islands, the Loyalty Islands, Samoa, and Viti (77).

Patma, *barrel drum of Burma, of wood, with 2 heads held by V- or Y-lacings. Tuning paste is applied to the center of each head. The drum is suspended horizontally and played with bare hands on both heads. *Ca.* 60 cm. (2 ft.) long (172, 178).

Patola (crocodile), syn. of mi gyaung (148).

Patouille, obs. Fr. term for xylophone, used by Mersenne.

Patpati, small *rattle drum of N. India, with 2 heads, attached to a handle. Sometimes it is filled with grain, sometimes small balls are tied to a cord so as to strike the heads when the drum is shaken. A child's toy (176).

Patsa, syn. of patbo.

Pattala (Burm.) [Sans. *pataha,* drum], royal xylophone of Burma, with 17–23 bamboo slabs of different lengths, tuned by affixing wax to the underside, and suspended over a carved trough that acts as resonator (138).

Patuweh, side-blown trumpet of the Canella Indians of Brazil, made of a section of cane to which an elongated calabash is affixed (176).

Pat waing, in Burma a set of 21 drums suspended in a circular frame (103).

Pau, Jew's-harp of the Kachin of Shan State, Burma, made of bamboo (172).

Pauke [MHGer. *pûke, bouke*], Ger.: kettledrum. The word has been in use since the 13th c., but as a generic term for any drum used as a signal instr. Virdung in 1511 still used it in this sense. Its specific use as a kettledrum is of comparatively modern date (169).

Pava (Sans.), *cross flute of India, with 6 front fingerholes (176).

Pavillion [Fr. *pavillon*], obs. Engl. for the bell of a wind instr.

Pavillon, Fr.: bell (of a wind instr.).

Pavillon chinois, Fr.: Jingling Johnnie.

Paxiuba, *vertical flute of the Tucano Indians of the Upper Amazon, made of paxiuba wood (176).

Paya, drum of Pukapuka, W. Polynesia (77).

Payecha, scraper of Spain (120).

Pazi, var. of hpa si.

Peacock sitar, syn. of mayurī.

Peau de bufle, Fr.: *buff leather.

Pea whistle, whistle in which a pea is enclosed to give a trilling effect.

Pecherz z grochem, Pol.: "bladder and peas," a folk instr. (89).

Pectis, see: pektis.

Pedal [Lat. *pedalis,* adj.] (Fr.: *pédale;* Ger.: *Pedal;* It.: *pedale*), **1.** foot lever, as on the piano; **2.** the component keys of an organ pedalboard; **3.** 17th-c. name of a harpsichord with registration pedals, so named "because it is contrived to give varieties with the foot" (Thomas Mace, 1676). See also: pedal harpsichord.

Pedal accordion (Fr.: *accordéon à pédales*), accordion patented in France by Brendel & Klösser, with bellows controlled by pedals (204).

Pedalboard (Fr.: *clavier de pédales;* Ger.: *Pedalklaviatur*), keyboard for the feet, as on organs, probably invented by Lodewijk van Walbeke of Brabant (d. 1318). Paulus Paulirinus, writing *ca.* 1460, mentions both organ and clavichord pedalboards. Early organ pedalboards had no pipes of their own, but were hung from the manual. See also: organ, pédalier.

Pedalcembalo, Ger.: pedal harpsichord.

Pedal clavichord (Fr.: *clavicorde à*

pédales; Ger.: *Pedalklavichord*), clavichord to which a pedalboard is attached, with or without strings of its own. Paulus Paulirinus, writing *ca.* 1460, describes one: then, as later, it was a practice instr. of organists. From Paulirinus' day on they were built intermittently up to the end of the 18th c. A 2-manual clavichord with independent pedalboard, built in 1760 by Johann David Gerstenberg, is still extant; the manuals are bichord, the pedalboard has 4 strings per note.

Pedal drum (Fr.: *timbale à pédale;* Ger.: *Pedalpauke;* It.: *timpani a pedali*), *machine drum with a pedal that acts on a central tuning screw. The farther the pedal is depressed, the more the pitch is raised. See also: timbalarion (170).

Pedale di fagotto, It.: bassoon stop.

Pedalflügel, Ger.: pedal piano.

Pedal harp (Fr.: *harpe à pédales;* Ger.: *Pedalharfe;* It.: *arpa a pedali*), see: harp.

Pedal harpsichord (Ger.: *Pedalcembalo*), harpsichord furnished with a pedalboard and used as a practice instr. by organists. The pedalboard may have its own independent strings and action, or it may be connected by pulldowns to the keys. The earliest record of a pedal harpsichord occurs in Crakow in 1497, according to Adolf Chybinski (SIMG XIII, 1911), described as a *clavicembale cum pedali.* The pedal harpsichord of which Mace wrote in 1676 was a harpsichord with registration pedals. He called it "the pedal": 4 foot levers, 2 for each foot, were housed in a box that could be closed by a door when not in use. When at rest, the pedals were in the "off" position and were brought into the "on" position by being depressed. The "pedal" is first recorded in 1664 and was made *i.a.,* by John Haward of London. But the time for such improvements was apparently not ripe, for we do not hear of pedals again until 1741, when Nils Brelin of Sweden used registration pedals on a clavicytherium of his invention.

Pédalier (Fr.), **1.** generally speaking,

a pedalboard attached to a piano, organ, etc.; **2.** pedalboard with its own strings and action; it can be connected to a piano. So named by its inventors, Pleyel, Wolff & Cie. of Paris (126).

Pedalklaviatur, Ger.: pedalboard.

Pedalklavier, Ger.: pedal piano.

Pedal organ, a division of the organ which is controlled from the pedal. Known since the late 14th c., the pedal organ originally was no more than a pedalboard hung from the manual; subsequently it drew its registers from the manual, or had a stop or two of its own and drew others from the manual, later becoming an independent division. Arnold Schlick in 1511 recommended a compass of F^0–c^1 on the pedal; Fr. pedalboards of that time generally had 7–9 keys, It. ones were hung from the manual, and Brit. ones were then nonexistent (they were introduced there in the 18th c. but did not become common until the 19th c.). See also: organ.

Pedalpauke, Ger.: pedal drum.

Pedal piano (Fr.: *piano à pédalier;* Ger.: *Pedalflügel; Pedalklavier*), grand piano with pedalboard. The piano is set upon a box containing the projecting pedalboard as well as an independent action and strings; it serves as a practice instr. for organists. Occasionally upright pianos are also combined with pedalboard, the latter being connected in such cases by pulldowns to the piano keys. See also: pédalier, pianoforte organistico.

Pedal zither, zither invented in 1891 by G. Schömig of Vienna, with strings that were shortened a semitone by means of pedals. Another version, invented by F. Wigand in the U.S. in 1894, had 12 pedals that raised the pitch of the accompaniment strings by 3 semitones (176).

Peddaganta, Tel. equivalent of kamsya.

Peduba, panpipes of the Kobéua Indians of S. America (105).

Pegbox (Fr.: *cheviller;* Ger.: *Wirbelkasten*), continuation of the neck of certain chordophones, in which the lateral pegs are inserted. (If the pegs are inserted from front or rear, we speak of a peg-disc.)

Pegdisc (Ger.: *Wirbelbrett*), see: peg-box.

Peigne, Fr.: string fastener (140).

Peixet [*peix,* fish], scraper of Cata-lonia, a folk instr. made of sheet metal in form of a fish, with raised scales that are scraped with a metal rod. Also called xifla (57).

Peking, syn. of saron panerus.

Pektis, chordophone of ancient Greece, identified by some authors as a *magadis; other writers mention it together with the magadis. We know that it was triangular in form and played with a plectrum (170).

Pe k'ung hu, syn. of k'ung hu.

Pelittifero, wind instr. invented by Giu-seppe Pelitti of Milan in 1843, of wood, covered with leather, with 3 rotary valves, played with a cup mouthpiece (158).

Pelittone, It. bass and contrabass tubas made by Giuseppe Pelitti of Milan and patented by him in Italy and Austria. The contrabass *flicorno is also known as pelittone.

Pellankovi, Tel. equivalent of the vāmsī.

Pellet bell (Fr.: *grelot;* Ger.: *Schelle*), despite its name the pellet bell is a *vessel rattle, not a bell. It consists of a small ves-sel, usually globular or oval, enclosing loose pellets, pebbles, etc., that rattle when shaken. Pellet bells were known to antiquity and probably originated in Asia, where they are still worn as ankle rattles and bracelets, much as they are in many parts of Africa, particularly by dancers. They were also known to pre-Columbian America; in ancient Peru they were made of metal and contained pebbles. They reached Europe *ca.* 500 B.C. Because of their magical power pellet bells were hung from the necks of domestic animals to protect them from evil spirits; for the same reason they were sewn to the hems of garments in ancient Israel, by S. Amer-ican Indians and Siberian shamans. In med. Europe they were also worn as pro-tective amulets, and from the 12th c. on they became indispensable objects of or-namentation to persons of elegance, often made of gold, either spherical or piri-form, worn on clothing or as necklaces. See also: arain(e), arxouxelas, bangkula, brimbale, bubbolo, cai nhac, carcan, car-quavel, cascabel, cascaveaux, cheh oc mazcab, chincha, chingraq, coyolli, ghunghunā, girellina, girgila, glegni, go-nongo, grelot, guiso, juljul, kalwaking, kaskabilo, kiskilla, klintingan, kuskulu, mjolo, mo, morenne, muyang, nzobo, nzolo, nzonga, oyualli, rizmoc, Rolle, Rollschelle, Schelle, sonnaille, sonneau, sonnette, suzu, tenabari, tivolu, zurgalău (169).

Pena, rustic *spike fiddle of Manipur, E. India, with coconut or gourd body, leather or palm-leaf belly, cane handle, and single string (172).

Penda, *musical bow of the Tshopi of S. Africa, with string looped to the bow, played by men only. Sometimes a rattle of calabash, tin, or other material is added to the bow (116).

Pendant rattle (Ger.: *Pendelrassel*), series of rattling objects hung from a frame (100).

Pendelrassel, Ger.: pendant rattle.

Pender, syn. of penser.

Pendibe, syn. of kweningba.

Penganak, gong of the Karo Batak of Sumatra, suspended by a cord and held in the player's hand (144).

P'eng chung, *finger cymbals of China, very deep, worn like thimbles on thumb and middle finger. *Cf.* hsing erh (1).

Penimba, xylophone of the Azande of the Congo (42).

Penitil, name of the saron panerus in Solo, Java (121).

Penna, Lat.: feather; by extension, quill.

Penny whistle, Engl. name of a small, high-pitched *whistle flute made of metal, with 6 fingerholes, fingered like the fife. Also called tin whistle.

Penontong, gong of C. and E. Java, with central boss and very broad rim, somewhat smaller than the kempul. It serves both as orchestral and as signal instr. Also called kenong penontong (121).

Penorcon, bass cittern mentioned only by Praetorius, according to whom it had 9 pairs of strings tuned $G^1 A^1 C^0 D^0 G^0 c^0 e^0 a^0 d^1$. Cf. stump (159).

Penser, magical drum of the Ostyak, a *frame drum with wooden frame and reindeer membrane, played with a beater covered with reindeer skin. Also called pender (169).

Pentaphone, *bowed zither invented by Henry Müller-Braunau of Hamburg in 1903, with 5 steel strings tuned $c^0 g^0 d^1 a^1 e^2$ that were bowed mechanically by as many wheels with rosined bands, one for each string. The wheels were controlled by a pedal, and the strings were stopped by the player's fingers on a fingerboard provided with 28 metal frets (115, 149).

Pentecontachordon [Gk. *pentekonta,* fifty + *chorde,* string], another name of the sambuca lincea.

Penting, idiochord bamboo *tube zither of Lombok, Indonesia (119).

Penuntung, syn. of ketipung.

Penyipu, *globular flute of the Sea Dayak of Borneo, with 2 fingerholes (176).

Pepa, hornpipe of Assam, a pastoral instr. with a cylindrical cane pipe in which 6 fingerholes have been burned; the single reed is protected by a mouth horn of buffalo horn. The lower end of the pipe is fitted into a large bell, also of buffalo horn (13).

Pe pan, see: p'ai pan.

Pepe, panpipes of the Nonama-Choco Indians of Colombia and Panama (105).

Pepéon, name of the dermenan in the Gayo district of W. Java (121).

Perce, Fr.: bore.

Percussion beam (Ger.: *Schlagbalken*), wooden beam treated as a percussion instr., often placed on the ground and drummed upon, distributed in Africa,

Surinam, Asia, S. Seas, and among the Negro population of Brazil (168).

Percussion idiophone (Fr.: *idiophone par percussion;* Ger.: *Aufschlagidiophon*), instr. sounded by being struck, either with a nonsonorous body (such as the hand, a stick) or against a nonsonorous object (the human body, the ground) (100).

Percussion plaque (Fr.: *disque sonore;* Ger.: *Aufschlagplatte*), percussion plaques may occur singly or in sets; they may be either lithophones or metallophones.

Percussion pot (Ger.: *Schlagtopf*), clay pot or gourd with an open mouth; either it is drummed upon, with bare hands or beaters, or the mouth is alternately opened and closed by hand or by flat beater, causing the air inside to vibrate. In some instances a lateral hole is perforated in the pot. See also: canarí, chang kun, chankun, ghadam, ghāta, ghatamu, idudu egu, ikokolo, kuku, okonko, udu, zeli, zin-li.

Percussion reed, metal reed struck with a small felt hammer. This principle of sounding a reed was discovered by Martin de Provens in 1841. The reed's vibrations were sustained by air pressure from a reservoir, but the importance of this discovery was not realized until Jacob Alexandre of Paris bought the patent in 1849. Today the percussion reed is used in certain *electrophonic instrs., including *electrophonic pianos (132).

Percussion stick (Fr.: *bâton frappé;* Ger.: *Schlagstab*), percussion sticks occur as individual sticks or in sets. As individual sticks, they are struck against a hard object or by another stick, used as rhythm instrs. in China, Ghana, and the S. Seas. Several percussion sticks may be united to form a single instr., such as a xylophone. See also: amagala, ana-batching, bulo lae-lae, bulo paseya-seya, bul tyang' apena, cai siñ, ganggereng, garabato, hula kalaau, ikú-achán, kagura sutsu, kalutang, klowa, lae-lae, lungóna, makata, pachán, pang tse, siya-siya (100, 168).

Percussion tube (Ger.: *Aufschlagröhre*), bamboo percussion tubes occur in Asia and the S. Seas, other types in Europe, such as *tubular bells or the tubaphone. The *slit drum is also a percussion tube. See also: stamping tube (100, 168).

Pereret, name of the selompret of Java in ancient Hindu-Javanese literature as well as in Bali today (121).

Perinet valve (Ger.: *Perinetventil*), improved *piston valve, patented by Étienne-François Périnet of Paris in 1839 and, with minor modifications, still in use today (15, 176).

Peripetika, *percussion beam of the Betsimisaraka of the Malagasy Republic. It corresponds to the tsikaretika (171).

Peristomion, syn. of phorbeia.

Pernanguma, 1. Afro-Cuban *vessel rattle. Also called prananguma (152); **2.** Afro-Brazilian rattle made of a tin can filled with pieces of lead or shot (7).

Pero, *ribbon reed of Slovenia, made of a leaf held taut between the thumbs (144).

Perroquette [Fr. *perroquet,* parrot], Fr. *bird organ, larger than the serinette (204).

Perubali, panpipes of the Karapaná Indians of Brazil (105).

Peruliababaro, panpipes of the Uaiana Indians of S. America (105).

Peruliro, panpipes of the Tuyuka and Uasona Indians of S. America (105).

Peteng, W. Java name of the sundari, 1 (121).

Petit bugle, Fr.: octave and/or sopranino saxhorn.

Petit jeu (Fr.), 18th-c. Fr. term for the 4′ register of the harpsichord.

Petit tambour, Fr.: snare drum.

Pfeife [MHGer. *pfife*], Ger.: pipe.

Pfeifenbrett, Ger.: rack board.

Pfeifenflöte, obs. organ stop of: 1) stopped cylindrical pipes, a syn. of gedackt; 2) a stopped quint (133).

Pfeifenkern, Ger.: languid.

Pfeifenstock, Ger.: upper board.

Pfife [Lat. *pipa,* pipe], MHGer.: pipe.

Phaamon, see: pa'amon.

Phagotum [Latinization of It. *fagotto*], obs. woodwind instr. devised by Canon Afranio of Ferrara *ca.* 1522, bellows-blown, with connected twin tubes made of a single block of wood in U form, each having a cylindrical bore. The bellows were strapped to the player's arm and fed the instr. through a single beating reed. The tubes, shaped like pillars, were about 53 cm. (21 in.) high and were called *"fagoto."* Altogether the phagotum was more like a bagpipe than a bassoon (the bassoon has a conical bore, is mouth-blown with a double reed). It is known to us through the canon's nephew, Teseo Afranio, who described and illustrated it in 1539 (125).

Phalaphala, horn of the Pedi and Venda of S. Africa, made of sable antelope horn, with lateral blowhole. The name is occasionally given to horns made of other material. See also: mpalampala, shipalapala (116).

Phan, mouth organ of Vietnam, corresponding to the khen (132).

Phen, mouth organ of Thailand, corresponding to the khen (47).

Philomela (Fr.: *philomèle*), **1.** bowed chordophone of mid-19th-c. invention, shaped like a soprano *viola da gamba, with 4 metal strings tuned like those of a violin; **2.** a form of monochord played in Hungary in the 19th c., possibly inspired by the *psalmodicon. Originally shaped like a box with 1 or even 2 strings, it was later made in form of a kite with 2 soundholes. Also called gypsy fiddle; **3.** organ stop made in different forms: a) as a *nightingale; b) of narrow-scaled, open cylindrical flue pipes; c) as an overblowing, double-mouthed flue stop (133, 149, 176).

Phin nam tao, *stick zither of Thailand, identical with the sa diu of Cambodia (118).

Phlaouton, flute of modern Greece.

Phlogera, end-blown cane flute of modern Greece.

Phoenician pipes, syn. of tibiae serranae.

Phoinix, unidentified instr. of ancient Greece, probably the same as the lyrophoinix (21).

Phone (Gk.: sound), the first inventor to use this word in naming an instr. (euphone) was Chladni in 1790 (169).

Phonéorgue [Gk. *phone,* sound + Fr. *orgue,* organ], *orgue expressif invented by Baron, of Maubourguet, Hautes Pyrénées, with pedalboard. It was patented on Nov. 16, 1869 (204).

Phoneuma [Gk. *phone + pneuma,* breath], name by which the *Zartflöte was introduced by Robert Hope-Jones in 1896, a softly intoned stop of stopped flue pipes at 16' or 8' pitch. Also built by Whitely (101, 133).

Phonikon, *barytonhorn invented by Vaclav F. Červeny of Königgrätz (Hradec Králové), with tulip-shaped bell (176).

Phonola, a variety of pianola formerly made by L. Hupfeld of Leipzig. See also: trifonola; not to be confused with Fonola (37).

Phonolith, musical stone. See: lithophone, musical stone.

Phonomine, pipe organ in form of a piano, with 4 registers imitating the sound of the human voice, invented by 1834 (204).

Phonorganon, automatic *trumpeter built by Robertson in 1812 (204).

Phorbeia (Gk.), leather band worn by aulos players across the mouth and the cheeks, tied at the back of the head, with a slit for introducing the reeds into the mouth. Called capistrum by the Romans. The phorbeia is first depicted on a proto-Corinthian vase of the 7th c. B.C. Also called peristomion. *Cf.* tarompet. See also: aulos (21, 170).

Phorminx [U.], Homeric term that probably denoted the kithara or early form of lyra (177).

Photinx, 1. aulos of ancient Greece, of Egyptian origin, believed to have been a

*cross flute corresponding to the sebet, possibly the Alexandrine name of the plagiaulos; **2.** a name of the crumhorn organ stop (21, 133, 144).

Phrygian auloi, syn. of auloi elymoi.

Phrygian pipes, 1. the auloi elymoi of Greece; **2.** the tibiae impares of Rome.

Phunga, trumpet of Nepal, of copper, *ca.* 125 cm. (4 ft.) long; it rests on a support while played (176).

Phusa, syn. of the täks (panpipes) among the Aymara and Chipaya Indians of the Andes (104).

Phusana mati, gourd trumpet of the Aymara Indians of the Andes (105).

Phusana ochulu, *marine-shell trumpet of the Aymara Indians of the Andes (105).

Phyen kyung, lithophone of Korea (168).

Physallis, unidentified instr. of ancient Greece (144).

Physharmonica (Ger.: *Physharmonika*), **1.** small *free-reed organ, invented by Anton Häckl of Vienna in 1818, designed to be played simultaneously with a piano under whose keyboard it was placed, in order to sustain the melody. A precursor of the harmonium, it had a 4-oct. compass. Its bellows were worked by 2 pedals. The name was subsequently applied to all precursor instrs. of the harmonium; **2.** organ stop of reed pipes made with harmonium reeds, and an imitation thereof with string tone, made of narrow-scaled flue pipes. See also: concordia, harmoniphon, harmoniphon-coranglais (89, 132, 133, 176).

Pi, shawm of Thailand, made of wood or ivory, with 6 fingerholes disposed in groups of 4 and 2. The middle of the instr. is slightly barrel-shaped (176).

Piah, *stick zither of Laos, made of a slender conical stick with half gourd resonator and 4 metal strings. The gourd is pressed against the player's chest. *Cf.* si so laos (173).

Piahanú, panpipes of the Uitoto Indians of Rio Japurá, Brazil (105).

Pianette, 1. Engl. name of a low *upright piano introduced by Bord of Paris in 1857 and made by several London firms. *Cf.* bibi; **2.** a name wrongly given to a *barrel piano (89).

Piani-flûte, *piano-organ patented by L. Duvivier of Nevers on March 2, 1868, with 2 stops of pipes (flute and panpipes) and a 6-oct. compass (204).

Pianino, name given by Pleyel & Cie. of Paris to Robert Wornum's *cottage piano, which they copied, so called to distinguish it from their *piano droit. Thereafter any small upright piano became known on the European Continent as pianino. They were not built in Germany until the 1840's (92).

Pianissimo stop (Ger.: *Pianissimozug*), piano stop similar to the 18th-c. *piano stop, 1, but with a piece of leather interposed full length to muffle the sound (92).

Pianista, device set in front of a conventional piano for mechanically depressing the keys. A set of horizontal levers extended from a cabinet and depressed the appropriate keys, driven by a hand crank acting on perforated cards. The player turned the crank with his left hand while the right controlled the dynamics. For a list of similar devices see: pianola. See also: player piano.

Pianito, Cuban syn. of ginebras (152).

Piano (Engl., Fr.) [see text], stringed keyboard instr. invented by 1709 by Bartolommeo Cristofori of Padua, then in Florence, characterized by a hammer action. Cristofori (pron. Cristófori) called his new instr. the *gravicembalo col pian e forte* (harpsichord with soft and loud), and our names piano and pianoforte are merely abbrs. thereof. In 18th-c. France and Germany the word was reversed to *forte-piano.* The modern piano is made in 2 forms: horizontal ("grand piano") or vertical ("upright," "spinet," or "console") piano, each maker having his own standards of length or height. Generally it has a compass of 7 octs. and a 3rd, A^2–c^5 (but Bösendorfer of Vienna makes a grand with an 8-oct. compass). When

not in use the keys are covered by the fall-board, which folds up against the nameboard. Behind this lies the pin block, or wrest plank, of laminated wood, drilled in its entire depth with holes for the tuning pins. The nut of its precursor, the harpsichord, is replaced by agraffes in the bass and a *capotasto bar in the treble. A narrow gap is left behind the pin block for the hammers to rise and strike the strings; this gap is closed to the rear by the belly rail, to which the front edge of the soundboard is glued. The latter bears a stout, S-shaped bridge, as well as a separate straight bass bridge, which is undercut on the side facing the tail and placed diagonally in order to facilitate cross-stringing. Stringing is trichord in the treble, bichord in the middle, and single in the bass, the change-over points being known technically as "breaks." A metal frame is set over the entire pin block and the soundboard: it takes the tremendous stress of heavy modern stringing—some 30 tons—and also carries the hitchpins. The belly, soul of the instr., is "crowned," *i.e.,* forced into a convex shape and heavily barred, before being inserted into the piano. Once the instr. is strung, the pressure of the strings on the bridge causes the belly to flatten out. The soundboard is made of softwood (increasingly, of laminated wood) and has been heavily varnished on both sides since the 19th c. Square pianos of the early 19th c. often have the upper surface varnished, and in 1826 a patent was taken out for a soundboard to be varnished on both sides. On grand pianos 3 pedals (in Europe 2) are suspended in a "lyre" (it is technically known as lyre even if not lyre-shaped). The left, or "piano," pedal is also called the "soft," or *"una corda,"* pedal; it shifts the key frame slightly to the treble so that the left string of each course is no longer struck by the hammer (in a few makes this pedal instead raises the hammer rail); the middle pedal, called sostenuto, immobilizes any raised dampers until the pedal is released, thus permitting a tone or chord to continue sounding even after other strings have been struck; the right, or sustaining, pedal, also called "damper" or "loud" pedal, raises all the dampers and holds them suspended until the pedal is released. The action is mounted on a bracket attached to the key frame (in grand pianos), and the whole is enclosed in a case of laminated hardwood.

In Vol. V of the *Giornale dei Letterati d'Italia*, 1711, the Marchese Scipione di Maffei published details of his visit in 1709 to the workshop of Cristofori, at which time he had seen 4 of the newly invented pianos, 3 in harpsichord form and 1 of "different" shape. Maffei added a drawing of the action. Two of Cristofori's pianos are extant, one dated 1720, preserved in the Metropolitan Museum of New York, the other, dated 1726, in the instrument collection of Leipzig University. The soundboard and hammers of the former are replacements. A comparison of the drawing made by Maffei with those of the 1720 piano action made in Italy and published in Leto Puliti's *Cenni storici*, 1874, shows that the actions were not identical, and the discrepancies between the 1720 and the 1726 actions are even greater. The earlier piano has a compass C^0–f^3, the later one C^0–c^3 (long octave); both have white natural keys, overhead dampers, leather-covered hammers attached to a hammer rail, and are bichord. The 1720 action has discarded an intermediate lever apparent in Maffei's drawing; it already has a back check, a hopper, or escapement, and dampers resting on the rear of the keys. In the 1726 piano the tuning pins pass through the pin block and the strings are secured to pins underneath it, and the intermediate lever is restored. More important is the presence of an *una corda* shift controlled by 2 hand stops and worked by iron levers underneath the key bed; here the keyboard is shifted toward the bass. (The 1720 piano has no shift.) The longest string has a speaking length of 195.5 cm.

(*ca.* 6 ft. 5 in.), the shortest, 14.5 cm. (5¾ in.).

The rigid dynamics of the harpsichord had been the subject of comments and complaints for at least a c., and the problem of creating a keyboard instr. capable of gradations of loud and soft was first solved by Hans Haiden, who produced the *Geigenwerk in the late 16th c. One of his instrs. was in the Medici instr. collection, of which Cristofori became curator in 1716, but which must have been known to him by 1709 (he had moved to Florence by 1693). It must be emphasized that the new piano was conceived as a harpsichord capable of dynamic modifications; there appears to have been no desire to change the timbre or even the volume. Dr. Harding reports that there was early opposition to the piano, its tone not being considered as distinct as that of the harpsichord (it is interesting to find that as late as 1802 Heinrich Koch criticized the piano as being *schwächer* (weaker) than the harpsichord). About the time Cristofori's invention took place, independent efforts were being made in France to solve the same problem. Cuisinié in 1708 had made a bowed keyboard instr. with *maillets* on the ends of the keys, thick, stumpy tangents, which instr. he submitted to the Paris Académie des Sciences. It may have been known to Jean Marius, who in 1716 submitted 4 different actions for *clavecins à maillets*. The first had stumpy wooden tangents on the rear of the keys, larger in the bass than in the treble; his second action was similar to the later *Tangentenflügel; the third was a trichord instr. with abstracts to which tangents were fixed at right angles, without any escapement; the fourth was a bichord piano-harpsichord (*clavecin à maillets et à sautereaux*), but the hammers of the piano were still attached to the keys. A year later Christoph Gottlieb Schroeter, a Dresden organist, designed—or claimed to have designed—2 hammer actions inspired by Hebenstreit's *Pantaleon, one with downstriking action, the other, upstriking. However, he did not publish his claim until after Cristofori's invention was known in Germany. Maffei's article had been translated into German and published in Johann Mattheson's *Critica musica* (1725). Schroeter published his claim in Lorenz Mizler's *Neu eröffnete musikalische Bibliothek* of 1747 (diagrams appeared in Friedrich Marpurg's *Kritische Briefe* of 1763). Meanwhile Ferrini, a pupil of Cristofori, continued making pianos in Italy. He made one for the Queen of Spain, who bequeathed it to Farinelli, the singer. Sonatas for *cimbalo di piano e forte* by Giustini were published in 1732, but Cristofori did not live to witness this recognition of his invention (d. 1731). After Maffei's article appeared in Germany, Ger. makers experimented with the new instr., apparently using the clavichord rather than the harpsichord form for their model, and producing the *square piano with a primitive type of *Prellmechanik. But they also produced grand pianos: Gottfried Silbermann started building grand pianos in the early 1730's and showed 2 of his instrs. to J. S. Bach, probably in 1733 or 1736. Bach commented adversely upon the touch and weakness of the treble (in 1747 Bach saw a later piano of his of which he approved). Silbermann's action was a developed form of the Cristofori action. The earliest known example of a square piano is one by Johann Socher, dated 1742. Early Ger. square-piano actions were simpler than those of the contemporary grand (see: *Prellmechanik, *Stossmechanik), and the instrs. often of cruder workmanship. The earliest record of an upright form of piano dates from 1739 (see: upright grand piano). In the 1750's Johann Andreas Stein (1728–92), one of the greatest of Ger. makers of stringed keyboard instrs., started devoting less time to the organ and more to the making and improving of pianos. He transformed the old Prellmechanik into the *German action, improved the touch, and generally

brought the art of piano making to a high degree of perfection. In France, Jean Marius had created the *piano-harpsichord in 1716, and our next record of a Fr. piano occurs in 1759, when Weltman submitted another piano-harpsichord, with *genouillères, to the Académie des Sciences. In 1772 L'Épine submitted a piano-organ to the Académie for approval, and it is not until 1777 that an "ordinary" piano was made in France, by Sébastien Érard, probably a square. Pascal Taskin, France's greatest harpsichord maker, also made grand pianos in the 1780's, and these are characterized by a system of bichord stringing well in advance of his time: a double length of string with a loop at each end was attached to the hitchpins, and the middle of the string was placed over a hook that passed horizontally through the pin block. It was pulled up to pitch by tightening a nut on the hook's threaded shank, the nut being situated on the keyboard side of the pin block, the hook on the soundboard side. In theory this system of tuning both unisons simultaneously prevented their going out of tune separately. The hammers are hinged to the belly rail, and the overhead dampers are attached to the hammers. But the normal method of stringing in harpsichord fashion continued in use, and it was not until 1827 that James Stewart, a partner of Jonas Chickering, discarded the looped unison strings in favor of double-length strings, each end of which was brought forward and threaded through a tuning pin, as today.

In England the first pianos were imported ones. Then a Silbermann pupil named Johann Christoph Zumpe migrated to England and devoted himself from *ca.* 1760 on to the manufacture of square pianos, of which he produced quantities. One of these, dated 1766, is the earliest British-made piano. Zumpe's action is known as the *single action; his dampers could be kept raised by means of hand stops. In 1768 the world's first piano recital was given in London: Johann Christian Bach played on one of Zumpe's squares (this was the same year that Taskin created his *clavecin à peau de bufle*, the *ne plus ultra* of harpsichord refinement). According to Dr. Burney, Bach's arrival had given British harpsichord makers the necessary impetus to turn to piano making. In 1770, if not earlier, Friderici of Gera invented means for transferring the clavichord *Bebung* to the piano in an attempt to gain better sustaining power. A couple of years later, probably in 1772, the *English action was invented by Americus Backers, a Dutchman working in England. John Broadwood of London (successor of Burkat Shudi, the harpsichord maker) started making pianos in 1773; until 1780 they were all squares, modeled on those of Zumpe. In 1780 he created his own model, patented in 1783, breaking with the tradition of clavichord disposition for tuning pins and pin block. His earliest known grand piano dates from 1781. The old harpsichord pedals for machine and swell he transformed into *piano* and *forte* pedals (patent of 1783); A. J. Hipkins was of the opinion that Broadwood was the first maker to attempt to equalize tension and striking point throughout the scale (in the 1780's). He aimed at a striking point of $\frac{1}{9}$ (Carl Kützing, writing in 1844, thought $\frac{1}{8}$ best), and built a separate bass bridge in his grands (1783 on) as a step toward equalizing the tension. In America the first piano was built by John Behrent of Philadelphia. By the end of the c. piano compass had increased from F^1–f^3 to 5½ octs., F^1–c^4 and was shortly to reach 6 octs. Square pianos were made with treble "extensions" (see: square piano). A number of stops and gadgets had been fitted, apparently in a desire to create a sort of one-man orchestra. Fr. and Ger. makers reversed both the name of the instr. (to *fortepiano*) and the traditional colors of the keys, using black natural and white accidental keys, one explanation being that the black keys showed the white skin of a lady's hand to better advantage, but a more down-to-earth argument pointed out that the price of ivory, with which natural keys were ordinarily covered, had gone up. The greater tension occasioned by the larger compass necessitated extra bracing of the instr., and from 1794 patents for metal braces of different kinds were applied for. In 1799 the earliest complete frame was patented, consisting of a series of braces united together. Broadwood applied tension bars to the treble of his grands in 1808 (they were not satisfactory), the same year that Sébastien Érard of Paris patented his first repetition action. His second repetition action, patented in 1821, remains the basis of virtually all of our double escapement actions of today. Also in 1808, Wachtel & Bleyel of Vienna began artificially seasoning their soundboards by steaming them for 48 hours, bringing the resin up to the surface in brown splotches, then drying them in drying boxes. The development of the modern piano was notably aided by the industrial revolution: invention of the telegraph led to vast improvements in wiredrawing, permitting both heavier stringing and an increase in scale. The "newfangled" hot-air furnaces installed in basements of private homes in the U.S. caused perfectly good pianos to curl up suddenly, and the great advances made by metallurgy permitted the casting of plates, at first partial, later whole ones, to offset the ill effects of the furnaces. In 1825 a complete cast-iron frame for square pianos was patented by Alpheus Babcock of Boston. Since 1822 metal hitchpin plates had been fitted to square pianos. A patent was granted to J. Muller of Paris on Apr. 17, 1823, for a metal pin block. In 1826 Carl Schmidt of Pressburg (Bratislava) invented a new kind of *gepresster Resonanzboden* (laminated soundboard) claimed not to split or sink. Numerous patents were taken out in the U.S. from then on for plates and frames, few in Europe, possibly because of its more benign climate. The first overstrung pianos were apparently produced by Bridgeland and Jardine of New York in 1833; in 1840, Jonas Chickering of Boston, patented a new cast-iron frame for square pianos, and in 1843 a frame for grand pianos in one solid casting. Europe meanwhile continued to build with the earlier bracings. Agraffes were invented by Sébastien Érard of Paris in 1838, and the *capotasto bar was introduced by Antoine Bord of Paris in 1843. Steinway of New York brought out an overstrung piano with complete iron frame in 1855. By then the compass had increased to 6½ or 6¾ octs. In 1826 Jean-Henri Pape of Paris patented felt for use in making hammers, but the prejudice against any material except leather was hard to overcome, and Gustav Schilling in 1835 criticized Broadwood for using felt; deer leather was still being used in Germany in the early 1850's—felt did not come into universal use until after 1855. Hipkins relates that Broadwood adopted intentional equal temperament in 1846. In our c. laminated soundboards are being made increasingly, both in upright and grand pianos; hammers with synthetic instead of felt heads are coming into use; plastic has replaced the ivory of keys (because ivory cracks and yellows with age; Pleyel bleached their ivory a c. ago); a grand is being manufactured in Holland in which case and frame are one, thus permitting a departure from the traditional shape (89 Harding; 92; Hipkins, A. J.: *History of the Pianoforte;* Chladni in: *Allgemeine musikalische Zeitschrift*).

Piano à archet, Fr.: bowed keyboard instr.

Piano à buffet, obs. Fr. term for an upright piano.

Piano accordion (Fr.: *accordéon-piano;* It.: *fisarmonica*), accordion with piano-type keyboard, patented on Sept. 16, 1852, by Bouton of Paris. Models in use today have a keyboard compass of 2–4 octs. and a series of bass and chord buttons. One row of buttons produces

bass tones, another row produces a series of chords. Large models have their bass buttons arranged in rows of 6 and can furnish major, minor, dominant 7th, and diminished 7th chords. *Cf.* harmoniflûte (151).

Piano achromatique (Fr.), piano patented by Behrens of Paris on July 22, 1892, with quarter tones in addition to the usual tones and semitones.

Piano à claviers renversés (Fr.: piano with reversed keyboards), grand piano with 2 keyboards, made by Mangeot Frères & Cie. of Paris in 1876, the lower keyboard of which was standard, but the upper was reversed in pitch, the lowest note being in the treble. A total of 6 were built, as well as a few uprights (176).

Piano-action glockenspiel, see: glockenspiel.

Piano à cylindre, Fr.: barrel piano.

Piano à double percussion, piano invented by 1844, with 2 hammers for each key, one for the key depressed and one for its lower oct. (204).

Piano africano, Sp.: marimba (152).

Piano à pédalier, Fr.: pedal piano.

Piano à prolongement, piano combined with free reeds to obtain greater sustaining of the tone, built by Alexandre of Paris in the 19th c. (176, 204).

Piano apythmolamprotérique [Gk. *apythemos,* bottomless + *lampros,* sonorous], piano without a (closed) bottom, "invented" in 1834, the object being to obtain greater clarity of tone.

Piano à queue, Fr.: grand piano.

Piano à queue à quart de ton, Fr.: quarter-tone piano.

Piano à queue mignon, Fr.: baby grand piano.

Piano armonico (harmonic plane), It.: soundboard.

Piano à sons soutenus (Fr.: piano with sustained sounds), piano built by Jean-Louis Boisselot of Marseille in 1843, with a special sustaining pedal (176, 204).

Piano autopanphone, see: autopanphones.

Piano basque (Fr.), invented by Paul-

Joseph Sormani of Paris in 1841, the piano basque was a set of tambourines (called *tambour de Basque* in Fr.)—the patent suggests 13 such—each provided with 2 drumsticks worked from a keyboard. Each drumstick corresponded to a separate key so that the keyboard consisted of 2 keys for every note (92).

Piano carré, Fr.: square piano.

Piano chanteur (Fr.), keyboard instr. patented by Gustave Baudet of Paris on Sept. 1, 1875, with a series of steel rods set in vibration by wind supplied by bellows. It was shown at the 1878 Paris Exposition (169, 204).

Pianochordia, *chord zither similar to the autoharp (149).

Piano-clavichord, a combination of piano and clavichord, such as that patented in 1792 by John Geib of London (27).

Piano clédi-harmonique [Gk. *kleides*, key], piano built by Jean-Louis Boisselot of Marseille in 1839; he suppressed the tuning pins and passed his double-length strings over a hitchpin, thus obviating the necessity for loops (156).

Pianoctave, piano of Jean-Louis Boisselot of Marseille, 1834, in which a depressed key and its oct. were sounded simultaneously. *Cf.* piano octave (204).

Piano de cauda, Port.: grand piano.

Piano de cola, Sp.: grand piano.

Piano de cuia (gourd piano), Afro-Brazilian rattle made of a gourd with natural handle, covered entirely by a network of cotton string threaded with small shells. Sometimes there are pellets in the gourd. Also called agé, agüé, amelé, cabaça, xaque-xaque, xere (7).

Piano diaphonique [Gk. *dia*, across + *phone*, sound], bichord piano built by Donald of Louisbourg in 1855, with 2 soundboards, 2 pin blocks, and 2 bridges. One string of each note was stretched over the upper soundboard, the other over the lower soundboard. Trichord pianos were also made, with 3 soundboards (158).

Piano diphone, 2-manual piano with

free reeds, patented by Rousseau on May 24, 1881 (204).

Piano droit (Fr.: upright piano), name of a small upright piano with diagonal stringing, shown by Roller & Blanchet in Paris in 1827. Subsequently this became the generic name for upright pianos in Fr. (149).

Piano duplex, piano made by the Ithaca Piano and Organ Co., first shown in Amsterdam in 1883, with 2 complete actions and 2 sets of strings, one above the other. They could be played separately or together (176).

Piano-écran, diminutive piano by Alexandre-François Debain of Paris, 1829, with forged iron frame (92).

Piano elliptique (Fr.), a combination of grand and square pianos built by Eulriot in 1825 (158).

Piano éolien, keyboard instr. similar to the anémocorde, devised in 1837 by Isouard. His patent was bought by Henri Herz of Paris. The strings were set in vibration by wind directed against them (149, 169).

Piano eutonophone, piano exhibited by Le Gay of Paris in 1889, with 2 soundboards (176).

Piano-exécutant, early *player piano patented by Fourneaux of Le Grand-Montrouge, France, on Apr. 23, 1883, played by means of perforated cardboard strips. See also: player piano (204).

Pianoforte (It.), see: piano.

Pianoforte a cilindro, It.: barrel piano.

Pianoforte a coda, It.: grand piano.

Pianoforte da tavola, It.: square piano.

Pianoforte guitar, obs. name of the keyed guitar (79).

Pianoforte organistico, *pedal piano of Abbé Gregorio Trentino of Venice, 1817, with a 2-oct. pedalboard provided with 2 x 8' and 1 x 4' sets of strings (178).

Piano giraffe, Fr.: giraffe piano.

Piano harmonicorde (Fr.), piano of Klepfer & Cie. of Paris, 1829, with soundboard above the strings and a 7-oct. compass, C^1–c^5 (176).

Piano-harmonium (Ger.: *Harmonium-klavier*), a combination piano and harmonium, built in the mid-19th c. The instrs. could be played separately or together.

Piano-harp, *electrophonic instr. invented by J. Béthenod by 1932, with electron-tube tone generators (W. Meyer-Eppler: *Elektrische Klangerzeugung.* Bonn, 1949).

Piano-harpsichord, a combination of piano and harpsichord, built from 1716 on. In that year Jean Marius submitted his *clavecin à maillets et à sautereaux to the Paris Académie des Sciences. In or by 1755 the Rev. William Mason had bought in Hamburg a piano-harpsichord with 2 x 8' on the harpsichord, the jacks serving as "mutes" when the piano was played. Weltman in 1759 submitted a piano-harpsichord to the Académie, but its piano action consisted of tangents rather than hammers. See also: clavecin mécanique, crescendo, Fortepianoclavier, Polytoni-Clavichordium (89 Harding, 92).

Pianola, device for the mechanical playing of pianos, invented by the American engineer Edwin S. Votley and patented in 1897. At first the player was made separately; subsequently it was incorporated into the piano. "Pianola" was the trade name of the device manufactured by the Aeolian Piano Co., but later it came to denote any automatic piano furnished with a pneumatic system. Earlier pianolas were worked by a harmonium-type double pedal, later replaced by an electric motor. Punched paper rolls were driven by clockwork in the first models, thereafter by a pneumatic device. The instr. was immensely pop. for decades; the Aeolian Co. attempted to revive the pianola after World War II, but without success, and production was discontinued in 1951. See also: player piano. Other player devices are: Duo-Art, Fonola, ludo, mélographe, mélotrope, Phonola, pianista, piano mécanique, Pleyela, trifonola, Welte-Mignon (37).

Piano mécanique (Fr.), automatic player attachment for *cottage pianos, exhibited at the London Exhibition of 1851. The device was an improvement of Alexandre-François Debain's *antiphonel. It fitted on top of the pianos and levers lifted the hammers. The music was pinned on a flat oblong piece of wood. For a list of similar devices see: pianola (92).

Piano-melodico-orchestrion, 19th-c. automatic piano worked by perforated paper strips driven by a motor, in form of a cupboard (149).

Piano mélodieux, a combination piano and harmonium of Léopold Guérin of Paris, *ca.* 1883, with a 7-oct. compass (176).

Piano-mélodium (Fr.), a combination piano and harmonium of Jacob Alexandre of Paris, shown at the Paris Exposition of 1855, with 2 keyboards, the upper for the piano, the lower for the harmonium (176, 204).

Pianon, harmonium in form of a small table with keyboard, invented by Carl Kuhn of Vienna *ca.* 1873. The bellows were worked by depressing the keys, so that no pedal was required (176).

Piano octave, piano of Alphonse Blondel of Paris, 1853–55, with a device for adding the upper oct. to the treble keys or adding the lower oct. to the bass keys. *Cf.* pianoctave (176).

Piano-organ (Fr.: *piano organisé, piano-orgue;* Ger.: *Orgelklavier*), a combination of piano and organ, very pop. at the end of the 18th c. Johann Andreas Stein of Augsburg built one in 1772, now preserved in the Göteborg museum, with 2 manuals, the upper for the piano, the lower for the organ; in the same year L'Épine of Paris built one, also with 2 manuals; another, by Zumpe & Buntebart, of 1778 is preserved in Paris. Most of the surviving specimens from 1785 on are in form of square pianos, such as the *organochordon of Abbé Vogler, built 1798. *Ca.* 1800 Friderici of Gera produced one in form of a grand piano. Soon thereafter free-reed instrs. became the great vogue (27, 92, 149).

Piano organisé, Fr.: piano-organ.

Piano-orgue, Fr.: piano-organ.

Piano-orphéon, *transposing piano patented in France in 1865 by Roz (204).

Piano planicorde, friction bar keyboard instr. invented by Jean-Louis Boisselot of Marseille in 1849 (176).

Piano pyramidal, Fr.: pyramid piano.

Piano quatuor (Fr.: quartet piano), improved *piano violon of Gustave Baudet of Paris, patented May 21, 1873; a keyboard instr. in form of a *cottage piano, with one string per note set in vibration by means of a metal cylinder covered with papier-mâché and rosined, rotated by a treadle (149).

Piano scandé (Fr.: accented piano), piano built by Lentz & Houdard of Paris in 1853, with special sustaining pedal for each oct. (176).

Piano secrétaire (Fr.: desk-shaped piano), piano introduced by Érard Frères of Paris in 1812, with 2 soundboards, 1 above the other, each with its own separate action and strings. Both were trichord. The upper set of strings was tuned an oct. higher than the lower ones. They could be coupled. The upper instr. had a movable bridge so that its string lengths could be changed to correspond with those of the lower. A second keyboard could be fitted if desired (92).

Piano stop, name given to 2 stops found in some pianos: **1.** in the 18th c. (Fr.: *jeu céleste;* Ger.: *Pianozug*) a strip of wood to which tongues of leather or cloth were attached. The strips were about 2½ cm. (1 in.) long and could be interposed between hammer and strings. Often made as a divided stop for treble and bass; **2.** 19th–20th c.: lever worked by a pedal that raises the hammer rail, thereby shortening the radius of the hammer's blow; nowadays known as the "piano pedal" of upright pianos. It has also been fitted to a few makes of grand pianos (92).

Piano stops, see: bassoon stop, buff stop, celestina stop, cembalo stop, dolce campana, forte stop, harmonica, harmonic swell, harpsichord stop, harp stop, jeu céleste, jeu de harpe, jeu de luth, Lautenzug, lute stop, mute stop, pianissimo stop, piano stop, sordin stop, una corda.

Piano transpositeur, Fr.: transposing piano.

Piano trémolophone (Fr.), grand piano with 2 keyboards, invented or improved by engineer Philippe de Girard and patented in 1842, but not shown until 1844. The piano had 5 strings per key and the upper keyboard produced a tremolo by quick repetition of the hammers (176, 204).

Pianotron, *electrophonic piano of the electroacoustical type, developed by Selmer of London in 1938.

Piano vertical, Fr.: upright piano.

Piano-viole, *bowed keyboard instr. built by Lichtenthal of Brussels *ca.* 1830 (176).

Piano violon (Fr.), *bowed keyboard instr. invented by Gustave Baudet of Paris and patented July 26, 1865. It had a continuous bow. In 1873 it was improved and its name was changed to *piano quatuor (176, 204).

Piatti, It.: cymbals.

Pi-bang, var. of pi-wang.

Pibat, free-reed *double pipes of the Kachin of Shan State, Burma; 2 cylindrical cane pipes containing metal reeds are tied together at both ends. The melody pipe has 4 front fingerholes and a rear thumbhole; the drone pipe is thinner and devoid of fingerholes (172).

Pibau, Welsh: pipes.

Pibcorn, Welsh *hornpipe, similar to the Scottish *stock and horn, believed to have been in use in the Middle Ages; it survived in N. Wales and Anglesey until the 18th c. Recently it has been revived. The only preserved specimens date from the 18th c. and were probably made by shepherds on Anglesey. A pibcorn is depicted in a 15th-c. window of St. Mary's Church, Warwick. Pibcorns were made of a single or double cylindrical chanter with idioglott beating reed, terminating in a cow-horn bell, with a mouth bell of cow horn protecting the reed(s). The chanters may be of bone, wood, or cane, with 6 front fingerholes and 1 rear fingerhole, *ca.* 50 cm. (20 in.) long. Also called cornicyll (14; 89 Rendall, 153).

Pibgorn, see: pibcorn.

Pibole, Fr.: *chalumeau; *flûte à trois trous; the chanter of a bagpipe, later the bagpipe itself. Cotgrave (in 1611) translates it as "a kind of bagpipe" (35, 197).

Pib-pib, clay flute of the Achin of Sumatra (176).

Piccolo (It.), **1.** name occasionally given to the sopranino *cornet; **2.** Fr.: piccolo flute.

Piccolo clarinet (It.: *ottavino*), in the 19th c. an oct. clarinet in high C existed in Italy (made by A. Tosoroni, 1850), but now the clarinet in high A♭ is the only surviving piccolo—a military instr. *Cf.* sestino, settimino, Sextklarinette (89 Rendall).

Piccolo Fagott, of Praetorius, the same as his single *curtal, with compass G⁰–f¹.

Piccolo flute (Fr.: *piccolo;* Ger.: *Pikkoloflöte, Oktavflöte;* It.: *ottavino*), small flute sounding an oct. higher than the ordinary, or concert, flute, with the same fingering and keywork as the ordinary (Boehm) flute. For military bands it is also made in E♭ and F. Orchestral models have a head joint and separate body, but no foot joint, and either a conical or a cylindrical bore. They are made of either wood or metal. In the past they have also been made with a foot joint. Piccolo flutes have been built since the late 18th c., with but one key originally, and were preceded by the flageolet. The words "flauto piccolo" in 18th-c. scores prior to Gluck designate the flageolet. Compass d²–d⁵, notated an oct. lower; 32–33 cm. (12½–13 in.) long (14, 89, 151).

Picco pipe, *zuffolo played by the blind It. peasant Picco in London from 1856 on, and made as a toy until the early 20th

c. Usually made of boxwood with 2 front fingerholes and 1 rear fingerhole, the conical bore terminating in a small bell, the total length not exceeding 9 cm. (3½ in.). Owing to its flexible playing technique this short instr. could be made to yield a compass of over 2 octs. from b⁰: it was played as an open pipe, as a stopped pipe, as a half-stopped one by closing all or part of the bell with the left hand, and it could also be overblown (79, 89).

Pi chawar (Thai: Javanese shawm), shawm of Thailand, of the zurna type (173).

Pie, Sp.: foot.

Pièce de rechange, syn. of corps de rechange.

Pied, Fr.: **1.** foot; **2.** boot (of organ pipes).

Piede, It.: foot.

Pien ch'ing, lithophone of China, consisting of 16 sonorous, L-shaped stone slabs (*t'e ch'ing) of identical lengths and widths but of different thicknesses, suspended in 2 rows of 8 each from a large rectangular frame. The upper row contains the male semitones, the lower row the female. The number of stones varied with the dynasties. The pien ch'ing is struck with hammers (89, 170).

Pien chung, *bell chime of China, of great antiquity. Its 16 bells are of identical lengths and widths but of different thicknesses. They are disposed in a frame in the same manner as the pien ch'ing. *Cf.* chung, p'yon chong.

Pierement [obs. Du. *pieren,* to make music], street organ of Amsterdam (80 VII).

Pífano [*pífaro*], Port., Sp.: fife. The term is recorded from the early 16th c. on.

Pífaro, Sp.: flute, fife. The word corresponds to the Cat. pifól (44).

Pife [*pífano*], *cylindrical flute of Brazil, of wood or cane, made as a blown or side-blown flute, without keys. Both versions have a compass of some 2½ octs., generally 5 or 6 fingerholes, but some specimens have 4 or 7; 2 pifes and 2 *zabumbas make up an ensemble called *cabaçal*. In some areas the pife is known as the gaita; 25–65 cm. (10–26 in.) long (7, 29).

Piffara, see: bifaria.

Piffaro (It.), **1.** name given to various It. woodwind instrs. at various times, etymologically related to the Ger. Pfeife and Engl. fife. In the 16th c. it denoted the shawm; it has also been used to designate flutes and is a syn. of ciaramella, a folk instr. of the Abruzzi. The term is often confused with piva, a bagpipe. Also spelled piffera; **2.** organ stop, also with a dual meaning: it occurs as a flue stop (piccolo flute) or as a reed stop (treble shawm) (80 IV Baines, 133).

Pifilka, wooden whistle of the Araucano Indians of S. America, 20–30 cm. (8–12 in.) long (192).

Pifól, Cat.: fife, flute. Also called pipe. The word corresponds to the Sp. pífaro (44).

Pigeon whistle, small *aeolian pipe attached to the tail of a pigeon to discourage attack by birds of prey (176).

Pignato (Prov.: pot), Prov. *friction drum consisting of a clay pot with a membrane affixed by a string, and friction stick (169).

Pihurne, folk trumpet of the Landes, France, made of wood in shape of a megaphone, without mouthpiece (136).

Pijp, Du.: pipe.

Pikkolo . . . , Ger.: see: piccolo . . .

Pilai, obs. Finn. bagpipe, with single drone (13).

Pileata [Lat.: wearing a cap (*pilleus*)], said of an organ stop, meaning stopped; *e.g.,* pileata major.

Pilgrim staves, early Renaissance name of the bourdon in England. "Flutes . . . caulled pilgrim staves" or "pipe" were among the instrs. of Henry VIII (79).

Pi li, cylindrical bamboo oboe of China, with metal bell, similar to the kuan, 2. Farmer believes it to be of Tatar origin (75 II, 142).

Pill, Estonian: musical instr. See: kiri

pill, molli pill, nutu pill, pilli, ruoko pilli, toru pill.

Pillängövi, Kan. equivalent of vāmsī (173).

Pillänkulal, Tamil equivalent of vāmsī.

Pilli, hornpipe of Finland, consisting of a cylindrical pipe with 4 fingerholes, a single reed that is mouthed, and a horn bell. Also called lavikko. Similar to the Sp. gaita madrileña. *Cf.* ruoko pilli (*Anuario musical,* 1956).

Pillui, syn. of palweh.

Piluli (Angami), straight trumpet of the Naga of Assam, slightly conical, of wood, without bell or mouthpiece; 135 cm. (53 in.) long (172).

Pimpa, OProv.: pipe.

Pim-pim, wooden kettledrum of the Mataco and Toba Indians of the S. American Chaco, made of a mortar with goatskin head, lapped with cord. It is partly filled with water when played (105).

P'in, *stick zither of Thailand, with 2 strings and 2 calabash resonators. The upper calabash rests against the player's shoulder; his left hand stops the strings while his right hand plucks them. *Cf.* p'in namao (170).

Pi nai (*pi,* oboe), cylindrical oboe of Thailand, slightly barrel-shaped, with cylindrical bore, 6 front fingerholes, and a metal staple, 5–6 cm. long, that carries a double reed. Compass f^0–c^3. *Ca.* 40 cm. (16 in.) long, with a diam. 4 cm. (1½ in.) at each end. *Cf.* pi orh (65).

Pināka (Sans., Beng.), *musical bow of N. India, without resonator, tapped with a little stick. The invention of the bow as a musical instr. is attributed to Siva. Also called pināka vīnā (17, 176).

Pināka vīnā, syn. of pināka.

Pin block (Fr.: *sommier;* Ger.: *Stimmstock;* It.: *somiere*), block of wood into which the tuning pins of stringed keyboard instrs. are driven. The word is an abbr. of wrest pin block and was formerly better known as wrest plank.

Pincullu (Quechua), *whistle flute of Bolivia and of the Aymara Indians. *Cf.* pingullo, pinkillo, tupa pincollo (105).

Pingoru, 1. idiochord *musical bow of the Orokaiva of Papua, usually made from a rib of the sago palm leaf. The bow is not bent, but kept straight, and is taken into the player's mouth almost at the middle; **2.** the name of the Jew's-harp there (77).

Pingullo, *whistle flute of the Jívaro and Sombesi Indians of Ecuador, with 2 front fingerholes and 1 rear fingerhole, and of the Chipaya Indians, with whom it has 6 fingerholes and is cylindrical, *ca.* 50 cm. (20 in.) long. *Cf.* pincullu, pinkillo, pinkui (89, 104).

Pinkillo, *whistle flute of NW. Argentina and of Bolivia, made of a bamboo internode *ca.* 30 cm. (12 in.) long. Also called tarka (192).

Pinkui, *nose flute of the Jívaro Indians of Ecuador, stopped at both ends, *ca.* 60 cm. (2 ft.) long (203).

P'in namao, *stick zither of Thailand, with slender stick and one string held by a large rear peg, mounted on a half-calabash resonator (149).

Piob, Irish: pipe.

Pioban, Irish: small pipe.

Piobmala, obs. Irish name for bagpipe (79).

Piob mor (Gaelic: great pipe), see: Highland pipe.

Pionne (Fr.), *bird organ with 2 or 3 ranks of pipes (132).

Pio poyo [?Sp. *pio pollo,* chirping chick], syn. of trompa de Paris.

Pi orh, shawm of Thailand and Cambodia, slightly barrel-shaped, with conical bore ending in a flare, 6 front fingerholes in groups of 4 and 2. Made of wood and said to exist also in ivory and even marble. *Cf.* pi, pi nai (173).

Pipa, Lat.: pipe.

P'i p'a, short-necked lute of ancient and modern China, with shallow piriform body, wooden soundboard, 2 crescent-shaped soundholes, fingerboard with 4 convex frets, 6–13 frets on the belly, and 4 silk strings fastened to lateral pegs in a reversed pegbox. The instr. is first mentioned in the 2nd c. A.C., when it had 4

strings and was about 90 cm. (3 ft.) long. The strings are usually tuned $e^1 a^1 b^1 e^2$, with a compass e^1–e^4, but other varieties of p'i p'a have 2–13 strings. It is held in an upright position on the player's thigh and is plucked with bare fingers. The *biwa of Japan is descended from it. Farmer has identified the p'i p'a with the ancient Pers. *barbat. See also: ch'in Han p'i p'a, ch'in kang t'ui, ch'in p'i p'a, ch'u tse p'i p'a, T'ang p'i p'a, ti ba (80 XII, 89, 170).

Pipaut, OProv. equivalent of pipeau.

Pipe, 1. (Engl., OFr.) (Ger.: *Pfeife*), generic term for a tube of wood or other material with or without fingerholes. The term occurs in Engl. and OFr. literature from the early 13th c. on. Pipes are sounded by whistle head, reed, or mouthpiece. A whistle head in its simplest form consists of a sharp edge against which the player directs an air stream that sets the air inside the tube in vibration. Pipes may be either open or stopped; they are said to be stopped if their lower end is closed. In that case its pitch will be an oct. below that of an open pipe of the same length. Open pipes overblow the second harmonic (the fundamental being considered as first harmonic), closed pipes the third harmonic, *e.g.*, an open c^0 pipe overblows its oct., c^1; a stopped c^0 pipe overblows its 12th, g^1. Vertically played pipes are held to be older than horizontally held ones. According to Galpin, the next step in the pipe's evolution was the provision of a notch in the upper rim (see: notched flute) which ultimately came to form the lip of the *whistle flute. For pipes played with a reed see: reed-pipe;

2. specifically, a small flute played together with the tabor; see: pipe and tabor;

3. (Fr.: *tuyau;* Ger.: *Pfeife*), in the organ, pipes are divided into *flue, *reed, and *regal pipes. Flue pipes may be open, stopped, or half-stopped, and assume a number of shapes, metal pipes usually being cylindrical, wooden pipes square; conical, inverted conical, and other forms also occur. In the Middle Ages both cylindrical and conical pipes were known, the latter being more usual in positives. Both open and stopped pipes occurred in antiquity (*cf.* Aquincum *organ), but stopped pipes were not made thereafter until the 15th c. Materials used are metal or wood; copper and bronze were used in early organs—copper from the 10th c. on —and Jerome of Moravia, *ca.* 1250, mentions pipes of silver and of lead. Later an alloy of tin and copper was used. Pure tin, being very expensive, was generally restricted in use to show pipes. Arnold Schlick still recommends it (1511). Show pipes were sometimes made of ivory, boxwood, ebony, and, in Spain, mahogany. For wooden pipes oak has been the favorite material historically, but many other woods have been used, including softwoods. Pipe metal, also called spotted metal, is an alloy of tin and lead, about 50 per cent tin, and has a mottled appearance. Pipes containing 75 per cent or more tin are nowadays called tin pipes. Formerly the alloy was expressed in terms of weight, and thus Henri Arnaut of Zwolle *ca.* 1440 speaks of a "⅔" tin content. In Andreas Werckmeister's day the usual alloy was ⅓ tin, but he recommends ½ and says that ⅔ is better yet.

Early pipes were all of uniform diam., thus varying in tone quality throughout the compass. The Bern Anonymous gives the diam. of a pigeon's egg as one suitable for organ pipes. In the 12th c. variable diams. were introduced. Med. organ builders calculated pipe lengths from either the bottom pipe up, or the top pipe down. In either case the first pipe served as standard for determining the length of the others, and the older sources give the top pipe as standard. Notker Labeo (d. 1022) seems to be the first author to indicate a scale proceeding from the bottom pipe up. Of 29 med. sources listed by Mahrenholz, 8 use only monochord lengths in their calculations, 12 use a combination of monochord lengths and end correction (Ger.: *Mündungskorrek-*

tur). Since most scales proceed downward, the correction is calculated as a lengthening of the taller pipes. Only 6 authors compute a scale from the bottom up. Since the same width could not be maintained for more than a 2-oct. compass or so, because of difficulty of speech, variable widths had to be introduced when the compass was increased. And with varying widths the higher pipes became relatively narrower and the lower ones relatively wider, thus reducing the end correction. See also: block, Blockwerk, boot, flue pipe, foot, languid, reed pipe, regal pipe, (62; 89 Galpin, 133; Mahrenholz, C.: *Die Berechnung der Orgelpfeifenmensur,* 1938).

Pipe and tabor, ensemble consisting of a 3-holed pipe accompanied by a small drum, both played simultaneously by one performer; it first appeared in S. France and N. Spain in the 12th c. and is still played there today. During the late Middle Ages and the Renaissance it seems to have been known to most of W. Europe. Its chief function was to accompany dances, and in England the so-called *whittle and dub accompanied morris dances until the late 19th c. In France the tabor is now usually replaced by a *tambourin à cordes (string drum), while the Basque people still use a snare drum. In Catalonia the sardana *cobla* employs a *flaviol and *tamboril player. See: tabor, tabor pipe for further details. See also: tutu-panpan, whittle and dub (14, 89 Baines).

Pipeau, Fr.: historically, a rustic reed-pipe; a *chalumeau (chanter of a bagpipe); a bird call. In the last sense it was also called *pipeau de chasse.* The term occurs from the 16th c. on. See also: pipet, pipaut.

Pipet, obs. Fr. term for a rustic pipe, recorded from the 13th c. on. In Normandy it denotes specifically a pipe made of wheat stalk. Later the word became syn. of pipeau, a bird call.

Pipette [Fr., dim. of *pipe*], Fr. term recorded since the 15th c.; in Bresse and the Vosges it is a small *whistle flute (35).

Pi-pi, unidentified instr. of Tibet, said to be a fife or flute (89 Picken).

Pipinë, double hornpipe of S. Albania, made of 2 wheat-stalk pipes, each with a single reed; it is mouth-blown. One pipe has 4 fingerholes; the other, none (13).

Pipiritaño, reedpipe of Spain, made of green cane, a child's toy. Cf. zamploña. See also: zampoña.

Pipiza, oboe of modern Greece, similar to the zurna, with equidistant fingerholes all of the same size. It is often replaced by a clarinet. Tuning is accomplished by partly stopping the holes with wax (144).

Pipo, Jew's-harp of the Ruro of Papua (103).

Pi pyu, *ring flute of the Shan of Shan State, Burma, made of bamboo with 7 front fingerholes and a rear thumbhole. The duct is formed by a lateral hole and a bamboo ring (172).

Pique, Fr.: spike (of a cello, etc.).

P'iri, oboe of Korea, made of bamboo. It corresponds to the Japanese hichiriki (66).

Piring būrū (brass trumpet), metal trumpet of Turkey, known by the 17th c. (76).

Piripity, drum of the Malagasy Republic (171).

Pirolo, It.: tuning peg.

Pirone, It.: tuning pin.

Pirouette (Fr.) (Sp.: tudel), wooden disc, cylinder, or cup-shaped attachment that partly covers the double reed of some older European wind instrs. and is still in use on folk oboes of Europe as well as on virtually all non-European double-reed instrs. It acts to protect the reed and provides a lip rest for the player, who takes the whole reed into his mouth. Height of the pirouette varies according to the length of the reed employed. In SE. Asia a *phorbeia type of (wooden) pirouette that fits right across the player's cheeks is known. Trichet ca. 1640 called the pirouette a rosette (89, 176, 190).

Pirutu (Quechua), small flute or panpipes of ancient Peru (80 XII).

Piščal, primitive wooden pipe of Slovenia (144).

Pisha, small *cross flute of Persia (89 Farmer).

Pi shanai [sānāyī], oboe of Cambodia, nowadays called sr̥lai (47).

Pisk, ribbon reed of Slovenia, made of a grass blade held taut between the ends of a split stick. Also called čivink (144).

Piskulice, syn. of trstenke.

Piston, 1. name sometimes given to the piccolo cornet; **2.** Fr.: cornet; **3.** Ger.: cornet; **4.** Fr.: piston valve, valve.

Piston à boîte carrée, Fr.: box valve.

Piston basse (Fr.), a large, valved brass instr. invented by Étienne-François Périnet of Paris in 1841, designed to replace the ophicleide (204).

Piston compensateur, Fr.: compensation valve.

Piston double, Fr.: Vienna valve.

Pistone, It.: **1.** piston valve; **2.** Eb alto cornet.

Piston flute (Fr.: flûte à coulisse; Ger.: Stempelflöte), flute with an adjustable stopper inserted in the lower end by means of which the pitch is altered. It occurs in Europe, Asia, and the S. Seas. Also called piston pipe. See also: bird warble, slide whistle (168).

Pistonkornett, Ger.: syn. of Kornett.

Piston valve (Fr.: piston; Ger.: Pumpventil; It.: pistone), valve having a piston, a metal cylinder of brass or phosphor bronze which is pierced so that the air stream can pass through it into the valve slide when depressed, thereby altering the length of the tube. An improved version is the Berliner Pumpventil, and a subsequent improvement by Étienne-François Périnet of Paris in 1839 produced the valve in use today (89 Morley-Pegge).

Pisui, idiochord bamboo *tube zither of Hainan, with up to 6 strings (119).

Pitch pipe (Fr.: choriste, diapason; Ger.: Stimmpfeife; It.: corista), pipe yielding a single standard pitch; or a wooden *piston flute designed to give various pitches by pushing the stopper in more or less, usually with a calibrated surface and used principally to give the pitch to singers. The piston pipe type was replaced in the 19th c. by a circular device with free reeds in which the length of the reed, and thus the pitch, is regulated by a rotating spiral. See also: harmonica-Jaulin (89).

Pitikilangy, *ground zither of the Malagasy Republic (171).

Pitjol cumui, *musical bow of the Pomo Indians of California, made of willow, with 2 strings. One end of the bow is taken into the player's mouth while the other is struck with a small stick (105).

Pito, 1. short *whistle flute of Galicia, Spain, with 3 front fingerholes and 2 rear holes, the latter being stopped by the thumb and the upper surface of the little finger. *Cf.* apito, pitu; **2.** a similar flute played in S. America, where it is *ca.* 30 cm. (12 in.) long, very slender, and is played as a one-hand flute together with a drum (57, 89, 137).

Pitorka, flat, clapperless bell of the Muria of Bastar, India, made of *semur* or *siuna* wood, apparently derived from the wooden cowbell. The aperture is no more than a slit. Roughly triangular in form and often carved, it is worn suspended in front of the player's waist. The open rim is beaten with 2 stout sticks. It accompanies marriage dances, producing a sharp, penetrating sound, and is also an object of worship before a wedding. Up to 68 cm. (27 in.) wide and 36 cm. (14 in.) high. Also called kutorka, thuturka, tudra. See also: piturka (68).

Pitu, 1. (Akk.) pipe of ancient Babylon, with upturned end; it appeared in the first millennium B.C. (89 Galpin); **2.** [Port. *apito*], stopped wooden pipe of the Lower Congo (176).

Piturka, word that designates 2 instrs. of the Muria of Bastar, India: **1.** large bell of the cowbell type; **2.** *slit drum in form of a canoe. A small hole is pierced in the bottom to improve the tone. The slit is long and deep, but the remainder of

the drum is not hollowed out. It is worshiped before a marriage ceremony. See also: pitorka (68).

Piva, a rare if not extinct bagpipe of N. Italy, mouth-blown. Its conical chanter has 7 fingerholes (some specimens also have a rear thumbhole) and a double reed. The single drone has a tuning slide and a single reed (13, 89).

Piva torto, It.: crumhorn.

Pivette, Fr.: reedpipe (197).

Pivone (It.) [aug. of *piva*], a large piva.

Pivora, syn. of mbombu.

Pi-wang, long-necked Tibetan lute with hollowed-out wooden body, related to the N. Indian lute. Its strings, variable in number, are tuned in 4ths and are played with a plectrum. Also called pi-bang (89 Picken, 176).

Pi-wang-rgyud-ysum, instr. of Tibet known by literary references only and believed to be a 3-stringed guitar (89).

Pizczalka, *whistle flute of Poland, made of a single piece of wood, with 6 fingerholes and a rear blowhole (91, 176).

Piztli, pipe of the Aztec (144).

Plagiaulos [Gk. *plagios,* oblique + *aulos,* pipe], aulos of late antiquity, a transverse monaulos held obliquely or like a cross flute, with the reed inserted into a lateral protuberance near the end. Several instrs. believed to represent plagiauloi have survived: 2 in the British Museum, sections of 1 in Boston. Those of the British Museum are of bronze, with vestiges of a wooden pipe inside 1 of the 2. The upper end of 1 pipe is stopped; the other is incomplete. On both an oblique tube projects from the main tube, inclined toward the upper end. Each has 3 front fingerholes, very unevenly spaced, and the complete pipe has a rear hole placed between the 2 top fingerholes. The oblique tube is presumed to have carried a double reed. Despite much investigation in recent years the nature of plagiauloi is still not clarified.

Planchette ronflante, Fr.: bull-roarer.

Plandang, bamboo flute of the Bagobo of S. Mindanao, Philippine Islands, with 5 fingerholes at the lower end and half-stopped at the upper. *Ca.* 1.50 m. (5 ft.) long (176).

Pläschprment [*pläschpern,* to make a noise], the cello-sized bass member of the *Klarfiedel quartet, made only in Jihlava (Iglau), Moravia. Its 4 strings are tuned C⁰ G⁰ d⁰ d¹. A thin metal plaque is glued to the belly at the height of the tailpiece; a peg is inserted vertically into the tailpiece, so as to leave a minute space between peg and plaque, and the peg rattles against the plaque when the instr. is played (86).

Platerspiel, Ger.: bladder pipe. See also: Blaterpfeife.

Platillos, Sp.: cymbals.

Plattflöte (Ger.: flat flute), **1.** *chord flute built in the 18th c. by C. Schlegel of Basel (169); **2.** organ stop of flue pipes, so called because of its flat form; a syn. of the Doppelflöte (133).

Player piano, piano fitted with an attachment or device for automatic playing, actually a 19th-c. adaptation of the *pneumatic organ action to a piano. The first players were separate cabinets set in front of the keyboard, hand cranked, the keys being depressed by finger-like levers (see: pianista). Later the mechanism was incorporated into the piano proper. The pneumatic system was controlled by perforated paper rolls. See: piano-exécutant, pianola, Welte-Mignon (37, 89).

Plectro-euphone, keyboard instr. of unknown construction, invented by Gama of Nantes in 1827, and presumably bowed (92, 204).

Plectrum [Gk. *plektron,* an object to strike with] (Fr.: *plectre;* Ger.: *Plektrum*), Lat. word used in several senses: it commonly designates a device for plucking strings and can be made of wood, ivory, metal, tortoise shell, quill, etc.; it may be held in the hand, worn around a finger, or form part of the action of certain keyboard instrs., as in jacks of a harpsichord. In med. times it

designated the languid of an organ pipe, the tangents of a hurdy-gurdy, the tuning key of a harp, and occasionally even the bow.

Plectrum ferreum, Lat.: clapper of a bell (188).

Plein-jeu (Fr.), large mixture organ stop found in Fr. organs, composed of *cymbale and *fourniture. It contains octaves and quints (20, 63).

Pléniphone (Fr.), a variety of guitar patented in Paris by De Zavala in 1881 (176, 204).

Pleret, ancient Hindu-Javanese name of the selompret (121).

Pless horn, see: Prince Pless horn.

Plettro-lyre, instr. with plucked strings, patented by Trajetta of Philadelphia, in 1833 (158).

Pleyela, a type of *pianola formerly made by Pleyel of Paris (37).

Plinthion, unidentified instr. of Byzantium, according to Jacques Handschin (*Zeremoniewerk*); large psaltery of Byzantium, with 32 strings, according to Amédée Gastoué.

Plockflöte, obs. spelling of Blockflöte.

Plucked drum (Fr.: *tambour par pincement;* Ger.: *Zupftrommel*), in its simpler form the plucked drum consists of a bucket-like container with an open top and with a membrane bottom, to the center of which a string is attached. The other end of the string is held taut by the player's left hand while his right hand plucks it. In more developed forms, such as the *tuntina, the human arm is replaced by a fixed wooden shaft carrying a tuning peg. The plucked drum has been classified as a membranophone, as the string's vibrations are transmitted to a membrane that is thereby also set in vibration. However, the string's share in tone generation is at least as great as that of the membrane, and thus the plucked drum can equally well be classified as a chordophone, a primitive form of zither with the player's arm acting as string bearer. Plucked drums occur only on the Indian subcontinent. See: ānanda laharī, ektār, gabuki, gopi yantra, kutam, than-thona, tuntina.

Plucked idiophone (Fr.: *idiophone par pincement;* Ger.: *Zupfidiophon*), idiophone in which elastic tongues or lamellae, fixed at one end, are vibrated either with the fingers or mechanically. The tongues can be of wood, bamboo, metal, or other material. Commonly called linguaphone nowadays. The sansa, Jew's-harp, and music box are the best known linguaphones (100).

Plumbe, large cowbell of Switzerland, made of copper or sheet iron. Lowest-pitched of the cowbells, it often reaches a diam. of 30 cm. (12 in.).

Pluriarc (Fr.) (Ger.: *Bogenlaute*), term devised by Montandon to designate a W. African chordophone, also known as bow lute. As its name indicates, the pluriarc is generally considered to be a multiple *musical bow. The single resonator is a wooden box, of irregular rectangular form; from its back project a number of flexible sticks, each held under tension by a taut string attached by one end to the belly of the resonator. These bow-like projections number from 2 to 8. They are approximately of equal length, the strings being tuned by differences in tension (causing different curvatures of the bows). Generally there is a nut on the belly. The pluriarc was known to Praetorius, who depicted it. In more recent times it has been called harp-zither, Congo guitar, westafrikanische Gitarre. See also: bolima, bompete, dumo, esandju, goukha's, gunge, imele, kalangu, kambi, kissanga, kissumba, kokolo, limele, lokombe, longombe, longombi, lukombe, lukonde, lunko, lusinga, mveul, ndongo, ndono, ngomfi, ngwen, ngwombi, ngwomo, njembo, nsambi, ovambu guitar, sabe, sambi, wambi (15 Wachsmann, 170, 185).

Pneumacorde, invention of Jean-Antoine Berger of Grenoble, 1762, presumably the mechanism for obtaining a crescendo on a harpsichord. *Cf.* épinette expressive (27).

Pneumatic lever (Fr.: *levier pneumatique;* Ger.: *pneumatischer Hebel*), a component of modern organ actions, invented in 1827 by Joseph Booth, organ builder of Wakefield, England, and developed by Charles Spackman Barker of Bath, later of Paris, *ca.* 1832. Its object was to ease organ touch. With the lever the keys no longer opened pallets, but opened valves of small, intermediary bellows. Unable to introduce the lever in England, Barker went to France, where it was promptly adopted by Aristide Cavaillé-Coll of Paris (89, 99).

Pneumatic organ, 1. name wrongly applied to the ordinary organ to distinguish it from the water organ or *hydraulos; **2.** organ with pneumatic action. See: tubular-pneumatic action.

Po, cymbals of China, made of bronze, with pronounced central boss and flat or slightly turned rim, in different sizes, up to some 60 cm. (24 in.) in diam. Introduced from Turkestan in the Middle Ages, they now play a prominent part in theatrical performances. They are equivalent to the Korean tong pal and the Jap. batsu. Also called t'ong po. See also: nao (89, 170).

Poari, clarinet of the Bororó Indians of Brazil (105).

Poche (Fr.: pocket), Fr.: *kit, so named because it was carried in dancing masters' pockets. The term is recorded from 1570 on. In 1575 a *poche de violon* is mentioned (80 VII).

Pochette [Fr., dim. of *poche,* pocket], syn. of poche.

Pochette d'amour (Fr.), 18th-c. kit with 4 sympathetic strings.

Po chung, single bell of China, suspended in a frame (66, 142).

Po fu, *barrel drum of China, with 2 nailed heads. Originally a grain drum, it used to be filled with rice hulls but became a temple instr. It is held horizontally on the player's knees and is played with the fingers of both hands. *Ca.* 46 cm. (18 in.) long (89, 170).

Poïkilorgue [Gk. *poikilos,* variegated +

Fr. *orgue,* organ], an improved *orgue expressif invented by Aristide Cavaillé-Coll of Paris and first shown at the Paris Exposition of 1834. Built in form of a small square piano, it had one rank of free reeds with a compass C^0–f^0, 2 pedals, large bellows worked by the left pedal, while the right pedal varied the air pressure, thus constituting an expression stop (132; catalogue of Paris Exposition, 1900).

Pointed flute, wooden flute with doubly notched mouthpiece, barrel-shaped at the upper end, with a cylindrical or inverted conical lower section. Used by buffalo hunters of Timor. Exactly the same instr. is found in Sokoto Province of Nigeria and among some peoples of the Upper Nile. See: dunda, feku (118, 123).

Pokakaa, said by Stewart Culin (*Hawaiian Games,* 1899) to be a *disc buzzer of Hawaii, made of bark (77).

Poketa danyakko, gourd rattle of the Toba Indians of the Chaco.

Pokido, sansa of the Lokele of the Congo, made of a human skull (19, 42).

Pok shu, cross flute of China (176).

Pokul-logun, tube zither of Nias (176).

Poliphant, string instr. resembling the modern *harp lute, invented *ca.* 1600 by Daniel Farrant, with 25–40 strings. An illustration of it appears in ms. Harl. 2034 of the British Museum. Apart from this and Playford's comment that it was not unlike a lute, little is known of it except that it was also called polyphon (79).

Polka, an improved accordion, patented by Jacob Alexandre of Paris on Dec. 12, 1849 (204).

Polnische Geige (Ger.), term used by Agricola (in 1545) to designate an unfretted bowed instr. tuned in 5ths, with strings stopped in the ONordic and Slav. fashion by lateral pressure of the fingernails. Agricola points out that lack of frets makes the fingering more difficult. In the 17th c. Praetorius identifies *polnische Geige* as a name given by musicians to the violin. Unfortunately we do not know what relationship, if any, existed between this and the *sistrum smiczocz of Paulus Paulirinus, and the *skrzypce. It may have been called "Polish" because it was played by Poles (*cf.* Schweitzerpfeife, for instance): the accounts of Neustift (Novacella) Monastery record the payment of *"item lb 1 pro libalibus tribus polonis qui fecerunt recreationem d. et f.* [*dominis et fratribus*] *in refectorio cum fidelis in die S. Anne 1511* (text kindly communicated by Professor W. Senn). An inventory of Kremsmünster Monastery dated 1584 lists 4 polnische Geigen without strings, as well as rebecs.

Polnischer Bock, Ger. name of the koza; a syn. of Bock.

Polo, drum of the Banza of the Congo, similar to the bia. *Ca.* 1 m. (40 in.) long (30).

Polychord [Gk. *poly,* many + *chorde,* string], 10-stringed violin invented by Friedrich Hillmer of Leipzig in 1799, the object being to facilitate the playing of chords. Between 1811 and 1818 the number of strings was reduced to 8 (176).

Polyharmonion, syn. of pansymphonicon.

Polyphant, see: poliphant.

Polyphon, 1. *music box made by the Polyphon Co. of Leipzig soon after 1886, with punched steel disc and star wheel plucking the comb (37, 43); **2.** syn. of poliphant (89).

Polyphone, 17th-c. chordophone of bass range, described by James Talbot (*ca.* 1700) as having a body 3½ ft. long, with scalloped profile, metal strings, 4 brass frets, nuts, and bridges. The number of strings seems to have averaged 40. Also called polythore (80 XV).

Polyphonion trumpet, wind instr. of unknown construction patented by William Close, a chemist of Dalton, Lancashire, on Nov. 2, 1811 (126, 158).

Polyplectron, *bowed keyboard instr. invented by Johann Christian Dietz, Jr., of Paris in 1827 (158).

Polythore, on Aug. 9, 1661, John Evelyn, then in Italy, saw at "Sir Fr. Prujean" (Francis Prujeane) the polythore, "an instrument having something of the harp, lute and theorbo, by none known in England, nor described by any author, nor used, but by this skilful and learned Doctor." *Cf.* polyphone.

Polytoni-Clavichordium, *piano-harpsichord invented by Johann Andreas Stein of Augsburg in 1769, believed to have been inspired by an instr. of Jean Marius that he saw in Paris. It consisted of a 2-manual harpsichord, separated from a lower piano by a central soundboard. The upper instr. had 3 sets of strings at 8′ pitch and 1 at 16′ pitch. The upper of its 2 keyboards plucked one 8′ only; the lower, all 4 strings. The lower instr. was a standard piano, with its own manual. The dampers were worked by a knee lever, and its case was built to look like the stand of a harpsichord (95).

Pometto, obs. It. syn. of pirolo.

Pomhart, 16th-c. corr. of Bombard.

Pommer, new-Ger. corr. of Bombard.

Pompa, It.: crook; slide.

Pomsa, small lute of "Saberma, Lower Niger," similar to the kambreh, but with 2 strings (176).

Pone, bowed *tube zither of the Ndebele of S. Africa; it corresponds to the tsijolo (116).

Ponga, syn. of apunga.

Ponggang, syn. of monggang.

Pong-pong, aeolian *slit drum of N. Celebes, made of a bamboo segment with a slit in the length of an internode. A pole is driven into the ground; from its upper end are suspended the slit drum, a piece of palm leaf or bark matting, and a striker. When the matting catches the breeze the striker keeps hitting the drum. It is used to scare away animals from fields under cultivation (112).

Ponitu, nose flute of the Maori of New Zealand (203).

Ponticello [dim. of *ponte,* bridge], It.: bridge (of bowed instrs.).

P'o pan, wooden clappers of China, consisting of 6 pieces of hardwood, all of the same size, tied at one end by a silk cord. *Cf.* haku han, pak (66).

Popó, syn. of cajita china.

Popondi, syn. of tuba pondi.

Poretu, flute of New Zealand, occasionally played as a nose flute. Also called e'wiu (203).

Porongo, maraca of the Cainguá Indians of Argentina (152).

Portable grand pianoforte, *upright piano invented by John Isaac Hawkins of Philadelphia in 1800 and patented by him there. His father, Isaac, patented it in England on his behalf in the same year. The piano was vertically strung, with strings reaching down to the ground, and the soundboard was set in a metal frame and braced with metal bars; the pin block was of metal. It had a 5-oct. compass, F^1–f^3. Height only 138 cm. (52½ in.) (92; A. J. Hipkins in: Encyclopaedia Britannica, 14th ed.).

Portativ, Ger.: portative organ.

Portative organ (Fr.: *orgue portatif;* Ger.: *Portativ*), small, portable organ that first appeared in the 12th c. and disappeared in the 16th c., used both for secular purposes and in church processions. Characteristically it was carried by its player, suspended from a band around his neck and held at right angles to the body. The bellows, in back of the instr., were worked by the player's left hand, the keyboard by his right. A treble instr., the portative originally had a compass of 2 octs., which by the late Middle Ages had increased to 3—presumably chromatic by then. All its pipes were flue pipes. Early in its existence it added a couple of tall bass drone pipes, placed at the treble end. Most portatives are depicted as having more than one row of pipes and usually more than one set of keys, which arrangement seems to have been merely a space-saving device, and does not indicate the presence of stops. The pipes were probably disposed somewhat like the C and C♯ divisions of the organ:

C♯ E♭ F G A B . . .
C D E F♯ G♯ B♭ . . .

Its key buttons were either T-shaped or in form of typewriter keys. Wooden pipes are sometimes discernible on later instrs. The portative organ was played monophonically (except for drones), and, owing to the position in which it was held, with 2 fingers only (62, 167, H. Hickmann: *Das Portativ*, 1936).

Portevent, Fr.: wind trunk.

Portunal [corr. of *Sordune*], organ stop of inverted conical flue pipes of medium scale, invented *ca.* 1600, at 8′ pitch and occasionally also 4′ pitch. Also called Bordunal (133).

Portunen, var. of Portunal.

Portvent, obs. Engl.: wind trunk.

Porutu, *end-blown flute of the Maori of New Zealand, usually made of kaiwhiria wood hollowed out by fire, and elaborately carved. Or it can be made of 2 half cylinders hollowed out and bound together. Generally it has 3 equidistant front fingerholes and a rear thumbhole, but some specimens are made of bone and lack a thumbhole. It is played by men with the object of attracting women. *Cf.* whio (8, 77).

Posaune [MHGer. *busîne, busune*, from Fr. *buisine*], **1.** Ger.: trombone. The word has been employed since the early 17th c. See also: pusaune; **2.** organ stop of reed pipes; it branched off from the trumpet stops at the end of the 15th c. Usually at 16′ pitch but also found at 32′ and 8′ pitches, almost invariably in the pedal. See also: trombone, 2 (2, 133).

Posche, Ger. corr. of poche.

Positie, obs. Du. and Flemish: mixture organ stop (167).

Positif de dos, Fr.: chair organ.

Positiv, Ger.: positive organ.

Positive organ [Lat. *ponere*, to place] (Fr.: *orgue positif, positif;* Ger.: *Positiv*), small, nonportable organ with flue pipework, lower in pitch than the *portative organ, in existence from the 10th to 17th c. Positives were furnished with short feet and were placed on a table or set on the floor and played with both hands by one person, while a second person worked the bellows (in contrast to the *portative organ). The bellows were worked either by hand or trodden. Trodden bellows were known to Byzantium by the 4th c. and appear in the West by the early 12th c. In its earlier days the keys of the positives were often T-shaped, as on some portatives, or they were elongated *slider keys. Both types still occur in the 14th c., when a clear distinction between the 2 types of organ is drawn: *"orgues seans et orgues portatives"* ("sitting" and portative organs). Early church organs were positives, and when larger organs were available, the positive was often retained. Thus Basel Cathedral in 1473 had 2 organs and 3 positives. The smaller table instrs. became secular house organs in the 16th c., prototypes of the later *chamber organ, while larger ones continued in existence in Italy until the 18th c. (62, 167).

Positiv im Stuhl, Ger.: chair organ.

Postclaves, 16- and 17th-c. Ger. expression, used chiefly by organ builders, for accidental keys. *Postfa* is F♯, for instance.

Post horn (Fr.: *cornet de poste;* Ger.: *Posthorn;* It.: *cornetta da postiglione*), valveless brass or copper horn made in a variety of shapes, the signal instr. of *postillons* and mail-coach guards. In the Germany of Praetorius' day they were coiled; in the France of Mersenne's, crescent-shaped. The Fr. model had acquired a diam. of 30–45 cm. (12–18 in.) by the late 18th c. and became identical with the *bugle horn. The coiled form was also known in France, where it assumed a single coil and looked like a small Fr. horn. In the 19th c. this model was transformed into the *cornet by the addition of valves. The *Reichspost* horns had 3½ coils, were pitched in C or A, had a compass of 2 octs.; those of Prussia were smaller and, according to Halle (in 1764), had a compass of a single oct. Koch wrote (1802) that except for its smaller size the post horn was identical to the Fr. horn. In 19th-c. England it assumed a straight form with narrow bore, 70–80 cm. (28–

32 in.) long, usually made in 2 sections, and also known as tandem horn; it was also made in coiled form for carrying in the pocket. These models produced 3 or 4 tones. See also: coach horn, tandem horn (89, 90, 150).

Potato, syn. in rhythm bands of ocarina. See also: sweet potato.

Pot drum (Fr.: *pot tambour;* Ger.: *Topftrommel*), clay pot with a membrane tied over its mouth. The membrane is sounded. Distributed in Asia, W. and C. Africa, whence it was carried to the New World. See also: gada, gātha, ilongo, intambula, kattivadiyam, khais, koda, kuta, tarra, wainkya.

Poti-poti, syn. of pu tatara.

Pot musical (Ger.: *Sprechtopf*), Fr. term for a clay pot or gourd into which the performer sings or speaks, thereby modifying the timbre of his voice, which may appear to him like that of a spirit or of an animal. A magical apparatus rather than a musical instr.

Pot tambour, Fr.: pot drum.

Potence, Fr.: the U-bend of a trumpet or trombone. The term dates back to the early 14th c.

Potuto, syn. of putoto.

Poukhan, OHGer.: drum, kettledrum. *Cf.* Pauke.

P'rad-gling, small *cross flute of Tibet, made of metal (89 Picken).

Prananguma, syn. of pernanguma.

Prasārinī vīnā [*prasārinī,* eleventh quarter tone of the Indian oct.], a 2-necked vīnā of India, with calabash body and the long fretted neck of a *sitar with 5 strings, parallel to which and to its left is a second, shorter neck, with 16 frets and 5 strings. The latter are tuned an oct. higher than those of the main neck. The shorter neck has no body of its own, but is attached to the main neck by 2 short horizontal struts; its upper end terminates in a flat pegdisc with frontal and lateral pegs (132, 173).

Prda, syn. of troba.

Prellmechanik (Ger.), piano action in which the hammers point toward the

player and are attached either directly or indirectly to the keys. The hammer shank is stopped by a *Prelleiste* (rail) when a key is depressed. In most actions fitted with a *Prelleiste,* be they square or grand, the hammers were pivoted on a *Kapsel* mounted on the key. See also: German action (92).

Prepared piano, a conventional piano, the sound of which is modified by the application of foreign bodies to strings or hammers, popularized by the U.S. composer John Cage.

Préstant (Fr.) [Lat. *prae stare,* to stand before], organ stop, historically the 4' position of the montre.

Prillarhorn, syn. of bukkehorn.

Primasica (first voice), syn. of tanburica (176).

Primbass (Ger.), syn. of Baroxyton; also called Tenorbass in Germany.

Primhorn (Ger.), valved brass instr. of alto range, first built by Vaclav F. Červeny of Königgrätz (Hradec Králové) in 1873, similar to the *French horn and the *ballad horn, the bore being wider than that of the French horn and narrower than that of the ballad horn. Its bell is wider than that of the ballad horn. Pitched in F, an oct. higher than the horn, for which reason it is also called Oktavhorn. It is played with a French-horn mouthpiece. Today the Primhorn is built in F and E♭. In Ger.-speaking countries it is also known as Konzerthorn.

Prince of Wales harp, psaltery of early-20th-c. England, a child's toy. *Cf.* Erato harp (79).

Prince Pless horn (Ger.: *Fürst Pless-Horn*), wide-bore *hunting horn in helicon form, named after Prince Pless. Made both as a natural and as a valved horn (169).

Principal [Lat.: *vox principalis*], in British and American organs a 4' diapason in the manual or 8' diapason in the pedal (corresponding to the Fr. préstant). Elsewhere the word, or its local equivalent, designates a foundation stop of open cylindrical flue pipes normally made of metal, rarely of wood. The principal scale became a standard scale for open flue pipes. *Cf.* Prinzipal.

Principale spezzato, It.: a divided principal (organ stop).

Principalino, syn. of prinzipal amabile.

Prinzipal (Ger.) [Lat. *vox principalis*], until approximately the end of the 15th c. Prinzipal denoted: a) the row(s) of principal pipes in an organ; b) the combined Prinzipal and Hintersatz. In the latter sense it was also known as Chorstimme, Flötenwerk. In the early 16th c. the Prinzipal in the pedal was at 16' pitch, that of the manual at 8', and that of the Positiv at 4' pitch. Ger. Prinzipals have historically had a narrower scale than other principals. See also: principal (133).

Prinzipal amabile, metal Flötenprinzipal at 8' pitch. Also called principalino (133).

Prinzipal Diskant (Ger.), also written Prinzipaldiskant. A Prinzipal in the upper half of the manual only, the object being to reinforce the treble (133).

Prinzipalflöte, syn. of Flötenprinzipal.

Prinzipaltrompete, the lower register of the *natural trumpet, usually e¹–c² (176).

Pritsche [MHGer. *Britsche*], modern version of the *Britsche, a switch used during carnival. Longitudinal saw cuts are made in a piece of wood, thereby creating lamellae. Grimm defines it as clappers, crepitaculum (88, 169).

Procession cello, see: violoncello.

Professional pianoforte, small *upright piano brought out by Robert Wornum of London in 1826, with a "pizzicato" pedal, details of which are unknown (92).

Progessio harmonica (Lat.), mixture organ stop invented by F. Wilke of Neuruppin in 1839, increasing in the number of ranks as the pitch rises, now virtually obs. In its original form it started on C⁰ with 1⅓' and 1'. See also: compensation mixture (133).

Prolongement harmonique (Fr.), device invented by Martin de Provins in the 19th c. for sustaining sound after the hands were removed from a keyboard. Applied to the harmonium, it was controlled by either a hand stop or a pedal (169, 198).

Proteus, *enharmonic harpsichord designed by Francisco Nigetti *ca.* 1650, each tone being divided into 5 microtones, and provided with 5 rows of keys. Also called cembalo omnicordo, cembalo omnisono, strumento omnisono. An Innsbruck inventory of 1665 records ". . . *ein anderes Instrument mit vielen Claviaturen von weissem helfenbein . . .*" bearing Nigetti's name (27, 64).

Psallmelodikon, an improved *Neu Tschang invented in 1828 by Weinrich of Heiligenstadt near Erfurt, in form of a flattened cylinder with free reeds, 26 keys, 6 front and 2 rear fingerholes. See also: Apollo lyre, 1; Melodica (178).

Psalmodicon, *bowed zither of Sweden, said to have been invented by Johann Dillner by 1829, when it was approved by the Swedish Academy. Originally it consisted of a flat rectangular box with single melody string of gut and several metal drone strings. The melody string passed over a ruler marked with stopping positions. The psalmodicon was intended as a substitution for the organ in accompanying church and, above all, school singing, and enjoyed great popularity as a school instr. With time it underwent further development: the body assumed cello shape, with long stick handle, and the number of strings increased to 4 melody strings, or to 1 or 2 melody strings plus a variable number of drone strings. Until the 1860's it remained in great demand, but the introduction of harmoniums in schools doomed it. Otto Anderssen was of the opinion that it might have been of considerable antiquity (see: bowed harp). Its pop. name was notstok. See also: keyed psalmodicon (9, 91, 149).

Psalmodicon à clavier, Fr.: keyed psalmodicon.

Psalmonica, var. of psalmodicon.

Psalter, obs. Engl.: psaltery.

Psalterie, OFr.: psaltery.

Psalterion (Gk.) [Gk.: *psallein*, to pluck], **1.** generic term for plucked instrs.; **2.** a name of the harp in ancient Greece.

Psaltérion, Fr.: psaltery.

Psalterium [Gk. **psalterion*], St. Jerome's Vulgate translation of **nebel.* The church fathers speak of it as triangular; Hippolytus says its advantages are that its exterior form has no curved line and that the resonator is on top (as opposed to the kithara), and since Cassiodore it is described as having the form of the Gk. letter Δ. The resonator is said to have been round and covered with skin. From the 9th c. on we also hear of a psalterium in form of a square shield with 10 strings (see: psalterium decachordum). The word is thought to have designated the vertical **angular harp or the cruit. During the late Middle Ages it came to mean psaltery and dulcimer. Paulus Paulirinus *ca.* 1460 describes it as triangular but sometimes made in harpsichord shape.

Psalterium decachordum (Lat.), the 10-stringed **psaltery of the Vulgate, of square shape, which Sachs compared to that of the Phoenician zither. The 9th-c. epistle to Dardanus by Pseudo-Jerome says that it was formed like a shield; Notker Balbulus complains in the 12th c. that its shape has been changed to triangular, the number of its strings increased, and that its name was changed to **rotta (cruit) (170).

Psaltery [Gk. **psalterion*] (Fr.: *psaltérion*), plucked zither known from med. times on. It may be plucked with bare fingers or with a plectrum. By the late Middle Ages it had assumed a variety of shapes, trapezoid, semitrapezoid, wingshaped, harp-shaped. For details see: ala, ala bohemica, armandine, arpanetta, 'asor, canale, caño, canon, canone, chang, décacorde, demi-canon, ele, Erato harp, gusli, kanala, kankles, kannel, kanon, kanón, kanonaki, kantele, ko erh nai, kohkles, kuakle, kuokle, mbanju, media ala, medicinale, medio caño, medius canon, meo canno, metzkanon, mezzo canone, micanon, Prince of Wales harp, qanum, qānūn, salmaharphâ, salmsang, saltere, salterio, salterium, saltirsanch, satatantri vīnā, sautier, shepherd's harp, soittu, trumpa.

Psaltery-viol, syn. of sultana.

Psantrīn (Aram.) [Gk. **psalterion*], chordophone of ancient Israel, of unknown identity. It is mentioned in the Book of Daniel, written in the Hellenistic era, and in the 13th c., when Saadi affirms that it was identical with the nebel.

Pseudo-arc, Fr.: harp zither (128).

Psycho, large orchestrion built in the U.S. in 1874 by J. A. Clark and Neville Maskeline (37).

Pu, generic term for wind instrs. among the Maori of New Zealand (8).

Pu-a, globular **nose flute of Hawaii, with 2 or 3 fingerholes (203).

Pualtem-puch, syn. of puch.

Puch, horn of the Cheremiss of the U.S.S.R., made of wood or spirally twisted bark. Also called pualtem-puch (146).

Puchero, Basque: large cowbell (56).

Puepava, panpipes of New Hebrides (176).

Pu hau re roa, syn. of pu tatara.

Pu heko heku, nose flute of the Marquesas Islands, Polynesia (203).

Pu hoho, syn. of pu torino.

Pühuri, marine-shell trumpet of the Alifu of Ceram, Indonesia (144).

Puíca, syn. of cuíca.

Pu ihu, cane **nose flute of the Marquesas, Polynesia (203).

Pu ili, **percussion tubes of Hawaii, one of which also serves as a rattle. Made of segments of bamboo, a longer and a shorter one. The bark is detached from the longer one, giving it the appearance of a switch; alternate sections of bark are removed to give freer motion to the others. This is then either shaken as a rattle or struck with the smaller tube, or it may be struck against the player's body (8, 132, 176).

Puita, 1. **friction drum of the Bambala

and Bahuangana of the Congo, with cylindrical body, laced membrane, and friction stick of palm rib. *Ca.* 50 cm. (20 in.) long; **2.** syn. of cuíca (16).

Pujāri kaichilambu, temple rattle of S. India, consisting of a pair of hollow, elliptical metal rings 2½ cm. (1 in.) in diam., containing small pieces of metal. One is held in each hand and shaken gently, providing rhythmical background (179).

Puk, generic term in Korea for drums (66).

Pukaea, straight wooden trumpet of the Maori of New Zealand, varying from 90 cm. (3 ft.) to 2½ m. (8 ft.) in length, made of totara or matai wood that is split, hollowed, and bound together. It terminates in a bell made by splitting open a portion of the tube and inserting pieces like gores. The mouthpiece is carved. Some pukaeas are conical throughout, others are cylindrical with a conical bell. A feature of the instr. is a free tongue of wood, called *tohe-tohe* (tonsil), placed inside the tube about 8 cm. (3 in.) below the mouthpiece or near the lower end. This is formed of 2 separate pieces, irregularly shaped, both attached to the tube and facing each other, with a windway between the 2; the smaller (upper) is a movable ulula, and its vibration is said to enrich the tone. Pukaeas serve as signal instrs. in wartime. Also called putahoro (8, 77).

Puke, MHGer.: drum, kettledrum.

Pu kihi, a local name of the tetere.

Pukin sarvi, horn of Finland, made of goat horn (89).

Pukku, see: ellag.

Pukuta yemnga, percussion board of the Andaman Islands, in form of an elongated shield. It lies on the ground and is struck from time to time by dancers with their feet (138).

Pukwulu, var. of pakwulo.

Pulala, bamboo shawm of the Montese of Mindanao, Philippine Islands (176).

Pulavan kudam, see: kutam.

Pulgaretes, pulgarillas [Sp. *pulgar,* thumb], Sp.: castanets.

Pulik, zoomorphic clay whistle of Malaya (18).

Pulluvam kutam, see: kutam.

Pulotu, small *slit drum of Samoa, with a loose wooden cover over the aperture. Also called fa'ali laiti (176).

Pulve, see: palweh.

Pumhart, corr. of Bombard.

Pu moana, syn. of pu tatara.

Pumpiang, bell of the Philippine Islands, imported from China (176).

Pumpventil, Ger.: piston valve.

Pungacuqua, tubular trumpet of wood, cane, or clay, of the Tarascan Indians of Michoacán State, Mexico, sometimes with a gourd bell. Also called puuaqua (170).

Pūngī (Hindust.), the tiktirī of N. India (its S. India equivalent is the magudi).

Pung ku, see: pang ku.

P'ung kyong, aeolian crystallophone of Korea, consisting of up to 20 rectangular pieces of glass suspended by cords, hung from verandas (66).

Puniu, small drum of Hawaii, with coconut body and with single sharkskin or fishskin head laced to the bottom. Tied to the player's knee, it was struck with a basketwork stick (8, 77).

Puo fu, see: po fu.

Pu pai, reedpipe of C. Celebes, made from a paddy straw 5–7 cm. (2–3 in.) long, closed by a node at the top. The lower end is fitted with a bell of spirally twisted pandanus leaves. One or 2 slits are cut in the upper end, which is taken rather far into the player's mouth. *Cf.* leléo (173).

Pupakapaka, pu tatara with an extremely elongated mouthpiece, several times that of the shell itself (8).

Pupui, bamboo clarinet of C. Celebes, with 3 or 4 fingerholes on its flattened front, a narrow single reed on a separate tube inserted into the larger one, and a disproportionately large bell of spirally twisted pandanus or lontara leaves. Also called bansi. *Cf.* mots (173).

Purfling (Fr.: *filet;* Ger.: *Äderchen, Flödel;* It.: *filetto*), narrow inlay usually formed of 3 strips of wood, glued into a groove that follows the outline of violins, viols, etc., the purpose of which is to prevent chipping of the edges.

Pusaune [MHGer. *busîne, busûne*], Ger. word, derived from words meaning trumpet, that first denoted that instr. but came to designate the trombone after the latter came into existence. Early references therefore pertain to the trumpet. See also: Posaune (169).

Putahoro, syn. of pukaea.

Putara, syn. of pu tatara.

Pu tatara, 1. *marine-shell trumpet of the Maori of New Zealand, made of *Triton australis.* The tip is cut off and a short, carved wooden mouthpiece is fitted on. Sometimes the sound is modified by placing a piece of hardwood in the upper portion of the shell's large whorl. In Tahiti the same instr. has a long bamboo mouthpiece inserted in a lateral hole pierced near the tip. The pu tatara is a signal instr. Also called ka ea-ea, kakara, poti-poti, pu hau re roa, pu moana, putara, putoto pu moana; **2.** syn. of tetere (8).

Pu torino, *end-blown flute of the Maori of New Zealand, tube and bore being widest at the middle, the lower end terminating in a point that may be open or stopped. It is made of wood that is first shaped, then split, hollowed, and bound with flax or other cord. Usually there is one large central fingerhole carved to represent a human mouth. Stopping this hole changes the pitch. The pu torino produces a booming sound. Double pu torinos also exist; they have a single blowhole, single lower section, but 2 center tubes with fingerholes opposite one another. Also called pu hoho (8).

Putoto, large *marine-shell trumpet of ancient Peru, also of modern Colombia and Peru. Also called botuto, fotuto, fututo, jututo (38, 89).

Putoto pu moana (putoto of the sea), syn. of pu tatara.

Putura-putura, wooden war trumpet in tuba form of the Maori of New Zealand, some 210 cm. (7 ft.) long (176).

Pututue, nose flute of the Marquesas Islands, Polynesia (203).

Puuaqua, syn. of pungacuqua.

Puwi puwi, 1. idioglott clarinet of Java, with conical bore and downcut reed, 6 front fingerholes and a rear thumbhole (121); **2.** oboe of S. Celebes, made of 4 bamboo segments slid one over the other, like a telescope, with a bell of coconut shell, 6 equidistant fingerholes, 1 thumbhole, a metal pirouette, and a very wide, fan-shaped double reed (112).

Pworu, 1. *double bell of the Bobati of the Congo, identical with the aporo; **2.** single bell of the same people, a war bell sounded to signal the attack (132).

Pwupworo, *conical drum of the Babanga and Mono-Bundu of the Congo, with 2 laced heads; 36–57 cm. (14–22 in.) long (30).

Pyē, Jew's-harp of Shan State, Burma, made of bamboo, long and slender. *Ca.* 13½ cm. (5¼ in.) long, and 0.6 cm. wide. A shorter one of metal bears the same name (172).

Pyi krap, *ring flute of the Kachin of Shan State, Burma, made of cane, with 4 front fingerholes and a rear thumbhole. A bamboo ring is set around the top of the tube (172).

Pyi sun, beaked *whistle flute of the Kachin of Shan State, Burma, of bamboo, with 4 front fingerholes and 1 rear fingerhole (172).

Pyon chong, *bell chime of Korea, consisting of 2 rows of 8 bells each, suspended in an elaborate frame. All the bells are of the same size but have different thicknesses. The oldest Korean chimes date from the 14th c. The pyon chong corresponds to the Chin. pien chung. Height of bells is 28 cm. (11 in.), diam. is 18 cm. (7 in.) (66).

Pyon kyong, lithophone of Korea that corresponds to the pien ch'ing of China. The oldest chime dates from the 14th c. The pyong kyong serves religious purposes exclusively. See: pien ch'ing (66).

Pypelys, *whistle flute of Lithuania, with 4 front fingerholes set in indentations. *Ca.* 32 cm. (12½ in.) long (174).

Pypine, short *end-blown flute of Lithuania, the lower end being stopped with rosin. The upper end is furnished with 2 saddle-like projections, one to rest the player's lip against, the other to create a sharp edge against which the breath is directed. The instr. yields one tone (174).

Pyramide, see: pyramid piano.

Pyramidon, organ stop of stopped wooden flue pipes, invented by Sir Frederic Gore-Ouseley in the 1840's and built by Flight. The pipes were about 4 times as wide at the top as they were at the mouth, and were constructed at 16′ and 32′ pitches. Now obs. (176, 186).

Pyramid piano (Fr.: *piano pyramidal;* Ger.: *Pyramidenklavier*), *upright grand piano in form of a truncated pyramid. Owing partly to its decorative effect, the pyramid piano remained pop. until *ca.* 1825, when it was replaced by the *upright piano. Earlier specimens had curved sides, later ones straight sides. For a long time Christian Ernst Friderici was said to have invented the pyramid piano in 1745, and even to have christened it "Pyramide." He may have christened it, but an older pyramid piano by Domenico del Mela exists, dated 1739, now in the Florence Conservatory (92, 144).

Pyrophone [Gk. *pyr,* fire], keyboard instr. invented by physicist G. F. E. Kastner in 1873, with glass tubes, of graduated lengths, that were caused to sound by means of gas flames. Compass C^0–c^2 (176).

Qabā (Arab.), zamr of modern Egypt, 58–60 cm. (23–24 in.) long (98).

Qabā zurnā (Turk.: tenor zurnā), obs. zurnā of Turkey that had 7 front finger-holes and a rear thumbhole and was *ca.* 60 cm. (2 ft.) long (89 Farmer).

Qabūs (Arab.), Arab. parchment-bellied lute made of a single block of wood, about 1 m. (40 in.) long, with a max. width of 25 cm. (10 in.), terminating in a sickle-shaped pegbox bearing 6 lateral pegs. It is played with a plectrum. See also: qūbūz (75 I, 89 Farmer).

Qachel, see: qākel.

Qadīb (Arab.), Arabian stamped stick (89).

Qākel, rattle of the Christian priests of Ethiopia. A cluster of *pellet bells is attached to a leather band worn on the priest's hand, or to a metal cylinder, and shaken (132).

Qalam [Gk. *kalamos*], Arab.: reed, pipe.

Qalqal, pl. **qalāqil** (Arab.), Arabian jingles, formerly hung on mules and camels (74).

Qanā [*qarna*], Ethiopian horn, made of cow horn or antelope horn; a shepherd's instr. (144).

Qanābir (pl.), court instrs. of unknown construction of a 14th-c. sultan of Mali, made of gold and silver (75 I).

Qanbūs, Hadramaut name of the qabūs.

Qand, see: qanā.

Qanda, drum of Ethiopia, *ca.* 80 cm. (32 in.) long (176).

Qanum [Arab. *qānūn*], name of the qānūn in N. India (89).

Qānūn, pl. **qawānim** (Arab.) [Gk. *kanón*], Arab. name for the psaltery in form of a trapeze or half trapeze, known in the 10th c. and still played. Depicted with 10 strings in the 10th c., it had acquired 64 in Persia by the 14th c., arranged in courses of 3. From the 12th to the 15th c. it was held vertically with its soundboard against the player's chest. One hand held it in position, the other hand plucked the strings. Although it is depicted as early as the 10th c., it is first mentioned in the 11th c. in Moorish Spain. By the 12th c. it had been introduced to non-Moorish Europe, where it assumed different shapes, being called canon and micanon in France, kanon and metzkanon in Germany, caño and medio caño or meo caño in Spain. Later it was simply called psaltery. The European canon was played in the same upright position as was the qānūn. In the 14th c. a Pers. treatise describes it in some detail: it was then trapezoid with a base of 81 cm. (32 in.) and sides of 40½ and 75 cm. (16 and 29½ in.) in height, with 64 strings in courses of 3. In the early 15th c. Ibn Ghaid describes it as being 9 cm. (3½ in.) deep, with 105 copper strings in courses of 3. It reached Turkey in the same c. In Europe the qānūn died out with the introduction of keyboard instrs., but it has survived in Arab.-speaking countries to this day, and even in India, where it is known as kanuna, qanum, satatantri vīnā, and in Indonesia (kanun). In the Near East it is played with a plectrum. In Turkey both the qānūn and the *santir are played. In the Maghrib it shows tendencies of becoming obs., but is still pop. there and in Egypt, Syria, and Iraq. Today it is gut-strung and is held horizontally on the player's lap, with the tuning pins pointing away from the player: a flat box zither with 17–25 courses of 3 strings and a belly half of wood, half of skin. The tuning varies according to the piece to be played, but is within a compass of c¹–g³. The right hand plays the melody while the left doubles it an oct. lower. In Egypt it is gut-strung, plectrum-played, and furnished with a series of movable bridges that permit retuning the strings a quarter tone higher. N. African specimens are from 75 by 50 cm. (30 by 20 in.) to 100 by 60 cm. (40 by 24 in.) (89 Farmer, 144 Chottin, 170).

Qānūn misrī (Arab.: Egyptian *qānūn*), name given to the qānūn in *The Arabian Nights* (75 I).

Qaramut, name of the garamut on the Gazelle Peninsula, New Britain (77).

Qarāqib, plate-shaped castanets of N. Africa, joined in pairs by leather thongs, *ca.* 30 by 10 cm. (12 by 4 in.) in size. Also called qarqabū (144).

Qarna, pl. **qurun** (Arab., Pers.), a successor to the *nafīr*; a long, S-shaped trumpet of Islam in use during and after the 14th c. The word corresponds to the Heb. keren.

Qarnā (Aram.), horn or trumpet of ancient Babylon (170).

Qarnai [dim. of *qarna*], small qarna. *Cf.* karranay.

Qarnu, Akk.: horn (170).

Qarqabū, syn. of qarāqib.

Qasa' (Arab.), small Arab. kettledrum, first mentioned in the 10th c. and still in use (170).

Qasaba, pl. **qasabat** (Arab.), *end-blown flute of the Maghrib; it corresponds to the nāy of Egypt, Persia, etc., and is made of cane, 60–70 cm. (24–28 in.) long, with 5 or 6 fingerholes in 2 groups. The qasaba was known to the Arabs by the 7th c., but was supplanted by the Pers. nāy in the 9th in the Islamic East. It continued in use in the Maghrib and in Moorish Spain, and is still a most pop. instr. of NW. Africa today. It is held obliquely to the player's right. *Cf.* qasba, qusaiba (89 Farmer, 170).

Qasba, vulgar form of the word qa-

saba in the Maghrib today (89 Farmer).

Qāshiq (Pers., Turk.: spoon, ladle), rattle of modern Persia, possibly also of ancient Persia, made of 2 hollowed, spoon-shaped pieces of wood, with *pellet bells placed in the hollow, then joined together (75 II).

Qassāba, see: qasaba.

Qatros, the *kithara of ancient Babylon, mentioned in the Book of Daniel. The word itself corresponds to kithara (170).

Qawal, flute of Morocco and Egypt. *Cf.* caval, qawūl (144).

Qawūl (Turk.), **1.** *end-blown flute of Turk. peasants and shepherds, made of wood with 6 front fingerholes and a rear thumbhole; **2.** the qawūl is also played as a reed instr. in Turkey. See also: caval, cavalche (76).

Qemqem, unidentified instr. of ancient Egypt, believed to have been a drum (147).

Qeren, see: keren.

Qisaba, pl. of qussāba.

Qītāra (Arab.) [Gk. *kithara*], Arab. word in use since the 9th c.; in N. Africa today (W. of Egypt) it denotes a lute of European, not Pers., origin. *Cf.* kaitara (75 II, 169).

Qīthāra (Arab.), syn. of qītāra.

Qīz, medium-sized modern Turk. nāy. *Cf.* mansūr, shāh (76).

Qobūz, see: gambus, qabūs, qūbūz.

Qquepa, see: quepa.

Quadragesima (It.: fortieth), repeating organ stop, a quint ⅛'.

Quadragesima terza (It.: forty-third), repeating organ stop, an oct. ⅛'.

Quadrille flageolet, a 19th-c. name of the French *flageolet (15 Baines).

Quagliere [It.: *quaglia,* quail], It.: quail pipe. Buonanni depicts one. *Cf.* courcaillet, Wachtelpfeife.

Quarquerel (kestrel), obs. Fr.: cog rattle. *Cf.* crécerelle (169).

Quarregnon [*carillon*], 13th-c. Fr. term for carillon, bell chime (197).

Quarta (Lat.: fourth), **1.** see: Rauschpfeife, 2; **2.** panpipes of the Surinam Indians (176).

Quart bassoon, see: Quartfagott.

Quarte, see: doublette; quarte de nazard (organ stops).

Quarte de nazard (Fr.), mutation organ stop of open flue pipes, so named because it is a 4th higher than the *nazard 2⅔', i.e., at 2' pitch. Dom Bedos explains that it was regarded as a mutation stop, as it was to be played with nazards and tierces (20).

Quarter-tone piano (Fr.: *piano à queue à quart de ton;* Ger.: *Vierteltonklavier*), grand piano made in the 1920's by the Grotrian and the Förster piano companies, so devised that 2 instrs. were superposed on each other, tuned a quarter tone apart, with 2 manuals played by 1 performer (64).

Quartfagott (It.: *fagotto quarto*), in Praetorius' day a bassoon pitched in G^1, a 4th below the ordinary bassoon (for pieces written in *"canto duro,"* as he says). In the 18th and 19th c. the term also denoted a bassoon pitched in F^0, a 4th above the ordinary bassoon. *Cf.* Quintfagott, tenoroon.

Quartflöte (Ger.), **1.** obs. *cross flute in F, also called the G flute; **2.** recorder of the 17th and 18th c. in C, with a compass c^2–c^4, the same as the larger Diskantflöte of Praetorius (Walther gives its compass an oct. too low) (176).

Quartgeige (Ger.), syn. of Halbgeige, according to Leopold Mozart.

Quartino (It.), small It. clarinet in D, E♭, or F above the ordinary clarinet. The name is derived from that in F, which is a 4th higher. See also: sopranino clarinet (176).

Quartposaune (Ger.), 17th- and 18th-c. term for the bass trombone in F, a 4th below the (ordinary) tenor trombone in B♭.

Quartventil (Ger.: fourth valve), valve that adds 5 semitones (the interval of a 4th) to a bass instr.'s low compass, to bridge the gap between pedal tone and lowest tone available by the other valves (25).

Quartzink (Ger.), small 18th-c. cornett pitched a 4th higher than the type cornett, with a compass d^1–d^3. Majer and Walther (in 1732) still mention it. Also called Kleinzink. See also: cornettino (134).

Qūbūz (Turk.), obs. lute of Turkey, with wooden body, skin belly, and short neck; it spread to Europe (see: cobza, koboz, koumpouzi) and to the east, its descendants now being found from Malaya to Madagascar and Zanzibar.

Qudūm (Turk.), kettledrum of 17th-c. Turkey, smaller than the *kūs but larger than the naqqāra (76).

Que, see: gue.

Quena (Quechua), **1.** generic name of flutes and pipes in Bolivia (89); **2.** *notched flute of ancient and modern Peru, also played in the Chaco, in Bolivia, and along the Amazon and its tributaries as far as Guiana. Formerly made of bone, clay, gourd, or metal, with up to 8 fingerholes, today it is fashioned only of clay, with 6 equidistant front fingerholes and with a rear thumbhole. As cane splits easily in a dry climate, those of the Chipaya, Aymara, and Quechua Indians are wound (104, 192).

Quenaquena, Aymara equivalent of quena (80 XII).

Queng, marine-shell trumpet of New Guinea (144).

Queniba, see: kweningba.

Quepa (Quechua), *marine-shell trumpet of ancient Peru that served chiefly as a military instr. See also: chil-chil, hayllaquepa (80 XII).

Quer . . . , Ger.: side-blown . . .

Quere-quexé, syn. of reco-reco.

Quereré, Afro-Brazilian drum, cylindrical, with single head secured by large wooden pegs (6).

Querflöte, Ger.: **1.** *cross flute. The term has been in use since the early 18th c.; **2.** organ stop of flue pipes of wood or metal, occasionally made as a stopped register; with low cutup, overblowing, at 16', 8', 4', or 2' pitch (2, 133).

Querflügel (Ger.), Ger. equivalent of *spinetta traversa.

Querpfeife (Ger.), **1.** fife (19th-c.

term); **2.** syn. of Querflöte, both instr. and organ stop.

Querriegel, Ger.: string fastener.

Quesse [Lat. *capsa,* box], Fr. 16th- and 17th-c. spelling of caisse.

Quia-quia, *vessel rattle of Haiti, made of a piriform gourd or other hollow object and filled with pebbles (132).

Quicahue, syn. of kunkulkawe.

Quijada (Sp.: jawbone), Afro-Cuban scraper made of the lower jaw of a mule, horse, or donkey, with all its teeth left in. It is also a rattle, as the teeth chatter when it is shaken, and a percussion instr., as it can be hit with the fist. Negroes of coastal Peru have used it as a musical instr. since the late 18th c. See also: jawbone (152).

Quijango, *musical bow of the Indians of Costa Rica and Nicaragua, with a small jar serving as resonator, and wire string with tuning loop. Both sections of the string are tapped with a stick while the jar, its mouth facing away from the bow, is opened more or less by the palm of the player's left hand. The Nahuatl of Nicaragua call it carimba (17, 105).

Quilando, scraper of the Ambundu of Angola, made of a large calabash with notches on one surface, played together with the *cassuto. The quilando was described by Girolamo Merollo in 1692 (185).

Quills, "the quills" is the name of a panpipe with 3 pipes of New Orleans Negroes (152).

Quinardophone, wind instr. patented by Quinard in France on June 14, 1893, designed to replace the saxophone (204).

Quincena, Sp.: fifteenth (organ stop).

Quindeze, corr. of quintadecima.

Quinquecahue, syn. of kunkulkawe.

Quint [Lat. *quintus,* fifth], **1.** (Ger.) in the 16th and 17th c. the highest string of the lute, etc., regardless of whether the instr. had 5 or 6 strings. When the sixth string was added (in the bass), the top string retained its old name. The word is an abbr. of Quintsaite and corresponds in this sense to chanterelle; **2.** prefix given

to members of certain instrumental families pitched a 5th above or a 5th below the type instr., *e.g.,* Quintfagott; **3.** (Fr.: *quinte;* Ger.: *Quinte;* It.: *quinta*), the oldest mutation stop of the organ, originally sounding a 5th above its fundamental, as the name indicates; later the third harmonic, a 12th higher. It occurs at 10⅔', 5⅓', 2⅔', 1⅓' pitches. On older organs this was expressed as 12', 6', 3', 1½'. Also called fifth; **4.** (Ger.), on older organs, syn. of Quintflöte; **5.** (Ger.) prefix or suffix to names of organ stops, indicating tonal position.

Quinta, It.: quint (organ stop).

Quintaclave, see: quinticlave.

Quintadecima, It.: fifteenth (organ stop).

Quintadena [Lat. *quintadenare*] (Fr.: *quintaton*), organ stop of cylindrical stopped metal flue pipes of narrow scale, in existence since the mid-15th c. According to Praetorius, it originated in the Low Countries. In addition to producing the fundamental, the Quintadena is characterized by the prominence of its twelfth. Built at 32', 16', or 8' pitch, rarer at higher positions. There exist numerous vars. of the word (133).

Quintaria, It. 14th-c. equivalent of quinterna or Quinterne (169).

Quinta strepida, Lat.: Rauschpfeife (organ stop).

Quintaton, Fr.: Quintadena.

Quintbass, Ger.: quint 10⅔' organ stop.

Quint bassoon, see: Quintfagott.

Quinte [Lat. *quintus,* fifth], **1.** (Fr.) coll. abbr. for quinte de violon (the viola) and for the viola part. In France the viola had many names up to the end of the 18th c. and was not called alto until the 19th c.; **2.** Fr. and Ger.: quint organ stop.

Quinte de hautbois (Fr.), obs. syn. of cor anglais.

Quinte de violon, obs. Fr. term for viola, so called because it was tuned a 5th below the violin. Commonly called quinte. Also called cinquième.

Quinterna, Lat.: gittern 1. and 2. Paulus Paulirinus describes it as smaller than the "cithara" (cittern) *ca.* 1460; some 20 years later the phrase *"lutina quinterna vocant"* occurs. To Praetorius it was a type of guitar with 4 pairs of strings, tuned c⁰ f⁰ a⁰ d¹, and a sickle-shaped pegbox.

Quinterne [Lat. *quinterna*], MHGer.: gittern. In Hans Burgkmair's *Triumph of Maximilian* it is depicted as a small lute; to Virdung and Agricola it is a mandola; in Roth's dictionary of 1571, a 9-stringed lute (169).

Quintfagott, Ger.: *quint bassoon, in Praetorius' day pitched in F¹, a 5th below the ordinary bassoon (for pieces written in *"canto b molli,"* as he says). In the 18th and 19th c. the term also denoted a bassoon pitched in G⁰, a 5th above the ordinary bassoon. The low-pitched Quintfagott was also called Doppelfagott. *Cf.* tenoroon.

Quintflöte, syn. of Hohlquinte.

Quinticlave [Lat. *quintus*, five + *clavis*, key], low-pitched keyed bugle in F or Eb invented by Halary (Jean-Hilaire Asté) of Paris, and submitted to the Académie des Beaux-Arts in 1817, so named to indicate its pitch, a 5th lower than the keyed bugle. Made in bassoon shape, it had 9 or 10 keys. Halary was unable to patent it before 1821. It was also known as quintitube and was later developed into the *ophicleide (89 Langwill).

Quintitube, syn. of quinticlave.

Quinto (Sp.: fifth), 1. Afro-Cuban drum similar to the conga, but smaller and higher-pitched. Played in rumba orchestras; 2. small guitar of Venezuela. *Cf.* cuatro.

Quinton (Fr.) [Lat. *quinta vox*, fifth voice], 1. Fr. 17th-c. syn. for the 5-stringed *pardessus de viole, according to Jean Rousseau (*Traité de la viole*, 1687), tuned g⁰ c¹ e¹ a¹ d²; 2. a late-18th-c. hybrid of viol and violin, with 5 strings, violin body except for sloping shoulders,

with fretted viol neck, about the size of a violin, and tuned g⁰ d¹ a¹ d² g².

Quintposaune (Ger.), 17th- and 18th-c. term for the bass trombone in Eb, a 5th below the (ordinary) tenor trombone in Bb, with compass Eb¹ or F¹ to bb² (176).

Quintsaite (Ger.), see: Quint, 1, chanterelle.

Quintspitze, see: Spitzquinte.

Quipa, syn. of chil-chil.

Quiquia [Araucano *quiqui*], piriform gourd rattle of S. America, with natural handle, filled with pebbles. *Cf.* quia-quia (57).

Quiquiztli, end-blown *marine-shell trumpet of ancient Mexico, also called tecciztli by the Aztec (170).

Quisanche, name of the marimbula in Montevideo, Uruguay (152).

Quitarra, var. of guitarra.

Quitarre, var. of guitarre.

Quiterne [Gk. *kithara], OFr. var. of guiterne, a gittern. The term is recorded from the 14th c. on (204).

Quitiplá, bamboo *stamping tube of Venezuela (103).

Qullal, goblet drum of the Maghrib (89).

Qūpūz, see: qūbūz.

Qurmah, *double clarinet of the argūl type, characterized by parallel tubes of equal length. (The illustration of a zummāra in Sachs's *Reallexikon* is in reality a qurmah.) (144).

Qurnaita, name given to all reed-blown aérophones in Syria (76).

Qurnāta, reedpipe of 17th-c. Turkey (76).

Qūrqah, see: kūrka.

Qurun, pl. of qarna.

Qusaiba [dim. of *qussāba*], small qasaba, also known as juwāq, called joch by med. Lat. chroniclers (89 Farmer).

Qūshnāy, see: kūshnāy.

Qussāba, pl. **qisab,** syn. of qasaba.

Quwāl, N. African *frame drum, called gullāl in Algeria (75 I).

R

Rabāb (Arab.), Near East name of the *spike fiddle, with small coconut body, divided or membrane belly pierced by a long stick, lateral pegs, and usually 3 strings. Its ancestor, the short lute of ancient Persia, was adopted by the Arabs and became a bowed instr. in the 10th c. As a lute, it had a piriform body, membrane belly, sickle-shaped pegbox, and 3–5 strings. When it became a bowed instr. it was called rabāb. It coexisted with the plucked lute, keeping the piriform body but reducing the number of strings to 3 or less, and discarding the sickle-shaped pegbox: the rabāb neck ends in a stump. In Arab. the word *rabāb* was formerly a generic term for bowed instrs.

The rabāb was mentioned by Al Farabi (d. 950) and was known in Byzantium by the 10th c. as lūrā (lyra). With the spread of Islam it was carried both E. and W. after modifying its form: a scaphoid instr. was introduced into Moorish Spain—it may have been the *rabé morisco—and is depicted in the *Cantigas de Santa María*. The piriform variety with parchment belly became widely distributed, and a type with circular body is described in the 18th c. Rectangular or trapezoid bodies were also common. In Europe the instr. was adopted as the rubeba, an early name of rebec. Jerome of Moravia describes it in the mid-13th c. as having 2 strings tuned a 5th apart, and in the mid-17th c. Al Fasi iterates that description. This tuning is standard in most areas today. By the early 15th c. the Arabs had reached Indonesia (they invaded Java in 1406), where the spike fiddle is still called rebab. Today the instr. is played in Afghanistan, Egypt, Ethiopia, Israel, Iran, Iraq, N. Africa, Syria, Turkestan, Turkey, by the Islamic population of the Indian subcontinent, Malaya, and Indonesia.

In N. Africa a primitive form of rabāb is found in 2 regions far apart: among the Algerian Tuareg and the Moroccan Sūs-Shluh. The Tuareg call theirs am'zad; the Sūs-Shluh call theirs ribab. The instr. has a membrane belly, lacks a fingerboard, has 1 or 2 horsehair strings at low pitch; a more developed form has the body carved out of a block of wood, generally rectangular. See also: arababu, arbab, erbabi, hapa'i, marbab, merdap, oreh, rababa, rabāba, rabōb, rebab, robab, tambur (89 Farmer, 144 Chottin, 173).

Rababa [Arab. *rabāb*], syn. of the odi, 1, a lyre (195).

Rabāba, the rabāb of Egypt, with rectangular or trapezoid body, membrane back and belly (144, 170).

Rabāb ash-sha'ir (Arab.: poet's *rabāb*), Egyptian rabāb with single string, used for accompanying the recitations of public narrators (144).

Rabāb el mogannī (Arab.: singer's *rabāb*), N. African rabāb with trapezoid body, round neck, lateral pegs, 2 strings tuned a 5th apart (91, 170).

Rabāna, 1. a small *frame drum of S. Celebes, of wood or clay, basin-shaped, with laced head. It corresponds to the rebāna of Sumatra (112); 2. frame drum of Malaya. It has been suggested (by Dr. Pijper) that the word may be derived from "rabbana," the Arab. vocative of "Our Lord," the opening words of many Arab. hymns of praise accompanied by drums (121). Cf. arabana, ravana, rebāna, terbang.

Rabé, Sp. name, used by Juan Ruiz in the early 14th c., for the European rebec, as opposed to the rabé morisco.

Rabeca [Prov. *rebec*], 1. obs. and modern coll. Port.: violin (7); 2. primitive violin of Brazil used for accompanying the *cantoria* (89).

Rabecão, Port.: double bass.

Rabel, 1. a small, homemade pastoral violin of Estremadura, Spain, with 4 strings; 2. Sp.: rebec; 3. Pietro Cerone, writing in 1613, uses the word for violin; 4. obs. Sp.: *bladder and string.

Rabel de arco (Sp.: bowed rabel), term recorded in 1571 in the municipal archives of Lequeitio (Basque). The word *rabetero*, rabel player, is already mentioned in 1507 (56).

Rabell, Cat.: rebec.

Rabé morisco (Sp.), the Moorish rebec of Spain, as distinguished from the European rebec, or rabé.

Rabequet, Cat. var. of rabell.

Rabequinha [dim. of *rabel*], Port.: small rebec.

Rabil, Port.: rebec.

Rabōb [*rabāb*], syn. of sarōd (170).

Rabube, Buonanni's spelling of rebube (1722) (39).

Rack board (Fr.: *faux-sommier, tamis;* Ger.: *Pfeifenbrett*), wooden board pierced with holes to hold the pipes of an organ in upright position.

Racket [Ger. *Rank,* a bend] (Fr.: *cervelas, cervelat;* Ger.: *Rackett, Rankett;* It.: *cortali* [pl.]), 1. obs. woodwind of the 16th and 17th c., made of a short cylinder of ivory (later models were of wood), in which a number of parallel cylindrical channels are bored up and down, connected alternately at top and bottom to form one continuous tube. The channel emerged at the top in the center. Rackets were played with a double reed, like that of a bassoon, partly enclosed in a *pirouette inserted in the opening of the channel. The bore is very narrow, being some 6–7 mm. wide; 10–12 very narrow

fingerholes are bored obliquely into the channels; they were covered by the tip and middle joint of the player's fingers. A number of ventholes and a water escape are bored along the cylinder also. The combination of double reed and cylindrical bore causes the racket to sound as a stopped pipe, an oct. deeper than its tube length. Owing to the limited control of the reed, caused by presence of the pirouette, the racket did not overblow. Praetorius lists 4 sizes of instrs., each having a compass of a 12th: soprano G^0–d^1, alto/tenor C^0–g^0, bass F^1–c^0, great bass D^1–A^0 or C^1–G^0. The soprano was but 12 cm. (4¾ in.) long, with 9 channels totaling 115 cm. (45 in.).

The racket is first mentioned in a Württemberg inventory of 1576, as "Raggett"; a year later in a Graz inventory several are enumerated as Rogetten or Cortali, the latter being their It. name. Mersenne reports use of the racket as a bass in various ensembles, but it did not outlive the 17th c. in its original form. Toward the end of the c. it was completely remodeled—by J. C. Denner of Nürnberg, one gathers from Doppelmayr (in 1730)—and emerged with conical tube and bore, its pirouette replaced by a bassoon-type bell, sometimes with a mute in form of a perforated cap, its reed carried on a bassoon crook. Some specimens even had keys. This later type became known as *racket bassoon or sausage bassoon;

2. for the organ stop see: Ranket (14, 36, 89 Langwill, 170).

Racket bassoon (Fr.: *basson à fusée, basson à raquette;* Ger.: *Rackettenfagott, Wurstfagott, Stockfagott, Faustfagott*), a late form of *racket, created by Johann Christoff Denner of Nürnberg, according to Doppelmayr (in 1730). Also called sausage bassoon. See: racket.

Rackettenfagott, Ger.: racket bassoon.

Racle, racleur, Fr.: scraper.

Radius, Lat.: wire (string).

Radius French horn, *omnitonic horn

built by John Callcott of London in 1851 (80 XII).

Radleier, Ger.: hurdy-gurdy.

Rad-Maschine, original name of the *rotary valve, patented in 1832 by Joseph Felix Riedl of Vienna (15 Morley-Pegge).

Raffle, cog rattle of Uri, Switzerland (102).

Raft zither (Fr.: *cithare en radeau;* Ger.: *Flosszither*), zither composed of canes tied together in the manner of a raft, the canes being either idiochord or heterochord. Found today in E. Africa, W. Africa, the Chittagong district of E. Pakistan (100, 195).

Raganella (It.: frog), *cog rattle of Italy and of the Ticino, Switzerland, used in churches during Easter week (102).

Rag-dung (brass pipe), monastic and ceremonial trumpet of Tibet, made of several sections of thin conical tubing, of copper, brass, or bronze, that telescope into one another, terminating in a large bell; it is played with a wide mouthpiece. Because of its great length the trumpet is supported on a frame or block of wood, or by a novice. It sustains long pedal tones in services and mystery plays. See also: cos-dung (89 Picken).

Ra gvin, syn. of ya-gvin.

Rahmenrassel, Ger.: frame rattle.

Rahmentrommel, Ger.: frame drum.

Rahmenzither, Ger.: frame zither.

Raita, Fr. colonial spelling of *ghaita in N. Africa. *Cf.* reïta, rheita.

- **Rajão,** Port. name of the guitar with 5 single strings (7).

Rali cultrun, see: cultrun.

Rälla, Rälle, cog rattle of Valais, Switzerland (102).

Raloba, *percussion beam of the Malagasy Republic; it corresponds to the tsikaretika (171).

Ramkie [*?rabequinha*], primitive guitar of the Hottentot, Bushmen, and other S. African peoples, with wood or calabash body, belly of skin or other materials, and 3 or 4 strings. A plucked instr. known to have existed since the first half

of the 18th c., presumably of Port. origin, it is now replaced by cheap European guitars (116, 185).

Rammelaar, Du.: rattle.

Ran, bronze *kettle gong of the Garo of Assam, 13 cm. (5 in.) high, 26½ cm. (10½ in.) in diam., of open bottom (172).

Ranasringa (Sans.: war horn), metal sringa of India, occurring under various names over the whole subcontinent. See: ekkalam, gala, jayasringa, kāhalam, kakalam, kalam, kōbe, narsringa (173).

Ranat ek, xylophone of Thailand, usually with 21 slabs of hardwood 29–39 cm. (11½–15½ in.) long, identical in width and thickness, strung on cords over an elaborate footed trough that acts as resonator. The trough is about 120 cm. (4 ft.) long. Compass f^0–f^3, with a skip of a 4th between the first and second slabs. It is played with 2 beaters having knobbed ends. It corresponds to the roneat ek of Cambodia (65).

Ranat lek, syn. of ranat thong ek (65).

Ranat thong ek, metallophone of Thailand, with 21 steel bars 23–27 cm. (9–10½ in.) long, identical in width and thickness, laid on a trough about 1 m. (40 in.) long. Compass f^0–f^3. It is played with 2 beaters. Also called ranat lek (65).

Ranat thong thum, metallophone of Thailand, similar to the *ranat thong ek, but of lower pitch. The 17 steel bars are 30½–35 cm. (12–14 in.) long and are suspended over a trough *ca.* 105 cm. (41½ in.) long. Compass d^0–f^2. Also called ranat thum lek (65).

Ranat thum, xylophone of Thailand, similar to the ranat ek, but of lower pitch. Its 17 wooden slabs are 34–42 cm. (13½–16½ in.) long; they are suspended above a trough resting on very short feet. Compass d^0–f^2. Also called ranat thum mai (65).

Ranat thum lek, syn. of ranat thong thum (65).

Ranat thum mai, syn. of ranat thum (65).

Rang, 1. gong of the Garo of Assam, with narrow rim (170); **2.** Fr.: rank (of organ pipes).

Rangertone, *electrophonic organ invented by Richard H. Ranger, with acoustically generated tone—wind-blown reeds—and photoelectric pickup.

Rang nat, Laos equivalent of the roneat ek (47).

Ranita (Sp.: little frog), obs. *friction drum of Cuba, with friction cord (152).

Ranjanī vīnā, Beng. var. of the mahati vīnā, the sole difference being that it has a gutter neck.

Rank (Fr.: *rang;* Ger.: . . . *fach*), set of organ pipes forming one stop.

Ranket, Rankett, 1. Ger.: racket; **2.** obs. organ stop of regal pipes or of reed pipes, encountered from the 16th c. on, usually at 16′ or 8′ pitch (133).

Rankoan, *nose flute of the Admiralty Islands, Melanesia (203).

Rapa [Mongolian: *rapal*], brass trumpet of Japan, similar to the siao t'ung kyo (170).

Rapakai, *marine-shell trumpet of Japan, played with a cup mouthpiece (178).

Rapal, brass trumpet of Mongolia. For description see: siao t'ung kyo.

Rapana [*rabāna*], tambourine of the Achin of Sumatra. Cf. rabāna, rebāna.

Rapapa, symmetrical lyre of the Bari of the Congo (128).

Raspadero, Sp.: scraper.

Rassel, Ger.: rattle.

Rasseltrommel, Ger.: rattle drum.

Ratsche, S. Ger.: cog rattle.

Rattle [MEngl. *ratelen*] (Fr.: *crécelle, hochet;* Ger.: *Rassel;* Sp.: *sonajero*), shaken idiophone that can assume a number of different forms. See: cog rattle, frame rattle, pendant rattle, sliding rattle, stick rattle, suspension rattle, vessel rattle. See also: acherē, adja, agbē, aggüē, agüē, akacence, akakyenkye, akayamba, alfandoque, amafandoque, amafohlwane, amahahlazo, amalē, amanqashele, amele, angklung, anukuē, anzolo, arbu, asakasaka, asok, assogui, as-

son, axatse, axmāl, ayacachtli, ayon chicuaztli, azibwasi, bagezege, bare, belapella, Bigopp, bin-sasara, brchak, buttori, cabaca, cabaça, cakot, caracaxá, carraca, carrau, cascavell, caxixi, chachá, chalapata, chanrara, charkhi, chekeré, chicahuaztli, chichikone, chocalho, ch'uan ling, chullo-chullo, churu, clacke, clapet, claquette, conguinho, crécerelle, dabbūs, dara, dichela, doka, dorje, durdavets, duruitoarea, dyanga, ekiro, ensansi, ensegu, erikunde, faray, firisai, fowa, ga, gabi, gadza, ganzā, gejjam, ghunghura, girugate, gorzia, grantang, grefelle, guache, gulung-gulung, herrach, hikile, hochet, huada, hulima, imiguza, injua, iselwa, isikunjane, jawbone, jhanjhana, jicotea, kāapolo, kaiamba, kajirei, kalaka, 2, karchilambu, karraka, katana, kechrek, kechruk, kekechrek, kepyak, 3, keriten, khakkhara, kharraka, kikori, kiliba, kin, 2, kindembo, kindja, kinkini, 2, kirrika, kitsarakara, kitsatsa, kiyamba, klimperküle, Knarre, kolokocho, korei, kraobi, kritsa-kritsa, kuchiru, kujamba, kuteru, kwakwa, laala, legwegwe, lien hua lo, ligoshu, lolo, lunyege, mafowa, mahea, makasa, makkow, mandileh, maraca, maruga, masacalla, masaka, mathlo, mathotse, matraca, matraqueta, mbaraca, mbugi, mena'anim, mohea, morothloane, mujegereza, mukwanga, musesegeto, mussamba, mutshakatha, mwakasa, nao chin chieh, napura, ngotad, njele, nsansi, nseke, nzau, okoco, olubeye, osun, oyualli, ozohahi, padatrong, pernanguma, piano de cuia, poketa danyakko, porongo, prananguma, pujāri kaichilambu, qākel, qāshiq, quarquerel, quia-quia, quiquia, Raffle, raganella, Rälla, rammelaar, Ratsche, ré-ré, rong ruyh, routelle, saccapa, sagaru, sakala, sake-sake, salangai, Schnarre, scīrtīitoarea, scrandola, sege-sege, sehgura, seistron, seke, seke-seke, sgrigias, shakshak, shaku gyo, shaq-shaq, shekere, shu ch'iu, silambu, sistrum, skellat, so'ktsoks, taletta, tartarie, tartavelle, tempella, terkotka, tervelle, thuzo, towa, tricca-vallacca, triquette, troccola, tsakaiamba, tschäderäggen, tsele, tsikatray, tsikiripika, tsikitray, ualu, uasapa, ubuxaka, uli-uli, vajra, voamaintilany, wansamba, xaquexaque, xeque, xequere, xere, yawina, yucuyu, zacapa, zichirei.

Rattle drum (Fr.: *tambour-hochet;* Ger.: *Rasseltrommel*), drum that is shaken or twirled; the membrane is struck by enclosed pebbles, pellets, etc., or by the impact of the knotted end of an attached leather strap. They are found in Asia (100).

Rau-rau, sistrum of Malaya, made of a piece of forked bamboo, the 2 prongs being held apart by a stick on which 4 coconut half shells are strung, disposed in 2 pairs facing one another. The coconut sections clash together when the sistrum is shaken. It is used only by fishermen (18).

Rauschflöte, syn. of Rauschpfeife (organ stop).

Rauschpfeife [?MHGer. *Rusch,* rush], **1.** family of Ger. Renaissance reed-cap shawms, with wide conical bore, 7 front fingerholes, and 1 rear thumbhole, terminating in a bell without flare, the double reed concealed in a wooden cap. A consort of 6 in the Berlin instr. collection was described by Sachs as: soprano, 42 cm. (16½ in.) long in e^1; tenors, 54 cm. (21 in.) long in c^1; and bass, 86 cm. (34 in.) long in g^0. Each of a set of 5 reed-cap shawms in the Prague National Museum (reed caps missing) has a swallow-tail key protected by a *fontanelle. Buchner has described them as: tenor, 85.5 cm. (34 in.) long, compass f^0–$f\sharp^1$; bass, 106 cm. (42 in.), compass d^0–$d\sharp^1$; great bass 127.5 cm. (50 in.) and 129.5 cm. (51 in.), compass B^0–c. This is the type of instr. depicted and named by Hans Burgkmair (in 1512), obs. in Germany by the mid-16th c., but that lived on in France as *hautbois de Poitou. The *taille* of Mersenne would correspond to the Berlin bass or the Prague tenor. See also: Russpfeif (36, 170, 178); **2.** (Du.: *ruispijp;* Lat.: *quinta strepida*), organ stop first mentioned by Arnold Schlick in

1511. It seems to have consisted originally of reed pipes with conical resonators; it became transformed in the course of the c. to a 2-rank stop of flue pipes at 4' and 2⅔' or at 2' and 1⅓'. This order was then reversed to 5⅓' and 4' or to 2⅔' and 2', etc. Since the mid-17th c. the stop was treated as a mixture, often 3-rank (4', 2⅔', 2'), rarely also 4-rank. In the 18th c. it was enlarged further, occurring as a 10-rank stop, as we know from Johann Samber. The original meaning of the word had long been forgotten: to Praetorius already it was a "rustling" pipe (from *rauschen,* to rustle). Some older builders called the stop Quarta because of the intervening interval of a 4th between the 2 ranks. Adlung knew it as an open metal stop of 3' and 2' or of 2' and 1½'. Also called Rauschquinte (133).

Rauschquinte, syn. of Rauschpfeife (organ stop).

Ra'us woja, name of the dermenan on Flores Island, also that of a similar instr. with a double reed (121).

Ravalement, see: clavecin à ravalement, clavecin à grand ravalement.

Ravana [*rabāna*], name of the rabāna on the Moluccas (173).

Ravanahasta (Sans.: Ravana's hand), sārangī of India, with neck terminating in an outstretched hand.

Ravanastron [king Ravana], fiddle of N. India, with small cylindrical body, wooden or skin belly, open bottom, long handle, and 2 strings held by rear pegs; counterpart of the S. India trāvanāttam. See also: rāvanatta (47).

Rāvanatta [king Ravana], fiddle of W. India, with hemispherical body of coconut, parchment belly, 2 strings attached to lateral pegs. The bow passes between the strings (144).

Rbairbe [*rebube*], metal Jew's-harp of the Freibergs, Switzerland (102).

Real, Ger. corr. of Regal (1596 Ambras inventory).

Realejo, Port., Sp.: regal; barrel organ, street organ (7).

Rebab [Arab. *rabāb*], *spike fiddle of

Java and S. Celebes, introduced by Islam, with flat, heart-shaped body of wood or coconut, soundholes pierced in its back, belly of buffalo gut or bladder, a turned neck and spike, no fingerboard, 2 elongated lateral pegs, copper or brass strings, and a very high bridge. The pitch is modified, not only by the position of player's fingers on the strings, but by the amount of pressure exerted; he can produce *Bebungen* by varying the pressure. On N. Celebes a similar instr. is found, but it has one string only and occasionally a circular body. It has no name. The rebab is equivalent to the tro khmer of Cambodia. Also called erbab (112, 121, 173).

Rebab batok besar, syn. of gihyan.

Rebab batok kechil, syn. of ohyan.

Rebāna [*rabāna*], *frame drum of Sumatra that corresponds to the Javanese terbang. The basin-shaped wooden frame has a head laced with rattan cords to a cane ring on the underside of the drum. Up to 60 cm. (2 ft.) in diam. Also called robana, redap. *Cf.* arabana, rabāna, rapana (121, 173).

Rebebe [Arab. *rabāb*], med. Fr. rebec. The word is recorded from 1391 on. At the time it was an instr. to which one danced. Numerous vars. of the word occur, such as rebeibe, rebesbe, reberbe, rebarbe, rebelle. *Cf.* rubebe (61, 85).

Rebec [Arab. *rabāb*] (Engl., Fr.: *rebec;* It.: *ribeca;* Sp.: *rabel*), bowed chordophone of the high Middle Ages and of the Renaissance, evolved from the Arab. rabāb, which can be traced back to the 11th c. From the 13th to 16th c. it was chiefly known as *rubeba; the early Fr. form was *rebebe,* and the Engl. form "rebeck" appeared in the literature of the early 15th c. Its small piriform wooden body and short neck were made of a single piece of wood; it took over the lateral pegs of the rabāb and also retained its rose for several c.; its 3 strings, tuned in 5ths, were rib-fastened. Later instrs. had a split-level soundboard, the raised upper portion of which was a continuation of the fingerboard, the bridge

being placed on the lower level. Although the *kit branched off from the rebec in the 16th c., the parent instr. continued in occasional use in France at least until the early 18th c. In France during the 17th and 18th c. (possibly already by the mid-15th) the rebec had sunk to the level of a street musician's instr.; Trichet (*ca.* 1640) reports, however, that there were still people who played it. In the 15th c. the nomenclature is perfectly clear: writers such as Gerson and Tinctoris refer to the rebec in unambiguous terms; but during the 16th c. the name was transferred to the violin, and until the end of the c., when the violin group had names of its own, it is often not possible to tell which instr. is meant. An exception occurs in the 1551 inventory of a deceased Parisian instr. maker; both rebecs and violins are mentioned. (See also: violin). Agricola in 1528 depicts and describes a family of 3-stringed rebecs that he calls *"kleine Geigen ohne Bünde"* (little fiddles without frets); each has a split-level belly and the neck is of one piece with the body. In his expanded edition of 1545 he calls them *"kleine 3 saitige Handgeigen"* (small 3-stringed hand fiddles) and adds *"jeder will jetzt damit umgehen"* (everybody now wants to play them). His tunings are: soprano $g^0 d^1 a^1$, tenor, $c^0 g^0 d^1$, bass $F^0 c^0 g^0$ The drawings show identical instrs. except for variations in size. That the true rebec was made in different sizes seems likely: the 15th-c. Orvieto poet Simone Prodenzani writes of the *rubechette* and the *rubicone.* A *ribecchino* and 4 *violini* were used in a Florence *intermedio* in 1565; 4 *grosse Rebebn* are listed in a 1584 inventory of Kremsmünster monastery. The word rebec is also in frequent use in the records of the courts of England and Lorraine. In 1518 a "rebecke" named John Severnac was employed at the court of Henry VIII; by 1526 the court employed 3 rebeckes; in 1538 there were 2 rebecks, and by 1552, under Edward VI, only 1. But in 1588 a rebeck is listed as one of Elizabeth's court musicians, and in 1633 there are 4 rebecks at court. The rebec is mentioned continuously from 1509 to 1528 at the court of the dukes of Lorraine; in 1568 the word is used there in the pejorative sense of street musician. Hercole Bottrigari, in his *Desiderio* of 1594, speaks of ribecchini, lire, and viole, adding that ribecchini and lire have no frets. He may be referring to violins. Praetorius, less than a quarter of a c. later, leaves us in no doubt about the identification of ribecchino with violin: "... *deroselben Bass- Tenor- und Discant-geig* (*welche Violino oder Violetta picciola auch Rebecchino genennt wird . . .*) *seynd mit 4. Saiten . . .*" (these bass, tenor, and discant Geigen [which are called violino or violetta picciola or rebecchino] have 4 strings). Rebecs of Fr. 18th-c. make are occasionally met with in museums. See also: hum-strum, marionetta, vialo, violin (80, 82, 106, 145, 180, 190).

Rebeca, Lat., Port.: rebec (61).

Rebecca [*rebeca*], obs. It. var. of ribeca.

Rebecchino, var. of ribecchino.

Rebelle, var. of rebebe.

Rebequín, Sp.: rebec (Cerone, *Melopeo,* 1613: "*los rabeles o rebequines*").

Rebhüppi, name of the bargialera in Canton Aargau, Switzerland (102).

Rebube, obs. Fr.: Jew's-harp. The word is first recorded in 1373, but does not necessarily apply to an instr. then. It reappears in the 17th c. Trichet uses it *ca.* 1640. Furetière in 1690 says that the *trompe is also called rebube. Gradually the word is replaced by *guimbarde in the 18th c. See also: guimbarde, rabube, ribeba, ributhe, trompe de Béarn, trompe de laquais (53, 82, 190).

Rebun, *whirled friction drum of Russia (169).

Récit, manual of Fr. organs and that section of the organ it controls, of late-16th- or early-17th-c. origin (62).

Récit expressif, récit with pipes placed in a swell box: a swell organ.

Reclain [?Lat. *clamare,* to call], med. Fr. bird call. The word occurs in Fr. literature up to the 17th c. See also: reclamo (204).

Reclam, var. of reclain.

Reclam de xeremias, pastoral *double clarinet of Ibiza, Balearic Islands, with 2 cylindrical tubes, each having 4 front fingerholes and a rear thumbhole, all situated opposite one another so they can be closed by the same finger. The single tube is called xeremia. *Cf.* xeremia besona (81).

Reclamo (Sp.: decoy bird), Cast. equivalent of the botet, in use from the 16th c. on. See also: reclain.

Recorder [see text] (Fr.: *flûte à bec;* Ger.: *Blockflöte;* It.: *flauto dritto,* Sp.: *flauta de pico*), **1.** a variety of flageolet, characterized by a wider, tapering bore, that became a classical instr. of the Renaissance and baroque. Prototypes of the recorder can be followed back to the 12th c., and Sachs mentions a Fr. miniature of the 11th c. on which an instr. with tapering bore can be seen. Known on the Continent as "flute" (1320: "*une flûte d'yvoire*"), later with qualifications derived from its timbre (flûte douce, flauto dolce) or form (Schnabelflöte), it was called "recorder" in England by the late 14th c. The earliest trace of this name was recently discovered by Brian Trowell in the household accounts for 1388 of the Earl of Derby, later Henry IV: "*i fistula nomine Ricordo*" (a flute called Keepsake); a "recorde" is mentioned in the *Squire of Low Degree, ca.* 1400. By the 15th c. the recorder was being built in several sizes, and by the end of the c. the consort included a bass. Virdung in 1511 describes and depicts 3 sizes: bass on f^0, tenor on c^1, soprano on g^1; the alto part could be played on either tenor or soprano. He further states that sopranos, tenors, and basses were each made in 2 different sizes, differing in pitch by a tone, the choice of size depending upon the tonality of the piece (much as our C and B♭ clarinets of today). Silvestro Ganassi in 1535 also lists 3 sizes; his *Fontegara* is the first tutor for the recorder and already includes tonguing exercises. The instr. of that time was made of a single joint, either wood or ivory, usually boxwood, with beaked mouthpiece, had a compass of about 2 octs.; the bore tapered slightly toward the lower end, later more markedly so, and terminated in a small flare. Up to the late 15th c. it had 6 front fingerholes and a rear thumbhole; a seventh fingerhole was added during the course of the 15th c., duplicated for left- or right-handed players, the unwanted hole being stopped with wax. Its total of 9 fingerholes caused it to become known in France as the *flûte à neuf trous,* the 9-holed flute. The bass instr. had one open key in lieu of the duplicated little-finger hole, protected by a fontanelle, needed by the wider spacing of the holes; 16th-c. authors give the fundamentals of the 3 sizes as $F^0 c^0 g^0$, but they sounded an oct. higher in reality. This custom of notating recorder music an oct. lower than it sounds has persisted until now (although today the alto and tenor are notated as they sound) and may derive from the fact that, because of the paucity of overtones, the recorder sounds lower than it actually is. Larger basses were being made by the middle of the 16th c., and when Praetorius wrote in 1618 he could list 7 sizes of recorders. The 2 largest sizes were played with crooks. Probably the most important event in the recorder's history was its complete remodeling, undertaken by Jean Hotteterre of Paris or his entourage of woodwind makers in the mid-17th c. The new model was made in 3 separate joints, with cylindrical head joint, tapering middle and foot joint. The degree of taper was about twice that of the older version. The little-finger hole was now placed on the foot joint, and since this was movable, duplication of the hole became unnecessary. At about the same time, possibly under the influence of the new Fr. instr., the English began using the word "flute"

instead of "recorder," and the old word gradually disappeared from the Engl. vocabulary, to be resuscitated early in our c. by writers such as Christopher Welch (*Six Lectures on the Recorder,* 1911). During the 18th c. recorder parts in England were marked "flute" or "flauto" (as they were elsewhere), whereas the cross flute was called German flute or flauto traverso. This terminology has caused much confusion in modern times. Early in the 18th c. the largest and the smallest sizes were dropped and a family of 3 or 4 instrs. was retained. The old soprano on G was transformed into an F instr. and became the type instr. of the family. Johann Mattheson mentions only 3 sizes in 1713, but Walther knew 4 in 1732, and the *Encyclopédie méthodique* gives 5 later in the c. But the recorder's compass was too restricted, and the sound that in 1668 had caused Samuel Pepys to rhapsodize about the "sweet tone" was deemed too weak in the latter part of the 18th c.; by the end of the c. the recorder had been totally discarded in favor of the cross flute.

The popularity of the recorder from a comparatively early date on was probably a factor in developing the system of cross-fingering. As fingerholes were equidistant, the intonation of several tones had to be corrected in order to produce accurate semitones, and this at a time preceding the availability of keywork. Revival of the recorder was started by Arnold Dolmetsch in 1919; he used an Engl. 18th-c. instr. for his model, and this type has been in common use ever since. Modern recorders are bored for 2 different fingerings, one known as the "English fingering," which is that of all old recorders, and the "German fingering," with a lowered fifth hole, not widely accepted. In connection with the following table it should be borne in mind that C in 1500 did not necessarily sound at the same absolute pitch as does our C today. In Britain the soprano recorder is called descant; the alto, a treble (see table on p. 440);

Modern	Approximate lengths:		16th c. all authors	1618 Praetorius	Approximate lengths:	
	cm.	(in.)			cm.	(in.)
Sopranino f^2	25	(9½)		Exilent g^2	20	(8)
Soprano c^2	33	(13)		discant c^2	30	(12)
Alto f^1	50	(19)	soprano g^1	alto g^1	· 43	(17)
Tenor c^1	66	(26)	tenor c^1	tenor c^1	60	(24)
Bass f^0	100	(38)	bass f^0	basset f^0	93	(26½)
Low bass c^0	122	(48)		bass c^0	125	(49)
				grt. bass F^0	193	(76)

ca. 1700 Talbot	1713 Mattheson	1732 Walther	18th c. Encyclopédie méthodique
f^2			dessus f^2
c^2		Quartflöte c^2	haute contre c^2
treble f^1	discant f^1	flûte douce f^1	taille f^1
tenor c^1	alto c^1	alto c^1	quinte c^1
bass f^0	bass f^0	bass f^0	basse f^0
double bass c^0			

Eisel in 1738 lists the same sizes and pitches as Walther, except that he calls the recorder in c^1 a tenor. Praetorius also lists a bass in Bb^0.

2. organ stop of flue pipes, built either as an open or as a stopped register, now obs. Also called tibia vulgaris. See also: double recorder, doucet, Quartflöte.

Reco-reco, scraper of Brazil, made of a bamboo segment with transverse notches, or small metal box, etc., scraped with a small stick. Also called quere-quexé. See also: reso-reso (7).

Recumbo, *musical bow of Brazil and Angola, with resonator (152).

Redap, name of the terbang in SW. Sumatra (121).

Redoblante, Sp.: tenor drum.

Reed (Fr.: *anche;* Ger.: *Rohr, Rohrblatt;* It.: *ancia;* Sp.: *lenguëta*), a thin, elongated piece of cane, wood, metal, plastic, or other material by means of which a number of instrs.—chiefly woodwinds—are sounded. Woodwind reeds are set in vibration by the player's breath. They may be *single reeds or *double reeds, the latter probably being the older of the 2. Single reeds are either idiochord or heteroglott and are divided into *beating, *retreating, or *free reeds. By idioglott we understand that the reed is cut from the body of the instr. itself; by heteroglott, that it is affixed to the body. If an idioglott reed is cut upward toward the top of the instr. (the end nearest the player's mouth) it is termed an upcut reed, if cut downward, a downcut reed. In classical antiquity, as in modern Europe and America, reeds were made of a cane called *Arundo donax* or *sativa* which grows in S. Europe and today comes chiefly from the Fréjus area of France. Reeds of organ pipes were of the single beating variety up to the 19th c. when free and retreating reeds were introduced, but after a flurry of popularity they were replaced, and most organ reeds of today are beating reeds again. The earliest organ reeds may have been of cane, but if so they were replaced by metal at a very early date, usually hard brass. Another type of reed is the metal *percussion reed, which is sounded by being struck, now used in certain electrophonic instrs. The primitive *ribbon reed should also be mentioned: here the reed itself forms the instr. See also: double reed, percussion reed, reed pipe, reedpipe, retreating reed, ribbon reed, single reed.

Reed cap, a small wooden cap with a blowhole on top; it enclosed the reed of some 16th-c. double-reed instrs.

Reed-cap shawm, shawms of the Renaissance provided with a protective reed cap, such as the hautbois de Poitou, Nicolo, Rauschpfeife.

Reed organ, 1. regal; **2.** an organ, such as the harmonium, American organ, etc., in which the sound is produced by wind acting on free metal reeds.

Reed pipe (Fr.: *tuyau à anche;* Ger.: *Zungenpfeife*), organ pipe sounded by the vibrations of a flexible metal tongue. The reed is either beating or free. In the former the tongue beats against the rim of a brass shallot (Fr.: *rigole,* Ger.: *Kehle*) and is enclosed in a tube usually of cylindrical or conical form. Since the tongue is the prime factor in determining pitch, the resonator serves above all to determine the timbre, less by its shape than by its length. Overblowing reeds were created by extending the resonator to 2 or even 3 times its normal length; originally this was done in order to assist the dynamically weak higher pipes of the 4′ stops. The top oct. of Andreas Silbermann's clairon 4′ in the Ebersmünster organ of 1730 is already an overblowing one. Dom Bedos also mentions the practice. Reed stops overblowing the entire compass are known from 1785 on (by Lohelius of Prague). Pre-baroque and early baroque tongues were extremely thin and very wide, construction that favored the upper partials. By Praetorius' time they were already narrower, and our reeds of today are, generally speaking, nearly twice as thick and far narrower. Efforts to replace the metal tongue by some other arrangement resulted in the leather *diaphone of 1888. *Free reeds were first introduced into the organ by Abbé Vogler in 1792, but without attracting attention at the time. It was not until after the spate of early-19th-c. free-reed instrs. had become known that the soft-toned free reed was imitated in the organ. After a period of great popularity it was virtually abandoned, except for the clarinet stop. Reed pipes are very sensitive to changes of pressure, particularly in the treble, and old organs with slider chests often suffered in the tutti from drops in dynamics and pitch. Reed pipes have been built from 32′ pitch to 2′ pitch. In Spain when they occur as front pipes they are placed *en *chamade.* The top oct. or so of reed pipes is often made of open, small-scaled flue pipes. As a *regal pipe, the reed existed already in the 12th c.; cylindrical reed pipes are known from the late 13th c., conical ones since the 16th. The earliest known reed stop is the Fr. *chalumeau, which was built in Dijon in the 13th c. Details of its scale are given by Arnaut of Zwolle *ca.* 1440. Reed pipes do not occur in Ger. organs before the 15th c.; the oldest Ger. reed stop is the Krummhorn, recorded from 1489 on (133, 167).

Reedpipe (Ger.: *Rohrpfeife*), any tubular aerophone sounded by a vibrating *reed, usually placed at the head of the instr., sometimes in its interior (in N. America) or, as a free reed, set in the wall of the tube (in SE. Asia). See also: pipe.

Reformflöte (Ger.), late-19th-c. flute of Schwedler & Kruspe of Leipzig: a C flute with a B♭ foot joint, conical bore, metal head joint, and a new ring-key system. It represents an attempt of flautist Maximilian Schwedler and maker Karl Kruspe to combine a conical "Vienna" flute with the Boehm system (183).

Regal [possibly Fr. *rigole*] (Fr.: *régale;* Ger.: *Regal;* It.: *organo reale;* Sp.: *realejo*), a small portable organ containing *regal pipes exclusively. Its relationship to the organ has been likened by Mahrenholz to that of the harmonium to our modern organ: an independent form of instr. The word "regal" is not encountered before the mid-15th c., and in Eng. literature it does not occur until a century later, from 1546 on. At first the regal was provided with a single row of horizontal reeds, then, in imitation of the organ, it took on ranks at other pitches, *i.e.*, at 4' and 16'. By 1500 this multirank regal was incorporated *in toto* into the organ, and the name came to denote the ranks of pipes. The reeds had also acquired short resonators made of brass, wood, etc., and this material is sometimes indicated in the name of a regal stop, as for instance in *Messingregal* (brass regal). As a church instr. it maintained itself on the European continent until into the 18th c. During the course of the 17th c. the short resonators were gradually abolished in favor of longer ones, thus transforming the regal pipe into a reed pipe. In Britain the word "regal" also designated the positive organ. References to "single" or "double" regals are not uncommon and refer to an instr. having a manual compass not descending below Γ ut (single regal), or descending below Γ ut (double regal). Pietro Cerone (in 1613) says that no instr. keeps its tuning less well than does the regal, that it goes out of tune from one hour to the other. See also: bible regal, book regal (20, 133, 180).

Régale, Fr.: regal; regal organ stop; abbr. of régale de bois.

Régale de bois, Fr.: xylophone. The expression has been in use since the late 16th c. Richelet reports that the instr. reached France from Flanders, and Majer calls it the "hölzernes Gelächter of the Flemings" (134, 166).

Régale de percussion, Fr.: xylophone.

Regal pipe, organ "pipe" in which the reed alone speaks, having either no resonator at all or an extremely short one. Originally the pipes had no resonators, but short resonators were acquired by the time regal pipes were incorporated into the organ. See: regal (20, 133).

Regency harp lute, *harp lute with added second fingerboard and 3 strings tuned e♭²g²b♭², notated c³e³g³, devised by Charles Wheatstones. The instr. is in E♭ (89).

Regent's bugle, *slide trumpet built by 1815 and thereafter to the specifications of Johann Georg Schmidt of Thuringia, solo trumpeter of the Prince Regent, by Thomas Percival and other London makers. The Regent's bugle is a short, widebore, slide trumpet in F, not a bugle, although it was designed to look and sound like one, and is played with a deep cup mouthpiece. The slide has a short extension 6–9 cm. (2½–3½ in.) long (80 IX).

Regent zither, 19th-c. *chord zither similar to the autoharp (149).

Regina, *music box that contained 20 punched steel discs 18 cm. (7 in.) in diam., each with a 2-minute playing duration, and 2 combs with a range of 7 octs. (89).

Registre, Fr.: **1.** stop; **2.** the slider of an organ.

Registre traînant, Fr.: slider.

Registro, It.: stop.

Regula, Lat.: organ register; stop.

Regula harmonica, Lat.: monochord.

Regula mixta (Lat.), an older designation of a mixture organ stop (133).

Regula tremula (Lat.), an older designation of tremulant (organ stop).

Rehu, flute of the Maori of New Zealand, made of matai or tupakihi wood, with 3 equidistant fingerholes near the lower end, stopped at the upper end, with lateral blowhole. Another type, also called rehu, has no fingerholes and is endblown (8, 77).

Rei, small hand bell of Buddhist Japan, with clapper (135).

Reibtrommel, Ger.: friction drum.

Reifchen, Ger.: lining.

Reihenrassel, Ger.: suspension rattle.

Reïta, keyless shawm, imitating the Arab. ghaita, made by Paul Evette and Ernest Schaeffer of Paris. *Cf.* rheita (176).

Rejong, see: reyong.

Remo-remo, *end-blown flute of the Ruro of Papua (103).

Rendang, misreading of gendang.

Rentang, bonang of Banten, W. Java, with one row of bonang kettles (121).

Reog, E. Java name of the dog-dog (121).

Repeating stop (Fr.: *jeu à reprise;* Ger.: *repetierende Stimme*), *mixture organ stop that does not proceed in a regular succession of ascending pitches because the treble pipes would become too small, but that "breaks" back periodically to a lower tonal position.

Repetierende Stimme, Ger.: repeating stop.

Req, see: riqq.

Requinta, Port.: treble guitar. *Cf.* quinto.

Requinto, Sp.: **1.** high-pitched clarinet; **2.** syn. of guitarra requinto.

Re-re, "tuning fork" idiophone of C. Celebes, similar to the genggong sakai but longer, its total length 40–70 cm. (19–27 in.). Some specimens have a third hole; some have rattan bindings on the cylindrical portion which can be used to modify the tone. It also occurs in other parts of Celebes. See also: druri dana, kakonti, parē, sasesaheng, talalo (112).

Ré-ré, cog rattle of the Ticino, Switzerland (102).

Resonanzboden, Ger.: soundboard.

Resonanzsaite, Ger.: sympathetic string.

Reso-reso [*reco-reco*], scraper of Western rhythm bands, of Latin-American origin. A bamboo tube is notched on one of its surfaces and is scraped with a stick. See also: reco-reco.

Resting bell (Ger.: *Standglocke*), cup-shaped bell without handle or clapper, placed open side up on the palm of the hand, a cushion, etc. (100).

Resultant bass, syn. of acoustic bass.

Retreating reed (Ger.: *ausschlagende Zunge*), **1.** reed that is closed when at rest, such as that of the Moroccan lira, or a slit in a piece of stopped cane, unlike the beating reed, which is open when at rest; **2.** organ reed introduced by Robert Hope-Jones (d. 1914); it lies on its frame when at rest (89 Galpin).

Revith (Heb.), percussion instr. of post-Biblical Israel, equated by the Vulgate with the Egyptian sistrum (89).

Reyong, bonang of Bali and Lombok, now extinct in Java, in shape of a dumbbell, 2 bonang gongs being connected by a tube. The reyong appears on 12th-c. reliefs (121).

Rezumbador, Sp.: humming top.

Rgya-glin, temple oboe of Tibet, with conical bore, expanding metal bell, 7 equidistant fingerholes, and bulbous mouthpiece with pirouette. The tube is bound with brass rings. Outside the temples it is known as surna or harib. *Ca.* 60 cm. (2 ft.) long (89 Picken).

Rgyud-mang, unidentified chordophone of Tibet (89).

Rheita, Fr. colonial spelling of ghaita in Algeria and Morocco. *Cf.* raita, reita (93, 170).

Rhombe, Fr.: bull-roarer.

Rhombos (Gk.), rhomboid piece of wood attached to a cord—the bull-roarer of antiquity.

Rhyton (Gk.: drinking vessel), drinking vessel of antiquity, horn-shaped, known as rhyton from the 4th c. B.C. on (as keras earlier), occasionally made as a musical instr., of clay, with or without fingerholes (48, 96).

Riabuh, *cross flute of Manipur, India, stopped at both ends, with single fingerhole. *Ca.* 80 cm. (32 in.) long (172).

Riang wulu baba, syn. of go beto.

Rib, 1. (Fr.: *éclisse;* Ger.: *Zarge;* It.: *fascia*), the side walls of a violin, etc.; **2.** (Fr.: *côte;* Ger.: *Spa[h]n*), the shuttle-shaped pieces of wood constituting the body of a lute, etc.

Ribab [Arab. *rabāb*], *spike fiddle of the N. African Sūs-Shluh, a primitive form of rabāb. See: rabāb.

Ribbon reed (Fr.: *anche à ruban;* Ger.: *Bandzunge*), ribbon, such as a blade of grass, stretched taut between 2 points and set in vibration by the player's breath. Often a child's toy held between stretched thumbs in front of cupped hands, the latter forming a resonator.

Ribeba, It.: Jew's-harp. *Cf.* rebube (190).

Ribeca, It.: rebec.

Ribecchino [dim. of *ribeca*], see: rebec.

Ribibe [Arab. *rabāb*], obs. Engl.: rebec. Also written rybybe.

Ribible [Arab. *rabāb*], obs. Engl.: rebec. The term was in use from the 14th c. on, together with numerous vars. The *Promptuarium parvulorum*, written *ca.* 1440, equates the rybyble with vitula.

Ributhe [Fr. *rebube*], var. of rebube. It occurs in *Houlgate*, a 15th-c. Scottish poem.

Riccio, It.: scroll.

Richik, Balinese name of the smallest-sized kechicher (121).

Ricungo, var. of urucungo (152).

Riedehorn [*Rüderhorn*], Ger. 18th-c. term for hunting horn (169).

Riethoorn, 14th-c. Flemish horn (169).

Rigabello (Lat.: *rigabellum*), according to Sansovino, a musical instr. used in churches before the introduction of the organ. His text (*Descriptio Venetiarum, Lib. 6*) reads: *"In aede Sancti Raphaelis Venetiis, instrumenti musici cujusdam forma extat ei nomen rigabello: cujus in ecclesiis usus fuerit ante organa illa pneumatica quae hodie usurpantur. Rigabello successit aliud quod Turcello dictum est, cujus Venetias usum induxit homo Germanus."* Rigabello has been proposed as etymon of *regal.

Rigol, rigoles, obs. Engl.: regal. Similar word forms (Rigal and Rygal) occur in 16th-c. Germany.

Rigole, Fr.: shallot.

Rigols [Fr.: *régale*], "a kind of musical instrument consisting of several sticks bound together, only separated by beads. It makes a tolerable harmony, being well struck with a ball at the end of a stick," *i.e.*, a xylophone played with a knobbed beater (Grassineau, 1740).

Rigu-ragu, friction sticks of Barcelona, Spain, used as a rhythm instr., 2 sticks being rubbed together (57).

Rijak, *spike fiddle of the Sart of Tur-kestan, with coconut body, fish-bladder belly, unfretted neck terminating in a peg-box, and 3 strings. The instr. is rested on its elongated spike (176).

Rilya, Russ. hurdy-gurdy, mentioned from the late 16th c. on, with 2 drone strings tuned a 5th apart, and 1 melody string tuned an oct. above the higher drone. The wheel is covered with rosin-coated leather. It is played chiefly in the Ukraine, also in C. and SW. Russia. In C. Russia it is also called lira or kobza. The body often assumes the form of a flat violin, complete with F holes. It was formerly carried by mendicants, suspended by a strap from the neck. *Cf.* gudok (206).

Rinchik, name of the bonang panerus in W. Java (121).

Rinda, bottle-shaped Jew's-harp of Bonerate, Indonesia, made of bamboo (173).

Rinding, small idioglott Jew's-harp of Java, of bamboo or wood. *Ca.* 8 cm. (3 in.) long and 1 cm. wide (121).

Rinding besi, Jew's-harp of Java, made of wrought iron, more or less circular, with tongue of brass or other metal; 5–11 cm. (2–4 in.) long (121).

Ring flute (Fr.: *flûte à bandeau*; Ger.: *Bandflöte*), flute with external duct; the latter is chamfered in the wall under a ringlike sleeve (100).

Ringtuba, see: Wagner tuba.

Ripienflöte, modern name for an organ stop of flute quality, made of open wooden pipes at 8′ pitch, the mouth wall being wider than the sides (131).

Ripieno (It.), mixture organ stop found in It. organs, similar to the fourniture (133).

Riqq (Arab.), tambourine of modern Egypt, without snares, *ca.* 25 cm. (10 in.) in diam.

Riti, *spike fiddle of Gambia, with heart-shaped calabash body, membrane belly, and single horsehair string held taut by a tuning ring. In Guinea the riti also occurs with 4 strings (141).

Ritorto, It.: crook.

Riū teki, classical *cross flute of Japan, originally made of monkey bone, nowadays of bamboo split lengthwise into strips and turned inside out, so that the bark is on the inside, and then bound with thin bark, usually cherry. The riū teki has a cylindrical tube with 7 equidistant fingerholes. Formerly it was made both in long and short versions, but only the short one has survived; 40 cm. (15½ in.) long. Also called o-teki, yoko fuye (135, 157).

Rivet cymbal, see: sizzle cymbal.

Rizmoc, *pellet bells worn as anklets by children of the Maya Indians of C. America (144).

Rkan-dung, trumpet of Tibet, made of a human femur and covered with human or yak skin, with brass mouthpiece. Often decorated with metal bands and semiprecious stones and sometimes terminating in a wide flange. Used in Bon incantations, village services, etc. (89 Picken).

Rkan-gling, trumpet of Tibet, similar to the rkan-dung but made from a human tibia. Used by mendicants (89 Picken).

Rnga-ch'un, *rattle drum of Tibet, in hourglass shape, made of human skullcaps (occasionally also of wood) connected by a wooden disc and covered with skin. A cord or strip of leather is wound around the waist, with pellets at both ends, and the drum is whirled so that these strike the heads. Also called chang-tu or by its Indian name, dāmaru (89 Picken, 173).

Robab, name of the rabāb in Kabul (144).

Robana, syn. of rebāna.

Rock gong, slab of rock played like a drum, distributed in Africa N. of the equator, Asia, and Europe. See also: musical stone (15 Wachsmann).

Rock harmonicon, lithophone made by a stonemason named Richardson, of Cumberland, England, in 1841, consisting of tuned basalt bars 10–120 cm. (4–48 in.) long, with a 5½-oct. compass. It was played with sticks. Richardson and

his brothers concertized extensively with the instr.

Rocking melodeon, syn. of lap organ.

Roding, tube zither of the Moi of Vietnam (103).

Roekua, *globular flute of Indians of the Peruvian Amazon, made of beeswax (103).

Rog, Bulg., Pol., Russ., Ruth., Serb., Slov.: horn. See also: rozhok, Russian horn.

Roga, bagpipe of Albania, with chanter and single drone pipe, found in the Lake Scutari region (144).

Rogett, corr. of Racket.

Rohr, Ger.: reed; cane; tube. See also: S-Rohr.

Rohrblatt, Ger.: reed.

Röhrenglocke, Ger.: tubular bell.

Röhrenpneumatik, Ger.: tubular pneumatic action.

Röhrentrommel, Ger.: cylindrical drum.

Röhrenzither, Ger.: tube zither.

Rohrflöte (Ger.) (Engl.: *chimney flute;* Fr.: *flûte à cheminée;* It.: *flauto a camino),* organ stop of large-scaled metal pipes covered by a flat, perforated cap and surmounted by a cylindrical tube (chimney) fitted into the center of the cap, *i.e.,* a half-stopped register. Made at 16′, 8′, 4′, 2′, 1′ pitches (2, 101).

Rohrpfeife, Ger.: **1.** reedpipe; **2.** med. Ger.: panpipes; **3.** flûte allemande (organ stop) (133, 189).

Rohrquintadena, organ stop of half-stopped flue pipes of medium scale. In older organs it appeared as Rohrschelle, Hohlschelle (133).

Rohrquinte (Ger.), Rohrflöte at quint pitch, *i.e.,* 10⅔′, 5⅓′ or 2⅔′ (2).

Rohrschelle, in some older organs the name of the *Rohrquintadena, at 1′ or, rarely, 2′ pitch, probably derived from its shrillness (133).

Rohrwerk, Ger.: the reed pipework of an organ. Also called Zungenwerk. *Cf.* Schnarrwerk.

Roiza, double reedpipe of the Kachin of Shan State, Burma, consisting of 2 cylindrical cane pipes with metal free reeds. The melody pipe has 8 front fingerholes and 2 rear thumbholes; 3 front holes and 1 rear hole are stopped with wax. The drone pipe is thinner and devoid of fingerholes (172).

Rojeh, cymbal of Java, thin and without a boss, mentioned in literary sources from the 11th c. on. Suspended vertically, it is struck with a mallet and is generally played in pairs (121).

Rojek, rojok, see: rozhok.

Roku-gen-kin, see: roku kin.

Roku kin (Jap.: six-stringed kin), 6-stringed koto of Japan, made of a flat board, hollow underneath, that rests on 2 short feet at its upper end. The 6 silk strings pass over 2 bamboo bridges. Stopping points for the melody string are marked by small inlays in the board. *Ca.* 116 cm. (46 in.) long (149, 157).

Rolle, Alemannic: *pellet bell. The term is used in S. Germany, parts of Switzerland, the Tirol and Styria (169).

Roller (Fr.: *rouleau, abrégé;* Ger.: *Welle*), in the organ a horizontal cylinder, a wooden or metal rod, that transfers motion between key and pallet to the left or right.

Roller action (Fr.: *abrégé;* Ger.: *Wellatur*), in an organ the ensemble of rollers, roller boards, stickers, etc., forming its action.

Roller board (Fr.: *table d'abrégé;* Ger.: *Wellenbrett*), the board to which the rollers of an organ are attached.

Rolliertrommel, obs. Ger.: tenor drum.

Rollschelle, Ger. term for pellet bell, coined by Curt Sachs.

Rolltrommel, Ger.: tenor drum.

Rol-mo, Tibetan cymbals of Indian origin, smaller than the sil-snyau and with larger bosses. Two are joined together by a cord or chain and are held vertically. They serve in the less important forms of worship (89 Picken).

Romanca, small kettledrum of Cambodia, with nailed head. *Ca.* 30 cm. (12 in.) in diam. (47).

Rombo sonore, It.: bull-roarer (152).

Rome, romy, *cylindrical drum of the Betsileo of the Malagasy Republic (171).

Rommelpot [Du.: rumble + pot], Dutch and Flemish *friction drum with friction stick, made of an earthenware pot sometimes containing water, closed at the top by an animal bladder. The friction stick penetrat∴s the center of the bladder and is rotated or pushed up and down. See also: Rummelpot, Rummeltopf.

Romuz, bowed chordophone of Persia, invented in 1875 by Khossor of Hamadan, a combination of tar and kamānja with 4 or 5 strings. *Ca.* 90 cm. (3 ft.) long (176).

Roncador (Sp.: snorer, droner), Sp.: disc buzzer (152).

Roncón, Sp.: drone.

Rondador, panpipes of the Quiche Indians of Guatemala, with 10 pipes; also known in Ecuador, where they have 9–13 pipes, and in Colombia (89, 105).

Rondro, percussion instr. of the Tanala of the Malagasy Republic. A wooden bar is placed in a rice mortar, the cavity of which serves as resonator. The bar is struck with sticks. Now a child's toy, the rondro was originally played by adults to welcome chiefs and to serve at other functions. See also: kakanika-kanika (171).

Roneat dec, metallophone of Cambodia, with 21 iron bars. *Cf.* ranat thong ek, ranat thong thum (173).

Roneat ek, xylophone of Cambodia, with 21 tuned bamboo slabs. It corresponds to the ranat ek of Thailand. *Cf.* rang nat (65).

Roneat thum, xylophone of Cambodia, equivalent to the ranat thum, but with bamboo slabs.

Rongo, 1. xylophone of the Golo of the Congo; **2.** ivory horn of Loango, Angola (19, 176).

Rong ruyh, rattle of the Moi of Vietnam (103).

Ronker (Du.: snorer), *whirled friction drum of Holland (176).

Ronmonea, small hand drum of Cambodia, *ca.* 38 cm. (15 in.) high (176).

Rootsikandel (Swedish kantele), a name by which the talharpa was known to the Estonians. Also a syn. of kannel.

Roria, obs. Jew's-harp of the Maori of New Zealand, made of a curved wooden tongue tied to a short stick so that its end is left free. Another form consisted merely of a piece of wood the size of a little finger, scraped thin at one end and held close to the teeth while it was plucked (8).

Rosace, Fr.: rose.

Rose [from similarity to rose-window] (Fr.: *rosace;* Ger.: *Rose*), openwork ornamentation placed in the soundhole of certain instrs.; of Oriental origin. Originally mere decoration, roses later were often used to identify the maker by incorporating his mark or initials. Also called knot in 17th-c. England, and Stern (star) in 16th-c. Germany.

Rosette, Fr. 17th-c. term for pirouette (190).

Rossignol (Fr.), **1.** a pottery whistle flute in vase form, partly filled with water —a child's toy; **2.** the nightingale organ stop (70).

Rota, Latinization of rote, OProv.: cruit (185A).

Rota campanarum (Lat.: bell wheel), see: horologium.

Rotary valve (Fr.: *cylindre à rotation;* Ger.: *Zylinderventil;* It.: *cilindro rotativo*), valve for brass instrs. probably invented by Joseph Felix Riedl of Vienna in 1832 (he called his invention Rad-Maschine), a short cylinder with 2 passages controlled by a metal spring; a later system (1866) is known as the American action or string action (15 Morley-Pegge, 25).

Rota tintinnabulis, see: horologium.

Rote, OFr. and MEngl. form of the word cruit. In France the term is recorded from the late 12th c. to the late 14th; in England it occurs in literary sources from *ca.* 1300 to *ca.* 1400 (180).

Rotllo [Lat. *rotella,* small wheel], in León Province, Spain, a small bell wheel of churches (57).

Rotsikandel, see: rootsikandel.

Rotta, OHGer., OProv., med. Lat.: cruit (185A).

Rotte, MHGer.: cruit (185A).

Rotumbes, MHGer.: tambourine. The word is recorded in the 13th and 14th c. It corresponds to *temple (189).

Rouchalo, bagpipe of Bulgaria (89).

Roue à clochettes, Fr.: bell wheel.

Roue flamande (Fr.: Flemish wheel), an 18th-c. degeneration of the horologium or rota campanarum, a noisy child's toy made of a wheel strung with small bells and turned on an axle. *Cf.* ruota fiamminga, hoepelspel (124).

Rouleau, Fr.: roller (organ action).

Routelle [Lat. *rotella,* small wheel], obs. Fr. *cog rattle used in some Fr. churches during Easter week (82).

Royal Albert transposing piano, *transposing piano with divided keys, the rear sections of which acted on the neighboring course of strings if desired. This system was invented by Sébastien Mercier, of Paris, who took out a British patent in 1844; the patent was worked by Robert Addison, who showed the piano at an 1851 exposition. A similar piano was patented in France in 1843 by Le Bihan of Carhaix, Finistère (92).

Royal crescendo, piano-organ of Hofrat Bauer of Berlin, 1786. A 4½-oct. piano was provided with flue pipes and 6 pedals. See also: crescendo (176).

Royal Kent bugle, see: keyed bugle.

Royal seraphine, see: seraphine.

Rozhok (Russ.) [dim. of *rog,* horn], folk cornett of Russia, made of 2 sections of hollowed wood bound with birch bark, straight, with slightly conical bore, 4 or 5 fingerholes, and a rear thumbhole. The mouthpiece is turned in the instr. like that of the *mute cornett. Until the 1870's 2 sizes were played, tuned an oct. apart, but today only one size is in use; *ca.* 40 cm. (16 in.) long. Rozhoks were played in small ensembles up to 1923. See also: vizgunok (14, 25).

Rr . . . (OSp.), see: R . . .

Ruba, bull-roarer of the Elema of Mei, Papua (201).

Rubāb (Pers., Turk.), short lute of ancient Persia, with piriform body, membrane belly, and 3–5 strings tuned in 4ths, attached to a sickle-shaped pegbox. Adopted by other Islamic countries from Egypt to Afghanistan and still a pop. instr. (75 II, 89 Farmer).

Rubbile, var. of rubebe.

Rubeba (Lat.) [Arab. *rabāb*], med. European word for the rebec, in use from the 13th to the 16th c. Jerome of Moravia describes it in the 13th c. as having 2 strings tuned a 5th apart; it is mentioned in Fr. literature in the same c., in Engl. literature in the 14th c. By the 16th c. the term was misapplied to other stringed instrs. and no longer designated the rebec. *Cf.* rebebe, rubebe (Note: rebube is the Jew's-harp) (53, 89).

Rubebe [Arab. *rabāb*], var. of rubeba.

Rubecca, corr. of rebec.

Rubechette, dim. of rubeba.

Rubembe, syn. of lubembe.

Rubicone, aug. of rubeba.

Rückpositiv, Ger.: chair organ.

Rucungo, var. of urucungo (152).

Rüderhorn, large Hiefhorn (169).

Rudien sulu, metal Jew's-harp of the Sea Dayak of Borneo, 10–12 cm. (4–5 in.) long (173).

Rudra vīnā (*rudra,* name of a quarter tone in the Indian scale), vīnā of Bengal, with body and neck made from one piece of wood, membrane belly, unfretted neck, lateral pegs, and 6 strings played with a very long wooden plectrum. Tuned $c^0 e^0 g^0 e^0 d^1 g^1$ (138, 173).

Ruganira, syn. of akakyenkye.

Ruhamo, large drum of the Wanande of the Congo, beaten only by order of the *mwami* (great chief) (30).

Rührtrommel, Ger.: tenor drum.

Rukinzo, drum of the Warundi of Urundi, with zebra-skin head. It accompanies the king, carried by members of the Basengo clan (30).

Ruliapa, panpipes of the Uanána Indians of Brazil (105).

Rumana, round *frame drum of Thai-land, with wooden frame and nailed head (132).

Rummelpot (rumble pot), Frisian *friction drum, a children's toy (16).

Rummeltopf, *friction drum of Germany.

Runche, runcho, disc buzzer of Venezuela (152).

Ruoko pilli, reedpipe of Finland. *Cf.* pilli (89).

Ruota fiamminga (It.: Flemish wheel), It. equivalent of the *roue flamande or hoepelspel; described by Buonanni in 1722.

Russian bassoon (Fr.: *basson russe; serpent-basson; serpent droit;* Ger.: *russisches Fagott, Fagottserpent*), upright serpent of the 19th c.; it originated with Regibo's upright serpent model of 1788. Made of wood in 3 or 4 detachable sections, 2 of which somewhat resembled the butt and wing joints of a bassoon, terminating in a straight brass bell or a painted animal head. The latter variety was also known as *ophibaryton. Six fingerholes and 3 or 4 keys were provided. The mouthpiece was carried on a crook. Compass and playing technique were those of the serpent, but the instr. was easier to hold. Also called bassoon serpent (89 Morley-Pegge).

Russian horn (Fr.: *cor russe;* Ger.: *russisches Horn;* Russ.: *ohotniche rogi*), **1.** straight or slightly curved wide-bore hunting horn of Russia, made of copper or brass in a large variety of sizes, about 30–210 cm. (1–7 ft.) in length. In 1751, J. A. Maresch, hornist of Empress Elizabeth, organized a band consisting only of these horns, making use of 37 different sizes. For tuning purposes a metal cap was affixed at the bell end. Each player sounded only one tone—the second harmonic of his instr. The band first performed in 1755 and was an immediate success; it lived on well into the 19th c., performing in Paris in 1833 (89, 169); **2.** organ stop of flue pipes, a loud Waldflöte (133).

Russisches Fagott, Ger.: Russian bassoon.

Russisches Horn, Ger.: Russian horn.

Russpfeif [?MHGer. *Rusch,* rush], according to Virdung and Agricola, writing in the early 16th c., a short, wide-bore recorder with 4 front fingerholes, terminating in a slight flare. If their terminology is correct, there would be no connection between Russpfeif and Rauschpfeife, but their identification is questionable.

Rūta, unidentified instr. mentioned by Al-Shaqandi (d. 1231) as being made in Seville (75 I).

Rutuk tundum, small tundum (176).

Rwa-dung, Tibetan horn of exorcism. It assumes various forms, usually that of a ram or antelope horn carved with symbols. It is thought to be of Indian origin (89 Picken).

Rybebe, 16th-c. Ger., var. of rebec.

Rybybe, rybyble, 15th-c. Engl., var. of rebec.

Rylya, see: rilya.

Ryong ko, small drum of Korea, played with 2 sticks, equivalent to the Chin. lung ku (66).

Ryū teki, see: riū teki.

Š . . . , see also: Sh . . .

Sabang, large *slit drum of the Bukar Dayak of Borneo (176).

Sabangan, *pigeon whistle of Java, made of wood, dried fruit husks, etc. (148).

Sabbeka [*sabaq,* intertwine], instr. of ancient Babylon, probably a horizontal *angular harp, identical with the (later) Gk. sambyke (21, 170).

Šabbur, Syrian: horn (98).

Sabcha, unidentified instr. of ancient Israel, mentioned in the Book of Daniel. We know only that it was a high-pitched instr. The word corresponds to the Gk. sambyke (89).

Sabdaghantikā, Beng. equivalent of saptaghantikā (173).

Sabe, pluriarc of the Bambala of the Congo (19).

Sabeca, see: sabbeka, sambuca.

Sabitu (Sum.), the 7-stringed lyre of ancient Babylon, first recorded in the third millennium B.C. Cf. shabitu (89).

Sabka, see: sabbeka.

Sacabuche [Fr. *saquer,* pull + *bouter,* push], Sp.: sackbut. In this sense the word has been in use from 1470 on. (It was also the name of a hooked lance.)

Saccapa (Aymara), rattle of ancient and modern Peru, made of dried fruit shells. Cf. zacapa (80 XII, 105).

Saccomuse, see: sacomuse.

Sac de gemecs (bag of moans), Cat.: bagpipe.

Sackbut [Fr. *saqueboute*] (Fr.: *saqueboute;* Sp.: *sacabuche*), **1.** early name of the trombone. The word was in use until the 18th c.; **2.** organ stop of reed pipes, introduced by William Hill in 1833, at 32′ pitch (198).

Sackgeige (Ger.: pocket fiddle), Ger.: kit.

Sackpfeife, Ger.: bagpipe.

Sackpipe, 15th-c. var. of Sackpfeife.

Sacomuse, the *Dictionnaire de Trévoux* (1704) says that the *cornemuse was formerly called by this name (35).

Sacqueboute, see: saqueboute.

Saddu (Akk.), curved signal horn of ancient Babylon, first recorded in the second millennium B.C. (89 Galpin).

Sa diu, *stick zither of Cambodia, with straight conoid stick, or stick that is up-curved at one end, a half-gourd resonator, and a single string of metal attached to a long rear peg. The resonator is pressed against the player's stomach. Cf. phin nam tao (47, 173).

Sa dueng, *spike fiddle of Thailand, made of ivory. A little shorter but otherwise identical to the cai ñi and t'i ch'in. See also: sa u, sō, sō u (173).

Saeng, *drum chime of Burma, composed of a number of *bung, usually 21, suspended in a low circular frame so that the player, in the center, can reach them all. It is played with bare hands. Cf. saing waing (176).

Safa ai, sistrum of Turkestan (176).

Sa fa fir, panpipes of modern Egypt, made of 24 pipes (176).

Safāqis (Arab.), instr. similar to the *kūbā, according to a 9th-c. Arab. source (75 II).

Safé, lute of the Dayak of Borneo, scaphoid, with open bottom, neck sometimes fretted, head usually carved, and 3 strings, formerly of rattan, now of metal. Also called jimpai, kasapi, sapeh. Cf. impai (120).

Saffaqātān (Arab.), Arab. cymbals,

mentioned in the 10th c. but not described until the 16th; round brass plates that were struck together (75 II).

Saffāra, see: sūfaïra.

Safīr-i bulbul [Arab. *sāfūra*], obs. Turk. nightingale whistle, probably of metal. *Cf.* sūfaïra (76).

Sāfūra, syn. of sūfaïra.

Sagaru, vessel rattle of the Dogon of Mali (103).

Saga-saga, syn. of yangong.

Sagbut, var. of sackbut.

Sage koto, 9-stringed koto of Japan, said to have been invented 3468 B.C. Small, ornate, with highly curved board, *ca.* 60 cm. (2 ft.) long (149, 157).

Saggat, see: sajjāt.

Saghana, *percussion stick of Persia, with 3 pellet bells. *Cf.* chaghāna (98).

Sāgo, sansa with wooden tongues, in Agni, a Sudanic language (93).

Sahib nahabat (master drum), huge kettledrum of India, always played in pairs, with a diam. of 1½ m. (5 ft.), mounted on elephant back. Each drum has its own player and is struck with a silver stick. See also: nahabat (170).

Saib-it, see: sebet.

Sain, early var. of sein; the term was in use in the 12th and 13th c. (204).

Saing, mouth organ of Korea, similar to the sheng (144).

Saing waing, *drum chime of Thailand, consisting of 17 drums suspended in a low circular frame so that the player, in the center, can reach them all. See also: saeng (176).

Saint, OFr., 15th-c. var. of sein (82).

Sa-it, panpipes of ancient Egypt, according to Victor Loret (98). See also: sebet.

Saite, Ger.: string.

Saitenhalter, Ger.: tailpiece.

Saitenharmonika, piano invented by Johann Andreas Stein of Augsburg in 1783, with an additional third string to each pair of unisons. When the keyboard was shifted, the hammers struck the third, or "Spinett," string (? at 4' pitch) while

the normal strings vibrated sympathetically. *Cf.* Spinettzug (92).

Saitenorgel, *upright piano furnished with a device for sustaining tone and controlling its dynamics, invented by C. Gümpel and built by Crasselt & Rähse of Löbau in 1890. Wind was supplied by pedal-controlled bellows to a series of reeds that in turn imparted their vibrations to the strings (176).

Sai t'o erh [*sitār*], Chin. name of the sitār (75 II).

Sajjāt, Syrian term for the ancient kāsāt (147).

Sakala, *vessel rattle of the Lower Congo, made of dried *strychnos* shells threaded on a cord or impaled on a stick. They contain seeds of *Canna indica* or other small bodies. Also called nsakala (185).

Sake-sake, name of the maraca, 1, among the Negroes of Surinam (105).

Sak ko, drum of Korea. See also: ung ko (66).

Salamine, organ stop of flue pipes, a Zartflöte introduced by Meyer of Hannover *ca.* 1850, at 8' or 4' pitch. A soft echo stop (133, 198).

Salamuni, shawm of Georgia, U.S.S.R., of wood, with cylindrical bore, 8 fingerholes, and a vent, according to Sachs (176); Montandon describes it as a beaked flute with 7 fingerholes, 29 cm. (11½ in.) long (141).

Salangai, rattle-anklet of S. India, made of *pellet bells threaded on a cord and tied around the ankles of dancers and some actors. Also called gejjim, kinkini (179).

Salāsil, Arab.: cymbals. See also: selslīm, sil, sil-sil, sil-snyau, zil (170).

Salbāq [?Gk. *sambyke*], Arab. harp, first mentioned by Avicenna (11th c.) (89 Farmer).

Salet, *nose flute of the Plee of the Malaya Peninsula (203).

Salicet, corr. of salicional; the word often designates a salicional at 4' pitch (3, 101, 133).

Salicetina, superoctave salicional organ stop (*i.e.,* at 2′ pitch) (101).

Salicional [Lat. *salix,* willow] (Ger.: *Salizional*), organ stop of cylindrical, narrow-scaled open metal flue pipes; it appeared in the late 16th c. Built at 16′, 8′ pitches, with soft tone (3, 133).

Sa-li-ne-lu (Sum.), chordophone of ancient Babylon, possibly a psaltery; equivalent of the Akk. pagie (89).

Salisīm, see: shalishīm.

Salizional, Ger.: salicional.

Salmaharphâ (psalm harp), OHGer.: psaltery.

Šalmaj, Czech: shawm.

Salmo, obs. folk zither of Spain, a tambourin à cordes similar to the chicotén. See also: salterio (165).

Salmodicon, see: psalmodicon.

Salmsang (psalm song), OHGer.: psaltery.

Salpingi, semanterion of Georgia, U.S.S.R. (178).

Salpingion [Gk. *salpinx*], free-reed *automatophone invented by Friedrich Kaufmann of Dresden after 1808, with 9 automatic trumpets and 2 kettledrums. See also: trumpeter (37).

Salpinorganon, free-reed automatophone built by Cornelius van Oeckelen of Breda in 1824, with 20 trumpets, 2 drums, and a triangle, presumably a copy of the salpingion. See also: trumpeter (204).

Salpinx (Gk.), **1.** straight conical trumpet of ancient Greece, with narrow bore, terminating in a slight flare. According to Gk. tradition, it was of Tyrrhenian origin and seems always to have been considered a foreign instr. In the *Iliad* it is mentioned twice, then not again until the 5th c. B.C. by Bakchylides. The earliest representation is on a slightly earlier vase, where it is shown played with a *phorbeia, playing technique perhaps taken over from the aulos, which it replaced as a military instr. Later the phorbeia is no longer shown. A surviving instr., now in the Boston Museum of Fine Arts, is made of ivory with a brass bell and measures 158 cm. (62 in.);

2. new Gk.: trumpet, trombone (21, 89, 170).

Saltarello, It.: jack.

Saltere, OEngl.: psaltery.

Salterio, 1. It., Sp.: psaltery, dulcimer; **2.** Sp. folk zither, a *tambourin à cordes of upper Aragon, with all its strings tuned to the same pitch and struck with a rod. It accompanies the one-hand flute. See also: chicotén, salmo.

Salterio tedesco (It.: German psaltery), the oldest It. name of the trapezoid dulcimer (149).

Salterium [Lat. *psalterium*], OEngl.: psaltery. The term occurs up to the early 13th c. (180).

Saltirsanch (psalter song), OHGer.: psaltery.

Salundi, ancient Javanese metallophone, a variety of gender (121).

Salunding wesi (*wesi* iron), name of the gender in Bali (121).

Salzburg zither, folk zither with semicircular projection of the body on the side opposite the fingerboard, made in the Salzburg area from the 1830's on. Those terminating in a helmet-like pegbox are known as Helmzither, which date from the 1840's and 1850's (117, 178).

Sama'a, clarinet of modern Egypt, with cylindrical tube and 6 or 7 fingerholes (144).

Samba, small *frame drum of the Yoruba of Nigeria. *Cf.* asiko (108).

Sambi, 1. pluriarc of the Songo of the Congo (128); **2.** *musical bow of Cuba, with tuning loop and gourd resonator. Also called burumbúmba (152).

Sambiut [Lat. *sambuca*], MHGer.: chordophone mentioned in Gottfried von Strassburg's *Tristan und Isolde,* probably a cruit. See: sambuca, 2.

Sambuca [Gk. *sambyke*], **1.** chordophone of ancient Rome, believed to have been a horizontal *angular harp. Its players, the *sambucistrae,* were girls of very low repute; **2.** in med. Europe it denoted a chordophone and was glossed in the 10th c. as *hruozza, the cruit. As the Lat. word *sambucus* means the elder tree, sambuca also stood for a woodwind. In an 8th-c. Saxon vocabulary, *sambucus* is glossed as *swegelhorn. In the 14th c. it is compared to a harp, with as many strings, also identified with a pipe, and is mentioned in regulations concerning players, apparently considered as a stringed instr.; in the 16th and 17th c. it is identified as hackbrett or arpicordo. The word also occurs as the occasional name of the hurdy-gurdy. See also: sambiut (21, 53, 79, 82, 170, 189).

Sambuca lincea [sambuca of the Lincei Academy], *enharmonic harpsichord designed by Fabio Colonna by 1618, each whole tone being divided into 4 microtones, with bichord stringing and 8 rows of keys. Also called pentecontachordon from its 50 unequal strings (27, 64).

Sambuca rotata, occasional Lat. name of the hurdy-gurdy.

Sambyke (Gk.), unidentified instr. of ancient Greece, possibly a horizontal *angular harp with very short strings. *Cf.* sabbeka, sambuca (170).

Samfonia [Gk. *symphonia], syn. of sinfoyna.

Samisen, a long-necked lute of Japan, the present-day form of the *jamisen. It has a square body made of 4 pieces of wood, preferably sandalwood, mulberry or Chin. quince, with catskin (or the cheaper dogskin) belly and bottom. The snakeskin belly of the Chin.-inspired jamisen did not stand up to the Jap. manner of plectrum playing and had to be supplanted by tougher material. The long, slender neck is now made in 3 sections for ease in transportation, and carries a reversed pegbox with 3 lateral pegs for the silk or nylon strings. The bridge is of ivory, wood, or plastic. Apart from 3 standard tunings there exist 2 special ones for comic music. The standard tunings are (relative pitch): $b^0 e^1 b^1$; $b^0 f\sharp^1 b^1$; $b^0 e^1 a^1$. Absolute pitch is determined by the range of the voice to be accompanied. The object of the various tunings is to permit the playing of open strings as often as possible. The samisen

is played with a wide *bachi* that first strikes against the belly, reinforced at this point with a piece of parchment. The samisen corresponds to the san hsien of China, the hyon cha of Korea. Its total length is 94 cm. (37 in.), of which 74 cm. (29 in.) are neck. The striking edge of the *bachi* is 9 cm. (3½ in.) wide. See also: chosen (135, 157).

Samisen no fuye, *cross flute of Japan, made of cane with 7 fingerholes. *Ca.* 40 cm. (16 in.) long (176).

Samphor, drum of Cambodia, identical with the tapone of Thailand (47).

Sampogna (It.), var. of zampogna.

Sampogne, obs. Fr.: zampogna.

Sampoña [Gk. *symphonia], obs. Sp. term for panpipes, first mentioned by Juan Ruiz in the early 14th c.; the term occurs also in the 16th and 17th c. (44).

Sampuegn [Gk. *symphonia], N. It. dialect: cowbell (44).

Samuius, *musical bow of the Zulu of S. Africa with short, wide, flat bow, a string of metal, gut, or fiber, without resonator or tuning loop. The bow is held in the player's mouth and the string is struck rapidly with a steel wire (17).

Samusi, the equivalent of the saz in Georgia, U.S.S.R.

San, var. of sein.

Sanafil, OProv. var. of añafil.

Sānāī, see: sānāyī.

Sanaporcs [Cat. *sanar,* geld], syn. of sanatrujes.

Sanātira, pl. of sintīr.

Sanatrujes [Cat. *sanar,* geld + *truja,* sow], Cat. equivalent of the Sp. castrapuercos. *Cf.* capador, capapuercas, sanaporcs.

Sānāyī (Sans., Beng.) [Pers. *surnā], conical shawm of N. India, of Islamic origin, made of wood, sometimes with a metal bell, with 7 equidistant fingerholes and a wide bore. The sānāyī has a pirouette but lacks a metal staple. Sometimes 2 sānāyīs are combined to form a double shawm, but generally the single instr. is accompanied by the *sruti upāngi, played by a second performer. The sānāyī corresponds to the nāgasuram of S. India and is also called shannāi. Average length 33 cm. (13 in.). *Cf.* sarnā, zurnā (170, 179).

Sanbomba, It. *friction drum with a friction stick. See also: simbomba, zambomba.

Sandau, bamboo flute of the Dayak of W. Borneo, with 6 fingerholes (176).

Sand drum, in ethnomusicology the name given to a bridge of sand between the 2 openings of a small tunnel. The sand is beaten by the player's hand (170).

Sanduhrtrommel, Ger.: hourglass drum.

Sanfoña [Gk. *symphonia*], accordion of the S. Brazil Gauchos, also called gaita (7).

Sanfonha, Port.: hurdy-gurdy.

Sanforgna, name of the zanfoña in Forez, France (44).

Sanfornia, according to Giustiniani, a Jew's-harp (80 VI).

Sanftflöte (Ger.), syn. of the Zartflöte organ stop (133).

Sanftgedackt, lieblich Gedackt organ stop in echo form (133).

Sanfthorn, 1. organ stop of reed pipes, a softly voiced horn stop, also called corno dolce; **2.** 18th-c. translation into Ger. of "cormorne," itself a corr. of Krummhorn (133).

Sang, 1. name of the santir among Turkoman peoples (89 Farmer); **2.** obs. clappers of Korea, made of 2 pieces of wood (66).

Sangboden, obs. Ger.: soundboard.

Sangboi, *goblet drum of the Mende of Sierra Leone, with hoop and lacings. *Ca.* 60 cm. (2 ft.) high.

San gen da kin, dulcimer of Japan, built in an ornate lacquered box, often scalloped, generally with 14 courses of 3 strings each, occasionally with 15 pairs of strings. It corresponds to the Chin. yang ch'in (149).

San gen kin (Jap.: three-stringed kin), 3-stringed koto of Japan, a development of the ichi gen kin, with which it is identical except for the number of strings.

These are tuned $c\sharp^1 f\sharp^1 c\sharp^1$. The first string is a melody string; the others are used for accompaniment (149, 157).

Sangkultap [Babylonian *zakkal,* chordophone], lyre of the Vogul of W. Siberia, called nares-jux among the Ostyaks. See nares-jux for description.

Sangna, drum of Cambodia, with 2 heads tuned a 5th apart. *Cf.* song na (176).

Sangoi, large *nose flute of the Kanowit of Borneo, with blowhole, 3 fingerholes, and a thumbhole. Over 1 m. (40 in.) long (176).

Sangona, *nose flute of C. Celebes, almost identical with the tulali except that it has 3 fingerholes (112).

Sangsaite, Ger.: chanterelle.

Sangu, Ewe word for the sansa. See also: afosangu, tresangu (93).

Sanguna, pl. of mir sang.

San hsien [Pers. *si tar,* three strings] (Chin.: three strings), long-necked lute of China, of W. Asian origin, with small square or rectangular frame body, usually of redwood, snakeskin belly and back. The body is pierced by a long, slender neck that carries 3 lateral tuning pegs. A capotasto permits changes of pitch according to the requirements of the singer to be accompanied. It is played with a broad plectrum. Also called hsien tse. The san hsien corresponds to the jamisen of Japan. See also: samisen, yon cha (170, 178).

Sanj, pl. **sunūj** (Arab.), Arab.: cymbal. The sanj has been confused with the harp *jank, due to Al-Farabi's describing it as having 15 strings. *Cf.* sanūj, sinj (89, 98).

Sanj-chini, see: sanj sini.

Sanj sini (Arab.: Chinese sanj), unidentified instr. mentioned by 2 11th-c. Arab. authors.

Sankh, Hindi equivalent of shanka.

Sankha, see: shanka.

Sanko, Pali equivalent of shanka.

Sanku, *harp lute of Upper Guinea, also of the Ewe and Ashanti, with skin belly, curved neck that pierces the resonator, strings running in 2 parallel planes, and bast tuning rings (176).

Sanmartín, hollow gong of Cuba, made of a piece of rectangular sheet metal bent into a cylinder but leaving a narrow aperture. It is played with an iron rod in pop. orchestras and certain Negro cults; 30–40 cm. (12–16 in.) long (152).

San no tsuzumi, large *hourglass drum of Japan, of Chin. origin, introduced through Korea and used only in *Koma* (Korean) music. The Jap. form is said to have evolved in the 8th c. Its heads are stretched over hoops and are laced, held by a central belt. The player grasps the cords with his left hand and strikes it with his right (144, 157).

Sansa, linguaphone consisting of tuned metal or split-cane tongues fitted to a wooden board or resonator, so that one end of the lamellae can vibrate freely. *Sansa* is the name of the linguaphone among the Marungu people of the Congo; by extension it has come to be used in a generic sense for all similar instrs. The lengths of the lamellae determine their pitch, and are easily adjustable. Some C. African specimens are attached to gourd resonators held against the player's body, but generally if there is a resonator it is in form of a box with soundholes. Söderberg is of the opinion that those having split-cane lamellae must be considered older than those of metal. The sansa is played by depressing and releasing the free ends of the tongues with thumbs and forefingers. The number of tongues varies considerably. Its age is unknown: João dos Santos mentioned the *ambira in 1586; Buonanni in 1722 refers to the sansa as *"marimba de Cafri,"* a term related to the 20th-c. expression "Kaffir piano" (it has also been called "African nail violin"). The sansa was introduced by Africans into the New World, where it is found in C. and S. America today (10, 15 Wachsmann, 19, 185). See also: abuboyo, afosangu, akadongo k'abaluru, ambira, bamboli, biti, chisanchi, deze, dimba, diti, ekende, geliti, ibeka, ikimbe,

insimbi, isanzi, jimba, kabarome, Kaffir piano, kalimba, kankobele, kansambi, kasanga, kasayi, kibanda, kibiti, kimbanda, kinditi . . . , kisachi, kisanchi, kisansi, likembe, lukembi, lukeme, lusukia, marimba, marimbula, maringa, mbichi, mbila, mbira, mbobila, modeku, molo, muzumbi, ndandi, ngala, nsansi, nsimbi, nzangwa, nzanza, ompochawa, pokido, quisanche, sāgo, sangu, sengwelembwe, sippi, tresangu, uadaku, valdímbula, zeze, zimba.

Santir (Arab., Pers.) [Gk. *psalterion*], dulcimer of the Arabs, Georgians, Kurds, and Persians, in form of a shallow trapezoid box with symmetrical sides, metal strings, played in horizontal position (whereas the *qānūn is played in vertical position). The usual number of strings is 14 courses of 4 each; these are secured by tuning pegs inserted into the right wall of the box, from which they project horizontally. Each course has its individual bridge. The strings are struck with 2 curved blade-shaped beaters. Literary references to the santir before the 17th c. are rare, although the instr. is known to have existed by the 15th c. By the 18th c. it was to be found in most Turk.-dominated areas, and possibly was adopted by the Chin. as their *yang ch'in. *Cf.* santouri, santūr, sintīr (89 Farmer, 170).

Santo, idiochord *tube zither of Maumere, Indonesia, with several strings. Also called nggonggri (119).

Santouri [*santir*], trapezoid dulcimer of modern Greece, played with a stick (89, 120).

Santung, 1. *bar zither of Soroako, SE. Celebes, identical with the dunde (112); **2.** idiochord bamboo *tube zither of Tolitoli and Bolaäng, Celebes (119).

Santūr (Turk.) [Gk. *psalterion*], dulcimer of Turkey and Iraq, known by this name since the 15th c. Today both European and Turk. models are played in Turkey. *Cf.* santir (76).

Santūr fransiz, santūr of modern Tur-

key, introduced *ca.* 1850, with 21 courses
of 5 strings each (89 Farmer).

Santuri, see: santouri.

Santūr turki, the Turk. santūr, as distinguished from the European dulcimer,
which is also played in modern Turkey
(89 Farmer).

Sanūj, *finger cymbals of modern
Egypt. *Cf.* sanj, sinj, sunūj.

Sanyōgī, fiddle of N. India, derived
from the sārangī. Body and neck are
made from a piriform calabash, the belly
is of membrane, glued to the body. Its 4
strings are tuned like those of the sārangī
and are supplemented by 3 or more sympathetic strings. *Ca.* 60 cm. (2 ft.) long
(173).

Sanzu, *board zither of the Azande of
the Congo, with bark resonator (128).

Sao, see: cai sao.

Sapeh, syn. of safé.

Saptaghantikā (Sans.: seven bells),
*bell chime of India, with 14 bells of different sizes, struck with small felted hammers connected to keys in piano fashion.
Sometimes it is also made as a metallophone. Formerly it had 7 bells, all struck
with 1 hammer. Also called saptasvāraba.
Cf. sabdaghantikā (138, 173).

Saptasvāraba, syn. of saptaghantikā.

Šaqef, see: shaqef.

Saqueboute, saquebute (Fr.) [*saquer*,
pull + *bouter*, push], **1.** sackbut. The term
occurs from 1466 on, often as *trompette
saqueboute,* and was still used in the 18th
c.; **2.** large size of cornett.

Sarada, Tamil equivalent of sarōd.

Sāradīyā vīnā (Sans., Beng.: autumn
vīnā), obs. name of the sarōd (173).

Sarala-vānsī, bamboo *whistle flute of
India, with 7 front fingerholes and a
thumbhole (176).

Sārangī (Beng.: fish), bowed chordophone of N. India, the whole instr. usually
being made of a single block of wood.
The large, clumsy body has a waisted
belly and very wide neck, with lateral
pegs for 3 gut strings to which 1 of metal
is sometimes added. From 11 to 15 sympathetic strings pass through small holes

in the fingerboard to reach their smaller
pegs set in the neck. The sārangī is held
vertically, the strings being stopped laterally by the player's fingernails. Today it
is played largely in dance and theater music, but as it was formerly an instr. of
dancer-prostitutes it is held in disregard.
See also: alābu-sārangī, ravanahasta, sārindā, sarong (144, 170, 179).

Sarasvati vīnā (vīnā of the goddess of
wisdom), vīnā of S. India, about 300
years old. The body is a large bowl hollowed out of jackwood or blackwood.
The hollow neck bears 24 fixed frets (12
for each of 2 octs.) and terminates in a
carved animal head. A large, detachable
gourd resonator with a hole cut in the
bottom is affixed to the vīnā. The metal
frets are adjustable. Four long strings are
stretched from the pegbox over a metal-
topped wooden bridge, and 3 shorter
ones, lying off-board, pass from pegs inserted in the neck over a bridge secured
to the main bridge. The vīnā is placed
across the player's knees, in a horizontal
position, its strings being plucked with
bare fingers (179).

Sarga, OEngl.: trumpet; glossed as
tuba, lituus. Syn. of truðhorn.

Sārindā, folk sārangī of India, with
thin wooden body of irregular shape, and
skin belly covering only the lower part of
the body, short neck, 3 gut or hair strings
that are bowed. Their tuning is $c^1 f^1 g^1$.
They are held by lateral pegs in a pegbox
surmounted by a carving. There are no
frets. The sārindā is played all over the
subcontinent by members of the lower
castes (170, 173).

Sārmandel, a Mar. name of the satatantri vīnā (173).

Sarnā [Pers. *surnā*], Hindust., Hindi
equivalent of sānāyī (173).

Sarnai [Pers. *surnā*], bagpipe chanter
of India, mouth-blown; a drone accompaniment is played by a second player on
a second chanter (89).

Sarōd (Hindust., Mar.), short-necked
fiddle of NW. India, usually bowed but
sometimes plucked, with very deep body

shaped to form a manner of center bout, tapering toward the neck, which is of one piece with the body. Four gut strings are usual, tuned $c^1 f^1 g^1 c^2$. The highest 2 may be geminated. In addition, there may be 8–12 sympathetic strings. Formerly it was known as sāradīyā vīnā. Also called rabōb (170, 173).

Saron, metallophone of Bali and Java, first depicted at Borobudur (*ca.* 800). In modern sarons the bars are set above a wooden trough resonator, frequently carved to resemble a dragon. They are usually of bronze, rarely of iron. Sometimes the larger ones are bossed; those of bronze are slightly arched on top. There exist 3 1-oct. sarons and 1 multioct. saron. Those of a single-oct. compass nearly always have 7 bars in *pelog*, and 6, 7, or 8 in *slendro*. See also: chelepita, chente, dempling, demung, gambang gangsa, kedempling, pantu, peking, penitil, selokat, tete lile (121, 170).

Saron barung, single-oct. saron of Java, the second highest in pitch (121).

Saronen [Pers. *surnā*], E. Java and Madura name of the selompret (121).

Sarong, 1. name of the sārangī in Assam; **2.** 4-stringed lute of the Khasi of E. Bengal; **3.** *harp lute of Sierra Leone, with 6 strings, hemispheric body, antelope-skin belly; **4.** harp lute of the Mandingo and Sarakole of W. Africa (132, 173, 176).

Saron jemblung, xylophone of Java, with 6 bamboo slabs laid side by side on a small, carved trough. Used in *jemblung* ensemble (121).

Saron panachah, syn. of saron panerus.

Saron panerus, single-oct. saron of Java, the highest in pitch. Also called peking, saron panachah. See also: chente, penitil, selokat, tete lile (121).

Saron slentam, bossed saron of Java, lowest pitched of the 1-oct. sarons, now somewhat antiquated (121).

Sarpa (snake), serpentine ceremonial horn of India, made of metal (144).

Sarrusophone (Ger.: *Sarrusophon;* It.: *contrabasso da ancia*), family of brass

instrs. with tube of wide conical bore ending in a flare, and played with a double reed. Invented by Sarrus, a Fr. bandmaster, and built by P. L. Gautrot, Sr., of Paris, who took out a patent for it on June 9, 1856. The 2 smallest sizes were made in straight form, the tube of the others was doubled back on itself. The sarrusophone was designed for use of military bands and was made in 8 sizes, all of which are notated from $b\flat^0$ to f^8.

sopranino in $E\flat$, compass $d\flat^1$–$a\flat^8$
soprano in $B\flat$, compass $a\flat^0$–$e\flat^8$
alto in $E\flat$, compass $d\flat^0$–$a\flat^2$
tenor in C, compass $B\flat^0$–f^2
baritone (actually bass) in $E\flat$, compass $D\flat^0$–$a\flat^1$
bass (actually contrabass) in $B\flat$, compass $A\flat^1$–$e\flat^1$
contrabass (actually subbass) in $E\flat$, compass $D\flat^1$–$a\flat^0$
subcontrabass in $B\flat$, compass $A\flat^2$–$e\flat^0$

The contrabass was also built in C, for orchestral use. The instrs. were furnished with 18 keys and had the same fingering as the saxophone. The smaller sizes are now obs. The larger ones proved pop. in wind and rhythm bands, and the contrabass has been scored for in orchestral works, chiefly Fr. ones. In Italy it is still a pop. band instr., going under the name of contrabasso da ancia.

Sarud [?Sans. *rudri*] (Arab.: king of *ruds*), a chordophone newly invented in Al-Farabi's day (d. 950). According to him it had a 3-oct. compass.

Sarune (Batak) [Pers. *surnāy*], *double pipe of the Land Dayak of Borneo, with pipes of unequal length, furnished with single reeds. The larger of the 2 is considered male and has 4 or 5 fingerholes; the shorter pipe, considered female, is a drone and has no fingerholes. Also called serubayi. *Cf.* srune, zurnā (144).

Sasesaheng, "tuning fork" idiophone of Talaud Island, Indonesia, identical with the re-re (122).

Sassandu, *tube zither of Timor, with

18 metal strings and an enveloping palm-leaf resonator; 57 cm. (22½ in.) long. *Cf.* susunu (141).

Sassofone, It.: saxophone.

Sa tai, *spike fiddle of Thailand, made of ivory and mother-of-pearl, with heart-shaped body, membrane belly, long neck, and lateral ivory pegs for 3 silk strings. Some specimens have a coconut body, but then the heart-shaped upper surface is preserved. The strings are attached to the spike, pass over a semicircular bridge, under a ligature that serves as nut, or capotasto. A small deposit of rosin for the bow is kept attached to the membrane. The spike is rested on the ground and the neck is held obliquely by the seated player (132, 173).

Satar [contraction of *sapta* + *tar,* seven strings], syn. of sitār.

Satatantri vīnā (Sans.: hundred-stringed *vīnā*), trapezoid *box zither of India, with 22–36 metal strings attached to tuning pegs along the oblique side. Actually it is a qānūn and is often so called. It is played while in a horizontal position; the strings are plucked with a plectrum and tuned to the pitches that may be required. Also called kanuna, katyayana vīnā, svaramandala. See also: churamantalam, kshudrā katyayana vīnā, sārmandal (138, 173).

Satong, idiochord bamboo *tube zither of Sarawak (119).

Satsuma biwa, biwa of Japan, named for Satsuma, and developed from the bugaku biwa in Kagoshima. Somewhat smaller than the bugaku biwa, and narrower than the heike biwa, but with a much larger pegbox. Its 4 strings may be tuned $e^1 b^0 e^1 b^1$ or $e^1 b^0 e^1 f\sharp^1$; other tunings are also employed. The melody is played on the upper string. Four high frets, with a large gap between the first and second, are attached to the fingerboard. The satsuma biwa is played with a very broad, fan-shaped plectrum; it accompanies the recitation of old epics and is held in an upright position (135, 157).

Sattel, Ger.: nut.

Satyrpfeife (Ger.), obs. term for pan-pipes.

Sa u, large sa dueng of Thailand, with heart-shaped body of a half coconut, skin belly, and 2 strings. *Cf.* sō, sō u (132).

Sauglufttharmonium, Ger. term for the *American organ, which works on suction wind (*Saugluft*).

Saukopf (Ger.: sow head), var. of Schweinskopf.

Saung, see: tsaung.

Sausage bassoon (Ger.: Wurstfagott), syn. of racket bassoon.

Sautereau, Fr.: jack.

Sautier, OFr.: psaltery.

Sautika vīnā (Beng.: mother-of-pearl *vīnā*), lute of Bengal of the sitār type, with mother-of-pearl body tapering to the head of an ibis. *Ca.* 1 m. (40 in.) long.

Sautry, obs. Engl. var. of psaltery.

Saw . . . , see also: Sa . . .

Sawangan dara, *pigeon whistle of C. Java, globular, made of wood, fastened to the tails of doves (121).

Sawangan dudan, *pigeon whistle of Java, cylindrical, made of bamboo, fastened to the tails of doves (121).

Sawangan gandok, double *pigeon whistle of C. Java, made of 2 whistles, 1 mounted above the other, fastened to the tails of doves. Also called sawangan renteng (121).

Sawangan gejilan, small *pigeon whistle of C. Java (121).

Sawangan layangan, syn. of sundaren (121).

Sawangan randan, *pigeon whistle of C. Java, with 1 or 2 ducts (121).

Sawangan renteng, syn. of sawangan gandok.

Sawergnil, generic name for bamboo flutes of the Kai Islands (119).

Sax-bourdon en mi♭, syn. of the saxhorn bourdon.

Saxhorn, a series of valved bugles introduced by Adolphe Sax of Paris in 1843, and patented in 1845, with medium conical bore and medium-sized bell, played with a funnel-shaped mouthpiece.

Saxhorns

Tonal position	Pitch	Original names	Other French names	U.S. equivalents	German equivalents
octave	B♭	saxhorn sopranino	petit bugle		Oktav Kornett
sopranino	E♭	saxhorn soprano	petit bugle, bugle soprano en mib, saxhorn sopranino	flugelhorn	klein Kornett
soprano	E♭	saxhorn contralto	bugle soprano, saxhorn soprano	flugelhorn	Flügelhorn, Kornett
alto	B♭	saxhorn ténor	bugle alto, saxhorn alto	althorn*	Altokornett, Althorn
tenor	B♭	saxhorn baryton	bugle ténor, saxhorn tenor	tenor horn	Tenorhorn
baritone	B♭	saxhorn basse	basse à pistons, saxhorn baryton	euphonium	Barytonhorn
bass	E♭	saxhorn contrebasse	bombardon contrebasse, contrebasse à pistons, saxhorn basse	bass tuba	Basstuba
contrabass	B♭	saxhorn bourdon	contrebasse à pistons, saxhorn contrebasse	BB♭ bass	Kontrabasstuba
subbass	E♭	saxhorn bourdon		EE♭ bass	Subbasstuba
subcontrabass	B♭	saxhorn bourdon		subcontrabass tuba	Subkontrabasstuba

* In Brit. usage: soprano saxhorn, contralto bugle

As valved bugles had been known for some 20 years, Sax's claim to the invention was heatedly attacked. However, it is now clear that his contribution consisting in blending a number of related but heterogeneous instrs. of his time (cornets, flugelhorns, tenor horns, tubas, etc.) into one homogeneous pattern, all built in upright form with valves fitted vertically on horizontal tubing. The whole series was intended primarily for military band use. Sax made 7 sizes originally, later augmented to 9 by the addition of sopranino and subbass. Initially all were fitted with 3 valves, and shortly after the whole series was also built with 4. The entire group was pitched alternately in E♭ and B♭ (see chart below). The subbass in E♭¹ was built in 1855 for the Paris Exposition; the subcontrabass was built in the same year. At about the same time, Sax changed the valve system, applying his own system of ascending valves (6 of them) to the group. These cut out a given length of tubing instead of adding to it. As band instrs. the saxhorns were very pop. and are still in use today. Confusion of nomenclature is almost complete, abetted by differences of opinion among Fr. and Belgian makers and writers in the past c. as to tonal positions. See also: contrahorn (89 Bates, 169).

Saxhorn bourdon (Fr.), subbass *saxhorn in E♭¹, built by Adolphe Sax in 1855 for the Paris Exposition. Also called sax-bourdon en mi♭. According to Sachs, it had a tube length of 49 ft. and was 10 ft. high (25, 176).

Saxophone (Fr.: *saxophone;* Ger.: *Saxophon;* It.: *sassofone*), **1.** family of wind instrs. invented by Adolphe Sax, then of Brussels, in 1841, and patented by him in France in 1846, with wide conical bore and slightly flared bell, made of metal, with oboe-like key arrangement, a mouthpiece similar to that of the clarinet, and played with a single reed. The 2 smallest sizes were built in straight form, the larger ones were bent back to form a curved bell and were fitted with a crook.

Sax devised this instr. for both orchestral and military purposes, and his patent thus covered instrs. of 14 different sizes: a group of 7, alternating in F and C (orchestral), and another group of 7, alternating in E♭ and B♭ (military), from sopranino to contrabass. All except the orchestral soprano (in C) are treated as transposing instrs., and all are notated from b♭⁰ to f³. Most pop., over a longer period of time, were the E♭ alto, a solo instr., the tenor in C, known in the U.S. as melody saxophone, and the soprano in C. Depending on its size, the saxophone is fitted with 18–21 keys, as well as 2 speaker keys. It overblows the oct. and has a compass of 2½ octs. By 1848 the family was completed from sopranino to contrabass (actually a subbass). A subcontrabass was added in 1904 by Conn of Elkhart, Ind. Desfontanelles of Lisieux had built a bass clarinet, with bell and bent mouthpiece, that has been considered a precursor of the saxophone, but it overblows the 12th. Compass and notation of the saxophone are the same as those of the sarrusophone. Leblanc of Paris is currently producing a Boehm-system saxophone. The saxophone family consists of the following members: sopranino f¹/e♭¹, soprano c¹/b♭⁰, alto f⁰/e♭⁰, tenor c⁰/B♭⁰, baritone (actually a bass) F⁰/E♭⁰, bass (actually a contrabass) C⁰/B♭¹, contrabass (actually a subbass) E♭¹, subcontrabass B♭²;

2. organ stop of either flue pipes or reed pipes, invented by Haskell of England. As a reed stop, it occurs at 16′ or 8′ pitch, chiefly in the pedal. As a flue stop, it is usually built of wood. It is found mainly in the U.S. (101, 131).

Saxotromba, see: saxtromba.

Saxtromba, a family of brass valved instrs. invented by Adolphe Sax of Paris and patented Oct. 13, 1845, designed for use by cavalry bands, with a bore intermediate between that of saxhorn and trombone; 7 sizes were built, from sopranino in E♭ to contrabass in B♭, pitched alternately in E♭ and B♭ except for one instr. in F, intended as a substitution for the French horn. Compass and notation were those of the saxhorns. Saxtrombas were played with a cup mouthpiece. The *Armeeposaunen of Vaclav Červeny are very closely related to the saxtrombas, but the proportions of their tubes differ (25, 89, 176).

Saxtuba, valved brass instr. of great power, built by Adolphe Sax of Paris in 1852 for the performance of *Le Juif errant,* of Halévy. It had the circular form of a Roman buccina. Sax offered it in 7 sizes, from a B♭ piccolo to a B♭ contrabass.

Saz (Pers., Turk.), a family of plucked chordophones of modern Anatolia, with small body, long neck, 16 movable frets, and a variable number of strings, 2 or 3 courses being the most common; these are tuned E D A or G D A, the lowest string being D, the center string. The melody is generally played on the A string, sounded simultaneously with its 5th (on the middle string), or the melody is played with a single or double drone. The family comprises the following members (from small to large): cura saz, baglāma, bozuk, achik saz, meydan saz; **2.** plucked chordophone of Armenia and Azerbaidzhan, with piriform body, 16 movable frets, 4 strings, and a neck encrusted with nacre; **3.** similar instr. of S. Yugo. towns; **4.** spike fiddle of NW. India, similar to the kamānja, with small calabash body, glued skin belly, long iron spike, and 3 strings as well as 14 sympathetic strings held by lateral pegs. The handle is surmounted by a wooden knob. See also: samusi (89, 173).

Saz-i alwah-i fūlad, metallophone of med. Islam, with iron bars (147 Farmer).

Saz-i kāsāt (Arab.), *musical cups of med. Islam, made of earthenware, the pitch being determined by the amount of water in each one. They were known to 14th-c. Persia (144, 147 Farmer).

Sbugs-nag, said to be a form of Tibetan bassoon with large, nearly globular bell (89 Picken).

Scabellum (Lat.), Roman equivalent of the kroupalon.

Scacciapensieri (It.: drive away thoughts), It.: Jew's-harp. Also called cacciapensieri.

Scagnello, var. of scannello.

Scale (Fr.: *diapason;* Ger.: *Mensur*), relative measurements of an instr., such as the inside diam. and length of a pipe in relation to its pitch; the length, thickness, and density of a string in relation to its pitch; also the proportions by which a series of organ pipes is constructed or the stringing of an instr. is determined. Makers of stringed instrs. seem to have striven for maximum scale ever since the Middle Ages. We read for instance in 1372, *"Tant comme les cordes de la guiterne sont plus seiches et plus tendues, de tant en font elles meilleur son"* (the drier and tenser the strings of a gittern, the better sound they make) (82).

Scannello, obs. It.: bridge.

Scappamento, It.: escapement.

Scarp, scarpa, corr. of scherp (organ stop).

Scattagnetti, Sicilian: castanets (169).

Scella [Gothic: *skaella*], OHGer.: bell.

Sch . . . , see also: Sh . . .

Schachtbrett, word that occurs in the *Minne Regel* (*Rules of the Minnesinger*) of Eberhart Cersne, of 1404, related to the Romance terms for chekker.

Schäferpfeife (Ger.), **1.** obs. Ger. bagpipe described by Praetorius (but depicted a c. earlier), with conoid chanter, compass f¹–f², 2 drones inserted into 1 stock sounding B♭⁰ and f⁰ (Praetorius gives their compass an oct. too high). Also called Schaperpfeiff; **2.** rustic pipe (13, 117).

Schalenleier, Ger.: bowl lyre.

Schallbecher, Ger.: bell (of a wind instr.).

Schallemelle [Lat. *calamus*], MEngl.: shawm.

Schallhorn, OGer.: (loud) horn (88).

Schalloch, Ger.: soundhole.

Schallstück, Ger.: bell (of a wind instr.).

Schalmei [OFr. *chalemie*], **1.** Ger.: shawm. Numerous var. spellings exist; **2.** 20th-c. wind instr. made by Martin, also known as Martintrompete, consisting of several straight conical metal horns, each provided with a metal beating reed controlled by a common mouthpiece, and with valves; **3.** organ stop of: a) reed pipes with conical resonators, dating back to the early 16th c., b) regal pipes, short, narrow, and conical. See also: bombard, deutsche Schalmei.

Schaperpfeiff, syn. of Schäferpfeife.

Scharf, see: acuta.

Scharfflöte (Ger.), organ stop built as: a) Prinzipal in high tonal position, b) loudly voiced Spitzflöte, c) a mixture, usually of wide-scaled pipes in high tonal positions.

Scharfonett, Scharf mixture stop in high position, built by Leyser in the late 17th c. (133).

Scharfzimbel, syn. of Zimbelscharf.

Scheide, Ger.: slide.

Scheitholt [*Scheit,* log + *holt,* wood], obs. folk zither of Germany, similar to the bûche, with 1–4 melody strings and several drone strings stretched over a slender rectangular box that had fixed frets fitted to its left long side, and that tapered to form a pegbox at the upper end. The metal strings were secured by lateral pegs. In some instances the back was half open or entirely absent. The strings were plucked with bare fingers; Praetorius says that they were strummed by the right thumb while the left hand held a small stick with which the strings were stopped. The Scheitholt was played up to the early 19th c. See also: tambourin à cordes.

Schella, med. Lat.: bell (61).

Schelle, Ger.: *pellet bell, in agricultural areas a cowbell or cattle bell.

Schellenbaum, Ger.: Jingling Johnnie.

Schellentrommel, Ger.: tambourine.

Scherp (Du.), see: acuta.

Schgara, cog rattle of the Oberland, Switzerland.

Schlagbalken, Ger.: percussion beam.

Schlagidiophon, Ger.: struck idiophone.

Schlagstab, Ger.: percussion stick.

Schlagtopf, Ger.: percussion pot.

Schlagzither, Ger. term for plucked zithers to distinguish them from bowed zithers (Streichzither).

Schlangenrohr, Ger.: serpent.

Schleife, Ger.: slider.

Schleiflade, Ger.: slider chest.

Schlitzgeige (Ger.), syn. of Scheitholt, according to J. J. Kachell (ms. 1792).

Schlitztrommel, Ger.: slit drum.

Schlotter, obs. Ger.: rattle.

Schlüssel, Ger.: obs. term for the key of a wind instr.

Schlüsselfiedel (Ger.), obsolete keyed fiddle of Northern Germany that corresponded to the *nyckelharpa of Sweden. Melody and drone strings were bowed; they were stopped by tangents activated by slider-keys. After the 17th c. they are no longer heard of in Germany. See also: nyckelharpa.

Schnabelflöte, Ger.: beaked flute, recorder.

Schnarre, Ger.: cog rattle.

Schnarrsaite, Ger.: snare.

Schnarrwerk, obs. Ger.: reed pipework of an organ. *Cf.* Rohrwerk, Zungenwerk.

Schnecke (snail), Ger.: scroll.

Schnurrassel, Ger.: strung rattle.

Schraper, Ger.: scraper.

Schreierpfeife, 1. Germanized form of Schryari; **2.** organ stop imitative of 1, with characteristically high overtones, consisting of a 2- or 3-rank mixture of octs., 2′ and 1′, or 2′, 1′, and ½′, repeating. Built infrequently after the mid-baroque but encountered up to the 19th c. (133).

Schryari [U.], wind instr. of the Renaissance of which no specimen has survived, played with a double reed. It is mentioned in several inventories from 1540 to 1686 but depicted only by Praetorius, mentioned for the last time by Martin Fuhrmann in 1706. In 1541 the Nürnberg trumpet maker, Georg Neuschel, offered Duke Albert of Prussia some "schreyende pfeiffen" he had received from Lyon and Venice which he said were far louder than pumharts. Schryari were made in consorts of soprano, alto/tenor, and bass; they had conical tubes with double reed protected by a reed cap. Bass and tenor had 2 keys to extend the compass upward (like the calandrone). We do not know whether the bore was contracting. The compass was limited to a 9th, as the instr. did not overblow. The sound was shrill and the pitch an oct. lower than that of a recorder of the same length: soprano *ca.* 22 cm. (9 in.) long in g^0; alto/tenor *ca.* 44 cm. (17 in.) in c^0; bass *ca.* 66 cm. (26 in.) in F^0 (36, 89 Baines, 114).

Schubventil, an early form of *piston valve, a hollow piston that deflects the air stream at right angles (25).

Schulitgas (willow), Romansh: rustic whistle flute (102).

Schulterharfe, Ger.: shoulder harp.

Schüttelidiophon, Ger.: shaken idiophone.

Schwanenhorn (Ger.: swan's horn), valved, circular bugle of Vaclav Červeny of Königgrätz (Hradec Králové), with curved bell. Built by 1846 (176).

Schwebung, Ger.: tremulant.

Schwegel (Ger.) [OHGer.: *Schwägel,* shinbone], **1.** woodwind instr. widely distributed on the European Continent from the Middle Ages on, in various forms: a) as a tabor pipe, with 2 front fingerholes and a rear thumbhole, an equivalent of the galoubet; it had a narrow cylindrical bore and was made in several sizes, the tenor being also known as Stamentienpfeife; b) in the Alemannic area the word also denoted a *cross flute; as such, it was depicted in the 12th-c. *Hortus deliciarum* (our first record of the cross flute in Europe). An Ambras inventory of 1596 enumerates soprano, tenor, and bass sizes. Praetorius says that these had a range of up to 2 octs., the soprano of *ca.*

50 cm. (20 in.) length from d^2 up, the tenor 65 cm. (30 in.) from g^1, and the bass 75 cm. (30 in.) from c^1; c) in the Austrian Alps, the word *Schwegel* denoted both transverse and vertical flutes, which were played there until the early 19th c., when the vertical model became extinct. The transverse Schwegel has traditionally been built with a cylindrical bore and is still so made today. A variety with inverted-conical bore is of later origin and now obs. Today's Schwegels are made in 4 sizes, the smallest, called Goasspfeiff, is 33 cm. (13 in.) long, the largest, Biripfeife, 43 cm. (17 in.), with 2 intermediary sizes 37 and 39 cm. (14½ and 15¼ in.); the last 2 are pitched in A and in B♭ or B and are the most commonly used. Each size has 6 equidistant fingerholes, occasionally arranged in 2 groups of 3. See also: Seitenpfeife, švegla, svirel (117, 170);

2. organ stop of flue pipes built in many forms, probably of Du. origin. At first it was wide-scaled with narrow cutup, built chiefly at 8' or 4' pitch; also built like a Prinzipal, chiefly at 1' pitch; then again of conical pipes, similar to a Gemshorn; finally of half-conical pipes like a Spillflöte. Adlung lists Schwegels at 8', 4', 2', 1' pitches. Also called Schwiegel (2, 133, 159).

Schweinskopf (pig's head), obs. Ger. expression for dulcimer or psaltery, with reference to its triangular shape with incurving sides; also used to designate a wing-shaped keyboard instr. Also called Saukopf. *Cf.* instrumento di porco.

Schweizerflöte, syn. of Schweizerpfeife.

Schweizerhorn, organ stop: a new name for the old overblowing tuba or tuba mirabilis (133).

Schweizerpfeife (Ger.: Swiss pipe), **1.** the fife of the Swiss infantry fife-and-drum corps, so named during the Renaissance. It had a cylindrical bore and, according to Praetorius, was 2 ft. long with a compass of g^1–c^3 or d^1–a^2. In 1732 Majer describes it as a soldier's instr. with a d^1–d^3 compass. Also called Feldpfeife, fistula helvetica (134, 170); 2. organ stop of overblowing flue pipes, of narrow scale, recorded from 1489 on. Built at 8', 4', 2', 1' pitches (133).

Schweizertrompete, organ stop: a new name for the overblowing reed trumpet stop (133).

Schweller, Ger.: swell.

Schwellkasten, Ger.: swell box.

Schwiegel, syn. of Schwegel organ stop. Adlung equates Schwiegel 2' or 1' with the *flageolet, 2.

Schwirrholz, Ger.: bull-roarer.

Schwirrscheibe, Ger. disc buzzer.

Scilla, Lat. var. of skella (61).

Scîrtîîtoarea, Rom.: cog rattle (5).

Sco-thom, barrel drum of Cambodia, *ca.* 50 cm. (20 in.) long (176).

Scottish Highland pipe, see: Highland pipe.

Scottish Lowland pipe, see: Lowland pipe.

Scrandola, It. cog rattle used during Easter week.

Scraped idiophone, see: scraper.

Scraper (Fr.: *racle, racleur;* Ger.: *Schraper;* Sp.: *raspadero*), also called scraped idiophone. A solid or hollow body of wood, bone, shell, gourd, or other material is notched on its surface and scraped with a stick. It is found in paleolithic and neolithic Europe, in modern times in Flanders and Italy, Africa, Asia, America, S. Seas. See also: ayotl, banga-banga, cansar, caracacha, carrasca, cassuto, chara, charrasca, chicahuaztli, congoerá, faray, guacharaca, guayo, guïra, guïro, gyo, hiohkat, huli-huli, jawbone, jicotea, joucoujou, kekreng, kemae, kirrkishi, kokkara, kwacha, morache, mukumbi, munkwaka, nkumbi, nkwagasho, nkwaka, nkwimbi, ō, omakola, omichicahuaztli, pandola, payecha, peixet, querequexé, quijada, quilando, reco-reco, resoreso, temraga, yü (168).

Scroll (Fr.: *volute, crosse;* Ger.: *Schnecke;* It.: *voluta, chiocciola, riccio*), the terminal volute of instrs. of the violin family and modern viols, used from the 16th c. on.

Sebet, unidentified instr. of ancient

Egypt, believed by some authors to have been an oblique flute, by others, a cross flute.

Sebizga, syn. of chebuzga.

Seburuburu, *bull-roarer of the Chwana of S. Africa, now a child's toy. *Cf.* sevuruvuru (116).

Seby, misreading of sebet.

Secreet, obs. Du.: wind chest.

Secret, obs. Fr.: wind chest.

Secrétaire, see: piano secrétaire.

Sedecemquinta, organ stop a 5th above the sedecima, *ergo* quint 1⅓' (133).

Sedecima (It.: sixteenth), organ stop, an oct. 2' (occasionally also an oct. 4' or 1') (133).

Sedetz, corr. of sedecima.

See saw laos, see: si so laos.

Sefinjolo, bowed *tube zither of the Chwana of S. Africa; it corresponds to the tsijolo. Also called segankuru, setinkane (116).

Segankuru, syn. of sefinjolo.

Sege-sege [Arab. *shaq-shaq*], in Kanga-Bonu (a Sudanic language) a calabash rattle filled with seeds. *Cf.* sekeseke (93).

Segi, large *cylindrical drum of Burma, with 2 heads and zigzag lacings (176).

Segundilla, Sp.: a small conventual bell.

Segwana (calabash), *musical bow of the Chwana of S. Africa, identical with the uhadi (116).

Sehem, syn. of iba.

Sehgura, *vessel rattle of the Mende of Sierra Leone, made of a gourd with a natural handle. The exterior is partly covered by a network of dried fruit seeds threaded on a cord. It is held by the handle while the player's right hand holds the ends of the cord, plaited into a rope, and agitates them (Collection of the Commonwealth Institute, London).

Sein [Lat. *signum,* sign], OFr.: church bell. There exist numerous vars. of this word. *Cf.* sino, tocsin.

Seistron (Gk.: a thing shaken), **1.** Gk. name of the ancient Egyptian temple rattle, later called sistrum in Lat.; **2.** new Gk.: bell clapper (176).

Sei teki, *cross flute of Japan, made

of bamboo, with 6 front fingerholes and an additional hole between blowhole and fingerholes, covered by a thin membrane —a mirliton device. It corresponds to the Chin. ti. *Ca.* 53 cm. (21 in.) long (157, 170).

Seitenbart, Ger.: ears.

Seitenpfeife (Ger.: side pipe), wooden *cross flute of Austria, without keys; a folk instr., particularly of the Salzkammergut, where 2 or 3 are played together. In other parts of Austria it is called Schwegel (117).

Sekatari, bowed *tube zither of the Sotho of Basutoland; it corresponds to the tsijolo (116).

Seke [Arab. **shaq-shaq*], in Gazu (a Sudanic language), rattle (93).

Se ken hsien erh, see: su ken hsien erh.

Seke-seke [Arab. **shaq-shaq*], calabash rattle of the Agni of W. Africa (93).

Sekgapa, 1. *musical bow of the Sotho of Transvaal, identical with the uhadi, 1; **2.** musical bow of the Sotho, Bakwele, and Balubedu of S. Africa, with tuning loop, identical with the dende, 2 (116).

Sekgobogobo, bowed *tube zither of the Sotho of Transvaal, identical with the tsijolo. Also called setsegetsege (116).

Sekitulege, ground bow of the Ganda of Uganda, a child's toy (195).

Sekund, Ger.: second (with reference to size or pitch).

Sekundfiedel, name given to the second fiddle in a Klarfiedel quartet (117).

Selantan, see: slentem.

Selăsil, see: salăsil.

Seljefløyte, Nor. rustic pipe, made of the bark of the sallow during May and June. *Ca.* 60 cm. (2 ft.) long (89).

Selokat, Jogya name of the saron panerus (121).

Selompret, wooden shawm of Java, with slightly conical bore, flaring bell, 6 front fingerholes, and a rear thumbhole. It is not found in *gamelan.* In the ancient Hindu-Javanese literature it was called pleret. *Ca.* 45 cm. (18 in.) long. Also called serompret, sompret. See also: sa-

ronen, serunen, tarompet, tetepret (121).

Selslīm (Heb.) [*salāl,* clash], cymbals of ancient Israel, in use *ca.* 1100 B.C., called slasal in Talmudic writings. See also: metziltāyīm, sil, sil-sil, salāsil, silsnyau, zil. *Cf.* shalishīm (170).

Semakkalam, bell-metal gong of India, without boss, suspended from a short wooden cylinder. It is played with the left hand while the right hand plays a thappattai. Both a temple instr. and that of mendicants and of the Dāsaris, Pandarams, and people of Panichavam caste. Also called sōmangalam (179).

Semanterion (Gk.: signal), wooden percussion board of considerable antiquity, struck with a hammer, used in the Gk. Orthodox Church in lieu of bells, particularly during Easter week. The church Lat. term for it is lignum sacrum. See also: agiosideron, han, klepalche, klepalo, klepavka, klepetalo.

Semantron, see: semanterion.

Sembe, small drum of the Basire and Abandya of the Congo, in form of a truncated barrel, with laced heads, only one of which is played. The lacings form a network over the body; 45–90 cm. (18–35 in.) long (30).

Sembilan, see: gong sembilan.

Semicontrabassoon (Ger.: *Halbkontrafagott*), modern expression that denotes a bassoon pitched a 4th or 5th lower than the ordinary bassoon.

Semi-luna, a name of the nail violin, from the shape of its resonator.

Senafil, see: añafil.

Sendaren, syn. of sundaren.

Sendari, var. of sundari.

Sendiu, *double clarinet of the Padaung Dayak of W. Borneo, consisting of 2 narrow tubes of slightly different lengths with idioglott reeds. One pipe has 5 fingerholes; the other has 1 fingerhole (176).

Sengwelembwe, sansa of the Ababua of the Congo (19).

Seno, panpipes of the Chayahuita Indians of Ecuador and Peru, with 12 pipes (105).

Šenterija, syn. of oprekelj (144).

Sentuang, bamboo *cross flute of Malaya, with 3 fingerholes (176).

Seny [Lat. *signum*], obs. Cat.: bell.

Septième (Fr.), see: seventh (organ stop).

Septime (Ger.), see: seventh (organ stop).

Ser, frame drum of ancient Egypt that first appears in the 18th dynasty (89, 96).

Seraphim [Heb., pl. of *seraph*], *musical glasses consisting of a set of graduated, stemmed glasses inserted by their stems into a special frame that could be used as a table when closed. They were made in Europe and America in the early 19th c.

Seraphine [*seraph*], free-reed keyboard instr. resembling the physharmonica, invented by John Green in England in 1833, with a compass of 5 octs., F^0-f^3, and capable of both crescendo and decrescendo. Later any free-reed instr. working on the principle of the *American organ was known in England as seraphine. Various improvements of Green's instr. were patented between 1839 and 1851. Also called Royal Seraphine. See also: organo-harmonica (80 XII, 89 Hipkins, 204, Oxford English Dictionary).

Seraphone, 1. free-reed automatophone with keyboard, patented by C. F. Pietschmann et Fils in France on Sept. 26, 1876; **2.** organ stop invented by G. F. Weigle of Stuttgart in 1901, with two mouths at right angles to each other. Depending upon its construction, the seraphone is classed as Seraphon-Prinzipal, Seraphon-Flöte, Seraphon-Gamba, etc. (133, 204).

Serbung, E. Java and Madura name of the gumbang (121).

Serēre, whistle of the S. American Choco Indians, also of the Chiriguano and Yurucare. It originated in Peru and consists of a piece of rectangular wood with conical bore, held vertically, suspended from the player's neck on a cord; 11–55 cm. (4–21½ in.) long (105).

Serimba, see: silimba.

Serinette [Fr. *serin*, finch], small *bird organ for teaching finches to sing; by extension, generic term for bird organs.

Seringonási, panpipes of the Kandoshi Indians of Ecuador and Peru (105).

Sernei (Mal.) [Pers. *surnāy*], shawm of Malaya, of the zurnā type (18).

Serompret, syn. of selompret.

Seron, *harp lute of the Malinke of the Republic of Guinea, with 15–19 strings. Those with 15 strings are played as follows: the right hand plucks $c\sharp^0 c\sharp^0 g^0 b^0 d^1 f\sharp^1 a^1 b^1$, the left hand, $B^0 d^0 f^0 b\flat^0 c^1 e\flat^1 g^1$. *Ca.* 1.50 m. (5 ft.) high. Equivalent to the bolon and kora (42, 103).

Seror-ē, heteroglott clarinet of the Warrau Indians of Venezuela, with gourd resonator (105).

Serpent (Fr.) (Ger.: *Serpent, Schlangenrohr;* It.: *serpentone;* Sp.: *serpentón*), **1.** woodwind instr. of bass register, so named because of its serpentine form, and said to have been invented in 1590 by Canon Edme Guillaume of Auxerre, France. Recent investigation of claims for greater antiquity and It. origin of the instr. have failed to upset this attribution. The serpent consists of an S-shaped wooden tube of extremely wide bore, the shape being necessary in order to bring the fingerholes of so large an instr. into playable position. The tube is about 2.10 m. (7 ft.) long, covered with black leather, and carries a crook *ca.* 30 cm. (12 in.) long, bringing the total length to some 2.40 m. (8 ft.). Two groups of 3 fingerholes each are spaced about 30 cm. (12 in.) apart, convenient for fingering if not in strict accordance with the laws of acoustics. In its early days the instr. was devoid of keys. It was played with a narrow-rimmed cup mouthpiece of ivory or horn, later, in military bands, often made of metal. The serpent is commonly referred to as the bass instr. of the cornett family, but should perhaps more correctly be considered as allied to the cornetts and serving as their bass. (In 1730 Bailey wrote of it as "serving as bass to the cornet or small shawm.") For the first c. of its existence, if not longer, the serpent was an ecclesiastic instr. exclusively; it doubled liturgical chant (men's voices) at the unison, and as far as we know its use was confined to France. From there it subsequently spread to Flanders, England, and Germany. Praetorius does not mention it, but Mersenne gives a description; the instr. was then shorter than the 18th-c. model and its fundamental was E. The occasions on which we learn of nonecclesiastic uses are rare, but Trichet, writing *ca.* 1640, informs us the serpent was used for bass parts in instrumental consorts; he calls it the true double bass of the cornett and describes it as generally 6 ft. in length without the crook, with a compass of a 17th, and 6 fingerholes of which the lowest was supplied with a key inside a fontanelle. He also says that mouthpiece and crook could be made of one piece, about a half a foot long, and that the best woods for making serpents were walnut, plum, or sorb. The serpent was known in England by the late 17th c. and is mentioned by Talbot writing at the turn of the c.; to Kircher in the mid-17th c. it was still a Fr. instr. (in Flanders keyless serpents were still to be found in churches a c. ago, though). Clumsy as it may have been, the serpent had the undisputed advantage of power and a wide dynamic range, and by the 18th c. military bandmasters were becoming aware of this. By the mid-18th c. it was gaining admission to military bands and began to be scored for in Ger. military marches, while continuing its existence in the church, thus ultimately leading to the *serpent d'église and the *serpent militaire. In the first half of the 19th c. the serpent took the part of the contrabassoon in France, as the latter was not made there until later in the c. With new life infused into it as a band instr., the serpent gradually was supplied with keys; by 1800 3 closed keys were standard, although in Engl. military bands 4 keys

had been adopted in the late 18th c. Keys continued to be added until a total of 14 was reached. Open extension keys were never used: the tendency was toward a higher, not lower, compass. Around 1800 metal serpents were occasionally made. The serpent remained in military grace until the advent of the tuba and bass-horn displaced it. In 1835, the year in which the tuba was introduced, Gustav Schilling could write (*Universal Lexikon der Tonkunst*) that the serpent should not be lacking among instrs. of bass register. Some bands retained their serpents until the mid-19th c., and Spain actually had serpents in 3 bands in 1884. Angul Hammerich reported having heard the serpent played in a Paris church in 1870, and it was still in use in many Fr. village churches in the first quarter of the 20th c. The first half of the 19th c. even saw its appearance in opera and symphony orchestras. In 1788, Regibo, a musician of the Collegiate Church of St. Peter, Lille, built the first bassoon-shaped serpent; little is known about it except that it was demountable in 3 sections, allegedly sounded louder and was easier to play than the conventional instr., and cost 3 carolins. He thus abolished the serpentine form and opened the way for a number of upright versions far easier to play, as they could be held bassoon-wise. The earliest of these was the *serpent Piffault. Owing to the interaction of huge bore, fingerholes, and cup mouthpiece, with concomitant degree of control exercised by the player's lips, considerable leeway was experienced in both compass and pitch. The former is said to have varied between 2½ and 3½ octs. From the 18th c. on the serpent was considered on the European Continent to have D as its fundamental, in England, C. However, by varying the lip tension it is possible to produce tones as much as a 4th lower than the fundamental. Morley-Pegge reports (in 89, "Serpent") that of 8 fingering charts published between *ca.* 1760 and *ca.* 1835, no 2 agree as to fingering or compass; most of them give C[0] as the lowest tone.

The serpent was made by hollowing out 2 blocks of wood, fitting and gluing them together, and covering them in leather. But in 19th-c. England they were made in short overlapping sections, permitting more acute curves, and Engl. instrs. are readily recognized by their compact form with U bends rather than S curves. Contrabass serpents twice the size of the ordinary serpent and sounding an oct. below it were devised in 19th-c. England. One such has survived: built in 1840, it was played in a church for over 20 years and measures 4.75 m. (15 ft. 7 in.). Another, pitched in E♭, by James Jordan of Liverpool, was shown at the 1851 London Exhibition. The contrabass serpent is also called contra-serpent. See also: basse-cor, euphonic serpentcleide, ophibaryton, serpent d'église, serpent Forveille, serpent militaire, serpent Piffault;

2. organ stop of reed pipes, known in the 18th c. and found chiefly in Fr. organs. It is built either in inverted conical or in cylindrical form (80 XII, 89 Langwill, Morley-Pegge; 91, 190, 133).

Serpent anglais, a Fr. name of the Engl.-made bass-horn.

Serpent-basson, Fr.: Russian bassoon.

Serpent bombardon, an improved ophicleide in F, invented by Vaclav Červeny of Königgrätz (Hradec Králové) ca. 1840 (176).

Serpentcleide [serpent + Gk. *kleides,* key], ophicleide of unknown construction, invented either by Beacham or by Charles Huggett of London, or by Thomas MacBean Glen of Edinburgh, said to have been made of wood. One was played in London in 1846, and serpentcleides with 11 keys were offered for sale in 1855 (89).

Serpent d'église (Fr.: church serpent), 19th-c. term denoting the serpentine form of serpent played in churches, as opposed to the upright serpent of military bands.

Serpent droit, Fr.: Russian bassoon.

Serpent Forveille, a variety of upright serpent devised by a Parisian maker named Forveille by 1833, when it was first exhibited. The instr. was of brass except for a wooden bell section and consisted of 2 sharp U bends. Earlier models had 3 keys, later ones 4, in addition to the 6 fingerholes. The mouthpiece was carried on a crook. Fingering remained that of the ordinary serpent. Turlot of Paris (fl. 1829–39), apparently a pupil of Forveille, also made them. Also called basson Forveille (89).

Serpent militaire (Fr.), upright serpent used in 19th-c. military bands, such as the *serpent Piffault, or those by Tabard of Lyon made of wood with a double bore, terminating in a copper bell and pitched in C (89, 132).

Serpentón, Sp.: serpent.

Serpentone, It.: serpent.

Serpent Piffault, serpent in upright form, devised for military bands by Piffault of Paris in 1806. Its form made it considerably easier to manage, especially when marching, than the serpentine model. Also called serpent militaire (126).

Serubayi, syn. of sarune.

Serulo, panpipes of the Omoa and Buhagama Indians of S. America (105).

Serunai [Pers. *surnāy], name of the surnāy in Sumatra. *Cf.* srune, zurnā (121).

Serunen [Pers. *surnāy], E. Java and Madura name of the selompret (121).

Serutu, *ring flute of W. Borneo, with bamboo ring and 5 fingerholes arranged in 2 groups, one of 3, the other of 2 (176).

Sesando, *tube zither of Timor that occurs in both idioglott and heteroglott forms. In the latter copper strings are strung pairwise all around the tube and secured by tuning pegs. The tube is surrounded by a palm-leaf resonator (119).

Sese, see: seze.

Seseri, panpipes of the Kuerutu Indians of Brazil and Colombia (105).

Sesheshet, sistrum of ancient Egypt,

shaped like a *naos* (temple), with a heavy frame resembling a small temple seen from the front. Wires were strung loosely across the frame, pierced on both sides for this purpose. At a later date jingling metal discs were added, taken over from the *iba. This form of sistrum is not found outside Egypt. Also called naos sistrum (170).

Sesquialtera (Lat.), mixture organ stop composed of 2 ranks of pipes, a quint 2⅔' and tierce 1⅗'. This represents a ratio of 5:3, not 3:2, as its name calls for (sesquialtera means 1½ to 1). Adlung knew it also as a 3-rank mixture with added oct. 4'. An oct. 2' can also be added (3, 133).

Sesquialtera bass, sesquialtera at 10⅔' and 6⅖' pitch (133).

Sestino [dim. of It. *sesto,* sixth], small It. clarinet in A♭, a 6th higher than the ordinary clarinet. *Cf.* Sextklarinette.

Setār (Pers.: three strings), **1.** Pers. long lute with 3 strings, similar in other details to the dutar; **2.** syn. of sitār.

Setara, Beng.: sitār.

Setinkane, syn. of sefinjolo.

Setolotolo, pl. **litolotolo,** *musical bow of the Sotho of Basutoland, with one string looped to the bow. Played by male persons only (116).

Setsegetsege, syn. of sekgobogobo.

Settimino [dim. of It. *settimo,* seventh], small It. clarinet in high B♭, a 7th above the ordinary clarinet. *Cf.* sestino.

Setukat, name of the bonang panerus in W. Java. Also called gembyang (121).

Setzstück (Ger.), loop-shaped crook of variable length, inserted between main tube and mouthpiece of brass instrs. in order to change their tonality.

Seventeenth, mutation organ stop of open metal flue pipes, a 17th above the fundamental, or an oct. above the tierce (1⅗' from 8').

Seventh (Fr.: *septième;* Ger.: *Septime*), mutation organ stop of open metal flue pipes, a 7th above the fundamental,

at 4⁴⁄₇', 2²⁄₇', or 1¹⁄₇' pitch. See also: flat twenty-first.

Sevuruvuru, *bull-roarer of the Sotho of Basutoland. *Cf.* seburuburu (116).

Sexquialtera, see: sesquialtera.

Sexta, tierce organ stop, so called because its tonal position is a 6th above the quint (*e.g.,* tierce 1⅗', a 6th above quint 2⅔') (133).

Sextklarinette (Ger.), clarinet in high A♭, a 6th above the ordinary clarinet, played chiefly in military bands. It corresponds to the It. sestino. *Cf.* piccolo clarinet.

Seze, Swah. term for the *bar zither. That of the Washambala of Kenya has 1 or 2 resonators of calabash neck or of gourd, and several strings, one of which passes over a bridge. The instr. is very reminiscent of the Indian vīnā. The open bottom of the resonator is held against the player's chest. That of the Baluba and Babembe has 1 string and 3 very high frets. The Mbanja of the Congo also call their stick zither by this name. See also: dyedye, enzenze, nzenze, zeze, 2 (19, 111, 128).

Sgra-snyau, bowed chordophone of Tibet, about two-thirds the size of a violin, with 4 strings of which the first and third, second and fourth are unisons, terminating usually in a carved horse's head. The bow remains attached to the instr. Its yak-hair strings pass between strings 1 and 2 and between 3 and 4, so that 2 strings are always sounded together (1 and 3 or 2 and 4). It serves purely secular functions and is possibly of Mongolian origin. Also called k'o-pong (89 Picken).

Sgrigias, cog rattle of Oberhalbstein, Switzerland (102).

Sguilla [Lat. *scilla*], It.: cattle bell (176).

Shabbāba, *end-blown flute of Islam, made of cane, half the size of the qasaba, with 6 front fingerholes and 1 rear thumbhole. In med. Spain, where it had been imported by the Moors, it became known as axabeba or ajabeba; in the

Malagasy Republic it is called sobaba (170).

Shabbai, flute of the Druse of Israel (103).

Shabitu, Akk. equivalent of sabitu.

Shabur, see: shyabur.

Shagbushe, 16th-c. Engl.: sackbut.

Shāh, medium-sized modern Turk. nāy. *Cf.* mansūr, nāy shāh, qīz (76).

Shāhrūd, archlute of ancient Persia, known from the 10th c. on, with an original compass of 3 octs. (147 Farmer).

Shaifur, see: shaipūr.

Shaing, horn of Cambodia (47).

Shaipūr (Pers.) [Aram. *shopara*], straight trumpet of Persia. *Cf.* shephor, shofar (98).

Shakbott, corr. of sackbut.

Shakbush, corr. of sackbut.

Shaken idiophone (Fr.: *idiophone par secouement;* Ger.: *Schüttelidiophon*), the same as rattle.

Shākh, Pers. shawm (98).

Shak-shak, name of the maraca among the Negroes of the Guianas (152).

Shaku byoshi, clappers of Japan, made of 2 thin squares of wood and used in *gagaku* (court music) and Shinto music (135).

Shaku gyo, *stick rattle of Japan. A number of small metal rings are strung on a large ring attached to the top of a wooden staff. An attribute of the god Jizo (148, 178).

Shaku hachi, *notched flute of Japan, introduced from China in 935. It is made of thick bamboo lacquered on the inside, with a small notch, wide bore, 4 front fingerholes, and a rear thumbhole, terminating in a slight flare. The pitch tone of Japan is taken from the lowest tone of the shaku hachi at 292 cps, with a standard length of 54.5 cm. (*ca.* 21½ in.). The shaku hachi is thicker and longer than the hitoyogiri. From the 16th c. on it has been played by the *komuso,* wandering priests wearing a basket over the head. See also: hitoyogiri (135, 177).

Shakwa, small drum of the Wanande of the Congo, reserved for the personal

entertainment of the *mwami* (great chief) (30).

Shalamo, obs. Engl. var. of chalumeau.

Shalishīm (Heb.), a disputed word mentioned once in the Bible (I Samuel 18:6), possibly a dance, possibly an instr. but *cf.* selslīm (89).

Shalme, var. of shawm.

Shalmeye [MEngl. schallemelle], early form of the word shawm.

Sha lo, gong of China, first mentioned in the 6th c., its introduction being ascribed by tradition to "barbarians" *i.e.,* aliens, of the West (144, 170).

Shaltva, pastoral, end-blown *whistle flute of Yugoslavia with 6 fingerholes (176).

Shalva, var. of shaltva.

Shambu kaw, *end-blown flute of Ethiopia, generally of bamboo, sometimes of metal, with 4 fingerholes. Played as a solo instr. (45).

Shamisen, see: samisen.

Shamshal, see: shemshal.

Shamshīr (Pahl.), unidentified instr. of ancient Persia.

Shandze, Mongolian chordophone of Chin. origin; it corresponds to the san hsien. Plucked with a plectrum or bare fingers (69).

Shank, a piece of straight tubing inserted between mouthpiece and body of a brass instr. to lower its pitch slightly. Also called tuning bit. See also: crook, Einsatzbogen, Setzstück.

Shanka (Sans., Beng., Kan.), endblown *marine-shell trumpet of India, usually made of a slim, white *Turbinella rapa,* pierced at the tip and frequently decorated. An attribute of Vishnu, the shanka is a sacred temple instr. Today it serves religious functions only, but formerly it was used as a signal instr. in wartime. See also: bakura, sankh (170, 179).

Shannāi, see: sānāyī.

Shantu, percussion gourd of the Hausa of Nigeria, with open top and bottom, and decorated. It is played by women only (185).

Shao, see also: hsiao.

Shao erh, clay toy whistle of China, made in a variety of forms, 6–7½ cm. (2½–3 in.) long. Some are provided with 2 fingerholes, others have none (142).

Shapar, bagpipe of the Chuvash of U.S.S.R. *Cf.* shyabur (13).

Shaqef, Arab.: tambourine (98).

Shaqira, see: al shaqira.

Shaq-shaq (Arab.) [Turk. *chaqchaq*], rattle of the Arabs and Moors of N. Africa (93).

Sharada, Tamil equivalent of sarōd.

Shāradīyā vīnā, see: sāradīyā vīnā.

Sharghy [Turk. **sharqī*], tanbūr of Croatia, Bosnia, and Herzegovina, with elongated body and 5 or 7 strings. These are tuned (relative pitch) $f^1 f^1 c^1 g^1 g^1$, with one shorter string, about half length, tuned an oct. above the lowest or the highest string. The same instr. exists in Bulgaria. *Cf.* sharqī (89, 144).

Sharp mixture, see: Scharf.

Sharqī, (Turk.: eastern) Turk. tanbūr with 3–5 strings, similar to the chartār. *Cf.* sharghy (76).

Sharqoqitha (Heb.) [*sharaq,* to whistle], name given in Talmudic times to the mashroqītā (147 Farmer).

Sharud, see: sarōd.

Shashkāna, long-necked, single-stringed lute of 17th-c. Turkey (76).

Shashtār (Pers.: six strings), small 6-stringed lute of the Near East, known since the Middle Ages, with piriform body and membrane belly. One variety was short-necked, another long-necked, and a third had 15 pairs of sympathetic strings. Today it is obs. except in Persia, Azerbaijan, and Caucasia. *Cf.* chartār, dutār, panchtār, setār (75 II, 76).

Shatatantri vīnā, see: satatantri vīnā.

Shautika vīnā, see: sautika vīnā.

Shawm [Lat. **calamus*] (Fr.: *chalemie, hautbois;* Ger.: *Schalmei;* It.: *piffaro;* Sp.: *chirimía*), **1.** obs. woodwind instr. consisting of a conically bored wooden tube, played with a double reed, introduced to Europe from the Near East in the 12th c., probably by way of Italy and the Balkans. It remained in use until the 17th c., when it was replaced by its offspring, the oboe. The shawm has survived in Spain, where it still flourishes as **tiple and **tenora. The European shawm was made of a single piece of wood terminating in a bell; its double reed was mounted on a conical metal staple, with a wooden **pirouette giving support to the player's lips. Of its 7 front fingerholes the lowest was duplicated for the accommodation of left- or right-hand players. All fingerholes were situated in the upper half of the instr., the lower portion being provided with ventholes. The reed is described by James Talbot (*ca.* 1700) as about 1.2 cm. (½ in.) wide at the top and 3 cm. (1¼ in.) long. In the course of the 13th c. the shawm came into common use and from the early 14th c. it is found in town bands. It played an important part as a component of "loud" music. From the mid-14th c. on a larger size, called **bombard, was also being made; in 1390 bombard and "shalemele" are mentioned together. By the 16th c. a whole family had appeared, whereupon the word "shawm" was reserved exclusively for the soprano instr. (for larger sizes see: bombard). Praetorius in the 17th c. also listed a sopranino (*klein Schalmey*) on b¹, the ordinary shawm being on d¹. In the last quarter of the c. a very slender model came into use in Germany, called **deutsche Schalmei, which maintained itself until *ca.* 1720.

During the 16th c. a new family of shawms appeared, often called "reed-cap shawms." They had a wide conical bore, and their reeds were enclosed in **reed caps. In France they were known as **hautbois de Poitou. The basset shawm (Nicolo) of Praetorius also shows a reed cap and is the only one of his shawms to do so. They do not seem to have had a wide diffusion. Surviving specimens of reed-cap shawms are preserved in the

Berlin and Prague museums; they have 7 front fingerholes, the lowest brought into the player's reach by a swallow-tailed key set in a fontanelle. The tube ends with no more than a suggestion of a flare;

2. the organ stop of this name is the same as the hautbois organ stop (36, 89 Baines, 180).

Shē, *long zither of China, with convex surface; in antiquity it had 50 strings, now reduced to 25, each with its own triangular bridge, and tuned to a pentatonic scale. The instr. is richly ornamented with lacquerwork. Ca. 2 m. (80 in.) long and 46 cm. (18 in.) wide (4, 142).

Shegandi (Tamil), metal percussion plaque of S. Indian temples; 20–30 cm. (8–12 in.) in diam. (173).

Shekere, gourd rattle of the Yoruba of Nigeria. Cf. chekeré (103).

Shem (Sum.) cylindrical *double pipe of ancient Babylon; it first appears in the third millennium B.C. and corresponds to the Akk. halhallatu (89 Galpin).

Shemshal, oboe of the Kurds (170).

Sheneb, see: chnouē.

Sheng, free-reed *mouth organ of China, mentioned ca. 1100 B.C. but not depicted until the 6th c. A.C. It is considered the ancestor of all our free-reed instrs. (see: free reed). The sheng's elegant form is traditionally said to be that of the phoenix. The instr. consists of a wind chest and pipes. Originally the wind chest was a small gourd or calabash, its natural neck serving as mouthpiece and wind trunk; today it is made of lacquered wood with a shorter mouthpiece. The bamboo pipes are usually 17 in number; their lower ends are fitted with metal free reeds and are inserted into the wind chest in circular fashion. They are of 5 different lengths, arranged symmetrically. Not all of the pipes speak: in a set of 17, 4 are not provided with reeds, but act as dummies to complete the symmetry. Some of the speaking pipes have slotted backs, and each pipe is pierced with a small

lateral hole just above the rim of the wind chest; this must be closed if the pipe is to speak. The sheng is played in slow chords, several holes being covered simultaneously by the player's fingers while it is held cupped in both hands. The reeds are set in motion both by inhalation and exhalation. See also: fong sheng, ho, ho sheng.

Shepherd's harp, name given in late-17th-c. England to a rectangular psaltery (79).

Shepherd's pipe, in the U.S. a simple whistle flute of bamboo. Cf. bamboo pipe.

Shephor, Armenian: trumpet (176).

Sher, var. of ser.

Sheshta, see: shashtār.

Shi chi gen kin (Jap.: seven-stringed kin), koto of Japan, with curved, lacquered board tapering in width, with lateral indentations, and 7 silk strings; one of these is a melody string, the others are drones; 13 small mother-of-pearl discs are inlaid in the soundboard under the melody string to indicate the stopping points. The strings are tied to silk loops fastened underneath the board. The drones are played in sweeping arpeggios of the right thumb. Ca. 120 cm. (4 ft.) long (157, 178).

Shidirghū, chordophone described in the 15th c. by Ibn Ghaibi as having 4 strings, the lowest 3 of which were tuned like those of the 'ūd; half of its belly was of skin. It was played chiefly by the Chinese (75 II).

Shidūrghūr, chordophone of E. Turkestan (176).

Shi gen, syn. of genkwan (170).

Shi gen kin, syn. of shi chi gen kin (176).

Shikolombane, drum of the Thonga of S. Africa, similar to the muntshintshi, with which it is played together, but devoid of legs and of more elongated form. Possibly influenced by the Venda (116).

Shime daiko, syn. of uta daiko (157).

Shin gane, small den sho (176).

Shinguvo, small cuneiform *slit drum

of the Congo, played by the Baloi, Bambole, Banziri, Kalunda-Kazembe, Kundu, Losakani, Mongo, Mussumba, Tofoke, Waruwa (19).

Shino fuye, cylindrical *cross flute of Japan, made of bamboo, with 7 equidistant fingerholes. *Cf.* take fuye (144).

Shin sō, syn. of gaku sō (144).

Shipalapala, side-blown horn of the S. African Thonga, made of the horn of the sable antelope, the kudu, etc. See also: mpalapala, phalaphala (116).

Shiragi koto, 1. 6-stringed *angular harp of Korea, of great antiquity; **2.** obs. koto of ancient Japan, introduced from Korea. It became obs. during the Heian period (9th to 12th c.). Also called kaya kin (144, 148).

Shishak, see: ghichak, ghizhak.

Shitiringo, see: tshitiringo.

Shitloti, *cross flute of the Thonga of S. Africa, identical with the tshitiringo (116).

Shiwaya, *globular flute of the Thonga of S. Africa, made of *strychnos* shell, with blowhole and 2 fingerholes—the only globular flute found in S. Africa. It is blown like a *cross flute (116).

Shkewa, bagpipe of Algeria, similar to the zūkra (13).

Shnb, see: chnouē.

Sho, free-reed *mouth organ of Japan, very similar to the sheng of China. Generally it has 17 bamboo pipes set in a cup-shaped wind chamber of lacquered wood in symmetrical order, forming a circle. Pipe Numbers 2 and 9 are dummies that complete the symmetry. All are so arranged that those opposite one another are of the same height. The speaking length of each pipe is determined by a slot in the back. The reeds are of metal and, as with the sheng, remain silent until a side hole in the pipe is closed by the player's hand (135, 157).

Shofar (Heb.) (Fr.: *chofar;* Ger.: *Schofar*), ritual horn of the ancient and modern Hebrews, the only Heb. cult instr. to have survived until now. Made

of a natural ram's-horn or ibex horn, the shofar has traditionally been played without a separate mouthpiece, and produces only 2 sounds—very rough ones at that. Of martial origin, the shofar was a priestly instr. in biblical times. According to the Mishna, 2 different forms were employed in the Temple: that sounded at New Year and during the Yovel Days was a straight ibex horn, its bell ornamented with gold; that sounded on fast days was a curved ram's-horn with silver ornamentation. After the destruction of the Temple it became a cult instr. of the synagogue—its only one, in fact. We learn from the Mishna and the Talmud that in the Hellenistic period no improvements or modifications that might affect the tone were permitted: no gold-plating of its interior, no plugging of holes, no alteration of its length (the minimum permissible length of a ritually approved horn was 3 handbreadths); the shofar tone was to be preserved unaltered. Nor was the process of steaming or boiling permitted. In C. and E. Europe a straight form of shofar with bent-back bell is in use, reminiscent of the Roman lituus; its bell is often serrated; nowadays such horns are immersed in boiling water to soften them sufficiently for bending to the required angle. Elsewhere the shofar has retained the unaltered animal-horn shape. Apart from its liturgical uses the shofar was closely connected with magical symbolism. Its blast destroyed the walls of Jericho, and in the Dead Sea scrolls we read that during battles shofar blowers sounded a powerful war cry to instill fear into the hearts of the enemy while priests blew the six "trumpets of killing." In the apocalyptic literature it assumed a new function, that of announcing doomsday, which function became symbolically associated with the resurrection of Israel. Historically the shofar has also served in a number of pop. usages: it was sounded during rites to bring rain, in **the event of local dis-**

asters, etc. In our times its liturgical use is restricted to New Year and the Day of Atonement. The word *shofar* is related to the Sum. *sheg-bar* or *zag-bar*, the male wild goat or ibex (84, 144 Hickmann, H. Avenary: "Magic . . . of the Old Hebrew Sound Instruments," in: *Collectanea historiae musicae*, II, Florence, 1957).

Sho hitsu no koto, very long koto of ancient Japan, with 25 strings, ornamented with precious stones. *Ca.* 2.20 m. (7 ft. 3 in.) long. *Cf.* hitsu no koto (157).

Shoko, bronze gong of Japan, with turned rim, suspended from a lacquered frame and played with 2 knobbed beaters, used in *gagaku* and *bugaku* music. It is made in several sizes (135, 157).

Sho ku, percussion trough of Japan, of wood or metal, with a movable clapper fixed inside with which the player strikes the sides (157).

Shong nong, Jew's-harp of Thailand (176).

Sho no fuye, panpipes of Japan that correspond to the p'ai hsiao of China, with 22 pipes arranged in raft form, the longest ones being in the center. Smaller models, with 12 or 16 pipes, are also made. The largest pipe is about 43 cm. (17 in.) long (157).

Short octave (Fr.: *octave courte;* Ger.: *kurze Oktave;* obs. It.: *mi re ut*), arrangement for saving space and pipes in the lowest octave of organs, both in manuals and pedal, by omitting unneeded keys and pipes. This arrangement seems to have been known by the 14th c. and was taken over by stringed keyboard instrs. by the late 15th c. (Ramis de Pareja); both types of instr. retained them in some instances as late as the 18th c. When manual and pedal compass of organs was extended downward from C or B to F, the accidentals of the lowest oct. (except Bb) were omitted as unnecessary, and the keys of that oct. were then rearranged as follows:

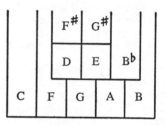

By the early 17th c. the missing low F♯ and G♯ were needed, and in order to supply these without enlarging the keyboard, 2 *split keys were introduced:

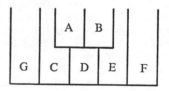

The front portions of the keys controlled the D and E pipes, the rear portion the F♯ and G♯ pipes. On stringed keyboard instrs. this type of keyboard is rarely met with before 1700. Although the C short oct., as the above version is called, was by far the most common, other arrangements of the low oct. existed, notably the G short oct.:

resulting from a downward extension to G, and also completed by split keys on occasion. Other patterns have been encountered on organs, but only in isolated instances.

Shotang, *angular harp of the Ostyak of the U.S.S.R., similar to those of ancient Egypt and Further India, made occasionally with a pillar. The resonator, *ca.* 1 m. (40 in.) long, continues in a swan's neck and often terminates in a carved bird's head. The metal strings, 6–10 in number, are fastened by turnable wooden pegs. *Cf.* torop-jux (144).

Shoulder harp (Fr.: *harpe epaulée;* Ger.: *Schulterharfe*), small *arched harp of the Middle and New Kingdoms of ancient Egypt, with 3–5 strings and membrane belly. It rested on the player's left shoulder, with its neck projecting behind.

Shringa, see: sringa.

Shruti, see: sruti.

Shu'aibīya (Arab.), panpipes of Egypt that correspond to the mūsīqāl (147 Farmer).

Shuang ch'in, flat lute of China, with octagonal body of hardwood, short neck with frets, 4 strings in pairs, tuned a 5th apart, and is played with a plectrum. It corresponds to the genkwan of Japan (142, 170).

Shu ch'iu, *vessel rattle of N. China, consisting of 2 hollow iron globes, *ca.* 4½ cm. (1¾ in.) in diam., each containing a small metal ball (142).

Shu ku, *frame drum of China with 2 nailed heads, tapped with the player's fingers. *Ca.* 20 cm. (8 in.) in diam. (142).

Shu k'ung hu, syn. of k'ung hu.

Shun, *resting bell of Chin. Buddhist temples, a heavy bronze basin of varying size, placed open side up on a cushion and struck with a round wooden stick on its edge. Its pop. name is ch'ing. When Moule wrote, the largest shun was in Hangchow and measured 75 cm. (2½ ft.) in diam. (142).

Shunga, ancient chordophone of Japan, bowed, similar to the kokyu, but with 4 strings and 5 frets (157).

Shu pan, clappers of China, made of redwood slabs, used in Confucian rituals. They replace the obs. *ch'ung tu. *Ca.* 40 cm. (16 in.) long (142).

Shupelka, flute of Yugo. Macedonia, without mouthpiece, provided with 6 fingerholes. *Ca.* 30 cm. (12 in.) long. *Cf.* Sopilka (89).

Shuqaifāt, word for clappers among the Syrian Arabs. The instr. corresponds to the musāfiq (147 Farmer).

Shutka, see: šutka.

Shutky, see: šutky.

Shuttle pipe, obs. bellows-blown bagpipe of Northumberland, of which only 2 specimens are known. They had short, Northumbrian-style chanters, and drones of the musette pattern with double reeds. They date from the late 17th c. (89).

Shwegu, syn. of mulizi. *Cf.* schwegel.

Shyabur, mouth-blown bagpipe of the Cheremiss of the U.S.S.R., with bag of cow bladder, and a double chanter consisting of 2 cylindrical pipes cradled in a gutter, and terminating in a common bell of cowhorn. The pipes are fitted with single reeds. The right pipe has 4 fingerholes, the left has 2, irregularly spaced. *Cf.* shapar (13).

Si, Burmese: drum (176).

Siao, see: hsiao.

Siao po, cymbals of China (91).

Siao t'ung kyo, straight trumpet of China, with conical tube made in 2 or 3 sections that telescope into one another, terminating in a large bell. Made of brass with bosses between the sections. A wide and shallow mouthpiece is attached to the upper end. The instr. came to China, where its pop. name is la pa, from Mongolia and Tibet. Originally its function was military, now a religious one. When not in use, or "folded," it measures about 1.50 m. (5 ft.). *Cf.* cha chiao, rapa, rapal (170).

Sibilus, Lat.: pipe, whistle.

Siblet [Lat. *sibilus,* whistle], OFr.: a whistle, particularly a bird whistle. The term was in use from the early 14th c. on. Also written sublet (82, 85).

Sibs, modern name of a small Egyptian oboe (170).

Sico (Aymara), small antara in form of single or double panpipes. *Cf.* ayarichi (192).

Side drum, Engl. equivalent of snare drum.

Sieb, Ger.: guide, lower guide.

Sierszenki, siesienki, *bladder pipe of Poland, with reed mouthpiece, 1 or 2 bladders, a pipe with 7 fingerholes and an upturned bell. An extant folk instr. (89).

Sifflet [Lat. *sifilare*], **1.** Fr.: whistle, pipe. The word has been in use from the 13th c. on, at which time small whistles of precious materials were made; **2.** organ stop of open flue pipes at 1′, ½′ pitches, known in France from the 16th c. on (62, 204).

Sifflet à eau (Fr.), a globular *rossignol flute (70).

Sifflet a roulette, Fr. equivalent of the penny whistle (70).

Sifflet coucou, Fr.: cuckoo, 1.

Sifflet de chauderonnier (Fr.: tinker's whistle), metal panpipes by means of which Fr. tinkers formerly made known their presence in the streets (78).

Sifflet de Pan, obs. Fr.: panpipes.

Sifflöte [Fr. *sifflet*], obs. organ stop of open cylindrical wide-scaled metal flue pipes, similar to the It. principale, at 2′, 1⅓′, or 1′ pitch, dating back to the baroque. There exist numerous var. spellings of this word. *Cf.* sifflet, 2 (3, 133).

Sigitot, *spike fiddle of the Sea Dayak of Borneo, with coconut body, palm-leaf belly, bamboo handle, and one fiber string that passes from a spike to a frontal tuning peg, via a bridge. The back is pierced with several small soundholes. It is played with a bamboo bow (176).

Signalhorn, Ger.: bugle.

Signalpfeife, Ger.: whistle.

Signulum [dim. of *signum*], Lat.: small bell (161).

Signum, med. Lat.: bell, a syn. of campana, nola. First mentioned in 513 by St. Cesaire of Arles, later in the c. by Gregory of Tours (in 576). *Ca.* 1290 it designated a tower bell; later the word was dropped in favor of *campana (61, 82).

Sigordang, drum of the Batak of Sumatra, made of a hollowed tree trunk, with single head fastened by rushes and tensed by wedge bracings (176).

Sigu mbava, reedpipe of Nias, made of bamboo, generally with 3 or 4 small fingerholes on the flattened front and without bell. The narrow reed forms part of a separately inserted tube.

Sigu nihu, *nose flute of Nias, made of cane, with 4 circular burned-in holes (176).

Si-im [Sum. *si*, horn + *im*, wind], ritual horn of ancient Babylon; it appears in the third millennium B.C. (89 Galpin).

Si-im-da, the same as si-im.

Siku (Aymara), see: sico.

Sikulu (Kikongo), drum of the Kongo people, almost spherical, with 2 membranes laced to each other. *Cf.* esikulu (30).

Sikunru, small clarinet of S. Celebes (121).

Sikwi, idiochord *raft zither of the Babale of the Congo, made of thin bamboo or raffia sticks attached to another by interweaving, with 16 strings (149).

Sil (Pahl.), cymbals of ancient Persia, possibly finger cymbals, played in pairs, the *sinj of modern times. *Cf.* zil, sil-sil, selslīm, salāsil, sil-snyau (75 II).

Sila, *conical drum of the Banza of the Congo with 2 laced heads. Identical with the nyi n'go of the Ngbandi (30).

Silambu, leg rattles of S. India dancers, made of hollow tubular silver rings containing small pellets. Also called karchilambu (179).

Silbador, modern name given to the *whistling pot of ancient and modern S. America (137).

Silbato, Sp.: whistle.

Silbo, syn. of chistu.

Silbote, the bass chistu, 60 cm. (24 in.) long, usually made of ebony with silver rings. The player does not accompany himself on a drum (as does the chistu player) and consequently has both hands free for playing the larger instr. (89).

Silimba, xylophone of the S. African Marotse, with 12 slabs and gourd resonators. Also called serimba (176).

Silingut, *nose flute of Borneo, made

of bamboo, with 4 fingerholes. *Ca.* 60 cm. (24 in.) long (176).

Sillet, Fr.: nut.

Silselim, see: selslīm.

Sil-sil, Tibetan: cymbals. *Cf.* sil, zil, selslīm, sil-snyau, salāsil (170).

Sil-snyau (pleasant music), cymbals of Tibetan abbots, of E. Asian origin, with small boss and wide rim, held horizontally; 30 cm. (12 in.) in diam. or larger. *Cf.* sil, zil, sil-sil, selslīm, salāsil (89 Picken).

Silvador, see: silbador.

Silvestris [Lat. *silva,* forest], abbr. of tibia silvestris. See: Waldflöte.

Simandre [Gk. **semanterion*], Fr.: semanterion.

Simbomba, Cat.: friction drum. *Cf.* sanbomba, ximbomba, zambomba.

Simfon [Gk. **symphonia*], var. of symphonie, mentioned *ca.* 1300.

Simfonia [Gk. **symphonia*], Jew's-harp of the Llusanés and Bergadá regions of Spain, played by shepherds. *Cf.* sanfornia (57).

Simha, Beng.: sringa (173).

Simikion [?Pers. *sim,* string], chordophone of ancient Greece, unidentified; Sachs suggested that it might have been a *board zither with 35 strings, held across the knees of a seated musician (170).

Simphonie, see: symphonie.

Simplification system, simplified organ devised by Abbé Vogler in the last decade of the 18th c., the object being to reduce cost and space. Its main features were: the omission of all show pipes and of all mixture stops, these being deemed unnecessary. The front row of pipes was no longer arranged symmetrically but in order of progressive size, in order to simplify wind supply and action. The entire pipework was enclosed in one large box provided with swell doors or roof. The lowest-pitched registers had no pipes of their own, but consisted exclusively of resultant tones (in order to obtain a 16′ tone, for example, an 8′ pipe and a softly voiced 5⅓′ pipe were played together). See also: acoustic bass.

Simpunia, see: symponia.

Simsimijah, 5-stringed lyre of the Egyptian fellahin, sometimes also called tanbur (144 Hickmann).

Sin, var. of sein.

Siñ, see: cai siñ.

Sineta [dim. of **sino*], Port.: small bell.

Sinfon, var. of symphonie.

Sinfonia [Gk. **symphonia*], obs. It.: hurdy-gurdy. Zarlino still used the term (in 1588).

Sinfoyna [Gk. **symphonia*], name of the Jew's-harp in Gerona, Spain. Also called pampa, samfonia (*Anuario musical,* 1946).

Sing, 1. var. of sein; **2.** Hindi: horn; equivalent of sringa; **3.** *musical cups of N. India (121); **4.** small cymbals of Laos (*Zeitschrift für vergleichende Musikwissenschaft,* II, 1934); **5.** small cymbals of China, corresponding to the ching of Thailand (46).

Sinğ, see: sinj.

Singa, horn of the Garo of Assam, made of curved buffalo horn (172).

Singam, Pali equivalent of sringa.

Singend (Ger.), a prefix to names of organ stops; when applied to flue pipes it denotes a stop with narrow scale and narrow mouth; when applied to reed pipes, the word is syn. with *geigend (133).

Singend Prinzipal (Ger.), syn. of Harfenprinzipal.

Single, as prefix to names of Renaissance and baroque instrs., single denotes an instr. of 8′ pitch or one whose bass compass does not exceed Γ ut.

Single action, name given to the square-piano action of Johann Zumpe, in which the jack is fixed to the key and the hammers are hinged to a hammer rail, pointing away from the player. The comb-like damper system was of whalebone. Érard and other makers also used this action, an adaptation of that of Cristofori (89 Harding).

Single curtal, see: curtal.

Single reed (Fr.: *anche simple;* Ger.:

einfaches Rohrblatt; It.: *ancia semplice*), single blade of cane, metal, or other material that serves as sounding apparatus of certain instrs. Single reeds are idioglott or heteroglott. Among the idioglott we distinguish between upcut and downcut reeds, *i.e.,* between those cut from the bottom up and left attached at the upper end, and those cut from the top down and left attached at their lower end. We also distinguish between *beating, *retreating, and *free reeds, as well as *percussion reeds. Of these the beating reed is the most common among Western single reeds (the clarinet reed, for example). The single reed is believed to be younger than the double reed (14).

Singwe, side-blown whistle of the Wasongola of the Congo, used as a signal instr. and also to chase away evil spirits. It is worn around the neck as an amulet (42).

Sinj (Pers.), cymbals of Persia and finger cymbals of modern Islam. *Cf.* hsing erh, sanj, sanūj, sunūj (75 II).

Sinkang imilyanga, drum of Rwanda (30).

Sinnitu (Akk.), 2-stringed lute of ancient Babylon that first appeared in the second millennium B.C. (89).

Sino [Lat. *signum*], Port.: bell. *Cf.* sein.

Sint, var. of sein.

Sintīr, pl. **sanātira,** dulcimer of Egypt and Syria. *Cf.* santir (89).

Sintubu, pl. of ntubu.

Sioulet, Béarnais: pipe, whistle. *Cf.* xiulet (176).

Sioulet cristedou, small panpipes of Pyrenean animal herders, made of a triangular piece of wood with 9 bores, 3½–6.7 cm. long (176, quoting Gustave Chouquet).

Sipa, bamboo *cross flute of the Naga of Assam, with 7 front fingerholes, one of them stopped; 52 cm. (20½ in.) long (172).

Sipi na pili, *board zither of the Bali of the Congo, without resonator (128).

Sipovka, *whistle flute of Russ. and Yugo. shepherds (132).

Sipowanamige, panpipes of the Nocomán Indians of E. Peru, with 7 pipes (105).

Sippi, sansa of the Mabali of the Congo (19).

Sirene, var. of syɩɔn.

Sirenion, *upright piano, invented in 1828 by Johann Promberger of Vienna, with short scale, thick strings, and a soundboard not attached to the case. It had a 6-oct. compass. *Ca.* 120 cm. (4 ft.) high (204).

Siri, panpipes of the Nonama-Choco Indians of the Pacific coast of Colombia and Panama. *Cf.* siru (105).

Siringa [Gk. *syrinx*], It.: panpipes.

Siroro, panpipes of the Bora Indians of the Upper Amazon (105).

Siru, panpipes of the Empera-Choco Indians of the Pacific coast of Colombia and Peru. *Cf.* siri (105).

Sirumee, panpipes of the Muinane Indians of the Upper Amazon (105).

Sisi, panpipes of New Ireland, open at both ends (176).

Si so laos, *stick zither of Thailand, similar to the piah but with 2 strings. *Ca.* 112 cm. (3 ft. 8 in.) long (17).

Sistema pneumatico tubolare, It.: *tubular-pneumatic action.

Sister [Fr. *cistre*], Ger.: cittern. The word has been in use since *ca.* 1800 (172).

Sistre, var. of cistre.

Sistro, It., Port.: sistrum. Pietro Cerone in 1613 uses the word in the sense of cittern and includes it in his "ordinary" stringed instrs. (*El Melopeo,* p. 1038).

Sistrum, pl. **sistra** (Lat.) [Gk. *seistron*] (It., Sp.: *sistro*), Roman name of the Gk. seistron. Known to ancient Sumeria by the third millennium B.C., the sistrum was then a rattle in U form with a short handle and 2 crossbars that rattled when shaken. Sistra of the same form have been found near Tiflis, Georgia, U.S.S.R., and still exist in Ethiopia in the Christian church. This same type is also found among the Yaqui Indians of Mexico and the U.S., and the Kaduveo Indians of Brazil, made of wood, with jingles strung on wires. The Egyptian sistrum is characterized by being closed at the top; it was sacred to Hathor, and when Hathor was later metamorphosed into Isis, it became sacred to Isis (and was then played by women). Gold and silver, metal, wood, and clay were used in making sistra. Two different forms occurred in Egypt: the *sesheshet, in shape of a temple; and the *iba, in shape of a horseshoe. The sistrum traveled to Rome with the cult of Isis, and specimens have been found as far away as France. In addition to the above-mentioned localities, the sistrum is also known in W. Africa. See also: iba, mena'anīm, rau-rau, safa ai, seistron, sesheshet, sistro, tsanatsel, tsnasin (15 Wachsmann, 137, 170, 192).

Sistrum smiczocz (Czech: bowed sistrum), instr. described by Paulus Paulirinus *ca.* 1460 as similar to the "cithara" (cittern) but bowed. (Pietro Cerone in 1613 also used the word "sistro" in the sense of cittern). Unfortunately we do not know whether it was related to the polnische Geige (Paulirinus came from Kraków) or the skrzypce.

Sitār [Pers. *si tar*, three strings], long-necked lute of India, of Pers. origin. It appeared in the latter part of the Middle Ages, invented, according to tradition, by Amir Khusru, poet and singer, *ca.* 1300, and is the most pop. instr. of N. India today. Its piriform body either is made of hollowed-out wood or consists of a gourd; the wooden belly is pierced with soundholes. A long neck, 7½ cm. (3 in.) wide, carries a flat fingerboard with 16–20 movable frets. These may be of gut or wire, brass or silver. If of brass or silver, they are secured to the neck by brass springs so as to retain their mobility, as frets are positioned for each required scale. The name sitār is misleading, as nowadays the instr. has between 4 and 7 strings (a sitār with 3 strings is called *tritantri vīnā). The

strings are of metal, held by frontal and lateral pegs, 2 generally being inserted in the neck and the remainder in a pegdisc. The melody is played on one string only, the others serving as drone accompaniments. Some specimens have additional, sympathetic strings. The tuning is $g^0 c^1$ $f^0 c^2$. The sitār is plucked with a wire plectrum worn on the player's right forefinger. One reason for its popularity is undoubtedly that it is easier to play than the vīnā. Also called satar (*i.e., sapta-tar,* seven strings), sundari. See also: achhrautī, charga, kachvā, kāncha bīnā, sai t'o erh, setār, setara (138, 173, 179).

Sitāra, name occasionally given the Kāmanja a'gūz in certain towns of India (173).

Siter, modern version of the kachapi, 3, of W. Java (121).

Sitlanjani, reedpipe of the Venda of N. Transvaal, made of 2 pieces of concave ivory 7½ cm. (3 in.) long, tapering 2½–1¼ cm. (1–½ in.), tied together by a piece of buckskin. One end of the buckskin passes between the ivories so as to form a vibrating reed. It serves in secret ceremonies. *Cf.* mantsakota (116).

Sitole, var. of citole.

Siurell, Balearic Islands: whistle.

Siya-siya, *percussion stick of S. Celebes, similar to the lae-lae. A bamboo pole 2 m. (6½ ft.) long is beaten with a piece of bamboo split for a portion of its length. It is used for expelling evil spirits (112, 173).

Siyem, see: gong siyem.

Siyu teki, *end-blown flute of Japan, generally made of bamboo (176).

Sizipán (pron.: sisipa), tambourine of Haiti, where it was introduced from Cuba (152).

Sizzle cymbal, cymbal used in rhythm bands, with jingles or rivets attached through holes drilled for this purpose. Also called rivet cymbals.

Skalapianino, upright *transposing piano, invented 1887 by Hermann Wagner of Stuttgart, with a keyboard that could be shifted to permit the playing of all tonalities as C major or A minor (176).

Sk'a'na, generic name of woodwind instrs. of the Indians of British Colombia, many of which are of Aztec descent. Among the most interesting are bladder or bellows blown double pipes (Galpin in SIMG IV, p. 661).

Skella [Gothic *skaella*], med. Lat., OHGer., Icelandic: bell (61, 176).

Skellach, var. of skellat.

Skellat [Gothic *skaella*], Scot.: small bell, hand bell; an iron rattle to make proclamations. The term, now rare, has been in use from the 14th c. (107).

Skellie, Scot.: hand bell used by public criers (107).

Skellilinum, OHGer.: small bell.

Skor, *goblet drum of Cambodia, beautifully decorated, with laced head. It corresponds to the darabuka, also the thōn of Thailand and gedombak of Malaya (47).

Skor thom, *barrel drum of Cambodia, with 2 nailed heads, only one of which is played. It is suspended by a ring and beaten with a stick. *Cf.* khong that (47).

Skripka [*skripietsh,* to squeak], **1.** bowed chordophone of the Caucasus, with rebec-shaped wooden body, 3 melody and 3 metal *sympathetic strings—a form of *lira; **2.** pop. Russ.: violin (68, 132).

Skruibka, Russ. var. of skripka.

Skrzypce, bowed chordophone of Poland, similar to the skripka.

Slapstick, clapper of modern rhythm bands, made of 2 slabs of wood hinged at one end and clicked together.

Slasal, cymbals of ancient Israel: the Talmudic form of selslīm (170).

Slegel, OEngl.: plectrum.

Slegil, OHGer.: "percussorium" (plectrum, beater).

Sleigh bell, orchestral percussion instr. consisting of a number of pellet bells strung on a hoop.

Slendang, name given erroneously to a Javanese tube zither.

Slentem, name given erroneously to a Javanese scraper by Mahillon (121).

Slentem gandul, Pasuran name of the *slentem gantung (121).

Slentem gantung (Solo: *slentem* with hanging bars), single-oct. gender of Java, at the same pitch as the lowest oct. of the gender barung (121).

Slide, 1. (Fr.: *coulisse;* Ger.: *Zug; Scheide;* It.: *pompa*), the U-shaped tube of a brass instr. which changes the length of the air column by its to-and-fro motion. See also: double slide; **2.** (Fr.: *coulisse;* Ger.: *Register*), perforated strip of wood into which the jacks of plucked keyboard instrs. are inserted; more properly called slider, as the word is taken over from organ terminology; **3.** see: tuning slide.

Slide cornet, see: soprano slide cornet.

Slider (Fr.: *registre, registre traînant;* Ger.: *Parallele, Schleife*), in an organ a thin, narrow strip of wood placed under a row of organ pipes, having holes corresponding to their apertures. It runs at right angles to the grooves and controls the admission of air to the pipes by its connection to the corresponding drawstop.

Slider chest (Fr.: *sommier à coulisses;* Ger.: *Schleiflade*), organ wind chest in which there is one groove for each key. Each groove serves all the pipes sounded by the corresponding key. This type of chest was in use in the Middle Ages and is still found in many organs today. *Cf.* spring chest.

Slider key (Fr.: *tirette;* Lat.: *regula, lingua*), term used to denote the mechanism by which pipes were sounded in med. organs from the 10th c. on. We do not know exactly when it ceased to be used. The slider key was a strip of wood terminating in a flat handle by which it was pulled out to sound the pipes, pushed back to silence them. The strip was perforated with either one hole or as many holes as there were pipes to make speak. Actually this device was a primitive form of register, as it controlled the admission of air to the pipes.

Slider-key chest (Fr.: *sommier à tiret-*

tes), organ *wind chest with longitudinal grooves, in use in antiquity and the high Middle Ages.

Slide trombone, see: trombone.

Slide trumpet (Fr.: *trompette à coulisse;* Ger.: *Zugtrompete;* It.: *tromba da tirarsi, tromba spezzata*), *natural trumpet provided with a telescopic slide in an attempt to give it a complete scale. Its earliest known form is the trombone, developed in the 15th c. From early 15th to mid-16th c. some It., Flem. and Ger. paintings show curious trumpets with elongated mouth pipes; the term *Zugtrompete* occurs in several late-16th-c. and in 17th-c. Ger. inventories; finally we have a surviving instr.: a trumpet by Veit, dated 1651, preserved in the Berlin instr. collection, with an elongated mouth pipe that can be pulled out for 56 cm. (22 in.) and that will lower any note by 2 tones. This is presumably the instr. for which Bach wrote; his *tromba da tirarsi* parts cannot be played on an ordinary (natural) trumpet. Later in the 17th c. the *flat trumpet made a fleeting appearance in England. Buonanni in 1722 mentions a trumpet in which a section, inserted into the other section, could be moved in order to change the pitch; Laborde in 1780 reports that in his day one built trumpets with slides in the manner of the new horns (see: cor à l'anglaise), thus rendering them easier to play; and in 1795 J. E. Altenburg compared the slide trumpet to an alto trombone, thereby clearly indicating that the 2 were not identical. At about the same time a modified version of the flat trumpet appeared in England, introduced by John Hyde, trumpet major, in his *Compleat Preceptor* of 1798; it was in F, provided with the same crooks as the ordinary trumpet, and the U bend nearest the player was made to telescope, being drawn back by the player's right hand and returned by a spring. In England it became the standard orchestral trumpet of the 19th c. Covent Garden still had slide trumpets in 1882, and they were

being taught as late as 1893 at Kneller Hall school of military music. This type of instr. was not played in continental Europe. A Fr. design appeared in 1821 with a slide that was pushed forward like a trombone slide, but usually either the natural or the valve trumpet was played. See also: flat trumpet, trombone snodato, trompette rompue, trompette-trombone (89 Baines, 124, 132).

Slide whistle, U.S. term for *piston flute.

Sliding rattle (Fr.: *tuyau basculant*), rattle in which objects slide up and down in the hollow of a pounded stick or grooves of a frame, such as the angklung (170).

Slit drum (Fr.: *tambour de bois;* Ger.: *Schlitztrommel;* Sp.: *tambor de tronco hendido*), *percussion tube, often erroneously called drum or gong. In its earliest form a stamped idiophone made of a hollowed-out tree trunk placed over a pit and stamped. The Uitoto Indians of Colombia still so use it. In the next stage of its development it was also a tree trunk, but one hollowed out through a narrow, longitudinal slit. Early types are struck with large sticks, later ones are drummed on the edges of the slit, purposely left of different thicknesses so as to yield different pitches. From giants 10 m. (*ca.* 30 ft.) long or more housed in roofed-over enclosures, the slit becomes increasingly smaller in later stages, until finally it is a very small, portable signal instr., such as those carried by Mal. watchmen. Apart from its uses as signal instr., news conveyor (*talking drum), and stamped log, the slit drum is also credited with magical powers in certain areas and participates in magical rites. It is distributed in Africa, the Americas, Asia, S. Seas. Larger forms of slit drum are also called log drum. See also: amejoni, angremut, antanatra, ao yü, bakilo, balah, bideru, bogir, cai mo, cai mo ca, cutín, dan, dangamut, daola-daola, do, dobon, duku, dyadiko, fa'ali, farara hazu, galamutu, gamti, ganang, garamo, garamudu, garamut, gasa-bin, geramo, gerom, giramo, gram, guggu, gul-gul, guruma, hatranatra, hatuntaqui, huare, iamut, ikuru, ka'ara, kaduar, kalah, karamut, katiboke, kele, kentongan, kentung-kentung, keplek, keprak, kereteta, kibudikidi, kikomfi, kilando, kilangay, kiondo, kiringi, kohkol, koko, kolamut, kolilo, kol-kola, koriro, kukulan gantang, kul-kul, lali, lalis, lepakusu, letlot, lokanko, lokole, lokombe, lolob, longo, manguare, mayohuacan, mbudikidi, me, mi, miaba, modimba, mo ko, mo kugyo, mondo, mongondo, mongungu, mukoko, mukonzi, mulimba, munkoko, mu yü, nafa, naffa, naramut, nawa, nemurambi, ngaramut, ngilamo, ngungu, nkoko, nkolenkole, nkonko, nku, nkumoi, nolipiru, nungungu, pahu, palo, palo hueco, pang, pang tse, pate, piturka, pong-pong, pulotu, qaramut, sabang, shinguvo, tambor mumbomba, tamtam, tarremut, tecomopiloa, tepanabaz, teponagua, teponaztli, tetekan, t'o, tokere, tonga, tong-tong, trocano, tunduli, ungar, valihambalo, yabó, yohuacán, yü pang (168, 170).

Slit tube (Ger.: *Spaltrohr, Blasspaltrohr*), tube of bamboo or other material with a lengthwise slit against which the player's lips are pressed, thus causing it to open and close rapidly (77).

Small-pipe, 1. bellows-blown bagpipe of Northumberland, an indoor instr. that first appeared in the late 17th c. and is believed to be descended from the musette. Originally it had a plain, cylindrical chanter and musette-like drone; another model had 3 drones on the same stock, tuned $g^0 d^1 g^1$ (keynote g^1). This model remained until the mid-18th c., when the characteristic feature of the small-pipe was developed: its chanter was stopped. (The small-pipe is the only extant Western bagpipe to have such a chanter. But see: surdelina.) This procedure reduced the compass by a tone but permitted staccato playing, as by covering all fingerholes the chanter was silenced. In 1805, 4 closed keys were added, increasing the compass to d^1-a^2,

and a fifth key was subsequently added for $c\sharp^2$, thus making D major available. A fourth drone was also added. Over a period of time up to 17 keys and 5 drones were fitted, but normally the chanter has only 7 keys now. Of the 4 drones usually supplied, not more than 3 are used simultaneously. The chanter is cylindrical not only in shape but also in bore; the drones have single beating reeds, the chanter a double reed. Although manufacture is not standardized, chanters are generally stopped with a piston stopper, the sound issuing from a small lateral hole. Its tone is soft; **2.** there exists also a Lowland smallpipe that is bellows-blown; **3.** mouthblown Highland small-pipe with cylindrical chanter, 7 front fingerholes, a rear thumbhole, and 3 drones tuned $a^0 e^1 a^1$ (13, 89).

Smyček, Czech: bow.

Smyczek, Pol.: bow.

Smyk, 1. obs. bowed chordophone of Russia, a folk instr. identical with the gadulka, played from med. times until the end of the 18th c. An 11th-c. fresco in the Sofia Cathedral of Kiev shows it held against the player's shoulder; **2.** syn. of luk muzycyny. *Cf.* gudok.

Snaar, Du.: string.

Snare (Fr.: *timbre;* Ger.: *Schnarrsaite*), gut string stretched over that head of a drum that is not struck. Tension of a snare can be regulated; the tighter it is, the more brilliant the sound. Snares were introduced to Europe from the East.

Snare drum (Fr.: *caisse claire, petit tambour, tambour militaire;* Ger.: *kleine Trommel, Militärtrommel;* It.: *cassa, tamburo militare, tamburo piccolo*), double-headed *cylindrical drum of indefinite pitch, characterized by snares stretched across its lower head; they add great brilliance when the upper head is played. Historically the body was of wood or metal, and the heads were stretched by lacings. The med. tabor is the earliest form of snare drum; during the 15th c. it gradually increased in size, to emerge by the 16th c. as a military instr., popularized by the fife-and-drum corps of the Swiss mercenary foot soldiers, a large instr. carried over the player's right shoulder, suspended on a strap. It is to this instr. that the Engl. word "drum" was first applied. From then on the snare drum has remained associated with the infantry and with the fife. In the 18th c. it was first used in the orchestra, and in the 19th c. it succeeded in replacing the *tenor drum in military bands. At that time it was made with a thin metal shell. The snare drum is played with 2 short wooden sticks on the upper head only (known as the batter head; the lower head is called snare head). A snare consists of a group of strings of gut or silk bound with wire; their tension is controlled by means of a screw. In Thoinot Arbeau's day (1588) a snare consisted of cords; 8–10 snares are now usual. The drum itself is made in several sizes nowadays, the orchestral version having a diam. of some 36–38 cm. (15–16 in.) and a depth of 13 cm. (5 in.). Its shell is of metal or laminated wood, the heads are tightened by tension rods and thumbscrews, on better instrs. by spring-loaded tension units. The heads are now often of plastic. In England the snare drum is known as the side drum.

Šneb, see: chnouē.

Snorrebot, Du.: bull-roarer.

Snug, see: sunūj.

So, panpipes of Korea, consisting of 16 stopped bamboo pipes arranged in raft form, with the smallest pipe in the center, the whole enclosed in a casing (66).

Sō, 1. fiddle of Laos and Cambodia, with 2 strings tuned a 5th apart. The hair of the bow is inserted between them so that they always sound together. See also: sa dueng, sō i, sō u; **2.** syn. of gaku sō (47).

Soalha [Port. *soar*, to sound], Port.: jingles (of a tambourine).

Sobaba [Arab. *shabbāba*], *end-blown flute of the Malagasy Republic, made of cane, with 6 front fingerholes and a rear thumbhole, an immigrated shabbāba; 30–35 cm. (12–14 in.) long (170).

Sō ban, gong of Japan, with a rough surface, made of thin metal, used in *kabuki* (135).

Sō bang, rustic bowed instr. of Laos, made of a bamboo tube affixed to a handle (47).

Socador (pounder), syn. of fungador (7).

Sock cymbals, modern orchestral cymbals attached to an upright stand so as to lie horizontally. The lower cymbal is movable, the upper fixed. The lower cymbal is moved up against the fixed one. See also: choke cymbals (151).

Sodelina, 17th-c. var. of sordellina.

Sódina [Mal. *suling*], *vertical flute of the Malagasy Republic, usually of cane and generally provided with 6 front fingerholes and a rear thumbhole, probably introduced by Arabian immigration. It is played by men only. Also called: antsódina, dretsa, fololitsy, kiatsódy, kitsódy, sódy, sóly (172).

Sō do, see: sa diu.

Sō dorang, see: sa dueng.

Sō dueng, see: sa dueng.

Sódy, syn. of sódina.

Sogo, *barrel drum of the Ewe of Ghana, with one head lapped over an iron hoop. The bottom is closed but may have a hole in it, covered by a cork, used for wetting (see: atsimevu). Its pitch is between that of the atsimevu and the kidi. It is played with drumsticks (109).

Sō hu, see: su hu.

Sō i, *spike fiddle of Laos, smaller than the sō u. The body consists of a wooden cylinder covered with a snakeskin belly. The 2 strings are tuned a 5th apart. It corresponds to the t'i ch'in of China, the cai ñi of Vietnam, the sō luang of Thailand, and the amrita of India (47).

Soifflöte, var. of Sifflöte.

Soinu, Basque folk zither of the Soule district, a *tambourin à cordes played together with a pipe. The strings are struck with a small stick, and are tuned to fundamental and 5th. The word is also applied locally to a fiddle (56).

Soittotorvi, horn of Finland, of animal horn, thick, straight, conical, having 4 equidistant fingerholes (169).

Soittu, Carelian name of the kantele (9).

Soko, bowed chordophone of the Guinea Republic, with a half-gourd body, a handle, and a single string held by a tuning ring (42).

So'ktsoks, deer-hoof rattle of the Klamath Indians of the Western U.S., consisting of a pole 1.20–2.10 m. (4–7 ft.) long with clusters of deer dewclaws attached to its upper end. Associated with adolescence rites for girls (105).

Soku, Mandingo (a Sudanic language): bowed chordophone (93).

Soku-sarv, horn of Estonia, made of animal horn, provided with fingerholes (169).

Sok yet, clappers of Malaya, used for accompanying dances (173).

So-la, name of the sona in SW. China (89).

Solo organ, organ manual and that section of the organ it controls. The solo manual was unknown prior to the 19th c.

Solophone, *bowed zither shaped almost like a wing, with fingerboard running along the left side and 2 strings stopped by means of buttons. A late-19th-c. invention (149).

Solor, syn. of bansurī.

Solotrompete, Ger.: song trumpet (organ stop).

Solovox, monophonic, imitative *electrophonic instr. of the electronic type, made by the Hammond Organ Co. from 1941 on. In appearance it is a piano attachment with 3-oct. keyboard that is clipped onto the keyboard of a conventional piano, with a separate cabinet for tubes and speaker. The Solovox is played with the right hand while the left hand plays an accompaniment on the conventional piano. Tone generation on earlier models was by means of vibrating reeds, but is now completely electronic.

Sō luang, *spike fiddle of Thailand, equivalent to the sō i of Laos, the t'i ch'in of China (47).

Sóly, syn. of sódina.

Sōmangalam, syn. of semakkalam (179).

Sombo, drum of the Gombe of the Congo (30).

Somiere, It.: **1.** wind chest; **2.** pin block.

Sommerophone, an early name of the euphonium (wind instr.) in England and France.

Sommier, Fr.: **1.** wind chest; **2.** pin block.

Sommier à coulisses, Fr.: slider chest.

Sommier à ressorts, Fr.: spring chest.

Sommier à soupapes, Fr.: spring chest.

Sommier à tirettes, Fr.: slider-key chest.

Som pho, barrel drum of Cambodia, with tuning paste on the heads.

Sompret, syn. of selompret.

Sona [Pers. *surnā], conical oboe of China, made of wood with a flaring brass bell, 7 front fingerholes, and a rear thumbhole, played with a flat metal lip rest; a most pop. instr. In Shantung, where it is called wa wa erh, it is made completely of metal. *Cf.* chi na, so-la. Also called hiang te (142, 170).

Sona cigales (cricket sound), disc buzzer of Catalonia (152).

Sonaglia [Lat. *sonus,* sound], It.: pellet bell.

Sonaja, Sp.: pellet bell, jingle. A *sonaja de azofar* (brass) was mentioned by Juan Ruiz in the first half of the 14th c. (44).

Sonajero, Sp.: rattle.

Sonall, Cat. equivalent of sonajero.

Sonarpfeife (Ger.), organ stop of flue pipes invented by Trautner of Kaiserslautern in 1911 and built by Walcker of Ludwigsburg. Its clarinet tone is achieved by narrowing and widening the pipes at points where nodes and antinodes are formed. Also called Sonarklarinette, Sonorklarinette (133).

Songka, marine-shell trumpet of ancient Java (121).

Song na, drum of Thailand, similar to the sangna of Cambodia, with tuning paste on the heads. During performance it is held on the player's lap and is played with bare hands. *Ca.* 56 cm. (22 in.) long (65).

Song trumpet (Ger.: *Solotrompete*), organ stop of reed pipes at 8′ pitch, designed for solo use (198).

Sonnaille [Lat. *sonus,* sound], Fr.: originally a pellet bell, jingle, clapperless bell; later, a bell hung around the neck of a domestic animal. "Sonnailler" is the bellwether. From the 16th c. on the term is used in the sense of herd animal bell; it is still so employed in Auvergne, where the bells are made of sheet metal (53, 127).

Sonnailles sur bâton, Fr.: stick rattle.

Sonneau, Fr.: tiny bell or pellet bell of the 16th c., worn as an ornament.

Sonnette (Fr.) [Lat. *sonus,* sound], bell or pellet bell of med. and Renaissance France, mentioned from the 13th c. on. Originally it denoted a small campaniform bell, from the 14th c. on a pellet bell, such as those sewn to fools' clothes or attached to birds' legs. Today it denotes a hand bell (53, 82, 190).

Sō no koto, ** long zither of Japan, equivalent of the Chin. cheng. A descendant of the hitsu no koto, it was a fashionable court instr. for over 1000 years, reserved exclusively for classical Chin. music. During the Heian period (9–12th c.) it was played with sweeping arpeggio technique. The upper surface of the koto is convex; its 13 strings pass over individual bridges and are played with a plectrum. *Ca.* 2 m. (6½ ft.) long. See also: gaku sō, tsukushi sō, zoku sō (144, 157).

Sonorophone, valved brass instr. of bass register, patented by George Metzler and James Waddell of London on Aug. 12, 1858, apparently made in Paris. Actually it was a *bombardon, 3, in E♭ with 3 valves, furnished with an innovation called "circular arrangement" (126, 132).

Sonorous stone, see: musical stone; also: lithophone, phonolith.

Sō o, syn. of sō u.

Sopella, see: sopila.

Sopelo, see: sopila.

Sopila, shawm of Yugoslavia, found chiefly on Krk Island and the Croatian coast, with head, middle, and bell joint of conical bore, pirouette, and 6 front fingerholes. Played with a short, wide reed. The sopila is made in 2 sizes and is always played in pairs of one long and one short instr. Before it is played, water is poured into the tube through the bell to swell the wood and thereby tighten the joints. In Istria it goes under the name of tororo (34).

Sopilka, *end-blown flute of the Ukraine, without mouthpiece but with fingerholes. Also called svirel. *Cf.* shupelka (169).

Sopjelka, see: sopilka.

Sopranino clarinet, clarinet pitched between the ordinary C clarinet and the *piccolo clarinet in high A♭. It may be pitched in D, E♭, E, F or G, one tone to a 5th above the C clarinet. Those in E and G, mentioned by 18th-c. writers, are now obs. That in F was formerly used in Ger. military bands and in England, where it is now replaced by that in E♭. The sopranino in D was in use in 18th- and 19th-c. orchestras. See also: quartino (89 Rendall).

Soprano slide′ cornet, name given by U.S. instr. makers to the soprano trombone played with a cornet mouthpiece (25).

Sora, *marine-shell trumpet of Korea. It corresponds to the hora of Japan and the hai lo of China (66).

Sordellina, 1. a small sordone; **2.** var. spelling of surdelina.

Sordino, 1. It.: mute; damper; kit; clavichord; **2.** the sordin stop.

Sordin pianoforte, Sordin fortepiano, piano with 6 variations of tone, invented in 1798 by Christian Gottlob Friderici of Gera, imitating flute and oboe (27).

Sordin stop (Fr.: *sourdine*), piano stop identical with the mute stop (92).

Sordone (It.) [aug. of *sordo,* mute] (Fr.: *sourdine;* Ger.: *Sordun*), a rare woodwind instr. of the late Renaissance, similar to the courtaut (without its *tétines*), an early form of bassoon, with a cylindrical bore running up and down 1 piece of wood 2 or 3 times and terminating in a lateral hole, played with a double reed. The sound was soft and muffled. Zacconi was first to mention the sordone (in 1592). An Ambras inventory of 1596 enumerates 2 basses, 2 tenors, 2 descants and 1 "smaller" descant. Praetorius describes and depicts a consort of 5 sizes: descant Bb^0–g^1, alto Eb^0–c^1, tenor C^0–a^0, bass Bb^1–g^0, great bass F^1–d^0, the compass being a 13th in each case. Four specimens have survived, housed in the Vienna Kunsthistorisches Museum. From them we know that the bass measured 87 cm. (34¼ in.), the great bass 90 cm. (35½ in.). The 3 larger sizes were played with curved metal crooks, and the bass and great bass were also furnished with keys (89 Langwill, 170, 183).

Sordun, Ger.: sordone.

Sordune, organ stop of narrow, cylindrical reed pipes of the *dulcian family, with soft tone, dating from the Renaissance. It was usually placed in the pedal at 16′ pitch, occasionally at 8′. Johann Samber, writing in 1707, mentions a 2-rank Sordune 8′, the nature of which is not known (3, 133).

Sosanru, syn. of dunde.

Sosoangan, *pigeon whistle of W. Java, corresponding to the sawangan (121).

Sostinente piano, 1. trade name of a *bowed keyboard instr. invented by Isaac Henry Robert Mott of Brighton, England, and patented Feb. 1, 1817, with rollers acting on silk threads that communicated vibrations to the strings; **2.** term applied in modern times to a whole series of keyboard instrs., including many that were in existence before the piano was invented, sounded by a continuous bow.

Since neither piano nor harpsichord action is involved, they are termed bowed keyboard instrs. in this book (79).

Sō tai, see: sa tai.

Sotharpa (soot harp), believed to have been a syn. of the narrow-holed *bowed harp of Sweden. The terms occurred in the 18th c. (9).

Sō u, sō of Laos and Thailand, with coconut body, wooden belly, long neck, and rear tuning pegs. A silk ligature below the pegs forms a nut, tying the strings to the neck. The sō u corresponds to the hu ch'in of China, the rāvanatta of India, the tro u of Cambodia. Also called sō o (47).

Soubasse, Fr.: subbass.

Soufflet, Fr.: bellows.

Soundboard, 1. (Fr.: *table, table d'harmonie;* Ger.: *Resonanzboden;* It.: *piano armonico, tavola armonica*), thin board of wood or other material over which the strings of stringed keyboard instrs. are stretched, corresponding to the belly of bowed and plucked chordophones. Up to the 19th c. it formed the top of a resonating chamber, but since then most keyboard instrs. are built with open bottom. Varnishing the upper surface of the soundboard started in the early 19th c.; a patent was taken out in 1826 for a soundboard to be varnished on both sides. Today piano soundboards are heavily varnished on both sides, as are those of most harpsichords, etc., although some makers prefer to varnish the upper surface only, to encourage formation of a "crown" to offset pressure of the strings. Soundboards are made of narrow strips glued together; the thickness varies virtually from maker to maker;

2. name formerly given to the grooved portion of an organ wind chest.

Soundhole (Fr.: *ouïe;* Ger.: *Schalloch*), the soundholes of chordophones are of great antiquity and appear in Egypt at least 3000 years ago. The oldest known types are very small, circular holes, a number of which were pierced in the belly, in the East often on the back or sides of the instr., forming definite patterns. Smaller soundholes have assumed a variety of shapes and patterns. Larger holes are usually single, placed in the center of the belly, or paired as on violins. Sometimes the center hole is covered by a rose. The C holes of older European bowed instrs. were placed facing each other ❯ up to the 16th c., when their position was reversed to ❰ . Sachs believed that this pairing of soundholes originated in the Middle Ages, when S. Slavs laid a bridge across the central soundhole of their *lira, thereby dividing it into 2 circle segments ultimately resulting in C holes. In the days when stringed keyboard instrs. had closed bottoms, a soundhole was generally cut in the soundboard—occasionally several were—a procedure taken over from *lutherie*. Kirby reports that some African gourd rattles have a number of soundholes drilled to increase resonance, and that these form fairly definite patterns.

Soundpost (Fr.: *âme;* Ger.: *Stimmstock;* It.: *anima*), dowel of Swiss pine, spruce, or other softwood inserted upright in the body of viols, violins, etc., set close to the right foot of the bridge, with the grain running at right angles to that of the plates. It serves to transmit the vibrations from belly to back. Its position is highly critical, as even a minute change will materially alter the tone. The soundpost is, or should be, kept in place solely by pressure of the strings, fitting the curvatures of back and belly very closely. Originally its purpose may have been one of supporting the belly to prevent its collapsing, but violins, etc., can be played quite safely without a soundpost; however, its absence muffles the tone completely. Up to the end of the 18th c. top and bottom of soundposts were arched and thus covered a far smaller surface than they do today, modern soundposts being flat at both ends.

Soupape, Fr.: pallet.

Souravli, *end-blown flute of modern Greece, made of cane, wood, or bone, with 6 front fingerholes and a rear thumbhole (132).

Sourdeline, Fr.: surdelina.

Sourdine [Fr.: *sourd,* mute] (Fr.), **1.** mute (mid-16th c. on); **2.** kit; **3.** sordone; **4.** clavichord; **5.** sordin stop; **6.** mute violin.

Sourdine pédale, violin mute invented by Jean-Baptiste Vuillaume of Paris by 1867 and shown at the Paris Exposition that year. Actually it was a very clever combination of mute and tailpiece: the player could mute his instr. by pushing with his chin without having to interrupt the performance (127).

Sousaphone, a form of helicon with a very long, detachable bell some 60 cm. (2 ft.) or more in diam., originally pointing upward but later made to point forward, made to the specifications and named in honor of John Philip Sousa, American bandmaster. Originally built for the Sousa band by C. G. Conn of Elkhart, Ind., and adopted 1908 by U.S. military bands. Two sizes only were made, a bass in E♭ and a contrabass in B♭. Both are still in use (15 Morley-Pegge).

Spadix, unidentified chordophone of ancient Greece, believed to have been a form of lyre.

Spagane, clappers of the Thonga of S. Africa, consisting of rectangular slats of wood, with a leather band attached to the narrow end, thus permitting them to be worn as mitts. They are played only by male dancers to increase the sound of hand clapping (116).

Spaltflöte, Ger.: duct flute.

Spaltrohr, Ger.: slit tube.

Span, Ger.: rib (of a lute, etc.); formerly spelled Spahn.

Spanish cittern, cittern with 5 strings tuned $A^0 d^0 g^0 b^0 e^1$, according to Joos Verschuere Reynvaan's dictionary, 1790 (176).

Spanish guitar, see: guitar, guitarra española, vihuela.

Spanrutengitarre, obs. Ger. term for pluriarc, coined by Sachs.

Spassapensieri, obs. It. syn. of scaccia-pensieri.

Speelfluit (Du.), see: Spillflöte.

Sphärophon, *electrophonic instr. invented by Jörg Mager in 1921, a monophonic instr. of the electrophonic type, originally designed for quarter-tone music. With the addition of a keyboard in 1928, the name was changed to Klaviatur-Sphärophon. Another variety was known as Kurbel-Sphärophon.

Spieldose, Ger.: music box.

Spielpfeife, Ger.: chanter.

Spieltisch, Ger.: console.

Spieluhr, generic Ger. term for smaller mechanical instrs. driven by clockwork, even though no timepiece is involved (144).

Spiessgeige, Ger.: spike fiddle.

Spiesslaute, Ger.: spike lute.

Spike (Fr.: *pique;* Ger.: *Stachel*), metal projection added in modern times to the cello and other instrs. to support them at a desirable height from the floor. Also called tailpin. The length of the spike is modifiable in the West; that of the Eastern *spike fiddle is fixed.

Spike fiddle (Fr.: *vièle à pique;* Ger.: *Spiessgeige*), fiddle with a round handle that pierces the body and projects at the lower end, forming a cello-like spike. The earliest fiddles seem to have been spike fiddles: Al Farabi mentions spikes in the 10th c. Traditionally of Kurdistan origin, spike fiddles are found in Egypt and Asia today. See also: amrita, amz'ad, arababu, arbab, arnaba, asmari, bēhālā, cai ñi, cai tam, chanuri, cherewata, dhusir, end-ingidi, enkerbap, erh hsien, erh hu, garadap, geso-geso, ghizhak, ghordjek, gughe, ha erh cha ko, hu ch'in, hu hu, hui hu, iqliq, kamānja, kāmanja, karan-ing, kauss, kei kin, khil, khil-khuur, ko kin, kokun, kongkeh, marbab, ngenge, pan hu, pena, rabāb, rebab, rijak, riti, sa dueng, sa tai, sa u, sigitot, sō i, sō luang, sō u, su hu, su ken hsien erh, sze hu hsien, ta hu ch'in, tan ch'in, tei kin, t'i

ch'in, tin thaila, tro duong, tro khmer, tro u (168).

Spike lute (Ger.: *Spiesslaute*), lute with a handle that pierces the body and projects at the lower end, known in the second millennium B.C., when it appears in W. Asia and Egypt. See also: dvitāra, ēka tantrikā, ēkatāra, ektār, yaktāra (168).

Spikharmonika, Swed.: nail violin.

Spikharpa, Swed.: nail violin.

Spillflöte, Spillpfeife (Ger.) (Du.: *speelfluit*), organ stop of open conical flue pipes, or cylindrical half-stopped pipes. In some areas the name was replaced by Gemshorn; elsewhere it was confused with the Spitzflöte, with which it then became identical. The nomenclature is extremely involved. The stop dates from the 16th c. and is now obs. It occurred at 16' and 8' pitch; in higher tonal positions it was generally known by other names (Schwegel, larigot, etc.). Praetorius and Adlung both knew it as Gemshorn. Also called Spindelflöte (3, 133, 159).

Spindelflöte, see: Spillflöte.

Spine (Ger.: *lange Wand, Basswand*), the straight long side of a horizontal stringed keyboard instr., roughly parallel with the bass strings.

Spinet (Fr.: *épinette;* Ger.: *Spinett;* It.: *spinetta*), stringed keyboard instr. with action identical to that of the harpsichord, differing from the latter by its form, usually by its lesser size, and by the direction of its strings, those of a spinet proceeding diagonally from left to right of the player. Direction and scale of the strings cause an irregular trapezoid, details of which are modified with each school of building. With few exceptions spinets have but one manual and one set of strings. As a means of saving space, all spinets with the normal disposition of one set of strings have their jacks placed in pairs, back to back, their plectra pointing in opposite directions; hence the strings are grouped in pairs also, as on a bichord harpsichord. The classical instr.

of 16th- and 17th-c. Italy was six-sided, with the longest side nearest the player, containing the keyboard, which projected like a balcony. The wrest pins were placed at the right; the jacks formed an oblique row from left front (bass end) to right rear (treble end). Both case and soundboard were made of very thin cypress, without lid or stand, housed in a separate, stouter case, usually painted, from which it was withdrawn for performance. The compass was either 4 octs., C^0–c^3, with a *short oct., but more often $4\frac{1}{2}$ octs., C^0–f^3, also with a short oct. Contemporary 4′ instrs., called spinettini or ottavine, were proportionately smaller and made in either rectangular or polygonal form. The rectangular ones had recessed (i.e., nonprojecting) keyboards and were built directly into their outer case. In many 4′ instrs. the tuning pins were placed immediately behind and parallel with the nameboard, as in a harpsichord, with jacks following closely, separated by a nut. Such spinettini formed an irregular trapezoid, with the front and back walls of equal length, but with the bass side shorter than that of the treble. This disposition of tuning pins and jacks was retained in another model the Italians evolved at the end of the 17th c.: here the spine is by far the longest side and the front, or keyboard, side is no longer parallel to it but is set obliquely, the old treble wall being transformed into a short cheekpiece connected at a 90-degree angle to a prolongation pointing to the player's right, or to a bentside. Exceptionally the spine was made as long as that of a harpsichord; this type had full harpsichord scale and was provided with more than one set of strings, but in general the cheek came to be replaced entirely by a bentside, thus giving it a pentagonal, wing-shaped form. In England the school of spinet making followed that of virginal building at the latter part of the 17th c., when the wing-shaped form was adopted, but most surviving Brit. instrs. date from the second half of the 18th c. Popularly

known as "leg of mutton," they are all alike and vary only in a few minor details. Made of walnut or mahogany, they were set upon stands of the same material, the latter conforming in design to that of the prevailing taste in furniture. Beautiful strap hinges of brass unite lid and body. Similar instrs. were also built in other European countries (and the U.S.) in the 18th c.: those made on the Continent retained a short bass wall, whereas in Britain this section was diagonal, meeting the spine at an acute angle and thereby giving the instr. a greater width in relation to its length than is found on Continental models. Compass of the "legs of mutton" was 5 octs., in England usually G^1–g^3, following Brit. organ-building practice, on the Continent F^1–f^3. Flanders prior to the 18th c. produced virginals rather than spinets, but the wing-shaped form was occasionally made there during the 18th c., as it was in France and Germany. We have little knowledge of Fr. spinets up to then: judging by Mersenne, the It. model prevailed in his day; the Fr. word épinette served as generic term for plucked keyboard instrs. and referred primarily to the harpsichord. In Germany a similar situation obtained: Praetorius' drawings show Italianate spinets; in the 17th and 18th c. both virginal and spinet were indiscriminately called Instrument, and in the 17th c. occasionally also Symphonie.

Both etymology and early history of the spinet are in need of future clarification. Concerning the former, we have the unsupported statement of Banchieri (Conclusioni, 1609) that the spinet was named after Giovanni Spina, the maker of a square instr., seen by Banchieri, dated 1501—a most unlikely derivation, as Sachs pointed out. Spinetta is an It. dim. of spina, thorn, and the instr. is also said to have been named for its thornlike plectra. This derivation goes back to Julius Caesar Scaliger (1484–1558), who implies that quill plectra came into use during his lifetime (which is not correct) and who says that the instr. called *clavicymbalum* and *harpicordum* (he is writing in Latin) when he was a boy "is now" called spinet from its plectra, thus indicating that the word was first used well after 1500. This also is erroneous: the household accounts of the Comtesse d'Angoulême for 1496 contain a payment for an *espinète* as well as for a coffer in which to place it. The instr. in question may have been a harpsichord; on the other hand, the *spineta sive gravicordi* mentioned in an Avignon contract of 1503 (in which a rose is also specified) was presumably shaped like a clavichord. In 1511 the Duke of Lorraine purchased an instr. *faisant eschiquier, orgues, espinette et flustes;* it is curious that Virdung, who wrote in that same year, should have been acquainted with the virginal and not with the spinet. A few years later, in 1514, an *espinette* is listed in the inventory of the effects of Charlotte, duchess of Valentinois, and an *espinette double* is mentioned in 1521. It may well be that the name is of Fr. rather than It. origin; it was the vernacular word applied to all plucked keyboard instrs. in France (the word "virginal" was but rarely used in France and *clavecin* is of 17th-c. date). In England the word was almost as rarely used as was virginal in France; indeed Cotgrave in 1611 translates *espinette* as "a pair of virginals." The height of confusion in terminology is perhaps reached by Bermudo in 1555: ". . . *llaman espinetas à otros clavicordios que son màs pequeños* . . . [but of the same shape]," literally: other clavicordios that are smaller are called spinets; meaning: 4′ instrs. are called spinets; this is echoed more than half a c. later by Praetorius, who says that spinets are small and are tuned a 5th or oct. higher than regular pitch, and are set on or in a larger instr.; in Italy, he adds, the larger ones also are called spinets. For Flem. 4′ spinets see also: virginal (24, 80 VI, 82, 106, 170, H. Havard: *Dictionnaire de l'ameublement*).

Spinetta traversa (It.) (Ger.: *Querflügel*), large wing-shaped spinet.

Spinettflügel (Ger.), name given in early-20th-c. Germany to the contemporary harpsichords of Hermann Seyfarth of Leipzig.

Spinettino (It.), oct. or 4′ spinet; syn. of ottavina. According to Athanasius Kircher, it was invented in Rome.

Spinettone [aug. of *spinetta*], It.: large spinet. The word has also wrongly been used to designate a harpsichord.

Spinettzug (Ger.), occasional 18th-c. Ger. designation of a course of strings at 4′ pitch on a harpsichord or piano. *Cf.* Saitenharmonika.

Spirafina, crystallophone built *ca.* 1850 by H. Spira (169).

Spitz (Ger.: pointed), reed organ stop, a syn. of the Zink organ stop in former centuries; later, of the Kornett organ stop. It was built at 2′ or 1′ pitch in the pedal, and is now obs. Also known as Kornettbass (133).

Spitzflöte (Ger.) (Fr.: *flûte à fuseau;* It.: *flauto cuspido;* Lat.: *tibia cuspida*), organ stop of open conical flue pipes at 8′, 4′, 2′, 1′ pitches, built since 1515 (from a Hagenau contract). In some cases it is identical with the Spillflöte (133).

Spitzgamba, organ stop of open conical flue pipes of narrow scale at 8′ pitch, of the gamba class (133).

Spitzgeige, Ger.: kit.

Spitzharfe, Ger.: arpanetta.

Spitzquinte, Spitzflöte organ stop at 5⅓′, 2⅔′, or 1⅓′ pitch, still in use. Also called Quintspitze.

Split keys (Fr.: *touches brisées;* Ger.: *gebrochene Tasten;* It.: *tasti spezzati*), the division of accidental keys into front and rear sections and their connection to organ pipes of different pitches was resorted to from the mid-15th c. on, in the interest of intonation. Later split keys were also applied to stringed keyboard instrs. for the same reason. Splitting the G♯ and E♭ keys was the most common way of eliminating the "wolf" of nonequal temperament. If the pitch of the E♭ keys were not satisfactory, they could be split into a D♯ and an E♭ key throughout the manuals; likewise, the G♯ was sometimes split to obtain an A♭. The contract of 1450 for the organ (completed 1484) of St. Martin's Church, Lucca, called for split D♯ and G♯ keys. In the 16th and 17th c. numerous organs were built with one or more split keys. Arnold Schlick wrote in 1511 that 12 years previously an organ had been built with *"doppelt semitonien"* in manual and pedal. It was customary to allot the front portion of the key to the sharps, the rear portion to the flats. Split keys in the lowest oct. of the compass are a result of other considerations, however: by the early 18th c. need began to be felt for the lacking low F♯ and G♯ of the *short octave; as a consequence, the accidental keys sounding D and E (they looked like C♯ and D♯) were split to give D/F♯ and E/G♯. In the bass oct. of a clavichord, split keys served to extend the compass downward: the F♯ was split to sound D also; the G♯ was split to sound E in some clavichords with an F compass. See also: short octave (64).

Sprechtopf, Ger. equivalent of pot musical.

Spring chest (Fr.: *sommier à soupapes; sommier à ressorts;* Ger.: *Springlade*), organ *wind chest in which each groove serves all pipes of the corresponding stop, with individual pallets for each pipe. The name is derived from the springs of the spring valves, *i.e.,* pallets. Spring chests were used chiefly by organ builders of the Low Countries, but slider chests were generally preferred as being simpler to maintain and repair. In 1842, Eberhard Walcker of Ludwigsburg transformed the spring chest into the *Kegellade.

Springer, Ger.: jack.

Springlade, Ger.: spring chest.

Square piano (Fr.: *piano carré;* Ger.: *Tafelklavier;* It.: *pianoforte da tavola*), piano in rectangular form, originally about the size of an 18th-c. clavichord,

finally an unwieldy giant with a 7-oct. compass. Claims for invention of the square piano in favor of Friderici of Gera or Zumpe of London have been abandoned, as a square piano dated 1742 by Johann Socher has come to light, the oldest known so far. With the immigration to England of Johann Christoph Zumpe, a former Silbermann pupil, the making of clavichord-shaped pianos was introduced there, and squares became immediately popular. In 1770 J. K. Mercken started making them in France, and by 1780 they had spread all over Europe. The early square pianos had a compass of 5 octs., F^1–f^3. Engl., Fr., and some Ger. makers used a simplified form of the Cristofori action known as *Stossmechanik, but most Ger. makers preferred the *Prellmechanik. During the last decade of the c. (1794 on) the compass was increased in the treble to c^4 by means of an "extension" consisting of a gap for the new hammers cut in the rear of the soundboard and a small additional key frame with keys and action slid underneath the soundboard. Also in this decade Broadwood invented the short-lived under-damper system, with a series of pivoted brass forks inserted in the keys, containing small pieces of thick material that damped the strings from underneath. In the 19th c. the compass was further increased and the stringing became trichord; in order to accommodate the larger number of tuning pins (hitherto situated to the player's right, as on a clavichord) it became necessary to move the pin block to the rear, parallel with the spine. Technical improvements in grand-piano making were of course also incorporated into squares, but by the middle of the 19th c. square pianos were gradually replaced by a newcomer: the *upright piano. American builders continued making square pianos longer than did their European competitors, their efforts culminating in a cross-strung, metal-plated monster with a 7-oct. compass that took up about the same amount of space as did a grand.

Squilla, med. Lat.: bell (61, 182).

Śr, frame drum of ancient Egypt (170).

Sralai [Pers. *zurnā*], oboe of Cambodia and Laos, of the zurnā type, with 6 fingerholes. Formerly called pi shanai (47, 173).

Sri churnam, syn. of tiruchinnam.

Sringa (Sans., Beng.), originally a cow horn, now a crescent- or S-shaped metal horn of N. India, made of several (2–5) curved brass sections that fit into one another, with bosses at the joints. The bore is conical. The crescent-shaped version has a thin brass rod connecting the extremities in order to give it greater stability—rather like the *cornu. Both a temple and watchman's instr.; 120–180 cm. (4–6 ft.) long. Cf. deren, kombu, ranasringa (173, 179).

S-Rohr, Ger.: S-shaped crook.

Srune [Pers. *surnāy*], Achin (Sumatra) name of the sarune. Cf. zurnā.

Sruni (Javanese) [Pers. *surnāy*], shawm of Indonesia, made of wood or bamboo with a slightly flared bell. As a temple instr. of Java, Bali, and Lombok, it is often carved and painted to resemble a dragon. Cf. sarune, serunai, srune, surnāy, zurnā (173).

Sruti, see: bajānā sruti; sruti upāngi.

Sruti upāngi (Tamil), bagpipe of S. India, a drone instr. only (in contrast to the N. Indian mashak and nāgabaddha), mouth-blown, with goatskin bag, cane blowpipe, and chanter, the last some 22 cm. (8½ in.) long, with cylindrical bore, large single reed of cane, and 6 fingerholes of which 5 are plugged with resin. It serves as a drone accompaniment to other instrs. Also called bajānā sruti, titti (13, 173).

Sruti vīnā (Sans., Beng.), vīnā of Bengal that differs from the *sitār only in that it has frets, usually 26, spaced for the 22 *sruti* (microtones) of the Indian oct. (138, 173).

Staafspel (bar chime), Du.: xylophone,

metallophone. Its first mention as a metallophone is in the 18th c. by Quirin van Blanckenburg, who described one made of bronze. It was probably of Javanese inspiration (169).

Staartstuk, see: staertstuk.

Stabrassel, Ger.: stick rattle.

Stabspiel (bar chime), Ger.: metallophone.

Stabzither, Ger.: stick zither.

Stachel, Ger.: spike.

Staertstuk [Du. *staert,* bend], Du.: harpsichord; so named from its *bentside.

Staffa (stirrup), 15th-c. It.: triangle. Cf. Stegereif.

Stag-dung, ritual trumpet of Tibet, similar to the rkan-dung but made of a tiger's femur (89 Picken).

Stahlgeige (Ger.: steel fiddle), Ger., generic name for a number of violin-type instrs. with 4 steel strings, dating from the mid-19th c. on (149).

Stahlklavier, Ger. designation of a keyboard metallophone.

Stahlspiel, Ger.: 1. metallophone; 2. bell lyre.

Stamentienpfeife (Ger.), syn. of Schwegel, particularly of the tenor instr. (159).

Stampfrohr, Stampftrommel, Ger.: stamping tube.

Stamping tube (Fr.: *bâton de rythme;* Ger.: *Stampfrohr, Stampftrommel, Stosstrommel*), tuned wooden or bamboo tube that is beaten rhythmically against the ground. Distributed in Africa, C. and S. America, Asia, and S. Seas. See also: akpateré, ambnuba, ayíguí, bazara, ch'ung tu, dikanmbo, din tenkhin, ganbo, iguíégun, juk jang go, kendang awi, kinchir, kya, muvungu, mzungu, ohe keeke, págugu, pah pung, quitiplá, tacuapa, tok, uana, wahlongka, waranga.

Stampun, Romansh: piston flute (102).

Standglocke, Ger.: resting bell.

Staple (Ger.: *Stiefel;* Sp.: *boquilla*), short, tapered metal tube on which a double reed is placed. The curved version of larger instrs. is called crook.

Stark . . . (Ger.), as a prefix to names

of organ stops, stark denotes loud intonation (133).

Steel drum, oil drum used as a musical drum in Trinidad, with one end divided into sections of different pitch by punched grooves (15 Howarth).

Steel guitar, syn. of Hawaiian guitar.

Steel marimba, syn. of marimbaphone.

Steg, Ger.: bridge.

Stegereif (stirrup), obs. Ger.: triangle. The term occurred as early as 1404 (Eberhart Cersne: *Minne Regel*) (169).

Steinharmonika, Ger.: lithophone.

Stella, *music box made by Mermod Frères of Ste. Croix from 1895 on.

Stempelflöte, Ger.: piston flute.

Stemvork, Du.: tuning fork.

Stentor . . . (Gk.), as prefix of an organ stop, stentor denotes a stop of flue pipes on exceptionally high wind pressure, usually with narrow mouth (133).

Stentorphone, organ stop of: 1) wide-scaled flue pipes at 8' pitch on high pressure, found in U.S. organs as early as the 1890's; 2) flue pipes invented by G. F. Weigle of Echterdingen at 8' pitch, with mouth extending halfway around the pipe (133, 198).

Stern, 16th-c. Ger.: rose.

Sticcado pastorale (It.), crystallophone pop. in England during the late 18th c., manufactured there *ca.* 1775, similar to the xylophone but with glass bars (89).

Sticcato, It.: xylophone (176).

Sticker (Fr.: *vergette;* Ger.: *Stecher*), **1.** in the organ a very slender vertical wooden rod between key and roller, and between roller and pallet. It communicates motion by pushing; **2.** in a piano, syn. of jack.

Stick rattle (Fr.: *sonnailles sur bâton;* Ger.: *Stabrassel*), rattle consisting of rattling objects strung on a bar or ring (100).

Stick zither (Fr.: *cithare sur bâton;* Ger.: *Stabzither*), rigid stick with one or more strings stretched between its two ends. Generally an added resonator is needed; this can be a gourd, the mouth of the player, an inflated vesicle, etc. See

also: akadingidi, bajah, banzie, baya, bīnsitar, bladder and string, bongele, carambano, carángano, devil's fiddle, dhenka, dunde, dyedye, dzendze, enzenze, gawukha's, gombi, isikehlekehle, jejy, jinge, kairata vīnā, king, kingira, kingwa ndikila, kinnara, kinnari, lokango voatavo, lusese, mongele, nengoniki, ngumbi, ngwomi, njenjo, nzenze, nzeze, phin nam tao, piah, p'in, p'in namao, pone, sa diu, santung, sefinjolo, segankuru, sekatari, sekgobogobo, setinkane, seze, si so laos, suleppe, talindo, tarimba, tsijolo, tuila, tutalo, tzitidoatl, ubhek'indhlela, udahi, villadi vādyam, vīnā, zenze, zeze, 2.

Stiefel, Ger.: boot (of an organ pipe); staple.

Stiefelstück, Ger.: butt (of a bassoon).

Stierhorn (Ger.: bull horn), see: cow horn.

Stiftgeige, Stiftharmonika, Ger.: nail violin.

Still . . . , (Ger.), as a prefix to names of organ stops, still is a syn. of echo (133).

Stiller Zink, Ger.: mute cornett.

Stillgedackt, an older name of lieblich Gedackt (133).

Stimmbogen, Ger.: crook.

Stimmbügel, Ger.: crook.

Stimme (Ger.), **1.** stop (of organ pipes); **2.** in the 18th c., soundpost (134).

Stimmer (tuner), Ger.: drone (pipe).

Stimmgabel, Ger.: tuning fork.

Stimmgabelklavier, Ger.: tuning-fork piano.

Stimmpfeife, Ger.: pitch pipe.

Stimmstock, Ger.: pin block; soundpost.

Stimmzug, Ger.: tuning slide.

Stive [OFr. *estive*], MEngl. and MHGer. term believed to denote the bagpipe or possibly the trumpet. The word appears in Engl. literature of the 13th c., and in *Parzifal* the stive is played with a buisine, flute, and tabor. *Cf.* estive (35, 189).

Stobung, brass *Jew's-harp of the Land Dayak of Borneo, with very thin frame and tongue, and a handle. *Ca.* 9 cm. (3½ in.) long (176).

Stoc, pl. **stuic,** Irish: trumpet. *Cf.* bemastocc.

Stock, in a bagpipe, the short wooden socket inserted into the bag for holding the pipes.

Stock and horn, obs. pastoral hornpipe of S. Scotland, similar to the Welsh pibcorn but not identical with the stockhorn. The tube was of wood or bone, with a horn bell, mouth bell, and single reed. Only 2 original specimens have survived: these have wooden tubes with 7 front fingerholes and a rear thumbhole, horn bells, and a wooden cap over the reed. One of them has a double bore, with 7 front fingerholes and 1 rear fingerhole on each pipe, so disposed that a pair can be closed by one finger (13, 89 Langwill).

Stockbüchel (OHGer.: *stock,* wood + *büchel,* horn), name of the alphorn in Uri and Schwyz, Switzerland.

Stockfagott, Ger.: walking-stick bassoon; racket bassoon.

Stockfiedel, 18th-c. Ger.: kit (Mattheson, *Orchester,* 1713).

Stockflöte, Ger.: czakan; walking-stick flute.

Stockgeige, Ger.: walking-stick violin.

Stockhorn, 1. in 16th-c. England, a forester's horn; **2.** in 18th-c. Switzerland, syn. of alphorn.

Stockklarinette, Ger.: walking-stick clarinet.

Stockoboe, Ger.: walking-stick oboe.

Stocktrompete, Ger.: walking-stick trumpet.

Stone chime (Ger.: *Steinharmonika*), syn. of lithophone.

Stop, 1. a control system of organs; when in the "off" position it "stops" the wind from entering the pipes; by extension, a rank or register of organ pipes; **2.** a control system on harpsichords and early pianos, taken over from organ terminology; **3.** a contrivance for altering the pitch of an instr., as pressure of a finger on a string, placement of a finger over an aperture in a tube, by extension the aperture itself; **4.** on instrs. of the vio-

lin family, the distance from the top of the belly to the emplacement of the cross stroke of the F holes, now standardized at 19.3 cm. (7⅝ in.) on a violin; **5.** obs. syn. of fret. See also: draw stop.

Stopftrompete (Ger.) (Fr.: *trompette demi-lune*), natural trumpet built in the first quarter of the 19th c. in elongated half-moon shape—hence its Fr. name—designed to accommodate the hand-in-bell playing technique that Anton Joseph Hampel had introduced for the horn. The Stopftrompete was provided with *corps de rechange (132, 169).

Stopped (Fr.: *bouché;* Ger.: *gedackt;* It.: *coperto;* Sp.: *tapado*), said of any pipe closed at the end farthest from the wind supply.

Stopped diapason, organ stop of flue pipes, originally of stopped rectangular wooden pipes, occurring at 16′ or 8′ pitch, rarely at 4′. It corresponds to the Fr. bourdon and the Ger. Gedackt. *Cf.* diapason, open diapason (129).

Stopped metallic, obs. organ stop of stopped flue pipes at 8′ and 4′ pitches, introduced by Edmund Schulze in London in 1851 (198).

Stopt, obs. spelling of stopped.

Stortino [dim. of *storto*], It.: a small or treble crumhorn.

Storto (abbr. of *cornetto storto*), It.: crumhorn.

Stossmechanik (Ger.), an early piano action in which the hammer was hinged to a rail (hammer rail) attached to the key frame: the hammers pointed to the back of the instr. and were set in motion by a jack or other device fixed to the key. A simplified form of Cristofori's action, without escapement (92).

Stosstrommel, Ger.: stamping tube.

Stosszungenmechanik, a developed form of Stossmechanik, with hammers set in motion by a form of escapement fixed to the key (the Stosszunge), usually with a check (92).

Strählorgeli, name of a mirliton in Hai, Switzerland (102).

Straight cornett (Fr.: *cornet droit;* Ger.: *gerader Zink;* It.: *cornetto dritto*), cornett with conical bore, made of a single piece of wood, usually boxwood, with rounded exterior (not octagonal, as the curved cornett), and 6 fingerholes. Also known as "white" cornett, owing to the light color of the wood, as opposed to the black leather-covered curved cornett. The Renaissance instr. had a 2-oct. compass, a^0–a^2, or higher, and was played with the same mouthpiece as the curved cornett. See also: cornett, curved cornett, mute cornett.

Stråka, Swed.: bow (9).

Stråkharpa, Swed.: bowed harp.

Stránčica, syn. of stranka.

Stranka [Serb. *strana,* side], *cross flute of Yugoslavia, found in N. Croatia and parts of Slavonia, made of maple or chestnut, with cylindrical bore and 6 equidistant fingerholes. Some shorter instrs. have only 5; 42 cm. (16½ in.) long, 2.7 cm. in. diam. Also called fayfarica, frula, stránčica (34).

Straw fiddle (Ger.: *Strohfiedel*), xylophone in which the slabs are separated from one another by straw.

Street organ, hand-cranked *barrel organ played on the streets, generally mounted on 4 wheels. See also: pierement.

Street piano, syn. of barrel piano.

Streich . . . , Ger.: bowed.

Streichbart, see: frein harmonique.

Streichklavier, Ger.: bowed keyboard instr.

Strike note, the first tone of a struck bell that is prominently heard, also called tap note or heard tone; often misnamed fundamental (155).

String (Fr.: *corde;* Ger.: *Saite;* It.: *corda;* Sp.: *cuerda*), strings have been made of a variety of materials: fiber, gut, horsehair, silk, metal, nylon. Those of fiber can be idiochord or heterochord. Idiochord strings are the older and are found today only in Further India, Indonesia, Malagasy Republic, and parts of Negro Africa: 2 longitudinal incisions are made in the outer surface of a piece of cane and are left attached at both ends; a tiny sliver of wood is pushed under

the extremities to raise and tension it. Gut strings were used in the ancient Mediterranean area and Asia Minor; now they are made chiefly of sheep intestines. The Engl. term "catgut" has still not been satisfactorily explained. Hindus do not make use of gut strings for religious reasons. Introduction of spun gut strings on the viola da gamba was attributed by Jean Rousseau (in 1687) to Sainte Colombe, but some forms of spun strings existed earlier, as Trichet, writing *ca.* 1640, relates that the lowest strings of the pandora were *retortillé* (twisted), and early in the 17th c. Hans Haiden's Geigenwerk had narrow parchment strips wound around its bass strings. Horsehair is used chiefly on bowed instrs.: the Slavic gusle still has a twisted horsehair string. Silk strings originated in Western Asia and spread from there both east and west, still very much in demand in the East. Metal has been employed ever since med. wire drawing made its use practicable. Our earliest treatise on the subject is by Theophilus, a monk now considered to have lived around 1100 (he does not mention the drawing of wire for musical instrs.). Nylon is a latecomer on the scene, but has been successfully used on both plucked and bowed instrs.

Strings may be classed as open or stopped; as melody, *sympathetic, or *drone strings; as *on-board or *off-board strings. Keyboard instrs. with 2 strings per note are said to be bichord; those with 3 strings per note trichord.

String bass, coll.: double bass.

String drum, see: tambourin à cordes.

String fastener (Ger.: *Querriegel*), flat wooden member, glued to the belly of some plucked stringed instrs., to which the strings are attached. Mersenne called it *peigne.*

String gamba, organ stop invented by Robert Hope-Jones (d. 1914), actually a viola stop voiced to imitate the viole d'orchestre of Michell and Thynne (101).

Strohfiedel, obs. Ger.: xylophone. See: straw fiddle.

Stroh violin, violin designed for recording purposes by Charles Stroh of London in 1901, with an aluminum plate instead of a body, and a trumpet bell (176).

Stromento . . . , see also: instromento . . . ; strumento . . .

Stromento d'ottone, It.: brass instr.

Struck idiophone (Ger.: *Schlagidiophon*), instr. made to vibrate by being struck (100).

Strumento d'acciaio, It.: bell lyre.

Strumento di penna, see: instromento di penna.

Strumento di porco, see: instromento di porco.

Strumento omnisono, syn. of Proteus.

Strumstrum, see: humstrum.

Strung rattle (Ger.: *Schnurrassel*), rattle composed of small objects such as shells, seeds, hoofs, etc., strung on cords or tied in bundles (170).

Stummes Klavier, Ger.: dumb piano.

Stumme Violine, Ger.: mute violin.

Stump, instr. invented by Daniel Farrant, according to Playford (in 661); an archcittern with 8 off-board and 7 on-board courses of wire strings (80 XV).

Sturgan, trumpet of ancient Ireland (144).

Stürtze, Ger.: bell (of wind instrs.).

Stutzflügel, Ger.: baby grand piano.

Stützharfe, Ger.: footed harp.

Stviri, bagpipe of Georgia, U.S.S.R., similar to the tulum but with a varying number of fingerholes, sometimes 6 on the left pipe, 3 on the right, sometimes 5 on the left, 1 on the right; or with a triple pipe composed of 2 drones and melody pipe with 7 fingerholes (13).

Su, generic term for drum in Tem (a Sudanic language) (93).

Suabe flute, organ stop of open wooden flue pipes at 4' pitch, with inverted mouths, invented by William Hill of London (d. 1871). It was of smaller scale than the claribel, but of similar tone; occasionally also made of metal (99, 198).

Suavial, organ stop of softly voiced open wooden pipes of narrow scale at 8' pitch. Also built in metal, with narrow-

mouthed, cylindrical pipes, occasionally also at 4' or 2' pitch; it is further built as a stopped Zartflöte and as an over-blowing flute. Also called flauto suabile, suabile (133).

Subbass (Fr.: *soubasse;* Ger.: *Subbass*), **1.** tonal position lying halfway between bass and contrabass; **2.** organ stop of stopped or occasionally open flue pipes of diapason scale, at 32' or 16' pitch.

Subbass viola da gamba, contrabass viola da gamba.

Subbourdon, organ stop identical with the *bourdon subbass, a 32' bourdon stop.

Subcontrabassoon (Ger.: *Subkontrafagott*), bassoon invented in 1873 by Vaclav Červeny of Königgrätz (Hradec Králové), in B♭, pitched an oct. below the contrabassoon, with a compass $B\flat^2 - B\flat^0$. No surviving specimen is known (89 Langwill).

Subcontrabass clarinet, a model in B♭, an oct. below the contrabass clarinet, is currently being produced on an experimental basis by Leblanc of Paris, designed by Houvenaghel (164).

Suber, see: shyabur.

Sublet, var. of siblet.

Sub-Prinzipal (Ger.), organ stop, a low-pitched Prinzipal.

Sudrophone, a short-lived family of valved brass instrs., invented by François Sudre of Paris, patented Feb. 18, 1892, made in sizes from soprano to contrabass, as well as 2 other sizes with modified bores. The tube was bent back on itself, with the valves, usually 3 in number, mounted on the side of the main tube, terminating in a slightly flared bell. The sudrophone was furnished with a gold-beater's-skin membrane controlled by a supplementary valve that permitted the player to modify the timbre. It was played with a cup mouthpiece (15 Morley-Pegge, 89 Bates).

Sudsu, see: suzu.

Suegala, OHGer.: swegel.

Su erh nai, Chin. name of the surnāy (75 II).

Sūfaïra, Pers., Arab.: generic term for flutes. Also called sāfūra (98).

Suga koto, syn. of wagon (144).

Su-ghosha (Sans.), *marine-shell trumpet of India (132, 144).

Sugs-pa, Tibetan whistle, taken completely into the mouth in order to sound it. Not strictly a musical instr. (89 Picken).

Sugugalli, great drum of ancient Sumer (170).

Su hu, *hu ch'in with hexagonal body of wood, snakeskin belly, and 4 strings looped to the handle, held taut by rear pegs. Called su ken hsien erh in Peking. *Cf.* dörwen chikhe khuur (142).

Suifloit, var. of Sifflöte.

Suka, obs. folk instr. of Poland, a fiddle with center bouts, F holes, stumpy neck, short and broad pegdisc, and 4 strings tuned in 5ths (89).

Suke, trumpet of Eddystone, Solomon Islands, made of 2 cylindrical tubes, of different lengths and diams., joined together. It serves as a combined vertical flute and trumpet (77).

Su ken hsien erh, name of the su hu in Peking (142).

Su ku, *frame drum of China, with 2 nailed heads. *Ca.* 9 cm. (3½ in.) high, 31 cm. (12 in.) in diam. (178).

Sul, large komunko of Korea that formerly had 25 strings. Its movable bridges are set in a diagonal line. It corresponds to the shē of China. *Ca.* 2 m. (6½ ft.) long (66).

Sula, drum of the Bwaka of the Congo, in form of 2 truncated cones joined at the smaller ends, and single head nailed with large wooden dowels (30).

Suleppe, *bar zither of Halmahera, Moluccas, very similar to the dunde. *Ca.* 66 cm. (26 in.) long (17, 173).

Suling, 1. *cross flute of E. and C. Java, with 6 fingerholes and silver mounts. Called bangsi in Batavia, Java (121); **2.** *ring flute of E. and C. Java, made of bamboo. The top is closed by a natural node; a notch is cut in this end and in the tube. A narrow bamboo ring is tied around the upper extremity, guiding the player's breath to the lower edge of the aperture; 4, 5, or 6 fingerholes are pierced at the lower end of the tube. This form of suling is the most pop. solo instr. of Java (121); **3.** the same instr. as 1, played as a *nose flute in Java (203); **4.** *whistle flute of Thailand, with rear duct; the upper end is almost closed by a wooden plug; it has 6 or 7 front fingerholes and a rear thumbhole. *Ca.* 45 cm. (16 in.) long (18).

Suling degung, suling of W. Java, with 4 fingerholes, the next to top one being much larger than the others (121).

Suling gede, very large, deep-pitched bamboo flute of Bali (J. Kunst: *The Music of Bali,* 1949).

Suling idong, *nose flute of the Sea Dayak of Borneo, made of bamboo. The lower end is open, or a lateral hole may be pierced near the bottom; it has 3 front fingerholes and a rear thumbhole and is 70–100 cm. (28–40 in.) long (176).

Suling kechil, small bamboo *ring flute of SE. Borneo, with 4 fingerholes (176).

Suling nyawa, bamboo *whistle flute of the Sea Dayak of Borneo, with 3 or 4 fingerholes. The duct is created by tying a small bamboo tube to the upper end, above the blowhole. It can also assume the form of a *ring flute (176).

Suling reog, *end-blown flute of Java, with 3 fingerholes (121).

Sultana, wire-strung viola da gamba of late-18th-c. Britain, made *ca.* 1780 by Perry of Dublin, with a body about the size of a viola d'amore and 5 pairs of metal strings, probably tuned $g^0 c^1 e^1 g^1 c^2$. Also called cither viol, psaltery-viol (79, 94).

Sultane durgi, name of the tabl turki in Nubia (176).

Suma koto, syn. of ichi gen kin.

Sumber (MHGer.: grain measure), **1.** med. Ger. name of a small *cylindrical drum; **2.** 16th-c. organ stop consisting of a few bass flue pipes that imitated the drum; first recorded in Zürich in 1507 and apparently known only in the Alemannic region. See also: drum pedal, Heerpauke, Hersumber (167).

Sumle, iron hand bell of the Namji of the Congo (19).

Summer, Ger.: drone.

Sumper, see: sumber.

Sumponia, see: symponia.

Sun, small hand bell of Korea, rarely used (66).

Sundar (Turk.), obs. Turk. lute with 10 sympathetic metal strings. *Cf.* sundari, 2 (76).

Sundaren, *aeolian bow of Java; a bamboo bow with a horsehair or rattan string is attached by its curved side to a kite that is then flown. Also called sawangan layangan, sendaren, sundari (121).

Sundari, 1. *aeolian pipe of C. Java, made of bamboo. Also called peteng, sendari (121); **2.** var. of sundaren; **3.** syn. of sitār (179).

Sung chung, former name of the po chung.

Suntūr, syn. of santūr.

Sunūj (Arab.), pl. of sanj. Cymbals of ancient Islam and of the Maghrib today. Two are held in the right hand, sometimes a single one is also held in the left. *Cf.* sanj, sanūj, sinj (144 Chottin, 147 Farmer).

Suomu duda (Finnish bagpipe), Latvian name of the bagpipe (13).

Suona-tutto, original name of the pantophone.

Šupeljka, *end-blown flute of shepherds in Yugo. Macedonia, also known in Bulgaria, made preferably of boxwood, with cylindrical bore and 6 equidistant fingerholes; it lacks a mouthpiece; 22–24 cm. (9–9½ in.) long (34).

Super . . . , as prefix to names of organ stops, super designates an oct. position.

Superoktave, Ger.: fifteenth.

Super-piano, *electrophonic piano of the electromechanical type, invented by E. Spielmann in 1927, with photoelectric tone generators.

Su pill, Estonian: Jew's-harp.

Sūpurga, smallest of the modern Turk. nāys.

Suqqara, see: zuqqāra.

Sūr, pl. **asvar,** judgment trumpet of Persia, also an instr. of dervishes (176).

Surauli, see: souravli.

Surbahar, Beng. equivalent of sur vāhara (89).

Surdelina, bellows-blown bagpipe of 17th-c. Italy, with 2 or 3 chanters and 2 drones. The chanters had narrow, cylindrical bores, were fitted with double reeds, and, according to Mersenne, had 6 and 4 keys, respectively, in addition to their fingerholes. The drones had 10 closed keys. Trichet, writing *ca.* 1640, gives the number of chanters as 3 *vs.* Mersenne's 2, each with a different number of fingerholes and keys, the object of having 3 chanters being, he says, to play 3-part music. He mentions that when the fingerholes were closed no sound issued from the pipes; thus they must have been stopped, like those of the Northumbrian small-pipe. He calls it a modern instr., gives its size as about 1½ ft., and says that it was also called *organine* (*cf.* Irish organ) (13, 190).

Suri gane, small gong of Japan (135).

Surilit, 1. W. Java name of the susurilitan; **2.** small whistle of W. Java, used by coachmen (121).

Surla [*zurnā*], **1.** *whistle flute of Hvar Island, Yugoslavia, very rare today. Similar in form to the recorder, it has 6 equidistant holes of which 5 are fingerholes, 1 a vent (34); **2.** shawm of Romania, made of wood or metal, usually with 6 fingerholes (5); **3.** Alb. word for zurnā; also called jura (12); **4.** syn. of zurla.

Surle [*zurnā*], oboe of Turkey (170).

Surma [?*zurnā*], Lith.: shawm.

Surna, syn. of rgya-gling.

Surnā (Pers., Hindi, Hindust.), conical shawm of Persia and N. India, identical with the sānāyī. *Cf.* zurnā (173).

Surnāy (Pers.), classical name of the small conical shawm of Persia, a martial instr. in the 9th c. Under Turk. influence its name was changed to zurnā.

Surnāya, Syrian word for surnāy (98).

Surrscheibe, Ger.: disc buzzer.

Sursanga, bowed chordophone of India, with body, pegbox, and scroll of the violin, but parchment belly, frets, and 4 metal strings tuned $f^1 c^1 c^1 g^1$. *Ca.* 120 cm. (4 ft.) long (173).

Sursringara, long-necked lute of S. India, with calabash body, metal belly, small gourd resonator set under the upper part of the neck, and 6 metal strings attached to lateral pegs. It is played with a plectrum (132 Tagore).

Surune, 1. *nose flute of Nias, Indonesia, made of cane with square fingerholes burned in (176); **2.** an oboe of Nias (203).

Sur vāhara (Sans.), esrar of N. India, having the gutter-shaped neck of a ranjanī vīnā, a modern bowed instr. Also called alapu vīnā (168).

Sur vīnā, vīnā of Bengal, with round, gourd body, wooden belly, and 4 or 6 strings tuned $c^0 g^0 c^1 c^1$ or $c^0 e^0 g^0 c^1 d^1 g^1$. *Ca.* 110 cm. (43 in.) long (138).

Suryā nai (Arab.), ancient Arab. reedpipe, first recorded in the 9th c. (75 I).

Sūryapirai, *frame drum of S. India, restricted to temples. A piece of parchment is stretched over a slender iron hoop and fastened by a handle to a person's forehead. Played with a stick. *Cf.* chandrapirai (179).

Susira, generic name of wind instrs. in India (147).

Suspek (nightingale), *whistle flute of the Cheremiss of the U.S.S.R., made of hollow twigs or of clay; the instr. must be moistened before use (146).

Suspension rattle (Ger.: *Reihenrassel*), perforated idiophones mounted together so as to strike against each other, as jingles, for instance (100).

Susunu, 1. heterochord *tube zither of Malaya, with a variable number of strings, movable bridges, and a palm-leaf resonator (176); **2.** name of the sassandu in the Moluccas (149).

Susurilitan, small *globular flute of Java, made of terra cotta and shaped like a bird. The blowhole is a slit in its tail. It has 2 fingerholes and 1 other hole and sounds $f^2 g^2 g\#^2 a^2$. *Cf.* surilit, taleot (121).

Sūt (Pers.), *whistle flute of Persia, with 6 front fingerholes and a rear thumbhole. Also called nāy labek (98).

Sutak, obs. bird whistle of Persia, consisting of a brass bowl containing water, to which a whistle was attached (76).

Šutka, mouth-blown bagpipe of Slovakia, a small, high-pitched dudy (13).

Šutky, obs. bagpipe with single drone, played in Moravia until the 18th c. (89).

Sutri nahabat, copper kettledrums of India, mounted on a camel, both played by the same drummer. *Cf.* nahabat (170).

Suwukan, see: gong suwukan.

Suxča, globular flute of pre-Columbian Peru, made of deer or guanaco skull (105).

Suzu, ovoid *pellet bell of ancient and modern Japan, used by female temple dancers, now a Shinto ceremonial instr. Made of copper or brass. A cluster is often affixed by metal rings to a handle, thus forming a rattle (144, 157).

Svarabat, large, clumsy lute of India, with bucket-like body continuing as neck and terminating in a carved head; it has a parchment belly, bridge, 6 strings held by lateral pegs in a pegbox, and gut frets. It is played with a small horn plectrum (179).

Svaragat, see: svarabat.

Svaramandala, syn. of satatantri vīnā.

Svardonica, double svirala, a Serb. *whistle flute made of a single block of wood divided for half its length into 2 pipes. The right pipe has 5 fingerholes, the left has 4. The 4 lower holes are parallel and can be stopped with one finger; they are slightly apart in pitch and produce beats (132).

Svegelhorn (OEngl.), see: swegelhorn.

Švegla, primitive wooden pipe of Slovenia (144).

Svigla, Gothic: swegel.

Svirala, pl. **svirale,** generic term for flutes in Serb., some of which have specific names. The specific name of the svirala of N. Croatia and Slavonia is *jedina, that of W. Serbia, *duduk (34).

Sviralina, dim. of svirala.

Sviralja, syn. of mali caval in N. Montenegro (34).

Sviraljka, dim. of sviralja (34).

Svirchitsa (dim. of svirka), Bulg. *whistle flute with conical tube and 6 fingerholes. *Ca.* 32 cm. (12½ in.) long (132).

Svirel, 1. *whistle flute of Russia, with 2 front fingerholes and a rear thumbhole, rarely with 6 fingerholes and a thumbhole—a Schwegel; **2.** syn. of sopilka, a Ukrainian flute; **3.** Russ.: shawm; **4.** Russ.: chanter of a bagpipe (176).

Svirka, Bosnian equivalent of the Serbian duduk, 3; it has a rear duct and is octagonal in cross-section. It is played by peasants and shepherds (34).

Svistulka, Russ. clay whistle with 2 fingerholes (132).

Svrdonica, see: svardonica.

Swalwe, term that occurs in MHGer. literature, believed to be a swallow-shaped harp, possibly of Engl. origin (189).

Swannee whistle (Fr.: *jazzo-flûte*), bird whistle of 19th-c. origin, used as a toy instr. and exceptionally scored for in orchestral works.

Swarabat, see: svarabat.

-**Sweet potato,** U.S., syn. of ocarina.

Swegel (OEngl., MHGer.: shinbone), earliest name of the *cross flute in Europe. See: Schwegel.

Swegelbalc (swegel bag), OHGer.: bagpipe.

Swegelhorn, in med. times a form of hornpipe with parallel double pipes, 1 or 2 horn bells and reeds mouthed directly, according to contemporary representations. An 8th-c. Saxon vocabulary translates *"sambucus"* as "swegelhorn." See also: swegel (14, 79).

Swell (Ger.: *Schweller*), device to give dynamic expression to keyboard instrs. Abraham Jordan in 1712 had produced the first *swell box, in which a portion of the organ could be enclosed. Roger Plenius built a keyboard instr. in 1741 called *lyrichord, with the lid divided into 2 sections, 1 of which could be opened and closed by means of a pedal. In 1769 Burkat Shudi patented his *Venetian swell for harpsichords, and his competitor, Jacob Kirkman, was obliged to fall back on Plenius' version of the divided lid. Upon his death in 1773, Shudi's patent was inherited by John Broadwood. On square pianos of the 18th and early 19th c. the swell was a device for lifting the front portion of the right side of the lid, or the wooden dust plate that rested over the strings (89 Hipkins, 92).

Swell box (Fr.: *boîte expressive;* Ger.: *Schwellkasten*), boxlike chamber furnished with shutters or louvers containing the pipes of a swell organ. The shutters open and close like a venetian blind, causing the box to be called occasionally *Venetian swell. The first swell box was built in 1712 by Jordan of London, a large sliding shutter forming the front side of the box (89).

Swell organ, the section of an organ inclosed in a swell box and controlled by a swell pedal.

Swesch, swische, 16th-c. Scottish word for the drum of the Swiss fife-and-drum corps, the later snare or military drum (79).

Swiss bells, modern percussion clapper bell of rhythm bands.

Swiss drum, early name of the snare drum.

Syao, see: siao.

Sylvestrina [Lat. *silva,* forest], see: Waldflöte (organ stop).

Symandre, var. of simandre.

Sympathetic string (Ger.: *Resonanzsaite*), a string that is not bowed or plucked but that vibrates in sympathy with others that are. Such strings reached England from the Near East in the 16th c. and spread from there to the Continent.

Francis Bacon (d. 1626) wrote of a viola da gamba with sympathetic strings, and Praetorius relates that the English used them on bowed instrs. In 1652 Playford wrote that the lyra viol with its sympathetic strings had been "set aside." The only European instr. to retain its sympathetic strings is the viola d'amore. Short-lived attempts have been made to add to the piano's resonance by applying sympathetic strings to part of the compass.

Symphonia (Gk., Lat.), **1.** in antiquity, see: symponia; **2.** in the early Middle Ages, a 2-headed drum, according to Isidore of Seville, who first used the word in this sense. See also: cylindrical drum; **3.** med. name of the organistrum, recorded (first in Fr. as *symphonie*) from the mid-12th c. to the early 16th c.

Symphonica [Gk. *symphonia*], an improved accordion, patented by Rouet of Paris on Aug. 21, 1857. Also called accordéon-symphonica (204).

Symphonie [Gk. *symphonia*], **1.** OFr. name of the organistrum from *ca.* 1155 to 1377; later it is used in a historical sense by writers such as Mersenne, who added *"qu'on nomme vielle"* (that one calls *vielle*). During this period and after it also was known as chifonie; **2.** occasional name of the drum, used in an antiquarian sense only (see: symphonia), by Arbeau, for instance, who in 1588 uses the word as syn. for tabourin; **3.** MEngl.: word occurring in literature from *ca.* 1330 to 1430, taken over from OFr.; **4.** Ger. generic term for spinets and virginals from the late 16th c. to the 18th c.

Symphonium [Gk. *symphonia*], **1.** an early form of *mouth organ, patented by Charles Wheatstone in 1829, with free reeds that operated on pressure wind only and were contained in a metal box, with a single blowhole in front and a finger button on each side. The reeds were first made of silver, then of steel (15 Howarth); **2.** automatophone invented by Friedrich Kaufmann of Dresden after

1838, an enlarged *chordaulion with automatic piano, flutes, clarinets, clappers, kettledrums, a forerunner of the *orchestrion (37); **3.** free-reed keyboard instr. that could be combined with a piano, patented by Alexandre-François Debain of Paris on Oct. 28, 1845 (204); **4.** *music box introduced by Paul Lochmann of Gohlis near Leipzig in 1885, mass produced from 1886 on, with perforated circular cardboard disc sounded by combs. Usually it assumed the form of an upright cabinet. The first musical "slot machine," it enjoyed considerable popularity in its day (37, 43).

Symphonium mélodique, free-reed keyboard instr., an improved mélophone in form of a violoncello, patented by Arthur Quentin de Gromard in France on March 9, 1861, and in England on June 3, 1863. See also: cécilium (176, 204).

Symphony [Gk. *symphonia*], in late med. England an organistrum or a 2-headed drum. In the 16th c. it was equated with dulcimer. *Cf.* symphonia, symphonie (Oxford English Dictionary).

Symponia, the symponia (also simpunia, sumponia) of biblical times was for a long time considered to have been a bagpipe (a nonexistent instr. in those days) and subsequently an orchestral performance rather than an instr. More recently Dr. Edith Gerson-Kiwi has suggested that it could have been a form of *magrepha, if we admit the possibility of the word being derived not from Gk. *symphonia* but from Gk. *siphon,* reed, artery, indicative of a wind instr., and that *zampogna might likewise be descended from siphon, the two terms (siphon and symphonia) having later become confused. The Book of Daniel uses the word form *siphonia*. See also: symphonia (84).

Synthematophone, organ stop of wide-scaled metal pipes, conical, with double mouths opposite each other, introduced by Walcker. They require high pressure and speak at 8′ pitch (131).

Syringe [Gk. **syrinx*], obs. Fr.: pan-pipes.

Syrinx, panpipes of ancient Greece, a shepherd's instr. with 3–13 pipes, commonly 7, arranged in raft form. Earlier representations show rectangular instrs.; in Hellenistic and Roman times the pipes are graduated in length (21, 176).

Syron, name given in early-17th-c. England to an archcittern having 7 pairs of on-board strings and 7 single off-board strings, therefore, also called "fourteen-course cittern." Its tuning was $G^1 A^1 B^{(b)1} C^0 D^0 E^0 F^0$ (off-board) $G^0 d^0 f^0 b^{(b)0} g^0 d^1 e^1$. Also called sirene (79).

Système à fourchettes, Fr.: fork action.

Sytole, sythol, sytholphe, MEngl.: citole.

Sze hu hsien, Peking equivalent of the hu ch'in (176).

Sztort [It. **storto*], Pol.: crumhorn (176).

T

T . . . , see: Ch . . .

Tabal [Arab. *tabl*], Hispano-Arab.
form of tabl. *Cf.* atabal.

Tabala [Arab. *tabl*], Khassonka (Sudanic) name of the tabl, a hemispheric
drum hollowed out of a block of wood;
it is carried by 2 persons on great occasions, the player walking behind them
(93).

Tabalde [Arab. *tabl*], Ful (a Sudanic language): drum (93).

Taballo [Arab. *tabl*], early It. form
of the word *timballo*, a kettledrum.

Tabalu (Akk.), generic name for
drums in ancient Mesopotamia (147
Farmer).

Tabang-tabang, name of the terbang in
ancient Hindu-Javanese literature (121).

Tabaq, Sudanese (Dongola) kettledrum, with clay body (176).

Tabaqa, frame drum of the Maghrib
(176).

Tabaque, var. of atabaque.

Tabbäl, Arab.: kettledrum (98).

Tabella, It. semanterion, sounded during Easter week instead of bells.

Tabir, tabira (Pers.), *hourglass drum
of ancient Persia. Firdusi (d. 1020) used
the expression. *Cf.* atambor, atämo, danbore, gatambore, gathanbore, katambore
(44).

Tabl, pl. **tubūl** (Arab.) [Aram.
tablā], generic name for drums in med.
and modern Arab. culture, also used in a
specific sense to designate a *cylindrical
drum. Vars. of the word occur from the
Iberian Peninsula to India. *Cf.* atabal,
atabale, atabule, atama, atukpani, atumpani, tabal, tabalde, tabbāl, tabla, tabule,
tamande, tamatama, tamba, tambana,
tambari, tumbul, tubbel (147 Farmer).

Tabla [Arab. *tabl*], drum of N. and
C. India, with body of metal, wood, or
clay, in shape of 2 truncated cones
joined at their widest part. The single
head is laced with thongs forming a zigzag pattern and tightened with cylindrical wooden dowels. The head is permanently treated with black tuning paste;
this accounts for its being compared to
the right head of the *mridanga. It is
generally played together with the bāmyā
(138, 179).

Tablā [Akk. *tabalu*], Aram.: drum
(93).

Tabl al bāz, see: tabli bāz.

Tabl al ġawīq, kettledrum of the modern Near East; a single, shallow metal
kettle with laced head, carried on horseback, struck with a single beater (170).

Tabl al kabir (Arab.: great drum),
large kettledrum of the Near East, successor to the kurga.

Tabl al markab, Arab. kettledrum first
mentioned in the 10th c., identical with
the naqqāra (170).

Tabl al shāwish, var. transcription of
tabl al ġawīq.

Tabl baladi, small wooden *cylindrical
drum of the Near East, with 2 heads; the
ancestor of our snare drum and tenor
drum (170).

Tabl dūrū'i, obs. double-headed drum
of the Near East (75 II).

Table, 1. (Fr.: *table;* Ger.: *Fundamentalbrett*), in an organ the board constituting the top of the wind chest, on
which the sliders are laid; **2.** the belly or
back of a stringed instr.; **3.** Fr.: abbr.
of table d'harmonie.

Table d'abrégé, Fr.: roller board.

Table d'harmonie, Fr.: soundboard.

Tablettes [dim. of *table,* from Lat. *tabella,* tablet], clappers of med. France. The term is replaced by *cliquette* from the 15th c. on (53).

Tabli bāz (hawking kettledrum), very small kettledrum of the Near East, made of metal and used for hawking. It existed in 17th-c. Turkey and is still played there; it is also played in Egypt, but only during Ramadan. Beaten with a strap. The name is also abbr. to bāz (25, 76, 144).

Tablilla [Lat. **tabella*], obs. Sp.: clapper.

Tabl migrī, shallow kettledrum of the modern Near East, of metal, with a laced head beaten with a strap (170).

Tabl mukhannath, hourglass drum of the Arabs. Syn. of kūbā (93).

Tabl shāmī, shallow kettledru;. of the modern Near East, of metal with laced head. Also known to med. Islam. It is played with 2 sticks (170).

Tabl turki (Arab.: Turkish drum), large, shallow, *cylindrical drum of the Near East, carried on donkey back. It is the ancestor of our bass drum (called Turkish drum up to the 19th c.). *Cf.* atabal turqués (170).

Tabolija, idiochord bamboo *tube zither of S. Nias, Indonesia (119).

Tabor [OFr. **tabur*], small drum, round and shallow, often provided with a snare, in use from the 12th c. on; the ancestor of our snare drum. In Engl. literature of the 14th c. it is commonly spelled tabour. Played together with a pipe (see: pipe and tabor), it is most often depicted suspended from the player's left arm, with the drumstick held in his right. During its long career it has assumed many sizes and even shapes, generally being rather shallow in relation to its diam.

Tabor au flahutel (MFr.), drum of the *pipe and tabor ensemble.

Taborel [dim. of **tabor*], 13th- and 14th-c. Fr.: small tabor.

Tabor pipe (Ger.: *Trommelpfeife*), the pipe of the *pipe and tabor ensemble.

The typical pipe is a flageolet type, with 2 front fingerholes and a rear thumbhole, narrow cylindrical or slightly tapering bore, usually made of boxwood, and held in the left hand. Commonly pitched in D, it is devoid of keys and has a length of some 30 cm. (12 in.). (These remarks do not apply to the *fluviol.) The pedal tone is not obtainable, and the scale starts on the second harmonic, so that 3 fingerholes suffice to bridge the gap between the second and third harmonics. See also: chistu, flageol, flahute, flûtet, fluviol, gaita, galoubet, jombarde, pipe, pipe and tabor, pito, Schwegel, Stamentienpfeife, Tämerlinpfeife (14).

Tabour [OFr. *tabur*], Engl., Fr.: drum. The term occurs from the 11th to the 15th c.

Tabouret [dim. of **tabour*], obs. Engl.; Fr.: small tabour.

Tabourin [dim. of **tabour*], in 15th-c. France a small tabour; during the c. the word changes to tambourin.

Tabourin de Basque (Fr.), tambourine. Thoinot Arbeau in 1588 and Cotgrave in 1611 describe it as a frame drum, the latter noting: "small bells and other jingling knacks of lattin . . ." *Cf.* tambour de Basque (204).

Tabret [dim. of **tabor*], small tabor, first mentioned in 1464.

Tabrwdd [**tabor*], in former times a drum of Wales used by minstrels on feast days and for dancing (79).

Tabuan veteh, syn. of tatabuan kavan (119).

Tabule [Arab. **tabl*], large drum of the Mandingo of Guinea and Senegal republics (176).

Tabur [prob. Pers. **tabir*], OFr.: drum. The word is first recorded in the 11th c.

Tabūrak (Pahl.), probably a dim. of tabir (75 II).

Taburn [OFr. **tabur*], MEngl.: drum (180).

Tacuapu, *stamping tube of the Apapocuva-Guaraní and Caingua Indians of Brazil, usually of bamboo, 75–130 cm. (30–51 in.) long (105).

Tad, fiddle of Punjab and Rajputana villages, with wooden body partly covered with a membrane belly, a square pegbox with lateral pegs, 4 melody strings and 3 sympathetic (173).

Tadumon, improvised drum of Upper Guinea, made only when no other drum is available. A rice mortar is covered with a tanned skin lapped on by a ligature (42).

Tafelklavier, Ger.: square piano.

Taga, see: taqa.

Taganing, small sigordang, *ca.* 48 cm. (19 in.) high (176).

Taganza, *frame drum of the NW. Sahara, made of goatskin stretched over a flour sieve and decorated with henna. It is played by women during wedding festivities (193).

Tagbuan, idiochord *tube zither of Buru Island, Indonesia, with 4–6 strings spaced close to one another. *Cf.* tatabuan kavan (173).

Tagelharpa (horsehair harpa), syn. of talharpa.

Tagong, *tube zither of Mindanao, Philippine Islands, with up to 6 idiochord strings distributed on both sides of a longitudinal gutter. Also called togo (119, 149).

Tahitahia, children's clay flute of the Malagasy Republic, with 2 fingerholes (171).

Tahona, syn. of tajona.

Ta hu ch'in, hu ch'in (Chin. spike fiddle), with piriform body of coconut, wooden soundboard, and lateral tuning pegs. It bears resemblance to the khilkhuur (69, 170).

Ta hu le, chordophone of China, with piriform body, rounded back, snakeskin belly, and neck terminating in a carved figure. Two rib-fastened strings are held by lateral pegs sometimes made of ivory. The neck and body are carved out of one piece of wood. Also called hu le (4).

Tahur, *marine-shell trumpet of Laur,

New Ireland, Bismarck Archipelago (176).

Taide, syn. of trompetica china.

Taiko, see: daiko.

Taille, Fr.: tenor; instr. of tenor range; abbr. for taille de violon, taille des hautbois, etc.

Taille d'amour, Fr.: Amorschall.

Taille des hautbois (Fr.), oboe of the late 17th and early 18th c., resembling the ordinary oboe except that it was larger and pitched in F, a 5th lower. In band music its part was often abbr. to "taille." Some models were made with the flaring bell of the oboe, others with a globular bell like that of the cor anglais. The reed was carried on a bent metal crook. In England the instr. was known as tenor hoboy (although it is an alto instr.). Henry Purcell scored for it in his *Dioclesian* of 1690. James Talbot, about a decade later, describes a tenor hoboy made in a single section. Whereas on the Continent a curved model came to be preferred, the Engl. model remained straight and was subsequently known as the vox humana (15, 89).

Taille de viole, Fr.: tenor viola da gamba.

Taille de violon, Fr.: tenor violin. The term is recorded from the mid-16th c. (1553) on (80 VII).

Tailpiece (Fr.: *cordier;* Ger.: *Saitenhalter;* It.: *cordiera*), piece of wood to which the strings of most European bowed instrs. are attached. Historically the shape has varied; it has been semicircular, crescent-shaped, a tapering rectangle, a triangle. The tailpiece can be traced to the 11th c.

Tailpin, syn. of spike.

Tai p'ing hsiao, *whistle flute of China, usually of bamboo, with 6 front fingerholes and a hole covered with a thin membrane—a mirliton device. The duct is formed by closing the top with a wooden plug and cutting a mouth in the back of the pipe. *Ca.* 40 cm. (16 in.) long.

Tairan [Arab. *tarayān,* to fly], name

given by the Arabs of Java to the terbang (121).

Taisen, large kirisen of Japan, with circular body and parchment belly, played with a small wooden plectrum. *Ca.* 38 cm. (15 in.) in diam. (157).

Tājira, small bowl-shaped drum of the N. African Berber (89 Farmer).

Tajona, Afro-Cuban drum made of a slender conical barrel, with single head stretched over a hoop and laced to projecting pegs. Also called tahona (152).

Take fuye, syn. of shino fuye.

Takhe (crocodile), wooden *tube zither of Cambodia, carved to resemble a crocodile. It corresponds to the mi gyaun of Burma and Assam and to the chakhe of Thailand. Its 3 strings are tuned $A^0 e^0 a^0$ (47).

Taki koto, koto of Japan, with 13 strings and as many movable bridges, tuned $d^1 g^0 a^0 b\flat^0 d^1 e\flat^1 g^1 a^1 b\flat^1 d^2 e\flat^2 g^2 a^2$, and played with an ivory plectrum (176).

Täks, 1. generic term for flutes among the Uro-Chipayan Indians; **2.** specifically, the name of panpipes of the Chipaya Indians of the Andes. They have raft form, are stopped by a natural node, and number 5 or 7 pipes. A peculiarity is that each pipe has tied to it a bamboo split, cut obliquely at its lower end. *Cf.* phusa (104).

Taku, bronze bell of ancient Japan. *Cf.* thak (144).

Tāla (Sans., Beng.), small cymbals of India. *Cf.* talam (173).

Talabalacco [Turk. *dumbelek*], 16th- and 17th-c. It., Moorish war drum. *Cf.* tichecombaco.

Talalo, syn. of re-re on Celebes and Banggai Island, Indonesia (122).

Talam, small basin-shaped cymbals of India, heavier and thicker than the jalra, and having a tinkling sound. See also: Brahmatālam, kayitalama, tāla (179).

Talambasi [Turk. *tulumbaz*], obs. small kettledrums of Yugoslavia, formerly played in pairs and carried on horseback on either side of the saddle. Up to 20

cm. (8 in.) in diam. *Cf.* tulumbas, tulumbaz (89).

Talancă, Rom.: bell (5).

Talberone, talbrone [*tabur*], Scottish: a drum. *Cf.* taburn (107).

Talburn [*tabur*], Scottish: tabour.

Talemon, syn. of chelempung, 1.

Taleot, 1. name of the susurilitan in W. Java; **2.** *cross flute of Banten, W. Java, made of bamboo (121).

Taletta, It. cog rattle used during Easter week (169).

Taleua, *end-blown flute of the Siusi of Brazil, made of cane or deer bone (176).

Talharpa [*tall,* pine, or *tagel,* horsehair], a form of *bowed harp preserved in the Swed. settlements of Estonia, that is, in the coastal area and islands settled not later than the 13th c. It corresponds to the Finn. jouhikantele, from which it may be derived. The handhole is very wide, often square. The 3 or 4 strings were formerly of horsehair, now are gut or metal; 2 are melody strings, the remainder, drones. They are secured by rear tuning pegs. The playing position is that of the jouhikantele. *Ca.* 44–55 cm. (17–21½ in.) long. Also called tagelharpa. See also: haarr gie, rootsikandel (9).

Talimpuen, syn. of chelempung.

Talindo, *stick zither of Banggai Island, Indonesia, with single string and resonator (119).

Taliuma, panpipes of the Tariana Indians of Brazil (176).

"Talking drum," drum of a portion of W. Africa (the "bend"), used for transmitting messages. This is done, not by tapping out signals, but by sounding the actual words on 2 drums of different pitches; R. S. Rattray discovered that the high and low pitches of the drums used for this purpose corresponded to the high- and low-pitched vowels of local speech. This procedure is of course possible only when dealing with tonal languages. For details and sample messages see Source 162.

Tallharpa, var. of talharpa.

Talon, Fr.: frog (of a bow). Also called hausse.

Tal tanbūr, obs. Turk. metal-strung tanbūr (76).

Talusuba, panpipes of the Desana Indians of the Guianas (105).

Tālyika, Sans.: cymbals (176).

Tam, 1. lyre of the Dinka-Agheer of the Congo. *Cf.* tohmu, tom, tum (19); **2.** see: cai tam.

Tama fuye, globular stone flute of ancient Japan, with single hole (144).

Tamande [Arab. **tabl*], Mandingo word for drum (93).

Tamarinpfeife, corr. of Tämerlinpfeife.

Tamatama [Arab. **tabl*], Tuareg word for drum (93).

Tamba [Arab. **tabl*], Mandingo: drum (93).

Ṭambal (pron. tsambal) [Gk. *kymbalon*], Rom. dulcimer, a cimbalom introduced from Hungary in the 19th c. Made in table form, but also as a smaller trapezoid that can be suspended from the player's neck (C. Prichici: *Metoda de ṭambal,* 1956).

Tambana [**tabl*], Jalonka (Sudanic) name for the tabl, an **hourglass drum with cord lacings. It is held under the player's left arm; the pitch is modified by grasping the cords (93).

Tambaque, var. of atabaque (5).

Tambari [**tabl*], kettledrum of the Hausa of Sokoto Province, Nigeria (93).

Tambattam (Tamil) [?**timbuttu*], large, circular **frame drum of S. India, possibly descended from the Babylonian **timbuttu. In some areas the head is nailed; in others it is laced with thongs that converge in form of a star at the center of the open bottom. This variety is used only by aboriginal peoples such as the Khota, Khondo, etc. It is played with a short stick while held horizontally in front of the player. Up to 1.25 m. (4 ft.) in diam. It corresponds to the Near Eastern daf. Also called thambatti. *Cf.* dafli, tambotta, tammittam, tappeta, temettama (170, 173).

Tambolo, bamboo trumpet of the Poso Toradja of Celebes, presumably a foreign word (112).

Tambor [?Pers. **tabir*], Cat., Port., Prov., Sp.: kettledrum; in Port. and Sp., also: drum.

Tambora, Cat.: kettledrum.

Tambor de fricción, Sp.: friction drum.

Tambor de tronco (Sp.: tree-trunk drum), Latin-American name of the **yuka (152).

Tambor de tronco hendido (Sp.: cleft-trunk drum), Sp.: slit drum.

Tamborí, Cat. equivalent of tamboril; it accompanies the **flaviol in *coblas.*

Tamboril, very small **cylindrical drum of Spain, with 2 laced heads and a snare; it serves to accompany the one-hand **gaita or **pito. Its diam. is about the same as its height. Also played on the Balearic Islands. It corresponds to the tabor (57).

Tamborim [dim. of **tambor*], Port.: small one-headed drum. In Brazil it often consists of a half barrel, held under the left arm and played with the right hand (7).

Tamborin, Prov.: tambourin à cordes.

Tamboritsa, see: tamburiṭe.

Tambor mumbomba, obs. Afro-Cuban **slit drum, formerly in use in Havana, with plain vertical slit, played with 2 small sticks. It disappeared during the late 19th c. *Ca.* 1.50 m. (5 ft.) high with a diam. of 25 cm. (10 in.). Very similar to the ikuru of Nigeria (152).

Tambor-onça, name of the cuíca (friction drum) in Maranhão, Brazil (7).

Tambor terrero, Sp.: ground drum.

Tambotta, Malayalam equivalent of the tambattam (176).

Tambour [**tabour*], generic Fr. word for drum, in use from the mid-14th c. on. In Trichet's day (*ca.* 1640) it could be used to denote a snare drum, tambourine, or kettledrum (190).

Tamboura, see: tanbura.

Tambour à friction, Fr.: friction drum.

Tambouras, see: tampouras.

Tambour d'eau, Fr.: water gourd.

Tambour de Basque, Fr.: tambourine. *Cf.* tabourin de Basque.

Tambour de Biscaye, syn. of tambour de Basque (79).

Tambour de bois, Fr.: slit drum.

Tambour de bronze, Fr.: kettle gong.

Tambour de Perse (more correctly: *tambour des Perses*), obs. Fr.: kettle-drum. Arbeau still used the term in 1588.

Tambour en cône, Fr.: conical drum.

Tambour en cylindre, Fr.: cylindrical drum.

Tambour en double cône, Fr.: double conical drum.

Tambour en goblet, Fr.: goblet drum.

Tambour en sablier, Fr.: hourglass drum.

Tambour en terre, Fr.: ground drum.

Tambour en tonneau, Fr.: barrel drum.

Tambour-hochet, Fr.: rattle drum.

Tambourin [dim. of *tambour*], **1.** 2-headed tabor drum of Provence, known from the 15th c. on, with long cylindrical body of walnut or beechwood, the upper head of stillborn calf, the lower of kidskin. Still played, together with the *galoubet, it is 70 cm. (28 in.) high, 35 cm. (14 in.) in diam.; **2.** Fr. abbr. of tambourin à cordes; **3.** name of the chicotén in the Basque country (23).

Tambourin à cordes (Fr.: string drum), European folk zither descended from the med. *chorus. Gerson in the 14th c. described it as having 2 strings; in the 15th c. it is depicted with 3. The instr. is formed of a rectangular box with a variable number of strings stretched over one of the long surfaces. They are struck, all at the same time, with a small stick. Frequently a one-hand-flute player accompanies himself on the tambourin à cordes, which he then suspends from his left forearm by a strap. The instr. is known by a number of names. See: alto-basso, bertz, bûche, chicotén, chorus, épinette des Vosges, salmo, salterio, soinu, tambourin de Béarn, tambourin de Gascogne, tamburina, tuntun.

Tambourin de Béarn, tambourin à cor-des played together with the one-hand flute in S. France. Its thick gut strings are tuned to tonic and dominant (170).

Tambourin de Berne, corr. of tambou-rin de Béarn.

Tambourin de Gascogne, tambourin à cordes of Gascony, played with the one-hand flute.

Tambourin de Provence, elongated 2-headed *cylindrical drum of Provence, played with the one-hand flute (136).

Tambourin de Suisse, 1. 15th- and 16th-c. name of the *snare drum in France; **2.** organ stop, imitative of 1, built at Rouen in 1515, equivalent of the Heerpauke stop (167, 169).

Tambourine [*tambour*]' (Fr.: *tambour de Basque;* Ger.: *Tamburin, Schellentrommel;* It.: *tamburino;* Sp.: *panderete*), modern name (1579 on) of the *timbrel, a shallow *frame drum of Near Eastern origin reintroduced to Europe with the Turk. music of the 18th c. It may have 1 or 2 heads, is often supplied with jingles, and is played with bare hands. The tambourine is a descendant of the hand frame drum of E. Mediterranean culture; its ancestor was an attribute of Astarte and it remained the sole female instr. of the Near and Middle East. The modern European form has a single head nailed over a wooden hoop 25–30 cm. (10–12 in.) in diam. and some 8 cm. (3 in.) in depth. Metal jingles *ca.* 5 cm. (2 in.) in diam. are inserted in holes cut in the frame. Tambourines may be played with the fingers or closed knuckles or simply be shaken to set the jingles ringing. The European form is devoid of snares. The Spanish type is made with either round or square frame and is hung with jingles and pellet bells. Tambourines are found on the N. coast of Africa, S. America (from Europe), Asia, ancient and modern Europe (84, 89, 168).

Tambour militaire, Fr.: snare drum.

Tambour par pincement, Fr.: plucked drum.

Tambour roulant, Fr.: tenor drum.

Tambour sur cadre, Fr.: frame drum.

Tambour sur pied, Fr.: footed drum.

Tambue (lion), *friction drum of the Luba of the Congo, with decorated globular body. The sound is said to resemble the roaring of a lion (16).

Tambula, med. Lat.: kettledrum (176).

Tambur [*tanbūr], **1.** long-necked lute of Afghanistan, with hemispheric body, fretted neck, and both melody strings and sympathetic strings. The melody strings are inserted in frontal pegs; the sympathetic ones are inserted into the neck by lateral pegs. Also called rabāb; **2.** bowed chordophone of the S. African Griqua, a European-inspired fiddle with skin belly. Cf. velviool (116).

Tambūr, 1. Pahl. equivalent of tanbūr; **2.** MHGer. [OFr. *tabor]: tabor.

Tambura, 1. LLat.: kettledrum; **2.** obs. tanbūr of Romania; **3.** Tinctoris' spelling of tanbūr (ca. 1490).

Tamburā [*tanbūr], classical drone lute of India, introduced from Persia during the late Middle Ages, similar to the sitār. The body is of wood or, in cheaper models, of a spherical gourd, with a flat or slightly arched belly, a long unfretted neck, and 4 metal strings tuned to tonic, 5th or 4th, and 2 oct. unisons, e.g., $c^0 c^1 c^1 g^0$. The strings are never stopped, but are gently plucked with the player's right forefinger. Plectra are not used. The tuning pegs are both frontal and lateral. A movable bridge of ivory is placed on the neck; as the tamburā accompanies the singing of ragas, its pitch is adjusted to the range of the singer's voice. Today, however, it is being replaced by the harmonium. The tamburā is held in upright position, with its body resting on the player's right thigh. Var. types include those with octagonal wooden body and carved head. Also called tumburu vīnā (138, 179).

Tamburello, It.: tambourine (187).

Tamburi, syn. of tamburā.

Tambūr-i mas (Pahl.), a large tanbūr of ancient Persia (75 II).

Tamburin, Ger.: tambourine.

Tamburina, a name of the tambourin à cordes in the Basque country (132).

Tamburino, It.: tambourine.

Tamburiţe [*tanbūr], long-necked lute of Romania, borrowed from the Serbs, with metal strings. It is played with a plectrum (5).

Tamburo, It.: drum; kettledrum.

Tamburo da rullo, syn. of tamburo rullante.

Tamburo grande, obs. It.: bass drum.

Tamburo militare, It.: snare drum.

Tamburone [aug. of tamburo], obs. It.: bass drum.

Tamburo piccolo, It.: snare drum.

Tamburo rullante, It.: tenor drum.

Tämerlinpfeife, Ger.: tabor pipe.

Tami, var. of dan.

Tamis, Fr.: rack board.

Tammarinpfeife, see: Tämerlinpfeife.

Tammittam, Malayalam equivalent of tambattam (176).

Tammuredda, *frame drum of Sicily, with single head and metal jingles, played by women only. Max. diam. 37 cm. (14½ in.).

Tamoa, percussion basket of the Papago Indians of the Western U.S. An ordinary medium-sized household basket is turned upside down and struck with bare hands like a drum (51).

Tampon (Fr.), in Engl. an obs. double-headed drumstick with a knobbed head at each end of a handle, in appearance rather like a dumbbell, and formerly used for playing rolls on bass drums. Today ordinary timpani sticks are used. Known in Fr. as maille double. In France tampon is the padding at the extremity of a maille.

Tampouras [Gk. *pandoura], long-necked lute of modern Greece, with 2–4 metal strings tuned $g^1 bb^1$ or $a^0 d^1 a^1$ or $g^0 gb^1 bb^1$ (176).

Tam-tam [Malayalam, *tammittam, drum], **1.** name given in Europe and America to gongs of indefinite pitch; **2.** gong used in Western rhythm bands; **3.**

more recently, name given to some African *slit drums. See also: tom tom.

Tamukku (Malayalam), small kettledrum of S. India, identical to the tarshā (176).

Tanābīr, pl. of tunbūr.

Tanbīk (Pers.), var. writing of tunbūk.

Tanborete [dim. of *tanbor*], OSp.: small drum.

Tanborín, small drum played simultaneously with the Basque chistu or chirula (one-hand flutes) by the same player; a Basque tabor.

Tanbur, syn. of simsimijah.

Tanbūr (Pers., Turk.) [Sum. *pandur*], long-necked lute of the Near East, with small piriform body, fretted neck without pegbox, and pegs for a variable number of thin metal strings inserted in the neck from both front and side. In appearance the tanbūr is similar to the lutes of ancient Babylon and Egypt. It has been a pop. instr. ever since med. times and is found today from the Balkans to the Middle East. *Cf.* tunbur (170).

Tanbura [Turk. *tanbūr*], 1. tanbūr of Bulgaria, with oval body and 2 pairs of strings tuned a 4th or 5th apart. Also called baylama, bulgaría, drunka; 2. tanbūr of Mohammedan Yugoslavia, built in several sizes, with fixed frets on the neck. *Cf.* bisernica, brač, bugariya (89).

Tanbūra, Hindust. equivalent of tumburu vīnā.

Tanbūr al mīzānī (measured tanbūr), 2-stringed tanbūr of the ancient Near East. In pre-Islamic times the string lengths were theoretically divided into 40 equal parts, but only the first 5 divisions were used in playing, giving a scale with microtones. By Al Farabi's time (d. 950) this tuning had been abandoned. Probably identical with the later tanbūr baghdadi (170).

Tanbūr baghdadi (tanbūr of Bagdad), see: tanbūr al mīzānī.

Tanbūr baglama, see: baglama.

Tanbūr bulgārī, Turk. name of the bulgaría. *Cf.* tanbura, 1.

Tanbūr buzuk, see: buzuk.

Tanburica [dim. of *tanbura*], next to smallest of the Yugo. tanburas, formerly with 3, now with 4 strings tuned $d^2 f^2 f^2 f^2$, frontal pegs, and fretted neck. *Ca.* 50 cm. (20 in.) long. Also called primasica (176).

Tanbūr kabīr tuıkī (large Turkish tanbūr), largest of the tanbūrs, with circular body and 8 strings inserted into the neck, tuned $a^0 a^1 c^1 c^2 d^1 d^2 d^0 d^0$.

Tanbūr küchük (Turk.: small tanbūr), small tanbūr of Turkey, with 8 strings (176).

Tanbūr sharqī (Turk.: Eastern tanbūr), see: sharqī.

Tan ch'in, *spike fiddle of China, a hu ch'in with cylindrical bamboo body, snakeskin belly, rear pegs, 2 strings looped to the handle by a cord. Diam. of the body is about 5 cm. (2 in.) (170).

Tanda, side-blown trumpet of the Bwende of the Congo, made of wood or horn (185).

Tandem horn, another name of the 19th-c. Engl. mail *coach horn. See also: post horn.

Tandilo, idiochord bamboo *tube zither of C. Celebes, with 2 strings (119).

Tandrokaka, horn of the Malagasy Republic (171).

Tangala, *conical drum of the Teke and Kuta of the Lower Congo, made of a hollowed trunk of *Ricinodendron africanum,* generally in pairs of unequal sizes and played with sticks. The Kuta also play it with bare hands. *Ca.* 1 m. (40 in.) long (185).

Tang chok, *cross flute of Korea, with 7 fingerholes, *ca.* 40 cm. (16 in.) long (66).

Tangentenflügel, keyboard instr. the invention of which is attributed to Jacob Späth the younger of Regensburg, made from *ca.* 1770 on. Its exterior is indistinguishable from that of a grand piano, but the action differs and is far simpler: wooden tangents resting on the rear of the keys are thrust against the strings by movement of the keys. This principle was not new, as one of the harpsichord models submitted by Jean Marius to the Académie des Sciences in 1716 had a similar action, and a piano invented by Christoph Gottlieb Schroeter of Dresden in 1739 had a tangent, not a hammer, action. Späth took his son-in-law Schmahl into his business, and from 1774 the firm name appears as Späth and Schmahl; extant instrs. date from these partnership days. (H. Herrmann: *Die Regensburger Klavierbauer Späth und Schmahl*, 1927).

Tanggetong, idiochord bamboo *tube zither of the Toba Batak of N. Sumatra (119).

Tang koa, bamboo "hydraulic carillon" of the Miau and Sedang of Vietnam, made of 50 bamboo pipes suspended vertically and struck by hammers; these are affixed to a frame similar to a water wheel and are moved by water from a waterfall. It can play 2 bars of music indefinitely. Also called tang gong (70, 103).

Tangkolnang, idiochord bamboo tube zither of the Dusun of N. Borneo (119).

T'ang ku, *barrel drum of China, with lacquered cowskin heads that are nailed, provided with 4 metal rings for ease of transportation. Made in various sizes, the max. diam. being equivalent to its length. It is played with 2 sticks (142).

Tang lo, brass gong of China, bossless, with turned rim, suspended from a wire ring. *Ca.* 20 cm. (8 in.) in diam. (142).

Ta ngo, drum of the Ngbandi of the Congo, identical with the bia, played at dances, when death occurs, or at wrestling. The ta ngo and to ngo are played by the same performer, one with a stick and the other with the player's bare hand. Also called mbonda (30).

Tang gong, syn. of tang koa.

T'ang p'i p'a, p'i p'a of the T'ang era, with 4 strings, now a Korean instr. Formerly played with a plectrum, it is now played with bare fingers. *Ca.* 110 cm. (43 in.) long (66).

Tang tse, flat gong of China, with turned rim. A temple instr. of *ca.* 30 cm.

(12 in.) in diam. and a 5th-cm. (2-in.) rim (142).

Tanguri, Jew's-harp of the Bariai of NE. New Guinea (176).

Tan pu la, Chin. name of the tanbūr, introduced from W. Asia (75 II).

Tanse, syn. of ekue.

Tanso, end-blown flute of Korea, with 4 fingerholes (66).

Tan-tabola, idiochord bamboo *tube zither of Bolaäng, Celebes. Also called ta-tabola (119).

Tantan (Fr. and Engl.), syn. of tentant.

Tanzmeistergeige (Ger.: dancing master's fiddle), Ger.: kit.

T'ao, small *cylindrical drum of China, with 2 nailed heads and a handle (80 VIII).

T'ao ku, small *rattle drum of China, impaled on a handle, with 2 snakeskin heads. Two small balls of wax are suspended from the drum by cords so as to strike against the heads when the drum is twirled. The t'ao ku dates back to the Sheng dynasty (*ca.* 1400–1200 B.C.) and in ancient times consisted of 2 or more small drums impaled on a stick, one above the other, or hung in a frame. It is now a Confucian instr. chiefly used by itinerant vendors or as a child's toy and popularly called yao ku; 5–30 cm. (2–12 in.) long, with the same diam. (89, 142, 170).

Taouat, oblique flute of the NW. Sahara, of cane, with 5 fingerholes. It is made and played by shepherds (193).

Tapado, tapadillo [Sp. *tapar,* to close], Sp.: stopped (said of organ pipes).

Tapan, see: tupan.

Taphon, *barrel drum of Laos that corresponds to the tapone of Thailand. See: tapone.

Tapil, clay drum of the Kurds of Iraq (103).

Tapone, *barrel drum of Thailand, hollowed out of a single block of wood, with heads of slightly different diams. The right head, of parchment, is the larger; the left is of calfskin. Each is laced in zigzag pattern with leather thongs and has a central tension ligature. The tapone is laid horizontally in a frame and tapped with the fingers. Tuning paste is applied to both heads. The tapone corresponds to the cai bon of Vietnam, mādalā of India, samphor of Cambodia, taphon of Laos (65, 173).

Tappeta, Tel. equivalent of tambattam.

Ta pu, Chin. name of the daf (75 II).

Ta pu la, Chin. name of the tabl (75 II).

Taqa, liturgical *percussion plaque of the Ethiopian and Egyptian Copts, with a series of metal rings strung along the edges; it is struck with a mallet (132).

Tār, pl. **tīrān** (Pers.), **1.** long-necked lute of Persia, also played in Azerbaijan, Tadzhikistan, Caucasia, and Armenia. The body is hollowed out of a single piece of wood, usually rounded, octagonal in Georgia, with membrane belly, spike, movable frets, and lateral pegs for 2–5 metal strings that are rib-fastened. It is played with a plectrum. Cf. tari, 1 (103, 178); **2.** *frame drum of the modern Near East, with jingles but no snares. It is held in the left hand while the player's right hand strikes it with the fingers, alternating between center and rim. In N. Africa it is played by both men and women. Cf. tari, 2, ta'riya, tarra (11, 144 Chottin).

Taraban [Turk. *balāban], Pol., Ruth.: drum. Cf. baraban, darabána.

Tarab angiz, bowed chordophone of Persia, introduced in 1883, together with the madilan, by Mirzā Ghulām Husain of Teheran (89 Farmer).

Tarabast, New Prov.: clapper (53).

Tarabat (Fr.) [?Lat. *trabs,* beam], according to Richelet (in 1680), an instr. used for waking up nuns at night; also a rattle sounded during Easter week, and a board that was struck, *i.e.,* a form of semanterion (53, 166).

Tarabilla [?Lat. *trabicula,* dim. of *trabs*], **1.** *bull-roarer of Argentina; **2.** Afro-Cuban drum, conical, with single head lapped over a hoop and laced (152).

Tarabouka [Arab. *darabuka], pottery drum of Bulg. gypsies (89).

Tarabrab (Pers.), small Pers. lute with 6 strings (75 II).

Taraf-i tar (*taraf,* sympathetic string), sitār with sympathetic strings (173).

Taragav, Wendish: tárogató (144).

Tarai, 1. straight trumpet of India, played in pairs at funeral ceremonies; **2.** copper *percussion plaque of the Dayak of Borneo (176).

Tarakava, see: taragav.

Tarambuke [Arab. *darabuka], drum of Bulgaria, identical with the darabuka, played with the fingers of the right hand on the center of the skin (11).

Taranta, name of the humming top among the Indians of Venezuela (152).

Tarantara (Ger.) [onom.], obs. pop. name of the trumpet (159).

Taravaka, syn. of taragav.

Taravangsa, bowed chordophone of W. Java, now in process of being replaced by the rebāb and the violin. Its large rectangular body is shaped like a punt; the neck is ornamented with carvings and lies on a plane parallel to the back of the instr. It has 2 or 3 strings; if 3, the third does not pass over the high bridge, but disappears into the body. Some specimens have C holes and center bouts, showing marked European influence. Cf. vihola (121, 173).

Tari [Pers. *tār], **1.** tār·of Georgia, U.S.S.R., with a wooden body made of a single piece of wood, octagonal in form, membrane belly, and 10 metal strings; 4 pairs are sympathetic, and all 10 are secured by 6 lateral pegs; **2.** Swah.: tambourine with handle.

Tarimba, *stick zither of the Guianas, with single string that passes over a high nut placed close to the tuning peg (149).

Ta'riya [Pers. *tār], clay *cylindrical drum of N. Africa, played in pairs (144 Chottin).

Tarka, syn. of pinkillo.

Taró, tarol, in Paraíba, Brazil, a name of the snare drum (7).

Tárogató, Hung. woodwind instr., originally a modified Eastern shawm, today resembling a soprano saxophone. Old and new versions have a wooden body and conical bore in common. The older type was played with double reed and pirouette and had an ornamental body without fingerholes, or a carved body and trumpet-like bell, or a straight body with flat bronze bell; the last 2 had variable numbers of fingerholes. The oldest type, that without fingerholes, is traceable to the 13th c. According to present-day research, the Arabs brought the tárogató to the Magyars by the Balkan trade routes. In the 18th c. the tárogató became associated with the Rákóczy movement, causing it, a good c. later, to be considered as something of a national instr. In the mid-19th c. a new mechanism was introduced, but the real change was brought about by Joseph Schunda of Budapest at the end of the 19th c.: he replaced the double reed with a single reed and a clarinet-type beak, with mouthpiece fitted inside the instr., and simple-system keywork, closely akin to that of the B♭ soprano saxophone, with a compass b♭⁰–d³. Today it is also built in E♭ and A♭; tenor and bass sizes have also been made. See also: taragav, torogoata (89, 132).

Tarole, small snare drum made by Grégoire of Nantes by 1861 (176).

Tarompet, name given to the selompret in the Sunda districts of W. Java, with long coconut "wings" attached to the mouthpiece, curved to fit the player's blown-out cheeks, reminiscent of the phorbeia (121).

Taro patch fiddle, ukulele with 8 strings, strung in pairs like a mandolin.

Taroro, Serb.: tárogató (176).

Tarot [U.], Fr. equivalent of curtal, forerunner of the bassoon. The term was in use in the 16th and 17th c. (190).

Tarota, pop. instr. of Catalonia, a member of the chirimía family (57).

Tarr, see: tār.

Tarra [*tār], clay or gourd *pot drum of Morocco, with goatskin head (176).

Tarremut [*garamut], slit drum of New Ireland, Melanesia (176).

Tarreña, tarrañuela, Sp.: castanet; flat clappers; "bones."

Tarro (Sp.), Latin-American word denoting a horn made of animal horn (152).

Tarsa, see: tarshā.

Tarshā (Beng., Mar., Punj.), small kettledrum of N. India, made of clay, with a thin skin head, usually glued, rarely laced. In Bengal the body is painted red. Formerly a wartime instr., the tarshā is played with sticks. Cf. tamukku (132, 170).

Tartarie, med. Fr. rattle. The term occurs in Fr. literature as a syn. of crécelle (85).

Tartavelle, obs. *cog rattle of France, in the 13th c. a beggar's instr. Also used during Easter week in lieu of bells (85).

Tartold, large 16th-c. rackets, carnival or masquerade instrs., with metal bodies painted like dragons, terminating in open mouths that served as bells. The body contained coiled cylindrical metal tubing, was pierced with 7 fingerholes and a thumbhole, the coiled tail acted as a crook, carrying a double reed. An Innsbruck inventory of 1496 enumerates a consort of *"Tartold wie Drachen geformirt"* (tartolds formed like dragons). The only surviving specimens are housed in the Vienna Kunsthistorisches Museum: 2 sopranos, 2 tenors, and a bass. The word has been derived from *torto,* It. for crooked, bent, by Schlosser, and from *Kurtholt,* a corr. of *Kurzholz,* or from *cortali,* by Sachs (183).

Tarumbeta [It. *trombetta*], Swah.: trumpet (176).

Tarunbata [It. *trombetta*], the European trumpet in 17th-c. Morocco (76).

Tary, *cylindrical drum of the Maintirano district of the Malagasy Republic, with single nailed head (171).

Tās, pl. **tasat** (Pahl.), small kettledrum of ancient Persia, mentioned *ca.* 600 A.C. (75 II, 170).

Tāsā (Pers.), kettledrum of ancient Persia and modern N. India. Cf. tarshā, tās, tasah (75 II, 170).

Tasah, Arab. equivalent of tāsā.

Tasarishe, bowed chordophone of the Caucasus, similar to the skripka (176).

Taschengeige, Ger.: kit.

Tāsha, syn. of tarshā.

Tasīnfak, carved side-blown horn of Mali (72).

Tasseau, Fr.: block (of violins, etc.).

Tasta, Tinctoris' expression for fret (ca. 1490), now called tasto in It.

Tastame, obs. It.: keyboard.

Tastatur, Ger.: keyboard.

Tastatura, It.: keyboard.

Taste, Ger.: key (of keyboard).

Tastencister, Ger.: keyed cittern.

Tastengitarre, Ger.: keyed guitar.

Tastenharmonika, Ger.: keyed harmonica.

Tastenmonochord, Ger.: keyed monochord.

Tastenpsalmodikon, Ger.: keyed psalmodicon.

Tastenxylophon, Ger.: keyed xylophone.

Tastiera, It.: keyboard, fingerboard.

Tasti spezzati, It.: split keys.

Tasto, It.: fret.

Tat, horn of Thailand, made of buffalo horn, with a cup mouthpiece cut out of the horn itself. The instr. is strongly curved; it serves as a signal instr. (18).

Tata, generic name for stringed instrs. in India (147).

Ta-tabola, syn. of tan-tabola.

Tatabuan, gong chime of the Moluccas, similar to the bonang of Java (173).

Tatabuan kavan (kavan, bamboo), idiochord *tube zither of Buru Island, Indonesia, made of bamboo, closed at both ends by natural nodes, with 5 strings. The player's left hand plucks the strings while the right drums on the head of the instr. Also called tabuan veteh, tagbuan. Cf. tattabua (119, 173).

Tataganing, wooden *barrel drum of the Toba Batak of Sumatra, with 2 heads laced in zigzag pattern and with central tension ligature. Only one head is played (122, 173).

Tatawak, syn. of tawak.

Tatekoto (Jap.: standing koto), a later name of the kugo (144).

Tattabua, idiochord *tube zither of Halmahera, Moluccas, drummed while its strings are being plucked. Now a child's toy. Cf. tatabuan kavan (173).

Tatung, xylophone of the Miau of Vietnam, with 9 bamboo slabs (103).

Ta t'ung kyo, tubular metal trumpet of China, so long that its end must be supported during performance. Instead of a bell it has a long, wide cylinder of wood, brass, or iron into which the main body slides telescopically when at rest. It is played with a flat, disc-like mouthpiece. The length is variable, often 120 cm. (4 ft.) long. It corresponds to the dodaku of Japan and is similar to the siao t'ung kyo (la pa) except for the bell. Popularly called hao t'ung; also called huang teh (142, 170).

Tau, *marine-shell trumpet of Jabim and Bukawa, New Guinea (176).

Taule, *marine-shell trumpet of the Barriai, New Ireland, Bismarck Archipelago (176).

Taure, *marine-shell trumpet of Siassi Islands, Bismarck Archipelago (176).

Taurea [Lat. taurus, bull], Lat.: a variety of tuba that sounded like the bellowing of a bull (61).

Taus, Punj.: peacock. See: mayurī.

Ta uto, "tuning fork" idiophone of Talaud, Indonesia, identical with the genggong sakai.

Tavalaika (frog), *whirled friction drum of S. India, made of clay, conical or cup-shaped, closed by a paper membrane, with a horsehair string smeared with rosin. Also called menghi (16).

Tavel (MHGer.) [Lat. tabula, board], med. Ger. *percussion plaque struck with a mallet by persons announcing their arrival (189).

Tavil, *cylindrical drum of S. India and Ceylon, hollowed out of a block of wood, with 2 heads lapped over projecting hoops, laced in W-pattern, with a central tension ligature. The right hand plays the right head, with wrist and fingers; the left head is played with a stick (179).

Tavola armonica, It.: soundboard.

Tawak, large gong of the Dayak of Borneo, with central boss. It is known as garantong in S. Borneo. Also called tatawak (173).

Ta wang, syn. of kang t'u.

Tawaya, idioglott Jew's-harp of the New Hebrides, shuttle-shaped, made of cabbage-tree bark (132).

Tawi, *marine-shell trumpet of St. Matthias Islands, Bismarck Archipelago (176).

Tawul, *marine-shell trumpet of Tami, New Guinea (176).

Taya, violin of Burma, of European influence and shape, but with 3 strings. An instr. of blind mendicants (172).

Tāyus, Beng., Hindust.: peacock. See: mayurī.

Tbel, see: tabl.

Tbn, see: teben.

Tch . . . , see also: Ch . . .

Tchatcha, Haitian equivalent of chachá, 2.

Tebashul, *cylindrical drum of Algeria, with wooden body and 2 laced heads (176).

Teben, *barrel drum of ancient Egypt, depicted and named on an inscription of the Great Temple at Karnak (as tbn). Possibly a hieroglyphic translation of the Gk. word tympanon (170).

Tebuni, term used erroneously in the 19th c. to denote the ancient Egyptian harp *bīnt, based on Flavius Josephus' designation, to'buni (170).

Tecciztli, syn. of quiquiztli. An Aztec name of the *marine-shell trumpet, named for the god Tecciztcatl (152).

Te chang, * long zither of Korea, corresponding to the cheng of China and the wagon of Japan. See also: komunko (66).

T'e ch'ing, *musical stone of China, consisting of a piece of marble, stone, or jade cut in shape of an obtuse L and suspended by a cord in a frame. The larger section is struck with a mallet; 16

t'e ch'ing form a pien ch'ing. *Cf.* thuk kyong (89, 132).

Technicon, mute practice keyboard invented in the U.S. in the 1880's (89).

T'e chung, obs. flat bell of China (132).

Tecla, 1. Sp.: generic term for keyboard instrs.; **2.** Port., Sp.: key.

Teclado, Sp.: keyboard.

Tecomopiloa, slit drum of the Aztec; it was partly filled with water (144).

Tede, whistle of the Cuna Indians of Panama, made of animal skulls and lengthened with bird bones. It produces 2 tones (105).

Tedoc, wooden cattle bell of Cambodia (176).

Teeter, see: lap organ.

Teiboro, *musical bow of Lake Kutubu area, E. New Guinea, played in 2 ways: it is held vertically, the upper end of the bow being taken into the player's mouth and the string plucked with his right hand; or it is held obliquely, one end of the string being taken into the player's mouth and the other end plucked (77).

Tei kin, *spike fiddle of Japan, similar to the kei kin but with 2 strings only, tuned a 5th apart (157).

Tejoletas [Sp. *teja,* tile], obs. pop. Sp.: small roofing tiles played as castanets.

Teki, Jap.: flute (176).

T'e k'ing, see: t'e ch'ing.

Telali, generic name for flutes in W. Borneo, both mouth-blown and nose-blown (176).

Telarli, *ring flute of the Land Dayak of Borneo, with 2 fingerholes on the same side as the blowhole, or 5 fingerholes on the opposite side.

Telein, Cornish: harp.

Télen, modern Breton: harp (153).

Telharmonium, *electrophonic instr. of the electromechanical type, invented by Prof. Thaddeus Cahill of New York in 1906, based on his development in 1897 of a rotating electromagnetic generator. The telharmonium was the first instr. to employ such a generator; it precedes applied electronics by several decades. The inventor intended transmitting its tones over telephone wires, but this did not prove feasible. Also called dynamophone.

Telinca, until recently the name of the Romanian tilinca.

Telio-chordon [Gk. *teleios,* perfect], grand piano invented by Charles Claggett of London and patented on Aug. 15, 1788, with 39 tones to the oct. Each key could produce 3 microtones, the retuning being done by pedals, as on a harp. Two additional, movable bridges were provided to this end (92, 176).

Tellimbilla, telumbilla (Kikongo), side-blown wooden trumpet of the Kongo people; also the name of a megaphone of theirs (185).

Telyn (Welsh: harp), **1.** a harp, the national instr. of Wales, mentioned in Welsh poetry by the 10th c. According to Welsh laws, known to us from the 12th c. although codified in the 10th c., the telyn was listed as one of the 3 indispensable possessions of a freeman. Originally with horsehair strings, it had sheep-gut strings by the 14th c., at which time it appears to have been made of wood and covered with leather. The pillar of early instrs. was curved: in postmed. times it became straight. Later models show a large, upright resonator, a comparatively short, curved neck, and straight pillar set at an oblique angle; **2.** harpsichord stop imitating a harp, patented on July 10, 1741 by Roger Plenius. Small pieces of buff leather glued to a strip of wood could be pushed up against the strings, giving a pizzicato effect (27, 153).

Telyn teirtud [*tair,* three + *tud,* land], said to denote a *triple harp, this term probably refers to Castell Teirtud (Trecastle in Brecknockshire) (89).

Tembelic, syn. of tumbelechiŭ.

Temettama, *frame drum of Ceylon, equivalent to the tambattam, with nailed head.

Tempella (It.), *cog rattle used in Italy

during Easter week instead of bells. According to Lodovico Antonio Muratori, a clapper to awaken monks (169).

Temple [Lat. *tympanum*], OProv.: *frame drum with jingles, in use from the early 13th c. on, chiefly by girls. Of Near Eastern origin, it was adopted during the Crusades; it corresponds to the rotumbes, timbre, timbrel, and our modern tambourine.

Tempuku, small *end-blown flute of Japan, made of bamboo (135).

Temraga, scraper of Torres and Banks islands, New Hebrides, used during death and funeral ceremonies. Also called werewere (77).

Temür-khuur, stirrup-shaped Jew's-harp of the Mongols, formerly a shaman's instr., now rare. Also called aman-khuur (69).

Tenabari, *pellet bells of the Yaqui Indians of Mexico, made of dried butterfly cocoons. Also called tenaboin (137).

Tenaboin, syn. of tenabari.

Tenora (Sp.: tenor), tenor chirimía of N. Catalonia, leading instr. of the *cobla* (band), shawm pitched in B♭, a tone below the oboe, with a compass e^0–c^3, notated f♯^{0}–d^3. In the 19th c. the tenora was fitted with keywork and now has 6 fingerholes and 9 keys. The wooden body terminates in a long metal bell. A short, wide double reed is recessed in the *pirouette. It is 84–86 cm. (33–34 in.) long. See also: tiple, 3 (80 VI Baines, 132).

Tenorbass (Ger.), syn. of Baroxyton.

Tenorbass . . . , Ger.: baritone.

Tenorbasshorn, Ger.: euphonium.

Tenor-Bass Posaune, Ger.: B♭/F trombone. See: trombone.

Tenor clarinet, name of the alto clarinet in F in Britain.

Tenor cor, Brit. name of the mellophone and the cor alto.

Ténor-cor, valved brass instr. built by Fontaine Besson of Paris *ca.* 1860, a cross between the French horn and the tenor horn, pitched in C or B♭. See also: cor alto.

Tenor cornett, see: cornone.

Tenor drum (Fr.: *caisse roulante, tambour roulant, caisse sourde;* Ger.: *Rührtrommel, Wirbeltrommel, Rolltrommel, Rolliertrommel;* It.: *cassa rullante;* Sp.: *redoblante*), *cylindrical drum slightly larger than the snare drum, with a diam. of some 45 cm. (17½ in.). Formerly a military drum but now replaced in most military bands by the snare drum. Its orchestral use is of recent date. In some countries, such as England and Spain, it is still used in both military bands and the orchestra (57, 170).

Tenore, a name of the guitarra tenor.

Tenore in si♭, It.: tenor horn.

Tenorgeige, Ger.: tenor violin.

Tenor hautboy, tenor hoboy, see: taille des hautbois.

Tenor horn (Fr.: *bugle ténor, bugle basse;* Ger.: *Tenorhorn;* It.: *tenore in si♭*), valved brass instr. of the cornet family, with narrow conical bore and medium-sized bell, 3 valves, played with a cup mouthpiece. It is usually built in B♭, but occasionally also in C and A, with a compass E⁰–b♭¹ for the B♭ instr., notated a 9th higher. Today the narrow cornet bore has been largely abandoned outside Italy, and the instr. now closely approaches the tuba. According to Sachs, Wilhelm Wieprecht introduced it into Prussian cavalry bands before 1829. In Bavaria it is called Althorn; in Austria, Bassflügelhorn; in England, baritone. The tenor bugle is also called tenor horn. In the U.S. the B♭ tenor horn is also called B♭ tenor (25, 169).

Ténor impérial, Fr.: Kaisertenor.

Tenor oboe, see: taille des hautbois.

Tenoroon, 1. 19th-c. term for a small bassoon of tenor range, pitched in f⁰ or g⁰, a 4th or 5th higher than the ordinary bassoon; it was at the same pitch as the single *curtal of the 16th and 17th c. By extension the name is also given to any 19th-c. bassoon of higher than normal pitch; it has also been misapplied to the *alto fagotto. Now obs., these instrs. were occasionally used to replace the cor anglais (89 Langwill); **2.** when affixed to names of organ stops in the 19th c., the word indicated that the stop did not descend below tenor C (Oxford English Dictionary).

Tenor shawm, Engl. name of the alto bombard in g⁰.

Tenor-viola, *tenor violin made in 1912 by Eugen Vitaček of Moscow to the design of A. von Glehn of Reval (Tallin), Estonia. *Cf.* viola tenore (26).

Tenor viola da braccio, in Praetorius' day our viola.

Tenor violin (Fr.: *taille de violon;* Ger.: *Tenorgeige*), large-sized viola in existence since the mid-16th c., tenor member of the violin family, as its name indicates. It became obs. in the 18th c. A tenor-sized 3-string violin is depicted on the fresco of Saronno Cathedral dome, painted by Gaudenzio Ferrari *ca.* 1535; a *taille de violon* is mentioned in France in 1553. Zacconi in 1592 listed a tenor viola da braccio tuned F⁰ c⁰ g⁰ d¹, and Banchieri in 1609 had a bass *viola da braccio* tuned G⁰ d⁰ a⁰ e¹, an oct. below the violin; a Cassel inventory of 1613 gives F⁰ or G⁰ as the lowest string of the tenor, but most baroque writers give its tuning as F⁰ c⁰ g⁰ d¹. Praetorius has a bass viola da braccio at this pitch (and a "Tenor Viol" at c⁰ g⁰ d¹ a¹, that of our viola). To Playford and Talbot, in England, the tenor violin was a viola. Attempts to revive the true tenor have been made sporadically ever since the reduction of 5-part polyphonic writing to 4-part writing spelled its doom. And, as by 1800 the instr. had fallen into oblivion, it was also reinvented around that time (proposals were made to build an instr. pitched between viola and cello and to call it tenor violin). Over-all length of the tenor violin is 70–75 cm. (27½–29½ in.), with a speaking-string length of some 50 cm. (19½ in.). See also: controviolino, Oktavgeige, Tenor-viola, viola nova, viola tenore, violetta, violonet, violon-tenor, 2 (26, 80 VII, 94).

Tentant [Lat. *tintinnus*], in med. France a small bell or pellet bell sewn on garments; later a cattle bell. Also spelled tantan, tentent, tentin.

Tenth, mutation organ stop sounding a 10th higher than the key played, labeled 3⅕′ on the manual or 6⅖′ on the pedal. Cf. Dezem (101).

Tentin, var. of tentant.

Téorbe, var. of théorbe.

Tepanabaz, *slit drum of Guatemala, with 2 or 3 slits on the upper surface and several holes in the bottom (176).

Tepanahuaste, drum of the Lacandón Indians of Guatemala (176).

Tepan-tepan, drum of MacCluer Gulf, NW. New Guinea, with head of sea porcupine (176).

Tepma, *globular flute of the Sepik area of New Guinea, made of a small coconut; it serves ritual purposes and may not be seen by women (202).

Teponagua, slit drum of the Chorti Indians of Guatemala (152).

Teponaztli, *slit drum of ancient and modern S. and C. America, made of wood; in pre-Columbian times some small specimens were also made of stone, beautifully carved, occasionally zoomorphic. Characteristic feature of the teponaztli is its H-shaped slit, creating 2 tongues facing each other. The interior is chiseled away so as to leave different thicknesses of wood, producing different pitches when struck. Smaller specimens are placed on tripod stands to avoid deadening the sound by contact with the ground. The tongues vibrate when beaten, and the body acts as resonator. The instr. is no longer known in S. America, its use being restricted to C. America, where it is used as a musical, not a signal, instr. and is played with rubber-coated beaters. It is 60–150 cm. (2–5 ft.) long (105, 137).

Tepuzquiquiztli, end-blown *marineshell trumpet of ancient Mexico (170).

Terbang, *frame drum of Sunda and Java, recorded from 1135 on, made in form of a basin with open bottom of thick, heavy wood, with goatskin head secured with rattan. The terbang is not used in the *gamelan* orchestra. On other islands of the archipelago it is known as arabana, rabāna, ravana, rebāna, redep, robana, and in ancient Hindu-Javanese literature it was called tabang-tabang. Cf. gembyung, kitimplik, tairan (121).

Terbang batok, W. Java name of a small terbang without jingles (121).

Terbang benjangan, W. Java name of the terbang besar (121).

Terbang besar, largest of the Javanese terbangs, with diam. up to 75 cm. (30 in.), and so heavy that it has to be carried on a pole by 2 persons and played by a third. The head is nailed (121).

Terbang gembang, terbang of W. Java with wedge bracings and rattan ring, 25–30 cm. (10–12 in.) in diam. (121).

Terbang genjring, terbang of W. Java with jingles (121).

Terbang ketimpring, flat terbang of W. Java, with jingles, 25–35 cm. (10–14 in.) in diam. (121).

Tercerola, Sp.: tierce flute.

Tergale positivum, Lat.: chair organ.

Terkotka, Pol.: rattle (89).

Terpodion, 1. friction instr. with keyboard, developed by Johann David Buschmann of Friedrichroda, near Berlin, in 1816, and improved by his sons in 1832, a successor to his earlier *uranion and similar to the *clavicylinder except for the material of the cylinder. The terpodion had the form of a square piano; when the keys were depressed they pressed tuned wooden bars against a rotating, rosin-coated cylinder of wood controlled by a pedal. It had a 6-oct. compass, F^1–f^4; **2.** friction keyboard instr. patented in England in 1821 by Daniel Loeschman and James Allwright, with brass springs and metal cylinder, and a compass F^1–f^4; **3.** organ stop of open cylindrical flue pipes of narrow scale, first built by F. Schulze after 1850 (132, 133).

Terpomele [Gk. *terpein,* gladden + *melos,* song], organ stop of free reeds, similar to the euphone (198).

Tertia (Lat. third), see: tierce.

Tertia manu (Lat.: third hand), a name of the octave coupler of an organ (133).

Tertian (Lat.: third), mixture organ stop containing a tierce, historically 2-rank, now 3-rank, an inversion of the *sesquialtera: 1⅗′ + 1⅓′ or, if 3-rank, 1⅗′ + 1⅓′ + 1′. Adlung also knew it at a lower tonal position as 3⅕′ + 2⅔′ (3, 133).

Teruding, Jew's-harp of the Dusun of Borneo; the end forms a handle (176).

Tervelle, term for cog rattle in Fr.-speaking Switzerland (102).

Terz, Ger.: tierce (organ stop).

Terzfagott (Ger.: tierce bassoon), obs. bassoon pitched in E♭, a minor 3rd above normal pitch. *Cf.* tenoroon.

Terzflöte, Ger.: tierce flute.

Terzgitarre, Ger.: chitarrino.

Terz-Heckelphone, see: Heckelphone.

Terzian, Ger.: tertian.

Terzina, It. treble cittern tuned a 3rd higher than the ordinary cittern; a tierce cittern (144).

Terzposaune, Ger.: tierce trombone.

Testudo (Lat.: tortoise), Lat. word applied to the Gk. lyra, with reference to its tortoise-shell body. In the 16th and 17th c. the term was applied to the lute.

Testudo major, 16th- and 17th-c. Lat.: lute.

Testudo minor, Lat.: mandora.

Testudo theorbata, Lat.: theorbo-lute.

Teteg, syn. of bedug (121).

Tetekan, *slit drum of Java, made of a bamboo segment. See also: kentongan (121).

Tete lile, a Solo name of the saron panerus (121).

Tetepret, name of the selompret in the Banyumas district of Java (121).

Tetere, aerophone of the Maori of New Zealand, made of long green blades of spirally twisted flax; the bell end is wound with flax strips. Sometimes a beating reed is inserted into slits cut in the wall. It is used chiefly as a toy but

also as a signal instr. Also called pu tatara. *Cf.* pu kihi (8).

Tetzilacatl, percussion trough of pre-Columbian America, made of metal in form of a coffer or tub and struck with a metal hammer (137).

Tevur, syn. of atvur.

Tewek, an E. Java name of the kemanak (121).

Texboya, panpipes of the Yupua Indians of S. America (105).

Thak, a rarely used bell of Korea. It corresponds to the to of China and taku of Japan (66).

Thambatti, syn. of tambattam.

Thandanda, clappers of the Venda of S. Africa, consisting of carved sticks clicked together in imitation of a drum (116).

Than kvin, cymbals of Burma, made of bronze, with central boss (172).

Than la, see: cai than la.

Thanthona, *plucked drum of the Tanjore region of India, very similar to the tuntina, but with 2 strings. A mendicant's instr. (138).

Thappattai, small *frame drum of India, with metal frame, sloping sides, and calfskin head, played with the right hand while the left plays a semakkalam. An instr. of the Dāsaris and Pandārams (179).

Thar, see: tār.

Thari, see: tari.

Theorbe, Ger.: theorbo.

Theorbencister, Ger.: archcittern.

Theorbenflügel (Ger.), harpsichord invented by Johann Christoph Fleischer in Hamburg in 1718, with 3 registers, a gut-strung 16′ and 8′, and a metal-strung 4′. It had a 4-oct. compass.

Theorbierte Laute, Ger.: theorbo-lute.

Theorbo [U.] (Fr.: *théorbe;* Ger.: *Theorbe;* It., Sp.: *tiorba*), **1.** archlute invented in Venice *ca.* 1575 by "il Bardella" (Antonio Naldi), according to G. B. Doni, and mentioned by Florio in 1598, by which time the word also occurred in France. The claim of invention has also been accorded to others of the period. The theorbo had its heyday in the 17th c. as a continuo instr. and survived into the second half of the 18th c. Its characteristic feature is a second pegbox set immediately above the regular pegbox and to its side, separated by a very short S-shaped neck, for accommodating the long off-board strings. The speaking length of its 14–16 strings is 75–100 cm. (30–40 in.). Because of the length of the fingerboard the frets were set farther apart, rendering impossible the fast finger technique of the lute, which was shorter. Until the late 17th c. the strings were single throughout; in the 18th c. they were geminated except for the top 2. Praetorius gives the following tuning: F^1 G^1 A^1 B^1 C^0 D^0 E^0 F^0/G^0 c^0 f^0 a^0 d^1 e^1. The *Dictionnaire de Trévoux* (1771) still mentions its 8 offboard strings. The theorbo maintained its existence longest in Germany and Sweden; in Sweden it was made in the first quarter of the 19th c. with a flat back and almost triangular outline. It also took on a number of auxiliary strings in the treble. Theorbos are believed to have been built first in Padua; an instr. subsequently known as the "Paduan theorbo" was very like the *chitarrone but had a larger body;

2. short-lived organ stop first built in 1721 in Spain (as tiorba), of regal pipes. Details of its construction are unknown (44, 82, 89 Prynne, 133, 169).

Theorbo-lute (Fr.: *luth théorbé;* Ger.: *Theorbenlaute, theorbierte Laute;* It.: *liuto attiorbato, tiorbato*), pop. doublestrung archlute (with single chanterelle), having either a second nut attached to the pegbox, for 1 or 2 off-board drone strings, or 2 pegboxes, the first being the normal lute pegbox set at right angles to the fingerboard, the second a straight continuation of the neck, set immediately above the first pegbox. The body was smaller and string length far shorter than that of the theorbo. The theorbo-lute is said to have been invented by Piccinini in 1593. Praetorius called it a new instr. and depicted it as a bichord

theorbo. The theorbo-lute was the instr. of the Fr. 17th-c. school of lutanists and their followers abroad, and several tunings were developed for it: Francisque's tuning *à cordes avalées:* $Bb^1 Eb^0 F^0 G^0 Bb^0 f^0 bb^0 d^1 g^1$; the "sharp" tuning: $G^0 c^0 f^0 a^0 c^1 e^1$; the "flat" tuning: $B^0 e^0 a^0 c^1 e^1 g^1$; the "new" tuning: $A^0 d^0 f^0 a^0 d^1 f^1$; and others. See also: French lute (15 Prynne, 89, 169).

Théorgue, portable *orgue expressif patented by Baron of Toulouse on Feb. 10, 1846, the entire instr. being contained in a box. *Cf.* phonéorgue (204).

Theremin, a monophonic, nonimitative *electrophonic instr. of the electronic type invented by Léon Thérémin in 1924 and first performed in public in 1928. The tone is generated by 2 supersonic oscillators, one of fixed frequency and the other of variable frequency. The latter is connected to a projecting metal rod that forms the frequency-determining element in conjunction with the proximity of the player's hand. Tone is produced by the heterodyne action of the fixed and variable oscillators, and is thus variable at the player's discretion. The theremin was formerly manufactured by Radio Corporation of America. Also called aetherophone.

Theuk . . . , see: thuk . . .

Thieu cañ, see: cai thieu cañ.

Thij, see: thith.

Thilo, panpipes of the Jebero Indians of Peru, with 12 pipes (105).

Thipinütsu, var. of eltzabor.

Thith, *nose flute of New Caledonia, Melanesia, usually of curved form. It occurs both as an open and as a stopped instr. (203).

Thlin-thli-no-me, tube zither of New Mexico, U.S., with single string (17).

Thof, see: tof.

Tho ko, drum of Korea, similar to the kal ko but with body of stone (66).

Thomo, pl. **lithomo** (voice), **1.** *musical bow of the Basuto of Basutoland, with central gourd resonator but without tuning loop. The gourd is turned away from the player, the string toward him; the string is tapped with a small stick; **2.** musical bow of the Sotho of S. Africa, similar to 1, except that it is held and played like the *uhadi (17, 116).

Thōn, *goblet drum of Thailand. It corresponds to the gedombak of Malaya, the skor of Cambodia, and the cai trong of Vietnam (173).

Thoti, end-blown trumpet of the Chipaya Indians of the S. American Andes, made of a cow horn with prolongation of dried cow tail, the narrow end sawed off to provide a blowhole (104).

Three-quarter fiddle (Ger.: *Dreiviertelgeige*), violin smaller than standard size for use of children.

Throat trumpet, familiar name of the nyastaranga.

Thuk chong, clapperless bell of Korea, with a small knob close to the rim; the knob is struck with a wooden mallet; occasionally used in orchestras. It corresponds to the po chung of China. *Ca.* 60 cm. (2 ft.) high, lower diam. 30 cm. (12 in.) (66).

Thuk kyong, *musical stone of Korea, in shape of an obtuse L; rarely used. It corresponds to the t'e ch'ing of China (66).

Thum, lyre of Kenya (120).

Thunder stick, syn. of bull-roarer.

Thung sŏ, *end-blown flute of Korea, with 4 or 5 fingerholes and 1 or 2 thumbholes, as well as 1 hole close to the lower end and covered by a thin membrane—a mirliton device. Its compass is a^1–a^4. It corresponds to the tung hsiao of China and the shaku hachi of Japan (66).

Thuorbe, obs. Fr.: theorbo.

Thüringer Zither (Ger.), cittern with 5 pairs of metal strings tuned $c^0 g^0 c^1$ $e^1 g^1$ and 2–10 off-board drone strings, open soundhole; the only surviving member of the C. European cittern family. Also called Bergzither, Harzzither, Waldzither (176).

Thurnerhorn [MHGer. *thurn,* tower], horn of med. tower watchmen, with which the hours of day and night were announced, and still depicted by Virdung

and Agricola in the early 16th c. The Ger. equivalent of *wait (161, 194).

Thuthaurn, Gothic: horn. *Cf.* truð-horn.

Thuturka, syn. of pitorka.

Thuzo, leg rattle of the Venda of S. Africa, worn by both men and women, identical with the mutshakatha (116).

Ti, *cross flute of China, made of a cylindrical lacquered bamboo tube, with 6 fingerholes and with another hole covered with a thin membrane—a mirliton device—plus ventholes. Today the ti is usually called ti tse and is always sideblown, but in former times it was endblown, with a variable number of fingerholes and 1 or 2 thumbholes. *Cf.* ch'ang ti, heng ti, hsiao, lung ti, sei teki, yü ti (142, 178).

T'i, heterochord *tube zither of the Orang Semang of Malaya, with 2 or 3 rattan strings (173).

Tiape, 3-stringed guitar of the Montese of Mindanao, Philippine Islands (176).

Ti ba, piriform lute of Vietnam, with 4 silk strings. It corresponds to the p'i p'a of China (70).

Tibbū, Akk. equivalent of the dub (177).

Tibia (Lat.: shinbone), **1.** Lat. equivalent of aulos, literally: pipe; **2.** bone flute; **3.** in late med. times a reed instr. in general, a shawm in particular. Tinctoris, in the late 15th c., glosses it as celimela, a shawm; **4.** organ stop of flue pipes, syn. of flute, hohlflute, on the European Continent; in Engl. and Amer. organs usually of rectangular, wide-scale pipes, with high mouths, on high pressure; foundation stop of the former theater organ. The upper partials are eliminated as much as possible (60, 101).

Tibia angusta (Lat.: narrow pipe), organ stop identical with the Dulzflöte. Also called tibia dulcis (133).

Tibia aperta (Lat.: open pipe), see: Offenflöte.

Tibia bifaris (Lat.: twofold pipe), see: bifaria.

Tibia clausa (Lat.: closed pipe), organ stop invented by Robert Hope-Jones (d. 1914), of stopped wooden flue pipes of wide scale, with the upper lip leathered, at 8' and 4' pitches (101).

Tibia cuspida (Lat.: pointed pipe), see: Spitzflöte.

Tibia dulcis (Lat.: soft pipe), syn. of Dulzflöte.

Tibia dura (Lat.: hard pipe), organ stop invented by Robert Hope-Jones (d. 1914), originally of open wooden pipes with square tops, later of modified design. Built at 4' pitch (198).

Tibiae impares (Lat.: uneven pipes), the ancient Roman equivalent of the auloi elymoi, divergent double pipes portrayed in Roman art chiefly in the 1st and 2nd c. B.C. The left pipe is longer than the right and terminates in an upturned bell of horn. Pollux also mentions 2 bells, one for each pipe (13).

Tibiae pares (Lat.: even pipes), syn. of tibiae serranae.

Tibiae phrygiae, see: auloi elymoi, tibiae impares.

Tibiae serranae, divergent double pipes of ancient Rome, of equal length and with identical fingerholes. Also called Lydian pipes, Phoenician pipes, tibiae pares. *Cf.* aulos (170).

Tibia incentiva, term used by Varro in the 1st c. A.C. for one of the pipes of Roman double tibiae, which term he does not explain. Sachs surmised that it might have been the melody pipe, played with the left hand; its counterpart, the tibia succentiva, a drone played with the right hand (170).

Tibia major, see: flauto major.

Tibia minor, organ stop invented by John Compton of Nottingham, of stopped pipes of wood or metal, with wide scale. See also: minor . . . (198).

Tibia mollis, organ stop of open flue pipes of the flute class, invented by Robert Hope-Jones (d. 1914), with vertical mouths (198).

Tibia obliqua, Roman equivalent of the plagiaulos.

Tibia plena, organ stop of very wide-scaled wooden flue pipes invented by Robert Hope-Jones (d. 1914), of powerful intonation. The mouth is placed on the narrow side of the pipe and the lips are usually leathered (198).

Tibia profunda, tibia plena organ stop at 16' pitch (101).

Tibia profundissima, tibia plena organ stop at 32' pitch.

Tibia silvestris, see: Waldflöte (organ stop).

Tibia succentiva, see: tibia incentiva.

Tibia tenor, Tinctoris' name (*ca.* 1490) for the bombard.

Tibia transversa, Lat.: cross flute.

Tibia utricularis, bagpipe of ancient Rome, known to have existed by the 1st c. A.C., possibly earlier.

Tibia vulgaris, Lat.: recorder; also, recorder organ stop.

Tible, see: tiple.

Tibu, see: tibbū.

Tibura, bull-roarer of the Barriai of NW. New Guinea (176).

Tibuu, cylindrical drum of Celebes, with palm-trunk body and single head (112).

Tichecombaco, Genoese var. of talabalacco.

T'i ch'in, *spike fiddle of China, with coconut body, wooden soundboard, long spike, and 4 strings held by lateral pegs. It corresponds to the sō i of Laos, the sō luang of Thailand, the cai ñi of Vietnam, and the amrita of India (4, 47, 170).

Tid, see: tad.

Tidinit, lute of the Moors of Mauretania, with shallow, oblong body, lambskin belly, and 4 strings. The neck is surmounted by a metal plaque with copper rings. Normally plucked, the tidinit can also be bowed (103, 193).

Tiduran, *ground zither of Java: a rattan string has its ends secured in the ground by bamboo pegs, and is held taut by a central bridge consisting of an upright stick resting on a reversed half coconut or wickerwork basket placed over a pit. Sometimes an earthenware jar in the pit acts as resonator (121).

T'ieh ma, syn. of yen ma.

T'ieh pan, *percussion plaque of China, consisting of a piece of iron about 30 cm. (12 in.) long, slightly curved, struck with a short iron bar by blind fortunetellers (142).

Tien erh, gong of N. China, similar to but smaller than the chin ku (142).

Tien ku, drum of China, with 2 heads, in form of "two soup plates tied rim to rim" and struck with 2 sticks. Max. diam. 20 cm. (8 in.) (142).

Tien tse, *percussion plaque of China, made of iron or brass, of fantastic shape, suspended in a frame; 30–120 cm. (1–4 ft.) in diam. (142).

Tierce (Fr.: tierce; Ger.: Terz; It.: decima; Lat.: tertia), mutation organ stop of open metal flue pipes a 3rd above the *fifteenth, sounding at 6⅖', 3⅕', 1⅗', or ⅘' pitch (99).

Tierce bassoon, see: Terzfagott.

Tierce flute (Fr.: flûte tierce; Ger.: Terzflöte; Sp.: tercerola), name given in the 18th c. to a *cross flute pitched a minor 3rd above the ordinary flute. As the latter was then considered to be in D, the tierce flute was said to be in F; today we consider the ordinary flute to be a C flute and the tierce flute to be consequently in E♭, although in military bands it is still referred to as an F flute. Its compass is 2½ octs.; 54–55 cm. (21½ in.) long (14, 89).

Tierce trombone (Ger.: Terzposaune), mentioned ca. 1600; probably a trombone pitched in G, a 3rd below the ordinary tenor trombone (176).

Tiercina, very narrow-scaled Quintadena organ stop invented by Robert Hope-Jones (d. 1914), designed to emphasize the nineteenth instead of the twelfth partial (133).

Tifa, single-headed drum of Java and the Moluccas (103, 121).

Tifal, wooden *goblet drum of Werinama and Gorong Islands, Moluccas, with parallel rattan lacings. Cf. tihal (173).

Tig, var. of tigi.

Tigi (Sum.), *vertical flute of ancient Babylon, also known in China. A temple instr. known to both countries by the third millennium B.C. It corresponds to the Akk. tigu. See also: gigid (89 Galpin).

Tigu, Akk. equivalent of tigi.

Tihal, wooden *goblet drum of E. Timor and of Leti, with parallel rattan lacings. Cf. tifal (173).

Tikārā, clay kettledrum of India, of ancient Pers. origin, with oval body (170).

T'i kin, see: t'i ch'in.

Ti ko tse (Chin.: pigeon on the ground), *humming top of China, made on the principle of the aeolian pipe, a bamboo segment with wooden top and bottom and an opening on either side of the body with beveled edges forming a whistle (142).

Tiktirī (Sans.), *double clarinet of the Indian subcontinent and Ceylon, a widespread pastoral and snake charmer's instr. The 2 parallel pipes are made of cane, glued together, with the mouthpiece end inserted into a globular gourd or a calabash, and made airtight with wax. This serves as wind chamber, its elongated neck as blowpipe. The right pipe is the melody pipe and has 7 or 8 fingerholes. The left pipe is a drone, with 3 or 4 holes that are plugged as required. In N. India the instr. is called pūngī, in S. India magudi, in Ceylon tūmerī. See also: bin-jogi, jingivi, nāsa jantra, pāngrā, tubrī, tūngbī (13, 173, 179).

Tilik abero, small ceremonial drum of Christian Ethiopia, barrel-shaped, with ends of different diams. Its single head is laced. The drum is suspended from the player's neck and is beaten with bare hands (144).

Tilinca, cylindrical *end-blown flute of Romanian shepherds and of Hungary, made of willow, elder, or other wood, without fingerholes. The pitch can be changed by more or less closing the open bottom with the fingers; 65–80 cm. (25½–31½ in.) long. Cf. telinca (5).

Tilinca cu dop, tilinca with fipple but without fingerholes (5).

Tilpanu, Babylonian name of the angular harp (84).

Timbalarion, a series of 8 *pedal drums invented by Colos and patented by him in France before 1855. They were tuned to a diatonic scale (204).

Timbale, timballe [Lat. *tympanum*], Fr.: kettledrum. The word has been in use since early 14th c.

Timbale à pédale, Fr.: pedal drum.

Timbales-chromatique (Fr.), a series of kettledrums without shells, constructed by Adolphe Sax in 1857, each consisting of 2 concentric hoops of metal, like an embroidery frame, with a cross member of wood or metal, and a taut membrane. Several of these were superimposed above a footed stand, with space between each for striking. The heads could be tilted as desired and were tuned to the diatonic scale (158, 204).

Timballe-trompette, see: trompette-timbale.

Timballo, obs. It.: kettledrum.

Timbalo (Prov.), large drum formerly used by the leaders of Provençal bands to give the rhythm (23).

Timbalou(n), Prov.: kettledrum.

Timbana, word for drum in several Sudanic languages: Huela, Dyoula, Degha, Siti, Kulango, Gã (93).

Timbano [Gk. *tympanon*], med. Lat. equivalent of timbrel.

Timbila, xylophone of the Rongo and Gusamba of Mozambique, and of the Tshopi workers in the Rand mines, imitative of the mbila. Those of Mozambique usually have 10 slabs on a horizontal frame, with dried *massala* fruit resonators. Each resonator has 2 holes covered with a bat wing—a mirliton device. Those of the Tshopi have pine slabs and tin resonators, with ox intestine covering the holes pierced in the latter (42, 116).

Timbirimba, musical bow of Colombia, without resonator (152).

Timbo, Galla word for the massaneqo and kerar (144).

Timbre (Fr.) [Lat. *tympanum*], the word has been in use from the 12th c. on and designates 2 instrs.: **1.** a small, clapperless bell; *cf.* appeau, tymbris; **2.** a frame drum, the equivalent of timbrel. It also denoted a snare (61, 190).

Timbrel [OFr. *timbre*], *frame drum with jingles, introduced to Europe during the Crusades, a Near Eastern instr. played chiefly by women, the Engl. translation of the biblical word *tof.* The term occurs in Engl. literature from the early 14th c. on (*King Alisaundre*). Today its use is chiefly biblical, and we usually speak of a *tambourine (Oxford English Dictionary, 170).

Timbuttu, Akk. equivalent of dub.

Timiri, a small variety of nāgasuram (179).

Timpan, 1. (?Celtic, OIcelandic) [U.], chordophone of ancient Ireland. Opinion is divided as to its identity: Otto Anderssen presented reasons for believing that it might have been a *bowed harp or an instr. with strings stopped laterally by the fingernails; Galpin described it as a wire-strung psaltery and derived the word from tympanum. It may have been a syn. of cruit (see: timpe). If timpan were a Nordic word, unrelated to Gk. *tympanon,* it would explain how the tympanum came to be identified as a stringed instr. Also called benn-crot, tiompan; **2.** [Lat. *tympanum*], kettledrum; the term occurs in Engl. literature from the early 13th c. on. Also spelled timpane. *Cf.* timpe (9, 89 Galpin, 180).

Timpane [Lat. *tympanum*], OFr.: bell. The term is recorded in 1370; also a var. spelling of timpan (82).

Timpani, pl. of **timpano,** It.: kettledrum. See also: electrophonic timpani. For the orchestral timpani, see: kettledrum.

Timpani a pedali, It.: pedal drums.

Timpano, It.: kettledrum. *Cf.* timpani.

Timpano, Sp.: dulcimer (169).

Timpe, var. of timpan. It occurs in 13th-c. literature as a translation of rotte.

Timple, corr. of tiple, a treble guitar.

The word is used on the Canary Islands (152).

Tin, lute of the Shan of Burma, with piriform body made of a single piece of wood, wooden belly, sickle-shaped pegbox, and 3 strings. *Cf.* tinse (172).

Tinbuk, xylophone of Gazelle Peninsula (New Britain), Duke of York Island, S. New Ireland, and Tami, Bismarck Archipelago, consisting of 2 slabs 60–100 cm. (24–40 in.) long and 10 cm. (4 in.) wide, laid across the player's thighs or over 2 logs. Sometimes a pit is dug underneath. Also called tutupele (77).

Tindi de kileru, ground zither of the Mamvu and Djodje of the Congo (128).

Tinding, idiochord bamboo *tube zither of Flores, Indonesia (119).

Tingka, cylindrical drum of Sumatra, with wooden body and 2 goatskin heads (171).

Tingning, *tube zither of the Miau of Vietnam, with 10 tuning pegs and 2 gourd resonators (103).

Tingotalango, ground bow of Trinidad, Cuba (152).

Tingšak, clappers of Mongolia (168).

Tinniolum, Lat.: small bell. Syn. of tintinnabulum (61).

Tin-sags, see: tin-tin-sags.

Tinse, lute of the Kachin of Shan State, Burma, with piriform body of one piece of wood, wooden soundboard, sickle-shaped pegbox, soundhole, lateral pegs, and 3 strings, played with a plectrum. *Cf.* tin (172).

Tinternel [Fr. *tintinele*], 16th-c. Engl.: bell.

Tin thaila, *spike fiddle of the Naga of Assam, with gourd body, glued skin belly, and a single string (172).

Tintinabulum, see: tintinnabulum.

Tintinele, tintinable, tintinnabule [Lat. *tintinnabulum*], 16th- and 17th-c. Fr.: bell.

Tintinnabulum (Lat.), bell of ancient Rome, in late antiquity a herd animal bell. Tintinnabula were put to this use in 397 in Nonsberg, S. Tirol. In early

med. times the word came to designate the hammer with which bells were struck from the outside, by the 13th c. either the bell or its (inside) clapper, later the bell itself. The term is recorded in France from the 7th c. on (63, 82, 188).

Tintinnus, Lat.: bell. The term was used *ca.* 600 by Venantius Fortunatus.

Tin-tin-sags, miniature cymbals of Tibet, played by hermits and in certain rites. They are sounded by contact of the rims. Also called tin-sags (89 Picken).

Tintinullum, Lat.: bell (61).

Tin whistle, see: penny whistle.

Tinya, abbr. of huancar tinya.

Tiompan [Lat. *tympanum*], in modern Irish a drum; also a dulcimer. In ancient times a var. spelling of timpan.

Tiorba, It., Sp.: theorbo.

Tiorbino, small theorbo, mostly of It. 17th- and 18th-c. manufacture. Stringing and tuning were not standardized.

Tiparu, bull-roarer of the Elema of Papua (201).

Tiple (Sp.: treble) [Lat. *triplum,* threefold], **1.** syn. of guitarillo, on the Canary Islands also called timple; **2.** in Cuba a small bandurria with 5 pairs of strings; **3.** treble chirimía of N. Catalonia, prominent in the *cobla* (band), pitched in F, a 4th above the oboe, treated as a *transposing instr., with a compass d^1–g^3 written a^0–d^3. Like the *tenora, the tiple was modernized in the 19th c. and fitted with keywork. Played with a wide double reed recessed in a *pirouette; 56 cm. (22 in.) long (80 VI, 89 Baines).

Tīrăn, pl. of tār.

Tire-cordes, Fr.: tailpiece (rare).

Tirette, Fr.: slider key.

Tiril, Turk.: humming top.

Tiruchinnam (Tamil), temple trumpet of S. India, with cylindrical bore and narrow, conical bell, the 2 being separated by a boss. Depicted as early as *ca.* 1300, the tiruchinnam is played in pairs, 1 player simultaneously sounding 2 instrs. As there is no mouthpiece, the end of the tube is pressed against the player's lips. *Ca.* 75 cm. (2½ ft.) long. Also called sri churnam (170, 179).

Tiryāl, Arab.: tambourine (98).

T'i tang, brass gong of China, made of thick metal, with turned rim. *Ca.* 11 cm. (4½ in.) in diam. Also called lo pan (142).

Titapu, 1. *musical bow of Raïvavaé, Tubuaï Islands, Polynesia, with one or more strings and a bridge. One end of the bow is held in the player's mouth. *Ca.* 60 cm. (2 ft.) long; **2.** Jew's-harp of the Marquesas Islands (77).

Țitera (pron. tsitera) [Ger. *Zither*], Rom.: zither (5).

Titimotiti (onom.), ground bow of the Andekote of the Congo (128).

Titir, syn. of kentongan.

Ti tse, modern name of the ti.

Titti, Tel., Kan., Malayalam, Tulu: equivalent of the sruti upāngi.

Tiu, see: cai tiu.

Tiumbelek [Turk. *dumbelek*], Bulg.: kettledrum.

Tiva, wooden *goblet drum of the Kai Islands, Indonesia, with laced, wedge-braced head; 13–34 cm. (5–13 in.) high (119).

Tival, single-headed *cylindrical drum of C. and N. Celebes, a temple instr. with body of palm wood (112).

Tivele, wooden *goblet drum of Sermata Island, Moluccas, with parallel rattan lacings (173).

Tivolu, *pellet bell of Kulavi, Celebes; small, of metal, more or less globular, containing a small piece of metal or a pebble. Clusters of these are suspended from a flexible stick and are tied around the waists of young girls. They are associated with the belief in spirits (112).

Tj . . . , see: ch . . .

Tlanquiquitl, clay *whistle flute of ancient Mexico, similar to the pito (176).

Tlapanhuehuetl, large war drum of the Aztecs, played in vertical position, made in either cylindrical or barrel form. It survives today as a cylindrical footed drum. *Cf.* huehuetl (105, 137).

Tlapiztalli, small beaked *whistle flute

of the Aztecs, cylindrical, made of bone or clay, with or without fingerholes. Those of clay usually have 4 fingerholes, a long beaked mouthpiece with narrow duct, terminating in a disc-like flare, upturned to a 90-degree angle. Also called Aztec flute. *Cf.* cocoloctli (80 XII, 137).

To, 1. hand bell of China, nearly cylindrical, with metal or wooden clapper. An instr. of Buddhist priests, it corresponds to the thak of Korea; **2.** *musical bow of the Jukum, Benue River area, Nigeria, without resonator or tuning loop. The string is placed between the player's lips and is struck with a small stick (17, 89).

T'o, syn. of pang, 2.

Toa, Kru harp of Africa (144).

Toaca, Rom. semanterion of wood or metal, used in Orthodox churches, also by children during carnival (5).

Toba [Hung. *dob*], Rom.: drum.

Toba mare, Rom.: bass drum.

Tobera, metal percussion bar of the Basque people, used at wedding ceremonies, when the men beat it with sticks.

Tobi no o koto, syn. of wagon.

Tobol [Arab. *tabl*], kettledrum of the Haratin of Mauritania, with hemispheric body covered with lambskin. It accompanies songs and dances of religious and civil ceremonies (193).

Tobshuur, plucked chordophone of Mongolia, similar to the khil-khuur, with triangular or trapezoid body and 2 strings held by lateral pegs (69).

To' buni, see: tebuni.

Tocsin (Fr.) [Fr. *toquer,* strike + *sein*], bell rung to sound the alarm, used in France from the 14th c. on. The term is also employed in Engl. *Cf.* toquassen, toxin.

Tof, pl. **tupim** (Heb.), the *frame drum of ancient Israel, made of a wooden hoop, probably with 2 membranes, no jingles, played almost exclusively by women, the timbrel of Miriam. The word corresponds to the Arab. duff, and was translated as *timbrel.

Togha, Sans.: cymbals (176).

Togmur, cross flute of E. Bengal, with 7 front fingerholes (176).

Togo, syn. of tagong.

Toheli, chordophone of the Muria of Bastar, India, similar to the sitār, with bamboo neck and gourd resonator (66).

Tohila, see: tuila.

Tohmu, lyre of the Mittu of the Congo. *Cf.* tam, tom, tum (19).

Tok, *stamping tube of Korea, made of a segment of bamboo split several times for part of its length, and stamped against the ground. It corresponds to the ch'ung tu of China. *Ca.* 2 m. (80 in.) long (66, 170).

Tokere, 1. *slit drum of the Cook Islands and Tahiti; **2.** obs. bone clappers of New Zealand (77).

To-ko, *rattle drum of Korea corresponding to the furi tsuzumi of Japan.

Tokoro, name given to a large pinkillo (192).

Tolombas [Turk. *tulumbaz,* drummer], Alb., Pol.: kettledrum.

Tolo-tolo, *musical bow of the S. African Basuto, with thick, straight central portion and slender, flexible ends notched at their extremities to hold a wire string. This is looped to the bow. Either the bow is made of a single piece of wood or the center section may be a tube; in the latter case the bow is fitted through it. The string is tapped with a small stick (17).

Tom, lyre of the Bari of the Congo. *Cf.* tam, tohmu, tum (19).

Tomangu, 1. *musical bow of the Jívaro Indians of Ecuador, held horizontally by its end in the player's mouth like a cross flute, so that the string faces away from the player. The string is struck with a stick; **2.** *musical bow of the Busintana Indians of Colombia (105).

Tomba, *hourglass drum of the Mandingo of Sierra Leone, with laced heads. Played with 2 curved sticks (176).

Tombura, Hung.: tanbūr (now obs.).

Tomo, *musical bow of the S. African Hottentot and Bushman, with gourd resonator in the center of the bow, played with a smaller bow *ca.* 30 cm. (12 in.)

long, having horsehair string. In Balfour's opinion probably an imitation of the European violin (17).

Tom-tom, 1. set of high-pitched, tunable drums in use in Western rhythm bands since the 1920's, imitations of African drums. The head is lapped over a hoop and has modern rod tensioning. The drums are usually double-headed, vertical, cylindrical, but the cheaper ones have one head only; 15–30 cm. (6–12 in.) in diam.; **2.** name of a single-headed bamboo drum of New Guinea, provided with a handle (89, 176).

Ton, Fr.: fret.

Tonabulum, med. Lat.: small bell (61).

Tonadion, small flute of Byzantium (63 Gastoué).

Ton de rechange, Fr.: crook.

Tonette, modern wind instrument similar to the flutophone.

Tong, 1. Jew's-harp of Borneo; **2.** side-blown wooden trumpet of the Fan of W. Africa (176).

Tonga, small slit drum of Samoa (176).

Tongbī (Hindust.), var. of tūngbī.

Tonggong, Du. name of the kentongan.

Tongkat krutak, N. Borneo name of the gulung-gulung (176).

T'ong ku, small gong of China with central boss (89).

To ngo, drum of the Ngbandi of the Congo, similar to the ta ngo. The 2 are played together by 1 person (30).

Tong pal, copper cymbal of Korea, made in different sizes. It is rarely used. Equivalent of the po of China, the batsu of Japan (66).

T'ong po, syn. of po.

Tong tieng, gong chime of the Miau of Vietnam (103).

Tong-tong, ancient Javanese bronze *slit drum, known by the 4th c. *Cf.* tong-gong (121).

T'ong tyen, small gong of China, with shallow rim (89).

Tonitru, acoustic bass organ stop invented by Robert Hope-Jones (d. 1914), at 64' pitch (198).

Tonkori, plucked zither of the Ainu of Japan, now becoming obs. It has a narrow, elongated body, with long, tapering lateral pegs for 2–5 strings. Those having 5 strings are tuned $b^0 e^1 a^1 d^1 g^1$. Only open strings are played and these are plucked with bare hands. The tonkori is played by women, either as a solo instr. or as a drone to accompany singing (135, 144).

Tonnant [Fr. *tonner*, to boom], Fr.: bass drum (rare).

Tontaqui, abbr. of hatuntaqui.

Tontarde, rustic oboe of the Vendée, France, made of spirally twisted bark. *Cf.* touta (136).

Ton-ton, idiochord *tube zither of the Land Dayak of Borneo, with 3 strings, wooden bridges, and rattan bindings (173).

Tonus faber [Lat. *tonus fabri*], see: Faberton.

Topan, name of the tupan among Macedonians, W. Bulgars, S. Serbians, and E. Albanians (11).

Topftrommel, Ger.: pot drum.

Toph (Heb.), see: tof.

Topona, great drum of Haiti (176).

Toquassen [OProv. *tocar*, strike + *sein*], OFr. spelling of tocsin, recorded from 1372 on. Also spelled toquesing (85).

Torban [*?théorbe*], theorbo-like instr. pop. in 18th-c. Poland and the Ukraine, obs. by 1825, possibly a modification of the theorbo; 6 pairs of strings were affixed to the main pegbox, 4 single off-board strings to a second pegbox, and 14 or 15 more strings called *pristrunki* were stretched over the treble side of the body and attached to pegs inserted in the edge of the body. The on-board strings were tuned $D^0 d^0 G^0 g^0 c^0 c^1 f^0 f^1 g^1 a^1$, the off-board ones $D^0 G^0 C^0 F^0$, the *pristrunki* b^1-a^3 (115, 132, 170).

Toré, idioglott bamboo clarinet of the Guianas, the Amazon, and its tributaries, with long mouthpiece containing the reed, sometimes terminating in a gourd

bell, devoid of fingerholes. Often played in sets of different sizes, each producing only one tone (105).

Tori, side-blown horn of the 'Belinyan Bari of E. Africa, made of animal horn, with a ball of plaited wickerwork stitched to the opening and a handle of the same material in the center (195).

Toriibakue, panpipes of the Uitoto Indians of Colombia, with 3 pipes (105).

Tori parra, syn. of parrang.

Torloroto, obs. Sp. aerophone, possibly a shawm. Borel in 1654 identified it as an "hautbois" of S. France. More recently it has been described as a crumhorn (35).

Torogoata, Rom. name of the tárogató, imported from Budapest. In the Banat it has replaced the clarinet in folk music (5).

Torogop-jux, syn. of torop-jux.

Töröksip (Turk.: pipe), a name given the tárogató.

Torop-jux, *frame harp of the Ostyak of the U.S.S.R., with swan neck and lateral pegs for 8–10 strings, very similar in form to an illustration in an 8th-c. Anglo-Saxon ms. and a 9th-c. Irish depiction on a reliquary, earliest representations of a frame harp on the British Isles. The Ostyak play the melody with one hand and accompany themselves with the other hand on the 2 highest strings (9, 169).

Tororo, name of the sopila in Istria, where it is very rare (34).

Torotok, bamboo clappers of C. Java (121).

Tortald, corr. of Tartold.

Tortil (Fr.: twist), Fr.: crook.

Toru pill, bagpipe of Estonia, with bag of seal stomach, cylindrical chanter with 6 fingerholes and single cane reed, and 1 or 2 bass drones (13).

Totoro, syn. of ndundu among the Gombe of the Congo (30).

Tot-tlapiztali (Nahuatl: whistle birds), *whistling pot of Ecuador and Peru; it imitates the warbling of birds (152).

Touche, Fr.: fingerboard; key (of a keyboard).

Touche brisée, Fr.: split key.

Toulouhou, whirled friction drum of the C. Pyrenees (70).

Tountouna, see: tuntun.

Toupie bourdonnante, Fr.: humming top.

Tournebout, Fr.: crumhorn.

Touta, rustic oboe of Fr.-speaking Switzerland, made of spirally twisted willow bark. *Cf.* tontarde (102).

Towa, *vessel rattle of the Baoule of the Ivory Coast Republic, consisting of a bead-covered gourd (103).

Toxin, Engl. var. of tocsin.

Traccaballà, Neapolitan: tricca-vallaca.

Tracker (Ger.: *Abzug*), part of a mechanical organ action consisting of a slender strip of wood in horizontal or vertical position, used to communicate a pulling motion (12).

Tracker action, a mechanical action of an organ, consisting of trackers, rollers, stickers, etc., which form the connection between keys and pallets.

Tralaballacco, syn. of tricca-vallacca.

Trampes, a pair of kettledrums of Gerona, Spain, mounted on horseback. The sing. word form is not used (57).

Transmission, in an organ, the transferring of stops from one manual to another. Its invention is usually said to date from the last third of the 18th c. However, Eugen Casparini (1623–1706), an organ builder, made claviorgana of cypress with up to 20 variations of tone by transmission of the "pneumatic stops" (*"die durch Transportirung der penumatischen Stimmen bis etliche 20 Variationes gehabt"*) according to his son, Orazio, writing in the *Breslauer Sammlungen* of 1718. This may indicate that organ transmission existed almost a c. earlier than hitherto believed (176).

Transponierpianino, transposing *upright piano of Hermann Wagner of Stuttgart, 1884 (89).

Transposing instruments, term generally designating those instrs. written for at a pitch other than that at which they sound, such as basset horn, cor anglais, cornets, oboe d'amore, saxophone, kettledrums, to name only a few. In the case of woodwind instrs. this treatment permits uniform fingering of an instr. built in several pitches, and in the case of brass instrs. it permits sounding the same partials regardless of absolute pitch.

Transposing keyboards (Fr.: *claviers transpositeurs;* Ger.: *Transpositionsklaviatur*), difficulties of transposition experienced by keyboard players of the past are said to have been responsible for the creation of a number of devices for transposing the pitch. But this is not always true. Transposing keyboards have been made for various reasons, the most common being: a) to enable the performer to accommodate singers or other instrumentalists by playing at a different pitch; b) prior to the adoption of equal temperament, to furnish accidental notes not otherwise available (*e.g.,* D$\sharp$ instead of E$\flat$), although this defect was often remedied by *split keys; c) to enable an unskilled performer to play in "easy" keys pieces having several sharps or flats in the key signature; d) at a time when the pitch of organs differed by as much as half an oct., to permit organists to play certain solo works, such as intonations, at the same pitch level but without change of fingering. The first of these conditions was most commonly met by shifting the keyboards of organs. This device was already known to Arnold Schlick (early 16th c.) and has been in use intermittently ever since; it was in use on harpsichords at a somewhat later date. In a letter to Constantin Huygens dated July 31, 1648, De La Barre writes of a 2-manual harpsichord with shifting keyboards *"pour jouer en touttes sortes de tons et demy tons: cette invention est de moy . . ."* (for playing in all tones and semitones: this is my invention . . .) it was also applied occasionally to harmoniums in the 19th c. and to pianos from the 18th c. on. In organs, transposition stops also brought different pipes into play without any shift of the keyboard: the many 18th-

and early-19th-c. *Kammerton* stops fall into this category; they sounded a tone or so lower than the rest of the organ. A variation on this theme was the patenting by Sébastien Mercier of Paris by 1844 of a piano with divided keys, the rear sections of which could cause the hammers to strike the neighboring course of strings. The second condition was met by devices such as that applied to the organ of the Foundling Hospital in London, whereby the accidental keys usually tuned C♯ D♯ G♯ A♯ could by means of a special register be changed to D♭ E♭ A♭ B♭. The third condition was met on pianos by the use of false keyboards; in 1801 Edward Ryley patented a piano with a false keyboard placed above the real one; this could be shifted to any semitone of the oct., thus making it possible for players to play constantly in C if they so desired. On Oct. 3, 1872, Pleyel, Wolff & Cie of Paris patented a false keyboard, with a 6-oct. compass, that could be applied to any piano with no greater inconvenience—according to Mahillon—than a slight stiffness of the keys. The last condition was met by creating as practice instrs. for organists, harpsichords with 2 manuals, 1 at the pitch of the high organ, the other at the pitch of the low organ, the F key of one manual being at the same pitch (and plucking the same string) as the C key of the other manual. Several Flem. harpsichords so disposed, dating from the first half of the 17th c., have survived. This system was used only by Flem. builders; the Italians seem to have solved the problem in a different manner, namely by pitching their spinets (normally a 4½-oct. compass) half an oct. lower than their harpsichords (normally a 4-oct. compass). That the transposing keyboard is not a dead issue is shown from the following passage, written by Wedgwood in the first decade of our c.: "[the transposition stop] is a valuable adjunct to small instruments for village or mission churches, unlikely to be able to command skilled performers." See also:

clavicymbalum universale, keyboard (De La Barre letter in: *Revue de musicologie*, XII, 1928).

Transposing piano (Fr.: *piano transpositeur;* Ger.: *Transpositionsklavier*), piano that saves the performer the need of transposing, generally by means of a shifting keyboard that causes the hammers to strike the neighboring strings. The first patent for such an action was granted 1801 to Edward Ryley. Roller of Paris made a model with a keyboard that could be shifted either up or down, from 1 to 3 semitones each way. See also: crescendo, piano-orphéon, royal Albert transposing piano, Skalapianino, Transponier-Pianino (92, 204).

Transpositionsklaviatur, Ger.: transposing keyboards.

Transpositionsklavier, Ger.: transposing piano.

Transverse flute, see: flute, cross flute.

Traste, Sp.: fret.

Trautonium, monophonic, nonimitative *electrophonic instr. of the electronic type, invented by Friedrich Trautwein of Berlin in 1930. The tone was generated by a neon tube and controlled by a keyboard. The Trautonium was designed for experimental purposes. See also: Mixturtrautonium.

Trāvanāttam (Tamil) [King Ravana], fiddle of S. India, corresponding to the N. Indian ravanastron. See also: rāvanatta (47).

Traversflöte (Ger.), organ stop of overblowing flue pipes, wide-scaled and cylindrical; also made with narrow-scaled pipes, and occurring at 8′, 4′, 2′ pitches (133).

Traverson, trombone built by Daniel Fuchs of Vienna by 1873, in F and B♭, with a detachable bell (176).

Tre, Cuban *criollo* dialect for tres (152).

Treble violin, obs. expression for the violin. *Cf.* Diskantgeige, Diskantvioline.

Trembita, alphorn of the Pol. Gorals and Ruth. Hutsuka, a wooden tube 140 cm. (4 ft. 7 in.) long, now obs. among the Gorals. Also called trombita. *Cf.* trîmbiţă (89).

Tremblant, Fr.: tremulant.

Tremblant à vent perdu, see: Bock, 2.

Trémolophone, see: piano trémolophone.

Tremulant [Lat. *tremulus,* shaking] (Fr.: *tremblant;* Ger.: *Tremulant, Schwebung*), auxiliary organ stop, a device for producing rhythmical pulsations in the wind trunk, thereby causing a slight change in the pipe's pitch so that beats are created. The frequency of the beats can be regulated: Esaias Compenius (17th c.) suggested 80 pulsations per minute. Organ tremulants have historically been of 2 kinds: the *tremblant à vent perdu,* the more violent of the 2, in which, as the name implies, part of the wind supply was lost, and the *tremblant clos* with a special valve in the wind trunk. The earliest recorded tremulant was built into the Hagenau organ, Alsace, in 1491, with Sorau following in 1496 (133).

Trepie [Vulg. Lat. *tripede*], obs. Fr.: triangle. The term is recorded from the 14th c. on.

Treppiede, obs. It.: triangle.

Tres (Sp.: three), small guitar of Cuba, with 3 pairs of metal strings (152).

Tresangu (*tre,* gourd), Ewe word for sansa, so named for the round gourd that forms its resonator. See afosangu, sangu (93).

Tres palos (Sp.: three sticks), drum of the Dominican Republic, equivalent of the yuka (152).

Triangle [Lat. *triangulum*] (Fr.: *triangle;* Ger.: *Triangel;* It.: *triangolo*), a steel rod bent into the shape of a triangle and struck with a metal beater. Owing largely to its many high inharmonic overtones, the triangle can be heard above a full orchestra; for the same reason its pitch remains indeterminate. The triangle first appeared in the early 14th c. but the word is not recorded before 1589. Early forms of triangle were often trapezoid or stirrup-shaped, and up to the 19th c. jingling rings were usually appended to

them; up to 1600, 3 such rings are seen, thereafter as many as 5, strung as on a sistrum. These were abandoned *ca.* 1810. Mersenne called the instr. a *cymbale* (cymbal), a fairly common name for it, and remarks that it was a beggar's instr. Through 18th-c. Janissary music it gradually gained acceptance and entered the regular orchestra in the same c. See also: staffa, Stegereif, trepie, treppiede (59, 140, 169).

Triangolo, It.: triangle.

Triccaballacca, syn. of tricca-vallacca.

Tricca-vallacca, rattle of Naples, with 3 or 5 mallets inserted in a wooden frame, so that the center one is fixed and the outer ones are free to strike against it. Also called traccabballà, tralaballacco, triccaballacca. *Cf.* trich varlach.

Trichordon (Gk.: three strings), Hellenistic name of the pandoura, 3-stringed lute of ancient Greece (170).

Trichter, Ger.: bell (of a wind instr.).

Trichterregal (Ger.: funnel regal), organ stop of regal pipes with funnel-shaped resonators, built as a trumpet and later also as a shawm at 4' or 2' pitch (133, 198).

Trich varlach, Laborde's spelling (1780) of tricca-vallacca (124).

Trifonola, a variety of pianola made in the 1920's by L. Hupfeld of Leipzig. See also: phonola (37).

Trigesima prima (thirty-first), It.: tierce ⅖' organ stop.

Trigesima sesta (thirty-sixth), It.: octave ¼' organ stop.

Trigesima terza (thirty-third), It.: quint ⅓' organ stop.

Trigonon (Gk.: triangle), unidentified instr. of ancient Greece, probably a harp or psaltery. See also: organon trigonon enarmonion.

Trikimaka, syn. of gabi.

Trilodeon, an improved "melodeon," patented by Cornelius van Oeckelen in France (204).

Trîmbiţă, Rom.: trumpet; also a shepherd's alphorn of pine wound with birch bark. *Cf.* trembita.

Trimmi, Trimpi, name of the Jew's-harp in Uri, Switzerland (102).

Trinklen, cowbell of Switzerland.

Trinona, organ stop of narrow-scaled flue pipes, usually of metal, rarely of wood, with string tone. The name does not occur before the mid-18th c. Built at 8′ or 4′ pitch. Also called Triuna (133, 198).

Triorganon, organ built by Abbé Vogler in 1810 in Munich, with trapezoid console at which 3 organists could play simultaneously (176).

Triphone (Ger.: *triphon*), bowed friction instr. in form of an *upright piano without keyboard, invented by Weidner of Fraustadt in 1810 (169).

Triphonium, a combination zither-harmonium invented by Robert Lechleitner of the Lechtal, Tirol, *ca.* 1878. It produced flute and harmonium tones by means of flue pipes and reeds, in addition to the string tone of the zither.

Triple flageolet, a form of English flageolet made in the early 19th c. by William Bainbridge of London. All 3 pipes were blown through a common mouthpiece; the third pipe acted as a drone (89).

Triple harp, see: Welsh triple harp.

Triplo (triple), Cat. term for a small guitar (165).

Triquette, 16th-c. Fr.: cog rattle (53).

Tristanschalmei, shawm in F built by Wilhelm Heckel of Biebrich to play the shepherd's pipe in Wagner's *Tristan und Isolde. Cf.* Heckelclarina (176).

Tritantri vīnā (Sans. three-stringed vīnā), the least common of the sitārs, with 3 strings tuned $c^0 e^1 f^1$ or $g^0 c^1 f^1$, with round body and fretted neck. *Ca.* 90 cm. (3 ft.) long (132, 173).

Tritonikon, copper contrabassoon patented in 1839 by Schöllnast of Pressburg (Bratislava), and also named Universal-Kontrabass. It had a tube length of 4.56 m. (*ca.* 15 ft.) doubled back on itself 5 times, 15 keys, all closed except for the first, and a crook to carry the double reed. The tube terminated in a bell. Its compass was D^1–f^0, notated an oct.

higher. By 1856, Vaclav Červeny of Königgrätz (Hradec Králové) had worked out an improved model and brought it out in tuba form, pitched in E♭. This was followed by a larger one, in B♭, first shown at the Paris Exposition of 1867, with a 2-oct. compass. See also: contrebasse à anche, Klaviaturkontrafagott (89).

Triuba, var. of truba.

Tro, generic name of bowed chordophones in Cambodia and Burma. An ancient form of tro appears on a 10th-c. monument of Tanjore, India, a Burmese instr. resembling a med. European fiddle (47).

Troba, aerophone of Slovenia, made of cane with idioglott double reed, a child's toy. Also called prda (144).

Trobec, primitive wooden pipe of Slovenia (144).

Trobenta, syn. of tul.

Trocano, slit drum of the Miraña Indians of S. America (105).

Troccola, cog rattle of Sicily, used during Easter week (176).

Trochleon, bowed friction rod instr. invented in 1812 by Johann Christian Dietz, Sr., of Paris, with metal bars bowed by a continuous felt-covered band and controlled by a keyboard (169).

Tro duong, *spike fiddle of Java, of ivory, a little shorter than the sa dueng but otherwise similar to it.

Trögel [*Trog,* trough], Ger. 16th- and 17th-c. term for kit (176).

Troïne [*troëne,* privet], signal instr. of med. France, mentioned in Fr. literature from mid-12th c. to the 14th c. In modern Auvergne it is a shepherd's wind instr. made of spirally twisted bark (35, 204).

Tro khmer, ornate *spike fiddle of Cambodia, of ivory and mother-of-pearl, with tubular handle, goatskin belly, lateral pegs, and 3 strings. The spike is stuck in the ground during performance. Equivalent to the rebab of Java (47, 173).

Trom, Du.: drum.

Tromba, 1. It.: trumpet; **2.** organ stop,

see: trumpet, 2; also a flue Dulzian organ stop.

Tromba a chiavi, It.: keyed trumpet.

Tromba a macchina, It.: valve trumpet.

Tromba contralta in fa (It.), valved trombone in trumpet form, played with a trumpet mouthpiece, pitched in F and sounding an oct. below the (natural) trumpet in F. It was devised and first introduced by Rimsky-Korsakov in his opera-ballet *Mlada,* in order to obtain fullness and clarity in the lower notes (25).

Tromba cromatica, It.: chromatic trumpet.

Tromba da caccia (It.), a hitherto unidentified 18th-c. brass instr. in F.

Tromba da tirarsi, obs. It.: slide trumpet.

Tromba di zucca (It.: gourd trumpet), Buonanni in 1722 depicts this as a pipe with calabash bell. The nature of reed or mouthpiece is not clear.

Tromba marina, 1. It.: trumpet marine; **2.** organ stop of pipes with free reeds (133).

Tromba-piano, piano with 2 superposed soundboards and a metal frame, shown by Greiner of London in 1851 (158).

Tromba spezzata, It.: slide trumpet.

Tromba ventile, It.: valve trumpet.

Trombe (Fr.), a late name of the basse-trompette.

Trombēt, modern Egyptian name of the bass drum (98).

Trombetta, early It. term for trumpet, probably corresponding to the Lat. *tubecta.* Dante used the word in this sense. Later Praetorius says that it is syn. with tuba minor, trombone piccolo, and with the trombone in general (159, 169).

Trombino, obs. It.: alto trombone (159).

Trombita, 1. syn. of trembita; **2.** Hung.: trumpet, bugle.

Tromboncino [dim. of *trombone*], **1.** It.: alto trombone; **2.** organ stop of reed pipes.

Trombone [aug. of *tromba*] (Fr., It.:

trombone; Ger.: *Posaune*), **1.** brass wind instr. with cylindrical bore, its characteristic feature being a telescopic slide, played with a cup mouthpiece slightly larger than that of a trumpet. The trombone started life as an improvement of the trumpet, perhaps at the court of Burgundy at the turn of the 14th/15th c. Its names "trombone" and "Posaune" bear witness to its ancestry, the latter name being derived from *buisine. The trumpet of that time was S-shaped and sometimes had a telescopic mouthpipe. The larger version, the new trombone, had the mouthpipe fixed to the parallel tube by a cross-stay, and one whole section was made to slide by means of parallel outer tubing, while the rest was held still. From the late 15th c. on the trombone has remained virtually unchanged except for the shape of its bell—the older one being conical, whereas from the 18th c. on the bell has flared out—and the thickness of the metal, that of our modern instrs. being thinner. When the slide is pulled back (to the player) all the way, it is said to be in first position. In a B♭ trombone this will sound the fundamental $B\flat^1$ and its harmonics; if the slide is pushed out a few inches, into second position, its fundamental will be a semitone lower, or A^1, and the harmonics will be those of A^1, and so on. Its 3 lowest fundamentals, or pedal tones, are very hard to produce.

The early trombone was known in England as sackbut, in France as saquebute. Its first unequivocal representation appears on a Florentine painting of *ca.* 1420. Later in the c. Tinctoris says that the trombone was used for the deep parts of the "loud music," and in 1495 there were "shakbushes" at the court of Henry VII. These instrs. could be dismantled for easy transportation. By the late 16th c. trombones were being made in 3 sizes: an alto in f^0 (with its slide pushed out, in B^0); a tenor in $B\flat^0$ (with its slide pushed out, in E^0); and a bass in $E\flat^0$ (with its slide pushed out, in A^1). A tierce trombone is mentioned *ca.* 1600,

possibly an instr. pitched in G⁰, a 3rd below the tenor (later a bass in G⁰ became
standard in England). Praetorius reports
in 1618 that a contrabass trombone
sounding an oct. below the tenor, *i.e.*, in
Bb^1 (with its slide pushed out, in E^1),
had been made by Hans Schreiber "four
years ago." In addition to alto and tenor,
the latter also called *gemeine* (ordinary)
or *rechte Posaune* in German, he says
that there existed (quart) basses in F^1
and (quint) basses in Eb^1. Later in the
c. a soprano was added, pitched an oct.
above the tenor, but it never gained wide
acceptance and was usually replaced by a
cornett; also, it was often confused with
the alto. The tenor was then, as now, the
type instr., the word "trombone" without
qualification denoting the tenor trombone.
In the 16th and 17th c. the pitch was adjusted by the insertion of crooks at the
U bend between slide and bell joint. In
the course of the 17th c. the contrabass
instr. was discarded, leaving alto, tenor,
and the basses. The lack of flare in the
bell and use of thicker metal were chiefly
responsible for the mellower and softer
tone of the old instrs., making them acceptable in small vocal or instrumental
ensembles, yet during much of the 18th
c. little is heard of the trombone. Mattheson in 1713 comments that it is rarely
heard outside the church; Dr. Burney reports on the difficulty of finding players
in 1784 for the Handel festival, and about
a year later Christian Schubart says that
the trombone was neglected and played
only by cornettists (*Zinkenisten*); indeed,
the *Encyclopédie méthodique* of 1751 declared that the name "trombone," used
by Italians, designated a sort of trumpet.
However, Halle in 1764 still knew the
soprano, alto, tenor, quart bass, and quint
bass, the quart bass (in F) being at organ
pitch, as he says, *i.e.*, at choir pitch. But
with a redesigned bell the trombone
made its entrance into the orchestra in
the late 18th c., as Eb alto, Bb tenor,
and Eb bass (the F bass is rarely used
and now only in Germany). In classical

scores they are notated in alto, tenor, and
bass clefs, now customarily in bass clef
only, and, except for the bass, as transposing instruments. The 19th c. saw in-
novations in trombone making, the most
important of which was the application of
valves. The first valve trombones were
made experimentally by Heinrich Stölzel
and F. Blühmel in 1818, and by 1830
several makers were turning them out.
By the mid-c. they had become pop. in
Germany and Italy. Today 3- and 4-valve
instrs. are frequently encountered in
many countries; in Italy they are made in
the following sizes: tenors in Bb with 3
valves, basses in F with 4 valves (the
fourth lowers the pitch by the interval of
a 4th), and contrabasses in Bb with 4
valves. Valved basses in G are built in
England. Mention should also be made of
a valved bass in F built by Adolphe Sax
à tubes independantes. In the 1830's a
combination Bb/F trombone (Ger.:
Tenor-Bass Posaune) was introduced:
this was a tenor instr. fitted with an "F
attachment," consisting of *ca.* 1 m. (40
in.) of coiled tubing brought into play by
a rotary valve, sometimes called the
thumb valve. It was normally in Bb, but
the valve lowered it to F. Likewise, the
Engl. G bass can be switched into D by a
"D attachment," giving it a compass of
$E^1–g^1$ or higher. The modern trombone
is made to 3 bore specifications: narrow,
medium, and wide. Wide bores are common in the U.S. and Germany, narrow
bores in France, medium bores in England and in most rhythm bands. Tube
length of the alto is 208 cm. (82 in.) to
the mouthpiece, that of the tenor 272 cm.
(107 in.), that of the G bass 330 cm.
(130 in.). These sizes are used in orchestras, in military, brass, and rhythm bands,
and in addition a soprano is used in
rhythm bands (see: soprano slide cornet).
The compass averages 2½ octs. See also:
Quartposaune, Quintposaune, soprano
slide cornet, tierce trombone (41, 59, 89
Baines, 159, 170);

2. organ stop of reed pipes, usually at

16' or 8' pitch, with inverted conical resonators. William Hill attempted a 64' contratrombone at Town Hall, Sidney (133).

Trombone à coulisse, Fr.: (slide) trombone.

Trombone all'ottava, 17th-c. It.: contrabass trombone (159).

Trombone à pistons, Fr.: valve trombone.

Trombone buxin à tête de serpent, see: buccine.

Trombone da tracolla (It.: shoulder-belt trombone), valved trombone built in helicon form, specially for mounted bands: it encircles the player's neck. Formerly used by Du. military bicycle bands (89 Baines).

Trombone de France, obs. organ stop, allegedly a trombone stop in echo form (133).

Trombone doppio, 17th-c. It.: contrabass trombone (159).

Trombone duplex (Fr.), trombone of Gustave-Auguste Besson of Paris, 1864, with both slides and valves (156).

Trombone duttile (It.), It. translation of tuba ductilis.

Trombone grande, obs. It.: bass trombone (159).

Trombone majore, syn. of trombone grande.

Trombone omnitonique (Fr.), see: omnitonic trombone.

Trombone piccolo, according to Praetorius, the tenor trombone.

Trombone saxchromatique, trombone invented by Adolphe Sax in 1850, with 6 pistons (204).

Trombone saxomnitonique, trombone invented by Adolphe Sax, provided with an omnitonic system.

Trombone snodato [It. *snodare,* to unknot], It.: (slide) trombone.

Trombone spezzato, It.: (slide) trombone.

Trombone ventile, It.: valve trombone.

Trombotonar, a huge contrabass *tuba patented by Gustave-Auguste Besson of Paris in 1855 and shown at the exposi-

tion there that same year. It stood 3 m. (*ca.* 10 ft.) high.

Trombula, 17th- and 18th-c. Lat.: Jew's-harp (169).

Tromett, obs. Ger.: trumpet.

Trommel [OHGer. *trumba*], **1.** Ger.: drum; **2.** organ stop, see: drum pedal.

Trommelpfeife, Ger.: tabor pipe.

Tromp, obs. Du.: horn.

Trompa, 1. Cat., Port., Sp.: a) horn, b) straight trumpet; the term is recorded in Sp. literature from the 13th c. on (137); **2.** obs. Basque: Jew's-harp (56); **3.** *musical bow of the Guajiro and Kichos Indians of S. America. The bow is held in the player's mouth and the string plucked by his finger. *Ca.* 140 cm. (55 in.) long (105).

Trompa de París, pop. name in certain parts of Spain for the Jew's-harp. Cervantes said that it was also called trompa gallega or pio poyo; today it is called guimbarda (57, 165).

Trompa de vocal, Sp.: ballad horn.

Trompa gallega, syn. of trompa de París.

Trompa goajira (Sp.: *trompa* of the Guajiro Indians), Jew's-harp of Venezuela.

Trompa inglesa, Sp.: Jew's-harp.

Trompa manedica, OProv. translation of tuba ductilis.

Trompe [OHGer. *trumpa*], **1.** generic Fr. term for horns and bugles, recorded from the 12th c. on (but later than *buisine). A 13th-c. *Art de chevalerie* describes it as being long and straight. During the same c. the word is taken into the Engl. language. The trompe served as a signal instr. in battle, at tourneys, and was used at weddings and other ceremonies. In 1606 Nicot differentiates between the hunting horn made of horn or ivory and the trompe made of brass. In the late 17th c. Furetière defines it as a horn with a single coil. The word is still in use; **2.** in the late 17th c. and during the 18th c. trompe came to denote the Jew's-harp (35, 53, 78, 82).

Trompeau [dim. of *trompe*], small trompe of late med. France (204).

Trompe de Béarn (Fr.), Jew's-harp (78).

Trompe de Berne, corr. of trompe de Béarn.

Trompe de chasse, Fr.: hunting horn; also called cor de chasse.

Trompe de laquais, see: trompe-laquais.

Trompe de Lorraine, *natural horn of Grégoire of Nantes, 1866, spirally wound, in a casing shaped like an animal horn, and pitched in D (176, 204).

Trompe Dufouilloux (Fr.), crescent-shaped *hunting horn with a small coil in the center, in use in 16th- and 17th-c. France. It corresponded to the Jägerhorn of Praetorius (89 Morley-Pegge).

Trompe-laquais, obs. Fr.: Jew's-harp (78).

Trompe Maricaux, name occasionally given in 17th-c. France to a closely coiled horn (89 Morley-Pegge).

Trompeta [Fr. *trompette*], Sp.: trumpet. The term is recorded from the 15th c. on.

Trompeta bastarda (It., Sp.) (Fr.: *trompette bastarde*), hitherto unidentified trumpet known in France, Italy, Spain, and Portugal from the 15th to the 17th c. Sp. literary sources of the 15th c. mention the trompeta bastarda together with the clarin trumpet, and *"trompetas bastardas e italianas"* are referred to by the chronicler Miguel Lucas in 1461. In the late 16th c. the Port. priest João dos Santos speaks of a Kaffir horn he had heard in Africa as having the "terrible and frightening" sound of a trompeta bastarda, and in the early 17th c. we hear of Sp. trumpeters applying for the job of town trumpeters who had to pass an examination in both trumpet and trompeta bastarda playing. *Ca.* 1640 Trichet wrote of the instr. that *"on leur baille quelques fois des replis"* (one sometimes gives them *replis*); the word *repli* means primarily fold, secondarily coil, and this remark is unfortunately the closest we come to a contemporary description: either it was occasionally folded, or it was occasionally coiled. Covarrubias (in 1611) defines it most unconvincingly as intermediary between a loud, low-pitched trumpet and a soft, high-pitched clarin. Modern reference works call it a trumpet of intermediate size or pitch. We know from the letters of Georg Neuschel (1541), a Nürnberg trumpet maker, that *welsche* or French trumpets cost about twice as much as German trumpets (Duke Albert of Prussia ordered from him *"12 deucze and 12 welsche oder franczosische"* trumpets); this can hardly have been because of a minor difference of pitch: there must have been far more tubing involved, or far more work, or both. To the confusion of all horn connoisseurs, a woodcut by the Strassburg humanist Sebastian Brant, illustrating a 1502 edition of Virgil, shows two men, one blowing a natural trumpet, another standing close to him playing a hoop-shaped horn with 3½ coils, terminating in a bell. It is hung around his neck and has a diam. of perhaps 40 cm. (16 in.) (reproduced in Source 144, article "Horn"). No such form of horn existed at the time, nor indeed before the mid-17th c. The instr. in question has been explained as a figment of Brant's imagination, as an early occurrence of a type of horn promptly forgotten and rediscovered subsequently. (It is not clear why and how a horn and a trumpet should be played or even portrayed together in the 16th c.: one would imagine that the trumpeters' guild would have rendered such association impossible.) But if this were a trumpet? Examples of 17th-c. hoop-like trumpets are occasionally met with in museums, and the bore of Brant's instr. is certainly more cylindrical than conical. Perhaps it represents a trompeta bastarda. The greater amount of tubing would permit "loud, low-pitched" tones, and if Trichet's bastarda was sometimes folded, then it must have been usually coiled (or vice versa).

Trompeta morisca, the añafil.

Trompete, Ger.: trumpet.

Trompetengeige, Ger.: trumpet marine.

Trompetenregal, obs. organ stop of conical regal pipes, little known outside Germany (133).

Trompetica china, oboe of the Chin. population of Cuba, yielding 5 high-pitched sounds, played in Eastern style, with the performer breathing through his nostrils while playing, so as to maintain uninterrupted sound. Also called dettoi, sona, taide. Ortiz calls the instr. a trumpet, but, judging by the playing technique he indicates and the fact that sona is a syn., it must be a form of oboe (152).

Trompetine, postillon's horn made by Stegmeier of Ingolstadt, 1854, with one valve (204).

Trompette (Fr.) [dim. of *trompe*], **1.** Fr.: trumpet; a short trumpe; the term is recorded from 1339 (Machaut) on; **2.** MEngl.: small trumpe; **3.** formerly a drone string on a hurdy-gurdy; **4.** organ stop of reed pipes of inverted conical form and medium scale, at 8′ pitch, the most brilliant of the organ reeds. In 4′ position it is called *clairon (20, 133).

Trompette à clefs, Fr.: keyed trumpet.

Trompette à coulisse, Fr.: slide trumpet.

Trompette à pistons, Fr.: valve trumpet.

Trompette bastarde, see: trompeta bastarda.

Trompette céleste, organ stop of reed pipes at 8′ pitch, invented by the Belgian organ builder Van Bever (131).

Trompette chromatique, Fr.: chromatic trumpet.

Trompette demi-lune, Fr. equivalent of *Stopftrompete.

Trompette duplex, trumpet having both slide and valves, built in 1884, with a compass g^0–c^3 and a fundamental of F♯. *Cf.* trombone duplex (176).

Trompette harmonieuse (Fr.), 18th-c. var. of trompette harmonique.

Trompette harmonique, 1. Fr. 17th-c. term for trombone. Both Mersenne and Trichet use the word in this sense; **2.** or-

gan stop of overblowing reed pipes, invented by Aristide Cavaillé-Coll of Paris in the 19th c., with medium scale. Called Harmonietrompete in Ger. *Cf.* clairon harmonique (133).

Trompette marine, Fr.: trumpet marine.

Trompette marine organisée (Fr.), *trumpet marine with sympathetic strings inside the body, an improvement of Jean-Baptiste Prin (*ca.* 1650 to *ca.* 1740) (89).

Trompette omnitonique, Fr.: omnitonic trumpet.

Trompette rompue, Fr.: trombone. Mersenne and Laborde use the word in this sense.

Trompette saqueboute, early Fr. name of the trombone.

Trompette thébaine, Fr.: Aïda trumpet.

Trompette-timbale (Fr.), kettledrum invented in 1855 by Adolphe Sax of Paris, based on Félix Savart's observations of vibrating membranes. Its feature was an elongated conical resonator, similar to a giant ophicleide mouthpiece; the pitch could be changed by a series of pedal-operated valves, slides, or keys that controlled the air volume. *Cf.* tubus timpanites (158, 176).

Trompette-trombone, *slide trumpet patented on Dec. 13, 1821, by André-Anthony Schmittschneider of Paris (204).

Trompettine, Ger. term for a trumpet in high D, E♭, or B♭ (176).

Trompille, 15th- and 16th-c. Fr.: trumpet.

Trompillon, obs. bridge of the trompette string on a hurdy-gurdy (25).

Trompo de guïro, humming top of E. Cuba, made from the fruit of the guïro gourd (152).

Trompong, a one-row bonang of Bali, tuned an oct. below the babarangan (121).

Trompo silbador, Sp.: humming top.

Trong, 1. see: cai trong; **2.** goblet drum of Cambodia (173).

Trong boc, see: cai trong boc.

Trong cai, see: cai trong cai.

Trong com, see: cai trong com.

Trong con, see: cai trong con.

Trong giang, see: cai trong giang.

Trong khan, see: cai trong khan.

Trong kuan, see: cai trong kuan.

Trong mañ, see: cai trong mañ.

Trong met, see: cai trong met.

Trong tien co, see: cai trong tien co.

Trong va, see: cai trong va.

Tronpa, Basque: trumpet; Jew's-harp.

Tronpeta, Basque: trumpet.

Trottola, It.: humming top (176).

Tro u, *spike fiddle of Cambodia, with 2 strings, equivalent to the sō u of Laos and Thailand and to the hu ch'in of China (47, 173).

Trough zither (Ger.: *Trogzither, Schalenzither*), chordophone in which the strings are laced up and down across the opening of a flat trough, found only in Africa (195).

Troumpeto de San Jean, Prov. horn made of glazed clay, formerly played by boys on June 23 (176).

Troynice, triple flute of Croatia; the right bore has 4 fingerholes, the middle bore 3, the left bore none. Playing technique is that of the dvoynice (34).

Trstenke, Slov. shepherd's panpipes in raft form, made of cane. Number and length of the pipes vary. They are arranged in 2 rows, held in position by little slats of wood, and tuned by ear with wax and resin. Also called orglice, piskulice. *Cf.* coštimaje (144).

Truand, see: instrument truand.

Truba, 1. Russ., Ruth.: trumpet; **2.** rural trumpet of Yugoslavia, made of ash tree bark in early spring, up to 1.50 m. (5 ft.) long; **3.** shepherd's trumpet of Lithuania, equivalent to the alphorn, made in 2 forms: a) a straight, conical tube made of a log that has been split twice, *i.e.*, into 4 sections, covered with bark and bound with cane. *Ca.* 1 m. (40 in.) long; b) an S-shaped tube similar to the 15th-c. European trumpet, also made of the split sections of a log, these being glued together with rosin and bound with

bark. A mouthpiece is carved into the tube proper. It was formerly used in processions, at weddings, etc. (89, 174).

Truc, largest of the sonnailles (herd animal bells) of the Auvergne, made of sheet metal, *ca.* 40 cm. (16 in.) long (127).

Trumba, OHGer.: drum; trumpet.

Trumbe (MHGer.), **1.** early med. metal trumpet of Germany, without bell; **2.** med. drum of Germany. Var. spellings occur, such as trumpe, trumme.

Trumbel, Trumel, MHGer.: drum.

Trumm, Estonian: drum.

Trumma, Swed.: drum.

Trumme, MHGer.: small *cylindrical drum. The word is used in this sense in med. Ger. literature (189).

Trump, Scot. and N. Engl.: Jew's-harp (Oxford English Dictionary).

Trumpa, 1. OHGer.: trumpet; **2.** in the old Swed. colonies of Estonia the trumpa is a rectangular psaltery with 11 strings of different lengths, played with or without a plectrum, and tuned $F^0 c^0 d^0 e^0 f^0 g^0 a^0 b^0 c^1 d^1 e^1$ (149); **3.** *musical bow of the Pánobo Indians of S. America, with the string taken into the player's mouth (105).

Trumpe [Fr. *trompe*], MEngl.: trumpet, made of brass, occasionally of gold. First recorded in *Cursor Mundi, ca.* 1300, the term is then used in literary sources together with *beme until the latter word disappears *ca.* 1500 (180).

Trumpel, earliest Ger. word for the Jew's-harp, mentioned by Virdung in 1511 (169).

Trumpet [Fr. *trompette*] (Fr.: *trompette;* Ger.: *Trompete;* It.: *tromba*), **1.** lip-vibrated wind instr. originally made of a tube of bamboo, cane, or wood—thus a straight instr.—later imitated in metal. Sometimes a gourd was affixed to the lower end to serve as a bell. (A horn, on the other hand, was originally made of animal horn or tusk.) Sachs pointed out in 1910 that in Europe trumpets are more cylindrical than conical, horns more conical than cylindrical, but this does not hold true elsewhere: ancient Egyptian trumpets, for instance, have a conical bore throughout. For problems in distinguishing between the 2 instrs. and for the classification employed in this dictionary, see: horn. The first trumpets served magical and not musical ends; they were used to distort primitive man's voice, and were shouted or sung into, very much like a megaphone, in order to ward off evil spirits. Megaphone-like trumpets are still in use in Switzerland and Brazil, devoid of mouthpiece and bell. Marine shells, usually conchs, are often blown as trumpets, and originally they also were used as voice disguisers. Both tubular and *marine-shell trumpets are either end-blown or side-blown. The earliest types of both were end-blown, and these were followed by primitive side-blown instrs. The latter are still found in Africa, S. America, and the S. Seas and existed in Ireland during the Bronze Age (which extended there far later than elsewhere). (The British Museum houses a bronze statuette from Campania, dated ca. 470 B.C., that patently if inexplicably is blowing a transverse trumpet.) More developed forms are end-blown. In the ancient Mediterranean area the trumpet was both a war instr. and a temple instr. Trumpets of ancient Egypt are first depicted ca. 1400 B.C.; they were of metal with conical bore and short, flaring bell. Surviving examples have wooden stoppers exactly fitting the whole bore, perhaps to protect the very thin metal. One found in the tomb of Tut Ankh Amon (d. 1349 B.C.) is made of silver, some 58 cm. (23 in.) long; another of bronze is about 50 cm. (20 in.) long. Ancient Etruscan trumpets were similar, also with conical bore. Egyptian, Israelite, Etruscan, and Roman trumpets were straight. We know that those of Egypt and Israel were played in pairs, as were those of Afghanistan, of ancient and modern India and Tibet, all of which were made of metal. Wood or bark trumpets of Lithuania, Romania, Chile, C. America, and the Amazon forests are also

played in pairs. The performances are antiphonal, each instr. yielding 1 or 2 rough tones: verdicts of ancient writers concerning contemporary trumpets are invariably uncomplimentary.

The trumpet of post-classical Europe first appears as a degeneration of the *tuba (8th c.), replaced by the 13th c. by a long, straight Saracen instr. that the Fr. called *buisine, and ca. 1300 by a shorter one with cylindrical bore and wide, flaring bell. These two may be identical with the tubae and a tubecta of silver ordered by Emperor Frederick II when he was in Arezzo in 1240; and the word tubecta may furthermore be the Lat. rendering of trombetta, mentioned shortly thereafter by Dante. The Fr. word buisine, given to the larger instr., was taken over into the Ger. language, first as busîne, ultimately as *Posaune (Ger. for trombone), with ensuing confusion of functions. By the end of the 14th c. the trumpet is folded into an S shape, and a c. later it had assumed the form we associate with the "natural" trumpet, wound into an elongated hoop. This was to become the classical trumpet of Europe, and it remained standard until the end of the 18th c. Originally an attribute of worldly power, the trumpet had been an instr. of princes and high dignitaries in the East, and was to retain this role in Europe. Only ruling princes, high nobility, cavalry forces (originally composed of noblemen) and the free cities of the German Empire were permitted to retain trumpeters (Augsburg in 1434; other cities followed), and these organized themselves into a privileged and powerful guild with jealously guarded rights. According to the range they specialized in, its members were classified either as clarin or as principal players, the former being the upper register of the trumpet, played with a special mouthpiece; the latter, its lower register (see: clarino). With the decay of the corporation system in the 18th c., the days of the guild were over and the trumpet was freed from restrictive practices.

The natural trumpet was made of brass, occasionally of silver, hammered on forms and soldered, its joints concealed under ornamental garnishes, with a boss on the last joint. The embossed rim of the bell is known as "garland," and it is here that the maker signs his instr. The brilliance of the trumpet's tone is caused by the narrow and mainly cylindrical bore. It was essentially an outdoor instr. when it first entered the orchestra; its role was that of a fanfare instr. By the 18th c. composers had taken advantage of its high register, and as long as the art of clarin playing flourished, this register was exploited for its brilliance. As late a writer as Christian Schubart associated its use with festive and majestic occasions. With a tube length of *ca.* 210 cm. (7 ft.) it was pitched in D in Praetorius' time; he writes that, shortly before, trumpets had been of larger scale and tuned to C. In 18th-c. Germany their pitch was chamber pitch D (identical with choir pitch C; according to Johann Mattheson, the trumpet was thought of as being in C choir pitch "so that *Kammerton* pieces are composed in D major"). They could of course be crooked to sound at lower pitches. In England the trumpet was usually in E♭, according to James Talbot, writing *ca.* 1700, and could be crooked to D C B B♭ A A♭, as desired. Later it was in G, according to Hermann Eichborn, and that of the French, in F. The same author stresses the fact that Germany was the only country to have the low-pitched trumpets (E♭, D, C, B♭) suitable for clarin playing. In the course of the 18th c. orchestral trumpets were made in several sizes and were provided with crooks; a *slide trumpet was also in use. Halle in 1764 says that the trumpet was in D♯, with shorter trumpets in E♭ or F for the military. The higher pitch of the (shorter) trumpets in the latter part of the c. is confirmed by many writers. Hermann Eichborn states that this was in

order to have them sound an oct. higher than the horns (in F). Around 1780 the *Inventionstrompete was brought out, followed by the *chromatic trumpet and French horn of Claggett in 1788, and the *Stopftrompete (called trompette demilune in Fr.) in the early 19th c.; in 1801 a keyed trumpet was built, but without success. The search for chromaticism did not end before the invention of the *valve, *ca.* 1815. (Leonardo da Vinci, who died in 1519, drew a straight trumpet with what looks suspiciously like valves. *Cf.* Folio 175 of the *Codex Arundel.*) Valves were fitted to the cylindrical section of the tube; at first 2, then 3; and by 1828 valve trumpets in F, E♭, and high B♭ were being produced. Eichborn relates that by 1840 valve trumpets had a place in most Ger. opera orchestras. The F trumpet became rapidly pop. in Germany, but was not adopted until later in France, where it had to meet the competition of the cornet à pistons. But by the end of the c. it was being abandoned again in favor of the C and B♭ trumpets. Today, that in B♭ is the most commonly used; its 3 valves not only fill the gap between the harmonics but also take the compass down from b♭^{0} (its second harmonic) to e^0. The "B♭ and C" trumpet is also much used in W. Europe and the U.S.; it is a normal C trumpet that can be lowered to B♭; similarly, there exists a combination E♭ and D trumpet. In the late 19th c. instrs. were specially made for the performance of clarin parts of classical scores: a straight trumpet in A, a 5th higher than the classical D trumpet, with 2 valves, was used for Bach performances; in 1890 Mahillon of Brussels introduced a sopranino in d^0 for the performance of classical obbligatos, made both in straight and in wound form, as is the "little F" trumpet a 3rd above it; and Otto Steinkopf of Berlin has now introduced a small, spirally coiled version. Piston valves are now in use everywhere except in Ger.-speaking countries and E. Europe, where rotary valves are still preferred. Trumpets are treated as transposing instrs. and are notated in C (41, Talbot in 80, 89 Baines, 90, 137, 168; H. Hickmann; *La Trompette dans l'Egypte ancienne*, 1946). See also: acocotl, adil, adjulona, agaita, ah tu, ahuri'au, Aïda trumpet, akawunde, alto trumpet, anafil, añafil, anafim, anjomary varahina, antsivambazaha, arupepe, asukusuk, atoros, Bach trumpet, bal, banku, bawwāqe, bazuna, belebān, bemastocc, beme, bher, bhuri, biglo, biludi, bingo, bonto, botuto, botzina, brofwe-awe, b'ru, buccina, buccine, budu, bughri, buisine, bulu, bunu, būq, būrghū, buri, burloir, buru, būrū, buruga, buse, busîne, butyu, cangueca, carnyx, cha chiao, chnouē, clairon, clareta, clarin, clario, clarion, claro, classicum, classique, cor crochu, corniard, cornu, cor sarrazinois, cos-dung, danafil, dbang-dung, deren, dhudka, didjeridoo, dodaku, dung, dung chen, eggwara, ekkalam, ekkondere, erque, fanfami, flat trumpet, gādar, gala, gangurih, ghunda, gwara me akuta, hahi, hao, hao talla, hao t'ung, hatzozroth, herald's trumpet, hom, hong, horesemoi, huang la pa, huang teh, icilongo, icombi, ika, jayasringa, ka, kabacha, kaha, kāhalam, kakati, kalam, kanga, kang dung, kang t'u, karan, karana, karnā, karnay, karranay, kawunde, ketsü, kivudi-vudi, kōbe, kombu, kommu,

kondere, kornai, k'rims-dung, labbanātu, la pa, lik haanga, limba, loku, lolkin, ludi, luru, maitai talla, makondere, malakat, manyinyi, mare, marine-shell trumpet, matabo, mpolomono, mushekera, nafari, nafīr, nāgaphani, nāgbin, na pal, narsringa, ngalir, nibiles, nkenke, nsiba, ntamba, ogo buru, olwet, pampame, panna, patuweh, phunga, phusana mati, pihurne, piluli, piring būrū, ˅ pukaea, pungacuqua, putura-putura, qarna, qarnā, rag dung, ranasringa, rapa, rapal, Regent's bugle, rkan-dung, rkan-gling, salpinx, sarga, shaipūr, shephor, siao t'ung kyo, simha, sing, singam, slide trumpet, sringa, stag-dung, stoc, Stopftrompete, sturgan, suke, sūr, tanda, tarai, tarantara, tarumbeta, tarunbata, ta t'ung kyo, taurea, tellimbilla, thoti, tiruchinnam, tong, trîmbiţă, tromba, trompa, trompeta, trompeta bastarda, trompette, trompettetrombone, tronpa, tronpeta, truba, trumba, trumbe, trumpa, trumpe, trutruka, tube, tuda, tuhunta, tulumbeta, turi, turulu, tūrumpata būrūsī, turuta, tūrya, tuum, uapida, uhuhuk, ulia, uluru, utgorn, yuge, yurupuri, zäns-dung, zozoloctli;

2. in France an organ stop of reed pipes having normal-length bodies, also a class of such stops, including the clairon 4', 2', bombardes 32', 16', basson 16', 8',

Tonal position	Fundamental	Valved trumpets	Natural trumpets
octave or piccolo	bb^0	modern	
sopranino	f^0	modern; straight or wound	
	eb^0		
	d^0	modern; straight or wound	
soprano	c^0	late 19th c.; standard in France	
	Bb^0	modern	
	A^0	late 19th c.; straight with 2 valves for clarin parts	
	Ab^0		19th-c. Fr. and It.
	G^0		19th-c. Fr. and It.
alto	F^0	19th-c. standard	19th-c. standard
	Eb^0	19th-c. military	classical and military
	D^0	orchestral	classical
bass	C^0	orchestral bass	pre-Praetorius
(really baritone)	Bb^1	military bass	Altenburg's lowest pitch
	A^1	military bass	

4', and hautbois. Elsewhere the term is reserved for a reed stop of inverted conical pipes at 8' pitch (63, 133).

Trumpeter (automatic) (Fr.: *orgue-trompette*), automatophone imitating one or more trumpets; some show human figures purporting to play the instrs., but these are dummies, as all automatic trumpeters employ free reeds. In 1808 Friedrich Kaufmann of Dresden built an automatic trumpeter that he named *salpingion; this was followed in 1812 by the *phonorganon of Robertson, and the *salpinorganon of Van Oeckelen in 1824, the same year that the Berlin clockmaker Kielblock produced a similar instr. See also: belloneon (37, 176).

Trumpet marine (Fr.: *trompette marine;* Ger.: *Trumscheit;* It.: *tromba marina*), bowed chordophone with a slender, 3-sided body made of thin boards, tapering to the top, usually provided with a single string. Characteristic of the instr. were its bridge and its playing technique. One foot of the bridge was suspended a hairsbreadth above the belly, against which it drummed rapidly when played. (Cf. the special drumming bridge of some later hurdy-gurdies. Inbuilt drumming or rattling devices are more frequently encountered in non-Western than in Western instrs.) The string was not stopped in the usual sense of the word, but touched lightly, mostly with the thumb, according to Glarean (in 1547), thus producing flageolet tones, while it was bowed with a short bow close to the nut, *i.e.*, between nut and stopping point. During performance it was held either with the upper end resting on the player's shoulder or chest, and the lower end on the ground, or with the lower end projecting obliquely upward, over the player's head.

The origin of this peculiar instr. remains to be investigated. It first appears on a 12th-c. Fr. sculpture, was called monochord in the Middle Ages (and later), and may originally have been plucked rather than bowed. By the 15th c.—its heyday—a second string had been

added, either of the same length as the first or half as long. Memling depicts it with 2 strings, but up to 4 are encountered. On early paintings it has a frontal peg, string fastener, no neck. Around 1500 the shape changes: the bottom develops a flare rather like a bell, and a neck is formed. L.ter the pegs are inserted laterally. Virdung in 1511 calls it a useless instr., but Glarean in 1547 uses a 2-stringed trumpet marine to demonstrate monochord ratios; he says that the French and Germans play an instr. called *"tympanischiza"* (his translation of the Ger. word Trumscheit), apparently it was not known by any other name at the time. He infers that it was an instr. of street musicians. In England it did not become known until the 17th c. Samuel Pepys heard a performance on one in 1667 and reported "it do so far outdo a trumpet as nothing more." Mersenne says that the second string was discarded by his day. Later in the 17th c. a number of sympathetic strings of brass, 12–24, were added inside the body by Jean-Baptiste Prin, all tuned at unison with the melody string. Prin also invented a regulator for the bridge to control the drummings of the short foot. This variety with added strings was known as *trompette marine organisée*. The instr. was also made far larger than before, attaining 180–210 cm. (6–7 ft.) in height. James Talbot, *ca.* 1700, gives the tones of the melody string as G^0 d^1 g^1 b^1 d^2 g^2 a^2 b^2 c^3 d^3 e^3 and also mentions the metal sympathetic strings. Leopold Mozart, writing in 1756, says that it was still in use, and in France the instr. even managed to maintain itself in the *Musique des Écuries* of the Fr. court until 1767. As an instr. of ambulant musicians, it was pop. in Germany, France, and Italy, and apparently also in Poland. Sachs pointed out that the triangular form and the technique of playing in flageolet tones are E. European, and in this connection it is interesting to note that Paulus Paulirinus of Prague described the instr. *ca.* 1460, calling it *tubalcana* (its earliest association with the trumpet?). Paulirinus taught at Cracow; its present Pol. name is tuba maryna. The trumpet marine is also called nun's fiddle (Ger.: *Nonnengeige*) because it is supposed to have substituted for the trumpet in convents. There is only sparse evidence to substantiate this. It is called "trumpet" in several languages because the harmonics of its melody string are those of the trumpet, but the qualification "marine" is not clear; the word has been derived from Mary, and the instr. is also called Marientrompete in Ger. Other names are Trompetengeige (Ger.), violetta marina (It.) and violitromba (also It.) (89, 94, 149, 169, 170).

Trumscheit [**trumpa* or **trumme* + *scheit,* log], Ger.: trumpet marine.

Trumway [*tramway*], pop. clarinet of Egypt, said to sound like the signal instr. formerly employed by tram conductors (144).

Trumway shubbuk, triple clarinet of Egypt, a folk instr. Two of the pipes terminate in a common bell of horn (144).

Truðhorn, OEngl.: horn. Glossed in the 11th c. as lituus. *Cf.* sarga, thuthaurn (89).

Trutruka, straight trumpet of the Araucano Indians of Argentina and Chile, made of wood, terminating in an upturned bell of oxhorn. According to Vega it is end-blown; according to Izikowitz, side-blown, possibly indicative of varying playing techniques in different areas; 2½–3 m. (8½–10 ft.) long (105, 192).

Trylodeon, an improved harmonium, patented in 1860 by Richard A. Brooman; the depth of the touch controlled a variable number of reeds so that registration was accomplished by the player's fingers (176).

Tš . . . , (Basque), see: Ch . . .

Tsakaiamba, rattle of the Morondava region of the Malagasy Republic (171).

Tsambal, see: ṭambal.

Tsampara, see: champara.

Tsampouna [*zampogna*], bagpipe of modern Greece, bellows-blown, with kid-skin bag and with 2 chanters of cane terminating in a common bell of cow horn. The right pipe has 5 fingerholes, the left pipe 1. The pipes are of equal length and are provided with single reeds. The left pipe is a drone and plays in the tonic of the right pipe. On some of the islands, the 2 pipes each have 5 equal holes, and 1 of the pipes plays pedal tones (13).

Tsanatsel, Ethiopian sistrum of iron, copper, silver, or even gold, shaped like a horseshoe with a handle, with 2 rods hung with rings connecting the arms. It is used by priests in religious ceremonies. See also: tsnasin (45, 144).

Tsang, Burmese: drum (176).

Tsaung [?Pers. **chang*], **1.** a slender, elegant *arched harp of Burma, with scaphoid body and leather belly, generally lacquered, and 13 strings. It is rare today (103, 178); **2.** idiochord *tube zither of the Shan State, Burma. On the underside of the bamboo tube is a rectangular hole covered with a piece of thin wood; this is drummed upon by the player's left thumb while he plucks the strings (138).

Tschäderäggen, cog rattle of Graubünden, Switzerland (102).

Tschake, see: chakhe.

Tschinellen [It. *cinelli*], Ger.: cymbals. The term is now obs. in Germany, but is still in use in Austria.

Tschivlots, Romansh: rustic *whistle flute (102).

Tsebu, lute of the Lisa of Shan State, Burma, with round wooden body, snakeskin belly, long neck, pegbox, and 3 lateral pegs. The strings are tuned to tonic, 4th, and oct. It is similar to the san hsien of China (172).

Tse king, see: t'e k'ing.

Tšeko, see: cheko.

Tsele, hand rattle of the Venda of S. Africa; it corresponds to the njele (116).

Tselo, panpipes of the Chamicura Indians of Peru, with 12 pipes (105).

Tseng, see: cheng.

Tshembe, syn. of nabita, 1.

Tshigwana, *musical bow of the Venda

of S. Africa, *ca.* 90 cm. (3 ft.) long, with one string looped to the stick near its center. The player's mouth acts as resonator, the wood being taken between his lips. Also called tshivhana (116).

Tshihoho, short, high-pitched side-blown horn of Bavendaland, S. Africa, made of the horn of small antelopes and used as signal instrs. by boys (116).

Tshikala, syn. of dende, 2, among the S. African Venda (116).

Tshikasa, syn. of kikasa.

Tshiniloi, see: chiniloi.

Tshiondo, war drum of the Bena Kanioka of the Congo (30).

Tshipendani, *musical bow of the Karanga of S. Africa, with the string looped to the bow near its center (116).

Tshitendje, syn. of dende, 1.

Tshitendole, *musical bow of the Tshopi of S. Africa, identical with dende, 2; it is played only by men (116).

Tshitiringo, *cross flute of the Venda of S. Africa, possibly of European origin, made of river cane with both ends closed, 2–4 fingerholes bored in the lower end and a blowhole in the upper (116). Montandon reports a double cross flute of this name, played by the Bakuna tribe of the Tonga, Transvaal; made of cane, stopped in the center and at one end by a node, at the other end by a cork. A blowhole was cut at each side of the central node, and 3 fingerholes close to each end. *Ca.* 60 cm. (2 ft.) long (141).

Tshivhana, var. of tshigwana.

Tshivhilivhi, *bull-roarer of the Venda of S. Africa, also called luvuvu (116).

Tshizambe, see: chizambi.

Tsiañe, *cylindrical drum of the Betsileo of the Malagasy Republic (171).

Tsigulka, syn. of gadulka.

Tsihali, globular *nose flute of the Paressi-Kabishi Indians of Brazil, made of 2 gourds glued together, with 2 fingerholes (176).

Tsijolo, bowed *bar zither of the Venda of S. Africa, made of a tube or hollow bar with single metal string and tuning peg. Originally the player's mouth

acted as resonator, but now a paraffin can is usually added to the lower part of the instr. The bow has cow-tail hair, is 15–18 cm. (6–7 in.) long. It is played by men and boys only. *Ca.* 75 cm. (2½ ft.) long. *Cf.* isikehlekehle, pone, sefinjolo, sekatari, sekgobogobo, ubhek'indhlela, udahi (116).

Tsikaretika, *percussion beam of the Diégo-Suarez region of the Malagasy Republic. A bamboo plank several meters long is either laid on the ground or suspended horizontally about 1 m. above it. Several persons beat it simultaneously, each with 2 sticks. It accompanies dances and is played at funeral wakes. *Cf.* farai, karatsaka, kimbolo, peripetika, ralobe, tsipetrika, volo (171).

Tsikatray, gourd rattle of the Malagasy Republic (171).

Tsikiripika, rattle of the Tuléar region of the Malagasy Republic (171).

Tsikitray, rattle of the Morondava region of the Malagasy Republic (171).

Tsimbi, cane *nose flute of the Bahuana of the Congo, end-blown, held obliquely, without fingerholes. Modifications of pitch are obtained by half-stopping the lower end (203).

Tsinda, drum of the Mbole, Bukutu, and Bosake of the Congo, similar to the bondundu (30).

Tsin ku, *barrel drum of China, *ca.* 2 m. (6½ ft.) long, with the same diam., suspended vertically in a frame. A Confucian temple instr., it corresponds to the da daiko of Japan and the chin ko of Korea (142).

Tsipakilangay, ground zither of the Malagasy Republic (171).

Tsipetrika, *percussion beam of the Malagasy Republic, played by the Tanala; it corresponds to the tsikaretika (171).

Tsipwali, drum of the Luimbi of the Congo (30).

Tsitsilo, syn. of kikilo.

Tsnasin, horseshoe-shaped sistrum of S. Ethiopia, also of the Galla and Somali. See also: tsanatsel (144, 176).

T'sögs-rol, Tibetan assembly cymbals of the monastic precentor; held horizontally and clashed by a vertical movement (89 Picken).

Tsong, see: saung.

Tsu ku, *barrel drum of China, supported in horizontal position by a pedestal. A Confucian temple instr. that corresponds to the choa ko of Korea (89).

Tsukushi sō, sō no koto of Japan, formerly made with 13 strings and in 3 sizes: 194 cm. (77 in.), 167 cm. (66 in.), 127 cm. (50 in.). Today's kotos are modeled on these. *Cf.* sō no koto, zoku sō (144).

Tsula, stopped, end-blown pipe of the Pedi doctors of S. Africa, made of the leg bone of an eagle or wildcat. The pipe is enclosed in a casing of leguan (lizard) and is suspended from its owner's neck; 12–13 cm. (5 in.) long (116).

Tsula ya noko, panpipe of the Pedi of S. Africa, made from the tail of a porcupine, with the quills acting as stopped pipes. They are not tuned (116).

Tsuma koto, koto with trapezoid body, 13 strings, and 13 tuning pegs on the upper surface of the board. *Ca.* 64 by 47 cm. (25 by 18½ in.) (149, 157).

Tsungali, panpipes of the Campa Indians of the Upper Amazon, with 5 pipes (105).

Tsuri daiko (Jap.: hanging drum), *barrel drum of Japan, made of zelkova wood with nailed heads and painted body and heads, suspended in a very elaborate circular frame. The center of the upper head has a patch of deerskin in the center, upon which it is beaten with knobbed sticks. It is a *bugaku* drum of variable size, the diam. being almost equal to the height. Also called daiko (135, 157).

Tsuri gane (Jap.: hanging gong), suspended gong of Japan (176).

Tsuzumi, generic name of *hourglass drums of Japan. The instrs. have 2 heads lapped over hoops that project well beyond the body, laced to one another, with central tension ligature. Generally they are lacquered black and ornamented with gold. See: furi tsuzumi, gaku no ts., ichi

no ts., ko ts., kune ts., ni no ts., okawa, oto ts., o-ts., san no ts. (157, 170).

Ttimba, royal drum of the Ganda of Uganda, pot-shaped, made of wood, with nailed head and a snake carved on the body. It hangs suspended from the player's neck and is beaten with bare hands (195).

Ttinya (Quechua), name given to the guitar and vihuela by the Quechua Indians of Peru (80 XII).

Ttun, dim. of tuntun.

Tuba, 1. trumpet of ancient Rome, identical with the Gk. salpinx, primarily a signal instr. of the legions (infantry troops). The straight body had a conical bore terminating in a slight flare. Tubae were made of bronze generally, rarely of iron, and were played with a detachable bone mouthpiece. They also played a part in temple services; temple trumpeters, *tubicines sacrorum,* had the rank of priests. *Ca.* 125 cm. (4 ft.) long. See also: tube, tubecta (21, 170); **2.** in ethnomusicology any straight trumpet; **3.** (Fr.: *tuba;* Ger.: *Tuba*) a family of valved brass instrs. with a wide conical bore terminating in a flared bell, played with a cup mouthpiece, actually wide-bore bugles. Built from 1835 on, if not earlier, by Johann Gottfried Moritz of Berlin to the specifications of Wilhelm Wieprecht, who was probably acquainted with the *ophicléide à pistons of A. G. Guichard —a *de facto* tuba. The tuba has been made in different sizes, from tenor to subcontrabass, and in different shapes. The terminology is extremely vague with respect to these instrs.: thus, F. L. Schubert, writing in 1862, does not discriminate between the cornet, flugelhorn, or tuba; the bass tuba in E♭ is still called bombardon, but, if it is built in circular form, helicon. The upright form, with bell pointing skyward, has been identified as the typical tuba shape, and any valved instr. so constructed may be termed tuba (and often is). Members of this family are used both in the orchestra and in military or other wind bands; they are fitted with 3–5 valves.

The tenor tuba, now obs., was built in B♭⁰ or c¹ by Carl Wilhelm Moritz of Berlin in 1838. It had 4 valves and a wider bore than its successor instr., the *baritone. The bass tuba in F⁰ or E♭⁰ (Fr.: *contrebasse à pistons, tuba contrebasse;* Ger.: *Bass-tuba;* It.: *tuba, basso tuba*), first built in 1835 by Johann Gottfried Moritz, spelled doom to the *serpent and *bass horn. As a band instr., it is simply called F bass or E♭ bass. Its compass is B♭¹/C⁰–e♭¹/f¹ or, with a fourth valve, a 3rd lower. In France and Belgium it is treated as a transposing instr.; elsewhere it is notated as it sounds. It is fitted with 3–5 valves. Both the F bass and the E♭ bass were formerly called bombardon. Moritz's patent covered only a 5-valve instr. and was soon infringed by makers who copied the instr., except for a modified valve system, and called the "new" creation "bombardon." Vaclav F. Červeny of Königgrätz (Hradec Králové) made a bombardon in F with 6 rotary valves. The name, already in use for a different instr., did not die easily: the tuba was still known as such in the 1860's, and in France today the contrabass tuba is occasionally so called. Early bass tubas had a relatively narrow bore.

The contrabass tuba in B♭¹ or C⁰, also called BB♭ bass (pron. double-B-flat bass) in bands, has a compass F¹/E♭¹–c¹/b♭⁰ or, with a fourth valve, a 3rd lower. This variety was invented by Červeny in 1845 and has been made in upright (tuba) form or in circular form. The latter may be *helicon shape, *sousaphone shape, or the more modern model with detachable bell and double bend in the bell joint. Its It. equivalent is called cimbasso. The first subbass tuba, in E♭¹, was built by Adolphe Sax of Paris in 1855 (see: saxhorn bourdon) and subsequently also by Červeny in 1873, in both E♭¹ and F¹. The subcontrabass tuba was also first built by Adolphe Sax in 1855, for the Paris Ex-

position, pitched in B♭², an oct. below the contrabass. Since then other giants have been built in C¹ and B♭², the largest of which assume the proportions of 2.40 m. (almost 8 ft.) height, with a tube length of 13.68 m. (45 ft.). Mahillon of Brussels made them in helicon shape. See also: alto tuba, basso tuba, BB♭ bass, bombardon, cimbasso, contrebasse à pistons, E♭ bass, F bass, flicorno contrabasso, ophicléide à pistons, taurea, trombotonar, Wagner tuba (89 Baines, 176); **4.** Pol.: trumpet; **5.** *goblet drum of Buru and Sula Besi Islands, Moluccas, of conical shape, with parallel rattan lacings (172); **6.** organ stop of overblowing reed pipes with funnel-shaped resonators at 8′ pitch (133).

Tuba aujota, idiochord bamboo *tube zither of Sula Island, Indonesia (119).

Tuba clarion, tuba organ stop at 4′ pitch.

Tuba curva, 1. syn. of the Roman cornu; **2.** an 18th-c. Fr. revival of the classical cornu, first used in 1791, when Voltaire's remains were transferred from the Abbaye de Scellières to the Panthéon, accompanied by an *"immense cortège."* The tuba curva was built in form of a semicircle by Jean-François Cormeri of Paris, and sounded A⁰ a⁰ e¹ a¹; 150 cm. (5 ft.) long, with a bell 19 cm. (7½ in.) wide.

Tuba de Wagner, Fr.: Wagner tuba.

Tuba ductilis (Lat.), a term believed to have denoted a trumpet made of drawn metal, as opposed to cast metal. Later the expression was also applied to the *sackbut (89 Galpin).

Tuba-Dupré, treble ophicleide with 6 keys, made by Pierre-Paul-Ghislain-Joseph Dupré of Tournai, made of wood, and exhibited in Haarlem, Netherlands, in 1825. Mahillon reports that Dupré was a very able builder who had a mania for making in wood all the instrs. that his colleagues made in brass (132, 169).

Tubaile [Arab. *tabl*], small kettledrum of Tunisia, with metal shell, *ca.* 14 cm. (5½ in.) in diam. (132).

Tubalcana, name used by Paulus Paulirinus *ca.* 1460 to describe the *trumpet marine (called tuba maryna in Poland; Paulirinus taught at Cracow).

Tubalflöte, syn. of Jubalflöte (organ stop).

Tuba magna, syn. of tuba major (organ stop).

Tuba major (Lat.), **1.** the bass trombone (159); **2.** organ stop, an 8′ tuba of great power on heavy pressure (198).

Tuba maryna, Pol.: *trumpet marine, now obs. in Poland, said to have been used as a signal instr. and to have had 2 strings. See also: tubalcana (89).

Tuba maxima, Lat.: contrabass trombone (159).

Tuba minor, 1. the tenor trombone; **2.** organ stop of reed pipes at 8′ pitch, less powerful and on lower pressure than the tuba (189).

Tuba mirabilis (Lat.), organ stop, a powerful, overblowing tuba stop on heavy pressure.

Tuban iotta, idiochord *tube zither of Sula Besi Island, Moluccas, with 4–6 strings (173).

Tuba oblonga, Lat.: trombone (176).

Tubaphone, metallophone, offspring of the Glockenspiel, but with metal tubes instead of steel bars, with a softer sound. It is used in military bands and has a compass c^2–c^4 (89, 169).

Tuba pondi, idiochord bamboo *tube zither of Sula Island, Indonesia. Also called kokondi, popondi (119).

Tuba profunda, tuba sonora organ stop at 16′ pitch.

Tuba profundissima, tuba sonora organ stop at 32′ pitch.

Tuba sonora, organ stop of reed pipes invented by Robert Hope-Jones (d. 1914), a tuba stop with thick tongues (198).

Tubasson, organ stop of reed pipes, similar to the trombone stop, at 32′ or 16′ pitch (198).

Tuba tympanodis, Lat.: swegel (124).

Tubbel [Arab. *tabl*], word occasionally used for drum by the Tuareg (93).

Tube [Lat. *tuba*], early Fr. term for a straight horn or trumpet, recorded from *ca.* 1200 to 1504.

Tubecta (LLat.) [dim. of *tuba*], med. term for a small straight trumpet, first recorded in the 13th c. It probably corresponded to the trombetta of Dante (159, 170).

Tube-indépendant (Fr.), bass trombone in F, patented by Adolphe Sax of Paris in 1852 and shown at the Paris Exposition of 1867. It had 7 independent tubes, each with its own bell, corresponding to the 7 positions of the slide, and 6 valves that controlled all but the largest tube, which was connected directly to the mouthpiece (25, 89 Langwill).

Tubette (Fr.), name given by Evette & Schaeffer of Paris to their tenor *Wagner tuba in B♭ with 4 piston valves (176).

Tube zither (Fr.: *cithare sur tuyau;* Ger.: *Röhrenzither*), primitive zither with string bearer having a vaulted surface. It may consist of a whole tube, such as a length of bamboo, in which case the tube acts as resonator; or the tube may be halved lengthwise, constituting a so-called *half-tube zither, with strings stretched over the convex surface of a gutter. Tube zithers are further divided into idiochord and heterochord instrs. In the former, a narrow strip of the bark is cut out lengthwise in such a way as to remain attached at both ends, and is given the necessary tension by raising it on 2 tiny sticks that act as nuts. See also: aeolian tube zither, agith, agong, amang, bemu nggri-nggo, be-orla, boletón, bumbung, chakhe, chanang triëng, dakado, danang, dinglye, doal doal bulo, dungga wo'o, entuning, gandang bavoi, garatē, gendang batak, gendang bavoi, gendang bulu, gendang-gendang, gettun-gettun, gingala, go beto, gobi-gobi, gondang bulu, gondra hao, gonra, goslice, gumbeng, guntang, haiau, harpa, jungga au, jurusian, kantom, kanun, 1, kechapi, kenadi, keranting, keteng-keteng, klung kung, kokondi, kolong-kolong, kranti, krob, krumba, lakado, laka do'o, lotong, mapa, maradika, mariri, marovany, mawahellis, mi gyaun, mukko, nungneng, ogung-ogung bulu, orglice, pagang, penting, pisui, pokul-logun, popondi, roding, santo, santung, sassandu, satong, sesando, susunu, tabolija, tagbuan, tagong, takhe, tandilo, tanggetong, tangkolnang, tantabola, tatabuan kavan, tattabua, thlinthli-no-me, ti, tinding, tingning, ton-ton, tsaung, tuba aujota, tuban iotta, tuba pondi, valiha (100, 170).

Tubrī, Beng. equivalent of tiktirī.

Tubūl, pl. of tabl.

Tubula, Lat.: small tuba.

Tubular bells (Fr.: *cloches tubulaires;* Ger.: *Röhrenglocken*), a modern substitute for real bells in the orchestra, theater and rhythm band, as well as in the organ. Those of the orchestra, etc., consist of a series of tuned metal tubes suspended by cords vertically in a frame and struck with wooden mallets. The usual compass is 1½ octs. c^2–f^3, notated an oct. lower. The tubes have a diam. of *ca.* 4 cm. (1½ in.) and are of varying lengths. They are provided with dampers operated either by hand or by a pedal connected to the damping bar. In organs tubular bells are controlled directly from the manual. The principle of resonant tubes comes from SE. Asia, where tuned bamboo segments are in use. *Ca.* 1885 John Harringon of Coventry started making bronze tubular bells that were struck with hammers. Today they are made of brass. See also: codophone, electrophonic carillon (151, 169).

Tubular-pneumatic action (Ger.: *Röhrenpneumatik;* It.: *sistema pneumatico tubolare*), organ action invented in 1872 by Henry Willis after earlier experiments by other builders (see: pneumatic lever) to take the place of the long tracker action and the magnetoelectric action, and devised as a connection between an organ separated from its console. When a key is depressed, a small wind chest is opened; this conveys wind through a lead tube to a small bellows that opens the pallet.

However, distance between organ and console is limited, as the action becomes slow and unresponsive if they are too far apart. Vars. of this type also existed. This action has now been replaced by electric actions (89, 99, 176).

Tubuphone, see: tubaphone.

Tubus timpanites, loud drum imagined in the 17th c. by Athanasius Kircher (*Phonurgia*), with the body extending into a sort of trumpet tube. If, as Pontécoulant says, Adolphe Sax based his trompette-timbale on Félix Savart's observations, then Savart may well have been acquainted with the description in *Phonurgia* (176).

Tuda, the sringa of the Khanda of E. India (176).

Tudel, Sp.: pirouette.

Tudelhorn, Swiss goatherd's horn, made of ram's-horn.

Tudi, syn. of udukkai.

Tudra, syn. of pitorka.

Tuduk, see: duduk.

Tudu kat, primitive xylophone of the Mentawai Islanders, Indonesia, with slabs laid across 2 hollowed tree trunks (173).

Tudung punduk, name of the kowangan in the Ampel district of Java (121).

Tugal, W. Borneo name of the gulung-gulung (176).

Tuhunta, Basque: trumpet. *Cf.* turulu, turuta.

Tuhuta, syn. of tuta.

Tui hsiao, *double clarinet of China, composed of 2 ch'un kuan (142).

Tuila, *stick zither of several aboriginal tribes of the Chota Nagpur and Orissa regions of India, made of a bamboo stick hooked at one end to keep the single string clear of the stick, and a half-gourd resonator. The tuila is held vertically, with the resonator resting against the right side of the player's chest. Also called bajah (17, 173).

Tuiter [Flem. *tuit,* pipe], clay bugle formerly played by children of the Dunkerque-Bergues district of France on the eve of St. Martin. With bugle in one hand and a primitive lantern in the other, they helped to "search" for the donkey that St. Martin, according to legend, had lost in the dunes (132).

Tujali, syn. of lolowe.

Tu kuan, syn. of kuan, 2 (89).

Tul, rustic shawm of Slovenia, made of spirally twisted strips of bark, with a double reed. *Ca.* 60 cm. (2 ft.) long. Also called trobenta (144).

Tulali, *ring flute of C. Celebes, with exterior duct. Made of bamboo, cylindrical, with 4 equidistant fingerholes, terminating in a bell of spirally wound pandanus leaves. The upper end is stopped by a natural node. A blowhole is cut underneath it, the surface is peeled, and a piece of pandanus leaf is knotted around the aperture, leaving an air duct; 50–72 cm. (20–28½ in.) long. Also called banchi-banchi, tujali. *Cf.* lolowe (112).

Tule, panpipes of the Oyana Indians of the Guianas (105).

Tu ling (Chin.: single bell), Hangchow name of the ma ling (142).

Tulnic, *alphorn of Rom. mountain shepherds, with straight conical tube, similar to the bucium. *Ca.* 2 m. (6½ ft.) long.

Tu loa, see: cai tu loa.

Tülök, Hung.: horn.

Tulum (bag), mouth-blown bagpipe of NE. Turkey, with double chanter of 2 cane pipes in a cradle that terminate as an upturned square bell. The pipes have 5 fingerholes each, opposite one another so that a pair can be stopped by the same finger. Sometimes 2 holes of the right pipe are plugged. Each chanter is furnished with a single reed and often has a bell of cow horn. *Cf.* tulumi (13).

Tulumbas [Turk. *tulum,* bag + *baz,* hawk], a newer spelling of tulumbaz, a Russ. infantry bass drum. *Cf.* talambasi (25).

Tulumbaz [see: *tulumbas*], kettledrum of Russia, made of iron, copper, silver, or steel, richly ornamented, used singly, mostly for hawking, and struck with a beater called voshaga. *Cf.* talambasi, tulumbas (25).

Tulumbeta [Swah. **tarumbeta*], Kikongo: trumpet (176).

Tulumbu, pl. of kalumba.

Tulum duduyi [Turk.: *tulum,* bag + *duduk,* pipe], Turk.: bagpipe. Mentioned in Turk. 17th-c. literature as a foreign instr. (76).

Tulumi [Turk. *tulum,* bag], modern Gk. equivalent of the tulum, also called aski, askaulos.

Tum, 1. *ground bow of the Lango of Uganda, used as a child's toy; **2.** *arched harp of the Labwor and Lango of Uganda, with tortoise-shell body and 5 or 6 strings (195); **3.** lyre of the Shilluk of the Congo (112). *Cf.* tam, tohmu, tom.

Tumba [*tambor*], Afro-Cuban drum, single-headed, played only in E. Cuba. Varieties of this drum include the tumba francesa, which accompanies the Haitian Creole (*francesa*) dances; tumba elemonte, made of palm tree trunk and tuned by heat. All tumba drums are vertical with 1 head, but they assume a variety of shapes (152).

Tumbak, Pahl. equivalent of tunbūk (75 II).

Tumbandera, ground bow of E. Cuba (152).

Túmbano [**tympanon*], modern Gk.: drum.

Tumbelechiŭ [Turk. **dumbelek*], Rom.: kettledrum of (former) Turk. music. Also called tembelic.

Tumbelek, see: dumbelek.

Tumbeleki [Turk. **dumbelek*], clay goblet drum of modern Greece (144).

Tumbi, *goblet drum of the Baholoholo of the Congo, with nailed head and an aperture covered with a thin membrane—a mirliton device (30).

Tumbukin, Sans.: drum (176).

Tumbul [Arab. **tabl*], Tuareg word for drum (93).

Tumburu vīnā (Sans., Beng.) [Pers. *tanbūr*], syn. of tamburā.

Tūmerī, equivalent of the tiktirī in Ceylon (132).

Tumpia-yot, panpipes of the Aueto Indians of Brazil (105).

Tümür, drum of the Cheremiss of the U.S.S.R. (176).

Tūnava, unidentified instr. mentioned in the *Atharva-Veda,* possibly a flute of ancient India (170).

Tunbak (Pers.), var. writing of tunbūk (75 II).

Tunbūk (Pers.), obs. *goblet drum of Persia, equivalent to the darabuka. See also: dinbik (75 II).

Tunbūr, pl. **tanābīr,** Arab. equivalent of tanbūr. In Al Farabi's time (d. 950) it had 2 or 3 strings and 5 frets set at the top of its long neck.

Tunbūra turkī, a 14th- to 15th-c. tanbūr of Islam, with small body and 2 or 3 strings tuned a 4th apart, plucked with bare fingers (147 Farmer).

Tunbūr-i shirvīnān, a 14th- to 15th-c. tanbūr of Islam, with deep piriform body and 2 strings tuned a 2nd apart, played with bare hands (147 Farmer).

Tunbūr Khurasānī (tanbūr of Khurasan), 2-stringed tanbūr with frets, mentioned by Al Farabi (d. 950); its strings were usually tuned in unison.

Tunde, see: dunde.

Tunduli, *slit drum of the Jívaro Indians of Ecuador, *ca.* 1½ m. (5 ft.) long (42, 176).

Tundum, *bull-roarer of Australia, with pointed ends, *ca.* 30 cm. (12 in.) long. See also: rutuk tundum (176).

Tungali, *nose flute of Luzon, Philippine Islands (203).

Tūngbī, Hindust. equivalent of tiktirī.

Tung hsiao, modern name of the hsiao (flute of China). It corresponds to the thung sŏ of Korea and the now obs. dŏ shŏ of Japan.

T'ung kyo, see: siao t'ung kyo.

T'ung lo, bronze gong introduced to China *ca.* 500 A.C. (121).

T'ung po, cymbals of China introduced from W. Asia (75 II).

Tungtungi, syn. of ektār.

Tuni, 1. *cross flute of the Fula of Sierra Leone, made of cane, slightly conical, tapering to the lower end, and bound with strips of snakeskin. It has 3 equidistant fingerholes near the lower end and a blowhole cut very close to the upper end. See also: fuli (Collection of the Commonwealth Institute, London); **2.** slightly conical reedpipe of the Fula of Sierra Leone, made of cane, with upcut idioglott reed. A bulbous gourd bell is attached at the lower end, with rectangular holes cut in the walls. A number of fine metal chains terminating in coins dangle freely from the bell (Collection of the Commonwealth Institute, London).

Tuning bit, syn. of shank.

Tuning fork (Fr.: *diapason;* Ger.: *Stimmgabel;* It.: *corista*), 2-pronged metal fork tuned to a given pitch, invented, according to Sir John Hawkins (in 1776), by John Shore, the trumpeter. Through a misreading of Hawkins' text the invention is generally dated 1711, too early by far. James Rivington, a New York music dealer, offered tuning forks for sale in 1773. When Reynvaan wrote (1787), they were being made at chamber and choir pitch.

Tuning-fork piano (*Stimmgabelklavier*), keyboard instr. in which the strings are replaced by a series of tuning forks set on a resonator and struck by hammers. Charles Claggett of London seems to have been the first to experiment in this direction (in 1788). A number of such instrs. were built during the 19th c. See: adiaphone, aiuton, dulcitone, euphonium, 2, euphotine, Melodikon, typophone.

Tuning peg (Fr.: *cheville;* Ger.: *Wirbel;* It.: *bischero, pirolo*), wooden pegs to which the strings of some chordophones are attached and by which they are tuned. In ancient Egypt and on some non-European instrs. of today (African arched harps, for instance) the pegs are immovable, their purpose being to prevent the strings from slipping.

Tuning pin (Fr.: *cheville;* Ger.: *Wirbel;* It.: *pirone, caviglia*), metal pin around which the strings of some instrs. are wound and by which they are tuned. From *ca.* 1820 on a hole has been drilled through the pin for threading the string.

Tuning slide, 1. (Fr.: *coulisse d'accord;* Ger.: *Stimmzug*), on brass instrs. a connecting slide invented by J. G. Haltenhoff of Hanau by 1776, graduated for tuning purposes; **2.** the tenon and socket of a flute head-joint made long enough to be pulled out for tuning purposes. It was originally devised to obviate the need for an extra *corps de rechange.* J. J. Quantz claimed the invention for himself; **3.** small metal tube fitted on top of a metal flue organ pipe (from 4′ C up) for tuning purposes. Also used on some reed pipes. The tuning slide succeeded the tuning cone (89, 101).

Tunkobele, pl. of kankobele.

Tunkul, *cylindrical drum of the Mayas, made of a hollowed log, with one sheepskin head. Held under the left arm, it is played with the fingers of the right hand. *Ca.* 1 m. (40 in.) long (105, 144).

Tunshinkidi, *cylindrical drum of the Baluba of the Congo, with 2 nailed heads, often made of a palm tree trunk, hollowed out at both ends but left intact in the center. It is suspended horizontally from the player's neck by a band and is played with bare hands. The drum has also been adopted by the Bayeke (30).

Tuntina, *plucked drum of India, a mendicant's drone instr. Made of a bucket-shaped resonator of wood or metal, with open top, the bottom covered with parchment. A pole is attached to the side of the bucket, projecting above it and carrying a tuning peg at its far end. A metal string is attached to this, then passed inside the bucket, through a hole in the center of the membrane, to be attached underneath it. The tuntina accompanies singing, its string being tuned to the keynote of the singer's voice. No plectrum is used. *Cf.* plucked drum (179).

Tuntun, small Basque tambourin à cordes, suspended from the player's left arm and struck with a stick. Also called tountouna. *Cf.* ttun (56).

Tuohitorvi, horn of Finland, made of birch bark (89).

Tuorba, obs. It.: theorbo.

Tuorbe, obs. Fr.: theorbo.

Tupan [?Gk. *tympanon*], double-headed *cylindrical drum of the Balkans, similar to the bass drum, played in Yugo. Macedonia, Serbia, E. Albania, and W. Bulgaria. Its heads are secured by zigzag lacings; the diam. is greater than the height; it is devoid of snares. In Yugoslavia the heads are tuned a 5th apart, and the instr. is now replacing the bubanj. The tupan is held in front of the player, suspended by a strap over his left shoulder, in tilted position. The right head is beaten with a drumstick, the left by a switch in the Turk. manner. Usually it is played together with a shawm. *Ca.* 75 cm. (30 in.) in diam. Also called goč, kasa, topan (11, 89, 144).

Tupa pincollo (Aymara), cane flute of ancient Peru. *Cf.* pincullu (80 XII).

Tupim, pl. of tof.

Tūra, Prakrit: tūrya.

Turaī, Hindust.: tūrya.

Turali, *nose flute of the Dusun of Borneo, with 3 front fingerholes and a rear hole, and a blowhole in the septum (176).

Turam, small kettledrum of the Hill Muria of Bastar, India, made of sago palm or bija wood (68).

Turburi, small earthenware kettledrum of the Muria of Bastar, India, with cowhide head. The drum is tied to its player's waist and is beaten with 2 small sticks; a more advanced form of turam. Also called kundri, kundur, kundurka (68).

Turcello, see: rigabello.

Ture angwa, short, side-blown horn of the Madi of Uganda, made of animal horn, played by men and boys during dances (195).

Ture turungale, syn. of turi.

Turi, straight conical trumpet of the Madi of Uganda, side-blown, made of 2 hollowed sections of wood covered with leather. Also called ture turungale (195).

Tūrī, Beng., Punj.: tūrya.

Turiyam, Pali: tūrya.

Turkish crescent, see: Jingling Johnnie.

Turkish drum, name by which the bass drum was known in Europe up to the early 19th c. Villoteau still described it as such in 1823. *Cf.* tabl turki (170).

Turlure(tte), OFr. term recorded in literary sources, chiefly in the 14th c.; it probably denoted a bagpipe. In Normandy today the turlurette is a flageolet (35).

Turlutaine [Fr.: *turlu,* curlew], Fr. *bird organ; a familiar name for bird organs in general in the 17th and 18th c. (33).

Turnerhorn [MHGer. *Thurnerhorn*], a cornet made by Vaclav F. Červeny of Königgrätz (Hradec Králové) from 1867 on, in 4 sizes: soprano in C, alto in F, tenor in C, and bass in B♭ (176).

Turturī, Hindust.: Tūrya.

Turullo, horn of Sp. shepherds, used for calling cattle (57).

Turulu, Basque: trumpet. *Cf.* tuhunta, turuta.

Turumba, musical bow of the Cocama Indians of the Upper Amazon (105).

Tūrumpata būrūsī, 17th-c. Turk. term for the European trumpet (76).

Turunta, var. of turuta.

Turuta, Basque: trumpet. *Cf.* tuhunta, turulu (56).

Turututela, *bladder and string of Olivone, Switzerland, with a gourd instead of a bladder, introduced by Italians (102).

Tūrya (Sans.), metal trumpet of India, of brass, virtually identical in form with the classical European natural trumpet, complete to bosses and bell. Probably of Asiatic origin, it is distributed on the whole subcontinent. Also called nāgaphani. See also: bher, gādar (170, 173).

Tūryam, Malayalam: tūrya.

Tusese, musical bow of the Basonge of the Congo (19).

Tusse fløyte, Nor.: recorder.

Tusūt (Arab.), *musical glasses of the Near East, mentioned by Ibn Ghaibi (d. 1435), played with little sticks (75 II, 147).

Tuta, 1. Basque horn, syn. of adar, tuhunta; **2.** Basque name of the gaita gallega.

Tūtak (Pers.), whistle flute of Persia (76).

Tutalo, stick zither of Ternate Island, Indonesia, identical with dunde (173).

Tutārī, Mar.: tūrya.

Tūtik, whistle flute of the Kurds, Tatars, and Turkomans. *Cf.* tūtak (76, 176).

Tutila, *conical drum of the Sundi of the Lower Congo, with 2 laced heads, in different sizes. A palm nut or other hard object is placed inside the drum. It is generally made in pairs of a larger (mother) and smaller (child) drum and is used chiefly at funerals (185).

Tuto [Kikongo *tutu*], primitive flute of Surinam (152).

Tuttārā, Tel.: tūrya.

Tutu, 1. (Kikongo) cane flute of the Kongo people, used as a child's toy (185); **2.** drum of the Washambala of Tanganyika, cylindrical, with head laced to projecting wooden pegs. Always used in pairs of a large and a small one (111); **3.** drum of N. Nias, Indonesia, cylindrical, with heads lapped over hoops and with zigzag lacings (176).

Tutumedjo, drum of the Bakwelo of S. Africa, identical with the murumbu (116).

Tutung, syn. of lotong.

Tutungulan, W. Java name of the bendrong (121).

Tutu-panpan, pop. Prov. appellation of the galoubet and tambourin (*i.e.,* pipe and tabor) ensemble (23).

Tutupele, syn. of tinbuk.

Tutūri, Kan.: tūrya.

Tuum, side-blown trumpet of the Acoli of Uganda, straight, conical, made of 2 hollowed sections of wood covered with leather; 80–165 cm. (32–65 in.) long (195).

Tuwung, word believed to have been an early name of the cheluring (121).

Tuyau, Fr.: pipe.

Tuyau à anche, Fr.: reed pipe.

Tuyau à bouche, Fr.: flue pipe.

Tuyau basculant, Fr.: sliding rattle.

Tuyau bouché, Fr.: stopped pipe.

Tuzu abe, friction sticks of the Lugbara of Uganda, rubbed by girls against a board placed over a pit and played during dances (195).

Twangl, in Styrian dialect, Jew's-harp.

Twelfth, mutation organ stop of diapason pipes a 12th above the fundamental, at 2⅔' in the manual or 5⅓' in the pedal.

Twenty-first, see: seventh.

Twenty-second, mutation organ stop of open metal flue pipes, a 22nd above the fundamental, at 1' pitch in the manual and 2' in the pedal (99).

Tx . . . (Basque), see: Ch . . .

Tymbalon [Gk. *tympanon*], small tambourine of Provence; it accompanies the galoubet during dances. Formerly the tymbalon was one of a pair of small kettledrums suspended from the player's neck and beaten with 2 sticks; the shells were of copper; *ca.* 20 cm. (8 in.) high (23, 132).

Tymbre, see: timbre.

Tymbris, Lat.: a clapperless bell. *Cf.* timbre (61).

Tympan [Lat. *tympanum*], 12th- and 13th-c. Fr.: drum. *Cf.* timpan, 2 (204).

Tympana, the name of the "recently" introduced copper kettledrum of Virdung's day (1511) (194).

Tympane [Lat. *tympanum*], OEngl., MEngl.: kettledrum (180).

Tympani, (modern) misspelling of timpani.

Tympani schiza, Glarean's attempt at clothing Trumscheit in classical garb. See: trumpet marine.

Tympanocorde, bowed chordophone patented in France by Bernard in July 1861, in form of a large banjo with 4 strings (204).

Tympanon (Gk.), **1.** Gk.: hand-beaten *frame drum of ancient Greece, held in one hand and struck with the fingers of the other, usually with 2 heads, occasionally with only 1. It corresponded to the Near Eastern tof and, like other Near Eastern frame drums, was played by women only. A cult instr.; **2.** Fr.: dulcimer. How the word came to designate a stringed instr. is not clear: in the 10th c. rotte is translated as tympanon, and the OEngl. term glēo-bēam was also glossed as tympanum. Furetière in 1690 describes the tympanon as a musical instr. in use in Germany, played with a plectrum and called psaltery in France: one mày gather that the dulcimer was played little, if at all, in France at that time (53, 78, 89 Galpin).

Tympanum, pl. **tympana** (Lat.) [Gk. *tympanon*], **1.** hand *frame drum of ancient Rome, taken over from Greece. In the later days of the empire it became an instr. of the joculators, who were probably responsible for spreading it outside the peninsula. They are sometimes depicted throwing it up in the air and catching it again. Around 600 Isidore of Seville gives a clear description of the single-headed frame drum: *"Tympanum est pellis vel corium ligno ex una parte extentum. Est enim pars media simphoniae in similitudinem cribri . . ."* **2.** later the word is applied to kettledrums; Virdung in 1511 relates that "recently" introduced kettledrums of copper were called tympana. The word lives on today as timpani.

Typophone, *tuning-fork piano invented by Victor Mustel of Paris in 1865, with 49 tuning forks (4-oct. compass) set in resonator boxes and struck by hammers played from a keyboard—a precursor of the celesta. On Dec. 22, 1868, Mustel took out a patent for improvements (204).

Typotone, free-reed pitch pipe invented by Pinsonnat of Amiens and patented in Paris on Jan. 17, 1829, tuned to A. The reed was attached to a plaque of nacre or silver. See also: harmonica Jaulin (154, 204).

Tz . . . , see also: Ts . . .

Tzambuna, see: tsampouna.

Tzit-idoatl, bowed *stick zither of New Mexico, made of a convex agave stalk and a single horsehair string held by a large wooden peg (149).

U

Uadaku, sansa of N. Uele, the Congo, with tortoise-shell resonator and 7 lamellae made of *Raphia vinifera,* 24 cm. (9½ in.) long, max. width 15 cm. (6 in.) (132).

Ualu, gourd rattle with handle, of the Carajá Indians of Brazil (176).

Uana, *stamping tube of the Catapolitani, Siusi, and Yukuma Indians of Brazil, made of hollowed-out *ambaúva* wood (176).

Uapida, small trumpet of the Tariana Indians of NW. Brazil (176).

Uasapa, ankle rattles of the Catapolitani Indians of NW. Brazil, made of dried fruit half-shells (176).

Ub (Sum.: skin), hand drum of ancient Babylon (89 Galpin).

Ube, in Uzaitui, a Sudanic language, a woman's drum, made in different sizes up to 120 cm. (4 ft.) long, struck alternately with drumstick and bare hand (93).

Ubhababa, syn. of mantshomane.

Ubhek'indhlela, bowed *bar zither of the Zulu of S. Africa; it corresponds to the tsijolo (116).

Ubuxaka, dancing rattle of the Zulu of S. Africa, consisting of a bundle of sticks some 45 cm. (18 in.) long tied together at one or both ends; played by women only (116).

Uche, drum of the Bambute of the Ituri Forest, the Congo (176).

Uchinarashi, syn. of kin, 1.

Uchiwa daiko, drum of Japan that plays an important part in Buddhist music. It has a single head lapped over an iron hoop attached to a wooden handle, and is beaten with a stick. Also used in *kabuki* (135).

'Ūd, pl. **'idān** (Arab.: wood), ancient and modern lute of the Near East, known from the 7th c. on, called barbat by Ibn-Sina (Avicenna) (b. 980). Originally its piriform body tapered toward the pegbox without distinct neck and it had 2 crescent-shaped soundholes in the belly. Then as now it had a bulging wooden body, frontal string fastener, lateral pegs in a reversed pegbox, and double strings. Up to the 9th c. it was furnished with 4 pairs of silk strings tuned in 4ths, named *bam, matlat, matnā, zīr, bam* being the lowest in pitch (the word means "high." This usage is reminiscent of kithara string names). During the course of the 9th c. a fifth pair of strings was added in the bass. It seems that, apart from purely theoretical purposes, frets were not in use then, nor are they now; and certainly the iconography of the 'ūd is a fretless one, despite the detailed rules of theorists for the placing of frets for various tunings (based on the Gk. system). The form of the 'ūd was later changed, assuming a distinct neck, almond-shaped body, and central soundhole covered by a rose; this transformation may have taken place in Spain, where it had been introduced by the Arabs. Certainly it retained its 4 pairs of strings there until the expulsion of the Moors. From Spain the instr. returned to Egypt, and from Egypt it traveled to Europe by other routes and in such a roundabout way that in 1555 Bermudo could call the lute *vihuela de Flandres.* In or after the 16th c. a sixth pair of strings was added, and since the 'ūd is played with a plectrum, a strip of tortoise-shell was glued to the belly below the soundhole, to protect it from damage by the plectrum. In performance it was held either horizontally, or obliquely with the body higher than the pegbox; only in Spain and Egypt was it played with the body resting in the player's lap. The modern 'ūd has a shorter neck than the European lute. Its pegbox is thrown back at a less acute angle, and it usually has 3 soundholes. Sizes are not standardized. Today it is played in Algeria, Morocco, and Tunisia, with 4 pairs of strings, tuned $G^0 e^0 A^0 d^0$, or with 6 pairs. In 19th-c. Egypt it boasted 7 pairs of strings, now reduced to 5 pairs. It disappeared from Iran and Turkey, to be reintroduced in the 19th c. into Turkey from Europe, where it now bears the name of *lauta and is tuned $c^0 g^0 d^1 a^1$. In the Balkans it is still called 'ūd (oud) or uti (74, 75 II, 89, 170).

Udahi, bowed *stick zither of the Xhosa of S. Africa; it corresponds to the tsijolo (116).

Udongwe (clay), *whistle flute of the S. African Pondo, imitative of the European instr., made of a short piece of thick grass inserted into a hollow clay globe while the clay is wet, with a transverse slit cut later across the grass (116).

Udre, var. of kudre among the Momvu of the Congo (30).

Udu, 1. *percussion pot of the Ibo of Nigeria; **2.** percussion pot in Edo, a Sudanic language (93); **3.** syn. of idudu egu (152).

Udukkai (Tamil), *hourglass drum of S. India, with body of brass, wood, or clay, and 2 parchment heads secured by W lacings and central tension ligatures. The udukkai is a temple instr., is held in the left hand and played with the fingers of the right hand. Also called idai surungu parai, tudi. See also: dāmaru (170, 179).

Uele [region of the Congo], rare Afro-Cuban musical bow with gourd resonator, used only during certain secret funerary rites of the Kongo people (152).

Uempompali, var. of ueopama.

Ueobaba, panpipes of the Bora Indians of the Upper Amazon (105).

Ueopali, panpipes of the C. Amer. Chola Indians (105).

Ueopama, panpipes of the Tukuna Indians of Brazil, also called uempompali (105).

Uérgano [Lat. *organum], OSp.: musical instr. The term is first recorded in 1294 (44).

Uerizu, small reedpipe of the Catapolitani Indians of Brazil, with 4 fingerholes (176).

Uffātah, *end-blown flute of modern Egypt and Morocco, with very wide bore, held obliquely (144).

Ufu-ufu, decoy pipe of N. Nias, Indonesia (176).

'Ugab (Heb.), generic name for wind instrs. of ancient Israel, excepting horns (i.e., for flutes and reedpipes). The name was also given to a pastoral instr. not played in the Temple. The Targum translates it as *abuba (84).

Ugagweng, *notched flute of Finschhafen, New Guinea, stopped at the lower end, with 2 fingerholes. Ca. 35 cm. (14 in.) long (178).

Uganga [*ganga], Bassa (a Sudanic language) for drum. See also: ganga (93).

Ugene, globular flute of the Ibo of Nigeria, with 2 fingerholes (152).

Ugubo, *musical bow of the S. African Zulu, identical with the uhadi. Also called gubuolukhulu, ngumbo (116).

Ugun, *marine-shell trumpet of the Solomon Islands, blown at the death of a man (176).

Ugwala, name of the gora among the S. African Zulu (116).

Ugwali, name of the gora among the S. African Xhosa (116).

Uhadi, 1. *musical bow of the Xhosa of S. Africa, with half-gourd resonator. The truncated side of the gourd is held close to the player's chest, and he can modify the dynamics by opening the resonator more or less. The string is struck near the bow's lower end. Cf. segwana, sekgapa, ugubo; **2.** the term is also applied by the Xhosa to modern instrs. such as the *American organ (116).

Uhuhuk, bamboo trumpet of the Carajá Indians of Brazil. A pierced node acts as mouthpiece. *Ca.* 45 cm. (18 in.) long, 7 cm. (2½ in.) thick (176).

Uillean pipes (elbow pipes), a designation of the *union pipes; its historical authenticity is questioned.

Ukeke, 1. obs. *musical bow of Hawaii, the bow being flat on top and convex underneath, with 3 strings originally made of sennit. After the white man's arrival the strings were of horsehair, later even of gut. One end of the bow was notched to hold the strings, the other carved. During performance it was held horizontally with one end taken into the player's mouth. The strings were tuned to fundamental, 3rd, and 5th and were plucked with either bare fingers or a plectrum; 40–60 cm. (16–24 in.) long; **2.** musical bow of the Marquesas Islands, with single string passing over a bridge. Up to 148 cm. (58 in.) long. *Cf.* utete; **3.** Jew's-harp of Hawaii (8, 77).

Ukeke-laau, *musical bow of Hawaii, with 3 strings of coconut fiber or gut, but no resonator. The bow is taken into the player's mouth between the teeth and is plucked with fingers or plectrum (149, 176).

Ukelele, Brit. spelling of ukulele.

Ukkalī, drum of Bengal (176).

Ukombe, *double flute of the S. African Xhosa, similar to the uveve, 2 (116).

Uku (Akk.), wind instr. of ancient Babylon, possibly a whistle (89 Galpin).

Ukulele (Hawaiian: flea), small guitar of Hawaii, resembling the machete, introduced by Port. sailors in the 1870's, and probably derived from the machete. Made preferably of koa wood, with 4 strings, tuned $d^1 f\sharp^1 a^1 b^1$ or $g^1 c^1 e^1 a^1$, held by rear tuning pegs set in a flat pegdisc, fretted neck, and frontal string fastener. It is not identical with the Hawaiian guitar. Spelled ukelele in Britain. *Cf.* taro patch fiddle (151).

Ulia, short straight wooden trumpet of the Opaina of NW. Brazil (176).

Ulili, nose flute of Hawaii (203).

Uli-uli, *vessel rattle of Hawaii, consisting of either a gourd, provided with a handle and filled with seeds or pebbles, or 3 small calabashes loosely impaled on a stick so as to strike against each other (8, 77).

Uluru, bamboo trumpet of the Madi of Uganda, with one or more large gourds affixed to one end, played during important dances. *Ca.* 60 cm. (2 ft.) long (195).

Umakweyana, *musical bow of the Zulu and Swazi of S. Africa, identical with the dende, 2 (116).

Umbrella flute, *walking-stick flute adapted to Brit. climatic conditions by flautist J. Clinton (14).

Umcunga, *musical bow of C. Brazil, with tuning loop at one-third the length of the string. The bow is held against the player's throat or vocal chords and the string is struck with a small stick. *Cf.* umqangala, umqunge (17, 105).

Umfece, syn. of amafohlwane, 2.

Umqangala, *musical bow of the S. African Swazi, Thonga, and Zulu, similar to the lugube; played only by women and girls (116).

Umqunge, *musical bow of the S. African Pedi. The string is "bowed" by a piece of stalk while the player's mouth acts as resonator, and the string is stopped by the first finger of his left hand. *Cf.* umrube, utiyane (116).

Umrube, *musical bow of the S. African Xhosa; it corresponds to the umqunge (116).

Umtshingo, *end-blown flute of the Pondo and Zulu of S. Africa, slightly conical, made of cane or bark, open at both ends. The cane is cut off at a 45-degree angle to form an embouchure always placed at the thicker end. It is devoid of fingerholes. By stopping the lower end a second tone can be obtained. *Cf.* ixilongo, lekolilo (116).

Umtshingosi, 1. *end-blown flute of

the Swazi of S. Africa; it corresponds to the umtshingo; **2.** *cross flute of the Swazi; it corresponds to the tshitiringo except that its lower end is open (116).

Umudende (tinkle), elongated, forged clapper bell of Uganda, made of sheet iron (195).

Umukunto, the ordinary drum of the Balamba of the Congo, goblet-shaped, held between the legs and played during dances. Also called kitumba (30).

Umutungu, drum of the Balamba of the Congo, made of a large calabash, played by women only (30).

Una corda (It.: one string) (Ger.: *Verschiebung*), a piano stop, a device for shifting the keyboard so that only one string of each pair of unisons was struck by the hammer. Bartolommeo Cristofori's piano of 1726—his later model—is already provided with such a contrivance. In England and the U.S. this stop was subsequently called "piano," and for a while it was also known in England as "harmonica" (92).

Unanga, board zither of the Warega of the Congo, with 5 or 6 strings (42).

Unda maris (Lat.: sea wave) (Ger.: *Meerflaut, Meereswelle*), beating organ stop consisting of 2 ranks of pipes tuned very slightly apart; from the 18th c. on also built as a single rank tuned slightly sharper than the rest of the organ (2, 133).

Undemoū [*unde,* illness + *moū,* change], *musical bow of the Balese of the Congo, with tuning loop but no resonator (128).

Unfretted (Fr.: *libre;* Ger.: *bundfrei*), see: clavichord.

Ung, *percussion tube of Korea, consisting of a hollowed-out pole *ca.* 2 m. (6½ ft.) long, the ends of which are struck with a hammer (66).

Ungar(a), name given to the gerom by the Monumbo of New Guinea (77).

Ung ko, *cylindrical drum of Korea, with 2 nailed heads, suspended in a frame together with a similar drum, called sak ko, one above the other but

at different angles. *Ca.* 66 cm. (26 in.) in diam. (66).

Union pipes, bellows-blown bagpipe of Ireland, intended for indoor music only, and played sitting with the drones lying across the player's knees. In its present form it dates back to the 18th c., with its 3 types of pipe: a) a chromatic chanter, with rather narrow conical bore, 7 front and 1 rear fingerholes, and up to 9 keys, played with a double reed and having a 2-oct. compass, d^1–d^3. The chanter is 36–45 cm. (14–17½ in.) long, hence is variable in pitch (from standard pitch to 2 tones below it); b) formerly 1 drone, now 3 drones in 1 stock, tuned D^0 d^0 d^1, with cylindrical bore, played with single reeds. Each drone is provided with a shutoff valve. The lowest ends in an upturned brass tube known as the "trumpet"; c) 3 or even 4 regulators of different lengths, with conical bore, played with double reeds, and provided with a number of large, heavily sprung closed keys; the lower end of each regulator is closed by a stopper. Their purpose is to provide chords by the striking of appropriate keys; they speak only when a key is opened. The union pipe is played: a) either with the lower end of the chanter stopped by holding it against the player's right knee (it has to be lifted off for the lowest tone, d^1, played with all fingerholes closed) or: b) with the chanter off the knee. Chords may be supplied by striking simultaneously one key of each regulator with the lower edge of the right hand while the chanter is being played. The keys are disposed so that any 3 in a row form a chord. Because of its complicated nature the union pipe is often called the Irish organ; the term uillean pipes (elbow pipes) has been questioned (13, 89).

Universal-Klavizimbel, see: clavicymbalum universale.

Universal-Kontrabass, see: Tritonikon.

Universalzither (Ger.), zither invented by E. Salomon of Aachen *ca.* 1880, said to have been a combination of an ordinary zither with the *Elegiezither (22).

Unkin, 1. Jew's-harp of Manipur, India, made of bamboo, *ca.* 15 cm. (6 in.) long (172); **2.** chordophone of Japan, similar to the gekkin, with 4 pairs of silk strings, elliptical body, and 7 frets on the neck (176).

Unkoka, syn. of inkohlisa.

Untersatz (Ger.), organ stop of flue pipes. The name was originally given to those large pedal pipes that were separated from the main chest and placed on a lower chest. Later the name of *unter* (below) changed from a designation of space to one of pitch, and the Untersatz became a low-pitched *Prinzipal, at first open, later also stopped. The stopped variety is at 32′ pitch and today is sometimes composed of differential tones $(16′ + 12\frac{2}{3}′)$ (133).

Upondo, mpalampala made of oxhorn, a substitute for kudu horn (116).

Upper board (Fr.: *chape;* Ger.: *Pfeifenstock*), in an organ the board over the wind chest, drilled with holes to hold the feet of the pipes.

Uppu (Akk.), the same as ub.

Upright grand piano, term applied to a vertical piano having the string length of a (horizontal) grand piano, built in the 18th and early 19th c., the earliest form of *upright piano, set on a stand. The oldest surviving example is that of Domenico del Mela of Gagliano, Italy, dated 1739, housed in the Florence Conservatory. Its action is an adaptation of that of Bartolommeo Cristofori, with hammers striking from behind the strings. By 1825 the huge rectangles then being made began to be replaced by the smaller upright pianos (92).

Upright piano (Fr.: *piano droit, piano vertical;* Ger.: *Pianino*), vertical piano, at first built like an upended grand piano (see: upright grand piano), later as a *pyramid piano, *giraffe p., *cabinet p., *cottage p. The tendency has been to build uprights less and less high, with an ever-increasing compromise in the scale, especially in that of the bass strings. The

low vertical pianos of today are often called spinet pianos or consoles, both misnomers. In 1800, John Isaac Hawkins of Philadelphia made an upright with metal plate; 2 years later Thomas Loud followed with a diagonally strung upright. Robert Wornum was first to make low, diagonally strung pianos in 1811, only 101.5 cm. (3 ft. 4 in.) high; our modern upright piano action goes back to the tape-check action of his pianos, used from *ca.* 1840 on. See also: cottage piano, euphonicon (92).

Uqwabe, syn. of inkohlisa.

Uranicon (Ger.: *Uranikon*), instr. consisting of 2 harps connected together, invented by F. von Holbein in 1805 (176).

Uranion, friction bar "piano" built by Johann David Buschmann of Friedrichsroda, near Berlin, in 1810, an imitation of the clavicylinder. The instr. was identical with his later *terpodion except in one respect: the uranion's cylinder was cloth-covered (176).

Urghanun, var. of arghanum.

Urheen, see: erh hu.

Urra-boi, var. of berra-boi.

Urucungo, Afro-Brazilian *musical bow, in which the string passes through a small gourd resonator attached to the bow. The gourd is held against the player's chest or stomach while he stops the string with his hand and taps it with a small stick. Another variety has no gourd, the string being taken between the player's teeth. Also called berimbao, bucum-bumba, gobo, gunga, macungo, marimba, matungo, mutungo, oricungo, ricungo, rucungo (7).

Urusa, panpipes of the Omagua Indians of S. America, with 12 pipes (105).

Urutsa, panpipes of the Cocoma Indians of the Upper Amazon, with 10 pipes (105).

Uta, *musical bow of Equatorial Africa, with tuning loop (100).

Uta daiko (Jap.: song drum), *barrel drum of Japan, with heads lapped over projecting hoops and laced. The body is of plain *kiri* wood, the heads of parchment. Used in orchestras, theaters, etc. *Ca.* 15 cm. (6 in.) high, 35 cm. (14 in.) in diam. Also called geza daiko, shime daiko (157, 178).

Uter (Lat.: leather bag), bagpipe (190).

Utete, 1. idioglott Jew's-harp of Samoa, Futuna, Uvéa, made from a leaf; **2.** heteroglott Jew's-harp of Tonga, made from a palm frond (77); **3.** *musical bow of Nukahiva, Marquesas Islands, one end of which is held between the player's teeth; it is played with a small stick. *Cf.* ukeke (17); **4.** Swah.: shawm, shepherd's flute (176).

Utgorn, Welsh: trumpet.

Uti [Arab. **'ūd*], short-necked lute of modern Greece, a bass instr. with 4 pairs of strings tuned in 4ths, unfretted; currently being displaced by the *lauto coming in from the West. It is played with a plectrum (144).

Utiyane, *musical bow of the Swazi of S. Africa; it corresponds to the umqunge. Also called ipiano (116).

Utricularium (Lat.), bagpipe of ancient Rome (169).

Utriculus, Lat.: bagpipe (190).

Utusitori, pl. of akasitori.

Uva, Lat.: languid.

Uvete, bamboo stopped *end-blown flute of Florida Island, Solomon Islands, with 3 fingerholes near the lower end (176).

Uveve, 1. Zulu flute corresponding to the luveve; **2.** double *whistle flute of the Zulu, an imitation of the European police whistle, with an interval between the pipes varying from a minor 6th to a major 7th. Up to 24 cm. (9½ in.) long (116).

Uvuru, disc buzzer of the S. African Xhosa (116).

Uzan, Egyptian lute, introduced from Turkey in Muslim times (89 Farmer).

Uzo, syn. of m'bia.

Vaccin, Haitian word for canuto (152).

Vadyam, see: villadi vādyam.

Vagon, see: wagon.

Vajra, syn. of dorje (1).

Valdímbula [*marímbula*], modern Afro-Cuban instr., now obs., an improved marímbula with a larger number of metal lamellae, invented by Gilberto S. Valdès (152).

Valdosa, see: baldosa.

Va let kyong (bamboo hand clapper), clappers of Burma and Laos, made of a bamboo internode with a large rectangular cut in the center, and the upper section split down the middle (112).

Valga, syn. of wambi (132).

Valiha, idiochord *tube zither of the Malagasy Republic, also of Ceram, Gorong, Halmahera, W. New Guinea, made of bamboo with 7–20 strings raised at both ends by small sticks forming individual bridges. It is played in an upright position, plucked with bare fingers. Also called marovany in the Malagasy Republic (119, 171).

Valihambalo, slit drum of the SW. Malagasy Republic (171).

Valiha vero, toy zither of the Malagasy Republic (171).

Vallhorn, folk instr. of Scandinavia, a *fingerhole horn made of horn (144).

Valtorna [Ger.: *Waldhorn*], Russ.: French horn.

Valve (Fr.: *piston, cylindre;* Ger.: *Ventil;* It.: *cilindro*), device applied to a brass instr. to alter its tube length by a fixed amount. Valves are of 2 kinds: descending or ascending. The former lowers the pitch, the latter raises it. Descending valves operate by bringing extra sections of tubing—loops—into play, thereby adding to the total tube length, whereas ascending valves operate by cutting out a section of the main tubing. The function of a valve is to create a new series of tones with their harmonics, so that a chromatic scale may be played throughout an instr.'s range. On instrs. fitted with descending valves, the first valve (with a loop length one-eighth that of the main tubing) lowers the pitch by one tone; the second valve (loop length one-fifteenth that of main tube) lowers it one semitone; the third valve (loop length one-fifth that of main tube) lowers it 3 semitones. The last-named valve is used chiefly in combination with one or both of the others to fill the larger gaps of the scale and has the disadvantage of sharpening the pitch. This can be obviated by use of *compensation valves. Piston valves are used today on all valved instrs. in Belgium, Britain, France, and the U.S. (except that rotary valves are used on horns in Britain and the U.S.). Elsewhere the rotary valve is in use.

The valve in the form we know it today was demonstrated in Berlin by Heinrich Stölzel, a horn player, in 1815. He and Friedrich Blühmel patented it jointly in 1818. Their patent describes a rectangular valve. (In 1920 Curt Sachs drew attention to a trumpet dated 1806 by A. and I. Kerner of Vienna, fitted with 2 valves, preserved in the museum of Tölz, Bavaria, presumably without examining it personally. According to R. Morley-Pegge, the horn authority, this is a composite instr. with trumpet bell by Kerner dated 1806 attached to the body of a 2-valve trumpet of *ca.* 1820.) The rectangular valve was soon succeeded by a tubular model known as the "Stölzel valve." In 1824 John Shaw of England patented a "transposing spring slide" with 2 original features: twin pistons and ascending valves. In 1830 Leopold Uhlmann of Vienna invented the "Vienna valve" (still used on French horns in Vienna) with twin pistons, hence also called the "double piston valve." The year 1832 saw the patenting of Joseph Riedl's *Rad-Maschine* in Vienna, probably the first rotary valve and basically the same as that in use today. The piston valve was improved in 1835 by Wieprecht and Moritz of Berlin and called *Berliner Pumpventil*. Étienne-François Périnet of Paris introduced his piston valve in 1839, and with slight modification this is still in common use. The so-called "American" or "string-action" rotary valve, also pop. today, was patented in 1866 by the Schreiber Cornet Manufacturing Co. of New York (Morley-Pegge 15 and 89; 169). See also: box valve, compensation valve, double piston valve, Perinet valve, piston valve, Quartventil, Rad-Maschine, rotary valve, Schubventil, Vienna valve.

Valve accordion, see: accordéon à pistons.

Valve horn (Fr.: *cor à pistons;* Ger.: *Ventilhorn;* It.: *corno a macchina, corno ventile*), horn provided with valves.

Valve trombone (Fr.: *trombone à pistons;* Ger.: *Ventilposaune;* It.: *trombone ventile*), trombone fitted with piston valves, first built experimentally in 1818. See: trombone.

Valve trumpet (Fr.: *trompette à pistons;* Ger.: *Ventiltrompete;* It.: *tromba a macchina, tromba ventile*), see: trumpet.

Valvonium, *electrophonic instr. with electromagnetic sound generation, invented by Dowding (W. Meyer-Eppler: *Elektrische Klangerzeugung,* 1949).

Valvula, It.: pallet.

Vāmsī (Sans., Hindi), *cross flute of India, made of cane with a node at the upper end and 3 or 4 fingerholes. Also played as a *nose flute. Also called

basulī, vansali. *Cf.* bāmsī, boisi, nāy, pellankovi, pillāngōvi, pillānkulal (173, 203).

Van (Pers.), term proposed by Farmer for a 7th-c. angular harp of the Near East (98).

Vāna, unidentified instr. mentioned in the *Rig-Veda,* possibly a flute. *Cf.* venu (170).

Vanjak (Pahl.), unidentified instr. of ancient Persia (75 II).

Vansali, syn. of vāmsī.

Vansikā (Sans.), see: vāmsī.

Vargan, pl. **vargani** [Gk. **organon*], 1. unidentified Turk. military instr. mentioned in Russia in 1453, possibly a type of chaghāna. We know that it was very noisy; 2. nowadays the Jew's-harp in Russia (25).

Variachord, *electrophonic piano designed by Pollak-Rudin, of the electroacoustical type, with conventional tone generation, in appearance a small, round keyboard instr. (W. Meyer-Eppler: *Elektrische Klangerzeugung,* 1949).

Varinette, mirliton similar to the *bigophone that enjoyed great popularity in the mid-1920's.

Vase siffleur, Fr.: whistling pot.

Vaso silbador, the same as silbador.

Vatana, panpipes of the Waurá Indians of S. America (105).

Vatanatu, vatanati, panpipes of the Mehinacu and Yaulapiti Indians of S. America (105).

Vazang, large lancet-shaped Jew's-harp of the Bampara of E. Bengal, made of wood, with a handle (176).

Velviool (Du.: hide violin), an earlier name of the tambur, a European-inspired violin of the Griqua of S. Africa, with a skin belly (116).

Venava, fiddle of Ceylon, with body of polished coconut, lizardskin belly and 2 strings, 1 secured to a rear peg, the other tied to the neck. It is played with a horsehair bow. An instr. of mendicant musicians (173).

Venetian swell (Ger.: *Jalousieschweller*), a harpsichord swell patented by

Burkat Shudi of London on Dec. 18, 1769, consisting of a series of small shutters, placed over the soundboard, that could be opened or closed by means of a pedal. A similar system, worked by a knee lever, was invented independently by Ferdinand Weber of Dublin at about the same time, possibly earlier. See also: swell (27).

Ventil, syn. of pallet; in Ger.: a valve.

Ventilfagotthorn, an improved *valve horn by Heinrich Zetsche of Hanover, 1841, with a 3½-oct. compass (176).

Ventilhorn, Ger.: valve horn.

Ventilkornett, the same as Kornett.

Ventilposaune, Ger.: valve trombone.

Ventiltrompete, Ger.: valve trumpet.

Ventura guitar, syn. of harp Ventura.

Venturina, small guitar introduced by Angelo Benedetto Ventura of London in 1851, with 4 strings. *Ca.* 50 cm. (20 in.) long (176, 191).

Venu (Sans., Pahl.: cane, bamboo), long, *end-blown flute of E. India, devoid of fingerholes. *Ca.* 130 cm. (4 ft.) long. *Cf.* vāna (170, 173).

Vergette, Fr.: sticker.

Verrillon, Fr.: musical glasses.

Verschiebung, Ger.: una corda.

Vertical flute (Fr.: *flûte droite;* Ger.: *Langflöte;* It.: *flauto verticale*), see: flute.

Vessel flute, see: globular flute.

Vessel rattle (Ger.: *Gefässrassel*), vessel enclosing small rattling objects that strike against each other or the walls of the vessel, such as fruit shells filled with seeds, pellet bells, etc. An important variety is the gourd rattle: a calabash held by its natural neck or by a wooden handle and filled with pebbles. In countries where there are no calabashes it is imitated in clay, wood, metal, basketwork. Basketry rattles occur in ancient Egypt, modern Africa, America, S. Seas (100, 168, 170).

Vèze [Lat. *vesicula*], *bladder pipe of 16th-c. France. In the 17th c. the word came to mean bagpipe, especially in Berry

and Poitou. Trichet *ca.* 1640 says that it is the same as *loure (35, 85, 190).

Viabò, according to Vincenzo Giustiniani, a term for the Jew's-harp in Lombardy (80 VI).

Viall, vialle, obs. corr. of viol.

Vialo (Croatian), small chordophone of Yugoslavia that corresponds to the lira of modern Greece. The piriform body is carved out of a single piece of wood, the flat pegdisc is either round or cloverleaf-shaped; 3 strings are secured by rear pegs and pass over a flat bridge. A nut is lacking. The strings are tuned $d^2 a^1 e^2$, the center string being a drone. *Cf.* rebec (117, 176).

Vibe, coll. for vibraphone.

Vibraharp, metallophone developed in the U.S. in the 1920's, with tuned, graduated metal bars arranged in 2 rows in the manner of piano keys, with tubular metal resonators suspended below them. These sustain the tone and also produce a characteristic vibrato by means of motor-driven propellers affixed to the top of each resonator. Both bars and resonators are suspended from a metal frame set on wheels. A damper pedal is provided. Vibraharps are built in low and high pitches, with a 3-oct. compass, the most common range being f^0–f^3. They are played with padded beaters. See also: harpa-phone (59, 89).

Vibraphone, name by which the vibraharp is known in Europe.

Vichitra vīnā, see: bicitrabīn.

Videl, MHGer. var. of fiedel.

Vidula [Lat. *vitula*], med. Lat.: fiddle. *Cf.* fidula.

Vidulice, syn. of dvoynice (in Croatia and Slavonia only) (34).

Viela, Lat.: fiddle; also syn. of organistrum. *Cf.* viella.

Viele, vièle (Fr.), var. of vielle; modern revival of vielle.

Vièle à pique, Fr.: spike fiddle.

Vièle à roue (Fr.), name given to the hurdy-gurdy in France from *ca.* 1600 on. *Cf.* chifonie, symphonie.

Viella, Lat., It.: early form of the word

viola, related to fiddle, fiedel, viele. Johannes de Grocheo wrote *ca.* 1300 that of all stringed instrs. he preferred the viella. See: fiddle.

Vielle [see: fiddle], **1.** med. Fr. word equivalent to fiddle. The term was in use from *ca.* 1180 to the late 14th c., when it was transformed into viole; **2.** an abbr. of vielle à roue.

Vielle à roue, var. of vièle à roue.

Vielle d'amour (Fr.), Fr. hurdy-gurdy with 3–6 sympathetic strings, usually 4. If there are 6 strings, they are tuned in pairs, $c^1 d^1 g^1$; if there are 4 single strings, they are tuned $c^1 e^1 g^1 a^1$ (149).

Vielle en guitare (Fr.), hurdy-gurdy of 18th-c. France, tuned $c^1 e^1 g^1 a^1$.

Vielle en luth (Fr.), hurdy-gurdy of 18th-c. France, tuned $c^0 c^1 d^0 d^1 g^0 g^1$.

Vielle organisée, see: organized hurdy-gurdy.

Vienna action (Ger.: *Wiener Mechanik*), name by which the *German action, a piano action, became known after Nanette Streicher and her brother, children of its inventor, Johann Andreas Stein, moved to Vienna (92).

Vienna barrel organ, see: Wiener Werkl.

Vienna flute, see: Wiener Flöte.

Vienna valve, valve patented by Leopold Uhlmann of Vienna in 1830, having twin pistons. Formerly used in Austria, Belgium, and France, now still fitted to horns in Vienna but obs. elsewhere. Also called double piston valve, Uhlmann valve (89 Morley-Pegge).

Viertel Orgel (Ger.: quarter organ), obs. Ger. term for an organ having as its foundation a register of 4' pitch. The expression was not in use after the mid-18th c. *Cf.* ganze Orgel, halbe Orgel (90).

Vierteltonklavier, Ger.: quarter-tone piano.

Vigalo, see: vialo.

Vigele, MHGer.: fiddle.

Vigesima nona (It.: twenty-ninth), It.: oct. ½' (organ stop).

Vigesima secunda (It.: twenty-second), It.: oct. 1' (organ stop).

Vigesima sexta (It.: twenty-sixth), It.: quint ⅔' (organ stop).

Vihola (Port.), bowed instr. of the Moluccas, with 3 strings, similar to the taravangsa.

Vihuela (Sp.) [see: fiddle], **1.** originally a generic term for chordophones in Spain, whether bowed or plucked. Bermudo wrote (in 1555) of the "vihuela that Mercury invented"; a *Libro de caballería* of 1460 mentions *"miges viules,"* small fiddles, and Tinctoris wrote (in 1484) that the guitar was called vihuela in Spain. Ultimately the different types were distinguished by qualifications such as *vihuela de mano* for the finger-plucked, *vihuela de peñola* or *de péndola* for the plectrum-plucked, and *vihuela de arco* for the bowed instr.; **2.** specifically, the classical plucked instr. of Sp. Renaissance society, identical in structure to the contemporary guitar, but with 6 courses of strings (against the guitar's 4) tuned like those of the lute, $G^0 c^0 f^0 a^0 d^1 g^1$, and plucked with bare fingers. Bermudo also shows a 7-course vihuela and gives its tuning as $G^0 c^0 f^0 g^0 c^1 f^1 g^1$; however, he is careful to point out that his tunings indicate relative pitches only. The vihuela for which Luys Milan wrote (in 1535/36) had 5 pairs of strings and a single chanterelle, an arrangement similar to that of the guitar. In fact the 2 instrs. were so alike that Bermudo could say it sufficed to remove the top and bottom courses from a vihuela to transform it into a guitar, and a year before, Fuenllana had written of the *"vihuela a cuatro ordenes que dizen guitarra"* (the 4-course vihuela called guitar). In the 17th c. we hear less and less of the vihuela, more and more of the guitar, until ultimately they merge (24, 144 Pedrell).

Vihuela bastarda (Sp.), Pietro Cerone's name (in 1613) for instrs. of the violin family.

Vihuela de arco (Sp.), Sp. equivalent of viola da gamba; also called viola de arco. Juan Ruiz mentions it in the first half of the 14th c., when it presumably denoted a fiddle. Two "old" vihuelas de arco were listed in the 1503 inventory of instrs. of Queen Isabella the Catholic (154).

Vihuela de braço (Sp.: arm vihuela), Pietro Cerone's term (in 1613) for the violin and viola, commonly called violeta, as he says, used when musicians played standing or walking, and of higher pitch than the gambas. His comments on stringing and tuning are those of Giovanni Lanfranco. See also: vihuela bastarda, violetta da braccio.

Vihuela de Flandres, 16th-c. Sp. name for the lute. It had 3 or 4 pairs of strings, each pair consisting of fundamental and its oct. (24).

Vihuela de mano, vihuela plucked with bare fingers, as opposed to the vihuela de peñola or vihuela de arco; the classical vihuela of Spain.

Vihuela de péndola, syn. of vihuela de peñola.

Vihuela de peñola (Sp.: plectrum *vihuela*), vihuela played with a plectrum, similar to the chitarra battente. Juan Ruiz mentions it in the first half of the 14th c.

Vihuela de piernas (Sp.: leg *vihuela*), Pietro Cerone's term (in 1613) for the viola da gamba; he says that it is more commonly known as vihuela de arco.

Vihuela sin trastes (Sp.: *vihuela* without frets), an early Sp. term for instrs. of the violin family.

Viiul, syn. of kantele in Estonian sagas, probably a corr. of viol (9).

Vijalo, see: vialo.

Viktoriaglocke, hemispheric bell with thin walls, patented by A. Appunn of Hanau on July 28, 1895, for use as a church bell (169).

Vilangwi, xylophone of the Washambala of Tanganyika and of the Usambara of Mozambique, rare today, with 10–15 slabs laid across 2 parallel banana trunks and played simultaneously by 2 persons (111).

Villadi vādyam, *stick zither of the W. coast of India, consisting of a long lac-quered stick with leather cord resting on a clay pot placed upside down on the ground, acting as resonator. Clusters of small bells, threaded on a string, are suspended from the stick; 4 or 5 persons alternately strike the cord with specially made short sticks (179).

Villukottu, *musical bow of the W. coast of India, made from a flat spathe of areca or coconut palm, provided with a small slit at each end, and with a strip of bamboo, knobbed at the ends, inserted into the slits. The bamboo "string" is struck with a small stick (179).

Vina, ancient Javanese name of the stick zither (123).

Vīnā (Sans., Pali), stringed instr. of ancient and modern India. In modern times the word has become a generic term for chordophones in S. India, the N. India equivalent being bīn. Originally it may have designated the arched harp, as the term is clearly related to bint, the harp of ancient Egypt. The harp itself disappeared from India some 1000 years ago and the word came to designate a stick zither. Thus the word is older than the form of instr. we know today. In Vedic literature the vīnā is referred to as a 7-stringed instr. The vīnās of our day are highly developed stick zithers, closer to the lute family than to the zithers (the *sitār is considered a vīnā), attributes of Sarasvati, goddess of wisdom. The calabash of the stick zither is replaced by a body, the stick by a broad neck often having a gourd resonator attached to its upper end, lateral pegs inserted in a peg-box, and frets. The S. India instr. is longer than that of N. India. Of the 7 strings 3 are drones. The melody strings are tuned $G^0 c^0 g^0 c^1$ or $F^0 c^0 f^0 c^1$ or $G^0 d^0 g^0 d^1$, and have a total compass of *ca.* 3 octs. They are plucked with the fingernails of the right hand, or with a plectrum, and the higher-pitched drones with the little finger. During performance the upper part of the instr. or the gourd resonator rests against the player's left shoulder. The word *vīnā* is frequently used as an abbr. of *mahati vīnā*. See also: alapini vīnā, alapu vīnā, bharata vīnā, bicitrabīn, bīn, bipanchi, churamantalam, gotuvādyam, kachapī vīnā, kācha vīnā, kairata vīnā, kāncha bīnā, kanuna, katyayana vīnā, kinnarī vīnā, kshudrā katyayana vīnā, mahānātaka vīnā, mahati vīnā, naradiya vīnā, pināka vīnā, prasārinī vīnā, ranjanī vīnā, rudra vīnā, sāradiyā vīnā, Sarasvati vīnā, satatantri vīnā, shautika vīnā, sruti vīnā, sur vīnā, tritantri vīnā, vīnā kunju, vipanchi vīnā (89, 168, 170).

Vīnā kunju, fiddle of the W. coast of India, with shallow circular body surmounted by shoulders forming a slender neck. A single fiber or twine string is secured to a lateral peg. It is an instr. of the Pulluvan of Malabar, India, a tribe of serpent worshipers (179).

Vīnā pināka, see: pināka.

Vioara, Rom.: violin (5).

Viol, 1. coll. Engl. for viola da gamba; **2.** as a translation of the Fr. viele, term loosely and erroneously applied to forerunners of the violin (see: fiddle); **3.** generic Engl. term for organ stops having string tone.

Viola [see: fiddle], **1.** (Fr.: *alto;* Ger.: *Bratsche, Viola;* It.: *viola*), an abbr. of viola da braccio, the alto member of the violin family tuned a 5th below the violin, *i.e.*, c⁰ g⁰ d¹ a¹, with a body length of 38–44 cm. (15–17¼ in.) and a speaking string length of 33.5–37.5 cm. (13¼–14¾ in.). (Larger instrs., with a body of 47 cm. (18½ in.) or more, are termed *tenor violins.) A comparison of these measurements with those of the violin will show that in relation to the violin the viola is proportionally small for its pitch; theoretically the viola should be half again as large as the violin, but so large an instr. would be difficult to play at the shoulder. Structurally the viola is identical with the violin, as are its fittings and the modifications they underwent in the past. For its early history see: violin.

The earliest surviving violas—of It. make—are of 2 virtually standardized sizes with body lengths of *ca.* 41 cm. (16¼ in.) and *ca.* 44 cm. (17¼ in.); those of Gasparo da Salò (1540–after 1600) measure 44 cm. (17¼ in.), and it seems that until the end of the 17th c. the larger pattern predominated. But from then on a smaller model was preferred, and because of this preference a number of old instrs. were cut down. The role of the viola was a very subordinate one until the latter part of the 18th c.; indeed as late an author as J. J. Quantz pointed out (in 1752) that the instr. was of little consequence in music and that its players lacked ability. Many viola players seem to have been indifferent violinists who were naturally more at ease with a small instr., and violas of this period were made with a body 37.5–39.5 cm. (14¾–15½ in.) long. When in the late 18th c. and in the 19th c. the viola was given more important parts, a larger pattern gradually came into favor again. Today a fairly large instr. prevails, with body 40–43 cm. (15¾–17 in.) long. The viola has been scored for under a variety of names: in the late 16th c. it was sometimes written for as violino; Banchieri in the first decade of the 17th c. enumerates it among his violini da braccio (tuned d⁰ g⁰ d¹ a¹, but Zacconi had already given the c⁰ g⁰ d¹ a¹ tuning in 1592). Later in the 17th c. the term viola da braccio was reserved for the viola. In Ger. scores the viola also appears as violetta. Its Fr. nomenclature was highly complex: the 1751 edition of the *Encyclopédie Méthodique* speaks, probably inspired by Mersenne, of 3 *altos,* of which the *hautecontre* is notated in C clef on the bottom line, the *taille* in C clef on the second line, the *quinte* in C clef on the third line, all 3 instrs. being at the same pitch. In other words, the viola was given the name of the part it played; and apart from these names it was also called cinquième, alto-viola, violette, or quinte de violon. Played as a folk instr. in a large part of Transylvania, the viola has

only 3 strings; its bridge is flat and all 3 strings are sounded simultaneously (5, 15 Skeaping, 41);
2. obs. abbr. of viola da gamba and of viola da braccio. Sébastien de Brossard says (in 1703) that in It. the word means *basse de viole* unless otherwise qualified; **3.** organ stop of cylindrical open flue pipes of narrow scale, known since the 16th c., at first usually built at 4' or 2' pitch, later the 8' became preponderant. It rarely occurs at 16'. In 1885, William Thynne introduced his string tone viola, and since then the viola stop has become identified with his in Engl.-speaking countries (101, 133); **4.** syn. of ligina; **5.** rare Afro-Cuban single-headed drum with circular frame from 8–10 cm. (3¼–4 in.) high, 30–40 cm. (12–16 in.) in diam.; 2 converging wooden arms project upward, united by a crossbar at the top in the manner of the yoke of a lyre. The arms serve as a handle to hold the drum while it rests against the player's shoulder. Some specimens are made of banjo bodies; **6.** occasional syn. of gadulka. See also: alto-moderne, alto-piano, alto-ténor, contralto, contraviola Paganini, Dessauerbratsche, viola alta, violalin, viola nova, violette, violon-alto.

Viola a cembalo, harmonium of Giuseppe Maria Pomi of Varallo, 1833 (176). *Cf.* violicembalo.

Viola all'inglese, 18th-c. It. expression, presumably equivalent to *English violet.

Viola alta, 1. in 17th- and 18th-c. Italy probably syn. of viola, 1; **2.** large viola made by Karl Adam Hörlein of Würzburg and introduced in 1876 by violist Hermann Ritter, who had a fifth string added to it in 1898 (for e²). Hörlein also called his instr. Altgeige. It had a body length of 48 cm. (19 in.). *Cf.* viola bassa, violon-alto (26, 191); **3.** organ stop of string tone, named after Ritter's instr.

Viola-arpa, see: violino-arpa.

Viola bassa, the bass instr. of a new quartet, designed by Hermann Ritter in 1905, twice the size of the *viola alta

and pitched an oct. lower. See also: viola alta, viola tenore (26).

Viola bastarda, viola da gamba of size intermediary between the bass and the tenor, with C or F holes, often an additional, circular soundhole under the fingerboard, and usually a scroll rather than a sculptured head. The earliest literary reference found so far occurs in Italy in 1589. Praetorius lists 5 tunings for the instr. The name *bastarda* probably derives from its tunings, which follow the principle of those of the lira da braccio (mixed 4ths and 5ths) rather than that of the viola da gamba; such tunings favored chordal playing, also reminiscent of the lira. The bastarda had a somewhat larger body than the bass lira, but a slightly shorter speaking string length. In England the instr. was known as the *lyra viol. For tunings and measurements see: lyra viol. See also: basse de viole d'amour, viola doppia.

Viola braguesa, syn. of viola d'arame.

Viola chuleira, syn. of viola d'arame.

Viola contralta, in 17th- and 18th-c. Italy, probably syn. of viola.

Viola da arco (It.), mentioned by several 16th-c. authors without further description; presumably the viola da gamba.

Viola da braccio (It.: arm viola), 16th- and 17th-c. designation of instrs. of the violin family, as opposed to those of the viola da gamba family. During the course of the 17th c. the term became reserved for the alto instr., our viola, still called *Bratsche* (from *braccio*) in German (Praetorius, however, equated it with violino da braccio). A Graz inventory of 1577 lists bass, tenor, and discant "*geigen da prazo*," and an Ambras inventory of 1596 a bass and 3 tenor "*viole di praz oder cleine geigen*," as well as a consort of 1 bass, 4 tenors, 1 discant, and 2 "*cleine Diskant*." Banchieri gives (in 1609) the pitches of a set of violini da braccio: his soprano has our violin tuning, the intermediary instr. is a viola tuned $d^0 g^0 d^1 a^1$, and the bass is tuned an oct. below the violin ($G^0 d^0 a^0 e^1$), *ergo* a tenor violin. Banchieri's pitches conform to those of a harpsichord, he says, indicating thereby that they are not relative pitches. The tenor viola da braccio of Praetorius was tuned a 5th lower than the violin, hence a viola (alto violin). See also: violin (159, 183).

Viola da gamba (It.: leg viola), **1.** a family of bowed chordophones that evolved from the med. *fiddle (known as viele, viola, viole, etc. in Romance languages). The "gambas" or "viols" as they are now usually called in Engl. became obs. in the 18th c. and were revived in the 20th. They have much in common with the violin family: their component parts are the same (see: violin), both have lateral pegs and rib-fastened strings. The viols differ in having 6 strings tuned in 4ths around a central 3rd, deeper ribs, sloping shoulders, a proportionately longer neck, belly and back usually set flush with the ribs without any projection (but many old It. gambas form exceptions to this rule), a flat back with sloping upper portion to reduce the depth of the ribs there, plain corners, C holes, wider bridge and fingerboard to accommodate the larger number of strings, often a carved head in lieu of a scroll, movable frets placed on the neck, and thinner strings. From bass to smallest size, the instrs. were held vertically by seated players, the larger ones being supported by the player's calves, the smaller ones resting on his lap. In common with the violins, they have soundpost and bass-bar. The traditional bowing technique has been with palm up. Today we play 4 sizes: soprano, with its 6 strings tuned $d^0 g^0 c^1$ $e^1 a^1 d^2$; alto, tuned $c^0 f^0 b^0 d^1 g^1 c^2$; tenor, tuned $G^0 c^0 f^0 a^0 d^1 g^1$; bass, tuned $D^0 G^0 c^0 e^0 a^0 d^1$.

The early history of the viola da gamba is still shrouded in darkness. A fiddle closely resembling a gamba is depicted in the Bible of Étienne Harding in the Dijon municipal library; the Bible was completed between 1098 and 1109 (illustration in Source 147, III; better in 185A):

it has rounded lower bouts, a marked waist, upper bouts with sloping shoulders characteristic of the later instr., and apparently 4 strings attached to an ill-defined pegdisc. Its over-all length is about 60 cm. (24 in.). It is being played by a seated performer, held between the thighs in a vertical position, bowed with the palm up (to become the classical bowing technique of the gambas). From here on there appears to be little development until the gamba emerges fully fledged at the beginning of the 16th c. As is the case with the violin, it would seem that the decisive transitory step from the fiddle was the exchanging of pegdisc (implying frontal or rear pegs) for a pegbox (implying lateral pegs). Judging by the iconography, this was accomplished by the early 16th c. Bernardo Prospero relates that in 1493 Spanish musicians came to Mantua from Rome who *suonano viole grande quasi come me*, but although these instrs. may have been gambas, we cannot be sure that they were not large fiddles. However, large-sized gambas appear to have preceded the smaller ones, and certainly the bass became the type instr. of the family in the first third of the 16th c. The smaller instrs. were not held against the player's shoulder or chest, but rested vertically on his lap, a position suggestive of Eastern influence. All other fretted instrs. were held horizontally or diagonally, so that many hypotheses have been advanced regarding the origin of frets on the gamba. No satisfactory answer has been forthcoming so far. Fretting was undoubtedly a question of expediency and was probably connected with the large size of the instr.: violin players did not exceed the first position for a long time, whereas by the time Ganassi wrote (in 1542) gamba players could play right up to the edge of the fingerboard. The fact that frets are responsible for the gamba's open-string timbre cannot have concerned the 15th or 16th c. Both fretting and tuning of the viola da gamba are shared with the Sp. *vihuela, a word that formerly designated plucked as well as bowed instrs., and it is possible that the gamba assumed its final form in Spain. Several It. Renaissance writers hint at this.

Extant 16th-c. instrs. have wider upper and lower bouts in relation to their body lengths than have later models; their C holes are placed almost vertically in the middle of the center bouts, whereas later they are slanted to follow the curve of this bout's lower portion (but vertical C holes are found on small 18th-c. instrs.); the bridge was lower and was placed below the soundholes, a fact confirmed by Mersenne and Jean Rousseau (1687) as well as by the iconography. By the mid-16th c. a whole family had developed, consisting of double bass, bass, tenor (a second tenor tuned to the same pitch played the alto part if needed), and soprano. Of these the bass had already become the type instr. and was the preponderantly important member of the group, being used for both solo and ensemble work. It is probable that a subcontrabass also existed by then: a *double basse contre de viole* was among the effects of a deceased Fr. instr. maker in 1557, although Praetorius stated (in 1618) that the 5-stringed subbass had been invented "recently." Adriano Banchieri (in 1609) gives the tuning of a *violone in controbasso con tasti*, the fourth member of his gamba consort, as $D^1 G^1 C^0 E^0 A^0 d^0$. Virtuoso players are mentioned by Ganassi in 1542, an indication of the degree of perfection that the instr. had attained by then. His is the first tutor for the viola da gamba (*Regola Rubertina*, 1542–43). The latter part of the c. saw the addition of the *viola bastarda, the 17th c. that of the *pardessus de viole, and the emergence in England of 2 separate sizes of bass: a larger one called *consort viol and a slightly smaller *division viol. A seventh string was added to the bass in France in the second half of the 17th c., apparently by Sainte-Colombe, usually tuned to A^1 (re-

quired, *i.a.*, for Bach's *St. John Passion*), the bass then being tuned $A^1 D^0 G^0 c^0 e^0 a^0 d^1$.

With the possible exception of Spain, about which we as yet know too little, viol making and playing first assumed importance in Italy. In 1526, 2 "vialls" were employed at the court of Henry VIII and in 1540 there were 6 new "vialls" (*i.e.*, performers), all of them Italians, from Cremona, Milan, and Venice. In his *Epitome musical* of 1556, Philibert Jambe de Fer says that gambas in France had 5 strings, all tuned in 4ths, although Italy had gambas with 6 strings. Jean Rousseau (*Traité de la viole,* 1687) confirms that the "first viols" in France had but 5 strings, all tuned in 4ths ($E A D G C$), and says that they were very large basses with very thick strings; subsequently, he relates, the viol's shape was changed and a sixth string was added. He goes on to say that the English reduced their viols to a convenient size before the French did, "as one can easily judge by ancient English viols for which we in France have a particular esteem," but that the French were the first to thin down the neck and set it at a slight angle to facilitate playing. Indeed, during the 17th c. England was the center of performance, and her players were sought and often met with on the Continent. In France the art of viol playing flourished into the 18th c., when the *quinton was introduced (the smaller-sized members of the family had already been abandoned in other countries), and as late as 1740, Hubert Le Blanc could write his fulminating *Défense de la basse de viole contre les entreprises du violon et les prétensions du violoncel*. But with the exception of Germany the only member of the original family still in use in the late 17th c. was the bass. In 18th-c. Germany only the bass was played. Ger. writers of the period gave its tuning as $D^0 G^0 c^0 e^0 a^0 d^1$ and called it *basse de viole* or simply *viola da gamba*. Carl Friedrich Abel played the viola da gamba in public until

1787, the year of his death, and the *Musikalische Realzeitung* of Oct. 11, 1788, reported that a Miss Thicknesse, a pupil of his, was then England's most notable gambist.

The vexed problem of tunings remains to be discussed: a number of writers, among whom Lanfranco, in 1533, Ganassi, in 1542, and Cerreto, Mersenne, Playford, Simpson, and Talbot in the 17th c., give the following tunings:

Soprano	d^0	g^0	c^1	e^1	a^1	d^2
Tenor	A^0	d^0	g^0	b^0	e^1	a^1
or	G^0	c^0	f^0	a^0	d^1	g^1
Bass	D^0	G^0	c^0	e^0	a^0	d^1

(Talbot's consort bass has a seventh string, tuned C^0, and he adds a double bass viol pitched an oct. below the tenor in G). Other writers, including Zacconi, in 1592, Banchieri, in 1609, Cerone, in 1613, and Praetorius, in 1618 (his chief tunings) give:

Soprano	G^0	c^0	f^0	a^0	d^1	g^1
Tenor	D^0	G^0	c^0	e^0	a^0	d^1
Bass	G^1	C^0	F^0	A^0	d^0	g^0

(Praetorius' soprano is 1 tone higher than the above; Banchieri calls his bass a *violone da gamba*). These 2 sets of tunings, lying a 5th apart, have perplexed the specialists. The relationship between them may be expressed thus:

Soprano	d^0–d^2	
Tenor	G^0–g^1	Soprano
Bass	D^0–d^1	Tenor
	G^1–g^0	Bass

With the exception of Cerone (who follows Zacconi) all the above writers are authoritative. Gerald Hayes pointed out that no literature exists for a bass at the lower of the given tunings, and that an instr. large enough to yield such low tones would indeed be unwieldy as a solo instr. The suggestion has been made that the set of low-pitched instrs. actually sounded a 5th higher, the G^1 string of one bass being at the same absolute pitch as the D^0 string of the other. Unfortunately this is impossible: Banchieri and Praetorius

elsewhere give the tuning of the violin as g^0 d^1 a^1 e^2, that of today, and Zacconi gives its compass as g^0–b^2. But, to conform to the above theory, these authors, who indicate the lower of the viol tunings, should state the violin tuning as c^0 g^0 d^1 a^1. Other modern writers have pointed out that absolute pitch was nonexistent in earlier times, and that as late an author as Jean Rousseau advises (in 1687) that gamba tuning be started by pulling a middle string (c^1) up to a "reasonable" pitch. But the "reasonableness" in such cases was limited upward by the breaking point and downward by the loss of tone quality, perhaps 3 or 4 semitones in all. Two possibilities remain: a) if no literature exists for the low bass, then it must either have been used for improvisation —unlikely because of its size—or it was played from music written for a different instr.; b) the pitches were exactly what their authors said they were, and the discrepancy lay in the nomenclature, a situation that still obtains in our times: the alto flute of the U.S. is called a bass flute in Britain, for example; the alto recorder a treble recorder in Britain, etc. One man's bass was another man's tenor. Contemporary literature tends to bear out both of these points. In comparing the works of those authors who list the higher tunings with those who list the lower ones, it will be noticed that the former are by and large more concerned with solo performance and the latter with concerted music. Banchieri and Praetorius in particular use gambas to double voices or other instrs., at unison or at the (lower) oct. Praetorius is more explicit, albeit in a rather muddled fashion. Writing of the gamba, he says of the English—in his day the foremost exponents of gamba playing—that when they *"allein damit etwas musizieren"* (literally, "make music alone therewith," meaning when they play viols only, *i.e.*, a consort of viols—as becomes evident a few lines later), they tune a 4th or a 5th lower; this is a slip of the pen and should obviously read "4th or

5th higher," as appears from the next sentence: ". . . *also dass sie die unterste Saiten im kleinen Bass vors D, im Tenor und Alt vors A, im Cantus vors e rechnen und halten; Do sonsten . . . ein Quint tiefer, als nemlich der Bass ins GG, der Tenor und Alt ins D, der Cant. ins A gestimmt ist. Und das gibt in diesem Stimmwerk viel eine anmutigere, praechtigere und herrlichere Harmonij als wenn man im rechten Thon bleibet* (so that they count the lowest string of the small bass as a D, that of tenor and alto as A, that of soprano as e; as otherwise . . . the tuning is a 5th lower, namely the bass in GG, the tenor and alto in D, the soprano in A. And that gives this consort a far more splendid . . . resonance than when one remains at the ordinary pitch). His Engl. consort tuning thus corresponds to the first set of tunings given above, and since viol strings just cannot be pulled up a 4th or a 5th (or let down, for that matter, if the instr. is still to sound like a viol —*cf.* Playford on this subject), the English must have played a consort of smaller instrs. tuned a 4th or 5th higher than Praetorius' corresponding instrs. As a matter of fact, the 2 terminologies subsist side by side today: in modern Fr. and Brit. usage (as in the U.S.) the bass is still considered the type instr., whereas in Ger. usage the tenor is considered the type instr. Many museum catalogues using the Ger. classification enumerate a

fair quantity of tenors and at best a stray bass, sometimes no bass at all. The Brit. bass and the Ger. tenor are both tuned D^0–d^1 and both have the same dimensions, needless to say.

Approximate speaking lengths of the gamba strings are: pardessus 28 cm. (11 in.), soprano 35½ cm. (14 in.), alto 39–40 cm. (15½ in.), tenor 48–53 cm. (19–21 in.), small (division) bass 63½–66 cm. (25–26 in.), large (consort) bass 71 cm. (28 in.), double bass 98 cm. (38½ in.). See also: consort viol, division viol, lyra viol, pardessus de viole, quinton, viola bastarda;

2. organ stop of open cylindrical (sometimes conical) flue pipes. Up to *ca.* 1700 called viol, viola, viole; then when the orchestral da braccio family displaced the da gamba family, the stop was named viola da gamba, later abbr. to gamba or viol. Originally built at 4′ and 2′ pitches, in which positions it remained for some time, later adding 16′ and 8′. The 2′ was also known as violet, violetta (133).

Viola da mano, a 16th-c. syn. of viola da braccio.

Viola d'amore (Fr.: *viole d'amour*), **1.** name given to 2 different stringed instrs.: a) an ordinary violin strung with metal strings, to which a fifth string was sometimes added (Praetorius had already praised the sound of metal-strung violins in 1618). John Evelyn is the first writer known so far to mention it. He called it

Lowest string	Modern	Modern Ger.	Classic "low"	Classic "high"	Praetorius
g^0	pardessus	pardessus			
d^0	soprano	soprano		soprano	
c^0	alto				
A^0		alto		tenor	Cantus
G^0	tenor		soprano	tenor	
D^0	bass	tenor	tenor	bass	Tenor
G^1		bass	bass		Kleine Bassgeige
D^1, E^1					(5-string) Violone; gross Viola da Gamba; contrabasso da gamba
D^1, E^1					(4-string) gar gross Bass-viola da Gamba; gross Contrabass Geig

a "viol d'amore" and said that it had 5 strings of wire that were bowed. Many later authors describe it, but none mentions sympathetic strings before 1741. Earlier in the c. its tuning is given as $g^0 c^1 e^1 g^1 c^2$. In 1738 Eisel wrote that the Italians had recently brought out a viola d'amore with 7 strings, tuned $F^0 Bb^0 d^0 g^0 c^1 f^1 bb^1$, all bowed. Then, in 1741, Majer writes of 2 varieties of viola d'amore, a smaller one like the violin and another, slightly larger than a viola, both with 6 strings. A footnote informs us of the existence of sympathetic strings. This is presumably the earliest reference to: b) a stringed instr. with viol-like body, held and bowed like a violin, without frets, having flame holes and often a circular soundhole as well, a long pegbox to accommodate pegs of the 6 or 7 gut melody strings and as many sympathetic ones. The latter pass through holes in the bridge and disappear underneath the fingerboard. *Ca.* 1740 Antonio Vivaldi wrote for this instr., requiring a tuning of $A^0 d^0 a^0 f^1 a^1 d^2$. A similar tuning is common today, $A^0 d^0 a^0 f\sharp^1 a^1 d^2$, with the sympathetic strings tuned arbitrarily, but accordaturas of the amore are very numerous. By the latter part of the 18th c. the instr. was almost forgotten. Giacomo Meyerbeer brought it back to life temporarily in *Les Huguenots* (1836), after which it slumbered again until the end of the 19th c. (67, 89 Hayes, 134, 170); 2. organ stop of cylindrical open flue pipes of narrow scale; also built in conical form as a solo stop (133). See also: arnolo, English violet, pardessus de viole d'amour, violetta marina, violon d'amour.

Viola d'amour, syn. of viola d'amore (organ stop).

Viola da orbo, It.: hurdy-gurdy.

Viola d'arame (Port.: wire guitar), Port. guitar with 6 pairs of metal strings and usually 10 frets. Also called viola braguesa, viola chuleira (7).

Viola da spalla (It.: shoulder viola),

early-18th-c. name for a small violoncello, first mentioned by Mattheson, who says in 1713 that it had 5 or 6 strings and was held against the player's chest by a band passed over the shoulder. Majer in 1732 echoed Mattheson, but added that it was also held between the legs, was written for in C clef on the fourth line, and was tuned $C^0 G^0 d^0 a^0$. At mid-c. Adlung equated it with the cello. It. 18th-c. writers used the expression in contradistinction to viola da gamba. *Cf.* Fagottgeige.

Viola de praz, corr. of viola da braccio.

Viola de rueda, Sp.: hurdy-gurdy (176).

Viola di bordone, see: baryton, 1.

Viola di braccio, a softly voiced viola organ stop built in 1850 by Sonreck (133).

Viola di fagotto, see: Fagottgeige.

Viola di gamba, organ stop, syn. of gamba. Built as a cylindrical stop of flue pipes or, in Praetorius' day, of conical pipes (2).

Viola doppia, Giustiniani's name (*ca.* 1626) for the viola bastarda (80 VI).

Viola fagotto, see: viola di fagotto.

Viola francesa, Port.: the Spanish guitar.

Violalin [*viola* + (*vio*)*lin*], 5-stringed viola of Friedrich Hillmer of Leipzig, first mentioned in 1800, the additional string being the violin e^2 string (169).

Viola major, organ stop, a powerful gamba at 8' pitch.

Viola michaelense, large viola d'arame (7).

Viola nova, large viola made by Hiller in 1926, tuned like a viola but held like a cello, with a body length of 54 cm. (21¼ in.) (26).

Violão, Port.: the Spanish guitar. In Brazil it denotes a large guitar with 6 strings, with 8-shaped body (7).

Viola organista, chordophone designed by Leonardo da Vinci (d. 1519) (but never made), with mechanically bowed strings. In an earlier drawing the strings are bowed by a revolving wheel, in a later one by an endless bow of horsehair. The viola organista is the first mechanically bowed instr. to be designed after the *organistrum and is a precursor, or perhaps one should say, a drawing-board precursor, of the *Geigenwerk. Leonardo wrote in his notebooks that he intended obtaining "unending" sounds from all kinds of instrs. and made drawings of a few others (G. Kinsky in *Zeitschrift für Musikwissenschaft* VI, 1923/4).

Viola paredon, corr. of viola di bordone. See: baryton.

Viola piccola, obs. term for the violino piccolo.

Viola pomposa, viola with an additional string, tuned e², in use from *ca.* 1725 to 1770. Its invention has been ascribed to J. S. Bach by various late-18th-c., *i.e.,* noncontemporary, writers, and the myth persists, even though Bach never scored for such an instr. But Graun, Telemann (in 1728), and Lidarti (in 1760) did, calling for a range of f⁰–e³. Two of the strings appear to have been tuned to g⁰ and d⁰ (these are found on both violin and viola). In his *Musikalisches Lexikon* of 1802, Koch remarks that occasionally one uses a viola with the addition of a violin E string, sometimes called violino pomposo. Graun used both terms. The instr. allegedly made for Bach by J. C. Hoffmann of Leipzig is believed to have been a *violoncello piccolo, for which Bach *did* write (89 Hayes, 170).

Viola tenore, 1. in 17th- and 18th-c. Italy, probably the *tenor violin; **2.** tenor violin introduced by Hermann Ritter in 1905, with a body length of 72 cm. (28¼ in.). The strings were tuned G⁰ d⁰ a⁰ e¹, and the instr. was played in cello position. *Cf.* Tenor-viola. See also: viola alta, viola bassa (26).

Viol barytone, see: baryton.

Violdigambe, corr. of viola da gamba. See: gamba (organ stop).

Viole (Fr.), word that occurs in Fr. literature from 1318 on, a var. of vièle, later used in the general sense of viola. For the organ stop see: viola da gamba.

Viole céleste, see: vox coelestis.

Viole d'amour, see: viola d'amore.

Viole d'orchestre, organ stop of small-scaled metal flue pipes, cylindrical, usually slotted, invented by Michell and Thynne and introduced in 1885. The stop is at 8′ pitch. Its 4′ equivalent is called octave viol or celestina-viol (129, 198).

Viole sourdine, organ stop of small-scaled conical metal pipes, invented in 1885 by Michell and Thynne, softly voiced, at 8′ pitch (101, 198).

Violet [dim. of *viol*], **1.** early Engl. word for violin, in use in the mid-16th c.; **2.** organ stop, syn. of violetta, 2. See also: English violet.

Violeta, 1. Port.: viola; **2.** Sp. equivalent of violetta; **3.** in old Sp. organs a narrow-scaled crumhorn, syn. of orlo.

Violeta chica (Sp.), Pietro Cerone's translation of (Zacconi's) violetta piccola, the soprano viola da gamba.

Viole-ténor, syn. of alto-moderne.

Violett, obs. name of an oct. viola da gamba organ stop at 4′ pitch (133).

Violetta [dim. of *viola*] (It.), **1.** in the 16th c. a small viola, fiddle, equivalent of kleine Geige; **2.** the viola, *i.e.,* alto violin. In this sense the term was in use chiefly in the 18th c.; **3.** in the 17th c. it also designated the soprano viola da gamba with 3, 4, or 6 strings; **4.** organ stop, a viola da gamba stop in 2′ position; in the 18th c. also syn. of viola. *Cf.* violette.

Violetta da arco (It.: bowed *violetta*), Giovanni Lanfranco mentions (in 1533) a family of "*violette da arco senz tasti.*" *Cf.* kleine Geige, violin.

Violetta da braccio (It.: arm *violetta*), Giovanni Lanfranco mentions (in 1533) a family of instrs. by this name, each having 3 strings except the bass, which had 4, tuned in 5ths, and without frets. *Cf.* violin.

Violetta marina, 1. bowed instr. invented by violinist Pietro Castrucci in England in the early 18th c. Dr. Burney reports it to have been a viola d'amore. Handel scored for it in his *Orlando* and *Sosarme* (176); **2.** It.: trumpet marine (rare).

Violetta piccola (It.), according to early It. and Sp. writers, a soprano viola da gamba, tuned (A^0) d^0 g^0 b^0 e^1 a^1; to Praetorius it was both a violin and a 3- or 4-stringed soprano viola da gamba.

Violette (Fr.), **1.** obs. Fr. term for the viola (alto violin); **2.** term recorded from 1527 on, equivalent of the It. violetta.

Violicembalo [*viola* + *cembalo*], **1.** bowed keyboard instr. of Abbé Gregorio Trentino of Venice, 1820. The strings were pressed against a continuous bow; **2.** It.: lute harpsichord.

Violin [dim. of *viola*] (Fr., OProv.: *violon;* Ger.: *Violine;* It.: *violino*), **1.** bowed chordophone, treble member of a family comprising violin, viola, and violoncello, with 4 strings tuned g^0 d^1 a^1 e^2. Its over-all length averages 60 cm. ($23\frac{1}{2}$ in.), its body length, from the late 18th c. on, 35–36 cm. ($13\frac{3}{4}$–14 in.), speaking length of its strings today 32.5–32.7 cm. (*ca.* $12\frac{3}{4}$ in.). The violin consists of the following parts: a top or belly, also called soundboard, and a back, the 2 sometimes being referred to as the tables. The top is made of softwood (spruce, pine), the back and ribs of hardwood (usually maple, sycamore, fruitwood). Both top and back are arched; they are glued to the ribs, with an overhang of a couple of mm., thus forming a resonating body, and may be made of 1 or 2 pieces of wood. The body is connected to the neck, which terminates in a pegbox and scroll. The strings are wound around lateral pegs, pass over an ebony nut, along the ebony fingerboard, over the maple bridge, to be attached to a tailpiece. This in turn is secured by a loop of gut to the end pin (also called button) inserted in the lower rib; a low saddle assists the tailpiece in keeping clear

of the belly. The neck was originally set at the same plane as the body, and the fingerboard was tilted upward by the insertion of a wedge. The incurved waist, which facilitates passage of the bow, forms the center bouts (often referred to as CC); the outward-curving upper and lower portions of the body constitute the upper and lower bouts. The F-shaped soundholes, also called FF or F holes, are cut into the belly near the edges of the center bouts. The bridge is placed between the FF, immediately in line with their cross-strokes. An inlay called *purfling is generally present. Inside the body are a *soundpost and *bass-bar, corner blocks, top and bottom blocks, and linings that furnish gluing surfaces. Since the latter half of the 19th c., it has been customary to attach a chin rest—introduced by Louis Spohr *ca.* 1820—to the left of the tailpiece. The exterior is varnished to protect it from the ravages of sweat, dust, and rosin. As to the alleged importance of varnish in enhancing violin tone, it should be borne in mind that the most sensitive part of plucked instrs., the belly, has traditionally been unvarnished (lute, guitar, harpsichord, etc.). Thus it would appear that the bellies of violins and other bowed instrs. were varnished of necessity rather than by choice, and the major preoccupation must have been to apply a flexible varnish that would not *impair* the tone.

Surviving examples by early makers have less pronounced corners and more elongated soundholes than later instrs. have, but not highly arched backs, as is often stated. Until the 18th c. violins were made in both small and large patterns, with the body $34\frac{1}{2}$–37 cm. ($13\frac{1}{2}$–$14\frac{1}{2}$ in.) long. During the last decade of the 18th c. and the early 19th c. the instr. was transformed to its present-day model because of demands for greater volume and brilliance of tone, which demands apparently originated in Italy in conjunction with the incipient use of large halls for public concerts. The neck, previously on the same plane as that of the body, was now thrown back at an angle and slightly lengthened—up to 1 cm. at most, usually less—the wedge was discarded, the fingerboard lengthened and redesigned, the bridge made correspondingly higher, the tops of bridge and fingerboard were made more convex, and the bass-bar was made considerably stouter. Although thinner strings were then used, the tension was greater than on the old model. (A modern term for the old model is "short-neck violin" in Engl., *Kurzhalsgeige* in Ger.) Very few instrs. indeed escaped this treatment. In the early 19th c. François Chanot of Mirecourt and Paris designed an experimental model (patented 1817) with a guitar-shaped body, small crescent soundholes, and a reversed scroll. The same year, Félix Savart, Parisian physicist, designed a trapezoid model with straight sides and sound slits. These attempts, as well as others to improve violin tone further by constructing instrs. according to acoustical principles, were short-lived.

The early history of the violin is unduly complicated by the fact that at first it had no name of its own at all, and later a plethora of names, so that until the end of the 16th c. we often cannot tell with certainty which of several instrs. our sources refer to. Because the word *viola* is fem., scholars have argued that violino (masc.) cannot be its dim., that the dim. of *viola* would be violina, and consequently that *violino* must denote similarity: *like* a viola, as, *e.g.*, the It. *lupino* from *lupo, marino* from *mare*, etc. Yet there are organological parallels that invalidate such arguments: a spinettino (masc.) is a smaller version of a spinetta (fem.), the trombino (masc.) is a small tromba (fem.), the small mandola (fem.) is known as mandolino (masc.), and the ribeca (fem.) itself becomes a ribecchino (masc.). Praetorius (*Syntagma*, III) gives a table of It. instr. names ending in the suffixes *one, ino, accio,* and considers trombino and violino as dim. forms denoting discant instrs.

That the violin evolved from the med. fiddle is now an accepted fact. Just when and how this transformation took place remain unknown. Judging from pictorial sources, the decisive step in the evolution of both violin and viola da gamba was the exchanging of a pegdisc (implying frontal or rear pegs) for a pegbox (implying lateral pegs); a number of pre-16th c. fiddles with outlines similar to those of violin or gamba are represented with pegdiscs and often show 3 strings. The most obvious reason for such a transformation would seem to be the greater tension obtainable with lateral pegs; and greater tension spells higher pitch and/or greater brilliance of tone. The violin's lateral pegs may have been taken over from the rebec; this at least would explain some of the confusion of terminology. A drawing of a musical group by Albrecht Dürer, *ca.* 1515, shows a harp, a lute, and an instr. that would be a very small violin if it were not for the pegdisc; it is held at the chest and may have had an over-all length of perhaps 40–45 cm. (16–17½ in.). But the first unambiguous records of the new instr. are the frescoes at Bergamo and Saronno by Gaudenzio Ferrari, *ca.* 1535. At Saronno, 3 angels are playing instrs. of violin, viola, and tenor violin size, each with 3 strings, yet true violins all, down to the FF. The alto member of the family is generally considered to have evolved prior to the treble (*i.e.*, violin) and to be the type instr. of the family, chiefly because it retained the name of viola, other members being called by dims. or augs. of this word, and this may indeed be the case. The earliest known *violino* part, by Giovanni Gabrieli (1597), is written in alto clef and descends below g⁰, and must therefore have been for a viola. By the time Praetorius (1618) and Mersenne (1636) wrote, the terminology was still not established:

Praetorius informs us that the "discant viol or violino" was tuned $g^0 d^1 a^1 e^2$ (a violin); he refers to the same instr. as *Discant-Geige, kleine Geige, viola da braccio, violetta piccola, violino da braccio, rebecchino,* and adds that the viole da braccio were called *Geigen* or *polnische Geigen* by musicians. And Mersenne's description of compass and tuning of the *dessus, cinquième, hautecontre,* and *taille* (the first three being syns., he indicates), as well as the nomenclature given the 3 lower instrs. by the 24 *violons du Roi* (*haute-contre, taille, cinquième*), shows no progress in the elimination of confusion. It is noteworthy that both authorities draw attention to var. names given the instr. by practical musicians.

Against this background we can attempt to trace the violin back further. When Virdung wrote in 1511 he depicted a rebec, called it *kleine Geige,* and classified it among the "useless" instrs. of his day. Agricola in 1528 depicted a whole family of rebecs that he called *kleine Geigen ohne Bünde* (small Geigen without frets). They are virtually identical with that of Virdung and have 3 lateral pegs, split-level bellies with bridge set on the lower section, body and neck of one piece. Lanfranco in 1533 (*Scintille di musica*) writes of 3 sizes of *violette da arco senza tasti* (bowed violette without frets), also called *violette da braccio.* They had 3 strings, except for the 4-stringed bass. He specifies that the bottom string of the soprano was at unison with the top string of the bass and of the middle string of the tenor. No pitch names are given. Silvestro Ganassi, in the second volume of his *Regola Rubertina* of 1543, devotes a chapter to the playing of *violette senza tasti* with 3 strings. Their tunings were: soprano $g^0 d^1 a^1$, tenor $c^0 g^0 d^1$, bass $F^0 c^0 g^0$. He disapproved of the lack of frets. In Agricola's expanded edition of 1545, he mentions *polnische Geigen* tuned in 5ths, without frets; their

strings were stopped laterally by pressure of the fingernails, and he comments that as there were no frets the fingering was more difficult. Unfortunately he gives no illustration. The rebec of his earlier edition has now become a family of "small 3-stringed hand fiddles," but here the text says that they are tuned in 5ths and that "*jetzt will jeder damit umgehen*" (now everybody wants to play them) and that they serve the same use as the *polnische Geigen.* He gives tunings identical to those of Ganassi. These pitches correspond, as Hayes points out (in Source 89) to those of the 3 lowest strings of our violin, viola, and tenor violin. In 1555 Nicola Vicentino (*L'Antica musica*) still speaks of the *viole da braccio senza tasti* or *viole con tre corde senza tasti,* but a year later the Frenchman Philibert Jambe de Fer (*Epitome musical*) describes the full-fledged, 4-stringed violin (which he calls *violon*), tuned in 5ths from g^0 up, and also clearly defines the respective spheres of violin and viola da gamba, that of the violin being restricted to dance and popular music. (Later the *Dictionnaire de l'Académie Française* of 1694 echoes: . . . "*il n'y a point d'instrument plus propre a faire danser que le violon* . . ." [there is no instr. more suited for dancing than the violin], a sentiment iterated in other countries). By the time Lodovico Zacconi wrote (in 1592), the family of *viole da braccio* had all acquired their fourth string. He specifies that the top string of the bass is to be in unison with the bottom string of the soprano, and to the second highest string of the tenor. His tunings are expressed as compasses, that of the soprano, which he calls *violino,* being $g^0–b^2$, *ergo,* with strings tuned $g^0 d^1 a^1 e^2$, the tenor is given as F–A, *ergo,* $F^0 c^0 g^0 d^1$, and the bass B–D, *ergo,* $B^1 F^0 c^0 g^0$. We can now compare the pitches and tunings of Lanfranco, Ganassi, Agricola, and Zacconi, marking the strings to be tuned in unison as ⊖ :

Lanfranco, 1533   Ganassi, 1543 / Agricola, 1545   Zacconi, 1592

—	—	𝇋	a¹——	d¹——	g⁰—𝇋	e²——	d¹——	g⁰—𝇋
—	𝇋	—	d¹——	g⁰—𝇋	c⁰——	a¹——	g⁰—𝇋	c⁰——
𝇋	—	—	g⁰—𝇋	c⁰——	F⁰——	d¹——	c⁰——	F⁰——
—						g⁰—𝇋	F⁰——	B¹——

| S | T | B | S | T | B | S | T | B |

(Zacconi refers to the soprano instr. both as *viola da braccio* and as *violino,* and although he explicitly gives its compass as g⁰–b², he states in another passage that ". . . *i violini ascendono sino a 17 voci, incominciando da C fa ut sino in Alamire.*" From c⁰ to a¹ would be 13 "voices" however; did he mean a *violino* tuned c⁰ g⁰ d¹ a¹ with compass c⁰–e², 17 notes? This would be our viola).

The relationships between rebec, polnische Geige, and viola da braccio are still in need of clarification: rebec players are mentioned at the court of the dukes of Lorraine continuously from 1509 to 1528; the Lyon archives frequently mention *menestriers, tabourins, rebequets, joueurs de rebec* during the first half of the 16th c. These professional designations disappear .from the moment the word *violon* occurs, and several musicians designated until *ca.* 1550 by one of the aforementioned names are called *violons* exclusively from then on. *Violons* are recorded in 1548 in connection with the entry of Henry II and Catherine de Médicis; whether they were violins or not we cannot tell, but they were probably played out of doors (details of the indoor theatrical performances have come down to us: no violin is mentioned). At the English court a "rebecke" was employed from 1518 on; 3 are mentioned in 1626. In 1563, under Elizabeth I, Francesco of Venice is referred to as "one of our vyolons"—the same year that the Duke of Lorraine's "violes" become "violons." Two years

later, the Engl. court records list 7 "vyolons": the same men had been called "violetts" in 1559. Unambiguous at last is a violin mentioned together with a rebec in the inventory of a deceased Fr. instr. maker in 1551, as well as Rabelais's early reference (in 1564) to *violons demanchés,* and the record of a *violon de Cremone* bought in France in 1572. The obviously important role that France played in the early development and diffusion of the violin remains to be investigated (in this connection reference must be made to the *violini piccoli alla francese* that Monteverdi scored for in his *Orfeo,* first performed in 1607). Viole of different sizes as well as 4 violini and a ribecchino were played at a Florence intermedio in 1565; an ensemble of 8 viole da braccio performed at the wedding of Duke William of Bavaria in 1568; a Graz inventory of 1577 lists bass, tenor, and soprano geigen de prazo. Banchieri, writing in 1606 (*Conclusioni,* published 1609), speaks of violini da braccio and gives their tunings as g⁰ d¹ a¹ e², d⁰ g⁰ d¹ a¹, and G⁰ d⁰ a⁰ e¹, corresponding to our violin, viola, and tenor violin. Shortly thereafter (in 1618) Praetorius listed the various members of a thriving family: *Gross-Quint Bass viola da braccio,* tuned F¹ C⁰ G⁰ d⁰ a⁰; *Bass* C⁰ G⁰ d⁰ a⁰ (our violoncello) or F⁰ c⁰ g⁰ d¹ (our obs. tenor violin); *Tenor Viol* c⁰ g⁰ d¹ a¹ (our viola), *Discant Viol* or *Violino* g⁰ d¹ a¹ e² (our violin), *klein Discant*

Geig c¹ g¹ d² a² (our violino piccolo), *gar klein Geig*, called *pochette* in Fr., g¹ d² a² or a¹ e² b² (the kit). In another passage the *klein Discant Geig* is described as being a 4th higher, the *gar klein Geige* as an oct. higher than the *rechter Discant Geig* or violin.

The country of classical violin making is Italy. Brescia was already a center of *lutherie* by the time Gasparo da Salò (1540–after 1600) formed his school there. The Brescian school was relatively short-lived and became overshadowed by Cremona. Reputedly founded by Andrea Amati (*ca.* 1505–before 1580), who is usually credited with having given the violin its final form by changing the emplacement of the soundholes to their present position, the Cremona school flourished as chief center of violin making from roughly 1550 to 1760, first under the aegis of the Amati dynasty, which culminated with Nicola Amati (1596–1684) and continued until 1740 when Gerolamo Amati died, then with Nicola's pupil Antonio Stradivari (1644–1737), and Giuseppe Guarneri del Gesù (1698–1744). The only non-Italian master of the classical period to gain an international reputation was Jakob Stainer (*ca.* 1617–1683) of Absam near Innsbruck. Contributions of less importance were made by maker of Venice, Rome, and other It. cities, France, England and the Low Countries.

As a folk instr. the violin is played in certain parts of Romania with 5 or 7 additional sympathetic strings, in Norway with 4 (see: Hardanger fele). In Oklahoma it is held against the chest or waist when played as a folk instr., and the first position is there rarely exceeded. For automatic violins, see: Dea-Violina, violina, violiniste, virtuosa. See also: contra-violin, fiddle, Geige, Hardanger fele, polnische Geige, polychord, rebec, suka, tenor violin, viola pomposa, violino piccolo, violon moulé, violon stentor, violon-vielle; bassbar, bridge, pegbox, purfling, soundhole, soundpost (80 VII, 106, 145, 170; Dürer

drawing reproduced in *Archiv für Musikwissenschaft* XVI, 1959; dates for Stainer: W. Senn: *Jakob Stainer,* 1951); **2.** organ stop of narrow-scaled open cylindrical pipes, having string tone, of 19th-c. invention, occurring at 4′ and 2′ pitches (133).

Violina, automatic violin by Stránský of Vienna, in 1911, consisting of 3 violins grouped around the same axis and pressed against a rotating bow. Each violin had only 1 or 2 strings, the tone being controlled by perforated paper rolls (37).

Violinar [aug. of violin], 18th-c. expression for double bass (176).

Violin diapason (Ger.: *Geigenprinzipal*), organ stop of narrow-scaled cylindrical open metal flue pipes at 8′ or 4′ pitch, rarely at 16′ (129, 131).

Violiniste, automatic violin designed by E. Aubry and G. Boreau in 1920, with pneumatic mechanism. A conventional violin is set in a mobile cradle and its strings are stopped by levers as the instr. revolves (37).

Violino, 1. It.: violin; **2.** organ stop of flue pipes having violin diapason character, at 8′ or 4′ pitch. Also called violina (131).

Violino armonico, see: violino harmonico.

Violino-arpa, bowed chordophone designed by Prince Grégor Stourdza in 1873 and built by T. Zach of Vienna, the same size as a violin but with an irregular contour for ease in bowing, similar to Vuillaume's *contralto. It had a max. width of 36 cm. (14¼ in.). Also called violino-chitarra (132).

Violino-chitarra, syn. of violino-arpa.

Violino da braccio, see: viola da braccio.

Violino di concerto, organ stop of reed pipes found in some It. organs; it has string tone (131).

Violino di ferro, It.: nail violin.

Violino harmonico, Violino-Harmonika, name given by Senal of Bohemia to his version of the *nail violin, with sympathetic strings, made in the 1780's and with which he concertized (83).

Violino piccolo (It.) (Ger. *Quartgeige, Halbgeige*), small violin tuned $c^1 g^1 d^2 a^2$, a 4th above the ordinary violin, and equivalent to the kleine Discantgeige of Praetorius. It must have existed by 1596, when an Ambras inventory enumerates 2 *"claine Discant viole de braccio"* as well as the soprano violin. Leopold Mozart writes (in 1756) that concerti had been written for the piccolo but that this was no longer necessary as "now" everything could be played on the ordinary violin in high positions. With the improvement of violin technique the piccolo was discarded except for use as a children's instr.

Violino pomposo, a syn. of viola pomposa.

Violin-zither, see: chord zither, 2.

Violitromba, It.: trumpet marine.

Violo-clave, harmonium of unknown construction, patented by Morin de la Guerrière in 1847 (176).

Violon, 1. OProv., Fr.: violin; **2.** Ger.: double bass, Violone; **3.** 16th-c. Sp.: viola da gamba; **4.** organ stop of flue pipes, usually open but occasionally stopped, built in the 18th c. at 16' or 8' pitch, of different scales. Also called violone, contrabasso, double bass, violon d'orchestre (101).

Violon-alto (Fr.), viola designed by Michel Woldemar of Orléans *ca.* 1788, with a violin e^2 string in addition to the ordinary viola strings. It represents one of several similar attempts in the 18th c. to make the viola more competitive. Woldemar was a violinist, not a builder, and it is thought that François Lupot of Orléans built it. See also: viola alta, violalin, viola pomposa (169, 191).

Violonbass, organ stop of narrow-scaled flue pipes of wood or metal at 16' pitch, a frequently used pedal stop (131).

Violoncelle-piano (Fr.), see: mélotétraphone.

Violoncello [dim. of *violone*] (It., also Engl., Ger.) (Fr.: *violoncelle*), **1.** the

bass instr. of the violin family, tuned $C^0 G^0 d^0 a^0$, an oct. below the viola, with a compass C^0–a^2. Its total length averages 120 cm. (47 in.), body length 74–76 cm. (29–30 in.), and a speaking string length of 69–70 cm. (27⅛–27½ in.). Although similar in construction to the violin, the "cello," as it is familiarly called, differs in having relatively deeper ribs and a shorter neck.

The cello originated in the 16th c., perhaps in the mid-c., as bass member of the da braccio family, and was tuned either as it is today or one tone lower, $B^1 F^0 c^0 g^0$, a 5th below the obs. *tenor violin. Most 17th-c. sources give the lower of the 2 tunings (in England, France, and Italy), but Praetorius indicates the higher. Many surviving 17th-c. instrs. are slightly longer and wider than later ones, probably indicative of a lower pitch. Up to the end of the 17th c. the cello was known, logically enough, as bass violin. The number of its strings at that time was not always restricted to 4; 5 strings were quite common then. Praetorius describes a 5-stringed *Bassgeig da braccio* tuned $F^1 C^0 G^0 d^0 a^0$, a cello with an additional string in the bass. During the first c. of its existence the cello's role was confined to supplying a bass line to concerted works, any solo passages being given to the viola da gamba. The earliest pieces for solo cello known so far are those of Domenico Gabrielli of Bologna (not to be confused with the better-known Gabrieli) and bear the date 1689. Until the end of the 17th c. the cello had no spike: large models were big enough not to require one, and smaller models were set on footstools. With the advent of solo playing, however, a spike was found to be a great convenience to the standing performer; 5-stringed instrs. continued in use in the early part of the 18th c. Mattheson describes the cello in 1713 as having 5 or even 6 strings, but in 1756 Leopold Mozart could report that the *Bassel* or cello "formerly" had 5 strings. In the sixth suite for solo violoncello J. S. Bach calls for a 5-stringed instr., the nature of which has been the object of much speculation. The added string is tuned to e^1, and on so large an instr. this could break easily, hence a violoncello piccolo has been suggested. A number of 18th-c. cellos have come down to us with traces of holes in their back. They are known as "procession cellos" (Ger.: *Prozessionscelli*); the holes formerly served to pass a band by which the cello was suspended from the player's neck, leaving both hands free for playing in processions. In parts of Transylvania a 3-stringed cello is in use today. The strings are either plucked or tapped with a small stick (5, 89, 94, 170);

2. organ stop of 18th-c. origin, consisting of open cylindrical flue pipes of narrow scale, formerly only at 8' pitch now also at 16'. See also: bass violin, cellone.

Violoncello alto, instr. scored for by Luigi Boccherini and Franz Joseph Haydn and thought to have been a *violoncello piccolo or a *Handbassl (94).

Violoncello piccolo, small violoncello in use in the first half of the 18th c., tuned like an ordinary cello and probably intended for solo playing; J. S. Bach scored for it in several of his cantatas, and his sixth suite for solo violoncello *"à cinq acordes"* (tuned $C^0 G^0 d^0 a^0 e^1$) may have been written for this instr. or for an ordinary cello with 5 strings. In 1732 J. C. Hoffmann of Leipzig built a 5-stringed instr., 76 cm. (30 in.) long with ribs 3.8 cm. (1½ in.) deep, allegedly at Bach's request. A later instr. of his, dated 1741, is 2 cm. longer and has ribs 8 cm. (3⅛ in.) deep ribs. These are believed to represent violoncelli piccoli.

Violoncello tenore, violin-type instr. made by Eugen Sprenger of Frankfurt in 1922, with a scale exactly double that of the violin and a total length of 116 cm. (45⅝ in.) (26).

Violoncellum, free-reed keyboard instr. in form of a violoncello, patented in France by Gavelle on Sept. 26, 1896 (204).

Violoncino [dim. of *violone*], It. 17th-c. name of the violoncello.

Violon d'amour, obs. small viola d'amore in use in the 18th c., with a variable number of gut melody strings and metal sympathetic strings. The melody strings were generally 5 in number, tuned $g^0 d^1 a^1 d^2 g^2$, with 6 sympathetic strings, but examples survive with 4 melody strings (tuned $e^1 a^1 d^2 a^2$) and 12 sympathetic strings (134).

Violon de fer, Fr.: nail violin.

Violon d'orchestre, organ stop, syn. of violone.

Violone [aug. of *viola*] (It.), in the 16th c. a syn. of viola da gamba, subsequently a double-bass viola da gamba, syn. of contrabasso in Italy. The word *violone* occurs in an Este inventory of 1520. In a 1543 Verona inventory *"una cassa cum sette violoni"* and another containing *"5 violoni"* are enumerated, together with *"uno libro da insegnar la regula deli violoni";* the latter was undoubtedly Silvestro Ganassi's *Regola Rubertina,* the first volume of which appeared in 1542, the second in 1543. In another Verona inventory, undated but of the same period, the above-mentioned instrs. appear as *"viole."* At the court of the dukes of Lorraine, players called *viol* and *violleur* in 1529 are termed *vyolons* in 1562. Diego Ortiz in 1553 uses the word *violones* as a collective designation for gambas. Zarlino (*Sopplimenti,* 1588) classifies the violone among the fretted instrs. By the end of the c. the word is reserved for larger-sized violas. Banchieri in the early years of the 17th c. speaks of a *violone da gamba,* tuned $G^1 C^0 F^0 A^0 d^0 g^0$, that he considers a bass (see: viola da gamba on this point), and of a *violone in contrabasso* tuned $D^1 G^1 C^0 E^0 A^0 d^0$, a true contrabass. Thereafter terminology becomes less clear. The name was given to an instr. the size of which was not standardized, occasionally made in violin form, that stood between double bass and violoncello and is still played today, and also to a contrabass viola da gamba, somewhat smaller and with less deep body. Perhaps it is safe to say that the 17th and 18th c. understood by the term 2 different instrs., one with 4 or 5 strings, and another having 6 strings tuned in 4ths. Praetorius depicts an instr. he calls *grosse Bassgeige*, about 4½ Brunswick ft. (*ca.* 125 cm.) high, with 5 strings tuned $F^1 C^0 G^0 d^0 a^0$—our first type of violone—and speaks of the violono and its syns. *grosse Viol de gamba, Contrabasso da gamba*, saying that this instr. is tuned in 4ths. He gives 3 tunings for it: D^1-d^0, E^1-f^0 (with 6 strings each) and E^1-c^0 (5 strings). Nearly a c. later Sébastien Brossard describes (in 1703) the violone as being twice the size of a *basse de violon* (violoncello) and pitched an oct. lower. Johann Philippe Eisel in 1738 probably sums up the situation best by telling us that *basse violon, basse de violon, grosse Bassgeigen* are all syns. of violone, that the instr. has 6 strings tuned $G^1 C^0 E^0 A^0 d^0 g^0$ (a 5th below the bass gamba, that is), and that there also existed 2 other kinds of violone, namely one with a larger body and strings tuned a 4th lower ($D^1 G^1 C^0 E^0 A^0 d^0$), and another large-bodied one with only 4 strings, the lowest being 16' C (C^1); some tune it $C^1 G^1 D^0 A^0$, an oct. below the violoncello, he says, but most people prefer to tune *"per quartam"* (in 4ths, *i.e.*, $C^1 F^1 B^1 E^0$). The term is still used on the European Continent, where it denotes a small double bass. In England it is used in a historical sense only, meaning contrabass viola da gamba. See also: contrabasso da gamba, Contraviolon, double bass.

Violone da gamba, see: violone.

Violone grosso, see: Contraviolon.

Violonet, violin-type instr. intermediary in size between viola and violoncello, of F. Battachon, early 19th c. *Cf.* baryton, 2 (191, 204).

Violon moulé (Fr.), trade designation of a machine-made violin turned out in Mirecourt, France, the wood being cut and steamed, and the tables pressed between hot plates to give them the required arching.

Violonparthon, Ger. corr. of viola di bordone. See: baryton.

Violon sourdine, Fr.: mute violin.

Violon stentor, name given to a low-priced violin of Nicolas I. Vuillaume (191).

Violon-ténor, 1. Fr.: tenor violin; **2.** tenor violin designed by B. Dubois, double-bass player of the Paris Opéra, with a body length of 43½ cm. (17⅛ in.), an over-all length of 71 cm. (28 in.), height of ribs 8 cm. (3⅛ in.). A surviving specimen in the Heyer Collection at the Karl Marx University, Leipzig, is dated 1833. The instr. was tuned $G^0 d^0 a^0 e^1$, an oct. below the violin (26).

Violon-vielle (Fr.), violin to which a wheel and hurdy-gurdy keyboard were adapted by D'Laine in 1773. The keyboard contained 24 sliders. The stringing consisted of 2 melody strings and 12 metal sympathetic strings; the latter could be silenced if desired (132, 204).

Violotta, tenor violin built by Alfred Stelzner of Wiesbaden from 1891 on, tuned $G^0 d^0 a^0 e^1$, with a body length of 41 cm. (16⅛ in.), an over-all length of 71½ cm. (28 in.) (26, 169).

Violuntze, obs. Ger.: viola. The term was in use *ca.* 1600 (176).

Viool, Du.: violin.

Vipanchi vīnā (Sans.), vīnā of India, with gourd body shaped somewhat in 8 form but otherwise similar to the kachapī vīnā. *Cf.* bipanchi (132, 173).

Virgil practice clavier, mute practice keyboard in form of a clavichord, patented by Almon K. Virgil in the U.S. in 1892 and introduced to Europe in 1895, made with different compasses. The weight of the keys can be regulated as desired, and a ticking mechanism provides for ticks either when the key is depressed or when it is released, at the player's choice, or they can be silenced.

Virginal [see text] (Engl., Fr., Ger.), stringed keyboard instr., characterized by its rectangular form and plucked strings running from left to right, formerly said to have been named for the Virgin Queen of England. When it became known that the word had occurred before her lifetime, its virginal aspect was extended to include popularity "among young ladies," as a recent lexicon so neatly puts it. An alternate explanation was suggested by Sachs, who derived the word from the Lat. *virga*, rod, with reference to its jacks. The virginal was first mentioned by Paulus Paulirinus of Prague *ca.* 1460; he taught at Cracow and visited Italy twice, and may have heard the word on his travels. It was also mentioned in Basel (by Virdung in 1511) before it occurred in England, and thus cannot be considered an Engl. term. Absurd as it may sound at first, the virginal was so named because the frame drum of ancient E. Mediterranean culture was traditionally played by women. The confusion of etymons *tympanon* (drum, later dulcimer) and *cymbalon* (cymbal, later dulcimer) and resultant ambiguity of the word *cembalo* are set forth under *cembalo. The old tradition was transferred to the new plucked keyboard instrs. and their nomenclature included such terms as virginal and the 17th-c. Ger. *Frauenzimmer, Instrument vors Frauenzimmer.* (Walther still uses the latter expression in his dictionary of 1732).

Paulirinus describes the virginal as a keyboard instr. in form of a clavichord, *i.e.*, rectangular, having the sound of a harpsichord, with 32 metal strings (2½-oct. compass), so named, he says, because its sound is like that of angels' voices. Virdung took the instr. to be derived from the psaltery and described it as an oblong instr. of clavichord shape, as was probably *ung grand instrument virginal* purchased in Antwerp in 1533. In England the word was used during the 16th and 17th c. as a generic name for all plucked keyboard instrs. Thus in 1673 Henry Purcell was appointed "keeper of regalls, virginals, flutes . . ." A notable exception to this usage is the mention in one sentence of virginal, spinet, and harpsichord, occurring in Samuel Pepys's diary (Apr. 4, 1668). On the Continent the name scarcely survived the 16th c.

The virginal has the form of a rectangular box; its action is identical with that of harpsichord and spinet, differing from the latter by its shape and the direction of its strings. It has a single set of strings and jacks; the tuning pins are to the player's right, and from there the strings pass over a curved bridge and over a straight nut, the latter placed behind and parallel to the diagonal row of jacks, and are secured to hitch pins to the player's left. The keyboard is placed, not in the center, but to the left or right, that of Flem. instrs. being markedly to one side or the other. Virginals have been built in Italy, Flanders, and England. Those of Italy usually have projecting keyboards, are made of thin cypress, without lid, and were inserted into a separate housing from which they were withdrawn for performance. The Flem. school, centered at Antwerp, made its instrs. of thicker softwood, and, with the exception of the 4′ instrs. of *double virginals, its keyboards were recessed; thus when lid and drop leaf were closed the instr. formed a neat oblong box that did not require further protective housing. All surviving examples of Engl. virginals date from the 4 decades between 1640 and 1680; they combine It. and Flem. elements and have as a characteristic feature a vaulted lid. A special form was the Flem. double virginal, which combined an 8′ and a 4′ instr., and in an Innsbruck inventory of 1665 (published by F. Waldner in *Studien zur Musikwissenschaft,* 1916) mention is made of a *"spinetta darinnen 2 claine Spinetgen liegen und man alle 3 aufeinander setzen und auf einmal schlagen kann,"* a triple virginal in which all 3 instrs. could be placed one above the other and played simultaneously.

Virginalregal, see: vox virginea.

Virtuosa, automatic violin produced in

the U.S. in 1908, in which the strings of a conventional violin were stopped by a row of levers worked by electromagnets, and were "bowed" by a revolving disc controlled by an electric motor (37).

Vis-à-vis (Fr.: facing), combination piano and harpsichord, designed by Johann Andreas Stein of Augsburg by 1777 for 2 players seated opposite each other. A surviving instr. dated 1777, preserved in Verona, consists of a very long rectangular case with 3 manuals at 1 end (the 2 upper manuals are for a harpsichord with 4 sets of strings), and a 1-manual piano at the other end. The piano can be played either from its own manual or from the lowest of the 3 at the opposite end, and is furnished with a *bassoon stop. The harpsichord can be played either alone or combined with the piano. A second instr., dated 1783, has also survived. The vis-à-vis was also made by Joseph Senft of Augsburg in the 18th c.; it is thought that he may have been a pupil of Stein. But the idea was not new: a harpsichord built by Philippe Denis, with 4 manuals, 2 at each end, was exhibited in Paris in 1712, intended for 2 players, 1 playing the solo part, the other accompanying. Hofmann of Gotha made a similar instr. in 1779, furnished with a coupler. Stein's vis-à-vis was also called harmonicon (27, 33, 95).

Vis-pianoforte, *bowed keyboard instr., patented in England by Robert Thomas Worton on Nov. 16, 1861. See also: lyro-vis-pianoforte (176).

Vitula, Lat.: fiddle. The word was in use from the 11th c. on. The *Promptuarium parvulorum,* written *ca.* 1440 identifies *rybyble with vitula (61, 89 Farmer).

Vivitone, *electrophonic instr., invented by L. Loar by 1932, of the electro-mechanical type; a polyphonic instr. with electromagnetic sound generators (W. Meyer-Eppler: *Elektrische Klangerzeugung,* 1949).

Vivo, 1. *nose flute of Mangareva, of the Marquesas Islands and of Tahiti, made of bamboo, frequently ornamented, and generally having 3 front fingerholes and a rear thumbhole; 30–45 cm. (12–18 in.) long; **2.** Jew's-harp of Pukapuka, Danger Islands (8, 77).

Vizgunok (Russ.: squealer), the larger of the 2 sizes of rozhok (25).

Vizugo, 1. hourglass-shaped *double bell of the Washambala of Tanganyika, made of a piece of wood hollowed out at both ends, with 3 clappers, used for driving out demons; 23 cm. (9 in.) long; **2.** rectangular bell, also of wood, of the same people, with monoxylous handle and numerous clappers suspended from a cord. The shape is that of a flat and deep trough. It also serves to drive away demons (111).

Voamaintilany, rattle of the Majunga region of the Malagasy Republic, identical with the doka (171).

Vocal horn, syn. of ballad horn.

Vocalion, harmonium invented by James Baillie Hamilton in 1885, with 3 manuals and a pedal (89, 176).

Vogara, see: fugara.

Vogelorgel, Ger.: bird organ.

Vogelpfeife, Ger.: bird flageolet.

Vogelsang, Vogelgeschrei, see: nightingale.

Voice horn, syn. of ballad horn, 1.

Voix céleste, see: vox coelestis.

Voix humaine, see: vox humana.

Volavuk adjulona, *globular flute of the Carajá Indians of Brazil, made of a calabash, with several fingerholes. Also called laku (176).

Volo, *percussion beam of Farafangana, Malagasy Republic. It corresponds to the tsikaretika (171).

Voluta, It.: scroll.

Volute, Fr.: scroll.

Volynka [Volyn, Russ. region], Russ. literary term for bagpipe, the instr. being called by its local name (duda, koza, etc.) (13).

Võn (Pahl.), see: van.

Vordersatz (Ger.), in late med. organs those pipes that stood on the front of the wind chest, equivalent to préstant or montre. *Cf.* Hintersatz (133).

Votivtimpani, kettledrum invented 1876 by Vaclav F. Červeny of Königgrätz (Hradec Králové) and improved by him in 1882. It had a freely suspended body in form of a truncated cone (176).

Vox amorosa (Lat.), see: amorosa.

Vox angelica, organ stop of varying construction. In former centuries it was built as a 4' or 2' reed stop, in N. Germany also as a regal stop at 16' or 8' pitch with half-stopped resonators; then as a type of vox humana, in England as a small-scale dulciana, finally, on the Continent as a tremulant stop of flue pipes at 8' pitch (101, 131).

Vox barbata (Lat.: bearded voice), Lat.: gedackt organ stop. The term occurs up to the mid-17th c. and is derived from the large beards of the old gedackt pipes.

Vox coelestis (Lat.: heavenly voice), organ stop, originally of regal pipes; after the mid-19th c., in France the name was transferred to a tremulant stop of 2 ranks of pipes at 8' pitch. Also called viole céleste, voix céleste (133).

Vox humana (Lat.: human voice), **1.** in 18th-c. England a straight form of tenor oboe (see: taille des hautbois) made in 2 sections, without bell, terminating in a slight flare, with its double reed carried on a crook. The pitch was that of the tenor oboe (15, 89); **2.** organ stop of regal pipes of Fr. invention, with short resonators covered by a lid. Mersenne gives the oldest known scale, a non-progressive one with a diam. of 27 mm. for all resonators. Gottfried Silbermann seems to have introduced it to Germany from Alsace. Originally built only at 8', now it occasionally occurs at 16' also. The 16' stop is usually called baritone or baryton in Engl. and Amer. organs. It was also built as a beating stop of flue pipes. Also called anthropoglossa, Menschenstimme, voix humaine (2, 133).

Vox jubilans, syn. of vox coelestis.

Vox obtusa, Lat.: Gedackt (organ stop).

Vox pileata, Lat.: Gedackt (organ stop).

Vox virginea, organ stop of regal pipes, with wide, covered resonators, at 4' pitch, identical with the Jungfernregal, Virginalregal (133).

Vudi-vudi (Kikongo), same as kivudivudi.

Vuhudendung, *musical bow of Pentecost Island, New Hebrides, small and flat, held between the player's teeth and tapped with a little stick (17).

Vulgaris, see: tibia vulgaris.

Vul mi myel, drum of the Alur of the Congo, played during dances (30).

Vumi (Kikongo), *globular flute of the Kongo people, made of dried fruits of the *vumi* tree, with 2–4 holes, including a blowhole. Played by women and young men (185).

Vunija, bagpipe of Serbia (144).

Vurumbumbum, syn. of wurumbumba among the Bunda.

Vyuela, see: vihuela.

W

Wa, name of the dermenan in Achin (121).

Wachtelpfeife (Ger.: quail pipe), quail decoy whistle of Ger.-speaking countries. *Cf.* courcaillet, quagliere.

Wa'di, flute of ancient Egypt, possibly identical with the photinx. Also written wadai, wadeni (147).

Wagner tuba (Fr.: *tuba de Wagner;* Ger.: Wagnertuba), valved brass instr. with conical bore, played with a funnel-shaped mouthpiece, built as tenor in B♭ and bass in F at the suggestion of Richard Wagner, as he wished to obtain a tone quality intermediate between that of the horn (as it existed then) and the tuba, for the performance of *Der Ring des Nibelungen* at Bayreuth in 1876. The result was an instr. resembling a wide-bore horn in oval tuba shape, with 4 valves. The compass of the tenor is $B\flat^1$–f^2 without using the valves; with valves it descends to F^1; compass of the bass, with valves, is $B\flat^1$ (*sic*) to g^1, the tenor having an easily playable pedal tone, but the bass lacking a pedal tone. The tenor has a tube length of 277 cm. (*ca.* 8 ft.), the bass, 372 cm. (over 12 ft.). The Wagner tuba is also called Waldhorntuba or Ringtuba. In Germany the tenor is falsely designated as althorn or as alto tuba. See also: tubette (25, 170).

Wagon, classical *long zither of Japan, a koto said to be indigenous and to have developed from 6 hunter's bows laid side by side. Such bows, placed strings uppermost, once played a role in persuading the sun goddess to issue from the cave she had hidden in. Today one end of the wagon's board still has 5 notches cut in it, the 6 silk strings being attached to the 6 projecting "bows" thus created. But the oldest extant specimens point to Korean influence. The wagon consists of a long and narrow board with convex surface, tapering toward the notched end, with 6 silk strings, each passing over a movable bridge of inverted V shape, 6 cm. (2½ in.) high. Their basic (relative) tuning is $d^2 a^1 d^1 b^1 g^1 e^1$. All the strings are plucked simultaneously with a plectrum, while the left little finger plays the melody and the left hand damps the strings. The wagon is rarely played in our times. Also called ame no nori koto, azuma koto, suga koto, tobi no o koto, yamato koto (135, 144, 157).

Wahlongka, stamping tubes of British Guiana, *ca.* 150 cm. (5 ft.) long (105).

Waikoko (tobacco pipe), reedpipe of the Cayapó Indians of Brazil, made of spirally twisted grass blades, blown through a narrow aperture; 7½–28½ cm. (3–11 in.) long (105).

Wainkya, kettledrums of the Lengua Indians of the S. American Chaco, made of clay pots over which wet deer hides are stretched. They contain varying amounts of water and thus produce sounds at different pitches (105).

Wait [Frankish: *wahten*], tower watchman and, by extension, his instr. A 15th-c. *Nominale* glosses *colomaula as "wayte pype"; in 1530 Palsgrave defines wayte as "an instrument, hauboys." Although the favorite instr. was a shawm, other wind instrs. were also played (cornetts, sackbuts, recorders, curtals) and even stringed instrs. are occasionally mentioned. But the word wait seems to have been identified with the shawm—when it denoted an instr. and not its performer—since the 15th c. James Talbot, writing *ca.* 1700, lists the treble wait as 2 ft. 1¾ in. long, and his tenor measuring 2 ft. 5¾ in. is close to the Altpommer of Praetorius. *Cf.* guet, Thurnerhorn, the Fr. and Ger. equivalents (79; L. G. Langwill: *The Waits*, Hinrichsen, 1952).

Waldflöte, organ stop built in several forms: **1.** as a cylindrical Hohlflöte, of open metal flue pipes at 2′ and 1⅓′, later of wood at 8′ and 4′ with wide mouths; **2.** of inverted conical open pipes of medium scale at 2′, 1⅓′, and 1′ pitches, also a Hohlflöte; **3.** Portunal at 8′ pitch; **4.** stop of wide-scaled conical flue pipes: its usual form today. Also called flautino, silvestris, tibia silvestris, Waldpfeife. The Engl. waldflute is always made of wood; the pipes are of wide scale, open, with inverted mouths; the stop occurs in the manual at 4′ pitch (99, 133).

Waldflute, see: Waldflöte.

Wald-Hautbois, see: oboe da caccia.

Waldhorn (Ger.), **1.** the French horn; a hunting horn. An Ambras inventory of 1596 mentions a *"Waldhorn mit messing beschlagen"* (Waldhorn with brass trim); **2.** englisches Waldhorn: see cor anglais; **3.** name of the alphorn in N. Tirol; **4.** organ stop, oldest name of the horn stop in Ger.-speaking countries; also built as a cylindrical Hohlflöte, *i.e.,* it occurs both as a flue and as a reed stop; furthermore the name was given by John Compton of Nottingham to a powerful reed stop of his invention. See also: allgäuisches Waldhorn (133, 183, 198).

Waldhorntuba, see: Wagner tuba.

Waldteufel (Ger.: forest devil), *whirled friction drum of Germany, consisting of a pasteboard or tin cylinder closed at one end by parchment. A horsehair string is passed through the membrane and tied to the notched handle of a stick by which it is rotated. Up to *ca.* 1850 it was in use at Christmastide (16).

Waldtuter, name of the alphorn in S. Tirol (144).

Waldzither, syn. of Thüringer Zither.

Walking-stick bassoon (Fr.: *canne-basson;* Ger.: *Stockfagott*), 19th-c. bassoon made in form of a walking stick.

Walking-stick clarinet (Fr.: *canne-*

clarinette; Ger.: *Stockklarinette*), clarinet made in form of a walking stick during the first half of the 19th c.

Walking-stick flute (Fr.: *canne-flûte;* Ger.: *Stockflöte*), 19th-c. flute made in form of a walking stick. See also: umbrella flute.

Walking-stick oboe (Fr.: *canne-hautbois;* Ger.: *Stockoboe*), 19th-c. oboe made in form of a walking stick.

Walking-stick recorder, see: czakan.

Walking-stick trumpet (Fr.: *canne-trompette;* Ger.: *Stocktrompete*), a trumpet in form of a walking stick, invented by T. Harper of London in the 1840's (176).

Walking-stick violin (Fr.: *canne-pochette;* Ger.: *Stockgeige*), *kit in walking-stick form, invented in the mid-18th c. by Johann Wilde of St. Petersburg, and resuscitated in the 1880's by A. Lutz & Co. of Vienna (176).

Walu, see: ualu.

Walze, Ger.: barrel, 2 (3).

Walzenorgel, Ger.: barrel organ.

Walzentrommel, Ger.: cylindrical drum.

Wambi, 1. pluriarc of the Congo, with 5 bows and wooden body. Also called kissumba (176); **2.** name given in the Balumbo-Lango region of the Congo Republic to a cross between pluriarc and lute: a straight neck splits at the end into 5 sticks, each bearing a string. *Ca.* 90 cm. (3 ft.) long (141).

Waṁzdis, wamzis, obs. Lith. flute of cane or willow bark.

Wana, hand bell of the Mandja of the Congo Republic (176).

Wanaj, unidentified chordophone of ancient Persia (75 I).

Wánamigi, *musical bow of the Nocomán Indians of E. Peru, held like the tomangu, the string being stroked with a small stick (105).

Wanes, large, lancet-shaped bull-roarer of Torres Strait (176).

Wani guchi (Jap.: shark mouth), ritual gong of Japan, gilded, hung at shrine entrances and struck by worshipers (157).

Wankar, see: huancar.

Wann (Arab.), see: van.

Wansamba, Mandingo name of the laala (Collection of the Commonwealth Institute, London).

Wao, cylindrical reedpipe of the Palaung of Shan State, Burma, made of bamboo with 7 front fingerholes and a rear thumbhole, metal free reed, surmounted by a calabash acting as air reservoir (172).

Wa'r, wa'ra, var. of wa'yr.

Waranga, *stamping tube of the Cricxana, Ipurucotó, Arekuna, and Makushi Indians of S. America (105).

Warbler, see: bird whistle.

War pipe, 1. obs. mouth-blown bagpipe of Northumberland that may have been identical with the *Highland pipe; **2.** obs. mouth-blown Irish bagpipe, concerning which little is known. According to Grattan Flood, it was used in the 16th-c. Border Wars in Scotland, and had a long chanter with bell and 2 drones of unequal length. In 1909 a revival was started, based on a 16th-c. description (13, 89).

Warup, large hourglass drum of W. Torres Strait (176).

Wask-trumm (copper drum), Estonian: kettledrum.

Water drum, see: water gourd.

Water gourd (Fr.: *tambour d'eau*), half gourd or half calabash that floats, open side down, in a pan of water and is struck rhythmically with small sticks. The instr. is sometimes called water drum, a misnomer; it is not a true drum and the term leads to confusion with those membranophones that are partly filled with water. The water gourd is a development of the cupped hand beating the surface of the water. It is found in Africa, C. and S. America. In Guinea a variant form appears, that of an oblong board slightly hollowed, with a handle at each end. In Guinea the gourds are used in tuned pairs. In Dahomey and the Americas they serve principally at funerary rites. See also: gui

dounou, guïro de jobá, jícara de agua, jícara de jobá (70).

Water organ, see: hydraulos.

Wa wa erh, name of the sona in Shantung Province (142).

Wa'yr, flute of ancient Egypt, of Semitic origin (147).

Wayte, see: wait.

Wedsa, *musical bow of the Mashona of S. Rhodesia, with gourd resonator (17).

Weidenpfeife (Ger.: willow pipe), organ stop, thought to have been originally an overblowing flute stop. Later, as the name indicates, a salicional [Lat. *salix*, willow]. Weidenpfeife is also the name of a beating stop made of salicional pipes (133).

Wei-shun (Chin.: monkey bell), obs. bell of China, an instr. of the Chou dynasty, suspended from a frame by a knob carved to resemble a monkey. A cluster of small bells served as its clapper. *Ca.* 40 cm. (16 in.) high (89).

Weleri, a W. Java name of the kempul (121).

Wellatur, Ger.: roller action.

Welle, Ger.: roller.

Wellenbrett, Ger.: roller board.

Welsche fioln (Ger.), literally, foreign fiddles; they are mentioned in a 14th-c. ms. of Heinrich von Neustadt's *Gottes Zukunft,* and *"welhisch videlen"* appear in a ms. of Hugo von Trimberg written before 1430 (88, article *"Zither"*).

Welsche Geige (Ger.), literally: foreign Geige. Apparently a 16th-c. Ger. term for the viola da gamba family. Agricola speaks of grosse welsche Geigen in 1545 to describe the fretted viole, in contradistinction to the polnische Geigen and small Hand-Geigen. In a letter from Antwerp dated March 1571, Wilhelmo Olivo writes in Ger. that he is expediting a case containing a consort of 6 grosse welsche Geigen made in London by the Bassani brothers (reprinted by Wallner in *Festschrift zum 50. Geburtstag Adolf Sandberger,* 1918).

Welsh harp, see: telyn.

Welsh triple harp, an early-17th-c. Welsh contribution toward the creation of a chromatic harp. Its 3 rows of strings generally totaled 98; the outer rows were tuned diatonically: 37 strings for the right hand (bass) and 27 for the left hand (treble), with the inner row of 34 strings supplying the accidentals (153).

Welte-Mignon, *player piano made by Welte & Sons of Freiburg im Breisgau from 1904 on, controlled by means of perforated paper rolls (196).

Welte-Philharmonie, automatic organ made by Welte & Sons of Freiburg im Breisgau from 1913 on, controlled by means of perforated paper rolls (196).

Were-were, syn. of temraga (77).

Wer-wer, *bull-roarer of Java, made of thin bamboo. Also called ower-ower, ereg-ereg (121).

Westafrikanische Gitarre, a name given by some Ger.-language writers to the pluriarc.

Wewet, see: huehuetl.

Wezai, panpipes of ancient Egypt, according to Sachs (98).

Wheel cymbals, obs. Engl. term for keyboard instrs. sounded by rotating wheels (such as the Geigenwerk) (79).

Whi, end-blown *piston flute of Thailand, made of wood, with cylindrical bore (18).

Whio (whistle), syn. of porutu (77).

Whirled friction drum, *friction drum whirled by a cord that rubs on a (rosined) notch in the holding stick. See also: arran, biciŭ, bourdon, cri de la belle-mere, diable des bois, hummer, locust, rebun, ronker, tavalaika, Waldteufel (100).

Whistle [OEngl. *hwistle*] (Fr.: *sifflet;* Ger.: *Pfeife, Signalpfeife;* Sp.: *silbato*), short *end-blown flute in which the air stream is directed through a flue against the sharp edge of a lateral aperture, devoid of fingerholes and sometimes containing a captive pellet. The lower end is stopped and the instr. yields only one tone. In older Engl. literature it is usually designated as a decoy pipe, and the word is used in that sense from *ca.* 1400 on.

Prehistoric gourd whistles have been excavated at Huaca Prieta, N. Peru, 47 cm. (1⅞ in.) in diam. See also: anuman, appeau, bikut, bird whistle, botet, bulowok, bulu decot, bumbun, chilitli, cohuilotl, courcaillet, cuckoo, dakut, hua mei chiao tse, makuku, mariouneto, mbamba nsia, mbambi, mwanzi, nanga ya ntsa, nsiba, pea whistle, penny whistle, pifilka, pigeon whistle, pulik, safir-i bulbul, serēre, shao erh, siblet, sifflet, silbato, singwe, sioulet, siurell, sugs-pa, suxča, svistulka, tede, xiulet.

Whistle flute, flute with a whistle head; the same as fipple flute.

Whistling pot (Fr.: *vase siffleur;* Sp.: *silbador*), a form of globular flute of ancient S. America, consisting of 2 communicating clay vases partly filled with water. When the player blew into one pot, water was driven into the second, where the increased amount compressed the air and sent it out through the whistle head. The blowhole was placed at the top of a narrow neck. Double whistling pots also existed; they produced 2 sounds simultaneously. Whistling pots were used from El Salvador to Peru in pre-Aztec, archaic culture. Also called vaso silbador. See also: botijito, silbador, tot-tlapiztali (137, 170).

Whithorn, obs. rustic Engl. shawm, made in Oxfordshire as a signal instr. for the Whitmonday deer hunt. The double reed was made of green willow bark, the instr. proper of stouter willow bark twisted spirally. It had no fingerholes (79, 170).

Whittle and dub, a name of the *pipe and tabor ensemble that was played at the Morris dances at Whitsuntide in Oxfordshire and neighboring counties until the late 19th c. Until the 1860's every district had its piper, but they were then displaced by fiddle and concertina (13, 89 Baines).

Whizzer, syn. of bull-roarer.

Wibukannel, Estonian: bowed harp.

Wic-horn [*wicwar,* battle], MHGer.: signal horn used in battle, nearly as tall as a man. *Cf.* herhorn (169).

Wiener flöte (Ger.: Vienna flute), modern organ stop of overblowing flue pipes, usually at 8' or 4' pitch (133).

Wiener Mechanik, see: Vienna action.

Wiener Ventil, Ger.: Vienna valve.

Wiener Werkl, *barrel organ made in Vienna in the 1860's, with both flue and reed pipes, the latter being incorporated in order to save space (37).

Wikongwe, kikongwe made of bamboo or horn points (111).

Wiles-pill, Estonian: flute.

Wilmurra, *bull-roarer of the Algamurra of N. Australia, made in 2 sizes (176).

Wilwil' axtü [*wilwil,* small bird], *cross flute of the Yuma Indians of the Western U.S., made of cane, with 4 fingerholes. *Ca.* 68 cm. (27 in.) long (52).

Wilwil' telhuku'p, *end-blown flute of the Yuma Indians of the Western U.S., made of cane with a natural node left at about half its length. An aperture is cut halfway between the node and upper end, some 3 cm. (1¼ in.) long and 2 cm. (¾ in.) wide, the upper end of which is wrapped with a piece of brown paper tied by a string. It has 3 fingerholes (52).

Wimmerorgel, *barrel organ made in Germany, having a tremolo stop (37).

Wind cap, see: reed cap.

Wind chest (Fr.: *laye, sommier;* Ger.: *Windlade, Windkasten*), in the organ a boxlike reservoir that receives wind from the bellows for distribution to the pipes by means of grooves in its upper portion. Audsley defined it as that portion of an organ on which the pipes are planted, and goes on to say that Engl. writers have illogically and incorrectly described it as "soundboard," applying the term "wind chest" only to a subordinate part thereof, usually the portion below pallets and grooves (12).

Wind gauge (Fr.: *anémometre;* Ger.: *Windwage, Windprobe*), device for measuring wind pressure in organs, invented *ca.* 1667 by Christian Förner, organ builder of Wettin. It consists of a glass tube shaped like an S lying on its side,

one branch being prolonged and inserted into a socket. To measure the wind, the gauge is partly filled with water and the socket is placed over a hole of the *upper board. The wind depresses the level of the water on one side of the U-bend, raising it by the same amount on the other side. The difference between the 2 levels is measured and expressed in centimeters or inches. Also called anemometer (99).

Wind harmonica (Ger.: *Windharmonika*), **1.** instr. of unknown construction, built by A. Böhme of Duisburg in 1804; **2.** name occasionally given to the aeolodicon (176).

Windharmonika, Ger.: wind harmonica.

Wind instrument, see: aerophone.

Windkanal, Ger.: wind trunk.

Windkapsel, Ger.: reed cap.

Windkasten, Ger.: (lower section of a) wind chest.

Windlade, Ger.: (upper section of a) wind chest.

Windpfeife, Ger.: aeolian pipe.

Windprobe (Ger.), syn. of Windwage.

Wind trunk (Fr.: *porte vent;* Ger.: *Windkanal*), wooden tubes that convey the wind of an organ from reservoir to wind chest. In the high Middle Ages called *fistula maxima,* as one central wind trunk was employed then.

Windwage, Ger.: wind gauge.

Windway, the flue of an organ pipe, recorder, etc.

Winkelharfe, Ger.: angular harp.

Wiol, wiolin, Estonian: violin.

Wiola, Pol., Estonian: viola.

Wirbel, Ger.: tuning peg, tuning pin.

Wirbelbalken, obs. Ger.: pin block.

Wirbelbrett, Ger.: pegdisc.

Wirbelkasten, Ger.: pegbox.

Wirbeltrommel, Ger.: tenor drum.

Wokkepot, friction drum of Jutland, with friction stick (169).

Wolawuk adjulona, see: volavuk adjulona.

Wol kum, flat lute of Korea, with circular body, medium-long neck, 10 frets, frontal string fastener, 2 pairs of silk strings, played with a plectrum or bare fingers. It corresponds to the yüeh ch'in of China and the gekkin of Japan (66, 170).

Wongang, drum of the Kate of Sattelberg, New Guinea, similar to the oñ (28).

Wood block, syn. of Chinese block, Korean temple block.

Wrestplank [MEngl. *wresten,* to turn, twist], an older name for pin block, now obsolescent.

Wu, generic term for drum in Ewe (Sudanic language) (93).

Wupu-wupu, *friction drum of the Marutse-Mambanda country of Africa, with friction stick (16).

Wurlitzer electronic piano, *electrophonic piano, the tone being generated by hammers striking *percussion reeds, made by the Rudolph Wurlitzer Co.

Wurstfagott, Ger.: sausage bassoon.

Wurumbumba, *musical bow of the Bunda of the Congo, and of the Bihe tribe of the S. Angola Mbundu, with gourd resonator held to the stomach. *Cf.* bum-bum, 1, vurumbumbum.

Wurzhorn [Ger. *Wurzel,* root], obs. S-shaped or (natural) trumpet-shaped alphorn of the Austrian Alps, extinct since the mid-19th c. (117).

X

X . . . (Basque), see also: Ch . . .

Xabeba, var. of axabeba.

Xaque-xaque, 1. term that denotes a number of different Afro-Brazilian rattles; **2.** syn. of piano de cuia (7).

Xenorphica (Ger.: *Xänorphika;* It.: *cainorfica*), bowed keyboard instr., invented by Carl Leopold Röllig of Vienna in 1800 and later improved by Matthias Müller of Vienna, in form of a *claviharp, with separate bow for each string (149, 169).

Xeque, name given to the ganzá in Amazonia and the NE. provinces of Brazil (7).

Xequere, Afro-Brazilian calabash rattle with wooden handle (6).

Xere, 1. term that designates a number of different Afro-Brazilian rattles made of metal; **2.** syn. of piano de cuia; **3.** name of the maraca (rattle) in Pernambuco (7).

Xere de ogun, Afro-Brazilian calabash rattle, covered with a network of beads (7).

Xeremia [Lat. *calamus*], folk clarinet of Ibiza, Balearic Islands, cylindrical with cylindrical bore, with 4 front fingerholes and a rear thumbhole. Some specimens have an idioglott reed. The double xeremia is called reclam de xeremias. See also: chirimía, xirimia (13, 81).

Xeremia besona, syn. of *reclam de xeremias on Ibiza, Balearic Islands (81).

Xifla, syn. of peixet.

Xilla, Basque equivalent of chilla.

Ximbomba, on Mallorca a friction drum. *Cf.* sanbomba, simbomba, zambomba.

Xin tien, see: cai xiñ tien.

Xincherri, Basque: bell for herd animals. *Cf.* cencerro.

Xirimia, Cat., OPort.: chirimía. On Mallorca the shawm is still known by this name.

Xirribita, Basque: violin.

Xiula, syn. of chirula.

Xiulet, Cat.: whistle. *Cf.* sioulet.

Xyleuphone, keyed xylophone invented by Culmbach of Heilbronn *ca.* 1835, worked by wind pressure provided by bellows (204).

Xylharmonicon, keyed *xylosistron by Uthe of Sangerhausen, with secret action and a compass F^1–c^4, the keys F^1–C^0 merely doubling the upper oct. An imitation of the clavicylinder (169).

Xylomelodichord, keyed friction instr. patented by Naeter of Demmin on Aug. 10, 1848, with a series of wooden bars and friction cylinder (169).

Xylophone [Gk. *xylon,* wood], *percussion idiophone of Asiatic origin, consisting in its developed form of a series of graduated, tuned wooden slabs, laid parallel to one another and supported at 2 points that form vibrational nodes. Xylophones are played with 2 sticks or knobbed beaters. In its simplest form the xylophone consists of a couple of slabs played across the player's outstretched legs (usually a woman's) and struck with a stick; the slabs may be tuned or not, depending upon the area in which they occur. Later in the development the slabs are laid loosely on 2 parallel logs; next they are fastened to logs that assume the shape of a frame; then the frame becomes a trough. Gourd resonators are often placed under the slabs of African xylophones to augment the sound, and often a membrane is glued over a hole cut in each resonator—a mirliton device affecting the timbre. The highest development of the xylophone was reached in SE. Asia, where trough xylophones are depicted in the 14th c. (Panataran Temple of Java), showing 2 slabs being struck simultaneously, just as they are in certain areas of Africa today. Similarities not only in playing technique but of tunings and of the music played have led investigators to conclude that the African instrs. were introduced from SE. Asia. Kirby has recently stated that African xylophones with resonators are definitely of Mal. origin. The playing of 2 or more xylophones at once is also common to both areas. The xylophone was taken to the Americas by Africans, possibly in pre-Columbian times (Izikowitz) or by the slave trade (Sachs), and is known there chiefly by the name of marimba, the xylophone's name among several African peoples. In Europe, Arnold Schlick (in 1511) was the first to mention it; he called it *huĺtze glechter* (wooden stick); Holbein was the first to depict it (*Totentanz, ca.* 1525); Agricola (in 1528) depicted it with 25 cylindrical slabs; and Praetorius was the first (in 1620) to show it with flat slabs. Mersenne (in 1636) took it for a Turk. instr. and depicted it with 12 graduated slabs strung on a cord and held vertically, like a ladder (called *echelette*); a keyed xylophone he calls *clavicymbalum;* here the backs of the keys terminate in hammers that strike the slabs when the keys are depressed. Kircher depicts a similar instr., and one gathers that they were used by Low Country carillonneurs as practice instrs. In 1780 Laborde also knew the keyed xylophone, with 17 slabs struck by key-operated hammers. By 1810 the word xylophone had come into use (it was preceded by xylorganum). In the 1830's the instr. became better known through the efforts of J. Gusikov, a Russian who concertized with it. From then on it was admitted into *musica regularis,* acceptable to symphony orchestra and variety entertainment audiences alike, ultimately to become an important component of rhythm bands. Up to 1923 xylophones were built with 4 rows of slabs isolated on straw (hence their name of straw fiddle). Today's instr. was made possible by the invention of the arcuate notch by Hermann E. Winterhoff in 1927: an arc cut underneath the slab to improve its tone and definition of pitch.

The modern instr. has a varying compass, that of the larger instrs. being c^1–c^4, with wooden slabs arranged in 2 rows like the keys of a piano, laid on strips of felt or rubber. Each slab is furnished with a tubular metal resonator suspended vertically beneath it, the whole arrangement being set in a wheeled metal frame. The slabs can be tuned by reducing the length to raise the pitch or by reducing the thickness to lower it. For the organ stop see: hölzernes Gelächter. See also: akadinda, amadinda, ambira, angklung, anzang, bala, balafo, balak, balangi, balingi, bangi, banjanga, baza, carimba, carrasquiña, chalung, chinditi, chontang, claquebois, clavitympanum, didimbadimba, dimba, dipela, doli-doli, echelette, embaire, endara, entaala, entara, gagambangam, gambang kayu, garanktum, gbingbe, gigelira, ginebras, gubu, handja, hölzernes Gelächter, ilimba, imbila, jimba, kalanba, kalangwa, kidimba, konkon, kpedimba, krotong, kundi, kwengwe, kweningba, ligo, lilimba, linz, madera y paja, madimba, madinda, madiumba, magondo, majimba, makaji, malimba, malume, manja, manjanga, manza, marimba, mbasa, mbila, medzang, menza, menzan, menzi, midimba, mokkin, morka, mozungu, muhambi, ndara, njaga, nsatong, paningba, patouille, pattala, pendibe, penimba, pianito, queniba, ranat ek, ranat thum, rang nat, régale de bois, rigols, roneat ek, roneat thum, rongo, saron jemblang, silimba, staafspel, sticcato, straw fiddle, tatung, timbila, tinbuk, tudu kat, vilangwi, xyleuphone, xylharmonicon, xylorganum, xylorimba, xylosistron, yo (89, 124, 144 Kirby, 169, 170, 194).

Xylophone à clavier, Fr.: keyed xylophone.

Xylophon-Mundharmonika (Ger.), *mouth organ with a wooden bell instead of the metal casing, patented by Hohner of Trossingen, in 1906 (176).

Xylorganum, 17th- and 18th-c. term for xylophone, used, *i.a.*, by Kircher and Adlung.

Xylorimba, xylophone used in rhythm bands.

Xylosistron, friction xylophone invented by Uthe of Sangerhausen in 1807 or 1808, a variation on Ernst Friedrich Chladni's euphone. It consisted of a set of graduated wooden bars laid horizontally and stroked by the player's rosin-coated gloves. *Cf.* triphone, xylharmonicon (169).

Y

Yabó, *slit drum of Cuba, with one straight slit. Also called palo or palo hueco (152).

Ya cheng, friction zither of China.

Yadok, syn. of pagang.

Ya gvin, bronze cymbals of Burma, with large central boss and turned rim; 9–29 cm. (3½–11½ in.) in diam. Also called ra gvin. *Cf.* ye gwin (172).

Yak (foot; measure), *notched flute of Korea, with 3 fingerholes. It measures exactly 1 Chin. foot (229.9 mm.) and corresponds to the yo of China (89, 170).

Ya koto (light[-stringed] koto), koto of Japan, said to have evolved from the *yamato koto, with highly convex body and 8 strings, strung in pairs. The strings are secured by tuning pegs to the underside of the board. *Ca.* 110 cm. (3 ft. 7 in.) long, string length 81 cm. (32 in.) (157).

Yaktāra (Punj.: one string), *spike lute of N. India, with small coconut or gourd body, skin belly, long bamboo neck that pierces the body and projects at its lower end, and single horsehair string. An instr. of religious mendicants. *Cf.* dvitāra, ēka tantrikā, ēkatāra, ektār (173).

Ya ku, former name of the hua ku (142).

Yakumo koto (light-cloud koto), koto of Japan, very similar to the ni gen kin, formerly made of bamboo with a closed wooden bottom, now made of paulownia or cedarwood; 13 small discs in the board indicate the stopping positions. *Ca.* 110 cm. (43 in.) long (144, 157).

Yamada koto, modern koto of Japan, rather plain, with 13 silk strings and high bridges, often of ivory. *Ca.* 180 cm. (6 ft.) long. Not to be confused with the yamato koto (157).

Yamato fuye, bamboo *cross flute of Japan, lacquered on the inside and bound with silk threads, believed to be an autochthonous instr. When 6 fingerholes are closed, a scale of D E G A B D is obtained, the actual pitch varying with the length of the instr. (135, 170).

Yamato koto, syn. of wagon.

Yamilango, large drum of the Bateke of the Congo, with head of laced buffalo or antelope hide. It is strictly reserved for use of a great chief, and then only played on official occasions. It is played with 2 sticks (30).

Yang ch'in (Chin.: foreign ch'in), dulcimer of China, introduced from Europe or possibly Turkey *ca.* 1800 and varied as to form, size, and number of strings. Usually, however, it resembles a trapezoid box furnished with a lid; 2 round soundholes are cut in the wooden soundboard. The stringing is 14–20 courses of 2, 3, or 4 strings each; half of these pass over 2 bridges, the other half over one bridge and through holes pierced in the other. Tuning pins are to the right, along the oblique wall. It is played with 2 bamboo sticks. The yang ch'in corresponds to the san gen da kin of Japan. See also yang kum, yan kin (89, 142).

Yang kong, syn. of pagang.

Yang kum, dulcimer of Korea, with 14 wire strings, very pop. today. According to tradition, it was introduced from India *ca.* 1725. It is played with one bamboo stick while the instr. is held by the player's free hand. It corresponds to the yang ch'in of China (66).

Yangong, Jew's-harp of Thailand, made

of carved bamboo that reaches more than 1 m. (40 in.) in length. Also called saga-saga (173).

Yangroi, Jew's-harp of the Lesa of E. Bengal, lancet-shaped, of wood (176).

Yan kin, apparently a syn. of san gen da kin.

Yan-ljin, unidentified Tibetan instr., said to be a dulcimer (89 Picken).

Yao ch'in, *aeolian bow of Shanghai, made of 7 strings stretched over as many bamboo fragments and tied parallel to each other to a light, piriform bamboo frame. This is attached to a paper kite and makes loud humming sounds when the kite is flown (142, 148).

Yao ku, 1. pop. name of the t'ao ku; **2.** former name of the hua ku (142).

Yao p'ien, *aeolian bow of China, similar to the feng cheng, consisting of a bamboo bow 1½ m. (5 ft.) long and of a string raised over a small cylindrical bridge at each end. This is attached to the end of a kite and is flown (142, 148).

Yapurutu, large flute of the Catapoli-tani Indians of NW. Brazil (176).

Yarā, Arab. reedpipe, identical with the lira (89 Farmer).

Yareito, small Afro-Cuban drum of Oriente Province, Cuba, with single head, made of 12 staves of *yarey* palm. The head is nailed and is played with bare hands. *Ca.* 40 cm. high, with about the same diam. (152).

Yaroul, name of the argūl among the Druse of Israel (103, 120).

Yatag, zither of W. and Chakha Mongolia, similar to the Chin. cheng and now rare. A long rectangle of wood with arched top, the lower end forming an obtuse angle, is usually strung with 12 silk strings, each with its individual bridge. Only open strings are played; they are plucked with either a plectrum or the player's bare fingers and are tuned to a pentatonic scale. Compass *ca.* 2 octs. The yatag is also in use among the Volga Kalmuk and the Kirghiz; the instr. of the latter is flat and has 7 wire strings. Also called itag, yitag (69, 170).

Yawi api (jaguar bones), bone flute of the Tariana Indians of NW. Brazil (176).

Yawina, rattle of the Tariana Indians of NW. Brazil (176).

Ye gwin, musical cups of Burma. *Cf.* ya gvin (121).

Yektar, see: ektār.

Yelo, bull-roarer of the Bakairí of Brazil (176).

Yen ma, aeolian chime of China, a "mobile" of small plaques of metal, stone, or glass, suspended by silk threads from roofs or over windows and doors. Called yü k'o in ancient times, now also known as t'ieh ma (142).

Yheku, bamboo Jew's-harp of the Naga of Assam, rectangular with rounded ends and obtuse tongue. *Ca.* 12 cm. (5 in.) long (172).

Yin ch'ing, hemispheric brass gong of China, struck with a brass rod; 5–7½ cm. (2½–3 in.) in diam. (142).

Ying ku, *barrel drum of China, with nailed heads, suspended in an elaborately ornamented frame. The upper head is beaten with 2 sticks. A Confucian temple instr. formerly known as chien ku. It is 90–112 cm. (36–44 in.) high, 76 cm. (30 in.) in diam. (121, 142).

Yin lo, see: yün lo.

Yitag, syn. of yatag.

Yo (Chin.: foot, measure), **1.** *notched flute of ancient China, first mentioned in the 8th c. B.C., so named because it measured exactly 1 yo (229.9 mm.), or Chin. foot. In ancient times it had 3 fingerholes and served as a dancer's instr. As such, it became transformed in the course of time into a dancer's wand, and has been no more than a wand used in ritual dances since the 16th c.; the modern instr., called yo, is a notched flute with 6 fingerholes. *Cf.* yak, yüeh; **2.** xylophone of the Mundang-Weima of the Congo (19).

Yoara, var. of joare.

Yo ch'in, small ch'in of China, with 13 single or double strings. *Ca.* 110 cm. (43 in.) long. *Cf.* yo kin (176).

Yóeri, *musical bow of the Amahuaca

Indians of NE. Peru, made of a small piece of flat cane (105).

Yohuacán, Indo-Cuban slit drum, occasionally called palo or palo hueco (152).

Yokeli, bull-roarer of the Baoule of the Ivory Coast Republic (103).

Yo kin, koto of Japan that rests on low feet, with 13 pairs of brass strings, each with its individual movable bridge. It is 66 cm. (26 in.) long, 25 cm. (10 in.) wide, and 10 cm. (4 in.) high (157).

Yoko fuye, syn. of riũ teki.

Yoraghayi, set of 2 dholas of Bengal, connected at the base and suspended from the player's neck. The one to his right is the larger of the 2 and is played with a drumstick, that on the left with the bare hand (176).

Yotsu dake (Jap.: four bamboos), clappers of Japan, made of split bamboo. A pair is held in each hand. They are played during theatrical performances, also by mendicants; on the Ryukyu Islands also for accompanying traditional dances (135, 157).

Ysis, name given to the organistrum by Paulus Paulirinus *ca.* 1460.

Yü (Chin.: tiger), *scraper of China of considerable antiquity, of carved wood in form of a crouching tiger, with 28 notches along the back. These are scraped with a bamboo stick split halfway down its length to form 12 or more switches. A Confucian ritual instr., it corresponds to the ŏ of Korea, the gyo of Japan. *Ca.* 60 cm. (2 ft.) long (142, 170).

Yucuyu, Afro-Cuban scraper, consisting of a pole 1½ m. (5 ft.) long with a short crossbar to which 4 spherical gourds are attached so as to form a cross. This is held in the player's left hand and is shaken. The lower portion of the pole is notched, and this section is scraped simultaneously with a small stick (152).

Yüeh, a former name of the yo.

Yüeh ch'in (Chin.: moon *ch'in*), short-necked lute of China. Its flat circular body has earned it the pop. name of "moon guitar." It has a wooden belly, 10

raised frets on belly and neck, lateral pegs, frontal string fastener, 2 pairs of silk strings tuned a 5th apart. A metal tongue vibrates inside the body, rattling against it when played. *Ca.* 35 cm. (14 in.) in diam. It corresponds to the gekkin of Japan, wol kum of Korea, cai dan nguyet of Vietnam, cha pei toch of Cambodia. *Cf.* China sampan (4, 142, 170).

Yuge, side-blown trumpet of the Kakwa of Uganda, also of the Bongo and Babwendi of the Congo, with cylindrical tube. In Uganda it is 138 cm. (54 in.) long, 23 cm. (9 in.) in diam. (195).

Yü hsiao, hsiao made of marble (89).

Yuka, Afro-Cuban drum used for accompanying *yuka* dances, made from a hollowed tree trunk, cylindrical, with single head tied on; 3 sizes are used. Also called fumabata ngoma. *Cf.* tambor de tronco (152).

Yü k'o, an ancient name of the yen ma (142).

Yü ku, drum of China, made of a bamboo tube *ca.* 50 cm. (20 in.) long, 7 cm. (2½ in.) in diam., and a single head of snakeskin. A vibrating metal tongue is placed inside. It is tapped with bare fingers, and is often played together with the chien pan, principally by blind men. Also called yü t'ung (142).

Yumeru, fish-shaped *bull-roarer of the Ipurina Indians of Brazil (176).

Yun hu p'i p'a, p'i p'a of China, with neck carved in form of a cloud (89).

Yün lo, *gong chime of China, consisting of 9 or 10 small bronze gongs shaped like soup plates, all having the same diam. but of different thicknesses, suspended in 3 rows from a wooden frame and beaten with a felt-covered mallet. A Confucian and social instr. formerly also played at court. Gong *ca.* 10 cm. (4 in.) in diam. Also called yun ngao (89, 142, 170).

Yun ngao, syn. of yün lo.

Yūnqãr, obs. 3-stringed lute of Turkey, invented in the 16th c. by Shamsĩ Chelebĩ (147 Farmer).

Yupana, panpipes of the Lamisto Indians of Ecuador and Peru, with 12 pipes (105).

Yü pang, *slit drum of China, carved to resemble a fish, with a slit along its back and a loose ball of wood in its mouth; found chiefly in temples and monasteries (142). *Cf.* mu yü.

Yurupuri, wooden trumpet played in pairs by youths of the Amazon forest region (137).

Yü ti, marble ti of China. *Cf.* ok che (89).

Yü tung, syn. of yü ku.

Yuxpána, panpipes of the Pánobo Indians of S. America, with 12 pipes (105).

Z

Zabs-dung, see: zäns-dung.

Zabumba, 1. Port.: bass drum, also called bombo, bumbo; **2.** *friction drum of Brazil and El Salvador, equivalent of the zambomba; **3.** tenor or bass drum of Brazil, made in different sizes. One large and one small zabumba combined with 2 pifes make up a *cabaçal* ensemble (7, 29, 152).

Zacapa, rattle of the Taino Indians of C. America, made of dried shells. *Cf.* saccapa.

Zacatan, vertical drum of the Mayas (144).

Zaduneni svirki, beaked whistle flute of Bulgaria (89).

Zag-sal (Sum.), *arched harp of ancient Babylon; it first appeared in the third millennium B.C. and was the chief temple instr. *Cf.* zakkal (89 Galpin).

Zagu, flute of Ethiopia, similar to the nāy (144).

Zakkal (Ass.), upright, vertically strung harp of ancient Babylon; it first appeared in the second millennium B.C. *Cf.* zag-sal (89 Galpin).

Zāmar, double hornpipe of Morocco, with 2 cane pipes *ca.* 42 cm. (16½ in.) long, tied together top and bottom and inserted into large cow-horn bells. Each pipe has a single reed and 6 front fingerholes opposite one another, in 2 groups of 3. Some specimens have a small mouth horn as well. It is played by the Berbers of the Riff Mountains. *Cf.* zummare (13).

Zambé, Afro-Brazilian drum (152).

Zambi, *musical bow of the Thonga of S. Africa; it corresponds to the nxonxoro except that the stick is strung with 1–4 dried globular fruits called *maronge,* filled with pebbles (116).

Zambomba [Sp. *bomba,* jar, drum], *friction drum of Spain, with friction stick, made of clay occasionally, but also made of a cylindrical tin can; in each case one end is covered with a membrane. *Cf.* sanbomba, simbomba, ximbomba, zabumba (16, 63 Schaeffner).

Zammāra (Arab.), **1.** double reedpipe of Iraq, a folk instr. (147 Farmer); **2.** earlier form of the word *zummāra* (75 I).

Zampara, see: champara.

Zamploña, Asturian equivalent of the pipiritaño.

Zampogna [Gk. *symphonia*], mouth-blown bagpipe of Calabria, Sicily, and Malta, known by this name since the 14th c. but not described until the 17th c. The zampogna of Calabria and Sicily has a sheepskin bag, blowpipe, 2 divergent conical chanters and 2 drones, all on 1 stock, and all fitted with double reeds. It occurs in 2 forms, as a solo instr. and as an accompanying instr. In the solo form the chanters are pitched in 4ths; in the accompanying form, in octs. The accompanying form is built in 2 sizes, 1 pitched an oct. lower than the other, with the left-hand (longer) chanter of the deeper model, called *trombone,* reaching a length of 1.50 m. (5 ft.). On both forms the right-hand (shorter) chanter has 4 front fingerholes and a rear thumbhole. The left-hand (longer) chanter of the accompanying form has 4 fingerholes, 1 of which is closed by a little-finger key protected by a *fontanelle. The drones are tuned an oct. apart. The accompanying form plays together with a *ciaramella. Zampognas are traditionally played by shepherds who at Christmastide come to the towns. The Maltese zampogna, also called "zapp," has chanters consisting of 2 cane pipes terminating in a serrated bell of cow horn. The right-hand chanter has 5 holes; the left, 1 hole. *Cf.* ciarameddari (13, 14).

Zampoña, Sp. term used to designate a number of instrs.: **1.** in certain areas of Spain it is syn. of gaita, a bagpipe; **2.** also syn. of caramillo and of pipiritaño; **3.** from the 14th c. on it has designated the panpipes; **4.** on the Balearic Islands it specifically denotes a mouth-blown bagpipe with sheepskin bag, chanter, and bass drone, also 2 small dummy drones; **5.** among the Huave Indians of Mexico it is a *musical bow struck with a small stick (13, 57, 105).

Zamr, pl. **zumūr** (Arab.), **1.** conical wooden shawm of the Near East, with flaring bell, 6–8 front fingerholes, and a rear thumbhole. The double reed is attached to a removable neck, one surface of which is cut away. This acts as a capotasto, as the upper fingerholes can be blocked off by turning it. The double reed is mouthed entirely; the player breathes through his nose while playing, his lips firm against a lip rest, producing uninterrupted sound. Conical oboes of this sort are known to have existed from the 2nd c. A.C. on (170); **2.** in N. Africa the zamr is a double pipe with single reeds, similar to the zummāra of Egypt (144 Chottin).

Zamr el soghair, Arab.: small zamr (11).

Zamr siyāh nāy, syn. of nāy siyāh.

Zanfoña [Gk. *symphonia*], hurdy-gurdy of Galicia and the Asturias, Spain. Although it is still played in Galicia, it is no longer being made. *Cf.* fanfóni, founfóni, sanfoña, sanforgno, zarrabete (165).

Zanfonía, syn. of zanfoña.

Zangak, zanakik, Armenian: small bells (98).

Zangora, xylophone of the Nzakara of the Union of African Republics (42).

Zangskar, cross flute of Kashmir; it corresponds to the muralī (176).

Zanj, Afghan: bell. *Cf.* jänk (98).

Zäns-dung, copper trumpet of Tibet, with wide bore, similar to the rag-dung; 2–3 m. (6½–10 ft.) long (89 Picken).

Zanza, see: sansa.

Zaouzaya, flute of Mauretania, made of bark, with 4 front fingerholes, played by shepherds (193).

Zapotecano [of the Zapotec Indians], a Mexican name of the *marimba xylophone.

Zapp, Maltese abbr. for zampogna (13).

Zaqqal, Babylonian word meaning chordophone (170).

Zaranda, humming top of Venezuela (152).

Zarbasnay, brass cross flute of the Sart of Turkestan (176).

Zarge, Ger.: rib (of a violin).

Zarrabete, Álava dialect (of Spain): zanfoña.

Zart . . . , as a prefix to names of organ stops, zart is a syn. of echo (133).

Zartflöte (Ger.), organ stop built in many forms, the most common being a narrow-scaled cylindrical rank of stopped flue pipes, very softly voiced. It also occurs as an overblowing *Dulzflöte or as an open conical *Spitzflöte. Usually at 8′ pitch, it is also found at 4′ or 2′, with metal treble and wooden bass. See also: flûte pastorale (133).

Zauberflöte (Ger.: magic flute), organ stop of narrow-scaled, overblowing, stopped cylindrical pipes, with an overblow hole at 9/16 of the pipe length, invented by William Thynne in 1885 and first built by Michell and Thynne. It is found at 8′ and 4′ pitches (129).

Zazah, Engl. mirliton, consisting of a cylindrical tube with a membrane covered by a perforated cap. *Cf.* kazoo (25).

Zedzilava, *musical bow of the Malagasy Republic, with cylindrical stick and a gourd resonator attached at about ⅓ of its length. The gourd is pressed against the player's chest; his right hand holds a palm-leaf rattle and a piece of split cane with which he taps the string (17).

Zeinu [Lat. *signum*], Basque: church bell; syn. of ezkila.

Zeli, *percussion pot of Dahomey, used during funeral ceremonies. The open mouth of the pot is struck with the player's bare hand. Cf. zin-li.

Zeng, Pers.: bell (98), clappers (168).

Zenk, Kurdish: bell (98).

Zenze, *stick zither of the Luba of the Congo, similar to the nzenze (128).

Zero, panpipes of the Paressi-Cabishi Indians of the Mato Grosso, with 5 pipes (105).

Zeze, 1. drum of the Mobati of the Congo, in form of a truncated barrel, with 2 laced heads forming a network over the body (30); **2.** a name given to the seze in parts of Tanganyika and Uganda (139) and by the Bali and Luba of the Congo (128).

Zezilava, see: zedzilava.

Zhaleika, see: jaleika.

Zicchignola, It.: rattle.

Zichirei, rattle of Japan, with 3 small bells attached to a handle. Cf. kajirei.

Ziehharmonika, Ger.: accordion.

Zifflöt, see: Sifflöte.

Zil (Arab., Turk.), cymbals of ancient and modern Islam, in ancient times probably *finger cymbals. In Turkey they were employed in military music for several centuries and spread from there to the Balkan peoples (cf. zile) and the Kurds. Today the Kurds and the Turks still call their cymbals by this name (75 II, 98).

Zile [Turk. *zil*], cymbals of Yugoslavia (89).

Zils, syn. of zile.

Zimba, sansa of the Babunda and Bakwese of the Congo (42).

Zimbalom, see: cimbalom.

Zimbel [Lat. *cymbalum*], **1.** MHGer.: cymbalum. The word occurs in med. Ger. literature, denoting a small bell of bronze struck on the outside with a hammer. Cf. Glocke (189); **2.** Russ.: dulcimer. A folk instr. suspended from the player's neck by a band (206); **3.** mixture organ stop composed of a small number of ranks, usually not more than 3, dating back to the

15th c. Adlung qualifies it as a sharp, i.e., high-pitched, mixture. It breaks at every oct. Cf. acuta, cymbale.

Zimbelrad (Ger.: cymbal wheel), syn. of Zimbelstern.

Zimbelregal, obs. organ stop composed of a single rank of regal pipes, at 2' pitch, repeating. Praetorius mentions it as an organ reed stop at 1' pitch.

Zimbelscharf (Ger.), a high-pitched *acuta mixture stop, usually of 4 or 5 ranks. Also called Grosszymbel, Scharfzimbel (133).

Zimbelstern [Ger. *Zimbel* + *Stern*, star], auxiliary organ stop of the German Renaissance and baroque, evolved from the med. *horologium, and as such the earliest known auxiliary stop, at present being revived. Originally the stop consisted of a number of very small bells attached to a revolving star on the organ front. For reasons of symmetry a second star was usually added, but devoid of bells. Before the application of pneumatics to the organs the star was set in motion by a wind wheel (similar to the water wheel of a mill) connected to a roller. Later the bells were removed from the star—which continued nonetheless to turn —and were caused to tinkle by wind supply, as heretofore, or 3 or 4 bells, generally tuned to a major scale, were struck by hammers. This form did not become common until the late baroque. Also called Zimbelrad. See also: cascabeles (133).

Zinburrin, rustic Basque pipe made of straw or bark.

Zinburruna, name of the Basque alboka (56).

Zindimga, pl. of ndimga.

Zingenmutti, term occurring in a Graz inventory of 1577, apparently an early form of Esperanto. The concoction should properly read either "*stille Zinken*" or "*cornetti muti*"; a (mute?) reminder that music was international even in the *secolo sedetz*.

Zinj, see: sinj.

Zink, 1. Ger.: cornett; in the 18th and

19th c. the *curved cornett; 2. the smallest size Hiefhorn; 3. organ stop of reed
pipes known since the late 15th c. (Lan-
gensalsa organ, 1499), with inverted conical pipes at 8' pitch. It became obs. in
the 18th c. Zink stops labeled 4' or 2'
are 8' Zinken starting on c⁰ or c¹. Also
built as a 2-rank sesquialtera (133, 167).

Zin-li, *percussion pot of the Fan of
Dahomey, and of Dahomey Negroes in
Brazil and Cuba. A clay pot is struck with
a flat, spoon-shaped beater formed to fit
the open mouth. It is used in funeral ceremonies. Cf. canarí, idudu egu, zeli (152).

Zinzerri [Arab. *jul-jul], Basque: bell
of herd animals. Cf. cencerro, cianciana,
cincerria.

Zither [Gk. kithara, via Ger. Cither]
(Fr.: cithare, Ger.: Zither), 1. organological term for any simple (i.e., not composite) chordophone, consisting solely of
a string bearer; if there is a resonator, this
must not be integral, but must be detachable without destroying the sound-producing apparatus. A typical example of the
zither in this sense is the *musical bow,
consisting as it does of a flexible stick
and a string; the player's mouth, a gourd,
basket, etc., may or may not be used as
resonator. According to form or composition, we distinguish *bar, *board, *box,
*frame, *ground, half-tube, *harp, *long,
*raft, *stick, *trough, and *tube zithers.
Musical bows as well as raft and tube
zithers, whether whole or half tube, may
be either idiochord or heterochord. Of all
these the board zither is the most highly
developed and from a Western viewpoint
the most important, as it includes all
stringed keyboard instrs.;

2. a Ger. name for the cittern until the
18th c. Thereafter it was used only to
designate: 3. a folk zither of the Austrian
and Bavarian Alps, a box zither descended from the *Scheitholt, now also
found in Slovenia. One of the oldest in
existence, dated 1675, was made in the
S. Tirol and still preserves the rectangular
form of the Scheitholt: it has 2 melody
strings and 2 accompaniment strings, the

former stretched over a fingerboard with
14 frets. Up to the 1830's rectangular
zithers were still being made. At that time
2 schools of building were developed, one
at Mittenwald (*Mittenwald zither) and
one in the Salzburg area (*Salzburg
zither). Until the late 18th c. the zither
was restricted to the Alpine regions, but
then the Alps were "discovered" by travelers, and, with them, the zither. This resulted in a flurry of building, and zithers
were made in different sizes for ensemble
playing, such as the Prim, Terz, and Alt
zither, and in different types, such as
*bowed zither, *Elegiezither, etc. During
the 19th c. the zither lost its Scheitholt-
like scroll and assumed its standard
forms. Basically it is a flat rectangular box
zither. One long side, that next to the
player, carries a fretted fingerboard, and
a large soundhole is cut into the center of
the soundboard. Two sets of strings are
used: one for the melody, the other for
accompaniment. Their number varies
considerably, but 4 melody strings are
common, tuned c⁰ g⁰ d¹ a¹, with up to
37 accompaniment strings. The steel melody strings are played with the player's
right thumb, wearing a ring plectrum,
while his left hand stops them by pressing
them against the frets. The gut accompaniment strings are played with the first,
second, and third fingers of the right
hand. Three sizes were commonly made,
the largest of which was known as concert zither (22, 100, 117, 151).

Zither banjo, banjo with parchment
belly stretched over a hoop, with machine head and 5 strings; 3 of these are
metal, 1 is gut, and 1 is spun silk. Not
to be confused with banjo zither (89).

Zitherelegie, harp invented ca. 1880 by
Raab. A zither in name only, it is not to
be confused with the Elegiezither (22).

Zither-Konzerttisch (Ger.: concert table zither), a combination of 3 zithers,
pipework with 25 flue pipes, metallophone, and drum, all in a table-shaped
housing, invented ca. 1873 by Franz
Böhm of Griesbach, Germany (176).

Zitherpiano, chord zither similar to the autoharp (149).

Zit-idoatl, see: tzit-idoatl.

Zitol, zittol, MHGer.: citole.

Zitter, obs. Ger.: cittern.

Zocchetto, It.: block (of a violin).

Zoku sō, a sō no koto evolved from the tsukushi sō, now simply called "koto" (144).

Zooglossa (Gk.: animal voice), name given by Athanasius Kircher in the 17th c. to the old (uncovered) Krummhornregal (organ stop) (133).

Zozoloctli, gourd trumpet of the Aztecs. *Cf.* cocoloctli (144).

Zuffolo [?Lat. *sibilus* via It. *zuffolare,* to blow], short It. *whistle flute, recorded from the 14th c. on, traditionally made of boxwood, with conical bore, 2 front fingerholes, and rear thumbhole, *ca.* 8 cm. (3 in.) in over-all length, terminating in a flare. The scale is completed by stopping the bell with the palm of the hand. By playing it as an open pipe, a stopped pipe, and a half-stopped pipe, and by overblowing, a total compass of b^0–c^3 is obtained. This is the pipe that was popularized abroad by Picco and became known as the *Picco pipe. Grassineau (in 1740) reports that it was also used to teach birds how to sing tunes. In the 18th c. the word was applied to any kind of whistle, today it refers only to a tin whistle. In Sicily, however, the term applies to a very widebore beaked flute with 6 equidistant fingerholes, played by shepherds, with a max. length of 29 cm. (11½ in.) (87, 89).

Zuffolo pastorale, name occasionally given to the panpipes in Lombardy. *Cf.* ciufolo pastorale (132).

Zug (Ger.), **1.** slide (trombone, etc.); **2.** stop (keyboard instrs.); **3.** speaking length of pipe or string; used in this sense by Praetorius apropos of viols.

Zuglum, imported chordophone played by the Bagolo of Mindanao, Philippine Islands, with neck and elongated body made of 1 piece of wood, and 2 strings;

1 of these passes over 7 bridges. It is 125–150 cm. (50–60 in.) long (176).

Zugposaune, Ger.: slide trombone.

Zugtrompete, Ger.: slide trumpet.

Zūkra, bagpipe of Tripoli and Tunisia, mouth-blown, with kidskin bag, 2 parallel chanters of cane, each terminating in a small cow-horn bell and furnished with a single reed. Each chanter has 5 fingerholes. Also called zuqqāra (13, 170).

Zulami [*nāy zunāmī*], med. double shawm of the Arabs (98).

Zumba, 1. Basque: large cowbell (56); **2.** in Spain and Lat. America, bull-roarer (152).

Zumbador (Sp.: buzzer), Sp.: bull-roarer (152).

Zumbidor, bull-roarer of Brazil (152).

Zummāra (Arab.), Arab. double clarinet, distributed all over the Near East, descended from the ancient memet. The 2 parallel cylindrical pipes are always of the same length and always have the same number of equidistant fingerholes. One hole of both pipes is stopped by a single finger. The single reeds are upcut. The sound produced is tremulant, caused by the roughly cut holes in uneven cane. It is 18–43 cm. (7–17 in.) long. See also: zāmar, zummare (89, 144 Hickmann, 170).

Zummāra arbawija [Arab. *arba,* four], zummāra with 4 fingerholes on each pipe (144, 168).

Zummāra chamsāwija [Arab. *chansa,* five], zummāra with 5 fingerholes on each pipe (144, 168).

Zummāra sattawija, zummāra with 6 fingerholes on each pipe (144, 168).

Zummare, double hornpipe of S. Albania, consisting of 2 cane pipes *ca.* 13 cm. (5 in.) long, tied together, and a bell of cow horn or chamois horn. Each pipe is fitted with a single reed that is mouthed directly, usually having 5 equal fingerholes (13).

Zumūr, pl. of zamr.

Zungenpfeife, Ger.: reed pipe.

Zungenstimme, Ger.: reed stop (in the organ).

Zungenwerk (Ger.), syn. of Rohrwerk.

Zupfgeige (plucked fiddle), coll. S. Ger.: **1.** grosse Zupfgeige: the harp; **2.** kleine Zupfgeige: the guitar.

Zupfidiophon, Ger.: plucked idiophone, linguaphone.

Zupftrommel, Ger.: plucked drum.

Zuqqāra, syn. of zūkra.

Zūqra, see: zūkra.

Zurgalău, Rom.: pellet bell (5).

Zurla [Turk. *zurnā*], shawm of Yugoslavia, introduced a relatively short while ago by gypsies from Persia, and made in 2 sizes from a single piece of maple or fruit wood, with the upper part of the bore cylindrical, the lower part conical, 7 front fingerholes, and a rear thumbhole, plus a number of ventholes. It is played with a pirouette in the Oriental manner, with blown-out cheeks. The same instr. is found in W. Bulgaria and in Albania. See: surla, zurnā (11, 34).

Zurna, name of the bagpipe in the Caucasus (13).

Zurnā (Arab., Kurdish, Slav., Turk.), shawm of the Near East, with conical bore terminating in a flared bell, 7 front fingerholes, and a rear thumbhole, plus several ventholes near the lower end. Under modified names, also found in the Balkans, India, Indonesia. *Cf.* sānāyī,

sarnā, sarnai, sarune, sernei, serunai, serunen, srune, sruni, surle, surna, surnā, surnāy, surnāya, zurnē, zurni.

Zurnē [Turk. *zurnā*], shawm of Albania. *Cf.* zurnā.

Zurni, shawm of Bulgaria. *Cf.* zurnā (89).

Zurr, end-blown flute of the Kalmuk, with 3 fingerholes, now rare (69).

Zurrumbera, bull-roarer of N. Spain (152).

Zuzu, ground bow of the Balese of Tshumunange, the Congo (128).

Zwerchflöte (Ger.), instr. mentioned in several Renaissance inventories, possibly identical with the Dulzflöte. Not identical with Zwerchpfeife, as both are mentioned separately in some texts.

Zwerchpfeife [MHGer. *twerch*, diagonal, across], obs. Ger.: *cross flute. The term is first recorded in the 14th c. and maintained itself longest in Bavaria; also an organ stop, syn. of Schweizerpfeife and Traversflöte (168).

Zwergpfeife, var. of Zwerchpfeife.

Zylinderventil, Ger.: rotary valve.

Zymbel, 1. obs. Ger.: cymbal; **2.** organ stop, see: Zimbel.

Zymbel . . . , see: Zimbel . . .

Zymbelrad, obs. Sp. of Zimbelrad.

SOURCES REFERRED TO BY NUMBER IN THE TEXT

1 Aarflot, Olav. *Kinesisk musikk*. Oslo, 1948.
2 Adlung, Jacob. *Anleitung zur musikalischen Gelahrtheit*. Erfurt, 1758.
3 Adlung, Jacob. *Musica mechanica organoedi*. Berlin, 1768.
4 Alender, I. S. *Musical Instruments of China* (in Russian). Moscow, 1958.
5 Alexandru, Tiberiu. *Instrumentele muzicale ale poporului romîn*. Bucharest, 1956.
6 Alvarenga, Oneyda. *Catálogo ilustrado do museu folclórico*. São Paulo, 1950.
7 Alvarenga, Oneyda. *Música popular brasileña*. Buenos Aires, 1947.
8 Andersen, H. *Maori Music*. New Plymouth, New Zealand, 1935.
9 Anderssen, Otto. *The Bowed-Harp*. London, 1930.
10 Ankermann, Bernhard. "Die afrikanische Musikinstrumente," in *Ethnologisches Notizblatt*, Vol. 3. Berlin, 1901.
11 Arbatsky, Yury. *Beating the Tupan in the Central Balkans*. Chicago, 1953.
12 Audsley, George A. *The Art of Organ Building*. New York, 1905.
13 Baines, Anthony. *Bagpipes*. Oxford, 1960.
14 Baines, Anthony. *Woodwind Instruments and Their History*. London, 1957.
15 Baines, Anthony, editor. *Musical Instruments Through the Ages*. London, 1961.
16 Balfour, Henry. "The Friction Drum," in *Journal of the Royal Anthropological Institute*, Vol. 37. London, 1907.
17 Balfour, Henry. *The Natural History of the Musical Bow*. Oxford, 1899.
18 Balfour, Henry. "Report on a Collection of Musical Instruments from the Siamese Malay States and Perak," in *Fasciculi Malayensis, Anthropology*, Part II. Liverpool, 1904.
19 Baumann, Hermann. "Die materielle Kultur der Azande und Mangbetu," in *Baesseler Archiv*, Vol. 2. Berlin, 1927.
20 Bedos de Celle, François. *L'Art du facteur d'orgues*. Paris, 1766–78.
21 Behn, Friedrich. *Musikleben im Altertum und fühen Mittelalter*. Stuttgart, 1954.
22 Bennert, J. E. *Die Technik der Zither*. N.d.
23 Benoit, Fernand. *La Provence et le Comtat Venaissin*. Paris, 1949.
24 Bermudo, Juan. *Declaracción de instrumentos musicales*. Osuna, 1555.
25 Bessaraboff, Nicholas. *Ancient European Musical Instruments*. Boston, 1941.
26 Besseler, Heinrich. *Zum Problem der Tenorgeige*. Heidelberg, 1949.
27 Boalch, Donald H. *Makers of the Harpsichord and Clavichord*. London, 1956.
28 Bodrogi, Tibor. *Yabim Drums in the Biró Collection*. Budapest, 1950.
29 *Boletín latino-americano de música*. Vol. 6, 1946.
30 Boone, Olga. "Les Tambours du Congo Belge et du Ruanda-Urundi," *Annales du Musée du Congo Belge*. Tervueren, 1951.
31 Boone, Olga. "Les Xylophones du Congo Belge," *Annales du Musée du Congo Belge, Ethnographie*, Series III. Tervueren, 1936.
32 Bose, Fritz. "Musik der Uitoto," in *Zeitschrift für vergleichende Musikwissenschaft*, Vol. 2. Berlin, 1934.

33 Brenet, Michel. *Dictionnaire pratique et historique de la musique.* Paris, 1926.
34 Brömse, Peter. *Flöten, Schalmeien und Sackpfeifen Südslaviens.* Brno, 1937.
35 Brücker, Fritz. *Die Blasinstrumente in der altfranzösischen Literatur.* Giessen, 1926.
36 Buchner, Alexandr. *Extinct Woodwind Instruments of the 16th Century.* Prague, 1952.
37 Buchner, Alexandr. *Mechanical Musical Instruments.* London, n.d.
38 Buchner, Alexandr. *Musikinstrumente im Wandel der Zeit.* Prague, 1956.
39 Buonanni, Filippo. *Gabinetto armonico.* Rome, 1722.
40 *Carl Claudius' samling af gamle musikinstrumenter.* Copenhagen, 1931.
41 Carse, Adam. *The Orchestra in the XVIIIth Century.* Cambridge, 1950.
42 Chauvet, Stephen. *Musique nègre.* Paris, 1929.
43 Clark, John E. T. *Musical Boxes.* London, 1952.
44 Corominas, J. *Diccionario crítico etimológico de la lengua castellana.* Madrid, 1954.
45 Courlander, Harold. "Notes from an Abyssinian Diary," in *Musical Quarterly,* Vol. 30. New York, July 1944.
46 Danielou, Alain. *A Catalogue of Recorded . . . Indian Music,* Introduction. UNESCO, Paris, 1952.
47 ———. *La Musique du Cambodge et du Laos.* Pondicherry, 1957.
48 Daremberg, Charles Victor, and Saglio, Edmond. *Dictionnaire des antiquités grecques et romaines.* Paris, 1873–1919.
49 Densmore, Frances. "Chippewa Customs." Bureau of American Ethnology, Bulletin No. 86. Washington, 1929.
50 ———. "Northern Ute Music," Bureau of American Ethnology, Bulletin No. 75. Washington, 1922.
51 ———. "Papago Music," Bureau of American Ethnology, Bulletin No. 90. Washington, 1929.
52 ———. "Yuman and Yaki Music," Bureau of American Ethnology, Bulletin No. 110. Washington, 1932.
53 Dick, Friedrich. *Bezeichnungen für Saiten- und Schlaginstrumente in der altfranzösischen Literatur.* Giessen, 1932.
54 Dincser, Oszkár. *Két cziki hangsza mozsika és gardon.* Budapest, 1943.
55 Disertori, B.
   a. "L'Arciviolatalira in un quadro del Secento," in *Rivista musicale italiana,* Vol. 44. Turin, 1940;
   b. "Pratica e tecnica della lira da braccio," in *Rivista musicale italiana,* Vol. 45. Turin, 1941.
56 Donostia, José Antonio de. "Instrumentos musicales del pueblo vasco," in *Anuario musical,* Vol. 7, 1952.
57 Donostia, José Antonio de, and Tomás, Juan. "Instrumentos de música popular española," in *Anuario musical,* Vol. 2. Barcelona, 1947.
58 Dorf, Richard A. *Electronic Musical Instruments.* New York, 1959.
59 Douglas, Alan. *Electrical Production of Music.* London, 1957.
60 ———. *The Electronic Musical Instrument Manual.* London, 1957.
61 Ducange, Charles. *Glossarium ad scriptores mediae et infimae latinitatis.* 1733–36.
62 Dufourcq, Norbert. *Esquisse d'une histoire de l'orgue en France.* Paris, 1935.
63 ———. (editor). *La Musique des origines à nos jours.* Paris, 1946.
64 Dupont, Wilhelm. *Geschichte der musikalischen Temperatur.* Kassel, 1935.
65 Duriyanga, Phra Chen. *Thai Music.* Bangkok, 1954.

66   Eckardt, Andreas, O.S.B. *Koreanische Musik*. Tokyo, 1930.

67   Eisel, Johann Philipp. *Musicus autodidactos*. Erfurt, 1738.

68   Elwin, Verrier. *The Muria and Their Ghotul*. Bombay, 1947.

69   Emsheimer, Ernst. *The Music of the Mongols*. Publication No. 21 of the Sino-Swedish Expedition. Stockholm, 1943.

70   *Encyclopédie de la musique*. Paris, 1958–61.

71   Farmer, Henry George. "Byzantine Musical Instruction in the 9th Century," in *Journal of the Royal Asiatic Society*. London, 1925.

72   ———. "Early References to Music in the Western Sudan," in *Journal of the Royal Asiatic Society*. London, 1939.

73   ———. *Military Music*. New York, 1950.

74   ———. *The Minstrelsy of the Arabian Nights*. Bearsden, Scotland, 1945.

75   ———. *Studies in Oriental Musical Instruments;* Series I, London, 1931; Series II, Glasgow, 1939.

76   ———. *Turkish Instruments of Music in the 17th Century*. Glasgow, 1937.

77   Fischer, H. *Schallgeräte in Ozeanien*. Strasbourg, 1958.

78   Furetière, Antoine. *Dictionnaire universel*. 1690.

79   Galpin, Francis W. *Old English Instruments of Music*. London, 1932.

80   *Galpin Society Journal, The*, Vol. 1. 1948–.

81   García Matos, M. "Las xeremies de la Isla de Ibiza," in *Anuario Musical*, Vol. 9. Barcelona, 1954.

82   Gay, Victor. *Glossaire archéologique du Moyen Age et de la Renaissance*. Paris, 1882–1928.

83   Gerber, Ernst Ludwig. *Historisch-biographisches Lexikon der Tonkünstler*. Leipzig, 1792, 1812–14.

84   Gerson-Kiwi, Edith. "Musique," in *Dictionnaire de la Bible*. Paris, 1950.

85   Godefroy, Frédéric. *Dictionnaire de l'ancienne langue française*. 1880–1902.

86   Götz, J. "Die Fidelmusik in der Iglauer Sprachinsel," in *Bericht des 3. Kongresses der IMG*, 1909.

87   Grassineau, James. *A Musical Dictionary*. London, 1740.

88   Grimm, Jakob, and Grimm, Wilhelm. *Deutsches Wörterbuch*. 1854–.

89   Grove's Dictionary of Music and Musicians, 5th edition. London, 1954.

90   Halle, Johann Samuel. *Werkstätte der heutigen Künste*. Vol. 3. Berlin, 1764.

91   Hammerich, Angul. *Das musikhistorische Museum zu Kopenhagen. Beschreibender Katalog*. Copenhagen, 1911.

92   Harding, Rosamund E. M. *The Pianoforte*. Cambridge, 1933.

93   Hause, Helen E. "Terms for Musical Instruments in the Sudanic Languages," *Supplement to the Journal of the American Oriental Society*, Vol. 68. New Haven, Conn., 1948.

94   Hayes, Gerald. *Musical Instruments and Their Music*. London, 1928–30.

95   Hertz, Eva. *Johann Andreas Stein*. Würzburg, 1937.

96   Hickmann, Hans. *Catalogue général des antiquités égyptiennes au Musée du Caire. Instruments de musique*. Cairo, 1949.

97   ———. *Les Harpes de l'Égypte pharaonique*. Cairo, 1953.

98   ———. *Terminologie arabe des instruments de musique*. Cairo, 1947.

99   Hopkins, Edward J. *The Organ*. London, 1855.

100   Hornbostel, E. M. von, and Sachs, Curt. "Classification of Musical Instruments," translated by Anthony Baines and Klaus P. Wachsmann, in *The Galpin Society Journal*, Vol. 14. N.p., 1961.

101   Hunt, N. A. Bonavia. *Modern Organ Stops*. London, 1923.

102 In der Gand, Hanns. "Volkstümliche Musikinstrumente der Schweiz," in *Schweizer Archiv für Volkskunde*, Vol. 36, 1937–38.

103 *International Catalogue of Published Records of Folk Music*, edited by K. P. Wachsmann. International Folk Music Council. London, 1960.

104 Izikowitz, Karl Gustav. "Les Instruments de musique des Indiens Uro-Chipaya," in *Revista del Instituto de Etnología*, Vol. 2. 1932.

105 ———. *Musical and Other Sound Instruments of the South American Indians*. Gothenborg, 1935.

106 Jacquot, Albert. *La Musique en Lorraine*. Paris, 1886.

107 Jamieson, J. Etymological Dictionary of the Scottish Language. Edinburgh, 1808, 1825.

108 Jenkins, Jean L. Personal communication.

109 Jones, A. M. *Studies in African Music*. London, 1959.

110 *Journal of the International Folk Music Council*, Vol. 13. London, 1961.

111 Karasek, A. "Beiträge zur Kenntnis der Waschambara," in *Baessler-Archiv*, Vol. 7. Leipzig and Berlin, 1918–22.

112 Kaudern, Walter. *Musical Instruments in Celebes*. Gothenborg, 1927.

113 King, Alexander Hyatt. "The Musical Glasses and Glass Harmonica," in *Proceedings of the Royal Music Association*. London, 1946.

114 Kinsky, Georg. "Doppelrohrblattinstrumente mit Windkapsel," in *Archiv für Mussikwissenschaft*, Vol. 7. 1925.

115 ———. *Musikhistorisches Museum von Wilhelm Heyer in Cöln. Katalog*, Vols. 1, 2. Cologne, 1910, 1912.

116 Kirby, Percival R. *The Musical Instruments of the Native Races of South Africa*. London, 1934.

117 Klier, Karl M. *Volkstümliche Musikinstrumente in den Alpen*. Kassel, 1956.

118 Kunst, Jaap. *The Cultural Background of Indonesian Music*. Amsterdam, 1949.

119 ———. *Een en ander over de muziek en den dans op de Kei-Eilanden*. Amsterdam, 1945.

120 ———. *Ethnomusicology*, 3rd edition. The Hague, 1959.

121 ———. *The Music of Java*. The Hague, 1949.

122 ———. *Muziek en dans in de Buitengewesten*. Amsterdam, 1946.

123 ———. "The Origin of the Kemanak," in *Bijdragen tot de tael-, land- en volkenkunde*, Part 116. 1960.

124 Laborde, Jean Benjamin de. *Essai sur la musique ancienne et moderne*. Paris, 1780.

125 Langwill, Lyndesay G. *The Bassoon and Double Bassoon*. London, 1948.

126 ———. *An Index of Musical Wind-instrument Makers*, 1st and 2nd editions. Edinburgh, 1960, 1962.

127 Larousse de la musique. Paris, 1957.

128 Laurenty, J. S. *Les chordophones du Congo Belge et du Ruanda-Urundi*. Tervueren, 1960.

129 Lewis, Walter, and Lewis, Thomas. *Modern Organ Building*. London, 1939.

130 Lindblom, G. "Die Stosstrommel, insbesondere in Afrika," in *Ethnos*, Vol. 10. Stockholm, 1945.

131 Locher, Carl. *Die Orgelregister*. Berlin, 1912.

132 Mahillon, Victor. Catalogue descriptif et analytique du Musée Instrumental du Conservatoire de Bruxelles. 1893–1922.

133 Mahrenholz, Christian. *Die Orgelregister, ihre Geschichte und ihr Bau*. Kassel, 1942.

134 Majer, Joseph F. B. C. *Museum musicum*. Halle, 1732.

135 Malm, William P. *Japanese Music and Musical Instruments*. Rutland, Vt., and Tokyo, 1959.

136 Marcel-Dubois, Claudie. Contributions in *La Musique des origines à nos jours*, edited by Norbert Dufourcq. Paris, 1946.

137 Martí, Samuel. *Instrumentos musicales precortesianos*. Mexico City, 1955.

138 Meerwarth, A. M. A guide to the collection of musical instruments . . . of the Indian Museum, Calcutta. Calcutta, 1917.

139 Merriam, Alan P. "Musical instruments . . . [of] the Bashi," in *Zaire*, Vol. IX. 1955.

140 Mersenne, Marin. *Harmonie universelle*. Paris, 1636; and *Harmonicorum libri XII*. Paris, 1635 and 1648.

141 Montandon, George. La généologie des instruments de musique. Geneva, 1919.

142 Moule, A. C. "A List of the Musical and Other Sound-producing Instruments of the Chinese," in *Journal of the North China Branch of the Royal Asiatic Society*, Vol. 39. London, 1908.

144 *Musik in Geschichte und Gegenwart*. Kassel and Basel, 1949.

145 Nagel, Willibald. *Annalen der englischen Hofmusik*, supplement to *Monatshefte für Musikgeschichte*, Vols. 26–27. 1894–95.

146 Nettl, Bruno. *Cheremis Musical Styles*. Bloomington, Indiana, 1960.

147 *New Oxford History of Music*. Vol. 1, "Ancient and Oriental Music." London, 1957.

148 Norlind, Tobias. "Beiträge zur chinesischen Instrumentengeschichte," in *Svensk tidskrift f. musikforskning*, Vol. 15. Stockholm, 1933.

149 ———. *Systematik der Saiteninstrumente*. Stockholm, 1936; Hanover, 1939.

150 Old Guard, An. *The Coach Horn*. London, n.d.

151 Olson, Harry F. *Musical Engineering*. New York, 1952.

152 Ortiz, Fernando. *Los Instromentos de la música afrocubana*. Havana, 1952–55.

153 Peale, I. C. *Welsh Musical Instruments*, in *Man*, Vol. 47. London, February 1947.

154 Pedrell, Felipe. *Emporio científico e histórico de organografía musical antiqua española*. Barcelona, 1902.

155 Peery, Paul D. *Chimes and Electronic Carillons*. New York, 1948.

156 Pierre, Constant. *Les Facteurs d'instruments de musique*. Paris, 1893.

157 Piggott, Francis. *The Music and Musical Instruments of Japan*. London. 1909.

158 Pontécoulant, Louis Adolphe. *Organographie. Essai sur la facture instrumentale*. Paris, 1861.

159 Praetorius, Michael. *Syntagma musicum*, Parts II, III. 1618, 1619.

160 Price, Frank Percival. *The Carillon*. London, 1933.

161 Quoika, Rudolf. *Altösterreichische Hornwerke*. Berlin, 1959.

162 Rattray, R. S. *Ashanti*. Oxford, 1923.

163 Reinhard, Kurt. "Trommeltänze aus der Süd-Türkei," in *Journal of the International Folk Music Council*, Vol. 13. 1911.

164 Rendall, F. G. *The Clarinet*. London, 1954.

165 Ricart-Matas, J. Personal communication.

166 Richelet, Pierre. *Dictionnaire françois*. 1680.

167 Rücker, Ingeborg. *Die deutsche Orgel am Oberrhein um 1500*. Freiburg i. Br. 1940.

168 Sachs, Curt. *Geist und Werden der Musikinstrumente*. Berlin, 1929.

169 ———. *Handbuch der Musikinstrumentenkunde*. Leipzig, 1920.

170 ———. *The History of Musical Instruments*. New York, 1940.

171 ———. *Les instruments de musique de Madagascar*. Paris, 1938.

172 ———. *Die Musikinstrumente Birmas und Assams.* Munich, 1917.
173 ———. *Die Musikinstrumente Indiens und Indonesiens.* Berlin, 1915.
174 ———. "Die Musikinstrumente Lithauens," in *Internationales Archiv für Ethnographie.* Vol. 23. 1915.
175 ———. *Our Musical Heritage.* New York, 1955.
176 ———. *Reallexikon der Musikinstrumente.* Berlin, 1913.
177 ———. *The Rise of Music in the Ancient World.* New York, 1943.
178 ———. *Sammlung alter Musikinstrumente bei der staatlichen Hochschule für Musik zu Berlin. Beschreibender Katalog.* Berlin, 1922.
179 Sambamoorthy, P. *Catalogue of the Musical Instruments Exhibited in the Government Museum,* Madras. 1931.
179A *Sammelbände der internationalen Musikgesellschaft.* Leipzig.
180 Schad, G. *Musik und Musikausdrücke in der Mittelenglischen Literatur.* Giessen, 1911.
181 Schaeffner, André. *Les Kissi.* Paris, 1929. Source unavailable at time of writing.
182 ———. *L'Origine des instruments de musique.* Paris, 1936.
183 Schlosser, Julius von. *Die Sammlung alter Musikinstrumente.* Vienna, 1920.
184 Schneider, Wilhelm. *Historisch-technische Beschreibung der musikalischen Instrumente,* Neiss, 1834.
185 Söderberg, Bertil. *Les Instruments de musique du Bas-Congo et dans les régions avoisinantes.* Stockholm, 1956.
185A Steger, Hugo. *David Rex et propheta.* Nürnberg, 1961.
186 Sumner, W. L. *The Organ.* London, 1955.
187 Szadrowsky, H. "Die Musik und die tonerzeugende Instrumente der Alpenbewohner," in *Jahrbuch des schweizer Alpenclubs,* Vol. 4. 1867/8.
188 Theobald, Wilhelm. "Technik des Handwerks im 10. Jahrhundert." *Des Theophilus Presbyter Diversarum Artium Schedula.* Berlin, 1933.
189 Treder, Dorothea. *Musikinstrumente in höfischen Epen.* Bamberg, 1933.
190 Trichet, P. *Traité des instruments (vers 1640).* Edited by François Lesure. Paris, 1957.
191 Vannes, René. *Dictionnaire universel des luthiers.* Brussels, 1951, 1959.
192 Vega, Carlos. *Los Instrumentos musicales aborígines y criollos de la Argentina.* Buenos Aires, 1943.
193 *Vie du Sahara, La.* Musée de l'Homme, Paris, 1960 (exhibition catalogue).
194 Virdung, Sebastian. *Musica getutscht.* Basel, 1511.
195 Wachsmann, K. P. (chapter on musical instruments), in Trowell, M., and Wachsmann, K. P.: *Tribal Crafts of Uganda.* London, 1953.
196 Walcker, Oscar. *Erinnerungen eines Orgelbauers.* Kassel, 1948.
197 Wartburg, Walther von. *Französisches etymologisches Wörterbuch.* 1928.
198 Wedgwood, James Ingall. *A Comprehensive Dictionary of Organ Stops.* London, 1905.
199 Wegner, Max. *Das Musikleben der Griechen.* Berlin, 1949.
200 Wiens, Heinrich. *Musik und Musikpflege am herzoglichen Hof zu Kleve.* Cologne, 1959.
201 Williams, Francis Edgar. *Bull-roarers in the Papuan Gulf.* Port Moresby, 1936.
202 Wirz, Paul. *A description of musical instruments from Central North-Eastern New Guinea.* Amsterdam, 1952.
203 Wolf, Siegfried. *Zum Problem der Nasenflöte.* Leipzig, 1941.
204 Wright, Rowland. *Dictionnaire des instruments de musique.* London, 1941.
205 Zamfir, C., and Zlotea, I. *Metoda da cobza.* Bucharest, 1956.
206 Zelenin, Dmitrij. *Russische Volkskunde.* Berlin, 1927.

NORTON BOOKS ON MUSIC
Norton Library and Liveright Paperbacks